SELIM PALMGREN

THE INTERNATIONAL LIBRARY OF MUSIC

FOR HOME AND STUDIO

MUSIC LITERATURE
VOLUME II

THE HISTORY OF MUSIC
Critical and Biographical Sketches of the
Epoch Makers of Music

The Modern and Contemporary Schools—National Groups

Containing Chapters by

Romain Rolland	Vincent d'Indy	Henry T. Finck
Pierre Lalo	Pietro Mascagni	Horatio Parker

and others

PRONOUNCING DICTIONARY OF MUSICAL TERMS
BIOGRAPHICAL DICTIONARY OF MUSICIANS

THE UNIVERSITY SOCIETY
NEW YORK

Copyright, 1948, by
THE UNIVERSITY SOCIETY
INCORPORATED

In addition to a wealth of new material, this new edition of The International Library of Music combines the best features of its highly successful predecessors; namely:

Famous Songs and Those Who Made Them	Copyright 1896
The World's Best Music	Copyright 1897
Paderewski—Century Library of Music	Copyright 1900
Modern Music and Musicians	Copyright 1912
La Mejor Musica del Mundo	Copyright 1917
The University Course of Music Study	Copyright 1920
The International Library of Music	Copyright 1925
A Melhor Musica do Mundo	Copyright 1930
The International Library of Music	Copyright 1936

MANUFACTURED IN THE U. S. A.

CONTENTS

CRITICAL AND BIOGRAPHICAL SKETCHES ON MODERN MUSIC

		PAGE
BRUCKNER, MAHLER AND THEIR SUCCESSORS	*Eugene E. Simpson*	393

A Modern Repository of Musical Mysticism—Outlines of Bruckner's Life—Conditions of Mahler's Youth—Bruckner and the Brahms-Wagner Controversy—Consideration of Bruckner and Mahler's Principal Works—The Younger Generation; Korngold—Arnold Schönberg—Estimate of Schönberg's Work—Future Aspects of the School Founded by Bruckner and Mahler.

RICHARD STRAUS	*Romain Rolland*	400

Strauss's Life—Salient Influences—An Estimate of His Art—His Symphonic Works—"Tod and Verklärung"—"Guntram"—"Till Eulenspiegel"—"Zarathustra"—"Don Quixote"—"Heldenleben"—Strauss and the Modern Teutonic Spirit—Strauss's Operas.

CAMILLE SAINT-SAËNS	*Pierre Lalo*	411

The Diversity of Saint-Saëns's Talents—Saint-Saëns as a Song Writer, Composer of Piano Pieces and Chamber Music—A Master of the Orchestra—His Symphonic Poems—Symphony in C Minor—His Dramatic Works—An Estimate of Saint-Saëns's Music.

CÉSAR FRANCK	*Vincent d'Indy*	420

Franck's Neglect by the Public of His Day—The Man: His Life and His Character; His Daily Habits—The Artist; The Rare Quality of Sincerity—A Genius of Pure Music; Predilection for Religious Themes and the Portrayal of Noble Traits—Melodic and Harmonic Qualities of His Music: Franck's Conception of the Cyclical Forms—"The Redemption"; "The Beatitudes"; The Quartet in D—The Last Three Organ Chorales—The Instructor—Appreciation and Personal Recollections.

THE MUSIC OF MODERN FRANCE		435

The French Spirit in its Relation to Modern Music—The Nineteenth Century in France—Effect of the War of 1870—Organization to Promote Native Art; The National Society of Music—Preparatory Forces: Berlioz, Bizet, Franck—Debussy and the Pupils of Franck.

THE LEGACY OF THE CENTURY	*Pietro Mascagni*	441

Introduction—Rossini and Verdi the Unbroken Line of Genius Through the Century—English Music Exotic—The Other Northern Nations Exhibit Well-Defined Schools—Italy, Spain, and Hungary—The Potency of Popular Melody Among Its Own People—Hungarian Music—Foreign Art Cannot Be Grafted Upon a Country—Music in Spain—On the Northern School—The New Russian School—Italian Sacred Music—Perosi, the True Genius—The Respective Influence of France, Germany and Italy Upon Music—Brahms, the Greatest Figure of the Century in German Music—A Review of Melo-Dramatists—Germany and Italy Contest the Field—Review of French Music—Boito, an Isolated Genius in Modern Italian Music—Shall Italian Music Be Germanized?—The Mischievous Modern Critic—Italian Music Will Progress—Wagnerism the Danger of Italian Music—Popular Melody the Solution of Our Enigma.

ARTHUR SEYMOUR SULLIVAN	*Charles Maclean*	464

The Significance of Sullivan in English Musical History—The Monodic Style in Relation to National Development—Sullivan's Use of British Folk Songs—The Development of His Talents; Biographical Facts; Study and Early Works—Sullivan and W. S. Gilbert—The Renascence of the Operetta—Sacred Works—Later Operas—An Estimate of Sullivan's Genius.

SAMUEL COLERIDGE-TAYLOR		471

Coleridge-Taylor in Relation to His Race—Biographical Facts—Early Works; His Use of Rational Material—The Samuel Coleridge-Taylor Society—The "Bamboula"—Personal Characteristics—His Efforts on Behalf of His Race.

AMERICA'S POSITION IN MUSIC	*Eugene E. Simpson*	476

Two Errors in the Consideration of the Question—Early American Composers; Lowell Mason, William H. Fry, George F. Bristow—Stephen Foster—State of Music in Europe During the Period of America's Musical Infancy—First Studies in Native Musical Material—Early Nationalists in American Music—Later Influences and Present-Day Endeavor in Musical Nationalism—Chronology of American Composers.

THE COMPOSERS OF AMERICA	*Frederick H. Martens*	491

Introduction—The Pioneers—MacDowell's Contemporaries: Chadwick, Kelley, Parker and Others—MacDowell's Successors—Oldberg, Arne and other Neo-Classicists—The Modernists: Nationalists and Eclectics; Ultra-Moderns; The Lighter Vein.

EDWARD MACDOWELL	*Henry T. Finck*	505

Biographical Facts—MacDowell's Use of Indian Themes—Stephen C. Foster and Edward MacDowell—MacDowell's Gift of Humor—His Relations with Raff—Recognition by Liszt—Return to America—MacDowell as a Teacher—The Estimate of MacDowell's Works: His Piano Pieces and Songs—The Last Years of His Life.

CONTENTS

PAGE

AFRO-AMERICAN COMPOSERS - *Grover Brower* 512
   Negro Folk Song and the Negro Composer—Harry T. Burleigh—Will Marion Cook—Nathaniel Dett—Carl L. Diton and Others.

ERNEST BLOCH - *Cesar Saerchinger* 515
   Ernest Bloch's Position in Contemporary Music; An Expression of the Jewish Race Spirit—Creative Influences—Bloch's Life—The Principal Works: The Jewish Poems; Settings of the Psalms; "Israel"; The String Quartet and Other Works.

CONTEMPORARY MUSIC - *Horatio Parker* 519
   The Three Essentials in the Pursuit and Enjoyment of Music—The Attitude of the Contemporary Public Toward the Music of Palestrina, Bach, Beethoven—The Modern Aspects of Absolute Music and Program Music—Modern Aspects of Opera—Strauss and Debussy as Champions of the Modern French and German Schools—A Consideration of Their Comparative Significance.

NATIONALITY IN MUSIC - *James C. Dibdin* 525
   Fashioning the Destinies of the Ages to Come—The Individualism of a Nation—The Polynesians and the Flute—Music Among the Hebrews—English Ballads—Opera in Italy—Counterpoint—Individuality and Science.

MUSICAL TASTE IN CHILDREN - *Arthur Elson* 535
   The Sedate Style of the 18th Century—Compass of the Child Voice—Exaggerated Sweetness—Guido and His Choir Boys—The Child Prodigy—The Preservation of Enthusiasm.

A HISTORY OF MUSIC

INTRODUCTION - 539
   Three Forms of Musical Instruments: the Drum, the Pipe, and the Lyre—Their Succession Established as the Law of Development of Musical Instruments in Prehistoric Times—The Stages of Early Musical History.

CHAPTER I.—THE DRUM STAGE - 540
   The Origin of Music—The First Musical Instrument—The Drum-god—Drum-worship—Musical Religions of Savage Races—The Structure of the Drum and its Gradual Progress to a Perfect Type of Instrument.

CHAPTER II.—THE PIPE STAGE - 541
   The Horn and the Flute the Leading Types of Wind Instruments—The Horn Invented for the Purpose of Warfare—Its Use in Warfare—Love and Origin of the Flute—The Courting-flutes of Savage Nations.

CHAPTER III.—THE VOICE - 542
   The Origin of Song—Its Development from Speech—Evolution of the Scale—The One-note Period in the History of Music—The Two-note Period—The Three-note Period—The Succeeding Periods—Dancing, and its Influence upon Song—Origin of the Minor.

CHAPTER IV.—THE LYRE STAGE - 544
   The Beginnings of Stringed Instruments—The Lyre the Instrument of the Barbarians—The Bards of Barbarian Nations—The Universality of Music in This Stage of Development—Music Coequal with Culture—Music as a Moral Power.

CHAPTER V.—THE EGYPTIANS - 546
   Music in Egypt During the Nineteenth Dynasty—Instruments of the Egyptian Orchestra—The Great Harp—Egyptian Music from the Times of Menes to the Times of the Ptolemies—The Music of the Temples.

CHAPTER VI.—THE ASSYRIANS - 548
   The War Music of the Assyrians—Character of Their Bands—Love for Shrill Sounds—Assyrian Dulcimers.

CHAPTER VII.—THE HEBREWS - 549
   The Minstrel Poets—The Prophets—The Form of the Hebrew Music, Elucidated by an Analysis of the Poetry—Hebrew Music at the Time of David—Music in the Schools of the Prophets—Rabbinical Traditions, etc.

CHAPTER VIII.—THE CHINESE, INDO-CHINESE, AND OTHER MONGOLOIDS - 551
   The Chinese Scale of Nature—The Scale of the Seven Substances—The Music of Drums, Bells, etc.—Legends of the Origin of Music in China—The Chinese Musical System—Similarities in Other Music of the East.

CHAPTER IX.—THE PERUVIANS AND MEXICANS - 553
   Music in Peru at the Time of the Conquest—Peru the Home of the Flute—Contrast with Music of the Mexicans—Mexican Instruments of Percussion and Wind—The Public Dances.

CONTENTS

v

PAGE

CHAPTER X.—THE ANCIENT ARYANS — — — — — — — — — — — — — — — — — 554
    The Vina—The Aryan Bards—Composition and Performance of Their Hymns.

CHAPTER XI.—THE GREEKS — — — — — — — — — — — — — — — — — — — 555
    Homer and the Minstrels of His Day—Reforms of Terpander—Sappho—Cultivation of Song—Greek Musical Notation—The Enharmonic Genus—Olympus and Phrygian School of Flute-playing—Stringed Instruments in Use in Greece—The Lyre—Wind Instruments—Greek Dances—The Choral Music of Greece.

CHAPTER XII.—THE GREEKS (CONTINUED) — — — — — — — — — — — — — — 557
    Organization of the Greek Musical System by Pythagoras—The Chromatic Genus—Greek Modes in the Form They Reached Under Aristoxenus—Greek Harmony—The Brotherhood of Pythagoras.

CHAPTER XIII.—THE GREEKS (CONTINUED) — — — — — — — — — — — — — — 558
    Three Specimens of Ancient Greek Music—Tragedy of Athens—The Great Theatre of Bacchus—The Actors—Methods of Performing the Tragedies—The Chorus—Choral Dances and Songs.

CHAPTER XIV.—THE ROMANS — — — — — — — — — — — — — — — — — — 559
    General Mingling of All the Music of the Ancient World at Rome—The Roman Pantomimes—Instruments in the Orchestra—Nero—His Performances at the Theatres—His Patronage of Organ-builders—The Water-Organ—Death of Nero—The Early Christians—Their Psalms and Services—Progress of Music Among Them.

CHAPTER XV.—EARLY CHRISTIAN MUSIC — — — — — — — — — — — — — — 562
    The First Christian Songs and Psalms—Weakness and Unsteadiness of the Singing—Indifference to These Points on the Part of the Worshipers.

CHAPTER XVI.—THE MUSIC OF THE MIDDLE AGES — — — — — — — — — — — 563
    Modes—Neumes—Theorists—Organum—Solmization—Measured Music—Counterpoint—Motets—Troubadours—Minnesingers—Music in England—Defay to Lasso in the Netherlands—Italian Choral Music—Early German Composers.

CHAPTER XVII.—ENGLISH MUSIC FROM THE TUDORS TO THE STUARTS — — — — 566
    Tudor Influence—Henry VII and Elizabeth—Early Church Music—Tallis and Byrd—Madrigals—Rise of Instrumental Music—Decline of Choral Music—Influence of the Stuarts and Puritans.

CHAPTER XVIII.—THE BIRTH OF OPERA AND ORATORIO — — — — — — — — — 568
    A Revolution in Art—Harmonic Music—Music-Drama and Oratorio—Monteverde—Carissimi—Schütz—The First Opera Houses Open—Cavalli—Cesti—Stradella—The First Important Operas.

CHAPTER XIX.—GENERAL DEVELOPMENT OF OPERA IN EUROPE — — — — — — 570
    Differences of the Music-Drama in France and Italy—Monteverde's Traditions Continued in France by Lulli—English Music and Purcell—German Opera—Scarlatti and the Neapolitans—Handel—Italian Opera Supreme.

CHAPTER XX.—ORATORIO IN THE TIME OF BACH AND HANDEL — — — — — — 573
    Different Lines Taken by Italians and Germans—Passion Music in Germany—Bach's Predecessors—His Choral Works—Italian Influence Upon Handel—His Oratorios.

CHAPTER XXI.—THE PROGRESS OF INSTRUMENTAL MUSIC UP TO THE TIME OF JOHANN SEBASTIAN BACH — 574
    Early Instrumental Music—In England—In France—Couperin—Organ Music in Italy—Frescobaldi—In Germany—The Great Italian Violinists—Suites and Sonatas—Handel—J. S. Bach—Domenico Scarlatti.

CHAPTER XXII.—THE PROGRESS OF INSTRUMENTAL MUSIC IN THE EIGHTEENTH CENTURY — — — 577
    The Great School of Italian Violinists—The Clavier Sonata—In Italy—In Germany—Karl Philipp Emanuel Bach—Rise of the Symphony—Alessandro Scarlatti Again—Stamitz—Haydn—Mozart—Nature of Changes in the Latter Half of the Century—Sonatas—Quartets, etc.

CHAPTER XXIII.—OPERA IN THE TIME OF GLUCK AND MOZART, AND IMMEDIATELY AFTER — — — 581
    Reaction from the Formality of Italian Opera—Gluck's Aims—Difference of Mozart's Position—"Idomeneo" a Turning-point—German Aspirations for a National Opera—"Entführung aus dem Serail"—"Nozze di Figaro"—"Don Giovanni"—"Die Zauberflöte"—Progress of French Opera—Spontini.

CHAPTER XXIV.—THE PROGRESS OF INSTRUMENTAL MUSIC TO BEETHOVEN AND HIS IMMEDIATE SUCCESSORS — 584
    Rise of Pianoforte Music—Clementi—Cramer—Other Prominent Composers of Instrumental Music—Beethoven's Early Circumstances—Predominance of Sonatas Among His Works—His Characteristics—Enlarging Principles of Design—Characteristic Expression—Program—Hummel—Weber—Schubert—Spohr.

CONTENTS

	PAGE
CHAPTER XXV.—MODERN INSTRUMENTAL MUSIC	588

Berlioz—Design—Program—Instrumentation—Mendelssohn—Chopin—Polish and Parisian Influences—Schumann—Teutonic Disposition—Virtuosity—Liszt—Other Representatives of Instrumental Music.

CHAPTER XXVI.—MODERN OPERA — 592

Opera in Italy Since Gluck's Time—Rossini—Opera in France—Meyerbeer—Gounod—Other Recent French Representatives—Germany—Continued Aspirations for National Opera—"Fidelio"—Spohr—Weber—"Der Freischütz"—Weber's Position and Influence—Wagner—Early Influences—Maturity First Attained in "Der Ring des Nibelungen."

CHAPTER XXVII.—MODERN VOCAL MUSIC — 597

Solo Song—Characteristic of the Modern Phase of Music—Schubert—Schumann—Brahms—Solo Song in France—In England—Revival of Oratorio—Haydn—Spohr—Lesser Lights—Mendelssohn—Thriving State of Choral Music in Combination with Orchestra.

CHAPTER XXVIII.—NEW WORKS IN RECENT YEARS — 601

The Close of the Nineteenth Century and the First Decade of the Twentieth—The Program Principle—Wagner's Influence—The Russian School—Richard Strauss—Later European Composers.

BIOGRAPHICAL DICTIONARY OF MUSICIANS

A GUIDE FOR THE PRONUNCIATION OF FOURTEEN LANGUAGES — 609
BIOGRAPHICAL DICTIONARY — 615

PRONOUNCING DICTIONARY OF MUSICAL TERMS

DIRECTIONS FOR PRONUNCIATION — 728
DICTIONARY OF TERMS — 729

BRUCKNER, MAHLER AND THEIR SUCCESSORS

BY

EUGENE E. SIMPSON

IN any consideration of the works of Anton Bruckner (1824-1896), his pupil, Gustav Mahler (1860-1911), and their successors, there is little need this late day to discuss the texture of their product, but it is pertinent to speculate upon the place which the world may grant them in the future. There is no problem as to the abstract value which their compositions represent, since those are seen to be wholly sincere and wholly worthy of a high place among the many forms of human discourse. There exists only the practical problem of the changing fashions in the concert life of the world—whether these composers and their strong contemporaries like Reger, Schönberg and Korngold will prove to be needed in future repertories. If among the thousands of prolific composers of the last two centuries the present day repertory holds fast only to Bach, Beethoven, Chopin, Liszt, Schumann, Tschaikowsky, and Brahms, with a little of Scarlatti, Tartini, Gluck, Mozart, Weber, Berlioz, Mendelssohn and Grieg, then one may easily question who it is that will remain as casual and welcome guest, and who may become the indispensable member of the household.

Even now it should be confessed that without regard to the exact degree of one's individual love for this music, there is danger in any direct answer, because as a futurity the matter is subject to all the musical world's vagaries, and in the past those have been legion. Nevertheless there is one strong premise which may be offered unqualifiedly—that the eighteen symphonies, and the usual choral by-products of these two composers, represent the greatest and most homogeneous of all repositories of music-religious mysticism. That statement is in nowise affected by the circumstance that Bruckner's works are strongly dominated by Richard Wagner, while Mahler, as a veritable stylistic omnibus, was enabled to carry influences, not alone of Bruckner and Wagner, but of all the world's other important music-dialectic sources, not even scorning those of the older Italian operas. Also, that Bruckner was a singularly devout adherent to the Catholic faith and that Mahler was a Jew alters nothing in the premise, for their thought in music was continually directed toward the celestial and the more somber relations of life, and it might seem that the technic of symphonic discourse did not yet differentiate the creeds.

For a broader understanding of the life currents which drove these men to the profuse expression of their moods, one should look briefly into the details of their musical training and their environment. Without wishing in any way to exaggerate the picture, it is shown that Bruckner was the son of a poor Austrian schoolmaster, as indeed all Austrian schoolmasters are poor. Upon the early death of his father, he became a chorister in a collegiate church, then succeeded his father in the needy profession of an assistant schoolmaster at Windhag, near Freistadt. Almost wholly through self-help, Bruckner gradually raised his musical knowledge to take part in an organist competition at Linz. This was in 1855, when he was thirty-one years old. The next twelve years of his homely yet potent genius, with a bit of study in trips to Vienna, sufficed to raise him to the organist post of the Vienna Court Opera and a teacher's post at the Imperial Music Institute, while the eleventh of those years had marked the creation of his first symphony. Henceforth his life was comparatively easy, still always marked by his great religious sincerity, marked modesty and a personal simplicity in perfect keeping with his homely beginning.

In the life of Mahler, who was born in the Bohemian town of Kalischt, the temporal conditions surrounding his youth seem not to have been severe, for he was at least enabled to attend the usual high school (Gymnasium) of the time, and even to study at Vienna University while carrying on music-theoretic training under Bruckner. It does not matter that the personal details of his early life are less known than the musical, for the world long since has come to see in the mere fact of his race sufficient basis for the idealistic in his music, with the tragic outlook upon life.

Going somewhat deeper into the position which Bruckner held in the world, the most salient group of circumstances is inseparable from those which touched the progress of Richard Wagner and Johannes Brahms, since all three of these composers came simultaneously to their finest periods of productivity. Typifying the arrival of nearly every great master of the musical world, each of these became the center of heated controversy. As usual, the various approbations and dissensions were not confined to the merits of any composer alone—his friends invariably assaulted some other artistic citadel, as if the right place to build a temple would be upon the ruins of the old.

As to the nonsensical rivalries of those times, it availed nothing that Wagner was solely a music-dramatist and Brahms solely a symphonist; their friends still projected these cross relations into a semblance of opposing interests. The direct result upon the affairs of Brahms was, that for about two generations his great symphonies remained coldly withheld from the highly important concert life of Munich, which city was for many years thus wildly employed in an exclusive idolization of Wagner. In the same connection, the Max Reger article in the present volume incidentally remarks that it was fifteen years after Brahms' death when Munich gave this great master the belated honor of a festival of his works.

From the innocent occurrence that out of the artistic turmoil which prevailed in the musical world, Bruckner's convictions could make him nothing but a pronounced champion of the complete Wagner, and that he was either unable or unwilling to prevent his own symphonies from partaking strikingly of the orchestral color and the very mood of the Wagner music dramas, it was inevitable that Bruckner was also projected into a false rivalry with Brahms. Though neither of these composers is thought to have had part in the agitation, there was at least a more reasonable ground for a contest, since symphony could be posed against symphony. In final judgment of such rivalries, after forty years it is difficult to say whether the world lost or gained. Had it not been for the intensification thus afforded, any one of the three composers mentioned might have waited much longer for recognition than he did, since nothing in art kills so surely as lethargy.

Before going further into the affairs of Bruckner, Mahler and those who grew up after them, it may be helpful briefly to indicate the character of some of their compositions, through the specific medium of contemporary concert reports. As concerns the Bruckner eighth symphony:

The Bruckner second symphony was conceived in much beauty, if already with the composer mannerisms that remained with Bruckner through his nine symphonies; but the second proved to be of the lightest spiritual power of all, and required but fifty minutes to play, while the eighth symphony has shown some of the finest inspiration, often in the highest degree Wagnerian, also fully withstanding the Wagnerian endurance test, and playing for an hour and fourteen minutes, in the authoritative Nikisch tempos. The Wagnerian relation was but barely noticeable in the first movement, where there was some particularly intense and noble inspiration in evidence. Strangely enough, the main figure of the second movement Scherzo would have been entirely impossible without the Mendelssohn "Midsummer Night's Dream" overture as forerunner, yet this strong Scherzo picture had for a contrasting theme, one of the slow, half-funereal moods which had so large a part in the Bruckner life. In the succeeding Adagio, which alone played for twenty-five minutes, it was impossible to disassociate Wagner, since his influence was in evidence in the musical texture and still more the typical use of the horns, the low strings of violins and violas, finally employing much tremolo and concluding in pronounced "Waldweben" writing. The fourth movement came in large array of Bruckner's own use of the horns, a beautiful and very individual assignment for the violins, the ever-recurring pizzicato of the contrabasses, and the most vigorous hammering of kettle drums in a long climax which again faded away to a close.

And summarizing on the composer's great E minor mass:

It is doubtful if any one of the Bruckner symphonies can show the composer's real genius more clearly than it is shown in this mass, where every contrapuntal line for orchestra is thrown upon the canvas with the sharpness of a steel engraving. Here it is once more the genius for simplicity, for a single clarinet or horn above the chorus may be responsible for the entire color. At any rate, an intellect of the highest power is necessary to the creation of so noble music in so plastic means, and the whole effect of the mass is therefore one of most striking individuality and sublime musical content.

In direct comparison with Bruckner, the following on Mahler's ninth symphony is to the point:

The symphony was first brought to the public ear at the Vienna festival in 1912, thirteen months after the death of the composer. In nearly all its hour and thirteen minutes actual playing length, it has exactly the element which is ever absent in Bruckner, and that is the one idea of logic and dogged devotion to treatment of the fixed thematic materials. In view of the sturdy type of work, which is the ideal type for all symphonic forms, Mahler's ninth symphony will have that much with which to furnish pleasure to many who have not yet felt sympathy for the strange, the Oriental or transcendental mood worlds in which he moved about through long episodes of his symphonies. Nevertheless, there is in his ninth symphony a feature tending to

ANTON BRUCKNER

disturb the idea of homogeneity first secured by industrious work in thematics. The fault lies in the unending stopping and starting, as if the movement were once complete, but that some other member of the orchestra had begged for one more chance to play. The first movement suffers perceptibly from this unfinished, eleventh-hour gossiping by every player who may happen to straggle in, so that the last few minutes of the movement are in thus far disturbing to the effect once gained from the beautiful materials employed.

The fault is likewise a specialty of another gifted composer who writes long works, and that is Max Reger. But in this, Beethoven was also an offender long before their time. Both the Reger interpreting art and composing art contribute to the disturbance, just as Mr. Walter's interpreting art failed to read out such false closes in the Mahler symphony. The musical content of this symphony is about that of any of his other works and that often represents high mood power, invariably taking expression in a very plain, at times homely, often borrowed dialect. Nobody who has heard Mahler's other symphonies will go wrong in surmise of the strange and wonderfully effective devices invented and employed, but there is one thing more to report as an item of progress. The strange effects here employed are not of such

GUSTAV MAHLER

nature as to annoy, as was true of those in every other symphony, even including his immensely impressive eighth.

Mahler's style may be further judged from a discussion of his six-movement "Lied der Erde" for solo and chorus voices with orchestra:

The three tenor numbers are by far the less earnest in content, as they also require only a total of seventeen minutes to give. The three numbers for contralto are of very great beauty, and it may be that the last section, requiring just thirty minutes to perform, is among the greatest mood monuments that has ever been set in tone. The musician can never forget the one reservation, and that is that Mahler's musical dialect is always one of the utmost simplicity, sometimes directly commonplace; yet in the dialect at his command, the composer had extraordinary impulses to convey. The contralto's first solo is already a picture of great power. Her second solo sings of beauty and grace, in many Oriental colors. The long finale sings of parting, and there is lyric tragedy of overwhelming intensity. Mahler has then brought to the orchestral palette some of his most wonderful colors.

Of the extreme elements which may have arisen after Bruckner and Mahler to continue or still further involve the harmonic and orchestral fabric of composition, the contemporaneous composers of Russia and France have been already considered in special articles in the present series. Particularly in the general article on Russia, there is set forth the fact that at the first and second decades of the twentieth century, the art of complex instrumentation and great harmonic intensity was property common to all. Then for Central Europe, and most directly associated with the traditions and the territory of Bruckner and Mahler, there were coming forward just at the death of Mahler, Arnold Schönberg (1874—) and Eric Korngold (1897—).

The boy Korngold had come into public notice with a stage pantomime, "The Snowman," written when he was about ten years old. There was still a great deal of Viennese operetta spirit in the music, though still an extraordinary performance for a child. Besides fantastic piano pieces, a piano trio, and two sonatas for piano, when he was fourteen years old Korngold wrote an "Overture to a Drama" (Schauspiel), which was of the largest modern orchestral scope, but was even more remarkable because written entirely in complete score or partitur—that is, entirely without sketches of any kind. It was simply a free discourse on which he wrote a page or two of score every day through the summer vacation of 1911. Again quoting from a concert report:

The Korngold overture plays for thirteen minutes in heavy modern scoring of great tonal brilliancy and polish. The present state of the boy's uncommon genius manifests itself in occasional rare touches, rather than in the main character of the musical dialect employed. Thus one would have to classify this work as one often related to the Richard Strauss type of phrase building, and it has the occasional ecstatic, lyric content of nearly every Strauss composition. Though these general features are perfectly easy of identification, the overture is none the less a remarkable example of beautiful music, written in steady inspiration and perfect sequence.

Among characteristics that one first hears in the Korngold overture are the strange throbbing effects produced by some mordent or short trill of the muted violins. The horns come into heavy modern operatic sighing to harp accompaniment, and the interrupted throbbing resumes over muffled horn, in beautiful slow song. After some kind of proclamation over the whole orchestra, the Strauss relation first becomes strongly apparent in the large episode directly ensuing. There is further a very beautiful piece in modern operatic spirit, played quietly by clarinet, then soon reinforced by the entire orchestra. A short, broad waltz, in full dance manner, is introduced and still later repeated. There is a good deal of the Strauss spirit again until near the close.

The Korngold music may be further indicated by discussion of his other works.

The progress from the piano trio to the sonata was very marked, with frequent strange harmonic effects in going by. For the composing of these works the boy had also employed the dominating musical dialect of his time, and that was the poorer dialect of phrase-building modeled after the operas and the symphonic poems, rather than after the better rhythmic and canonic type of Beethoven and the rest of the symphonic classics. However unlucky may have been the choice, one must never forget that the boy still represents an individuality of the highest rank, which is still more abundantly shown in the rare freedom of the fairy pictures. The proverbial wildness of youth is shown here in full bloom, and no musician is able to sit through a recital of these works without feeling himself in the presence of a unique gift, still manifesting itself in reasonable health and order.

Among the first occasions on which the musical world began hearing of Arnold Schönberg as a modern apparition, was when the great master and critic, Ferruccio Busoni, wrote that here was a composer who would have to be considered in future calculations. At about the same time, musicians were hearing of some very vague piano pieces, and almost simultaneously a committee of Schönberg pupils and admirers were taking definite steps toward having some of the composer's larger orchestral works performed. Then Schönberg changed his residence from Vienna to Berlin, and received pupils while giving a series of lectures in which he discussed his own views of composition.

In the Schönberg piano pieces earliest heard, their tonal complications were in part exaggerated by their reflective, non-

ARNOLD SCHÖNBERG

rhythmic playing manner. The composer's early string sextet, "Transcendent Night" (Verklärte Nacht), on a title of a Dehnel poem, was found to be a work of very great beauty, possibly in the mood of Wagner's "Tristan," where the ever firm harmonic fabric was a highly satisfying feature. However, his orchestral "Chamber Symphonie," and the string quartet, Op. 7, soon arrived, in such revolutionary intricacy as to vex the conservatives and cause even some of the strong admirers of Schönberg's former works to hesitate.

When the public doubt thus aroused was at its highest, there came a series of reassuring performances of the very beautiful "Gurrelieder," comprising an all evening entertainment for orchestra, chorus and vocal soloists. The composer had begun these some years before, had laid them aside, then completed them at a time when his style had undergone a decided change. The difference was apparent to their composer and to the average gifted amateur who studied them, yet to the ordinary concert visitor they still constituted an imposing entertainment. The work is divided into twenty parts, to require about two hours and a half for performance. The chorus has nothing to do but look on for the first two hours, an intermission having occupied twenty-five minutes between the first and second large divisions. Quoting further:

Proceeding at once to a consideration of the music, it is only fair to say that throughout the work it is seldom possible to forget Richard Wagner, either for the actual musical feeling or the main school and color of the instrumentation. Notwithstanding an overwhelming amount of Wagnerian music, there is still an overwhelming amount of the purest Schönberg. The phenomenon is felt at its highest, while observing how remarkably the Schönberg instrumentation springs up out of the sublime reflection and the depth of the Schönberg inspiration. In this stated spirit and strongly Wagnerian type of instrumentation, Schönberg goes much further and calls up fabulously interesting and fanciful mood and tone pictures of forest and field. On the purely musical side he has written for the solo voices a material often representing the highest attainable stage of concert repose and poetic reflection.

The Jacobsen poem on which the songs are written depicts King Waldemar's journey to the Gurre Island, to visit the maid Tove Lille. Later the forest dove proclaims Tove's death, which was brought about through the Queen's revenge. Because of the loss of Tove, Waldemar blasphemes the Lord, and he becomes a type of the wandering huntsman of Northern legend.

In the Schönberg composition these choruses are employed to depict the wild hunting scenes of the dead. The first two sections predominate in music of the forest and the many phases of the deeply inspired love scenes. Notwithstanding Schönberg's abstract musical talent, the first ten songs occasionally lapse to modern romantic conventional, and the auditor instinctively wishes again for the wild instrumentation and rhythmic change which are then later delivered in plenty. Whoever finds it difficult to understand how so much true Wagner can mix with so much true Schönberg may find voluminous precedent in the Mozart-Haydn of Beethoven; the Mozart-Schumann of Tschaikowsky; the Wagner-Liszt-Tschaikowsky of Richard Strauss, and the Bach-Schumann-Brahms-Palestrina of Max Reger—all noble combinations which have given out prodigally of that which inspires and elevates.

As to the Schönberg string quartet, Op. 7, it required fifty-one minutes for performance, given without pause. It was music of extraordinary beauty and individuality, if also suffering the public disadvantage which every long work undergoes at a first hearing. In all the discussion for and against and about Schönberg, there will be this much permanently valid—that he is a composer of very unusual musical gift and great accomplishment.

The very strange "Chamber Symphony," following the performance of a Richard Strauss orchestral preludium, is said to have ushered in real guessing. It was so radical as actually to have angered many of the auditors, so that there was hissing with right good will,—and still the hissing could not affect the large musical value of the work. Compared with the quartet, the chamber symphony is in slightly easier hearing, on account of the broader canvas, yet this work had incidents which were really difficult for the ear to take. Nevertheless, when the music had proceeded for some minutes, it was possible to feel that in instrumentation Schönberg was not very many leagues in advance of his near contemporaries, Strauss, Bruckner and Mahler. The art of instrumentation, even in its most striking forms, had become indeed universal.

Returning briefly to speculate upon the possible future of Bruckner and Mahler's vast fund of musical mysticism, one must restate the conviction that the world's literature furnishes as yet absolutely no counterpart. There was hope that a similar fund might rest in the works of Scriabin, who was cut off in a comparative youth of forty-four years. Certainly Scriabin was avowedly seeking exactly that which Bruckner and Mahler sought, and it must be said that the outward conditions of success were largely on his side. If in fact, many of his piano works in the larger classic forms still partook slightly of the nature of miniature, his orchestral writing in such as the "Poème Divine," "Poème Extase" and "Prometheus" was infinitely more concise and compact in form than the massive creations of the two music-religious Austrians. Notwithstanding all this in his favor, as

WAGNER AND BRUCKNER
Cartoon by Becker

has been already suggested in the paper on Modern Russian Music, in the present volume, Scriabin might still have failed because time may prove that he lacked in those qualities of poetic grace and mood necessary to move the musical public. On the other hand, if Bruckner and Mahler had possessed the acumen to create their works in the practical logic and conciseness of their sublime contemporary, Brahms, they would have been occupying ere now the place of the choicest strongholds in the world's music repertories.

For the rest, there remains the question, whether in the usual evolutions of practical fashion in concert going, the public may occasionally revert to a condition of willingness to sit all evening at an entertainment. As yet the extremes, aside from the Bruckner and Mahler symphonies, have been found in the Wagner operas of "Siegfried," "Götterdämmerung" and "Die Meistersinger," each of which requires from four and a half to five hours. It is certain that upon the appearance of the Strauss one-act operas, "Salome" and "Elektra," each occupying a single period of an hour and forty minutes, that length of entertainment was ideally gauged to the hurried spirit of the time; yet in theory one should welcome the principle that nearly any length were justifiable if only the discourse were of such consistent and unbroken power as to command attention, while providing at the same time the most necessary and rational elements of relief.

Finally it is not entirely impossible to discern a saviour in the future Schönberg. Korngold is as yet too well at home in the ways of youth to have begun bothering with religious and philosophical problems of life. Schönberg may be just now at the age of his greatest desire for technical complexity, and in the usual history of an art mentality, age tempers and clears up the intellect. It is at least true that his past performances in mood and abstract musical beauty are voluminous proof of his great gifts. Possibly the succeeding years will allow him to create a large and useful repertory in fields related to those already powerfully touched by Bruckner and Mahler. Meantime the world's concert map shows here and there a bit of territory long since strongly occupied by these two great spirits, and time may increase their power.

RICHARD STRAUSS

BY

ROMAIN ROLLAND

RICHARD STRAUSS was born in Munich on June 2, 1864. His father, a well-known virtuoso, was first horn in the Royal orchestra, and his mother was a daughter of the brewer Pschorr. He was brought up among musical surroundings. At four years old he played the piano, and at six he composed little dances, *Lieder*, sonatas, and even overtures for the orchestra. Perhaps this extreme artistic precocity has had something to do with the feverish character of his talents by keeping his nerves in a state of tension and unduly exciting his mind. At school he composed choruses for some of Sophocles' tragedies. In 1881. Hermann Levi had one of the young collegian's symphonies performed by his orchestra. At the University he spent his time in writing instrumental music. Then Bülow and Radecke made him play in Berlin; and Bülow, who became very fond of him, had him brought to Meiningen as Musikdirector. From 1886 to 1889 he held the same post at the Hoftheater in Munich. From 1889 to 1894 he was Kapellmeister at the Hoftheater in Weimar. He returned to Munich in 1894 as Hofkapellmeister, and in 1896 succeeded Hermann Levi. Finally he left Munich for Berlin, where at present he conducts the orchestra of the Royal Opera.

Two things should be particularly noted in his life: the influence of Alexander Ritter —to whom he has shown much gratitude— and his travels in the south of Europe. He made Ritter's acquaintance in 1885. This musician was a nephew of Wagner's, and died some years ago. His music is practically unknown outside of Germany, though he wrote two well-known operas, "Fauler Hans" and "Wem die Krone?" and was the first composer, according to Strauss, to introduce Wagnerian methods into the *Lied*. He is often discussed in Bülow's and Liszt's letters. "Before I met him," says Strauss, "I had been brought up on strictly classical lines; I had lived entirely on Haydn, Mozart and Beethoven, and had just been studying Mendelssohn, Chopin, Schumann and Brahms. It is to Ritter alone I am indebted for my knowledge of Liszt and Wagner; it was he who showed me the importance of the writings and works of these two masters in the history of art. It was he who by years of lessons and kindly counsel made me a *Zukunftsmusiker*, and set my feet on a road where now I can walk unaided and alone. It was he also who initiated me into Schopenhauer's philosophy."

The second influence, that of the South, dates from April, 1886, and seems to have left an indelible impression upon Strauss. He visited Rome and Naples for the first time, and came back with a symphonic fantasia called "Aus Italien." In the spring of 1892, after a sharp attack of pneumonia, he traveled for a year and a half in Greece, Egypt and Sicily. The tranquillity of these favored countries filled him with never-ending regret. The North has depressed him since then, "The eternal gray of the North and its phantom shadows without a sun." When I saw him at Charlottenburg one chilly April day, he told me with a sigh that he could compose nothing in winter, and that he longed for the warmth and light of Italy. His music is infected by that longing; and it makes one feel how his spirit suffers in the gloom of Germany, and ever yearns for the colors and laughter and the joy of the South. Like the musician that Nietzsche dreamed of,* he seems "to hear ringing in his ears the prelude of a deeper, stronger music, perhaps a more wayward and mysterious music; a music that is super-German, which, unlike other music, would not die away, nor pale, nor grow dull beside the blue and wanton sea and the clear Mediterranean sky; a music super-European, which would hold its own even by the dark sunsets of the desert; a music whose soul is akin to the palm-trees; a music that knows how to live and move among great beasts of prey, beautiful and solitary; a music whose supreme charm is its ignorance of good and evil. Only from time to time perhaps there would flit over it the longing of the sailor for home, golden shadows, and gentle weaknesses; and toward it would come flying from afar the thousand tints of the setting of a moral world that men no longer understood; and to these belated fugitives it would extend its hospitality and sympathy." But it is always the North, the melancholy of the North, and "all the sadness of mankind," mental anguish, the thought of death, and the tyranny of life, that come and weigh down afresh his spirit hungering for light, and force it into feverish speculation and bitter argument. Perhaps it is better so.

Richard Strauss is both a poet and a musician. These two natures live together in him, and each strives to get the better of the other. The balance is not always well maintained; but when he does succeed in keeping it by sheer force of will the union of these two talents, directed to the same end, produces an effect more powerful than

RICHARD STRAUSS

any known since Wagner's time. Both natures have their source in a mind filled with heroic thoughts, a rarer possession, I consider, than a talent for either music or poetry. There are other great musicians in Europe, but Strauss is something more than a great musician, for he is able to create a hero.

When one talks of heroes one is thinking of drama. Dramatic art is everywhere in Strauss's music, even in works that seem least adapted to it, such as his *Lieder* and compositions of pure music. It is most evident in his symphonic poems, which are the most important part of his work. These

---

* "Beyond Good and Evil," 1886. I hope I may be excused for introducing Nietzsche here, but his thoughts seem constantly to be reflected in Strauss, and to throw much light on the soul of modern Germany.

poems are: "Aus Italien" (1886), "Macbeth" (1887), "Don Juan" (1888), "Tod und Verklärung" (1889), "Till Eulenspiegel" (1894), "Also Sprach Zarathustra" (1895), "Don Quixote" (1897), "Heldenleben" (1898), "Symphonia Domestica" (1904), and "Natursymphonie" (1915).

I shall not say much about the earlier works, where the mind and manner of the artist is taking shape. The "Wanderer's Sturmlied," the song of a traveler during a storm, op. 14, is a vocal sextette with an orchestral accompaniment, whose subject is taken from a poem of Goethe's. It was written before Strauss met Ritter, and its construction is after the manner of Brahms and shows a rather affected thought and style. "Aus Italien" (op. 16) is an exuberant picture of impressions of his tour in Italy, of the ruins at Rome, the seashore at Sorrento, and the life of the Italian people. "Macbeth" (op. 23) gives us a rather undistinguished series of musical interpretations of poetical subjects. "Don Juan" (op. 20) is much finer, and translates Lenau's poem into music with bombastic vigor, showing us the hero who dreams of grasping all the joy of the world, and how he fails, and dies after he has lost faith in everything.

"Tod und Verklärung" ("Death and Transfiguration," op. 24) * marks considerable progress in Strauss's thought and style. It is still one of the most stirring of Strauss's works, and the one that is conceived with the most perfect unity. It was inspired by a poem of Alexander Ritter's, and I will give you an idea of its subject.

In a wretched room, lit only by a night-light, a sick man lies in bed. Death draws near him in the midst of awe-inspiring silence. The unhappy man seems to wander in his mind at times, and to find comfort in past memories. His life passes before his eyes; his innocent childhood, his happy youth, the struggles of middle age, and his efforts to attain the splendid goal of his desires, which always eludes him. He had been striving all his life for this goal, and at last though it was within reach, when Death, in a voice of thunder, cries suddenly, "Stop!" And even now in his agony he struggles desperately, being set upon realizing his dream; but the hand of Death is crushing life out of his body, and night is creeping on. Then resounds in the heavens the promise of that happiness which he had vainly sought for on earth—Redemption and Transfiguration.

Richard Strauss's friends protested vigorously against this orthodox ending, and Seidl, Jorisenne and Wilhelm Mauke pretended that the subject was something loftier, that it was the eternal struggle of the soul against its lower self and its deliverance by means of art. I shall not enter into that discussion, though I think that such a cold and commonplace symbolism is much less interesting than the struggle with death, which one feels in every note of the composition. It is a classical work, comparatively speaking; broad and majestic and almost like Beethoven in style. The realism of the subject in the hallucinations of the dying man, the shiverings of fever, the throbbing of the veins, and the despairing agony, is transfigured by the purity of the form in which it is cast. It is realism after the manner of the symphony in C minor, where Beethoven argues with Destiny. If all suggestion of a program is taken away, the symphony still remains intelligible and impressive by its harmonious expression of feeling. Many German musicians think that Strauss has reached the highest point of his work in "Tod und Verklärung." But I am far from agreeing with them, and believe myself that his art has developed enormously as the result of it. It is true it is the summit of one period of his life, containing the essence of all that is best in it; but "Heldenleben" marks the second period, and is its corner stone. How the force and fullness of his feeling has grown since that first period! But he has never refound the delicate and melodious purity of soul and youthful grace of his earlier work, which still shines out in "Guntram," and is then effaced.

Strauss directed Wagner's dramas at Weimar from 1889. While breathing their

---

* Composed in 1889, and performed for the first time at Eisenach in 1890.

atmosphere he turned his attention to the theatre, and wrote the libretto of his opera "Guntram." Illness interrupted his work, and he was in Egypt when he took it up again. The music of the first act was written between December, 1892, and February, 1893, while traveling between Cairo and Luxor; the second act was finished in June, 1893, in Sicily, and the third act early in September, 1893, in Bavaria. There is, however, no trace of an oriental atmosphere in this music. We find rather the melodies of Italy, the reflections of a mellow light, and a resigned calm. I feel in it the languid mind of the convalescent, almost the heart of a young girl whose tears are ready to flow, though she is smiling a little at her own sad dreams. It seems to me that Strauss must have a sacred affection for this work, which owes its inspiration to the undefinable impressions of convalescence. His fever fell asleep in it, and certain passages are full of the caressing touch of nature, and recall Berlioz's "Les Troyens." But too often the music is superficial and conventional, and the tyranny of Wagner makes itself felt—a rare enough occurrence in Strauss's other works. The poem is interesting; Strauss has put much of himself into it, and one is conscious of the crisis that unsettled his broad-minded but often self-satisfied and inconsistent ideas.

"Guntram" was the cause of bitter disappointment to its author. He did not succeed in getting it produced at Munich, for the orchestra and singers declared that the music could not be performed. It is even said that they got an eminent critic to draw up a formal document, which they sent to Strauss, certifying that "Guntram" was not meant to be sung. The chief difficulty was the length of the principal part, which took up by itself, in its musings and discourses, the equivalent of an act and a half. Some of its monologues, like the song in the second act, last half an hour on end. Nevertheless, "Guntram" was performed at Weimar on May 16, 1894. A little while afterward Strauss married the singer who played Freihild, Pauline de Ahna, who had also created Elizabeth in "Tannhäuser" at Bayreuth, and who has since devoted herself to the interpretation of her husband's *Lieder*.

But the rancor of his failure at the theatre still remained with Strauss, and he turned his attention again to the symphonic poem, in which he showed more and more marked dramatic tendencies, and a soul which daily grew prouder and more scornful. You should hear him speak in cold disdain of the theatre-going public—"that collection of bankers and tradespeople and miserable seekers after pleasure"—to know the sore that this triumphant artist hides. For not only was the theatre long closed to him, but by an additional irony he was obliged to conduct musical rubbish at the opera in Berlin on account of the poor taste in music—really of Royal origin—that prevailed there.

The first great symphony of this new period was "Till Eulenspiegel's lustige Streiche, nach alter Schelmenweise, in Rondeauform" ("Till Eulenspiegel's Merry Pranks, according to an old legend, in rondeau form"), op. 28.* Here his disdain is as yet only expressed by witty bantering, which scoffs at the world's conventions. This figure of Till, this devil of a joker, the legendary hero of Germany and Flanders, is little known to non-Teutonic peoples. And so Strauss's music loses much of its point, for it claims to recall a series of adventures which we know nothing about—Till crossing the market-place and smacking his whip at the good women there; Till in priestly attire delivering a homely sermon; Till making a fool of the pedants; Till tried and hung. Strauss's liking to present, by musical pictures, sometimes a character, sometimes a dialogue, or a situation, or a landscape, or an idea—that is to say, the most volatile and varied impressions of his capricious spirit—is very marked here. It is true that he falls back on several popular subjects, whose meaning would be very easily grasped in Germany; and that he develops them not quite in the strict form of a rondeau, as he pretends, but still with a certain method, so that apart from a few frolics, which are unintelligible without

* Composed in 1894-95, and played for the first time at Cologne in 1895.

THE WEIMAR HOFTHEATER
Where "Guntram" was first produced.

a program, the while has real musical unity. This symphony, which is a great favorite in Germany, seems to me less original than some of his other compositions. It sounds rather like a refined piece of Mendelssohn's, with curious harmonies and very complicated instrumentation.

There is much more grandeur and originality in his "Also Sprach Zarathustra, Tondichtung frei nach Nietzsche" ("Thus spake Zarathustra, a free Tone-poem, after Nietzsche"), opus 30.* Its sentiments are more broadly human, and the program that Strauss has followed never loses itself in picturesque or anecdotic details, but is planned on expressive and noble lines. Strauss protests his own liberty in the face of Nietzsche's. He wishes to represent the different stages of development that a free spirit passes through in order to arrive at that of Super-man. These ideas are purely personal and are not part of some system of philosophy. The sub-titles of the work are: "Von den Hinterweltern" (Of Religious Ideas), "Von der grossen Sehnsucht" (Of Supreme Aspiration), "Von den Freuden und Leidenschaften" (Of Joys and Passions), "Das Grablied" (The Grave Song), "Von der Wissenschaft" (Of Knowledge), "Der Genesende" (The Convalescent—the soul delivered of its desires), "Das Tanzlied" (Dancing Song), "Nachtlied" (Night Song). We are shown a man who, worn out by trying to solve the riddle of the universe, seeks refuge in religion. Then he revolts against ascetic ideas and gives way madly to his passions. But he is quickly sated and disgusted and, weary to death, he tries science, but rejects it again, and succeeds in ridding himself of the uneasiness its knowledge brings by laughter—the master of the universe—and the merry dance, that dance of the universe where all the human sentiments enter hand-in-hand—religious beliefs, unsatisfied desires, passions, disgust and joy. "Lift up your hearts on high, my brothers! Higher still! And mind you, don't forget your

* Composed in 1895-96, and performed for the first time at Frankfort-on-Main in November, 1896.

legs. I have canonized laughter.* You super-men, learn to laugh!" And the dance dies away and is lost in ethereal regions, and Zarathustra is lost to sight while dancing in distant worlds. But if he has solved the riddle of the universe for himself, he has not solved it for other men; and so, in contrast to the confident knowledge which fills the music, we get the sad note of interrogation at the end.

There are few subjects that offer richer material for musical expression. Strauss has treated it with power and dexterity; he has preserved unity in this chaos of passions by contrasting the *Sehnsucht* of man with the impassive strength of nature. As for the boldness of his conceptions, I need hardly remind those who heard the poem of the intricate "Fugue of Knowledge," the trills of the woodwind and the trumpets that voice Zarathustra's laugh, the dance of the universe and the audacity of the conclusion which, in the key of B major, finishes up with a note of interrogation in C natural, repeated three times.

I am far from thinking that the symphony is without a fault. The themes are of unequal value: Some are quite commonplace; and, in a general way, the working up of the composition is superior to its underlying thought. I shall come back later on to certain faults in Strauss's music; here I only want to consider the overflowing life and feverish joy that set these worlds spinning.

"Zarathustra" shows the progress of scornful individualism in Strauss—"the spirit that hates the dogs of the populace and all that abortive and gloomy breed; the spirit of wild laughter that dances like a tempest as gaily on marshes and sadness as it does in fields."† That spirit laughs at itself and at its idealism in the "Don Quixote" of 1897, "fantastische Variationen über ein Thema ritterlichen Charakters" (Don Quixote, fantastic variations on a theme of knightly character), opus 35; and that symphony marks, I think, the extreme point to which program music may be carried. In no other work does Strauss give better proof of his prodigious cleverness, intelligence, and wit; and I say sincerely that there is not a work where so much force is expended with so great a loss for the sake of a game and a musical joke which lasts forty-five minutes, and has given the author, the executants, and the public a good deal of tiring work. These symphonic poems are most difficult to play on account of the complexity, the independence and the fantastic caprices of the different parts. Judge for yourself what the author expects to get out of the music by these few extracts from the program.

The introduction represents Don Quixote buried in books of chivalrous romance; and we have to see in the music, as we do in little Flemish and Dutch pictures, not only Don Quixote's features, but the words of the books he reads. Sometimes it is the story of a knight who is fighting a giant, sometimes the adventures of a knight-errant who has dedicated himself to the services of a lady, sometimes it is a nobleman who has given his life in fulfilment of a vow to atone for his sins. Don Quixote's mind becomes confused (and our own with it) over all these stories; he is quite distracted. He leaves home in company with his squire. The two figures are drawn with great spirit; the one is an old Spaniard, stiff, languishing, distrustful, a bit of a poet, rather undecided in his opinions but obstinate when his mind is once made up; the other is a fat, jovial peasant, a cunning fellow, given to repeating himself in a waggish way and quoting droll proverbs—translated in the music by short-winded phrases that always return to the point they started from. The adventures begin. Here are the windmills (trills from the violins and woodwind), and the bleating army of the grand emperor, Alifanfaron (tremolos from the woodwind); and here, in the third variation, is a dialogue between the knight and his squire, from which we are to guess that Sancho questions his master on the advantages of a chivalrous life, for they seem to him doubtful. Don Quixote talks to him of glory and honor, but Sancho has no thought for it. In reply to these grand words he urges the superiority of

---
* Nietzsche.
† Nietzsche, "Zarathustra."

sure profits, fat meals, and sounding money. Then the adventures begin again. The two companions fly through the air on wooden horses; and the illusion of this giddy voyage is given by chromatic passages on the flutes, harps, kettledrums, and a "windmachine," while "the tremolo of the double basses on the keynote shows that the horses have never left the earth."*

But I must stop. I have said enough to show the fun the author is indulging in. When one hears the work one cannot help

RICHARD STRAUSS
Charcoal drawing by Farrago

admiring the composer's technical knowledge, skill in orchestration, and sense of humor, and one is all the more surprised that he confines himself to the illustration of texts † when he is so capable of creating comic and dramatic matter without it. Although "Don Quixote" is a marvel of skill and a very wonderful work, in which Strauss has developed a suppler and richer style, it marks, to my mind, a progress in his technic and a backward step in his mind, for he seems to have adopted the **decadent conceptions of an art suited to playthings and trinkets to please a frivolous and affected society.**

In "Heldenleben" (The Life of a Hero), opus 40, ‡ he recovers himself and with **a stroke of his wings reaches the summits.** Here there is no foreign text for the music to study or illustrate or transcribe. Instead, there is lofty passion and an heroic will gradually developing itself and breaking down all obstacles. Without doubt, Strauss had a program in his mind, but he said to me himself: "You have no need to read it. It is enough to know that the hero is there fighting against his enemies." I do not know how far that is true, or if parts of the symphony would not be rather obscure to anyone who followed it without the text; but this speech seems to prove that he has understood the dangers of the literary symphony and that he is striving for pure music.

"Heldenleben" is divided into six chapters: The Hero, the Hero's Adversaries, the Hero's Companion, the Field of Battle, the Peaceful Labors of the Hero, the Hero's Retirement from the World and the Achievement of his Ideal. It is an extraordinary work, drunk with heroism, colossal, half-barbaric, trivial, and sublime. **An** Homeric hero struggles among the sneers of a stupid crowd, a herd of brawling and hobbling ninnies. A violin solo, in a sort of concerto, describes the seductions, the coquetry, and the degraded wickedness of woman. Then strident trumpet-blasts sound the attack; and it is beyond me to give an idea of the terrible charge of cavalry that follows, which makes the earth tremble and our hearts leap; nor can I describe how an iron determination leads to the storming of towns, and all the tumultuous din and uproar of battle—the most splendid battle that has ever been painted in music. At its first performance in Germany I saw people tremble as they listened to it, and some rose up suddenly and made violent gestures quite unconsciously. I myself had a strange feeling of giddiness, as if an ocean had been

---

* Arthur Hahn, *Der Musikfuhrer: Don Quixote*, Frankfort.

† At the head of each variation Strauss has marked on the score the chapter of "Don Quixote" that he is interpreting.

‡ Finished in December, 1898. Performed for the first time at Frankfort-on-Main on March 3, 1899. Published by Leuckart.

upheaved, and I thought that for the first time for thirty years Germany had found a poet of victory.

"Heldenleben" would be in every way one of the masterpieces of musical composition if a literary error had not suddenly cut short the soaring flight of its most impassioned pages at the supreme point of interest in the movement, in order to follow the program; though, besides this, a certain coldness, perhaps weariness, creeps in toward the end. The victorious hero perceives that he has conquered in vain: the baseness and stupidity of men have remained unaltered. He stifles his anger, and scornfully accepts the situation. Then he seeks refuge in the peace of nature. The creative force within him flows out in imaginative works; and here Richard Strauss, with a daring warranted only by his genius,

MANUSCRIPT OF THE FIRST PAGE OF THE SCORE OF "SALOME"

represents these works by reminiscence of his own compositions, and "Don Juan," "Macbeth," "Tod und Verklärung," "Till," "Zarathustra," "Don Quixote," "Guntram," and even his *Lieder,* associate themselves with the hero whose story he is telling. At times a storm will remind this hero of his combats; but he also remembers his moments of love and happiness, and his soul is quieted. Then the music unfolds itself serenely, and rises with calm strength to the closing chord of triumph, which is placed like a crown of glory on the hero's head.

There is no doubt that Beethoven's ideas have often inspired, stimulated and guided Strauss's own ideas. One feels an indescribable reflection of the first "Heroic" and of the "Ode to Joy" in the key of the first part, E-flat, and the last part recalls, even more forcibly, certain of Beethoven's *Lieder.* But the heroes of the two composers are very different. Strauss's hero is more concerned with the exterior world and his enemies, his conquests are achieved with greater difficulty, and his triumph is wilder in consequence. If that good Oulibicheff pretends to see the burning of Moscow in a discord in the first "Heroic," what would he find here? What scenes of burning towns, what battle-fields! Besides that there is cutting scorn and a mischievous laughter in "Heldenleben" that is never heard in Beethoven. There is, in fact, little kindness in Strauss's work; it is the work of a disdainful hero.

In considering Strauss's music as a whole, one is at first struck by the diversity of his style. The North and the South mingle, and in his melodies one feels the attraction of the sun. Something Italian had crept into "Tristan"; but how much more of Italy there is in the work of this disciple of Nietzsche. The phrases are often Italian and their harmonies ultra-Germanic. Perhaps one of the greatest charms of Strauss's art is that we are able to watch the rent in the dark clouds of German polyphony, and see shining through it the smiling line of an Italian coast and the gay dancers on its shore. This is not merely a vague analogy. It would be easy, if idle, to notice unmistakable reminiscences of France and Italy even in Strauss's most advanced works, such as "Zarathustra" and "Heldenleben." Mendelssohn, Gounod, Wagner, Rossini and Mascagni elbow one another strangely. But these disparate elements have a softer outline when the work is taken as a whole, for they have been absorbed and controlled by the composer's imagination.

His orchestra is not less composite. It is not a compact and serried mass like Wagner's Macedonian phalanxes; it is parcelled out and as divided as possible. Each part aims at independence and works as it thinks best, without apparently troubling about the other parts. Sometimes it seems, as it did when reading Berlioz, that the execution must result in incoherence, and weaken the effect. But somehow the result is very satisfying. "Now, doesn't that sound well?" said Strauss to me, with a smile, just after he had finished conducting "Heldenleben."*

But it is especially in Strauss's subjects that caprice and a disordered imagination, the enemy of all reason, seem to reign. We have seen that these poems try to express in turn, or even simultaneously, literary texts, pictures, anecdotes, philosophical ideas, and the personal sentiments of the composer. What unity is there in the adventures of Don Quixote or Till Eulenspiegel? And yet unity is there, not in the subjects, but in the mind that deals with them. And these descriptive symphonies with their very diffuse literary life are vindicated by their musical life, which is much more logical and concentrated. The caprices of the poet are held in rein by the musician. The whimsical Till disports himself "after the old form of rondeau," and the folly of Don Quixote is told in "ten variations on a chivalrous theme, with an introduction and finale." In this way Strauss's art, one of the most

---

* The composition of the orchestra in Strauss's later works is as follows: In "Zarathustra": One piccolo, three flutes, three oboes, one English horn, one clarinet in E flat, two clarinets in B, one bass-clarinet in B, three bassoons, one double-bassoon, six horns in F, four trumpets in C, three trombones, three bass-tuba, kettledrums, big drum, cymbals, triangle, chime of bells, bell in E, organ, two harps, and strings. In "Heldenleben": Eight horns instead of six, five trumpets instead of four (two in E flat, three in B); and, in addition, military drums.

literary and descriptive in existence, is strongly distinguished from others of the same kind by the solidarity of its musical fabric, in which one feels the true musician —a musician brought up on the great masters, and a classic in spite of everything.

And so throughout that music a strong unity is felt among the unruly and often incongruous elements. It is the reflection, so it seems to me, of the soul of the composer. Its unity is not a matter of what he feels, but a matter of what he wishes. His emotion is much less interesting to him than his will, and it is less intense, and often quite devoid of any personal character. His restlessness seems to come from Schumann, his religious feeling from Mendelssohn, his voluptuousness from Gounod or the Italian masters, his passion from Wagner.* But his will is heroic, dominating, eager and powerful to a sublime degree. And that is why Richard Strauss is noble and, at present, quite unique. One feels in him a force that has dominion over men.

It is through this heroic side that he may be considered as an inheritor of some of Beethoven's and Wagner's thoughts. It is this heroic side which makes him a poet— one of the greatest, perhaps, in modern Germany, who sees herself reflected in him and in his hero. Let us consider this hero.

He is an idealist with unbounded faith in the power of the mind and the liberating virtue of art. This idealism is at first religious, as in "Tod und Verklärung," and tender and compassionate as a woman, and full of youthful illusions, as in "Guntram." Then it becomes vexed and indignant with the baseness of the world and the difficulties it encounters. Its scorn increases and becomes sarcastic in "Till Eulenspiegel"; it is exasperated with years of conflict, and, in increasing bitterness, develops into a contemptuous heroism. How Strauss's laugh whips and stings us in "Zarathustra!" How his will bruises and cuts us in "Heldenleben!" Now that he has proved his power by victory, his pride knows no limit; he is elated and is unable to see that his lofty visions have become realities. But the people whose spirit he reflects see it. There are germs of morbidity in Germany to-day, a frenzy of pride, a belief in self and a scorn for others that recalls France in the seventeenth century. "Dem Deutschen gehört die Welt" (Germany possesses the world) calmly say the prints displayed in the shop windows in Berlin. But when one arrives at this point the mind becomes delirious. All genius of many contemporary Germany artists is an aggressive thing, and is characterized by its destructive antagonism. The idealist who "possesses the world" is liable to dizziness. He was made to rule over an interior world. The splendor of the exterior images that he is called upon to govern dazzles him; and, like Cæsar, he goes astray. Germany had hardly attained the position of empire of the world when she found Nietzsche's voice and that of the deluded artists of the Deutsches Theater and the *Secession*. Now there is the grandiose music of Richard Strauss.

APPENDIX

In the above article, by Romain Rolland, Strauss is treated essentially as a symphonist. In recent years the composer has, however, devoted himself more especially to the composition of music dramas, which signalize a radical departure from his earlier ideals as exemplified in "Guntram," above described. The first of these, "Feuersnot" (Fire Famine), the text of which was written by Hans von Wolzogen, and which was first produced in Dresden in 1901, represents a transition to his later style. It adopts the concise one-act form to which he adheres in the two subsequent works, but does not abandon the spirit of romanticism which pervades the earlier work. It is, in fact, a poetic episode based on a simple mediæval folk tale, and is aptly called by its composer a "Singgedicht," or song-poem.

But in the next work, "Salome," produced in 1905, Strauss adopts an unprecedented kind of musical realism, amply suggested by the text, which is an almost literal translation of Oscar Wilde's drama. There are in this work passages of great

---

* In "Guntram" one could even believe that he had made up his mind to use a phrase in "Tristan," as if he could not find anything better to express passionate desire.

THE BERLIN ROYAL OPERA HOUSE

beauty, but the love music of "Salome" is frankly passionate and sensual, and the brutality of her blood-orgy is pictured forth with all the resources of modern orchestral tone-painting of which Strauss is master. This work established the composer's reputation as a musical dramatist, and was followed in 1909 by another one-act opera of very similar character, "Elektra," based on the drama of Sophocles, rearranged by Hugo von Hofmannsthal. In the musical portrayal of the psychological phenomenon of hate Strauss here uses even more complex and cacophonous means than in "Salome." Yet, if he sets himself no limits in the production of sheer ugliness to reach realistic effects, he also reaches heights of beauty rarely attained in his previous works.

A reaction from these expressions of passion and violence is represented by the comparatively romantic, sensuously beautiful and often frankly melodious "Rosenkavalier." This three-act work, also a setting of a Hofmannsthal libretto, was first produced in 1911 and has already become a favorite almost the world over. There are in it scenes of pictorial charm and of historical interest, impressions of eighteenth century life which ring true in spite of inherent anachronisms. There is love music of supreme beauty, tone-painting of the utterest *raffinement,* and, most important perhaps, a true inwardness of conception, a fine portrayal of the nobility of a human character capable of renunciation, a portrayal of the kind in which Wagner was master. "Rosenkavalier" has not unjustly been hailed as a worthy successor to "Die Meistersinger."

In his next work, "Ariadne auf Naxos," Strauss has made the somewhat dubious experiment of providing a sort of Italian intermède to be sung with a condensed version of Molière's "Bourgeois Gentilhomme." This piece has not had the success of its predecessors. A still later opera, "Die Frau ohne Schatten," has been completed since the outbreak of the war and is unknown outside of Germany.

Meantime Strauss, stirred by the success of the Diaghilev Russian Ballet, has written "The Legend of Joseph," a ballet pantomime, which, produced in Paris and London, does not seem to have added to the composer's reputation. The same may be said of his most recent essay in the symphonic field, the "Natursymphonie," a realistic portrayal of the scenery of the Alps, the beauty of which has presumably made a deep impression on the composer, whose summer home is in Switzerland. In its reflective moods this work has moments of beauty which recall in a measure Strauss's more youthful inspiration.   C. S.

SAINT-SAËNS IN 1846.
From "L'Illustration" in 1846.

CAMILLE SAINT-SAËNS

BY

PIERRE LALO

WORTHY persons sometimes regret that men of the present period reveal an ever-increasing tendency to confine themselves to the study of one single art or one single science, and despair of ever again beholding a Michelangelo or a Leonardo da Vinci. It must lighten their sorrows to think of M. Saint-Saëns, for he is possessed of genius of marvelous diversity. He has been, with somewhat unequal success, a poet, a dramatist, a mathematician, a naturalist, a philosopher, a critic, and a musician. His music itself — limiting one's self thereunto — is as varied as is his mind. There is no style that has not allured him: he has produced piano compositions, melodies, vocal numbers, symphonies, symphonic poems, concertos for all sorts of instruments, oratorios, cantatas, and operas. If one seeks to define his artistic personality, one is promptly embarrassed by contradictory qualities and defects. M. Saint-Saëns is classical by race and education: the firmness of his style, the strength of his architecture, the poise of his development, at once proclaim it. And yet the classicist readily expends himself in capricious fancies: he is the author of several celebrated harmonic acerbities, and his finest symphony

LAS PALMAS, GRAND CANARY,
Where Saint-Saëns has a summer home.

has scarcely any tonal scheme. Many of his works, in their perfect precision and clearness, suggest something petty, thin, cramped. But who can deny the grandeur and power of the symphony in C minor, or of "Samson et Dalila"? The latter achievement is admirable through its broad lines and its free motion, but nothing can be more fragmentary, more *sautillant* or skippy, than "Proserpine" or "Ascanio." M. Saint-Saëns has melodic ideas which are not devoid of savor, and others in which neither substance nor character is discoverable. But — and herein the contradictions are effaced — he presents these melodies of unequal worth with the most even and sure-handed art; develops and renovates them with the rarest abundance of resource, with the most subtle fecundity of imagination; shades them, varies them, transfigures them through the medium of instrumentation of prodigious suppleness and wealth. No one knows more than he, or better than he, how to use his skill. He can impart charm and brilliancy to the most ordinary things; of this he is, perhaps, too well aware. And all these qualities and defects make up one of the most complex and brilliant characters that France has ever possessed.

A study of all the works of M. Saint-Saëns could not be accomplished within the limits of the present article; a whole volume would not suffice.

I must confine myself to viewing his most significant and representative productions — those that will best serve to define the nature of his art and embody the most marked traits of his personality. To that end, I shall not busy myself with his songs. Although M. Saint-Saëns has composed a large number of melodies, many of which are beautiful and graceful, they in no way occupy the place melody holds in the work of a Schumann, a Schubert, or, to speak of a contemporary and a Frenchman, in that of M. Gabriel Faure. The melodies form no essential part of M. Saint-Saëns's talent; they add nothing to it. Nor shall I take into consideration his compositions for piano; although they are numerous, and written with extreme dexterity, and with the surety and perfect knowledge of the instrument one can expect from such a virtuoso, they are not sufficiently characteristic to exact much attention. The composer's chamber music claims closer observation, though it does not contain any of his master works. In France M. Saint-Saëns was one of the first artists that undertook to revive the cult of chamber music, suppressed during more than half a century by the exclusive predominance of the opera. He is the author of

SAINT-SAËNS IN TRAVELING COSTUME, 1869.

several sonatas, trios, and quartets, of a quintet, and of a septet; most of these are excellent works, solidly constructed, skilfully developed, and conforming in the most legitimate manner to classical tradition. These excellent works, however, have not generally much breadth or force; they are somewhat superficial; their musical substance is light and deficient in richness and density.

Summary as this review may be, it prompts one observation and conclusion: in works of this sort, intended for the voice, for one instrument or a few instruments, or written for "chamber" performance, in the production of which the composer's resources are limited, M. Saint-Saëns is not wholly himself, and is not revealed in his entirety. In order that his talents may develop in all freedom, he requires more abundant and complicated media: he needs the orchestra.

SAINT-SAËNS'S ROOM IN THE MUSEUM AT DIEPPE.
Presented to the museum by the composer.

When the orchestra is at his disposal the situation changes. Look at the second part of the oratorio "Le Déluge"—the division describing the covering of the earth by the waters. Here is nothing of pettiness, frailty, or lightness; the vast and mighty picture is adequate to the subject that inspired it; it is grandiose and formidable, and, despite the amplitude of its proportions, one never feels that the musician has exceeded his resources. This is proved by the ease with which he produces, varies, and renews his effects. The richness and might of the picture are really admirable. Of what, however, is "Le Déluge" fashioned? One can scarcely discern in it a melodic idea worthy the name, a theme that impresses itself upon the listener, or a decisive and impressive rhythmical form, such as often sufficed Beethoven for the construction of a whole division of a symphony. There is nothing in this entire long section but the orchestra. The orchestra gives the variety and imparts the grandeur;

the orchestra, inexhaustible in felicitous "finds" and novel contributions of timbres, sustains to the end the full weight of the task.

One might suspect that the composer was striving to win a wager; how few musicians could carry the feat to a victorious conclusion! "Le Déluge" is unquestionably the most brilliant and significant of M. Saint-Saëns's triumphs of this sort; it is by no means the only one to his credit. The instrumental works of M. Saint-Saëns include concertos, symphonic poems, and symphonies. One need not dwell upon the concertos, although they are certainly among the best that have been written since Beethoven, reconciling, too, very ingeniously the requirements of virtuosity, which must be considered in efforts of this description, with those of musical interest.

On the other hand, the symphonic poems merit special attention. The friendship and admiration that M. Saint-Saëns has always proclaimed for Liszt have from the first inclined him to follow the example set by the Hungarian celebrity, and impelled him to compose symphonic poems. It were useless to enumerate the drawbacks and defects of "program music"; the works of many contemporary composers have proved with sufficient clearness that by following a literary program too closely symphonic music loses its special form and worth, and ends by consisting of a series of disconnected fragments only. Liszt's own symphonic poems are not free from this defect, and many are, as to structure, vague and incoherent. M. Saint-Saëns, whose musical nature is not as exuberant as was Liszt's, but who possesses more taste, more poise, and a nicer sense of proportion, has in his works avoided excess. His four symphonic poems, composed upon very simple subjects, are from a musical standpoint constructed with great vigor. Literature does not direct or lead astray their music; it inspires it only, endows it with a special picturesque and poetic color, and opens new vistas to the auditor's imagination. "Program music," thus understood, escapes the slightest charge that may be brought against it. Its rights are established, in M. Saint-Saëns's performances, by perfection of detail, clearness and skill in the writing, and incomparable spirit and brilliancy in the instrumentation. "La Danse Macabre" is particularly admirable through the finesse, the supple lightness, and the brilliant vivacity of its build, as also through its logic and unity as a composition. It needs no program, and may be listened to as a division of a symphony.

Symphony. This word leads us to a still more important work, to one of M. Saint-Saëns's essential productions: the symphony in C minor. M. Saint-Saëns has composed five symphonies. Of the first four, two have not been published, and two others appear to have been neglected and disparaged by the composer himself. The fifth survives, and makes M. Saint-Saëns glorious in this domain. The formidable words "C minor" do not overwhelm the composer, and if his work must yield pre cedence to its immortal rival, it is at least worthy of following in its path. In point of form it is divided, in classical fashion, into four parts, connected two by two, thus concealing the traditional order. This, however, is but a superficial indication. The most remarkable characteristic of the score is that it grows, in its entirety, out of the expansion and transformations of a single fundamental theme, which serves as a center for the four divisions, and about which accessory ideas gravitate. The theme in question, uneasy and sorrowful as first presented by the quartet, enters into the most diverse symphonic and instrumental combinations. It mingles with the reverie of the adagio, sometimes passing from instrumental group to instrumental group, sometimes veiled beneath transparent variations. It is metamorphosed to take part in the fanciful scherzo, and again spreads out in flights and showers of brilliant tones. Then the finale commences, and a new change of rhythm makes of the original theme a chant. It is divided, broken up into fragments once more, and then brought together and gradually broadened out, while the vibrant blasts of the brass appear to acclaim its triumph. In its first form, this theme, like many other themes of M. Saint-Saëns's, impresses one as quite indifferent; but it is varied, developed, and adorned by an imagination so abundant and fecund that it takes on unexpected savor and worth; through its numerous transfigurations it assumes splendor, significance, almost grandeur. Instrumentation is in this instance, as usual, M. Saint-Saëns's mightiest and most precious ally; the soft richness, the clear solidity, the supple dexterity, and the sparkling diversity of the composer's orchestration cannot be too loudly eulogized. Two new elements add to its resources: the piano, employed as an orchestral instrument, and the organ. M. Saint-Saëns introduces them resolutely into the symphony, and does well, for they produce special effects, the piano by legato passages for two and four hands, impracticable for the harp, and the organ by sustained tones and sudden and magnificent reinforcements of orchestral sonority. Through its magical instrumentation, and its supple, ingenious, and elegant architecture, the C minor symphony is the most important of French symphonies, and one of the most memorable works of that order written in any land since the death of Beethoven.

The vocal and instrumental works of M. Saint-Saëns are of two kinds: oratorios and operas. The most noteworthy of the oratorios, with "Le Déluge" already mentioned, is undoubtedly "La Lyre et la Harpe," a very noble and fascinating score, which may be regarded as one of the composer's best works.

In our musician's productions in the dramatic genre one marks the most obvious contradictions as characteristic of his talent. The list includes five or six achievements such as "Proserpine," "Ascanio," "Henri VIII," and "Etienne Marcel," all cleverly written works, no doubt, but inconsistent, divided into numerous small and ill-matched fragments, treated in different fashions, and leaving upon the auditor a confused impression. It includes, too, a masterpiece in point of symmetry, breadth, and unity: "Samson et Dalila." The strange fondness that M.

SAMSON.
From the painting by G. F. Watts.

Saint-Saëns has usually shown for historical and melodramatic librettos may have some bearing on this contradictory condition of things. Either through natural inclination, or in order to array himself in opposition to the Wagnerian theory as to the need of simple legendary subjects in which the feelings and passions are dominant, M. Saint-Saëns has always insisted upon transforming into operas romances of adventure or chapters from French or English history; in other words, upon setting to music many things that are not suited to music. Only once has he happened upon a good libretto, and on this he wrote "Samson et Dalila." The book of this opera, whatever may be said upon the subject, is a good lyric book. Music requires action rather than a plot, and especially internal action, bringing into conflict essential feelings. These must not be too numerous or complicated; they need only be profound. Such are the principal conditions of a good opera book. They are found in the story of Samson; in the example — one of the oldest and most pathetic known — of female treachery. M. Saint-Saëns has made admirable use of it. "Samson et Dalila" is about sixty-five years old. It was disregarded for a long time, then came forth at the Eden Theater, and was transferred two years later to the Grand Opera. Time has neither enfeebled nor aged it; the flight of years has not lessened the respectful admiration it commanded from the first. It is, in truth, one of the most substantial, earnest, and noble efforts that modern lyric art has produced; it is one of the most classic, too, if the qualities of a classic work are order, proportion, regularity, clarity, and reason. It may be somewhat deficient in passion; or, rather, the passion expressed is less violent, less savage, in its accents than might be expected of a Delilah. But if passion is now and then lacking, the work is never wanting in style, and the style is superbly beautiful and elevated, always eloquent, always forceful, and of equal might in the expression of all sentiments. There are few feeble points in "Samson et Dalila," and the habitual weakness of the composer in respect to melodic invention is less apparent than in his other works; M. Saint-Saëns's most striking themes are found in "Samson et Dalila."

Such is, to our vision, in its most characteristic traits, the musical personality of M. Saint-Saëns. He is one of the greatest of French, one of the greatest of modern musicians. If he has not the steady nobleness and the depth of Cæsar Franck, the sensual ardor and melodic grace of M. Massenet, or the concentrated force and rigorous scholasticism of Johannes Brahms, he has more suppleness, ease, and dexterity than has any one of these musicians; his genius has more resource and fancy. I use the word "genius" intentionally: for a long while many persons, because M. Saint-Saëns's melodic imagination often lacks definiteness or personality, have affected to deny him the innate qualities of inspiration, and recognized in him only the qualities acquired by study and knowledge. This because, for the masses, melody proceeds only from inspiration, and all else in musical art is the product of the musician's trade. There prevails no more erroneous opinion. The musician invents not only in the realm of melody, but in that of harmony and of the orchestra; there is, too, invention in rhythm, and invention — which I almost incline to proclaim the noblest, most precious, and rarest — in the realm of musical development, construction, and architecture. One does not learn to compose beautiful harmonies, beautiful orchestral sonorities, ingenious or impressive rhythms, or vast and mighty symphonic structures, any more than one learns how to find pleasing melodies. None of these things, in its essence, is the outcome of knowledge or of a trade; all are the offspring of art and inspiration. And melody, in the totality of music, is not a much more considerable element than are its other components. It is, of course, the most easily comprehended; but it enjoys no privileges of divine right, and harmony, rhythm, orchestration, and structure are equally important factors in the art of sounds, and equally useful for the greatness of an artist. M. Saint-Saëns possesses in an eminent degree at least two of the essential qualities: he has orchestral inspiration and "architectural" inspiration, if I may so put it; these are sufficient for his glory.

THE SINGING BOYS

From the Painting by Frans Hals

A DANCE OF BOY ANGELS.
In the Salon at Houghton.

CÉSAR FRANCK

BY

VINCENT D'INDY

THE 9th of November, 1890, there died, in the full vigor of his talent, an artist of genius, whose name was then almost ignored by those we know as the "great public." This name has gained little by little in celebrity, and now commands the respect and admiration of all musicians, in an equality with those of our greatest masters.

His obsequies were as simple as his life: no official delegation from the ministry or from the administration of the Beaux Arts accompanied his remains to their last resting-place. Even the Conservatory of Music, although he had belonged to its corps of instructors,—the Conservatory, whose directors were accustomed to make it a duty to recite dithyrambics over the graves of empirical professors of singing or of obscure monitors of solfeggii,—was not represented at the funeral ceremony of this organ-professor, whose "advanced" theories had been reported dangerous to the tranquillity of the official establishment.

Only his many pupils, and the musicians whom his boundless affability had attracted to him, formed a crown of reverent admiration around the bier of this lamented master; for César Franck, dying, had left to his adopted country a school of symphony, alive indeed, and of such vigorous constitution as France had never before produced.

To obtain a good idea of the character of this great musician we should study him from three points of view—as man, as artist, and as educator; in other words, should consider his life, his work, and his instruction.

I. THE MAN

CÉSAR AUGUSTE FRANCK was born at Liège, Belgium, on the 10th of December, 1822. A few lines sum up his biography, because his career was without shocks or romantic convulsions, but flowed along in such calm of incessant labor as one loves to think of as belonging to the lives of the great artist-workmen in that beautiful time when art itself was new —lives to which that of Franck bore more than a resemblance.

Without fortune, brought up by a father whose extreme severity bordered upon egotistical cruelty, César habituated himself from infancy not to remain unoccupied a single moment. At fifteen he had finished his studies in the school of music in his native city and entered the Conservatory of Paris, where he won in a few years the prizes for piano, fugue, and organ, the last under peculiar circumstances which deserve to be related.

The competition for the organ prize includes, among other tests, a fugue upon a subject furnished by one of the members of the jury, and an improvisation in a free style upon a given theme.

César Franck, having observed that the two subjects admitted of being treated simultaneously, improvised a double fugue in which he led as second subject progressing with the other, the theme to be treated in free style, thus forming combinations for which the examiners were in no wise prepared. This might have ended badly for him, since members of this jury, for all that it was presided over by the aged Cherubini, understood nothing of this *tour de force*, accustomed as they were to the methods of the Conservatory, and it was necessary for Benoist, the titulaire of the class, to explain the matter to his colleagues in person, after which they decided to award to the young contestant the *second* organ prize!

It was perhaps from this moment that to those in office César Franck became "suspect."

After a short stay in Belgium, where he went to offer to King Leopold I his first trios, without obtaining any mark of thanks for the same, not even the traditional snuff-box in silver-gilt, he returned to Paris, where from that time he commenced that career of organist and professor which he carried on without cessation until his death. Thus it happened that from the beginning of the year 1859 the church (newly built) of Ste. Clotilde saw him every Friday morning and all day Sunday

VINCENT D'INDY.
From a photograph by Reutlinger, Paris.

seated on the tribune of the organ. Those whom the kindness of the master authorized to assist at these offices will never forget the great artistic pleasure which they received from his inspired improvisations.

In 1872 Franck succeeded his old master Benoist as titulaire of the organ class in the Conservatory; but never did the majority of his colleagues consider as one of themselves this instructor who saw other things in art besides a profession. They made him suffer much.

Franck was, as I have already said, a worker; winter and summer he was on foot at six o'clock in the morning. He consecrated his first two hours to composition, which he called *working for himself*. At eight o'clock he took a light repast, and departed immediately afterward to give his lessons in all the corners of the capital, because, up to the end of his life, this great man used the greater part of his day in educating amateurs in the piano, even pupils in the pensions for young girls. He did not ordinarily reënter his home until supper-time, and then, though his evenings were disposed of in favor of his organ or composition pupils, he still found time to copy parts for the orchestra. Thus it was that during only two hours of morning work and a few weeks of vacation he thought out and wrote his most beautiful compositions.

If Franck was a worker, he was also a modest man. Never did he strive after honor and distinctions; never, for example, did it occur to him to canvass for a place as member of the Institute; not because, like a Puvis de Chavannes, he disdained this title, but because he did not consider that he had done enough to merit it, even though at this epoch the Institute counted in its ranks a number of musicians whose worth was very contestable, and certainly infinitely inferior to his own.

His modesty, however, did not preclude confidence in himself, a primordial quality for a creative musician when it is supported by a healthy judgment and exempt from vanity. When, at the opening of the course, the master, with his face illumined by his great smile, would say to us, "I have worked *well* during the vacation, you will see, you will see; I think that you will be content," we were certain that a chef-d'œuvre would soon come to light.

It was his pleasure to find in his busy life a few leisure hours,—a thing not easy to accomplish,—when he would assemble around him his favorite pupils, Henri Duparc, Camille Benoît, Ernest Chausson, and him who writes these lines; to them he would play on the piano some work which had been lately finished, singing all the vocal parts with a voice as grotesque as painful. And it did not appear to him below his dignity not only to ask our advice, but to conform to it if our criticisms appeared to him just and well grounded.

The foundation of Franck's character was goodness, calm and serene goodness, and his nickname *pater seraphicus* was just. His soul could not conceive of evil; he never believed the low jealousies which his talent had excited in the minds of his colleagues. He passed through life with eyes elevated toward a high ideal, without suspecting the inherent baseness of human nature—baseness from which, alas! artists are far from free.

This disposition was intensified in him to such an extent that he never perceived that his works were much too elevated and were conceived on too high a plane to be understood by his contemporaries; and that they were not comprehended when he brought them before the public. The applause of his friends, scattered here and there through the audience, produced on him the effect of unanimous approbation; and delighted at having procured them the pleasure of hearing his own works played by himself, he never failed to bow profoundly to an assembly which, if not hostile, was at least indifferent, because it had been forced out of its usual habit of mind.

In the summer of 1890, during one of his daily walks in the streets of Paris, the master, absorbed, no doubt, in the inception of a musical idea, did not awake in time to save himself from the shock of an omnibus, the pole of which struck him violently on the side. Indifferent to physical pain and unaccustomed to worry about himself, he made no break in his ordinary life of labor and fatigue. But soon pleurisy set in; he was forced to take to his bed, and not long after succumbed.

Such was the man.

As to physique, any one who had encountered this being in the street, with his coat too large, his trousers too short, his grimacing and preoccupied face framed in his somewhat gray whiskers, would not have believed in the transfiguration which took place when, at the piano, he explained and commented on a beautiful work of art, or when, at the organ, he put forth one of his inspired improvisations. Then the music enveloped him like an aureole; then one could not fail to be struck by the conscious will expressed in the mouth and chin, by the almost superhuman knowledge in his glance; then only would one observe the nearly perfect likeness of his large forehead to that of Beethoven; and then one would feel subdued and almost frightened by the palpable presence which reigned around the noblest and greatest musician which France has produced since Rameau.

CÉSAR FRANCK.
From a photograph by Pierre Petit, Paris, made in 1888.

II. THE ARTIST

To leave an enduring milestone on the pathway of art, which stretches out to infinity, all the poetry of thought, of color, of form, or of sound must add to invention and science, those two pillars of an artistic monument, a quality more rare than all others—*sincerity*.

In music, for example, it is incontestable that the great works which time has not deprived of value, from the "Selectissimae Modulationes de Vittoria" to the "Ninth Symphony" of Beethoven, and including the chorals and the "Passions" of J. S. Bach, have emanated, all of them, from artists sincerely expressing their inmost thoughts without considering glory and immediate success. The dramas of Gluck which will remain immortal are those he wrote after his evolution toward the expression of truth. "Iphigénie en Tauride" has aged less than many an opera composed in our day; but one now can no longer read the "Artamène" or "La Chûte des Géants" by the same composer. And it is curious to observe, in regard to the philosophy of art, that some thousands of operas in the Italian school, since Scarlatti,—a school which despotically ruled all the theaters of Europe during the greater part of the eighteenth century,—have fallen into a profound abyss—a fate the more merited because these mediocre works were composed with an eye to fashion, effect, and virtuosity only. This school continued through the beginning of the nineteenth century, contemporaneously with the pernicious Jewish school, and lived almost entirely because of its pecuniary success with the public. The operas of Halévy are now insupportable to the listener; it will soon be the same with those of Meyerbeer.

Sincerity is the necessary condition for the endurance of all manifestations of art, and it is the most important of all the qualities of a

the choruses of the unjust and the rebels in "Les Béatitudes," also the rôle of *Satan* in the same work.

It is then entirely natural that, besides composing pure music, wherein he excelled, César Franck was impelled by a talent, which his sincerity rendered conformable to his charac-

"AROUND THE PIANO."

The friends of César Franck. From a painting by Fantin-Latour (Salon of 1885), belonging to M. Adolphe Jullien. Reproduced by his permission.

creative artist. No modern artist has been more sincere in his life and in his works than César Franck, and none has possessed a higher degree of that touchstone of genius, artistic conscience. We may find in many works of this master the proof of this assertion.

An artist truly worthy of the name expresses well only what he has felt himself, and finds it difficult to reproduce sentiments foreign to his nature. Thus it is remarkable that purely on account of his disposition, too noble to suspect evil, Franck never succeeded in satisfactorily depicting human perversity. In each of his works those parts where he was forced to represent sentiments like hatred, injustice,—in a word, to express evil,—were incontestably the most feeble. In proof, read

ter, into the depicting of Biblical and Evangelical scenes ("Ruth," "Rebecca," "Rédemption," "Les Béatitudes," "L'Ange et l'Enfant," "La Procession," "La Vierge à la Crèche"), in which radiant throngs of angels, such as a Lippi or an Angelico might have dreamed of, mingled charmingly with one another to chant together the praises of the Most High.

Even when he was treating profane subjects, Franck could not depart from this, so to speak, angelic conception. "Psyché," in which he endeavored to paraphrase the antique myth, has a peculiar interest on this account. The work is divided into choral parts, in which the voices recite the fable while recounting and commenting upon it;

and into parts for the orchestra only, little symphonic poems designed to express the drama which ensued between *Psyche* and *Eros*. Now, without speaking of its charming descriptive parts, like the carrying away of *Psyche* by the *Zephyrs*, or the enchantment of the gardens of *Eros*, the principal piece, the love scene, if I may be allowed to say so, never seemed to me anything but an ethereal dialogue between a soul, such as the mystic author of the " Imitation of Christ" conceived of, and a seraph, descended from heaven to instruct her. Other French masters, Saint-Saëns and Massenet, for example, if called upon to illustrate this same subject musically, would infallibly have endeavored to depict, the one, physical love in its most realistic aspect (*vide* "Le Rouet d'Omphale"), the other, discreet erotism, very much à la mode in certain salons of the Quartier Monceau (compare "Eve" and "La Vierge"). I think that Franck chose the better part, and I even dare affirm that, in acting thus almost unconsciously, he has come the nearest to seizing the real significance of that ancient symbol which has received so many expositions in medieval and even in modern times, in a series which reaches up to and comprehends "Lohengrin."

It is perhaps because of this tendency of his talent toward the purely mystic that the two operas "Hulda" and "Ghisèle," although containing very beautiful music, are far from being as perfect works as Franck's vocal and instrumental pieces.

Passing to a point of view more especially musical, the real character of Franck's music arises from three very well handled properties: the expressive nobleness of the melodic phrasing, the originality of harmony, and the unattackable solidity of the synthetic conception.

César Franck was a melodist in the highest meaning of the word; with him everything sings, and sings constantly. He could no more conceive music without melodic line carefully defining the contours obtained by it and very clean, than Ingres could imagine a painting without impeccable drawing. And this melody derived a great deal of its expressive charm from the skill shown in the grand variation, such as only Bach, in his *chorals d'orgue*, and Beethoven, in his last quartets, have known how to write.

To the abundance of his melodic vein Franck's harmony owes its peculiarly original quality, because he considered music horizontally, following the *fécond* principles of the contrapuntists of the sixteenth century, and not merely vertically, as do the composers of the harmonic epoch. The contours of his melodic phrases give, by their superposition, aggregations of notes which produce a style that is interesting for other qualities than are displayed by the banal or incoherent suites of chords written by those who have only harmony as objective.

It is principally, however, in the domain of musical architecture, the basis of all composition, that the innovating genius of Franck knew how to create a place absolutely apart. He was the first to consider the works of Beethoven from the point of view of a cyclic style (works which no successor of the father of the noble symphonic form had dared to assimilate), and to employ a new mode of construction according to orderly and logical principles. In 1841, at the age of nineteen, he built his first work, the Trio in F Sharp, on two generating themes, which, combining with the special themes of each number, were enlarged according to and in the measure of their successive expositions, and thus formed a solid foundation for the whole musical cycle.

Furthermore, the preoccupation of his whole artistic life was to find new forms, while always respecting in the highest degree the immutable principles of tonal construction laid down by his predecessors. For the rest, it is almost impossible to explain by a literary medium, satisfactorily and clearly, in what his innovations consisted, and one will be more easily convinced of the progress which the Master of Liège accomplished in musical art by reading his music than by description. I should like to dwell for a moment, however, on certain compositions which merit particular mention and study.

"RÉDEMPTION"

"RÉDEMPTION," a symphonic poem in two parts and an intermezzo, was the first work in which the genius of Franck clearly demonstrated itself. As I assisted intimately at the evolution of this oratorio, as different from a classical oratorio as is a *poëme* of Liszt from a symphony of Mozart, I subjoin some details not to be found in the biographies of the master.

The poem is simple. Part first: people moving about in the shadows, which are the evil passions engendered by paganism; suddenly a flight of angels illumines space, an archangel announces the coming upon earth of a redeeming Saviour, and the people, filled with enthusiasm by this promise, repudiate their hatreds and unite their voices in a Christmas chant.

Part second: humanity, having forgotten the precepts and benefits of the Redeemer, delivers itself afresh to its evil ways, but cries out its misery to the Christ; the angels veil their faces with their wings so as not to see the crimes of the people; then comes the archangel, prophesying in a graver tone than before a new redemption for the repentant, and the quieted people chant in a canticle the union of love and mercy.

Between the two parts an intermezzo for orchestra serves to synthesize the new evolution of humanity, proclaiming by an enlargement of the prophetic theme the final triumph of sublime love.

In order to express by music this progress toward the light, Franck imagined it as beginning in a neuter tone, A minor, symbolizing pagan darkness; then rising little by little into the exceedingly clear tonalities of E and B major, he used in a unique way sharpened notes through the length of the work. The effect of gradual illumination due to this tonal disposition is magical.

Long was the elaboration of this beautiful poem into music, into the expression of which the master put all his heart and all of his naïve and pious enthusiasm; it was commenced before the war of 1870, but not finished until 1872, and suffered a large number of successive remodelings.

Originally the first part ended in F sharp major, but at the first performance the violinists, according to a tradition dear to orchestral artists which happily shows a tendency to disappear, having declared that this unaccustomed tonality rendered their part unplayable, Franck felt himself obliged—a little, too, because of our advice (we were sorry for it afterward)—to transpose to E major the fulgurous air of the archangel and the final chorus. This, although it facilitated the execution, diminished the luminous effect as it was dreamed of by the master.

The intermezzo of the orchestra was also subjected to retouches so numerous and important that the second version bears scarcely any relation to the first. This complete making over of a long symphonic movement, which was already finished and engraved, is a very interesting example of an artist's conscience; but it is to this conscience that we owe the blooming of the superb melody which constitutes the principal idea of this intermezzo.

Finally, a chorus, somber in its very striking harmonies, was added to the commencement of the second part to make a contrast to the brightness of its close. The first hearing of this composition, so novel in all respects, took place in the theater of the Odéon, on Holy Thursday of the year 1872, under the direction of Colonne, who at the same time made his début as leader of the orchestra; but as Massenet, whose sensual opera, "Marie Madeleine," was on the same program, absorbed to his profit the major part of the applause, the performance of "Rédemption" was mediocre and made no impression upon the audience, who waited impatiently for the mystico-sensual sweets then so much à la mode.

"LES BÉATITUDES"

WE touch here upon one of the crowning works of Franck, one of those splendid edifices which range themselves on the highway of art as if to show the charm of a new departure, and which disdainfully withstand the injuries of man and time.

A paraphrase of the Sermon on the Mount, this oratorio, a concise expression of the moralities of the Evangelist, is divided naturally into eight parts, each one representing antithetically a double tableau; for example, the violent and the gentle, the simple and the proud, the cruel and the charitable. Toward the end of every part a song arises, calm and grand; it hovers over the miseries of mankind. It is the voice of Christ which we hear, commenting briefly upon the text of the beatitude. This divine melody, so intensely expressive that one cannot forget it from the moment that it appears in the prologue, does not attain to its complete development until the end, but it becomes then so sublime that when one hears it rolling out so majestically it is as if one saw the clouds of incense mounting up under the vaults of a cathedral, veritably assisting the radiant ascension of happy souls to the celestial mansions.

Notwithstanding these dazzling splendors, it is permissible to make a few reservations in considering this colossal work. It presents, in fact, inequalities of style which are sometimes shocking. Thus, as I have already indicated, when it is necessary to depict the climax of evil the characters of tyrants, of the cruel, and even of *Satan* himself, are a little conventional. Franck, not being able to find in himself the power of expressing what he does not understand at all, borrows from Meyerbeer's opera style, which makes a truly unpleasant contrast to the rest of the work.

Although it contains these few feeble points, "Les Béatitudes" is, none the less, the most noteworthy musical monument, in the genre of religious concerted music, which has been created since Beethoven's "Missa Solemnis," and this lofty and expressive work makes up for the emphatic bombast which certain modern composers, with an eye to effect, have heaped up under the disguise of sacred drama.

So great was the modesty of the author of this beautiful commentary on the Evangelist that he never imagined the work capable of being brought out otherwise than in fragments, and it was not until 1893, three years after his death, that it was given in its entirety at the *Concerts du Châtelet*, under the direction of Colonne. It made such a profound sensation in its ensemble that it was immediately adopted by most of the concert societies, French, Belgian, and Dutch, and still remains in their repertories.

THE QUARTET IN D

THE first movement in this Quatuor, for two violins, alto, and violoncello, is certainly the most astonishing piece of symphonic composition since the last quartets of Beethoven. The essentially novel form of the first movement consists of two pieces of music, each living its own life and possessing a complete organism, which mutually penetrate each other, without confusion, thanks to the absolutely perfect ordering of their various parts.

All the composers who follow the Beethoven epoch keep, as to form, to the types already established in the eighteenth century; neither a Mendelssohn, nor a Schumann, nor a Brahms dared to take the twelfth or the fourteenth quartet of Beethoven for a point of departure, and even Richard Wagner based his entire symphonic system upon the imperishable Ninth Symphony. It took an architect of sound as sure of himself as was César Franck to undertake a renovation of forms, while preserving in the movement a general classical style.

Finally, the Quintet in F Minor, and the superb Violin Sonata which Ysaye has made popular, are constructed, like the Quatuor, by the aid of a generative theme which becomes the germ of expression in the musical cycle; but nothing in Franck's work, nor in that of his predecessors, equals in harmonious and audacious beauty the Quartet in D, a type of chamber music unique, not only in the merit and elevation of its ideas, but also in its esthetic perfection and its novelty of form.

THE LAST THREE ORGAN CHORALS

I WILL pass rapidly over these chefs-d'œuvre of Franck, which were, as I have said, the last emanation of his genius, and the registration of which, though already in the grasp of the disease which was to carry him off, he fixed at his organ in Ste. Clotilde some days before taking to his bed, never to rise again. These chorals are written in the form of the amplified variation created by Bach and taken up again by Beethoven; but two of them, at least, have the peculiarity that the theme, though at first hardly more than a sketch, is the germ from which the variations develop, and which, at the end of the piece, brightens into triumphant completeness.

I will not speak of the other poems, "Ruth," "Rebecca," "Psyché"; the two operas "Hulda" and "Ghisèle"; the two morceaux for the orchestra, "Les Eolides" and "Le Chasseur Maudit"; the very beautiful "Symphonie en D"; the compositions for piano with and without orchestra; the nine great pieces for the organ; and the religious melodies. I will pass to the third aspect of the master, that of instructor.

III. THE INSTRUCTOR

CÉSAR FRANCK was, to all of the generation who had the happiness of being nourished by his healthy and solid principles, not only a clear-sighted and sure instructor, but also a father in art. I do not fear to use this name to characterize him who gave the light of day to the French symphonic school, because all of us, the artists who came in contact with him as well as his scholars, have always called him unanimously, and with one, though unconcerted, accord, *Father Franck*.

While the professors of the conservatories, especially of the Conservatory of France, to which one hardly applies except to compete for the first prizes, obtained as a result of their system of competition young people who were veritable rivals in their classes, and who often therefore became genuine enemies, Father Franck studied only to form artists truly worthy of this beautiful and liberal name. He radiated such an atmosphere of love that his scholars not only loved him as a father, but, which is more, through him, they loved one another, and during the eleven years that the good master has no longer been with us, his beneficent influence has so perpetuated itself that all his disciples have continued intimately connected, without a cloud to darken their friendly relations.

Yes, what an admirable professor of composition was César Franck! What sincerity, what integrity, what conscience, did he carry to the examination of the sketches which we presented to him! Unpitying toward vices of construction, he knew without hesitation where to place his finger, and when in the process of correction he arrived at passages which we ourselves would consider doubtful (though we took good care not to show it), instantly his large mouth would become serious, his forehead would wrinkle, his attitude express suffering, and after playing the passage at the bar two or three times on the piano, he would look at us and let escape the fatal "Je n'aime pas." But if in our stutterings we had chanced upon some harmony new and logically treated, some trial of an interesting form, then, satisfied and smiling, he would lean toward us, murmuring, "J'aime, j'aime." And he was as happy to give us this approbation as we were to merit it.

Permit me to add a personal anecdote relative to the manner in which I made the acquaintance of Father Franck.

After having ended my course in harmony and having aligned some troublesome counterpoints, without having studied either fugue or composition, I fancied that I was sufficiently instructed to write, and having with great trouble placed upon music-paper a quintet for piano and string instruments, I begged my friend Henri Duparc, one of the oldest of the master's scholars, to present me to the great artist whom I revered without knowing, in the firm belief that my work could not fail to win his felicitations.

When I had played the quintet to him, he remained silent a moment, then turning to me with a sorrowful air, he said these words, which I have never forgotten, because they had a decisive influence upon my life: "There are some good things; the ideas would not be bad, but—you don't know anything *at all!*" Then, seeing that I was much mortified by this judgment, which, I confess, I had not in the least expected, he added, with a corrective intention: "If you wish that we should work together, I could teach you composition."

While returning home that night,—for this interview had taken place at a late hour,—I said to myself, smarting with wounded vanity: "Certainly Franck is a spirit of the past; he understands nothing of the beauties of my work." Nevertheless, in a calmer mood the next morning, and re-reading this unhappy quintet and recalling the remarks the master had made to me while underlining, according to his habit, words in pencil, like arabesques, upon the manuscript, I was forced to own to myself that he was absolutely right: *I did not know anything.* So, almost trembling, I went to beg him to be so good as to admit me to the number of his pupils, and he placed

A MANUSCRIPT OF CÉSAR FRANCK.

Nocturne for the Voice, taken from the collection of M. Ch. Malherbe, in charge of the archives of the Paris Opera. Copy made by César Franck for M. Malherbe.

me in the organ class to which he had just been assigned as professor.

This organ class, of which I retain a vivid memory, was for a long time the real center of the study of composition in the Conservatory. At this epoch (I am speaking of the years 1872-73), the three courses called "advanced composition of music" (courses which hardly received actual instruction, but which led to the writing of a cantata for the prix de Rome) had for professors: Victor Massé, a composer of the second rank, having no leanings toward symphony, absorbed as he was all his life in the perpetration of mediocre operas comiques; Henri Reber, a musician advancing in years, narrow and behind the times; and, finally, François Bazin, author of some vulgar operettas, and also of a treatise

429

MONUMENT ERECTED BY SUBSCRIPTION TO THE
MEMORY OF CESAR FRANCK

In the Square Ste. Clotilde in Paris. The work of Alfred Lenoir.

on the fugue, a strange thing from a man who, as I can testify, was not capable of discerning whether a response in a fugue was false or exact.

[1] The monument to the memory of César Franck, the work of M. Alfred Lenoir, is to be erected in the Square Ste. Clotilde, in Paris. Subscriptions have been received from many French, Belgian, and German artists, and from the admirers and friends of César Franck. Additional subscriptions may be sent to M. Vincent d'Indy, treasurer of the César Franck Committee, 7 Avenue de Villars, Paris.

It is not astonishing, then, that the noble instruction of César Franck, founded upon Bach and Beethoven, but admitting all the passions, all the novel and generous aspirations, drew to him all the youthful spirits endowed with elevated ideas and really devoted to their art.

One of the precious peculiarities of Franck's lesson was the demonstration by example. When we found ourselves embarrassed in the construction of a musical idea or in the course of its development, the master would at once go to the library to search out some work of Beethoven, Schumann, Mendelssohn, or Wagner. "See," he would say to us, "this author found himself in the same situation in which you are. Read attentively the manner in which he got out of it; and while guarding carefully lest you imitate him, receive the inspiration which will aid you to correct the fault in your work."

It is thus that unconsciously the master drained, so to speak, all the sincerely artistic forces which were scattered through the different classes of the Conservatory, without counting the scholars from outside, who took their lessons in a quiet salon on the Boulevard St. Michel, where large windows opened upon a garden full of shade, a rare thing in Paris. It was there that we assembled once a week, because Father Franck, not content with instructing us in the science of counterpoint, fugue, and improvisation in his class at the Conservatory, made those of us whom he considered worthy of particular instruction come to him. This was absolutely disinterested, and not the ordinary rule with the professors of the official establishment, in which instruction is inscribed at least in the rules as gratuitous, though it is, alas! far from being so in reality.

When one had finished with Franck the study of counterpoint, which he wished to be always intelligent and melodic, and that of the fugue, in which he allowed a wide liberty of expression, then one undertook the study of composition, based entirely, according to him, upon *tonal* construction.

No art, in fact, has a nearer connection with music than architecture. To build an edifice it is necessary at the very beginning to choose the materials and to have them of good quality: it is the same with musical ideas, in the choice of which the composer must take infinite pains if he wishes his work to be of value.

But it is not sufficient to employ good and beautiful materials in construction; there must follow the knowledge how to dispose of them so that they will act together powerfully and harmoniously. Stones, carefully chiseled, but put simply in juxtaposition without order, will not constitute a monument; nor will musical phrases, however beautiful each may be, added together end to end make a piece of music. It is necessary that their place and their connection be regulated by an ordering sure and logical; at this price only will the monument endure; thus, if its elements be beautiful, and the synthetic order harmoniously combined, the work will be solid and lasting. The composition of music involves nothing but this.

This is what Franck, and he alone at this time, knew so well how to convey to his disciples. Accordingly, though for the first three quarters of the nineteenth century the symphonic production in France had been absolutely *nil*, there has been seen arising, suddenly, in the last thirty years, a new French school, full of creative vigor and daring, expert in the symphonic art and in chamber music, and surpassing artistically, by its solidity of construction, its clearness of form, and even its ideas, the symphonic school of Germany of the same period, which still drags along in the rut marked out by Mendelssohn. Father Franck's beneficent influence did not confine itself to the musicians who worked especially under his direction. It made itself felt also upon those scholars of the Conservatory who received his advice in the organ class: Samuel Rousseau, G. Pierné, A. Chapuis, Paul Vidal, G. Marty, Dallier, Dutacq, Mahaut, Galeotti, and others; upon the virtuosos who came in contact with him, among whom I will cite only the incomparable violinist Eugène Ysaye, to whom he dedicated the celebrated Sonata for Violin in A; and also upon those artists who, without being precisely his pupils, yet felt from contact with him the ascendancy of his probity and of his artistic sincerity: for example, Gabriel Fauré, Paul Du Kas, the illustrious organist Alexandre Guilmant, and Emmanuel Chabrier, who, in the name of the Société Nationale de Musique, of which Franck had been president, gave an address full of feeling at the tomb of the master.

The principal disciples who had the happiness of receiving directly this precious instruction were, in chronological order: Henri Duparc, the successor of Schubert and Schumann in the genre of song; Arthur Coquard

CÉSAR FRANCK AT THE ORGAN OF STE. CLOTILDE.
From the painting by Mlle. Jeanne Rougier, made in 1888.
Reproduced by permission of the owner, Georges Franck.

Albert Cahen; Alexis de Castillon, who died in 1873, at the age of thirty-six years, and who, after having received for many years lessons from Victor Massé (who seemed to try to annihilate the marvelous gifts of this beautiful nature), had the courage to recommence his entire musical education with Franck, and, having destroyed all his previous essays, wrote a great amount of symphonic and chamber music of the first order; Vincent d'Indy, the writer of this study; Camille Benoît; Madame Augusta Holmès; Ernest Chausson, author of "Le Roi Arthus," a lyric drama, and of very beautiful symphonies (he was prematurely taken away from the affection of his friends in 1899); the delicate worker Pierre de Bréville; Paul de Wailly; Henri Kunkelmann; Louis de

Serres; Charles Bordes, the young and already celebrated director of "Les Chanteurs de Saint Gervais," who are reviving in France the knowledge of real religious music; Guy Ropartz, now the director of the Conservatory of Nancy, to whom we owe some very remarkable symphonic compositions; Fernand Le Borne; Gaston Vallin; and, finally, poor Guillaume Le Keu, who died at twenty, leaving a considerable legacy of works of an intensity and expression almost amounting to genius.

It was principally to continue instruction such as Franck's and to perpetuate it that three men, scholars or admirers of this lamented master, Alexandre Guilmant, Charles Bordes, and Vincent d'Indy, founded, now some years since, La Schola Cantorum, a school of music whose principles are uniquely grounded upon love and veneration of art, without other prejudice. But even if pious friends had not been found to continue the work of didactic propaganda, nothing could have hindered the healthy and honest doctrine of César Franck from fructifying and spreading from one to another, because it is the verity of art.

Besides, nothing will prevent the productions of the master's genius from living in the future; and while the names of certain composers, who worked only for glory or for money, and strove for immediate success as their most desired good, are even now commencing to retire to the shadows from which they will never again emerge, the seraphic figure of the author of "Les Béatitudes" floats high and ever higher in the light toward which, without compromises or fatigue, he strove all his life.

Le Directeur du Conservatoire de Musique
et de Déclamation,

MARIA LUIGI CHERUBINI

Le Directeur du Conservatoire de Musique et de Déclamation

THE MUSIC OF MODERN FRANCE

THE century of alternation in lethargy and turmoil which evolved the exquisite musical art of Modern France presents interesting aspects that are wholly of France, besides many that are interwoven with musical progress in other countries. Of the historical features involved, none are more striking than those of asylum occasionally furnished to gifted foreigners while blindly ignoring, even opposing, some of the most gifted of her own. Neither Chopin, Liszt, Thalberg, nor Gottschalk was native to France, yet they were all taken up as would have been becoming to her own children. At times, between 1839 and 1861, even Richard Wagner found a few friends there. Then the great neglect of Berlioz—in a smaller degree also the fine genius of such composers as Alkan and Bizet, came with just so much force against the French spirit which could hate as violently as it could love.

The history of music in France for the nineteenth century also shows some strange analogies, principal among which is that between Glinka and Berlioz. Both were born in 1803 and their respective masterpieces for Russia and France were produced within the half decade beginning about 1835. The latter year marked the arrival of Berlioz's great opera, "Benvenuto Cellini," followed in two-year intervals by the "Requiem" and the "Romeo and Juliette" symphony. Glinka's "Life for the Czar," composed in 1834 and 1835, was first given in 1836, and his much more even and potent "Russlan and Ludmilla" came to the public in 1842. Upon the failure which was the temporary fate of "Russlan," Glinka went out into the world, and in Paris found Berlioz, whose own battles for recognition allowed him to sympathize to the highest degree. Berlioz helped Glinka to secure performance for some of his works, and life for the stranger became much more endurable. Within a short time, Berlioz also went out into foreign lands to find the success which was wrongfully denied in France, and in Austria and Russia he found some of the comfort which Glinka had secured in France and Spain.

At the beginning of the nineteenth century music in France was at a very enthusiastic stage through the recent organization of the Paris Conservatory, a distinctively Republican institution as against the old Monarchical institution of the Grand Opera. Violin playing especially was in high fame there through the co-operation of Rode, Kreutzer and Baillot. The newest symphonies by the young Beethoven were being given in Paris with the most creditable promptness. On that general momentum French musical life proceeded at a good pace for a couple of decades, until Meyerbeer and Halévy appeared and attained a popularity which for a time obscured not only Berlioz, but the young Wagner of "The Flying Dutchman" and "Tannhäuser." Wagner's earlier "Rienzi" had been very well received at Dresden in 1842, but his succeeding operas were to meet with difficulties, both in securing performance and the understanding of the people.

Henceforth France was to settle down into a lethargy of thirty years, until the death of Berlioz in 1869 and the first full realization of his genius through Reyer's festival of March, 1870. In our present view of the evolution, we know positively that the neglect of Berlioz in those years was paralleled by that accorded his own countryman, Ch. V. Alkan (1813-1888), who modestly preferred the career of a teacher-composer to that of the piano virtuoso, at a time when Paris was largely occupied with Chopin and Liszt. Meantime Alkan was composing works of so great content and character as to represent a complete revolution in the piano literature of that day, just as they have in part a potent meaning for ears of the twentieth century. As to Wagner, he lived in Paris for three years, 1839 to 1842, struggling against poverty. In 1849, upon his flight to Paris from Germany, the city was at a low ebb musically and there was no encouragement. He went to Zurich. He was in Paris again from September, 1859, until the failure of his "Tannhäuser," after three renditions, in March, 1861. Though he had the close friendship and artistic appreciation of many musicians and literary celebrities, the public would not yet follow. Then for the thirty years before the war with Germany, only the pianists Liszt and Chopin, re-enforced in 1841 by the coming of Gottschalk, had enjoyed the great popularity which was denied the genius of Alkan and Berlioz, although deserved. From 1835, for a few seasons, the Swiss, Sigismund Thalberg had already shared the popularity of Chopin and Liszt.

The history of musical progress in France for the period since 1870 has other aspects of the greatest moment and they should never be overlooked, since they are of a type likely to mark the history of every nation's progress. The prime lesson therein is this—that having had for a time no active art of her own, she borrowed from the furthermost parts of the world until her own gifted sons came forward with an art wholly individual, and the peer of any. In France the war of 1870 aroused the people to a sense of nationalism which was willing to accept Berlioz in his most extreme flights. It was the later combination of Berlioz and Wagner, adding a bit of Tschaikowsky and Grieg with the intense classicism of Franck, which prepared France for the peaceful revolution accomplished in 1902 by Debussy's "Pelléas et Mélisande."

Direct proof of the educative power and the occasional need of foreign influences is seen in the unfortunate experience of Bizet's "Carmen." From 1870 to 1875, the five years of willingness in musical nationalism, and the important success of the "Arlésienne suite," in 1872, were yet insufficient in public education to save the finest fruit of the life, which from earliest childhood, Bizet had given devotedly to

EMMANUEL CHABRIER

music. But when the hatred which war engendered had, by 1882, receded far enough to permit Lamoureux's playing of Wagner, "Carmen" also came into the esteem and full understanding which should have been accorded while the composer still lived, in 1875.

Nevertheless the extraordinary progress which musical France made after 1870 had not been possible either to foreign or domestic influences alone; rather it was accomplished through the most intense application of every imaginable force which could lead, coax or educate the French public to the acceptance of new and extreme conditions in music.

As early as 1851, Jules Pasdeloup had made an attempt to improve and intensify Parisian concert life by establishing the "Society of Young Conservatory Artists." After some success and many vicissitudes in this concert giving, he was enabled ten years later to reorganize for the famous "Concerts Populaires," which rather happily existed until the outbreak of war. Meantime, in 1869, during a brief directorship of the Théâtre Lyrique, Pasdeloup had given Wagner's "Rienzi," though under conditions of heavy financial loss. After the war he was enabled to resume concert-giving by the aid of an annual government subsidy of twenty-five thousand francs, and his activity thus extended to 1884, when the competition long since arisen through the finer artistic results of the Colonne and the Lamoreux concerts, made it no longer necessary nor advisable to continue.

Before proceeding to notice the activity of various other organizations which strongly contributed to progress, it should be observed that before 1870 there was no place where a modern composer could get a hearing for his works, except by hiring his own orchestra and hall. Even Berlioz and Wagner were constrained to undergo this responsibility and in nearly every instance with heavy loss. Then aside from Pasdeloup's earliest concert-giving by conservatory students, the one other important organized attempt at concert culture had been Emile Lemoine's Society for Chamber

VINCENT D'INDY

Music, established in 1860, which had but a short existence.

Briefly stated, the most potent organizations and forces contributing to the final redemption of musical France, were the Société Nationale of 1871, and the "Concerts de l'Association artistique," founded in 1873 by Colonne, and where honor to Berlioz reached its highest in about 1880. The Lamoreux concerts also began in 1882 a brisk promotion of the public acquaintance with Wagner, and, after the usual years of contention, by 1885 the Wagnerian philosophy dominated all discussions of art and literature in Paris; by the year 1890, when César Franck died, the time had come to rebel against so much Wagner, and there were introduced new elements represented by such as Tschaikowsky and Grieg. In 1892 the "Chanteurs de St. Gervais" were organized to perpetuate the César Franck traditions in the new-classicism. The Schola Cantorum, in further opposition to Wagnerian influences, was organized in 1894, by Vincent d'Indy and Charles Bordes. Within the next ten or eleven years, there came also the "Ecole superieure de Musique," under d'Indy; the "Nouvelle Société Philharmonique de Paris," under Emanuel Rey, and in 1905

Victor Charpentier's series of free concerts known as "L'Orchestre."

All of the above named activities had been unavailing but for the powerful and all-permeating agencies enlisted for the enlightenment of the masses. In 1871 music lectures were instituted at the Conservatory of Paris, and in 1893 the presentation of musical theses was begun at the Sorbonne. In 1889 the French Government sent Charles Bordes to assemble the folk songs of the Basque country and he issued a highly valuable report entitled "Archives de la Tradition Basque," besides giving modern orchestral setting in a "Fantaisie" and a "Rhapsodie Basque." In 1895 valuable collections of French folk songs were distributed to the pupils of the common schools of the Republic. From 1900 to 1906 Maurice Buchor was busily engaged in the revolutionary and quasi-vandalistic process of setting the great German choral classics to modern, French-nationalistic poems. In this radical manner he soon had children all over France singing the choruses from Beethoven's "Fidelio," Schumann's "Faust" and Handel's "Messiah." The years 1903-1904 found the national attitude so changed that the music periodicals were presenting such topics as "Influence of German Music on France" and "Present Conditions of Music in France." Nevertheless, at any time within the two decades just preceding those years, one might have found music-literary discussions by such strong leaders as Saint-Saëns, d'Indy and the much younger Debussy, all lending the most valuable aid through the technical and daily press.

Ignoring for awhile the history of public prejudice and gradual conversion as indicated in the foregoing exposition, it will be of interest to examine the inner character of compositions which emanated from the different schools within the French nation itself. For it is certain that on the way from Berlioz to César Franck, music harmonic texture had a long journey, and from Franck to the Debussy of "Pelléas et Mélisande," lay another great stretch in evolution, though in chronology it was but little more than a decade.

Going back to the Berlioz of 1840, the texture and the message he had to convey in music was sufficiently new to repel the French public, yet it was not in advance of his contemporary, Robert Schumann; and though Berlioz could not succeed in his native land, he was promptly taken up in Central and Eastern Europe, just as Schumann was also enabled to bring his works before the German public with seldom a delay or a disappointment. Furthermore, Schumann had the power greatly to influence Tschaikowsky and Rubinstein, not to speak of the horde of his own countrymen who drank at the same fount. Doubtless the Berlioz influence upon the instrumentation of Wagner and Liszt, still further upon that of Bruckner, and yet a full half-century later upon Gustav Mahler, was ultimately as great as Schumann's, but Berlioz did not live to receive credit, either in honor or in this world's goods.

As for Bizet, there was no valid excuse for the failure of his "Carmen," except that as drama the moral status of the heroine may have been given consideration over all other problems of music or tragedy; thirty years later the tremendous musical and dramatic inspiration of the Richard Strauss "Salome" was put to the same test, but the great lyric beauty of the music and the better education of the public rightly prevailed, and the work ran to hundreds of performances throughout Europe. Judged for the respective modernity in the periods of their creation, and for the innate power of their messages, there is hardly anything to choose between them, and they should both maintain themselves for long generations to come.

One of the most striking of all aspects in the late nineteenth century of music history in France is the suddenness with which César Franck (1822-1890), as a radical harmonist, was superseded by Debussy; for within three years after the death of the old master, the very year in which "The Beatitudes" was first heard, Debussy was already occupying the ground with his much more radical string quartet, and only one year later there appeared his high color "Afternoon of a Faun." In the quarter of

CLAUDE DEBUSSY

a century that has elapsed since the appearance of those works the world has witnessed a veritable succession of other fine music-revolutionary feats, and still one feels a sense of amazement that compositions of such intricate texture were in existence so long ago. This impression is all the stronger for the fact that, notwithstanding the still more evanescent "Pelléas et Mélisande," of 1902, the outer world came to its highest point in Debussy worship only within the five years which began at about 1905. Through all such circumstances as the above, César Franck's fine place in history stands wholly unaffected, for he exerted a timely and a tremendous force in diverting French thought away from the general operatic and Wagnerian exclusiveness, back to the enduring uses of symphonic and chamber forms. Added to it all, there is the permanent fund of beautiful and vital discourse represented in his own compositions. There is further the rich fund of characterful and enduring compositions that have been written by his pupils, as by d'Indy, Chausson, Ravel, Dukas, Chabrier and de Ropartz.

Looking for a moment to the externals of Parisian concert life, up to the beginning of the world war, the French capital was showing a very large vogue in the appreciation of the Brahms *Lieder*. Simultaneously the great German lyricist was similarly honored throughout the intense musical life of Russia; now there have been thoughtful musicians who were in fullest sympathy with these various elements of Russian and French geography and German music, who felt that the Brahms cult could have only a brief existence in those lands, since the psychology of the peoples was so unlike that of Brahms. At first flush that argument seemed plausible, yet time may prove it erroneous, since the Brahms nature was pre-eminently lyric, and there has never been a time when either the Russians or the French were not susceptible to lyric beauty when presented in a language whose technic they understood.

In final comment upon phases of French music history for the nineteenth century, there appears a very striking fact relating to the particular nativity of the nation's composers—in effect, that among a mere thirty of the most gifted and best known, fully thirteen were born in the one city of Paris. In the study of the nativity of the world's other composers, this grouping within one city the birth of so large a percentage of the entire nation's gifted sons is an instance wholly unparalleled. It is a crushing argument against the French systems of education in vogue for that century—the lack of opportunity, not alone for Berlioz, Alkan, Bizet and Franck, but of the thousands who happened to be born away from the metropolis. For it is simply unbelievable that during the period in which Paris produced thirteen, the rest of the nation gave birth to no more than the twenty who were permitted to come to maturity.

SIGNATURE OF DEBUSSY

GIOACHINO ROSSINI

THE LEGACY OF THE CENTURY

THE EVOLUTION OF MUSIC FROM THE ITALIAN STANDPOINT

BY

PIETRO MASCAGNI

AT the mere thought of my broad and varied field a spontaneous enthusiasm incites me to the expression of ideas that have long tenaciously beset me — ideas by which I guide myself in that infinite realm of art wherein the soul vainly seeks peace and rest. I shall be sincere, but it is not my aim to diffuse dissatisfaction.

Let us consider the matter. "The Legacy of the Century" is the gift of the dying age to a new era, with no indication whatever as to whether we stand face to face with the dead or with the heir. I firmly believe that the new century will accept the inheritance of its predecessor in bulk and without reserve, because, as a whole, it is by no means a bad one. But if we of the new school (so called) desire to draw up an inventory of the bequest, how should we proceed? May we not be taxed with having sought to squander the patrimony of our grandparents, of our ancestors — treasures of rarest worth, resplendent with gems of "purest ray serene"? Happily, our guide into the new century is our great-grandfather Giuseppe Verdi; he holds us by the hand: our inheritance is safe.

ROSSINI AND VERDI THE UNBROKEN LINE OF GENIUS THROUGH THE CENTURY

I LOOK back, and to my searching gaze appears a vision of clearest light; one single line, unbroken, scarcely knotted, midway, by the impact of genius, encircles the nineteenth century. Rossini, Verdi: behold the symbolic vision of the century of melody, and beneath it, beneath that luminous heaven, see how numerous the other names of genius, how marked a continuity in the evolution of music.

I purpose to deal with our Italian art, especially the art melo-dramatic, neglecting nothing cognate to the general evolution of music, but giving prominence to the Italian melo-drama which in the nineteenth century has been the lever of all musical activity. I cannot imagine an Italian musician that is not a writer of melo-dramatic music; the blood of the symphonists courses not in his veins, but the need of producing melo-drama impresses me as natural, as imperative, to any composer born under our fair skies. There can be but two kinds of music, melo-dramatic and symphonic Chamber-music always belongs to one sort or to the other; the romance, the duet, the quartet, slender though the tie may be, can never be isolated from the parent root; and as in the trio and in the quartet one encounters the forms and developments of the classic symphony, so one always finds in the romance and in the duet the germ of melo drama. The construction of the symphony involves few ideas connected and developed by science; the melo-drama, on the other hand, requires many ideas and little science. One readily comprehends why the Italian, by

VERDI

his geniality and volubility, should naturally incline to melo-drama. No one will deny that Italians have always had an abundance of ideas.

These two radical characteristics of musical composition appear in accordance with the character of each several nation. The Latin races, in general, neglect and despise science in art; the Northern and Teutonic races make science the basis of art.

The nineteenth century has beheld the efflorescence of a new musical culture in Northern lands; it has christened and confirmed Russian, Swedish, and Norwegian composers, but the appearance of these new and valiant champions in the field of music has been greeted by the homage exclusively due to the will and power of science. England, on the other hand, has felt the influence of the French and Italian schools, and has sent forth operas and operettas impressed by the elegance and volubility of the former and the geniality of the latter.

ENGLISH MUSIC EXOTIC

A STRANGE country is England, considered from the musical standpoint. She has produced excellent composers, but without ever expressing a distinctly national character in her style of music. The invasion of German, French, and Italian musicians into the wealthy British Isles, undertaken unquestionably rather at the call of the *lira sterlina* than of the *lira musicale*, may account for the fact.

I witnessed in London the astounding success of a sort of operetta written by an English composer, who, in a twinkling, had scaled the heights of fame. The composer in reference, encouraged by his triumph, composed a serious melo-drama, a genuine one. Queen Victoria, desiring to have the new work performed in Berlin, wrote a brief note to her grandson, the Emperor William, warmly commending the effort of her favorite composer. One can easily imagine the care and pains with which the new opera was made ready and the importance given the first performance. I had the good fortune to be a spectator. This work met with complete failure.

It seemed to me, as I thought over the case of English musical evolution, that the English musician seeks to force himself beyond the limit of his powers, and that under the influence of foreign *maestri* to whom he has given hospitality, and encouraged by the success of artists from other lands, who are always admirably received in London, he does not measure his steps. Thus it comes that the music of the English people faces the new century void of any special character and with no definite goal assigned to its unsteady and sinuous course.

THE OTHER NORTHERN NATIONS EXHIBIT WELL-DEFINED SCHOOLS

ON the other hand, the other Northern nations present themselves with strength and compactness and with a definite purpose; they already tread a well-marked path. And why? Because their music takes its origin in their national folk-songs. In Russia, Denmark, Norway, the basis of musical culture is popular melody. I am thoroughly awake to the great influence of folk-song upon the musical development of nations. Music is a universal language; its purpose is to be understood by the people. It must, therefore, be born of the people's feelings, must be people's music.

A distinguished authority, writing in 1765, in the journal "Il Caffè," then published in Milan, observed that almost no nation of the world found pleasure in music foreign to it. How much of nationality, how much of popularity, lies in these words! I do not refer to such symphonic or melodramatic music as requires for its comprehension a certain intelligence common to all nations. I mean music imbued with popular sentiment, with national spirit; music that, freed from all discipline and formula, aims exclusively at uplifting the hearts of the people; music that must be the foundation, the principle, the affirmation of any school.

I have not time to consider the influence that popular music has had upon the artistic and intellectual evolution of such countries as Scotland, Russia, Denmark, Poland, and Bohemia. The development and progress of that musical culture, always based upon their folk-song, may some day be a potent factor in their artistic development. The theme is admirably suited to bear out the assertion that all principles of music must originate in the spontaneous expression of the people. Pietro Lichtenthal, in his golden dictionary of music, says that if in war-time soldiers were led to battle singing their folk-songs in chorus, victory would be secure. In the soul of every warrior the enthusiasm aroused by the familiar melody would have no limits; national melody would make each man a hero. We recall the ancient Spartans following limping Tyrtæus, the Athenian. In Italy, at least, the monotonous and anti-melodious drums have, in the nineteenth century, been done away with, and a broad and vigorous impulse has been given in our regiments to the bands, which are among the most beautiful and efficient expressions of patriotic, national, and popular feeling.

ITALY, SPAIN, AND HUNGARY, THE THREE COUNTRIES WHERE POPULAR MUSIC BEST FLOURISHES

THERE are, in Europe, three countries in which popular music flourishes with particular luxuriance: Italy, Spain, and Hungary. The three differ from each other in respect to manners and customs, and one is unlike the other two in point of race, and yet in their people's music there is something that imparts the same attractiveness and awakens the same enthusiasm. Does it lie in the expression, in the rhythm? I know not; but I do know that the music of each is born of the same feeling.

ITALIAN MUSIC

I WAS in Venice a few years ago. The weather was lovely, the skies were glorious, the *laguna* was fraught with ineffable charm. I was to depart by the evening train; a gondola awaited me on the Canal Grande, in front of the Grand Hotel. I hastily bade farewell to a few friends, for I wished to be alone. I felt, I know not why, strangely impressed. Perhaps I was grieved at leaving all this enchantment of art and nature. The gondola glided noiselessly over the middle waters of the Canal Grande, whose exquisite airy walls gradually passed from my ecstatic vision. The moon diffused its white and misty light, bestowing new colors and new shapes upon the dark waves and their marvelous surroundings. The cadence of the oar marked every instant of delight that swept past the heart as the indescribable picture unfolded. A soft harmony, gentle and suave as a caress, fell upon my ear from afar. I listened attentively; yonder, in the Canal Grande, they were singing a popular song, one of those sentimental Venetian mel-

A MEMORY OF VENICE.
Drawn by Robert Blum.

odies that draw their inspiration from the beautiful and amorous eyes of the women of the people. My heart overflowed; I sought about me for some object that should divert my attention, that might quickly arouse me from the ecstasy of body and soul. In vain, in vain! Everything was beautiful and sublime, everything added to my emotion. The sweet song continued; my eyes were full of tears. Oh, fascinating might of popular melody! How thou dost stir the soul to its depths and arouse a sentiment of pain almost physical! I have never escaped it while listening to a *canzone* of Piedigrotta's, a *bolero*, or a Tzigane "elegy."

THE POTENCY OF POPULAR MELODY AMONG ITS OWN PEOPLE

LET no one reproach me with my cosmopolitan enthusiasm by quoting an adverse axiom. The feeling that a people displays sis, will always remain incomprehensible to the foreigner who seeks to study it technically.

The enjoyment of a people in the music of its own land is, according to my own observation, far superior to that which can be given it by any foreign music. The Venetian *canzone* and *barcarole* instantly render the most ferocious Venetian gentle, soft, and kindly, though they would not even attract the attention of a slave-dealer. A Neapolitan *melodia* may be potent to arrange the marriage of a native pair, though it might pass unnoticed by the watchers of a seraglio. A dulcet Spanish dance has power to dissolve a throng of Spaniards into the abandon of a Southern siesta, but to the ears of the Chinese opium-smoker it would remain but a noise

HUNGARIAN MUSIC

THE effect of Hungarian national and popular music is strange and intense. It may be

MUSIC IN A PUBLIC GARDEN, BUDAPEST.
Drawn by Joseph Pennell.

in its character, its habits, its nature, and thus creates an ever-privileged type of music, may be apprehended by a foreign spirit which has become accustomed to the usages and expressions common to that particular people. But popular music, void of any scientific ba- defined as the gentlest of spasms, as agonizing suavity, as voluptuous pain. To comprehend this clearly one must have been in one of those night taverns of Budapest, when the Tzigane band madly strikes up a patriotic song, or tearfully sighs out a popular elegy

The first violin sings in strange and penetrating accents; the seconds, the violas, the cellos, and the double bass accompany capriciously and fancifully; the clarionet trills; the *cymbalon* compasses the whole gamut of sound and whirls it madly up and down, violin, sees, feels, imagines which of the auditors is the most stirred, the most ecstatic; he turns to him when he reaches the *cadenza* of the elegy and kisses his brow. The listener closes his eyes; perhaps he faints away. The players strike up the *csardas* with in-

SONTAG.
From a lithograph published in England in 1828.

welding and completing the characteristic polyphony into a natural and lovely harmony.

Thus the band sadly intones the "Hallgato nota." The few listeners drink no more; they seem to drowse; really, they think, with half-closed eyes, of their ideal; they behold a vision of the loved object, feel the delight of the coveted kiss, the shudder of the fancied embrace. The leader of the band, the first credible *slancio*. The listeners are roused; their eyes open wide; their hands clutch the locks of hair about their ears; their bodies are irresistibly convulsed. The music has changed, the scene has shifted, the feeling is transformed for the dance. Oh, the magnificent power of these expressions!

While I was in Budapest with an Italian friend, a Southerner from Bari, we dined at a hotel celebrated for its band. The drawing-room was nearly filled by a distinguished and richly attired throng; the band was tuning its instruments. I observed to my companion: "You will soon be able to determine which are the Hungarians and which the foreigners." My friend, like a true Southerner, silently expressed more by a motion of the head than words could say. The band was sighing forth a mournful chant. We beheld, with surprise, a part of the hearers, who were slowly laying knives and forks upon the table-cloth, almost imperceptibly raising their heads and closing their eyes in ecstatic sensuous indolence, while the remainder of the guests tranquilly and indifferently continued their repast. My friend understood at once; touching my elbow and smiling, he asked: "What, you? Are you, too, perchance a Hungarian?" He was right; the sweetness of the strains had overcome me also. When, according to usage, the youngest of the band walked around the dining-room to take up the collection, which constitutes the only salary of Tzigane musicians, in gratitude for the heavenly delight given me I offered something more than the usual fee. To my surprise, the Tzigane withdrew the plate and would take nothing. A waiter, acting as interpreter, explained the motive of his refusal. "We cannot accept anything from a colleague." How happy I felt over the title conferred on me with so much sincerity by the generous Tzigane! My bosom swelled with pride. Would to heaven I could find the rare song, could create the phenix-like melody that could, like popular Hungarian music, conjure such triumphs of enthusiasm! But I awoke to a sad disillusion. The Tzigane had used the word "colleague" in its closest, narrowest sense. A few nights previous he had beheld me, in a tavern, blindly whirled along in the vortex of a maddening csardas, snatch the violin from a musician and join furiously, despairingly, in the performance of music that has, in truth, been familiar to me since early childhood.

Must not popular and national melody of such strength and potency have tremendous influence upon the development and evolution of music?

I confess, however, that this germ which could produce other and far more savory fruit has been too little cultivated. Hungary, compared with Spain and Italy, has received most from its popular melodies, inasmuch as the national Hungarian opera, first created in the nineteenth century,— to be precise, by Ruzsieska, in 1826,— may be said to be the genuine outcome of folk-music. Erkel, the most celebrated Hungarian composer of the age, and regarded in his native land as the true creator of the national opera, has even employed in his works popular instruments such as the *cymbalon* and the *tilinko*, the latter a sort of *piffero*. I do not think I am wrong in asserting Erkel to be the most celebrated Hungarian composer of the century. Hungary has given other illustrious musicians, such as Hummel, Heller, Liszt, and Goldmark, but none of these is a national composer. It is impossible to find any influence of race or land in Heller's music, or, if we except the adagio of the "Sonata in A Flat," anything of genuine Hungarian character in Hummel's compositions. Goldmark discloses only the characteristics of the German school, and Liszt himself, in spite of the famous Hungarian rhapsodies, cannot, in my opinion, be included in the array of national Hungarian composers. Nor will his less celebrated and familiar efforts, such as "Le Carnaval de Pesth," "The Legend of St. Elizabeth of Hungary," or the symphonic poem, "Hungary," admit Liszt into the national Hungarian school. Without attempting a critical study of the genre of his music, and speaking of the evolution of art and its necessary influences only, I must ask how it comes that Liszt has had no influence upon the musical evolution of his country, or, I might add, upon that of any other nation? What trace has his music left in the history of art? What mile-stones has his art erected on the long road the musician traversed? I see nothing. There remains of Liszt the fascinating echo of the exceptional, well-nigh incredible executant. It may be said of Liszt, in the words of Albert Soubiès, that "he belonged to no school and held in art a unique position." By a courteous concession to the author of the "History of Music," he may be proclaimed a *génie à part*— a separate and isolated genius; but this does not make me discover in Liszt— it rather implies the reverse— any element of influence upon the musical evolution of the century. His Hungarian rhapsodies are nothing but artful acrobatism gyrating around original Hungarian themes which completely lose their character in the composer's skilful paraphrases. When one has once heard this music performed in its original form one can never adapt it to the oleographic paraphrases of Liszt.

Per contra, how admirably has Brahms known how to preserve the genuine national character of his Hungarian dances, and what a monument of perfect reproduction is offered by Berlioz in the superb Rakoczy march in "The Damnation of Faust," that imperishable national march which Hungarian patriotic spirit and the imagination of the people made a woman sing as she traversed Hungary to awake the populace and summon it to the rescue, to the redemption, of their land! But Brahms and Berlioz were not two separate geniuses; they were men of real and authentic genius who brought an incalculable contribution to the musical evolution of the century. Isolated and barren genius is inadmissible; genius, if it be genius, naturally and unconsciously finds the light not only in the shape of works that spontaneously germinate from its seed, but through the influence which these works themselves diffuse in an art epoch which, as the result of the evolution of genius, becomes historical.

SCIENTIFIC MUSIC NOT FRUITFUL

A DISTINCTION might, perhaps, be made: admit that artistic evolution implies a technical progress for which no genius is required, but merely a studious musician skilled in

GOLDMARK IN HIS STUDY.
From an amateur photograph lent by Mr. Adolph Goldmark of New York.

writing canons. I mention this distinction because nowadays one beholds a great many learned men, exalted in high positions and greatly honored, who would persuade people that art can be manufactured by scientific dogma. Poor visionaries! These very dogmas, these canons that are your sole means of creation, have been dug out of and scraped off from true works of art. No theory has ever been invented that can create art; but art in its development, in its evolutions, its new creations, produces the new theories that you, step by step, exhume and scratch off. You contribute to history your studies of art works, analyses, coördinations, lists of recovered formulas, but to art itself you tender nothing. Genius has been the sole donor to art and to history.

HUNGARY POSSESSES A NATIONAL OPERA, BUT IS THREATENED BY GERMAN INFLUENCE

THE nineteenth century has witnessed the dawn of Hungarian opera, which has undergone a notable evolution through the efforts of the composers Ruzsieska, Erkel, the brothers Doppler, Albert, François, and others, down to Mosounyi, who may justly be cited as the most faithful interpreter of popular Hungarian sentiment. I recall the fact that many foreign composers have found inspiration in popular and national Hungarian music. The magical influence exercised upon the souls of artists by this characteristic music may, when it is more generally studied and cultivated, bear unexpected fruit. The balance-sheet of the century in Hungary, however, does not arouse much hope. German influence begins to exert itself even in that broad and typical land, and Conductor Mikalovich, the present director of the Budapest Opera House, represents, perhaps, the great danger menacing national Hungarian music. May the evil omen be averted! May strong and noble Hungary decisively cut itself away from all foreign schools and affirm itself anew in its glorious national music!

FOREIGN ART CANNOT BE GRAFTED UPON A COUNTRY

I HAVE written at length of Hungary, while I have been brief in dealing with Spain and Italy. It is not sufficient for the national character of a country to raise a *bolero* or a *siciliana* to the dignity of a recognized poem in order to establish the influence of popular music in the evolution of art — I refer to periods preceding the nineteenth century; otherwise, what could be said of the *polacca*, which in its season of popularity invaded even Germany, France, and Italy? The history of art awaits far different fruits from the influence of national music. Nothing is more useless to the artistic evolution of a country than foreign influence. In so far as genius imposes itself upon the whole world, it is true that art has no country; but the production congenial to one country, informed with its personal and natural character and bearing the stamp of its origin and race, will always exercise a negative influence upon a land foreign to it. Such lands will submit to its potency with effort and reluctance. I do not admit that grafting can be practised in art. Each nation must progress and develop itself through its own forces and germinate from its own seed.

MUSIC IN SPAIN

I DEPLORE the ill-prepared and disjointed conditions which England presents to the new century, and, similarly, I observe that Spain has submitted to the absolute dominion of Italian music during the entire nineteenth century, giving no sign of a desire to shake off the yoke or to gather strength for freedom in the memories of her glorious musical past. In the words of Albert Soubiès, "her once vigorous national art which formerly produced masterpieces has been replaced by a superficial and conventional Italianism." I see no reason to be proud of this Italian invasion. I have already proclaimed Rossini to be the most celebrated man in Europe, from Naples to St. Petersburg. In Spain his influence was so great that he found imitators even among the composers of church music. While his incursion never took very deep root, we find few indications during the nineteenth century of the return of Spanish music to its national color, and these consist exclusively of works of buffo character. The apathy of Spain is quite incomprehensible in view of the glorious past of her national music. Even as we must inscribe a few names on the credit side of England's balance-sheet (I include among them that of Mackenzie, a Scotchman), names that do honor to the art of their native land and will have no slight influence upon the development of its national music, so I am glad to place upon the credit side of Spain's account the name of Pedrell. Pedrell has been almost alone in point of influence upon the evolution of music in Spain, but he stands well prepared, well schooled, and self-reliant. His spirit is wholly national, and he does battle for the complete artistic redemption of his country. I can only express my sincere and reverent feelings of admiration for his noble work, without foreshadowing what fruits his sacred campaign may bear. I can, however, speak of his preparation and of the music he purposes to employ to attain the ideal he has set himself.

ON THE NORTHERN SCHOOL

But here a digression, and not too brief a one, is apposite. At the beginning of this paper, referring to Northern musicians, I observed that their achievements had been greeted with the exalted honors due to science. I have been perhaps too absolute and too sweeping in my statement, for throngs of listeners have had opportunities to admire the genial and melodious compositions of Tschaikowsky, Grieg, and Rubinstein. The uncompromising character of my opinion is, however, strengthened as to the opinion itself. I did not speak with reference to a special case. I intended to embrace a whole art system that, from my point of view, is appreciable only for its theoretico-scientific qualities. Here again I make use of an odious term, "art system," as though artistic production could be subordinated to a system — to a series of formulas; yet, speaking of Northern music, the term impresses me as fitting. Be it as it may, it came to me spontaneously.

ANTONIO TAMBURINI.
Celebrated bass-baritone (1800–1876). Sang with Grisi, Rubini, and Lablache at the Théâtre Italien, Paris, during 1831–42.

I except Norway, with Svendsen, a pure and masterly symphonist; and Grieg, the suave, amorous poet, the eternal singer of the soft language of his fatherland. I except Denmark, with Hartmann and Gade. I come to Russia, which, abandoning whatever influence might be exerted by the Polish music of Elsner, Kurpinsky, and Glinka, during the nineteenth century founded the "new school" with the composers Cui and Balakirew.

THE NEW RUSSIAN SCHOOL

I REVERE Russian music when it is the expression of national sentiment — when its vibrant and expansive accents penetrate my heart and seek its most responsive fiber. Then I feel that this music has something to express. But what place can Russian music (and there is much of it) hope to occupy when desperately void of all ideal or inspiration?

GIOVANNI BATTISTA RUBINI.

A famous Italian tenor (1795–1854), Director of Singing in Russia. From a French lithograph.

It may be argued that it is well written, but this convinces me the more that it is utterly useless and, therefore, harmful to the artistic development of its native land. I am certain that the young Russian school has had from its origin that defect the reverse of which would have been its greatest merit — complete preparation. The new school entered the lists armed *cap-a-pie* with formulated dogmas, canons, systems, and perhaps even weights and measures.

I recently attended the concert of Russian music given in Rome, under the conductorship of the director of the Conservatory of Music of Moscow. I except from the program a symphony of Tschaikowsky and a movement of a quartet of Rubinstein. Despite my uncompromising views, I admit the existence of exceptions, and how eloquent were the exceptions in this instance! But during the remainder of the program the most recondite and extravagant harmonic and polyphonic combinations succeeded one another without rest, without a ray of light. Every instrument was used in the strangest positions, to bring forth tones least familiar, the intervals least frequent, the modulations least in use. It was a very pandemonium of sounds, now fearfully acute and again bellowing in the depths of madly plunging dissonances and wildly distorted rhythms. All this was fashioned with art, with great art, but with that studied astuteness that gives to art, in Italian, the name of artifice. Let us admire and praise this artifice. But where is the ideal, where the inspiration, where the strength of influence upon the artistic awakening? It has been said that the young Russian school was founded on an independent basis, without puerile regulations, and with full freedom for its composers to choose and follow their own paths, while always keeping in view a goal where all were to meet to establish a new objective point, and then continue their individual advance. The idea is a graceful and seductive one; but we wonder whether in their progress somebody has not lost his reckoning. The new Russian school, in my opinion, is imbued with all the evils of technic and science — evils which, in its abundant productiveness, it keeps on developing to exaggeration and excess.

It is easy to talk of choosing the path of one's preference; but following such a path implies advance, unless we are to find the last stage of the journey, the final ideal to be attained, at the limits of the technical and mechanical methods that the Russian school apparently wishes to master. If so, let her give over this forced march; whether she reaches the goal set, or not, her progress will mark no point of importance in the intellectual evolution of the nations. Far different is the ideal which Russian music, possessed of much natural strength in itself, in its people, in the glory of its past, must finally attain. And if the limit assigned it by its own desire appears too close, let the gaze extend beyond the slender boundary line and behold the deep oases that attract the far-reaching and luminous vision. Let the mind recur to its true goal, its final stage; at the sight of the splendid vision of life and serenity which awaits it, let not the soul sink in despair; let it break forth in a spontaneous, irresistible aspiration toward the sublime ideal. A pale and gentle presence stands silent and sorrowful in the midst of the iridescent oasis. It is Chopin — Chopin, the great poet of music, the most lyrical of the lyrists of the century, as Sanzacchi has said. Hush! He sings — sings the woes of his oppressed Poland, though he seems to sing the sorrows of all suffering lands and all bleeding hearts. Chopin! Chopin! What a guide for the new school! what a future! what an aspiration! In Chopin's name I embody the evolution, the redemption, of Russian music. I trust that the first period of the existence of the new school will have for its sole object the extirpation of all foreign influence upon the nation. Russia can, and must, aspire to a great musical future.

SPANISH MUSIC, LIKE RUSSIAN, TOO LABORED

HERE I bring to a close this long digression, with the preconceived idea of wondering whether Pedrell did not appear in the arena armed with weapons identical with those of the new Russian school. In all his admirable esthetic studies Pedrell distinctly reveals a strong sympathy for the theories of the young Russians. Like them, he aims with great energy at emancipating his country from foreign influence. But one must remark that if foreign, and especially Italian, influences only retarded in Russia (perhaps by exacting it) the birth of a national art, which was still groping in the obscure conscience of the nation and had not yet issued from the prehistoric limbo, the same influence in Spain reduced to submission — literally put to sleep — the national art once so proud and great. Hence the double merit of Pedrell if he succeeds in the task he has set himself.

Soubiès, who has written intelligently and industriously of the music of the different countries, offers a characteristic comparison between Pedrell and the new Russian school. He thinks that Pedrell follows César Cui, one of the founders of the new Russian school, in his reservation in respect to Wagner. Pedrell would have what is sung by the characters on the stage well in the foreground, not covered by the orchestra and eclipsed by the complicated polyphony of the instrumentation. As to the *leit-motif*, he accepts it, but not without resorting to all kinds of precautions and restrictions. Wagner has composed the German lyric drama; Russia, declining to Germanize itself, seeks, above all, to be Russian. Even so, Pedrell, in the presence of the German masterpieces, sustains the rights of the Southern races. Face to face with the works of the artists of the North, he invokes the names of Calderon and Lope de Vega.

These are fine words, unquestionably, but to me they appear as so many systems that can add no power to the influence that should agitate an artistic evolution impelled solely by the breath of a creative and innovating spirit. May the genius of art assist Pedrell! Musical Spain to-day awaits everything from him. Happy am I to send him a greeting from that fair Venice that was first to listen to "The Pyrenees," with which Pedrell has endeavored to realize the ideal of his esthetic study, of his protracted aspiration.

ITALIAN SACRED MUSIC

I HAVE not yet reached the kernel of my subject. A special episode in the evolution of music claims consideration. I cannot neglect nor hint incidentally at the evolution of sacred music. I shall not ask why Italy has had but few and barren examples of great performances of the classic oratorios of celebrated composers when during the entire century Germany and England have admired them. In reaching the logical conclusion I purpose to establish, I shall deal exclusively with Italy itself, which offers a remarkable and characteristic example of evolution.

Sacred music has been treated in Italy, during almost the entire century, with general and unpardonable neglect. Despite the influence of Cherubini, even his contemporaries began to write church music that savored too much of the theater. Perhaps the faithful may have derived enjoyment and religion may have profited; but the error grew to such proportions that the temples of God often sank below the plane of the lowest and most trivial playhouses.

Pacini himself, Mercadante even, could not

stem the tide. A few glimpses of clearing skies followed those lightning-flashes of genius — Rossini's "Stabat Mater" and his Mass. But the foundation of the religious music of the period was theatrical. Rossini, perhaps, felt this with the intuition of his great mind, when, on the last page of his Mass, he asks of the *Buon Dio* whether his music was sacred or damned, words that in French constitute a witty *bisticcio*, one of those "final conceits" to which Rossini cheerfully sacrificed even his "Petite Messe."

What, I may be asked, do I understand by the term "sacred music." Music, I reply, which satisfies the requirements of Lichtenthal:

"*First*: THE CANTILENA OR MELODY should be simple and dignified in a high degree, free from all frivolous motion (rhythm). Its character, be it gay or sad, should always be noble; hence the forms peculiar to dance music should be avoided.

"*Second*: THE HARMONY should be so chosen as to produce the effect of solemnity, grandeur, and simplicity. Rapid and startling transitions, marked digressions, should occur only where the text expresses strong contrast. The legato style is preferable, because, while possessing most importance and variety, it serves at the same time to express the sublime, which must have the first place in sacred music. Choruses and numbers for several voices acquire much greater impressiveness when the counterpoint, of which the fugue is the capital portion, is adequately handled.

"*Third*: THE SONG, besides being simple, should contain no difficult or far-fetched passages, nor vain and useless ornaments.

"*Fourth*: THE INSTRUMENTATION should bear a due proportion to the character of church music; for the gay, brilliant orchestration; for the serious and sad, less lively measures."

The quotation is somewhat long, but it is the foundation for my whole argument. Observe, for the sort of music intended for the admiration and praise of the omnipotence and goodness of God, as Lichtenthal defines sacred music, are needed all the things which on the surface appear to be formulas and systems, but which are really esthetic indications of an ideal sentiment. When he speaks of melody and of the style suited to the expression of the sublime, which in sacred music must have first place, there is no system in question; we are clearly in the domain of genial creativeness. Since in the class of sacred music to which I first referred there is nothing of sublimity, either in the style or melody, and as we find ourselves in its form at the very antipodes of the esthetic ideas of Lichtenthal, in which I concur, I must pitilessly condemn the whole production, as hurtful as it is enormous, that has marked the finest part of the nineteenth century. And let it not be thought that the morbid influence of this sort of music has completely exhausted itself in Italy. If in some provinces it has weakened, in others it still proudly wields power, and it is painful to concede that in some ecclesiastical institutions connected with the government the sacred cabaletta[1] still reigns.

In 1888, when I was *maestro* at Cerignola, I was summoned to try a new church organ. I went to the place at night; the church was closed to the public and dimly lighted with a few wax tapers set in old discarded candelabra, placed on sundry impedimenta to prevent my breaking a limb in my progress. Equipped with the contract and the detailed description of the instrument I was to test, I climbed into the organ-loft, accompanied by the blower and the builder of the organ. The builder was somewhat excited. He never wearied of telling me that he had added a stop to the number agreed upon, and that there were four reeds more than the contract called for; and he explained the matter with a wealth of gesture and such an expenditure of melted wax from the taper in his hand that I bore home the most unpleasant of impressions, represented by numerous spots on my poor garments. The tone of his voice, too, astonished me; he shouted like a maniac when he assured me that he had made sacrifices innumerable out of deference to his most reverend patrons. All of a sudden he said to me, in a whisper, that he would not forget me if my report were to his complete satisfaction.

I was beginning to understand, but meanwhile my mind was turning from material

---

[1] "A song in rondo form, with variations, often having an accompaniment in triplets, intended to imitate the galloping of a horse."

LUCRETIA BORGIA'S FAMILY.
From a painting by Dante Gabriel Rossetti.

and mechanical considerations. Perhaps it was the surroundings, new to me, in the soft, religious light; perhaps the darkness that weirdly enlarged the arches and made prominent in the gloom many golden, glittering objects; perhaps the ever-lighted lamps that burned more than dimly before the high altar; perhaps the scene as a whole as beheld from the organ-loft: the fact remains that a feeling of soft, devout contemplation had stolen into my heart. Almost unconscious of what I was doing, I seated myself at the organ, drew out the principal stops, and began to prelude, with my thoughts still beset by celestial visions. I know not, and knew not then, what I played. Perhaps I followed, without overtaking it, an idea that then appeared, for the first time, on the horizon of my mind; perhaps my fingers pursued it in its meandering, unending course. I improvised—I dreamed. I was aroused by a sonorous barytone voice; it was that of a handsome, stout, and jovial chaplain, who had ascended to tell me that what I was playing was tedious and put people to sleep, and that something lively was expected of me, something from an opera or operetta. Confound it! The worthy reverend had issued invitations; there was a throng of intelligent people below; no need of boring them! The dream, the vision, vanished as by enchantment. Reality in its limpid clearness entered my mind. The jovial chaplain had been too kind; he might have added that, while I was paid to try the organ, I was especially engaged to entertain the guests. I turned mechanically toward the builder, who stood transfixed at my right, taper in hand, anxiously awaiting the moment when, at a sign from me, he should loose all the forces of his instrument. His expression was that of a man under sentence of death; his face was pallid, his eyes and lips were tremulously suppliant; his hand was dripping with wax, and his brow damp with perspiration. I took pity on the poor devil, who, as soon as the chaplain disappeared down the little stairway, said to me with tears in his voice, "You are ruining me!"

He was right. Away with the dreams, away with the visions; out with the stops, the clarionet, the octave flute, the cornet, the *bombarda*, the bells; let loose the delights of the joyous, shrill, and sonorous voices, and all the powers of the mighty fabric! "There are still the cymbals and the big drum," suggested the builder. Capital! Excellent! Hurrah for the tempest of sound!

The trial was a magnificent success for the organ, and also for myself. How ashamed I felt when I descended the stairs, followed by the enthusiastic builder, and when the good priests marveled at my skill and, deeply moved, thanked me! On the plea of being overheated, I turned up the collar of my coat as high as possible, and blessed the gloom that concealed my crimson blushes. One more disconsolate look at the high arches, at the lamp always lighted in front of the Madonna, and I departed, contrite and crushed. I pause at this incident, which amply illustrates to what a depth a class of music that should aspire to sublimity has fallen.

A NEW SCHOOL OF REFORM IN CHURCH MUSIC NOT SUCCESSFUL

BUT the evolution commenced. A few studious youths stood forth with a firm determination to check the sacrilegious invasion, and restore to Italy the splendor of her past glory in sacred music. How grand the cohort which, in serried ranks, gathers under the holy banner! Observe the weapons of combat. Lo, the error—the same error! Drawing their inspiration from the German school of Regensburg, they enter the lists with formulas, canons, and systems; they seek to attain their ideal by means of a revival of liturgic music, of the Gregorian chant and the ecclesiastical modes. What profit shall they derive? Is the evolution, the awakening, the progress of art, brought about by making it retrace its steps, glorious though they may be? No; art always needs new vitality, new force to accomplish its ascent. Art requires the lightning-flash, the flame of creative genius. Let us respect the patrimony of long study and great culture, but hope not for victory without the aid of the spirit of genius. Out from this band of daring spirits no genius wings its upward way, and if some timid trial of wings is essayed, the oppressing weight of theory at once bears them down. Thence it comes that no effort of these young men has achieved aught save the partial destruction of pernicious prejudices which permitted the diffusion of sacred music that ministered too much to profane delight without inspiring the devotion which informs those mysteries of religion that dwell in the temples of God.

From one excess we have fallen into another; from sacred expression fashioned out of *motivetti* we have passed to the manufacture of counterpoint. I ask not, where is the sublime, for no one would understand me; I inquire only, where is sincerity. Diligent study and extended culture may be proved by ingenious combinations of notes, but these will never convey to us that contemplative and spiritual enjoyment which the interpretation of the sacred mystery should always instil into the souls of the faithful.

Musical expression in its spontaneous interpretation should correspond with the sentiment of the hearer, whether a word or an idea, the human verb or the divine Word, is concerned. Only then does art, the pure and exclusive emanation of genius, exist. Otherwise we have another example of science which has nothing to do with art, and no place whatever in any period of its evolution. The new students have simply offered us an attempt at a fair reproduction of set forms—this, and nothing more. Verdi himself sought to demonstrate the error of the new school of music by freely interpreting the words of the "Stabat Mater" and the "Te Deum" as though to give rise to a musical polemic between barren doctrine and creative genius.

PEROSI, THE TRUE GENIUS

THE close of the century, however, has brought us a moment really important in the evolution of sacred music. A slight, timid figure has appeared alone, unarmed, to combat for the ideal. He has conquered the soul of the throng by wondering admiration, has thrown down all obstacles, and gathered the palms of victory. What secret weapons aided him? What concealed shield protected him? Who were the invisible heroes that watched over him? He fought unaided with the unbidden might of genius.

THE RESPECTIVE INFLUENCE OF FRANCE AND GERMANY AND ITALY UPON MUSIC

I ENTER upon the final division of my paper with an examination into the artistic influence on the musical evolution of the century exerted by the three great countries, France, Germany, Italy. The theme would furnish material for ten lectures. But melo-dramatic music will mainly occupy my attention, for melo-drama constitutes the real musical charm of the century. When I said, at the outset of this paper, that I could never imagine an Italian musician who was not a composer of melo-drama, I might have added that all musicians of all nations are subject to the attraction, to the suggestion, of melody. Melo-drama arrived betimes to the waiting army of musicians, vainly panting for an ideal.

Farewell, Symphony! Farewell, Sonata! Farewell, Quartet! All are wiped out in the great dedication to that temple of melo-drama, the theater. From the Rossinian period to the present the influence of theatrical music on symphonic music during the nineteenth century has been enormous. Were

PEROSI.
From a photograph by Guigoni & Bossi, Milan.

there not at hand eloquent exceptions, foremost among which, great and admirable, is Brahms's music, it might be affirmed that no composer who could aspire to melo-drama has composed symphonic works.

BRAHMS, THE GREATEST FIGURE OF THE CENTURY IN GERMAN MUSIC

BRAHMS, standing alone, represents a whole and glorious epoch of symphonic music. Brahms, in my judgment, is the greatest of

LUIGI LABLACHE.

A famous bass opera-singer. His most noted part was *Leporello* in "Don Giovanni." 1794–1858. Drawn from life by F. Salabert. Reproduced from a French lithograph.

the German musicians of the age, and the influence of his work will be imperishable on the future of musical history. Persisting in my impenitent affection for the melo-drama, how can I refrain from deploring that Brahms was never willing to compose anything for the stage? For what hidden reason did he decline to attempt melo-drama, though living in a period that most flourished through music of this genre? Brahms, when handling voices with the orchestra, has furnished us genial, powerful, and perfect creations, of which his celebrated "German Requiem" is the most luminous example. Of vocal compositions of precious quality, he has also brought forth an infinite number. Why, then, his obstinate ostracism of melo-drama? He felt, perhaps, the full individual strength of his genius to be able victoriously to resist the impetuous current which hurried along so many strong men and swept away so many weaklings. Or did he, unconsciously, follow the dictate of some higher power in a secret resolution to behold the classical and purest of eras, inaugurated by Haydn, Mozart, and Beethoven, continued and made eternal?

A REVIEW OF MELO-DRAMATISTS

To reach the kernel of my discourse, let us return to the symbolic vision of the school of melody — to that bright and uninterrupted line that, beginning with Rossini, awaited from Verdi the supreme moment of its connection, under garlands of roses, with the new century.

It has been affirmed that the Rossinian melo-drama, the natural root of the great evolution of the century, decisively marked the end of classicism. Be it so. I note the date, and now address myself exclusively to the task of considering the romantic melo-drama, as it has been called in opposition to classic music. This constrains me to neglect the great *maestri* who, while living in the century of romanticism, have kept intact their faith in the classicism of their fathers. But observe that, because the influence of the romantic drama has been preponderant upon all schools and nations, Germany included, the number of pure symphonists is relatively small. Tschaikowsky, Rubinstein, Raff, Goldmark, Dvořák, D'Indy, and other symphonists, in the fullest sense of the term, have paid their tribute to melo-drama. Not even Richard Strauss has withstood the temptation. Strauss, respected for the style of his instrumental music, appears bent upon reviving the glories of his forebears. The sublime duel between Gluck and Piccini shall not detain me in Paris for an instant, not even to note the first steps of the centennial evolution of dramatic music that received its earliest impulse from these two worthies; that gathered from illustrious legions the continuous and mighty motion which conducted it, ever quickening, to the present period — a motion which now forces it onward, enwrapped in the gloom of the future, in its irresistible and fatal course.

Nor shall I be delayed by the important melo-drama of Mozart, nor be turned from my path by the Neapolitan school, originated by Scarlatti, and developed and exalted by Cimarosa and Paisiello; nor shall my progress be retarded by Cherubini, Spontini, Mayer, Paër, Flotow, Paresi, or Generale; nor by Goldmark, powerful and original; nor by the Czech Smetana; nor shall the musical drama of Weber, the last classical resistance in the domain of the stage, turn me from my purpose; nor even my passion for Schubert and Mendelssohn, gentle and melodious, nor for Schumann, the ever divine.

The heart cannot withstand the memories of all these soft, undying sensations; the mind sways and loses its track. All mental strength weakens and ebbs away in this painful abandonment. I need assistance. Oh, for the supreme vision that shall arouse me from a contemplation that fills me with longing desire — the supreme vision, the ideal, the purpose!

GERMANY AND ITALY CONTEST THE FIELD

The faculty and the potency revive; the supreme vision is disclosed, the struggle between the two great schools, Italy and Germany. France almost disappears in comparison with the two Titanic forces which, in a superbly heroic contest, give to history the most beautiful period of the artistic evolution of the nineteenth century. The struggle to-day is confined to the two strong races, the German and the Latin, the latter represented by the array of soldiers first led by Rossini and since marshaled by Verdi; the former represented by one combatant — by one man, Wagner. Every other nation, every other school in the present struggle, bows to one or the other of these forces. And it is most regrettable that France should be absent from this Homeric battle of art.

REVIEW OF FRENCH MUSIC

France — how many geniuses did the nineteenth century behold rising from her fruitful soil! The glorious light they brought forth is indeed light — sunlight; but in her splendid and glowing course there has been no fecundity, no imparting of fire or warmth, where her planets, in their own splendor, remain motionless and isolated.

France reveals to us an admirable array of the elect, a splendid continuity of purely genial art, but no well-defined movement of evolution. Where are the followers of Berlioz, founder of a school that could be and should be the opulent and coveted inheritance of national art? Berlioz opened to the world the new paths of instrumental music which before his days had never been explored. He is the son of a land that had no symphonists in the eighteenth century. Berlioz is the creator of a new style of composition that is even now much discussed, and still appears too modern. Berlioz is the true genius, misunderstood in his day, and perhaps not understood even in ours. But Berlioz is a genius, and will his work remain barren? I behold already a youthful cohort proudly advancing to do battle in his name. In the valiant group I recognize Messager, D'Indy, Laborne. Courage, brave youths! It is late, but Berlioz's art has lost none of its power.

And Gounod? From the clearness of his sentiment, whence the national spirit is ever soaring, it would seem as though he desired to bring forth a shadow of the art of Weber and Wagner. But where are the fruits of his school? Bizet, too, stands isolated in his country — the great, the mighty Bizet, who has given so much development to the modern Italian musical drama, the victorious course of which has even tempted the Germanic race. And Meyerbeer himself, who, though born in Berlin, must be regarded as a French composer, what effect has he produced upon the musical century beyond exciting admiration for his own power, shown in the progress of instrumentation, and the genial and mighty creativeness that has furnished one of the best exemplars of generative romanticism in the new dramatic music? France, in the nineteenth century, has given a garden to each of her flowers. From Méhul and Auber, from Hérold and Halévy, through Reyer, and Saint-Saëns the worshiper of classicism, one reaches sentimental Massenet and the throng of new youths, a constellation of brilliant and generous minds, but each separated, distinct, and isolated. How great a future might be in store for France if all the richness of her art could have that complete development which has been till now too limited! Its very opulence and exuberance of power constrains it. How great the future of the quickening action of the germs of genius if these had not been scattered, but strewed broadcast, in the nineteenth century!

At the opening of the new century, however, the world takes a passionate interest in the struggle between Italy and Germany only, and France herself offers, in lordly and disinterested fashion, the most favorable battle-field while seeking to renew the epic and memorable war between Gluck and Piccini, who, on the same field, breathed the first breath of life into the great era of dramatic music.

I shall forget Flotow, who, like Meyerbeer, might well be credited to the French school; and Nicolai and Marshner, and the Alsatian Adam, and the Austrian Kienzl, and Reinecke and Max Bruch and Martin Roeder and Humperdinck. I shall forget them all, to dwell upon great and resplendent Wagner.

In the Italian school I shall attempt no elimination; our opera-writers are all equally Italian (I do not include the so-called young school), and form that admirable melo-dramatic world, the luminous poles of which are Rossini and Verdi. A single exception among these Italian musicians should be noted.

BOÏTO, AN ISOLATED GENIUS IN MODERN ITALIAN MUSIC

At the moment of the great efflorescence, the complete ripeness, of Italian melo-drama, conceived and developed by Rossini and enlarged by Bellini, Donizetti, Verdi, and Ponchielli, a young *maestro* presents himself to public opinion, and it seems as though he would defy, with new forms and new acts of boldness, the tastes and habits of the multitude. Was his opera the spontaneous outcome of his creative genius? was it the fruit of his vast and admirable culture? was it the product of the musical and dramatic reforms of Wagner? The opera failed, the public hurling the wildest imprecations at the rash composer, but the *maestro* remained calm; faith strengthened his spirit; the vision of the future sustained him. His work, burning with powerful originality, was beheld anew, and resumed its course so suddenly and brutally interrupted. It continued in its path, now freely opened to it, until it won the laurels with which a glorious span of thirty years is crowned. What fair, fallacious hopes were centered in that bold and genial *maestro!* And art awaited anxiously and long; it still awaits the new opera of Arrigo Boïto.

THE ITALIAN SCHOOL

I have reached the last stage. Before us are the two schools in combat: here Wagner, there Rossini and Verdi, with the legion that has come into existence and grown in their great shadow. I need not give the biography of all our great composers; it would be irreverent to speak of Donizetti, of Bellini, incidentally and laconically. Each of our great masters merits for himself not merely an essay, but whole volumes. The individual genius of those great men that first followed Rossini glowed with the splendor of its own light, but did not depart from a renewed style; rather strengthened this, by a great creative power; amplified, developed, modified it, little by little, naturally, involuntarily, through its own genial creativeness. Thus was born the magnificent and perfect opera; the final outcome of that Italian school of melo-drama which is the fairest artistic page of the nineteenth century.

Hence no more names; the two only nations, the two only schools, that contend with each other, that struggle frantically for — for — for what?

In Italy all is excitement; they write and repeat that Germany is winning from us supremacy in respect to melo-drama; that we have indeed lost it; and some rejoice, and others weep. On one side men deplore the complete exhaustion of Italian genius; on the other the triumph of the German opera is acclaimed. They prate of preponderating influence, of depraved taste, of discarded forms, of progress and decadence, of the past and of the future, of glory and of obscurity. Passions are kindled, the fancy is stimulated; men rack their brains, and the national literature is enriched with strange books, with stranger ideas, and with the strangest of opinions. To what end all this tumult? Wherefore this pandemonium, this obsession? I see nothing beyond the natural movement of an ascending period of the evolution of music. New Italy, the new school,— one must perforce speak of it,— now that it is in the mood, lovingly studies the Wagnerian music-drama. It studies it from the standpoint of form, of the technical progress that it yields, and also, if you will, from the point of view of the whole and perfect musical conception; but in Wagner's music-drama the *feeling itself* cannot be studied, for the feeling is in the blood of the artist, and in Wagner one cannot study *the idea*, because in art the idea is the spontaneous and unconscious expression of genius in the act of creation.

SHALL ITALIAN MUSIC BE GERMANIZED?

WHY are we not willing to permit the Italian school to study the new models of melo-drama calmly, and why do we grow weary of proving that the Italian lyric drama must make way for the German opera? Do we seek to convince ourselves that the Italian lyric drama of Rossini, Bellini, and Donizetti has aged in comparison with the new German melo-drama? *But does genius grow old?* Do the melodies that moved our fathers and grandparents no longer stir us as deeply, even through the medium of that sad and untruthful interpretation that appears to delight in slighting our masterpieces? Do we wish to prove that the great Italian lyric drama *has grown old as to form?* Then let us put our treasures in safe places; let us remove them from modern profanation; let them be kept intact for future generations, when spirits tired and exhausted by vain Byzantine strife shall seek consolation, rest.

RICHARD STRAUSS.
From a photograph by Fr. Müller, Munich. Published by Jos. Aibl.

Let us consider Wagner. Born of the germination of Gluck and of that of the first romantic period, he stood forth with all the most manifest signs of the originative influence, and in his first efforts revealed himself a follower of that romanticism which in France had Meyerbeer for its high priest. Wagner was great, but not sincere. Then his disposition and nature led him into other paths, and Wagner gave to his country the melo-dramatic theater. I shall not stop to discuss whether his genius — for Wagner is a real genius — was, in the continuance of his work, sacrificed to systems and programs, nor do I wish to investigate whether in his last work he sought, as it were, to change his belief. I aver that Wagner in making the German lyric drama was sincere.

and light in true and pure art. If, however, it is form which we would renew, let us allow our youths to study; let us permit them to traverse freely the new period of evolution they themselves have begun. Now they grope, they stumble in the dark, they clutch at things hither and thither. Let us leave them in peace; it is the acute period of the evolution. Who knows but they may give to Italy the melo-drama renewed in form, but in substance and idea ever and sincerely Italian. Verdi lived through the epoch of the evolution, and upon each period left the indelible impress of his genius, but, through all influences, he remained marvelously Italian.

In his famous book entitled "Opera and Drama," Wagner wrote that the ancient melo-drama was founded upon an equivocation, because the drama serves for writing the music. I do not quote the phrase with the thought of bringing it into discussion, but only to show that all the movement carried on about Wagner rests on this aphorism. We note more ostentation than sincerity in Italian appreciation of Wagner's music; and persons that have never comprehended the easiest and most melodious *canzonetta* have felt the need of understanding at sight all the vast achievements of Wagner, in whose formula they have fancied that they discovered the real cause of their intellectual inferiority. To this day they know nothing of music, but they can grasp, with tolerable facility, the reasons for this or that fragment or prelude, aided in their wearying diligence by a guide, a sort of railway time-table, which has for some time seemed indispensable to the enjoyment of Wagner's operas.

THE MISCHIEVOUS MODERN CRITIC

POOR unfortunates! That which you apprehend and appreciate is but the program of Wagner. Would that it were even the esthetic purpose of his work? The best of Wagner, represented by the whole genial creation, admits of no system; you, perhaps, regret and despise it, being unable to understand it and not finding it mentioned among the stations in your time-table. And this ostentation, this simulation of intelligence and competence, has made possible the unwholesome efflorescence of those musical critics that, with ferocious facility, seek to destroy in an hour's work what has cost the assiduous mind years and years of effort.

Contemporary criticism — what a task it would be to enumerate its blunders! Criticism, in my opinion, can exist after the historic period only, when its duty is much simplified, because the goal has been reached by works only that are sound, vital, and bearing the seal of genius. Weak and false achievements cannot outlive their age. But contemporary criticism in every artistic evolution is always a venomous reptile. The deviation of the artist, the ruin of the mind, the persistence of error, are sometimes due to its influence.

And if the Italian school now advances with uncertain and faltering steps, it is largely attributable to certain pseudo-artists that vainly endeavor to direct its course. Our young musicians would have felt the influence of Wagner's art far differently if they had not been deafened and misled by so many false theories. Let us leave our young writers to think and write in peace. We know not yet whether their performances may not survive and bear to the history of art their share of the worthy part of its evolution. Your work, ye critics, in any case, will always remain unfruitful, for it will never represent aught but your pretentious and not dispassionate personal opinion. Descend from the pulpit and sit ye down on the stool of the reporter. There, at least, you will be sincere and true and of some service to the future.

The appearance which the great struggle between the two great schools presents to me, in the opinion that long ago shaped itself spontaneously in my thoughts, will not coincide with every one's views. No absolute conquest is reserved for one party or for the other, no influence will change the nature of a people, no human power sterilize the root of a national art. The German lyric drama, in its highest ascension, is now victorious. But I do not see how, in the future, it can have development and continuation. Wagner began it, and Wagner completed it. It seems to me impossible to carry it on on a different basis and to make it progress by other paths. Its track is too clearly defined. It is alike impossible to follow it or to imitate it. This would be the profanation of opera, the degradation of the type. Wagner accomplished his work and made it perfect. The grandiose period of Wagner's achievement will endure, an everlasting and glorious token of the highest point of the parabola in German dramatic music, which must fatally follow its descending course.

Because the great Italian public, blinded by the reforming art of Wagner, no more sees its past glories, and has no faith in the pygmies that, scattered and uncertain, are engaged in combat. But Italian art will be born anew; it will live again, strengthened by the influence of the evolutionary period that now witnesses its slavery. Italy awaits her coming genius; and that genius will come. The soul of Giuseppe Verdi awaits him, to

ITALIAN MUSIC WILL PROGRESS

WHY, on the other hand, does the Italian school now appear overcome, prostrated?

tender to him the chain of laurels and flowers that Rossini intrusted to him, and that will stretch through all future ages, to perpetuate the supreme glory of music. This will be the luminous continuation of the work made perfect by our great men. But the perfection of Italian art lies not in form. It lies wholly in ideal creativeness, and every new work that derives its inspiration from this liquid font increases the flow of its invading tide.

WAGNERISM THE DANGER OF ITALIAN MUSIC

I WOULD fain close with this expression of a sincere and roseate wish, but reality summons me. A great peril threatens. The youth of the period have gone astray, and, persisting in the error into which they have been led by evil counsel, will end by completely destroying Italian melo-drama. Disconcerted by criticism and by the fickle taste of the public, assailed in every direction, they have sought salvation by clutching desperately at the Wagnerian formula. But they have grasped it at its weakest point. They have thought: "Wagner reproaches the old opera with having used the drama to make music; this means that we shall use music to make the drama." And, because of their Italian nature and because of the nature of the germ that created them, they can never conceive of composing music such as Wagner has poured forth in his Northern legends. They will exaggerate the formula and use little music to make much drama. I do not discuss the genus, but I say that, keeping up the pace, we may reach the stage when the violin will calmly accompany a sentimental song recited by Eleanora Duse. This will not be wanting in emotion, nor will tears be lacking; but the melo-drama will be missed, and the music and the word, the two sister arts that have been locked in one embrace since the days of ancient Greece, will be parted, and one will be the humble slave of the other. In the presence of such an intensely dramatic and touching scene as that in which *William Tell* is bidden to shoot the apple from the head of his son, our young composer will find the situation so interesting in itself as to need no added music. A simple roll of the kettle-drums will suffice, instead of which Rossini (how ingenuously!), stirred by the incident, dictated that sublime page, "Jemmy, pense à ta mère!" that makes one weep even when one hears it sung by a barytone in a black dress-coat and a white tie.

Back to the faith of our fathers, back to the purity of our origin! Let us be Italians once more. Let the new genius, the genius we await, stand forth to marshal us again in the path that leads to all conquests. In the enthusiasm of invocation and of joyful hope the mind pursues an immense vision, that seems an ideal synthesis of our dreams — the vision of a great evolution accomplished in the splendid triumph of our dramatic and our popular music.

POPULAR MELODY THE SOLUTION OF OUR ENIGMA

INSPIRATION and strength! The latter is bestowed with largesse by the production of our great masters; the former flows freely from the songs of our people, the songs that are the pride of our honest and cheerful national instinct, and that we allow to languish and disappear through neglectful desertion. Let us keep intact this art patrimony of the nation; keep it for future generations; keep it to transmit to new ages in the purest and most expressive language the glories of the epoch, the modern story of our redemption and the glorious narrative of the Italian revival. Oh, how marvelously shall our popular music relate to the youth of the future the enterprises of their grandparents, and how the national and patriotic songs shall carry the pride of the race into the hearts of future nations! How our songs shall express the glad and scornful feelings of so many historical episodes! How our melodramatic stage shall represent the whole heroic drama of the epoch of fable!

THE LAST PHOTOGRAPH OF SIR ARTHUR SULLIVAN.
From a photograph by Elliott & Fry, London.

ARTHUR SEYMOUR SULLIVAN

BY

CHARLES MACLEAN

SULLIVAN was born to show that the gods have not grown old. Through a side-venue he has given his country a share in the romantic tendencies of the music of the last half-century. More specifically he has built on the foundations of English national sentiment and laid more than one course in the edifice of a new national musical style.

That Sullivan was a genius, and one of a very high order, no one can doubt who either has instinct to see in a flash or will survey the facts. Simple natural melodies revolved incessantly in his brain, and could be evoked at any moment. His sense of adjusting labor to imagination was as keen as a knife-edge. In the transmutation of unpromising material so as to adapt it to subtle art (a theme which is the basis of the present article), he more than in any other respect showed his genius. As to Sullivan's romanticism, it was only of that class which yokes together sentiment and the precepts of art on equal terms. He had nothing to do with esthetic whims about the "ulterior meanings" of music; he was with the stanch

Hanslick, who attacked "vision-producing medicines," and with Schumann, who said, "Critics always wish to know what the composer himself cannot tell them." He was romantic because his own personal feelings were intense, but his products remained law-abiding and wholly sane. As Ruskin in his "Queen of the Air" puts it, "Music is thus, in her health, the teacher of perfect order; it is the voice of the obedience of the angels, and the companion of the course of the spheres of heaven." As to Sullivan's partly unconscious function of building up national material into a style, his merit is in proportion to the extraordinary difficulty of his task: a matter which has perhaps not yet been sufficiently considered. And this must be spoken of in detail.

Ever since the monodic style in music made its first effectual inroads upon the purely contrapuntal style, the national art-style of each particular country has more and more been determined in the last resort by the character of its folk-songs. One might cite a number of examples, as for instance in Russia, where short phrases, very free rhythms, a tendency to Lydian and Dorian scales of melody, and in general an absence of the feeling for tonality which we at the present day are disposed to regard as indispensable, have been transferred from the folk-songs to the art products. But it is enough to consider the case of the Colossus which has stridden from the Rhine to the Danube, and which even now wields almost undisputed authority in music. The German Volkslied (in which are included patriotic songs, students' songs, and soldiers' songs) originated in the fourteenth century, came to its zenith in the fifteenth and sixteenth, declined under the influence of the Thirty Years' War, was revived in the eighteenth century, and is still persistent. It rivaled the Gregorian chant; it went to school with and was molded by the congregational hymn of the Catholic and Protestant churches. Above all, the natural capacity of the Germans for singing in parts governed its growth. In structure it has always consisted of thesis and antithesis; the former generally moving harmonically to dominant, less frequently to subdominant or relative minor. This, in combination with the strophic and tripartite principles of meter as accessories, is the protoplasm out of which the whole of the great modern Teutonic art has been formed. So far has this been carried that in Brahms, the last of the great German masters, the use of the set forms has been extended to all choral and vocal works, most of which had hitherto been thought exempt.

When Sullivan opened his career the English art world, even apart from the Mendelssohnian prepossession, was wholly dominated by the influence of the German masters. All good music (so esteemed) followed such models as a matter of course. Sterndale Bennett broke away once in his eminently beautiful and successful and thoroughly English "May Queen,"—but once only. But this state of things was utterly powerless to develop a national style; and a composer like Sullivan, whose instincts and career led him to appeal to the heart of the people, had perforce to turn to native material.

Of what, then, did this consist? English national airs were terribly tampered with in an earlier part of the nineteenth century. Their distinctive modes — Dorian, D to D; Mixolydian, G to G; and Æolian, A to A — were "majored" and "minored"; they were fitted with accompaniments having no affinity whatsoever to them, and merely reflecting the harmonies taught in the thorough-bass handbooks of the period; even their rhythms were mangled and cut down to uniform four-measure periods. This unintelligent treatment created almost a jungle. Yet the original plants are still discernible, and certain broad statements as to our national material can be made. The English love a simple sentiment, particularly in the shape of their ballads and hymn-tunes, although these do not possess the German strength of form. Their national airs, not excluding Irish, Scottish, and Welsh, fail to show thesis and antithesis as in the Volkslied; and in so far as they betray any decided harmonic attribute, for they were not adapted for singing in parts, they hug the tonic. During a considerable period, since the Elizabethan era, the semi-national tunes composed by musicians have shown a cross between an amorphic madrigal and a metrical air. This was the material which our Mendelssohn Scholar, educated in Tenterden street and at Leipsic, had at his back in his native country; and until its utter incongruity with the dominant German art is realized, no point in his career can be understood, nor can his greatness as a musician be in the least appreciated. If a single concrete example is wanted, let it be considered that the English populace proper of the nineteenth century were brought up on such airs as "Pretty Polly Oliver," "The Keel Row," "The Girl I've Left Behind Me," "Hearts of Oak," and "Rule Britannia"; and however excellent these things may be in their way, they have naught in common with "sonata form" or any other form of the Teutonic art. The more the matter is considered technically, the more it will be seen that in the heights to which he raised his purely national art Sullivan achieved that which very few musicians in the world have done in a single lifetime.

It must not be supposed that Sullivan accomplished his task without opposition. He was the richest composer, enriched by his own labor, who ever lived. For the last twenty years of his life, at least, he was worshiped by the people at large. Yet though there were not two actual camps proclaimed, though there was no Delphi answering Dodona, nevertheless a considerable body of opinion among the cultivated classes harassed him with well-meant but ignorant suggestions that he was abusing his talents in the particular line in which he did the most work. When his body was scarcely cold the ordinary leader-writer lectured him on this head in terms quite fatuous. This might be ignored, but that it exactly focussed a cant long prevailing among irresponsible dilettanti and seldom checked; and it exactly focussed the inner trouble of Sullivan's mind. There were many who, while adulating Sullivan, intimated that they knew more about the functions of art than he did. He said nothing; he set his back against the wall. What he might have said was: "This is a national matter, in which it is better to level up what we have than to ape the inaccessible."

The history of Sullivan's art career, the history of the development of his talent, may be divided for convenience into five sections: the period of his pupilage, till he was twenty-one years old; the period when he was forming his general individual style, or about seven years, till he was twenty-eight; the period when he was grappling with the comic-opera problem, or about fifteen years, till he was forty-three; the period of further development of the same, or about seven years, till he was fifty; and the period of his restful maturity, or the last eight years of life. It will be seen that this division falls into groups of seven years, though that has not been intentional.

The father's father of Sullivan was an impoverished Irish squireen and a soldier in the army. His father was from 1845 to 1856 bandmaster of the small band at the Military College, Sandhurst, thirty-five miles from London; and from 1856 till his death in 1866 clarinet professor at the Bandmaster's School, Kneller Hall, Hounslow, not far from London. The mother's maiden name was Coghlan, and that of her mother was Righi (Italian) Sullivan was thus a slightly Italianized Celt.

Sir Arthur Sullivan was born May 13, 1842, in London, and was from the age of three till the age of eight at Sandhurst, being then sent to a school at Bayswater, but spending his holidays still at Sandhurst. When nearly twelve he obtained a choristership (which means board and lodging) in the Chapel Royal, St. James's. When he was fourteen the family moved into Pimlico, on the father's appointment to Kneller Hall. Thus till the age of fourteen he had constant or occasional access to the Sandhurst military band, and he showed a child's quickness in learning to play the different wind-instruments there. Otherwise he has not been claimed as a musical prodigy. In 1856 the trustees of the "English Mendelssohn Scholarship," who had been collecting money for the preceding ten years, announced a competition. There were seventeen candidates, and Sullivan, the youngest, tied with Joseph Barnby, the eldest, but was preferred to him at the final examination. The trustees kept him at the Chapel Royal till his voice broke, but sent him meanwhile to take lessons at the Royal Academy; in 1858 they sent him to Leipsic to attend the Conservatorium, which he did for four years. His output in composition during this seven years of direct tuition was nothing extraordinary in quantity or quality (a concert overture at the Academy, and a "Lalla Rookh" overture and romanza for string quartet at the Conservatorium), until he made his final and great effort with the incidental music to the "Tempest." He was then twenty years of age.

THE EARLIEST KNOWN PORTRAIT OF SULLIVAN.

Sir Arthur Sullivan standing, John Henry Barnett seated. A photograph made just after entrance to Chapel Royal.

No great individuality is noticeable in the "Tempest" music, but it showed the perfected musician and it hit the Mendelssohnian taste in London. The handsome youth had won his spurs, and was much fêted.

If during the above period his talent was not unhealthily pressed either by others or by himself, the following septennium was of extraordinary importance in the history of English music and of some brilliance in his personal career. He lived in his father's house, and made a small income as a church organist at St. Michael's in Chester Square; but the publishers captured him to write songs, and he at once developed that English quality which was his characteristic for the rest of his life. In 1864 his secular cantata "Kenilworth" was accepted for the Birmingham Festival, the subject being a supposed pageant before Queen Elizabeth. The music was most delightfully fresh and rhythmic, and more English in vein than anything since Bennett's "May Queen" of six years previous. The work constituted Sullivan's début as a national composer, and it is strangely and unwisely neglected. Meanwhile Costa allowed him to act as organist behind the scenes at Covent Garden, and he wrote a ballet for the company. In 1866 Sullivan was commissioned to write for the Norwich Festival, and, his father dying, he prepared an overture, "In Memoriam." This overture has much analogy to Wagner's "Faust" Overture, a work of which Sullivan as likely as not had never heard, though it had been written before he was born. In each case the sonata form is nominally retained, but rather as a scaffolding for the exhibition of certain melodies entirely characteristic of the composer, which appear in the situation of the "second subject" consecutively and without much cohesion. The "first subject," especially with Sullivan, shows little development, and is not much more than necessary "business" for maintaining the sonata form. The end justifies the means in each case, and each is a masterpiece in its respective national style. With Wagner the "second-subject" themes are just such as might appear in "Lohengrin"; with Sullivan they are simply Sullivanesque hymn-themes. In the Sullivan overture the introduction and coda are an English hymn (not chorale) played straight through.

LENT BY MR. HERBERT SULLIVAN.
SULLIVAN AT EIGHTEEN
This photograph was taken in 1860 at Leipsic, where he composed the music for "The Tempest."

With very unnecessary diffidence the composer did not publish his perfectly individual "Symphony in E minor," also brought out in 1866. In this same memorable year he wrote with F. C. Burnand the comic "Cox and Box, a new Triumviretta," from a business point of view the germ of his subsequent career in operetta. Viewed as a creation, it is only a facile parody of Cimarosa, though very delightful to listen to. In 1869 he wrote an oratorio, "The Prodigal Son," for the Worcester Festival. Here the Mendelssohnian tendencies of the day were too much for him, and the result is not invigorating. In 1870, at the Birmingham Festival, he again exhibited his own proper style in the "Di Ballo" overture. On the whole, he was now still poor in pocket, but he had made his style.

In 1871 Sullivan met W. S. Gilbert, destined to play Scribe to his Auber, and wrote with him the unpublished "Thespis" for Hollingshead at the Gaiety. Gilbert, a civil servant, barrister, militia captain, etc., was an extremely prosperous comedy dramatist. In 1875 R. D'Oyly Carte, manager of Selina Dolaro's Royalty Theatre, commissioned the pair to write "Trial by Jury," a skit on the law-courts; and from this point the London comic stage bifurcated decisively from the old "burlesque" into "operetta" on the one side and "variety entertainment" on the other. The vein which had run out in Vienna with Johann Strauss reappeared not in Italy, but in London. At the end of 1877 a "comedy-opera syndicate," composed of a few music-publishers and men of means and managed by D'Oyly Carte, brought out "The Sorcerer" at the Opera Comique Theatre in the Strand. By this time Sullivan had completely abandoned the quasi-classical stage style, and was writing in his own vein. In 1881 the Savoy Theatre was built specially for the Gilbert and Sullivan operetta. Briefly, in the fifteen years from 1870 to 1885, the pair wrote "Trial by Jury," "The Sorcerer," "Pinafore," "The Pirates of Penzance," "Patience," "Iolanthe," "Princess Ida," and "The Mikado," the last being high-water mark. All this time Sullivan was wrestling with the style of the Savoy, to purge it from the dross incidental to an appeal to the masses, and to bring it into the domain of pure music, Gilbert's words neither helping nor marring him in this aim, for he was by far the dominant partner.

Meanwhile he developed his powers elsewhere. In 1873 he wrote for Birmingham the oratorio "The Light of the World," an advance on "The Prodigal Son," though much in the same style. In 1880, succeeding Costa as conductor at Leeds, he wrote "The Martyr of Antioch," which the elect said was too frivolous, but which in point of fact was much better music than either of its predecessors. In 1883 his general reputation was such that he was knighted.

The next septennium opened with that extraordinary work, the cantata "The Golden Legend" (Joseph Bennett from Longfellow), and closed with the grand opera "Ivanhoe" (Julian Sturgis). The new version of "Der arme Heinrich" has no vogue in Germany, because the long, formless stretches are filled up with English and not with Teutonic sentiment. It was sketched by Sullivan in his former house at Sandhurst, where he took lodging. Space forbids a detailed analysis, but in short Sullivan here finally threw over Mendelssohnianism in the concert-room and relied on his own vein, bringing up purely English art to a level never dreamed of before. To a mind not over-warped in favor of German art the whole will appear very beautiful; and one may say of it, with Andrew Marvell:

Then Music, the mosaic of the air,
Did of all these a solemn noise prepare,
With which she gained the Empire of the ear,
Including all between the earth and sphere.

Technically it is a gorgeous production, and Sullivan handled the orchestra as he never did before. A well-known example is in the introduction: the slow chromatic sequence of chords of the seventh ($\frac{4}{3}$), accompanied in turn by rushing chromatic sequences of other chords of the seventh ($\frac{4}{3}$), the whole giving the surge of the tempest through the steeple. Of this, by the by, a learned critic once said that the "Golden Legend" "opened with a chord of the seventh," a primitive description certainly. Another well-known instance is where *Lucifer* offers the draught, analogous to, without actually resembling, the *Flackerlohe* in the "Valkyrie."

"Ivanhoe" was written when opera in English, beginning with Cambert's "Ariadne," was just two hundred years old. It was the immediate successor of such works as Cowen's "Pauline," Goring Thomas's "Esmeralda" and "Nadeshda," Stanford's "Canterbury Pilgrims," Mackenzie's "Colomba" and "Troubadour," and Corder's "Nordisa." An English opera-house was built for it in Cambridge Circus, and it had a long run. It just missed being strong enough to create an English operatic style. Sullivan would have been a miracle if he had built equally high in each department which he essayed. This period saw, in operetta, "Ruddigore," "The Yeomen of the Guard," and "The Gondoliers," after which last Gilbert's long-sustained powers appeared to wane.

The final period began with "The Foresters," an utterly delightful lyric piece to Tennyson's words, written for Daly's Thea-

AN EARLY PORTRAIT OF SULLIVAN.
From a photograph by H. M. King.

tre, New York. This period included "Haddon Hall" (Grundy), "Utopia" (Gilbert), "The Grand Duke" (Gilbert), "The Beauty Stone" (Pinero), and "The Victoria Ballet" for the Alhambra. The first three were moderate successes; "The Beauty Stone," a serious play with a comic devil, was a dead failure. The period ended with Sullivan's comic masterpiece, "The Rose of Persia" (Basil Hood). In the biography of Sullivan published not long before his death it was stated that the musical style was identical in all the Savoy operettas. If that were so, there would be little point in the present article. On the contrary, most distinct stages of purely musical development are shown at the points indicated by "Pinafore," "Mikado," "Gondoliers," and "Rose of Persia" respectively. Sullivan at the time of his death had in hand an Irish operetta (Basil Hood), which is to be finished by Edward German and produced in usual course at the Savoy.

Sullivan was essentially a melodist, and succeeded best lyrically. His vocal melody was based on an intense study of the meter of the words. His harmony was the simplest flowing, without anything of what has been called "akkordegoismus." His counterpoint was clean and clear; his orchestration just sufficient to be pointed, and never extravagant. His products seem very simple and obvious until an attempt is made to imitate them. His processes in "sketching" were known only to himself, but it is plain that in scoring he was extremely rapid. His musical handwriting was very distinct and rather formal, and apparently there was little erasure. All the Savoy operettas were experimentally rehearsed on the skeleton score principle, and orchestrated when all was settled at the last moment, to save labor in scoring and to avoid piracy. In his national position Sullivan most resembled the Bohemian Friedrich Smetana. The works by which he has most specifically raised the level of English music would seem to be: many songs; the two concert overtures and the symphony; "Kenilworth," "The Golden Legend," and "The Foresters"; "The Mikado," "The Yeomen of the Guard," "The Gondoliers," and "The Rose of Persia." Like many composers, he knew very little about other people's music, and scarcely ever went to a concert. He had no personal patrons—no Mæcenas, Lorenzo de' Medici, or Karl August of Weimar. He did not marry, and might have said with Michelangelo, "I have espoused my art, and it occasions me sufficient domestic cares." He must have had an income at one time of over £20,000 a year, but he spent or lost the greater part of his fortune. He had suffered half his life from gall-stones, and he died, worn out, on November 22, 1900. He left the residue of his fortune—some £35,000, and rights which may yet bring in several thousands a year—to an adopted nephew, a young stockbroker. His personal character was absolutely lovable. Grossmith the actor lately offered in print an unaffected tribute to it.

LENT BY MR. HERBERT SULLIVAN.

THE ROOM IN WHICH SIR ARTHUR SULLIVAN DIED.

As it was when he died. It has since been dismantled.

SAMUEL COLERIDGE-TAYLOR*

THE life of Coleridge-Taylor is inevitably sprinkled with references to his connection with his own race, and any notice of the man would be inadequate as well as unjust which did not recognize his relation to the Negro and his accomplishment for him. Pride in and his championship for his people developed with his manhood. The little dark-skinned lad who played the fiddle to his white schoolmates was perhaps scarcely conscious of the gulf which tradition had endeavored to place between himself and them; but the student at the Royal College had all the passionate irritability of genius, combined with an inordinate sensitiveness, and he seemed to look upon his color as an added tragedy, without which his cup was already overfull. He hated the early criticisms which dealt equally with his skin and his music; so much so that he told Colonel Walters that he was a British musician with an English education, and that he desired to be estimated in his relation to music and not to the music of the Negro only. Later on, the atmosphere of the Royal College, his growing success, and the interest aroused through actual contact with his own people, combined in early manhood to show him the nobler course of accepting the will of Providence and of devoting himself to the uplift of the colored race in so far as his art allowed. Once taken, the resolution became one of the passions of his life.

Its expression was both subjective and objective, conscious and unconscious. It was not merely fancy which discovered to the critics a strain of barbaric splendor in these early works which in their intention had no relation to the barbaric; the barbaric note was undoubtedly there, just as much as the barbaric splendor is generally present in the imagination of the older Dumas. It came out not only in the rich, unusual character of his orchestration, his short, often staccato, musical phrasing and new rhythms. It was even more apparent in an atmosphere which is peculiarly his own, and is undoubtedly racial. A facet of this race characteristic is his love of queer-sounding names, such as he found early in "Zara's Ear-rings" and in Longfellow's "Hiawatha," and ultimately in Alfred Noyes's "A Tale of Old Japan," where, as was the case with "Hiawatha," the strange names

---

*This article is based on W. C. Berwick Sayers' "Samuel Coleridge-Taylor, Musician," published by Cassell & Co., Ltd.

Yoichi-Tenko, Sawara, O Kimi San, were the first factor of attraction in the poem. A cursory study of the Negro shows how true this is to his temperament, and a glance at a list of the names chosen for themselves by Negroes will increase the assurance. These works are not our concern at the moment, so much as those which are consciously upon Negro subjects.

"The production of such men as Mr. Washington, Mr. Dunbar, and Mr. Taylor by the Negroid race gives a new complexion to the problem of black and white." This declaration of a well-known London journal illustrates the point of view which was gradually developing in Coleridge-Taylor; and his earliest conscious connection with his race as a musician was his collaboration with Paul Laurence Dunbar as early as 1897 in the series of songs, "The Corn Song," "At Candle Lighting Time," and the "African Romances," which first secured him an audience as a song writer whose work could not be neglected; as, also, in "The Dream Lovers," the slender but interesting operetta which was their joint work in 1898. The whole significance of Dunbar lies in his expression of the "souls of black folk," and Coleridge-Taylor recognizes and utters his affinity with him in his music.

His earliest orchestral piece on a more ambitious scale which was consciously directed to the expression of Negro ideas was also inspired by a poem of Dunbar's. This was "Danse Negre," which was afterward to be incorporated into what is one of the most important compositions of our times, partly because of its own musical quality, but more because it represents the successful entering of the highest field of creative music by the Negro—the "African Suite." His rhythms were deliberately drawn from the folk music of his people; and "Danse Negre" has a general resemblance to its source, but in its fulfilment it is upon a much more advanced plane, as is natural to the composer who is familiar with all the resources of modern harmony and the modern orchestra.

The "African Suite," the appearance of which was the unique event in music in the last generation, was published in 1898. It consists of four numbers, "Introduction," "A Negro Love Song," "Valse," and "Danse Negre," and is scored for full orchestra. The suite exhibits in miniature many of the characteristics of Coleridge-Taylor's work as a whole, and it is rather remarkable that this suite, which is a microcosm of his methods, and which is worthy of comparison with the "Peer Gynt Suite" in its strange and peculiar beauty, is not heard far more frequently at concerts than is the case.

The idea of doing for Negro music—to quote his own words—"what Brahms has done for Hungarian folk music, Dvořák for the Bohemian, and Grieg for the Norwegian," came early into his mind. In common with Dvořák he held that great racial music is to be found in germ in the folk songs of a people. Classical forms are highly civilized, and therefore largely artificial developments, and the new race, imagining such there be, that begins its higher musical expression with these, is of necessity unoriginal and imitative merely. The elements of all that differentiates it from the well-defined schools of other races are to be found in the everyday utterances of the people nearest to their mother earth. Like Dvořák, therefore, he turned to the folk music of his race, and found valuable material in the Jubilee Songs which had been collected in the seventies by Theodore F. Seward.

Among the Jubilee Singers who visited England in 1875 was Frederick J. Loudin. He came again to England in the late nineties with a new generation of Fisk Jubilee Singers, who revived the tradition of the old choir in London and in the larger British towns. Coleridge-Taylor attended some of the Jubilee concerts, and was deeply affected by the singing; the airs, indeed, struck a chord responsive in him; but in particular it was the quality of the voices that impressed him. The traditional reedy singing voice, which it is admitted was conspicuous in himself in later years, was absent, and the purity of the tenor tones and the deep forward tones of the bass, united with the power of using them to convey the whole range of emotion, were marked characteristics. Thereafter Negro themes occur frequently in his work. After the "African Suite," which is Negro in intention rather than its direct use of Negro themes, the most important early work in which such a theme was used deliberately was the "Overture" to the "Song of Hiawatha." This is built up upon the Jubilee song, "Nobody Knows the Trouble I See, Lord!" A curious choice, and one which removes the resultant work in character from the pagan Indian cantatas to which it is ostensibly the introduction. It is very undesirable, however, to press the importance of the originating theme too far. The hymn is of the most primitive character and very limited in range; the "Overture," on the other hand, is the work of the highly conscious, fully equipped artist, who has at his disposal and employs every modern medium. It is doubtful whether or not the slaves who sang the hymn at their camp revival meetings would recognize their old favorite in its highly civilized form. Be that as it may, his employment of the theme at the moment when his reputation was at its highest point is significant of his attitude.

His symphonic poem, "Toussaint l'Ouverture," written in 1901, is again directly the outcome of his racial sympathies. The music was designed to interpret and illustrate the character and tragedy of one of the most striking personalities that the Negro race has given to the world. Whether this composition is based upon original themes or themes derived from Negro folk songs is not certain. It is a subjective study of "Toussaint l'Ouverture's" character, his warlike prowess, and his strong family affections. The first theme and its accessories illustrate his sterner virtues, the second his gentler qualities.

Brief mention must be made of his relations with the Samuel Coleridge-Taylor Society, in the founding of which his race laid special claim to him, a claim which had his ready acquiescence. It was natural, when he was asked to contribute something original to the Washington Festival in 1904, that he should choose a subject closely linked with the mutual race of himself and the Coleridge-Taylor Society. The descendants of slaves could not but be interested in Longfellow's "Songs of Slavery," from which Coleridge-Taylor drew the words of his "Five Choral Ballads," three of which were presented at Washington. His treatment of these songs is of the simplest; his own idiomatic phrasings and repetitions with slight harmonic variations are present, but there is that remarkable restraint in his use of material and in his orchestration which only the master-hand shows.

It was in connection with his first visit to America that he received an invitation from a publisher to arrange a volume of "Negro Melodies Transcribed for the Piano," published in 1905, in which he attempted to show the main currents of native negro music, and which was, according to Dr. Booker T. Washington, who contributed a prefatory appreciation, "the most complete expression of Mr. Coleridge-Taylor's native bent and power." "Using," continues Dr. Washington, "some of the native songs of Africa and the West Indies with songs that came into being in America during the slavery régime, he has in handling these melodies preserved their distinctive traits and individuality, at the same time giving them an art form fully imbued with their essential spirit. It is especially gratifying that at this time, when interest in the plantation songs seems to be dying out with the generation that gave them birth, when the Negro song is in too many minds associated with the 'rag' music and the more reprehensible 'coon' song, that the most cultivated musician of his race, a man of the highest æsthetic ideals, should seek to give permanence to the folk songs of his people by giving them a new interpretation and an added dignity."

He also employed Negro melodies for the theme of a work which he considered better, "stronger and more modern altogether" than "Hiawatha." This was his "Symphonic Variations on an African Air," which formed the first item on the program of the Philharmonic Society on June 14th, 1906, and the air is "I'm Troubled in Mind," another Jubilee song. Although, as Coleridge-Taylor said in explaining the work, the tune is well-known in America in connection with the plantation hymn, there is reason to believe that it consists in large part of a much older native Negro melody. In the form in which it reached the composer, it is one of the most pathetic numbers in Seward's collection. Those who listen to Coleridge-Taylor's work, with its great range of pathos, strength, and at times almost weird beauty, may care to be reminded that the original tune was taken from the lips of a slave in Nashville, who first heard it from her father. The original tune is as follows:

and at the outset, without alteration of note or time, but with a simple transposition, Coleridge-Taylor uses this tune, and upon it builds a series of variations of progressive complexity and beauty.

Among the "Negro Melodies" was the "Bamboula," a West Indian dance, and this formed the groundwork of an orchestral rhapsody which he wrote in the early spring of 1910, and which he conducted at the Litchfield County Choral Union at Norfolk, Connecticut, on his third and last visit to America. The following particulars of the origin of the composition are from the pen of Mr. Carl Stoeckel:

I saw Coleridge-Taylor in London, in September, 1909, and arranged with him to come over and conduct his "Indian Music" at our recent concert. As I was talking with him, the thought came to me what he might do in a musical way in his mature manhood, as compared with the "Indian Music" of his student period. We could not use a choral work, so I proposed that he compose a work for full orchestra, using as a basis some African and American air, such a work to require not over fifteen minutes for rendition, to be brilliant in character, and suitable for a "closing piece" for our concert. There was not the slightest condition about all this; it was only a suggestion on my part—the only stipulation being for an orchestral work not to exceed fifteen minutes. Coleridge-Taylor accepted the commission, and evidently thought well of the proposition, for in the spring he wrote: "The orchestral piece is finished. It is a rhapsody dance on matter contained in my 'Bamboula,' a West Indian melody. Of course, it is very much amplified and enlarged and, in fact, quite different, but the actual four bars of the motto remain the same. I should say it will take ten to twelve minutes in performance. It is very brilliant in character, as you will see by the subject, which is taken from my collection of twenty-four Negro melodies. The work is scored for full orchestra, and is dedicated to Mr. and Mrs. Stoeckel." Coleridge-Taylor brought the score and parts with him when he came to America in May; the work was corrected on the steamship, and tried for first rehearsal at Carnegie Hall, New York, May 27th, second rehearsal at Norfolk, June 2nd, first concert rendition under the composer the same evening. The composer was much impressed by the ability of our players to give such a fine rendition after only two rehearsals. The "Bamboula" seemed to hit the fancy of the musicians present as "the best thing in an orchestral way yet done by the composer."

One of the most charming works of his later life, his "Fairy Ballads," is a setting of six lyrics by Miss Kathleen Easmon, a young West African girl. For the amusement of some child friends Miss Easmon had written little verses, enshrining pretty conceits. These her mother showed to Mrs. Coleridge-Taylor, who in turn showed them to her husband. He took the copy without expressing any intention in regard to them, and a short while later Miss Easmon was delighted to learn that he had clothed them in his most characteristic style in some of the most charming of recent music. Given a skilled accompanist, they are peculiarly adapted to the singing of little children.

The last considerable work produced during his lifetime, the "Violin Concerto," was built upon Negro tunes. Mr. Carl Stoeckel gives an account of the occasion of its origin during Coleridge-Taylor's visit to conduct "Bamboula" at the Norfolk Music Festival.

After supper my wife went into the library, and Coleridge-Taylor and I went into another room to have a smoke. She began playing on the piano, and suddenly Coleridge-Taylor dropped his cigarette, jumped to his feet, and said, "What is that lively melody?" It was an African slave song called "Keep Me From Sinking Down, Good Lord," which has never been in the books, as it was taken from the lips of a slave directly after the war by a teacher who went South and who gave it to my late father-in-law, Robbins Battell. Coleridge-Taylor went into the library and asked my wife to play it again, which she did, singing the melody at the same time. He said, "Do let me take it down. I will use it some time." For several days some of the violin passages in the "Bamboula" rhapsody had been running in my head, and the thought came to me that perhaps Coleridge-Taylor might be induced to write a violin concerto, using this African melody in the adagio movements. I proposed the matter to him then and there. He said that he was delighted with the idea, and would undertake it. In due season the manuscript of the violin concerto reached me. I took it at once to Madam Maud Powell, as the work was dedicated to her, and she was to give the first rendition. My original suggestion to Coleridge-Taylor was that the concerto should be founded on three African melodies characteristic of our so-called Southern Negro airs. When we went over the concerto, we found that the second movement was based on an African melody, but not on "Keep Me From Sinking Down," which Coleridge-Taylor had found that he could not use, and he had substituted "Many Thousands Gone" for this movement. In the third movement he had used "Yankee Doodle" quite frequently, which, of course, is not an African melody. We agreed that the second movement of the concerto was a beautiful piece of music, but both the first and third movements seemed to us rather sketchy and unsatisfactory. While I was considering what to write about this work to Coleridge-Taylor, I received a letter from him, requesting me to throw it into the fire; and saying that he had written an entirely new and original work, all the melodies being his own, and that it was a hundred times better than the first composition. I returned his first composition to him at once, as it seemed a pity to lose the second movement; and a few weeks later the score of the second concerto arrived. It was tried and found highly satisfactory. Its first rendition was at the Norfolk Festival of 1912, by Madam Maud Powell, under the directorship of Arthur Mees.

Almost to his last hour, Coleridge-Taylor was occupied with the welfare of his race; and his contribution to humanity takes its significance from his book. Other and greater musicians have lived, but he was the first of his race to reach recognition as a world musician. In the interval between the Negro folk songs and his work lie only the works of one Negro composer of consideration, W. Marion Cook, whose talents, however, reach mainly in the direction of musical comedy, which in modern days has not been rich in permanent music. Both he and Coleridge-Taylor's friend, Harry T. Burleigh, have written songs which, according to Professor B. G. Brawley, "satisfy the highest standards of art, as well as those that are merely popular music." But to neither does criticism award a place approaching that held by Coleridge-Taylor, the greatness of whose style is only equalled by the many and advanced forms in which it revealed itself. One such man is a complete answer to all the biologists who generalize on the limitations of the Negro:

Nations unborn shall hear his forests moan;
  Ages unscanned shall hear his winds lament,
Hear the strange grief that deepened through
    his own,
  The vast cry of a buried continent.

Through him, his race a moment lifted up
  Forests of hands to Beauty as in prayer;
Touched through his lips the sacramental Cup,
  And then sank back—benumbed in our bleak
    air.

True as they are, the beautiful lines of the poet speak for us to-day and for the past, but Coleridge-Taylor's work is prophetic as well. He has shown that the "buried continent" is capable of producing the highest in at least one art.

In any future discussion of his possibilities, the Negro may take heart in remembering that in the perfecting within itself of the race physically, morally, and intellectually, in an unswerving devotion to the higher human ideals, in a determination to stand upon its own achievements, lies the justification of the race. In the songs of a Paul Laurence Dunbar, the eloquence of a DuBois, the practical contributions of a Booker Washington, in the color dreams of a Henry Ossowas Tanner, in the world-embracing genius of a Dumas or a Pushkin, and perhaps even more than in these, in the melodies of a Coleridge-Taylor, which thrill the heart-strings of mankind irrespective of creed, caste, or color; in these lies the ultimate triumph of the oppressed people. More and more as the race produces examples of the highest human genius and achievement, more and more will the race be lifted to the level of those who until now have been regarded as "more advanced."

AMERICA'S POSITION IN MUSIC

BY

EUGENE E. SIMPSON

FOR more than a generation, in discussions about America's position in music, it has been the fashion to hold two pronounced views: the one, as it concerned the problem of our best procedure in study; the other, as it concerned the actual potency of our elemental forces, compared with the elements inherent in the music of other lands. During all that time both of those strongly represented views have been erroneous, as we will show.

The two errors rested, first, in the assertion that it was no longer necessary to go abroad for musical study; and second, that we had as yet no truly American music. The latter view has even persisted in face of the circumstance that for full twenty years European critics have been decrying, sometimes praising, those "Americanisms" they heard in musical compositions. Fortunately, also, the former view has remained unheeded by some thousands of musical youth who have annually flocked to Paris, London, Berlin, Vienna, even to Leipsic, Dresden, Cologne, Prague, Petrograd, Munich, Geneva, Milan, Florence and Rome.

The habit of going to Europe has immeasurably intensified our step and inestimably shortened the period of our apprenticeship. The whole process has been one of continual visiting about, plucking the best from every garden, soon discerning to reject all that had become antiquated and unworthy. With the possible exception of the Russians, in less degree those from Scandinavia and Finland, who visited central and western Europe rather more from necessity than from choice, the youth of the other European countries have not been accustomed thus to go from one country to another.

Norway, Sweden, Denmark and Finland sent their musical students to the South purely through lack of advantages at home. The case of the young Russians, who were overwhelmingly of Jewish parentage, hinged upon the two powerful forces of poverty and the restrictions which race and religion settled upon them at home. Thus were there many of those without means of the barest subsistence who went westward, and, by force of their great talent, often obtained free tuition while the wealthy of their own blood helped them to the modest and most actual necessaries of student life.

Meantime peregrination by the Americans resulted not only in finding that which was directly sought, but guaranteed for life the attitude and habit of "the open mind."

In fact their very presence abroad was a flaming and indelible sign of "the open mind," and for its influence upon the whole course of an intellectual life, that was of vastly greater importance than any group of technical principles that could be assimilated during the years spent in an academy.

America, as an item of attention in international musical life, may have begun with the work of Lowell Mason, who was born eleven years before Michael Glinka, twenty-one years before Richard Wagner and sixty-nine years before MacDowell. At about the time American statesmen were setting up the international policy of the Monroe Doctrine, in 1821, Mr. Mason was issuing the first of a series of hymn collections which were to have a very important home influence for the succeeding half century, besides earning notice and the profound respect of European musicians. Mr. Mason went abroad for a brief stay in 1837. When his son William, as a twenty-year old youth, went to Leipsic Conservatory in 1849, Hauptmann received him cordially, saying that he had been long acquainted with the elder Mason's excellent work.

Four years before this modest incident, Philadelphia had achieved the honor of presenting the first grand opera by an American, the "Leonora" by William H. Fry. As has happened to many other American manuscripts since then, the "Leonora" next waited the thirteen years to 1858, before coming into the quasi-internationalism implied by its New York presentation in the Italian language, which in 1858, as in A. D. 1918, was the prevailing operatic language in New York. Though Fry's "Leonora" and his later masterpiece, "Notre Dame de Paris" (1864), had not the vitality to earn revival in any American repertory, they gave pleasure through numerous performances accorded them in their day.

The problem of native opera had found other mild solution in 1855, by George F. Bristow's setting of the all-American "Rip van Winkle." However, there is no record of performance, either of that or other operas written by Bristow in the long life from 1825 to 1898, yet at the very close of his life he witnessed the fine success of his cantata on another American theme, "Niagara."

One year after Fry's American "Leonora" had been promoted, in its thirteenth year, to the grade of a New York opera in Italian, western America became the scene of another bit of musical internationalism; this time in a Polish-Indian combination, with Milwaukee as a background. Probably late in the year 1858 there came to Milwaukee the Polish conductor and composer, Edouard Sobolewski, who immediately set about to write an opera on the Indian title, "Mohega, Flower of the Forest." The composer is thought to have employed some real Indian themes, at any rate the work was completed and given performance in Milwaukee in 1859. The inaugural performance is said to have been met with a full house, the second by empty benches. The composer soon gave up Milwaukee for St. Louis, and after some years of great usefulness and partial artistic recognition, he died on a farm near St. Louis in 1872, almost wholly unsung.

At this late day, in the absence of Sobolewski's scores, and he had various others, there may stand open the question as to whether his talent was sufficient to constitute him a true martyr to a new world's

LOWELL MASON

WILLIAM H. FRY

unappreciativeness. If he had talent, then his failure in the pre-eminently German colonies of Milwaukee and St. Louis stands as a permanent indictment against the vaunted musical discernment there. The circumstance might have remained unchronicled except to prove what exaggeration the German attitude constituted; and this particularly in view of the fact that Milwaukee and St. Louis were among the very last American cities of long standing commercial importance to establish symphony orchestras. As to Sobolewski, if the qualities of his genius did not warrant his expectation of a first-class future in the new world, they had at least attained a first-class past in the old. Upon his arrival in America, at the age of fifty, he brought the rich tradition of a studentship under Weber; he had been for years conductor of opera in his native city of Königsberg, and from 1854 to 1858 at Bremen; his opera "Comola" had been honored with production at Weimar under one of the greatest of connoisseurs, Franz Liszt. By reason of his residence in the strongly Russian city of Königsberg, it was inevitable that he had viewed at close range the birth of Russian tradition in musical art—the production of Glinka's "Life for the Czar" (1836) and "Ruslan and Ludmila" (1842). He was said to be a Wagnerian, which would have been a most natural circumstance in view of his acquaintance with Liszt at a time when Wagner's works had not passed the complexity of "Lohengrin" and "The Flying Dutchman."

In view of all the above, it is seen that if Sobolewski's talent had been only of the most meager, and his music the veriest "Kapellmeister" product of the day, still his opera should have been accorded a worthy place for the delectation and the advancement of musical life in the new world.

When, in 1842, the American Stephen G. Foster's first song, "Open Thy Lattice, Love," was coming into print, the European cult which had already grown up around the artist and person, Felix Mendelssohn, at Leipsic, was of an enthusiasm and good-will almost without parallel. Schumann was also present there and in his prime, whole-heartedly enjoying the success of his colleague while busily composing his own works, which time proves to have been of much greater individuality and power. Two years before the death of Mendelssohn, in 1847, and four years before the death of Chopin, Foster had further brought his "Oh, Susannah" and "Old Uncle Ned," to be followed six years still later by "Old Folks at Home." In view of the present fashion in concert literature, it is seen not only that those first Americanisms by Fry, Bristow and Sobolewski have suffered the ignominy of the unused, but in all reverence to a great artist it must be said also that in the seventy years since the death of Mendelssohn his cause, still worthy, has fallen into a state of almost complete lethargy. Thus the songs of Foster, so modestly conceived, have met the better fate, since their hold extends to this day; they help to constitute one of the sturdy elements of Americanism which has been all too long occupied in stealing into our critical vision.

Let us further see how affairs of the musical world invoke patience. Going back again to the time of the Monroe Doctrine and Mason's hymnal, Johann Sebastian Bach had been dead and in the most pronounced oblivion for seventy-one years, and eight years more were to elapse before his rediscovery and Mendelssohn's revival of the St. Matthew Passion. Though the next few years saw Mendelssohn's enthusiasm rewarded by the erection of a small Bach statue near the Thomas Schule in Leipsic, still the Bach art had by no means come into its own. Professor Robert Teichmüller has shown that nearly up to the last decades of the nineteenth century, Bach was not played in Germany except through the most elementary and tuneful of his preludes and fugues. Thus the whole depth of appreciation due him was finally attained through the radical tonalities of Wagner and the musical army which directly succeeded him.

In 1821 Weber was universally recognized for his service in having created an operatic Germanism, not alone by the potency of his musical fancy but in the tradition represented in the texts, and though he had but five years more to live, his works survived, and bore still greater fruit in the inspiration they gave to Wagner. Beethoven died in 1827, recognized as a great personality and mentality, yet also not nearly understood for such as his great violin concerto and ninth symphony. For that matter the Herculean strength of his B-flat sonata, Op. 106, has not come to proper appreciation in the ninety years, to the present day. Schubert, only thirty-one years old, died a year after Beethoven, but miserably poor in the recognition to which we now see his genius entitled. His luster as song writer had been kept strangely dimmed by the popularity of a contemporary—Carl Loewe, who had undoubted talent and produced many works of permanent value, yet in nowise could those few works give him rank with a giant like Schubert. Still worse, Schubert's place as a symphonist was almost entirely unestablished, and the greatest of his eight compositions in this form, the one in C-major, was not even known to exist until Schu-

GEORGE F. BRISTOW

mann found the score in 1839, eleven years after its composer's death.

There is particular need to study the musical activity of Europe for the period of 1820 to 1850, because of the extraordinary enthusiasm with which the art went forward there. If for the same period the new America was not yet awake and following in that progress, then the need for an alibi is by just so much the greater.

When Mason's hymnal was issued, Paganini, fourteen years younger than Beethoven and eight years older than Mason, was thirty-five years old; eight more years were to elapse before Paganini's tour into Germany which resulted in electrifying Schumann. It was probably still later that Paganini cast his spell over Liszt. For America, the time of Paganini's death in 1840, found at least that the new world had already had a couple of seasons' portentous experiments in public school music, in Boston.

Whatever may be recorded of the whole time necessary for America to have found her real self in music, those Boston classes likewise stand as a record of an enduring wisdom. The eighty years of usage and experiment, sometimes of violent contention, have not sufficed to prove other than that the theory of music instruction then laid down was the right one. The ground principle involved, and thus long ago rightly discovered, was that the teacher in every schoolroom should conduct her own class in the daily music period, regardless of any particular talent she might have in music. The one need was that the teacher be rightly and effectively routined in the usual processes of pedagogy. The music classes would then progress in ratio with the other branches.

Briefly sketching further on the picture of music in Europe, to the middle of the century, the Leipsic cult of Mendelssohn and Schumann was reinforced by the veteran violinist, Ferdinand David, and the youthful Joachim, soon to be followed by the greatest of them all—Johannes Brahms. However, in that period of his career Brahms did not remain indissolubly associated with Leipsic, since his friends, Robert and Clara Schumann, and Joachim, spent most of their later lives in other cities. Many years later Brahms was often brought to Leipsic through his extraordinary friendship with the distinguished Leipsic pair, the Von Herzogenbergs; still later, with Arthur and Amelie Nikisch. All this time Nikisch was earning a particularly strong place in history, as well for his great gifts as conductor, but even more as the chief of all apostles of the Brahms symphonies.

Shortly before Mendelssohn's death, in 1847, the cult had absorbed a genial stranger, the Dane, Niels W. Gade. Incidentally, in a life of seventy-three years, Gade wrote eight symphonies, but in view of the whole world's attention which Leipsic's activities had centered upon itself, the more difficult attainment was the honor of conducting some years at the Gewandhaus. However little value the world now places upon the Gade symphonies, the Gewandhaus experience stands as eloquent testimony to the composer's tact among strangers. His tenure there might have extended over other years, but for the German-Danish political difficulties which were then developing.

In final estimate of Leipsic's early position, one will observe that of the numerous connections with the Mendelssohnian era, only Schumann and Brahms are seen to have had messages of power enough to interest posterity. Just as Weber's own potent compositions bore new fruit through their influence on Wagner, Schumann's had the honor markedly to influence Tschaikowsky, and Brahms, whose four symphonies are in themselves a rich and abundant heritage to the world, was destined to exert a most tenacious hold on Max Reger, who became at least the greatest polyphonist born in the nineteenth century.

One should not forget to add that the peculiarly strong local position of Leipsic's classic interests in music, found a wonderfully opportune auxiliary on the side of comic opera, since the very period under discussion witnessed the birth there of Lortzing's most beautiful examples in comic opera. They may well lead that branch of the literature for the nineteenth century, and eighty years have not sufficed to weaken them. Lortzing had been able to bring himself fully into the writing manner and the spirit of Mozart, and he added the technical routine of one whose life was spent on the stage.

Before returning directly to the work of America's native composers, one is reminded that against Leipsic's final tradition of Mendelssohn, Schumann and Brahms, the outer world had still Chopin, Berlioz, Liszt and Wagner, not to speak of Spohr, Paganini and Glinka. Whatever may be the exact value of their output, which reaches its highest in Chopin and Wagner, the combination Berlioz-Liszt-Wagner largely monopolized attention at the close of the century in which they lived, especially in view of the Wagnerian continuation through Richard Strauss, and in less degree, even through Bruckner and Mahler.

If America's chief values in music creative activity were represented, until 1850, by Lowell Mason and Stephen C. Foster, the alibi for the rest is found in many valid details. Up to the time that the Monroe Doctrine was born into the family of international councils, but forty years had elapsed since the American eagle completed its title to freedom. In 1812 there had arisen the need and the successful occasion to reassert the principle of liberty.

Then, happily, the Monroe Doctrine proved to be the culmination, rather than the beginning, of an international crisis, and Americans became free to consider grave problems which were growing up at home. In direct contrast, the very year of setting out the above principle in internationalism brought the Missouri Compromise, which proved to be, not the culmination, but the beginning of a crisis which grew for nearly forty other years and ended in our War of the Rebellion. Meantime we had controverted the individual rights of states, and on an entirely different set of causes, had fought the war with Mexico. Then who shall not say that the finest genius for the period was fully employed, once for all, at tracing out in blood the domestic relation which each should forever bear to the other.

Since 1850 nearly or quite a half hundred Americans are known to have composed music in the larger symphonic or operatic forms. About fifteen of our earliest composers were born before that date. Careful survey of the works by the younger group will show that individuals from among the fifty, not only employed traditional American titles but made desultory use of actual Negro or Indian themes. Still the last quarter of the century was more than half gone before there was issued the result of any organized study of our primitive resources.

It remained the privilege of a woman, Miss Alice M. Fletcher, to inaugurate the movement, and to find immediate response in a widespread interest and a new hope of progress in American nationalism. Her first report on the music of the aborigines was a monograph on "Omaha Indian Songs." This was made in 1893 for the Peabody Museum of Cambridge, Mass. She followed with various magazine articles and a book of "Indian Story and Song"; and finally a report to the United States Ethnographic Bureau, on "The Hako, A Pawnee Ceremony." For these works Miss Fletcher had valuable assistance from John C. Fillmore, who added harmonizations and included discussion of music theoretical principles involved.

The timeliness of Miss Fletcher's first study was accentuated by the appearance in the same year of Dvořák's New World symphony, which embodied Negro themes. the first-fruit of the Omaha Indian themes was MacDowell's Indian Suite, which is thought to be the best of all the composer's orchestral works. In the numerous subsequent collections and discussions of Indian music, doubtless the most valuable is the late Frederick R. Burton's "American Primitive Music," published in 1909. Mr. Burton was not only a trained composer, an ethnographic expert of the Chicago Field Columbian Museum and the American Museum of Natural History in New York, but a man of life-long routine as a *littérateur;* and because of the combination in talent and routine, his work will not be easily surpassed. Nevertheless, Miss Nathalie Curtis has issued a remarkable work called "The Indians' Book," which is a compendium of songs and textual interpretations assembled from among eighteen Indian tribes of the Southwest.

Aside, yet in continuation of the foregoing, at least three other musicians have personally gone among the Indians to study for their highly specialized composing on Indian themes. These were Arthur Farwell, a native of St. Paul; Charles Wakefield Cadman, of Pittsburgh; and the Kansas City Philharmonic conductor, the Dane, Carl Busch, who has ever held a good allegiance both to his native and to his adopted countries.

Of this group, Farwell doubtless has the priority in time, for he was already issuing Indian compositions at the turn of the century, and Cadman began in 1906. The latter gave out "Four Indian Songs," and has written other idealized pieces which have had a very wide circulation, yet the first great climax to his studies probably will be found to rest in his first Indian opera "Shanewis," wherein he has employed some forty aboriginal themes. Farwell established, in 1901, the Wa-Wan Press at Newton Centre, Massachusetts, and at about that time issued piano pieces called "Dawn," "Navajo War Dance," and "Pawnee Horses." He has also set Shelley's "Indian Serenade," has made various

STEPHEN FOSTER

tours lecturing on Indian lore, and has recorded Indian folk songs of the Southwest for the American Institute of Archæology.

More than twenty years ago, Busch had made idealized settings of American home song, as the "Old Folks at Home," for string orchestra, and an American rhapsody, besides having given much orchestral and choral attention to subjects from Tennyson. His later specializing on Indian themes came to their most comprehensive result in an orchestral five-movement Indian Suite, which he tried out in private hearing at Leipsic, 1906. At that time it was strangely noticed that of all the movements, entitled "Greeting of Hiawatha," "Chibiabos," "Omaha Funeral Procession," "Indian Love Song," and fantasia, variations and fugue on an Indian air, the least individual of the five was one in which the composer had kept closest to the original form of the Indian love song. The explanation may rest in the fact that at that point in the entertainment a slower movement was needed, and the composer found greater difficulty in obtaining a theme strong enough to be introduced. Other Indian works by Busch include songs, dances and choruses, besides the highly important cantata of "The Four Winds."

Other musicians who have at least paid compliment to Indian tradition, without having gone deeply into it, include Hugo Kaun (born in Berlin, and again resident there), who wrote symphonic poems, "Minnehaha" and "Hiawatha"; Victor Herbert (born in Dublin), represented by Indian melody in his opera, "Natoma"; Giacomo Puccini (Italian), who used Indian material in his "Girl of the Golden West"; Rubin Goldmark, who wrote a "Hiawatha" overture; Louis Adolf Coerne, with a symphonic poem, "Hiawatha"; Ernest R. Kroeger, author of a "Hiawatha" overture and "Ten American Sketches." S. Coleridge-Taylor set portions of Longfellow's "Hiawatha" in the form of a four-movement cantata. As to Frederick R. Burton's own composing in Indian materials, it was by choice largely on Ojibway themes, his most comprehensive work represented by the dramatic cantata "Hiawatha," and many Ojibway songs.

There is the highest probability that much other youthful enthusiasm, accompanied by talent and routine, may exist without yet having been formally introduced to the public. An example of this is found in Israel Amter's three opera manuscripts, all on his own texts and themes, at least one of which is on an Indian subject. Amter was reared in Colorado, though previous to his coming to New York in 1914 he had spent some years in the utmost retirement at Leipsic, partly in study, but chiefly in the quiet he desired for his own writing. Incidentally his young wife occupied herself with painting, and without having there any real Indian girl for model, she utilized an Alsatian friend and produced good "Indian" results.

Turning for awhile from consideration of the American aboriginal, the Negro element in music has been much oftener noticed by composers, and American bibliography shows a far earlier interest in the subject. Since the Negroes, unlike the Indians, are not looked upon as a vanishing race, there has been no occasion for our government to enter upon an intensive musico-ethnographical study among them. Meantime the stage of their own musical education has become so high that they easily help themselves. Latterly they have realized the nature of the change which an ever-moving civilization, and their own progress, may crowd upon their traditional music, and at least six of their higher institutions are taking care to gather and record the whole treasury of their song. These schools include the pioneer, and still most active among them, the Fisk University of Nashville, Tennessee; also the Hampton Institute, Atlanta University, Talladega College, Tuskegee Institute and the Calhoun School.

The "Coal Black Rose" of 1829 may have marked the first song publication on a Negro subject. Continual agitation of the slavery question, and the Dan Rice minstrels of 1834-35 greatly popularized the Negro as a topic for treatment on the stage, yet the literary discussion of the Negroes' music seems to have been deferred until the time of the war which so largely grew out of the controversy over slavery. Thus Mr. Frank Kidson's chapter for Grove's Dictionary suggests Miss McKim's letter in Dwight's Journal of Nov. 8, 1862, as the first which called public attention to the slave songs.

For the first artistic elaboration of songs on the Negro topic, a cursory glance falls upon a product of 1850—F. H. Williams' "Petit fantaisie for the harp, on the celebrated Ethiopian melodies 'Louisiana Belle,' 'Uncle Ned,' and 'Susanna.'" It may be looked upon as a noteworthy coincidence that in the retreatment of these three songs, Stephen C. Foster, then as now, was promising potentiality as one who might live again through those who would come after.

In the next important steps in utilizing the Negro tone, the palm for priority rests with G. W. Chadwick (1854—) and Henry Schoenefeld (1857—) who were students together at Leipsic conservatory, in the late seventies. The Scherzo of Chadwick's second symphony (1885) is the first example of his having written in this specific manner, yet the title of his public examination overture of 1879, "Rip van Winkle," indicates that thus early the composer's glance was turned toward home. Schoenefeld's first formal essay on the Negro topic is the overture, "In Sunny South," but he had already touched the Southern vein with his "Characteristic Suite." Hard after

LOUIS MOREAU GOTTSCHALK

Chadwick and Schoenefeld's Southern excursions, Maurice Arnold (1865—) takes credit for having proposed in 1883 to embody the plantation spirit in a suite which he would have written during his Berlin study under Urban. If Urban then advised against it, the intention came to maturity in a series of "Plantation Dances," which

Arnold wrote after Dvořák's coming to New York. Just as in Arnold's later use of this element in two movements of a sonata for piano and violin, these dances were not written directly on Negro themes but they sought to find the spirit of the South.

Among many who have followed, Harry T. Burleigh, himself of the Negro race, has had the honor to centralize his people's interest in their music, and as a pupil of Dvořák during that great master's sojourn here, Burleigh helped to find the materials which were embodied in the New World Symphony and the string Quartet, Op. 96. Burleigh's own efforts were greatly augmented by the American visits of the English subject, S. Coleridge-Taylor, of but half Negro blood, yet the most prolific and powerful composer who has sprung from the race. Doubtless the most intensive study of the music of the Negro race is embodied in a collection of songs then transcribed by Coleridge-Taylor and issued as brief variations for piano, with each theme first separately shown in its aboriginal form. The collection was accompanied by Booker T. Washington's Introduction, and the composer also prefaced the works with his own highly authentic discussion of the related character of the African aboriginal and American slave song. Other African works by Coleridge-Taylor were a set of orchestral variations, an orchestral suite, an overture, various other songs, and a number of dances for violin and piano.

The two distinguished, wholly non-American composers, Cyril Scott and Claude Debussy, have complimented the Negro tradition, while the late Bruno Oscar Klein, a native of Germany, but many years a citizen of New York, wrote numerous violin, song and piano pieces in which he sought the spirit of the American South.

MacDowell wrote a suite, "From Uncle Remus"; John Philip Sousa included "Darkest Africa" in his suite of "Quotations"; J. A. von Brockhoven, formerly of Cincinnati, wrote an orchestral suite on Creole melodies; John Powell, of Richmond, has a piano suite, "In the South"; E. R. Kroeger has treated the South in his "American Sketches"; Henry K. Hadley has a symphony entitled "North, East, South and West"; Henry F. Gilbert composed a comedy overture on Negro themes; and most recently, the New York woman, Mana Zucca, has brought out a short but modern and immensely effective orchestral fughetto on "Dixie."

For some years the spirit of the South has attracted Mortimer Wilson (1876—) who promises to qualify, not only as the strongest composer who has written in that tradition, but as the most facile and powerful symphonist America has yet afforded; and since Wilson's manuscripts already include five symphonies, his cause is seen to exist, not in the uncertain future, but in the present. His output is even now ready for adjudication—there remains only the problem of making these symphonies known.

Though Wilson by no means commits himself to write solely in this vein, he has lately said that therein he was coming to feel himself at his best, and he now realizes that his earlier works had this element even before he knew. As yet they include a four-movement piano suite, "In Georgia," a half dozen piano and violin ensembles, called "Suwanee Sketches"; his third sonata for piano and violin is the "Dixie"; while this intended Southern manner is very pronounced in the last movement of the G-minor piano trio, Op. 16, and the last movement of his fourth symphony. For that matter, a slight relation to ragtime rhythm may be found in any of his compositions, and in view of the composer's considerable attention to the subject, it will be of interest to embody here his characteristic position with regard to it.

"There is perhaps no more distinct tonal portrait of any people than that element of American national music which suggests the southern portion of these United States. Not that the Negro is to be considered the originator of that quaint style of lyric song which is inseparable from the South; but rather, he is the temperamental medium through which the white race of this portion of the United States has spoken, and the plantation song is a reflection of the white race through the voice of the darkey."

After the aboriginal and the Southern, there remain at least two other elements which have come up in our American music. In greater degree this is John Philip Sousa's influence upon the nation's music; in the smaller degree, two very intense performances in translating American bird song. The latter include Edgar Stillman Kelley's Andante Pastorale of the New England Symphony, and W. B. Olds' "25 Bird Songs," which are soon to be followed by about fifteen more. Mr. Kelley's entire symphony is of such power as forever to stand well among the world's worthy productions, and still a particular merit rests with this fine symphonization after the birds he heard in New England. Likewise, Mr. Olds has given the finest conscience toward the translation of bird song, as if truly he would give the bird the first chance; but because he had not yet any initiation into bird philological circles, neither a firm hold on any one of those dialects, he took the liberty to supply his own texts in English, still further enriching the discourse with finely conceived imagery for the accompanying piano.

Mr. Sousa's influence has ramified in a number of directions, and while the public of every continent is first taken by the individual rhythm and mood of his melodies, the musician also discovers that this great favorite of the people has been a real innovator in the technic of his trade. His earlier marches followed the old form of bringing four subjects without a return to either. Later he established the precedent of going back from the fourth to the third material and ending with that. This form has become universal among all writers of the practical military march. Furthermore, two of the composers above cited for their work in Indian and Southern vein, Charles Wakefield Cadman and Mortimer Wilson, have recently thanked Mr. Sousa for their first knowledge of instrumentation, learned from his scores while living in Western towns, out of range of any classes of instruction.

In general consideration of all those who have particularized, even to a small extent, in the nation's own, also further including about a hundred others who may have composed in the larger forms without any nationalistic intent, it will be noted that not one has sought the harmonically *bizarre* or the complex for its own sake. The work of most of them might have come to a better longevity if they had. Nevertheless, it should be chronicled that for eleven years there has lived in America a young Russian, Leo Ornstein, born at Kremyenchug, 1895, the most radical tonalist who has yet appeared on either continent, Schönberg, Korngold, Stravinsky and Scriabin notwithstanding. Brief examination of Ornstein's cause shows at least, that he has already the appreciation and sympathy of a number of highly capable musicians who have carefully examined and heard many of his most radical works. As in every instance of art or other intellectual revolution, or progress, there is a much greater army of violent dissenters than of those who, in a small measure, understand. At this stage one may grant the composer the courtesy of his own word, wherein he professes the complete sincerity of his aims.

With respect to Ornstein's hitherto unknown frequency of notes employed within the chord, termed clusters of notes, the composer claims them as a means for expressing color, and then he says: "Strip the color elements from one of my chords and you will find its actual structure one of Grecian severity of outline; but it requires study to distinguish between the fundamental tones and those purely incidental." At another time he expresses the belief that his music is continually under the influence of the Oriental Church, and says: "There is hardly a composition of mine which fails to offer proof of the lasting impression which Greek ritual music and the Asiatic chant have made upon me, though I have never exploited traditional themes or material." The above quotations are from Frederick H. Martens' book, "Leo Ornstein," published in New York, 1918.

With the distinctive elements of our primitive and nationalistic traits already under view, it will be pertinent to suggest that there is no valid reason why they all should not dwell here and increase, like one great family, each individual maintaining his own particular interest while contributing to the total of America's musical treasure. Yet it is true that, even within recent date, one has sometimes inveighed against the other. While the one thought that the Indian music constituted the more searching and intimate picture of the daily life of a race, the far more numerous group has decried the Indian in order to build up the cult of the South. Still others would have nothing to do with either of those elements, but expected that a musical saviour would some time arise and establish our Americanism at a stroke.

For two examples of the most authentic appeals for the respective nationalism represented by the Negro and Indian materials, we may review Mr. Burton's abovementioned "American Primitive Music," and J. W. Work's "Folk Song of the American Negro." The latter is issued from the press of Fisk University, which, in 1871, became the pioneer in the promotion of Negro music, and which still holds an advanced position in the same interest. Mr. Work, a Negro professor of Latin at the university, first notes that the Negro religious music had been always their best, while their secular songs had been poor. Then he directly presents the claims for five of the Stephen C. Foster songs to be accepted as the secular music of the Negro, as follows:

"Sometimes they are called plantation melodies. They were composed by a white man, and therefore cannot be placed in the catalogue of Negro Folk songs; still it can be correctly stated that in spirit and pathos they bear the Negro stamp, and it is not improbable that they are composed of stories and airs Mr. Foster learned from the Negroes he knew so well, and among whom he lived during the days of slavery. Consequently it is not out of place to state here the paradox that these are the finest secular Negro songs in existence. There have been many imitations of Negro music and some of it has been enjoyable, but these songs of Stephen Foster stand out as the best of that class, in fact they stand alone in a class between all other imitations and the genuine Negro Folk song."

Mr. Burton, as one of the broadest and most liberal of all those who have written on the topic, strongly sets forth his belief in the innate power of the Indian music, and further believes that the Ojibways will be proved to be the most musical of all the tribes. And still he presents a singularly charitable view toward Foster, when in reviewing respective arguments, he says, "I am still more in sympathy with those who would approximate as closely as possible to the beginnings of an American Folk song made for us by Stephen C. Foster."

Other phases of Mr. Burton's writing on the Indians show that his principal study of their music had been almost wholly among the Ojibways, and only the fact that he needed to compare with music of other tribes accounted for his not issuing this book as an Ojibway special. Primarily his thought was to notate and preserve our primitive music while it was still in the memory of Indian singers. He believed that the songs had positive art value, and not to make a statement of his convictions would be lacking in courage. In selecting twenty-eight Ojibway songs for publication he had kept a respect for ethnology by setting down also the crude and ugly, and he had tried to give an exact expression of Indian thought. Incidentally he noted that archæologists were recognizing fifty-eight distinct ethnic families of American aborigines living north of our Mexican border. For the Indian himself, music was not only an important but an essential feature of life. It entered more intimately into their lives than into the lives of any white nation. It touched every phase of daily life, and in that the vocally gifted Indian youth were taught by their elders he thought that the people of no nation loved music as did the North American Indians.

Finally bringing to a close the discussion of America's position in music, it remains to be stated that for a quarter of a century there has been at least an American longing, analogous to that of Chrysosthemis in the

Strauss "Elektra"—she yearned for a child of her own. The foregoing evidence discloses that during this entire period of longing, America had already, not one but several musical children, and it remained only for a progressive and discerning world to legitimatize them. No future art direction can vary the inherent merit of their claims.

For a last word in behalf of those nineteenth century Americans who are now seen to have written large musical forms without attaining the honor of performance for their works, one must question that justice was in any right degree accorded them. If, from among the European output played in America during this long period, there had not been included vast numbers of selections of no permanent worth, then the status might have represented a semblance of justice. It is impossible that the best of the American music has been less valuable than the poorest from abroad.

May the future soon make good the wrong which has been too long standing.

CHRONOLOGY

For the convenience of those who may not have facilities for finding the more important American composers for the period since 1820, the following list is appended, though it is inevitable that this, too, may disclose unintentional omissions:

LOWELL MASON   1792–1872
The Handel and Haydn Collection, and more than a half dozen other collections of anthems, hymns and songs.

EDOUARD SOBOLEWSKI (Polish)   1808–1872
Operas, "Mohega, Flower of the Forest," "Imogen," "Velledo," "Salvator Rosa"; symphony, "North and South"; cantatas with orchestra; choruses.

WM. H. FRY   1813–1864
An overture; operas, "Leonora," "Notre Dame de Paris"; three symphonies; cantatas; a Stabat Mater and many shorter vocal and instrumental works.

GEORGE F. BRISTOW   1825–1898
Operas, "Rip Van Winkle," "Columbus"; "Arcadian" symphony; symphony in F-sharp minor; two oratorios; two cantatas with orchestra; the descriptive "Niagara" for chorus and orchestra; and material to total about eighty opus numbers.

STEPHEN C. FOSTER   1826–1864
Composed about one hundred and seventy-five songs.

LOUIS M. GOTTSCHALK   1829–1869
The symphony "La nuit des tropiques"; an overture; a triumphal cantata; an unfinished opera; also for orchestra, "Montevideo," Grand triumphal march, "Gran marcha solennelle," "Escenas campestres Cubanos," and Gran Tarantella, besides many pieces for solo-piano.

C. C. CONVERSE   1832–1918
Overtures, "Hail Columbia" and "In Spring"; oratorio "Captivity"; two symphonies; ten sonatas; three symphonic poems, and other works.

B. J. LANG   1837–1909
Symphonies; overtures; oratorio, "David"; chamber music.

SMITH N. PENFIELD   1837–1920
Overture; orchestral setting of "Psalm XVIII"; string quartet.

JOHN K. PAINE   1839–1906
Two symphonies; symphonic poems, "Tempest," "Island Fantasy," "Lincoln" (unfinished); opera, "Azara"; oratorio, "St. Peter"; Mass in D; music to "Œdipus"; duo concertante for cello, violin and orchestra.

DUDLEY BUCK   1839–1909
Symphonic overture, "Marmion"; opera, "Deseret"; two sonatas for organ; cantatas, "Don Munio," "Voyage of Columbus"; oratorios, "Golden Legend," "Light of Asia," "Psalm XLVI."

GEORGE E. WHITING   1842–1923
Symphony; overture; piano concerto; one-act opera, "Lenore"; cantatas, "Tale of the Viking," "Henry of Navarre," "March of Monks of Bangor," "Dream Pictures," "Midnight."

JOHN C. FILLMORE   1843–1898
Collaborating with Miss Fletcher and F. La Flesche, one of the first to study music of the Indians.

JOHN NELSON PATTISON   1845–1905
"Niagara" symphony and piano works.

OTIS B. BOISE   1845–1912
Symphony; two overtures; piano concerto.

W. W. GILCHRIST   1846–1916
Symphony; quintet; trio; nonet for piano and strings; "Psalm XLVI"; suite for piano and orchestra; half dozen large works for chorus and orchestra; about two hundred songs.

HOMER N. BARTLETT   1846–1920
Orchestral Spanish caprice; concertstück for violin and orchestra; cantata, "Last Chieftain"; opera "Hinotito."

SILAS G. PRATT   1846–1916
Two symphonies; symphonic sketch, "Magdalena's Lament"; operas, "Antonio," "Triumph of Columbus"; symphonic suite, "Tempest"; grotesque suite, "Brownies"; serenade and canon for strings; orchestral, "Paul Revere's Ride," "Battle Fantasia," "Battle of Manila"; cantata, "The Last Inca"; many shorter works for orchestra; piano pieces and songs.

FREDERICK GRANT GLEASON   1848–1903
Operas, "Otho Visconti," "Montezuma" and others, sealed by his will until fifty years after

CHRONOLOGY—Continued

his death; three piano trios; piano concerto; triumphal overture for organ; symphonic poem, "Edris"; half dozen large odes and cantatas.

JULES JORDAN   1850–1927
Romantic opera, "Rip Van Winkle"; dramatic scene, "Joel" for soprano and orchestra; three works for chorus and orchestra, "Windswept Wheat," "Night Service," "Barbara Fritchie."

ALBERT A. STANLEY   1851–1932
Symphony, "Soul's Awakening"; symphonic poem, "Attis"; Ode for Providence Centennial.

JOHN A. BROECKHOVEN   1852–1930
Creole Suite for orchestra; "Columbia" overture.

ARTHUR FOOTE   1853–
Suite in D-minor; two smaller suites; serenade for strings; symphonic poem, "Francesca da Rimini"; overture, "In the Mountains"; piano quintet; piano quartet; two piano trios; two string quartets; violin sonata; two piano suites; organ suite; many large choral works with orchestra.

G. W. CHADWICK   1854–1931
Three symphonies; symphonietta; symphonic sketches; a Dedication Ode; symphonic poem, "Cleopatra"; overtures, "Rip Van Winkle," "Euterpe," "Melpomene," "Thalia," "The Miller's Daughter"; much chamber music and numerous cantatas.

CARL V. LACHMUND   1854–1928
Japanese overture; trio for harp, violin and cello.

ADOLPH M. FOERSTER   1854–1927
Orchestral character piece, "Thusnelda"; prelude to "Faust"; "Dedication March"; two piano quartets; piano trio; piano suite; suite for violin and piano; many piano pieces and about one hundred songs.

GEO. TEMPLETON STRONG   1855–
Symphony, "An der See," "In the Mountains"; symphonic poems, "Le Roi Arthur," "Undine" and "Sintram"; suite, "Die Nacht"; elegie, for cello and orchestra; many other small forms.

JOHN PHILIP SOUSA   1856–1932
Symphonic poem, "Chariot Race"; historical scene, "Sheridan's Ride"; the suites "Three Quotations" and "Last Days of Pompeii"; eight or more comic operas.

JOHN HYATT BREWER   1856–1931
Orchestral suite, "Lady of the Lake"; sextet for flute and strings; cantatas, "Hesperus," "Birth of Love," and numerous others.

EDWARD STILLMAN KELLEY   1857–
"New England symphony"; symphony, "Gulliver in Lilliput"; Chinese suite; orchestral pictures, "Christmas Eve with Alice"; melodramatic music to "Macbeth," "Jury of Fate" and "Ben Hur"; piano quintet; string quartet.

BENJAMIN CUTTER   1857–1910
Cantata, "Sir Patrick Spens"; a Mass; many smaller works.

HENRY SCHOENFELD   1857–
"Rural Symphony"; ode, "Three Indians"; overture, "In Sunny South"; "Characteristic Suite"; piano concerto; violin concerto; sonata for violin and piano.

F. VAN DER STUCKEN   1858–1929
Lyric drama, "Vlasda"; suites, "The Tempest," and "Pagina d'Amore"; a festival march; symphonic prolog, "William Ratcliff"; orchestral, "Pax Triumphans," and many songs.

HARRY ROWE SHELLEY   1858–
Two symphonies; orchestral suite; symphonic poem, "Crusaders"; fantasy, piano and orchestra; dramatic overture, "Francesca da Rimini"; one-act extravaganza; opera, "Leila."

BRUNO OSKAR KLEIN (German)   1858–1911
Opera, "Kenilworth"; orchestral variations; violin sonata; many songs and piano pieces seeking American folk spirit.

VICTOR HERBERT (Irish)   1859–1924
Operas, "Natoma" and "Madeleine"; symphonic poem, "Hero and Leander"; orchestral suites, "Woodland Sketches" and "Columbus"; numerous comic operas.

REGINALD deKOVEN   1859–1920
Comic operas, "Robin Hood," "Maid Marian," "Don Quixote," "Fencing Master."

GERRIT SMITH   1859–1912
Cantata, "King David"; ten-piece piano cycle, "Colorado Summer"; twenty-five "Song Vignettes" for children.

HOMER NORRIS   1860–1921
Overture, "Zoroaster"; cantatas, "Nain" and "Flight of the Eagle"; many songs and small forms.

ALFRED G. ROBYN   1860–1935
Four string quartets; a quintet; piano concerto; orchestral suites; a Mass.

E. A. MACDOWELL   1861–1908
Numerous orchestral and piano suites; two piano concertos; four piano sonatas; symphonic poems, "Hamlet," "Ophelia," "Launcelot and Elaine"; "Saracens," "The Lovely Alda"; many piano pieces and songs.

CHARLES MARTIN LOEFFLER   1861–1935
Orchestra, "Les Veillees de l'Ukraine"; fantastic concerto for cello and orchestra; divertimento for violin and orchestra, "La Mort de Tintagiles," "La Vilanelle du Diable," "Pagan Poem"; poem, "Memories of Childhood"; choral, "Hora Mystica," "Canticum Fratris Solis," "Evocation," "By the Rivers of Babylon"; chamber music; music for four string instruments; octet; two rhapsodies for oboe, viola and piano.

FREDERICK R. BURTON   1861–1909
"Inauguration Ode"; dramatic cantatas, "Hiawatha," "Legend of Sleepy Hollow"; notated and issued many Ojibway songs; book on "American Primitive Music."

ARTHUR WHITING   1861–
Concert overture; suite for strings; fantasia for piano and orchestra; piano quintet; piano trio; sonata piano and violin; many small forms.

ETHELBERT NEVIN   1862–1901
Pantomime for piano and orchestra; piano suites, "May in Tuscany," "A Day in Venice," "In Passing"; many songs and piano pieces.

CHRONOLOGY—Continued

WALTER DAMROSCH 1862—
Operas, "Scarlet Letter" and "Cyrano de Bergerac"; incidental music to dramas "Electra" and "Medea."

ERNEST R. KROEGER 1862–1934
Symphony, symphonic suite; overtures, "Endymion," "Thanatopsis," "Sardanapalus," "Hiawatha," "Atala"; piano concerto; three string quartets; two piano trios; piano quintet; sonatas for violin, viola, cello; for piano, ten "American Character Sketches"; "American Tone Pictures"; "Twenty Moods."

CARL BUSCH (Danish) 1862—
Five-movement orchestral "Indian Suite"; a symphony; Indian cantatas after Longfellow; elegy for strings; American rhapsody; orchestral prologue to "Passing of Arthur," and various cantatas after Tennyson.

HENRY HOLDEN HUSS 1862—
"Idyl" for small orchestra; Rhapsody, piano and orchestra; Polonaise, violin and orchestra; piano concerto; violin concerto; Festival "Sanctus" for chorus and orchestra; festival march, organ and orchestra; string quartet; piano trio; violin sonata; soprano aria, "Death of Cleopatra."

JESSIE L. GAYNOR 1863–1919
Operettas, "House that Jack Built," "Toy Shop," "First Lieutenant," "Man with a Wart," "Harvest Time," "Christmas Time," "Blossom Time"; many songs for children.

HORATIO PARKER 1863–1919
Opera, "Mona"; an operetta; a symphony; string quartet; overtures, "Regulus," "Count Robert of Paris"; two concertos for organ; choral works, "Hora Novissima," "Psalm XXIII," "St. Christopher" and others.

HUGO KAUN (German) 1863—
Symphonic poems, "Hiawatha," "Minnehaha"; festival march, "Star-Spangled Banner," and various symphonic forms.

FREDERICK F. BULLARD 1864–1904
Melodrama on Tennyson's "Six Sisters"; three vocal duets in canon form; many songs and important dramatic ballads.

HARVEY WORTHINGTON LOOMIS 1865–1931
Piano concerto; a MS. opera; burlesque operas, "Maid of Athens," "Burglar's Bride"; violin sonata; melodramatic, "Tragedy of Death"; "Norland Epic" for piano; nearly five hundred other works.

ALVIN KRANICH 1865–1921
Fantasia for piano and orchestra; opera, "Doctor Eisenbart"; five or more "American Rhapsodies" for orchestra.

MAURICE ARNOLD (STROTHOTTE) 1865–1933
Symphony; "Plantation Dances"; orchestra works on Oriental topics; dramatic overture; piano sonata; violin sonata; cantata "Wild Chase"; tarantelle for strings; six duets for viola and violin; ballet music; two comic operas.

NATHANIEL CLIFFORD PAGE 1866—
Opera, "First Lieutenant"; an Oriental opera; music to the play "Moonlight Blossom" on Japanese life, with overture on Japanese themes; orchestral, "Village Fête," and incidental music to "The Japanese Nightingale."

ARTHUR M. CURRY 1866–1908
Symphonic poem, "Atala"; overture, "Blomidon"; an elegiac overture; a Celtic legend, "Winning of Amarac" for chorus and orchestra.

ROSSETTER G. COLE 1866–1935
Orchestral melodramas, "King Robert of Sicily," "Hiawatha's Wooing"; cantata, "Passing of Summer"; violin sonata; ballade for cello and orchestra.

MRS. H. H. A. BEACH 1867—
Gaelic Symphony; piano quintet; piano concerto; violin sonata; a Mass for organ and small orchestra; a "Jubilate"; piano variations on a Balkan Theme, a French Suite and four Eskimo pieces on real Eskimo themes.

MARGARET RUTHVEN LANG 1867—
Three overtures; two arias; many piano pieces and songs.

WILLIAM E. HAESCHE 1867—
Symphony; symphonietta; "Forest Idyl" for orchestra; tone poem, "The South"; symphonic poem, "Frithjof Saga"; overture, "Spring Time"; two orchestral cantatas.

HENRY F. GILBERT 1868–1928
Comedy overture on Negro themes; orchestral "Legend" and "Negro Episode"; "Negro Rhapsody," "Americanesque," symphonic prologue, "Riders to the Sea," for orchestra; ballet pantomime, "Dance in Place Congo"; five Indian scenes for piano.

CHARLES SANFORD SKILTON 1868—
Orchestra, "Suite Primeval," "Legend," "Mt. Oread"; operas, "Kalopin," "The Sun Bride"; incidental music for "Electra"; oratorio, "The Guardian Angel."

WILLIAM HENRY HUMISTON 1869–1923
Southern Fantasy for orchestra; overture to "Twelfth Night"; dramatic scene for soprano, chorus and orchestra; songs.

HOWARD BROCKWAY 1870—
Symphony; a scherzo for orchestra; ballade for orchestra; orchestral, "Sylvan Suite"; cavatina for violin and orchestra; violin sonata.

LOUIS A. COERNE 1870–1922
Operas, "Woman of Marblehead," "Zenobia"; fairy ballet, "Evadne"; tone poems, "Hiawatha," "Liebesfrühling," "George Washington"; two overtures; orchestral fantasy; suite for strings; organ concerto; double concerto for cello and violin.

HENRY K. HADLEY 1871—
Symphonies, "Youth and Life," "Four Seasons," "North, East, South, West"; grand opera, "Azora"; three comic operas; three ballet suites; three orchestral suites; symphonic poems, "Lucifer," "The Ocean," "Salome," "Culprit Fay"; overtures, "Hector and Andromache," "Bohemia," "Herod"; piano quintet, quartet, trio; violin sonata.

CHRONOLOGY—Continued

Frederick S. Converse 1871—
Symphony; symphonic poems, "Festival of Pan," "Endymion's Narrative," "Ormazd," "Night," "Day"; overture, "Youth"; two string quartets; violin concerto; violin sonata; one-act opera, "Pipe of Desire," three-act opera, "Sacrifice," Fantastic, "Beauty and the Beast"; music to "Joan of Arc."

Percy Lee Atherton 1871—
Tone poem, "Noon in the Forest"; various symphonic movements; two violin sonatas; violin suite; comic operas, "Maharajah," "Heir-Apparent."

Arthur Nevin 1871—
Opera, "Poia," "Daughter of the Forest"; orchestra suites, "Lorna Doone," "Love Dreams," "Springs of Saratoga"; symphonic poem; string quartets.

Arthur V. Farwell 1872—
Orchestral pictures, "Dawn," "Domain of Hurahan," "Navajo War Dance"; "Cornell" overture; a setting of Shelley's "Indian Serenade"; many songs and piano pieces utilizing Indian themes.

Rubin Goldmark 1872—
Orchestral theme and variations; "Hiawatha" overture; symphonic poem, "Samson et Dalila"; cantata, "Pilgrimage to Kevlaar"; piano trio; violin sonata.

Edwin F. Schneider 1872—
Symphony, "Autumn Time"; "Triumph of Bohemia" for chorus and orchestra.

Edward Burlingame Hill 1872—
Two symphonies; Sinfonietta; two Stevensonia suites; three piano sonatas; two orchestral pantomimes; sonata for clarinet with piano; sonatas for flute and piano; sextette for wind and piano; choral works; many works for piano.

Henry Eichheim 1873—
Orchestra, "Oriental Impressions," "Java"; chamber music, sextet; string quartet; "Malay Mosaic" from chamber overture, "Chinese Ballet."

Daniel Gregory Mason 1873—
Symphony; orchestral music for Cape Cod Pageant; piano quartet; Pastorale for clarinet, violin and piano; violin sonata.

Arne Oldberg 1874—
Four symphonies; variations for orchestra; Festival overture and overture, "Paola and Francesca"; piano concerto; horn concerto; organ concerto; string quartet; string quintet; quintet, piano and woodwind; piano quintet; many other large forms written in youth.

Joseph Henius 1874–1912
Symphony; sonata, piano and violin.

Louis Campbell-Tipton 1874–1921
Piano sonatas, "Eroica," "Romantic"; pastoral suite for violin and piano; piano suite, "Four Seasons"; many piano pieces and songs.

Charles Ives 1874—
Two symphonies; two overtures; symphonic suite; works for chorus and orchestra; string quartet; violin sonata; many songs and piano pieces.

Ernest Schelling 1876—
Orchestra, "Suite Fantastique," "Symphony in C-Minor," "Legende Symphonique"; concerto for violin and orchestra; "Impressions of an Artist's Life"; "Victory Ball"; "Morocco"; pieces for piano.

Frederick Ayres 1876–1926
Overture, "From the Plains"; string quartet; two trios; violin sonata; cello sonata; piano fugues; piano pieces and songs.

Carl Ruggles 1876—
Orchestra, "Men and Angels," "Toys" (with voice), "Men and Mountains"; Vox Clamans in Deserto" (with voice), "Portals," "Sun-Treader."

Mortimer Wilson 1876–1932
Symphonic suite; four symphonies; piano trio; three sonatas for violin and piano; eight orchestral miniatures, "From My Youth"; six chamber sketches for violin and piano; four-movement orchestral suite, "In Georgia"; forty "Mother Goose" song settings; quartet forms for unaccompanied violins.

John Alden Carpenter 1876—
Orchestral, "Adventures in a Perambulator," "Skyscrapers," "Birthday of the Infanta," "Song of Faith," "Little Dancer and Little Indian"; string quartet; piano sonata; violin sonata; many songs.

David Stanley Smith 1877—
Orchestra, three symphonies, "Prince Hal," "Four Melodies, 1929," "Fête Galante" (for flute and orchestra), "Cathedral Prelude" (for organ and orchestra), "Tomorrow"; concerto for violin and orchestra; opera, "Merrymount"; choral, "Rhapsody of St. Bernard," "Vision of Isaiah"; chamber music, five string quartets, piano quintet, string sextet; sonata for violin and piano, sonata for violoncello and piano, "Sonata Pastorale" (for oboe and piano).

Benjamin Lambord 1879–1915
Opera, "Woodstock"; symphonic overture; piano trio; piano pieces; songs with orchestra; "Verses from Omar" for chorus and orchestra; part-songs; songs.

Arthur Shepherd 1880—
Overtures, "Joyeuse," "Nuptials of Atilla," "Horizons," overture to a "Dream," "Triptych" for soprano and string quartet; orchestral cantata, "City in the Sea"; symphonic poem, "Marsyas"; humoresque for piano and orchestra; piano theme and variations.

Eric Delamarter 1880—
Orchestra, overture, "The Faun," suite from "The Betrothal"; violin sonata; many songs and pieces for piano and pipe organ.

Charles Wakefield Cadman 1881—
Opera, "Shanewis"; numerous Indian songs, and songs on Persian, Japanese and South Sea Island topics.

CHRONOLOGY—Continued

GENA BRANSCOMBE   1881—
Orchestra, "Festival Prelude," "Quebec"; chorus and orchestra, "Pilgrims of Destiny"; many song cycles, piano and violin pieces and songs.

JOHN POWELL   1882—
Orchestra, "In Old Virginia," "Negro Rhapsody," "At the Fair," "Natchez-on-the-Hill"; Set of Three; symphony; choral, "Chorus and Finale"; chamber music, "Sonata in A-Flat" (for violin and piano); "From a Loved Past" (for violin and piano); also pieces for piano.

LOUIS GRUENBERG   1883—
Operas, "The Witch of Brocken," "The Bride of the Gods," "The Dumb Wife," "Emperor Jones," "Jack and the Beanstalk"; orchestra, "Jazz Suite," "Symphony," "Enchanted Isle," "Music to an Imaginary Ballet," "Vagabondia," "Moods," "Serenade"; chamber music, "Four Indiscretions," "Daniel Jazz," quintet.

EDWIN GRASSE   1884—
Symphony; suite; two piano trios; violin concerto.

JAMES PHILIP DUNN   1884—
Symphonic poem, "We"; "Overture on Negro Themes"; cantata, "The Phantom Drum"; opera, "The Galleon"; symphony; two string quartets; piano quartet; violin sonata; many songs and piano pieces.

CHARLES TOMLINSON GRIFFES   1884–1920
Orchestra, "The Pleasure Dome of Kubla Khan"; poem for flute and orchestra; piano, "Roman Sketches"; three tone pictures; many songs.

EMERSON WHITHORNE   1884—
Orchestra, "New York Days and Nights"; concerto for violin and orchestra, "Dream Peddler"; poem for piano and orchestra, "Moon Trails," "The Aeroplane," "In the Court of the Pomegranates," "Fata Morgana"; incidental music to "Marco Millions"; ballet, "Sooner and Later"; chamber music, "Greek Impressions," "Saturday's Child" (for tenor, soprano and chamber orchestra), "Grim Troubador" (for voice and string quartet); quintet for piano and strings.

DEEMS TAYLOR   1885—
Operas, "King's Henchman," "Peter Ibbetson"; choral, "The Chambered Nautilus," "The Highwayman"; orchestra, "Portrait of a Lady," "Through the Looking Glass," "Jurgen," "Circus Day," "A Kiss in Xandu"; piano pieces.

WALLINGFORT RIEGGER   1885—
Orchestra, "American Polonaise," "Rhapsody for Orchestra," "A Study in Sonority," "Frenetic Rhythms"; chamber music, "Chromatic Quartet," "La Belle Dame Sans Merci," "Trio in B-Minor"; divertissment; dichotomy; canons for woodwinds; suite for flute solo; also pieces for piano.

EDWARD BALLANTINE   1886—
Orchestra, "Prelude to the Delectable Forest," "The Eve of St. Agnes," "From the Garden of Hellas."

W. FRANK HARLING   1887—
Opera, "A Light from St. Agnes," produced in Chicago in 1925; light opera, "Deep River"; symphonic ballade, "The Miracle of Time."

ALEXANDER HULL   1887—
Symphony; orchestral suite; "Java" for piano and orchestra; piano sonata; operas, "Paola and Francesca," "Merlin and Vivien."

PHILIP G. CLAPP   1888—
Symphony; tone poem, "Norge"; orchestral prelude, "Summer"; string quartet; dramatic poem for trombone and orchestra.

CLARENCE LOOMIS   1889—
Piano concerto; opera, "Yolanda of Cypress."

HAROLD MORRIS   1890—
Orchestra; poem; concerto for piano and orchestra, "Dum-a-Lum"; symphony; chamber music, trio; string quartet; quintet; violin and piano sonata; also pieces for piano.

EDWIN J. STRINGHAM   1890—
Symphony; three symphonic poems; two orchestral suites; concert overture; many shorter pieces and songs.

JOSEPH WADDELL CLOKEY   1890—
Orchestra, "Ballet Suite"; symphonic pieces for piano and organ; two operas; opera comique; operetta; many anthems and organ pieces.

C. HUGO GRIMM   1890—
Orchestra, "Erotic Poem," 1927 M. F. M. C. prize work; two other symphonic poems; choral work, "The Song of Songs," 1930 MacDowell Club prize; other choral works; pieces for organ and chorus and songs.

PHILIP JAMES   1890—
Symphonic suite, "WO2BX," 1932 NBC prize; twelve large symphonic works; choral works; chamber music and many songs.

JOHN BEACH   1890—
One-act opera "Pippa"; string quartets; piano pieces; pieces for wind instruments.

FREDERICK JACOBI   1891—
Orchestra, "Eve of St. Agnes"; symphony; "Indian Dances," "Two Assyrian Prayers" for voice and orchestra; concerto for violoncello and orchestra; choral, "The Poet in the Desert," "Sabbath Evening Service"; chamber music, string quartet on "Indian Themes," "Nocturne"; second string quartet.

BERNARD ROGERS   1893—
Symphony, "Adonais"; orchestral tone poems, "To the Fallen," "The Faithful," "Fuji in the Sunset Glow," "Prelude to Hamlet"; "Soliloquy" for flute and string quartet.

DOUGLAS MOORE   1893—
Orchestra, "Museum Pieces," "Barnum Suite," "Moby Dick," "Symphony of Autumn"; music for "Twelfth Night," "Much Ado About Nothing"; chamber music, sonata for violin and piano.

CHRONOLOGY—Continued

Charles Haubiel 1894—
Symphonic work, "Karma," Schubert centennial prize; suite for strings and woodwind; many piano pieces and songs.

Walter Piston 1894—
Orchestra; symphonic piece; orchestral suite; symphonic poem; chamber music; first string quartet; three pieces for flute, clarinet and bassoon.

Robert Russell Bennett 1894—
Symphony and many symphonic works; operas, "Malibran" and "An Hour of Delusion"; string quartet; ballet, "Endymion"; many songs.

Albert Stoessel 1894—
Orchestra, "Cyrano de Bergerac," "Hispania"; orchestral suite in ancient style; chamber music; sonata for violin and piano; piano pieces and songs.

Albert Elkus 1894—
Orchestra, "Impressions from a Greek Tragedy," 1935 Juilliard Publication award; chamber music, works for chorus.

William Grant Still 1895—
Symphonic poems, "Darker America," "From the Land of Dreams"; symphony, "Africa"; many songs.

Leo Ornstein 1895—
Orchestra, "The Life of Man," "The Fog"; two piano concertos; chamber music, "Impressions of Switzerland"; quartet; two piano quintets; miniature string quartets; choral, "Thirteenth Psalm," "Three Russian Choruses"; songs, pieces for piano.

Leo Sowerby 1895—
Orchestra, "Irish Washerwoman"; concerto for violin and orchestra, "A Set of Four," "King Estmere," "From the Northland," "Monotony," "Synconata," "Symphony in B-Minor," "Prairie," "Florida," "American Rhapsody," "Passacaglia," "Interlude and Fugue"; concerto for piano and orchestra, "Comes Autumn Time"; chamber music, trio for flute, piano and violin; quintet for woodwinds; sonata for violoncello and piano; sonata for violin and piano; quartet in D-Minor; oratorio, "The Vision of Sir Launfal."

Richard Hammond 1896—
Orchestra, "Six Chinese Fairy Tales," "Voyage to the East," for voice and orchestra; sonata for oboe and piano; many songs and piano pieces.

Robert Braine 1896—
Operas, "The Eternal Light," "Virginia," "Diane"; orchestral episode, "S. O. S."; many chamber works, piano pieces and songs.

Howard Hanson 1896—
Opera, "Merry Mount"; orchestra, "Nordic Symphony," "North and West," "Lux Aeterna," "Pan and the Priest"; concerto for organ and orchestra; romantic symphony; choral, "Lament for Beowulf," "Heroic Elegy," "Beat! Beat! Drums!"; chamber music, "Quintet in F-Minor," "Concerto da Camera"; string quartet; many piano pieces.

Roger Sessions 1896—
Orchestra, "The Black Maskers"; two symphonies; concerto for violin and orchestra; also pieces for piano and organ.

Henry Cowell 1897—
Orchestra; synchrony; Two Appositions; reel; concerto for piano and orchestra; suite for chamber and orchestra; six casual developments; Ostinato Pianissimo; Exultation; Sinfonietta; chamber music, quartet pedantic; quartet; paragraphs for violin, viola, cello; ensemble for string quintet and thunderstick; ensemble for eight woodwinds; many piano pieces.

George Gershwin 1898—
Orchestra, "Rhapsody in Blue," "Piano Concerto in F," "American in Paris," "Cuban Overture," "Variations on an Original Theme"; operas, "135th Street," "Porgy and Bess"; many musical comedies.

Roy Harris 1898—
Symphony; symphonic piece, "When Johnny Comes Marching Home"; two string quartets; trio; concerto for two violins, two violas, and two cellos; concerto for piano, clarinet and string quartet.

Werner Janssen 1900—
Orchestra, "New Year's Eve in New York," "Louisiana Suite"; chamber music, five string quartets; wind octet; Obsequies of a Saxophone.

Aaron Copland 1900—
Symphony for organ and orchestra; dance symphony; symphonic ode; concerto for piano and orchestra; works for string quartet and piano.

George Antheil 1900—
Two operas; jazz symphony; "Ballet-Mechanique"; piano concerto; string quartet; piano sonatas; other orchestral and ensemble works.

Abram Chasins 1903—
Two piano concertos; orchestra, "Parade," "Introduction and Passacaglia"; songs and piano pieces.

THE NEW YORK SYMPHONY ORCHESTRA
Walter Damrosch Conducting

SYMPHONY HALL
Boston

Copyright, Detroit Photographic Co.

JOHN KNOWLES PAINE

THE COMPOSERS OF AMERICA

BY

FREDERICK H. MARTENS

AMERICA is the latest comer into the circle of musical nations, and its composers, in contrast to the racially unified representatives of European countries, represent a variety of diverging individual trends and tendencies. The fact that our nation embodies a great number of race factors and mental viewpoints, and that the European influence has until recently—and quite naturally—dominated our creative spirits, has delayed the unfolding of a truly national style, such as we find in the older countries. But by the use of localized folk material, such as the negro spirituals, the melodies of the Indian aborigines, the songs of the cowboys of the West, and the Appalachian mountaineers, we have now begun to develop the approaches to a national idiom which by the fusion with other cosmopolitan elements bids fair to become the foundation of a distinctively American school of musical art.

THE PIONEERS

Ever since William Billings, the Boston tanner (d. 1800), wrote his hymn-tunes, there has been a steady processional, onward and upward, of Americans who have felt the creative urge, and whose work and activities have laid the foundation for much of the subsequent effort and accomplishment which in our own day has given the American composer standing, far beyond the confines of his own land. The most striking exponents of individualism in American music during the first half of the nineteenth century are Stephen Collins Foster (1826-1864), and Louis Moreau Gottschalk (1829-1869). Stephen Foster, a composer whose simple, touching melodies have in the course of time come to be looked upon as a species of genuine American folk song, still lives in the unaffected music of "Old Folks at Home," "Old Black Joe," "Nellie Bly"

GEORGE W. CHADWICK

and their like. Gottschalk's Creole temperament and emotional gift gave his piano pieces and transcriptions an expressive quality which, as in the case of the Foster songs, lent them a vitality which carried them along into another age.

John K. Paine (1839-1906), who has been called "the dean of American music," was a composer of another type. Born in Portland, Me., he studied in Berlin, and after his return to his native land became professor of music at Harvard. His symphonic and large choral works, his incidental music for plays of Sophocles and Aristophanes, his grand opera, "Azara," show dignity, lofty concept and the soundest musicianship. But they have not survived as have the more "popular" compositions of Foster and Gottschalk.

Besides Paine other American composers experimented with grand opera in these early days. William Henry Fry (1813-1864) wrote "Leonora" and "Notre Dame de Paris"; George F. Bristow (1825-1898) composed "Rip Van Winkle," and Frederick Grant Gleason (1848-1903), besides his symphonic poem, "Edris," and works in other forms, also wrote the romantic grand operas "Otho Visconti" and "Montezuma." W. W. Gilchrist (b. 1846) is known as the composer of many important choral works, including a cantata, "The Rose," songs and instrumental music. Templeton Strong (b. 1855), Otis B. Boise (b. 1845) and Henry Schoenefeld (b. 1857), Adolph M. Foerster (b. 1854), Charles Crozat Converse (b. 1832) and Frank van der Stucken (b. 1858), have also written much for orchestra and for chorus. Silas G. Pratt (1848-1916) has contributed symphonies. symphonic suites, an opera-cantata, and two operas, "Zenobia" and "Lucille," to the record of senior accomplishment. Dudley Buck (1839-1909) is best known as a composer of church music. His numerous and effective anthems, cantatas and sacred songs, very melodic in style, though they have been largely supplanted by more recent compositions, still hold their own to a degree. With Dudley Buck might be mentioned his pupil, Harry Rowe Shelley, who has written symphonies, symphonic poems, instrumental pieces and much popular church music. Buck also wrote much for the organ, and in this connection the names of George E. Whiting, Samuel B. Whitney, Samuel P. Warren (who made a number of admirable Wagner transcripts for his instrument), George B. Warren, W. R. Bristow, Gerrit Smith, Henry M. Dunham and George B. Nevin should also be instanced. William Mason (1829-1908), and William H. Sherwood (b. 1854) are prominent among those Americans who wrote chiefly for the piano. The former, a native of Boston, Mass., was a pupil of Hauptmann and

Richter in theory and such famous keyboard artists as Moscheles, Dreyschock and Liszt, after a European and American career as a concert pianist, established himself in New York as a teacher in 1855, and in addition to "Touch and Technic," a method for artistic piano playing, and other pedagogic works, issued various pieces rich in pianistic effect. Of these his "Silver Spring" and "Spring Dawn" are justly considered to be among his best. The religious hymn-tunes of Bradbury, Sudds, Ira B. Sankey and Danks, have, strictly speaking, little musical value, and now that their day is done, are chiefly interesting as a passing phase in the growth of religious musical appreciation in the United States. Representing permanent national ideals, Dan Emmett's "Dixie," George F. Root's "Battle Cry of Freedom" and Henry Clay Work's "Marching Through Georgia," however, are patriotic songs which will live as long as the land which inspired them. Meantime, John Philip Sousa, "the march king," and other composers have done excellent work in the lighter vein.

In this brief mention of the best known Americans who were active as composers before MacDowell, whose works may be said to represent the highest point reached in original composition in this country, and who will be considered in a separate article. Many of MacDowell's most distinguished elder contemporaries have not been included. These will now be considered.

MACDOWELL'S CONTEMPORARIES

Foremost among those who, though his seniors, have outlived him, are Arthur Foote, George W. Chadwick and Edgar Stillman-Kelley—all New Englanders. Foote, though of American training, was reared in the "classic" traditions by his teachers, Stephen A. Emery and J. K. Paine. He is most successful in chamber music, piano music and songs, of which some, giving evidence of a truly lyric talent, have met with wide popularity, even in Europe.

Chadwick, a product of the scholarly education of the Leipsic and Munich conservatories, has given expression to a conservative but increasingly modernistic tendency in a series of programmatic symphonic works, chiefly distinguished by musicianly workmanship, a rather severe formalism and at times a remarkable dramatic power and pleasing orchestral color. His more recent works, "Adonis," "Euterpe," "Cleopatra," "Aphrodite" and "Tam O'Shanter" (a symphonic ballad), are distinctly modern, though untouched by French impressionism and similar tendencies.

Edgar Stillman-Kelley, too, was reared in the traditions of the German school, and his early successes were achieved in Berlin, which he had made his residence. Never-

EDGAR STILLMAN-KELLEY

theless, a hint as to his personal sympathies is given by his championship of Tschaikowsky, and his highly appreciative study of Chopin, recently published. Kelley has to his credit a number of highly imaginative works for orchestra. There is a suite, "Aladdin," of highly sophisticated orchestral texture, in which he uses Chinese themes; an earlier suite arranged from incidental music to "Macbeth," and a "New England Symphony," in which he has sought to embody "something of the experiences, ambitions and inspirations of our

Puritan ancestors." Kelley's clear and logical style is especially successful in chamber music, and in this field his piano quartet is best known.

To be included in this earlier group, though born after MacDowell, are Horatio Parker (b. 1863) and Arthur Whiting (b. 1861). The former has done his best work in the field of choral music, his "Hora Novissima" being a standard number in the repertory of American and English choral societies. His operas "Mona" and "Fairyland" are chiefly important in a historical sense, since both won prizes as the best American opera submitted, the first in New York in 1911, the second in San Francisco in 1915. His consummate skill in vocal polyphony, which have made his choral works effective, could hardly be applied with success to opera, and his scholarly and lofty, though often unemotional style were bound to militate against a gripping dramatic expression. Parker nevertheless represents a worthy conservative force in our native music.

Arthur Whiting represents an increasingly potent element in American composition, namely, the influence of Brahms, not in the narrow musical sense, but in the matter of general tendency, in the direction of a higher intellectuality and the preference for abstract musical thought. His works are chiefly for the piano and in the smaller forms, though a Fantasie for piano and orchestra, vocal quartets and songs give variety to the list.

William Harold Neidlinger (b. 1863), a pupil of Dudley Buck and Müller, has been active successively as a composer and teacher of singing in Paris, Chicago and New York. Though the author of a mass and various deservedly popular collections of children's ditties, he is best known as a song composer. The easy lyric spontaneity of his style is well exemplified in his "Sweet Miss Mary" and "The Weary Hours." Neidlinger was born in Boston and now lives in New Jersey.

Standing aside from all these, yet not without influence upon the general course of musical development in America, stand the works of Ethelbert Nevin. Essentially a lyricist, unschooled in the more sophisticated forms of musical composition, Nevin's appeal is directly to the hearts of his hearers and the genuine feeling which resides in such popular songs as "The Rosary" and "Mighty Lak' a Rose," or such pieces as "Narcissus," from the "Water Scenes," and other numbers from his various suites have given them a large place in the affections of the people. Among the least educated of American composers, Nevin was nevertheless one of the most gifted, and under other circumstances and at a later time could have produced works of real lasting value.

MACDOWELL'S SUCCESSORS

In considering the younger contemporaries and the successors of MacDowell we are confronted by such a large number of names that merit attention, that we are forced to adopt some form of classification in order to systematize in our minds, to some extent, the musical activity that is now going forward in America. It is, of course, too early to arrive at any sort of ultimate

HORATIO PARKER

ARTHUR FOOTE

judgment or to assay the relative value of this extraordinary output.

This present-day endeavor may be divided into two classes, according to the avowed purposes of the composers themselves. On the one hand we have those who aim to avail themselves of the native material which has been and is still being reclaimed, in order to give their work a distinctly national character. On the other hand there are all those who either ignore these native elements, though frequently they cannot forego at least an unconscious reflection of them, and are content to follow the traditions of some European country, or to achieve the amalgamation of several. These eclectics, as we may call them in contradistinction to nationalists, are again to be divided according to their influences. There are those who follow the classic traditions of pure music, eschewing the radical realism and impressionistic influences of more recent origin. Then there are what we may simply call the romanticists, and finally those who adhere to the modernistic and ultra-modern tendencies of the present day.

Prominent among the neo-classicists is Arne Oldberg (b. 1874), an Ohioan of Norse extraction. A pupil of Rheinberger, he has kept aloof both from the harmonic and polyphonic sophistications of the ultra-modern Germans, and from the impressionism of the modern French school. His works, cast from the most part in the cyclic forms, are, in the phrase of Arthur Farwell, "bafflingly absolute." Devoid of technical complications, they are nevertheless modern in spirit and show a complete mastery of means. A string quartet, two piano quintets, a woodwind quartet, two symphonies, overtures and other works constitute his output to date.

Rubin Goldmark, a nephew of the Hungarian composer Carl Goldmark, also follows the German tradition in the main, though he was largely influenced by Dvořák, whose pupil he was during that master's sojourn in America. His works, including a "Hiawatha Overture," a tone poem, "Samson," a trio, and string quartet, which won the Paderewski prize, are characterized by warm harmony, fluent melodic line and rhythmic distinction.

Another composer who betrays his allegiance to classical ideals is Howard Brockway (b. 1870). He produced a symphony before he returned from his studies in Germany, and subsequently composed a piano quintet, a 'cello and piano sonata, and a piano concerto, besides many piano pieces and songs. A ballade and suite for orchestra and a cantata, "Sir Olaf," are among his larger works; and recently he has achieved a popular success with some rather modernistic settings of American mountaineer songs, published under the title of "Lonesome Tunes."

A composer who worships a severely classic ideal and whose finely wrought works embody a protest against the sensational tendencies of the present, is Daniel Gregory

ETHELBERT NEVIN

Mason (b. 1873), a nephew of William Mason, the distinguished piano pedagogue. His most potent influences are Brahms, César Franck and Vincent d'Indy, with whom he studied for a time. Most important among his larger works are his Sonata in G minor, a string quartet and a piano sonata, all of which show great ingenuity in thematic development, more than ordinary technical mastery, and adherence to the highest forms of modern musical thought.

Frank Ward (b. 1877), a pupil of MacDowell, is another of those who prefer the classic forms. His recently published string quartet won the prize of the National Federation of Musical Clubs, and his sacred cantatas, "The Divine Birth" and "Saviour of the World," are frequently heard in churches. Among his works there is also an orchestral suite, a piano sonata, pieces for piano and organ as well as much church music.

The senior member of the group which we may, for want of a better term, call the romanticists, is Homer A. Bartlett (b. 1846), whose output has been enormous and ranges from salon music to opera. Genre pieces for the piano, Nocturnes, Reveries, Romances, etc., perhaps reveal his true métier, though he has been successful also in songs, violin pieces, organ pieces and choral works.

Henry K. Hadley, a native of Massachusetts (b. 1871), must be classed among the romanticists, though he still adheres to classical forms in many of his works, notably in four symphonies and three overtures, which have been heard in many places here and abroad. A pupil of Chadwick and of Mandycewski in Vienna, he has worked rather in the direction of the modern school of which Strauss is a leading representative, though he has not altogether yielded to the realistic tendencies of that school. His recently produced opera, "Azora," has aroused much divergent criticism, and his best work is thought by many to be an earlier tone poem, "Salome." A more recent and successful example of this form is his "Lucifer," first produced in 1914.

Frederick S. Converse, a pupil of J. K. Paine and Rheinberger, follows somewhat similar tendencies, though he abandoned classic forms rather early in his career. A symphony, a piano sonata and a string quartet must be regarded as works of his formative period. His orchestral romance, "The Festival of Pan," and the tone poems, "Endymion's Vision," "The Mystic Trumpeter," after Whitman, and "Ormazd," betray his romantic leanings. Two operas, "The Pipe of Desire" and "The Sacrifice," have been produced in Boston, the first also in New York, and a more recent essay of large dimensions is the music for the Pageant and Masque of St. Louis, performed in that city in 1914.

Reared in the Germanic traditions, Ernest R. Kroeger, of St. Louis (b. 1862), has given expression to a distinctly romantic imagination in several overtures and a suite, "Lalla Rookh," in which he uses Oriental color with considerable effect. A number of pieces, piano pieces, organ pieces and songs have also been published.

THE MODERNISTS

Composers of more outspokenly modernistic tendencies may be considered in two classes: those following the ideals of the modern German school on the one hand, and those the followers of French impressionism on the other. This classification must, however, be accepted with reservation; as in most of these composers' works the fusion of both elements is discernible and usually also an admixture of other, largely individualistic, elements.

Among outspoken nationalists, Arthur Farwell (b. 1872) occupies the position of a pioneer. As the founder of the Wa-Wan Press he was among the first to encourage Americanesque tendencies among native composers, and himself made some notable contributions to our nationalistic musical literature. Among these is a set of "American Indian Melodies," "Dawn," "Ichibuzzi" and "The Domain of Hurakan," also a "Navajo War Dance," as well as harmonizations of negro spirituals and cowboy songs. Notable among his larger works are the "Symbolic Sketches," described by the composer as "program" music in which the program is merely suggested." Among his songs "A Ruined Garden," with orchestra, is especially effective. Recently Mr. Farwell has devoted himself to a large extent in the writing of music for various community pageants, and he has espoused the cause of community music with remarkable results.

The most assertive and uncompromising as well as one of the most successful nationalists is Henry F. Gilbert. While a pupil of MacDowell, he owes little to the influence of his master, and, indeed, recognizes no school but that of his own experience. His frank admiration of Richard Wagner and his preference for the more picturesque and characteristic elements of modern music, as exemplified in the works of Chabrier, Rimsky-Korsakov and Grieg nevertheless betrays his true sympathies, and it is significant that after the rough-and-tumble existence of his earlier years, in which there was no definite artistic purpose, a hearing of Charpentier's "Louise" determined his future career as that of a composer. A rugged sincerity is the keynote of Gilbert's music. His inspiration, though objective, finds its sources in close personal associations. Thus an early attachment to the Irish literary revival, based on racial grounds, is reflected in a number of works that have an unmistakably Celtic flavor; his enthusiasm for Poe's fanciful verses found inspiration in a beautifully atmospheric piano piece, "The Island of the Fay," and his genuine love for the songs of the American negroes led him to embody a number of such folk themes in a series of orchestral compositions which thus far constitutes the most important section of his works. These include a "Comedy Overture on Negro Themes," a "Negro Rhapsody" and "The Dance in Place Congo," recently produced as a ballet-pantomime at the Metropolitan Opera House. Equally vigorous in its

ARTHUR FARWELL

HENRY F. GILBERT

Americanism are the "Humoresque on Negro Minstrel Tunes," an earlier "Negro Episode," a series of "Negro Dances" for piano, and a set of "Indian Scenes." The Celtic element in the composer's racial makeup has found expression in a symphonic prologue to Synge's "Riders to the Sea," a set of very individual "Celtic Studies," for voice and piano, and "The Lament of Deirdre." Equally characteristic is the setting of Stevenson's "Pirate Song," made popular by David Bispham, and another of Manley's "Fish Wharf Rhapsody" —a bit of Whitmanesque savagery that savors of real personal experience. Whatever the ultimate judgment of Gilbert's music may be it is in a very special sense American, and will endure as an ethnographic record of unquestioned authenticity. The fact that Gilbert commands all the resources of modern harmony and orchestration appears as an unimportant detail in comparison.

Not so with the music of John Powell. Equally suffused with Americanism, this music appeals to us first of all as ultra-modern in spirit and technic. The basic matter is not only American, but often more especially Virginian. Powell uses negro tunes and other folk material, clothes them in modern harmonies and develops them according to the most sophisticated methods of modern music. While discarding classic thematic styles he still retains the cyclical forms. The "Sonata Virginianesque" for violin and piano, the "Sonata Noble" for piano, two suites for piano, "In the South" and "At the Fair," and a string quartet, are all derived from the soil of America. Among other works, the "Sonata Teutonica," and a set of variations and double fugue on a theme of F. C. Hahr, are important.

The nationalism of Charles Wakefield Cadman is of a more obvious sort. American Indian tunes are his particular penchant, but in the diatonic and rather simple harmonic garb which he gives them they retain little of their original savage flavor. His distinctly lyric talent welds these materials into a pleasing, facile style which sometimes borders on the banal, but frequently attains a delicate charm, as in the popular "Land of the Sky-Blue Water." His recently produced opera "Shanewis" is based on an Indian subject, and in it he utilizes some Indian material effectively, but the work as a whole is lyric rather than dramatic in quality. Among other avowed nationalists mention must be made of Henry Schoenefeld with his "American Flag," "In the Sunny South" and "Rural Symphony"; and Maurice Arnold with his symphony in F minor and his "Plantation Dances."

A nationalist by association rather than performance is Harvey Worthington Loomis (b. 1865), though he has made occasional use of native thematic material. His ultra-refined, delicately impressionistic medium is not unrelated to the achievements of the modern French school, though to interpret it as the result of "influence" would be unjust, since it was developed independently and at least synchronously. His position in American music is so unique as to be almost anomalous. Hardly unusual in its technical procedure, his music is nevertheless highly original in effect. Songs and piano pieces, part-songs and children's songs are the best known of his works, but besides these "The Traitor Mandolin," and two comic operas, a setting of Verlaine's "L'Heure exquise," entitled, "In the Moon-shower," for singing voice, speaking voice, piano and violin, may be cited as an apt example of Loomis's exquisite style.

Of the native-born Americans none is better equipped than Mortimer Wilson. Born in Iowa, in 1876, his earlier music study was guided by the late Frederic Grant Gleason, S. E. Jacobsohn, and William Middleschulte in Chicago. At a later period he became a pupil of Hans Sitt and Max Reger in Leipsic, where a number of works which he took with him attracted considerable serious attention, and were even published abroad. Returning to the United States, he was for several years the conductor of the Atlanta Symphony Orchestra, and while there became more than ever imbued with the spirit of the Southern folk idiom, even though he did not become conscious of the influence until in later years. His spontaneous mastery of contrapuntal technic has, however, enabled him to infuse his entire harmonic texture with a lyric element, strongly felt but still not predominating, and which adds to his work an individuality that causes many critics to characterize it as marking the next epoch in the field of American composition after MacDowell. Included in the list of his writings are five symphonies, violin and piano sonatas, organ sonatas, and many other chamber music and piano pieces in smaller form.

One of the few Americans who have had the distinction to have an opera performed in Europe (Berlin, 1910) is Arthur Nevin, a brother of Ethelbert Nevin. This opera, "Poia," based on a sun legend of the Blackfeet Indians of Montana, definitely places the composer in the nationalistic category, and this tendency has recently been confirmed by another opera, "A Daughter of the Forest," performed by the Chicago Opera Company. His style is freely lyrical and based on the Germanic idiom, except for the infusion of native Indian material. Nevin was born in Pennsylvania in 1871, and is now professor of music at the University of Kansas. Orchestral and choral works as well as chamber music and songs have come from his pen in considerable quantity.

The so-called San Francisco group of composers, to which William J. McCoy, Edward F. Schneider, Humphrey J. Stewart, Edward G. Stricklen, Wallace Sabin, Herman Perlet and others belong, represent a rather special phase of American national life.

Of the ultra-modernists it is possible only to mention the best known. Charles Martin Loeffler, an American by adoption, being a native of Alsatia (b. 1861), stands preëminent among those who represent preponderantly French tendencies. In the mastery of technical resources, and in artistic maturity in general, he is easily at the head of living American composers. Though he makes use of modal harmonies and atmospheric effects, his own strongly poetic individuality so dominates the spirit of his work that no definite outside influence is discernible.

His serious claims as a composer were first made known through his "Veillées de l'Ukraine," for violin and orchestra, a suite based upon tales by Gogol, which was heard in Boston, with the composer as soloist, in

CHARLES WAKEFIELD CADMAN

CHARLES MARTIN LOEFFLER

1891, although an earlier string quartet in A minor had been previously heard in Philadelphia. A sextet, two violins, two violas and two cellos, next came into notice, and after that a "Fantastic" concerto for cello and orchestra. The "Divertimento in A Minor," for violin and orchestra, the composer played at a Boston symphony concert in 1895. Loeffler's fame has rested chiefly upon his remarkably imaginative tone-poems, "La Mort de Tintagiles," after Maeterlinck; "La Bonne Chanson" and "La Villanelle du Diable," after Verlaine and Rollinat, respectively, and the "Pagan Poem," after Virgil, which includes a piano and three trumpets behind the scenes. To these was recently added "The Mystic Hour," a symphonic interpretation of the Roman Catholic liturgy. His songs are exquisite reflections of the composer's subtle imagination. Among them are: "Harmonies du Soir," "Dansons la Gigue," "La Cloche felée," "Timbres oubliés," "The Hosting of the Sidhe," "The Host of the Air," and "To Helen." There are also an octet for strings, clarinets, and harp; a quintet for three violins, viola and cello; two rhapsodies for oboe, viola and piano;

"By the Waters of Babylon," and women's chorus, two flutes, cello, harp, and organ, and other works.

John Alden Carpenter owes a similar allegiance, though in his work also the individual note is strong, and, moreover, his impressionism is reinforced by more vigorous elements, which derive rather from Germanic than Gallic sources. Imaginative, at times whimsical, and always refined, Carpenter's music is distinguished by a consistent and self-confident modernity. Aside from songs, of which the "Ghitanjali" of Tagore are perhaps best known, and a violin sonata, he has written a symphonic suite, "Adventures in a Perambulator," which has met with much success.

Perhaps most definitely allied with the modern French school of any native American composer is Edward Burlingame Hill (1872). His choice of medium is, however, in no sense an imitation. It is spontaneously induced by the composer's own highly fastidious personality. He studied at Harvard under J. K. Paine, and is now an instructor at that institution. In his earlier works he was influenced by MacDowell, and in that period produced several piano sonatas, songs, and set of "Country Idyls" for piano. The atmospheric tendency becomes evident in a choral work, "The Nuns of the Perpetual Adoration," and in the exquisitely wrought music for the dance pantomime, "Pan and the Star." Later works include a symphonic poem, "Launcelot and Guinevere," after Stephen Phillips, and the subtle and whimsical "Stevensoniana" for orchestra.

Avowedly an adherent of the French school, though in his earlier period strongly influenced by Germans, is Louis Campbell-Tipton (b. 1877), for years a resident of Paris. His "Germanic period" culminated in a programmatic "Sonata Heroic," in one long movement, solid in structure and brilliant in effect. In his more recent "atmospheric" vein he had produced piano pieces and songs, a "Lament" for violin and piano, an opera, and other works.

Another American now resident in Paris is Blair Fairchild, whose choral settings of texts from the "Song of Songs," as well as his chamber music, orchestral sketches, "Tamineh," songs, etc., all reflect his French sympathies, though they are more frankly melodious than the more characteristic examples of impressionism.

More pronounced in the adoption of modal and whole-tone effects, the music of Walter Morse Rummel appears as a genuine product of the modern French school. He has found inspiration in troubadour songs and other mediæval folk music, and has published a collection of such songs as "Hesternæ Rosæ." A string quartet, a violin sonata, piano suites, other pieces and songs, constitute the bulk of his work to date.

In close relation to this group stands the young Leo Sowerby, whose works for orchestra and for string quartet have recently been performed with success, and Charles T. Griffes, who has found an apt vehicle for his talents in the intimate ballet.

Carl Engel, a composer of ultra-modern songs in the impressionistic vein, should also be mentioned here.

The list of those composers of the younger generation whose inclinations have led them in other directions than that of impressionism is, of course, a large one. Moreover, it is difficult to find any more exact designation for it than that of the much-embracing term "eclectic," for, though the Germanic heritage is still clearly traceable in the work of many, it would obviously be wrong to classify as "German" all that is not French. It is not unlikely, perhaps, that exactly these composers, who have not consciously excluded from their works any elements that readily fused with their own individuality are as truly American as any of those who have consciously striven for "Americanism" above everything else.

On the borderland of this region, showing impressionistic tendencies as well as elements of neo-classic solidity, is the music of David Stanley Smith (b. 1877), associated with Horatio Parker at Yale University. His solidity and power of coherent thematic development is shown especially in the symphony in F minor recently produced, and the string quartet in E minor. More pictorial qualities reside in the symphonic sketch "Prince Hal" and an overture, "Joyeuse," while certain works of smaller calibre, such as the popular women's

BENJAMIN LAMBORD

chorus, "Pan," have a rhythmic and harmonic piquancy that suggest a poetic imagination and a fine sense for color. A mixed chorus, "The Fallen Star," won the Paderewski Prize.

One of the first winners of that prize, but in the field of orchestral composition, was Arthur Shepherd (b. 1880), with his "Ouverture Joyeuse." Unusually accomplished in the command of ultra-modern technic and one of the most daring in his use of it, his is notably free from the Debussyan influence. His harmonies are original in the extreme, and there is no trace of sentimentality and little melodic suavity in his work, though it does not lack subjectivity. Though he employs cow-boy themes he does not feature the nationalistic element. His piano sonata, which won the National Federation prize, is among his most important creations, also a "poem" for orchestra, mixed chorus and baritone solo, "The City in the Sea," besides many piano pieces and songs.

Benjamin Lambord (1875-1915), whose untimely death robbed America of one of its most poetic creative spirits, frankly acknowledged the influence of the masters of modern Germany, especially Wagner and Strauss, though his partially French training and his enthusiasm for French literature also left their traces upon some of his later work. A pupil of MacDowell, he was early imbued with a fine romanticism, which, distilled through a personality of almost ascetic refinement and rare nobility, was expressed in a medium always lofty, yet full of sensuous beauty and genuine feeling. This spirit animates especially his songs, of which some combine a simple lyricism with a remarkable richness of harmonic and polyphonic texture. Among these a setting of André Chénier's "Clytie," with orchestra, is the most remarkable. A mood of mystery and deep reflection dominates the "Verses from Omar," for chorus and orchestra, while in an overture and a ballet scene for orchestra, pictorial and rich coloristic effects are achieved by spontaneous melodic development and a remarkably discriminating employment of modern orchestral resource.

More purposely ultra-modern is the work of T. Carl Whitmer, whose work is, like Shepherd's, remarkably free from sensuous elements. It is, on the other hand, full of psychological subtleties and animated by a spiritual quality, which has been said to give it often "a sense of overearthliness." Aside from a number of songs and piano pieces, he has written an "Elegiac Rhapsody" for chorus and orchestra, a set of "Miniatures" for orchestra, a violin sonata, women's choruses, etc. More unusual are his "Symbolisms," readings of original texts with piano accompaniment, and, still in manuscript, his so-called "mysteries"—spiritual music-dramas, of which form the composer is perhaps the sole exponent in America.

Other names to be attached to this group of eclectics are those of Henry Clough-Leighter, who, besides many songs, has written a number of choral works of large dimensions, also a symphonic ballad for tenor and orchestra and much Anglican church music; Frederic Ayres, whose essays in chamber music have been acclaimed by Arthur Farwell and others in enthusiastic terms; William H. Humiston, who has made an excursion into nationalistic territory with an effective and successful "Southern Fantasy," besides which he has written an overture to "Twelfth Night"; a dramatic scene for soprano, chorus and orchestra, and a number of fine songs; Marshall Kernochan and Homer Norris, whose styles are chiefly known through a number of published songs, and Noble Kreider, who, much influenced by the genius of Chopin, has chosen the piano as his principal medium. Similarly devoted to the violin is Cecil Burleigh, with a sonata, "Characteristic Pieces," "Rocky Mountain Sketches" and "Indian Sketches."

A special niche should be reserved for the courageous men who have successfully stormed the citadel of opera. Beginning with Converse's "Pipe of Desire," in 1910, an American opera has been almost an annual feast at the Metropolitan Opera House. Victor Herbert, with "Natoma" and "Madeleine"; Horatio Parker with "Mona," Walter Damrosch with "Cyrano," Reginald de Koven with "The Canterbury Pilgrims," and most recently

Charles Wakefield Cadman, with "Shanewis," have been the honored guests at this feast. It should be remarked, moreover, that Mr. Damrosch made his début in opera a number of years before, with his less successful "Scarlet Letter." More recently he has given new evidence of his creative ability in incidental music to Sophocles' "Elektra" and Euripides' "Medea." Victor Herbert's successes in comic opera are too well known for comment, and Mr. de Koven's light opera "classics" of an earlier day—"Robin Hood," "Maid Marian," and their companions—will live long in the hearts of the American public. In this connection mention should also be made of John Philip Sousa, already spoken of as a potent influence in a preceding chapter, and the recent writers of light operas who, while reaping the rich emoluments of that school of musical entertainment which conforms to the current taste, are raising so-called "popular" music to a higher level of distinction. These include Jerome Kern, Louis A. Hirsch, Rudolf Friml, and others.

Among those who have not been mentioned in this necessarily cursory review are many whose work merits favorable comment, though only the merest biographical notice is possible here.

Henry Holden Huss (b. 1862) is best known as a composer of songs, though he has composed and performed two piano concertos, a violin concerto played by Ysaÿe, a cello sonata, a trio, a rhapsody for piano and orchestra, choral pieces and other works. He was a pupil of the American, O. B. Boise, in Berlin, and of Rheinberger in Munich.

Louis A. Coerne (b. 1870) has the distinction of being the first to win the degree of Ph.D. from Harvard for work in music, his valuable treatise on orchestration being the thesis. After years as violinist, organist and conductor he turned to composition and supplemented his studies in Munich and Stuttgart. A symphonic poem in Longfellow's "Hiawatha" was produced in Europe and by the Boston Symphony. He has also written two operas, one of which was performed in Germany; a ballet, and smaller works.

Amy Marcy Cheney Beach (Mrs. H. H. A. Beach; b. 1867) ranks as America's foremost woman composer. A pupil of E. Perabo and K. Baermann (piano), and of Junius W. Hill (harmony), entirely self-taught in composition and orchestration, she has composed notable works in nearly every form, excepting opera. Among her numerous works are a Gaelic Symphony for orchestra, a mass, many choral works, piano pieces, songs, etc. Her "Indian Lullaby"

REGINALD de KOVEN

is one of the best of what have been termed her "expressive songs."

Among the other women composers of special note is Fay Foster, who has recently sprung into considerable prominence, especially as a result of her songs, which have a vocal appeal which has won for them a place on the programs of many concert artists. As a child Miss Foster was musically precocious, and might have been classed as a *Wunderkind*, studying harmony at eight, playing the organ at twelve, and touring the country as a pianist at seventeen. She studied theory with Frederick Grant Gleason in Chicago, and later went to Europe, where for twelve years she continued her musical studies under Rosenthal, Reisenhauer and Jadassohn. She has also won a number of prizes, such as the *Die*

Woche prize of 1911, and also one of the Federation of Women's Clubs' awards in 1917. One of the most popular of Miss Foster's songs is "Dusk in June," which is contained in the present collection.

Mrs. Lulu Jones Downing, another of this growing group of American women composers, was for a time musically active in Richmond, Ind., and of late has been established in Chicago as a teacher and composer. An example of her work contained in this collection is "June," one of her best known songs.

Nicholas deVore, a native of Ohio, is well known as a composer, organist, teacher and writer on musical subjects. He has written much music of notable individual quality in the various forms. Among his works are many charming songs, part-songs, anthems, and compositions for the piano, organ, violin and orchestra. His "Love and Life" is a characteristic example of his lighter works. As an educator his influence is chiefly felt through the pedagogic works issued by the National Academy of Music, of which he is president.

While in every creative field the American composer has come to the fore with music that is not unworthy of the land he represents, he has been especially prolific as a song writer. Among the names to be remembered in this connection only a few can be mentioned here. Charles Gilbert Spross, James H. Rogers, Will C. Macfarlane, Charles Fontaine Manney, William Lester, Mana Zucca, Sydney Homer, Whitney Coombs, Harry Burleigh, Clayton Johns, Philip James, Alexander Russell, William Arms Fisher, A. Walter Kramer, are a few among many lyric composers of distinction.

Representative composers of choral music are almost as numerous. Those not previously mentioned include James P. Dunn ("The Phantom Drum"); Franz C. Bornschein ("Onoa," "Maypole Bell," "Thyre"); N. Clifford Page ("Contest of the Nations," "Old Plantation Days," "Lord Howe's Masquerade"); Philip James, R. Nathaniel Dett, Deems Taylor ("The Highwayman").

The names included above give no more than an outline of American effort in the compositional field. They must be taken as representing thrice as many more creative musicians of distinction whose works have been published, even leaving out of account many composers of foreign birth who have made this country their home, and have become Americans to all practical intents and purposes. The field of American composition is wide, and the American composer who has a really valid art message of one sort or another need not despair of obtaining a hearing. Since the outbreak of the world war and the strengthening and unification of the spirit of nationalism in the United States, his prospects have grown even brighter. The American composer would at last seem to have come into his own, and, in some degree at least, to be esteemed "a prophet in his own country." And as the empire of Alexander was once shared among his successors, who spread the ideals of Greek civilization through the Orient; so the heritage of ideals left by Edward MacDowell, taken up by *his* successors, has done its share in bringing Americans as composers to the high plane of the deserved appreciation they have reached to-day.

FREDERICK S. CONVERSE

EDWARD MACDOWELL

BY
HENRY T. FINCK

BIOGRAPHICAL NOTE.—Edward Alexander MacDowell was born in New York, December 18, 1861, and died there February 24, 1908. He studied the piano with Teresa Carreño in New York, and in 1876 continued his studies at the Paris Conservatory. From 1879 he studied in Frankfort—piano with Heymann and composition with Raff. At twenty he was appointed principal piano teacher at the Darmstadt Conservatory and at twenty-one had a number of his works performed on the recommendation of Liszt. After several years' residence in Wiesbaden he returned to Boston in 1888. In 1896 he became professor of music in Columbia University, and retained that position till 1904. For a time he also conducted the Mendelssohn Glee Club. In the following year he fell victim to a cerebral disease, and, faithfully tended by his wife, lingered in increasing mental darkness until his death.—ED.

IN the summer of 1895 I spent a few days with Edward MacDowell in a hotel on the shore of Lake Geneva, near Vevey. He was at work on his "Indian Suite," which caused him so much trouble and perplexity that, as he confessed to me afterward, he was sorely tempted to ask my advice about various details, but refrained for fear of breaking into my vacation. When this suite had its first performance in Boston, one of the critics, while praising it highly for its artistic workmanship, found fault with the composer for trying to make a silk purse out of a sow's ear. That was rather a rude way of putting it—rude to the Indians—for the aboriginal Iroquois and Iowan songs which form its main themes are in themselves by no means without charm; yet it is undoubtedly true that MacDowell's own creative imagination would have easily yielded melodies more beautiful in themselves and more readily adapting themselves to thematic elaboration and orchestral coloring.

It is significant that the experiment of blending red and white music was never repeated by him, except in a short piano piece, "From an Indian Lodge"—one of the "Woodland Sketches"—in which original and aboriginal strains are commingled. He never indorsed the view—of which Harvey Worthington Loomis and Arthur Farwell are at present two most eloquent exponents—that a great American Temple of Music might and will be built with Indian songs as the foundation stones. Nor has he ever countenanced the widely prevalent opinion that Negro melodies form the only other possible basis of a distinctively American school of music. Dr. Dvořák adopted this view when he first came to New York as Director of the National Conservatory; but subsequently he abandoned it. It is unquestionable that the Negro has received credit for things that are not his. What is really unique in his music is an inheritance from Africa, wherefore it cannot be made the basis of an *American* school of music; while the rest of what is usually regarded as Negro or plantation song is partly a crazy-quilt made up of patches of tune from the stores of European nations, for the Negro is an imitative and quick as a mocking-bird, and partly the voice, or the echo, of the individual genius of Stephen C. Foster, a writer of true American folk songs, the best of which are equal to any German, Italian, French, Irish, or Russian folk music.

Foster's songs are unmistakably American—unlike any European folk songs. If an unknown one from his pen should come to light, say, in a remote Turkish village, an expert would say to himself, "That's American, that's Foster." If, therefore, an American composer feels inclined to write a symphony or a suite based on melodies borrowed from Stephen C. Foster, he is of course at liberty to do so, but he will show himself a greater master by creating his own melodies; and his music will be none the less American, provided he is himself sufficiently *individual* to be able—as Foster was—to write melodies different from those of Europeans.

It is time to drop the ludicrous notion that a truly national art can be built up on folk songs only. All that we need for the making of an American branch of music is *individuals* of real creative power. In the music of Wagner there is hardly a trace of German folk song, yet it is great and it is German because he was a great German *individual*. Mendelssohn and Schumann are real Germans, too, in their music, though they differ radically from Wagner and from each other. Even the nationalists among the great masters—Haydn, Chopin, Grieg, Dvořák—owe their position in the musical world much less to what they imbibed from the folk music of their countries than to their preëminent *individualities*.

In searching for such individualities in our own country we find at least two concerning whom there can be no dispute—Stephen C. Foster and Edward MacDowell, the latter representing our art music as Foster represents the folk music. I would recognize a new piece of MacDowell's anywhere, as I would the face of a typical American girl in any part of Europe. It is unlike the music of any European master, and it has on every page the stamp of his individuality as unmistakably as most two-cent stamps have the face of Washington. To be sure, there are European influences perceptible in it—the influence, particularly, of Grieg, Liszt, and Wagner, representing Norwegian, Hungarian, and German art. But the foreign influence in his compositions is less pronounced than it is, for instance, in the works of Handel, Gluck, and Mozart, who nevertheless remain Germans. What constitutes nationality, musically speaking, is very difficult to say. There is an impression that melody is the Italian element in music, harmony the German. But the greatest melodists that ever lived were Schubert and Wagner, and the greatest harmonists, apart from Bach, Wagner, and Schubert, are the Polish Chopin, the Hungarian Liszt, and the Norwegian Grieg. Music has many styles, some national, some personal.

Individuality is somewhat easier to describe, and when we examine the individuality of Edward MacDowell we find something that any American may feel proud to discover in a compatriot. To his friends his droll and truly American gift of humor has always seemed one of his most charming traits. In a letter to me he once recurred to his student days at the Paris Conservatoire. Life in Paris seemed to him "a huge but rather ghastly joke." His fellow-students "never seemed to miss the absence of the word 'home' in their language. Most of them looked as if they had been up ever since they were born. They seemed to live on cigarettes, odd carafons of wine, and an occasional shave."

That "occasional shave" is delightfully characteristic of MacDowell's wit. In his conversation he always kept the listener amused with such unexpected turns—as he does in his music. *Scherzo* is Italian for joke, and it is in his *scherzo* movements that we often hear him at his best. His famous teacher, the Venezuelan pianist, Teresa Carreño, hardly ever plays his second pianoforte concerto without being compelled to repeat the *presto giocoso*.

Another of his traits was revealed during

his Conservatoire days. Though but fifteen years old, he soon discovered that it was not the right place for him. There was too much striving for effect for its own sake, and not sufficient reverence for the masters, to suit this American lad. Famous professors like Marmontel, Mathias, and Ambroise Thomas did not hesitate to mutilate a composition or to insert measures of their own to make it what they deemed effective. He packed his trunk and went to Stuttgart. Here there was no lack of reverence for genius, but there was what throughout his life he hated quite as much—pedantry; so, after six weeks, he moved on again, a real American, in quest of the best wherever it may be found, and bound to find it.

He found it at last at Frankfort, where there was a pianist, Carl Heymann, who "dared play the classics as if they had actually been written by men with blood in their veins." Under his fingers "a sonata was a poem." The eminent composer Raff was director of the Frankfort conservatory; by him MacDowell was confirmed in his tendency toward writing music with a pictorial or poetic background. The death of Raff revealed the emotional nature of the American youth. His first pupil, Miss Marian Nevins, who became his wife two years later, says regarding this tragic event:

"He came to me at the hour for my lesson, looking so white and ill that I was frightened. His voice broke as he said only the words, 'Raff is dead.' There was a sweet hero-worship of a shy boy for an almost equally shy man, and for months after Raff's death he was in a morbid condition. He gave me eighteen marks—all he had at the time—and said, as I knew more about flowers than he did, would I get some for him to send? So I bought a mass of roses, and, what was unusual for Germany, had them sent not even bound together; and these were put about Raff, nearer than the grand beautiful floral things sent by the dozen."

Like all students of the pianoforte, MacDowell always adored the personality and the works of Liszt, to whom his first concerto is dedicated. Following the advice of Raff, he had visited Weimar, where he was greatly encouraged by the cordial praise Liszt bestowed both on his playing and his compositions, and by the invitation to play his first piano suite at the next convention of the Allgemeine Musik-Verein, over which

EDWARD ALEXANDER MACDOWELL

Liszt presided. There was, to be sure, more honor than profit in this. A man cannot live on compliments and applause, and MacDowell, like most other musicians, found it extremely hard to make a living in Germany unless he used up all his vitality in teaching, leaving none for creative work. Luckily, his wife had a little money, so they took the daring risk of dropping everything but composition and settling down to a quiet life in and near Wiesbaden. It was here that MacDowell wrote the compositions from op. 23 to op. 35.

Those were idyllic days. "The one dark spot," Mrs. MacDowell writes, "was a long and severe illness of mine brought on by overanxiety and trying to do work which I was not well used to; but in spite of it all, we were very happy. The six 'Idylls,' op. 28, of which I am very fond, I associate with our little flat in the Jahnstrasse. I had been ill a long time, and felt Edward was neglecting his work in his care of me. So I made him promise he would write a daily sketch for a week, and these six were the result of this promise. I in bed, and he writing music in the next room! Of course he changed and 'fixed' them later on, but the actual music was written in these six days."

After nearly four years of Wiesbaden it became imperative to replenish the exchequer, and an attempt was made to secure a position as local examiner for the London Royal Academy of Music. MacDowell had been specially recommended for this position, and the matter really rested in the hands of Lady Macfarren. She was a nice old lady, and things seemed certain until she suddenly said: "I hope you have no leaning toward the school of that wild man Liszt." The American had to confess sorrowfully that he had; and when he got home he found a note saying the place was not suited for him! It was not the first time, and far from the last, that devotion to an ideal cost him a worldly advantage.

He now resolved to try his luck in America, and he chose Boston instead of New York, his native city, partly because in 1880 Boston was still reputed the musical center of America, and partly because Paris had inspired him with an aversion to very large cities. He was soon in great demand as a teacher. His technical studies, in several volumes, which are not so well known as they will be by and by, reveal him as one of the most practical and successful pedagogues of all time. In the preface to Vol. I of his "Technical Exercises" he says: "In my opinion, physical development and music are two different things, and although musical talent is a *sine qua non* in pianoforte playing, it cannot reach its full expression without a thorough command of the muscles of the hand, wrist, and arm. I have found it advisable to keep the purely physical part of piano-playing entirely separate from its musical side, as this allows a concentration of the mind not otherwise practical. I therefore beg the student who may use these exercises to consider them from a purely 'athletic' standpoint."

When he accepted the professorship of music at Columbia University in 1896, little time was left for private instruction, and he could take only the most advanced students—pupils who were better suited with exercises like those in his "Twelve Virtuoso Studies," in which, as in his two concertos and in the "Études" of Chopin and Liszt, brilliant virtuosity is allied with poetic thoughts and moods. He had no use for pupils who had more money than talent; $12 a lesson would not tempt him to take such a one, while he would devote himself to others who could not adequately remunerate him. Once a week, indeed, for years, he gave a day to his free class; and when his mental collapse became imminent, he kept this class longest of all, despite the protests of friends and relatives. His pupils adored him for his kindly interest, his helpful hints, his illuminating remarks, his generosity and self-sacrifice.

On the whole, he probably enjoyed his teaching, as he did his composing, more than he did playing in public. His divers other duties made it impossible for him to practice six or more hours a day, like the professional virtuosi, and this made him nervous in view of possible technical slips. He was always handicapped, too, by an excessive diffidence, a lack of faith in himself as pianist and as composer. When he came on the stage and sat at the piano, he looked like a school-boy who has been sent to the blackboard on exhibition day and doesn't feel quite sure of himself. But soon, especially if he found the audience sympathetic, he warmed to his task and played as only a composer can play. He has had his superiors in those things in which a piano-player excels all pianists—brilliancy of execution—but none in the higher sphere of art. As regards beauty and variety of tone color, artistic phrasing, poetic feeling, dramatic grandeur in a climax, he was the greatest pianist this country has produced—an American peer of Paderewski.

It was doubtless a mistake—in which, I am sorry to say, I encouraged him—to accept the Columbia professorship. Although

MACDOWELL'S HOME AT PETERBORO, N. H.

he soon gathered large classes of devoted students about him, making music one of the most popular and prosperous of the university departments, few of the students were sufficiently advanced to need the instruction of a man of genius. In other words, most of his duties were such as a lesser man might have done, and they left him no time or energy for composing, except in summer, when, in view of his highstrung organization and tendency to headaches and insomnia, he should have rested absolutely. Had he but accepted Hamlin Garland's repeated and urgent invitations to spend a summer with him among the Indians in the Far West, he might have been saved. But the impulse to compose was irresistible, and the opportunity to rest was lost.

The time came when it was felt necessary for him to give up the arduous professorial duties or else sacrifice the higher mission of his life. After seven years of service he left, the more eagerly because the authorities hesitated to accept his plan of uniting literature and the fine arts in one faculty, or school, and possibly making some of the courses compulsory for every student in the college, in the hope of turning out fewer "barbarians" than the universities do at present. It was about the time that Professor Woodberry also left Columbia; there was some acrimonious discussion, which aggravated MacDowell's insomnia and hastened his breakdown. But the germs of his mental disease were busy long before that. More than a decade previously he would say and do strange things when in the throes of composition. I have elsewhere commented on the striking similarity of his case to Schumann's. But while Schumann hastened his collapse by intemperance, beer and cigars, MacDowell was intemperate in one thing only—his passion for work.

His career came to a close before he reached his forty-fourth year; yet he has written enough to place himself at the head of American composers. As a writer for orchestra the late Professor Paine may dispute the first place with him, and Paine also wrote a grand opera; but neither he nor any other American can for a moment contest his supremacy as a writer of songs and of pianoforte sonatas and short pieces. In these—particularly the songs—he ranks with the great masters of Europe—with Schubert, Franz, Grieg, Chopin, Schumann. Anton Seidl ranked him in point of originality above Brahms, while the eminent French composer Jules Massenet exclaimed: "How I love the works of this young American composer, MacDowell! What a musician! He is sincere and individual!—what a poet! What exquisite harmonies!''

MacDowell was not a juvenile prodigy. He was not like Schubert and Mendelssohn, who wrote some of their most mature things before they were out of their teens; but rather like Beethoven and Wagner, in so far as his genius matured slowly. Of his orchestral works only one belongs to the period when his genius had fully ripened—"The Indian Suite"—"one of the noblest compositions of modern times," as Philip Hale has aptly called it. Of the others, one, "Lamia," has never been printed or played;* the remaining ones—"Hamlet and Ophelia," "Lancelot and Elaine," "The Saracens and Lovely Alda," and the "First Suite"—are all distinguished by exquisite orchestral coloring and artistic workmanship, but thematically they are less individual than his later works. It is this evolution of his real self, this gradual maturing of his genius, that made his early death the greater calamity.

In the early pianoforte list there is much that is dainty, brilliant, and fascinating; among others, the two concertos, "The Eagle," "Clair de Lune," "Dance of the Gnomes." Most of these pieces, however, might have been written by other men; but with op. 45, the "Sonata Tragica," MacDowell's individuality begins to assert itself so strongly that thenceforth no expert could fail to recognize his seal on every page. Unlike most of his contemporaries, he always put melody in the first place, refusing to write unless he had a new melodic curve to guide his harmonies. In the German days he had many a dispute with his friend, Templeton Strong, as to the relative importance of harmony and melody. Yet his harmonies are no less original than his melodies; and for young composers he is a much better model than Richard Strauss and the other modern Germans who make dissonance an end instead of a means. MacDowell had a strong aversion to these cacophonists, who ladle out tabasco sauce with a soup-spoon. He used a much finer brand, and a few drops sufficed to give each of his pieces that agreeable but not too strong "bite" which the modern palate demands.

A trait which distinguishes MacDowell's pieces is the frequent alternation of exquisite feminine tenderness with outbursts of robust, overwhelming virility. "Tenderly" is the expression mark that occurs, perhaps most frequently on his pages; and, like a true American, he writes his expression marks in English, which means so much more to us than the worn old Italian stencils. Of his sturdy, manly spirit the four pianoforte sonatas afford the most numerous instances. Just to read the directions for the playing of one of his movements—say, the last of the "Keltic" sonata—"very swift and fierce"; "very emphatic"; "gradually increasing in violence and intensity"; "with tragic pathos"—makes one eager to witness this musical affray. To another frequent characteristic of his pianoforte music attention is called by the London *Times's* comments on the "Tragica": "The difficulties of the sonata are prodigious, for the music is orchestral. The ideas are big, but they seem to call for an orchestra to make themselves fully felt. Yet with all this the tragic note resounds with ten times the force of Draeseke's 'Tragic Symphony.'"

Pianists who wish to become familiar with MacDowell's genius should begin with his "Woodland Sketches" and add to these the "Sea Pieces," "New England Idylls," and "Fireside Tales"—collections of short pieces with those poetic titles and superscriptions that are so characteristic of their composer. The verses are usually his own; they have the concise, pictorial suggestiveness of Japanese poems. A specimen: "From a Wandering Iceberg" has these lines prefixed:

> An errant princess of the North,
>   A virgin, snowy white,
> Sails adown the summer seas
>   To realms of burning light.

In conversation with William Armstrong, Edward MacDowell once said: "A song, if at all dramatic, should have climax, form, and plot, as does a play. Words to me seem so paramount, and, as it were, apart in value from the musical setting, that, while

---

* "Lamia" has been played by the Boston Symphony Orchestra.—Ed.

I cannot recall the melodies of many of those songs that I have written, the words of them are indelibly impressed upon my mind." It stands to reason that, in view of this, and of the fidelity of the music to the prefixed verses in the pianoforte pieces, his songs must be characterized by a thorough blending of the words and the music; and this is indeed, apart from their spontaneous and individual melody, their most striking trait; it is admirably illustrated in what are perhaps his best five songs: the romantic "The Sea," the melancholy "Menie," the lovely Scotch "My Jean," the exquisitely poetic "Idyll" (op. 33), and the ravishing "The Swan Bent Low to the Lily," which is almost his own swan song (op. 60). Those who would know the best that America has produced in art song should get his op. 33, op. 60, and above all, the "Eight Songs," op. 47, every one of which is worth its weight in radium.

The best of MacDowell's songs and pianoforte pieces were composed in a log cabin buried in the woods near his hillcrest home at Peterboro, New Hampshire, facing Mount Monadnock. Here, before his illness, he was visited daily, in his dreams, by fairies, nymphs of the woods, and the other idyllic creatures of the romantic world about whom he tells us such strange stories in his compositions. He was taken up to Peterboro one May because he was so impatient to get there. All summer, however, he did not comprehend that he was there; and when I saw him, on October 4, he did not know it; yet he asked me if I had been in the log cabin! I never before realized so vividly what a mysterious, inexplicable organ the brain is—dead in some parts, alive in others. A framed photograph of myself was hanging on the wall, and Mrs. MacDowell told me that for a long time he had spoken daily with an air of distress of how uncomfortable it must be for me in that position. The day before we arrived he suddenly declared his conviction that it was, after all, not myself, but only my picture. When told of this, I said to him: "Don't worry, Edward, about my being stuck up on the wall, for you know I always was stuck up"; whereat he laughed in his hearty, boyish manner. He always enjoyed a pun, the worse the better, and was himself an inveterate punster. Later on he read to us the lines prefixed to the piece "From a Log Cabin," which sum up the whole tragedy of his life and the loss to American music:

A house of dreams untold,
It looks out over the whispering tree-tops,
And faces the setting sun.

It was almost prophetic. A few months afterward this sun of American music had set.

AUTOGRAPH OF MACDOWELL

AFRO-AMERICAN COMPOSERS

BY

GROVER BROWER

ONE of the most significant evidences of a healthy musical life in this country—perhaps the most significant—is the sudden and widespread interest in our national musical resources, that is, our folk music. Two decades ago the idea that America might possess rich possibilities in the field of folk music was one which either met with supercilious contempt or downright derision. Of the two main sources, Indian music and Negro folk songs, the first was unknown, the second neglected and despised. The fact that both might be powerful factors in the development of a national school was slow in attaining recognition, but after the pioneer work of MacDowell and Cadman, of Dvořák and Coleridge-Taylor, an impetus was given to the study of our native resources, with the result that at the present time both have attained their rightful place as important wellsprings of future American musical art.

The contributions of Indian folk song, and the way they have been utilized by American composers, are discussed in another article, but before dismissing this subject it may be worth while to call attention to the fact that Indian music has as yet developed no Indian composer. "Poor Lo's" native music furnishes inspiration to his white brother—to him is intrusted the task of making it the vehicle of artistic expression—whereas Negro folk songs, besides their utilization by white composers in the same manner, have been largely instrumental in the development of a group of native composers whose productions rank among the most worthy of our time. The causes of this peculiar state of affairs are partly to be found in the superior versatility and power of adaptability of the Negro over the Indian, but still more so in his greater native musical talent, which is a well-known race characteristic. Technically considered, this talent manifests itself in the broad, lyric quality of his melodies, the mixture of the grave and gay, plus that elusive factor, probably due to obscure psychological causes, which is the soul of all national folk song. Native Indian music also exhibits these same characteristics, but in quite a different manner, and in ways which render its utilization for artistic purposes more difficult.

Although a notable group of Negro composers have enriched the world with their works, the music historian of the future will no doubt prefer to break down the color line and to regard them as members of existing national schools, and not as forming a special racial school. There is nothing to warrant the latter classification. In England, as well as in other European countries, Negro themes have been used by composers, regardless of their color; on the other hand, Negro composers have not confined themselves to this material, but have, like others, also depended upon original inspiration or have taken their material from whatever sources suited their artistic purposes. Viewed in this way, Coleridge-Taylor appears as a distinguished representative of the English school of composition, as well as a distinguished member of his race, but not as a representative of the Negro school of composition, for none exists any more than does a Jewish school of composition. Whatever his race or nationality, any composer will inevitably assimilate the customs and ideals of the country in which he lives and works, and the matter of color then assumes an aspect of little or no importance.

It is from this point of view, therefore, that we regard Burleigh, Cook, Johnson, Dett and Diton, five Negro composers who have enriched American music with many compositions of interest and value. To what extent the elements of permanence exist in their work is a question for the future to decide: Time knows no distinctions either of color or nationality, and the chances that their contributions to art will survive are at least equal to those of other composers, whether of Europe or America. We are indebted to *The Crisis* for much of the following material regarding their lives and work.

One of the most important song-writers of the present day is Harry T. Burleigh. His work in this department of musical composition commands universal admiration. Touching practically every phase of lyric expression and often rising to a broad, quasi-symphonic sweep, his songs have been accorded a hearty welcome by both professional artist and amateur. Among the most popular may be mentioned "In the Wood of Finvara," "One Year," "Saracen Songs," "The Soldier" and "Five Songs" to words by Laurence Hope. They are art songs of as high quality as any that are being written at the present time. His settings of Negro folk music, of which "Deep River" is the best known example,

HARRY T. BURLEIGH

are not only of great musical value, but also of much historical interest, inasmuch as they perpetuate in an artistic form a phase of folk lore which is rapidly becoming extinct. He has crystallized, as it were, the Negro folk tunes for the voice, as Coleridge-Taylor did for the piano.

Harry T. Burleigh was born in Erie, Pa. He attended the grammar and high school there and was graduated in 1887. He sang in Erie churches and in the Synagogue there until 1892. He came to New York and was given a scholarship at the National Conservatory of Music, where he studied voice with Christian Fritsch, harmony with Rubin Goldmark, and counterpoint with John White and Max Spicker. He played double bass and later timpani in the Conservatory Orchestra under the late Dr. Anton Dvořák, and was librarian for the orchestra. For three years he was a teacher in the conservatory. He associated a great deal with Dvořák and copied many of the orchestral parts of his "New World" symphony for its first performance by the Philharmonic Society of New York.

Will Marion Cook was born in 1873 in

Washington, D. C. His mother was a woman of deep religious tendencies and, with her son, attended the emotionally expressive services of a small sect of Negroes whose children she was serving as teacher. The plaintive melodies and harmonies of the old Negro hymns exerted a lasting influence on young Cook. His first musical effort was as a boy soprano, and afterward he began the study of the violin. He went to Oberlin College for three years, and his advancement and promise were so marked that an opportunity to study abroad was arranged for him. He was sent to Berlin, entered the Hochschule, and made a splendid impression on Joachim, who invited him to his home for special lessons on the violin. On account of delicate health he was forced to abandon his studies in Berlin and return to America. At the time of his return the "ragtime" craze was at the height of its popularity, but nothing had been done for the development of these melodies in ensemble form. It was suggested to Cook by the late George W. Walker, of Williams and Walker, that he write some Negro songs with arrangement for choral effects; and Paul Laurence Dunbar, the Negro poet, furnished him with a set of characteristic lyrics which he set to stirring and inspiring tunes founded upon the old Negro melodies of the plantation and camp meeting. The little operetta was entitled "Clorindy, or the Origin of the Cakewalk"; it was produced upon the Casino Roof Garden, where it created a furore.

Cook has composed the music for the Williams and Walker productions, "In Dahomey," "Abyssinia" and "Bandanna Land"; also for Mr. George W. Lederer he composed the score of the Casino Theatre productions, "The Casino Girl" and "The Southerners." Among the distinctive Negro songs which he has composed are "Emancipation Day," "Lover's Lane," "Swing Along" and a score of others.

Cook's present serious work is the development of Negro folklore in dance forms for chamber music. He feels that the Negro in music will have to take his place through the development of the old melodies, the songs of the slaves and old religious croonings.

Another Negro composer, born in the same year as Will Marion Cook, is J. Rosamond Johnson. Until comparatively recent years his talent was directed toward the less serious phases of music as exhibited in light opera, but unlike most composers of this style, he is possessed of a versatility which enables him to attempt the more enduring forms. Well-known examples are the songs "I Told My Love to the Roses" and "Morning, Noon and Night," and a set of Negro melodies, freely transcribed for concert use, for piano.

R. Nathaniel Dett, one of the younger generation of Negro composers, is a native of Canada. He studied at the Oberlin Conservatory of Music, graduating from there in 1908, and afterward teaching. He has written a number of important choral works, both sacred and secular, among them "Listen to the Lambs," "Weeping Mary" and "I'll Never Turn Back No More"; also two characteristic suites for piano, entitled, "In the Bottoms" and "Magnolias."

Carl L. Diton is probably better known as a pianist, organist and teacher than as a composer, yet, if his works thus far published are regarded as a fair promise of what to expect in the future, American music is likely to be enriched by some highly important contributions from his pen. His "Jubilee Songs" for chorus have been greatly admired, and his transcription for organ of the Negro spiritual, "Swing Low, Sweet Chariot," is one of the finest pieces of organ writing published in this country within recent years. Melville Charlton is another organist whose work in composition has been recognized for its intrinsic value, entirely independent of any racial considerations.

Other Negro composers whose work demands recognition, and from whom much may be expected, are Wellington A. Adams, Thompson De Koven, Frederick J. and John W. Works and Clarence C. White, all of whom are doing noteworthy work in the development of the folk music of their race as well as in the stricter art-forms.

ERNEST BLOCH

BY
CÉSAR SAERCHINGER

THE music of Ernest Bloch defies classification, largely because it constitutes a class by itself. To the French it has appeared too German; to the Germans, too French. Of course, it is neither. It belongs to no school; it is not even calculated to found one—it certainly betrays no purpose to do so. It is a direct, vital, ungoverned expression of an indomitably free spirit, a spirit aflame with the passions of his race and of his age. More especially of his race. For Bloch has conceived his peculiar mission to be a musical expression of the racial soul of the Jew.

This racial color in the music of Bloch is not, primarily, a matter of intellectual endeavor. It is, rather, an intuitive recognition of self, a consciousness of personal characteristics which are the result of racial synthesis; a knowledge that we are not only ourselves but also our forefathers for generations upon generations. A certain violence, a certain childlike, almost naïve simplicity, a religious fervor, a deep compassion for humanity, a passionate sense of justice, all of which are a part of the composer's character, he simply conceives as the components of his racial soul and gives voice to them as such. To Bloch, a work of art is the soul of the race speaking through the voice of the prophet in whom it has become incarnate. This expression of race feeling, it will be seen, has little to do with the nationalism that animated musical endeavor in Europe before the war, which, in Bloch's own words, was an "affair of the will, of the intellect."

It is important to know this attitude of the artist toward his art, for it must determine our frame of mind in approaching it. Bloch believes art to be a matter of feeling, of instinct rather than intellect. He has no sympathy with merely brain-begotten works.

Hence it is little to the point to consider the technical characteristics of his works. It is enough to state that he is not an apostle of simplicity for simplicity's sake, neither does he affect harmonic, polyphonic or orchestral complexity for purposes of effect. He uses the resources of the modern composer according to the demands of his ideas. The matter at all times must determine the procedure. If we have new and complicated conceptions, a new language, new terms may be needed to express them. If the ideas are simple, broad truths, they should be simply expressed. "If you can say a thing in three words, it is wrong to use four."

Little may be said by way of description of Mr. Bloch's style. If, as he says, music cannot be described in words, that is especially true of his own works. Mr. H. F. Peyser has found a kinship between Bloch and Sibelius. But since Bloch had not heard the Finnish composer's music when most of his works were written, there can be no thought of "influence."

Among modern composers that may have made an impression upon Bloch one might name Moussorgsky, whose works appeared to him like a revelation of nature itself, by which contact could be re-established with the very mainsprings of human expression, a primary force ignoring all precedent and convention. An admiration for Strauss' orchestral mastery, a deep sympathy with Mahler as a man and a musician, and a fine appreciation of Debussy's art founded upon a just valuation of its merits and its limitations—all these merely attest Bloch's cosmopolitanism. His inspiration finds its roots rather in the works of the old masters, from Palestrina to Bach and Beethoven, even further back in Josquin and his successors, and, back of that, in nature herself.

HIS LIFE

Mr. Bloch was born in Geneva in 1880, the son of a Jewish merchant. He began to study music at the age of ten, and at once made a childish vow to devote his life to the art—which was, of course, quite contrary to the wishes of his parents. Jaques-Dalcroze was his teacher in solfeggio, Louis Rey in violin playing. At sixteen he went to Brussels to study violin with Ysaÿe, and also composition with Rasse, a pupil of César Franck. After three years he went to Frankfort and found his "real teacher" in Iwan Knorr. Strictly classical in his predilections, Knorr was, nevertheless, able to impart to his "revolutionary" pupil the true principles of constructive technic. Æsthetically teacher and pupil did not agree at all, and after a year and a half Knorr refused to continue the lessons.

After a few lessons with Thuille in Munich, Mr. Bloch traveled along paths of his own choosing. His First Symphony, begun in Frankfort, was completed, and it was promptly refused by all the conductors of Europe because its composer was "unknown." Despairing of any material success, with the affairs of his family in very bad condition, he himself almost in actual want, Mr. Bloch was driven to become bookkeeper in his mother's shop in Geneva, and to abandon all hope of "being heard." Thus for years he went on writing music in his spare hours, sustained only by an inextinguishable creative force and the sympathy of a few friends. During this time he completed an opera, "Macbeth," which, after a series of disappointments, was finally produced at the Opéra Comique in Paris. It was a popular success, but was deliberately killed by the critics.

After more years of weary drudgery and hopeless waiting, and piling up of "silent scores" ("Hiver-Printemps," a symphonic poem, was finished in 1904, and "Poèmes d'Automne," for voice and piano or orchestra, in 1906) there came the performance of the First Symphony in Geneva and Romain Rolland's encouragement. Rolland wrote:

Your symphony is one of the most important works of the modern school. I do not know any work in which a richer, more vigorous, more passionate temperament makes itself felt. It is wonderful to think that it is an early work. If I had known you at that time, I should have said to you: "Do not trouble yourself about criticisms or praises, or opinions from others. You are master of yourself. Don't let yourself be turned aside or led astray from yourself by anything whatever; either influence, advice, doubts or anything else!" From the very first bars to the end of such music one feels at home in it. It has a life of its own; it is not a composition coming from the brain before it was felt.

With the "Trois Poèmes Juifs" (1913) began Mr. Bloch's "Jewish Cycle." Of this are completed, besides the "Three Poems," three Psalms (the 114th, the 137th, and the 22nd) for solo voice and orchestra, two movements of the symphony "Israel" (1913-16), the Hebraic Rhapsody, "Schelomo" (Solomon) for cello and orchestra, and the String Quartet in B major, completed in America in 1916, and played by the Flonzaley Quartet in New York, Boston and Chicago. There are, besides, a "Symphonie Orientale" on Jewish themes (1916), an "Orientale" for orchestra

(1917), and parts of a Biblical drama, "Jézabel," on a text by Edouard Fleg.

Aside from the conducting of orchestral concerts at Lausanne and Neufchâtel in 1909-10 and frequent lecturing on æsthetic subjects at the Geneva Conservatory, 1911-15, there remains to be recorded only Mr. Bloch's coming to America. This was occasioned by the tour of Maud Allan, the dancer, who engaged Mr. Bloch as her conductor. The tour ended rather disastrously in Dayton, Ohio, and Mr. Bloch's subsequent successes were made possible largely through the good offices of Mr. Pochon of the Flonzaley Quartet, and the Society of the Friends of Music. Dr. Karl Muck, after hearing his music, placed the "Jewish Poems" on the Boston Symphony program of March 23-24, 1917, and they were conducted by the composer with great success. At a concert of his compositions in Carnegie Hall, New York, given under the auspices of the Society of the Friends of Music in May, 1917, his reputation as a symphonic composer of the first rank was established and the concert was followed by individual performances of his works in New York, Philadelphia, Chicago, San Francisco, and elsewhere. The composer himself accepted a post as teacher of composition at the David Mannes Music School in New York, where he is now living.

WORKS

Of his Jewish poems, Bloch himself has written as follows:

The "Jewish Poems" are the first work of a cycle. I do not wish that one should judge my whole personality by this fragment, this first attempt, which does not contain it. The "Psalms," "Schelomo," "Israel" are more representative, because they come from the passion and the violence that I believe to be the characteristics of my nature. In the "Jewish Poems" I have wished in some way to try a new speech, the color of which should serve my future expression. There is in them a certain restraint; I hold myself back; my orchestration is also guarded. The "Poems" are the first work of a new period; they consequently have not the maturity of the "Psalms" or of "Israel."

It is not easy for me to make a program for the "Poems." Music is not translated by words. The titles "Danse," "Rite," "Cortège funèbre," it seems to me, should sufficiently inform the hearer.

The form is free, but it is really there, for I believe that our constitution demands order in a work of art.

The Hebraic Rhapsody for cello and orchestra, entitled "Schelomo" (Solomon), is hardly to be taken as a musical portrait of King Solomon, certainly not of the "cynical old ruler to whom 'Ecclesiastes' was falsely attributed" (the words are those of Mr. Philip Hale). "I am not an archeologist," says Mr. Bloch, "and the Solomon of the archeologists does not interest me. It is the legendary figure, the author of 'Ecclesiastes,' that I had in mind." It is perhaps better to regard the Rhapsody simply as a discourse upon the theme, "Vanity of vanities, all is vanity." The form is exceedingly free, as the title "rhapsody" indicates.

The following notes on Bloch's settings of the three psalms mentioned above (114th and 137th for soprano and orchestra, 22nd for baritone and orchestra) by Mr. H. K. Moderwell give a fine idea of these remarkable compositions.

They are scored for a large orchestra, treated in a symphonic manner, while the solo voice carries a melody of declamatory character. The first of the three, using the text of Psalm 137, is a heroic lament. With the first bars the listener is in another world, in a Jewry nowhere existing now, with a tribe not so far from savagery that it cannot proclaim as its curse: "O daughter of Babylon, happy shall he be that taketh and dasheth thy little ones against the stones." The elegiac quality with which the work opens, on the words, "By the rivers of Babylon we sat down and wept," soon gives place to sterner emotions. With the words, "Remember, O Lord, the children of Edom in the day of Jerusalem," the fury of the coming curse approaches. After this the elegy returns, and the work finally glides into the second part, the 114th Psalm.

If the first of these Psalms is the lament of a people in bondage, the second is the pæan of a people escaping from slavery. "When Israel came out of Egypt," run the words, recalling the days of the Exodus. With exultant pride the triumph is recalled, and the emotion culminates in the words, "Tremble, thou earth, at the presence of the Lord, at the presence of the God of Jacob." This army of people, as Mr. Bloch imagines them, is no band of pilgrims journeying to a promised land. It is rather a wandering Bedouin tribe, moving slowly along the desert, with its bullocks and sheep, with its gaudy tents packed upon its beasts of burden, its trumpeters cracking the air with their blasts and its patriarchs surveying the whole scene from the backs of the largest camels. In great swaying masses of tone the desert is depicted. Then come enormous blocks of tone in the brass, the fierce strength of a primitive people. The trumpets are heard screeching as the great caravan moves on. Finally, above the monotonous but resistless motion of the music, rises the declamatory voice. The recitative, exotic yet rugged, has a crude expressive power which is indescribable. After the defiant voice has ceased the trumpets are heard once more, then the caravan slowly moves out of sight across the boundless desert.

The third of the Psalms is David's cry, "My God, my God, why hast thou forsaken me?" The general character of the music is the same, but its expression is more individual, more of the soul. As the speaker's depression turns into faith, the music surges up to a great climax. Yet here, as in the other Psalms, in spite of the dramatic movement in the text, Mr. Bloch has preserved a very evident form. Each movement ends as it began, and the free development carries with it, as it seems, a necessity to return to its starting-point. This instinctive sense of form is to be found in all Mr. Bloch's work.

The introduction and the first movement, which are predominantly in the keys of F major and D minor, are scored for the usual modern orchestra. The second movement is mainly for strings, with woodwind instruments sparingly used, and with the addition of human voices (four parts), used as an instrumental "choir," the words (a Hebrew prayer) being without importance.

The symphony "Israel," of which only the first part, in two movements, has been completed, symbolizes the spiritual significance of the sacred festival of Yom Kippur—the Day of Atonement. The introduction opens in an introspective mood. We may picture to ourselves a man about to question his conscience, to search the recesses of his heart. Impressive voices, short, rising motives, are sung by different instruments, polyphonically treated, like conflicting strands of thought. They form soft dissonances, and finally die away, having created an atmosphere of ominous expectancy.

The emotional storm breaks with the opening of the first movement proper. The man has come to a realization of his sins. There are gnashing of teeth and tearing of hair, a despair that bursts forth with all the traditional vehemence of the race. There are other themes, less violent, picturing, perhaps, a deeper remorse, the resolve for a new, purified life. There are conflicting rhythms, independent movements of themes, clashes of dissonance—all combining into a great, passionately uttered lament.

In the second movement the strife has ceased. The soul, cleansed through its confession, looks upward to God in a prayerful spirit. At times the music rises to a mood of passionate imploring. The choral parts are broad and sustained. Sometimes a great, summoning voice rises from the basses and is answered by renewed invocations.

There is not space to speak here of the earlier orchestral works, of the beautiful "Chansons d'Autômne" with orchestra, nor the String Quartet, in some respects the most significant of Mr. Bloch's works. In this work, though Jewish characteristics are still discernible, other forces are at work pointing the way to a new rhythmically free and poignantly dissonant style, a polyphony singularly free and spontaneous, a tone-painting in vivid colors, but colors that are the reflection of a deep and vital emotion. A return to the more reflective mood of some of his earlier works is seen in the slow movement, a beautiful "Pastorale" which seems to give voice to the very soul of those wonderful mountains that are the composer's native heath. If ever nature translated itself into music it is here. It is music so free from externals that it seems to be felt rather than heard. Here we are, it seems to me, in the threshold of the new generation in art evolution, signalizing a new and better readjustment "between nature and law"; in other words, between pure inspiration as it reveals itself to the composer's soul, and the artifice by which he must communicate it to the world.

CONTEMPORARY MUSIC

By HORATIO PARKER

A FAMOUS orchestral conductor once told me that he was glad he would be dead in fifty years, so that he would not have to hear the music of that time. It is needless to say that he was conservative, but it should be stated that he was, and is, one of the best-known and most efficient conductors we have ever had in this country. Although his remark is typical of the critical attitude of many who have to do with new music, yet it does not in the least represent the attitude of the public, which is interested and pleased as never before with the music of our own time. There have always been people to declare that the particular art in which they were interested, at the particular time in which they lived, was going to the dogs, and there seem to be peculiar excuses for this belief in music-lovers just now. But there ought to be some way of reconciling the pessimism of the critics and the optimism of the public, which expresses itself eloquently in the buying of many tickets. By critics I do not mean merely the journalists. I mean rather essayists and those accustomed to give well-deliberated judgment on matters of permanent importance. The journalists have been so often, so rudely shocked that they not only fear to tread, but fail to rush in, and at a first hearing of new things are fain to give forth an uncertain sound, which, in the light of subsequent developments, may be taken for approval or censure.

The pursuit and enjoyment of music call for the exercise, on the part of its devotees, of three principal functions widely different. These are the functions of the composer, of the performer, and of the listener.

The composer is the source and motive power of all art-music, the producer who draws his inspiration from the recesses of his inner artistic consciousness, whose desire and aim are to realize as well as possible the ideals with which his brain is filled. He seeks to give expression to musical ideas which shall call forth sympathetic feeling in those to whom the utterance is addressed. Although in some cases it is apparently meant for an ideal audience which has no existence, nevertheless, if the utterance be true and skilfully made, it will in no case fail of audience or of effect, even though the time be delayed.

The second function necessary to the practice of music is that of the performer or reproducer. This activity is closely allied to the first, which is in truth dependent upon it. It is of high importance, and in ideal instances may be artistic activity of a kind hardly lower than that of the composer, though wholly different in character. This also is at root a manifestation of a desire for utterance, of the craving to awaken sympathetic feeling in others; but it is different in that it seeks and gives expression to ideas which are already in existence. The composer seeks those which do not yet exist. The performer gives utterance to the thought of another; the composer, to his own. But the work of the performer is for most people the only actual embodiment of the results of the first function, and he frequently clarifies and enhances the composer's work in a measure beyond expectation. It calls for self-control as well as for self-abandonment, for sympathy in the highest degree, and a twofold sympathy—with the composer and with the audience—and for personal, magnetic power to such an extent that it is wholly quite natural that people should frequently, even usually, lose all sight and sense of the composer or producer, who is remote from them, and admire the work of the reproducing artist, who is always near.

The third function is of equal importance with the other two, but differs from them more than they do from each other. It is the function of the audience or the listeners. This function is largely misunderstood and usually undervalued. It is the exact opposite of the other two essentials of music-making in that it calls for receptive activity, if one may so express it, for intelligent, passive sympathy. This sympathy of the audience is the mark at which both composer and performer are aiming. It has no public or open reward, though it well deserves one. Audiences certainly should receive credit for intelligent listening, though it is hard to know just how or when to give it. The quality of sympathy is elusive and difficult to appreciate. To most audiences it seems unimportant whether it be given or withheld; the only matter of consequence is the applause. Genuine appreciation is often hard to identify or recognize. It is quite impossible to know whether a smooth, impassive, self-restrained Anglo-Saxon face hides the warmest appreciation or the densest ignorance or indifference. Such emotions often resemble one another. Nor can one ever tell whether the heightened color and brightened eyes are caused by the long hair and hands of the performer or by beautiful music. A particularly good luncheon or dinner preceding the concert may have the same outward effect. So the successful listener is a mystery, but a pleasing and very necessary one. His work is as important as that of the composer or performer, and his rewards are none the less real because they are not counted out to him in cash, because he pays and does not receive a tangible medium of exchange. They lie in the listening itself and in the consciousness of improvement which is the result of his effort.

In speaking of modern music, we can omit personalities concerning classical composers. Their works fall entirely to the exercises of the second and third functions mentioned; but since the bulk of contemporary music is by classical composers, it may be well to speak briefly of the attitude of performers and audiences toward music of this kind. In an ideal world the performer and the listener would have the same kind and degree of pleasure in music except in so far as it is more blessed to give than to receive. "We are all musicians when we listen well." It may be laid down as a general principle that performers of classical music have more enjoyment than listeners.

Palestrina is a pre-classical composer with distinct limitations, and it is quite reasonable that he should appeal under ordinary conditions to a small audience, and to that imperfectly. He is a religious composer, and most audiences prefer to keep their religious feelings for Sunday use. He is a composer of church music to be sung in church, so that his work must miss its effect in a modern concert-room. We have very few churches in our country fit for the performance of Palestrina's music. I know a jail or two where it would sound wonderfully effective, but there are obvious reasons for not going so far in the pursuit of art. It follows, therefore, that Palestrina in a concert-room is enjoyed by the average listener only by means of a lively exercise of the imagination, with frequent, perhaps unconscious, mental reference to what he has read or heard about it.

If there is enthusiasm, it is surely for the performance, because the music itself is so clear, so pure, so absolutely impersonal, that it is hardly reasonable to expect it to appeal to the listener of to-day. He is too remote from it, and should not think less of himself because he does not feel an immediate response. In proper circumstances, in a real church, he would surely respond at once. For this music is the summit of a great wave of musical development. Nothing exists of earlier or later date which may be compared with it. It is ideal church music, ideal religious music, the greatest and purest ever made; and it can never be surpassed, for we have gone by the point in the history of the art at which such effort as Palestrina's can bring forth such fruit.

The public attitude toward Bach is much more natural and unconstrained. He is nearer to us and is an instrumental composer. Although in somewhat archaic terms, his music is personal expression in a much higher degree than that of the absolutely impersonal Palestrina. The vigor, the life, and the animation which inform the whole texture of his work are so obvious that we cannot miss them. Again, in his greatest work the feeling of design is so clear, the upbuilding and the resulting massiveness are so faultless, that the devout and habitual lover of music has the reposeful and at the same time exciting conviction that he is hearing the inevitable. Enjoyment is easy even to the unlearned. In those works which are less massive than the greatest, the pleasure we have from Bach is more subtle, more refined, and perhaps less acute, but we always feel that we listen to a master. Bach gives, perhaps, the highest satisfaction in his chamber-music. Much of his work is so very intimate that we find the balance of expression and form most easily when we are near enough to hear every note. The church cantatas in church, the great organ works in a comparatively small place, or the orchestral music in a hall of moderate size, are among the keenest enjoyments for performers and audience. Applause, if it is given, must be for the performers or for their work. The compositions are above approval. To praise them is like speaking well of the Bible.

In the work of his contemporary Handel, whose texture is less purely polyphonic and instrumental, the enjoyment of performer and listener comes nearer to a point of coincidence. The audience can love it more nearly as a performer does. We feel that the vitality in Handel is of a more human kind; that it is nearer our level, less supernal: but it is convincing and satisfying even when most popular, and is not disappointing upon intimate acquaintance, even though it lack the nearly superhuman fluidity and the marvellous texture of Bach.

The music of Beethoven is so well known, so frequently heard, and so clearly understood that we may take it for granted, and go on to music which is modern in every sense, made in our own time, and addressed to our own personal feelings. Our present-day music is twofold in character, a direct result of the labors of Beethoven and his successors in pure music, and of Wagner and the romanticists in music which is not absolute. The symphony or sonata form is now archaic in the same sense that the fugue is archaic. Beautiful music may be, will be, made in both forms, but that is no longer the general problem.

It is probably true that since the four symphonies of Brahms, no symphonic works carry the conviction of the symphonic poems of Richard Strauss. Although these are cast in a modification of the symphonic form of Beethoven, they always have a psychological basis or an original impulse outside of music. They are intended to characterize in musical speech or language things which can only by vigorous effort be brought into any connection with music itself. The question naturally arises, Has the power of making absolute music entirely disappeared? I am loath to think so, but surely the practice has dwindled in importance.

We need not be concerned to examine these extra-musical bases. Granting them to be necessary, one is much the same as another. But that is just what many are reluctant to grant. Many are brazen enough to enjoy programme-music frequently in spite of, not on account of, the programme; and some people prefer the advertisements, which are usually in larger print. Both save thinking. But the underlying programme is not what most critics object to. The commonest criticisms which we hear of strictly modern music charge it with a lack of economy, amounting to constant extravagance; a lack of reserve, amounting almost to shamelessness; and a degree of complexity entirely incomprehensible to the average listener, and, if we are to believe careful critics, out of all proportion to the results attained. Of course economy is a great and essential virtue in art, but it is not incompatible with large expenditures. It depends on the size of the fund which is drawn upon. Nor is explicit and forceful utterance incompatible with reserve. As for complexity, it may sometimes be beyond the power of any listener to appreciate. Perhaps only the composer and the conductor can see or hear all the subtleties in an orchestral score. But is such complexity a waste? Not necessarily, for good work is never wasted. Although beauties in a viola part or in the second bassoon may not be obvious to the casual listener, however hard he may listen, they are not necessarily futile. They may, perhaps, be noticed only by the composer, the conductor, and the individual performer, but they are there and they constitute a claim on the respect and affection of future musicians. If all the beauties were hidden, they would be useless, but as gratuitous additional graces they call for approbation. But one may not admire complexity for its own sake. It is far easier to achieve than forceful simplicity.

At a recent performance of a modern symphonic work which was very long and called for nearly all possible familiar musical resources, I recall wondering whether or not it is a bad sign that a composer gets respectful hearing for pretentious trivialities and vulgarities uttered at the top of the many times reinforced brazen lungs of an immense orchestra. There were, indeed, a few minutes of exquisite beauty, but after more than an hour of what seemed an arid waste of dust and dulness. Meanwhile, there were long *crescendos,* with new and cruel percussion instruments working industriously ever louder and faster, but leading up time after time to an absolute musical vacuum. One's hopes were raised to the highest point of expectation; but they were raised only to be frustrated.

It is such unsatisfying work as this which elicits pessimistic forebodings as to the future of music as an independent art. Serious critics and essayists have made vigorous attempts to oust the music of the future from existence as an independent art and to relegate it to the position of a sort of language which is to be used, when it is quite grown up, to express more or less pictorially human happenings or emotions. And there have not been wanting composers to support this hopeless view. The application of pure reason to such emotional phenomena as our pleasure in music results occasionally in something very like nonsense. The arts have different media of expression, but excepting the art of literature, the medium is no spoken or written language. Indeed, artists are apt to regard with some degree of suspicion one who expresses himself well in any other than his own peculiar medium. Amateur is a dread term often applied to such men; and they are very likely to be amateur artists or amateur writers, perhaps both. It is consoling to think that all the words written and spoken about art have never yet influenced creative artists to any discernible extent. Their inspiration or their stimulus must come from within, and, after the preliminary technical progress over the well-trod paths of their artistic forefathers, which progress no great artist has ever yet evaded or avoided, their further advancement is always by empirical and not by logical processes, not logical except in an artistic sense, for logic in art, although very real, is not reducible to words until after it has already become an accomplished fact through empirical or instinctive practice. The evolution of logic in art cannot be foreseen or foretold.

The opera is just now the largest figure on our musical horizon, and opera, always responsive to the latest fashion, has undergone very important typical changes of late years. "Salomé," by Richard Strauss, for instance, is more an extended symphonic poem than opera in the older sense. It is as if scenery, words, and action had been added to the musical resources of such a work as Strauss's "Zarathustra." It is only about twice as long as "Zarathustra." Strauss's "Salomé" and Debussy's "Pelléas and Mélisande" are typical modern musical achievements. In spite of the suavity and popularity of Italian operas of our time and of the operatic traditions of the Italians as a nation, they do not appear to have the importance of the German and French works just mentioned. The two men spoken of seem just now the most active forces in our musical life, and it may throw light upon the music of our own time to compare the two operas with each other, not with other classic or modern works of the same nature; for from such they differ too widely for a comparison to be useful. Old-fashioned people seek in opera a union of speech and song, and each of these two composers has renounced the latter definitely. No human voice gives forth any musically interesting phrase in "Pelléas and Mélisande." In "Salomé" the voices, when used melodically, which is seldom, are treated like instruments, and it is no exaggeration to say that song is relegated entirely to the orchestra. The voices declaim, the orchestra sings. Each opera is a natural continuation of its composer's previous work. Each is an independent growth. Neither composer has influenced the other to a discernible extent. Yet it seems impossible to find any other notable musical work of our own day which does not show the influence of one or the other of these two men.

"Salomé" is in one act and lasts an hour and a half; "Pelléas and Mélisande" is in five acts and lasts about three hours. The difference in time is largely due to the underlying play which determines the form and length of each opera. It may be granted that each of these two works reflects conscientiously the spirit of the text. The shadowy, wistful people of Maeterlinck's drama are faithfully portrayed in the uncertain, keyless music of Debussy, as are the outrageous people of Wilde's play in the extravagant, vociferous music of Strauss. "Pelléas and Mélisande" as a play is perhaps the extreme of mystic symbolism. When reduced to its simplest terms in every-day speech, it may mean anything, everything, or nothing. The motive of the play "Salomé" is frankly an attempt to shock Herod, as tough a sinner as ever was drawn. The object is attained, and it is small wonder that the audience is moved. There seems to be throughout Debussy's work, to speak pathologically, a preponderance of white blood-corpuscles. In our day and generation we want red blood and plenty of it, and we find it in "Salomé," a whole cistern spattered with it. At its first performance in New York so much got on the stage that ladies had to be led out and revived.

There is a great difference in the matter of pure noise. Throughout the whole of "Pelléas and Mélisande" one feels that the orchestra has its mouth stuffed with cotton wool lest it should really make a noise. Most people want a healthy bellow from time to time to show that the orchestra is alive. And in "Salomé" we have an orchestra with its lid entirely removed. The hazy, indeterminate, wistful vagueness which is so much admired in Maeterlinck's poem some people resent in the music. That is too much like an Æolian harp, too purely decorative, too truly subordinate. The orchestra never gets up and takes hold of the situation as it often so frankly does in Strauss's "Salomé." "Pelléas" is a new sensation, perhaps a new art; but it is a little like looking at the stage through colored glass. Undoubtedly the play is the thing.

The musical vocabulary of the two men differs immensely. Many admirers of the modern French school think Strauss's music vulgar because it really has tunes, and because one can almost always tell what key it is in. In the French music the continual evasion of everything we consider obvious becomes monotonous, and after an hour or two furiously unimportant. One longs in vain for a tonal point of departure, for some drawing; but there is only color. In passing it may be said that the play in its form and vocabulary is the exact opposite of the music. Points of departure are not lacking in its construction, and the language is marvellously simple, lucid, and direct.

The matter of tonality remains. The six-tone scale which Debussy loves and uses so much divides the octave into six equal parts. The augmented triad, which he uses with the same frequency, divides the octave into three equal parts. Both devices constitute a definite negation of tonality or the key sense; for we need the recurrence of semitones in any scale which is to be recognizable as having a beginning and an end. It may be that our grandchildren will not want tonality in our sense, and again it may well be that they will prize it more highly than we do. It is hard to imagine what can take its place; certainly there is no substitute for it in music, for the essence of musical form consists chiefly in a departure from and a return to a clearly expressed tonality. A substitute for tonality outside of music would seem a hopeless abandonment of nearly all that makes the music of Beethoven, Bach, and Wagner great to us. Compare Strauss and Debussy in this respect. Each composer has a rich, individual, personal, melodic, and harmonic vocabulary; each offers new and satisfying rhythmic discoveries; each shows us a wealth of new and beautiful color. The differences in melody lie in the greater directness of Strauss's work. His tunes are sometimes garish in their very baldness and simplicity. This is never true of Debussy, to whom a plain tune like the principal dance tune in "Salomé" would seem utterly common and hateful. Polyphony is regarded as the highest, the ultimate development of melody. There seems to be vastly more polyphonic and rhythmic vitality in Strauss's work than in Debussy's. "Salomé" is as alive as an ant-hill. "Pelléas" is more like an oyster-bed, with no actual lack of life, but not much activity.

Harmony has become an attribute of melody, and our harmonic sense, a recent growth, furnishes the only means we have of definitely localizing formal portions of musical structure. Total absence of form is inconceivable in music, and form implies inevitably some degree of formality. This element is always clearly present in Strauss and always purposely absent in Debussy, who steadfastly avoids the indicative mood and confines himself apparently to the subjunctive. At great climaxes Strauss ordinarily seeks a simple triad, Debussy some more than usually obscure and refined dissonance. The harmonic element in Strauss is, perhaps, less refined, but it is less subtle. In Debussy this element is less direct and perhaps less beautiful, but quite distinctly less obvious or common, even if less varied.

Fully aware of inviting the warmest kind of dissent, I venture to suggest that Strauss may be a positive and Debussy a negative force in music, the one greatest in what he does, the other in what he avoids. After all, we cannot get on without the common things of daily life, and, admitting his occasional lapses into the commonplace or something lower, Strauss is the most consummate master of musical expression the world has ever seen; not the greatest composer, but the one most fully able to realize in sound his mental musical conceptions. In the last analysis it is, of course, what a man has to say, not entirely how he says it, which furnishes the basis for a sound judgment of him. We should not be too much impressed by Strauss's skill in writing for great orchestral masses. In itself that signifies little more than ability to use the wealth of orchestral material now available in Germany. Strauss's appetite for orchestra is a little like the Eastport man's appetite for fish. It is easily satisfied and not too extravagant. Much more convincing is the accuracy with which he finds rhythm, melody, harmony, and color to express just the shade of meaning he wishes to convey. To repeat, no musician was ever so well equipped to give to the world his musical creations, and yet since he was a very young man Strauss has produced no pure music, nothing without an extra-musical foundation; and although many of his friends and admirers hope still that he will, he admits frankly that he does not intend to.

Are we, therefore, to believe that music must be pinned down henceforth to its illustrative function? One prefers to think that our living composers are unconsciously intoxicated by the luxuriance and wealth of new and beautiful musical resources which have only recently been placed at their command. They confuse the means with the end. They have not yet learned to use their wealth. They are *nouveaux riches*. The more perfect performers, the more intelligent listeners, the new riches on every side tempt them to concrete rather than to abstract utterance. I believe that in the future the highest flights of composers will be, as they have been in the past, into those ideal, impersonal, ethereal regions where only imagination impels, informs, and creates. As for illustrative music, it must always have one foot firmly fixed on earth. How, then, can it rise to the heavens? Although not yet with us, the new vision will come in the fulness of time; and when it does, the whole world will know and follow it.

NOTE.—Professor Parker's well-balanced ideas and wise conclusions are of the utmost value. The suggestion that present composers are working in the new medium of modern orchestral color, and have not yet gone much beyond the mastering of the technique of composing in the new style, is most pertinent. The great masters of music amount to less than two dozen in number, so that we need not lose hope if we have had no commanding genius of the pioneer type since Wagner. Debussy and Strauss have prepared the way by experiments. In addition, it is harder to write pure music than to illustrate a programme in tones. One may mention again the case of Brahms, who wrote absolute music of the greatest value in his symphonies, in spite of the programme influence of the romantic school. What he did with the classical orchestra will very likely be done in the future with the fuller modern forces. Professor Parker's words, too, are not those of a speculative dreamer, but come from the pen of a great composer, well informed in the classics, and echoing an earlier school nobly in his own great oratorio, "Hora Novissima."—ED.

BERCEUSE.

DRAWN BY MAXFIELD PARRISH.

NATIONALITY IN MUSIC

By JAMES C. DIBDIN

FEW more useful lessons can be gathered from the teachings of recent discoveries in Science than this, that man is incapable of existence without leaving indisputable marks of his identity behind him. It matters not what he may lay himself out to occupy his time with during life's brief span—he may even fondly imagine that he is capable of doing absolutely nothing that will leave the slightest trace behind: but he miserably deceives himself; and although, of the vast majority among the billions of cases safely recorded on Nature's page, no direct evidence whatever can possibly be adduced, the fact remains that the individual man must take his share, infinitesimally minute though it be, in fashioning the destinies of the ages to come. And this entirely by the amount of individuality he may possess; for it must be distinctly understood that the above proposition does not at all refer merely to the part the human brain has played in the forward march of civilization. That is a thing entirely by itself, and in nowise connected with the part played by individual character, save it be the influence swayed by the latter over the former. At first sight such a statement may appear to be somewhat of a paradox, but we must bear in mind that hitherto undue value has mostly been given to the mere intellect or brain-power of man in estimating his work. Given two men with equal intellect but different amounts of individuality, it is not difficult to foretell which will achieve the more success. In fact, character or individuality may well be likened to the leaven that leavens the whole lump in man's actions and the results thereof.

If this be true of the individual, how much more so must it be in the case of nations. In the former the distinctive individual character of a man, save in extreme cases, seldom varies very much from that of his neighbor; but it is quite different with nations, where dissimilar sources of origin, variations of climate, soil and scenery, different conditions of life brought about by the other factors, and many other considerations, all tend to make and to keep the various races and nationalities of mankind separate and distinct, one from another, in every particular of national character or individuality.

In every occupation and enterprise, the peculiar bent of the national mind is more or less reflected. One nation is vindictive and cruel in warfare, another brave when driven to fight, but not hasty in quarrel; still another lazy and indolent to its own undoing, and so on through many other historical characteristics easily recalled to memory. But it is in art, applied art, the art that is part and parcel of the daily life of a nation, and not that spurious dilettante article so much in vogue just now among humbugs and fools; in a word, in real living art that the individualism of a nation is most vividly reflected. Turn to what country we like, of those at least of which there are any records, and we are sure to find the impress of national individuality stamped on its art; and in no department of art more surely than that of music.

From east to west and north to south we find it the same: whether we trace examples of it through the misty records of the past, or go afield to countries where the primitive life of the savage is still practised, or stay at home content with an examination into what our own country can bring forward in confirmation of the hypothesis, we find the same deductions have to be drawn, namely, that national temperament has invariably made its impression on the music of the country—left its stamp upon the very heart and soul of it.

In tracing back, so far as lies in our power, the chief characteristics of ancient or uncivilized nations, we at once find that a great deal is to be gleaned from a proper consideration of the favorite instruments of the people. We know that in old days those fond of sensuous and more especially sensual life, encouraged the use of the flute to an enormous extent. Cleopatra has claims to be appointed the patron saint of that instrument; while, on the other hand, Plato, who would have banished flutes from his republic, might well be termed their "John Knox." The Polynesians are ardent admirers of the flute and pipes, while in combination they use the drum with a remarkable degree of skill. The uses of the latter instrument are most varied under different national requirements. By the Polynesians it lends rhythmical beats to sensuous dancing, voluptuous feasting and idling. The North American Indians and the Esquimaux use drums to express their passions—joy, grief, love, hate, and lust for blood. Catlin speaks of the former people "touching their drums at times so lightly that the sound is almost imperceptible." In this we can easily trace the deep yearning nature, full of passion, kept under splendid self-restraint, that these people infuse into their strains, just as the Troubadours of the South of France carolled their lackadaisical loves, under the casements of their beloved, to the accompaniment of the insipid and soulless guitar.

As already mentioned, the Polynesians are slaves to the sensuous strains of the flute—they are by nature a soft and enervated people at best; but not so the Papuans, whose natures are decidedly of a spiritual complexion: with the latter tattooing is unknown, and only the rudest description of carving practised. They despise art for art's sake, and do not use it to make life more beautiful; or, on the other hand, "they are the only savages," says Pickering, "that can give a reason." They are eminently superstitious and imaginative, and they throw their whole spiritual nature into the chant. Rough and wild it may be, and of an uncouthness scarcely to be tolerated by cultivated ears, but nevertheless, it tells its story: it is the reflection of the inner thoughts, passions, and aspirations of the people, as distinguished from the merely sensuous enjoyment of rhythmical sounds. In the same way we can take the Chinese as compared to the Hebrews, the one living for color, beautiful form, and all that stimulates the indulgence of the senses, and the other whose whole history is one long protest against sensuality in every form. Here, however, we meet an apparent anomaly; for while we know, on excellent ground, that the music of the Hebrews was majestically severe and sombre, we cannot shut our eyes to the fact that, at any rate during one period, the Israelites were well acquainted with quite a number of musical instruments, and that the Temple service was instrumentally, as well as vocally, quite of an elaborate character. This, however, may well be accounted for by the regular commerce carried on between Israel and Egypt, where instrumental music was the fashion. In Egypt great orchestras of stringed and wind instruments were in daily attendance at the palaces of the nobility, and it is inconceivable that large quantities of Egyptian instruments would not be exported to Palestine.

We even have direct Biblical evidence of the Israelites having carried such with them out of captivity, but with the great majority of the sons and daughters of the favored people, their inartistic and superstitious nature prevented them from cultivating music apart from the offices of religion. Miriam among the women, and David and Solomon among the men, were evidently less straitlaced than their contemporaries; and the two latter chiefly were responsible for the lavish use of instrumental accompaniments to the antiphonal chanting of the service.

The Hebrews were a people who were able to think, and their minds were given up to problems of a deeply psychological nature. When they once gave vent to their feelings, their song came from the heart. It rushed out with uncontrollable force, and there was little chance of any time or attention being wasted on strains intended solely as sweet pabulum for the ear. The Egyptian might lie for hours dreamily listening to the long-drawn-out and luscious notes of his beloved flutes, or revel in the pageantry of large bands of musicians; the Assyrian might glory in the martial ring of the trumpet, and in imagination such warlike strains would carry his mind into the tented field, there to revel in war and all its paraphernalia; but to the Hebrew the sound of the flute could not convey ideas of love from his soul to the heart of his beloved, nor the trumpet's martial sound a sufficient defiance to his enemies. It was words only that could do these things; and splendidly did they employ their uncouth language in the one and the other. Like the old Hebrews the Scots also have unquestionably a dual nature. Remember that in this relation it is the Lowland Scot that is being spoken of. The sturdy psalm-tune could no more have been the product of French soil, or of the French people, than the vine-trees of the latter could grow in the Lothians or the Vale of the Clyde. There is almost a grim determination of bigotry and inartisticness pervading some of the "tunes" used in the Scottish kirks, that is not altogether redeemed by the majesty and grandeur of such strains as the "Old Hundred" and "French."

Unlike the Hebrews the Scots can scarcely be said to have ever imported instruments or instrumental music of any kind. At least such as were imported never became part and parcel of the beatings of the national pulse. They were purely exotic. The Reformation wave swept away almost all inborn love of art; sculpture, painting, music (save for the droning Kirk psalm), architecture, and everything artistic became practically a dead language in the nation; and yet, as we have seen, a glimmering of better things gradually prevailed, and out of the very grimness of the national character there arose, for instance, that splendid style of architecture, the Scottish Baronial. In the same way the feeling of national mourning for the disaster of Flodden was nobly crystallized in the "Flowers of the Forest." The full nobility of "Scots wha hae," or the depth of pathos in "Land o' the Leal," are splendid examples of the inability of the morose doctrines of the Reformation to stamp out the true national character.

The bagpipe music cannot be taken into account, as it is in origin distinctly Celtic,[1] and has only since Sir Walter Scott's time come to be regarded with anything like favor out of the Highlands. Nevertheless, it is in itself a splendid example of the influence of nationality in music. It is essentially a savage music which becomes the vehicle of the whole gamut of the more essential human passions.

One point that strongly illustrates the quantity, if it may be so called, of Nationality in Music is, that it requires a person to be of a particular country, or, at least, to have been very long and very intimately associated with people of that country, before he can properly appreciate the national music in its fullest meaning. Any typical Scotch song, the "Mar-

[1] The primitive bagpipe, although now used by comparatively few nations, ranks as one of the most cosmopolitan instruments known to the musical historian, and was formerly in almost world-wide use.

seillaise," "Die Wacht am Rhein," the "Rákóczy March," speaks each one its own special language, a language that is practically untranslatable in its real essence. It requires a Scot, a Frenchman, a German, and a Hungarian to grasp their full meaning and inner significance, although the people of all these four nations may, in addition to the mere enjoyment of the music as such, be able also to understand the more hidden meanings, in so far as they have national peculiarities in common. This is, of course, applicable much more to national or "Folk" music than to what may be termed cosmopolitan, although it is doubtful if the French people as a body, for instance, will ever properly appreciate and value Beethoven's or Brahm's symphonies or Wagner's operas. In the same way much of the French school of music is equally incomprehensible to the German family; its lightness and sparkle, as clear and brilliant as the country's champagne, its lack of even a tendency toward the ponderosity of deep thought, its occasional flippancy—all unite in taking it out of the sphere of comprehension of your heavy lager-beer-drinking German, who has no trouble in entertaining himself out of the resources of his own brain, where the Frenchman requires his amusements to be served up to him incessantly to save him from ennui. An Englishman does not experience the same difficulties; and in fact it is his happy lot to be able to appreciate the beauties of the music of both France and Germany; perhaps not so thoroughly as the natives of each do their own, but much more thoroughly than these do each other's. It is perhaps this fact that has unconsciously led many people who should know better, English as well as foreign, to assert that England is without any definite school of music of its own. Such statements of course are sheer nonsense, especially in retrospect. What is true, however, is that, although we have plenty of music full of English individuality composed in the past, it is more than questionable if as much can be said concerning our present-day music. Cosmopolitanism has done its work with a vengeance, and left us apparently high and dry with every indication that national characteristics will now be no longer found in our music; yet at the same time there is every sign of a modern English school with strong German tendencies uprising in our midst. One very curious feature of English national individuality must here be noted —the spontaneous manner in which the Oratorio was welcomed by the people and instantly took root, flourished, and is flourishing to this very day. And yet it is German in origin, and although not exactly "made in Germany" altogether, in the past, has been the outcome, in its highest reaches, of German brains. Perhaps in the same way as the Hungarian was too lazy to keep the performing of his music in his own hands, and allowed the Czigány to monopolize that branch of the art, so perhaps Englishmen were too lazy or too busy to create that great musical form for themselves, and allowed the industrious German within his gates to do it for him. The Oratorio is the Art-manifestation of the deepest and most deeply rooted religious sentiments and beliefs in the Englishman's breast; it speaks forth his holiest thoughts and aspirations; and yet he himself did not take the initiative in creating it, or even do very much since that day to keep up the supply. This is one of those anomalies that crop up in such an inquiry as the present that must give the student pause. The English, of course, are great otherwise in sacred music; and while much of it breathes forth a deeply religious tone, it must be confessed that it also shows clearly the influence of national prejudice and blind observance of the established order of things ecclesiastical.

While the English ballad is as different from the Scottish song as night is from day, it yet mostly expresses the same human passions, sympathies, and longings. Nor do we find it one jot the less in catholicity of subjects. All the passions and feelings common to mankind are portrayed with a fidelity and insight into the human heart, quite as true as in the case of its northern equivalent; and yet, notwithstanding all these similarities, there is as little resemblance between the one and the other as there is between the Scots fir and the English oak. That is precisely where the influence of Nationality in Music comes in. The English ballads suggest the expressions of a people not driven by adverse circumstances and continual warfare against climate and other foes into deeply heart-searching self-communings. They are rather the expressions of a people full of joyous self-reliance, full of natural affection for country, friends, and kindred, accustomed to plenty, and unacquainted with the horrors of war being brought to their doors. Eminently loyal and patriotic above all things, not a too deeply thinking people, fond of work, of play, and of mingling together in friendly talk, taking their religion on trust without much self-questioning—these were the people whose national characteristics were so truthfully proclaimed by Purcell, Arne, Dibdin, Shield, Bishop, Carey, and many others of the same type; and in almost every one of these we find characteristics which have no parallel in Scottish life. Hence the difference in the song productions of the two countries, and hence may be deduced the enormous influence nationality has on music.

Language as defining different races has a certain influence on national music. This is best illustrated, perhaps, by observing that as they loosen their Indo-Germanic ties and gravitate toward the East, unmistakable signs of national originality make their appearance. There are the Czechs among the Slavic races, who, bordering on Germany, may in their music be reckoned as a sort of transition between Western and Eastern national music, although, it seems, the former predominates in their strains. The southern Slavs, such as the Servians, Croatians, and the Roumanians, have, all of them, airs of pronounced

Eastern flavor, although there is also a tinge still of their Indo-Germanic relationship. Going back to the Romans, we find that great people singularly destitute in music of any kind. They imported it along with their slaves and their mistresses. Living, as a nation, in the first place, entirely for conquest, and afterward for sensual pleasure, it is scarcely to be wondered that they remained devoid of melodic outbursts. *La bella Italia,* however, could not remain forever without some music of its own; and so we find the Italians among the earliest in the field after the Renaissance spreading the gospel of melody to all the lands. The Italian folk-songs appear to vary in character as much as there are dialects spoken in the land. The Canzones and Gondolieras of the Venetian are entirely different from those of the Neapolitan; and each of course is in keeping with, and reflects the peculiarities of, the home of its birth. But Italian music, although certainly not the leading school in the great modern advance in the Sciences, has for ages been looked up to as the school *par excellence* of melody and a certain refinement of feeling. Nor could it well have been otherwise with a land where warm sunshine floods the landscape, where the choicest flowers are to be found growing wild, and birds tune their lays in the joyous consciousness of warmth and light. In Italy, from quite an early period, there can be traced, whether among churchmen or nobles, indication of a gracious, liberal, and sympathizing spirit as regards Art in all its branches. Italian art, so to speak, had grown early in the dawning of the new civilization, out of the Roman lack of the same. The Romans had no music, save such as they imported and paid for as a luxury. Their architecture was borrowed from Greece, and their literature, especially their drama, was much in the same category. Precisely as out of the old Roman nature there was evolved the new Italian (from the wreck of the luxurious and sensual living descendant of the determined warrior of the early days of Rome, the new, sanguine, quick-tempered, and eager Italian individuality had its rise), so out of the mass of wreck of imported art, scattered all over the land, there rose up a new form of creative art, which, whether in music, architecture, literature, or painting, at once gave breath to the new nationality. All classes took part in this renascence, and participation at once took the place of patronage, and music acquired a life, an aspect, and a position very different from what it had in countries where it was a mere exotic. While the ballad or folk-song of the people gave the note of the national feeling in its crudest state, the nobles and clergy, with the same genial and artistic temperament, refined and educated by the "modes" of Greece, and their sympathies and desires widened by a knowledge of the instruments of the East, were able at once to inspire, if not to establish a great school of cosmopolitan music, which, as already said, has served pretty well as a foundation for most European nations to build upon. In accomplishing this great work, their hereditary instinct of taking full advantage of all that came to their aid was not idle; and the examples of the Low Countries, as well as England, were not neglected in the matter of counterpoint. Still, even in its highest flights, the Italian school of counterpoint, for many years, was grim and almost ungracious to the ear—lacking, to an enormous extent, in the vitality necessary to make any save the antiquarian remember it in after-ages, except for its place in religious services.

Such a statement may at first seem little short of an exaggeration; but mature consideration of the works of all the early Italian masters must lead to a speedy acquiescence in its truth. Even the well-nigh perfect works of Palestrina, whether regarded as cosmopolitan or purely national music, cannot be pronounced as being still living, in the sense that Handel's oratorios or Tallis's responses live. So far as they, along with the works of other early Italian composers, are cosmopolitan, it is difficult not to imagine that either the amount of patronage and participation were not equal, or that the latter, on the part of the nobles and clergy, was on too high a platform for its perfect realization. In other words, that the learning of the nobles was of too exalted a nature to freely commingle and produce not only a national school of music, which none can dispute it did, but, in addition, a national music reflecting and typifying the aspirations and characteristics of the whole people. What, however, was not accomplished in this manner was eventually in another, although less artistic way.

It was quite in the early days of the kingdom that the opera—which had sprung from the still earlier mysteries and miracle plays—became so powerful an attraction among the people. The pity was that those responsible allowed, and in fact encouraged, meretricious panderings to the uneducated populace, in place of endeavoring to unite the higher school of music that the country had already produced, with the popular canzonet and similar forms. This brings us to another phase of the subject, namely, how did the nationality of the Italian people show itself in their music? It has already been pointed out that the things responsible for peculiarities in national character are very varied.[1] Climate, scenery, history (ancient as well as modern), religion, pursuits, soil, may be mentioned as among the chief. Now it is curious that wherever Southern influences have leavened the literature and art of any given country, there is always to be found some communicated torpor in regard to the picturesque; if so, then how

---

[1] A marvellous proof of this is that the music of mountain people, such as the Tyrolese, the Swiss, and the Norwegians, is all much the same. Your mountain pastorals or ditties, or by whatever local name they may be known, have all a character quite their own. Concerning their exquisite charm and beauty, especially when heard amid their native surroundings, it would be out of place to enlarge upon in a footnote; but the fact of such uniformity in character shows very clearly the tremendous influence of configuration of land or nationality.

much more should the feeling of indifference for scenery be in the land of the South itself. The Italians must have had eyes that either could not or would not see. Their indifference to the beauty of nature, as exhibited in that lovely land, is as great as their poverty in such descriptive faculty, which imparts so much racy variety to the forms taken by Northern national art. The Italians seem from the first to have become the slaves of two agents in life, namely sunshine and love. Their canzonets, whether of Venice or Padua, although differing in detail, are full of these two potent agents in life's economy. In Calabria and the Roman Campagna we find the same Pifferari tunes droned out from the pipes that may, with almost certainty, be regarded as the legitimate offspring of the primitive and mythological Pan's pipes. We know how this expression of the Italian nature has been congenially transplanted into many countries until its very name has become a musical term. Corelli employed it, "with a difference," in his "Nativity Concerto;" Handel did the same in his "Pastoral Symphony," and J. S. Bach in his Christmas Oratorio; so that, by a strange freak, what is really an Italian bagpipe tune, has become associated in the popular mind in England and Germany with Palestine, and what shepherds of that country were wont to play to beguile their time while tending their flocks by day.

What is true of the canzonet is also true of Italy's opera—dramatic instinct and interest has always been its weak point. The composers have pandered to the love of the people for melody; and that melody is either breathing full of passionate Southern love or of a sickly species of melodramatic writing. These remarks do not apply to quite recent years, which have seen the later Verdi, as well as a distinctly new and younger school, start up and take, as it were, the musical world by storm. Curiously, not thirty years since, a then eminent critic said, speaking of Verdi, "The waning of the coarse light of his star is pretty distinctly to be observed."

It is worth noting that men like Clementi, Cherubini, and Spontini have never been taken kindly to by their countrymen. The utterances in music of these masters to the Italians are, apparently, a dead letter, unless indeed, recent years have altered all that. But the most curious thing about them is how they, Italians born, so completely identified themselves with other schools. In the first named the wonder is perhaps not so great, as he was transplanted to England at quite an early age; but with Cherubini it is different. For thirty years he was Italian to the backbone, and only showed his new development in art when he composed "Lodoïska." True, his earlier efforts did have their day and fame, but, like most Italian compositions, had soon to resign in favor of newer favorites. The same of Spontini. It was only after he had quitted the land of his birth that this clever composer commenced writing those works by which he was to be remembered.

When we strike across the Alps and find ourselves in France, we immediately notice the difference of the national characteristics in music—as unlike those which we have just parted with as are the two peoples in manners, customs, and methods. The love-breathing canzonet, with its drone bagpipe accompaniment, and the love-scenes that go chiefly to make up the opera of the one people, are no more. Love-songs we have in plenty, and opera too; but forms are of little account, whereas as the spirit breathing through these forms is everything to the consideration of the present subject. The world of sentiment we shall see is left behind, and instead we find an enormous amount of intellectual vivacity, varied during later times almost everywhere by graftings or borrowings from other nations.

All French art is peculiarly French, and it takes a Frenchman rightly to understand it, or at least to appreciate it. Take their drama, for instance. Surely there is nothing so monotonous as the rules of French tragedy, nor yet anything so *piquant* as the working out of these rules by the performers. Take the grand *tirades* of Corneille and his successors. They are all rhymed—in a rhyme which may not be broken or bent; yet we know that the French actors and actresses not only did, but do "point such monotony," as one writer observes, "by a lacerating finesse of *accent,* sufficient to carry off the platitude of the verse, and its deficiency in idea, and to support the situation of the scene."

In music this phase of art, which is purely national, takes the form of a dry limited melody as applied to the setting of words, but, on the part of the executant, there is no doubt an intention to pay strict attention to time, tone, and accent for the real effect or, failing these methods, to catch the ear by disappointment or suspense. This general definition may fairly be said to apply to both serious and comic music; and it is this peculiar characteristic (love of effect, so thoroughly French) that seems unable of thorough appreciation by any one save a Frenchman. To him, on the other hand, it has a perfect fascination.

The French have always been a nation of song singers, but the charm of the performances, from the early romantic period of the Troubadours till long afterward, must have rested much more with the singer than the song. A certain charm or interest, of course, attached to the words; warlike feats, picaroon adventures, and romantic exploits, all had their share; but the real effect was left to the singer to infuse into the composition. Provided that the tune has a certain piquancy, let it be otherwise ever so commonplace, and if it has a burden to which men can stamp their feet, or march, or otherwise make a noise in keeping time—then it is sure to "catch on" in France, and afford intense delight to all who come beneath its influence. Added to these satisfying qualities an extra amount of pungency or accent that the singer can throw into his or her work, and the intense delight of the audience becomes at once transformed into the wildest enthusiasm. An enormous number of such ditties, as was only natural, appeared at the time of the Revolution—"La Marseillaise" at once recurring to the mind; and it indeed is as good an example as could well be found.

Like "God save the King," there has always been a dispute as to its authorship. One side claims it as part of an ancient Mass at Meersburg, and the other as the composition of Rouget de Lisle, a gentleman of great talents although little fortune, who certainly wrote many stirring songs of the same kind. Indeed the very style of the "Marsellaise" had been anticipated by him in some of his former works. It is possible that De Lisle heard the Mass at Strasburg in 1792, but it is much more probable that he did not, in which case, of course, the coincidence of the same tune, or nearly the same, having been twice independently composed, remains. The Germans no doubt would like very much to have it proved that De Lisle did take the great French national hymn from the Meersburg Mass—just as the French would equally like to palm off their adopted musician Lulli as the composer of "God save the King," but although there is little chance of the Fatherland ever being credited with the origination of the "Marseillaise," it is a curious fact that there are several German student-songs containing a phrase which is virtually identical with the fourth line of the song.

The importance of the dance tunes in French national music is at once apparent. There may even yet be English people, living in remote country districts, who still think of their Gallic neighbors as a nation of dancing-masters; and, although they do not go to that nation now for dances, they certainly did at the time when such an idea as the above first became prevalent in the land. The Scots, as was only natural, early began to import the French dances, and it was to the strains of one of these, a *Braule,* or "Brawl," that Mary Stuart chose to dance on the evening her husband was blown up in the Kirk-o'-Field House. The *Bourrée* comes from Auvergne, where the songs, curiously enough, are inclined to be doleful, although the dance is brisk enough, and has become so popular among composers as to have established a *tempo* in music.

The *Pavane,* the *Passacaille,* and the *Ronde* and the *Gavotte,* are also characteristic measures, the two latter being particularly illustrative of the national temperament. And there is another dance, which, it has been said, it is almost impossible to attempt anywhere out of France, namely, the *Galop,* although it has been asserted that this had a German origin.

In speaking of the noble patronage that prevailed, along with participation in Italy during the early days of that country's musical existence, it was pointed out that the attendant success of the combination was pretty well one-sided. Perhaps it was too early in the history of the birth of the New Art World, or its partial success may have arisen from other causes. Be that as it may, in Germany there was patronage only—and that too, one must conclude from the majority of evidence, not by any means calculated to encourage or stimulate talent in anything save the meanest spirit; and yet this same patronage was the indirect means, there is little doubt, of greatly hastening and strengthening the growth of that greatest of all schools of music, which, not only will, but has now, practically dominated the civilized world. "This world," some one neatly remarks, "is chiefly made up of anomalies," and here is one of the many cases. In Italy we find precisely that state of things to have obtained which should have brought about in time the greatest results, but failed. In Germany we find diametrically opposite circumstances that do bring about such results. In the first-named country musicians were honored guests and friends of the nobility, and their art was not only admired and appreciated, but felt; for several of its distinguished composers were nobles themselves. So were some of the German patrons, it may be contended. There was Frederick the Great of Prussia, for instance, and a Saxon Empress who composed operas; but these, like most other royal and noble people throughout the world, ran entirely after foreign models and schools; and although there have been exceptions in such circles of society during recent years, they are but few and far between, it is to be feared.

While the German small kings and dukes patronized music by paying miserable stipends to men of colossal brains, they can scarcely be said to have encouraged native art; or else, how was Weber permitted to play his compositions as an accompaniment to the gastronomic orgies of those who considered themselves his betters? Why was Spohr, after he had startled the rest of Europe by his genius, allowed to go down on his knees in order to tear up a carpet, which had been placed there expressly that the sound of the music might be deadened, and so those who were playing cards might not be disturbed by undue noise? These are not solitary cases—they are typical. Think of Mozart's struggles to obtain, from the Prince Archbishop of Salzburg, a wage somewhat lower than many of that nobleman's lackeys would be making. Think of all Beethoven's trials and poverty—he certainly had friends, upon some of whom it seems to have dawned that they were entertaining, well, not an angel, but perhaps somebody who might become a little famous. Besides, any one who can read between the lines can see that all this tale of friendship to the great master has been wonderfully exaggerated. To name a single German musician who had to earn his own living, and at the same time had not to submit to degradation and insults in receiving starvation wages, is, to put it mildly, a difficult task. Think of poor Schubert, and consider afterward if there was any good in the German patronage; yes, one, but not direct. It was the great lesson of self-reliance and industry. Work the composers had to, or starve; believe in their own abilities, or speedily lose all self-esteem and desire to succeed. In this way it threw the musicians' minds back upon themselves; and happily, their longings and desires being kept far removed from any contamination by the sensual and depraved Court life going on around them, they were fully able to enter with double intensity into the feelings and thoughts of their fellow-people—the great German nation. They went on as the Prophets of Israel had done before, sending forth their message to all the world. It was the message of musical sounds, linked together in harmony and melody, and one and all proclaiming the deep strivings after truth, love, and the ideal in life and eternity that filled the minds of that deep-thinking people. The grasp of conception that the German musicians must have possessed as a birthright is really almost beyond the sphere of contemplation. As in infinite space we cannot reckon up the height, or the length, or the breadth thereof; so, when we come to those colossal art creations of the Teutonic race, and think of the wonder of their conception, the depth of their meaning, the vastness of their design, and the catholicity of their form, we cannot but pause in silent admiration.

All the modern European nations had the same facilities to attain the post of master builder in the music structure of the earth. All of them had their peculiarities of nationality. England started early in the race, and was soon able to dictate the sovereignty of counterpoint over all other methods to all the nations. Italy followed close, and after working at the opera form, and twisting it this way and that way to suit passing whims—thinking of what is desired to be spoken, and not what has to be spoken—it, too, sank like England to being able only to express its national musical mind in mere songs and such trifles. Then France had its chance. It struggled hard to build up the opera form where it had been left off by its originators, and of what lasting result has it all come to now! A few operas of Auber, Halévy, Boieldieu, Bizet, Herold, and one or two more will occur to one's mind as pleasing enough in their way, and Gounod left a great masterpiece in "Faust." It might be said that France did build up a school of opera; but did it ever reach or include the highest possible attainment in this glorious branch of musical art? That is a question, we fear, must be answered by a monosyllable of only *two* letters. But France being a nation of born dancers could not have failed, even if it had tried, to bring to perfection that charming department of music; and so to them have we not the highest expression, in their captivating ballet suites, of the music that gives both motion to the limbs and charm to the heart?

In France there was an enormously lavish Court that encouraged or patronized music munificently. Gold was to be had by cart-loads, so to speak, if—there was an "if" attached—the composer could hit the vitiated and sickly taste of those who paid him. No wonder, then, that the nation did not get nearer the highest attainments. When the people, the real French nationality, at last got a chance, they were too much occupied for years with political murdering, as an amusement, to do more than express themselves musically in songs such as have been considered. Order came at last, but it was too late. Berlioz found that the great forms of musical expression had already been thought out, and, although even the apparently exhaustless limits of the symphony seemed to be all too small for his genius, yet to such musical forms as he found he had to confine himself. The great German introspective mind had already been over all the available ground, and left well-nigh unquestionable directions for the chief features of all buildings that were to follow.

It is an undeniable fact that in cosmopolitan music, it is only possible to show nationality of feeling or temperament by means of settled forms. No one could mistake Saint Saëns's music for anything but French; and so long as he is rushing us along with his wonderful suites, of course everything is French, even form. But not so anywhere else. In symphony, concerto, or overture he has so far at least to confine the bent of his own free genius, and remember the finger-posts.

These finger-posts are mostly written in German. The whole of the country thus finger-posted, however, was not originally discovered by Germans.

Englishmen did not at first discover America—there is a deal of English spoken there now, however; and most of the "finger-posts" are in that language. Columbus only saw scraps of the land he had risked so much for; and so it is in the other case.

Italy, England, and France had been allowed to see fractions of the complete symphony, concerto, etc.; but when the poor, underpaid, hard-working German master took the matter in hand, he at once produced it "with a difference"—a mighty difference it was too. The new forms rose up—created out of chaos—as if the rod of a musical Prospero had been in his hand. He left no holes, no slovenly workmanship, no weak points; what he undertook he finished; and then, looking at the beautiful image in music that he had made out of his own brain, he touched it anew, and breathing the breath of life into its form, made it living, an immortal witness to the highest attributes of the God-like that dwell in man.

The stability as well as the vitality of the present dominant Art-music forms—qualifications which can scarce be denied them—have, as a rule, been attributed by writers to the superior intellectual powers of the German nation. People have exercised themselves tremendously over scientific calculations regarding both the quantity and quality of the brains of famous musicians. The vast intellectual gifts of Beethoven, Weber, Schumann, Schubert, Wagner, and all the rest, have been a continual theme of argument, debate, and controversy. But the "mighty brain" and the "colossal intellect" have played bogey quite long enough, and it is about time that both critics and the public generally were beginning to recognize the fact that intellect unwedded to individuality, like most other things in the state of single blessedness, may be very nice and pretty, and at times even startling, but can never attain the dignity of being life-giving. Nobody will deny the great German masters more than a full share of brain power; but equally are there any prepared to state, far more to prove, that the great English, French, Italian, Russian, and Hungarian musicians were blessed in a less degree? To say the least of it, it would be presumptuous to assert as much. It may have been well within the power of the mere intellect to conceive and build up the structure of the Art-music form; but, without the life-giving breath of individuality, would not these forms have been left on the desert of time musical pyramids, colossal undoubtedly, but useless, mere monuments of misdirected zeal and labor. So far back as 1600, Giacomo Peri wrote a little sinfonia for flute, which contains the germ of the full symphony, inasmuch as it has the important feature of repeating a little characteristic figure of the cadence of the first half to complete the whole. In this we at once see Italy commencing to build up the dry bones of this Art-music form; and between that early date and Haydn's magical transformation, to be followed by Mozart and Beethoven's practical completion of it, scores of interesting examples may be found; but of what value are they now in the living world of Art?

As every musical student is aware, the art of counterpoint is nearly as old as is the practice of writing music. To what state of perfection, too, it was carried by Byrd, Tallis, Palestrina, and other masters, is also matter of common knowledge. From a purely scientific point of view nothing more complete or perfect can possibly be conceived than many of the compositions of these masters; and yet, where now in the Art world are they to be found save carefully arranged on an upper shelf of the inner museum of musical curiosities. Was there any deficiency in the brain power that wielded all these notes into such complicated forms? He would be a bold man who would affirm as much. Does not this evidence compel us to draw the conclusion that where brains alone are brought to bear upon the creation of Art-produce, the result may be infinitely clever, startling in its complexity, and at first sight apparently the work of true genius; but the structure is built of bricks made without straw, and crumbles and crumbles until it becomes useless and unattractive. These same composers, mentioned immediately above, were, however, more than mere thinking machines for the production of wonderful essays in counterpoint and elaborate canons. Sometimes their individuality got the better of their science, and then there came forth something that lives. Take, for example, Tallis's responses, Byrd's "Non Nobis Domine," and the former composer's well-known hymn-tune canon.

Again, so long as the early masters worked away at the fugue from a purely scientific point of view, how very little did they accomplish. The moment Bach and Handel, not to mention Albrechtsberger, touched the familiar form, it sprang at once into life—one of the first of that glorious constellation of Art-music forms which the world owes to German individuality linked together with brains.

Had brains only been requisite for the formation of a universal school of music—as only the German is—England and Italy might have come very near the goal. England, in fact, may even be allowed to have left a great, if not a universal heritage to musical posterity. English individuality was at times too strong even for the mania that existed for strict scientific treatment of everything. Examples of this have already been quoted, and others could easily be found, while England really has the distinction of having given to the world the completed and perfect form of the Madrigal, the Part Song, the Anthem, and the Glee—all as characteristic of English individuality as is the music of all the finer specimens of these forms of composition. Through the early death of Purcell, his country missed giving to the world a distinct Art form of English opera; there was almost more than the promise of it.

In ballad work in an ordinary way, it cannot be said that England in any respect went a step in advance of other nations, although the nationality displayed in the majority of examples is most marked. This is particularly the case with Purcell and Dibdin. In the works of these composers we seem to feel every phase of English life, while the solitary examples of "God save the King," by Henry Carey, and "Rule Britannia," by Arne, are monuments of English national loyal feeling which have no parallels in any other nation under the sun. In the ballad line England can also justly claim to have given to the world the first essays of the Art song; but, alas! as in so many other cases, it was Germany that took up the crude idea, and gave to the world the exquisite creations of Schubert, Loewe, Schumann, Lassen, and others. Poor Henry Lawes thought, no doubt, that it was very little trouble to endeavor to give utterance in the music to the same ideas and feelings as were conveyed by the words he was setting. It seems a simple enough thing, but English ballad composers do not seem to have had the inclination—even when they were their own poets—to study to set "words with just note and accent."[1] There seems to have been too much independence of character among our ballad writers to trouble themselves with thinking twice what their words were about. They simply set them to an attractive tune—in every way reflecting the national or individual temperament, but not subjected to that intro-retrospection and deep craving for perfect poetical expression in music, which are the primary characteristics of the German composers.

The Scots invented no Art-music form; but al-

---

[1] This is how Milton spoke of Lawes' work.

though their songs are no nearer the Art-song standpoint than the English ballads, it must be allowed that in many cases the wedding of the feeling of the words to the music is better than in the latter. This, as well as the preservation of the tunes at all for that matter, is due to an accident—the glorious accident of Robert Burns rewriting the words to most of them.

As already pointed out, when we come to the Art-music forms which the nationality of other nations, besides the English and the German, has been responsible for, we are at once struck by the poorness of the record. In fact, apart from the great family of dance forms which have recently been brought to great Art perfection in several countries, although in none so notably or to such perfection as in France, there are very few Art-music forms of any importance. In Italy opera had its rise, to be transplanted in due course to France, but finally brought to perfection in Germany, where the mighty individuality—German national individuality—of Richard Wagner at once placed it upon a platform of perfection as an Art-form. What Gluck, Weber, and Meyerbeer had struggled with, a struggle compared to which the twelve labors of Hercules were as but nothing, Wagner only accomplished. Gluck and Meyerbeer failed because they allowed their individuality to be lost in pandering to please popular taste; when fashion was forgotten their genius at once rose to the surface. With Weber it was different. In some respects he did more; but his life was too short, too busy, and too grinding for him to reach the supreme goal. Wagner had a superabundance of individuality. Everything else was made subordinate to it; and so, step by step, he raised himself and his national art until he attained the summit, where his work is likely to remain by itself for many ages.

It is the same with nearly all the great German masters. In symphony Beethoven still reigns supreme; in overture Beethoven, Mendelssohn, and Weber are hard to touch; and through the works of all of them there is that wonderful feeling of the national characteristics, that deep individualism which was the direct result of nationality.

The subject of Nationality in Music is one that may be studied in many respects. It covers a large field, and is quite beyond exhaustive treatment within the limits of the present article—which has been penned more as a general introduction to this particular study, than with any intention of supplying a manual of its many ramifications. The subject has hitherto been little regarded; and anything like an exhaustive treatise has still to be written. Even writers of analytical programmes—literary scavengers, as a rule, to whose nets all that comes is fish—have seldom if ever touched upon the theme of Nationality in Music. It is a glorious chance for them, as the registered facts concerning the classical composers and their works have, by this time, become decidedly monotonous. The hint to vary the stereotyped facts and deductions in this manner is given in the pure spirit of charity; and, in the interests of long-suffering concert-goers, it is to be hoped it will be accepted in the same Christian manner. Whether it is or not, Nationality in Music is a factor that will have to be reckoned with in the future.

INSPIRATION.

DRAWN BY MAXFIELD PARRISH.

534

MUSICAL TASTE IN CHILDREN

By ARTHUR ELSON

IT is only in recent days that the education of children in music, and their appreciation of the art, has been scientifically studied. Even Germany, the land of musical culture, did not study the child-mind or its development, in this field, until comparatively modern times. One can turn back with astonishment to the moral and sedate style of Johann A. Hiller, at the end of the eighteenth century, and note his strange attempts to write music and musical essays for the young. His choice of subjects was sometimes calculated to frighten off his juvenile students. Here is one of the gems of his book, which was expected to be sung by children—

TO DEATH.

"Old men have perished,
Whom no one cherished,
For whom no single being grieved.
When in death they were lying
Men said of their dying—
'Quite long enough, for sure, they've lived.'

"Be my endeavor
To act thus never.
If I die young let some be grieved.
Let not my friends forget me,
Let pious men regret me,
And say,—'Oh, had he longer lived!'"

We can scarcely imagine any normal child taking much delight in the above commendable but rather priggish and funereal sentiments.

In the same work the composer writes—

"Songs for children must be easy. They must be flowing and free from all artificiality. They ought to be of limited compass, so as not to tax the strength of the children. They ought also to be genial and attractive, that they may be easily caught up and retained in the mind."

In this connection we may state that only recently have investigators discovered that the compass of children's songs has been too restricted. The great majority of children's songs were kept below the two-lined E. But it has been discovered that almost every child can easily take F or G, so that the most modern juvenile songs will be found to range higher than those of a generation ago.

Every educator knows that normal children resent baby-talk or an exaggerated sweetness. Modern teachers will therefore be amused by J. F. Reichardt's preface to his collection of children's songs published in 1781. He begins as follows:

"My intention in publishing these songs, dear children, is to cheer you up, that you shall try to sing clearly and correctly. But before one gives one's self trouble or labor in any matter, one desires to know of what use it may be. Is it not so, my dears? See, then, I will explain it to you at once of how much use it is to sing sweetly and agreeably.

"Often in church you are disturbed by the false and bad-sounding screaming of children, and sometimes even of older people. You look around and sometimes you even laugh. Are you not worried by this, and is not your own singing disturbed by it, my loves?"

There is much more of the same kind of ridiculous twaddle, but fortunately the songs are better than the preface.

While dealing with the subject of juvenile vocal education in old times one may add that such education is as old as ancient Rome, where the children were trained to sing choruses at certain public festivals. Julian, the old Roman emperor who went back from Christianity to Paganism, endeavored at the end of the fourth century to establish children's music training schools at Alexandria, in Egypt, that the Roman youth might be educated to take a musical part in the sacrifices to the gods. He died before his aim was accomplished.

Guido of Arezzo delighted in the training of his choir-boys, about A.D. 1000, or a little later. He first taught sight-singing, by means of solfeggio, which he invented, and even exhibited his boys in Rome, before the Pope. Children were also trained in the Middle Ages to take part in the Mysteries and Moralities, the early religious musical plays which preceded the Oratorio.

Much ancient history is imbedded in children's songs. The juveniles of all nations have round-dances with song. "Little Sallie Waters" can be traced in various guises and through various countries, through the dance of the Israelites around the golden calf, through the dance of the Egyptians around the bull-god Apis, even to the sacrificial dances of the sun-worshippers. "Ride a cock-horse" introduces the hippo-griffus, the dragon of ancient days. "London Bridge is falling down" was sung centuries ago in another guise, as a satire against the great bridge which Peter of Colechurch was building. "Three Blind Mice" goes back as far as 1609. "Turn again Whittington" was sung by the London watermen on the Thames, in praise of Sir John Norman, in 1453.

We may learn something of the development of the child-mind in music by studying the youthful days of some of the great composers. The first recorded child-prodigy appears as a tiny organist at the court of Charles the Bald, in the tenth century. Some of the great composers, but not all of them, have been prodigies. Weber wrote very respectable *fughettas* when he was eleven years old. Beethoven composed a good two-voiced fugue at ten years. Mozart composed an attractive Minuet when he was five years of age.

Liszt, at ten years of age, could play any of the fugues of the "Well-tempered Clavichord" and transpose them into any key. Robert Franz remembered music that he heard when he was two years old. Gounod could name any note that was struck on the piano, when he was four years old. In view of some of these facts the question becomes pertinent, "How early ought the musical education of a child to begin? And what form should it take?"

In the first place let us speak a word against prodigies. If one discovers a gifted musical nature in a child, let the growth go steadily on without being interrupted by public appearances. The craze for such appearances is working great harm. It is even being pushed to the point of absurdity. A child of five years is at present allowed to conduct great orchestral works, in Italy. Smaller and smaller grow the musical prodigies, and younger and younger. By and by we shall have the musical infant composing and directing its own orchestral cradle-songs.

Very few prodigies grow into great artists. Josef Hofmann is an exception, and even he has not quite fulfilled the hope that a second Mozart had arisen,—a hope freely expressed when he electrified the world with his performances in his childhood. Music often becomes mere routine to the child who has been overforced, as he grows to maturity. Schumann and Wagner would never have become the masters that they were had they studied young. They both entered their musical career rather late, but they had an enthusiasm at twenty that the prodigy has long outgrown.

Yet late study is not advisable. On the contrary, the musical education may begin even with the youngest child. But it must not be a task in the earliest years; the idea of displaying the child must be absolutely renounced; the growth must be normal and continuous; the enthusiasm must never be extinguished. At the very beginning the youngest child may be allowed to use the keyboard of the piano, but should be taught from the first to pick out chords or intervals that sound well. Mere idle drumming is not to be encouraged.

Most important, however, is the question of a musical atmosphere. We are not all born Mozarts, but if the growing child is kept in constant touch with good music, he will gradually learn to appreciate and understand it. Atmosphere means much, even with prodigies. Mozart might not have developed nearly so early if he had not been born into the musical home of the great teacher Leopold Mozart, who was his father. With those who are less gifted, a continual training is necessary; and good taste cannot be developed without a constant hearing of good music. If the parents care for nothing higher than rag-time, the child, unless exceptionally gifted, will never rise above that level—at least not as long as he is subjected to home influences. When children take lessons, their faculties are put in charge of a teacher, who gives them something of the right atmosphere; but this brief article is a plea for the proper training of listeners as well as others—the large class who will get their knowledge of music only by hearing it.

John Stuart Mill's advice, "First a healthy animal," cannot be too strongly insisted upon. There is no need for the musician or music-lover to grow up an anæmic sentimentalist. If a child shows itself too sensitive, its musical development may be postponed until it grows more vigorous. Some infants are very easily affected by music, and the art should not be used to produce too strong impressions upon them at first.

More common, however, is the reverse error. Just as some people think that children never outgrow baby-talk, so there are many who do not realize that a child's musical appreciation may grow. The London *Punch* recently printed an anecdote illustrating the first point. A child having been brought home from the country on a train, its uncle asked, "Did ums ride on the choo-choo?" Thereupon the sage youngster replied about as follows: "Yes, we came up on a train. The engine had two cylinders, an extra-weighted driving wheel, and a new link-motion valve-gear." Too many people act on this principle in music, and think that the child must be trained forever on too simple material.

The music that a child hears should include all grades, from the simplest to that which is too complex for him to understand. The latter is most important. If the child hears only such music as that which does not demand its full faculties of appreciation and a little more, its taste will not grow. In literature we take care that the children of grammar and preparatory schools should be trained to appreciate the great masterpieces, even if they do so only imperfectly. The same principle should be adopted in music.

You will find helpful articles in Volume 3, "The Pianist's Guide." Consult the Table of Contents for instruction on theory, musical touch, hints on Piano Study, Harmony, Imitation, Canon, and Fugue, How to Study Scales, and a wealth of other items to help you. At present the school children sometimes expend their energy on collections of singing books of doubtful value and heterogeneous character. Our national music, too, is hardly of a high grade. For purposes of patriotism, the conventional "America," the overpompous "Hail Columbia," and the rather unsingable "Star-Spangled Banner" must form part of the curriculum; but the other songs might be chosen for their musical value as well as for their simplicity, in a greater degree than is the case at present. Also a part of the singing time might be well spent in having the pupils listen to a brief concert of good music. Short pieces by Schubert, the Mendelssohn "Songs Without Words," Handel's

THE FIRST PIANO-LESSON

From the Painting by J. A. Muenier

Largo, Schumann's many piano pieces, and others of the sort might give much pleasure, while being at the same time an education in good taste. Sonatas and other ambitious works might be included to a judicious extent. It would even be possible, with some skill in choosing illustrations, to interest the children a little in contrapuntal works, and give them an idea of what polyphony means. Not all pupils would rise to these opportunities; but we do not lower the literary standards because not all the pupils can rise to the level of the written masterpieces.

So much for the school. Another chance for developing taste comes with the possibility of taking children to public concerts. Here, too, the parents should not worry if part of the programme is beyond the child's comprehension. If he enjoys only a little of a classical programme at first, he will appreciate a little more at his next concert, and gradually grow to understand. But he will never understand if he is not given the opportunity.

If the home is one in which the parents themselves are unmusical, and the child is taking no lessons of a regular teacher, then little development of taste can be expected. But in those homes where the parents are musical, the child will have the advantage of learning to appreciate constantly higher things by repeated hearing; and this opportunity should never be curtailed.

At first the average child will care mostly for rhythmical melody. Gradually the taste for harmony will become evident. Then more and more advanced homophonic works will be appreciated, and finally polyphony.

Few young children care at first for contrapuntal treatment and devices. The taste for this must come gradually. Yet there are exceptionally gifted musical children who can appreciate some of these touches very early. With such young artists, when one has reached the Bach Two-Part Inventions, care should be taken to explain the points of treatment, the idea of canon and of double counterpoint (see No. 2 of the set), without, however, giving too involved laws regarding the creation of these; the mere hearing and recognition will be quite sufficient at first.

As regards an induction into the works of Bach, it is a fact that many a child has been turned from the great master by the lack of judgment of the teacher. If the Two-part Inventions are not appreciated (and very few children love them) let the first taste of Bach come from the Suites. And do not give these in their entirety. Choose a few of the most melodious Sarabandes (either to be played or merely listened to) for a beginning.

Be careful to remember that the cultivation and preservation of enthusiasm is worth as much as the technical advance. Not all children are alike in ability. Some may not take fire easily; they may even be indifferent for a while, yet they may become splendid students later on. Remember that Sir Walter Scott was regarded as a very dull student at school. Much introspection is necessary for the teacher himself. It is painful to watch the old-fashioned music teacher, excited, nervous, without definite plan, not understanding his pupil's nature nor how to appeal to it.

In execution demand of the pupil only what he can properly give. The great Dr. Arnold, of Rugby, was once about to punish a pupil whose dulness had provoked him greatly. "Please, Dr. Arnold," said the young delinquent, "I am really doing the best that I can." Dr. Arnold put by the cane, and afterward stated that he never forgot the lesson that this honest dullard had given him.

There are some teachers who imagine that they are doing their duty by treating all pupils alike, which is the greatest mistake that they can make. They must come down to the pace of the snail, and rise to the speed of the greyhound, among their pupils. They are unjust to both the superiors and the inferiors by any other plan. The pouring of an exact quart into every bottle leaves the gallon ones unfilled and the pint ones losing half of the allowance.

There has as yet been no Pestalozzi, or Froebel, or Montessori, in musical education, but a good beginning is being made in this generation. Let the individual teacher remember that the Public Schools and the Conservatories are with him in this modern uplift, and let him always bear in mind that the earliest stages may often be the most important, for "Just as the twig is bent the tree is inclined."

A HISTORY OF MUSIC

Courtesy Metropolitan Museum of Art, N. Y.

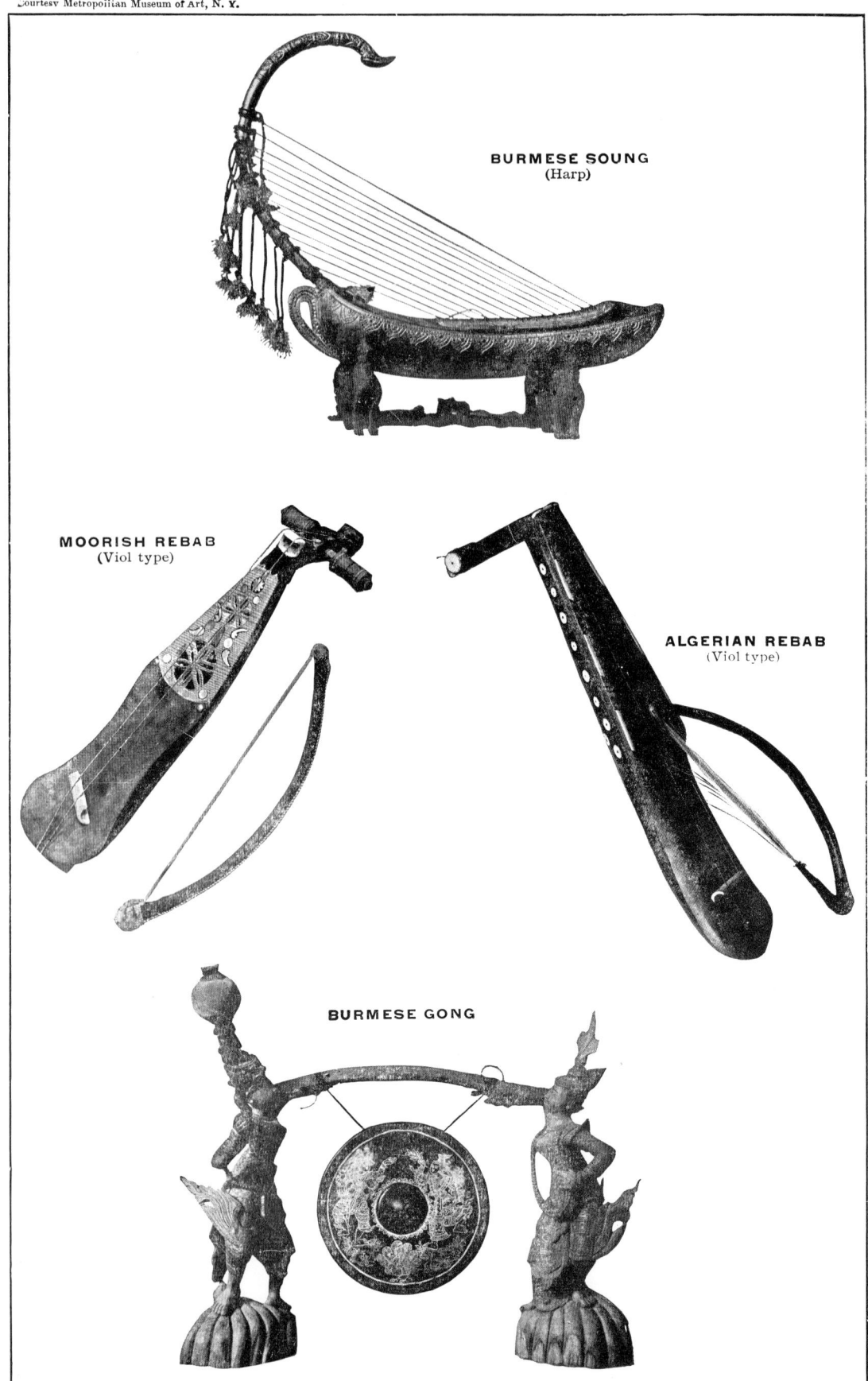

BURMESE SOUNG
(Harp)

MOORISH REBAB
(Viol type)

ALGERIAN REBAB
(Viol type)

BURMESE GONG

SOME PRIMITIVE MUSICAL INSTRUMENTS
from the Crosby-Brown Collection

A HISTORY OF MUSIC

PRIMITIVE AND ANCIENT MUSIC

INTRODUCTION

Three Forms of Musical Instruments: the Drum, the Pipe, and the Lyre—Their Succession Established as the Law of Development of Musical Instruments in Prehistoric Times—The Stages of Early Musical History.

MUSICAL instruments, though their varieties may be counted by hundreds, are yet readily reducible to the drum type; the pipe type; and the lyre type. Under the first head fall drums, rattles, gongs, triangles, tam-tams, castanets, tambourines, cymbals—in a word, all instruments of percussion. Under the second head fall flutes, oboes, clarinets, bassoons, horns, trumpets, trombones, bugles—all wind instruments. And under the third head fall all stringed instruments, comprising the harp, lyre, lute, guitar, the violin (with all its varieties), the mandolin, dulcimers, pianos, etc., etc. These three types are representative of three distinct stages of development through which prehistoric instrumental music passed, and the stages occur in the order named. The first stage in the development of instrumental music was the drum stage, in which drums, and drums alone, were used by man; the second stage was the pipe stage, in which pipes as well as drums were used; the third stage was the lyre stage, in which lyres were added to the stock.

Savages sometimes have the drum alone, but never the pipe alone, or the lyre alone; for if they have the pipe, they always have the drum too; and if they have the lyre, they always have both pipe and drum. We find the drum to be the only musical instrument known among the Australians, the Eskimos, and the Bering nations generally, the Samoyeds and the other Siberian tribes, and, until a comparatively recent date, the Laplanders.

With the Polynesian Malays and the Papuans the pipe makes its appearance, while in no single instance is the drum found wanting. Both pipe and drum are in use among the tribes on the Upper Amazon, the Indians of the Rio Negro and the Uaupes, the Tupis, the Omaguas and neighboring tribes, the Artaneses, and Tacunas, and generally the rest of the Brazilian tribes; the aborigines of Guiana, the Aymara Indians of Bolivia and Peru, the Gauchos of the Platine region, the Abipones of Paraguay, the Patagonians. What is true of the South American Indians is equally true of the North American Indians.

Where the lyre appears, both pipe and drum are found as its never-failing complements, as with the Dyaks of Borneo, the Khonds of Khondistan, the Finns, the Tatars, the Cossacks, the Turkomans, the Hindus, and the nations of history.

Throughout the Pacific Islands the drum is the instrument of the priests. Catlin mentions it as appropriated to religious ceremony among the Assiniboins, Mandans, Crows, and Sioux, and his assertion may be extended to all the North American Indians. It is the instrument of the priests in Guiana, and forms an essential element in the ritual of the Patagonian wizards; similarly used among the Abipones and other South American tribes, particularly the Guaycurus, at that beautiful ceremony with which they every morning welcome and adore the rising sun. The drum is depicted on the walls of the holy places in the ruined temples of Copan and Palenque; and, not to speak of its use in ritual among the Peruvians and Mexicans, a glance at ancient nations will remind us of the sistrum of the Egyptian priests, and the cymbals of the Assyrian and Hebrew priests. With the Greeks, the drum in its various forms of drum, tambourine, cymbal, and rattle was customarily employed.

The evidence of mythology is chiefly valuable for the hints it gives us about the order of succession—we are now speaking of the mythology of civilized peoples. Athena invented the flute, but afterward threw it away because it distorted her features, and took to the lyre instead. When Apollo received the lyre from Mercury, he praised the wonderful sound which neither gods nor men had heard before, for up till then he had been contented with the amorous sighing of the flute. But long before Athena's flute or Apollo's lyre was heard, music had come into being with the cymbals of the Curetes, says the legend in Herodotus, and from these simple elements all Greek music, it avers, was subsequently derived.

Legends of Egypt tell the same tale as those of Greece. Osiris invented the flute, and Isis the sistrum; but it was the Egyptian Hermes or Thoth, a deity of later date than either of these, who invented the lyre. Indian legend keeps up the order of succession. Vishnu was the inventor of the trumpet, and, in his avatar as Krishna, of the flute; but it was Nareda, the son of Brahma, who belongs to the second generation of gods, that first invented the lyre.

CHAPTER I

THE DRUM STAGE

The Origin of Music—The First Musical Instrument—The Drum-god—Drum-worship—Musical Religions of Savage Races—The Structure of the Drum, and its Gradual Progress to a Perfect Type of Instrument.

THE savage who for the first time in our world's history knocked two pieces of wood together, and took pleasure in the sound, had other aims than his own delight. He was patiently examining a mighty mystery; he was peering with his simple eyes into one of nature's greatest secrets. The something he was examining was rhythmic sound, on which roots the whole art of music.

The great seat of drum-worship was South America. Even at the present day it is to be found in full vitality in the interior of Brazil; but a hundred years ago it could be said that "the drum was the only object of worship from the Orinoco to the Plata." This is two-thirds of South America, and as it is more than probable that the great Southern region formerly designated as Patagonia should be added too, this would make the area of the cult nearly coequal with that of the continent. The fetish, though it belongs to the genus "drum," is strictly of the rattle species. The maraca, as it is called, is a hollow gourd, with small stones or hard corn-seeds inside it, generally the former, which rattle when it is shaken. Without his drum the Lapland sorcerer was powerless; but with it, and by its aid alone, he could do all his wonders. The Laplanders used the drum to find out what sacrifice their gods desired; but the Brazilians, who believed "that their devil dwelt in the maraca," offered sacrifice to the maraca itself. The Laplanders believed that the drum put them in communication with spirits, and had the power to predict the future.

Though Lapland and South America were the great seats of drum-worship, it was not confined to these countries by any means; for, stretching in an unbroken line along the entire extent of Northern Siberia to Bering Strait, passing over into the New World, trending right into Greenland, and descending in full force through the whole of North America, interrupted for a moment by the ancient civilizations of Mexico and Yucatan, but taking up the running again at the Orinoco, and never stopping till it gets to the bottom of Patagonia, an unbroken series of traces of the same idea extends. So unmistakable is the family resemblance that the constant repetition of the same phenomena through all the countries enumerated would seem to warrant the conclusion that from the North Cape down to the Strait of Magellan, at some period in the history of mankind, an organized system of religion prevailed in which the drum was worshiped as a god.

Among North American Indians the prophetic art is attained by the agency of the drum.

The history of the bell is a counterpart to the history of the drum. Whoever cares to peer into the records of that era of naïve credulity which we call the Middle Ages will find the same superstitions which were connected with the drum reappearing in connection with the bell. He shall read of bells being thought to speak, of bells thought to be alive, of bells dressed, and arrayed with ornaments not unlike the fetishes we are now considering. Maracas could influence the "fertility and sterility of the ground," and bells were rung "to make a good harvest." The Natchez used rattles to conjure the weather, and our own forefathers hung bells in their churches, "to break the thunderbolt and dispel the storm."

The drum was used for other purposes than worship. It was used to mark rhythm in dancing, and in the absence of any other instrument was put to most striking use as a means of human expression. The Eskimos use their drum "to express their passions"; the Manganjas "to express their joy and grief."

It is to Australia, which has been happily termed "the asylum for the fauna and flora of past ages"—to the "poor winking New-Hollanders," as Dampier calls them—that we must turn if we would find the living resemblances to the musical instruments used by primitive man. In that tranquil continent not only has the animal and vegetable world stagnated, but human life "set" early and was fossilized; and so in the present aborigines we may see very well what we were ages ago.

Their musical instruments are all extemporized for the occasion—thrown away as soon as used, most of them. Sometimes they beat two pieces of stick together, or two green branches, or shake bunches of boughs. At other times their instruments are still more elementary, being simply those which nature has given them. The bystanders accompany the dances at times by stamping their foot on the ground or clapping their hands, a method of drumming carried to its esthetic climax by the Andamanese. This same naïve use of "natural instruments" is to be found among many tribes far in advance of the Australians in point of civilization. A considerable advance on the boughs and sticks was made when spears were used in the same way, or when the women "rolled their skin cloaks tightly together into a hard ball, and beat them upon their laps with the palms of their hands."

Preambles, as we may call them, to the drum proper may also be studied in the clubs of the New Caledonians, the paddles of the New-Zealanders, the clubs of the Makololos, the paddles of the Tonga Islanders. A still nearer approach to the drum proper was made when such a thing as a spear-board was "beaten with a short stick held in the middle." Here the isolation

540

of the sound-generator had so far advanced that a generator was employed "which required some practice to play it." Yet ages wore away before any such thing as extra resonance was seriously sought after. In the hollow inverted bowl of the Hawaiians, which is struck by the foot, we first find ourselves in the transitional stage when man had awakened to the fact that hollowness is the first condition of resonance. This idea is wrought to its logical completion in the hollowed-out logs which serve the Samoans, many of the Amazon tribes, the Ugoma negroes, and the Fijians as very good drums.

Covering these hollowed-out logs with a skin head was a mighty step in the history of music.

With the invention of a stretched skin over a hollowed-out log—the form of drum to be found on the very earliest Egyptian sculptures, and clearly existent long before any historic record—the instrument reached its perfection, and man has never been able to improve upon it since. Mechanical ingenuity might strike out new shapes, artistic genius might adorn it with devices cut on the barrel, but the principle that the drum must be a hollow cylinder, with some sort of skin stretched over the end, has never been questioned from that day to this.

The resonance of the drum became in due course of time the prime object of admiration with its rude manufacturers. So man set himself to work to increase its resonance, either by enlarging its bulk or making a hole in its side, or by using particular kinds of wood for it, or, better still, by getting a more resonant drumhead.

CHAPTER II

THE PIPE STAGE

The Horn and the Flute the Leading Types of Wind Instruments—The Horn Invented for the Purposes of Warfare—Its Use in Warfare—Love the Origin of the Flute—The Courting-flutes of Savage Nations.

THE pipe stage speaks of a far higher intellectual development than the drum stage did. Unlike the drum, which became out of the darkness of nothing we can scarcely tell how, the pipe was made consciously to satisfy purely human needs.

First let us consider the elder branch of the pipe family, that is, the horn and trumpet species, for there is good evidence that these saw the light considerably earlier than the smaller members of the family to whom the term "pipe" is more properly applied. Among modern savages the use of the horn is in nearly every case limited to warfare. Savages of many tribes commence their attacks with a blast of horns and trumpets.

This use of the horn in warfare is plainly an infringement on one of the uses of the old drum, for the drum was supposed "to give victory over enemies." All panic is derivable from trumpet-like sound, if we may trust the derivation of the word which refers the first panic to the time when the great god Pan put to flight an army of Indians by a sudden shout, just as he set the Titans running on another occasion by a similar means.

Though we might well hesitate to say that the savages looked for a result so entirely miraculous, we may suppose that their horns and trumpets were designed to increase the terror of their onset, and contribute to scaring the foe, since we find them all doing their best to increase the sound of their horns and trumpets to unparalleled heights, and apparently having no other object in the manufacture of them than the production of "hellish sound."

Once proved efficacious for scaring the foe, what so natural that man should employ his horn as a weapon again his arch enemies the spirits? That it was on the frightening power of the horn, and no other, that man relied for its ability to influence the spirits may be seen from the ceremony which is practised by the lamas of Tibet, and which may be taken as a representative of similar ones among other peoples. At stated periods, M. Huc tells us, four thousand lamas assemble on the roofs of the various monasteries, and blow trumpets and conch-shells all night long. An old lama gave him the following explanation of the rite: It had been established, he said, to drive away demons by which the country had formerly been infested. They had caused all kinds of maladies among the cattle, corrupted the cows' milk, disturbed the lamas in their cells, and even carried their audacity so far as to force themselves into the choir at the hour of prayer. During the night these evil spirits used to assemble at the bottom of the ravine and frighten everybody in the neighborhood out of their wits by the noises they made, till at last a learned lama hit upon the idea of fighting them with their own weapons, and imitated their cries with horns and conch-shells—most successfully, it would seem.

The magic horn of the South African rain-maker gets its magic on precisely the same terms, for the louder the sound, the more potent is the spell. To the same category must be referred those ceremonies which take place in many nations at the time of the new moon, or at an eclipse—in either case for the same reason, and whether the spirits are to be frightened from the young crescent, or from the sick and blackened disk they have bewitched, trumpets will be equally efficacious. Of these the ceremonies of the Peruvians may be taken as good illustrations, of the ancient Mexicans, and of the Romans as described by Tacitus.

The origin of the flute, or smaller form of "pipe," must be sought on other grounds. It is impossible that its soft velvety tone should have the same origin as the sound of the trumpet, which frightened enemies and evil spirits. The Greeks, who were nearer the first movements of human civilization than we are, assigned its invention to the great god Pan. The heart of their legends is generally sound, and we may presume that whenever the great god Pan —the gayest Lothario of Olympus—comes prominently forward as an actor in the human drama, we are on the verge of an amour.

The flute is not only the darling instrument of those savage nations who are renowned for their gallantry, but there are also cases of the original use of the instrument surviving in all its purity. Among the North American Indians we find what is called the Winnebago courting-flute. "In the vicinity of the Upper Mississippi," says Catlin, "a young man will serenade his mistress with it for days together"— they sit on a rock near the wigwam and blow without intermission—"until she accedes to his wishes, and gives him her hand and heart." The ancient Peruvians had a regular love-language for the flute, and so powerful an appeal could it make to the female heart that there are stories of girls being drawn from a distance by the sound of the flute, and throwing themselves into the arms of the man who played it.

The mere fact that the love-call, to borrow an expression of Darwin's, is the only definite purpose for which the flute is employed among savage races, outside of its later employment as a musical instrument, is sufficient to communicate a peculiar character to the instrument, and there need be no hesitation in assigning its origin to the love-call. Darwin finds the origin of all instrumental music in the love-call. We content ourselves with referring the flute and the pipe to that origin.

It is highly probable that the flute was first played by the nose. This, at least, is the manner of playing which prevails in the Society Islands, the Friendly Islands, the islands of the Samoan group, the Marquesas, and generally throughout Polynesia, which is *par excellence* the home of the flute. That idiotic grimace into which one playing the flute with his mouth is compelled to contort his features, and because of which Greek sculptors were afraid to represent their flute-players in the act of playing, means a highly artificial pose of the features, and we may be sure that anything highly artificial is not primitive. Long practice is necessary before the art of blowing the flute with the mouth can be even tolerably acquired, but it can be played easily at the first attempt by blowing with the nostril, as the breath comes from that at the precise angle necessary to produce the tone.

CHAPTER III

THE VOICE

The Origin of Song—Its Development from Speech—Evolution of the Scale—The One-Note Period in the History of Music—The Two-Note Period—The Three-Note Period—The Succeeding Periods—Dancing, and its Influence upon Song—Origin of the Minor.

THE origin of vocal music must be sought in impassioned speech. Song is an outpouring of the heart, and an artistic embodiment of the language of emotion. Joy, grief, love, hope, despair, heroism, fortitude, despite the universality of music, will remain her favorite themes to the end. Moved by such feelings as these did primitive man first raise his rugged voice in the accents of passion. With primitive man emotional speech was far more common than with us. Hence the otherwise inexplicable fact that savages can extemporize song after song with the greatest ease.

But impassioned speech is not singing, and the points of difference between the two are many. In singing we use the whole range of our voice; in speaking we use only a part of it. When we sing we single out certain tones and keep to them; when we speak we never rest on any one tone; indeed, the subtle inflections of the voice between one tone and another become the means of expression. How did the conversion of speech into song proceed? There were certain influences at work from a very early period indeed, and the first and most important was the influence of the story, reciting the deeds of the past, the events of the chase or of the war-trail, and the like. These things were told round the camp-fires or in the gloom of the caves, and somehow in such narration men acquired the habit of confining the voice much to one note. In the rise and development of story-telling we hail the rise of the chant. The practical effect of the chant, or practice of intoning, would be to correct that fluctuation and unsteadiness of tone which is so essentially the characteristic of speech.

First, men were content with one note. The spoken

phrase at the normal pitch of the speaking voice would of itself settle down into this one note under the influence of the chant. It is probable that the first musical note was near to g, and for a long time the whole musical art lay in embryo in that note. At the present day the songs of savages are nearly all at this pitch, that is to say, with g for the keynote; and those savages who have only one note in their music usually have g for that one note.

The practical effect of chanting on impassioned speech would be to isolate the tone from the words; and the struggling into being of the one note would bring the isolation clearly before men's minds. We may suppose that the next step would be to treat the tone objectively, to make it the subject-matter of art. Men would come to enjoy the sound of itself, and study to give it variety, and while this object would be first secured by variety of rhythm, the tendency would ultimately result in the addition of another note to the compass of the chant. A one-note period would be succeeded by a two-note period. There is nothing improbable in the assumption that there was a period, and probably a very long period, in the history of primitive man, when the whole resources of vocal music at his command consisted of two notes.

After a period of two notes one more note was added to the compass of the chant, and, as was natural, it was the next note above. In the one-note period variety could only be gained by rhythmic means. In the two-note period the same means would be principally employed. But when three notes came to be used, there was the temptation to gain variety by the melody. It is easy to see what a complete reformation the addition of one note to the existing two would work in the art of music. For besides the scope it would give to melody, three notes would form a scale.

The early development which the scale passed through was not, as for example we might imagine, the addition to c', d', e', of the next note above, f', but the superposition of a new and smaller scale of two notes, g' and a', on the old scale c', d', e'.

We may term the old scale of three notes the great scale; the new scale of two, the little scale. That this was the progress of development we have positive evidence, not merely from the songs of savages, but from the musical systems of the civilized nations of antiquity, in all of which, without exception, there are obvious traces of a well-defined scale of five notes: c', d', e', g', a'. The best evidence of the five-note scale is that afforded by the Chinese, who at the present day use no other; and the same remark applies to the Indo-Chinese.

If all language passes through three stages, the first monosyllabic or isolating, the second agglutinative, and the third inflectional, we may similarly assert that music passes through three stages in its evolution of the scale. The first stage is isolating: c', d', e', g', a', where the great scale and the little scale remain isolated from one another, as is found in the most ancient music of the nations of antiquity, the music also of many savages and of the Chinese. The next is the agglutinative stage, when these two scales are agglutinated by the insertion of the fourth: c', d', e', f', g', a'. Last comes the inflectional stage: c', d', e', f', g', a', b', when, by the insertion of the seventh, the scale is enabled to pass naturally to the octave above, and to modulate to a new scale on the keynote of its fifth.

We have considered the influence of the chant in turning speech into song, but all the while there has been another influence at work. Perhaps more strongly noticeable than the steadiness of the notes in all specimens of primitive song is their rhythmic character, due to the influence of dancing. Men singing when dancing would naturally accommodate their song to the beats of their feet, so bringing two species of rhythm to bear upon their song. In every dance there are two kinds of rhythmic movement: the rhythm of the steps and the rhythm of the motions— foot rhythm and figure rhythm.

That frolic of the body or wanton enjoyment of motion called dancing expresses itself by a certain movement of the foot which is peculiarly its own, and must have been natural to it from the very first. The step and the stride belong to the walk, but the property of the dance is the skip. But besides the skip—which we may take to be the general and typical motion in dancing—there are other motions which seem all more or less to be derived from the skip. There is the shuffle, which may be called skipping without moving from the place; there is the trip, which is the moving shuffle, for in it each foot makes a short and long, and still the body moves, going straight along as it does in skipping; and there is the double skip, which consists in right heavy, left light, right heavy, and left heavy, right light, left heavy. All these steps are what children use as soon as they have learned to walk and run, and are almost as primitive as walking itself. Thus we have four rhythmic movements of the feet—the skip, the shuffle, the trip, and the double skip.

Besides the steps that the feet make in the dance there are the motions of the body to be taken into account; that is to say, besides foot rhythm there is also figure rhythm to be considered, which plays its part in all these motions of stepping.

Singling out the skipping form of dance as the simplest one wherein to show its influence, we shall easily see how the development of song proceeded. After the dancer has skipped forward for some distance in any given direction, he suddenly pauses and skips away in the other, goes backward and forward, now to one side, now to another, keeps up an alternation of right foot leading, left foot leading, and skips in sets of skips without knowing he does so. At the end of each set a step is lost, for except by missing a step there could be no change of feet. So each set is marked off from the other by a pause, and it will be plain what effect this will have on the song the man is singing; for it will produce in it a rhythm outside a rhythm. The melody will be cleanly divided into sets or groups of notes; for the first of each group, being the first skip of a new set, would have a stronger emphasis than all the others that followed, the foot being fresher when it struck it. And so the man would have divided his song into bars, and his words he would have divided into lines. This is how verse began.

Names are sometimes the best conservators of the traditions of the past, and as the term "feet" in poetry shows us clearly enough the source whence verse has sprung, so the term "rest" in music speaks equally plainly of short moments of repose in the hurry of the dance.

By the help of these considerations, and by reference to the songs of savage nations, it will be seen how great has been the influence of the dance upon impassioned speech, and to what artful and even intricate forms it has molded the natural inflections of the voice. Those songs, on the other hand, which do not exhibit the rhythmic contour so strongly, we must consider to have grown up under the influence of the chant. Indeed, we might almost divide all primitive songs into dance songs and chant songs.

The minor scale is in use in primitive songs no less than the major. Every one is familiar with the character of the minor key—its plaintiveness, its solemnity, its pathos. As the major expresses in an artistic form the joy and the elation of impassioned speech, so the minor is an artistic embalming of the language of grief. When a man grieves, his voice does **not** rise so buoyantly as usual—it droops as the spirits do —it is sluggish and weary, and shirks the pleasant trouble of free exertion. So it speaks short of its usual intervals, and in declaiming it will do the same. It should seem that this failure of the voice, though showing through all the intervals of the scale, would be likely most to show in the highest note of it, for there it is that the effort lies. Wherefore, if this be true, the great scale would be sung c', d', e' flat, instead of c', d', e', and the little scale g', a' flat, instead of g', a'.

By means of the minor scale the dirge of the savage is reëchoed in profounder strains by the great composers who move us with the contrasted effects of lamentation and triumph expressed through minor and major modes. Indeed, some composers have adopted savage themes and elaborated them in works at once reminiscent of primitive culture and inspired with the soul of art.

CHAPTER IV

THE LYRE STAGE

The Beginnings of Stringed Instruments—The Lyre the Instrument of Barbarians—The Bards of Barbarian Nations—The Universality of Music in this Stage of Development—Music Coequal with Culture—Music as a Moral Power.

THE lyre stage speaks of far higher culture than the two preceding stages, and is contemporaneous with the emergence of man from the savage state into that higher condition of development to which the name "barbarism" naturally applies.

The lyre was the dower which the great Aryan race brought to Europe. It was developed and invented in that wonderful Bactrian home of our ancestors where so many great and beautiful things were nursed into life. In studying the history of the lyre among the hordes of Central Asia, we shall not merely be studying a reflection of it, as in the case of the pipe and the drum, but we shall be studying it in the very place of its birth.

The Tatars are the troubadours of Asia—and of Asia in the widest sense of the word—penetrating into the heart of the Caucasus on the west, and pacing the country eastward to the shores of the Yellow Sea. "The wandering bards in Circassia" (this brings Europe, too, into the computation), says Herbert Spencer, "are generally Kalmucks." "They are often met with in Tatary," writes M. Huc; "very numerous in China"; "nowhere so popular as in Tibet." "They are called Toolholos, and remind us of the minstrels and rhapsodists of Greece." Marco Polo tells us that the Great Khan had so many of these minstrels at his court that, in order to get rid of a few of them, he sent an expedition against the city of Mien composed entirely of superfluous minstrels. When we read that they took this strongly fortified town, we may imagine the extent of the superfluity.

The minstrels are "the greatest delight of the Circassians," "the chief pleasure of the Kirghiz hordes," "the delight of the Crim Tatars," "every house open to receive them," "everywhere a corner for the bard," "every one favored by a visit from him," "all through Persia received with joy." Often each chief has his minstrel.

M. Huc's description of a performance will give us the picture: "For as he was speaking the minstrel was preluding on the chords, and soon commenced in a powerful and impassioned voice a long poetical recitation on themes taken from Tatar history. Afterward, on the invitation of our host, he began an invocation to Timur. There were many stanzas, but the burden was always: 'O divine Timur, will thy great soul be born again? Come back! come back! we await thee, O Timur!'"

Here the voice is everything, the instrument nothing—often not used at all, or at best to strike a short prelude announcing the entry of the voice. If we assume, as we have reason to do, that the primitive method of playing the lyre was such as we find here, we shall see why the lyre first saw light among the nomadic tribes of ancient Asia; for in the tranquillity of the nomadic life there comes a great gush of poetry from the human heart such as can never come again after the hum of cities begins to sound, and the bustle of business to occupy man's mind. And we shall further see why it was that the lyre has its particular form—strings stretched on pegs and twanged with the fingers—in other words, why such a form as the lyre succeeded to the pipe; for the pipe bound the mouth, the lyre set it at liberty, and enabled it to utter the great thoughts that filled the heart. Do not seek, then, to find the first idea of the lyre in the twang of the bowstring which the savage heard as he shot his game. Far from being a connection of the bow's, the lyre would seem to be inimical to it, if it is really an outcome of the nomadic state, when bows and arrows are laid aside.

The lyre, then, came into being as an instrument of accompaniment. In its rudest form it was probably a string or two stretched over a board or a stick, and twanged with the fingers—a small light instrument that would lay the least possible tax on the player and allow him to give his best attention to the song. Its form was the first easy development of the Jew's-harp form, that is to say, more like a lute than a lyre.

Such an instrument would be quite sufficient for the purpose for which it was intended—to prelude or strike a note or two by way of accompaniment to the song. Strings would be added in course of time; for the art of stopping had not then been discovered, nor how one string contains all harmonies as one ray of light all colors; but each new note meant a new string: the history of the pan-pipe repeated itself, in which each new note meant a new reed. After four strings were added, there was a pause; for none of the primitive stringed instruments that we know of have more than four strings.

The next development of this primitive instrument or lute was to take the step by which the true lyre came into being. This was effected by cutting away part of the board at the back of the strings and leaving an empty space, from one end of which to the other the strings ran, having now the benefit of a frame to be fastened to, and thus allowing far tighter stringing than when they were merely confined by pegs at each end of the board. Or perhaps the object of the cutting was to allow the strings to be struck instead of twanged, and struck, that is to say, by something else than the fingers, as a piece of bone or metal, which would deal a sharp blow and make the strings sound louder. The Scythians struck the strings of their lyre with the jawbone of a goat, and the Massagetæ struck theirs with the splinters of spears, and perhaps this may have been the reason. Now the development, having proceeded thus far, instead of going on regularly through the lyre to the other stringed instruments, breaks into two branches.

These are (1) the lute and its descendants, including the lyre, etc., and (2) the lyre's descendants.

The lute is the parent of all instruments whose strings are plucked by the fingers; and the lyre is the parent of all instruments whose strings are struck by a plectrum or hammer. The lute gave birth to the harp, and the lyre gave birth to the dulcimer; or, in other words, the lute obtained its increase in power by increasing the size and the tension of the strings themselves, the lyre by increasing the force with which they were struck.

This is how the lute produced the harp. The stick or board on which the strings lay pegged was bent a little, so that the strain might be divided between the pegs and the board or stick itself; and then this bending went on more and more, till at last it was found that the strain might be thrown wholly on the board or stick by bending it into the form of an arch. When that was done, the lute had grown into a harp. But the lyre never changed its form.

The stopping of the lute's strings was discovered as soon as the lute got a neck. In the primitive form of a piece of straight board with strings lying over it, there was no likelihood that the art of stopping would be learned, but the instrument would be played as nowadays we should play an Æolian harp (which, indeed, it very much resembled), or as the Chinese play their lute at the present day, resting on the knee, or on some artificial support, or perhaps on the left arm, while the thumb of the right hand steadied it underneath and the four fingers twanged the strings. When, for convenience of holding, one end of the instrument was made narrower so as to be grasped by the left hand—directly the left hand went round the strings, it could not help pressing them sometimes as it held them, and the difference of tone which the pressure caused would be at once noticed, and in course of time would be acted on.

The new music which came into being as the direct consequence of the appearance of stringed instruments in the world was the music of harmony; and its spirit was the disciplining of the instrumental by the reason of the vocal. The musical instrument, which in the pipe stage was used but to fling a cataract of idle sounds, now became the means by which actual thought could be expressed. At first it was only used to strike a prelude independently before the voice began to sing. Its development had several stages, and when the last stage was reached, when the instrument and the voice went hand in hand, note for note, and word for word, the instrument would be almost as skillful as the voice itself in expressing the minutest flickering of thought.

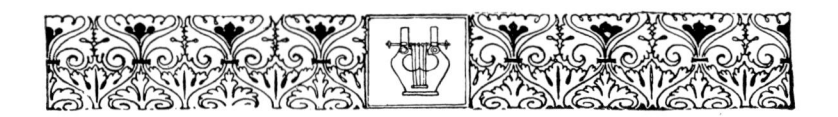

CHAPTER V

THE EGYPTIANS

Music in Egypt during the Nineteenth Dynasty—Instruments of the Egyptian Orchestra—The Great Harp—Egyptian Music from the Times of Menes to the Times of the Ptolemies—The Music of the Temples.

PASSING now from the fastnesses of the barbarian to the lawns and enclosures of civilized man, it will behoove us to see in what guise our art appears under these new conditions. Let us enter the land of the pyramids at the beginning of the nineteenth dynasty, about 1350 B.C., when the power of Egypt, which had been steadily mounting during the eighteenth dynasty, had now reached its height under Rameses II. Passing down the crowded streets, where, through the open shop-fronts, we may see the artisans in thousands at work at their laborious daily tasks, let us go in quest of music. We may traverse the busy streets of Thebes or Heliopolis in vain, and it is not till the shades of evening fall, and the entertainments of the wealthy begin, that we discover the existence of music in Egypt at all. We have to penetrate some brilliantly lighted hall full of guests and attendant slaves; and at the far end of the luxurious room we shall see a band of men and women playing on their instruments, amid all the clatter of the dishes and the chatter of the guests. They are all slaves, and before every piece they play they do obeisance to the master of the house. The business of these slaves was to attend the banquets of the great, and play and sing for the amusement of the company. We find them constantly represented in the sculptures in groups of from two to eight persons—some women and some men—playing on various instruments, as the harp, pipe, flute, etc.

Let us not forget that we are in the land of hieroglyphics, and that besides the figures on the surface a hidden meaning may remain behind. The sculptors who gave us these books of stone, which we have lately read off into words, are indeed the historians and annalists of Egypt. But in reading the books that they left us, we must remember that we are perusing the words of men who had only a limited space to express themselves in. When, therefore, they would speak of an army, they sculptured four men—this had to do duty for as many thousands. Their records are essentially abridgments, and in the pictures of the concerts we must not necessarily suppose that one harper, one piper, one flute-player, and one singer form the entire band, but that they are only the typical representatives each of a whole division of performers.

As a mere mechanical result of grouping various instruments together, some form of harmony must have grown up. Whether this partook of the nature of a mere single-part accompaniment, or whether it was a regular three or four part harmony, may admit of conjecture.

A full Egyptian orchestra was thus composed: twenty harps, eight lutes, five or six lyres, six or seven double pipes, five or six flutes, one or two pipes (rarely used), two or three tambourines (seldom used).

If vocalists were added, which was not necessarily the rule, they would number about three-fourths as many as the harpers.

The harp was the foundation of the Egyptian orchestra. Now the harp is essentially anti-chromatic. It is plain, therefore, that the Egyptian harmony was purely diatonic, such a thing as modern modulation utterly unknown, and every piece from beginning to end played in the same key.

The compass of the orchestra was considerable and may have been nearly as great as our own, even though not possibly used for harmonies.

An Egyptian instrument that may be called musical was the sistrum. This was a set of metal bars in a frame, so arranged that when shaken they gave a sound like modern sleigh-bells. The sistrum was used for rhythmic effects and played an important part in ancient dances. It may have been used also for giving signals, in some working-choruses.

Let us now go back to the supposed founder of the first Egyptian dynasty, about 5000(?) B.C. Up to this time the only rulers of Egypt of whom we hear were mythological gods and demigods. We are told that they went about among the people, instructing them in the arts of peace. They were accompanied everywhere by troops of musicians. What instrument these musicians played we are not informed, but we may imagine that they played the oldest of the Egyptian stringed instruments—the lute of Thoth—the only instrument which appears in the hieroglyphics. It was a little lute, shaped like the ace of spades, with an elongated neck, and fitted with three strings.

Then came Menes, "the strong man," and with him came Egypt's oppression. The people got their civilization and lost their music. Now that they adopted settled habits, and left their wandering life, their tents and leaf huts began to pass into permanent stone houses, and so did the portable lute of Thoth into the non-portable harp. Its form was slightly bent so as to admit of greater tension being applied to the strings by the benefit of the curve, which would partially remove the pressure from the pegs on to the body of the wood.

By the fourth dynasty the change was complete, and the connecting link between the lute and the harp had dropped out of sight altogether. The harps of this dynasty had six strings instead of three, which were fastened, as they had been in the lute, to pegs at the top and to the body of the instrument itself at the bottom. They were all bass, the place where the treble strings come being left quite bare; so that in these harps we see the progenitors of the great harps of Rameses's time. The orchestras of Cheops's time were very simply composed—bass harps, tenor or alto flutes, and single pipes formed the *tout ensemble*.

During the fifth dynasty the frame of the harp was bent still more—into a perfect semicircle; the lower part of it was greatly thickened, and had its bottom flattened, by virtue of which the harp could stand alone. In the thickening of the lower part we may see the first dim gropings after a soundboard.

By the twelfth dynasty this tendency was carried to its completion, and the harp furnished with a perfect soundboard. In the dark period between the close of the fifth dynasty and the opening of the twelfth the thickened and flattened pillar of the harp had been first thickened still more, then hollowed out, then rounded, and finally finished off into the shape of a kettle-drum. Thus was the harp provided with a regular soundboard, which greatly increased the volume of its tone. Small harps were now made as well as great harps; lightness was studied in the orchestras as well as massiveness. Sweetness also was an object of study, and the long-necked lutes now began to appear, affording another foil to the boom of the great harp.

Harps were now made of a particular sort of wood —sycamore—which was specially imported from distant countries for the purpose. The frame was covered with all sorts of fancy devices to attract customers, and the mechanical ingenuity of the craftsmen suggested a new method of fastening the strings, which bears a close resemblance to the way in use at the present time. Egypt, which was now the center of the civilized world, was brought into contact with many foreign nations, products of all parts of the earth flowed into its markets, and among the rest a Semitic lyre, an instrument never seen in Egypt before. It was merely a battered old square board, of which the top part was hollowed out into a kind of gibbous frame, on which seven strings were strung. There was no attempt at decoration; even the edges of the board were all left rough; the strings were simply twisted round the frame and tied in knots. Primitive though the thing was, it caught the public fancy. Its tenure of favor was lasting, but would probably have been brief had not its advent been shortly succeeded by the arrival of the Shepherd Kings, who probably brought a still ruder form of their national instrument with them.

By the beginning of the eighteenth dynasty the lyre had become a recognized component of the Egyptian orchestra, having undergone many improvements, not only in the increase of the number of its strings, but also in the finish of its make. The rude board had by this time given place to a handsome instrument of from ten to twenty-two strings. At this time we may find a sure trace of Semitic influence in the introduction of the dulcimer, which appears for a moment, but never took root as did the lyre.

The Semitic lyre in the eighteenth dynasty began to dispute the soprano place in the orchestra with the indigenous small harp. That the quality of its tone was rather sweetness and softness than strength, we may infer from its always being played by women.

And since the small harp, which was played by men, was fast giving place to it, we may fairly conclude that sweetness and beauty had become the leading characteristics of the music itself by this time. Another fact also points in the same direction—the alteration which was taking place in the form of the harp. The old curved form was now being fast abandoned, and the small harps were constructed with a frame of triangular shape, with strings strung obliquely across it. In this harp we have the parent of the notorious sambuca.

The great harp, however, still remained true to its old form, and like a rock kept back the unwholesome current. Standing nearly seven feet in height, and fitted with eighteen sonorous bass and tenor strings, it must have ruled the orchestra like a king, and have served as a standing protest against the meretricious tendencies of the time.

Other characteristics of this age were the growing fondness for female singers and instrumentalists; the daily increasing popularity of the double pipe, which was played almost exclusively by women; the more frequent use of the tambourine than in former dynasties—all pointing to an increased prominence of the sensuous side of the art.

The art of the twenty-first dynasty was remarkable for the feminine intricacy of its finish. The lyre played by women had completely banished the small harp from the orchestra, and the great harp was now being distorted into the triangular form. In the twenty-second dynasty the capital was removed to Bubastis, the most luxurious city in Egypt, and it is a sign of the times that the popular deity of the people was now a goddess. Of orchestras we no longer hear mention; they had been supplanted by dancing-girls and tambourine-players. The great harp had become a mummy, like its masters, and the attention of the musical world in Egypt was concentrated on a newly invented instrument—the treble flute.

If the flute owed its origin to the amorousness of primitive man, there was considerable reason for its supremacy at present; for the orgies of Bubastis had now become matters of wide notoriety. There is another point about this flute, which may give us an additional reason for the demise of the old harp—it was chromatic. Here, then, is the break-up of the Egyptian orchestra accounted for. The harp could only play a diatonic scale, and as long as the people were simple-minded enough to be contented with such simple melodies and harmonies as the diatonic scale could give, so long was the Egyptian orchestra possible; but directly the jaded taste required a new and more pungent stimulus, and the chromatic scale came, then great harps, small harps, and even the effeminate lyres, could no longer play the fashionable music, and the orchestra collapsed in consequence.

Let us pass on to the last stage of Egyptian music as we find it under the Ptolemies. In those days the Egyptians were accounted the greatest musicians in the world. Every man in Alexandria could play the flute and lyre, the flute always being the favorite instrument. The most untiring efforts were made to attain dexterity on it: bandages were bound round the cheeks to counteract the strain on the muscles, and veils were worn by the crack players to hide the contortions of the countenance. Through all grades of society, even to the king, ran this mania for flute-playing. And this is the last we hear of ancient Egyptian music.

One word more, however, should be added. Looking further into it than we have done, we shall find that there was a certain section of Egyptian life where music was allowed air, and where it was unpatronized and free. In the temples of Thebes, Memphis, Arsinoë—those twilight retreats of a sublime pantheism—amid clouds of incense and the flash of gold and white robes, was heard the music which might have been Egypt's, had Egypt been free—crowds of priests winding along the aisles of sphinxes, and chanting the praises of him who lives for ever and ever, God of the evening sun, God of the morning sun, bright Horus. There was the pulse of Egypt's spirit. But the religious music, like the religion itself, never spread its influence among the people at large.

For the rest, if we would find the exact contribution of Egypt to the general history of music, we must find it in the mechanical excellence of its instrument-makers, under whose dexterity and skill the harp gained sufficient power to be able to be played as a solo instrument. Everything else has perished, but the solo harp has remained.

CHAPTER VI

THE ASSYRIANS

The War Music of the Assyrians—Character of their Bands—Love for Shrill Sounds—Assyrian Dulcimers.

BY contrast with the music of the Egyptians, the music of the Assyrians was essentially martial. Drums, trumpets, and cymbals brayed and clashed in the Assyrian concerts. We must cease to talk of orchestras now, and speak of "bands" instead, for we are to speak of a music in which we seem to hear the war-horse neighing. The whole spirit of it seemed to come from the armies; the players, grouped in concise bodies and arranged in lines, have all the air of marching bands; the instruments, too, were all portable, strapped to the body or carried in the hand, the harps all so small that they could be held in the hand, the dulcimers strapped to the shoulders, and the drums strapped on the chest. The beating of time in the concerts was not by clapping the hands, but by stamping with the foot—as if learned from soldiers marching.

That a love for shrill sounds should be joined to this love of martial effect was but natural. The Assyrian bands were remarkable for the preponderance of the treble. The harps could scarcely contain any notes below alto compass. Of the other instruments, which were the lyre, the lute, the dulcimer, the flute, the double pipe, the trumpet, the single pipe, there is not one which is not small in make and probably treble in pitch, with a similar compass, no doubt, to that of the lyre-shaped harp. Agreeably to the composition of the instrumental portion of their bands was the composition of the vocal element, which was supplied principally by women and boys; that is to say, by treble voices. Eunuchs also are frequently found among the singers. There is no imagining any harmony in the music, which must have been an air in octaves, with all the stress on the high octave. The instrumental bands were analogous in their composition to the vocal choruses; nearly all the instruments were soprano, those of the bass and tenor order being rarely employed. To take off the edge of the disproportionate treble element the Assyrians employed loud instruments of percussion like the drum and cymbals.

But more than all other instruments, the dulcimer, their favorite, is a remarkable testimony to the nature of Assyrian music. The dulcimer, indeed, was such a favorite with the Assyrians, that it appears on the bas-reliefs twice as often as any other instrument. And of this instrument, which we must especially notice since it is the undoubted parent of the modern piano, there were two kinds, one of a horizontal form, with the strings lying flat, and the other of a vertical form, with the strings strung upward, but above one another; the first an exact model of our grand piano, the second not quite so good a one of the upright, because the strings were strung one above another instead of side by side.

These instruments had ten strings on an average, though sometimes one or two more are found, and sometimes less. They were strapped to the person, like so many of the musical instruments of the Assyrians, and being small, sat most conveniently to the figure, and allowed the player the greatest freedom of motion. Of the two kinds of dulcimer, the vertical is much the commoner. The player struck the strings with the rod which he held in his right hand, and used his left hand at the same time as a damper for the lower strings, in order to prevent their sounds running into one another, by which we may conclude that the music was as a rule very rapid, since in slow music the sound of each string would have died away in time.

CHAPTER VII

THE HEBREWS

The Minstrel Poets—The Prophets—The Form of the Hebrew Music, Elucidated by an Analysis of the Poetry—Hebrew Music at the Time of David—Music in the Schools of the Prophets—Rabbinical Traditions, etc.

THE Hebrews were lacking in feeling for the sensuous and artistic side of life, but they exalted its spiritual side to a wonderful height. Unlike the Assyrians, the beauty of whose carvings has seldom been surpassed, the Hebrews not only despised sculpture, but accounted it irreligious. Painting fared no better with them. Architecture was so poorly represented that Jahveh's tabernacle was for centuries a tent, and Solomon had to hire a foreigner to build the temple. Equally deficient were the Hebrews in dramatic genius. The one outlet by which their wild formless emotion could find a congenial vent was in the passionate outbreaks of lyric poetry and extemporized song.

It is here, therefore, that we must look for the import of the Hebrews in musical history. Their relation to instrumental music is a purely subordinate one, and scarcely merits remark. They had but few instruments, and of these all but one were borrowed from other nations, principally, it should seem, from the Egyptians. There was not a drum to be found from Dan to Beersheba, nor a dulcimer either; and flutes, if used at all, were very rarely used. The only instrument that attained much favor, and this was the indigenous one, was the harp, which should more properly be described as a lyre than a harp, since it was a small portable instrument which the player carried about with him wherever he went. This little lyre was the great instrument in Israel, and the reason it could be so was that the music of the Hebrews was in every sense of the word a vocal music. The voice transcended and outdid the instrument, and instrumental development stood still. With the Hebrews, therefore, we pass from the heated atmosphere of bands and concerts to a far higher and purer air, and the center of interest directs itself to a single typical figure, the minstrel poet.

To "prophesy" meant to sing, and there is little doubt that Isaiah, Jeremiah, and others like them, uttered their prophecies in song, no less than in verse, both alike being extemporized. To such men as these music could never be an art—it was a form of speech, closely knit up with poetry. It is most probable that the use of an instrument for accompanying was only occasional. Their song, no less than their verse, was purely unpremeditated, being in the first instance the same impassioned speech which we have noticed as the original of song among primitive men; but with the Hebrews this impassioned speech received a very peculiar development from the parallelism of sentences in which their language delighted. The effect of this was to divide every poetical expression into two similar or contrasted parts, and the music which accompanied the poetry naturally received this arrangement likewise. This peculiarity of structure may still be noticed to-day in the religious chant of our churches, and while the patriarchs were living in the plains of Mesopotamia it had begun:

Adah and Zillah, hear my voice: Ye wives of Lamech, hearken unto my speech.
For I have slain a man to my wounding: And a young man to my hurt.
If Cain shall be avenged seven fold: Truly Lamech seventy and seven fold.

That Lamech, the poet, should be the father of Jubal, the minstrel, is natural, and that the minstrelsy which arose in company with such a form of poetry should wear the same peculiar stamp was also to be expected.

The plain result of the establishment of such a form of poetry and song was this: When the minstrel of the old patriarchal times gave place to the choruses of city life, the division of the verse into two parts, each reflecting the other, would obviously suggest the division of the chorus into two parts, each responding to the other, as, for instance, the men to the women, or two companies of women, or it might be a solo-singer and a chorus.

That this style was developed in the city life in Egypt we may imagine, since the first mention of it in the Bible is immediately after the passage of the Red Sea, when "Miriam, the prophetess, took a timbrel in her hand, and all the women went out after her with timbrels and dances. And Miriam *answered* them:

Sing ye to the Lord, for he hath triumphed gloriously:
The horse and his rider hath he thrown into the sea.

The latter half was probably the response of the women. We may conjecture that the other song which immediately precedes this, sung by Moses and the children of Israel, was treated in a similar manner, and that the parts were distributed thus:

Moses. I will sing unto the Lord, for he hath triumphed gloriously:
Children of Israel. The horse and his rider hath he thrown into the sea.
Moses. The Lord is my strength and my song:
Children of Israel. And he is become my salvation.
Moses. He is my God, and I will prepare him an habitation:
Children of Israel. My father's God, and I will exalt him.
Moses. The Lord is a man of war:
Children of Israel. The Lord is his name.
Moses. Pharaoh's chariots and his host hath he cast into the sea:
Children of Israel. His chosen captains also are drowned in the Red Sea.

If we were to write a history of the Hebrew chorus from that time till the time of the Captivity, it would be but to enumerate the various occasions on which such performances are chronicled in the Bible, and the various personages who took part in them. For instance, in the services of the tabernacle, the priests formed one chorus, the Levites the other. Miriam and her women find their parallel in later times in the two choruses of women who came out to meet David after his victory over Goliath, one chorus singing, "Saul hath slain his thousands," the other answering, "And David his ten thousands"; and while Miriam and her damsels only used timbrels to accompany their voices, the women who went to meet David employed not only timbrels but also other instruments of music, so that there would be a distinct advance in musical feeling to chronicle here. It will be found to have had very important effects indeed, since not only would it imply two choirs of singers, but also two bands of instrumentalists, and very likely would affect the internal arrangements of the temple itself, on which we are left to speculate, in necessitating two rows of seats facing one another. That this was the arrangement in Solomon's temple we may judge from the arrangements in Nehemiah's time at the ceremony of the dedication of the wall of Jerusalem, which probably partook of the nature of the temple service.

It should seem that there were two choirs of Levites —or possibly one of priests, the other of Levites— stationed opposite one another at either side of the temple, who sang in antiphon the psalms and canticles which went to make up the service. The singers were flanked by instrumentalists, composed in like manner partly of priests, partly of Levites, who each had their peculiar instruments; for while the Levites had cymbals and psalteries and harps, the priests had trumpets—an instrument which appears to have been exclusively reserved for them. Appearing in its oldest form as a trumpet of ram's-horn, by the time we are speaking of it was made of brass and gold.

We are not to think of any elaborate harmony in the Hebrew temple services, such as characterized the performances of the Egyptians. To the Hebrews, music was not an art, but a voice in which they poured forth their soul to Him "that inhabited the praises of Israel." "The singers and the trumpeters were as *one* to make *one* sound to be heard in praising and thanking the Lord." "One hundred and twenty priests blowing with trumpets"—a scream of sound! Harshness is forgiven to that enthusiasm which so wrestles for expression, and sees heaven open before its eyes.

The reign of David is an idyllic episode in the history of Israel. The sternness of the national temper is seen much softened in him, and in thinking of the minstrel king we are apt to forget that we have before us the rare and short-lived bloom which appeared but once or twice on Hebrew history. We gain a truer conception of the features which were likely to dominate their music by thinking of the prophets of old, Moses, Joshua, Samuel; by remembering the harshness of the Hebrew language, with its abundance of aspirates and sibilants and gutturals, its plethora of consonants and feebleness in vowels. Their chants and psalms we must imagine they intoned or recited in an elevated voice, with but little to distinguish the delivery from ordinary recitation, except the monotony of the tone and the markedness of the cadences.

During this time the Levites who were these regular singers, were suffered to become completely disorganized, and eventually to degenerate into a half-mendicant order wandering up and down Israel, and dependent for their bread on the hospitality of chance entertainers; nor was it until the time of David that they were restored to their former position. That this restoration of the Levites should take place under the minstrel king was natural, and, generally speaking, as we have remarked, in David's reign there are everywhere signs of a musical renaissance, and for the first time the conception of music as an art begins to appear. To the same period also we must refer the establishment of those schools of the prophets in which music and poetry were the leading subjects of instruction. Standing out as these men did in bitter opposition to the tendencies of the age, and as embodiments of that ascetic spirit which was now beginning to wax faint in Israel, it was natural that they should inveigh against the art of the court life, which could seem to them little better than effeminate trifling. Even the temple services did not escape their invective. "The songs of the temple shall be howlings," says the prophet Amos. And in him and others like him spoke the real spirit of the Jewish people, which is doubtless the reason why they were tolerated and respected. If we would follow the track of the purely Jewish music, we must turn from the courts of Jerusalem and Samaria to these very schools of the prophets, secluded in the mountain fastnesses of Gilead or Bethel.

The prophetic ecstasy was doubtless necessary in a greater or less degree for the attainment of all prophecy. And since one of the features of all high spiritual exaltation, and particularly of this prophetic enthusiasm, was the morbid acuteness of the hearing, we may easily suppose that the prophetic ecstasy should be frequently brought on by music. The fact of all prophecy being delivered in the form of chanted verse will at any rate show how essential an element music was to the visionary condition of the consciousness.

If we turn to Saul we shall find what prophesying in its most exalted form actually was, for in his exaltation "he would tear off all his clothes, and lie stretched on the ground for a night and a day together." The condition of a man under the ecstasy, said Montanus, was like that of "a lyre swept by the plectrum." He was unconscious of what he said or did.

Numerous are the miraculous effects that have been ascribed to music by rabbinical tradition, but to suggest that the high estimation which the art enjoyed in Israel was in any way due to its supposed miraculous virtues would be to go too far. The Hebrew minstrels would never have risen above the social status and importance of their brethren in other lands, had not their subject been the noblest that man can aspire to sing of, and had it not been in such thorough harmony with all the highest feelings of their nation. These poets of God sang the praises and the might of God to a nation intoxicated with Deity, and this is why the fame of the brightest minnesinger shrinks to a speck before the majesty of Isaiah.

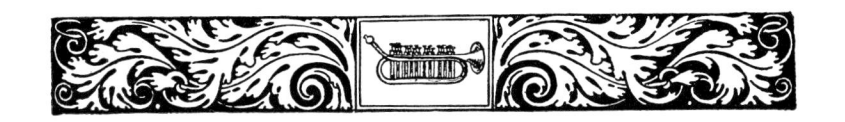

CHAPTER VIII

THE CHINESE, INDO-CHINESE, AND OTHER MONGOLOIDS

The Chinese Scale of Nature—The Scale of the Seven Substances—The Music of Drums, Bells, etc.—Legends of the Origin of Music in China—The Chinese Musical System—Similarities in other Music of the East.

TO the Chinese mere sensuous delight in tone presents such attractions that their musical system is occupied mainly with the analysis and classification of the different qualities of sound, and only secondarily with those sequences of sounds which we call notes.

According to the Chinese, there are eight different musical sounds in nature, each possessing a well-marked character peculiar to itself.

There are: the sound of skin, the sound of stone, the sound of metal, the sound of baked earth, the sound of silk, the sound of wood, the sound of bamboo, the sound of gourd.

Nature having so contrived, man has treated these substances for his own use, and has fashioned skin into drums, stone into cymbals, metal into bells, baked earth into horns, silk into lutes, wood into castanets and vibrating instruments, bamboo into flutes, gourd into mouth-organs.

The sound of skin has eight varieties, and there are therefore eight different kinds of drums, which vary in minute points of construction, as in having a longer or a fuller barrel, or in general bulk, or even in the method of beating; for the eighth variety has two different names, according as it is struck by the right hand or the left. This eighth variety has another peculiarity; for while the others give the sound of skin alone, this qualifies the sound of skin with the sound of rice, which is a subordinate sound of nature, and does not come into the universal gamut. The barrel of the drum is filled with the husk of rice, which has been beaten from the grain in a mortar, and by this means the sound of the rice is united to that of the skin.

The sound of stone is extolled by Chinese theorists as one of the most beautiful of all the sounds. It is said to give a sound midway between the sound of metal and the sound of wood, "less tart and rasping than the sound of metal, much brighter than the sound of wood, more brilliant and sweet than either." To make the stone instruments, of which there are two varieties, the tse-king and the pien-king, both being comprised under the general name king, the stone is sliced into thin plates, about the size and something of the shape of a carpenter's square. The term "cymbals" is misleading, for the stones are not clashed together, but struck like drums with a mallet. The bells likewise present a similar discrepancy with ours, being not rung with a clapper inside, but struck on the outside like the drums and cymbals with a mallet. The cymbals are of various sizes, according to the note they give, are arranged sixteen together on a frame, and played as we should play a dulcimer. When one of them goes out of tune, it can be flattened by taking a thin slice off the back, or sharpened by cutting a piece off the end. In the year 2200 B.C. we read that the Emperor Yu assessed the various provinces in so many stones each, which were to be taken in part payment of their regular tribute. These stones were destined for the palace instruments.

The sound of metal has three varieties, and consequently there are three kinds of bells manufactured to produce it—the po-chung, the te-chung and the pien-chung. Of these, the po-chung is the largest, and gives the richest tone; and the pien-chung the smallest, and produces the most piercing. The te-chung comes midway between the two. The small bells, however, are of more importance in Chinese music than the large ones; for while the large ones are only used occasionally in a piece, the small bells are arranged in sets, and are played solo. There are sixteen bells in all, hung by hooks to two cross-beams on a frame, eight on the top cross-beam, and eight on the bottom one, each bell giving one of the notes of the musical scale.

The sound of baked earth was first extracted by striking a flat piece of baked earth against some hard substance; but the sound thus produced was very unmelodious and harsh. The next attempt to extract it was by infringing on the domain of the drum, and stretching a piece of tanned skin over a vase of baked earth. These vases of baked earth were made in the shape of drums, and struck with drumsticks. These and similar experiments proving unsatisfactory, it was decided to attempt the extraction of this sound from an instrument of wind. A certain quantity of earth was therefore taken, the finest that could be procured. It was made still finer by washing it in several waters, and then worked into the consistency of liquid mud. Two eggs, one of a goose, the other of a hen, served as the models, and the liquid mud was thrown over these and allowed to set. Then the egg on the inside was broken and picked out, and an exact mold of the egg remained. The opening made at the end for the purpose of extracting the egg was next enlarged to serve as a mouthpiece, and five holes were pierced in the bowl, three on the front, and two on the back. Five musical notes were now possible, each giving the desired sound of baked earth.

The sound of silk has two leading varieties and seven minor varieties. It was produced by twisting silken threads into cords and twanging them with the fingers. Little by little it came to be noticed that the sound of silk gave definite musical notes. The cords were then pegged down on a flat board, and the number of threads in each cord counted, so as to preserve the note unaltered for the future. The board was gradually curved to bring the strings nearer together, and the number of strings was limited to seven, which gave the gamut. Of the instrument thus formed, which is called the kin, there are three varieties, and it is one of the most esteemed in China. The other instrument which gives the sound of silk, called the che, used to have fifty strings, but now has twenty-five. Each string has its own separate bridge, so that there are twenty-five bridges. In this instrument the sound of silk attains its greatest perfection; "its sound far excels that of any European clavichord," says Amiot. Nevertheless, the seven-stringed kin is more esteemed in China, probably in deference to its antiquity, for it is much the older instrument of the two.

The sound of wood is given by instruments which are the strangest of all. One has the shape of a bushel, another of writing-tablets, and the third of a tiger.

The sound of gourd went through somewhat similar experiences to the sound of baked earth, for there were many unsuccessful attempts to extract it before a satisfactory result was attained. It was found necessary to trench on the sound of wood and the sound of bamboo to aid the sound of gourd. Bamboo is by nature the most musical of all substances, for the hollow tubing between one knot and the other, the distance between each knot, and the proportions of the distances, the hardness of the cane, etc., all seem to invite man to blow into it, and the instruments made of bamboo were by consequence the earliest that were invented, and served as pitch-pipes for tuning the other instruments, especially those of silk. The instruments of bamboo are pan-pipes and various kinds of flutes. The instruments of bamboo attain a technical importance above the instruments of all the other seven substances; for not only does the bamboo pan-pipe regulate the tuning of the other instruments, but the succession of sounds which it gives serves as the foundation of the Chinese scale.

It was in the reign of Hoang-ty, runs the legend, that the famous musician Lyng-lun was commissioned to order and arrange Chinese music, and bring it from being a confused array of sounds into a regular system. Without knowing how to proceed with his task, Lyng-lun wandered, deep in thought, to the land of Si-joung, where the bamboos grow. Having taken one of them, he cut it off between two of the knots, and, pushing out the pith, blew into the hollow. The bamboo gave forth a most beautiful sound. It happened that this sound was in unison with the sound of his voice when he spoke; and at the same moment the Hoang-ho, which ran boiling along a few paces off, roared with its waves, and the sound of the great river was also in unison with the sound of his own voice and the sound of the bamboo. "Behold, then," cried Lyng-lun, "the fundamental sound of nature! This must be the tone from which all others are derived."

While he was musing on this, the magic bird, Fung-hoang, accompanied by its mate, came and perched on a tree near and began to sing. The first note it sang was also in unison with the sound of the Hoang-ho, and with the voice of Lyng-lun, and with the sound of the bamboo. Then all the winds were hushed, and all the birds in the world ceased singing, that they might listen to the song of the magic bird, Fung-hoang, and its mate. As they sang, Lyng-lun, the musician, kept cutting bamboos and tuning them to the notes of these magical birds, six to the notes of the male, and six to the notes of the female, for they each sang six notes; and when they had done singing, Lyng-lun had twelve bamboos cut and tuned, which he bound together and took to the King.

The bamboos gave the following sounds when they were blown into: f', f' sharp, g', g' sharp, a', a' sharp, b', c'', c'' sharp, d'', d'' sharp, e''.

The six notes with the odd numbers were given by the male bird, and those with the even numbers by the female. Each pipe received a name, and the notes given by these pipes constitute the scale of the Chinese, which, according to Chinese mythology, originated in the manner described.

It is hard to imagine that the Chinese bestow much attention on the actual notes that are struck or sounded—as little, perhaps, as they do on the actual forms and figures of their painting—and so their music is best described as a fanciful play with sound, as their painting is a play with colors. If this is the attitude of their musical sense to their music, we shall now have an explanation why their musical system should be taken up primarily with classifying qualities of tone, and only secondarily with musical notes.

When we think of the instruments themselves, it would seem as if they were not merely made to gratify the ear with their tones, but in quite as great a measure to please the eye with their form and their colors. The stones, for instance, of the stone organ, which is perhaps the typical instrument of China, are sorted in degrees of excellence, more out of regard for their colors than for their qualities of tone. They say that certain timbres go with certain colors, and profess to recognize the flavor of a tone by the color the stone has; but this looks like an afterthought, and as if the stones were ranked in order of excellence primarily on account of their colors, for certain colors would please the eye more than others. The stones are worked into all sorts of patterns, such as a carpenter's square, a heart, a shield, a man's face, a fish, a bat.

The characteristics of Chinese music repeat themselves in the music of the Indo-Chinese and other civilized Mongoloids of the Old World, and we may say generally that the music we have been describing just now is the music of the whole of Southeastern and Eastern Asia.

CHAPTER IX

THE PERUVIANS AND MEXICANS

Music in Peru at the Time of the Conquest—Peru the Home of the Flute—Contrast with Music of the Mexicans—Mexican Instruments of Percussion and Wind—The Public Dances.

THE most beautiful songs in ancient Peru were those which the reapers used to sing in the maize-fields as they were cutting the crops of the Inca. Whether they were reaping or binding up the sheaves, all the motions of their bodies were in time to the measure of their songs. Except a few of the very best love-songs, there was nothing that could equal these reapers' songs.

The Peruvians, as a rule, were not great singers. "In my time," says Garcilasso, "the people of Peru never sang at all, but they used to play their songs on the flute instead, which came to much the same thing, for the words of the songs being well known, and no two songs having the same tune, the melody of the flute immediately suggested the words to the mind." Flute-playing, it appears, had put singing quite out of court in Peru in Garcilasso's time, and while it had always been in high favor there, just before the conquest it amounted to a positive passion.

There could be no better commentary on the national character than this perpetual flute-playing, which is always a sign of effeminacy; and that the home of the flute should surrender without a blow to Pizarro is only what might have been expected. The flutes which the Peruvians played upon had four or five stops, and were often wrapped in embroidered needlework. The reason the stops were so few was that only songs were played on the flute, and five stops, which gave the complete vocal scale, were therefore sufficient. In the same way many of their pan-pipes only sounded the five-note scale, so that probably the pan-pipes were also used to play the melodies of songs. But most of the pan-pipes were tuned to a fanciful instrumental scale: e', f', f' sharp, g', g' sharp, a', c", c" sharp, d", e", f", a", and these would no doubt trifle with sweet sound and play music not unlike the instrumental music of the Chinese. The Peruvians were such skillful players on the pan-pipe, and delighted in the instrument so much, that they used to form bands of pan-pipes alone.

The idyllic music of Peru is a great contrast to the music of Mexico, where barbaric pomp and joy in the roar of sound reappear again. Copper gongs, copper rattles, conch-shells, trumpets, drums, cymbals, bells, bell-rattles, rattle-organs—these were the instruments the ancient Mexicans delighted in. If the music of Peru was founded on the flute, the music of Mexico was founded on the drum. The Mexicans developed the drum in a manner quite peculiar to themselves. It was an instrument of melody with them, as it is with the Chinese, the Burmese, etc.; but instead of resorting to the somewhat clumsy contrivance of combining a number of separate drums to produce the melody, the Mexicans had discovered how to elicit different melodic notes from the same drum. This they did by the use of vibrating tongues. In the top of the drum, which was an oblong, trough-shaped block of hollowed wood, they made two long incisions, one at each side, reaching nearly the whole length of the drum, and then a cross slit from one to the other. This gave them two tongues of wood, which were tuned c to e, c to f, c to g, and some c to e flat.

These tongued drums were called teponaztlis, and had a very deep tone. When they were played with other instruments, they served as the double bass. But they were also played solo; for teponaztlis of various pitches might be so arranged as to play a consecutive melody between them, much as the Peruvian pipe-players did with their pan-pipes.

The great drum of the ancient Mexicans was called veuetl, and it could be tuned to any pitch by tightening or loosening the drumhead. The copper gongs were struck with copper drumsticks, but the drums with drumsticks tipped with india-rubber. They had musical stones like the Chinese, but they used them in a different way, clashing them together like cymbals. The copper rattles were made like small oil-flasks, the neck being the handle, and the rattle itself filled with small stones. Sometimes these rattles were made of silver, and sometimes of pure gold. Strange instruments were the Mexican rattle-organs, of which there were two kinds—the small rattle-organ and the great rattle-organ. The second, of which the first was only a diminutive copy, consisted of a board twelve feet long and a span broad, on which were fastened, at certain intervals, round pieces of wood something of the shape of drumsticks, and when the board was moved these pieces of wood rattled against one another.

The variety of external form which the Mexicans gave to their instruments was very great. They made their whistles in the shape of birds, frogs, men's heads; their teponaztlis, even the ordinary ones, were covered with carvings. But those used in war were cut in the figure of a man crouching on his knees: his back was the drum, and he had eyes of bone, beautifully braided hair, earrings, necklaces, and boat-shaped shoes on his feet, all carved in a mulberry-colored wood, and highly burnished. The tambourines were constructed in the form of a snake biting a tortoise's head.

The Mexicans had rattles made in the shape of a snake crushing a toad in its coils—instruments very much like the Chinese egg-flutes, which were flageolets with two mouthpieces, giving a bass and a treble at the same time; and pipes and rattles combined in the form of three human heads supporting a pedestal, the pedestal being the pipe, and the heads, which were filled with stones, the rattles.

A highly plastic and sensuous music we might expect to find among such an artistic people, and such the Mexican music eminently was. In the vocal music, "meter and cadence were attended to most fastidiously." Perfect time, perfect unison, are the invariable eulogies passed on the Mexican music, and it is quite in keeping with such a character that dancing was its constant attendant. The Mexicans were the greatest dancers of the world. The princes, the nobles, and the elders of the city, all joined in the public dances with the women and little children. Mendieta describes five thousand dancing at once in two rings, both whirling round, but the outer one going at double the pace of the inner one, composed of elders and others who moved with deliberation and dignity. In the center of all were the drums, teponaztlis, and veuetls on mats. These were beaten in time to the dance and the song. After a while the children of the nobles came running in—little creatures of seven and eight years, some only four or five. These danced with their fathers, and began to sing the song in a high treble. Then the women joined in, and the musicians blew trumpets and flutes, and whistled on bone whistles. Meanwhile, the two rings were whirling round and round, never stopping or slackening for an instant.

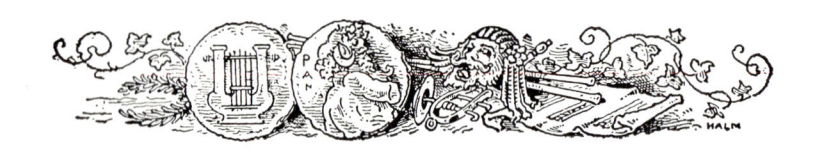

CHAPTER X

THE ANCIENT ARYANS

The Vina—The Aryan Bards—Composition and Performance of Their Hymns.

WHEN we first hear of the Aryans they were on the frontiers of India, and lived in the simplicity of the patriarchal state. The musical instrument which they used was called the vina or been. It was a lute of more highly developed form than the primitive lyre which was the ancient national instrument of the Mediterranean races, for the flat board had by this time been considerably curved—not longways, but broadways, until it resembled the segment of a water-pipe that has been cut in two. Then another similar board had been attached underneath, and so the frame came to resemble a pole—this hollow pole furnishing an excellent sounding-board. For a similar purpose two gourds were fastened, one at each end of the pole underneath, each about as big as a melon.

This was the chosen instrument of the Rishis, a class of holy bards in ancient India, who were not unlike the bards and minstrels of the Hebrews. They were said to be under the special protection of Heaven. "Indra loved their songs"; "Agni bethought him of their friendship." They were "the sons of Agni," "the associates of the gods," "they conversed about sacred truths with the gods of old." They were considered more venerable than the priests themselves.

It was their office to compose the hymns sung at the sacrifices, and to their tuneful lutes the Vedas saw the light. The worshipers joined hands about the altar, and moved in a slow religious dance round and round while the sacrifice was consuming. The length of the hymns was determined by the natural phenomena to the celebration of which they were devoted. Thus the hymn to the goddess of the dawn was commenced when the first streaks of light began to whiten the sky, and ended before the sun appeared. The hymn to the sun began when the tip of his disk showed above the horizon, and was finished when the entire circle was visible in the sky.

The composers of the hymns were credited with supernatural powers, and no greater honor could be paid, even to a god, than to bestow on him the epithet of bard. The myth of the Word admirably exemplifies the power of language and song over the ancient Aryan mind. They fabled how the Word walked in heaven before the gods were there. The subtlety of a later age added a pendant to this legend: how the Word escaped from heaven and hid among the trees, and how her voice was ever after heard in the lutes that were fashioned from their wood.

Thus these ancient singers, the Rishis, passed among the Aryan tribes with their inspired hymns. The number of the Rishis was sometimes given as seven, sometimes as nine, while Manu, the great mythical sage of India, speaks of ten.

CHAPTER XI

THE GREEKS

Homer and the Minstrels of his Day—Reforms of Terpander—Sappho—Cultivation of Song—Greek Musical Notation—The Enharmonic Genus—Olympus and the Phrygian School of Flute-playing—Stringed Instruments in Use in Greece—The Lyre—Wind Instruments—Greek Dances—The Choral Music of Greece.

VERY low was the estimation of the bard in those Ionian cities of Asia Minor where Homer sang; the bardic age had been followed by a heroic age, in which strength, not art, was the object of man's reverence. It was on the skirts of this heroic age that Homer lived, like other minstrels of his time, poor and despised.

It is a matter of tradition that the lyre to which Homer sang his poems had but four strings. It was customary to strike a few notes on the lyre as a prelude to the song, but not to employ it during the song itself. Homer is believed to have been the first who combined short songs or rhapsodies into one long poem. We may perhaps believe that he sang the "Iliad" and the "Odyssey" entire before he died, as we know they were sung in their entirety in later times, but with greater pomp. In later times the minstrels sat crowned with laurels and arrayed in gorgeous dresses, the "Iliad" being sung in a red dress, and the "Odyssey" in a violet one. Homer sang them in a beggar's gown. A boy would lead him into the center of the hall, and seat him on a stool in the midst of the banqueters, and taking down a lyre from a peg would place it in his hands. He would run his fingers over the strings, turn his sightless eyes heavenward, and begin to sing.

A long roll of minstrels extended from the time of Homer until the days of Terpander—a musician whose reforms are universally acknowledged by the Greeks as the starting-point of their later and more elaborate art. His first innovation was the separation of the prelude from the recital which followed it, and its constitution as an independent piece of music. Next he added words to the instrumental part, creating a new and terse musical form, containing pleasing melody. His next reform was the regulation of tune, presumably by a system of musical mnemonics.

The construction of the Dorian mode is likewise attributed to Terpander by the Greek musical historians. Probably this so-called construction consisted in joining the Æolian and Dorian modes, which in their earliest form existed as independent tetrachords. The Æolian mode—the oldest in Greece—was precisely identical, except in the omission of the lowest note, with the five-note scale of the Chinese and other nations, and that primitive and original scale of uncivilized man which we call the isolating scale. It had a break in the middle, and the notes which composed it were a, b, d', e'. The union of this with the Dorian tetrachord—the four notes from e to a below—produced the Dorian mode in its earliest form, or, as it is more generally called, "the scale of Terpander," according to which all lyres in Greece until the very latest period were tuned.

Singing, thus released from trammels, attained its perfection in Greece under the Lesbian school of musicians, founded by Sappho, who has been credited with as many improvements in Greek music as Terpander made. The invention of the Mixolydian mode has been assigned to her; likewise the introduction of the plectrum, with which the strings of the lyre were struck, besides numerous reforms in the measures of Greek song. Her life as the president of a college of women devoted to the cultivation of music and poetry has been well depicted by Maximus Tyrius.

The law of melody at that period of Greek art was this: Every note must be either equal to its fellow or double of it. The song of the singer, therefore, proceeded tranquilly along, while variety of expression on the part of the vocalist was secured by the application of certain graces. The principal grace was the prolepsis or slur, which consisted in singing one syllable to two notes. The prolepsis might occur in two ways. It might be *di grado* or *di salto*. The procrusis consisted in skimming lightly over two short syllables, and bringing the full emphasis on the long one. The kompismus or "saucy grace" was the staccato. The melismus was the "connected staccato."

That which we now regard as the dream of theorists, and an ideal beauty or delicacy which can never be realized in practice, was an everyday thing with Greek singers; namely, the enharmonic genus, or the correct intonation of quarter-tones. We have caught a gleam of its existence among primitive men, but only for a moment, for it soon vanished away, being but the spangles which speech flung off in its passage to song, and scarce destined to outlive the transit. Directly song began, by benefit of the chant, from that moment did the diatonic scale begin. As harder things will always give way to easier ones, so did the enharmonic pass away before the bold and simple diatonic song.

The Greek enharmonic divided the semitone, where it occurred in the scale, into two enharmonic demitones, which were preceded downward and succeeded upward by the interval of a major or minor third. Strange and unmelodious as it may appear to us, the enharmonic was esteemed one of the greatest ornaments of music. Nor was its compass ever extended so as to subdivide all the notes of the scale, but was limited to the partition of the semitones.

The honor of introducing the enharmonic into Greek music is universally attributed to Olympus, a Phrygian flute-player. Olympus came playing the flute from Phrygia to Greece. His flutes wept as he played them, by virtue of this beautiful mode. Romance and sentiment began to color the white light of the Greek music. The Phrygian satyr, Marsyas, whom Apollo had vanquished and crushed, lived again in the beautiful Olympus, who founded a school of flute-players in Greece.

We must now consider what effect dissemination of the enharmonic would have on the make and structure of the Greek instruments. It would plainly lead to an increase in the number of their strings or stops. The chief stringed instrument at this period was the magadis—a lyre with a bridge across the middle of its strings, so that the notes could be sounded in octaves. The strings of the magadis under the influence of the enharmonic were tuned: a, b flat, b, b sharp, c', d', e', e' sharp, f', g', with the octave below for each tone.

The pectis and barbitos, which were smaller varieties of the magadis, possessing five strings apiece instead of ten, were tuned: the pectis, e', e' sharp, f', g', a', and their octaves below; the barbitos, b, b sharp, c', d', e', and their octaves.

Doubtless similar concessions to the enharmonic were made by others of the numerous instruments which between now and the times of Sophocles were invented or introduced from various quarters into Greece. Of these we will now mention and describe some of the principal: The scindapsus was a high-stringed instrument to accompany women's voices. It had a willow frame, and was very light to hold. The enneachordon had nine strings, as its name implies. The phœnix and the lyrophœnix were plainly the Phœnician lyre, introduced as a novelty from Phœnicia. Ibycus, the poet, has the credit of introducing the small Egyptian triangular harp, the sambuca, at this period. It became notorious in later times as the instrument of the courtesans. The spadix was such another—a woman's lyre—and had the reputation of being an effeminate instrument. The epigonion was a great lyre of many strings, invented by Epigonus of Sicyon. The simicium was likewise a large lyre. The monochordon was a one-stringed lute introduced from Arabia. The primeval bin or kin was introduced as a curiosity from foreign parts, and the story current to account for its simplicity of shape was to the effect that it was made by the Pygmies, who lived on the shores of the Red Sea, out of the laurel that grows there.

The trigonus and the heptagonon were foreign instruments, of which the former was triangular, and the latter seven-sided. All the rest of these instruments, except the sambuca, had been assimilated more or less closely to the shape of the national lyre. For the lyre was the king and sovereign in Greece, and despite this crowd of interlopers still held its own. Its shape had not altered, nor had its strings been increased, since the time of Terpander.

And since the lyre has so glorious a race to run, and young Apollo played it, we may well pause to describe it minutely and relate with care its every part. Let us preside at its making. Hermes, walking by the sea-shore, found a tortoise, and he killed it, and made the shell empty. Then turning to some reeds that were growing near, he cut pieces off them, all of a length, and, drilling holes in the tortoise-shell, put these pieces of reed through, pushing them into the body of the shell, for they were to serve as blocks to take off the strain from the shell. He next covered the shell with a piece of bull's hide, and fastened two horns to one end of the shell, one on each side. Then he fixed a piece of wood to be a crosspiece, from the tip of one horn to the tip of the other, tied seven strings of gut from the crosspiece to the bottom of the shell, and the lyre was complete.

In later times some additions were made to this form, and one or two variations. The additions were pegs in the crosspiece, to fasten the strings to; a bridge to prevent the strings touching the shell; and two sound-holes cut in the shell, in order to add to its resonance. The variations were in the materials of which the body of the instrument was made, for sometimes it was made of wood.

The lyre reigned supreme in Greece itself. But there was one Greek city which was an exception to the rule. And this was the luxurious city of Sicyon, where the women were the handsomest in all Greece. Sicyon, the mart of Asiatic merchandise, and the Sicyonians, accustomed to the pomp and luxury of their merchant princes, could not be content with the simplicity of the lyre, nor with the smallness of its tone. They preferred and delighted in a variety of lyre called the cithara, whose horns were broader and hollowed out to act as sound-boards, and the belly of which was larger and broader. These two variations were plainly introduced for no other object than to increase the resonance of the strings. The cithara, from Sicyon, spread through Greece, and gradually attained wide popularity; but only the great and illustrious singers could employ it as the accompaniment of their voice, owing to its sonorous tone drowning all ordinary utterance.

The cithara was decked out with carving and paint; it was one of Greece's "sweetly-sounding carvings." The cithara-player was arrayed in a long flowing robe, and, crowned with a garland, he stood on an eminence among the people, and sang his beautiful song. The long flowing robe was what Arion arrayed himself in when he was told to prepare to die, having to cast himself in the sea to escape the malice of the sailors. Appareling himself in his robe, and with his cithara in his hand, he stood on the poop, and sang the Orthian song. And even those sailors retired awhile to hear him, for he was the finest cithara-singer in the world.

So the cithara was the instrument of the great and splendid singers, and it was thus the instrument of the Agon (the musical contests at the Olympian, Pythian, and other games). But on all other occasions the lyre was nearly universally employed: at banquets, revels, at the gymnasia, in domestic life; used by women, boys, and men alike.

Turning from the stringed instruments of Greece to the wind, we shall be aware of as numerous a variety. Flageolets, flutes, clarinets, and oboes were all represented. To the first class belonged the monaulos, the nightingale of the pipes, and the Lydian flute; to the second the photinx and the lotus pipe; to the third the Phrygian pipe and the elymus; to the fourth the gingras and the nablas.

The materials of which the pipes were made were reeds, copper, lotus wood, boxwood, horn, ivory, or laurel. Many of them were double. The Phrygian pipes were double, being double clarinets, and the Lydian pipes likewise were double flageolets. The pipes were not joined, but were held loosely in the hand. The right flute, which was the deeper one,

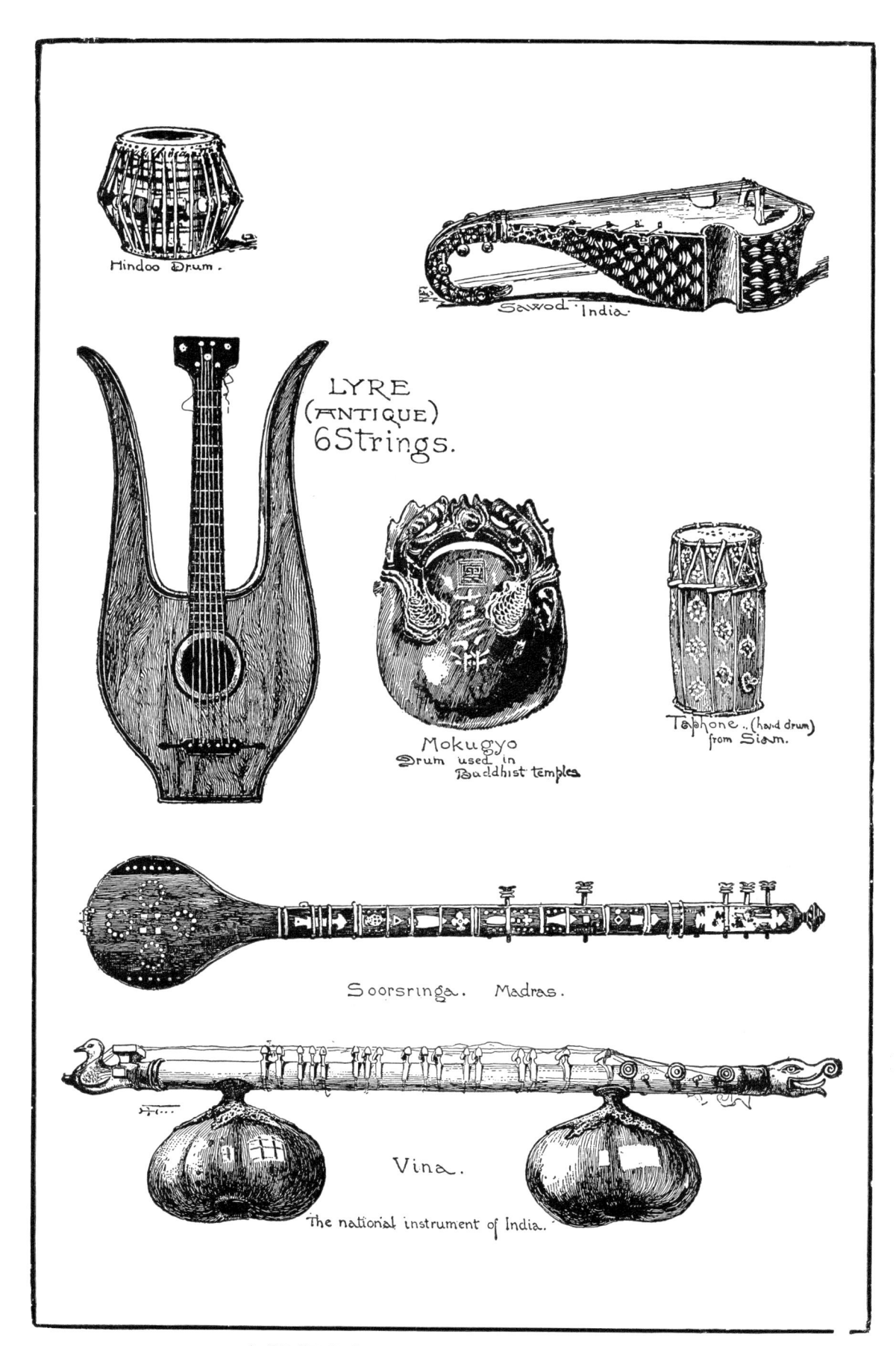

A GROUP OF PRIMITIVE INSTRUMENTS

From Drawings by Harry Fenn

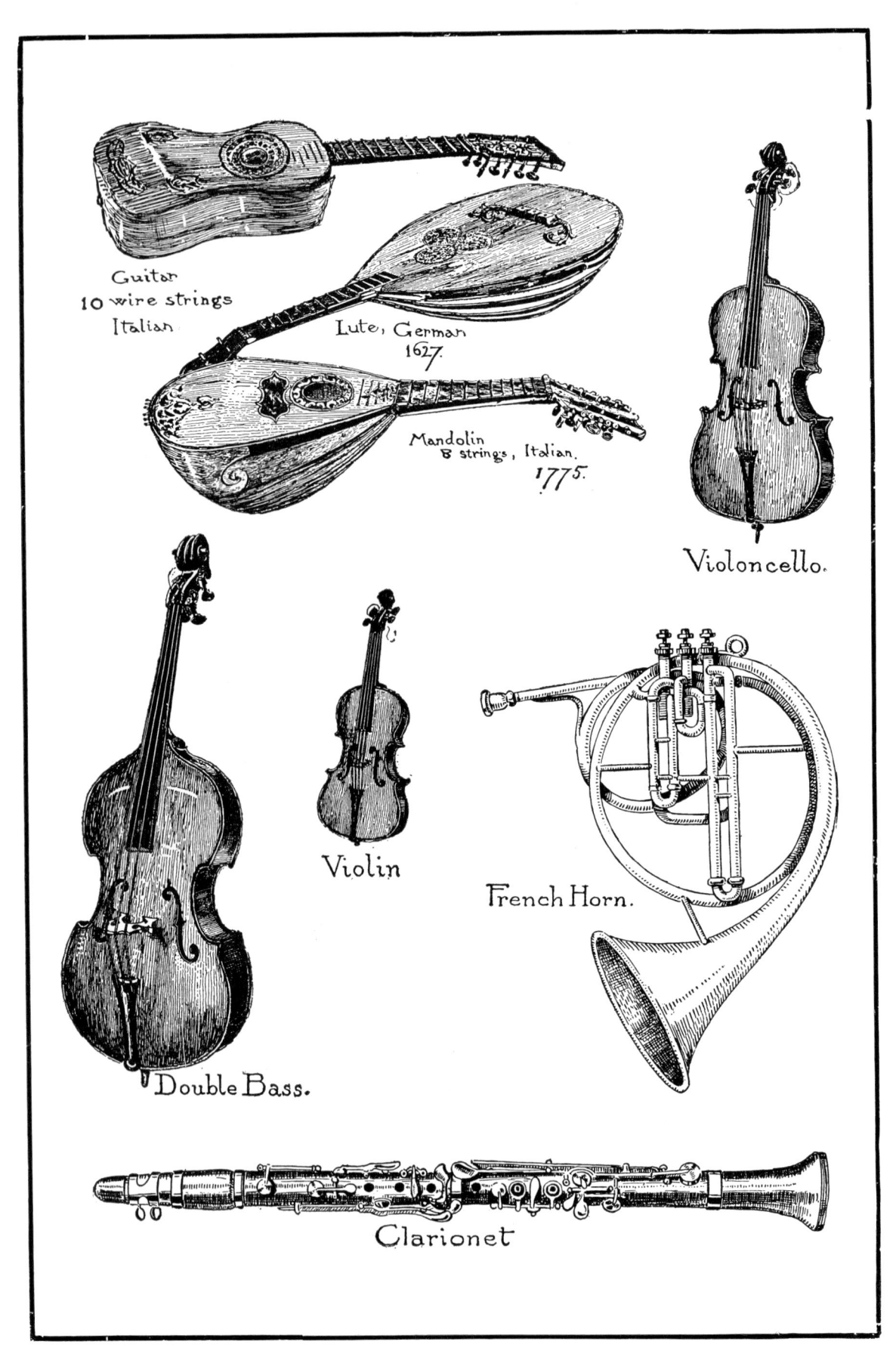

A GROUP OF INSTRUMENTS

From Drawings by Harry Fenn

played the melody, and the left, the higher one, performed the light accompaniment to it.

Such was the Greek method of accompanying, not only in the case of two flutes supplementing one another, but even with the lyre and the voice. The "melody," which was assigned to the latter, habitually traveled at a low pitch by comparison; while the lyre flung its artless harmonics "above the song." This was the method of accompaniment which had been introduced by the poet Archilochus at an early period of Greek music, and remained as the regular form throughout the whole history of the art.

Accompaniment and harmony had thus grown up; the instruments had been perfected and multiplied; the graces of song had been carried to a height of excellence, while the elaboration of time and rhythm was being worked out in the dances. The musicians who now came forward as the exponents of Greece's best music were the choral poets, such as Ibycus, Bacchylides, Simonides, and Pindar, whose compositions were designed with a view to the evolutions of a vast body of dances no less than the delivery of the music by song and instrument. Dancing had always been the most popular of pastimes in Greece. It passed, indeed, beyond a pastime, and became a great and serious art.

The Cretic foot was first devised in the dances of Crete, where Apollo himself was said to have led the measure, striking his lyre as he led the dances, with his hair wreathed with leaves, and twined with threads of gold, and his arrows rattling on his shoulders. With such a picture before us, we shall cease to wonder at that expression of Simonides, who says that the dance is dumb music, and music is speaking dancing.

The construction of the choral songs flowed naturally from the form of the ancient round dance, being arranged in a strophe sung in one key, an antistrophe delivered in another, and an epode (a later addition, during which the dancers stood still or marked time) probably in the key of the strophe.

In 250 B.C. at a festival to Apollo, a band of several hundred musicians played a five-movement piece representing Apollo's victory over Python. Such programme-music indicates a far more advanced school than many writers admit.

CHAPTER XII

THE GREEKS (CONTINUED)

Organization of the Greek Musical System by Pythagoras—The Chromatic Genus—Greek Modes in the Form they Reached under Aristoxenus—Greek Harmony—The Brotherhood of Pythagoras.

BY the time of Pythagoras the following modes were in use in Greece: the Æolian or Hypodorian or Locrian mode, the Hypophrygian mode, the Hypolydian mode, the Dorian mode, the Phrygian mode, the Lydian mode, and the Mixolydian mode. These modes differed in pitch, the lowest being the Æolian, which ranged from b to b; and the highest the Mixolydian, with a compass of from a to a'. The three genera of Greek music, the diatonic, chromatic, and enharmonic, of course prescribed the order of the intervals in every case.

The problem which lay before Pythagoras was the union of these various modes into one scale, which might be of any complexion, provided only it exhibited in a lucid and convenient form all the modes here recorded. He took the Dorian mode, and to each end of it he added two tetrachords; namely, a tetrachord to the lower e—b to e, and a tetrachord to the upper e—e' to a'. The scale as now constituted was b, c, d, e, f, g, a, b, c', d', e', f', g', a'. While the extreme tetrachords here are conjunct, the interior ones, it will be observed, are disjunct.

Pythagoras, having thus a scale of two octaves, all but a note, before him, took the Mixolydian mode, and applied it to the lowest note, b, and since the semitones of the Mixolydian mode are between the first and second notes, and the fourth and fifth notes, it will be seen that the Mixolydian mode exactly coincides with the notes of this great scale from b to b. Pythagoras called the octave in this great scale from b to b the Mixolydian octave. Next he took the Lydian mode, in like manner, and applied it to c, which is the second lowest note of his great scale. Since the semitones of the Lydian mode occur between the third and fourth notes, and also between the seventh and eighth, it will be seen that the Lydian mode exactly coincides with the octave from c to c, as the Mixolydian had with the octave from b to b. Pythagoras called the octave from c to c the Lydian octave. He applied the Phrygian mode in like manner to d. The Dorian mode stood as it was. The Hypolydian he applied to f; the Hypophrygian to g, and the Æolian to a. He named these various octaves by the names of the modes.

In order that his scale might have perfection, which it could not have if not rounded off by octaves, he added a note (a) to the bottom of it. This he called the "added note." In order to accommodate the scale to the workings of the enharmonic genus, Pythagoras adopted a simple and effective device. The two middle notes of each tetrachord, beginning from b, he called movable, the other notes he termed fixed. The chromatic genus could also be expressed by this scale written with the movable notes altered as needed. The chromatic genus made a leap of a tone and a half, and divided by two chromatic semitones.

By the time of Aristoxenus, who lived some centuries after Pythagoras, various new modes had sprung up in Greece in addition to the seven for which Pythagoras had made allowance in his scale. Room had to be found for these—the new ones were eight in number—and the scale of Pythagoras was augmented by the intrusion of as many chromatic semitones.

The Greek harmony, which had partaken more of the nature of improvised accompaniment up till the time of Pythagoras, was by him organized and laid down on scientific principles. He admitted as concords the octave, fifth, and fourth; to these were afterward added the double octave, the twelfth, and the eleventh. As discords, the second and third were permissible, and perhaps the ninth and tenth.

More interesting, perhaps, to general sympathy than the technical labors of Pythagoras for the cause of Greek music was his institution of a musical brotherhood in the south of Italy, among whom he sought to realize his doctrine that music is the great means of education in life, and the guide to all moral virtue. The members of its confraternity all rose together at an early hour in the morning, and having assembled, sang many songs and hymns in chorus, which freed their spirits from heaviness, and attuned them to harmony and order. This was sometimes varied by instrumental music for a change, without the accompaniment of singing.

It was their custom to meet together in some selected spot, generally in a temple, or in a portico, or avenue, and there they walked and conferred together, teaching and receiving instruction from one another in music, arithmetic, and geometry, the arithmetic and geometry being designed to educate their intellect, and the music their passions and feelings. In this conclave they made use of ineffable melodies and rhythms, not only to correct any perturbations of mind which might have arisen in spite of all their care, but also to sink deep into the soul, and subdue any lurking tendency to jealousy, pride, concupiscence, excess in appetite, angry feelings, looseness of thought, and other weaknesses of soul, for all of which there were sovereign musical specifics, that Pythagoras had prepared like so many drugs. After some hours they betook themselves to lawns and gardens, to exercise their bodies in various ways. In the common hall, toward noon, they had their first meal of the day, only eating bread and honey, or a piece of honeycomb. When evening came, they again occupied themselves with musical concerts for some hours.

It was amid the privacy of this ascetic brotherhood that the mysterious doctrines of Pythagoras were elaborated touching the creation of the world by music and the harmony of the spheres.

CHAPTER XIII

THE GREEKS (CONCLUDED)

Three Specimens of Ancient Greek Music—Tragedy at Athens—The Great Theater of Bacchus—The Actors—Method of Performing the Tragedies—The Chorus—Choral Dances and Songs.

WHERE are the melodies that filled the clear air of Athens in the heyday of its music? They are all perished, like its glory. Inscriptions cut in stone endure from the days of Egypt; sounds, that have an affinity with breezes, will scarce fetch a century's antiquity. Time, that has spared the treatise of Aristides, has wafted away the melodies of Sappho.

Three poor fragments alone remain from the Roman period: the first is from a hymn to the Muse by Dionysius, who was a poet of the Greek revival under Hadrian; the second is a hymn to Apollo by the same; and the third a hymn to Nemesis by the poet Mesomedes, who was probably a contemporary of Dionysius, but whose date we do not certainly know.

In Athens itself the center and meeting-ground of the musical life of the city was at the great theater of Bacchus, where the tragedies—or, as they should be more correctly termed, the operas—were performed at stated seasons of the year in honor of the god to whom the theater was dedicated. They were part of a religious observance connected with the worship of Bacchus, having originated in their most primitive form from the dithyramb, or sacred hymn in honor of that god, which was danced round his altar with appropriate mimic gestures by the worshipers.

The great theater of Bacchus was constructed on a hillside, the seats being cut in tiers on the hill. Thirty thousand seats were provided for the spectators, and in a great open space below them, not unlike the arena of our circuses, was a large flat piece of ground, called the orchestra, where the chorus went through its evolutions. In the center of this rose the altar of Bacchus, on which an aromatic gum was kept burning during the performances, in remembrance of those ancient times when the blazing altar was circled round by the dithyramb. Fronting the seats, on the other side of the orchestra, rose the stage, which was as high as the lowest seat of the tiers. Behind the stage there was a large saloon for the actors and chorus, with property rooms and dressing-rooms to the right and left of it.

Behind all there was a large park or lawn, set with trees, with a portico round it, for the chorus to rehearse their parts in, and wherein promenaders might expatiate between the pieces.

The actors all wore masks, inside of which was an apparatus resembling a speaking-trumpet, the object of this being to make the voice carry to the farther verge of the spectators. The actors declaimed their parts in the manner of the epic rhapsodists, reciting in a sort of exalted monotone. When they had finished their dialogue or harangue, the chorus, preceded by a line of flute-players, came dancing through the side wings into the large arena of the orchestra singing a most harmonious and plastic song. The flute-players ranged themselves on the steps of the altar, fronting the stage, while the chorus, in time to their song, performed their dances and evolutions. At the conclusion of the song and dance of the chorus, the actors began their chants again, which were followed by another choral song and dance, and in this graceful interchange of melodies, music, and impassioned or chanted declamation, the structure of the drama consisted.

The chorus entered through the wings of the orchestra with all the pomp of a mimic army. When they were fifty in number, which was during all the prime of Æschylus, marching with their band of flute-players before them, they were an exact representation of the Spartan company of fifty called a pentecostys. They marched either in column or in ranks, like a body of soldiers in battle array. Proceeding down the large open space of the orchestra, they took up a position round the altar of Bacchus, where their leader, like the captain of the Spartan company, stood on the steps, and led the song which they had been singing as they entered. When it was a chorus of women, they would enter in a style less martial, as in the "Prometheus," where the fifty daughters of Oceanus, the nymphs of the sea, are drawn in through the air in a car, with all their azure wings rustling.

The action of a tragedy was diversified with various choral dances and songs; the lyre often accompanied the declamation of the action, but the flute was the instrument *par excellence* of the dances. At certain places of the tragedy, principally at its most impassioned moments, the actors themselves broke out into melodious song. But these instances were rare, and when they became common in the decline of the art under Euripides, who invented the monody or "florid solo," they met with reprehension from the best critics in Greece. During the epoch of Sophocles and Æschylus, the palmy days of the Athenian music, the florid and melodious effects of song were reserved for the chorus alone, the actors being forced to content themselves with chanted declamation. In the graceful and frequent alternation of these two forms, the main beauty and sublimity of tragedy, in the opinion of Aristotle, consisted.

CHAPTER XIV

THE ROMANS

General Mingling of all the Musics of the Ancient World at Rome—The Roman Pantomimes—Instruments in the Orchestra—Nero—His Performances at the Theaters—His Patronage of Organ-builders—The Water-Organ—Death of Nero—The Early Christians—Their Psalms and Services—Progress of Music among Them.

IN Rome we find, after centuries had passed away, not only the reappearance of the gay Greek music, but in that capital of the earth a general mixing and blending of all the musics of the pagan world. Under the arches of the Campus in Imperial Rome might have been heard the sambucas and gingrases of the Syrian dancing girls, and beating in the taverns hard by the drums and cymbals of the tipsy priests of Tyre; in the theaters the flutes and lyres, and songs of Grecian chorus-singers, and winding along to the temples of Isis and Serapis, bands of Egyptian musicians with harps and sistrums—all the world's minstrelsy was there, in that great churning-press of nations which men called Rome.

The theaters, where we shall find the central point of the music, no longer served as the temples of a national religion, but were places of spectacle and amusement. Not only had the plays lost their religious significance, but they had also greatly changed in character. Tragedy had in a great measure passed away, and the pantomime reigned as the popular entertainment in its room. As in the tragedy, there were chorus and actors in the pantomime, but the chorus took no part in the action of the play. Stationed on the stage, they formed a kind of orchestra, partly vocal and partly instrumental, which accompanied with music and song the gestures and dancing of the performers.

The instruments used by the chorus were worthy of the pomp and pageantry of Rome, and also of that Oriental love of din and roar, which in Rome appeared so strongly, being cymbals, gongs, flutes, pipes, gigantic lyres, castanets, rattles, clattering shells, and foot-castanets. The cymbals, small and concave, almost fitted in the palms of the hand, yet made a loud clashing noise. The gongs were generally known by the name meaning "vinegar-jar gongs," because in shape they were much like vinegar-jars. They were made of brass, or sometimes of silver, and give a rich sonorous sound when struck. The flutes and pipes were much like the Greek pipes, some of them, however, being bagpipes. Long ago in the fields of Latium had the shepherds discovered the art of fitting their pipes into a bladder or bag, which should act as a wind-chest, and greatly lighten the labor of blowing. The gigantic lyres were also like the Greek in shape, but much larger and more powerful. The rattles were brass rings attached to iron rods. The castanets were sometimes made of brass, and decorated with bits of crockery, wood, etc. The shells were rattles of crockery-ware or shells. But most remarkable were the foot-castanets; they were great clattering fans, or clogs of wood, that were worked by the foot, and generally in exact time to the steps of the dancer; for all the time that the orchestra was singing and playing, the actors were carrying on their dumb show to the audience, endeavoring to express by their motions and gestures the action of the narrative that the chorus was singing.

These chorus pantomimes were produced on the most stupendous scale. Sometimes more people were on the stage than there were in the theater itself, for what with the immense pageants of actors, and the great choruses of singers and instrumentalists, the stage was full. "The passages are full of singers," says an eye-witness; "the orchestra is thronged with trumpets, and every kind of pipe and musical instrument peals from the stage." There were interludes of instrumental music, *entr'actes,* and overtures of flutes alone. The scenic displays were licentious; and Roman music lacked the chastity of Greek art.

Its chief patron was the Emperor Nero, who was celebrated as a professional singer in the theaters. His favorite parts were Orestes, Canace, Œdipus, and Hercules Furens. He had made his début at Naples in the third year of his reign. Scarcely had he stepped on the stage and begun the opening *scena* of the tragedy, when the shock of an earthquake was felt in the theater. Some said that the gods were angry that the emperor of the world should be seen in such a character. During all the time that he was singing at Naples, he would scarcely allow his voice any rest, and only left the theater for the baths. From Naples he went to Greece, and sang at the principal theaters there, entering into public competition with all comers at some of the games, and several times receiving the prize. Such diligence did he use to improve his voice, that he would sit up with his singing-master, Terpnus, till late in the night, practising his arias and roulades for the next day. He slept with plates of lead on his chest to correct unsteadiness of breathing and give him the power of sustaining his notes in equal volume. He would also abstain from food for days together in order to purify his voice, often denying himself fruit and sweet pastry, which are known to be prejudicial to singing. He was not only a cultivated singer, but a skillful performer on many instruments as well, and eminently a connoisseur. He could play the flute with the best players of his day, and was no mean performer on the trumpet. He was also a skilled lyre-player, but affected particularly that small Assyrian instrument the pandura, with three or four strings, which was now making its way along with other musical oddities to Rome.

During a musical tour of his through Greece, a revolt broke out among the Gallic legionaries, who put their general, Vindex, at their head, and began to march on Rome. Their disaffection was joined by the legions in Dalmatia under Galba, a more experienced general than Vindex, and a more powerful opponent. The news of this rebellion drew Nero reluctantly from the theaters of Greece, and after many delays on the route he appeared at last in Rome. The armies were not far off, and prompt action was essential; but instead of haranguing the senate, and issuing orders for calling out the troops, he spent the first day of his arrival in examining a new instrument, which had just been brought to Rome. It was called an organ, and had been made after the designs of Ctesibius of Alexandria, who derived the first idea of his water-organ from the clepsydra, or water-clock. The water in this mechanism was made to drop upon wheels, the motion of which was communicated to a statue, which gradually rose as they went round, pointing with a stick to the hours marked on a pillar. At night it sounded the hours on a flute instead, the air being forced through the flute by the agency of water. Taking his hint from this, he had made the hydraulis, or "water-flute," and eventually the water-organ, which, after various improvements, had traveled to Rome.

Having seen the instrument, Nero was well pleased with it, and determined to introduce it into the theaters, saying that it would make a most agreeable addition to the orchestras of the pantomimes, and would also come in well for tragedy. The same evening he banqueted, meaning to commence his preparations against the rebels next day. But the next morning brought news that another legion had revolted, and that three armies were marching on Rome. Nero assembled the singers and dancers from the theaters, and had them dressed like Amazons. Then putting himself at their head, he ordered the gates of the city to be flung open that he might go to meet the foe. He believed that perhaps some prodigy would be worked in his behalf, or that the soldiers, amazed at so strange an equipment, might return to their allegiance. But when the push came, and the armies were close to the city, his friends all abandoned him. Only a freedman of his, named Phaon, and the boy Sporus, whom he loved, and two slaves, still remained faithful, and with these he set off to Phaon's country house, in a storm of thunder and lightning. He was there introduced into a small chamber underground. He made them dig a grave, and Sporus begin the funeral lament. Nero looked at the grave, and cried, "What an artist dies in me!" But while he was yet speaking the hoofs of his pursuers' steeds were heard clattering in the distance, every minute growing louder and louder. He burst into a verse of Homer's:

The gallop of swift-footed horses strikes on my ear,

and, when he had finished singing, set a dagger to his throat, which by the help of Epaphroditus, his slave, he plunged in, and so he died.

Pagan music died with him; for though those theaters and pantomimes and great orchestras of many nations still survived, and a long line of emperors were still to come, yet a new music had begun. About this time a belated wayfarer, coming home at night through the Flaminian or Latin Way, or other road on the outskirts of the city, might have seen lights among the tombs, or glimmering from the catacombs underground; and muffled voices would strike his ear, as of men engaged in secret prayer and forbidden rites. The Christians had come, and these were their assemblages. Food for the torches of Nero, as the years wore on they waxed stronger and more numerous; but at first, and for a long time, they were obliged to hold their gatherings in such places as these. They met always in the evening, and sometimes at the dead of night, for fear of the law which prohibited all secret assemblages. They were the dregs of the people, many of them slaves, and all poor and despised and friendless.

At these meetings they would sing psalms, and in their psalms they were all unconsciously framing the new music of the world. It grew, as all musics originally grow, from the bosom of speech. Their psalms had no meter, and would fit no tunes, none of the gay tunes of Greece and Rome, that were fluttering on the golden surface of life, if indeed they had sorted with the mood of these poor outcasts. But a new style of strain, quite different from all we have hitherto been speaking of, must be born in the world to express them.

Greek music was born amid the patter of the dancers' feet, in showers of sunlight, and swimming of the senses. But Christian music had its birth in subterraneous vaults, among desperate men, to whom sorrow was a sister, and fear their familiar. The psalms in their services they muttered and mumbled, rather than sang. On happier days they would exalt their voices and declaim a little the words, but still it was far from singing. The only approach to the regularity of musical contour was the parallelism of parts in each verse, like that peculiar to the Hebrew psalms.

The congregations were accustomed to divide themselves into two groups, and declaim verses about, or else the halves of verses, first one group singing, and then the other answering them. This was called the antiphonal method of singing—the Semitic manner of choral declamation.

In addition to this comparatively organized method of singing, the congregations were accustomed to give vent to their emotions in the words "alleluia," "amen," "hosanna," etc., which they would exclaim in ecstasy of worship.

The primitive Christian idea of music may be gathered from the following utterances of the Fathers of the Church: "As David sang psalms on a harp to the Lord, so do we, too, sing, but on a harp whose strings are alive—our tongues are the strings; and more the Lord does not require." "The only instrument we use is the voice. The Word, and the Word of peace, is enough for us. Let syrinxes be given to silly clowns, the pipe to superstitious men, who pay honor to idols. Such instruments are to be banished from all sober company, and are more fitted for beasts than men. How entirely, then, must they be kept from the assemblages of Christians! Be far from us those florid songs and dissipated music, that corrupt the morals!"

Yet there was no preserving this simple music in its infant purity for long, and shutting out completely the influences of the world.

As it was the custom to have a president of the meeting to preach and take the lead in the prayers, so it was also the practice in the psalmody to have a precentor who should lead the psalmody; this seems to have been the habit from very early times. It was natural that this leader, feeling himself looked up to by the others, should sometimes be vain of his duties, and introduce a touch of art into the simplicity of the Christian psalms. Yet this did not have much effect on the congregations until largeness of numbers, or a growing respect for ceremony, which even their simplicity could not quite be free of, made them choose certain members of their body as regular psalmists in their services, who should follow readily the lead of the precentor and act with him, and whom in their turn the general congregation should follow. Toward the end of the second century after the beginning of Christianity, we find among the regular officers of their gatherings—doorkeepers, exorcists, readers, etc.—the names of singers also appearing, by which we may be sure that actual choirs had begun to be employed. Among these singers women as well as men were usual.

As the Christians grew stronger and more numerous, and numbered wealthy converts in their ranks, they began to worship more openly and with greater pomp. They would hold their services in basilicas, or public halls, which were the halls that the magistrates sat in during the daytime. Here would the Christians assemble, and conduct their services; and "the roofs reëchoed with their cries of alleluia"; and the sound of their psalms, as they sang them in immense congregations, "was like the surging of the sea in great waves of sound."

CHAPTER XV

EARLY CHRISTIAN MUSIC

The First Christian Songs and Psalms—Weakness and Unsteadiness of the Singing—Indifference to these Points on the Part of the Worshipers.

AT the services of the early Christians, the utterances by the congregation of "alleluia," "amen," and "hosanna" became much extended, for they loved to linger over them as they said them. Repeating the alleluia, they would dwell upon it, and declaim it, "alle------luia........," as if they were loath to let it go. As they sustained the tones, what waverings and tremblings would there be of their untaught voices! no long-drawn notes, such as practised singers give, but wayward dwellings on their loved words, and sighs of earnestness and emotion. "Amen" in like manner they would dwell on—"A------men"—as if it were never to be done, so much they longed to express its meaning. But besides these, actual chants and psalms had grown up, often they knew not how. First there was the angelic hymn. They called it a hymn indeed, but how far was it from being what we think of when we speak of "hymn"! It was rude and shapeless, like their psalms, with no meter to form or adorn it, and was the very utterance of their souls. Its words were those beginning: "Glory to God in the highest, and on earth peace, good will toward men." This was the angelic hymn they sang, and as they sang they thought the angels in heaven sang with them every morning. There was also the cherubic hymn, or trisagion, which was revealed in a vision to an ancient Hebrew prophet. Also, there was a verse of song, not so extended as these, which had grown up more like the "amen" and the "alleluia," as a passionate exclamation in the services, "Lord, have mercy on us," or "Kyrie eleison," which was much lingered on, in the utterance, "Ky-------rie........eleison."

Let us now examine more closely these Christian chants and psalms. First, they would have no tonality, for what were tones and scales to earnest men, who also were in the main ignorant men, knowing little more than how to praise God, and whose psalms were but the overflowings of an earnest heart? Even if the precentors had been skilled enough to check off the psalms in apt tonalities, what scope had they to make their knowledge good among such simple singers? But the absence of instruments from the psalmody was another reason why they would find it difficult to make much musical precision. Next, their psalms would suffer from all the failings of uneducated voices. If we examine the behavior of such a voice, we shall notice first that it has the greatest difficulty in lighting on a steady note. An uneducated voice will always anticipate a note it rises to, or a note it falls to, by two or three others on the way. Whether it does so because it cannot yet wholly shake off the influence of speech, which seldom makes intervals, but covers all up, or because there is a greater ease and less effort in sliding up or down than in jumping, may well admit conjecture.

How would this unsteadiness of tone be made evident in the unpractised Christian singing, especially in those exclamations of praise and fervor, the "alleluia," the "amen," and the "Kyrie," etc., where they dwelt so lovingly on the syllables as if they were loath to let them go!

The real truth is that the main aim of the early Christian song was not the exposition of musical tune, but the fervent utterance of holy thought, to the detriment and contempt of the tones in which it was uttered. St. Basil, who describes Christian music at this time, saying that the Holy Ghost was the author of it, considers that its main title to praise is that it profited the soul by the holy thoughts it expressed and the holy words it declaimed. "For through it," he says, "high advantage comes to one and all; for those who are old and steadfast in the faith, with what delight do they hear the music mixed with holy mysteries! and those who are young in years, or touching perfection of virtue as yet not grown to ripeness, while they think they sing, in reality learn."

St. Basil was the Bishop of Cæsarea, and we hear of the singing at his services, how they would pass the night in a vigil of prayers and weeping, and then, when the day broke, would begin the singing of their psalms. St. Basil, more than any other man of his time, was the supporter of the early Christian spirit, and in his ordinances about music he followed the pattern of St. Athanasius, or the Alexandrian style of Christian song, which was the best and purest exponent of the Christian spirit; for now another style of song was growing up in Italy, called the Italian style. But Alexandria, and Egypt generally, had been the stronghold of the primitive Christian spirit. There the monks preserved the earliest and simplest style of Christian song, singing antiphonally, and rather speaking than singing. St. Athanasius would have it also so at Alexandria, making the people rather read and speak than sing; this was the style which St. Basil upheld at Cæsarea. There was an intimate communion between the Church of Cæsarea and the Church of Armenia, which was an offshoot from the Church of Cæsarea. Armenia in its seclusion had preserved the earliest Christian traditions, having been founded in the second century. The influence of St. Basil was in course of time extended to Constantinople, and a service that he had written began to be used there.

562

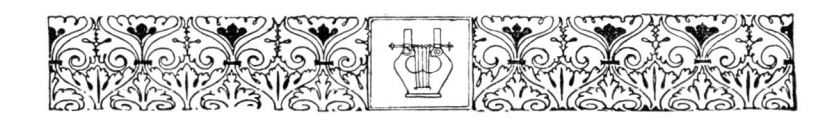

MEDIEVAL AND MODERN EUROPEAN MUSIC

CHAPTER XVI

THE MUSIC OF THE MIDDLE AGES

Modes — Neumes — Theorists — Organum — Solmization — Measured Music—Counterpoint—Motets—Troubadours—Minnesingers—Music in England—Dufay to Lasso in the Netherlands—Italian Choral Music—Early German Composers.

DURING the centuries in which the Roman Empire was falling to pieces, and until some of the modern states began to emerge from the chaos of barbarism and bloodshed, the development of any art was impossible. Music was only cultivated by churchmen and was of the simplest description—confined to melody only, and indefinite in pitch and rhythm.

A certain number of scales or modes, and a few simple traditional formulas of melody, were authorized for Church use about the fourth century; and a few more modes, which were really only extensions of the earlier ones, were added some centuries later. The modes of the earlier group are always associated with the name of Ambrose, Bishop of Milan, who died 397 A.D., and are called authentic; the later ones are traditionally attributed to Pope Gregory the Great and are called plagal modes.

The methods of writing music were extremely scanty and imperfect. The sources of the modern system of writing were the neumes, which were marks put over the words to be sung, and indicated vaguely the inflections or changes of pitch to be used. They were made more definite as time went on by drawing colored lines through the haphazard open order of the neumes, which were thereby made to indicate definite relations of pitch and definite intervals; and the shapes of some of the neumes, through which the lines were drawn, gradually changed into some of the notes which are used in modern times.

In the absence of composers, the early Middle Ages were plentifully supplied with theorists. One of the first important theoretical works of the medieval dispensation is the work called "Musica Enchiridiadis," formerly attributed to Hucbald, but now to Otger, Abbot of St. Pons de Tomières, of the tenth century. It contains information about notation, and also about the organum or diaphony, which was the first form of harmony, and consisted at that time chiefly of consecutive octaves, and fifths or fourths, added to the plain song of the Church.

To Guido d'Arezzo (about 1000-1050 A.D.), another monk, is attributed the distribution of the twenty notes then used into groups of six, which were called hexachords. To him also is attributed the invention of "solmization," which is the naming of the notes of each hexachord by the syllables, ut, re, mi, fa, sol, la.

The origin of these syllables was a verse of a hymn to St. John, each line of which began with one of them, and each of which was sung to phrases beginning successively a note higher each time. This system of naming the notes has persisted into modern times; but ut, as a bad syllable to sing, has been altered to do, and the syllable si, to complete the necessary seven notes in each octave, has been added.

In the early days there appear to have been no means of defining the relative length of notes; and it was not necessary to find any so long as music was purely melodic. But when men began to sing in parts some means had to be devised to keep the voices together. The first work of mark attempting to deal with this subject was by Franco of Cologne. It was called "Cantus mensurabilis," or "Measured Song," and was probably written about the middle of the twelfth century. He adopted four standards of length, and called them —(1) maxima, or duplex longa, (2) longa, (3) brevis, (4) semibrevis. Their relations to one another varied in accordance with a time-signature which was put at the beginning of the music, which showed whether each long note was to be equal to two or to three shorter ones. In course of time the long notes dropped out of use, and the longest note now in common use, the whole note, is the shortest in Franco's series. He also indicated an advance in feeling for harmony by expressing his preference for mixing up thirds and sixths with the so-called perfect consonances, instead of going on in rows of fifths and fourths.

This development of harmony implies the transition from diaphony to descant; as the former consisted chiefly of mere doubling of a melody or plain song at the fifth or fourth, and the latter entailed more freedom of the parts. The improvement was chiefly arrived at through the attempts of the singers to vary the monotony of the organum by the addition of ornamental notes, such as in modern times are called passing notes. These extempore attempts were imitated by composers, and hence arose the distinction of "contrapunctus a mente," which was the extemporaneous descant of the singers, and the "contrapunctus a penna," which was the written counterpoint of the regular composers.

The musicians of those days adopted also another method of singing in parts, which was to sing several tunes at once. They accommodated them by modifying the tunes a little when the roughnesses and dissonances were too conspicuous; but none of the many examples which survive sound anything but ludicrous to a modern ear.

The center of musical development in the twelfth and thirteenth centuries was Paris, which in those days was the chief focus of every kind of intellectual activity. The most distinguished musicians of the time were Léonin, Perotin, Robert de Sabillon, and Walter Odington, an Englishman.

Progress in the line of serious music was extremely slow and laborious. The efforts of composers for centuries continued to be crude and barbarous, and their compositions bore distinct traces of the diaphony from which their methods of part-writing were derived in the profuse successions of fifths with which they abounded. But in secular circles and among the people valuable progress was made by troubadours, trouvères, jongleurs, and minnesingers, who cultivated poetry and music under less restricted and less theoretic conditions, and with valuable results to art.

The troubadours (from about 1087 till late in the thirteenth century) cultivated lyric poetry and the tunes which are best adapted to it. Their center was mainly Provence and the south of France. Among the most notable were William of Poitiers, Richard Cœur de Lion, Marcabrun, and Guiraut Riquier.

The trouvères cultivated epic as well as lyric poetry, and also the drama. Their center was in the northern parts of France, and extended to the south of England. Thibaut, King of Navarre and Count of Champagne, was a noteworthy trouvère; and so was Adam de la Hale, who wrote the play of "Robin and Marion," in which music is interspersed with dialogue. So was the English Walter Map, who wrote the story of Lancelot; and Chrestien de Troyes, who wrote its continuation; and Luc de Gast, who lived near Salisbury, and wrote the story of Tristan. The trouvères took a very important share in the development of part music, and cultivated the composition of secular chansons for several voices, in which a rhythmic element sometimes makes its appearance.

The jongleurs or ménestrels (minstrels) were the singers and story-tellers of the common people, as distinguished from the courtly and aristocratic connection of the troubadours and trouvères. They wandered about the country and attended fairs and markets, and had a regular guild or organization, the center of which was in Paris, where their headquarters continued to exist till quite modern times.

The minnesingers occupied the same position in Germany as the troubadours in France, and flourished later, from about 1150 A.D. till about 1260. Their most famous representatives were Heinrich der Beldecke, Walter von der Vogelweide, Wolfram von Eschenbach, who wrote the first German poem of "Parsifal," and Heinrich von Meissen, sometimes called Frauenlob. The meistersingers, who were the burgher poets and musicians of the towns, were of a later time still. Their most famous representative was Hans Sachs (1494-1576).

In England the remains of early musical art are much scantier, and the traditions are vague and unreliable. But there are distinct proofs that the country was fully up to the level of the continental nations; and one conspicuous but isolated instance, the famous round "Sumer is icumen in," is very far ahead of any other production of its time (about 1228 A.D.), both in tunefulness and management of the voice parts.

The earliest period of medieval musical development, which culminated in the twelfth and thirteenth centuries, was succeeded by a pause in artistic progress. Various causes, social and political, disturbed the wellbeing of European nations, and brought back a state of distress and confusion most unfavorable to all things intellectual and artistic. The fourteenth century was barren of musical productions of any value. Such relics as the fragments of works of Guillem de Machault (1284-1369) show but little advance on the standard of the previous century. The age was more conspicuously marked by the activity of theorists, such as De Muris (1300-70), who wrote the "Speculum Musicæ"; Tunstede (born at Norwich, and died in Suffolk in 1369), who wrote "De musica continua et discreta" in 1351; and De Handlo, who flourished about 1326.

The first sign of reawakening energy was manifested in England, and its proofs are the works of John Dunstable (about 1390-1453), a composer and musician hitherto chiefly known through the appreciative allusions made to him by later writers on music—as, for instance, by the Netherland theorist, John Tinctoris (about 1445-1511), who speaks of the "source and origin of the new art being among the English, the foremost of whom is John Dunstable." In recent years a considerable quantity of his music has been unearthed in the cathedral libraries of Trent, Bologna, and elsewhere, and it is clear that he was in his time regarded as the greatest composer in Europe. The style of his works is for the most part crude, but here and there passages are found which are quite intelligible and interesting to the modern ear. An English contemporary of his, who was an important representative of the art and well known in Italy as well as his own country, was John Hothby. He wrote several treatises on music, the most important of which is the "Calliopea legale." He died in 1487. Unfortunately, the good beginning made by England was arrested by causes of which the Wars of the Roses were the most conspicuous, and but few indications of further musical progress can be traced in the country till the Tudor times. The equally disturbed state of France caused the center of musical activity to pass from Paris northward to the Netherlands, which held the preëminence thenceforward for a century and a half.

The first representative composer of the Netherlands period was Dufay, the dates and circumstances of whose life have only recently been traced and verified. He was a choir-boy at Cambrai about 1410, a member of the Papal Choir in 1428, rose to first rank as a composer, was a long while in the service of Philip le Bon of Burgundy and of his famous son Charles the Bold, became a canon of Cambrai in 1450, and died in 1474. His work is far in advance of the crude style of the earlier Parisian school, both in technique and expression, but he shows the influence of John Dunstable in sundry peculiarities of style and diction, though his work in general is more mature. He is reputed to have been the first composer who used secular tunes for canti fermi in the place of the old ecclesiastical plain song—a practice which attained unfortunate notoriety in later days.

Among his most prominent fellow-composers were Faugues (born 1415), Firmin Caron (about 1460), and his own personal friend, Binchois, who died at Lille in 1460. The most distinguished composer of the next generation was Antoine Busnois, born in 1440, in Flanders. He was in the service of Charles the Bold, and died 1482. In his works is found a further progress in smoothness and equality of style, and specimens of well-managed imitation. The latter feature soon attracted composers so strongly that they began to lose sight of expression in their search after ingenuity, and expended all their powers on the contrivance of futile and mechanical canons. Of this kind of misplaced labor, Okeghem was the principal representative. He was born in Flanders early in the fifteenth century, and lived till 1513. He was looked upon as one of the greatest of European composers, and was in the service of Charles VII and Louis XI of France. But, notwithstanding his reputation, nearly everything to be found of his is marred by features of positive ugliness, probably owing to the misdirection of his energies. He was famous as a master, however, and especially as the master of Josquin de Près (born about 1440), the greatest composer of the next generation, and among the first who shows the characteristics of genius. In Josquin's works there are many examples of the most exquisite vocal effect and passages of noble and sympathetic musical expression. He excelled alike in Church music and in secular chansons. He was one of the numerous Netherland composers who found employment in Italy, and was in the Papal Choir from 1471 to 1484. He died at Condé in 1521. Among his pupils the most famous were Jean Mouton (died 1522) and Nicholas Gombert (born 1495). The latter carried the traditions of the school to Madrid, where he was in the service of Charles V. He was a very prolific composer, and a good one.

A composer of scarcely less gift and feeling than Josquin was Obrecht, who was chapel-master at Utrecht when Erasmus was a choir-boy there, and lived from 1430 to 1506. With him may be fitly mentioned Brumel, Compère (died 1518), and Pierre de la Rue (died 1510), who were pupils of Okeghem.

During the lives of Josquin and Obrecht the first development of the art of printing took place, which soon had great influence in the diffusion of music; and their compositions were among the first that were printed.

In the latter part of the fifteenth and throughout the sixteenth century the Netherlands and Belgium produced a large number of great musicians, most of whom found employment in Italy. Among these Adrian Willaert (1480-1562) was famous for the choral works for a double choir which he wrote for use at the Cathedral of St. Mark's at Venice, where he was maestro di capella; also for his madrigals, from which he won the reputation of being the first madrigal-writer. Contemporary with him, and also attached to St. Mark's, was Philip Verdelot (about 1500-67), who was early in the field as a composer of madrigals, canzonas, and other works of the kind. He also had some claim to be considered the first of the madrigal-writers, as examples by him were published in a collection which came out in Venice in 1533. Jacques Arcadelt (about 1495-1560) was also famous for his madrigals, of which he published several sets in Venice, beginning in the year 1538, which met with great favor.

The first Italian to come prominently before the world was Constanzo Festa (about 1490-1545). Madrigals of his were included in the same early collection with Verdelot's, and also in Arcadelt's. His advent marked the beginning of the time when the preëminence in music passed from the Netherlands to Italy. Netherland composers of great power still came before the world, such as Jacques Clement, commonly known as Clemens non Papa, who died about 1558; Cyprian van Rore (1516-65), who succeeded Willaert at St. Mark's; Waelrent (about 1518-95); Philippus del Monte (about 1521-1600), and the famous Orlando di Lasso (1520-94); but the Italians rapidly surpassed them, and before the end of the century had wrested the supremacy from them. Lasso's reputation overtopped that of all his countrymen. He was a man of interesting personal character, and a lover of strange experiments in music. The most famous among his very numerous works is his setting of the seven penitential psalms, which contains some of the most curious effects ever contrived for unaccompanied voices, and a great deal that is both characteristic and beautiful.

The spread of Italian musical gift was as rapid as its rise; and before the end of the century Venice produced Zarlino (1519-90) the theorist, and the two Gabrielis, Andrea (1510-86) and Giovanni (1557-1612), great masters of choral art and experimenters in instrumental music; while from other parts of Italy came Claudio Merulo (1533-1604), the famous organist; Marenzio (1550-99), the greatest of the madrigal-writers, and Giovanni Pierluigi da Palestrina, the greatest master of the old pure choral style, in whom the progress of the previous centuries came to a final climax. Palestrina was born at the town from which he takes his name, about 1524. The obscurity of his origin and the greatness of his ultimate fame have combined to produce the usual crop of myths, but little is really known about him till he entered the service of Pope Julius III in 1551. His compositions are characterized by a quiet nobility and dignity of expression, which make them the most perfect and serenely beautiful religious music ever written; while his extraordinary instinct for choral effect of the purest kind enabled him to produce exquisite and subtle effects of sound with the voices, which in that particular style have never been surpassed. His death, in 1594, marked the turning-point to the decadence of the old choral style and the beginning of a new epoch in art, of which the first experimenters in opera and oratorio were the earliest representatives.

Among Palestrina's contemporaries who are worthy of being honorably remembered are Morales the Spaniard, who entered the Papal Choir about 1540, and the Italian Nanini (1545-1607), one of the foremost representatives of the Roman school. Another Spaniard, Vittoria, a little younger than Palestrina, was a very great master of choral art, and so was Giovanni Croce (1559-1609). Orazio Vecchi (1551-1605), Anerio (1560-1630), and Allegri (1586-1662) were also very important Italian representatives of the latest phase of the pure choral style.

As sometimes happens in human affairs, the nation that was destined to go farthest was slow to develop. In these early times Germany was not so liberally represented by great composers as some other nations.

But the country had produced a few remarkable representatives of the art, of whom the most notable was Heinrich Isaak, who lived in the fifteenth century, contemporary with Busnois and Okeghem. He produced a large quantity of fine Church music and some secular songs, among which was "Innspruch ich muss dich lassen," which in later times became one of the most famous of chorales. Johann Walther (1496-1570), the friend of Luther, took an important share in starting the music of the Reformed Church, and brought out the first Protestant hymn-book in 1524. Soon after followed Ludwig Senfl, Jacob Händl, commonly known by his Latinized name of Gallus; Antonius Scandellus, Thomas Stolzer, and Paulus Hofheimer. The latest important representative of the early form of choral art in Germany was Hans Leo Hassler (about 1564-1612), who was a pupil of Andrea Gabrieli in Venice.

CHAPTER XVII

ENGLISH MUSIC FROM THE TUDORS TO THE STUARTS

Tudor Influence—Henry VIII and Elizabeth—Early Church Music—Tallis and Byrd—Madrigals—Rise of Instrumental Music—Decline of Choral Music—Influence of the Stuarts and Puritans.

WHEN the Wars of the Roses came to an end in 1485, and the astute government of Henry VII gave England time to regain her balance, music began to be cultivated to some purpose in that country. The Tudors appear to have been a genuinely musical family, and their influence upon all kinds of arts was uniformly good. Henry VII himself had a large musical establishment, and the taste and skill of his son, afterward Henry VIII, were favorable to the state of music at court. The standard of musical composition in this reign was not very high, but excellent purpose is shown in the works of Dr. Robert Fayrfax, Sheryngham, Turges, Newark, Phelyppes, and others.

In Henry VIII's reign these somewhat tentative beginnings passed into vigorous exercise of musical faculty. The King himself produced some excellent compositions, and set a good example by his ability in singing at sight, which accomplishment came before long to be considered a necessary part of the equipment of a properly educated gentleman.

Various fortunate circumstances caused the transition from Roman Catholicism to Protestantism in England to be gradual and moderate, with the happy result that the noble style of the Roman Church music of that age passed without change into the music of the Reformed Church. Before the Reformation became an accomplished fact, there were already a number of composers and musicians of great ability in the country, most of whom gave the Reformed Church the benefit of their powers, sometimes without forsaking the old Church themselves.

Of those who came earliest into the field at this time, the most noteworthy are John Taverner (organist of Christ Church, Oxford, about 1530), John Redford (1491-1547), Robert Johnson, John Sheppard (organist of Magdalen at Oxford, 1542), Robert White (organist of Ely, 1562-67; died 1575), and Christopher Tye (organist of Ely, 1541; died 1572). The last-named held a most prominent position among musicians, and did great service to the cause of the art of the Reformed Church by the dignified and masculine style of his compositions. He was appointed music-master to Edward VI, in whose reign the movement toward Protestantism, under Archbishop Cranmer's guidance, became more rapid and decisive.

When the English Service-Book was compiled in 1550, the traditional plain song used in the old Church was adapted to it by John Merbecke, thereby confirming the musical identity of the old and new services.

In the next generation of composers, Thomas Tallis (born soon after 1510, died 1585) occupied a foremost place. He wrote works for both Roman and Protestant use which are solid and masterly, and have a distinct character of their own. His pupil, William Byrd (born about 1538, died 1623), had still more comprehensive talents, as he wrote admirable madrigals and instrumental music for keyed instruments, as well as Church music of the finest and noblest quality. Both Tallis and Byrd maintained their sympathy with the old Church till the end of their days, and the character of the music written for both the new and the old ritual is so similar as often to be indistinguishable; indeed many of the works used in the English service as anthems were merely adaptations from motets and *cantiones sacræ*, or similar compositions, with the words translated from the original Latin into the more familiar English tongue.

In Elizabeth's reign the progress of the previous years came to a brilliant climax. Tallis and Byrd by her time were men of mature years, and were followed by a younger generation fully worthy of the traditions they had established. Music has never been held in greater honor, nor cultivated with more judgment and high artistic sense, than at the time when the vigor of the nation in enterprise, adventure, and war was at its highest. The memorable year 1588, in which the huge Spanish Armada, with its 130 ships and 29,000 men, was defeated and dispersed, is marked in musical history by the definite beginning of the English madrigal period. A few isolated examples had made their appearance previously, such as the madrigal "In going to my lonely bed," attributed to Edwards (1523-66), and some secular part music published by Thomas Whythorne; but the publication of the first series of the "Musica Transalpina," by Nicholas Yonge, in this year, was the decisive beginning of a series of publications of madrigals and similar works which followed in rapid succession for a quarter of a century. This work was a collection of the finest madrigals, chiefly by Italian composers of the time, and the editor, Yonge, appended a preface which comments on the growing taste for part singing and the general appreciation of madrigals among cultivated musical amateurs. His venture and his views were thoroughly justified by what followed.

The first new composer who made his appearance in the field was Thomas Morley, who excelled in all the known forms of art, whether in Church music or in madrigals, or in the charming ballets in which he combined the subtleties of the madrigal style with the brightness and freshness of the Italian balletti. His first publication was a collection of canzonets, which came out in 1593. In 1594 followed a set of madrigals, and in 1595 the first set of his ballets. In 1597 he published his "Introduction to Practical Music," which contains invaluable information about the state of music in his time. In the same year that admirable master, Thomas Weelkes, made his first appearance in print with a set of fine madrigals; and in the same year also appeared the first set of the beautiful "Songs or Ayres of Four Parts," by John Dowland (1562-1626), which mark, by their simple character and the definiteness of their form, the approach of the new era in music; a characteristic which may have come about through the fact that Dowland was a great lute-player.

In the next year, 1598, appeared the first set of madrigals by the greatest of English madrigal-writers, John Wilbye; in which we find the richest development of the madrigal form combined with wit, vigor, and poetic feeling. The next year saw the appearance of ballets and madrigals by Thomas Weelkes and others, and the year 1599 the appearance of madrigals by John Bennet, one of the most versatile and expressive of composers in this line. In 1601 appeared a superb monument of the skill and artistic sense of the musicians of Elizabeth's reign in the "Triumphs of Oriana," which was a collection of twenty-five madrigals by English composers, made in honor of the Queen; almost all of which have distinct merit, while some are of the highest order. Of the composers who appeared first after this time the most important were Thomas Bateson, whose set came out in 1604; Michael Este, also 1604; and Orlando Gibbons (born at Cambridge, 1583, died at Canterbury, 1625), whose set came out in 1612—that is, nine years after the death of Elizabeth. The energy generated in Elizabeth's days lasted on into the days of the Stuarts, and the last-named writer was the greatest and most comprehensive composer of all the school, excelling even more in his superb music for the Church than in his fine madrigals. Of all the Church music of this period, indeed, Gibbons's is the highest type, and marks the culmination of the genuinely English branch of the polyphonic school, which came about a quarter of a century later than that of the Italian school.

The survey of the music of the Elizabethan period would not be complete without reference to the work of a few composers who devoted their energies almost exclusively to Church music, such as Richard Farrant (about 1530-80), Elway Bevin, who published a "Shorte Introduction to the Art of Musicke" in 1631; and Adrian Batten (about 1590-1640).

Reference is also due to the very serviceable work done in the line of instrumental music in the pieces written for "Virginals," by a considerable number of composers, the most ingenious of which, from a technical point of view, were written by John Bull (about 1563-1628)—an organist of universal fame—and the most interesting by Orlando Gibbons. Mulliner's manuscript collection of such music (about 1565) was probably the earliest made. More famous is the manuscript known as "Queen Elizabeth's Virginal Book," containing over 290 pieces, mainly by English composers. It could not, however, have belonged to Queen Elizabeth, as several of the pieces in it were certainly written after her death. Another collection is "Lady Nevill's Book," of forty-two pieces, all by Byrd. W. Forster's "Virginal Book," dated 1624, contains seventy-eight pieces, and Benjamin Cosyn's, ninety-eight. The first printed book of such music was the "Parthenia," which came out in 1611, and contained a number of pieces by Byrd, Bull, and Gibbons—some of those by the latter composer being specially fine. The pieces in all these collections consist mainly of old dances, such as pavanas and galliards, and preludes, fantasias, and arrangements of choral works. They indicate a considerable taste for such music and no little development of technique.

England was indeed very brilliantly represented in every department of art then known. Music for sets of viols of as good quality as any in Europe was produced by such composers as Thomas Morley, Michael Este, Alfonso Ferrabosco (about 1580-1652), and Orlando Gibbons. Lute music was represented by John Dowland, who was lute-player to Christian IV of Denmark. Organ music was represented by John Bull and Peter Philipps. The latter lived abroad most of his life, chiefly in Flanders. He was one of the foremost representatives of organ music of the day, and a notable musician in every respect. He produced admirable madrigals, motets, and other choral music, besides organ music.

During the unfortunate rule of the Stuarts the standard of music rapidly declined. But though Stuart taste had considerable influence upon the direction taken by music, especially in the case of the second Charles, the lowering of the standard of choral music cannot fairly be laid to their charge any more than to the Puritans. Musical historians are fond of holding the fanaticism of the latter answerable for the extinction of choral music; and no doubt they put the finishing blow to a crumbling edifice. But the decadence began long before the Civil War broke out. The last great representative of the choral epoch in Europe died in the very week Charles married Henrietta Maria. And though the complete change which had come upon music about the year 1600 was slower in influencing the art in England than in other countries, it was bound to bring the great era of pure choral art to an end there as elsewhere, without the assistance of either Stuarts or Puritans.

It is noteworthy that though the cultivation of the choral style came to an end, the wave of musical enthusiasm and ability did not by any means cease abruptly. It was deflected, as in other countries, into new channels; and England continued to be ahead of all the countries of Europe in the new lines of art, such as instrumental music and theatrical music, till the death of Purcell. Lute music was brilliantly represented by Thomas Mace, who brought out his famous book, "Musick's Monument," in 1676. Christopher Sympson carried the art of viol-playing to the highest pitch then known, and brought out his most important book, "The Division Violist, or an Introduction to the Playing on a Ground," in 1659, the year after Cromwell died. Music for sets of viols was represented by the "Fancies" and sets of "Ayres" and other pieces by John Jenkins (1592-1678), William Lawes (born about 1590, killed at the siege of Chester, 1645), Matthew Locke (born early in the seventeenth century, died 1677), Thomas Tomkins (about 1590-1656), and many others; while the new style of incidental music to masques and stage plays was written with much success by Henry Lawes (1595-1662), Matthew Locke, Simon Ives (died 1662), and others.

In these secular directions the short period of civil war did not have any great effect upon music. Many musicians who had been active before it began undoubtedly carried on their artistic work while it was going on, and came forward with undiminished luster after the Restoration. The wave of musical enthusiasm and ability which began in the Tudor times may therefore fairly be considered to have lasted on almost till the time when Handel went to England. For though the line of music to which composers gave their minds was changed, and Church and choral music practically fell from a grand and mature style to an almost infantile condition of experimental crudity, an equal standard of ability, comparable to the best in other countries, was still displayed in instrumental music, solo music, and music for the theater.

CHAPTER XVIII

THE BIRTH OF OPERA AND ORATORIO

A Revolution in Art—Harmonic Music—Music-Drama and Oratorio — Monteverde — Carissimi — Schütz—The First Opera Houses Open—Cavalli—Cesti—Stradella—The First Important Operas.

THE last quarter of the sixteenth century witnessed the culmination of pure choral music in the works of Palestrina, Lasso, Marenzio, and their fellows. It also witnessed the beginnings of a new movement, which amounted to no less than a complete artistic revolution.

About this time a certain group of artistic and musical enthusiasts entered into speculations on the possibility of developing a new kind of musical art, in the form of solo music with instrumental accompaniment. Their central idea was to revive the style of performance of the ancient Greek dramas; and in connection with this they made experiments in the musical declamation of sonnets and poems of various kinds.

The most prominent of those who took part in the earliest stages of the movement were Vincenzo Galilei, the father of the famous philosopher and physicist Galileo; Emilio del Cavalieri, a composer; Rinuccini, a poet; Giulio Caccini, a singer and composer; Jacopo Peri, a musical amateur of ability and taste; and Giovanni Bardi, Count of Vernio, in whose house at Florence they used frequently to meet. The first recorded examples of their experiments were three pastorals by Cavalieri, called "Il Satiro" (1590), "La disperazione di Fileno" (1590), and "Il giuoco della cieca" (1595). These were looked upon as containing the first successful examples of recitative, with the invention of which Cavalieri is accordingly sometimes credited. They were followed by the drama "Dafne," which was written by Rinuccini and set by Peri in 1594 or soon after.

These early experiments have unfortunately been lost; the first example of their reforming energy which has survived is the "Euridice," which was written by Rinuccini and set by Peri, and performed on the occasion of the marriage of Henry IV of France and Maria de' Medici in Florence, in 1600. This work is of a very slender description, consisting mainly of formless recitatives interspersed with short passages of instrumental music called "ritornelli," and equally short and unimportant choruses. The object of the composer appears to have been mainly to declaim the poem without attempting striking musical effects, and to look to the drama to supply the interest. Caccini also set the poem of "Euridice," and wrote a book on the new movement, called "Le Nuove Musiche."

In the same year (1600) Cavalieri's oratorio "La Rappresentazione di anima e di corpo" was first performed in Rome, shortly after the death of the composer. The work was a product of the same order of ideas which gave birth to the first music-dramas; but its immediate antecedents were different. It appears to have been suggested by the performances of plays founded on Biblical subjects and combined with simple music, which had been given in the Oratory of Santa Maria in Vallicella at Rome. These had been instituted by Filippo de' Neri, the founder of the Congregation of the Oratory, for religious purposes; and it appears that Cavalieri's oratorio had also a religious purpose, and that the familiar name which has become universal was derived from the place where these earlier works had been performed. The name "oratorio," however, did not come into use till considerably later. The first to use it in a published work is said to have been Francesco Balducci, who died 1642. The earlier examples were sometimes described as "dramma sacra per musica." In style Cavalieri's work appears to be finer than Peri's, as the prologue is a noble specimen of the early kind of declamation. The choruses are short and simple; some are like the "Laudi spirituali," and others have a histrionic character. The new movement was carried on by a good many energetic composers in the same line, and several more sacred musical dramas were produced in the early part of this century, as, for instance, "The Lament of the Virgin Mary," by Capollini, 1627; Mazzocchi's "Martyrdom of St. Abbundio," etc., 1631; "St. Alessio," by Landi, 1634; and others.

The most important work of the time was done in the line of the secular music-drama, which made great strides in the hands of Claudio Monteverde. This remarkable composer (born 1568) began his career as a violist in the Duke of Mantua's band, and afterward served him as maestro di capella until the time that he was advanced to the more important post of maestro at St. Mark's in Venice. His genius was of the revolutionary and experimental order; and the limitations and refinements of the old choral music were little to his taste. Even in his works for voices alone he endeavored to obtain dramatic and theatrical effects, and used more harsh and striking chords than had been usual in choral music. His success in this line was much less marked than in his works for the theater. The first two of these, "Arianna" and "Orfeo," which appeared in 1607, at once made him the most prominent of living composers. The former is lost, all but a fragment—the latter has survived complete, and gives a clear indication of the direction in which the art was moving. Monteverde in this shows daring and force in the treatment of his subject. He uses a large group of instruments for his accompaniments and ritornelli, with a certain crude sense of effect. As in the works of Peri and Caccini, there is a very large quantity of formless recitative, and very little that is constructively definite; but he evidently endeavored to intensify the dramatic situations by the character of the music, and to follow the varying shades of feeling expressed in the dialogue by characteristic intervals and harmonies.

He also had a considerable instinct for histrionic music, and worked rather for stage purposes than for purely musical effect. These early operas of his were written for special occasions, such as the marriage of the Duke of Mantua's eldest son; but he lived long enough to witness the opening of public opera houses in Venice by Manelli and Ferrari (1637), and wrote his last two operas, "L'Adone" (1640) and "L'Incoronazione di Poppea" (1642), for them. His singular preëminence has put the works of his contemporaries into the shade. But the "Dafne" of Gagliano, which was first performed in Mantua, and published in Florence in 1608, deserves to be remembered as representing a higher artistic conception of the form of art than the earliest examples.

The line of oratorio was worthily carried on by Giacomo Carissimi, a composer of powers in some ways equal to Monteverde's, and gifted with more artistic judgment and reserve. He was the first master of the new school who brought the experience of a thorough training in the old artistic methods to bear upon the new forms of art; and his oratorios, such as "Judicium Salomonis," "Jephte," "Jonas," and "Baltazar," contain really fine choruses, as well as most expressive and well-written solos, and many features which show a considerable sense of dramatic effect. He also wrote several secular cantatas for solo voice, and motets and masses and other Church music. He lived till 1674.

In his time the budding German school was brought into contact with the new Italian movement through Heinrich Schütz (1585-1672), who came from Saxony to study under Giovanni Gabrieli (1557-1612), at St. Mark's in Venice, early in the seventeenth century. He here became acquainted with the theories of the new school as well as with Gabrieli's own original experiments in direct musical expression by choral and instrumental means; and when he went back to Germany he gave characteristic evidence of his Teutonic love of the mystic and pathetic as well as of his Italian training in his oratorio "The Resurrection" (1623), and in his noteworthy settings of the "Passion" according to the four Evangelists, and in various psalms. He also set a German translation of Rinuccini's drama of "Dafne," which had served Peri as a libretto in the earliest years of the new movement.

The earliest composers of mark who profited largely by the opening of public opera houses were Monteverde's pupil, P. F. Cavalli (1599-1676), and Carissimi's pupil, Antonio Cesti (about 1620-69). They both show the influence of their masters, as the former had the greatest instinct for stage effect and the latter the more general musical instinct.

Cavalli wrote an enormous number of operas. At least twenty-six are still preserved in the library of St. Mark at Venice. The most famous was "Giasone" (1649), which contains a few strong points of dramatic effect and some characteristic and forcible passages of declamation. His later works indicate the tendency toward definite forms, and he even produced examples of the familiar aria form. His fame spread to foreign countries, and he was summoned to Paris, in 1660 and 1662, to superintend the performance of his "Serse" and "Ercole amante" for certain court festivities.

Cesti practically represents a later generation, for though he was busy with opera writing at the same time as Cavalli, his general standard of art shows a decided advance in all departments. His treatment of instruments is much freer and more effective; his general style of writing is more mature; while his sense of tune and construction is so good that he takes rank as one of the most successful melodists of his time.

Among many excellent operas his best was "Orontea," which was brought out in 1649 in Venice, for the opening of one of the new theaters, and maintained a vigorous popularity for thirty years. "La Dori" (1663) and "Pomo d'Oro," written for the Viennese court, also contain excellent music. He also wrote many cantatas for solo voices, which contain charmingly melodious arias.

A noteworthy contemporary of these composers was Legrenzi (born about 1625), who was maestro di capella at St. Mark's in Venice from 1685 to 1690, where he did good service by reorganizing the instrumental forces into something resembling the scheme of modern orchestras, and wrote a number of good operas.

One of the most interesting figures in the musical history of the century was Alessandro Stradella. He also was a pupil of Carissimi's, and his powers excited the imagination of his contemporaries to such an extent that he became the hero of one of the most remarkable romances in musical history. He was undoubtedly a composer of great powers, which are shown in his oratorio "San Giovanni Battista," by very free treatment of instruments, well and clearly designed arias, fine and broad choruses, and a considerable power of dramatic expression. His work shows the artistic thoroughness of the Carissimi school, combining respect for the old choral traditions with mastery of the new artistic theories. His work is more mature than that of any other composer of the century before Alessandro Scarlatti, and is rather suggestive both of his style and of Handel's.

CHAPTER XIX

GENERAL DEVELOPMENT OF OPERA IN EUROPE

Differences of the Music-Drama in France and Italy—Monteverde's Traditions Continued in France by Lulli—English Music and Purcell—German Opera—Scarlatti and the Neapolitans—Handel—Italian Opera Supreme.

THE new movement, which gave birth to modern opera and oratorio about 1600, soon branched out into two distinct lines, which have maintained their characteristics till the present day. The first prominent representatives of these were Monteverde and Carissimi. The former stands at the head of the modern composers who study effect more than art; the latter at the head of those who study art more than effect. Monteverde ostentatiously rejected the traditions of his predecessors, to leave himself free to carry out his dramatic ideals. Carissimi endeavored to make use of the accumulated wisdom of earlier generations to guide him to the fittest artistic expression of his musical ideas.

The traditions of Monteverde were handed on to his pupil Cavalli (1599-1676), who became the foremost operatic composer of his time; and by him they were introduced into France, whither his great reputation had penetrated. But the characteristics of French opera were different from the ideals of the Italians, being founded mainly on ballet and spectacular display. The Italians in those days cared little for ballet; and to make Cavalli's operas palatable to French audiences, ballet airs had to be supplied. The task fell to the lot of Jean Baptiste Lulli, a young man who had been sent from Italy to the French court and had ingratiated himself with King Louis XIV by his talent for supplying dance music for the "mascarades," in which the King and his court took pleasure in dancing. Lulli was by this means brought into direct contact with Cavalli's works, and the experience stood him in good stead when he came to write operas some ten years later. In the meanwhile he kept in touch with the stage by writing incidental music to several of Molière's "Comédies ballets," in which he himself sometimes acted; and by composing "divertissements dansés," in which line he had made considerable success as early as 1658 with "Alcidiane."

The foremost French composer of the time was Robert Cambert (1628-77), who is sometimes described as the first composer of French opera. He made his first appearance with noteworthy success in a work called "La Pastorale," in 1659, which is described in the language of the time as "the first French comedy in music." It was followed by "Ariane" in 1661. In 1669 Louis founded the "Académie Royale de Musique" for the performance of operas and gave the management into the hands of Perrin, who, being a kind of poet, provided the librettos and associated Cambert with himself as composer; and they produced "Pomone" with success in 1671.

Lulli, however, had the ear of the King, and persuaded him to abrogate Perrin's rights and hand them over to him; giving him sole power for the performance of opera in Paris. Cambert, by this means, was driven out of France and took refuge at the court of Charles II, where he remained till his death in 1677.

Lulli then began his important operatic career with the pasticcio "Les fêtes de l'Amour et de Bacchus" in 1672, and followed it up with his first complete opera, "Cadmus," in 1673. From that time till his death, in 1687, he continued to supply operas year after year: the most noteworthy being "Alceste" (1674), "Thésée" (1675), "Atys" (1676), "Bellérophon" (1679), "Persée" (1682), "Phaëton" (1683), "Amadis" (1684), "Roland" (1685), and "Armida" (1686). The last was "Acis et Galatée" (1686). The scheme of his operas was well contrived for spectacular effect, apparently on the same plan as that adopted in Cambert's works. The plays were interspersed with ballets and choruses, and scenes in which a number of persons were effectively grouped on the stage; and the development of each act shows considerable power of artistic management and insight for stage effect, which are made the more available by the allegorical character of the subjects. The best features of the works are the overtures, which are solid and dignified, and the many fine passages of declamatory music, which comprise some high qualities of dramatic expression. Lulli's work is immensely superior to Cavalli's in technical mastery of resource; its drawbacks are the heaviness and monotony of his instrumental accompaniments, and his carelessness of artistic finish. He had no rivals in France, and left no one capable of immediately carrying on the development of French opera. But he set his seal upon the form of art, and French opera has maintained its distinctive features ever since. He had a very keen eye for business, and left a fortune of 800,000 livres behind him when he died in 1687.

The influence of the French style became powerful in England when Charles II was recalled to the throne in 1660. He brought with him from foreign countries an enthusiasm for it, and when he restored the establishments of the chapels royal he endeavored to replace the grand old style of Tallis and Byrd and Gibbons, for which he had no taste, by the music of viols, and solos, and things generally of a livelier cast, like French music.

Most of the singing men and organists and composers of the old régime, such as Captain Cook and Christopher Gibbons and W. Child, were not sufficiently in touch with the new movement to supply him with what he wanted. So he took advantage of a manifestation of great talent among some of the choir-boys of the Chapel Royal to send one of the most gifted of them, Pelham Humfrey (born 1647), to France to learn his business there. After a year or so this boy came back thoroughly imbued with the French style, and became a fit leader to the younger generation of composers, represented by John Blow (1648-1708) and Michael Wise (born about 1648, died 1687), who were among the choir-boys of the same standing as himself. Unfortunately Humfrey himself only survived to the age of twenty-seven, and made no more than a beginning, with some singular and sometimes interesting experiments in Church music. But among the choir-boys of the next generation appeared the remarkable genius Henry Purcell (1658-95), who readily assimilated the influences of the new movement, both in its French and Italian aspects, and in the short space of the thirty-seven years of his life produced an enormous quantity of music of every kind, both instrumental and vocal, comprising operas, songs, sonatas for strings, suites, and Church music.

England had already at this time a distinct type of stage piece associated with music, which became the model of the occasional early experiments in opera. A kind of entertainment called a masque had been popular at court for many generations. All the Stuarts were fond of theatrical performances, and in Charles I's reign the court constantly entertained itself with such masques, in which the Queen and her ladies and little Prince Charles took part. The words of these works were written by the most distinguished poets, and the music by the ablest musicians attainable. These performances occurred annually almost up to the outbreak of civil war. Among their characteristics is a certain literary flavor, and a preponderance of fanciful elements over dramatic; and these qualities reappeared in the operatic experiments which were made after the Restoration.

It was in music for plays, operas, and dramatic scenes that Purcell's highest genius was ultimately shown, and the tradition of a national style, which had been manifested in the music of the earlier masques, was revived. But the legend hitherto universally accepted, that Purcell's career began with music for the theater, has recently been discredited through the careful and exact researches of Barclay Squire; for although he undoubtedly wrote music for "Theodosius" and "The Virtuous Wife" in 1680, his admirable music for various plays which were first performed shortly before that time has been considerably antedated, because it was evidently written for later revivals. It was not till about 1688 or so that opportunities for exercising his genius in connection with the stage became more frequent.

When Purcell died, in 1695, he left the country without any composer of sufficient powers to carry on the work he had so well begun, till the advent of Handel in 1710 put a new aspect on affairs. Purcell's style is very individual, and his powers most comprehensive; but the immature state of music at the time when he lived, as well as the absence of good models in the new style of art, militates against the general equality of his work, and prevents his holding as high a position in public favor as his genius deserves.

Germany shared the same fate as England at this time, as far as the establishment of any characteristically national opera was concerned. For though many composers took in hand the form of art known as the Singspiel, and though Reinhard Keiser (1673-1739) produced no less than 116 operas, mostly for his theater in Hamburg, no one was able to maintain a characteristically German quality of work, and in the next generation opera in Germany fell under the spell of the Italian style.

In Italy the highest position among opera composers at this time was held by the great Alessandro Scarlatti (1659-1725). He was a pupil of Carissimi, and carried on the artistic traditions of the line of art he represented.

His first opera, "Gli Equivoci nel Sembiante," came out in Rome in 1679. But most of his works were written for Naples, and with him began the great days of the Neapolitan school, whose composers were celebrated for the excellence of their writing for the voice.

In the course of his career Scarlatti produced over 100 operas, most of which have been lost. Those that remain show great advance on the work of his predecessors in maturity of technical workmanship and style. The instruments are much more effectively and freely used, the arias are better balanced and better developed, and his fund of melody is richer and more varied. He also did his art signal service by frequently adopting a form of instrumental overture in three or four movements, which was the ultimate source of the modern orchestral symphony.

The drawback of his type of opera is the constant and wearisome alternation of recitatives and arias, which latter are always in the same form, with a leading portion and a contrasting portion, and a "da capo," or simple repetition of the first portion to conclude with. Scarlatti was doubtless not the inventor of the form, but he used it with monotonous persistence, to the detriment of his works as wholes.

He was the last Italian of the early period who occupied the foremost place in the world as an operatic composer. In succeeding generations the German composers learned their art in the school of the Italians, and for some time maintained preëminence as writers of Italian opera.

The first to wrench the scepter from the hands of the Italians was G. F. Handel (1685-1759). When, in 1710, he went to England, that country was sorely in need of a man of sufficiently comprehensive powers to supply the fashionable world with operatic performances. But he did not at first devote much of his time to opera, as he had to attend to his duties as kapellmeister to the Elector of Hanover (afterward George I), and to his duties as kapellmeister to the Duke of Chandos at Cannons. Later he accomplished a vast amount of operatic work.

The period of his oratorio work slightly overlaps the operatic time. The greater part of the works by which he is best known were produced after the long effort of his operatic career was over.

His operatic works form the climax of the first stage in the history of opera. In plan they are much the same as Scarlatti's; and though his arias are characterized by a greater wealth of melody and a greater resource of treatment and expression, the same monotonous alternation of recitative and aria ruins the general effect of the works. The materials in detail are often superb; and though he played into the hands of the singers, who were already beginning to feel and show their power, he did not fall into the degree of empty conventional insincerity which characterized the works of the writers of Italian opera in the next generation. His position was that of a caterer for the public, but the quality of what he gave them was intrinsically worthy of his great powers. (See the biography of Handel in another section of this series.)

Meanwhile the popularity of opera in Italy evoked a perfect flood of fairly artistic works by a great variety of composers, all of whom had more feeling for suitable writing for solo singers than for dramatic effect. The influence of the Neapolitan school, of which Alessandro Scarlatti was the greatest representative and progenitor, became enormous. Most of the leading composers were either pupils of his or pupils of his pupils—such as Gaetano Greco—or pupils of his successor, Durante (1684-1755). Among those were Leonardo Leo (1694-1746), a composer of really solid and notable powers; Leonardo Vinci (born 1690, poisoned 1732); Niccolo Porpora (1686-1766); David Perez (1711-78); Niccolo Jomelli (1714-74); Domenico Scarlatti, Alessandro's son, and famous as a player on and writer for the harpsichord (1683-1757); the writer of native Neapolitan opera buffa, Logroscino (1700-63); and the short-lived but brilliant G. B. Pergolesi (1710-36). The composer who enjoyed the widest European fame was Adolph Hasse (1699-1783), a German, who began his career as a singer, and learned the arts of Italian opera under Neapolitan influences, and spread the subtle seductions of its easy fluency with too much success throughout his own country. He married the famous singer Faustina Bordoni. Among the few prominent Italian composers who were not of the Neapolitan school, Steffani (1655-1730), Lotti (1667-1740), Caldara (1678-1768), and Galuppi (1703-85) honorably represented Venice; and G. Bononcini, Handel's rival (1672-1752), and Sarti (1729-1802) came from Bologna.

The stiffness and formality of the Italian grand opera were very happily relieved by the influence of the opera buffa and the light pieces called "intermezzi," which were performed between the acts of the grand operas, act for act alternately. Their light humor and gaiety maintained a happy savor of human nature which the solemn and mechanical complacency of the grand opera tended to obliterate. Among the most famous of these was the "Serva Padrona," by Pergolesi, in which the source of much of Mozart's lighter style in the humorous situations of his operas may plainly be traced.

Music in France at this period had no great artistic importance, and only one name of conspicuous interest makes its appearance. J. P. Rameau (1683-1764), the son of the organist of Dijon Cathedral, was intended for the law, but he determined to devote himself to music, and gave his attention at first to musical theory, and wrote an important treatise on the subject; notwithstanding which, he kept his artistic freshness sufficiently unimpaired to write very successful operas in the later years of his life. His first was "Hippolyte et Aricie," which came out in 1733, and met with great opposition in Paris. "Castor and Pollux" appeared in 1736, and his most important work, "Dardanus," in 1739. He was a man of character and originality, and the genuine verve of his musical ideas cannot be gainsaid. It is shown very happily in the dance tunes with which his operas are interspersed, which are remarkably spirited and vivacious.

About the middle of the century Italian opera buffa was introduced into Paris by an Italian company. It was much opposed on the ground that it was not French, but the French composers imitated the style and improved upon it, and from this source sprang that most successful form, the opéra comique of later days.

CHAPTER XX

ORATORIO IN THE TIME OF BACH AND HANDEL

Different Lines Taken by Italians and Germans—Passion Music in Germany—Bach's Predecessors—His Choral Works—Italian Influence upon Handel—His Oratorios.

THE Italians enjoyed the distinction of giving the start to oratorio, as they did to most of the other forms of modern musical art; but, after their composers had developed it to the excellent artistic standard of Carissimi and Stradella, a blight seems to have settled on it, and it rapidly became even more mechanical and pointless than contemporary opera. There were many composers who were fully capable of writing effective and fluent choruses, such as Colonna (1640-95), Lotti (1667-1740), Durante (1684-1755), and Leo (1694-1746), but they reserved their powers in that line for their psalms, hymns, masses, and motets, and submitted to the public preference for solo-singing and fluent melody so far as to reduce the choral part of oratorios to a minimum, and to seek for their effect mainly in strings of formal and conventional arias. It remained, therefore, for other countries to develop this great form of art to its highest standard of interest and artistic completeness.

The mood of Germans was eminently favorable. They had more appreciation of choral effect, and regarded the oratorio form with much more serious feelings than the Italians. Moreover, it happened that the form which they especially cultivated lent itself naturally to very serious and earnest treatment. Italian oratorio dealt with a variety of subjects; sometimes Old Testament heroes, sometimes allegorical personages, sometimes famous saints. But German religious intensity showed itself by laying hold of one subject, and concentrating almost all its fruitful energy on the story of the Passion, as told by the four Evangelists. The source of their treatment of the subject was the traditional mode of reciting the story in Holy Week so as to give it more telling effect; by distributing the words of different characters to different readers, and giving the utterances of the masses of people to the choir, which went technically by the name of the "turba." John Walther wrote a musical setting of the tragedy on such lines as early as 1530. Heinrich Schütz followed with a very interesting and expressive treatment of the "Resurrection" in 1623, and of four "Passions" later in his life. More advanced stages of art are shown in settings by Giovanni Sebastiani in 1672, and Funcke in 1683, and by Keiser in 1703. The art of dramatic choral-writing was meanwhile developed in the kindred form of Church cantatas, by such masters as Tunder, Buxtehude, Johann Christoph Bach and Johann Michael Bach. The Italian aria form was also imitated by German composers, and introduced with effect into the settings of the "Passion"; so that by the time of Johann Sebastian Bach (1685-1750) the artistic scheme was tolerably complete; and no man was ever more ideally fitted to treat a subject at once mystical and dramatic with the highest intensity and genuine sincerity.

Bach wrote his first setting according to St. John in 1723, just before his move from Köthen to Leipzig. Beautiful and sincere as this work is, it falls considerably below the great setting of the "Passion" according to St. Matthew, which is far the noblest and most expressive example ever produced. In this complete state of the form it is noticeable that it takes the nature rather of a religious exercise than of a mere musical and dramatic entertainment. The story itself occupies comparatively small space, being told in the recitatives allotted to the Evangelist and the other characters, and in the short dramatic outbursts of chorus. What marks the form as ultra-German is the manner in which each step of the tragedy is weighed upon and brought home to the hearer and worshiper by the poetical reflections given either in the form of expressive arias or in the chorales, in which latter the audience in earlier days had been accustomed to take part. These are introduced at each step of the story, and serve to emphasize each successive situation; the whole being rounded off by the great reflective choruses which come at the beginning and end of the complete work. In Bach's hands the result is one of the most pathetic and deeply imaginative works in all the range of music. It was too characteristic and serious even for the German general public of that time; and its performance was restricted to Leipzig in the eighteenth century, and ceased altogether for a time at the beginning of the nineteenth. Mendelssohn revived it at Berlin in 1829, and the first performance in England was that under Sterndale Bennett in 1854. Bach wrote at least two more settings of the "Passion," but they have been lost. The rest of his sacred choral works consist mainly of the numerous Church cantatas written for weekly performance in Leipzig, the superb motets, the Magnificat in D, the great B minor mass, and the "Christmas Oratorio" written in 1734, which is really a series of cantatas for Christmas day, New Year's day, New Year's Sunday, and the Epiphany.

Handel, at the beginning of his career, came under similarly serious influences. He set the "Passion" as early as 1704, and employed in it the highest resources of choral effect and solos. But when he went to Italy he fell in with the Italian taste in oratorio for a time; and in the two examples of oratorio which he produced for performance there—the "Resurezzione" and the "Trionfo del Tempo e della Verita"—he reduced the choral portions to a minimum. He nevertheless learned much from the Italians in the art of smooth and fluent writing for chorus, and put it to excellent use at a later period.

Masques had long been popular in England. They were theatrical entertainments in which the interest was more literary than dramatic; the poems of which were contrived to serve for pretty pageants, enhanced by choruses and solos and incidental music. The general aspect of Handel's "Acis" and "Esther" shows that he followed the usual scheme of masques in them, the main difference being that as he was far the greatest and maturest composer who wrote music for anything of the nature of an English masque he naturally expanded and enriched the individual movements almost beyond recognition. In its more primitive form it had served as the model for experiments in English opera; in this more expanded form it also served as the principal model upon which the English form of oratorio was designed. The continuity is the easier to follow because till Handel's time the English people had never troubled themselves about oratorio at all, and its place in the scheme of English music was void. The manner in which the void came to be filled has something of the character of a chapter of accidents; but the accidents are quite coherent, and the fact that "Esther" was at first called a masque and later on an oratorio serves to unite the two types conclusively together.

The year 1738 marks the decisive turning of Handel's mind toward the oratorio form, for in this year he produced both "Saul" and his most monumental work, "Israel in Egypt." In "Israel in Egypt" he used music by Stradella, Gaspar Kerl, and Urio, and many movements from a Magnificat which was probably by Erba, though some people cling to the belief that it may be an early work of Handel's own. A great deal of the borrowed portions is distinctly dull, but what remains of Handel's own is so supremely fine that the oratorio as a whole is likely to be always regarded as Handel's most important achievement.

His most famous work, "The Messiah," differs from his other oratorios in its abstract nature, and the predominance of the reflective element gives it an affinity to the German form of Passion music. It is much more of an act of worship or a glorified anthem than a dramatic oratorio. This also evidently suits English moods, and though it did not lay hold of public taste at once, it seems now to be more firmly rooted in the national affections than any other musical work whatever.

The departure of two such great masters as Bach and Handel left the musical world very blank. They had summed up the possibilities of choral music so far, and, till instrumental music had developed a great deal, there was not sufficient field to give another great composer a chance, and the oratorio form almost completely collapsed for a long time. Arne and Boyce (both born in 1710) produced some artistic oratorios with distinctly English qualities about them, and Arne left a permanent mark upon the nation by his admirable tunes, such as "Rule Britannia" (1740) and "Where the bee sucks" (1746). His most successful oratorio was "Judith" (1773). Arne died in 1778, Boyce in 1779.

In Germany, Karl Philipp Emanuel Bach, who was keenly in sympathy with the modern tendencies of art, and excelled equally in symphonies and sonatas, produced two really interesting oratorios, "The Israelites in the Desert" (1775) and "The Resurrection and Ascension of Christ" (1787). Both of these works are designed on lines similar to those of the German Passions, and both are most significant in the qualities which show the progress of the art of instrumentation; and a treatment of chorus which has more kinship with the harmonic tendencies of modern times than with the grand and characteristic elaboration of his great father's work.

In Italy oratorio ceased to have any significance, and Church music became for the most part conventional and operatic. Italian composers wrote fluent counterpoint in their choruses, but their Church works have a singular lack of point and character. Besides those mentioned at the beginning of the chapter a few merit reference: Astorga (1681-1736) for his charmingly musical and expressive "Stabat Mater"; Marcello (1686-1739) for his famous psalms; Pergolesi (1710-36) for his "Stabat Mater."

CHAPTER XXI

THE PROGRESS OF INSTRUMENTAL MUSIC UP TO THE TIME OF JOHANN SEBASTIAN BACH

Early Instrumental Music—In England—In France—Couperin—Organ Music in Italy—Frescobaldi—In Germany—The Great Italian Violinists—Suites and Sonatas—Handel—J. S. Bach—Domenico Scarlatti.

THE history of instrumental music divides naturally into three well-defined periods. The first extends from the early experiments in the fifteenth and sixteenth centuries up to the time of J. S. Bach, the second up to Beethoven, and the third till the present day. They are each marked by consistent distinguishing traits: the first by contrapuntal methods akin to those of choral music; the second by the development of pure harmonic forms of the sonata order, which are shown in their highest perfection in the sonatas and symphonies of Beethoven; and the third by a striving after greater freedom than the pure sonata forms seem to allow, or an extension of its scheme by intellectual devices, and new kinds of contrapuntal methods; and by more decisive adoption than formerly of ideas and programmes as the basis of art.

In the early days of the first of these periods modern instruments were not available. The stringed instruments played with bows were the various viols—treble, mean, tenor, viola da gamba, and violone or double bass. And for this set a quantity of music, both in the shape of dance tunes and of movements imitated from choral canzonas and similar choral works, was written. Lutes of various sizes were conspicuously popular and useful, and the style of music written for them has permeated many types of more modern music written for other instruments. The position now occupied by the pianoforte was held by the harpsichord and the clavichord, and an immense quantity of music of permanent value was written for them in various countries.

All the forms of instrumental music then known throve in England in the time of the Stuarts. The last and greatest representative of this early English school was Henry Purcell, who had the advantage of knowing something of French and Italian models. His most important instrumental compositions are the suites or lessons for harpsichord and two sets of sonatas for strings. These sonatas are on the regular Italian plan familiar in Corelli's works. The admirable dance music he wrote for various plays ought also to be counted as representative of his skill as an instrumental composer.

Instrumental music throve also in France in those days, and early showed distinctive traits. The familiar inclination of the French for expressing their feelings by gestures has its counterpart in their predominant taste for dance rhythms in music and their love for ballet on the stage. Their own particular form of opera, which was set going by Cambert and Lulli, was mainly founded on ballet and kindred kinds of stage effect. Lulli no doubt gave considerable impulse to French instrumental music by the profusion of dance tunes he wrote for his operas. And he did good service to art by the type and style of overture he adopted, which was followed by Handel in the overtures to his operas and oratorios, and by other composers in the same line even in quite modern times, such as Spohr and Mendelssohn.

The department of instrumental music in which the French especially excelled was that of music for the harpsichord. Among the early masters was Jacques Champion de Chambonnières, who was harpsichordist to Louis XIV in the early part of his reign, and published harpsichord music in 1670. A collection of "Pièces de clavecin," by Le Bègue, also deserves mention, which was published in Paris in 1677. The greatest of the French school was François Couperin (1668-1733). He wrote a profusion of little movements full of grace, fancy, and character, grouped into sets called ordres, such as are now commonly called suites. He showed his most solid gifts in his allemandes, sarabandes, and preludes, and his lighter and more popular vein in his rondos, and the numbers of pieces with fanciful names which generally formed the latter part of these ordres. He is the prototype of an essentially French school, which has continued till the present day to supply the world with little pieces based on some dance rhythm, or a title which explains and supplies the motive of the pieces.

Couperin also wrote a book called "L'Art de toucher le clavecin" (1717), which is a most invaluable and complete explanation of harpsichord playing in its prime, and is often referred to by him in editions of his compositions as "Ma méthode." Similar to Couperin's works are the many pieces for harpsichord by J. P. Rameau (1683-1764). His first "Book of Pieces for the Clavecin" came out in 1706. The plan of his suites is much the same as Couperin's, comprising a few solid movements at the beginning and a number of lively tunes and rondos in the latter part. There is even more directness and point about some of Rameau's picture-tunes than Couperin's, and the connection with the stage is more obvious, inasmuch as some of those which are still familiar to modern pianists appear also as ballet pieces in his operas.

Before the end of the sixteenth century organs had arrived at a fairly complete state. It was natural that the associations of the organ should cause organists to imitate choral works in their compositions; and they improved upon them first by introducing a great variety of turns and runs and ornaments. These ultimately developed into a special kind of composition, somewhat like the products of extemporization, consisting mainly of runs, accompanied by simple successions of chords. This form was commonly known as a toccata; and though crude and elementary, it has considerable historical importance as one of the first of the large musical forms which established a sort of individuality, as an instrumental composition independent of choral models. Its earliest representative composers were Andrea Gabrieli (1510-86), and his famous nephew, Giovanni Gabrieli (1557-1612), and Claudio Merulo (1533-1604), all of whom were organists of St. Mark's in Venice.

The most important of the early northern organists was Jan Pieterszoon Sweelinck, organist of Amsterdam (1562-1621). His work, consisting of fugues, variations, toccatas, is marked by a considerable inventive gift, and talent for speculation, which were remarkably helpful to the progress of his branch of the art. He was the prototype of the northern group of organists, some of whom, such as Reinken and Buxtehude, were among the models of J. S. Bach. The greatest of the early organists, and the first who arrived at any real maturity of style, was Girolamo Frescobaldi (1583-1644), organist of St. Peter's at Rome. His works comprise some of the earliest examples of well-developed fugues of the modern kind, as well as specimens of all the forms known in his time; which show that he had great mastery of resource and inventiveness, as well as firm grasp of artistic principles.

The earliest of the great German organists was Samuel Scheidt, born in Halle in 1587. He wrote a large quantity of remarkable music for his instrument, and died 1654. Soon after him came Frescobaldi's pupil, Froberger, who was born early in the seventeenth century, and died 1667. He was even more important as a writer of harpsichord music than for his organ music: since he adapted the methods of the organ composers to the smaller domestic instrument, and was a special prototype of J. S. Bach in that respect. Caspar Kerl, who is thought to have been a pupil of Carissimi and of Frescobaldi, was born in 1628. A composer of greater scope was George Muffat, who not only wrote effective and genial organ music, but also some excellent suites for strings. He died in 1704. Johann Pachelbel (1653-1706) was especially successful as a composer of "choral vorspiele," a very characteristic form of German art. Reinken (1623-1722), another very remarkable musician, was organist of Hamburg for sixty-six years; the Danish organist Dietrich Buxtehude (1637-1707) was the most brilliant and interesting of this group of composers and exercised considerable influence on J. S. Bach.

The most important and fruitful line of instrumental music emerged from the obscurity of indefinite experiment into the light of a promising dawn in Italy in the latter part of the seventeenth century. The name with which the decisive awakening of violin music to life is always rightly associated is that of Arcangelo Corelli (1653-1713). In his time the art of violin-making was brought to perfection. Niccolo Amati was his senior by many years, and Antonio Stradivarius and Joseph Guarnerius, the two greatest of violin-makers, were his contemporaries. Corelli represents the essentially solid and expressively musical school of violin-playing. He was in nowise greatly expert in mechanical difficulties, but the traditions of his solid style have been handed down from master to pupil through successive generations of famous players till the present day. His works consist entirely of sonatas and concertos for stringed instruments, with accompaniment of figured bass for archlute, or harpsichord, or organ. The first set, consisting of twelve "Sonate da Chiesa," was published in Rome in 1683; the second set, twelve "Sonate da Camera," in 1685. The distinction between these Church and chamber sonatas is important, since the former represent (in an antiquated disguise) the modern abstract sonata, while the latter represent the dance suite. The whole of his compositions amount to no more than five sets of such sonatas and a set of concertos. What gives them their permanent attraction is their artistic equality and fluency, combined with simplicity, sweetness, a vein of poetic expression, dignity, and an admirably even flow of easy part writing. He set the seal of an evenly balanced individuality upon his works in such a manner as to make them one of the landmarks of musical history

Immediately after his time the great Italian school of violinists bloomed into wonderful vigor and perfection—several of Corelli's own pupils occupying an important position among them, such as Somis (1676-1763), Locatelli (1693-1764), and Geminiani (1680-1761). Other great players, more or less independent of Corelli, also made their appearance, such as Veracini (1685-1750) and Vivaldi (born in the latter part of the seventeenth century, died 1743), and Tartini (1692-1770). The school continued to flourish till the days of Mozart and Beethoven, and their works and deeds belong mostly to the second period of instrumental music, as their compositions are mainly of the sonata kind, and illustrate harmonic principles. Vivaldi, however, occupied a peculiar position, both as the early representative of the brilliant school of players and as a writer of a great number of concertos for stringed instruments, which served as the models to J. S. Bach for his compositions of that description.

Among early German violinists must be mentioned H. J. F. von Biber (1638-98). He was a famous performer and a worthy composer, and published a set of sonatas as early as 1681.

Handel's position in respect of instrumental music is comparatively unimportant. His most famous instrumental composition is the first set of lessons or suites, which came out in 1720. As types of the suite form they are irregular, and combine features both of Church and chamber sonatas of the Italian kind. The former is illustrated by the number of fugues, which correspond to the canzonas in the early Church sonatas; while interspersed with regular accepted dance tunes are sets of variations, which are unusual features in such works. The next most familiar are his violin sonatas and his organ concertos, which are mainly on Italian lines, and in their way admirable. The least familiar are his many concertos for orchestral instruments, which again are based on Italian models, and do not look as if he had taken much pains with them. Several are made up for occasions out of movements from other works, such as oratorios and operas; and movements have sometimes been used at least three times in different works. They are generally instinct with Handel's usual vigor and breadth, but occupy no very important position in musical history.

The position of J. S. Bach in relation to instrumental music is in strong contrast to that of Handel. Handel wrote most of his instrumental music for occasions, Bach chiefly to find the most perfect artistic expression of his ideas in the various forms of instrumental art existing in his time. He studied the works of all the recognized masters of different schools so minutely and carefully that his works became the sum of all the development hitherto attempted in instrumental music. He always applied himself in accordance with his opportunities. In his younger days, when organist of various towns, he studied organ works and the performances of Buxtehude and Reinken, and Georg Boehm. In his first important post as organist at Weimar, he composed a great part of his famous organ works, and some of his best Church cantatas. When, in 1717, he was made kapellmeister to the Prince of Anhalt-Köthen, who had a special taste for instrumental music, he devoted himself specially to that branch of art, and it was at that time that most of his important work in instrumental music was done.

In all Bach's most successful instrumental compositions his leaning toward the methods of the old school is evident. The elasticity and expansiveness of such old forms as the fugue, the canzona, the toccata, and the early type of fantasia made them more attractive to him than the sonata types, which seemed to limit the range of harmony and modulation. He very rarely attempted anything important in regular sonata form, and when he did the result is not very characteristic of him. He must therefore be regarded rather as the culminating representative of the polyphonic period of instrumental music than the forerunner of the harmonic period, whose representatives, until Beethoven's time, almost ignored both his music and his principles. (See the biography of Johann Sebastian Bach in another section of this series.)

Among composers who distinguished themselves in Germany in the early stages of instrumental music the following must also be remembered: Johann Kuhnau (1677-1722), Bach's predecessor as cantor at the

School of St. Thomas, who led the way in composing both sonatas and suites for clavier; Johann Mattheson (1681-1722), Handel's friend, who wrote suites and several very valuable works on music; August Gottlieb Muffat (born about 1690, died in 1742), who wrote a large quantity of instrumental music of various kinds. And the survey will not be complete without reference to that unique figure the Italian Domenico Scarlatti (1683-1757). He was a son of the famous Alessandro, and in the earlier part of his life followed much the same career as his father, writing operas and Church music. The direction in which his special gifts of harpsichord-playing lay was not fully appreciated by Italians, but after 1721 he settled in Lisbon, and found there and at Madrid a congenial audience among the people of the court; and it was this encouragement which induced him to produce the mass of his harpsichord music. Only thirty pieces were published in his lifetime, under the name of "Exercises for the Gravicembalo"; but altogether he produced several hundreds. In later times they are always spoken of as sonatas, and for their self-dependent nature they are rightly so named, though they only consist of one movement apiece. They are remarkable as being among the first works of the kind in which neither the fugue principle nor dance rhythms are essential features. They are based on very definite ideas and a grouping of keys similar to that found in modern sonata movements of the completely harmonic type; and his manner of repeating phrases again and again has its counterpart in Mozart's works. His devices of execution have been imitated by great writers for the pianoforte up to the most recent times.

CHAPTER XXII

THE PROGRESS OF INSTRUMENTAL MUSIC IN THE EIGHTEENTH CENTURY

The Great School of Italian Violinists—The Clavier Sonata—In Italy—In Germany—Karl Philipp Emanuel Bach—Rise of the Symphony—Alessandro Scarlatti Again—Stamitz—Haydn—Mozart—Nature of Changes in the Latter Half of the Century—Sonatas—Quartets, etc.

IT is from the Italians that our modern style of instrumental music springs. Their inclination for simplicity of design and for easing the labor of attention seems to have led them, first of all people, to cultivate those simple kinds of harmonic contrast upon which the whole system of modern instrumental music rests. The contrapuntal style of art which culminated in the works of Bach and Handel was full of vigor and variety, but it showed signs of being toned down into more easy and obvious moods, in the choral works of even such early Italian masters as Leo, Durante, and Colonna; and this tendency is shown in a more marked degree in instrumental works such as the concertos of Vivaldi. Early in the eighteenth century composers of Italian operas and of Italian instrumental music moved in the same direction. The writers of operas simplified their airs to the utmost to satisfy the taste of their indolent audiences. They made them as much as possible on one uniform pattern, in which simple contrast of the harmonies of tonic and dominant was essential to success; and they planned their overtures and preliminary symphonies on much the same principles.

The great school of Italian violinists, whose artistic aims were much higher and nobler, were insensibly drawn in the same direction, and conveyed their ideas more and more in uniform harmonic designs. Some of them introduced allemandes and gigas, and other movements more characteristic of suites, into their sonatas, but even these soon became more and more harmonic in character and more distinctly uniform in plan. In Corelli (1653-1713) the contrapuntal style was still predominant; in the works of his pupils and immediate successors the balance began to lean toward the harmonic style. Passages founded on chords made more and more frequent appearance in them, and so did those figures of accompaniment which are among its most decisive indications.

The great school of Italian violinists came to its zenith very quickly. Corelli's style was noble and pure, but his technical resources were limited. His immediate successors extended the technical resources of the instrument, and adopted a much more modern style of expression. The eldest of his most famous pupils was Somis (1676-1763), who was born in Piedmont, and became a pupil first of Corelli and afterward of Vivaldi. He settled in Turin, and is considered the head of the Piedmontese school. Among Somis's most famous pupils was the Frenchman Leclair (1697-1764), who began life as a ballet-master and writer of ballet music. He attracted Somis's attention while acting in that capacity at Turin, and under his guidance developed into a great violinist. Nevertheless he had not the good fortune to win any high position as a player, though he left some admirable sonatas of the Italian type.

A more famous pupil of Corelli's was Geminiani (1680-1761), a man of great abilities, but gifted with a temperament so excitable and ill-regulated that it prevented his attaining the position as a performer which his powers seemed to warrant. He, however, immensely enlarged the technique of the instrument, both by his compositions—such as sonatas and concertos—and by his teaching. His compositions were considered extremely difficult, and are not exactly child's-play even now, despite the advances made in technique; and they often present strikingly modern features of harmonization and expression. He also wrote a very valuable book on violin-playing which was far ahead of its time. He went to England in 1714, and spent a great part of his life there. One of his most famous pupils was the Englishman Dubourg (1703-67), who from 1728 was leader of the Viceroy's band in Dublin, and in that capacity led the orchestra on the occasion of the first performance of "The Messiah," in 1741. It was in his house that Geminiani died. Another famous pupil of Corelli's was Locatelli (1693-1764), who was born in Bergamo, settled in manhood at Amsterdam, and made a great reputation as a virtuoso. Some of his compositions are often blamed for artificial effects which are purely eccentric; but he was also capable of writing really admirable music, as his violin sonatas sufficiently prove.

In the same generation appeared, if report speaks truly, one of the greatest violinists of the world. This was Giuseppe Tartini (1692-1770). He was a Florentine by birth, and first studied law, but some matrimonial complications caused him to hide for two years in a monastery at Assisi, during which time he devoted himself to music and taught himself the violin. Soon after leaving the monastery he happened to hear Veracini in Venice, and was so struck with his own shortcomings by comparison that he went to work again for another two years in Ancona. Padua ultimately became his home. He was a man of large feeling and cultivated mind. As a player his style is said to have been particularly noble and expressive, and his sonatas of the Italian type—thoroughly harmonic in plan—are the best of all that fine group of highly artistic works; especially the famous "Trillo del Diavolo," and the one in G minor known as "Didone abandonnata." Tartini was one of the first musicians to draw attention to some acoustical phenomena known as "combination tones," which he called "Terzi tuoni." His influence was mingled with the direct Corellian traditions through his pupil Pugnani (1727-1803), who was also a pupil of Somis.

This famous violinist and teacher was born in Piedmont, and traveled in many European countries giving concerts. He wrote a good deal of violin music, and had a very famous pupil in the person of Viotti (1753-1824). Viotti was also of Piedmont, and studied under Pugnani in Turin. Later he traveled with him, and after that settled for some time in Paris, occupying himself mainly with teaching; for, though an extraordinarily fine performer, he greatly disliked playing in public. When the French Revolution came to its crisis, he crossed over to England, and led at various concerts in London, including some of those at which Haydn's symphonies were first performed. He is particularly notable for the large quantity of violin music he wrote, comprising concertos, quartets, duos, etc., which, though not of any great mark as actual music, are so admirably suited to the nature of the instrument and range over so wide a variety of technique that they are particularly valuable for teaching purposes.

His pupils, Rode (1774-1830) and Baillot (1771-1842), were famous representatives of the French branch of this school, all of whose members occupy an honorable position in the history of art and did most valuable service in furthering it.

In the department of clavier sonata the Italians were not so prominent, since their best composers of instrumental music were more attracted by the singing qualities of the violin. But they exerted much influence on its character and history, partly because the operatic style was more frequently used by composers of clavier sonatas than violin sonatas. The great Italian violinists wrote their sonatas for themselves to play; the writers of clavier music too often wrote their sonatas for fashionable pupils, whose tastes were mainly in the operatic direction. In the generation after the famous Domenico Scarlatti Italy was fairly well represented. The opera composer Galuppi wrote many sonatas for clavier, which have excellent points, and another of the best writers of the early clavier sonatas was Paradisi (1710-92), who was born in Naples, but settled in London, where he brought out a successful opera, "Phaëton," and a set of sonatas for "gravicembalo," as the harpsichord was sometimes called. Among these are some of the best examples of the early sonatas—neat, elegant, finished, and well balanced, and very clear and complete in form. Of less enviable fame is Alberti (died 1740), an amateur and a good singer, who published a set of sonatas which became popular. These contained such a profuse amount of one particular formula of accompaniment that it has been generally known in later years as the Alberti bass.

The clavier sonata was cultivated with greater musical success by the Germans. They, in their turn, were not so highly successful as violinists, and rather preferred the keyed instruments; perhaps because they were less attracted to melody than to harmony. Bach's sons and pupils were distinguished for their works of this order, more especially the second son, Karl Philipp Emanuel (1714-88). Like all the representatives of his generation, he was affected to a certain degree by the Italian influence, springing from the universal popularity of the Italian opera throughout Europe. But he kept more of the artistic vigor and genuineness of his father than any of his brothers and contemporaries. He wrote an immense number of sonatas, which are the best representative works of their kind in the interval between the days of Bach and Handel and the time of Haydn; and it was his sonatas which Haydn specially studied in early years as models for his own efforts in the same line. He also wrote some very curious, and sometimes interesting, experimental works, in a fantasia form, full of abrupt changes of time and strange modulations, and long passages without any bars; also some excellent and vigorous symphonies, the "symphony" being at that time like a prelude or "invention." He contributed, among his other services to art, an invaluable treatise on the way to play keyed instruments. His youngest brother, Johann Christian Bach (1735-82), also made a considerable mark as a composer of instrumental music. He was only fifteen when his father died, and felt his influence least among the brothers. He went early to Italy and was for a time organist of Milan Cathedral. Later he settled in England and obtained a great position, both as a fashionable teacher and as a composer of sonatas, symphonies, and operas. His style was ultra-Italian. He is sometimes called the English Bach, and sometimes the Milanese Bach. He exerted considerable influence on Mozart, who made friends with him when he went to England as a youthful prodigy. Many other composers added to the enormous mass of clavier music without greatly furthering the cause of art, though without discredit to themselves. Some few clung to the traditions of the ancient school, and wrote solid works of the suite order, and toccatas and fantasias and fugues; such as Krebs (1713-80), one of Bach's favorite pupils, and Eberlin (1702-76).

Meanwhile a much larger and more important form of art was progressing to maturity. In the next generation the general progress of mastery of design and instrumental resource advanced the standard of clavier sonatas and brought into being other forms of solo compositions, such as quartets, trios, etc. But the phases of progress which appear in them are all comprised in the progress of the grand form of the symphony, which is the highest and most perfect art-form of modern music.

The ultimate rise of this form of art was in the instrumental movements which were used for the overtures of operas. These were at first very short, and little more than simple and somewhat pointless successions of chords. By the latter part of the seventeenth century they had developed into a group of movements something like the group which at that time frequently constituted sonatas and concertos. In Alessandro Scarlatti's time this "sinfonia avanti l'opera" consisted of either three or four short movements, alternately slow and fast; and the order adopted uniformly by almost all composers soon after was a group of three, consisting of—first, a solid allegro, then a short slow movement, and lastly a light and lively allegro. In course of time these groups of movements began to attract some little attention, and as they improved in musical interest and artistic completeness they were often played apart from the operas. They were found very serviceable in this independent form, and to meet the demand an enormous number were produced by all manner of composers. They were usually scored for a group of eight instruments—that is, the complete set of strings and two pairs of wind instruments, such as two horns and two hautboys, or two horns and two flutes. Sometimes they were published as "overtures in eight parts," as were Abel's and Johann Christian Bach's, and sometimes as "symphonies in eight parts," as were Michael Esser's, Wagenseil's, Richter's, etc. The difference in name implies no difference in the works; as they might or might not have originally been attached to an opera.

The quality of the music was for the most part very flat, common, and empty, and very little attempt was made at either refined phrasing or effects of instrumentation. But every now and then a composer tried to put something genuine into his work, and a most important step was taken by the violinist and composer Stamitz (1719-61). He became leader and conductor of the band of the Elector of Mannheim in the early half of the century, and, being evidently a man of taste, set about making the performance more refined and artistic. Burney speaks of him as discovering the effect of crescendo and diminuendo, "and that the *piano*, which before was chiefly used as an echo, as well as the *forte*, had their shades as well as red and blue in painting." From which it may be divined that in the dreary period between J. S. Bach and Haydn music of this kind had been played in a most slatternly manner. The effect of Stamitz's reform was very great. The Mannheim band won the reputation of being the best in Europe, and kept up its standard of excellence long enough (after Stamitz's death) to exert a powerful influence on Mozart.

In point of form all these early symphonies were distinctly harmonic, representing the same scheme as the movements of modern sonatas, with but trifling deviations. In the hands of German composers the primitive outline of the design was enriched by degrees and developed to a more artistic standard of interest. Karl Philipp Emanuel Bach alone took a line of his own, which was more akin to his father's method in concertos. He commonly adopted some striking principle of effect as his cue, and alternated his subjects irregularly, distributing the modulations on quite different principles from those in his sonata movements, except in so far as the movements made digressions from the starting key, and returned to it finally at the conclusion to establish the unity. His material, at all events in the symphonies of 1772, is immensely more vigorous and animated than that of his contemporaries, and his treatment of instruments original and often ingenious. In the end his manner of dealing with form was abandoned by other composers for the sonata type, which was almost universally adopted. In that respect his younger brother, Johann Christian, stands more in the direct line of the descent of modern symphony, though his musical material is less vigorous. However, he had some excellent ideas of orchestral effect, and similar gifts were shown by the Belgian Gossec (1733-1829), who pushed the cause of instrumental music vigorously in Paris in the middle and latter half of the century.

But all these numerous early writers of symphonies were completely put in the background before the end of the century by Haydn and Mozart. For Prince Esterhazy and his guests Haydn wrote an immense number of symphonies, and found encouragement to make them more artistic, by raising the standard of the ideas and developing the resources of orchestral effect; and by degrees his fame began to spread abroad. But he did not come to the perfection of his mastery of this great form of art till Mozart had come and completed his share of active work and passed away. (See the biography of Haydn in another section of this series.)

In his early days Mozart might have learned from Haydn; in the latter part of his life Haydn learned, willingly, from him. Haydn's fame by about the end of Mozart's life had become universal, and several efforts had been made to induce him to come to England; but he would not desert his master or his duties. In 1790 Prince Esterhazy died, and then Haydn went to London, and the twelve symphonies which are the crowning glory of his life-work were written. His long experience and the example of Mozart lifted him to his highest level, and he produced for Englishmen the series that shows to the full all the natural geniality, humor, vigor, and simple good-heartedness which were his characteristics, in those terms of perfect art which, though not so delicately poised and finished as Mozart's, are fair parallels in point of artistic management.

The nature of the change which had been effected in the symphony since Haydn began to write may be summarized. In his early days it was a type of rather slight artistic importance. The ideas used were generally rather vapid, the design of the movements simple but uninteresting, the group of instruments used small, and the method of their employment blunt and crude. By the time Haydn and Mozart arrived at the climax of their work the group of instruments was much more highly organized, the element of powerful tone in trumpets and drums had been added, and the group of wood-wind was expanded in many cases to the full variety of flutes, oboes, clarinets, and bassoons, which is familiar in the full modern orchestra. Both composers used clarinets rarely, but they knew how to use them with effect. The whole treatment of the orchestral forces had become transformed. In early times the wind instruments were occasionally used for solo purposes, and often did no more than crudely fill up and reinforce the mass of sound; but in their later symphonies they were used with much more independence, as well as with far more coherence and sense of balance.

Then the ideas and subjects themselves had attained to a much more definite character and a much higher degree of beauty and individuality; and the resources of modulation had been applied to enhance and give extra variety and interest to the designs of the movements. The old number of three movements had in many cases been increased to four, and the relation of the movements to one another in point of contrast as well as coherence of style had become artistically perfect. It only remained for Beethoven to apply all these elements of art to the expression of a higher range of ideas and completely to balance the idea and the form in which the idea was expressed, so as to make one of the most perfect forms of art the world has ever seen.

The connection of Haydn and Mozart with the development of the clavier sonata and such forms of solo art as the quartet is of great importance, and the progress they made moves on parallel lines with that of the symphony. In the clavier sonata the improvement made by them was mainly in the matter of design; for before their time a group of only two movements was common, and the design of the movements was at once less concise and less interesting than it had become at the end of the century. But the improvements made were not by any means only owing to them. A very large proportion of their sonatas were of but slight importance, and were probably written for the use of pupils; and a lack of decided musical purpose in them makes them on an average of less historical importance than either Philipp Emanuel Bach's work in their own time or Domenico Scarlatti's in the earlier time.

The progress of the type of works for keyed instruments has been always rather dependent on the feeling for effect which composers, who were also performers, gained from their practical experiences; and Haydn and Mozart, being limited by the nature of the instrument for which they wrote, which was mainly the harpsichord, did not expand the limits of the form so notably as they did in other branches. It was not till the improvement of the pianoforte came about that the new and richer opportunities for effect thereby offered gave a fresh spur to the development of this form of art.

With the quartet for solo strings the case was different; such a form hardly existed before their time, and their work with it was such as almost to complete its artistic maturity in the course of one generation. The growth of the system of harmonic design, and the development of the technique of the violin, were the causes that brought about the perfecting of the quartet and kindred forms of chamber music. Haydn's first quartet was written in 1755. It was of slender proportions and no great interest. But he soon infused vigor and artistic value into his later works of the kind, giving the instruments more and more independence, and finding how to express more with such simple means. He continued composing them all through his life and was actually engaged on one when his powers finally broke down with failing health in old age. Mozart took up the form at a higher level, and though he did not do so much for its earlier development, he set even a nobler seal upon it in the superb group of six which he wrote in 1782 and dedicated to Haydn. It shows how great an advance they represent upon the average standard of the time that they were generally received with dislike even rising to indignation. To later generations they appear as perfect in artistic moderation as they are in mastery of design and skill in the use of the four solo instruments.

There were several other composers who did good service in Haydn's time in the development of the quartet form; notably Boccherini (1740-1805), who was a native of Lucca, and early made a great reputation as a composer and violinist. His facility in composition was extraordinary, and he produced altogether over 360 instrumental compositions, of which a large number are quartets and quintets. The German Dittersdorf (1738-99) was a most voluminous and successful composer in every branch of art.

The progress of modern instrumental music caused it to branch off into various lines, such as concertos, divertimenti, overtures, and numerous varieties of chamber music; but these all developed in their respective lines parallel to the greater and more central types to which they are akin; each received good measure of attention from the greatest composers, and before the end of the century progressed from the cruder types of the early days into most finished and artistic products, the most important phases of development being in all cases the improvement of design, and the more appropriate, independent, and characteristic use of the instruments. The highest phase of all in instrumental music had still to wait till the early years of the nineteenth century for its consummation.

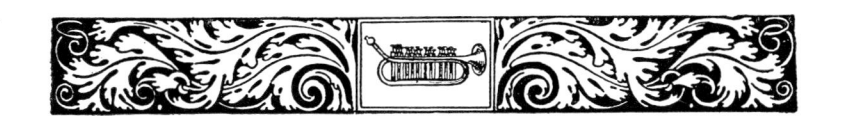

CHAPTER XXIII

OPERA IN THE TIME OF GLUCK AND MOZART, AND IMMEDIATELY AFTER

Reaction from the Formality of Italian Opera—Gluck's Aims—Difference of Mozart's Position—"Idomeneo" a Turning-point—German Aspirations for a National Opera—"Entführung aus dem Serail"—"Nozze di Figaro"—"Don Giovanni"—"Die Zauberflöte"—Progress of French Opera—Spontini.

ABOUT the middle of the eighteenth century the indolence of fashionable audiences and the short-sighted egotism of popular singers had reduced the opera to such a state of monotonous and mechanical dullness that a reaction was inevitable. Slight changes and improvements were frequently attempted by various composers, but the name with which the most definite attempts at general reform are associated is that of Christoph Willibald Gluck (1714-87).

Gluck's position in musical history, particularly with respect to the development of the opera, is very similar to Wagner's in recent times. His indictment against contemporary opera made much the same points as the modern composer's. But he labored under the obvious disadvantage of living at a time when the development of resources, such as are characteristic of regular modern music, was yet slender. The arts of orchestration were only just beginning to be understood, and the arts of dramatic expression of the modern type were both limited in amount and but vague in general character, while the subtler possibilities of modulation were hardly thought of. Like Wagner he was not gifted with musical powers of any very exceptional caliber to start with, nor with any marked individuality, but he developed what he had with exceptional success under the influence of great dramatic and poetic sympathy and insight. His later work is unique in style and in the dignified sincerity with which he treats great and pathetic situations. Even when he had to compromise with popular taste, as in the excessive use of the ballet which was required by French audiences, he succeeded in making it tell as part of the dramatic effect. And the same may be said of his use of arias, which he dispensed with as much as possible in favor of a shorter and more concentrated form of solo, while he raised the recitative whenever possible to a high degree of dramatic interest.

A fact which marks his position well is that he is the earliest opera composer who can arouse the sympathies of a modern audience, in strong contrast to the utterly defunct formality of Hasse, Galuppi, Jomelli, and hundreds of other composers of that class.

Mozart's career as an opera composer overlaps that of Gluck. The early operas of Mozart only serve to illustrate the strength of the Italian influence to which he was subjected. The European fame which Mozart attained when almost a child led to his having plenty of invitations to write operas, and he wrote them in rapid succession.

In his early years he could hardly have heard any operas which were not of the conventional Italian pattern, and indeed very little music of any kind which did not come from the southern source. This Italian influence was paramount through his lifetime, and illustrates the shifting of the highest level of musical composition from the vigorous North German Protestantism of Bach and Handel to the region in which Southern German gaiety and expansiveness adopted the Italian style and forms of music, and ultimately developed them to the very highest point which the new school could attain. The completeness of this change is chiefly owing to Mozart's genius, but it was not till the flood of prosperity which attended his youth had given place to the troubles and crosses of the latter part of his short life that he produced works of sufficient mark to change the course of history. (See the biography of Mozart in another section of this series.)

His unfortunate visit to Paris in 1778 marks the turning-point of his career. On his way there he made a prolonged stay at Mannheim, and became intimate with the traditions of Stamitz and with a group of sincere and earnest-minded musicians, of whom Cannabich was foremost; and here he heard, possibly for the first time, really refined performances of orchestral music, which clearly made a great impression upon him.

He arrived in Paris just in the heat of the excitement about Gluck and his rival Piccinni, and though he stayed several months he never gained any notice, or any opportunity of distinguishing himself except by the production of his Parisian symphony. This was by far the best he had yet written, but in Paris it did not bring him any particular repute, and, failing altogether to get a chance of producing an opera there, he returned to Salzburg in 1779.

His disappointments and troubles in Paris, where as a child he had been wildly petted and caressed, may have had something to do with his being so little affected by the controversy about Piccinni and Gluck. It is clear that Gluck's works made no great impression either upon his style or his methods of composition; but the trials of the journey and the change from the too easy success of his early years to the severe struggle of his maturity seem to have braced him to a higher standard of work. After a pause in opera-writing for some years, he was invited to write an opera for the carnival at Munich in 1781. For this occasion he wrote "Idomeneo," which is the first example of his more mature style. It is particularly noteworthy for the very rich and elastic treatment of the orchestra and for the effective choruses which are introduced. Its success bettered his position somewhat, and was followed by a request from the Austrian Emperor for a genuine German opera.

The Emperor had long had it in mind to make an effort for the cause of National Opera, which had hitherto been in a very backward state. The vigorous efforts Keiser had made at Hamburg had collapsed with his death, and all Germany had been again occupied with Italian operas, frequently written by her own composers. The only German form which had a sustained popularity was that of the "Singspiel" or song-play, a rather insignificant kind of work, consisting mainly of an ordinary theatrical piece interspersed liberally with songs and incidental music, like the English plays of Purcell's time and a little later. The most successful composers of such works (which were chiefly light and lively) were the following: Adam Hiller (1728-1804), who won considerable success with "Die verwandelten Weiber," a version of an English play, "The Devil to Pay," and with "Der Dorfbarbier," "Die Jagd," and many others. Dittersdorf (1739-99) was particularly successful in his "Doctor und Apotheker." Neefe (1748-98), Beethoven's master in Bonn, won success in the same lines, as did also Johann Schenck (1753-1836); and Kauer (1751-1831) is said to have written over 200 examples of this kind. It was for the development of a slender form of this sort into a type more worthy of being nationally representative that Mozart at the invitation of the Austrian Emperor produced his "Entführung aus dem Serail." It came out in 1782, and for once raised a Singspiel into the loftier region of first-rate art. It was the best work of its kind which Mozart had produced, and was too good for "Singspiel" audiences. The result was that Mozart received no encouragement to repeat the experiment for some time, and resumed the writing of Italian operas. His success in the Vienna experiments cannot be said to have been great.

"Figaro" and "Don Giovanni" will always remain the representative examples of Mozart's Italian operas, and are utterly different from the works of his predecessors in every particular which gives musical and artistic value. Mozart was not by nature a reformer like Gluck, neither could he have expounded a systematic theory. His reforms were the direct fruit of spontaneous genius and quickness of perception. In "Figaro" and "Don Giovanni" the plays are not mere excuses for making collections of pretty tunes, but are amusing in themselves; and Mozart's quickness has made the music reinforce every point of the story, even to mere slight details of theatrical business, which he seems to have had in his mind while composing. The human interest in them is immensely assisted by the element of comedy which Mozart illustrated with unsurpassable skill in the style of the Italian opera buffa and the intermezzi. In his hands instrumentation rose for the first time to a condition of mature and complete art. He was the first composer who had a refined feeling for orchestral color, and in opera he used this faculty with a natural ease and readiness; while his general power and mastery of his craft enabled him to develop ensembles and finales to a degree of effectiveness and dramatic relevancy which no previous composer had approached. Gluck surpassed him only in intensity in the situations which were suitable to the peculiar cast of his poetic temperament.

Quite at the end of his career Mozart had one more chance to make a stroke for German art, and the stroke was lastingly effectual. Not long after the successful launch of "Don Giovanni" he was applied to by Schikaneder—a man who combined the gifts of actor, playwright, manager, and man of enterprise—to set a fairy play which he had put together, and believed would attract the genuinely German masses. This was "Die Zauberflöte" (The Magic Flute), a play which is certainly not easily intelligible to the uninitiated, but contained enough mystery and magic and opportunities for scenic display to attract a German audience. Mozart set it to music in a manner which differs to a considerable degree from all his earlier works, as much of it is on a higher level. The peculiarity of the play has hindered its popularity in other countries, but Schikaneder rightly gauged its fitness for a thorough German audience, and the great success it ultimately won may fairly be said to be the definite starting-point of the successful development of the modern German music-drama, of which Weber, Beethoven, and Wagner are the foremost representatives.

A few contemporaries of Mozart deserve record for creditable and occasionally brilliant work in the operatic line. Sarti (1729-1802, organist of Faenza, 1748) produced his first opera, "Pompeo in Armenia," there in 1751; his best opera is said to have been "Giulio Sabino." He met Mozart in Vienna in 1784 and spoke of him afterward as a musical barbarian. Paisiello (1741-1815) belonged to the school of Naples, where he was a pupil of Durante. His music was elegant and successful, and was specially admired by Napoleon. He wrote a "Barbiere di Seviglia," which was so popular that when Rossini endeavored to get his setting performed the attempt was considered nothing less than presumption on his part and was at first vigorously hissed. Paisiello wrote in all ninety-four operas. Sacchini (1734-86) was also one of the Neapolitan school, and a pupil of Durante. He traveled to England and also to Paris, where he became very popular. His best operas were "Olimpiade," "Dardanus," "Œdipus," and "Tigrane."

The most brilliant member of this group was Cimarosa, born near Naples, 1749, and a member of the Neapolitan school. He early won reputation by his lively intermezzi. His first opera was "Le Stravaganze del Conte," 1772, his most famous was the "Matrimonio Segreto," one of the best and most brilliant opera buffas ever written. It came out first in Vienna in 1792, the year after Mozart died. His most successful serious opera was "Gli Orazii e Curiazii." He lived till 1801.

Salieri (1750-1825), Gluck's pupil, is most familiarly remembered for the reputation he won for scheming to prevent Mozart's success, but it may be remembered as a set-off that he acted to a certain extent as Schubert's master, and was held in some respect by Beethoven, who actually took lessons from him. He superintended most of the music of the court and opera of Vienna, and wrote many successful operas.

The Belgian Grétry (1741-1813) also requires notice as a representative of the Parisian section of opera writers. He was a poor musician, but made success through a certain gift of tune and expression, and a delicate sense of humor. Born at Liège, he went to Rome for musical study, and became the despair of his master. But he was quite confident of himself, and in 1767 applied to Voltaire for a libretto, which was declined. He was the first representative composer of operas comiques, and wrote some fifty operas for Paris, of which "Le Huron" was the first (1768) and "Le tableau parlant," "Zemir et Azor," and "Richard" were the best.

Of Mozart's junior contemporaries, the most notable was Cherubini (1760-1842). He was brought up in the atmosphere of Italian music, but his disposition caused him to take a more serious view of the art than most of his fellow-countrymen, and this has given him a position which is quite unique among them. His views were so extremely severe that he appeared pedantic even to Mendelssohn; but, notwithstanding, his works have a genuine freshness and vitality. He began opera-writing with "Quinto Fabio" in 1780. He went to England in 1784, and brought out some operas there, and finally settled in Paris in 1788. The first of his operas which won permanent fame was "Lodoiska," which came out in 1791. The light opera "Les deux journées" came out in 1800, and the famous "Médée" in 1797. These two represent extremes of different character, as the former is sparkling and bright and the latter a very severe tragedy. In both he succeeded equally well. His sense for dramatic effect was strong, but was always kept within bounds by a very sensitive taste, and his orchestration is often admirable. He was so much revered by musicians in Paris that in old age he was looked upon as a sort of autocratic censor.

Méhul (1763-1817) was a composer who held a great position in Paris about the same time. He was looked upon as the foremost French composer of the Revolution period. His best work, "Joseph," was his last, and came out in 1807. He had a genuine feeling for dramatic effect of a refined quality, and his orchestration was good.

Another composer of more striking caliber was Gasparo Spontini. He was born at Majolati in 1774, and educated at Naples. His first opera, "I puntigli delle donne," was brought out in Rome in 1796. His early works were in the light Neapolitan style. He went to Paris in 1803, but did not make the mark he hoped for in the light style, and therefore changed his tactics completely for a style of the utmost grandioseness. "La Vestale" was finished in 1805, and first performed in 1807. The excellent libretto by Jouy was much in its favor, and the music is also remarkably fine. Spontini here displayed a great gift for rich orchestration, and a sense of broad and large effect, and a mastery of resource combined with a very considerable power of dramatic expression which give him a high place among composers. "La Vestale" thoroughly deserved the estimation in which it has since been held all over Europe. He followed it up by "Fernand Cortez," which is on much the same grandiose lines, in 1809. He was made conductor at the Italian Opera in Paris in 1810, and brought out Mozart's "Don Giovanni" for the first time in that city. His next large work was "Olympia," which occupied him many years, but did not succeed in Paris.

When he went to Berlin to manage operatic affairs as kapellmeister and general director of the music of the court of King Frederick William, he remodeled "Olympia" and brought it to a hearing there in 1821 with triumphant success. Unluckily for Spontini, Weber's "Der Freischütz" came out soon after in Berlin and took such a hold of the hearts of Germans with its thoroughly Teutonic flavor, that Spontini's supremacy was checked. He brought out several more operas, such as "Nurmahal" (1822), "Alcidor" (1825), "Agnes von Hohenstaufen" (1829), but by degrees he became very unpopular, partly owing to his autocratic disposition, and after a period of tension, in which he seems to have shown some force of character, he finally left Berlin in 1842 and returned to Italy, where he died in 1851. He was a commanding and conspicuous figure, and his works have grand and impressive qualities. They belong to the class of French grand opera, and stand midway between the statuesque beauty of Gluck and the pomp of Meyerbeer, who was his successor in Berlin.

CHAPTER XXIV

THE PROGRESS OF INSTRUMENTAL MUSIC TO BEETHOVEN AND HIS IMMEDIATE SUCCESSORS

Rise of Pianoforte Music—Clementi—Cramer—Other Prominent Composers of Instrumental Music—Beethoven's Early Circumstances—Predominance of Sonatas among his Works—His Characteristics—Enlarging Principles of Design—Characteristic Expression—Programme—Hummel—Weber—Schubert—Spohr.

WHILE Haydn and Mozart were applying their great powers to the advancement of the highest forms of instrumental music, some very valuable work was being done in various subordinate branches by other composers and performers, of considerable though less comprehensive powers. The prominent position taken by the pianoforte in modern music gives special importance to the work of Muzio Clementi, who was the first composer to show a clear perception of the style of performance required by that instrument as distinguished from the old harpsichord. Till he applied his mind to the subject composers had mainly kept to the quiet gliding style suitable to the older instrument, and hardly realized the effects and contrasts which were obtainable by the more forcible and energetic treatment which was invited by the use of hammers instead of jacks as a means of producing the sound.

Clementi was born in Rome in 1752. He was solidly grounded in contrapuntal studies, and came before the public as a composer, with a mass, at the age of fourteen. He was brought to England by a rich amateur while still quite young, and made his first appearance in London in 1777; and with the exception of a few professional tours through Europe he remained in England for the rest of his life. He was of a practical turn of mind, and, besides establishing a very good position as a teacher and a performer and a conductor at the opera, he founded a pianoforte business, which still exists. He wrote a very large quantity of sonatas of very solid and artistic quality, but his best known work is the "Gradus ad Parnassum," a collection of his most excellent pianoforte studies, which he completed in 1817, when about sixty-five years old. He survived till 1832. The comprehensive quality and vigor of his work, and its perfect fitness for the pianoforte, justify his being called the father of modern pianoforte music.

Among his pupils the most important was J. B. Cramer, whose "Studies" hold so honorable a position among works of their class. They are more genial than Clementi's, though not so masculine. Cramer, like his master, was a thorough musician, and his insight into the requirements of the pianoforte is remarkably acute. He came of a family of musicians; and both his grandfather, as flute-player, and his father, as violinist, were members of the famous Mannheim band. He himself was born in Mannheim in 1771, but was brought to England by his father when one year old, and settled permanently in that country, where he also founded a music business, and held a distinguished position as a pianist and a teacher. He died in 1858.

Another famous pupil of Clementi was the Irishman John Field (1782-1837), who was a very able pianist, and wrote a large quantity of pianoforte music, of which his nocturnes still enjoy the appreciation of musicians. He settled in St. Petersburg. Among those who did good service in developing the resources of the pianoforte was J. L. Dussek, born in Bohemia in 1761. He began his career as an organist, but ultimately became one of the greatest pianists of his time and enjoyed a European fame. He was for a time a pupil of Karl Philipp Emanuel Bach's, and wrote a large quantity of sonatas in a graceful and fluent style, which exerted no little influence upon some later composers for the instrument. He lived till 1812. His contemporary Daniel Steibelt had a considerable vogue as a player and composer and fashionable teacher in Paris and London successively. The date of his birth was 1755; he died 1823.

Among the prominent representatives of instrumental music of this intermediate stage, Ignaz Pleyel deserves mention. He was born in Austria in 1757, became one of Haydn's favorite pupils, and showed such good promise in early years as to have his quartets highly spoken of by Mozart. He wrote a large quantity of symphonies and chamber music, went to England for a time in 1791, simultaneously with Haydn's first visit with Salomon, and ultimately settled in Paris, where he founded a successful pianoforte factory. He died in 1831. Madame Pleyel, the famous pianist, was his daughter-in-law.

A composer who enjoyed great popularity for a time was Adalbert Gyrowetz, born in Bohemia in 1763. He studied in Prague and then went to Vienna, where he received friendliness and encouragement from Mozart. His reputation was so good that he was engaged as a composer by Salomon at the same time with Haydn. He ultimately settled in Vienna and lived till 1850. So that having been born but a few years after Mozart, and having known him and Haydn intimately, he survived Mendelssohn and might have heard several of Wagner's operas. He also survived his own popularity. He wrote a large quantity of operas and cantatas and an immense number of symphonies and quartets. The symphonies are on a larger scale and more freely and intelligently scored than those of the previous generation, but they have not the distinction and artistic completeness of Haydn's and Mozart's, though they were sufficiently good for some of them to be passed off as Haydn's in Paris, till Gyrowetz went there and established his title to their authorship.

A family which did distinguished service in the cause of modern instrumental music was that of the Rombergs. Bernhard Romberg (1767-1841) was one of the earliest of great German cello players, and did a great deal to advance the technique of that instrument. He wrote quartets and a number of cello concertos, which are so admirably suited for the instrument as to be still valuable for teaching purposes. His cousin, Andreas Romberg (1767-1821), was a famous violinist and composer. He began his successful career as a player at the age of seven, and produced in the course of his life a great variety of compositions, such as operas, cantatas, symphonies, and quartets, which had wide popularity and no inconsiderable merit.

The greatest representative of pure instrumental music is Ludwig van Beethoven (1770-1827). His youth had none of the opportunities nor the brilliancy of Mozart's, and he developed slowly, in circumstances which forced him to get such musical education as he could by his own exertions. The music performed during his youth was not of the highest class, though of fair average merit of the time. Under the well-known theorist Albrechtsberger, after previous study, he worked energetically at counterpoint, fugue, and canon, with the result that his master declared him to be a very unsatisfactory and unpromising pupil. His relations with his fellow-musicians were not very friendly, for he thought poorly of most of them and did not disguise his opinion. But he won many ardent friends among aristocratic amateurs. The opportunities of Beethoven's youth had been singularly meager. He could have heard but very little choral music of good quality, and though his experiences were more rich in the line of operatic music, he could have heard very few operas that were better than second rate till he was nearly twenty; and his knowledge of orchestral works was equally limited, both through his living at Bonn and by the obvious fact that hardly any first-rate and mature symphonies existed before the year 1786. His musical education was also to all appearances very backward, but that may possibly have been a minor drawback, as he was forced to develop his own powers and find out his own way in art, and was thereby strengthened in individuality and character. (See the biography of Beethoven in another section of this series.)

The most obvious feature of his compositions as a whole is the immense preponderance of works in the form of sonatas. At the beginning of his career he published thirty consecutive works, every one of which is in sonata form; and in the whole list of his works—including masses, songs, variations, fugues, cantatas, and an opera—more than one-half are of the same order. The explanation lies in the fact that the artistic progress of music for nearly two hundred years had centered round the development of harmonic forms, of which the sonata is the highest type; and Beethoven, as the most highly gifted musician of his time, endowed with the keenest feeling for design and expression, naturally adopted the form which afforded him the richest opportunities; and circumstances being in every way favorable, he carried the treatment of the sonata to the highest perfection of which that form of art seems capable. He infused into it a new element of meaning and expression, without losing hold of the perfect balance of the design, and he immensely enriched and widened the scope of art in all directions to make room for the force and variety of his ideas; so that in the end the lover of strong impressions finds all he longs for, while the worshiper of abstract perfection in art rests satisfied that Beethoven was essentially a master of form.

In his early period, up to Opus 50, the influence of the style of the previous generation is more obviously apparent. This period, lasting till about his thirty-third year, comprises his first two symphonies in C and D, three concertos, the well-known septet, and a number of fine sonatas, such as that in C sharp minor, Opus 27, that in A flat with the variations, the remarkably rich and interesting one in D minor, and the superb "Kreutzer" sonata for pianoforte and violin. In some few of these, such especially as the last two, he gives a foretaste of his finest qualities; a variety and a scope, and a power for manipulating his design which no man ever showed before. After Opus 50 he passed into a new and more emotional and vigorous manner—the style of his best and happiest years. The mass of his best known and best loved works succeeded each other in rapid succession. They form a remarkable list, even if we consider only those representing his most important achievements up to about the year 1810, when he was forty years old.

Meanwhile he had been gradually passing under the influence of the two greatest trials of his life, which permanently affected his moods and character. The first and most obvious was his deafness. The other was the trouble with his nephew, which brought upon him lawsuits and many vexations. His work was for a time seriously interfered with, and constant worries caused him to become more morose and isolated than ever. His deafness reacted upon his art and more than ever intensified his originality and depth of thought, while his other troubles intensified his earnestness and style of utterance. To these two influences may be chiefly attributed the final change of his style, which began to be apparent soon after Opus 90 in such works as his E minor sonata (Opus 91) and his F minor quartet, and found its highest expression in the last five sonatas, the last quartets from Opus 127 onward, the great mass in D, and the final and greatest triumph of his life, the "Choral" symphony (Opus 125).

Beethoven was impelled to widen out and enrich his scheme in every respect. His thorough appreciation of the pianoforte, with its new opportunities of effect, derived in a measure from the important adjunct of the pedal, caused him to adopt, in writing for that instrument, a much more powerful style, and to employ means which at once widened the range of sound and produced a far greater volume of it than had ever been heard or thought of before; while his instinct for harmonic variety and the effects which are obtainable by new and striking progressions and subtle use of modulation enhanced to the highest degree his power of expression. In his symphonies he adopted from the first a larger group of instruments than his predecessors—invariably including clarinets with oboes as an additional element of color—and he soon found out how to use the various instruments, wind, strings, and drums, with more genuine independence, and with more real sense of their respective characteristics, and a more perfect blending into one complete whole than his predecessors had done. In grouping his movements, too, he soon became more free than they had been. At first he adopted a scheme of four movements, but soon found that much was to be gained by varying their order, number, and character. In some of his finest sonatas he adopted a group of three movements, and even sometimes reduced it to two, as better adapted to give individual character to the complete work; while he sometimes extended the scheme to five movements, as in the "Pastoral" symphony. But he set his impress equally upon all the movements His first allegros became more definite in character, and more closely knit by the use of short incisive figures instead of long melodious subjects; his slow movements passed out of the phase of being like the old opera arias into the most romantic and impassioned forms, full of human feeling and even dramatic effect.

His last movements grew more serious and solid and dignified than had been usual with earlier composers, while in changing the minuet movement (which had represented the dance type in a graceful and uniform manner) into the scherzo, he gave to art one of the most vivid, characteristic, and effective of all modern art-forms—one eminently calculated to express his sense of humor, fun, wit, irony, and subtlety of thought; and at the same time supplying a much more complete counterpoise to the sentiment of the slow movement than had before existed in the group of sonata movements. The slow introductory movements he sometimes adopted were quite a new departure in art. Previous to his time such movements had been extremely limited in range of harmony, and mainly formal in character. He entirely transformed them by introducing remarkable modulations and interesting ideas and devices of form; and sometimes developed them to a high pitch of importance. The introductions to the "Kreutzer" sonata, to the symphonies in B flat and A, and to the overtures to "Leonore" Nos. 2 and 3 are indeed among the most wonderful of his achievements. In the internal organization of the larger movements a like power of expansion is shown in the wonderful episodes, and the unexpected digressions (which are always perfectly coherent to the design), and the novelty and interest and wide range of his codas.

His tendency toward direct and decided expression is marked by his frequent adoption of a recognizable purpose in composing his works, as illustrated most remarkably in the "Eroica" symphony, in the "Pastoral" symphony, and in the two sonatas which bear distinct names. In the C minor symphony and the seventh in A an equally strong impression of something behind the music is apparent, and in all these respects he became the first notable exponent of the modern tendency toward what is sometimes called programme —which really means illustrating by music some definite conception, or circumstances which have a poetic or dramatic import external to the music itself. But with him the work never depends upon the programme for its effect, and he is careful to avoid attempting to paint scenes in musical figures; and some of those movements which are most obviously founded on an idea external to music are specially perfect and beautiful in form. He understood art too well by instinct to be misled into thinking that mere force, or vehemence, or definiteness of expression can make good works of art; and the greatness of his effects consists even more in the perfect management of the relative parts of his entire works, and their bearing upon one another, than in the mere ideas themselves.

His methods of composition were also very different from those of his predecessors, except J. S. Bach, for he rewrote and remodeled everything over and over again. Even his ideas were recast and reconsidered many times over before he was satisfied with them, and the contents of his numerous sketch-books bear eloquent testimony to his patience and self-criticism. His methods of work were much more like those of *littérateurs,* poets, painters, and sculptors than those usual with musical composers, and his works accordingly bear the marks of a higher degree of concentration and a wider range of expression and design; and the sum of the result is the richest and most perfect form of abstract instrumental art which exists in the whole range of music.

Contemporary with Beethoven, but representing an earlier state of art in many ways, was Johann Nepomuk Hummel (1778-1837). He had the great advantage not only of being Mozart's pupil, but of living for two years in his house. In his prime he was considered the most brilliant of German pianists, and had a very high reputation as a composer. He had a great talent for the ornamental part of music, and produced many large works which have a certain elegance and finish, but comparatively little substance. He exercised considerable influence upon many composers for the pianoforte in the succeeding generations, including Chopin.

The composers who came after Beethoven tended more and more to aim at direct expression of ideas external to music, but they immediately began to lose hold of full mastery and control of design. This is strongly noticeable even among his junior contemporaries.

Karl Maria von Weber (1786-1826) is chiefly important through the position he occupies as the first representative of true German national opera, in spirit and in method; but his instrumental music also has a position of some importance in history. He had great gifts, considerable sense of effect, and a highly strung and imaginative temperament. His sonatas illustrate the tendencies of modern instrumental music, in the skillful use of pianoforte effects, the scope afforded for the display of virtuosity, and the predominance of sentiment over closeness and concentration of design. In such things Weber shows the insight of the performer rather than the musician, of the elocutionist rather than the genuine orator; but his methods and treatment of the instrument undoubtedly impressed very distinguished composers in later times, and his influence upon art in that respect cannot be gainsaid. His impulse for adopting a definite external idea is most strongly emphasized in his "Concertstück" for pianoforte and orchestra, written in 1821, which was avowedly written to illustrate a fanciful episode about a knight and a lady in the days of the Crusades.

His genius shone at its brightest in the management of orchestral effect, as illustrated most happily in his famous overtures to "Der Freischütz," "Oberon," and

"Euryanthe." In his use of the characteristic qualities of tone of different instruments to illustrate special dramatic or poetic ideas he is one of the foremost of modern composers. He specially delights in things weird and magical—the music of the "Wolf's Glen," the magic music of fairies. In these things he expresses a trait of the Teutonic disposition, and also shows strongly the influence of the theater. Here again it is perceptible that the influence which raises him to his best achievement is a conception external to music, and not the spontaneous musical impulse such as commonly impelled composers before Beethoven's time.

The position of Franz Schubert (1797-1828) in the history of art is centered mainly upon his songs; but his position as a writer of instrumental music is by no means insignificant. His opportunities in youth were even less favorable than Weber's. His natural impulse was to look for external inspiration in poems, and under such influence he was at his best, and produced magnificent songs in quite early years. His models in instrumental music were not of the best, and his early efforts in the line of symphonies are comparatively tame; but as his experience of music enlarged, he found the way to express his ideas more completely in instrumental form. He was always uncertain in the management and control of design, but ideas of every kind were always ready in profusion, and take the hearer with them by qualities which are more direct and more in consonance with modern spirit than such purely artistic considerations as beauty and balance of design.

Of all great composers Schubert is the one who depends most on the actual attractiveness of his musical ideas and his musical personality; and these qualities have exercised great influence upon many composers of high rank in later times. The charm lies far more in his spontaneity than in his power of development or mastery of form. Judged from the abstract point of view as absolute music, his works of the sonata order are often obviously redundant and imperfect in design and bear cutting without much injury. Schubert in his profusion attacked all branches of instrumental music, and the best of his works of this kind belong to his later years, when his experiences had been enriched by hearing more first-rate music, such as some of Beethoven's most inspiring works. He set his seal upon this branch of art especially by his last two symphonic works—the delightful fragment known as the "Unfinished Symphony" in B minor and the grand symphony in C major. These are the first orchestral works on a large scale in which his genuine characteristic musical nature shows itself, not only in the ideas and the manner of treatment, but even in the scoring—which is quite modern in its effect. The B minor fragment was written in 1822, and therefore preceded Beethoven's Ninth symphony, while the C major symphony was written in 1828, after the appearance of that immense work; and the influence of Beethoven here appears most strongly, alike in the vigorous and full treatment of a large orchestra, in the characteristic scherzo, and in the romantic tendency of almost every movement. Of his other instrumental works the most impressive are the "Rosamunde" *entr'actes,* the quartets in D minor and G, the quintet in C, the octet, the pianoforte trio in B flat, and some of the sonatas. But it is also noticeable, as a sign of the times, that among the most permanently interesting are works which are definitely outside the circle of sonatas, such as the great fantasia in C, and some of the small impromptus and "Moments musicaux."

Ludwig (or Louis) Spohr (1784-1859), owing to the length of his career and the late date of the appearance of his most important works, seems to belong to a later generation than Weber and Schubert, although he was born before either of them. He showed his powers as a violinist very early, and, combining natural aptitude with singular perseverance, he rightfully won the reputation of being the greatest German violinist before he had long passed the years of his youth. His first large composition, a symphony in E flat, was soon followed by works in almost every form—operas, oratorios, cantatas, concertos, quartets, and symphonies. He wrote effectively, though not always judiciously, for the voice, but his chief importance lies in his connection with violin music and orchestral music, and among his firmest titles to fame is his invaluable "Violin School."

In the matter of style he was quite out of sympathy with Beethoven, adopting a chromatic and sentimental manner which is curiously at variance both with his own personal character and the best spirit of his age. But his impulse was as much to seek inspiration and motive external to purely musical considerations as Beethoven, and he had a very predominant taste for new experiments.

Spohr's labors have a very wide range, but he is historically most important in matters connected with the violin and the orchestra. The perfection of his instinct for his own instrument gives his compositions for it very high technical value; while his skilful orchestration marks a distinct advance in the use of variety of color and effect of a modern kind. The influence of Mozart is more apparent than that of any other master, but his sentiment and his use of varieties of color for distinct ends are essentially modern. He was a man of strong character, and his reputation in his lifetime was extraordinarily high; but his style was too deficient in genuine breadth and nobility to exert much permanent influence on his successors.

CHAPTER XXV

MODERN INSTRUMENTAL MUSIC

Berlioz—Design—Programme—Instrumentation—Mendelssohn—Chopin—Polish and Parisian Influences—Schumann—Teutonic Disposition—Virtuosity—Liszt—Other Representatives of Instrumental Music.

THE most notable composers who were born in the early years of the nineteenth century illustrate in a marked manner the general tendencies of artistic progress in instrumental music since Beethoven. Hector Berlioz, born 1803; Mendelssohn, 1809; Chopin, 1809; Schumann, 1810; Liszt, 1811; Henselt, 1814; Stephen Heller, 1815; Raff, 1822; Rubinstein, 1830, all show a disposition to drop the sonata form, and to seek new principles of procedure and greater variety of design, to meet the requirement of new types of musical ideas, and new ways of looking at music.

The works of the first member of this group seem to emphasize most forcibly the tendencies toward "programme" and independence of form. But it must be observed that the French had never shown any aptitude for pure instrumental music, and needed the stimulus of external ideas to excite them to musical utterance. The stage was their natural field of artistic activity, and the only music they had succeeded in at all conspicuously was in some way connected with it, either as actual operas or as ballet tunes. The fact that Berlioz wrote large instrumental works on theatrical lines is, therefore, less significant historically than the fact that a programme was so frequently adopted by Teutonic composers. All the traditions of classical art were distasteful to his eager and impatient temperament. He regarded them as superfluous, and sought to employ music of the largest caliber, with the most profuse resources of the orchestra, to express stories and human circumstances which struck him as likely to be effective and interesting in a musical dress; and he hoped to attain, by following the working and sequence of the extra-musical ideas, an orderliness and aspect of design which should satisfy the mind as well as the classical types of form and development which he gladly dispensed with.

His gifts were strongest in the direction of rhythm and color. His excitable disposition was particularly susceptible to the qualities of tone of instruments, and he set himself deliberately to develop remarkable effects of instrumentation, and succeeded so well that it has given him a unique place among the foremost representatives of modern art. The masters he worshiped were Beethoven—for the force of his expression—and Gluck—for his dramatic power and insight. He was also under the influence of Spontini to some extent, and, in a lesser degree, of Mozart. But he was more influenced by the style of their utterances than by their artistic principles. He always depended upon the stimulus of a strong programme for his guide in action. (See the biography of Berlioz in another section of this series.)

Though Mendelssohn's instrumental works are much less conspicuously of the programme order, his position as an essentially classical composer intensifies the inferences which his attitude in instrumental music suggests. Of all his numerous and popular solo works for the pianoforte and organ, hardly one belongs essentially to the sonata order. He infused new life into the elastic and perennial forms of prelude and fugue, both for organ and pianoforte, and he produced one admirable example of the variations form in the "Variations sérieuses" (1841). He was conspicuously successful in what he called "Songs without Words," which are short characteristic pieces in various forms, written at different times in his life from 1830 till the end. He was equally successful in organ works, and it is specially significant that most of those which are called sonatas are so only in name, and rarely have anything of the typical sonata character or principle of design about them. He was less successful in his capriccios and fantasias for the pianoforte, for in them his taste for brilliancy is shown at the expense of the musical material. The same gifts of brilliancy are applied, with much happier results, in his concertos for pianoforte and orchestra in G minor (1831) and D minor (1837), and in the concerto for violin and orchestra (1844), which is one of the very finest of all his works. In pure orchestral music he appears at his best in the music for the "Midsummer Night's Dream." Though comprising a certain quantity of vocal music, the most important parts of this work are the instrumental movements, such as the overture, scherzo, and notturno, which are among the most characteristically effective of modern orchestral works.

For all his most successful symphonies he adopted distinctive names. He wrote a great number in youth which have not survived. Only the thirteenth, in C minor, is occasionally played. The earliest which has maintained any hold on the musical world is the "Reformation" symphony, in which he endeavored to carry out something of a programme by the use of such features as the famous formula for the "Amen," used at the Roman Church in Dresden, and familiar to musical audiences in later days by its use in Wagner's "Parsifal"; and also by the use of the famous chorale of Luther, "Ein' feste Burg."

Mendelssohn was a classicist by nature, but even he fell in with the tendencies of his time; and though he was too wise to think weakness of design could be compensated for by programme or obviousness of meaning, he nevertheless in these most important cases allowed his inspiration to be impelled and nourished by a definite purpose.

The branch of chamber music is the one in which the traditions of the sonata persist most conspicuously. In combinations of pianoforte with other solo instruments, composers seem to find opportunities to do something new in that form which are less attainable in other branches of art. Mendelssohn was very successful in that line, and his trios for pianoforte and strings in C minor and D minor are among the most universally popular of all works of that class. His quartets, quintets, and octet for strings, though sometimes rather orchestral in style, are also favorite examples of that refined class of art.

Chopin was born less than a month after Mendelssohn. It illustrates the branching out of music into many different forms and styles that men so preëminent in art and yet so different in musical character should have been born so near together. Chopin is one of the most conspicuous representatives of the most modern type of music, for he is thoroughly independent of the conventions of classicism in art; but he is so far from being inartistic on that account, that the perfection of delicacy with which he applies all the richest resources of technique to the expression of his thoughts is almost without parallel. Moreover, though so specially notable as a master of the technique of performance, he really has musical thoughts which are worth expressing, and a genuine musical personality; and even the ornamental parts of his work— which form so important a feature in the stock in trade of virtuosi—in his case generally have real musical significance and beauty.

A great deal of the individuality of Chopin's music comes from the race to which he belonged and his early surroundings. His native country, Poland, had a long tradition of misfortune to look back upon; and nations in such circumstances commonly relieve their feelings in poetry and pathetic song. It appears to intensify the instinct for things imaginative, as well as racial characteristics. Chopin, who was born near Warsaw, imbibed the spirit of the Polish national music and dancing from early years, though their influence did not bear full fruit till experience had matured his powers. He began his career as a pianist, and before he was twenty had almost surpassed all rivals. He journeyed to Vienna and other musical centers, giving concerts, and finally settled in Paris in 1831, just at the time when that city was fermenting with romanticism in literature and art.

His compositions up to that time had comprised the set of studies, Opus 10, which are undoubtedly the finest examples of their kind ever written for any instrument, and some of the preludes, which are among the most interesting and poetical of his works. He had also written two concertos for his own use and a few movements representing or reflecting the style of the national dance music. But the mass of his mature and completely characteristic music was produced after he settled in Paris. Closer contact with musicians of high attainments, opportunities of hearing more music, and the romantic and intellectual ardor of the time widened his horizon and raised his standard, and he rapidly enriched the art with his great chivalric polonaises, the romantic ballades, the poetical nocturnes, the brilliant scherzos, the interesting and original sonatas, and many other types of very characteristic art. He uttered his thoughts with complete certainty only through the medium of the pianoforte. He never became master of orchestration even sufficiently to write the accompaniments to his concertos with due effect. But his work for the pianoforte is so marvelously perfect in its adaptation to the idiosyncracies of the instrument, that it beccmes historically important on that ground alone. His work is not often great in conception, or noteworthy in design, but it is the spontaneous expression of a poetical, refined, and sensitive temperament, and his style has exercised an almost universal influence upon writers of pianoforte music since his time, except in the case of a few specially strong-natured composers.

The very next year after Chopin, Robert Schumann was born. He represents a phase of music as characteristically modern as Chopin's, but of different quality. The points where the two composers touch is in the romantic and poetical character of their ideas, the warmth of color and richness of tone, and the strongly marked diversity of method from the old sonata type. They differ in depth of feeling and intellectuality. Chopin is at once lighter and more quickly sensitive— combining the poetry of the Pole with the alertness of a Parisian. Schumann is more reflective and intellectual, and saturated with Teutonic earnestness. Schumann indeed was the higher type of man, of purer aims, though of less brilliant skill. He fell under the influence of the romantic movement in German literature—especially under the spell of Jean Paul Richter —and he transmitted the figurative and metaphorical methods of this literature to his music.

Schumann's work was divided into a series of definite periods, as had been the case with Bach. He devoted himself at first mainly to writing sets of short and vivid pianoforte pieces, of wonderful variety of character and form. With these were interspersed a few works on a larger scale. In all lines he endeavored to find new and more elastic methods of applying musical art to the purposes of expression; and most of his pieces have definite names and special meanings, which are sometimes indicated by a verse of poetry. In the year 1840 he devoted himself mainly to songwriting. That was the year of his marriage with Clara Wieck. In the following year he wrote several symphonic works. The first which can be said maturely to represent him is that in B flat. It is the one of all his works which is most nearly on classical lines. In the second he tried experiments in new lines, and endeavored to unify the whole work by using characteristic figures throughout. It was subjected to much alteration before it was finally published as symphony No. 4, in 1851. In the year 1842 he occupied himself mainly with chamber music, and produced two of his most popular works—the pianoforte quintet and the quartet in E flat, besides string quartets and other examples of the same order of art.

In later years Schumann addressed himself to choral music and completed the series of his great instrumental compositions with the fine symphony in C major (1845-46) and the one in E flat, known as the "Rhenish" (1850), and the music to "Manfred," the overture to which is one of his finest and most complete orchestral works. But fine and noble in spirit as these are, he set his seal most effectually upon works in which the pianoforte takes the most prominent position; and especially those in which he endeavored to develop a new scheme or method of artistic procedure, and to use music as a vehicle for poetical thought. Much of the music of his later years suffers from the gradual increase of disease in the brain which caused his death.

It would be hard to find a more conspicuous contrast to Schumann than Franz Liszt, who came into the world but a year after him. He is mainly important in musical history as the representative of the most advanced standard of pianoforte technique, and the most brilliant virtuoso of his instrument who ever lived. He, as it were, summed up the labors of all previous players and inventors of devices of performance, and crowned them by his own special gift for contriving new and yet more brilliant effects. In his original compositions he was noteworthy as a prominent representative of radical theories for devising new principles of design and development; abandoning deliberately the classical principles of form, and trying to make movements intelligible by employing characteristic figures in a manner like the use of *Leitmotiven* by Wagner in music-dramas. His most important contributions to art in the line of programme music are the "Faust" and "Dante" symphonies and the thirteen symphonic poems, which are specially remarkable on the score of orchestral effect; for his sense in that direction is of a kindred nature to his instinct for pianoforte effect. His pianoforte concertos also are remarkable for their brilliancy and novelty of treatment, and so are his pianoforte studies. Although a great proportion of his works consists of transcriptions of songs, opera airs, and national tunes, these are noteworthy for the truly extraordinary and intricate skill with which the resources of the instrument are applied.

In the same year with Liszt was born Ferdinand Hiller, who was an efficient pianist, and a successful writer of pianoforte music, symphonies, and other kinds of music, of artistic but not very characteristic quality. He was a great friend of Mendelssohn's, but long survived him. He died in 1885.

As the pianoforte has become the familiar domestic instrument of the whole world it is natural that composers who aim at supplying music for it should spring up in legions. But not many have impressed sufficient individuality into their works to make them of any real historic importance. Among famous players of modern times Sigismund Thalberg takes high rank; in his time he was thought worthy of being compared with Liszt himself. He was a year younger than that master, being born in Vienna in 1812. He had an inventive gift for pianoforte effects and technical feats similar to Liszt's, though on a smaller scale. His style was brilliant, but much quieter, and his compositions were proportionately tamer than Liszt's. They are, indeed, more considerable in quantity than quality, though some of his studies are happily conceived and refined in style. He died at Naples in 1871.

Of far more poetical and real musical temperament was Adolf Henselt, who was born at Schwabach, in Bavaria, in 1814. He was a pupil of Hummel, and became a very considerable pianist in his early years. He played with great success in St. Petersburg in 1838, and was made court pianist, and that capital became his home from that time till his death in 1889. He had a distinctly individual way of treating his instrument, both as composer and performer; obtaining great effects of sonority without vehemence, through the actual fullness and spread of his harmony and the genial warmth of his ideas. His works are few, confined to two books of études, some lyrical pieces, and a concerto. As a warm admirer of Weber he devoted great pains to editing and adapting his instrumental works to the capacities of the modern concert pianoforte.

Stephen Heller was born in Pesth in 1815, and is one of the most widely popular of pianoforte composers. He combined a wealth of graceful, poetical, and refined ideas with a very considerable sense of finish and a capacity to knit little movements into compact unity. Without being great, he certainly occupies an honorable position in his own field. He settled in Paris in 1838, and rarely moved from there till 1888, when he died. His works are mainly études of a not very advanced standard of difficulty, and collections of short pieces known as "Promenades d'un solitaire," "Nuits blanches," etc.

Among representatives of instrumental music must also be counted William Sterndale Bennett, who was born in 1816, at Sheffield, England. He began his musical career as a choir-boy in King's Chapel at Cambridge, and his conspicuous talents caused him to be sent to the Royal Academy of Music, of which he ultimately became principal in 1866. He was an admirable and refined pianist, of a quiet school, and wrote a considerable quantity of delicate and artistic pianoforte music, including the sonata called "The Maid of Orleans," in which a programme is very definitely indicated. His works on a larger scale comprise some poetical overtures, such as "Parisina," "The Wood Nymph," and "Paradise and the Peri," and an effective concerto for pianoforte. He was one of the first Englishmen in modern times to develop any sense for orchestration. He died in 1875.

A conspicuous composer in all branches of instrumental music was Joachim Raff, born at Lachen, in Switzerland, in 1822. He began life as a schoolmaster, and was a man of culture and considerable general knowledge. From 1850 onward he enjoyed a remarkable degree of popularity all over Europe. He had a certain fund of poetry and romantic feeling, considerable instinct for effect, and extraordinary facility. He was a good deal in contact with Liszt, who was kind and helpful to him, and he avowedly allied himself with what was considered the advanced school of those days. He was fond of giving names to his works, and endeavoring to treat them as poems. Of his ten symphonies several bear distinctive names, such as "Im Walde," "Lenore," "Frühlingsklänge," "Im Sommer"; but in reality they do not break away from the traditions of sonata form in any very marked degree. His orchestration is effective and full of color, and in many works of different types the texture is rich and elaborate, as, for instance, in his violin sonatas. His works in general show considerable gifts of invention, but are very unequal, both in style and intrinsic value. He died in 1882.

Anton Rubinstein, the Russian composer—the most poetical and imaginative of modern pianists—was a prolific writer in every branch of art, and gifted with genuine musical ideas. One of his chief characteristics was impetuosity, and it is possibly owing to this circumstance that he was more successful in ideas than in construction. His work resembles in those respects the literature of his great fellow-countryman, Tolstoi. Indeed, it seems to be the rule with the artistic work of Slavs that the power of creating intrinsic interest is considerable, but that the faculties which are needed for concentration and systematic mastery of balance of design are proportionately weak. This is equally true of the very national composer Tchaikovsky (1840-93), whose gifts were exercised with characteristic results in concertos and other forms of instrumental art. Mention should also be duly made of the Russian composer Borodin (1834-87), who illustrates the same impetuous ardor, combined with a sense for technical feats in pianoforte playing of the same brilliant and surprising order as Liszt's.

The one great representative of the highest forms of instrumental music in recent times was Johannes Brahms (1833-97). The austerity and sternness of his musical character caused the public to be very slow in recognizing him; though he had for constant champions such great exponents as Madame Schumann and Joachim. Brahms had no sympathy with the methods of the modern music-drama, nor with the theories of composers who attempt to apply those methods to instrumental music. He was at once a musical intellectualist and a man of powerful and concentrated feeling. He seemed to judge instinctively that self-dependent music is artistically intelligible only on grounds of design and development; and he applied all the artistic resources which the long period of musical development had made possible to the expounding of his musical ideas in lofty and noble symphonies, in splendid examples of all kinds of chamber music, such as pianoforte quintets and quartets, trios, string quintets and quartets, and other combinations of solo instruments. It must be confessed that his powers were so great that he found how to do something new and individual in the old forms of the sonata order.

He did not attempt symphonies till comparatively late in life, No. 1, in C minor, being Op. 68, and the date of its appearance 1876, though it was actually written much earlier. The second, in D, followed in 1877, a third and fourth in F and E minor followed in later years, as well as two fine, difficult concertos for pianoforte, one violin concerto, one double concerto for violin and cello, and two overtures. His treatment of the orchestra was austere but powerful; as though he disdained the subtle seductions of color, and used only such grave and almost neutral tints as befitted the self-contained dignity of his ideas. He obviously eschewed programme even in pianoforte pieces; but his numerous capriccios, intermezzos, ballades, and rhapsodies are as full of genuine impulse as the best works of the programme composers, and are often very original in design. He is also one of the few great masters of the variations form—which is one that only the very greatest composers have excelled in—and has produced superb examples for orchestra as well as for pianoforte.

The branching out into variety of style and method which is so characteristic of the progress of music is illustrated by the increase of the influence of various national styles of expression upon notable composers. Hungarian music led the way in this respect, and influenced Schubert as well as Liszt and Brahms. Russian music followed, as above indicated, and in later times Norwegian and Bohemian music have come prominently forward. The former is conspicuously illustrated in the person of Edvard Grieg (1843-1907). He adopted in all his compositions certain fantastic and piquant traits of harmony, rhythm, and melody, which appear to be drawn from the national style of his country. He had a very happy gift for knitting his little lyrical movements into compact and deftly finished wholes, and his sense for effect both with pianoforte and orchestra was very keen. Though the intellectual processes of concentrated development were not much in his line, the piquant novelty of his diction gained also for his violin sonatas and for his pianoforte concerto a wide popularity.

Bohemian music is represented by Antonin Dvořák, who was born in 1841 at Mühlhausen, Bohemia, where his father was butcher and innkeeper. He played in town bands, and in the National Theater at Prague, and did not come into public notice as a composer till comparatively late. But when once started, about 1877, his progress to world-wide fame was very rapid. He is to be credited with several admirable symphonies, and a great deal of fine and interesting chamber music. He is generally at his best in the national style, which is his true sphere, and in the expression of such romantic folk-stories as "The Specter's Bride," and in the superb sets of "Slavische Tänze." He is one of the greatest recent masters of orchestration; and though in mastery of design and consistency of style he is a little uncertain, the profusion and freshness of his ideas place him very high among the composers of his time. He died in 1904.

Of composers who have done honorable and skillful work in the instrumental lines there are in modern times too many even to catalogue. The above have so far made most mark upon history, and can only be supplemented by reference to names of such high distinction as Niels Gade, the Dane; Max Bruch, an admirable master of choral as well as instrumental effect, and the writer of justly popular violin concertos; Karl Reinecke, a prolific and successful composer; Felix Draeseke, a composer gifted with highly original and romantic ideas; Xaver Scharwenka, a very successful composer of artistic pianoforte music; Johann S. Svendsen, the Norwegian composer of overtures, symphonies, and chamber music; the admirable organist and writer of organ and chamber music, Joseph Rheinberger; the popular composer of brilliant pianoforte music, Moritz Moszkovski; the highly gifted but unfortunately short-lived Hermann Goetz; the Polish born Jean Louis Nicodé, a very highly gifted composer of instrumental music of various kinds; and the British born Eugen d'Albert, one of the finest pianists of the age, and possessed of very high gifts as a composer.

In France, purely instrumental music has been less cultivated, but a few of her composers have written some effective music, mostly of a light and unclassical character; among others, Delibes, who wrote such charming ballet music as the "Coppélia" and "Sylvia"; Lalo, who wrote chamber music, and very effective violin concertos, as well as orchestral music; Saint-Saëns, who attacked classical forms of art in an unusually serious mood for a Frenchman. Italy is mainly represented by Sgambati, a pupil of Liszt, and the composer of much effective chamber music and other instrumental music, including two symphonies. The natural field for English composers seems to be choral music, but instrumental music has also thriven remarkably well of late in the hands of such composers as Mackenzie, Stanford, Cowen, Cliffe, and several younger composers, some of whose works are well entitled to serious consideration and study.

CHAPTER XXVI

MODERN OPERA

Opera in Italy since Gluck's Time—Rossini—Opera in France—Meyerbeer—Gounod—Other Recent French Representatives—Germany—Continued Aspirations for National Opera—"Fidelio"—Spohr — Weber — "Der Freischütz" — Weber's Position and Influence—Wagner—Early Influences—Maturity First Attained in "Der Ring des Nibelungen."

THE composers of Italian opera after Gluck's time, unaffected by his exhortations to reform, continued to concentrate their efforts on pleasing their audiences. In this direction they succeeded extremely well. The most conspicuous proof of the fact was the career of Gioachino Antonio Rossini (1792-1868). He won his first great success in opera seria with "Tancredi" in 1813. The music, though often borrowed from familiar sources, exactly hit the taste of typical opera audiences, and from that time what is known as the Rossini fever began, and spread by degrees over the greater part of Europe. Several buffa operas followed "Tancredi," and he had one or two checks before he arrived at the full measure of his popularity. "L'Italiana in Algeri," produced in Venice in the same year as "Tancredi," was a success, "Aureliano" was a failure, so was "Torvaldo e Dorlinska," and so at first was the famous "Barbiere" (1816). But this last failure was merely owing to the fact that the Romans, for whom it was written, were much attached to a setting by Paisiello, and regarded it as an impertinence of the young composer to use the same subject. In the end the superior verve and tunefulness of Rossini's work won its way, and it still holds a prominent place in the class of opera buffa.

His next important opera seria was "Otello," which came out at Naples in 1816, and the rest of his most successful works in the purely Italian style consisted of the opera buffa "Cenerentola" (Rome, 1817), "Gazza Ladra" (Milan, 1817), "Mosè in Egitto," a sort of dramatic oratorio (Naples, Lent, 1818), "Ricciardo" (Naples, 1819), "Ermione" (1819), "Donna del Lago" (Naples, 1819), "Bianca e Faliero" (Milan, 1819), "Maometto Secondo" (Naples, 1820), "Zelmira" (Naples, 1820), "Semiramide" (Venice, 1823).

The facilities for producing operas in Naples were brought to an end in 1820 by an insurrection which got rid of the King, and at the same time reduced the resources of the famous opera manager Barbaja, who had hitherto combined the operatic business with the farming of gambling houses. Rossini, therefore, was induced to go to Vienna, and "Zelmira" was written with more care than usual, with a view to performance there. In 1823 he went to London, under contract with the manager of the King's Theater, Benelli, to produce a new opera. He was extravagantly fêted, and made a large sum of money by playing the accompaniments for singers at fashionable parties for £50 a night; but the opera manager failed, and his new opera was never completed.

He then went to Paris, where all the world again fell at his feet; and fortunately the Parisian traditions of French opera, which had always kept the dramatic elements well in sight, influenced him very happily. He began his career there with old works refurbished, some of them with new names. "Maometto" appeared again as "Le Siège de Corinthe," and "Mosè in Egitto" was revised as "Moïse." His most important work, "Guillaume Tell," with libretto by Scribe, was produced at the Académie in 1829, and it was his last. The superior type of audience he addressed in Paris made him more careful, and the result showed how great his powers were in all directions, in respect of orchestration as well as mere vocal effect. Even the style is more genuine and sincere than in his earlier productions. But he went no farther. It may have been his notorious indolence of disposition or jealousy of Meyerbeer.

It is greatly to his honor that Rossini appreciated Mozart and Haydn. His ardor for their music in his youth caused him to be called "il Tedeschino"—the little German. Their influence upon his work is conspicuous in all its better aspects and also in his use of their melodic phrases. He was much better and more artistic in his orchestration than other Italians, and was distinctly inventive in the matter of effect. He deserves credit for trying to improve the treatment of the ordinary parts of the dialogue, and for making the recitative musically a part of the work, as Mozart had often done. Whatever his shortcomings, he towered over most of his compatriots in the following generation both in ability and artistic sincerity.

His contemporary, Mercadante (born 1797), was very popular in Italy. He was educated at Naples, and wrote both buffa and serious operas, such as "Elisa e Claudio" (1822), "Il Giuramento" (1837). He died blind in 1870. Donizetti (1797-1848), following Rossini's lines without his higher gifts, had great success with "Anna Bolena" (1830), "L'Elisir d'Amore" (1832), "Lucrezia Borgia" (1834), "Lucia di Lammermoor" (1835), "Favorita" and "Fille du régiment" (Paris, 1840), "Don Pasquale" (Paris, 1843). He was educated at the Conservatorio at Naples, and paid much attention to solo singing of the tuneful order, and was consequently very popular with opera singers as well as their audiences; and he had the advantage of being interpreted in his time by the finest singers in the world, such as Grisi, Rubini, Tamburini, Lablache, and Mario.

Bellini, born at Catania in Sicily (1802), was also educated at Naples, and learned early to concentrate his attention upon the requirements of solo singers; and they were consequently much at his service. The first of his operas to make any mark was "Il Pirata" (1827), which was written under the actual supervision of the famous tenor Rubini, who sang in it with immense success. "Sonnambula" came out in 1831, at the Scala in Milan; "Norma" in 1832, "Puritani" in 1835. He died in the latter year.

Giuseppe Verdi was born in 1813, at Roncole, where his father was an innkeeper. He had very slender opportunities to cultivate music till his eighteenth year, when he went to Milan and studied energetically for a time and learned to appreciate Mozart's music. His first public appearance as an opera composer was with "Oberto" (1839). "Proscritto" followed in 1844, and was better known later under the name of "Ernani"—the name of the famous play by Victor Hugo. His fame grew by degrees and he took an important position as an opera composer of better stamp than the immediately preceding Italian composers, with "Rigoletto"—founded on Victor Hugo's impressive play "Le roi s'amuse"—in 1851. "Trovatore" and "La Traviata" followed in 1853, "Les Vêpres Siciliennes" (1855), "Ballo in Maschera" (Rome, 1857), "Don Carlos" (Paris, 1867). These were mainly of the class popular with fashionable opera audiences, though they contain much skillful work, such as the famous quartet in "Rigoletto," where the characters are kept very clearly distinct. The influence of the sincerer type of German art began to tell upon him as time went on, and its effect is shown in "Aïda," written for the Viceroy of Egypt for performance at Cairo, in 1871. The same influence, and that of his friend Boito, are even more apparent in his "Otello," which is eminently dramatic, and shows his great powers in all branches of musical effect alike, especially in dramatic expression. His "Falstaff," which came out in February, 1893, exhibits the same characteristics. He died in 1901.

In France, in recent times, the fruits of the national instinct for the stage have been most happily shown in operatic comedies and light comic operas. These branches of opera originated from the Italian opera buffa which made its appearance in Paris a little before Gluck's time. The French composers imitated and improved upon it. Their natural wit, sense of finish and neatness, and lightness of skillful handling, all found a most suitable province for exercise, and the result in the hands of the later composers is singularly artistic and good of its kind.

One of the most successful of the early representatives of this kind of art was Boieldieu, born at Rouen in 1775. He began his career in Paris in 1797, with the opera "La famille suisse." Among his chief successes was "Le Calife de Bagdad," which came out in 1800. The most famous of all was "La dame blanche" (1825), which has had the most pronounced success of any opera of its kind. The thousandth performance was celebrated in 1862. It appears to be still alive in France at the present day. Boieldieu himself lived only till 1834.

Auber, whose successes are of a wider scope, and whose artistic powers were of a much higher order, was born at Caen in 1782. He began as an amateur, and was for a time a clerk in an office in London. He began composing little operas for Parisian theaters in 1811. Associated with the brilliant librettist Scribe, he came more into prominence with "Leicester" (1822), "Le Maçon" (1825), "Fra Diavolo" (1830), and "Les diamants de la couronne" (1841). The greater part of his work belongs to this light class of French opera comique, of which it is most brilliantly representative. His one serious opera, "Masaniello," or "La Muette de Portici," also had very conspicuous success. It came out in 1828, and made a great impression on quite different grounds from his lighter works; as he proved himself to have great dramatic powers, and used his orchestral forces for such purposes well. The opera had the singular honor of precipitating a popular revolution in Brussels, in 1830. Auber lived till after the German siege of Paris. The horrors of the Commune are reported to have hastened his end, and he died in 1871.

Another more short-lived composer of this light kind of opera was Hérold, born in Paris in 1791. He wrote much popular music for the pianoforte, and ballet music, and many operas, solid as well as light. The most famous were "Zampa" (1831) and "Le pré aux clercs" (1832). He died in 1833 of consumption. Halévy, whose original name was Levi, was born in 1799. He also wrote various operas of diverse calibers. The best of his grand operas were "La Juive" (1835) and "La reine de Chypre" (1841). They both show considerable sense of effect and skill of orchestration. Among his comic operas, "L'Eclair" (1835) was notable. He was also remarkably successful in ballet music. He died of consumption, like Hérold, in 1862.

The impulse toward scenic display, which was always liable to become prominent in French opera, even in Lulli's time, and is peculiarly noticeable in the works of Spontini and Halévy, came to a head in the works of Meyerbeer, the son of a German banker in Berlin, where he was born in 1791. He was extraordinarily clever in many ways, for in early years he was chiefly famous for his brilliant abilities as a pianist and for his remarkable gift for reading from score. He began his career as an opera composer with some German operas, which were not successful. After that he went to Italy and produced a great number of operas in a regular Italian style (much to his friend Weber's regret), and won considerable success. He also tried a combination of Italian and German styles in "Il Crociato in Egitto" (The Crusader in Egypt), which came out in 1826 in Paris.

His coming into contact with Parisian tastes turned his views in a new direction. The susceptibilities of the French to imposing spectacular display possibly indicated to him that they would be just the audience for gifts of his order. He studied French character and history carefully, and, with the congenial assistance of the librettist Scribe, made his first venture in the new line with "Robert le Diable," in 1831. He had calculated so well that the result gave him at once a commanding European reputation. He was very cautious and slow in maturing his work, calculating and testing his effects with infinite patience, and his successive operas therefore came far apart. "Les Huguenots" was produced in 1836, "Le Prophète" in 1849, having been finished as early as 1843 but kept back; "L'Etoile du Nord" came out in 1854, "Dinorah" in 1859. "L'Africaine" was kept by him for over twenty years, as he never could finally satisfy himself that he had got it all sufficiently up to his idea of effect. It was not performed till 1865, the year following that of his death.

Meyerbeer tried many styles and won popular favor in more than one, but it is as a representative of French grand opera that he is specially known to fame. He had great sense of theatrical effect without much real dramatic power. His operatic work dazzles and astonishes the senses, but does not appeal to deeper feelings or express any noble emotion. He carried the French taste for display to a climax and surpassed every one who preceded him in supplying fit music for crowded scenes and pompous spectacles. He wielded great resources with remarkable success, and used all the old conventions of arias, flourishes, and set movements without scruple.

Of very different caliber was Gounod (1818-93). His genuine sensibility is conspicuous, and his feeling for beauty of orchestral color, and even for genuine choral effect is remarkable. He studied at the Conservatoire in Paris under Halévy. Going to Rome in 1839 he became enamored of the old ecclesiastical style for a time. Then he fell in love with German music and with Berlioz, who exercised a permanent influence upon him. He won great and eminently deserved success in both kinds of opera. His lighter operas are worthy of association with the best types of this admirable branch of French art; and his great success in grand opera with "Faust," for which he had to wait so long, is too familiar to need comment. In this last the wholesome influence of German romanticism is clearly displayed, and his efforts in the direction of genuine expression are as conspicuous in his best works as they are conspicuously absent from Meyerbeer's productions. "Sapho" was his first opera (1851), and the most important of those which succeeded it are "La nonne sanglante" (1854), "Le médecin malgré lui" (1858), "Faust" (1859), "Philémon et Baucis" (1860), "La reine de Saba" (1862), "Mireille" (1864), "Roméo et Juliette" (1867), "Polyeucte" (1878).

Among the many successful representatives of modern French opera of various kinds, the following also deserve honorable recognition. Lalo (1823-92), whose comprehensive powers have been referred to above in connection with instrumental music, has also produced considerable impression with his "Roi d'Ys." Delibes (1836-91), whose brilliant gifts were most effectually shown in ballet music, was also very successful in the line of opera, especially in "Le roi l'a dit" (1873) and "Lakmé" (1883). Bizet (1838-75), whose characteristic and dramatic "Carmen" has given him such worldwide fame, was born in Paris, studied at the Conservatoire, and wrote several operas which were not very successful till "Carmen," which was his last, and came out in the year of his death. The remarkable instinct for effect possessed by Massenet (born 1842) has brought him into considerable prominence as a representative of modern French tendencies. His most celebrated operas are "Don César de Bazan" (1872), "Le roi de Lahore" (1877), the semi-religious opera "Hérodiade" (1881), "Manon" (1884), "Le Cid" (1885). A composer who has attracted attention is A. E. Chabrier (1842-93), who produced several operas, such as "Gwendoline" (1886) and "Le roi malgré lui" (1887). Ambroise Thomas (1811-96) was a most prolific composer of operas; and won conspicuous success with "Mignon" (1866) and "Hamlet" (1868). He succeeded Auber as director of the famous Conservatoire in 1871. Among the most recent composers of French opera André Messager (born 1853) is a happy representative. His "Basoche" is a very refined, artistic, and genial example of its class.

While France and Italy were already busy producing numbers of operas of all kinds, the Germans were still looking for the type of opera which should adequately represent the high standard of their taste and musical intelligence. After "Zauberflöte" a considerable time elapsed without any noticeable achievement, till Beethoven had at last found a subject which satisfied his scrupulous taste, and brought out "Fidelio" in 1805. In the interim since the "Zauberflöte" a good deal of progress had been made in orchestral art and in the development of the resources of expression. Beethoven himself had written his first three symphonies and a large number of sonatas, and the whole development of his first period lay behind him, so that "Fidelio" represents a very much more modern type of expression than Mozart's work. The treatment of the orchestra is much more rich and copious in variety, and the quality of the melody much less formal.

As might be expected, the scenes which are best, musically, are those in which there is a great deal of real human feeling, as in the prison scene. In parts like the duet between Marcellina and Jacquino, and in Rocco's song, the traces of the old traditional operatic style are more apparent. As a whole the standard is too high for average operatic audiences, and this, joined with the fact that when the opera was first brought out in Vienna in November, 1805, the Austrians had just suffered serious reverses at the hands of the French, who were even in occupation of the city, caused the opera to be but a moderate success. After three performances it was laid aside till May, 1806, and then again till 1814, when it was produced in a considerably revised state. It won its way slowly in Europe, but has never had any popular success, though to intelligent musicians it represents the highest standard of noble art that has ever been put into an opera. "Fidelio," however, did not finally solve the problem of national opera, for though written to German words and of the lofty type consistent with the dignified attitude of Germans toward music, the subject is not German, and the music still has touches of the earlier manner, and is not distinctly Teutonic throughout.

Neither did Spohr, with the most excellent purposes, completely satisfy German aspirations, as his dramatic sense was much too limited. He had good opportunities for studying operatic requirements, as he had great experience of orchestral music, and was appointed conductor of the Vienna Opera House for a time in 1812. But his strong impulse toward music of the classical type, like sonatas and concertos, prevented his hitting the right vein in operas. The first which he brought to successful performance was "Der Zweikampf mit der Geliebten," or "The Lovers' Duel," which came out at Hamburg in 1810. The most notable of those which succeeded were "Faust" (completed 1813, performed at Prague under Weber in 1816), "Zemire und Azor" (1819), and "Jessonda" (1823). The latter was far the most successful of all, and indeed was highly appreciated in Germany for the excellent use of artistic resources and the generally pleasant texture of the whole. He wrote several more, but none of them are of any real dramatic importance.

The composer with whom the solution of the problem of national Teutonic opera is always associated is Weber. The circumstances of his early years were not very promising, but his father's aspiration to have a prodigy producing operas in childhood, at least afforded him early experience of theatrical work. The son was drilled with the view of pushing him rapidly forward by Vogler, and produced his first opera, "The Dumb Girl of the Forest," at the age of fourteen. After that he was made a secretary at the court of the King of Würtemberg at Stuttgart, and when that part of his career was unexpectedly and abruptly closed, he resumed the occupation of music and went for concert tours round Germany as a pianist, his gifts in that line being very remarkable. He was first prominently touched by the national spirit when aspirations for independence seized on the Germans after Napoleon's conspicuous failure in the expedition to Moscow. Weber's own enthusiasm was expressed in his splendid national songs and part songs to Körner's words, in the sets of the "Leyer und Schwert," which went the length of the land.

He was further identified with the national spirit through being appointed to organize a really German opera, first at Prague in 1813 and then at Dresden in the following year, where hitherto Italian opera had had a monopoly. And, finally, his Teutonic impulse found its full expression in the opera "Der Freischütz," which came out in Berlin in 1821. This, at last, was German work through and through. The style is the style of "Volkslieder" expanded so as to meet the requirements of the situation. The traces of Italian traditions have at last evaporated, and all is genuinely Teutonic, in subject and treatment alike. Moreover, the treatment is of the highest artistic quality. The orchestration was the finest and the most perfectly adapted for such purposes hitherto seen; the musical characterization of the various actors in the drama is singularly clear and happy; and the expression is of that warm and sincere kind which essentially distinguishes the German style from that of all other nations. The dialogue is still spoken, as was traditional in the earlier German forms, such as the "Singspiel"; but the continuous texture of the ultimate type of Wagner is prefigured in many parts of the work.

In Weber's next important opera, "Euryanthe," which came out in Vienna in 1823, the dialogue was set as well as the more important parts of the work, and in some respects it rises to higher levels than "Der Freischütz." But the libretto itself is so foolish that it has prevented its having general success.

Weber's last opera, "Oberon," was written by invitation for England. It is a fairy play, and not much more fortunate in respect of the libretto than "Euryanthe." Weber went over to England to launch it. He was already in a broken state of health. He lived to see the first few successful performances, in April, 1826, and had just made up his mind to return to his family in Germany on June 6, when, on the morning of June 5, he was found dead in his bed in Sir George Smart's house. Wagner only expressed the general feeling when in the year 1844, on the removal of Weber's body to Germany for reburial in Dresden, he described him as the most German of composers. The vices and virtues of his manner are alike German. His style is saturated with the Teutonic spirit. Even the vagueness and irregularity of his form in instrumental music come from his aspiration after expression, which from the first had been the conspicuous aim of Germans.

His style had much effect upon German composers generally, even outside operatic work, as, for instance, on Mendelssohn. Marschner (1796-1861) was also much influenced by him, and most naturally so, as he was associated with him for some time in the opera work at Dresden. He produced several very successful operas, all rather in Weber's style, and some of them on the same supernatural lines which Weber liked. Among the best were "Der Vampyr" (1828), which had a great success, and even a long run in England; another was "Der Templer und die Jüdin," founded on Walter Scott's "Ivanhoe." His last was "Hans Heiling" (1833), regarded as his masterpiece.

Schubert also wrote some operas, but none of them ever took any hold of the theater. His instinct was too essentially lyrical, and his susceptibilities too delicate for theatrical work. Schumann also made his effort in "Genoveva" (1850, Leipzig), which contains superb music, but does not apparently hit the standard of the stage; which, considering Schumann's introspective disposition, is not surprising.

Other German composers who did successful work for the stage are Kreutzer (1782-1849), who wrote "Das Nachtlager in Granada"; Lindpaintner (1791-1856), a good conductor, who wrote a great many solid operas; Lortzing (1803-52), a composer of good light comic operas, such as "Czar und Zimmermann" (1837), "Wildschütz" (1842), "Undine" (1845), and many others; Nicolai (1810-49), who wrote the admirably artistic and effective opera "Die lustigen Weiber von Windsor"; and Peter Cornelius (1824-74), who identified himself with the "new German" movement of the days when Liszt was at Weimar, when Wagner's career was but beginning, and produced "Der Barbier von Bagdad," which was brought out by Liszt in 1859.

The composer on whom the influence of Weber and Beethoven was exerted with most important results was Richard Wagner. This greatest representative of music-drama was born at Leipzig in 1813. His father died when he was but a few months old, and his mother was soon married again to an actor named Ludwig Geyer; so he was surrounded by theatrical influences from his childhood. He early showed a passion for things dramatic, such as Greek plays and Shakespeare, and attempted to write plays of very tragic cast himself. He heard Weber's works in Dresden and learned to worship them and Beethoven's symphonies. He began his actual career in 1833 as a chorus-master at a theater in Würzburg, where an elder brother was engaged as an actor. After this he was successively conductor at the theaters of Magdeburg, Königsberg, and Riga.

In these early years he wrote several operas in different styles, none of which were successful; and finally determined to try his fortune at the Paris Opera House, which was then regarded as the center of the operatic world. As Meyerbeer's influence was paramount there he wrote his first grand opera, "Rienzi," very much in Meyerbeer's manner, with every kind of resource he could think of which ministered to spectacular and sensational effect. But, unfortunately, though he got an introduction from Meyerbeer to the director of the opera house, he never succeeded n getting a hearing for it. The only work of his which was heard by the Parisians was the libretto for his opera "The Flying Dutchman," which the opera-manager took and gave to one of his band to set, and then performed that setting, but not Wagner's. After waiting for a long while, and enduring many privations and disappointments, Wagner had to give up all hope of a hearing in Paris.

Ultimately "Rienzi" was accepted at Dresden and performed there in 1842, and met with success; and it was followed after a little while by his appointment as conductor there. His own setting of "The Flying Dutchman" then obtained a hearing, but did not meet with so much success as "Rienzi." The latter had been more in the style people were accustomed to, and the pomp and display dazzled them, while "The Flying Dutchman" was more of the real Wagner, extremely dramatic, and unlike the familiar operas of either Italian or French pattern, and people were too much puzzled by it to enjoy it. In the end its great dramatic power, and the genuine interest of the story, as well as the very striking and characteristic music, have won it a firm position, and it is recognized as the first of Wagner's works which approximately represents him. Wagner realized the advantage of using traditional stories and national legends as the basis of his works, since they necessarily represent things out of the range of common everyday experience, and are free from the hackneyed associations which make the singing of dialogue (except in comic scenes) seem ridiculous.

He also realized that it was an advantage to choose subjects which were of special Teutonic interest— and the next he undertook after "The Flying Dutchman" was "Tannhäuser," the story of the Hill of Venus; he completed it by 1844 and brought it out in the next year. Being still more uncompromising than the previous opera, it was not received with favor; to his great surprise, since he himself did not realize that his methods would be so unintelligible to minds accustomed to conventional things. However, he was not the man to go back or write at a lower level to please a public, and went on with "Lohengrin" and completed it in 1846. Unfortunately, in 1849 he was implicated in certain revolutionary proceedings in Dresden, and had to escape to avoid imprisonment. He fled to Liszt at Weimar first and thence to Paris. This episode caused him to lose his appointment at Dresden, and he had to remain in exile from Germany for many years. Liszt meanwhile, with the ardor which characterized him, was bringing out all sorts of operas of special interest at Weimar, and among them produced "Tannhäuser," soon after Wagner's flight, and then "Lohengrin" for the first time, also in 1850. Wagner himself never heard the latter till many years later.

During his exile Wagner mainly lived at Zurich in Switzerland. He occupied himself with much literary work, which caused him to consider the possibilities of the music-drama more carefully. He also took up the earliest forms of the myths of the Nibelungs and the gods of Valhalla, and the national hero Siegfried, which are embodied in Norse as well as ancient Teutonic legends; and finding them too rich in materials for one opera, he resolved on developing them into a great cycle of music-dramas, like the ancient trilogies of the Greeks. The first, which is a sort of preface to the series, is "Das Rheingold," which was completed in 1854. "Die Walküre" followed in 1856, "Siegfried" was not completed till 1869, and "Götterdämmerung" (Twilight of the Gods) was only brought to perfection in 1874. This series forms the group comprised under the general name "Der Ring des Nibelungen" (The Ring of the Nibelungs).

His work upon the great cycle was frequently interrupted. While he was still at work on "Die Walküre" he received an invitation to conduct at the Philharmonic concerts in London for the season of 1855. His reputation was at this time a very curious one; so few people understood his music that his determination to be true to himself and act according to his convictions appeared like a sort of lunacy of conceit, and his energy to be the mere self-assertion of a charlatan. It was impossible for his visit to that country to be anything but a mockery. He tried to insist upon some necessary reforms in the arrangements, and gave his full energies to making the performances as good as possible; but, of course, he was not invited again.

A more serious interruption followed. It dawned upon him while he was in the middle of "Siegfried" that it was already a long time since he had brought anything new before the public, and that it might be unwise to let the ten or twelve years pass before the whole of the "Ring" could be completed without showing any sign of continued activity. So he set to work on "Tristan und Isolde" and completed it before going farther with the "Ring." The poem was finished in 1857, and he worked on steadily till the whole was complete in 1859. After its completion he resolved to make a new assault upon Paris to try and get his works heard. He gave concerts there with excerpts from various works, and finally, through some influence at court, got "Tannhäuser" ordered for performance. Immense sums were spent on the preparation, and after 150 rehearsals it was received with a pandemonium of uproarious opposition got up by a Parisian clique, which prevented its even being audible.

A turn of better fortune followed. He received permission to return to Germany, and about this time he took in hand the composition of the delightfully genial "Meistersinger von Nürnberg." But things had gone so hardly with him that he was on the verge of throwing up the struggle for good. Just at the right moment came a message from the young King of Bavaria, offering him a small but sufficient pension and a home in his dominions where he could work in peace. This was followed by more reassuring events. "Tristan" was performed at Munich in 1865 and "Die Meistersinger" in 1868. In 1872 he settled in Bayreuth, and the foundation of the great theater was laid. He again took up the composition of the great trilogy, and when the whole thing was complete and the theater finished it was performed for the first time in 1876. About that time he completed the poem of "Parsifal," and went on with the composition shortly afterward, and finished this last of his great music-dramas in 1882. The first performances took place at Bayreuth in the same year. He did not long survive them, for his death occurred in Venice in 1883.

Wagner's impulse was at first mainly dramatic. His musical powers grew as his career proceeded and they scarcely arrived at maturity till the beginning of the "Ring." His great advantage lay in his control of all the factors of operatic art—as he attained a high degree of mastery of dramatic, theatrical, and musical effect, and in his hands each served to enhance the effect of the others. His reforms consisted mainly in getting rid of the old formulas, such as arias, recitatives, finales, and all the set movements which disturbed and hindered the action; and in thus making each act continuous music throughout. He developed the principle of the *Leitmotiv* to the fullest extent, giving a definite musical figure to each character and situation; and using the figures all through the orchestral part of the work, instead of the old formulas of accompaniment. He enlarged the bounds of tonality so as to give himself as much room as possible for expression, and developed the resources of effect in the orchestra to the utmost. His treatment of the voice was the natural outcome of modern musical development. He reserved the finer melodic phrases for the occasions when much expression was required, and treated the rest like the old declamatory recitative, but with richer accompaniment.

CHAPTER XXVII

MODERN VOCAL MUSIC

Solo Song—Characteristic of the Modern Phase of Music—Schubert—Schumann—Brahms—Solo Song in France—In England—Revival of Oratorio—Haydn—Spohr—Lesser Lights—Mendelssohn—Thriving State of Choral Music in Combination with Orchestra.

NO branch of modern music is more characteristic or more illustrative of prevailing tendencies than the solo song, for none illustrates more clearly the relation between music and the thought expressed, or the aim of the musician to be guided by the idea rather than the conventions of classical form. The typical modern song has only become possible through the long development of the resources of art, and only through long experience and innumerable experiments have men learned what to do and what not to do in dealing with a poet's language. Songs existed from the beginning of musical time; but until the beginning of the nineteenth century they consisted either of regular definite tunes which had to be fitted to all the verses, whatever change of sentiment or accent occurred, or of crude elocutionary experiments like the settings of lyrics made by the composers of the Restoration period in England.

Many tendencies combined to bring about the close wedding of music to word and sentiment, which began to be adopted at the beginning of the century. Gluck's theories had some influence, for they caused people to pay more attention to the meaning of the words and the declamation. The development of instrumental resources and of pianoforte technique put fresh powers in the hands of composers. Mozart and Haydn both approached to the ideal of modern song here and there, and Beethoven in several cases actually attained it. Weber, through his intense sympathy with the Teutonic Volkslied, likewise produced both in his operas and in separate songs perfect examples of the true modern song; but the first composer whose personality was specially expressed in this branch of art was Franz Schubert, and he consequently stands out as the first representative song-composer of modern times.

Schubert was one of the most spontaneous and one of the least systematically educated of musicians; and his musical nature was particularly open to follow external impressions. Knowing very little of any theory of form, he was particularly amenable to the guidance of a poet, and he seems to have written his songs under the immediate impulse which the poems he read produced in him. There was hardly any development of his powers in this respect, for some of his very finest songs were written in early years. "Gretchen am Spinnrade" was written when he was but seventeen (1814) and "The Erlking" when he was eighteen (1815). "Schwager Kronos" and "The Wanderer" followed soon after. Throughout the whole of his life he poured out song after song, and it was more the chance of a poem coming in his way than any other consideration which led to a composition. The beautiful set of twenty called "Die schöne Müllerin" belongs to the year 1823, "Die junge Nonne" to 1825, "Sylvia" to 1826, "Die Winterreise" to 1827, and "Liebesbotschaft" and "Der Doppelgänger" to the last year of his life, 1828. In all he wrote over 600, many of them long, rich, and deeply expressive works.

Scientific writers on music are fond of classifying songs into certain categories in accordance with the nature of the musical treatment. Schubert, of course, had no idea of such classification. The poems suggested to his mind the method of treatment. If the words were simple, he was satisfied to write a tune with a simple accompaniment and repeat the same for different verses; if the words were subtle and intricate in meaning, he adopted a more subtly artistic way of dealing with the musical material; if he had to tell a dramatic story he made the voice part declamatory and put the illustrative effects into the pianoforte part. It is rare that the special methods indicated by the scientific analysts persist through a song. Even the simplest have neat turns of artistic finish and subtleties of suggestion in detail, the most richly organized often have passages of vocal tune, and in the ballad-like songs every means is used to convey the musical counterpart of the words. He uses realism, color, striking harmony, polyphony, modulation, as well as melody to bring home the poet's meaning. Melody is relegated to its right place as only one of the factors of effect, and a great deal of his expression is produced by striking harmony and modulation.

Under such conditions the old idea of song has become almost obsolete and the word "accompaniment" a misnomer. The modern type of song is a complete work of art of a much more highly organized character than the old type. Harmony is an immensely more powerful means of expression than melody, and in bringing it to bear as a factor in the art-form the pianoforte necessarily occupies a far more important place than it used to do. It is through the treatment of what is technically called the accompaniment that the effects of harmony, modulation, and the rest become possible, and the resources of the composer for intensifying the poet's meaning and faithfully following his artistic intentions are immensely enhanced.

Schubert's songs were very slow in winning popular acceptance. Their very perfections were regarded as utter extravagance at first, but at the present day the best examples are regarded as the complete solution of the problem of song and are the prototypes of all modern products of the kind.

It is not necessary to discuss the songs of distinguished composers who are not particularly identified with the department of song. Spohr and Mendelssohn wrote some pleasant songs, but they were not by nature song-writers, and the same may be said of a large majority of able and conscientious composers who have shown themselves successful in other lines.

Of genuine song-writers since Schubert, Schumann is one of the foremost. His literary tastes and his poetical views on art were in his favor. He did not begin writing songs till after he had written a considerable portion of his best pianoforte music. In 1840, the year of his marriage, he suddenly threw himself with ardor into song-writing, and in one year produced over a hundred, comprising nearly all the best he composed. Schumann, like Schubert, adapted his methods to the poems he set. He was less happy than Schubert in the descriptive line, but he touched a deeper vein of emotion and reached a higher pitch of warmth in color and expression. He is most notable for his faithfulness to the poet's declamation, and the intense sympathy with which he follows every turn of thought and feeling.

Among composers whose fame is mainly centered in song-writing is Robert Franz, who was born in 1815 at Halle. Without the warmth or verve of the two greater composers, he won the affection of his fellow-countrymen by the faithful care and insight with which he followed the poet's meaning and diction—fitting his music close to every word. He died in 1892.

One of the greatest of song-writers was Johannes Brahms. A set of his early songs was among the things which first attracted the attention of Schumann, and throughout his life he was constantly pouring out songs of an infinite variety of style and form and caliber. In no department is he more thoroughly great. He is completely in touch with his poet, and applies his immense artistic resources to the ends of expression without a trace of superfluous artifice or pedantry. In later years he simplified his methods of treatment considerably. The finest songs belong to his early days and middle age, but out of many volumes of songs there are very few that have not decided point and genuine merit of the true song order.

The feeling for song-writing increases as music becomes more elastic and free in its adaptability to varieties of expression, and the number of genuine song-writers has of late become very large indeed. Among the most remarkable is Hugo Brückler (1845-71), whose settings of the songs in Scheffel's "Trompeter von Säkkingen" are of a very high order. The Norwegian, Halfdan Kjerulf (1815-68), has won a wide and well-deserved popularity for refined expression and well-varied songs. Rubinstein showed a very exceptional gift for song-writing, and produced some of the best examples of modern times; and Taubert, Lassen, Grieg, Dvořák, Jensen, and Henschel have all contributed their share.

The French conception of song is much more superficial than the German, and concentrates much more attention on the voice part. But they have an admirable literature of modern lyrics, and the foremost composers of the country have supplied the world with a vast collection of refined and pleasant settings of them. Berlioz stands at the head of these French song-composers with very characteristic examples, some of which are speculatively treated, and interesting on that account, as being out of the common line. Of modern composers Gounod was specially successful in England as well as in France, and not far behind come F. David, Massenet, Godard, and Widor.

In England song-writing reached, in the past generation, a pitch of degradation which is probably without parallel in all musical history. Mercantile considerations and the shallowness of average drawing-room taste produced a luxuriant crop of specimens of imbecility in which the sickly sentiment was not less conspicuous than the total ignorance of the most elementary principles of grammar and artistic construction, and of the relation of musical accent to poetical declamation. In those days the songs of Hatton (1809-86), and of Sterndale Bennett, and the early songs of Sullivan and those of F. Clay (1840-89), were honorably conspicuous for real artistic quality and genuine song-impulse. Though there are a good many representatives of the old school still active, the present day is represented by mature masters of their craft who can write genuine songs; such as Mackenzie, Stanford, Cowen, and Maude Valérie White, also a few younger composers, such as MacCunn and Somervell, who produce songs as genuine and as beautiful as are to be found anywhere in Europe. The impulse is certainly going in the right direction, and if the public can be persuaded not to insist so exclusively upon songs being either vulgar or trivial and vapid, the future of English song will undoubtedly be such as the nation may be proud of. (The development of music in America is fully treated in a succeeding section.)

A branch of art which is most characteristically modern, and seems to have a great deal of life in it, is the combination of orchestra with choral music and solos, independent of the stage, such as is familiar in modern oratorios, cantatas, odes, and so forth. The collapse of oratorio after the time of Handel and Bach was mainly owing to the spread of Italian operatic taste, which had moved rapidly away from choral music as soon as the Neapolitan school of composers gained hold of the world, and cared for nothing but solo-singing of the formal aria type. The influence of the prima donna was even more pernicious in the line of oratorio than in opera, for chorus is truly an essential of the latter form; and when chorus was reduced to the minimum possible, that form of art collapsed. Indeed, the Italian influence was fatal to serious and sacred music all round, and it was only in Protestant countries that the traditions of grand oratorio lingered on, and it was in Protestant countries that the resuscitation was achieved.

A sort of forlorn hope in this period is the work of Karl Philipp Emanuel Bach in that line. His two oratorios, "The Israelites in the Desert" (1775) and "The Resurrection" (1787), are both very interesting, and contain passages of great beauty and vivid expression. It is noteworthy that they foreshadow the very lines on which the resuscitation was cast, as there is an unusual amount of orchestral work in them, some of it very happily conceived.

It was, indeed, the development of orchestration, and the splendid opportunities which the combination of orchestra and chorus affords to composers, which led to the revival. In old days the instrumental accompaniment was purely secondary and subservient. The development of orchestral style and effect doubled the resources of composers in works of this class, and supplied them with a very interesting problem to solve. Mozart was in the forefront of the new development with his "Requiem," which is the most earnest and sincere of all his works. It was not finished at his death in 1791, but was very successfully completed afterward by his pupil, Süssmayer, partly from memory, and partly by repeating one of the first movements and adding new music where necessary.

The "Requiem" was soon followed by Haydn's "Creation," which forms a kind of landmark for the real commencement of the new movement. Haydn had been in England and had heard some of Handel's choral works for the first time in the last decade of the eighteenth century. Salomon had offered him an arrangement of Milton's "Paradise Lost" to set, and when he returned to Germany he had it revised and translated, and set it forthwith. It was first performed privately in the Schwarzenberg Palace in Vienna, in 1798, Haydn at that time being sixty-five years old. It spread with marvelous rapidity to all musical centers, and was received with special enthusiasm in England. He followed it up two years later with "The Seasons," which goes by the name of an oratorio and contains choruses, but is, for the most part, much too light and secular to accord with the usual idea of that form. The next work of the kind by a great master was Beethoven's "Christus am Oelberge," known also as "The Mount of Olives" and sometimes as "Engedi." Here the resources of the orchestra are even more richly used than by Haydn, but the style is rather florid and operatic. It is a comparatively early work of the great master, as it came out in 1803.

The most prominent composer in the field in the early years of the nineteenth century was Spohr, the great violinist. He began composition with the view of supplying himself with concertos, and succeeded so well that his powers as a composer were soon much in demand. He was invited to compose an oratorio for the Fête Napoléon at Erfurt, in 1812, and for that occasion wrote his first version of "The Last Judgment," under the German name of "Das jüngste Gericht." He prepared himself deliberately by borrowing a copy of Marpurg's "Art of Fugue" from one of his own pupils and studying like a neophyte; and the result seems to have justified his labor at the time, though the oratorio in question is not one that is familiar. His principal work in this line was "Die letzten Dinge," which is also well known as "The Last Judgment." This was produced in 1826. It is remarkable as the first oratorio which has the modern romantic character about it. There is a certain vein of poetry and a thoroughly modern color throughout, which comes partly from Spohr's skillful orchestration and partly from his chromatic manner; which, however, is not quite so pronounced in this work as in many others—as, for instance, in his oratorio "Calvary," which came out in 1835. Spohr's last composition of this class was "The Fall of Babylon," which was written for the Norwich Festival of 1842.

Contemporary with Spohr was F. J. C. Schneider (1786-1853), who wrote fourteen oratorios between 1810 and 1838, which at the time had much popularity. The best is said to have been "Das Weltgericht"; another is called "Sündfluth" (The Deluge). Another composer who had very remarkable success for a time was Neukomm (1798-1858). He was a pupil of Michael and Joseph Haydn. His oratorios "Mount

Sinai" and "David" were much in vogue in England before Mendelssohn's "St. Paul" came out. They are not without artistic merits, though the treatment of the commandments in "Sinai" is extremely funny. "David" was written for the Birmingham Festival of 1834. The advent of Mendelssohn caused Neukomm to disappear in the background. Mendelssohn brought the skill of a complete master of both orchestral and choral effect to bear upon oratorio. He began with "St. Paul," which was first performed at Düsseldorf in 1836, and was soon taken up in England. Its success naturally led to his seeking for another subject, and he finally settled on "Elijah." But before that came out the "Lobgesang" or "Hymn of Praise" was produced at Leipzig on the occasion of the celebration of the fourth centenary of the invention of printing. This work combines the qualities of a symphony and of an oratorio, and very emphatically illustrates the value of the combination of orchestral and choral effect.

The famous "Elijah" was completed in 1846, and first performed at Birmingham on August 26 in that year. Mendelssohn began another oratorio, "Christus," but died in 1847 before completing it. It seems to have been intended to be on the lines of the typical "Passions" of J. S. Bach. The influence of this form is very prominent in all his works of this class. He had taken up Bach's Matthäus Passion as early as 1827 and gave in Berlin the first performance it had received out of Leipzig since Bach's death. Its remarkable scheme came upon the world like a novelty, and it exercised an influence upon Mendelssohn's mind which was most powerful for good. He seized upon the salient principles of the "Passion" type, such as the admixture of narrative, reflective and dramatic principles in the solo parts, the use of types of choruses which represent masses of people who are personally engaged in the action of the drama, and the types of reflective choruses which express the mood of the spectator, and he applied these and other features of the old form with the happiest results. "St. Paul" is the more nearly on the "Passion" lines of the two, but the influence of the type is strong in both of them.

About the end of Mendelssohn's time composers became very busy with oratorios and similar works. Schumann produced the "Paradise and the Peri" in 1843 and the "Faust" music in 1848. In France the movement was early and brilliantly represented by Berlioz's remarkable "Damnation de Faust" and "L'Enfance du Christ." H. H. Pierson's "Jerusalem" was brought out at the Norwich Festival of 1852. Sterndale Bennett's principal work, "The May Queen," came out at Leeds in 1858; and his "Woman of Samaria" in 1867. Sullivan brought out his "Prodigal Son" at the Worcester Festival of 1869, and his "Light of the World" at Birmingham in 1873; Macfarren his "John the Baptist" in 1873 and "Joseph" at Leeds in 1877, and both composers followed up their successes with more in the same line, the most popular of its kind being Sullivan's "Golden Legend" (Leeds, 1886). For England also were written Gounod's "Redemption" and "Mors et vita." In Germany the highest standard of this type of art is represented by Brahms's "Schicksalslied," "Triumphlied," "Nänie," "Gesang der Parzen," and "Deutsches Requiem." Bohemia is well represented by Dvořák's beautiful "Stabat Mater," his picturesque "Specter's Bride," "Ludmila," and the "Requiem." Denmark is represented by numerous works of the kind by Niels Gade; Italy by Verdi's notable "Requiem" for Manzoni, and Mancinelli's "Isaiah"; and Belgium by Benoit's "Lucifer."

Choral music seems to thrive best in countries where independent democratic spirit is strong and tempered with common sense. England has always been happiest in such music, and it is most natural that this characteristic form of modern art should thrive in her soil. Her composers have been extremely active and extremely successful in this line of late. Indeed, in the past thirty years the standard of such work has risen to a truly surprising degree. The richness and variety, the poetry and masterly craftsmanship of such works as Mackenzie's "Rose of Sharon," Bantock's "Omar Khayyam," Stanford's "Eden" and "Revenge" and "Voyage of Maeldune," mark an awakening in English art which is most hopefully significant.

These indeed stand out as landmarks of the time; and they are worthily supplemented by many other fine works by the same composers, and by a flood of works by their fellow-composers which are all honorably artistic, and many of very high excellence, either for orchestral effect or choral effect, or for both together—such as Stainer's "Daughter of Jairus," "St. Mary Magdalen" and "Crucifixion," Lloyd's "Hero and Leander" and "Andromeda," Corder's "Sword of Argantyr," Bridge's "Callirhoë" and "Nineveh," Cowen's "Sleeping Beauty" and "Ruth," Williams's "Bethany" and "Gethsemane," MacCunn's "Lay of the Last Minstrel" and "Lord Ullin's Daughter," Gray's "Arethusa," and a great many others. The constant increase and improvement of the musical intelligence of choral societies all over the country invites good work on the part of composers; and undoubtedly good music wedded to good poetry makes an artistic combination as worthy of intelligent beings as any that exists.

CHAPTER XXVIII

NEW WORKS IN RECENT YEARS

The Close of the Nineteenth Century and the First Decade of the Twentieth—The Programme Principle—Wagner's Influence—The Russian School—Richard Strauss—Later European Composers.

THE few years intervening between the completion of the works previously discussed and the close of the year 1909 afford such striking illustrations of the tendencies of art latterly observable that they present almost the appearance of the summing-up of an argument. But in order to realize fully their confirmatory nature a short retrospect is necessary.

It is a curious coincidence that the last decade of the eighteenth century had analogously summed up the artistic tendencies of the latter part of that century by the appearance of Haydn's finest symphonies and Beethoven's earliest instrumental compositions, as well as Mozart's "Requiem" and "Die Zauberflöte"; thereby indicating the complete establishment of harmonic principles and the scheme of absolute art of which the sonata, the quartet, and the orchestral symphony were the highest types.

In the first quarter of the nineteenth century Beethoven brought the sonata type to its highest perfection, and at the same time signed its ultimate death-warrant, by indicating the road along which the art was destined to travel to reach the so-called Romantic phase. He not only occasionally resorted to programme, but in his later works of the sonata order showed a marked inclination to abandon the forms usually employed in such classical works and to exceed the limitations of self-contained types, by infusing a human quality, a subconscious emotionalism, which proved in the end to be incompatible with the conception of music which was to be beautiful and interesting of itself without reference to external ideas. In this manner the type of art which was destined to serve the purposes of the newly awakening democracy was planted in the very being of the aristocratic sonata.

The Romantic phase then appears to be a transitional episode between the highly ideal abstract art of the sonata type and the familiar type of programme music which was reached at the end of the nineteenth century. The Romantic movement had been undisguisedly human, but human with reservations. It was full of the fervor of beautiful ideals, of fancies tender and subtle, of elevating aspirations, and of all such human inwardnesses as had a touch of distinction and even of sacredness, implying that art was a thing to be revered and cherished with respectful devotion. But the wide diffusion of the art, which was such a striking feature of the last quarter of the century, tended to obliterate reticence and respect. Its intrinsic qualities were affected by the lack of discrimination of the general audience; and the types of beauty which had been its fit attributes when it was the appanage of a small, cultured and luxurious class, no longer satisfied the minds of a wider public whose outlook on life was very different from that of the old privileged classes.

The art which is to appeal to an immense range of people of very different grades of intelligence and culture must speak plainly to them of things they can readily understand. Most of them have neither time nor disposition to cultivate insight into artistic subtleties and refinements or to develop their taste and powers of concentrated attention; and they look for something which has a tangible, practical reality behind it; so in order to be acceptable, music has to talk less about itself, and more about subjects of general interest. Thus what is called the programme principle —which was dimly discernible in a very lofty phase in Beethoven's work, and became more definite and tangible in the Romantic period—appears in its frankest and least reserved guise in the music which met with the widest general favor in the last decade of the century, and its development represents the decisive outcome of recent artistic evolution.

Many causes combined to this end. Among the most powerful must be counted the overwhelming profusion of performances of excerpts from Wagner's operas in concert-rooms all over the civilized world. When the fierce and bitter animosity which Wagner's music at first aroused died down, public taste swung over, and people could never hear enough of it. But as frequent performances of his entire works with the full panoply of theatrical representation presented insuperable difficulties in most countries, the public craving had to be satisfied with the presentation of the music by itself, without the theatrical adjuncts. Then the effect on the public of listening in concert-rooms to so much music which represents definitely indicated stories and human situations in a very vivid and exciting manner, was to induce an attitude of mind inapt to listen to real concert music, which spoke for itself without reference to things external. It is also worth observing that Wagner's systematic adoption of the device of the *Leitmotiv* has not only been followed by operatic composers, but when also adopted by composers of instrumental music it has tended to replace the older methods of classical and tonal form.

Another influence which has told in the same direction is the enormous development of mere technique in the performers of recent years. Men have been busy finding out ways of overcoming difficulties and enlarging the store of the practicable resources of instruments for over three hundred years; but, as in the department of applied science, the advance has been greater in the last fifty or sixty years than in all the antecedent time. This has placed at the disposal of composers instrumental effects of extraordinary brilliancy and vivacity—a veritable plethora of opportunities for producing exciting contrasts of color and variety of tone; and this just happens to adapt itself to the trend of the development of general intelligence and taste. For it is to be observed that the greater diffusion of musical opportunities appears of late to have developed quickness rather than understanding, the capacity to enjoy the moment rather than to be deeply interested, and the disposition to delight in dexterity and dazzling superficialities of presentment rather than beauty or nobility of thought and feeling.

The gravitation of public taste and its influence upon art is shown in the reaction toward primitive emotional expression, and the art of the less critically self-conscious races such as the Czechs and the Russians. The Czechs have always been among the most spontaneously musical races of Europe, and the fiery vivacity of some of the music of Friedrich Smetana (1824-84), such as his overture to "Die Verkaufte Braut," and his string quartet in E minor, which he called "Aus meinem Leben," illustrates their disposition very happily; while his pupil Antonin Dvořák as their foremost representative composer greatly enhanced their distinction on this account, and illustrated in a very attractive manner the characteristics of a race more primitive and unsophisticated than those among whom art had attained to its greatest and noblest manifestations. These facts are patent in the liveliness of Dvořák's rhythms, his dexterous manipulation of figures of accompaniment, and the native freshness and directness of his tunes, many of which might have been borrowed from the lips of his own peasants or the emancipated negroes of America; while the exuberance and verve of his orchestration betray the Oriental strain in his disposition. The interest which had been aroused by his interesting and expressive "Stabat Mater" and his weird cantata "The Specter's Bride," the "Requiem," and several genial and attractive symphonies, has since been sustained by the "Carneval," "In der Natur" and "Otello," by his "New World" symphony, a violoncello concerto, and some fine quartets and songs.

The qualities of races but little advanced from primitive temperamental conditions are even more conspicuous in the Russian music which almost submerged the world, especially England and America, in the closing years of the last century. The music has naturally appealed to the awakening intelligence of the musical masses by vehement emotional spontaneity, orgiastic frenzy, dazzling effects of color, barbaric rhythm, and unrestrained abandonment to physical excitement which is natural to the less developed races. The first notable presentment of a work in England by Tchaikovsky was the performance of his concerto in B flat minor at the Crystal Palace, London, on March 12, 1876; but the time was scarcely ripe for his work to exert its full fascinations. The exact date when the Russian musical invasion commenced may be given at the performance of his "Pathetic" symphony (in B minor, No. 6) by the Philharmonic Society under the conductorship of Sir Alexander Mackenzie on February 28, 1894. From that moment Wagner's supremacy in the concert-room ceased to be uncontested. Public taste gravitated from the subtle emotionalism of the great Teutonic musical dramatist to the more obvious and highly accentuated passion of the more primitive and plain-speaking Russian. But, as has been before pointed out, Wagner had prepared the way, and had unintentionally led public taste away from the purity of abstract art and created a craving which could only be satisfied with draughts of stimulants of ever-increasing strength.

Tchaikovsky admitted that the "Pathetic" symphony had a programme, and he had intended to call it decisively a programme symphony, but was dissuaded by his brother. But at any rate the public recognized the singular intensity of its emotional expression, ranging from the exaltation of rapture to the depths of almost comatose collapse. As a human document the work was unmistakable, and the interest generated by such a graphic study of subjective states induced a desire for more of the same kind, and for a time the Russian composer became the central object of musical public interest. Several of his other symphonies, especially those in F minor, No. 4, and E minor, No. 5, were eagerly welcomed, though they never attained to the extreme popularity of the "Pathetic" symphony. Of his other works the sparkling and fanciful "Cassenoisette" suite of ballet tunes most nearly touched the high-water mark of public favor, while much interest was excited by his overture "1812," which, as a musical expression of the frenzy of national joy, is remarkably frank and graphic. Of his other numerous works the vivid fantasia for orchestra "Francesca da Rimini," written as early as 1880, is one of the most notable. It was recognized that the composer represented a new type, and the public having gained the clue to it were eager for enlargement of their experience, and chamber music, songs, pianoforte pieces, all characterized by the same profusion and spontaneity of utterance, rich color and excessive sensibility, were welcomed.

The taste thus generated led to acquaintance being desired with the works of other Russian composers, such as Alexander Borodin, whose symphony in B minor appears to have been first performed in England in 1896, while many other works won favor in various branches of art. Rimsky-Korsakov (1844-1908), composer of operas and brilliant orchestral music, enhanced the Russian prestige with his "Capriccio Espagnol" and his "programme" symphony "Antar," performed in England in 1896 and 1900 respectively. Among living Russian composers most attention has been deservedly attracted by Alexandre Glazunov (born 1865), who stands out with distinction among his fellows as being more in touch with the ideals of the great art of the past. Though capable of great force of expression, and gifted with the remarkable instinct for instrumental effect which seems to be characteristic of an Oriental strain, he holds his passion more under control; showing more sense of proportion, continuity of development, love of design, and purity of style than other notable composers of his race. The works which attracted most attention before the end of the last century were his fine symphonies in B flat and C minor, Nos. 5 and 6.

But by the time the musical public were becoming familiar with the Russian type and their interest was ready to transfer itself to fresh developments, the most extreme form of programme music yet presented to the world was just ready to satisfy their craving for a further new experience. The remarkable composer Richard Strauss (born June 11, 1864) may be admitted to have explored the region of programme music in a manner which was new at least in its uncompromising frankness. He had begun his career more or less within the range of the old order with interesting and effective chamber music, and it was not till comparatively late that he found the field in which he could demonstrate his full powers. The works which in the last century represent him in the later phase began with the symphonic poem "Don Juan," produced under Hans von Bülow at Berlin in 1888; "Tod und Verklärung" followed in 1890, and "Macbeth" in the same year. "Till Eulenspiegel" came out at Cologne in 1895; "Also sprach Zarathustra" at Frankfort in the same year; "Don Quixote" at Frankfort in 1897, "Ein Heldenleben" at the same town in 1899; and later his "Symphonia Domestica." (His principal works produced since the opening of the present century are considered in the biographical section of the present series.) The nineteenth century thus completed itself, and summed up the outcome of its musical proclivities.

Richard Strauss is a man of fine intellectual conceptions, who endeavors to expound them in the most vivid terms the complex possibilities of the modern orchestra afford. Gifted with deep feeling, a great sense of humor, with phenomenal resourcefulness, and the conviction that the ends justify any means which tend to complete and striking characterization, he so far represents the most uncompromising manifestation of musical art as a means to express vividly something outside itself. Abandoning the hope that music can any longer have full measure of vitality while produced in accordance with the old ideals of abstract beauty and interest of development, he frankly faces the problem of finding ideas external to music which are sufficiently rich in interest and sufficiently typical and comprehensive to be worth expending the fullest resources of art in their emotional and quasi-pictorial presentment.

With the view of making his intention clear and unmistakable he resorts to realistic devices of the most graphic description, and to combinations of sounds which show frank disregard of euphony; but at the same time he shows mastery of design of a new kind in the laying out of his work in broad and even impressive lines, in which the sequence of moods and the contrasts between them are employed as much as the old principles of the relations of keys to give the effect of design, and he has the gift of presenting his material in a manner which arrests attention. He also illustrates in the fullest degree the advanced evolution of orchestral style—wherein the dazzling variety of passages which illustrate the idiosyncrasies and characteristic capacities of the various instruments employed, are effectually welded into artistic unity.

While the attention of the widest general public was especially drawn to the more urgent forms of novelty, the main stream of serious artistic work continued in ample volume and fine quality. In England Sir Alexander C. Mackenzie produced his merry and vivacious overture "Britannia" in 1894 and his oratorio "Bethlehem" in the same year, and he added to the copious list of his compositions the suite "From the North" in 1895, his "Scottish Concerto" for pianoforte and orchestra in 1897, and his music to the dramatized version of Barrie's "Little Minister" in the same year. The remarkable facility and artistic perception and resourcefulness of Charles Villiers Stanford were illustrated by his fine symphony "L'Allegro ed il Pensieroso" and his pianoforte concerto in G, both of which came out in 1895; by his "Requiem," which was produced at the Birmingham Festival in 1897; by his "Te Deum," which came out at the Leeds Festival in 1898; by his variations for pianoforte and orchestra on the old tune "Down among the Dead Men," produced in 1899, and his setting of Henley's poem, "The Last Post," produced in 1900, and many other characteristic and admirable works. Frederic H. Cowen enhanced his eminent position among English composers by his cantata "The Water Lily," which came out in 1893, his "Transfiguration," his suite "In Fairyland," his "Dream of Endymion," his fine "Ode to the Passions," and his "Idyllic" symphony.

Edward German (born 1862), who had won deserved popularity by the characteristic freshness and spontaneity of his ideas and the effectiveness of his orchestration, gave further proof of the range of his powers by his symphony in A minor (produced at the Norwich Festival of 1893), his effective suite for orchestra in D minor, his English fantasia, since known as "A Rhapsody on March Themes," his symphonic poem "Hamlet," and by much admirable and appropriate music to plays, such as the music for "Henry VIII," "The Tempest," and "Romeo and Juliet." Frederick Cliffe, whose brilliant first symphony had attracted much attention in 1889, followed it up with a second in E minor (produced at the Leeds Festival in 1892) and with a violin concerto successfully played by M. Tivadar Nachez at the Norwich Festival in 1896. Sir Frederick Bridge brought out his cantata "The Flag of England" in 1897, and his "Ballad of the Clampherdown" in 1899. Charles Harford Lloyd produced "A Song of Judgment" at the Hereford Festival in 1891, a "Ballad of Sir Ogie and the Ladie Elsie" at the Hereford Festival in 1894, a masterly concerto for the organ at the Gloucester Festival in 1895, a Festival Overture at Gloucester in 1895, and a "Hymn of Thanksgiving" in 1897. Hamish MacCunn (born 1868) brought out "Queen Hynde of Caledon" in 1892, and the suite "Highland Memories" in 1897. Arthur Somervell (born 1863), who had delighted the lovers of imaginative and finished art by his characteristic songs, produced the orchestral ballad "Helen of Kirkconnel" in 1893, a cantata, "The Forsaken Merman," at the Leeds Festival in 1895, and "Ode to the Sea" at the Birmingham Festival, 1897.

H. Walford Davies first began to attract interested attention by a symphony in D and the choral ballad Hervé Riel" in 1895, and a setting of Psalm xxiii and a motet, "God Created Man," in 1900. W. H. Bell produced the symphonic poems "Canterbury Pilgrims" in 1898 and "The Pardoner's Tale" in 1899, and a symphony, "Walt Whitman," in 1900. William Wallace, an ardent sympathizer with the phases of art which represent its characteristic movement in recent years, produced the symphonic poem "The Passing of Beatrice" in 1892, a strenuous prelude to the

"Eumenides" of Æschylus in 1893, an overture "In Praise of Scottish Poesie" in 1894, a symphonic poem, "Amboss oder Hammer," in 1896, a symphonic poem, "Sister Helen," in 1899, a symphony, "The Creation," and a cycle of "Freebooters' Songs" in 1899, and a suite of five movements having reference to Maeterlinck's "Pelléas and Mélisande" in 1900, works which show a poetic and cultured mind, and keen and genuine feeling for orchestral expression.

The young composer Coleridge-Taylor (born 1875) sprang to a prominent position in the musical world with his "Hiawatha," the first part of which was performed for the first time at a concert given at the Royal College of Music in November, 1898. Two more parts were afterward added to complete the work, and in that form it has since been everywhere in request. His powers have also been illustrated by other popular works in various branches of art, such as his Orchestral Ballade (1898) and his "Scenes from an Everyday Romance" (1900). A new light of exceptional brilliancy came rapidly to the forefront in the last five years of the nineteenth century in the person of Edward Elgar (born 1857), whose fine cantatas "King Olaf" and "Caractacus" came out respectively at Hanley in 1896 and at Leeds in 1898. And yet more convincing proofs of his fertility of invention and exceptional mastery of orchestral effect were afforded by his remarkable Orchestral Variations (1899); and he completed the century and aroused the interest of the musical world even more effectually by his vivid and imaginative oratorio "The Dream of Gerontius," a presage of further striking works which duly made their appearance as the first-fruits of the new century.

Besides cultivating these larger forms of art, English composers showed an awakening to the artistic opportunities afforded by chamber music, and works of high quality in this branch were produced during the last decade of the century by the older composers, as well as by many of the later generation, such as H. Walford Davies, Richard Walthew, and Ernest Walker.

The volume of fine music represented by such copious productivity of British composers in all branches of art (for opera has yet to be touched upon) is a most significant feature in the closing years of the last century. For while in earlier days the manifestations of their higher energies had been overmuch centered in Anglican Church music—which stood by itself as a self-contained branch of art, presenting some fine compositions here and there, but barely in touch with the general movement of art in the world—this branch of Church music itself began to expand into wider significance in the first half of the century, as in the works of John Goss (1800-80), Henry Smart (1813-79), Thomas Attwood Walmisley (1814-56), and Samuel Sebastian Wesley (1810-76), whose justly beloved anthem "The Wilderness" was performed with orchestral accompaniment at the Birmingham Festival in 1852; and while the secular branches of art were often illustrated by W. Sterndale Bennett, as before noted, the growth of respect for music and a more liberal and appreciative attitude toward musicians encouraged composers of serious aims and higher capacities to take a line more independent of the cogency of ephemeral recognition, and in the last decade of the century the music produced by native composers attained to the cosmopolitan condition which successfully illustrates all its various branches, and takes its place worthily in the grand scheme of general art.

European composers of various nationalities were also very active in the latest years of the last century, and many striking works were produced. In Italian music the most conspicuous manifestation in the range of the concert-room was the attention bestowed upon the young composer Lorenzo Perosi (born 1872), whose oratorios "La Transfigurazione di Gesù Cristo," "La Risurrezione di Lazzaro," and "La Risurrezione di Cristo" aroused considerable excitement by a certain novelty and ingenuousness of treatment, which was maintained by the oratorio "La Passione di Cristo." The traditional predisposition of Italian composers for opera leaves them comparatively little energy for concert-room music; but among the works which illustrate the powers of the most distinguished Italians of the time may be mentioned the symphony "Epitalamio" of Giovanni Sgambati (born 1843), produced in Italy in 1888, and his "Requiem," which came out in 1896. The brilliant overture "Cleopatra," which the composer Luigi Mancinelli (born 1848) brought to its first hearing in England at the Norwich Festival of 1893, was in reality an early work, and the vivid "Hero and Leander" had its first performance as opera in New York at the Metropolitan, 1903. Of more decisively concert-room works by the same composer the "Scene Veneziane" may be mentioned, which came out in 1890. Among distinguished examples of the highest forms of art the admirable symphony in D minor by Giuseppe Martucci (born 1856) is also worthy of record, a work first performed in England at a concert given at the Royal College of Music in 1898. Among other works by this able composer and conductor a pianoforte concerto, a pianoforte quartet and trio, and a violoncello sonata are included.

In connection with French music of the concert-room the most interesting feature in recent years was the late revelation of the high qualities of the works of César Franck (1822-90), which had hardly even attained to a hearing in his lifetime. The recent performances of his symphony in D minor, his choral work "The Beatitudes" (first performed at Glasgow in 1900), and his violin sonata, pianoforte quintet, and string quartet made apparent their high qualities of sincerity, deep feeling, and artistic interest, and aroused a natural astonishment that a composer of such rare powers should have been entirely without recognition while he lived. Among well-known French composers the versatility of Charles C. Saint-Saëns has been illustrated by his cantata "Nuit persane," produced in 1893, a new trio for pianoforte and strings, which came out in 1892, and a fifth pianoforte concerto in 1896. Charpentier (born 1860) illustrated the tendencies of the day in his suite "Impressions d'Italie," his symphonic poem "Napoli" (1891), his opera "Louise," now well known in America, and his symphonic drama "La vie du poète" (1892), while Vincent d'Indy produced his symphonic poem "La forêt enchantée" and the music to "Karadec" in 1892, and a string quartet in 1898.

As illustrating the activity of Scandinavian composers, the symphony in D minor of the Norwegian C. Sinding (born 1856) may be referred to, which was performed in Berlin in 1895 and at the Crystal Palace in 1898, and attention has also been attracted to the same composer's pianoforte concerto, pianoforte quintet, and quartet for strings; and Edvard Grieg added to his earlier well-known compositions a scene "Der Einsame" in 1892.

The Belgian composer Edgar Tinel (born 1854) in the later years of the century attracted interested attention by his oratorio "St. Francis," performed at the Cincinnati Festival of 1894 and at the Cardiff Festival in 1895, and he has also written a mass (1892), entr'actes to Corneille's "Polyeucte," the cantatas "Kollebloemen" and "De drie Ridders," and a Te Deum.

In Germany the veteran Max Bruch brought out a third violin concerto in 1891, "Leonidas" in 1893, and "Moses" in 1895. Karl Goldmark (born 1830) produced a sonata for pianoforte and violoncello and a second suite for violin and pianoforte in 1893, and an overture, "Sappho," and a scherzo for orchestra in 1894, and a setting of Psalm cxiii in 1897. The popular composer Moritz Moszkovski brought out a second pianoforte concerto in 1898, and Engelbert Humperdinck, who had won such deserved favor in the department of opera, produced a Moorish rhapsody, which was performed at the Leeds Festival in 1898. In the latest years of the century Felix Weingartner (born 1863) came into considerable prominence both in Germany and in England, the works by which he gained much honorable reputation being the symphonic poems "King Lear" (1897) and the "Gefilde der Seligen" (1897), a symphony in G major (1899), and a symphony in E flat major and several string quartets and songs. The British-born composer known as Eugen d'Albert not only maintained his reputation as one of the finest living pianists, but gave to the world "Der Mensch und das Leben" in 1894, and a second pianoforte concerto in 1897, besides several operas which will be referred to later.

It is noticeable that the most conspicuous and interesting features of the music of the later years of the nineteenth century were in the range of music for the concert-room. In the operatic field the preëminent achievements of Richard Wagner left comparatively little room for anything of the nature of new departures, but the influence of his theories and examples has been universally perceptible in the comparative abandonment of set forms and the adoption of a style and method better adapted to the requirements of continuous dialogue and dramatic development. The most notable work in this sphere of art was Verdi's "Falstaff." In this work the veteran composer again manifested the vigor and distinguished style which had come with such a surprise upon the musical world with his "Otello." Here indeed was one of the most remarkable instances of a composer's arriving at his highest standard of fine artistic thought and diction at the age of eighty, maintaining all the freshness of humor and gaiety and warm feeling of his youth, and addressing himself, with full measure of success, rather to musicians of culture and taste than to the wider public he favored in earlier years.

Of almost equal importance and significance has been the phenomenal success of the opera "Hänsel und Gretel," by Engelbert Humperdinck (born 1854), which began its happy career in 1894. Something of the success may have been attributed to the folksongs and tunes of that type which are embodied in the work, which illustrate the disposition before referred to, in connection with Czech and Russian music, to seek for the renewal of spontaneous vitality in the primitive foundations of music, though it is true that in Humperdinck's case the reversion is in a more natural and healthy phase. But the opera also won its way by the attractiveness of the subject and the singular aptness with which the composer adopted and maintained a style perfectly and consistently adapted to the innocent sweetness of a children's legend.

Apart from these two specially prominent works, operas were produced in all countries in great profusion in the last decade of the century. Of the younger Italian composers Giacomo Puccini (born 1858) deservedly attracted attention by his admirable opera "Manon Lescaut" in 1893. He enhanced the estimation in which he was held by "La vie de Bohème" in 1896, added another remarkable work in "La Tosca" in 1899, and began the new century with "Madame Butterfly." Ruggiero Leoncavallo (born 1858) brought out the highly dramatic "Pagliacci" in 1892, "I Medici" in 1893, "Tommaso Chatterton" in 1896, another "La Bohème" in 1897, and "Zaza" in 1900. Umberto Giordano (born 1869) produced "Mala Vita" in 1892, "Regina Diaz" in 1894, "André Chénier" in 1896, and "Fédora" in 1898. Pietro Mascagni (born 1863), who had made such a mark with his dramatic "Cavalleria Rusticana" in 1890, followed it up with "Amico Fritz" in 1891, with "William Ratcliffe" and "Silvano" in 1895, and with "Zanetto" (1896) and "Iris" (1898); and Alberto Franchetti (born 1860) produced "Cristoforo Colombo" in 1892, "Fior d'Alpe" in 1894, and "Il Signor de Pourceaugnac" in 1897.

The profuse operatic facility of French composers was illustrated by J. E. F. Massenet's "Werther" in 1892, by his vivid "La Navarraise" in 1894, by "Thaïs" in 1894, by "Sapho" in 1897, and by "Cendrillon" in 1899; by Saint-Saëns's "Phryne" in 1893, "Antigone" in 1894, the ballet "Javotte" in 1896, and the music to "Déjanire" in 1898; by Alfred Bruneau's "Le Rêve" (1892), "L'attaque du moulin" (1893), and "Messidor" (1897); by Vincent d'Indy's "Fervaal" (1895); and by Debussy's "Pelléas et Mélisande" (1902).

In Germany also there was a profuse outpouring of operas during the short period under consideration. Richard Strauss gave the world further evidence of his copious facility in "Guntram," which came out at Weimar in 1894, "Feuersnot," at Dresden in 1901, "Salome," at Dresden in 1905, and "Elektra" (1908). Goldmark produced "Das Heimchen am Herd" in 1896, and "Die Kriegsgefangene" in 1899; Hugo Wolf, "Der Corregidor" in 1896; Hans Pfitzner, "Der arme Heinrich" in 1895; H. Zöllner made a mark with "Bei Sedan" and "Der Ueberfall" in 1895, and with "Das hölzerne Schwert" in 1897, and "Die versunkene Glocke" in 1899; and Felix Weingartner with "Genesius," which was produced in 1895; while Eugen d'Albert illustrated the spirit of the country of his adoption in "Der Rubin" in 1893, in "Ghismonda" in 1895, "Gernot" in 1897, "Kain" in 1899, and "Tragabaldas" and "Tiefland" in 1907.

In England the long and successful story of the so-called Gilbert and Sullivan type of Savoy operas came to an end with "The Rose of Persia" (produced in 1899), for which Basil Hood supplied the libretto. The composer herein showed all his old vivacity, gaiety, and tunefulness. He died, widely lamented throughout the whole country, in the following year. "The Emerald Isle," part of which had been written before his death, was completed by Edward German and produced in 1900. Of other achievements in the line of opera in England the most notable was Charles Villiers Stanford's brilliant "Shamus O'Brien" (1896), an Irish opera full of native humor and sensibility and dexterous artistic work. Frederic H. Cowen also produced several serious operas of large dimensions toward the end of the century, as "Signa" in 1893 and "Harold" in 1895. Sir Alexander Mackenzie adventured into the province of humorous Savoy opera with "His Majesty" in 1897. Hamish MacCunn also produced the opera "Jeanie Deans" in 1894 and "Diarmid" in 1897. Granville Bantock illustrated the tendencies and abilities of the younger generation in "Rameses II," 1891, "Cædmar," 1892, "The Pearl of Iran," 1894, and works of a dramatic cast for the concert-room.

In the United States the only important operatic works that have come to light in recent years were Walter Damrosch's "Scarlet Letter," Arthur F. Nevin's "Poia," Converse's "Pipe of Desire" and "The Sacrifice," Chadwick's "Judith" and Paine's "Azara," the last two having been heard only on the concert stage.

A GUIDE TO THE PRONUNCIATION OF FOURTEEN LANGUAGES

REVISED BY W. J. BALTZELL

A GUIDE TO THE PRONUNCIATION OF FOURTEEN LANGUAGES

(Note.—Letters not included are to be pronounced as in English. In general, and in most languages, accented vowels are long.)

1. GERMAN.

a—like a in far.
ä (ae)—like a in fate.
ai—like i in fine.
au—like ow in cow.
äu (aeu) and eu—like oy in boy.
e long—like a in fate.
e short—like e in met.
ei—like i in fine.
i long—like ee in meet.
i short—like i in pin.
o—like o in note.
ö (oe)—between a in fate and e in err.
u long—like oo in mood.
u short—like oo in foot.
ü (ue)—like ee in meet, pronounced with lips bunched as in whistling.
c—like ts before e, i, or ä; otherwise like k.
ch is a hissing k (the Greek Chi), derived from c, just as th comes from t. The hissing ch sound is represented by kh in the dictionary.
d or dt final—like t in pet.
j—like y in yet.
qu—like qv.
r—strongly rolled, as in most foreign languages.
s before a vowel is like z.
st and sp are like sht and shp.
sch—like sh in shop.
v—like f in fate.
w—like v in vat.
y—like ee in meet.
z—like ts.

2. FRENCH.

a long—like a in far.
a short—somewhat like a in fat.
ai—like a in fate.
aï—pronounced ah-ee.
au and eau—like o in note.
é—like a in fate.
è—like a in fare.
ê—like e in met.
e—like e in err.
e or es final—is usually silent.
ent final—in verbs is silent.
ei—is like e in met.
eu—is like the German ö, or the a in fate pronounced with the lips bunched as if for whistling.
i long—is like ee in meet.
i short—is like i in pin.
o long and ô—like o in note.
o short—much like o in not, with a trace of the u in but.
oi—much like wa in swat.
oei—like the e in err, followed by the ee in meet.
oeu—much like the e in err.
ou—like oo in mood.
u—like ee in meet, pronounced with the lips bunched as if for whistling.
y—like ee in meet.

At the end of a word, or of a syllable, if the next syllable begins with a consonant, French vowels followed by m or n are made nasal:

an—is between ahng and ohng, with the ng sound not exactly made, but the nasal quality of the vowel kept throughout.
in, ein, ain—like the ang in fang, made nasal throughout without the ng.
en—like ong in song, with wholly nasal vowel and no actual ng sound.
on—like the aw sound in long, nasal throughout and without ng.
un—like the u of urn, made nasal throughout.
ç, or c before e, i, or y—like s; otherwise like k.
g before e, i, or y—like zh, as of s in measure; otherwise like g in get.
h—always silent.
j—like zh, as of s in measure.
ll—between two vowels is often like y.
m final—after a vowel, or at ends of syllables, treated as if it were n final, and made to disappear in the nasal quality of the vowel.
qu—like k.
sc—like s.
x final—is silent.

3. ITALIAN.

a long—as in father.
a short—as in tufa.
e long—as a in fate.
e short—as e in met.
i long—as ee in meet.
i short—as i in pin.
o long—as o in note.

ó—between o in note and oo in took.
u long—like u in rule.
u short—like u in pull.
c or cc before e or i—like ch in chat; otherwise like k.
ch—like k.
g or gg before e or i—like g in gem; otherwise like g in get.
gli—like lee.
gn—like ni in pinion.
gh—like g in get.
j—like y, or if used as a vowel, like ee in meet.
z—like ts.
zz—like ds.

In general, double consonants are given more time than single ones.

4. SPANISH.

a long or å—like a in far.
a short—like a in hat.
e long—like a in fate.
e short—like e in met.
i long—like ee in meet.
i short—like i in pin.
o long—like o in note.
o short—like o in not.
u long—like u in rule.
u short—like u in full.
ue—like wa in wade.
y—like ee in meet.
Every vowel pronounced separately.
b—somewhat like v in very.
c before e, i, or y—like th in thank; otherwise like k.
ch—like ch in chat.
d—somewhat like th in then.
e before e, i, or y—like the German ch; otherwise like g in get.
j—like ye in yet.
ll—like lli in thrillium.
ñ—like ni in pinion.
qu—like k.
initial x—in some names like h; otherwise like x in fix.
z—like th in thank.

5. PORTUGUESE.

Some of the vowels are like the Spanish vowels, but ä, ö and ü are made very strongly nasal.
c before e, i, or y—like s; otherwise like k.
cc before e, i, or y—like ks; otherwise like k.
g before e, i, or y—like g in gem; otherwise like g in get.
h—is silent.
j—like j in jog.
lh—like lli in trillium.
m and n at the end of syllables often made nasal, as in French.
ph—like f in far.
qu before e or i—like k; otherwise like qu in quit.
s between vowels—like z.
x after e—like x in fox; otherwise like sh in shop.
z—at the end of syllables like s.

6. RUSSIAN.

a accented—like a in far.
a unaccented—like a in fat.
a initial—has a slight y sound before it, as in yard.
e—like e in met.
e initial, if accented—like yo in yodel.
e initial, if unaccented—like ye in yes.
i after labials (b, f, m, p, or v)—like i in pin; otherwise like ee in meet.
o—like o in not.
u—like ew in few, or like oo in loon.
y—like ee in meet.
Diphthongs as in German.
b—like a hard v.
c—like s or z.
ch final—like the German ch; otherwise like ch in chat.
g—usually like g in get; but a g final, and sometimes initial, like the German ch.
j—like y in yes.
qu before e or i—like k; otherwise like qu in quote.
s between vowels—like z.
tsch—like sh in shop, followed by ch in chat.
v—like f.
w—like f.
z—like ts, or sometimes like ch.

Russian names are usually spelled phonetically in English, the K of Konstantin, for instance, being replaced by our C.

7. NORWEGIAN.

a—like a in far.
aa—somewhat like o in north.
au—like o in note.
e final—like e in err; otherwise like a in fate.
i—like ee in meet.
o long—like o in note.
o short—like o in not, or like u in pull.
oe—like a in fate.
ö—like the French eu.
u—like u in rule.
y—like the French u.
g—always like g in get; except that g before j or y is like y in yet.
j—like y in yet.
k—before i or y is made somewhat like h.
kv—like qu in quit.
qu—like qu in quit.
z—like ts.

8. SWEDISH.

a long—like a in far.
a short—like a in tufa.
å long—like o in note.
å short—like a in what.
ä—like a in fare.
e long—like i in film.
e short—like e in met.
er—like air in fair.
i—like ee in meet.

o long—like o in move.
o short—like o in not.
ö—like the German ö.
u long—like u in rule.
u short—like u in pull.
c before **e, i,** or **y**—like s; otherwise like k.
ch—like the German ch.
d—is silent before j or t.
f—at the end of a syllable is like v.
g before **ä, e, i, o,** or **y,** or after **l** or **r**—is like y in yet.
j—like y in yet.
qv—like k.
sk, sj, or **stj**—somewhat like sh in shop.
th—like t.
tj—like ch in chat.
w—like v.
z—like s.

9. DANISH.

a—like a in far.
aa—like a in fall.
e—like a in fate, or like ai in fair.
ej—like i in mite.
i—like ee in meet.
o long—like o in move.
o short—like o in not.
o—like the German ö.
ö—like e in err.
u long—like u in rule.
u short—like u in full.
y—like y in myrrh.
ae—like ai in sail, or like ai in said.
ai—like i in mite.
au—like ow in cow.
c before **e, i,** or **y**—like s; otherwise like k.
ch—like k.
d final—like th in this.
ds—like ss in miss.
g after **e** or **ö**—like y in yet; otherwise like g in get.
j—like y in yet.
qv—like qu in quit.
x—like z.

10. DUTCH.

a long (aa)—like a in far.
a short—like a in mat.
aai—like the vowel sound of why.
e long (ee)—like a in fate.
e short—like e in met.
i long—somewhat like ee in meet.
i short—like i in pin.
ei (ij)—like e in met, followed by i in pin.
o long (oo)—like o in note.
o short—like o in not.
ooi—like o in note, followed by i in pin.
u long (uu)—like u in rule.
u short—like u in nut.
y—like i in slide.
ae—often replaces aa, with the same sound.
au—like a in fat, followed by oo, as in loon.

eu—like the German ö.
eeu (ieu)—like the a in fate, followed by a faint **v**.
ie—like ee in meet.
oe—like oo in loon.
ou—like the o in not, followed by the u in rule.
ui—almost like the sound of why.
b final—like p.
d final—like t.
g—like g in get.
j—like y.
kw—like qu in quit.
l—before a consonant is followed by a slight e sound; i.e., our word eld would be pronounced "el-ed."
ph—like f.
sj—like sh in shop.
ch—like the German ch, but much exaggerated.
sch initial—like stch (s before the ch of chat).
v final—like f.
w—like w in wet.

11. POLISH.

a—like a in far.
ą—like a in fall.
e—like e in met.
ę—like the French nasal in see.
é—like a in fate.
i—like ee in meet.
o—like o in note.
ó—between the o in note and the o in move.
u—like u in rule.
yj—like ee in meet.
oe—like a in fate.
c—like ts.
ch—like the German ch.
cz—like ch in chat.
dż—like dge in ledge.
j—like y in yes.
sz—like sh in shop.
w—like v.
z—like z in zone.
ż—like zh, as the s in measure.

12. BOHEMIAN.

a—like u in fun.
á—like a in far.
e—like e in met.
é—like ai in fair.
ĕ—like ya in yam.
i long—like ee in meet.
i short—like i in pin.
o—like o in note.
ó—like o in wrong.
u—like u in pull.
ú—like u in rule.
y—like i in pin.
ý—like ee in meet.
All vowels pronounced separately.
c—like ts or ds.

j—like y in yes.
ñ—like ni in pinion.
q—like qu in quit.
ř—like rzh or rsh.
š—like sh in shop.
ž—like zh, as the s in measure.

13. HUNGARIAN.

a—like a in what.
á—like a in far.
e—like e in met.
é—like a in fate.
i—like i in pin.
í—like ee in meet.
o—like o in note, sounded briefly.
ó—like o in note, prolonged.
ö—like the German ö.
u—like u in pull.
ú—like u in rule.
ü—like the French u.
cs—like ch in chat.
cz—like ts.
dj—like gy in orgy.
djs—like j in joy.
gy—like dy.
ggy—with a little extra vowel sound, as gygy.
j—like y in yes.

jj—like y prolonged.
ll or ly—like y prolonged.
nny—with an extra vowel sound, as nyny.
s or sz—like sh in shop.
tty—with an extra vowel sound, as tyty.

14. WELSH.

a—like a in mat.
â—like ai in air.
e—like e in met.
ê—like ee in meet.
i—like ee in meet.
o—like o in gone.
ô—like o in note.
u—somewhat like i in pin.
û—like ee in meet.
w (here a vowel)—like oo in loon.
y final—like y in pity; otherwise like y in myrrh.
c—always like k.
ch—like the German ch.
dd—like th in then.
f—like v.
ff—like f.
g—always like g in get.
ll—like l, with a suggestion of th.
ph—like f.
th—like th in thin.

BIOGRAPHICAL
DICTIONARY
OF
MUSICIANS

REVISED AND ENLARGED BY NICHOLAS DEVORE

ABBREVIATIONS

Acad.	Academy	mbd.	Member of the Board of Directors
Amer.	American	mss.	manuscripts
arr.	arranged; arrangements	N. Y. Phil.	New York Philharmonic-Symphony Society Orchestra
b.	born		
c.	about	orch.	orchestra
cath.	cathedral	org.	organist
cf.	compare	perf.	performed; performer
ch.	church	p.	pupil (of)
chamb. mus.	chamber music	pcs.	pieces
coll.	college	pf.	pianoforte
collab.	collaboration	Phil.	Philharmonic
comp.	composer (of)	prod.	produced
conc.-m.	concert-master (of)	prof.	professor
cond.	conductor; conducted	q.	quartet
Cons.	Conservatory	q. v.	which see—
d.	died	R. A. M.	Royal Academy of Music, London
dir.	director	Rus.	Russia
ed.	edited; editor; edition	Soc.	Society
edu.	educated (at)	Sp.	Spain
Eng.	England	SPAM	Society for the Publication of American Music
estab.	established	st.	studied under
fac. mem.	faculty member	str.	string
fd.	founder of; founded	str. q.	string quartet
fest.	festival	succ.	successor (to)
Fr.	French	symph.	symphony; symphonic
Ger.	German	symph. p.	symphonic poem
gr.	graduated (from)	t.	teacher (of) (at)
h.	Maintains home (at)	u.	under
ib.	in the same place; there	U.	University
incl.	including	v.	vide; see
It.	Italian	w.	with
m.	married	wks	works
mus.	music; musical	wr.	wrote
Met. op.	Metropolitan Opera House, New York		

BIOGRAPHICAL DICTIONARY OF MUSICIANS

A

Abbot, Jane Bingham. Composer; *b.* Charlotte, Va., 1851; *d.* Chicago, Feb. 20, 1934. Comp. ballads, incl., *Just for Today* (1893).

Abbott, Emma. Soprano; *b.* Chicago, Dec. 9, 1850; *d.* Salt Lake City, Utah, Jan. 5, 1891. Celebrated opera prima donna.

Abeille (*Ah-bay-yeh*), **Johann Christian Ludwig.** Pianist, composer; *b.* Bayreuth, Feb. 20, 1761; *d.* Stuttgart, Mar. 2, 1838. Some of his songs still in use in schools.

Abel (*Ah-bel*), **Karl Friedrich.** Viola da gamba player, composer; *b.* Köthen, Ger., 1725; *d.* London, Jun. 20, 1787; *p.* J. S. Bach.

Abel, Ludwig. Violinist, composer; *b.* Eckartsberge, Ger., Jan. 14, 1835; *d.* Neu-Pasing, Ger., Aug. 13, 1895.

Abendroth, Hermann. Conductor; *b.* Frankfort, Jan. 19, 1883. 1903, cond., Orchester-Verein, Munich; 1914, succ. Fritz Steinbach as dir. Gurzenich concerts, Cologne; 1922, dir. Konzert-Gesellschaft, Cologne.

Abert, Hermann. German musicologist; *b.* Stuttgart, Mar. 25, 1871; *d.* ib., Aug. 13, 1927. 1920, succ., Riemann at U. of Leipzig; wr. many theoretical and aesthetic treatises on mus.

Abert (*Ah-bert*), **Johann Joseph.** Composer; *b.* Kochowitz, Boh., Sept. 21, 1832; *d.* Stuttgart, 1915. Comp. operas, overtures, symphonies.

Abott, Bessie Pickins (Mrs. T. W. Story). Soprano; *b.* Riverdale, N. Y., 1878; *d.* New York, Feb. 9, 1919. Successful opera and concert singer.

Abranyi, Emil. Opera composer; *b.* Budapest, Sept. 22, 1882. Son of Kornel A. Cond. music. *h.* Budapest.

Abranyi (*Ah-bran-yee*), **Kornel.** Composer; *b.* Szent Györgz Abranyi, Hun., Oct. 15, 1822; *d.* Budapest, Dec. 20, 1903. Promoter of national music.

Abt (*Ahbt*), **Franz.** Composer; *b.* Eilenburg, Ger., Dec. 22, 1819; *d.* Wiesbaden, Mar. 31, 1885. Comp. many songs and part-songs which were widely popular in his day.

Achron (*Ak-ron*), **Joseph.** Composer, violinist; *b.* Lodzeye (now Lithuania), May 1, 1886; *p.* Liadow; 1925, to U. S. for première of *Salome's Dance* at Met. op.; perf. violin concerto with Koussevitzky and Boston Symph. *t.* Los Angeles. Comp. operas, 3 violin concertos, chamb. mus., all in modern idiom; also violin pcs., incl. *Hebrew Melody* and *Romanesca*.

Ackermann, A. J. Organist, composer; *b.* Rotterdam, 1836. *t.* The Hague.

Ackté-Renvall, Aino (*Ahk-tay, I-no*). Soprano; *b.* Helsingfors, Fin., Apr. 23, 1876. 1904-6 Met. op.; 1911, estab. Finnish Opera Festivals.

Adam, Adolphe Charles. Composer; *b.* Paris, Jul. 24, 1803; *d.* ib., May 3, 1856. Best known through opera, *Le Postillon de Longjumeau*.

Adam de la Hale (*Hahl*). Trouvère; *b.* Arras, Fr. c. 1240; *d.* Naples, c. 1287. Comp. *Robin and Marian*, possibly the first comic opera.

Adamowski, Antoinette Szumowska (*Shoo-moff-skah*). Pianist, teacher; *b.* Lublin, Pol., Feb. 22, 1868. Wife of Josef A.

Adamowski, Josef. 'Cellist; *b.* Warsaw, Jul. 4, 1862; *d.* Cambridge, Mass., May 8, 1930; bro. of Timothée A.; 1883, debut, Warsaw; 1889-1903, Boston Symph.; 1903, prof. New England Cons.

Adamowski (*Ah-dahm-off-skee*). **Timothée.** Violinist; *b.* Warsaw, Pol., Mar. 24, 1858. *t.* N. E. Cons., Boston.

Adams, Charles R. Tenor; *b.* Charlestown, Mass., 1848; *d.* West Harwich, Jul. 3, 1900. Successful in opera. 1861, in Europe. 1877, *t.* Boston.

Adams, Mrs. Crosby. Pianist, composer; *b.* Niagara Falls, N. Y., Mar. 25, 1858. Specialist in teaching methods for children.

Adams, Ernest Harry. Composer, teacher, pianist; *b.* Waltham, Mass., Jul. 16, 1886. *p.* Benj. Cutter. Comp. pf. pcs., incl. *Tone Fancies After Famous Paintings;* also songs, orch., chamb. mus.

Adams, Stephen. See **Maybrick, Michael.**

Adams, Suzanne. Soprano; *b.* Cambridge, Mass., 1872. Popular in England.

Adgate, Andrew. Concert impresario, author; *d.* Phila. 1793, during yellow fever epidemic. Fd. Uranian Academy (showing he was student of astrology); 1786, gave concert for Penn Hospital, with chorus of 230, and orchestra of 50. Author of musical textbooks and collections.

Adler, Clarence. Pianist, teacher; *b.* Cincinnati, O. *p.* Joseffy. 1907, debut, Berlin. 1913, New York; fd. New York Trio.

Adler (*Ahd-ler*), **Guido.** Theorist, author; *b.* Eibenschütz, Aus., Nov. 1, 1855; *d.* Vienna, Nov. 1, 1925; st. Bruckner; prof. mus. history in Vienna U.

Adler, Vincent. Pianist, composer; *b.* Raab, Hun., Apr. 3, 1826; *d.* Geneva, Switz., Jan. 4, 1871.

Aegidius, Johannes. Spanish monk in thirteenth century. Wr. *Ars Musica.*

Aerts (*Airtz*), **Egide.** Flutist, composer; *b.* Antwerp, 1822; *d.* Brussels, 1853.

Aerts, Félix. Violinist, conductor; *b.* St. Trond, Bel., 1827; *d.* Nivelles, 1888.

Afanassiev, Nicolai Jakovlevitch. Composer; *b.* Tobolsk, Sib., 1821; *d.* Petrograd, Jun. 3, 1898. Comp. operas, symph. and chamb. mus.

Afferni (*Ahf-fair-nee*), **Ugo.** Pianist, conductor; *b.* Florence, Jan. 1, 1871. Comp. opera *Potemkin.* Returned to Italy at outbreak of World War.

Afranio (*A-frah-nee-o*). Canon at Ferrara, Italy, in sixteenth century. Invented the bassoon.

Afzelius (*Ahf-zay-lee-oos*), **Arvid.** Writer; *b.* Enköping, Swed., May 6, 1785; *d.* Sept. 25, 1871. Folk-song collector.

Agnelli (*Ah-nyel-lee*), **Salvatore.** Composer; *b.* Palermo, 1817; *d.* 1874. Comp. operas.

Agostini, Paolo. Composer; *b.* Valerano, It., 1593; *d.* Rome, 1629.

Agramonte (*Ah-gra-mon-teh*), **Emilio.** Conductor, vocal teacher; *b.* Puerto Principe, Cuba, Nov. 28, 1844. *t.* New York.

Agricola, Johann Friedrich. Organist, writer; *b.* Dobitz, Ger., Jan. 4, 1720; *d.* Berlin, Dec. 1, 1774.

Agricola (*Ah-grik-o-la*), **Martin.** Theorist; *b.* Sorau, Ger., 1486; *d.* Magdeburg, Jun. 10, 1556. Author of important theoretical wks.

Aguilar, Emmanuel Abraham. Pianist, composer; *b.* London, 1824; *d.* ib., 1904. Comp. symph., cantatas, ballad operas.

Agujari (*Ah-goo-yah-ree*), **Lucrezia.** Soprano; *b.* Ferrara, It., 1743; *d.* Parma, It., May 18, 1783. Admired by Mozart; range of three octaves above middle C.

Ahlström, Jacob Niklas. Composer; *b.* Wisby, Swed., 1805; *d.* Stockholm, 1859. Son of Olaf A. Comp. operas.

Ahlström (*Ahl-straym*), **Olaf.** Composer; *b.* Stockholm, 1762; *d.* 1835. Collected folk-mus.

Ahna, Heinrich Karl Hermann de. Violinist; *b.* Vienna, Jun. 22, 1835; *d.* Berlin, Nov. 1, 1892. Member of famous Joachim String Quartet.

Aimon (*Ay-mong*), **Pamphile.** Composer; *b.* Paris, 1779; *d.* ib., 1866. Comp. chamb. mus., operas.

Akimenko (*Ah-kee-men-ko*), **Theodor.** Composer; *b.* Kharkov, Rus., Feb. 20, 1876. Comp. opera, *The Snow Queen;* orch., chamb. mus., pf. pcs. Prof. Petrograd Cons.

Alabieff (*Ah-lah-byoff*), **Alexander.** Composer; *b.* Moscow, Aug. 16, 1787; *d.* ib., 1851. Comp. operas; best known by songs, incl. *The Lark.*

Alard (*Ah-lar*), **Jean-Delphin.** Violinist, composer; *b.* Bayonne, Fr., Mar. 8, 1815; *d.* Paris, Feb. 22, 1888. Prof. Paris Cons., succ. Baillot, taught Sarasate. Author of Violin Method.

Albanesi (*Al-bah-nay-zee*), **Carlo.** Pianist, composer; *b.* Naples, Oct. 22, 1858. 1893, prof. R. A. M., London. Comp. orch. and ch. mus.

Albani (*Al-bah-nee*), **Marie Louise Cecile Emma Lajeunesse.** Famous soprano; *b.* Chambly, nr. Montreal, Nov. 1, 1850; *d.* London, Apr. 3, 1930. World career as operatic and oratorio soprano. 1911, retired to teach in London. An organist and choirmaster in Albany, N. Y., she became the decorated idol of royalty, immortalizing Albany as Albani, as Melba had for Melbourne.

Albeniz (*Al-ben-ith*), **Isaac.** Composer, pianist; *b.* Camprodón, Sp., May 29, 1860; *d.* Cambo les Baines, Fr., May 19, 1909. Comp. operas, *Magic Opal, Henry Clifford, Pepita Ximenes;* also many piano pcs. Popularly known by his *Tango in D.*

d'Albert (*d'ahl-behr*), **Eugen Francis Charles.** Pianist, composer; *b.* Glasgow, Apr. 10, 1864; *d.* Riga, Mar. 3, 1932; son of the dance composer Claude d'A. (1809-1886). A celebrated Beethoven interpreter. 1905, toured U. S. Comp. two piano concertos, two overtures, a symph., chamb. mus.; also operas, incl. *Tiefland,* 400 perf. to 1917.

Alberti, Domenico. Composer, singer, pianist; *b.* Venice, 171–; *d.* 1740. First to utilize the broken chord bass now known as the "Alberti bass."

Alberti, Solon. 'Cellist, composer, teacher; *b.* Mt. Clemens, Mich. 1914-1920 cond. Kansas City Grd. Opera Soc. 1914-1920, *t.* Kansas City Cons., Horner Institute of Fine Arts. 1918, Cond. Kansas City Little Symph.

Alboni, Marietta. Contralto; *b.* Cesena, It., Mar. 10, 1813; *d.* Paris, Jun. 23, 1894. Famous for beauty of voice.

Albrecht, Karl A. Violinist, conductor; *b.* Posen, Aug. 27, 1807; *d.* Gatchina, Rus., Feb. 24, 1863. 1838, cond., St. Petersburg Opera; 1842, led first performance of Glinka's *Russlan and Ludmilla;* 1845, cond. of Phil. concerts, St. Petersburg.

Albrechtsberger (*Al-brekhts-bairg-er*), **Johann Georg.** Organist, theorist; *b.* Klosterneuberg, Aus., Feb. 3, 1736; *d.* Vienna, Mar. 7, 1809. His *Guide to Composition* and *School of Thoroughbass* have outlived his compositions.

Alda, Frances Davis. Soprano; *b.* New Zealand, May 31, 1883. Former wife of Gatti-Casazza, retired impresario of Met. Op. Co., N. Y. 1904, debut, Paris; 1908, Met. Op., N. Y.

Alday, Paul. French violinist; *b.* 1764; *d.* 1835; *p.* Viotti; a celebrated virtuoso; fd. Dublin Conservatory; comp. violin sonatas and concertos.

Alden, John Carver. Composer, teacher; *b.* Boston, Sept. 11, 1852. *t.* Converse College, Spartanburg, S. C.

Alder, Richard Ernst. Conductor, composer; *b.* Herisan, Switz., 1853; *d.* Paris, 1904.

Aldrich, Perley Dunn. Teacher, composer; *b.* Blackstone, Mass., 1863; *d.* Phila., Nov. 20, 1933; *p.* Sbriglia. *t.* Curtis Inst.

Aldrich, Richard. Author, critic; *b.* Providence, R. I., Jul. 31, 1863. 1885, A.B., Harvard u. Paine. Author of *Guide to Parsifal,* and other wks. Music critic, Washington Star, N. Y. Tribune, N. Y. Times.

Alfano, Franco. Composer, conductor, pianist; *b.* Posilipo, nr. Naples, Mar. 8, 1877; *p.* Jadassohn; 1919, dir. at Bologna; completed *Turandot,* Puccini's unfinished opera. 1926, dir. Turin Cons. Comp. opera, incl. *Resurrezione;* orchestral and chamb. mus. wks., all in the modern idiom.

Alfarabi. Arabian musician theorist in the tenth century.

Alfvén, Hugo. Composer, conductor; *b*. Stockholm, May 1, 1872. Dir. of Mus., U. of Upsala. Comp. symph. p. *Swedish Rhapsody*, violin wks., piano pcs., and songs.

Alkan (pseudonym of Charles Henri Valentin Morhange). Composer, pianist; *b*. Paris, Nov. 30, 1813; *d*. ib., Mar. 29, 1889. Comp. études and pf. transcriptions.

Allegri (*Al-lay-gree*), **Gregorio.** Composer; *b*. Rome, 1584; *d*. ib., 1652. Comp. celebrated *Miserere,* for two choirs, sung in the Sistine Chapel, Rome, which the youthful Mozart wrote from memory, since copies were forbidden to those outside the choir.

Allen, Charles N. Violinist; *b*. York, 1837; *d*. Boston, Apr. 7, 1903. Distinguished as a teacher.

Allen, George Benjamin. Organist, composer; *b*. London, 1822; *d*. Brisbane, Australia, 1897. Comp. operas, incl. *Castle Grim.*

Allen, Nathan Hale. Organist, composer; *b*. Marion, Mass., Apr. 14, 1848; *d*. Hartford, Conn., May 9, 1925. Comp. ch. mus., organ, piano and violin pcs.

Allen, Paul. American composer of operas in Italy; *b*. Mass., 1882. Comp. opera, *The Last of the Mohicans;* also symph., *Pilgrims.*

Allen, Thornton Whitney. Composer; *b*. Newark, N. J., Jun. 26, 1890. ed. Intercollegiate Song Book. Specialist in College Songs.

Allen, Warren D. Organist, educator; *b*. California. *p*. Widor. Since 1919 dir. mus., Stanford U.

Allitsen, Frances. Composer; *b*. 1849; *d*. London, Oct. 1, 1912. Comp. many songs, incl. *Song of Thanksgiving.*

Alpheraky (*Ahl-fer-ah-kee*), **Achilles Nikolaievitch.** Composer; *b*. Kharkov, Rus., Jun. 21, 1846. Comp pf. pcs. and songs based on folk melodies of the Ukraine.

Alshalabi, Mohammed. Spanish-Arabian writer of the fifteenth century.

Alsleben, Julius. Composer; *b*. Berlin, Mar. 24, 1832; *d*. ib., Dec. 9, 1894. Comp. overtures.

Altes (*Ahl-tes*), **Joseph Henri.** Flutist, composer; *b*. Rouen, Fr., 1826; *d*. Paris, 1895.

Althouse, Paul. Tenor; *b*. Reading, Pa., Dec. 2, 1889; 1913, debut Met. op., as first American without European training to win leading rôles; 1929, toured Ger.

Altschuler (*Ahlt-shoo-ler*), **Modest.** Conductor, 'cellist; *b*. Mohilev, Rus., Feb. 15, 1873. *p*. Arensky; 1895, to U. S.; 1903, fd. Russian Symph. Orch., New York. Cond. for Anna Pavlova; 1927, cond. Hollywood Bowl.

Alvarez (*Ahl-vah-rez*) (pseudonym of Albert Raymond Gourron). Tenor; *b*. Bordeaux, Fr., 1861; *d*. Nice, Feb. 1, 1933.

Alvary (*Ahl-vah-ree*), **Max** (pseudonym of M. A. Aschenbach). Tenor; *b*. Düsseldorf, May 3, 1858; *d*. Datenburg, Nov. 7, 1898. Son of Andreas A., famous painter. Noted in Wagnerian rôles.

Alypios. Greek musical writer, fourth century; authority on Greek modes.

Amadei (*Ah-mah-day-ee*), **Roberto.** Composer, organist; *b*. Loreto, It., Nov. 29, 1840. Comp. opera and sacred mus.

Amani (*Ah-mahn-ee*), **Nicolai.** Composer; *b*. Rus., 1875; *d*. 1904. Comp. pf. pcs., songs.

Amati (*A-mah-tee*), **Andrea.** Violin-maker; *b. c*. 1530; *d*. Cremona, Apr. 10, 1611. First of famous family of violin-makers at Cremona. Sons: **Antonio,** 1550-1638; **Geronimo,** 1551-1635.

Amati, Nicolo. *b*. Cremona, Sept. 13, 1596; *d*. Aug. 12, 1684. Son of Geronimo.

Amato, Pasquale. Baritone, vocal teacher; *b*. Naples, Mar. 21, 1878. La Scala, Milan; 1908-1924, Met. Op. Retired to private teaching.

Ambros, August Wilhelm. Historian, writer; *b*. Mauth, Boh., Nov. 17, 1816; *d*. Vienna, Jun. 28, 1876. Frequent contributor to Schumann's *Neue Zeitschrift für Musik.* His unfinished *Musical History* is a valuable work.

Ambrose, Paul. Organist, composer; *b*. Hamilton, Ont., Oct. 11, 1868. Org., Trenton, N. J. Son of R. S. A.

Ambrose, Robert Steele. Organist, composer; *b*. Chelmsford, Eng., 1824; *d*. Hamilton, Ont., Mar. 31, 1908. Best known by his setting of the hymn *One Sweetly Solemn Thought.*

Ambrose, Saint, Bishop of Milan, church musician; *b*. Trèves, Ger., 333; *d*. Milan, Apr. 4, 397. Devised a system mus. notation, based on his understanding of the Greek modes.

Ambrosio, Alfredo d'. Composer, violinist; *b*. Naples, It., Jun. 13, 1871; *d*. Nice, Fr., Jan. 2, 1915. Comp. many popular violin compositions, incl. *Canzonetta.*

Amiot (*Ah-mee-o*), **Father Joseph Maria.** *b*. Toulon, Fr., 1718; *d*. Pekin, 1794. Jesuit Missionary to China; authority on Chinese mus.

Ancona, Mario. Baritone; *b*. Florence, It., 1870. 1893, in N. Y.; 1910, Chicago Op.

Andersen, Arthur Olaf. Teacher, theory and composition; *b*. Newport, R. I.; *p*. Guilmant. Fac. mem., Amer. Cons. of Mus., Chicago.

Andersen, Carl Joachim. Flutist, composer; *b*. Copenhagen, Den., 1847; *d*. ib., May 7, 1909. Cond., Tivoli concerts.

Anderton, Thomas. Composer; *b*. Birmingham, Apr. 15, 1836; *d*. Edgbaston, Sept. 18, 1903. Comp. cantatas.

Andrade, Francesco d'. Baritone; *b*. Lisbon, Jan. 11, 1859; *d*. Berlin, Feb. 9, 1921. Popular in opera in Ger.

Andrews, George Whitfield. Organist, composer; *b*. Wayne, O., Jan. 19, 1861; *d*. Honolulu, Aug. 18, 1932. Many years on faculty of Oberlin U.

Andrews, J. Warren. Organist, composer; *b*. Lynn, Mass., Apr. 6, 1860; *d*. N. Y., Jan. 18, 1932. Many years org. Ch. of Divine Paternity, N. Y.

Andrews, Mark. Organist, composer; *b*. Gainsborough, Eng., Mar. 31, 1875. New York org. and mus. ed.

Anério (*Ah-nay-ree-o*), **Felice.** Composer; *b*. Rome, *c*. 1560; *d*. ib. *c*. 1630. Comp. sacred contrapuntal wks., so good that some were attributed to Palestrina.

Anet (*Ah-nay*), **Baptiste.** French violinist; *b*. 1650; *d*. ——; *p*. Corelli. Popular virtuoso in Paris during his time. 1724, pub. book of sonatas for violin.

d'Angeli (*Ahn-jay-lee*), **Andrea.** Composer, writer; *b*. Padua, It., Nov. 9, 1868; *t*. Liceo Rossini, Pesaro, It. Comp. sacred wks. and an opera.

Anger (*An-jer*), **Joseph Humphrey.** Organist, composer, theorist; *b*. Ashbury, Eng., 1862; *d*. Toronto, Ont., Jun. 11, 1913. Author of valuable text-books on harmony.

d'Anglebert (*Ongl'-bare*), **Jean Baptiste Henri.** Composer, claveçinist; *b. c.* 1628; *d.* Paris, Apr. 23, 1691.

Animuccia (*Ah-nee-moot-chee-ah*), **Giovanni.** Composer; *b.* Florence, *c.* 1500; *d.* Rome, 1571. Comp. masses in fluent style, and *Laudi Spirituali* for Neri's lectures in his Oratory, thus leading the way to oratorio.

Ansermet, Ernest. Conductor; *b.* Vevey, Switz., Nov. 11, 1883. 1912, cond., Montreuz Kursaal; cond., Diaghilev Russian Ballet, touring Eng., It., Sp., North and South Americas.

Ansorge (*Ahn-sohr-geh*), **Conrad.** Pianist, composer; *b.* Liebau, Ger., Oct. 15, 1862. *p.* Liszt. 1887, toured U. S. His compositions utilize a strongly mystic idiom.

Antheil, George. Composer, pianist; *b.* Trenton, N. J., Jul. 8, 1900. St. Stravinsky. 1927, *Ballet-Méachanique,* scored for anvils, player-pianos and sundry noise machines, perf. Paris, and hissed. 1932, awarded Guggenheim Scholarship. 1934, opera, *Helen Retires,* to libretto by John Erskine, perf. in N. Y. The "bad boy" of Modernistic composers.

Antipov (*Ahn-tee-poff*), **Constantin.** Composer; *b.* Rus., Jan. 18, 1859. Piano and orch. wks.

Apthorp, William Foster. Author, critic; *b.* Boston, Oct. 24, 1848; *d.* Vevey, Feb. 19, 1912. 1869, A.B., Harvard; 1874-86, *t.* N. E. Cons.; 1881-1903, critic, Evening Transcript; 1892-1901, program annotator, Boston Symph.; 1903, retired to Switz. Author of many books on mus. subjects, and of an *Encyclopedia of Music.*

Aptommas, John. Harpist; *b.* Bridgend, Wales, 1826; *d.* Mar. 19, 1913. **Thomas.** Harpist; *b.* Bridgend, Wales, 1829. Both remarkable harpists and teachers; wr. a history of the harp.

Arban, Joseph Jean Baptiste. Cornetist; *b.* Lyons, Fr., Feb. 28, 1825; *d.* Paris, Apr. 9, 1889. Wr. a celebrated *Method* for the cornet.

Arbos, Enrique Fernandez. Violinist, conductor, composer; *b.* Madrid, Sp., Dec. 25, 1863. Cond. Madrid Symph. orch.; g. cond. N. Y. and Boston Symph. Orchs. Comp. mus. comedies and violin pcs.

Arcadelt, Jacob. Composer; *b.* Netherlands, *c.* 1514; *d.* Paris *c.* 1570. Comp. masses, motets, madrigals.

d'Archambeau (*Dar-sham-bow*), **Iwan.** Violoncellist; *b.* Liege, Belgium. St. Conservatory of Verviers. mem. Flonzaley Quartet, 1903-28.

Archer, Frederick. Organist, conductor; *b.* Oxford, Eng., Jun. 16, 1838; *d.* Pittsburgh, Pa., Oct. 22, 1901. Distinguished concert org.

Arden, Cecil. Mezzo-soprano; *b.* N. Y., Dec. 15, 1895. *p.* Buzzi-Peccia; 1918, debut, Met. op.; 1926-28, European concert tours.

Arditi (*Ar-dee-tee*), **Luigi.** Composer, conductor; *b.* Crescentino, It., Jul. 16, 1822; *d.* Brighton, Eng., May 1, 1903. Comp. songs, incl. *Il Bacio.*

Arens, Franz Xaver. Conductor, teacher of singing; *b.* Neef, Ger., Oct. 28, 1856; *d.* Los Angeles, Jan. 29, 1932. 1909, cond., Peoples Orch., N. Y.

Arensky, Anton Stepanovitch. Composer; *b.* Novgorod, Rus., Aug. 11, 1862; *d.* Terioki, Fin., Mar. 11, 1906. 1882, prof. Moscow Cons. Comp. operas, a ballet, two symphs., chamb. mus., piano pcs. and songs. Best known by *Trio in D Minor.*

Aria, Cesare. Composer, teacher of singing; *b.* Bologna, It., Sept. 21, 1820; *d.* ib., Jan. 30, 1894.

Arienzo, Nicola d'. Composer; *b.* Naples, It., Dec. 23, 1842. Comp. realistic operas; author of scientific wks. on mus.

Armbruster, Carl. Pianist, conductor; *b.* Andernach, Ger., Jul. 13, 1846; *d.* London, Jun. 10, 1917. Authority on Wagner operas.

Armes, Philip. Organist, composer; *b.* Norwich, Eng., Aug. 15, 1836; *d.* Durham, Eng., Feb. 10, 1908. Comp. oratorios.

Armitage, Merle. Impresario; *b.* Mason City, Iowa, Feb. 12, 1893. Manager of Los Angeles Grand Op. Asso.

Armsheimer, Ivan. Composer; *b.* Petrograd, Mar. 19, 1860. Comp. operas, orch. wks., cantatas. Author of a treatise on instrumentation.

Armstrong, Harry. Songwriter. Wr. *Sweet Adeline,* for variety q., the Quaker City Four. The "Adeline" after Adelina Patti, then making a final farewell tour. Even Volsteadism failed to kill its popularity.

Armstrong, William Dawson. Organist, composer; *b.* Alton, Ill., Feb. 11, 1868; *t.* Alton, Ill. Comp. opera, orch. pcs.

Arne, Thomas Augustine. Composer; *b.* London, Mar. 12, 1710; *d.* ib., Mar. 5, 1778. Comp. some thirty operas, two oratorios, and many glees and songs, incl. *Rule Britannia.*

Arneiro, Jose Agusto Ferreira Veiga, Vicomte d'. Portuguese composer; *b.* Macao, China, Nov. 22, 1838; *d.* San Remo, It., 1903. Comp. operas, ballets, and a *Te Deum.*

Arnold, Karl. Composer; *b.* Mergentheim, Mar. 6, 1794; *d.* Christiania, Nov. 11, 1873. Comp. chamb. mus., piano wks., and the opera *Irene.*

Arnold, Maurice Strothotte. *b.* St. Louis, 1865; *d.* Brooklyn, 1933. Comp. symph., *Plantation Dances;* orch. wks. on Oriental topics; cantata, *Wild Chase;* chamb. mus.

Arnold, Youri von. Composer; *b.* Petrograd, Nov. 1, 1811; *d.* Simferopol, Crimea, Jul. 19, 1898. Comp. opera, *Last Days of Pompeii.*

Arnoldson, Sigrid. Soprano; *b.* Stockholm, Mar. 20, 1861. Sang in principal opera houses of the world.

Arrieta (*Ar-ree-ay-tah*) **y Corera, Don Pascual Juan Emilio.** Spanish composer; *b.* Punta la Reina, Sp., Oct. 21, 1823; *d.* Madrid, 1894. Comp. an opera and numerous zarzuelas.

Ars, Nicolai. Composer, conductor; *b.* Moscow, Rus., 1857. Comp. operettas, symph. p.

Artchiboutchev (*Ar-chee-boot-cheff*), **Nicolai Vassilievitch.** Composer and arranger; *b.* Tsarskoë-Selo, Rus., Mar. 7, 1858. 1920, dir. Editions Belaief, Paris. Comp. songs, piano pcs., and many transcriptions.

Arthur, Alfred. Teacher of singing, theorist; *b.* Pittsburgh, Pa., Oct. 8, 1844. Dir. Cleveland School of Mus. Comp. ch. mus., songs.

Artôt (*Ar-to*), **Alexandre Joseph Montagney.** Violinist, composer; *b.* Brussels, Jan. 25, 1815; *d.* Paris, Jul. 20, 1845. 1843, toured U. S. Comp. orch., chamb. mus.

Artôt, Marguerite Josephine Désirée Montagney. Mezzo-soprano; *b.* Paris, Jul. 31, 1835; *d.* Berlin, Apr. 3, 1907.

Asantchevski (*Ah-sahnt-sheff-skee*), **Michael Pavlovitch von.** Composer; *b.* Moscow, 1838; *d.* ib., Jan. 24, 1881. Comp. overtures, chamb. mus., pf. pcs.

Ascher, Joseph. Composer; b. Groningen, Hol., Jun. 24, 1829; d. London, Jun. 4, 1869. Comp. popular salon mus. and teaching pcs.

Ashmall, William Edwin. Organist, editor; b. Eng., 1860; d. Arlington, N. J., Mar. 2, 1927. 1893, played at Chicago Fair; ed., *The Organists Journal.*

Ashton, Algernon Bennet Langton. Pianist, composer; b. Durham, Eng., Dec. 9, 1859. 1863-1880, Leipzig; 1885-1910, prof. R. C. M. An inveterate writer of letters to the press, more than a thousand of them published in book form. He made a hobby of seeking out and keeping in repair the graves of distinguished persons. Comp. over 150 wks., incl. chamb. mus., symphs., concertos, and small pcs.

Astorga, Emmanuele Gioachino Cesare Rincon Baron d'. Composer; b. Palermo, It., Dec. 11, 1681; d. Prague, Boh., Aug. 21, 1736. Comp. sacred mus.

Atherton, Percy Lee. Composer; b. Boston, Sept. 25, 1871. Comp. orch. wks., comic operas, violin sonatas, piano pcs., and songs. Career largely assoc. w. Boston.

Atkins, Sir Ivor Algernon. Composer; b. Cardiff, Wales, Nov. 29, 1869. 1920, Mus. Dir., Oxford; 1921, knighted; org., Worcester Cath. Comp. sacred mus., incl. *Hymn of Faith* to libretto by Edw. Elgar.

Atterberg, Kurt M. Composer, conductor, critic; b. Gothenburg, Dec. 12, 1887. p. Hallen, Stockholm. 1919, critic, *Stockholm Tidningen.* Subsidy from Swedish government enabled him to abandon engineering in favor of mus. Two symphs. were perf. by the Phila. Symph., prior to 1928, when he won $10,000 Columbia Phonograph Schubert Memorial award for his sixth Symph., which nevertheless was not received favorably by the critics. Besides symphs., comp. concertos, three operas, two str. quartets and a cantata.

Attrup, Karl. Organist, composer; b. Copenhagen, Den., Mar. 4, 1848; d. ib., 1892. Comp. organ mus.

Attwood, Martha. Soprano; b. Cape Cod, Mass. p. Felix Leroux. Created rôle of "Liu" in première of opera, *Turandot* in her debut at Met. Op.

Attwood, Thomas. Organist, composer; b. London, Nov. 23, 1765; d. ib., Mar. 24, 1838. p. Mozart. Org., St. Paul's Cath., London.

Auber (*O-bare*), **Daniel François Esprit.** Composer; b. Caën, Fr., Jan. 29, 1782; d. Paris, May 12, 1871. Comp. operas, incl. *Masaniello, Le Maçon, Fra Diavolo, Zanetta.*

Aubert (*O-bare*), **Louis Francois Marie.** Composer; b. Parame, Fr., Feb. 15, 1877. Edu. Paris Conservatoire. 1913, Opera, *Le Foret Bleue,* prod. Boston. After the World War, lived in unproductive retirement on the outskirts of Paris. Comp. orchestral and choral wks.

Audran (*O-drong*), **Edmond.** Composer; b. Lyons, Fr., Apr. 11, 1842; d. Tierceville, Fr., Aug. 17, 1901. 1862, org. at Marseilles. Comp. over 40 operettas, incl. *Grand Mogul* (1877) and *Mascot* (1880).

Auer, Leopold. Violinist; b. Veszprim, Rus., Jun. 9, 1845; d. New York, Jul. 15, 1930. p. Joachim. Missed the dedication of Tschaikowsky Concerto because he considered it unplayable. 1868-1911, prof. Petrograd Cons. The success of his pupils of the Elman-Heifetz class made him the most sought for violin teacher of the world. 1918, to U. S.

Aulin (*Oh-lin*), **Tor.** Violinist, composer; b. Stockholm, Sept. 10, 1866; d. ib., Mar. 1, 1914. Comp. violin pcs., incl., *Humoreske.*

Auric, Georges. Composer; b. Lodève, Fr., Feb. 15, 1899. st. d'Indy at Schola Cantorum. Strongly influenced by Eric Satie, he became a member of Satie's French-six group of modernists. After the dissolution of this group, Auric comp. his best works, *Les Matelots* and *Les Facheux.* Mus. critic, *Nouvelles Litteraires.* Comp. wks. for theatre and orch., incl. mus. for Rene Claire's motion picture *A Nous la Liberti.*

Aus der Ohe (*Ous-der-Oh-eh*), **Adèle.** Pianist; b. Ger., 1865. p. Liszt. Comp. piano suites.

Austin, Ernest. Composer; b. London, Dec. 31, 1874. Comp. orch. wks., and cycle of organ pcs. founded on Bunyan's *Pilgrim's Progress.*

Auteri-Manzocchi (*O-tay-ree Man-zok-kee*), **Salvatore.** Composer; b. Palermo, It., Dec. 25, 1846; d. Parma, 1924. Comp. melodrama, *Dolores.*

Averkamp, Anton. Composer, conductor; b. Langerak, Hol., Feb. 18, 1861. Comp. orch. mus.

Avison, Charles. Composer; b. Newcastle-on-Tyne, Eng., 1710; d. ib., May 9, 1770. Popular in his day. Recalled by Browning in one of his poems; also by Avison edition of Soc. of British Comp.

Axman, Gladys. Soprano; b. Boston, Mass. 1915, recital debut, Boston; 1917, San Carlo Op.; 1919, Met. Op., created part of *La Joie de Comprendre* in Wolff's *Blue Bird.*

Ayres, Frederic. Composer; b. Binghamton, N. Y., Mar. 17, 1876; d. Colorado Springs, Nov. 23, 1926. Comp. orch. and chamb. wks., pf. pcs., songs. Career largely assoc. w. Colorado Springs, Colo.

B

Bach Family. Most famous of musical families, including over twenty well-known musicians; descendants of **Hans Bach,** b. 1561; **J. S. Bach** himself had nineteen children, seven of whom became professional musicians; his grandson, **Wilhelm Friedrich Ernst,** lived until 1845.

Bach, Johann Christoph Friedrich. Composer, called the "Bückeburg Bach"; b. Leipzig, Jun. 23, 1732; d. Bückeburg, Ger., Jan. 26, 1795. In style of comp., he approached his brother Emanuel.

Bach, Johann Sebastian. Composer; b. Eisenach, Ger., Mar. 21, 1685; d. Leipzig, Ger., Jul. 28, 1770. Father of modern mus. Equally great as comp., org., and player on the clavichord. His wks. constitute the fountain-head of modern mus. It is a notable fact that Bach and Handel were born in the same year. Comp. organ sonatas, preludes and fugues, comp. for clavichord, *Passion* mus., sacred cantatas, of which latter no fewer than 226 are still extant, masses.

Bach, Karl Philipp Emanuel. Composer, pianist; b. Weimar, Mar. 8, 1714; d. Hamburg, Dec. 14, 1788. Third son of J. S. B. 1767, dir., Hamburg. His comp. mark the transition from his father's style to that of Haydn and Mozart.

Bach, Wilhelm Friedemann. Organist, composer; b. Weimar, Nov. 22, 1710; d. Berlin, Jul. 1, 1784. First son of J. S. B.; talented but dissipated.

Bache, Walter. Pianist; b. Edgbaston, Eng., Jun. 19, 1842; d. London, Mar. 26, 1888. p. Liszt.

Bachmann, Alberto. Violinist, composer; b. Geneva, Switz., Mar. 20, 1875; d. ———. Comp. violin pcs.; author of *Encyclopedia of the Violin.*

Bachmann, Georges. Composer; *b.* 1848; *d.* Paris, Dec. 1894. Prolific piano comp.

Bachrich, Sigismund. Violinist, composer; *b.* Zsdmbókreth, Hungary, 1841; *d.* Vienna, 1913. Comp. operettas.

Backer-Gröndahl, Agathe Ursula. Norwegian composer, pianist; *b.* Holmestrand, Nor., Dec. 1, 1847; *d.* Christiania, Jun. 6, 1907. *p.* Liszt. 1871, toured Europe. Comp. songs, piano pcs.

Backhaus (*Bachaus*), **Wilhelm.** Pianist; *b.* Leipzig, Mar. 26, 1884. 1905 *t.* Manchester Coll. of Mus., Eng.; won Rubinstein prize. Has toured U. S.

Badarczewska (*Bad-ar-chef-skah*), **Thekla.** Composer; *b.* Warsaw, Pol., 1838; *d.* ib., 1862.

Bagby, Albert Morris. Musical author; *b.* Rushville, Ill., Apr. 29, 1859. 1891, fd. Bagby Mus. Mornings. Author, mus. novel, *Miss Traumerei;* magazine articles.

Bagge, Selmar. Organist, writer; *b.* Coburg, Jun. 30, 1823; *d.* Basel, Switz., Jul. 15, 1896.

Bailey-Apfelbeck, Marie Louise. Pianist; *b.* Nashville, Tenn., Oct. 24, 1876. *p.* Leschetizky. *t.* Vienna.

Baillot (*Bi-yo*), **Pierre Marie Francois de Salles.** Violinist, composer; *b.* Passy, Fr., Oct. 1, 1771; *d.* Paris, Sept. 15, 1842. *p.* Viotti; last of the classic school. The principal French violinist of his day; member of Napoleon's private band; taught in the new Cons.; prepared method *w.* Rode and Kreutzer. His études and *L'art du violon* belong to the classics of violin playing.

Baini (*Bah-ee-nee*), **Giuseppe.** Composer, writer; *b.* Rome, Oct. 21, 1775; *d.* ib., May 21, 1844. Comp. sacred wks. Author of a monograph on Palestrina.

Bainton, Edgar L. Composer, pianist; *b.* London, Feb. 14, 1880; *p.* Stanford. Comp. orch. pcs., *Pompilia* and *Celtic Sketches;* also pf. pcs. 1912, dir., Cons. at Newcastle-on-Tyne. 1914-18, interned in Ger.

Bajetti (*Bah-yay-tee*), **Giovanni.** Composer; *b.* Brescia, It., 1815; *d.* Milan, It., 1876. Comp. operas.

Baker, Benjamin Franklin. Composer, teacher of singing; *b.* Wenham, Mass., Jul. 16, 1811; *d.* Boston, Mar. 11, 1889. Succ. Lowell Mason as *t.* of mus. in Boston public schools. Comp. cantatas, incl. the *Storm King;* and collections of vocal mus.

Baker, Dalton. Baritone; *b.* Merton, Eng., Oct. 17, 1879. 1919, *t.* Toronto Cons.; 1921, to N. Y. Successful oratorio and concert artist.

Baker, Theodore. Writer; *b.* New York, Jun. 3, 1851; *d.* Leipzig, Oct. 13, 1934. Authority on Indian mus.; 1874-1891, in Ger.; 1892, literary ed. Schirmer mus. publishing house; author *Dr. Baker's Dictionary of Musicians.*

Balakireff (*Bah-lah-kee-reff*), **Mily Alexeievitch.** Composer; *b.* Novgorod, Rus., Dec. 31, 1836; *d.* Petrograd, May 29, 1910. At twenty became the center of the Russian five, a group of nationalists *w.* Cui, Borodin, Moussorgsky, Rimsky-Korsakoff. Comp. symph., the symph. poems *Tamara* and *Russia,* mus. to *King Lear,* and many songs and piano pcs.

Balart (*Bahlahr*), **Gabriel.** Composer, conductor; *b.* Barcelona, Sp., 1824; *d.* ib., 1893. Comp. zarzuelas.

Balatka, Hans. Conductor, 'cellist; *b.* Hoffnungsthal, Aus., Mar. 5, 1827; *d.* Chicago, Apr. 17, 1899. The vogue of the Balatka concerts in Chicago waned with the coming of Theodore Thomas; yet he gave the first Chicago performances of eight Beethoven symphonies.

Baldwin, Minor Coe. Organist; *b.* Middletown, Conn., Feb. 21, 1856. Concertized extensively. Comp. of organ pcs.

Baldwin, Ralph Lyman. Composer, organist, conductor; *b.* Easthampton, Mass. *p.* Chadwick. 1899-1904, dir. pub. sch. mus., Northampton, Mass. 1904-25, Hartford, Conn., Schools. Org., Congregational ch.

Baldwin, Samuel Atkinson. Organist; *b.* Lake City, Minn., Jan. 25, 1862. edu. Royal Cons., Dresden. 1907, prof. C. C. N. Y.

Balfe, Michael William. Composer; *b.* Dublin, May 15, 1808; *d.* Rowny Abbey, Eng., Oct. 20, 1870. Best remembered by opera *The Bohemian Girl* (1843).

Ball, Ernest R. Pianist, ballad composer; *b.* Cleveland, Jul. 21, 1878; *d.* Beechurst, L. I., May 5, 1927. 1905, wr. mus. to James J. Walker's lyric *Will You Love Me in December as You Do in May.* Restores sentiment and eclipses ragtime to such an extent that years later the lyricist was inducted into office as New York's Mayor to the strains of his own song. An earlier success was *Love Me, and the World Is Mine.*

Ballanta, Nicholas G. J. Composer; *b.* Freetown, Sierra Leone, Mar. 14, 1893. St., Inst. Mus. Art, N. Y. 1925-26, research, African mus., West Africa and U. S.; 1927-28, Guggenheim Fellowship. Comp. *Prelude for Organ;* cantata, *Belshazzar's Feast;* overture, *Africa and the Africans.*

Ballantine, Edward. Composer; *b.* Oberlin, O., Aug. 6, 1886. 1907, gr. Harvard U.; 1912, prof. Harvard. *p.* Ganz. Comp. orch., *Prelude to the Delectable Forest* (1914), *Eve of St. Agnes* (1917), *From the Garden of Hellas* (1923).

Balthasar, Henry Mathias. Composer; *b.* Arlon, Bel., 1844. Wr. operas, symph., cantatas, concertos.

Baltzar (*Bäl'tsär*), **Thomas.** Violinist; *b.* 1630; *d.* 1663. One of the finest artists of his time; the first violin virtuoso heard in England. 1653, leader of the King's Band, London.

Bampton, Rose E. Operatic contralto; *b.* Cleveland, O., Nov. 28, 1909. Nov. 28, 1932, debut, Met. Op; oratorio and concert singer.

Bang, Maîa (Baroness Hoehn). Violinist; *b.* Tronsö, Apr. 24, 1877. *p.* Auer. Fd. of the Oslo Mus. Sch., Christiania. Author of violin method based on the Auer principles.

Banister, Henry Charles. Theorist, writer; *b.* London, Jun. 13, 1831; *d.* ib., Nov. 20, 1897. Wr. cantatas, overtures, chamb. mus., mus. literature.

Bantock, Granville. Composer, conductor, writer; *b.* London, Aug. 7, 1868. edu. Royal Acad. *u.* Corder; won Macfarren scholarship. 1893-6, edited *New Quarterly Music Review;* cond. Runcorn Phil. Soc.; 1908, prof. of mus., U. of Birmingham. Prolific modernist, with Oriental tendencies. Brought Sibelius to England. Comp. long list of orch. and choral wks., chamb. mus., and small pcs., incl. many songs, to texts by his wife, Helen von Schweitzer.

Barbieri (*Bahr-bee-ay-ree*), **Carlo Emmanuel di.** Composer; *b.* Genoa, It., 1822; *d.* Budapesth, 1867.

Barbieri, Francisco Asenjo. Spanish musicologist, composer; *b.* Madrid, Sp., Aug. 3, 1823; *d.* ib., Feb. 17, 1894. perf. prodigious researches of folklore from ancient tablatures. Comp. over 70 popular zarzuelas embodying a wealth of 18th century folk literature. *Pan y Toros,* although a light work, possesses marked national significance.

Barblan, Otto. Organist, composer; *b.* Scanfs, Switz., Mar. 22, 1860. 1887, org. St. Peter's Cath.; cond. Oratorio Soc., and *t.* at Cons. 1909, comp. cantata, *Post Tenebras lux* for Calvin jubilee. Comp. cantatas, choruses and organ pcs.

Barbour, Florence (neé Newell). Pianist, composer; *b.* Providence, R. I., Aug. 4, 1866. 1891, *m.* Clarence Augustus Barbour, later pres. Brown U. Comp. long list of pf. pcs., and some chamb. mus. Comp. pf. pcs., songs.

Barcewicz (*Bär'tsĕ-vĭtz*), **Stanislaus.** Violinist, teacher; *b.* Warsaw, Apr. 16, 1858. *p.* Hrimaly. Won success as a concert violinist, then became cond. of opera at Warsaw and *t.* at Warsaw Cons.

Bardi, Giovanni, Conte del Vernio. *c.* 1534-1612; a wealthy Florentine, at whose house Peri and others made the first experiments in opera.

Bargheer, Karl. Violinist; *b.* Buckeburg, Dec. 31, 1831; *d.* Hamburg, May 19, 1902. *p.* Spohr. concertmaster *u.* Hans von Bülow; a virtuoso of high rank.

Bargiel, Woldemar. Composer, pianist; *b.* Berlin, Oct. 3, 1828; *d.* ib., Feb. 23, 1897. Wr. symph., concert overtures, and much piano mus. Step-brother of Clara Schumann.

Barlow, Howard. Conductor; *b.* Plain City, O., May 1, 1892. 1919, cond., MacDowell Colony Fest.; cond., Columbia Broadcasting System.

Bärmann (*Bare-man*), **Heinrich.** Clarinetist; *b.* Potsdam, Ger., Feb. 14, 1784; *d.* Munich, Ger., Jun. 11, 1847. Wr. technical works for the clarinet.

Bärmann, Karl. Pianist, teacher; *b.* Munich, Jul. 9, 1839; *d.* Newton, Mass., Jan. 17, 1913. Grandson, Heinrich B. *t.* Boston.

Barnard, Mrs. Charlotte Alington. Composer; *b.* Dec. 23, 1830; *d.* Dover, Eng., Jan. 30, 1869. Comp. songs, incl. words, under pseud., *Claribel.*

Barnby, Sir Joseph. Composer, conductor; *b.* York, Eng., Aug. 12, 1838; *d.* London, Jan. 28, 1896. Wr. excellent ch. mus.

Barnekow (*Bahr-neh-koff*), **Christian.** Composer; *b.* St. Sauveur, Den., Jul. 28, 1837; *d.* Copenhagen, Mar. 20, 1913. 1895, pres. Copenhagen Mus. Soc. Comp. chamb. mus., pf. pcs., songs.

Barnes, Edwin N. C. Music educator; *b.* New Brunswick, Canada. *p.* Am. Inst. Normal Methods, Boston. 1924, prof. mus., Wash. (D. C.) Coll. of Mus.

Barnes, William H. Organist, organ architect; *p.* Clarence Dickinson. 1914, A.B., Harvard; org., Evanston, Ill.; Assoc. Ed., *The American Organist.*

Barnett, John. Composer; *b.* Bedford, Eng., Jul. 1, 1802; *d.* Cheltenham, Apr. 17, 1890. Comp. operas, incl. *The Mountain Sylph;* also other wks., incl. nearly 4,000 songs.

Barnett, John Francis. Pianist, composer, conductor; *b.* London, Oct. 16, 1837; *d.* London, Nov. 24, 1916. Nephew of John B. *t.* R. C. M., London. Comp. cantatas.

Barnhouse, C. L. Composer, publisher; *b.* Grafton, W. Va. Comp. wks., for band and orch.; *h.* Oskaloosa, Ia.

Barns, Ethel. Composer, violinist; *b.* London, 1879. *p.* R. A. M. 1899, debut Crystal Palace; *m.* Charles Phillips. Comp. violin concerto, sonatas, pcs. for violin, pf., songs.

Baromeo (Sikes), Chase. Basso; *b.* Augusta, Ga., Aug. 19, 1892. 1917, A.B., U. of Mich.; 1923-26, LaScala, Milan; 1927, Chicago Opera; 1935, Met. Op., N. Y.

Barrère, Georges. Flautist; *b.* Bordeaux, Oct. 31, 1876. Solo flautist of Colonne concerts in Paris; first flautist of N. Y. Symph. So., and Phil.; 1914, fd. Barrère Little Symph. Orch.

Barrett, Reginald. Composer; *b.* London, Jan. 12, 1861. Edu. Darmstadt and Guildhall Sch. of Mus., London. 1888, to U. S.; org., St. Petersburg, Fla.; 1898, won *The Musician* prize for best song. Comp. ch. mus., piano, organ pcs., songs.

Barrett, William Alexander. Writer; *b.* London, Oct. 15, 1836; *d.* ib., Oct. 17, 1891. Ed. of *Musical Times.*

Barstow, Vera. American violinist; *b.* Celina, O., Jun. 3, 1893. *p.* von Kunits. Concert tours in Europe and America.

Bartay (*Bahr-tye*), **Andreas.** Composer; *b.* Szeplak, Hun., 1798; *d.* Mainz, Ger., 1856. Comp. operas.

Barth, Karl Heinrich. Pianist, conductor; *b.* Pillau, Ger., Jul. 12, 1847; *d.* Berlin, Dec., 1922. *p.* von Bülow. 1871-1921, *t.* Hochschule; fd., Barth Trio, *w.* de Ahna and Hausmann.

Barth (*Bärt*), **Richard.** Violinist; *b.* Grosswanzleben, Jun. 5, 1850. *p.* Joachim. Due to an accident he was compelled to play the violin with his right hand and bow with the left; nevertheless he became an excellent perf.; concertmaster at Münster; Dir. of Mus. at Warburg U.; cond. Hamburg Phil.

Bartlett, Floy Little. Composer; *b.* Burlington, Ia. *p.* Dannreuther, Paris. Comp. pf. and violin pcs., songs, incl. *Sweet Little Woman O' Mine.*

Bartlett, Homer Newton. Composer, pianist, organist; *b.* Olive, N. Y., Dec. 28, 1845; *d.* Hoboken, Apr. 2, 1920. His best selling piece, *Grand Polka di Concert,* was comp. at the age of 18. Comp. an opera; the cantata *The Last Chieftain;* sextet for strings and flute, and 250 songs and pf. pcs. Ex-President, National Association of Organists.

Bartlett, James Carroll. Tenor, composer; *b.* Harmony, Me., Jun. 14, 1850; *d.* Apr. 3, 1920. Best known by his song, *A Dream.*

Bartok, Bela. Composer, pianist; *b.* Nagyszentmiklos, Yugoslavia, Mar. 25, 1881. Edu., Budapest. His mus. is entirely Hungarian, largely based on folk material, of which he is an active collector, in collaboration with Kodaly. 1907-13, prof. of piano, Royal Hungarian Mus. Acad.; 1917, Ballet, *The Woodcut Prince,* prod. Budapest, brought world recognition. Prolific comp. of orchestral suites; four str. quartets; an opera, *Bluebeard's Castle;* besides piano pcs. and arr. of folk songs. Career largely assoc. *w.* Budapest.

Barzin, Leon. Violist, conductor; *b.* Brussels, 1900. Violist, N. Y. Phil.; 1930, cond. of National Orchestral Assoc., N. Y.

Bassford, William Kipp. Pianist, composer; *b.* New York, Apr. 23, 1839; *d.* ib., 1902.

Bassi, Amedeo Vittorio. Tenor; *b.* Florence, Jul. 20, 1874. Sang in premiere of Puccini's *Girl of the Golden West;* at Costanzi Th., Rome; also Met. Op., and Chicago Op.

Bastiaans, J. G. Organist, composer; *b.* Wilp, Hol., 1812; *d.* Haarlem, Hol., 1875.

Batchelder, John C. Pianist, organist; *b.* Topsham, Vt., 1852. *t.* Detroit Cons. of Mus.

Bath, Hubert. Composer, conductor; b. Barnstaple, Eng., Nov. 6, 1883. 1913, cond. Quinlan Opera; 1923, Carl Rosa Op. t. Guildhall Sch., London. Comp. operas and orchestral suites.

Batiste (*Bah-teest*), **Antoine-Edouard.** Organist, composer; b. Paris, Mar. 28, 1820; d. ib., Nov. 9, 1876. His organ *Offertoires,* once extremely popular, now almost forgotten.

Batta, Joseph. 'Cellist, composer; b. Maestricht, Hol., 1824.

Bauer, Harold. Distinguished virtuoso, pianist; b. London, Apr. 28, 1873. 1883, debut as violinist; 1892, st. piano w. Paderewski; 1900, Amer. debut w. Boston Symph.; 1919, fd. Beethoven Soc., N. Y.

Bauer, Marion Eugénie. Composer, writer; b. Walla Walla, Wash., Aug. 15, 1887. p. Pugno. bd. of dir., League of Composers; Mus. Comm., MacDowell Club. Comp. chamb. mus., pf. pcs., songs.

Baumbach, Adolf. Composer, teacher; b. Ger., 1830; d. Chicago, 1880.

Baumfelder, Friedrich. Pianist, composer; b. Dresden, Ger., May 28, 1836; d. ib., 1916. Cond. Dresden Singakademie.

Baur, Bertha. Musical educator; b. Cleveland, O., St. U. of Mich. 1912, dir., Cincinnati Cons. of Mus.; 1932, retired.

Bausznern, Waldemar von. Composer, conductor; b. Berlin, Nov. 29, 1866. 1923, t. Berlin Acad. for Ch. and Sch. Mus. Comp. operas, incl. *Der Bundschuh;* also completed Cornelius's opera *Grunlöd,* prod. in Cologne in 1906.

Bax, Arnold. Composer, pianist; b. London, Nov. 6, 1883. p. R. A. M.; an English neo-romantic w. Celtic sympathies. By his disciples, claimed to be the successor to Elgar. 1922, tone poem *The Happy Forest* perf. at Queen's Hall by Sir Henry Wood. Comp. 5 symph., and other symph. and chamb. wks., ballets, songs and piano pcs.

Bay, Emanuel. Pianist; b. Kovno, Rus. p. Leopold Godowsky. 1919-20, t. Odessa Cons.; 1922-3, t. Russian Cons., Berlin; 1924, to U. S.

Bayer, Josef. Composer; b. Vienna, Mar. 6, 1852; d. ib., 1913. Comp. ballets, operettas.

Bazin (*Bah-zang*), **François-Emanuel-Joseph.** Theorist; b. Marseilles, Fr., 1816; d. Paris, 1878. t. comp., Paris Cons.

Bazzini (*Bat-zeen-ee*), **Antonio.** Violinist, composer; b. Brescia, Mar. 11, 1818; d. Milan, Feb. 10, 1897. dir. Milan Cons. Comp. overtures, cantata, opera, chamb. mus., and violin pcs., incl. *Ronde des Lutins.*

Beach, Mrs. H. H. A. Pianist, composer; b. Henniker, N. H., Sept. 5, 1867. Chief wks., *Gaelic Symphony,* cantatas, mass with orch., piano concerto, and many beautiful songs and piano pcs. Her most unique work is a set of piano pcs. on real Eskimo Themes. Her setting of *The Year's at the Spring* is her best known song. Divided her time for many years between Boston, Cape Cod, and New York.

Beach, John Parsons. Composer, teacher; b. Gloversville, N. Y., 1877. 1900, Minn.; 1904, New Orleans; 1907, Boston; 1910, Paris. Comp. operas, incl. *Pippa's Holiday;* chamb. mus., pf. pcs., songs.

Beale, Kitty. Coloratura soprano; b. Washington (D. C.). 1932, debut, Met. Op. in Puccini's *Suor Angelica.*

Beattie, John Walter. Music educator; b. Norwalk, O., Nov. 26, 1885. 1923, M.A., Columbia U. 1925, t. Northwestern U. Ed. of song collections.

Beaumont, Paul. Composer; b. Mainz, Ger., Jan. 13, 1853. Salon and teaching pcs. for piano.

Beazley, James Charles. Composer, teacher; b. Ryde, Isle of Wight, Eng., 1850. Comp. cantatas, violin, piano pcs.

Beck, Conrad. Composer; b. Schaffhausen, Switz., Jun. 16, 1901. p. Honegger, Paris. Comp. four symphonies, other orchestral wks., and three st. quartets. h. Paris.

Beck, Johann H. Violinist, composer; b. Cleveland, O., Sept. 12, 1856; d. ib., 1924. Edu. Leipzig. 1882, t. Cleveland. Comp. overtures *Lara* and *Romeo and Juliet,* mus. drama *Salammbo,* cantata *Deucalion,* chamb. mus.

Becker, Albert Ernst Anton. Composer; b. Quedlinburg, Ger., Jun. 13, 1834; d. Berlin, Feb. 10, 1899. Comp. symph., mass, oratorio, violin concertos.

Becker, Gustave L. Theorist and teacher; b. Richmond, Tex., May 22, 1861. p. Moszkowski. 1894-1907, dir., Hasbrouck Mus. Sch., Jersey City. t. N. Y.

Becker, Hugo. 'Cellist; b. Strassburg, Feb. 13, 1864. The classical 'cellist of the Germany of his epoch. t. Berlin Hochschule.

Becker, Reinhold. Composer; b. Adorf, Saxony, Aug. 11, 1842; d. ——. Comp. symph., ch. mus., operas, and songs.

Becker, René Louis. Pianist, organist, composer; b. Bischheim, Alsace, Nov. 7, 1882. Comp. pcs. for organ.

Beddoe, Dan. Tenor, teacher; b. Wales. 1885, debut, Aberdare, Wales. t. Voice, Cincinnati Cons. of Mus.

Bedford, Herbert. Composer, painter; b. London, June 23, 1867. m. Lisa Lehmann (q. v.). Comp. opera, symph., ch. mus., songs.

Beebe, Carolyn. Pianist; b. Westfield, N. J. p. Mosenthal, Moszkowski, Harold Bauer. 1904, debut at Berlin Singakademie; perf. w. Kneisel Q., Olive Mead Q., Longy Club, Barrère Ensemble; 1914, fd.-dir., N. Y. Chamb. Mus. Soc.; 1914-24, annual series in Aeolian Hall, N. Y.; 1924, began series of Sunday Salons, in Hotel Plaza. Premières of 200 chamb. wks., incl. mss. by Griffes, Deems Taylor, Ernest Bloch, Harold Morris, Lamar Stringfield, Henry Hadley, and others.

Beecham, Sir Thomas, Bart. Conductor, opera impresario; b. Liverpool, Apr. 29, 1879. 1906, fd. New Symph. Orch., London; 1916-1919, cond., Royal Phil.; 1919, cond., London Symph. and Covent Garden; 1935, g.-cond., N. Y. Phil. Introd. to England many new composers, particularly Delius. Accomplished more than any man of his generation to establish opera in Great Britain.

Beel, Sigmund. Violinist; b. California, Mar. 13, 1863. t. San Francisco.

Beethoven, Ludwig van. Composer; b. Bonn, Ger., Dec. 16, 1770; d. Vienna, Mar. 26, 1827. Distinguished himself first as a pianist. 1781-1796, made various concert tours. Although a number of his youthful compositions had already been published it was not until his twenty-fifth year (1795) that Beethoven attached an opus number: the three pf. trios, Op. 1, and the three piano sonatas, Op. 2, dedicated to Haydn—the beginning of Beethoven's influence on mus. art. Of wks. bearing a separate opus number, Beethoven left 138, including 9 symphonies, 7 concertos, 1 septet, 2 sextets, 3 quintets, 16 quartets, 32 piano sonatas, 16 other sonatas, 8 piano trios, 1 opera, 2 masses.

Behr, Franz. Composer; *b.* Lübtheen, Ger., Jul. 22, 1837; *d.* Dresden, Feb. 14, 1898. Comp. salon mus. and teaching pcs. for beginners. Used pseudonyms Cooper, Charles Morley, Francesco d'Orso.

Behrend, Arthur Henry. Composer; *b.* Danzig, Ger., Oct. 21, 1853; *d.* London, Nov. 30, 1935. Grandson of Michael Balfe. Comp. ballads, incl. *Daddy.*

Beliczay (*Bay-li-tchay*), **Julius von.** Composer; *b.* Komorn, Hun., Aug. 10, 1835; *d.* Pesth, Apr. 30, 1893. Comp. a mass, symph., and smaller wks.

Bell, William Henry. Composer; *b.* St. Albans, Eng., Aug. 20, 1873. Prof. of mus., U. of Cape Town, South Africa. 1924, F. R. C. M. Prolific comp. of operas, symph., ch. mus., choral mus., much perf. in Britain and S. Africa.

Bellincioni (*Bel-lin-chee-oh-nee*), **Gemma.** Coloratura soprano and actress; *b.* Como, It., Aug. 18, 1866. One of the most celebrated operatic singers of her epoch. Sang in première of *Cavalleria Rusticana.* Author, *Myself and the Stage.*

Bellini, Vencenzo. Composer; *b.* Catania, It., Nov. 1, 1801; *d.* Puteaux, Fr., Sept. 23, 1835. The centenary of his death was extensively celebrated in 1935, showing the unabated charm of melodies which are contained in his operas, *Il Pirata, La Sonnambula, Norma,* and *I Puritani.*

Bemberg (*Bem-bair*), **Henri Herman.** Composer; *b.* Paris, Mar. 29, 1861. Comp. opera, *Elaine,* a comic opera, songs, incl. *Chant Indoué, Nymphs and Fauns.*

Benda, Georg. Composer; *b.* Jungbunzlau, Boh., Jun. 30, 1722; *d.* Kostritz, Boh., Nov. 6, 1795. Comp. *Singspiele,* melodramas.

Bendel, Franz. Pianist, composer; *b.* nr. Rumburg, Boh., Mar. 23, 1833; *d.* Berlin, Jul. 3, 1874. *p.* Liszt. Comp. piano pcs., incl. *Am Genfer See,* songs.

Bendix, Max. Violinist, conductor; *b.* Detroit, Mich., Mar. 28, 1866. 1904, cond. St. Louis Fair Orch.; 1906, Manhattan Op.; 1909, Met. Op. H.; 1915, San Francisco Expo.; 1920, St. Louis Municipal Op.; 1933, Century of Progress Expo. Comp. incidental mus. to productions by Jane Cowl, Fokine, Hobart.

Bendix, Otto. Pianist, teacher; *b.* Copenhagen, Jul. 26, 1845; *d.* San Francisco, Mar. 1, 1904.

Bendix, Theodore. Conductor; *b.* Detroit, Jul. 25, 1862; *d.* Bayshore, L. I., Jan. 15, 1935. Brother of Max B. Cond., *Balle of New York; Ben Hur; Beauty and the Beast;* and other Broadway productions.

Bendix, Victor Emanuel. Pianist, composer; *b.* Copenhagen, May 17, 1851. *p.* Gade. Cond. Danish Concert Soc. Comp. symph. and pf. wks.

Bendl, Karl. Composer; *b.* Prague, Apr. 16, 1838; *d.* ib., Sept. 20, 1897. Comp. operas, masses, cantatas, symph., songs, and pf. pcs.

Benedict, Allan. Organist. *b.* Chicago, Mar. 10, 1883. *p.* Harrison Wild. Since 1902, ch. org. Comp. songs, operettas for young singers, incl., *In Old Vienna, Robin Hood Incorporated,* and *Blow Me Down.*

Benedict, Julius. Composer; *b.* Stuttgart, Nov. 27, 1804; *d.* London, Jun. 5, 1885. Protégé of VonWeber; lived in London for 40 years; 1871 knighted. Of his numerous light operas, he is best recalled by *The Lily of Killarney* (Covent Garden, 1862); also the oratorio, *St. Peter.*

Benedict, Milo Ellsworth. Pianist, teacher; *b.* Cornwall, Vt., Jun. 9, 1866. *p.* Liszt. *t.* Concord, N. H.

Bennett, George John. Organist, composer; *b.* Andover, Eng., May 5, 1863. *p.* R. A. M.; 1888, *t.* ib.; 1895, org., Lincoln Cath. Comp. anthems, cantatas.

Bennett, Joseph. Writer; *b.* Berkeley, Eng., Nov. 29, 1831; *d.* Purton, Jun. 12, 1911. Mus. critic, London *Telegraph.*

Bennett, Robert Russell. Composer; *b.* Kansas City, 1894. st. w. Nadia Boulanger, Paris; 1927, awarded Guggenheim Fellowship; 1930, won R. C. A. Symph. award for *Sights and Sounds,* and *Abraham Lincoln;* 1935, opera *Malibran* perf. by Juilliard Graduate School. Comp. str. q., ballet, *Endymion;* songs.

Bennett, Sir William Sterndale. Composer; *b.* Sheffield, Eng., Apr. 13, 1816; *d.* London, Feb. 1, 1875. 1891, perf. his piano concerto, and was commended by Mendelssohn. Prof. of mus., Cambridge U.; cond., Phil. Soc., London; 1866, prin., Royal Acad.

Benoist, François. Organist, composer; *b.* Nantes, Fr., Sept. 19, 1794; *d.* Paris, 1878.

Benoit (*Ben-wah*), **Pierre Léonard Léopold.** Composer; *b.* Harlebecke, Bel., Aug. 17, 1834; *d.* Antwerp, Bel., Mar. 8, 1901. Leader in Belgian mus. 1867, fd. school which in 1898 became Royal Flemish Cons. of Antwerp. Comp. cantatas, operas, sacred choral wks., and numerous pcs. in all forms.

Bentonelli, Joseph (really **Benton**). Tenor; *b.* Sayre, Okla., 1903. 1923, gr. U. of Okla.; *p.* J. de Reszke. 1928, debut, Bologna, It.; 1934, Chicago Op.; 1935, Met. Op.

Berber, Felix. Violinist; *b.* Jena, Ger., Mar. 11, 1871. Distinguished virtuoso. *t.* Munich.

Berens, Hermann. Pianist, composer; *b.* Hamburg, Apr. 7, 1826; *d.* Stockholm, May 9, 1880. Comp. pf. studies, operas and chamb. mus.

Berezowski (*Be-re-soff-skee*), **Maxim.** Composer; *b.* 1745; *d.* 1777. Comp. ch. mus.

Berezowsky, Nicolai. Composer, conductor, violinist; *b.* Leningrad, May 17, 1900. 1916, gr., Imperial Capella; 1921, dir., School of Modern Art, Moscow; 1922, violinist, N. Y. Phil. Orch., and student at Juilliard Graduate School; 1926, *Sextet for Strings, Clarinet and Piano,* perf. at Mrs. Coolidge's Chamb. Mus. Fest. in Washington; 1929-31, g. cond. in Europe. Assistant cond., Columbia Broadcasting System. Comp. opera, *Prince Batrak;* symphonies, violin concerto, 9 chamb. mus. wks.; a cantata.

Berg, Alban. Composer; *b.* Vienna, Feb. 9, 1885; *d.* ib., Dec. 24, 1935. *p.* Arnold Schonberg. 1910, *t.* composition. 1922, completed opera, *Wozzeck,* prod. in Berlin (1926) which startled the mus. world with its radicalism. Anticipating a hostile demonstration, fifty policemen were stationed about the hall during the Vienna performance in 1930, but the audience hailed it with a frenzy of enthusiasm. 1932, prod. in U. S., by Stokowski. In spite of his atonalism the critics generally consider it represents the mus. of the future. Another opera, *Lulu,* remained unfinished at his death. *Symphonic Pieces from Lulu* were perf. by Koussevitsky in Boston in Mar., 1935, and later in N. Y. by Klemperer. His str. q. was perf. in N. Y. in 1926 by the League of Composers.

Bergé (*Bear-zjay*), **Irénée** (*Ear-ray-nay*). Composer; *b.* Paris, Feb. 1, 1867; *d.* Jersey City, N. J., July 30, 1926. Ed., Paris Cons., *u.* Massenet; asst. to Jean de Reszke; Maitre du Chant at Covent Garden Op., London; 1900, fac., National Cons., N. Y.; 1923, won NFMC prize for *Spring in Sicily.* Comp. operas, incl. *Corsica;* symph. p., *E Pluribus Unum;* orch. pcs., ch. cantatas, anthems, piano pcs., incl. *Chant d'Amour.*

Berger, Francesco. Pianist, composer; b. London, Jun. 10, 1834; d. ib., Apr. 26, 1933. Prof. R. A. M. Comp. incid. mus. to plays, and over 100 songs, incl. *Night, Lovely Night.*

Berger, Ludwig. Pianist, teacher; b. Berlin, Apr. 18, 1777; d. ib., Feb. 16, 1839. t. Mendelssohn; comp. pf. studies, and opera, *Oreste.*

Berger, Wilhelm. Composer; b. Boston, Aug. 9, 1861; d. Jena, Jan. 16, 1911. 1888, t. Klindworth-Scharwenka Cons., Berlin. Comp. symph., choir mus., chamb. mus., and songs.

Berggren, Andreas Peter. Composer, teacher; b. Copenhagen, Mar. 2, 1801; d. ib., Nov. 9, 1880. Advocate of Danish mus.

Bergh, Arthur. Conductor, composer; b. St. Paul, Minn., Mar. 24, 1882. Cond. for Columbia Phono., gained public notice by mus. setting to Poe's *Raven,* as recited by David Bispham.

Bergmann, Karl. Conductor; b. Ebersbach, Ger., 1821; d. New York, Aug. 16, 1876. Leader of Germania Orch., and N. Y. Phil. t. Theodore Thomas. Responsible for first N. Y. perf. of Wagner's *Tannhäuser.*

Bergquist, John Victor. Organist, music educator; b. St. Peter, Minn., May 18, 1877. p. Scharwenka. 1918, t. McPhail Sch. of Mus.; summer, Northwestern U. Comp. oratorio, *Golgotha,* prod., 1906, Minn. Symph. and chorus 250.

Bergson, Michael. Composer; b. Warsaw, 1820; d. London, 1898.

Beringer, Oscar. Pianist, teacher; b. Furtwangen, Ger., Jul. 14, 1844; d. London, 1922. 1885, prof., R. A. M., London. Author of technical wks. for pf. instr.

Bériot (*Bay-ree-o*), **Charles Auguste de.** Violinist, composer; b. Louvain, Feb. 20, 1802; d. Brussels, Apr. 8, 1870. One of the great violinists of the 19th century. His compositions, now relegated to students, once held an important place in the repertory of every violinist.

Bériot, Ch. Vilfride de. Composer; b. Paris, 1833; d. ib., 1914. Son of Ch. deB. Comp. orch., chamb. mus.

Berlin, Irving (really Baline). Song writer; b. Russia, May 11, 1888. 1893, to U. S.; 1926, m. Ellin, daughter Clarence H. Mackay. Fd. own publishing house; wr. many popular ballads, beginning w. *Alexander's Ragtime Band.*

Berlioz (*Bair-lee-oz*), **Louis Hector.** Composer; b. Côte St. André, Fr., Dec. 11, 1803; d. Paris, Mar. 8, 1869. Sent to Paris to study medicine, he rebelled and pursued music, and in consequence was left to support himself as best he could. He made a number of successful concert tours, which he describes in his *Autobiography.* As a composer, the full extent of his influence has not yet been determined. His widening of the color scheme of the modern symph. orch. in itself gives his name immortality as an epoch-maker, even though his mus. may appear a bit bombastic to 20th-century listeners. Among his numerous compositions are the symphonies, *Symphonie Fantastique, Harold, Roméo et Juliet,* the dramatic legend *Faust,* the operas *Benvenuto Cellini* and *Les Troyens;* the choral *Requiem,* and lesser compositions in all forms.

Bernacchi (*Bare-nack-kee*), **Antonio.** Singer, teacher; b. Bologna, It., c. 1690; d. ib., Mar., 1756. Famous master of Italian *bel canto.*

Bernard (*Bare-nahr*), **Emile.** Composer, organist; b. Marseilles, Fr., Nov. 28, 1843; d. Paris, Sept. 11, 1902. Comp. concertos, suites, cantatas, chamb. mus.

Bernecker, Konstanz. Composer; b. Darkehmen, Oct. 31, 1844; d. Königsberg, Jun. 9, 1906. t. Königsberg Cons.; 1907, Bernecker Soc. formed to publish his operas and oratorios. Comp. *Judith* and *Hero and Leander.*

Berners, Gerald Hugh Tyrwhitt-Wilson (Lord Berners). Composer; b. Bridgnorth, Eng., Sept. 18, 1883. p. Casella and Stravinsky. His style is ultra-modern and unorthodox. *Valses bourgeoises* for piano, perf. at Salzburg Fest. (1923); comp. one-act opera, *Le Carrosse de Saint-Sacrement;* pcs. for orch.; *Fragments Psychologiques* and other pcs. for piano; and songs. The barony of Berners to which he succeeded in 1918, dates from 1455.

Bertini, Henri Jerome. Composer, pianist; b. London, Oct. 28, 1798; d. Meylan, Fr., Oct. 1, 1876. His études for the early grades of piano study are still in use.

Berumen, Ernesto. Pianist, teacher; b. South America. p. Robert Teichmuller. 1918, debut, New York; t. LaForge-Berumen Studios, New York.

Berwald (*Bair-valt*), **Franz.** Composer; b. Stockholm, 1796; d. ib., 1868. Opera comp.

Berwald, William Henry. Composer; b. Schwerin, Ger., Dec. 26, 1864; d. Syracuse, 193–. p. Rhemberger. 1889, cond., Phil. Soc., Libau, Rus.; 1892, prof. of mus., Syracuse U. Comp. overture, *Walthari,* over 70 pf. pcs., anthems and songs.

Besekirsky, Vassily Vassilievitch. Violinist, teacher; b. Moscow, Jan. 27, 1835. t. Moscow Cons.

Besson (*Bes-song*), **Gustave August.** Musical instrument maker; b. Paris, 1820; d. ib., 1875. Improved the manufacture of wind and brass instruments.

Best, William Thomas. Organist; b. Carlisle, Eng., Aug. 13, 1826; d. Liverpool, May 10, 1897. One of the foremost English org. of his day. Author of an organ method.

Besuner, Pearl. Soprano; b. Cincinnati, O., Nov. 4, 1904. 1928, Met. Op., N. Y.

Betti, Adolfo. Violinist, teacher; b. Bagni di Lucca, It. p. Cesar Thomson. 1900-1903, asst. t., Thomson, Brussels Cons.; 1903-29, fd. and dir., Flonzaley Quartet.

Bevan, Frederick Charles. Composer; b. London, Jul. 3, 1856. Concert singer and song writer. 1906, to Australia.

Bevignani (*Beh-vi-nyah-nee*), **Cavaliere Enrico Modesto.** Conductor; b. Naples, It., Sept. 29, 1841; d. ib., 1903. Italian opera cond. Comp. one successful opera, and abandoned composing.

Beyer, Ferdinand. Composer, pianist; b. Querfurt, Ger., Jul. 25, 1803; d. Mainz, May 14, 1863. Author of a piano Method.

Bianchi (*Bee-ang-kee*), **Chaitas Bianca (Bertha Schwarz).** Soprano, teacher; b. Heideberg, Jun. 27, 1858. t. Akademie der Tonkunst, Munich.

Biber (*Bee-ber*), **Heinrich Johann Franz von.** Violinist, composer; b. Wartenburg, Boh., Aug. 12, 1644; d. Salzburg, May 3, 1704. Comp. violin sonatas.

Biedermann, Edward Julius. Organist, composer; b. Milwaukee, Nov. 8, 1849; d. Freeport, L. I., Nov. 26, 1933. Comp. masses and sacred mus.

Biehl, Albert. Composer; *b.* Rudolstadt, Ger., Aug. 10, 1833. pf. t., Hamburg. Comp études and teaching pcs.

Bignami (*Been-yah-mee*), **Carlo.** Violinist, composer; *b.* Cremona, It., 1808; *d.* Voghera, It., 1848. Called by Paganini "the first violinist of Italy." Cond., Cremona. Comp. violin concerto.

Bilbro, Anne Mathilde. Composer, writer; *b.* Tuskegee, Ala. Writer of 50 books and 200 pcs. of easy teaching material. Lives at Gadsden, Ala.

Billings, William. Composer; *b.* Boston, Oct. 7, 1746; *d.* ib., Sept. 29, 1800. First Amer. comp. to pursue mus. as a profession. 1786, fd. Stoughton Mus. Soc., oldest U. S. singing soc. now in existence. Made six collections of mus., containing many original pcs., which in their day enjoyed wide popularity.

Billington, Elizabeth. Soprano; *b.* London, *c.* 1768; *d.* St. Artein, Aug. 25, 1818. Celebrated English singer.

Bimboni, Alberto. Conductor, composer; *b.* Florence, 1882. 1911, to U. S., to prepare Savage company for tour with Puccini's *Girl of the Golden West.* Cond. opera in Washington. 1926, opera *Winona,* prod., Portland, Ore.

Binchois, Egidius (or **Gilles de Binche**). Composer; *b.* Binche, Fr., *c.* 1400; *d.* Lille, 1460. Comp. sacred and secular mus. of Flemish contrapuntal school.

Birchard, Clarence C. Music publisher; *b.* Cambridge Springs, Pa., 1867; *d.* ———. 1900, fd., C. C. Birchard & Co.; set new Amer. standard w. his *Laurel Song Book* for sch. use.

Bird, Arthur. Composer; *b.* Cambridge, Mass., Jul. 23, 1856; *d.* Berlin, Dec. 22, 1923. *p.* Liszt. 1886, cond., Milwaukee mus. fest.; 1897, comic opera, *Daphne,* perf. at Bagby conc.; 1902, won Paderewski prize, w. *Decimette* for wind instr.; lived life in Germany. Comp. symph., chamb. mus., pf. pcs., organ pcs.

Birge, Edward B. Music educator; *b.* Northampton, Mass., Jun. 12, 1868. 1891, A.B., Brown; 1904, Mus.B., Yale; 1901-1920, mus. superv. Indianapolis sch.; 1921, prof. school mus., Indiana U.

Bischoff, J. W. Organist, composer; *b.* Chicago, 1850; *d.* Washington, D. C., Jun. 2, 1909. Blind from infancy.

Bishop, Anna. Soprano; *b.* London, 1814; *d.* New York, Mar. 18, 1884. Wife of Henry R. B.

Bishop, Sir Henry Rowley. Composer; *b.* London, Nov. 18, 1786; *d.* ib., Apr. 30, 1855. 1809, prod. *Circassian Bride.* Its success made him cond. at Covent Garden. A succession of successful dramatic wks. and songs made him one of the most popular composers of his day. Now chiefly remembered for his part songs, and as the composer of *Home, Sweet Home.*

Bishop, John. Organist, theorist; *b.* Cheltenham, Jul. 31, 1817; *d.* ib., Feb. 3, 1890. Translated Spohr's *Violin School* and Czerny's *School of Composition.*

Bispham, David Scull. Distinguished operatic baritone; *b.* Phila., Jan. 5, 1857; *d.* N. Y., Oct. 2, 1921. 1876, A.B., Haverford; 1891-1909, alternated Covent Garden, London, and Met. Op., N. Y.; sang 50 rôles, and created many rôles; 1909, retired to concertizing and teaching; advocate of opera in English. Author, *A Quaker Singer's Recollections.*

Bittner, Julius. Composer, writer; *b.* Vienna, Apr. 9, 1874. Abandoned law for music under influence of Gustav Mahler and Bruno Walter. 1907, the Frankfort première of his first opera, *Die Rote Gret,* established him as a successful opera composer. Ed. of the Vienna mus. magazine, *Merker.* With some eight successful operas to his credit, he is the opera hope of modern Germany.

Bizet, Georges. Composer; *b.* Paris, Oct. 25, 1838; *d.* Bougival, Fr., Jun. 3, 1875. Comp. operas, *Le docteur miracle, Les pêcheurs des perles, La jolie fille de Perth, Numa, Djamileh,* and *Carmen;* incid. mus. to *L'Arlésienne.*

Blahetka, Marie Léopoldine. Pianist; *b.* Guntramsdorf, Aus., Nov. 15, 1811; *d.* Boulogne, Fr., Jan. 12, 1887. Comp. opera, concerto, pf. pcs., songs.

Blake, John W. Songwriter; *b.* N. Y., 1862; *d.* ib., May 24, 1935. Wr. words to *The Sidewalks of New York,* immortalizing childhood playmate Mamie O'Rourke.

de Blanck, Hubert. Composer, educator; *b.* Holland, 1856; *d.* Havana, Nov. 28, 1932. Assoc. w. Theodore Thomas in early days in N. Y.; fd. Cons. in Cuba w. over 25 branches, and many thousands of students. *m.* a Menocal. Comp. pf. pcs., incl., *Vistas Cubanas.*

Bland, James. A banjo troubadour; *b. c.* 1860. Offspring of former Virginia slaves; page boy in House of Representatives at Washington. Comp. *Carry Me Back to Old Virginny* and *In the Evening by the Moonlight.*

Blanco, Pedro. Composer; *b.* ———; *d.* Oporto, Portugal, 1920. Edu., Madrid Roy. Cons. Located at Oporto. Assoc. w. E. de Fonseca, mus. ed. Comp. orch. pcs., several pf. and violin suites, and songs.

Blangini, Giuseppe, Marco Maria Felice. Tenor, composer; *b.* Turin, It., Nov. 18, 1781; *d.* Paris, Dec., 1841. 1814-30, t. Paris Cons. Author of *Autobiography.* Comp. thirty operas.

Blaserna, Pietro. Teacher, writer; *b.* Aquileia, It., Feb. 29, 1836; *d.* Rome, 1917. Famous acoustician. Prof., U. of Rome. 1890, Elec. Senator. Author, *The Theory of Sound.*

Blauvelt, Lillian Evans. Soprano; *b.* Brooklyn, Mar. 16, 1873. Studied violin; became opera and concert singer.

Blaze (*Castil-Blaze*), **François-Henri-Joseph.** Writer; *b.* Cavaillon, Fr., Dec. 1, 1784; *d.* Paris, Dec. 11, 1857. Pioneer among French critical writers; author of numerous treatises on opera, the dance; also a *Dictionary of Modern Music.*

Blech, Leo. Composer; *b.* Aix, Ger., Apr. 21, 1871. 1923, general musikdirektor Berlin State opera; 1925, g. cond. in U. S. Comp. operas, incl. *Versiegelt* (1908); operetta, *Die Strohwitwe* (1920); three symph. poems; pf. pcs., and songs.

Bleichmann, Julius. Composer, conductor; *b.* Petrograd, Dec. 5, 1868; *d.* ib., 1909. Comp. operas, orch. wks., songs.

Bleyle, Karl. Composer; *b.* Feldkirch, Ger., May 7, 1880. Prolific comp. in all forms. *h.* Stuttgart.

Blind Tom (Thomas Greene Bethune). Pianist; *b.* Columbia, Ga., *c.* 1849; *d.* Hoboken, N. J., Jun. 17, 1908. Father a slave of James Bethune. Celebrated for his improvisations.

Bliss, Arthur. Composer, conductor, pianist; *b.* London, Aug. 2, 1891. Edu., Cambridge, R. C. M. *u.* Stanford. 1923, took residence in New York. Comp. orch. wks., incl. *Rhapsody* and *Color Symphony;* chamb. mus., incl. *Rout;* pf. pcs., and songs.

Bliss, Philip Paul. Singer; *b.* Clearfield Co., Pa., Jul. 9, 1838; *d.* Ashtabula, O., Dec. 29, 1876. Wr. Hymn, *Pull for the Shore.*

Bliss, P. Paul. Organist, editor; *b.* Chicago, Nov. 25, 1872; *d.* Oswego, N. Y., Feb. 2, 1933. Mus. ed., J. Church Co., Willis. Comp. cantatas.

Blitzstein, Mark. Composer, pianist; *b.* Phila., Mar. 2, 1905. *p.* Siloti and Schoenberg. Comp. ultra-modern orchestral wks., incl. *Romantic Piece;* opera, chamb. mus., incl. *Gods;* songs, incl. *Is Five;* piano pcs. *h.* New York.

Bloch, Alexander. Violin teacher; *b.* Selma, Ala. *p.* Sevcik.

Bloch, Ernest. Composer, teacher; *b.* Geneva, Switz., Jul. 24, 1880. 1915, cond. for dancer Maud Allen on U. S. tour; 1917, *t.* Mannes Sch., N. Y.; 1920, Cleveland Inst. of Mus. Comp. symph. and chamb. mus., and choral wks., in an avowedly Jewish idiom.

Bloch, Josef. Violinist, composer; *b.* Pesth, Hun., Jan. 5, 1862. Fac. memb., Budapesth Cons. Comp. *Hungarian Rhapsody,* suites and violin pcs.

Blockx (*Block*), **Jan.** Composer; *b.* Antwerp, Jan. 25, 1851; *d.* ib., May 26, 1912. 1901, succ. Benoit as dir., Antwerp Cons. Comp. operas, incl. *Princess of the Inn, Bride of the Sea;* ballet, *Milenka;* cantatas, symph. and many wks. in all forms.

Blon, Franz von. Composer, conductor; *b.* Berlin, Jul. 16, 1861. Popular military marches.

Bloomfield-Zeisier, Fanny. Pianist; *b.* Bielitz, Aus., Jul. 16, 1866; *d.* Chicago, Aug. 20, 1927. *p.* Leschetizky. Distinguished virtuoso. Prominent Chicago mus. leader.

Blow, John. Organist, composer; *b.* Westminster, 1648; *d.* ib., Oct. 1, 1708. One of the many distinguished musicians trained in the Chapel Royal during reign of Charles II.

Blum, Elias. Tenor, organist, composer; *b.* Eisdorf, Hun., Feb. 22, 1881. 1891, to U. S.; edu., N. E. Cons., Boston; 1909-17, dir. Mus., Whitman Coll., Walla Walla, Wash.; 1917, prof., Grinnell (Iowa) Coll. Comp. anthems, choruses, songs.

Blumenfeld, Felix Michaelovitch. Composer, pianist, conductor; *b.* Kovalevska, Rus., Apr. 23, 1863. Prof. Petrograd Cons., until 1918. Comp. symphs. and chamb. wks., pf. pcs., songs.

Blumenthal, Jacob. Composer; *b.* Hamburg, 1829; *d.* London, May 17, 1908. A prolific song writer.

Bobinski, Heinrich Antonovitch. Pianist; *b.* Warsaw, Pol., Feb. 1, 1861. Prof. Kiev Cons. Comp. overture, piano concerto.

Boccherini, Luigi. Composer, 'cellist; *b.* Lucca, Feb. 19, 1743; *d.* Madrid, Sp., May 28, 1805. Comp. much chamb. mus.; best known by his *Minuet.*

Bochsa, Robert Nicholas. Harpist, composer; *b.* Montmédy, Fr., Aug. 9, 1789; *d.* Sydney, N. S. W., Jan. 6, 1856.

Bodansky, Artur. Conductor; *b.* Vienna, Dec. 16, 1877. 1912, cond. Mahler Fest., Mannheim; 1914, cond. *Parsifal* in London; since 1915, cond. Met. Op., N. Y.

Boehm (*Baym*), **Theobald.** Flute-maker; *b.* Munich, Apr. 9, 1794; *d.* ib., Nov. 15, 1881. Developed the improved or "Boehm System" flute.

Boekelman, Bernardus. Pianist, teacher; *b.* Utrecht, Hol., Jun. 9, 1838; *d.* New York, Aug. 2, 1930. 1866, to U. S. Inventor of analytical edition of Bach Fugues issued in colors.

Boëllman (*Bo-ell-man*), **Léon.** Organist, composer; *b.* Alsace, Sept. 29, 1862; *d.* Paris, Oct. 11, 1897. Career of promise curtailed by early death. Comp. organ mus.

Boepple, Paul. Music educator, conductor; *b.* Basel, Switz. 1918-26, *t.* Dalcroze Institute, Geneva; 1926, dir., Dalcroze Sch. of Mus., New York.

Boëtus (*Boëthius*), **Anicius.** Philosopher, writer; *b.* Rome *c.* 475; *d.* ib., *c.* 524. Author of *De Musica,* the chief authority on Greek mus. Executed for alleged treason by Theodoric, whose counsellor he had been.

Bogert, Walter Lawrence. Singing teacher, baritone; *b.* Flushing, N. Y., Dec. 7, 1864. 1889, B.A., M.A., then LL.D., Columbia U.; 1908, gr., Inst. Mus. Art. 1890, mem., N. Y. Bar Assn.; 1898, *t.* Natl. Cons. Mus.; 1907-09, *t.* Inst. Mus. Art; 1920-21, *t.* Yale. Author of articles on mus.

Boguslawski, Moissaye. Pianist, lecturer, teacher; *b.* Nov. 1, 1887. *p.* Ganz. 1909-19, dir. Kansas City Cons.; 1921, *t.* Chicago Mus. Coll. Since 1931, pres. of Bog. Coll. of Mus.

Bohlmann, Henry Frederic Theodor. Pianist; *b.* Osterwieck, Ger., Jun. 23, 1865; *d.* Memphis, Mar. 18, 1931. 1890, *t.* Cin. Cons.; 1919, fd. B. Sch., Memphis.

Bohm, Carl. Composer; *b.* Berlin, Sept. 11, 1844; *d.* Apr. 19, 1920. Prolific comp. of salon mus. for piano, violin, voice. Best known by song, *Calm as the Night.*

Bohm, Joseph. Violinist, teacher; *b.* Pesth, Hun., Mar. 4, 1795; *d.* Vienna, Mar. 28, 1876. *p.* Rode. Prof. Vienna Cons.; *t.* Ernst, Joachim, Hellmesberger.

Bohnen, Michael. Baritone; *b.* Cologne, 1888. 1911, Berlin opera; 1913, Met. Op. *m.* Mary Lewis (divorced).

Boieldieu, François Adrien. Composer; *b.* Rouen, Fr., Dec. 16, 1775; *d.* Jarcy, Fr., Oct. 8, 1834. Comp. operas, incl. *Le Calif de Bagdad, La dame blanche.*

Boisdeffre (*Bwa-defr*), **Ch.-Henri-René de.** Composer; *b.* Vesoul, Fr., 1838; *d.* Veselize, Fr., 1906. Comp. symph., oratorio, *The Song of Songs;* orch., *Scères Champêtres;* chamb. mus., violin pcs.

Boise, Otis Bardwell. Organist, theorist; *b.* Oberlin, O., Aug. 13, 1844; *d.* Baltimore, Dec. 2, 1912. Taught harmony and composition, Peabody Cons. Comp. symph., two overtures, piano concerto.

Boito (*Bo-ee-to*), **Arrigo.** Composer, poet; *b.* Padua, Feb. 24, 1842; *d.* Milan, Jun. 10, 1918. Distinguished both as poet and opera composer. Wrote many of Verdi's librettos, incl. *Otello* and *Falstaff;* also *La Gioconda* for Ponchielli. Exercised a profound influence upon mus. in It. for a half a century. Only opera, *Mefistofele,* prod. Mar. 5, 1868 at La Scala, was poorly received. Revised and abbreviated, it had a triumphal revenge in Bologna in 1875. His uncompleted opera *Nerone* was produced at La Scala in 1924.

Boix, Manuel Polan. Composer; *b.* Valencia, Jan. 4, 1893. *p.* Ravel. 1927, won prize for suite, *Congoriana.* 1935, *Laboradores,* from suite, *Siluetas,* perf. N. Y. by Iturbi. Comp. orch. wks.

Bolck, Oscar. Pianist, composer; *b.* Hohenstein, Mar. 4, 1837; *d.* Bremen, May 2, 1888.

Bonawitz, Johann Heinrich. Pianist, composer; *b.* Dürkhein, Ger., Dec. 4, 1839; *d.* London, Aug. 15, 1917.

Bonci, Alessandro. Tenor; *b.* Cesena, It., Feb. 10, 1870. One of the most celebrated operatic tenors of his day. 1908, Met. Op.; 1912, Chicago Op.

Bond, Carrie, née Jacobs. Composer; b. Janesville, Wis., 1862. Best known by her song, *The Perfect Day.*

Bonelli, Richard. Baritone; b. Port Byron, N. Y. Edu., Syracuse U. p. J. deRezke. 1925, Chicago Op.; 1935, Met. Op.

Bonetti, Mary. Contralto; b. Lynnbrook, L. I., Nov. 23, 1902. 1923, debut, Florence; 1925, Met. Op.

Bonnet, Joseph Elic Georges Maria. Organist, composer; b. Bordeaux, Mar. 17, 1884. p. Guilmant. 1906, org. St. Eustache, Paris; and concert tours in Europe; 1910, England; 1916, America; t. Eastman Sch., Roch. Comp. organ pcs.

Bononcini (*Buononcini*), **Giovanni Battista.** Composer; b. Modena, It., 1660; d. 1750. Opera comp. and rival of Handel.

Bonvin, Ludwig. Composer, conductor; b. Siders, Switz., Feb. 17, 1850. 1887, to U. S. Comp. Catholic ch. mus.

Booth, Christopher Henry Hudson. Organist, composer; b. Accrington, Eng., Sept. 5, 1865. 1895, to U. S.; 1900, Victor accompanist; 1909, org., Ch. of the Advent, N. Y. Comp. masses, songs, anthems.

Boott, Francis. Composer; b. Boston, Jun. 24, 1813; d. Cambridge, Mass., Mar. 1, 1904. Comp. mass and sacred mus.

Borch, Gaston. Composer, conductor, 'cellist; b. Guines, Fr., Mar. 8, 1871; d. U. S., 192–. p. Massenet. 1899, to U. S.; cond., Boston Symph. Comp. operas, symph., piano concerto, pf. pcs., and songs.

Bordogni (*Bor-dohn-yee*), **Marco.** Singer, teacher; b. Gazzaniga, It., 1788; d. Paris, Jul. 31, 1856. Comp. of vocalises.

Bori, Lucrezia (Family name Borja, originally Borgia). Operatic soprano; b. Valencia, Dec. 24, 1888(9). p. Vidal. 1908, debut, Rome; 1913, Met. Op. Formed committee that saved the opera in 1934. Foremost prima donna of her epoch.

Bornschein, Franz Carl. Violinist, composer, conductor; b. Baltimore, Feb. 10, 1879. t. Peabody Cons., Baltimore. Comp. *Three Persian Poems* for orch.; orch. suite, *Sea God's Daughter;* symph. poems incl. *Rime of the Ancient Mariner.*

Borodin, Alexander Porphyrievitch. Composer; b. Petrograd, Nov. 12, 1834; d. ib., Feb. 28, 1887. Member of Russian Nationalist group. Comp. incl. two symphonies, orch. tone-picture, *In the Steppes of Central Asia;* opera, *Prince Igor;* chamb. mus., pf. pcs. and songs.

Borowski (*Bo-roff-ski*), **Felix.** Composer, writer, teacher; b. Burton, Eng., Mar. 10, 1872; d. Chicago, 1897. t. Chicago Mus. Coll.; wr. erudite music criticism for Chicago newspapers; program annotator, Chicago Symph.; 1916-25, pres. Chicago Mus. Coll., succ., F. Ziegfeld. Comp. *Elegie Symphonic,* perf. Chicago Symph. (1917); ballet, *Boudour,* perf., Chicago Op. (1919); orch. tone-p., *Le Printempo Passionne,* perf. North Sh. Fest. (1920); also pf. concerto, organ sonatas, pcs. for organ and violin. Best known by *Adoration.*

Bortnianski (*Bort-nyan-skee*), **Dimitri.** Composer; b. Gloukov, Rus., 1752; d. Petrograd, Oct. 8, 1825. Comp. Russian ch. mus.

Bos, Coenraad V. Pianist; b. Leyden, Hol., Dec. 7, 1875. Distinguished accompanist. 1908, to U. S. w. Ludwig Wüllner.

Bossi, Marco Enrico. Organist, composer; b. Salo, It., Apr. 25, 1861; d. at sea, enroute It., Feb. 22, 1925. 1916-22, dir., St. Cecilia, Rome. An esteemed Italian musician. Reformed organ teaching in Italy. Long list of compositions in all forms, esp., organ concertos, cantatas, operas.

Bott, Jean Joseph. Violinist, composer; b. 1826; d. 1895. p. Spohr. 1885, to New York. His violin had a varied history and is still known as the "Bott" Strad. Comp. operas.

Botta, Luca. Tenor; b. Amalfi, It., Apr. 16, 1884; d. New York, Sept. 29, 1917. 1915, Met. Op., N. Y.

Bottesini (*Bot-te-see-nee*), **Giovanni.** Double-bass player; b. Crema, It., Dec. 24, 1823; d. Parma, Jul. 7, 1889. A virtuoso on the double-bass. Comp. operas, symphonies, concertos, quartets.

Boughton, Rutland. Composer, author; b. Aylesbury, Eng., Jan. 23, 1878. Edu. Royal Coll. Mus., u. Stanford; 1902, *Imperial Elegy* intro. by Sir Henry J. Wood, Queen's Hall; t. Midland Inst. Mus. till 1911; 1914, fd. Glastonbury Fest., prod. opera, *Immortal Hour,* but fest. proved a failure, blasting a life-long ambition; 1922, revised by Barry Jackson in London, it had the longest run of any English romantic opera; 1935, opera, *The Ever-Young,* prod. Bath. Comp. some six other operas, incl. *Alcestis* (1922); ballets, incl., *Snow-White;* symphonies, incl., *Deirdre;* chamb. mus. and chor. wks.; author of *Bach, The Reality of Music, The Nature of Music* and other wks.

Boulanger, Lili (Juliette-Marie-Olga). Composer; b. Paris, Aug. 21, 1893; d. Mezy, Fr., Mar. 15, 1918. Sister of Nadia B. 1913, gr., Cons.; Prix de Rome, for *Faust et Hélène.* A marked talent, marred by ill health, and cut short by an untimely death.

Boulanger, Nadia (Juliette). Composer, teacher; b. Paris, Sept. 16, 1887. p. Paris Cons.; 1908, won Second Prix de Rome w. cantata, *La Sirene;* prof., Cons., Ecole Normale de Musique, and Amer. Cons., Fontainebleau; 1925, perf., Aaron Copland's symph. for organ and orch., u. Damrosch; collab. w. Pugno in incid. mus. for d'Annunzio's *Citta Morte.* Taught Roy Harris, Aaron Copland, Samizky, Rich. Hammond, Bern. Rogers, Douglas Moore, and others of the ultra-modern sch. Comp. orch. wks., songs.

Boult, Sir Adrian Cedric. Conductor; b. Chester, Apr. 8, 1889. 1914, asst. cond., Covent Garden; 1918, cond., Royal Phil.; 1920, cond., B. B. C. Symph. and Diaghilev Ballet; 1923, cond., Birmingham Fest. Chorus, and London Bach Choir; mus. dir., B. B. C.

Bourgault-Ducoudray (*Boor-goh Du-cooh-dray*), **Louis Albert.** Composer; b. Nantes, Feb. 2, 1840; d. Vernouillet, Jul. 4, 1910. 1862, Prix de Rome; 1874, wounded in Franco-Prussian War, was sent to Greece on official mission, and became interested in folk-song research; 1878-1908, prof. mus. hist., Paris Cons. Comp. operas and orch. wks., and collections of folk-songs.

Bourskaya, Ina. Contralto; b. Gitomar, Rus., Sept. 9, 1888. 1913, Kieff Op.; 1922, Chicago Op.; 1935, Met. Op.

Bovy, Ch.-Samuel (pseudonym Lysberg). Composer, pianist; b. Lysberg, Switz., Mar. 1, 1821; d. Geneva, Switz., Feb. 15, 1873. Comp. salon mus.

Bowen, George Oscar. Music supervisor; b. Castle Creek, N. Y., 1873. 1917, mus. dir., Flint, Mich.; 1920, U. of Mich.; 1924, mus. supv., Tulsa, Okla.

Bowen, York. Composer, teacher; *b.* London, Feb. 22, 1884. A leading English pianist. Comp. pf. wks., also symph. and chamb. wks.

Bowman, Edward Morris. Organist, teacher; *b.* Barnard, Vt., Jul. 18, 1848; *d.* Brooklyn, Aug. 27, 1913. 1883-1905, pres. M. T. N. A.; 1891-5, prof., Vassar Coll.

Boyce, William. Organist, composer; *b.* London, Feb. 7, 1710; *d.* ib., Feb. 7, 1779. 1749, Mus.D., Cambridge U. Ed. of *Cathedral Music*. Comp. symph., oratorios, ch. mus., pf. pcs., songs, incl. *Hearts of Oak*.

Boyd, Charles N. Organist, conductor, editor; *b.* Greensburg, Pa., 1875. 1915, dir., Pittsburgh Mus. Inst.; author of musical wks.; assoc. ed., Groves Dict., Am. supplement.

Boyle, George Frederick. Pianist, composer; *b.* Sydney, N. S. W., Jun. 29, 1886. *t.* Peabody Cons., Baltimore. Comp. orch. incl. *Slumber Song, Aubade,* pf. pcs.

Bradbury, William Batchelder. Composer; *b.* York, Me., Oct. 6, 1816; *d.* Montclair, N. J., Jan. 7, 1868. Fd. Bradbury pf. factory. Comp. two cantatas and many hymns, incl., *He Leadeth Me*.

Bradley, Kenneth McPherson. Musical educator; *b.* Campbellsville, Ky., Sept. 27, 1872. Edu. Cincinnati Coll. of Mus.; 1902-25, pres., Bush Cons. of Mus., Chicago; 1925, Pasadena, Cal.; organizer and pres., Natl. Assn. of Schs. of Mus.

Bradsky, Wenzel. Composer; *b.* Hakovnik, Boh., 1833; *d.* ib., 1881. Comp. operas and songs, incl., *Thou Art Mine All,* once popular in U. S.

Braga, Gaetano. 'Cellist, composer; *b.* Giulianova, Jun. 9, 1829; *d.* Milan, 1907. Comp. of once popular *Angel's Serenade*.

Braggiotti, Isidore. Vocal teacher; *b.* 1864; *d.* Los Angeles, Sept. 16, 1934. Father of the ballet producer, Francesca (Mrs. John Cabot) Lodge.

Braham, David. Composer; orchestra director of Harrigan and Hart, celebrated minstrel pair. Comp. mus. for many of their songs, incl. *The Mulligan Guards,* first intro. in 1873, at Chicago Acad. of Mus., a song that afterwards was immortalized by Kipling. It spelled the doom of the post-civil war target parties.

Braham, John [Abraham]. Tenor; *b.* London, 1774; *d.* ib. Feb. 17, 1856. Opera and oratorio singer of unusual range. 1840, toured U. S. Comp. ballads.

Brahms, Johannes. Composer; *b.* Hamburg, Ger., May 7, 1833; *d.* Vienna, Apr. 3, 1897. Attracted attention of Schumann at early age, as accompanist to Wilhelmj. 1869, Vienna. With the exception of opera, there is scarcely a form in which he has not made his influence felt. Brahms is best known by his four symphonies, the first of which was called the "tenth," following after the classicism of Beethoven.

Braine, Robert. Composer, pianist, organist, editor; *b.* Springfield, O., 1896. St. Coll. of Mus., Cin. Comp. three operas, *The Eternal Light, Virginia, Diana;* 1924, mus. comedy, *Top Hole;* orch. episode, *S. O. S.;* also, orch. suite; overture; songs; sonatas; piano pcs.

Brambach, Kaspar Joseph. Composer; *b.* Bonn, Jul. 14, 1833; *d.* ib., Jun. 20, 1902. Best known by his cantatas.

Brandeis, Frederick. Pianist, composer; *b.* Vienna, Jul. 5, 1835; *d.* New York, 1899. Comp. salon mus.

Brandt, Marianne (really Bischoff). Contralto; *b.* Vienna, Sept. 12, 1842. 1882, Bayreuth, and New York; 1899, retired.

Branscombe, Gena (Mrs. John F. Tenney). Composer; *b.* Picton, Ont., Nov. 4, 1881. *p.* Borowski, Chicago. Comp. orch. wks., instrumental pcs., song cycles, songs, and choruses for women's voices. Career largely assoc. w. New York.

Branzell, Karin. Mezzo-soprano; *b.* Stockholm. 1919, Berlin Statsoper; 1924, Met. Op.

Braslau, Sophie. Contralto; *b.* New York, Aug. 16, 1892; *d.* ib., Dec. 22, 1935. 1913, Met. Op. H., N. Y.

Brassin (*Bras-sang*), **Louis.** Pianist, composer; *b.* Aix, Ger., Jun. 24, 1840; *d.* Petrograd, May 17, 1884. Wr. études, a piano method, salon pcs., etc.

Brauer, Max. Conductor, composer; *b.* Mannheim, Ger., May 9, 1855; *d.* Karlsruhe, 1918. Comp. a suite for strings, operas, violin pcs.

Braunfels, Walter. Composer; *b.* Frankfort, Ger., Dec. 19, 1882. *p.* Leschetizky. 1924, opera, *Don Gil von den grünen Hosen,* prod. at Munich, with success; 1925, dir., Cologne Stattlichen Hochschule; 1933, ret. to Godesberg. A romantic, but devoted to Bach and Beethoven. Comp. opera, incl., *Galatea;* orchestral wks., incl., *Neues Vederspiel;* choral wks., piano pcs., songs.

Brecher, Gustav. Composer, conductor; *b.* Eichwald, Boh., Feb. 5, 1879. Opera imp., Frankfort-a-M. Comp. symph., *Aus unserer Zeit;* str. q. and pf. sonata; author of biography of Richard Strauss.

Bree (*Bray*), **Johann Bernard van.** Violinist, composer; *b.* Amsterdam, Jan. 29, 1809; *d.* ib., Feb. 14, 1857. Best known by cantata, *St. Cecilia's Day*.

Breil, Joseph Carl. Composer; *b.* Pittsburgh, Jan. 29, 1870; *d.* Los Angeles, Jan. 13, 1926. 1919, opera, *The Legend,* perf. at Met. Op. H., N. Y. Comp. incid. mus. to *The Climax,* incl., *Song of the Soul*.

Breithaupt, Rudolph Maria. Pianist, teacher; *b.* Brunswick, Ger., Aug. 11, 1873. 1918, *t.* Stern Cons., Berlin, succ. M. Krause. Authority on pf. methods, and exponent of weight-technic; author of numerous books on technical branches of mus.

Brema (*Bray-ma*), **Marie** (pseud. for Minnie Fehrmann); Operatic mezzo-soprano; *b.* Liverpool, Feb. 28, 1856; *d.* Manchester, Mar. 22, 1925. *p.* Georg Henschel. Famous Wagnerian singer; 1892, Met. Op., in the *Ring u.* Mottl and Seidl. *t.* Royal Coll. of Mus., Manchester.

Breton, Ruth. Violinist; *b.* Indianapolis, Dec. 5, 1902. *p.* Auer. 1924, debut, N. Y. Phil. Orch.

Breton y Hernandez (*Her-nan-deth*), **Tomas.** Composer; *b.* Salamanca, Sp., Dec. 29, 1850; *d.* Madrid, Dec. 2, 1923. Opera, *Dolores* ran for 63 consecutive perf. in Madrid and 112 in Barcelona. Comp. many zarzuelas, incl., *La Verbena de la paloma,* which has gone closer to the Spanish heart than any lyric work of the modern times, also *Andalusian Scenes* for orch., and other symph., and chamb. wks.

Bréval (*Bray-vahl*), **Lucienne** (née Bertha Brennwald. Became Fr. citizen as L. B. Later known as Lizette Schilling). Soprano; *b.* Maennedorf, Switz., Nov 4, 1869; *d.* ib., Aug. 15, 1935. For 30 years contrib. to the glamour of the Paris opera, creating many rôles in Wagnerian and French operas. 1901, Met. Op., *u.* Grau.

Bréville (*Bray-veel*), **Pierre de.** Composer, teacher; *b.* Bar-le-Duc, Feb. 21, 1861. *p.* César Franck. *t.* Schola Cantorum; mus. critic, *Mercure de France.* Comp. choral work, *St. Rose de Lima;* orchestral piece, *Nuit de Décembre;* overture, *Princess Maleine;* incidental mus. to Maëterlinck's, *Sept Princesses,* besides organ pcs., songs, and piano wks.

Brewer, Alfred Herbert. Organist, composer; *b.* Gloucester, Eng., Jun. 21, 1865; *d. ib.,* Mar. 1, 1928. Cond., Three Choirs Fest., Gloucester. Comp. orch. wks., organ pcs., and songs.

Brewer, John Hyatt. Organist, composer, conductor; *b.* Brooklyn, N. Y., Jan. 18, 1856; *d. ib.,* Nov. 30, 1931. 1903, succ., Dudley Buck as cond., Apollo Club. Org., LaFayette Ave., Presby. Ch., for over 30 years. 1914, Mus.D., N. Y. U. Comp. organ pcs., cantatas, songs and choral wks. Career largely assoc. *w.* Brooklyn.

Bricken, Carl Ernest. Composer; *b.* Shelbyville, Ky., Dec. 28, 1898. 1922, B.A., Yale. *p.* Alfred Cortot. 1928-29, *t.* Inst. Mus. Art, N. Y.; 1929, Pulitzer Prize in Mus.; 1930, Guggenheim Fellowship; 1931, asst. prof. of mus., U. of Chicago; 1934, g.-cond., Chicago Symph. Comp. *String Quartet, Songs for Children, Variations for Two Piano on an Old English Theme.*

Brico, Antonia. Conductor. Only woman student of Karl Muck at Berlin State Acad. 1930, debut as cond. *w.* Berlin Phil.; g.-cond., Hollywood Bowl, Detroit and Buffalo Symph. 1934, fd. N. Y. Women's Symph.

Bridge, Frank. Violinist, composer, conductor; *b.* Brighton, Eng., Feb. 26, 1879. 1899-1903, edu. Royal Coll. Mus., *u.* Stanford. Member Grimson, Joachim, English String Quartets. 1906, succ. Wirth as vla. of Joachim quar.; 1923-4, g.-cond., Rochester Symph., and other Amer. orchs. Comp. orch. wks., incl., *Sea Suite,* and *Lament for Strings;* also chamb. mus.

Bridge, Sir John Frederick. Composer, organist; *b.* Oldbury, Eng., Dec. 5, 1844; *d.* London, Mar. 18, 1924. 1874, Mus.D., Oxford; 1875-1918, org., Westminster Abbey; 1897, Knighted; 1902, prof., London U., from its founding; lectured extensively. Author, treatises on Counterpoint, and other books, incl., *Shakespearean Music.* Comp. oratorios, cantatas, organ pcs.; also humorous part-songs.

Bridgetower, George Augustus Polgreen. Violinist; *b.* Biala, Pol., 1780; *d.* London, *c.* 1845. Son of African father and European mother. Gave first public perf. of the *Kreutzer* sonata.

Brink, Jules ten. Composer; *b.* Amsterdam, Nov. 4, 1838; *d.* Paris, Feb. 6, 1889. Comp. orch. wks.

Brinkman, Herman Philip. 'Cellist; *b.* Germany, 1861; *d.* Englewood, N. J., Jun. 20, 1934. Toured *w.* Patti; mem., Met. Op. Orch.

Bristow, George Frederick. Composer; *b.* Brooklyn, Dec. 19, 1825; *d.* N. Y., Dec. 13, 1898. His opera, *Rip Van Winkle,* was the second Amer. opera to be prod. It ran four weeks at Niblo's, following its première, Sept. 27, 1855. Historically important as early champion of Americanism in mus.

Britton, Thomas. Musical amateur; *b.* Northamptonshire, Eng., 1651; *d.* London, Sept. 27, 1714. A musical enthusiast, commonly known as the "Musical Small-coals Man."

Broadwood, John. Piano-maker; *b.* Cockburnspath, Eng., Oct., 1732; *d.* 1812. Contributed improvement to the piano mechanism.

Brockway, Howard A. Pianist, composer; *b.* Brooklyn, Nov. 22, 1870. St., Berlin. 1895, concert of his works; 1895-1903, *t.* N. Y.; 1903-10, *t.* Peabody Inst., Baltimore; 1907, Symph., perf. Boston Symph.; 1910, *t.* Mannes Sch., N. Y. Comp. symph. and chamb. wks., instr. pcs., songs.

Brodsky, Adolf. Violinist, teacher; *b.* Taganrog, Rus., Mar. 21, 1851. 1902, Mus.D., Victoria U. A powerful figure in violin history. Memb., Hellmesberger st. q.; 1870-80, Rus.; 1880-82, Ger.; 1883, soloist, Richter concerts, London; 1883-91, prof., Leipzig Cons.; 1891-4, conc.-m., N. Y. Symph. Soc.; 1895, prof., Manchester Coll., Eng.; cond., Hallé Orch.; fd. Brodsky Quartet. First to perf. Tschaikowsky concerto, and won the dedication.

Broekhoven (*Breck-ho-fen*), **John A.** Theorist, harmony teacher; *b.* Beek, Hol., 1852; *d.* Columbus, Aug. 4, 1930. *t.* Coll. of Mus., Cin. Comp. *Creole* suite, *Columbia* overture. Author of theoretical treatises.

Bronsart, Hans von. Pianist, conductor, composer; *b.* Berlin, Feb. 11, 1830; *d.* Munich, Nov. 3, 1913. His wife, Ingeborg Starck (1840-1913), comp. operas, concertos, and chamb. mus.

Brower, Grover Ackley. Pianist, teacher; *b.* Newburgh, N. Y., Nov. 17, 1884. *p.* Goetschius. Assoc. ed., *University Course of Music Study.* Instructor, Cadek Cons. of Mus., Chattanooga, Tenn.

Brown, Albert Edmund. Music educator; *b.* Derby, Eng., Dec. 9, 1874. 1886, to U. S.; 1912-13, *t.* Chautauqua Inst.; 1916-17, *t.* Boston U. Assoc. ed., *Musical Courier.*

Brown, Eddy. Violinist; *b.* Chicago, Jul. 15, 1895. *p.* Hubay. Distinguished virtuoso. *t.* N. Y.

Brown, Wade R. Music educator; *b.* Venice, O., Feb. 14, 1866. 1912, dean, Sch. of Mus., N. C. Coll. for Women, Greensboro; 1905-12, dir., N. C. mus. fest.

Brown, William Earl. Singing teacher; *b.* Milton, Ind., 1863. *p.* Gleason. *t.* King Cons., San Jose, Cal. Author of *Vocal Wisdom.*

Browne, John Lewis. Organist; *b.* London, May 18, 1866; *d.* Chicago, Oct. 23, 1933. 1875, to Amer. Prolific organ recitalist. Since 1912, org. and choirmaster, St. Patrick's Church, Chicago; head of theory dept., Fine Arts Cons. of Mus.; since 1928, dir. mus. pub. schs., Chicago. 1925, Bispham medal for opera, *La Corsicana,* prod., 1923, Chicago Playhouse; secular mus.; piano, organ pcs., songs.

Bruch, Max. Composer; *b.* Cologne, Ger., Jan. 6, 1838; *d.* Berlin, Oct. 2, 1920. 1863, opera, *Lorelei,* prod., Mannheim; 1878, cond., Stern Chor. Soc., Berlin, succ. Stockhausen; 1880, cond., Liverpool Phil., succ. Benedict; 1883, cond., Breslau Orch.; 1891, *t.* Berlin Acad.; 1893, Mus.D., Cambridge. His G. minor *Violin Concerto* has been one of the cornerstones of the violin repertoire for a generation. Comp. wks. in all forms, especially cantatas for male chorus and orch.; and pcs. for violin and orch., as *Romanze.*

Bruckner (*Brook-ner*), **Anton.** Organist, composer; *b.* Ansfelden, Aus., Sept. 4, 1824; *d.* Vienna, Oct. 11, 1896. The consummation of Austrian classicism, utilizing the complete resources of the modern orch. The almost formidable proportions of his 9 great symphs. retarded for a generation public recognition of their merits. A quintet and a few choral wks. complete the record of his life.

Brüll (*Bril*), **Ignaz.** Moravian pianist, composer; b. Prossnitz, Aus., Nov. 7, 1846; d. Vienna, Sept. 17, 1907. Contemporary and associate of Brahms. Comp. symph. and chamb. mus., but achieved popularity through his lighter operas, such as *The Golden Cross.*

Brune, Adolf Gerhard. Pianist, composer; b. Hanover, Jun. 21, 1870; d. Chicago, Apr. 21, 1935. 1889, to U. S.; 1898, t. Chicago Mus. Coll. Comp. orch. and chamb. mus., organ and pf. pcs., songs.

Bruneau, Alfred. Composer, writer; b. Paris, Mar. 3, 1857; d. Paris, June 15, 1934. Mus. critic on *Le Figaro.* Comp. symph. poems, incl., *La Belle au bois dormant;* but chief fame rests on his opera, incl., *L'enfant Roi,* to libretto written by Emile Zola. His first success was in *Le Rêve,* prod. 1891, to libretto by Louis Gallet based on the Zola novel.

Bruni, Antoine Barthelemy. Violinist, conductor; b. Coni, It., 1759; d. ib., 1823. 1789, cond., Opera Comique. Author of a Method for violin and viola.

Bucalossi, Ernest. Composer; b. London, May 27, 1867. Comp. songs, dance mus.

Büchner, Emil. Composer; b. Osterfeld, Ger., Dec. 25, 1826; d. Erfurt, Ger., Jun. 9, 1908. Comp. operas, overtures.

Buck, Dudley. Organist, composer; b. Hartford, Conn., Mar. 10, 1839; d. Orange, N. J., Oct. 6, 1909. For many years org. of Holy Trinity, Brooklyn; also Apollo Club. Comp. the opera *Deseret,* orch., organ, ch., and piano mus.; cantatas, *King Olaf's Christmas, Voyage of Columbus, Hymn to Music, The Light of Asia, The Christian Year,* a cycle of five cantatas.

Buck, Gene. Producer and playwright; b. Detroit, Mich., Aug. 8, 1885. St., Detroit Art Acad. Librettist for Ziegfeld Follies since 1912. Pres., A. S. C. A. P.

Buhlig (*Boo-lig*), **Richard.** Pianist; b. Chicago, Dec. 21, 1880. p. Leschetizky. 1901, t. Berlin; 1907, Amer. debut w. Phila. Symph.; 1918-22, t. IMA, N. Y.

Bull, John. Organist, composer; b. Somersetshire, Eng., c. 1563; d. Antwerp, Mar. 13, 1628. The great English musician of the Elizabethan epoch.

Bull, Ole Bornemann. Early violin virtuoso; b. Bergen, Nor., Feb. 5, 1810; d. Lysö, Nor., Aug. 17, 1880. 1843-5, first Amer. tour netted $400,000; 1852-7, toured from Me. to Cal. w. Adelina Patti; 1867-71, attempted to found a colony, *Oleana,* but was defrauded by land-sharks; 1879-80, last Amer. tour, w. Emma Thursby. Nor. mourned his death; Grieg and Björnson spoke at his grave. 1901, statue by Stephan Sinding unveiled in Bergen. Comp. violin pcs., songs, incl. *Upon the Sun I Gaze.*

Bullard, Frederick Field. Composer; b. Boston, Mass., Sept. 21, 1864; d. ib., Jun. 24, 1904. Comp. melodrama on Tennyson's *Six Sisters,* ch. mus., male choruses, and songs; known to fame by his *Stein Song.*

Bülow, Hans Guido, Freiherr von. Pianist, conductor; b. Dresden, Ger., Jan. 8, 1830; d. Cairo, Egypt, Feb. 12, 1894. 1848, st. Leipzig; 1849, an early advocate of Wagner; 1850, p. Wagner and Liszt; 1853-55, concertized; 1855, t. Stern Cons., succ. Kullak; 1875-6, Amer. tour. Held a variety of posts, w. frequent changes, helped by a querulous disposition. Issued historic edition of the Beethoven sonatas.

Bungert, August. Composer; b. Mühlheim, Mar. 14, 1846; d. Leulersdorf, Ger., Oct. 26, 1915. Comp. songs to texts of Carmen Sylvia, Q. of Roumania. Attempted a cycle of Homeric operas along lines of the Wagner Trilogy. Comp. other operatic and symph. wks.

Bunnett, Edward. Organist, composer; b. nr. E. Dereham, Eng., Jun. 26, 1834; d. Norwich, 1923. Comp. cantatas, ch. mus.

Bunning, Herbert. Composer, conductor; b. London, May 2, 1863. 1892-3, as cond., Lyric Th., prod. Albeniz opera, *Magic Opal.* Comp. opera, *La Princess Orsa,* prod. Covent Garden (1902); also other operatic and orch. wks., and songs.

Buonamici (*Bwoh-nah-mee-chee*), **Carlo.** Pianist; b. Florence, It., Jun. 20, 1875; d. Boston, 1920. Son of Giuseppe B.

Buonamici, Giuseppe. Pianist, teacher; b. Florence, Mar. 12, 1846; d. ib., Mar. 18, 1914. p. von Bülow. Powerful educational influence in It.

Burchard (*Boorkh-art*), **Karl.** Pianist; b. Hamburg, 1820; d. Dresden, Feb. 12, 1896. Made four-hand pf. arrangements of the classics.

Burdett, George Albert. Organist, composer; b. Boston, Jun. 17, 1856. Comp. ch. mus., organ pcs.

Burgmüller, Johann Friedrich. Composer; b. Regensburg, Ger., 1806; d. Beaulieu, Fr., Feb. 13, 1874. Comp. études and salon pcs. for piano.

Burgmüller, Norbert. Composer; b. Düsseldorf, Feb. 8, 1810; d. Aix, May 7, 1836. Schumann wrote that since the early death of Schubert nothing more deplorable had happened than that of Burgmüller.

Burgstaller, Alois. Tenor; b. Holzkirchen, Ger., Sept. 27, 1871. Wagnerian opera singer; 1902-9, Met. Op., N. Y.

Burke, Hilda (née Hopkins). Soprano; b. Baltimore, 1904. p. George Castelle. 1927, NFMC prize; 1928, debut, Chicago Op.; 1929, Juilliard fellowship to Dresden opera sch. 1931, m. Desiré Defrere, stage mgr., Met. Op. 1935, Met. Op.

Burleigh, Cecil. Composer, violinist; b. Wyoming, N. Y., Apr. 17, 1885. 1921, t. U. Wisconsin. Comp. violin pcs.

Burleigh, Harry Thacker. Baritone, composer; b. Erie, Pa., Dec. 2, 1866. p. Dvořák, who never tired of listening to Burleigh's singing of traditional Negro melodies, and was doubtless greatly influenced by them. Soloist, St. George's Ch., N. Y. First Amer. Negro to win recognition as composer. Comp. many songs; arr. Negro spirituals, notably *Deep River.*

Burmeister (*Boor-my-ster*), **Richard.** Pianist, composer; b. Hamburg, Ger., Dec. 7, 1860. p. Liszt. Comp. concertos and piano pcs.

Burmester (*Boor-mes-ter*), **Willy.** Violinist; b. Hamburg, Ger., Mar. 16, 1869; d. ib., Jan. 16, 1933. Distinguished concert violinist. Arr. from the classics many small pcs. for violin.

Burney, Charles. Organist, historian; b. Shrewsbury, Eng., Apr. 12, 1726; d. London, Apr. 12, 1814. p. Arne. Org., Lynn Regis, Norfolk. Toured the continent in search of materials for his *History of Music,* the first volume of which appeared in 1776.

Burrian, Karl. Tenor; b. Prague, Boh., Jan. 12, 1870; d. ib., Sept. 26, 1829. Famous Wagnerian tenor. 1905, sang in première of *Salome;* 1907-12, Met. Op., N. Y.

Burrowes, Katharine. Music educator; b. Kingston, Ont. 1895-1903, fd., Burrowes Piano Sch., Detroit. Prolific author of musical text wks., incl., *Burrowes Course of Music Study for Beginners* (1895).

Burton, Frederick Russell. Composer; b. Jonesville, Mich., Feb. 23, 1861; d. Lake Hopatcong, N. J., Sept. 30, 1909. Comp. cantata, *Hiawatha*, on Indian themes. Author of book on American Primitive Music.

Busby, Thomas. Organist, writer; b. Westminster, Dec., 1755; d. London, May 28, 1838. Author of wks. on mus. subjects, incl., a *History of Music*, based upon the larger wks. of Burney and Hawkins.

Busch, Adolf. Violinist, composer; b. Westphalia, Aug. 8, 1891. Brother of Fritz B. (1918-20). t. Berlin Hochschule, succ. Marteau. Comp. large list of wks. in all forms.

Busch, Carl. Composer, violinist, conductor; b. Bjerre, Den., Mar. 29, 1862. 1887, to U. S. and settled in Kansas City. Comp. symph wks., violin mus., cantatas, and small pcs. Cond., Kansas City Symph.

Busch, Fritz. Conductor; b. Westphalia, Mar. 13, 1890. 1909, cond., Riga Opera; 1918, dir., Stuttgart, succ. Schillings; 1922, dir., Dresden Opera, succ. Reiner; 1927, g. cond., N. Y. Symph.; 1934, exiled by Nazis; cond., Colon Th., Buenos Aires.

Busi (*Boo-si*), **Alessandro.** Composer; b. Bologna, It., 1833; d. ib., 1895. Comp. masses with orch., cantatas, songs, violin wks.

Busoni, Ferrucio Benvenuto. Pianist, composer; b. Empolim, It., Apr. 1, 1866; d. Berlin, Jul. 27, 1924. As a master class teacher, a disciple of Liszt; concertized extensively; 1910-11, 1914-15, to U. S.; 1915-19, in Switz., in self-imposed neutrality; 1920, master class in comp., Berlin Acad. of Arts. A powerful personality, and the most significant keyboard interpreter since Rubinstein and Liszt. Comp. opera, *Die Brautwahl*; incidental mus. to *Turandot*, chamb. wks., and many piano pcs. Best known as Bach ed., and transcriber for piano.

Busser, Paul Henri. Organist, conductor; b. Toulouse, Jan. 16, 1872. 1893, Prix de Rome; cond., Paris Opera. Comp. operas; also ballet, *Le Ronde Les Saisons* (1905).

Bussler, Ludwig. Theorist, teacher; b. Berlin, Nov. 26, 1838; d. ib., Jan. 18, 1901. Author of text-books.

Buths (*Boots*), **Julius.** Pianist, conductor; b. Wiesbaden, May 7, 1851. 1908, Kappelmeister, Düsseldorf. Comp. orch., chamb. mus.

Butler, Harold Lancaster. Opera basso, music educator; b. Silver City, Idaho, Jun. 18, 1874. 1923, dean, Coll. of Fine Arts, Syracuse U. Appeared in over 500 recitals, and in the operas.

Butler, John Vernon. Organist, conductor; b. Birmingham, Eng., Aug. 24, 1868. Fd. and cond., free oratorio concerts, Worcester (Mass.) introducing many important wks.

Butt, Clara (Mrs. Kennerley Rumford). Contralto; b. Southwick, Eng., Feb. 1, 1873; d. London, Jan. 23, 1936. p. Gerster. The most popular ballad interpreter in England in her epoch.

Butterfield, James Austin. Composer; b. Hertfordshire, Eng., May 18, 1837; d. Chicago, Jul. 6, 1891. Comp. cantata, *Belshazzar*; songs.

Buxtehude (*Boox-te-hoo-deh*), **Dietrich.** Organist, composer; b. Helsingör, Den., 1637; d. Lübeck, Ger., May 9, 1707. Most famous org. of his day; Bach traveled on foot to hear him play.

Buzzi-Peccia (*Boo-tsee Pet'-chee-ah*), **Arturo.** Composer, teacher; b. Milan, It. St. Royal Cons., Milan. t. New York Cons. of Mus. Comp. opera and songs.

Byrd, William. Organist, composer; b. London, 1542; d. ib., Jul. 14, 1623. The "Father of Musicke." Celebrated for his ch. mus. and madrigals.

C

Caballero (*Kah-vahl-lyair-oh*), **Manuel Fernandez.** Composer; b. Murcia, Sp., Mar. 14, 1835; d. Madrid, Feb. 26, 1906. Awarded many honors; zarzuelas enjoyed popularity in Sp. and Latin-Amer. Some 200 musico-dramatic wks., besides ch. mus. and songs; last wks. dictated during years of total blindness.

Cabezon (*Cah-be-thon*), **Antonio de.** Organist, harpsichordist; b. Madrid, Sp., Mar. 30, 1510; d. ib., May 24, 1566. Blind; called the "Spanish Bach."

Caccini (*Cat-chee-nee*), **Giulio.** Composer; b. Rome, c. 1550; d. Florence, 1618. In Florence, w. Peri, was the originator of opera.

Cadek, Joseph Ottokar. Violinist, teacher; b. Prague, 1868; d. Chattanooga, Nov. 3, 1927. 1903, fd. Cadek Cons. of Mus., Chattanooga.

Cadman, Charles Wakefield. Composer, pianist; b. Johnstown, Pa., Dec. 24, 1881. 1918, opera, *Shanewis*, on an Indian subject and using Indian themes, prod. at Met. Op. (Mar. 23, 1918). Comp. song-cycles, choral wks., and short pcs. chiefly based on Indian melodies. Popularly known by songs, *At Dawning*, and *Land of the Sky Blue Water*. Career largely assoc. w. California, with many lecture-recital tours in U. S. and abroad.

Cady, Calvin Brainerd. Teacher; b. Barry, Ill., Jun. 21, 1851. 1872-4, Leipzig Cons.; 1874-9, t. Oberlin Coll. Mus.; 1880-88, t. U. of Mich.; 1908-13, Inst. Mus. Art; 1922, t. Portland, Ore. Author wks. on normal instruction for children.

Caffarelli (*Ca-fa-rel-lee*), **Gaetano Majorano.** Singer; b. Bari, It., Apr. 16, 1703; d. Santo Dorato, Feb. 1, 1783. Artificial soprano. Became wealthy and bought a dukedom.

Cagnoni (*Can-yo-ni*), **Antonio.** Composer, conductor; b. Godiasco, It., 1828; d. Bergamo, It., 1896. Comp. over twenty operas.

Cahen (*Kaa-en*), **Albert.** Composer; b. Jan. 8, 1846; d. Cap d'Ail, Fr., Mar., 1903. p. César Franck. Comp. operas and songs.

Cahier, Mme. Charles. Contralto; b. Nashville, Tenn. p. de Reszke. Debut, Nice, Fr; 1911-12, guest artist, Met. Op.

Caldicott, Alfred James. Composer; b. Worcester, Eng., Nov. 26, 1842; d. Gloucester, Oct. 24, 1897. Comp. cantatas, operettas and glees.

Calkin, J. Baptiste. Organist, composer; b. London, Mar. 16, 1827; d. ib., Mar. 15, 1905. Comp. anthems, organ pcs.

Callaerts, Joseph. Organist, composer; b. Antwerp, Aug. 22, 1838; d. ib., Mar. 3, 1901. Comp. opera, a prize symph., cantatas, organ pcs.

Callcott, John Wall. Organist, composer; b. Kensington, Eng., Nov. 20, 1766; d. Bristol, May 15, 1821. Comp. many celebrated glees.

Callcott, William Hutchins. Composer; b. Sept. 28, 1807; d. Aug. 5, 1882. Son of J. W. C. Comp. anthems and songs.

Calvé (*Cahl-veh*), **Emma.** Soprano; b. Madrid, 1864. 1882, debut, Brussels in *Faust;* interpretations always individual and dramatically consistent; her *Carmen* deemed unapproachable; created many rôles in Rome and Paris. Long at Met. Op., N. Y.

Calvocoressi, Michael D. Music critic; b. Marseilles, Oct. 2, 1877. p. Leroux, Paris Cons. Has translated into Eng., Fr., or Ger., numerous operas and other wks. Contributor to British papers. 1907-10, collab. w. Diaghilev. Author of biographical wks., incl. Liszt (1915), Moussorgsky (1917, Eng.), Glinka (1911), Schumann (1912).

Cambert (*Cam-bare*), **Robert.** Composer; b. Paris, 1628; d. London, 1677. First writer of Fr. opera.

Cameron, Basil. Conductor; b. Reading, Eng., Aug. 18, 1885. Cond. at Torquay, Harrogate, Hastings; Royal Phil., London; Czech National Orch., Prague; also in U. S., at San Francisco and Seattle.

Camp, John Spencer. Organist, composer; b. Middletown, Conn., Jan. 30, 1858. p. Dvořák. 1902-12, cond., Hartford Phil. Orch.; 1921, Mus.D., Trinity Coll.; assoc., Austin Organ Co. Comp. orch. wks., cantatas, organ pcs.

Campagnoli (*Kam-pa-nyo-lee*), **Bartolomeo.** Violinist, composer; b. Cento, It., Sept. 10, 1751; d. Neustrelitz, Nov. 6, 1827. p. Nardini. Author of a *Violin School,* and *Caprices* that are still used.

Campanari, Giuseppe. Baritone; b. Venice, It., Nov. 17, 1858. At first a 'cellist w. Boston Symph.; then baritone w. Met. Op. Brother of Leandro C.

Campanari, Leandro. Violinist, teacher, conductor; b. Rovigo, It., Oct. 20, 1857. 1883, t. N. E. Cons., Boston; 1890-97, t. Cin. Cons.; 1906, cond., Manhattan Op., N. Y.; 1907, t. San Francisco.

Campanini, Cleofonte. Conductor; b. Parma, Sept. 1, 1860; d. Chicago, Dec. 19, 1919. World-famed opera cond., La Scala, Nice, Argentina, Spain, London, United States. 1908, cond., Hammerstein's Manhattan Op., N. Y.; 1913, cond., Verdi Centenary at Parma; 1920, cond. and impresario, Chicago Opera. Instrumental in estab. McCormack-Campanini annual competition for Italian opera composers.

Campanini, Italo. Tenor; b. Parma, It., Jun. 29, 1846; d. Vigatto, It., Nov. 22, 1896. Distinguished in Italian opera.

Campbell-McInnes, James. British baritone; b. Holcombe, Jan. 23, 1874. p. Henschel. Rec. by Joachim, because of his Brahms interpretations; did war service; 1919, to Toronto. Has given hearing to many new British composers.

Campbell-Tipton, Louis. Composer; b. Chicago, Nov. 21, 1874; d. Paris, May 1, 1921. 1900-5, t. Chicago Mus. Coll.; lived in Paris from 1906. Comp. piano and violin pcs., and songs. Best known for his song, *Spirit Flower.* Career largely lived in Paris.

Campo y Zabaleta, Conrado del. Composer; b. Madrid, Oct. 28, 1879. The outstanding figure in modern Spanish mus., expressing sincere Romanticism in an advanced technic. Comp. many operas, orch. pcs., masses, songs.

Campra, André. Composer; b. Aix, Ger., Dec. 4, 1660; d. Versailles, Fr., Mar. 29, 1744. Early French opera comp.

Canal, Marguerite. French composer; 1920, Prix de Rome; t. Conservatoire. Comp. symph. pc., *Don Juan,* violin sonata, and 100 songs and instr. pcs.

Cantu, Agostinho. Pianist, teacher; b. It., 1879. t. Sao Paulo (Braz.) Cons. Comp. pf. pcs., songs.

Caplet, André. Composer, conductor; b. Le Havre, Nov. 27, 1879; d. Paris, Nov., 1925. 1897, Paris Cons. u. Leroux; 1901, Prix de Rome. Cond., Boston Op. Comp. chamb. mus., chorus pcs.

Capocci (*Ca-pot-tchee*), **Filippo.** Composer, organist; b. Rome, May 11, 1840; d. ib., 1898. Comp. oratorio, *St. Atanasio,* and organ pcs.

Capron, Henry. 'Cellist, composer; b. Fr., 1757. 1785, gave concerts in N. Y. and Phila.; 1788-92, New York; 1793, partner with J. C. Moller in Phila. mus. store.

Capuzzi (*Ca-poot-zi*), **Giuseppe Antonio.** Violinist; b. Brescia, It., 1753; d. Bergamo, It., 1818. Comp. operas, ballets, chamb. mus.

Caraccioli, Luigi. Composer, teacher; b. Andria, It., Aug. 11, 1847; d. London, Aug. 22, 1887. Comp. ballads of great popularity in his era.

Carafa (*Ka-rah-fa*), **Michele Enrico.** Composer; b. Naples, It., Nov. 17, 1787; d. Paris, Aug. 26, 1862. Comp. operas, pf. pcs.

Carey, Henry. Composer, singer; b. London, 1685 (1692); d. ib., Oct. 4, 1743. 1740, probably composed words and music of *God Save the King* (*America*) at Cornhill Tavern, for a dinner to celebrate Admiral Versons' capture of Porto Bello.

Carissimi, Giacomo. Composer; b. Marini, It., c. 1604; d. Rome, Jan. 12, 1674. One of the earliest of oratorio composers.

Carl, William Crane. American organist, teacher; b. Bloomfield, N. J., Mar. 2, 1865. p. Guilmant. Toured U. S. and Orient as concert org.; org., First Presby. Ch., N. Y.; fd. Guilmant Organ Sch., N. Y.

Caro, Paul. Composer; b. Breslau, Oct. 25, 1859. Comp. four symphs., operas, *Hero and Leander* and *Ulfosti's Wedding;* symph. poems, str. quartets.

Caron, Rose Lucile, née Meuniez. Soprano; b. Monerville, Fr., Nov. 17, 1857. Wagnerian rôles in French. 1902, t. Paris Cons.

Carpenter, John Alden. Composer; b. Park Ridge, Ill., Feb. 28, 1876. 1897, A.B., Harvard, u. Paine; 1922, M.A.; came first to public notice by his characteristic orchestral suite, *Adventures in a Perambulator,* perf. Mar. 19, 1915, by Chicago Symph. Ballet, *Birthday of the Infanta,* perf. Dec. 23, 1919, by Chicago Op. *Krazy Kat,* a jazz-pantomime, perf. Dec. 22, 1921, by Chicago Symph. Comp. orchestral wks. in modern style, also chamb. mus., and songs.

Carr, Benjamin. Composer, conductor, organist, music publisher; b. London, 1769; d. Phila., 1831. Well edu. in Eng. 1793, opened Carr's Musical Repository, Philadelphia's first mus. store. Published much of the contemporary wks. of his day. Apr. 24, 1821, cond. first concert of Musical Fund Soc., and probably first Amer. perf. of Beethoven's First Symph. His setting of Schiller's *William Tell* as a ballad opera, prod., Apr. 18, 1796, in New York, antedates by 33 years Rossini's setting. NYPL and Arthur Billings Hunt library of Americana contain many of Carr's wks. St. Peter's Ch., Phila., holds a monument to his memory.

Carr, Frank Osmond. Composer; *b.* Yorkshire, Eng., Apr. 23, 1858; *d.* N. Y., Aug. 29, 1916. 1886, M. A. Cantab.; 1901, Mus.D., ib. Comp. operettas, incl., *In Town* (1892).

Carreño, Teresa. Pianist; *b.* Caraccas, Venezuela, Dec. 22, 1853; *d.* New York, Jun. 12, 1917. *p.* Rubinstein. Distinguished virtuoso who enjoyed worldwide recognition. *t.* McDowell, and exerted important influence on his career.

Carrillo, Julian. Conductor, composer, violinist; *b.* San Luis Potosi, Mexico, 1875. *p.* Jadassohn. 1902, debut, Leipzig; 1915, cond., Amer. Symph. Orch.; 1906-15, dir., National Cons. of Mus., Mexico. Comp. four symphs., three operas, chamb. mus. Author of theoretical treatises.

Carrodus, John Tiplady. Violinist, teacher; *b.* Brathwaite, Eng., Jan. 20, 1836; *d.* London, Jul. 13, 1895.

Carse, Adam (von Ahn). English composer; *b.* Newcastle, May 19, 1878. 1922, prof., R. A. M., London. Comp. orch., chamb. mus., songs. Author technical treatises.

Carter, Ernest. Composer; *b.* Orange, N. J., Sept. 3, 1866. 1888, A.B., Princeton; 1889, M.A.; 1934 (as of 1890) LL.B., Columbia; 1891-2, practised law N. Y.; 1892-4, *t.* Thacher School, Cal.; 1894-98, st. Berlin; 1899-1901, org., Princeton; 1932, Mus.D., Princeton. 1931, *Blonde Donna,* prod. N. Y. Opera Comique. Comp. opera, songs, anthems.

Carter, Russell. Music educator; *b.* Brooklyn, N. Y., Sept. 17, 1881. 1910, gr., Inst. Mus. Art, N. Y.; 1931, Mus.D., Chicago Cons. of Mus.; 1910-19, supervisor pub. sch. mus., Amsterdam, N. Y.; since 1923, N. Y. State supervisor, pub. sch. mus.

Carter, Stanley (Frederick J. Redcliffe). Wrote, to lyric by Harry Braisted (Berdan), *He Was Bred in Old Kentucky,* which was sung to a world success by Lottie Gilson.

Cartier (*Car-tee-yea*), **Jean Baptiste.** French violinist, dramatist and composer; *b.* 1765; *d.* 1841. *p.* Viotti.

Caruso, Enrico. Tenor; *b.* Naples, Feb. 25, 1873; *d.* ib., Aug. 2, 1921. Sang in first perf. of *Fedora* (Giordani), and *Germania* (Franchetti); drew caricatures as a hobby. At Met. Op., N. Y., commanded highest fees ever paid to a singer. The greatest tenor of his epoch.

Carvalho, Caroline Miolan. Soprano; *b.* Marseilles, Fr., Dec. 31, 1827; *d.* Puys, Fr., Jul. 10, 1895. Celebrated prima donna of the Paris Grand Opéra.

Cary, Annie Louise. Contralto; *b.* Wayne, Me., Oct. 22, 1842; *d.* Norwalk, Conn., Apr. 3, 1921. Opera debut in San Francisco, Sept. 19, 1877. Sang oratorio, concert.

Caryll, Ivan (pseud. of Felix Tilken). Operetta composer; *b.* Liège, 1861; *d.* N. Y., Nov. 28, 1921. His *Pink Lady* (1911) had a popular success in U. S.

Casadesus, Francis. Composer; *b.* Paris, 1870. 1918-22, dir., Fontainebleau School of Amer. Acad. Comp. symph. and operas.

Casals, Pablo. 'Cellist, composer; *b.* Veudrell, Sp., Dec. 30, 1876. Cond., Barcelona Orch.; has toured U. S. Distinguished virtuoso. An epoch-making figure; fd. a new school of 'cello playing. Restored Bach 'cello sonatas to the concert repertoire.

Case, Anna. Soprano; *b.* Clinton, N. Y., Oct. 29, 1889. 1909-16, Met. Op. *m.* Clarence Mackey and retired. Comp. songs.

Casella, Alfredo. Pianist, composer, conductor; *b.* Turin, It., Jul. 25, 1883. 1915-23, *t.* St. Cecilia Cons., Rome; *g.* cond. *w.* all important orchestras, incl. U. S. Mus. critic to French, Italian and American periodicals. Comp. long list of wks. in all forms.

Castelnuovo-Tedesco, Mario. Pianist, composer; *b.* Florence, It., Apr. 3, 1895. An infant prodigy; edu., Cherubino Royal Inst. Mus. *u.* Ildebrando Pizzetti. *h.* Florence. Career chiefly in Paris. Comp. orch. wks., incl. *Rioretti* and *Overture to Taming of the Shrew;* operas, incl. *Machiavelli;* instrumental pcs., and songs.

Castro, Juan Jose. Composer, conductor; *b.* Buenos Aires, Mar. 7, 1895. *p.* d'Indy. 1929, fd. Renacimiento Orch., B.A. 1931, *Allegro, Lento, and Vivace,* prod. by Internat'l. Soc. for Contemp. Mus. Fest., London. Comp. orch. wks., incl. *Dans le Jardin des Morts;* pcs. for piano, violin and violoncello.

Castrucci (*Cas-troot-chee*), **Pietro.** Violinist; *b.* Rome, 1689; *d.* Dublin, Feb. 29, 1752. *p.* Corelli. Leader of Handel's opera orch. in London.

Catalani, Alfredo. Composer; *b.* Lucca, Jun. 19, 1854; *d.* Milan, Aug. 7, 1893. *t.* Milan Cons. Comp. symph. and choir mus., operas, incl. *La Wally,* perf. at Met. Op.

Catalani, Angelica. Soprano; *b.* Sinigaglia, It., May 10, 1780; *d.* Paris, Jun. 12, 1849. One of the most brilliant sopranos known to history.

Catel, Charles Simon. Composer, teacher; *b.* L'Aigle, Fr., Jun. 10, 1773; *d.* Paris, Nov. 29, 1830. *t.* Paris Cons. Comp. operas.

Cavalieri, Emilio del. Composer; *b.* Rome *c.* 1550; *d.* Florence, It., Mar. 11, 1602. Comp. the first oratorio.

Cavalieri, Lina. Soprano; *b.* Rome, Dec. 25, 1878. A celebrated beauty; 1906, Met. Op. H.; 1908, Manhattan Op. H.; 1915, Chicago Opera Co.; 1913, *m.* Lucien Muratore, tenor.

Cavalli, Francesco (really Caletti-Bruni). Composer; *b.* Cremona, 1599; *d.* Venice, Jan. 14, 1676. *p.* Monteverde. Comp. operas, incl. *Giasone, Serse,* and *Ercole Amante.*

Cavos, Catterino. Composer; *b.* Venice, 1776; *d.* Petrograd, 1840. Comp. operas, in Russian, incl. *Ivan Sonsanin,* a subject later used by Glinka.

Cellier, Alfred. Composer, conductor; *b.* London, Dec. 1, 1844; *d.* ib., Dec. 28, 1891. Wr. successful light operas, incl. *The Mountebanks.*

Cesti, Marco Antonio. Composer; *b.* Florence, 1620; *d.* Venice, 1669. Early opera composer.

Chabrier (*Shab-ree-ay*), **Alexis Emmanuel.** Composer; *b.* Ambert, Fr., Jan. 18, 1841; *d.* Paris, Sept. 13, 1894. Asst. cond., Lamoreux. One of the most significant of Fr. composers, whose life was beset by perpetual ill luck. *Rhapsodie España,* and other orch. wks. perf. at Lamoreux concerts. Perf. of opera *Gwendoline* at Brussels cut short by bankruptcy of impresario; comic opera, *Roi malgré lui,* by burning of the theatre; Paris perf. of *Gwendoline* (1893) brought recognition too late. Broken in health and spirit by a life of delays, he died the following year.

Chadwick, George Whitfield. Composer; *b.* Lowell, Mass., Nov. 13, 1854; *d.* Boston, Apr. 4, 1931. *p.* Rhemberger. Dir., New England Cons. of Mus. At the outset he found a ready hearing for his wks.: comic opera, *Tabasco,* and *Viking's Last Voyage;* lyric drama, *Judith;* symph. and chamb. mus., choral ballads, songs, and anthems. Leader of the New England group throughout his generation; a loyal conservative of the Old Guard.

Chaliapin, Feodor Ivanovitch. Russian operatic bass singer; b. Kazan, Feb. 13, (o. s.) 1873. After severe struggle, rose from obscurity and became one of the most dramatic of operatic interpreters; 1901, first season outside Russia, sang *Mefistofele* (Boito) 10 times at La Scala; 1912, Met. Op., N. Y.; 1913, London. Domiciled in U. S. after Revolution.

Chambonnières (*Sham-bon-ee-air*), **Jacques.** Claveçinist, composer; b. c. 1600; d. 1670. Comp. pcs. for the clavichord.

Chaminade, Cécile. Pianist, composer; b. Paris, Aug. 8, 1861. Comp. ballet-symphony, *Calirrhoë;* lyric symphony, *Les Amazones;* suites, concerto. Best known by her graceful songs and piano pcs., incl. *Scarf Dance* and *The Flatterer.*

Chamlee, Mario. Operatic tenor; b. Los Angeles, May 29, 1892. 1924, M.Mus., U. of S. Cal.; 1920, debut, Met. Op. w. Scotti and Farrar in *Tosca.*

Chapi, Ruperto. Composer; b. Villena, Sp., Mar. 23, 1851; d. Mar. 25, 1909. Edu. Madrid Cons. 1882, first success w. zarzuela, *La Tempestuo.* 1892, organized Soc. of Authors for collection of performance fees. His prolific output of 168 wks. for the stage, besides symph. and chamb. mus., have occasioned endless strife as to his place in Spanish musical history. Many place his name along side of Albeniz, while others consider him a blot on the pages of time. At least his wks. manifest a strong individuality. His death occasioned a popular demonstration, and his memory is perpetuated by a statue in the Jardines del Retiro.

Chapman, William Rogers. Organist, conductor; b. Hanover, Mass., Aug. 4, 1855; d. ——. Cond., Maine Fest. Chorus; Rubinstein Club, N. Y.

Chappell, William. Historian; b. London, Nov. 20, 1809; d. ib., Aug. 20, 1888. Author of a *History of Music,* from the earliest records to the fall of the Roman Empire; also *History of the Popular Music of the Olden Times.*

Charpentier (*Shar-pon-tyay*), **Gustave.** Composer; b. Dieuze, Lorraine, Jun. 24, 1860. Edu., Paris Cons., u. Massenet; 1887, won Prix de Rome. Opera *Louise* prod., 1900, by Opéra Comique, a protest against the life of the working-girl, brought to N. Y., 1907, by Mary Garden at Oscar Hammerstein's Manhattan Op. H. Comp. suite, *Impressions d'Italie;* cantata, *La Vie de Poète,* and smaller wks.

Chasins, Abram. Virtuoso pianist, composer; b. New York, Aug. 17, 1903. St. Curtis Inst., Phila. 1931, *Parade* and *Flirtation in a Chinese Garden,* perf. by Toscanini and N. Y. Phil. 1931-32, European concert tour. 1933, N. Y. recital debut. Comp. orch. wks.; piano pcs., incl. *Twenty-four Preludes;* songs, incl. *Offering to Eros.*

Chausson (*Show-song*), **Ernest.** French composer, conductor; b. Paris, Jan. 21, 1855; d. Limay, Jun. 16, 1899. 1880, p. C. Franck. Comp. operas, symph., and chamb. mus., and songs. *Poème,* for violin and orch., is much perf.

Chavez, Carlos. Composer, conductor; b. Mexico City, 1899. Cond., Mexico City Symph. Orch.

Cheatham, Catharine Smiley. Diseuse; b. Nashville. World-wide reputation as authority on and interpreter of songs of childhood. Concertized leading cities U. S. and Europe.

Cherubini, Maria Luigi. Composer; b. Florence, Sept. 14, 1760; d. Paris, Mar. 15, 1842. p. Giuseppe Sarti. 1873, comp. a successful mass; 1780, his first opera, *Quinto Fabio,* prod.; 1788, to Paris; 1821-41, dir., Paris Cons. Comp. operas, incl. *Ifigenia in Aulide, Lodoïska, Médée, Les deux journées,* and *Anacreon;* also four masses, a requiem, str. quartets, many lesser compositions, and a masterly work on counterpoint.

Chevé (*Sheh-vay*), **Emile J. M.** Teacher; b. Douarnenez, Fr., 1804; d. Paris, Aug. 26, 1864. Inventor of simplified system of solfége.

Chevillard (*Shev-ee-yar*), **Camille.** French conductor, composer; b. Paris, Oct. 14, 1859; d. ib., May 30, 1923. 1887, assisted at first Paris perf. of *Lohengrin;* 1897, succ. Lamoreux as cond. of L. concerts; 1907, prof., Cons. Comp. ballade, symph., and chamb. wks.

Chickering, Jonas. Veteran American piano-maker; 1798-1853.

Chipp, Edmund Thomas. Organist, composer; b. London, Dec. 25, 1823; d. Nice, Dec. 17, 1886. Comp. oratorios, organ pcs.

Chittenden, Kate Sara. Pianist, teacher; b. Hamilton, Ont., Apr. 17, 1856. Dir., Amer. Inst. of Applied Mus., N. Y.; pf. faculty of Vassar Coll. Author, *Synthetic Method;* assoc. ed., *University Course of Music Study.* Career largely in N. Y.

Chladni (*Khlat-nee*), **Ernst Florens Friedrich.** Physicist; b. Wittenberg, Nov. 30, 1756; d. Breslau, Apr. 3, 1827. Profound researcher in acoustics.

Chopin, Frédéric François. Pianist, composer; b. Zelazowa Wola, Pol., Feb. 22, 1810; d. Paris, Oct. 17, 1849. Of French and Polish parentage. 1829, first public appearance in Vienna. King of pf. composers.

Chorley, Henry F. Writer; b. Blockley Hurst, Eng., Dec. 15, 1808; d. London, Feb. 16, 1872. Eminent mus. critic.

Christian, Palmer. Organist; b. Kankakee, Ill., May 3, 1885. p. Guilmant. 1924, dir., organ dept., U. of Mich.

Christiansen, F. Melius. Conductor, composer; b. Eidvold, Nor., Apr. 1, 1871. St. Leipzig Cons. 1903, dir. mus., St. Olaf Coll., Northfield, Minn.; fd. St. Olaf Choir. Comp. cantata, religious choral wks. Author, *Practical Modulation.*

Christie, Winifred. English pianist; Played in public at age of six. Edu., R. A. M. 1915-19, soloist, w. Boston Symph. tour; 1921, began using Moor Double-Keyboard Piano, which (as widow of Moor) she continues to exploit.

Christy, E. P. Early American minstrel singer. 1884, Albany, N. Y.; 1850, took British Isles by storm. Of interest only from fact that many of Stephen Foster's early songs were first published under Christy's name, at Foster's suggestion, thus becoming a historic "song-plugger."

Chrysander, Friedrich. German musicologist; b. Lübtheen, Jul. 8, 1826; d. Bergedorf, Apr. 13, 1901. Distinguished writer on mus. subjects. 1859-94, edited complete edition of Handel's wks. Author of Handel biography and many monographs containing the fruits of his painstaking researches.

Chubb, John Frederick. English organist; b. Hastings, 1885. Edu., Cambridge; 1910, org., Harrogate; 1912, org., Christ Ch., Vancouver, B. C.; important educational force in Canadian Northwest.

Chueca, Federico. Spanish composer; b. Madrid, May 5, 1848; d. Jun. 20, 1908. Usually collaborated w. Valverde. Of the *Pick-pockets' Song* from his *La Gran Via,* Nietzsche said, "the people that produced this music is beyond salvation." This zarzuela took Sp. by storm and afforded Spanish organ-grinder mus. for a generation.

Chwatal (*Shvah-tal*), **Franz X.** Composer; b. Rumburg, Boh., Jun. 19, 1808; d. Soolbad, Jun. 4, 1874.

Cilea (*Chil-a-ah*), **Francesco.** Italian composer; *b.* Palmi, Jul. 23, 1866. 1902, opera, *Adriana Lecouvrier,* perf. in Milan, and repeated around the world. Caruso's first Milan appearance was in Cilea's *Arlesiana.* Dir., Cons., Naples. Comp. chamb. mus., and songs.

Cimara, Pietro. Conductor; *b.* Rome, Nov. 10, 1887. *p.* Respighi. 1916, cond., Teatro Costanzi, Rome; 1935, Met. Op.

Cimarosa (*Chee-ma-ro-sa*), **Domenico.** Opera composer; *b.* Aversa, It., Dec. 17, 1749; *d.* Venice, Jan. 11, 1801. *p.* Piccinni. After three years at the court of Catharine II of Russia, he went to Vienna as court conductor. Of many operas, *Il Matrimonio Segreto* was his greatest.

Citkowitz, Israel. Composer; *b.* ——. *t.* Dalcroze Sch. of Mus. Comp. chiefly quartets; song cycles, to verses by Blake and Joyce; and choral mus.

Claassen, Arthur. Conductor, composer; *b.* Stargard, Ger., Feb. 19, 1859; *d.* S. F., Mar. 16, 1920. 1884, cond., Brooklyn Arion Soc.; 1910, cond., San Antonio Symph. Soc. Comp. choral and chamb. mus.

Claessens, Maria. Mezzo-soprano; *b.* Brussels, May 20, 1881. 1903, debut, Barcelona; since 1916, identified *w.* Chicago Opera.

Clapisson (*Clah-pee-song*), **Antoine Louis.** Violinist, composer; *b.* Naples, Sept. 15, 1808; *d.* Paris, Mar. 19, 1866.

Clapp, Philip Greeley. Composer; *b.* Boston, Aug. 4, 1888. 1908, A.B., Harvard; 1909, A.M.; 1911, Ph.D.; 1909, Symph. p., *Norge,* perf. Boston Symph.; other symphonies perf., 1914 and 1917, composer conducting. Comp. 12 major symph. wks., str. q., and misc. pcs.

Claribel (pseud. of **Charlotte Alington Barnard**), (q. v.).

Clark, Frederick Scotson. Organist, composer; *b.* London, Nov. 16, 1840; *d.* ib., Jul. 5, 1883. Comp. many organ pcs., chiefly Marches.

Clarke, Hugh A. Composer, theorist; *b.* Toronto, Can., Aug. 15, 1839. Prof., U. of Penn.

Clarke, Rebecca. English composer; *b.* Harrow, Aug. 27, 1886. *p.* Stanford. Plays viola in str. q.; 1916, to U. S.; won second prize in Coolidge competitions, 1919 and 1921; 1923, comp. 'cello work for Pittsfield Fest.

Clarke, Robert Coningsby. English song-writer; *b.* Old Charlton, Eng., Mar. 17, 1879. *p.* Bridge, at Westminster Abbey. Edu., Marlborough Coll.; 1902, org., Trinity Coll., Oxford; 1902, B.A.

Clarke, William Horatio. Organist, composer; *b.* Newton, Mass., Mar. 8, 1840; *d.* Reading, Mass., Dec. 11, 1913.

Claussen, Julia. Operatic prima donna; *b.* Stockholm, 1883. 1903, Royal Opera, Stockholm; 1912-17, Chicago Opera; 1917-27, Met. Op., N. Y.

Clay, Frederick. Composer; *b.* Paris, Aug. 3, 1840; *d.* Great Marlow, Eng., Nov. 24, 1889. Comp. light operas, incl., *Princess Toto;* also songs, incl., *I'll Sing Thee Songs of Araby.*

Clemens, Charles Edwin. Organist; *b.* Plymouth, Eng., Mar. 12, 1858. Edu. R. C. M. 1889, *t.* Klindworth Cons., Berlin; 1896, org., St. Paul's, Cleveland; 1899, prof., Western Reserve U., Cleveland; 1916, Mus.D. Author of technical wks.

Clément (*Clay-mahng*), **Edmond.** Tenor; *b.* Paris, Mar. 28, 1867; *d.* Nice, Feb. 22, 1928. Sang much in U. S. Operatic and concert interpreter of distinction.

Clement, Franz. Virtuoso violinist; *b.* Vienna, Nov. 17, 1780; *d.* ib., Nov. 3, 1842. Began as a child prodigy, but later became a matured artist; for him Beethoven wrote his violin concerto, first perf., Dec. 23, 1806.

Clementi, Muzio. Pianist, composer; *b.* Rome, 1752; *d.* Evesham, Eng., Mar. 10, 1832. 1761, accepted position as org.; 1766, visited London, where his pf. playing excited general admiration. 1817, wr. his celebrated studies for piano, *Gradus ad Parnassum.* His compositions display lucidity of construction, but few traces of originality. Survive only for educational value.

Cleve, Halfdan. Norwegian composer; *b.* Kongsberg, Oct. 5, 1879. 1898, to Berlin; 1907, played Grieg concerto *w.* Berlin Phil., the composer conducting; 1909, retired to Christiania. Comp. 5 pf. concertos, misc. pcs., songs.

Cliffe, Frederic. English pianist; *b.* Bradford, May 2, 1857; *d.* London, Dec., 1931. 1883, prof., R. C. M. Comp. for orch.

Clifton, Chalmers. American conductor; *b.* Jackson, Miss., Apr. 30, 1889. 1912, A.B., Harvard; 1912-14, *p.* d'Indy, on Sheldon fellowship; cond., Nat'l. Orch. Ass'n.; succ. by Barzin.

Clippinger, D. A. Conductor, voice teacher; *b.* Ohio, Sept. 2, 1860. Cond., Chicago Madrigal Club. Author of treatises on singing.

Clokey, Joseph Waddell. Composer, organist; *b.* New Albany, Ind., Aug. 28, 1890. 1915, gr., Cin. Cons. of Mus. *t.* Oxford, O., to 1926; *t.* Claremont, Cal., since 1926. Comp. 5 operas, 8 cantatas, orch. and organ suites, pf. pcs., anthems and songs.

Clough-Leighter, Henry. Organist, composer; *b.* Washington, D. C., May 13, 1874. 1892-1900, org., Washington, D. C.; 1901-1908, ed. *w.* Ditson; 1908-1921, *w.* Boston Mus. Co.; 1921, ed. of E. C. Schirmer Mus. Co., Boston. Comp. orch., songs, choral wks., symph. ode, *Christ of the Andes;* cantatas.

Clutsam, George H. Australian composer; *b.* Sydney, Sept. 26, 1866. Toured Orient, and settled in London; 1908-18, mus. critic, London *Observer;* 1910, opera, *A Summer Night,* prod. Beecham; 1923, operetta, *Lilac Time,* based on Schubert themes, prod. Lyric Th. Comp. also orch. and pf. pcs., songs.

Coates, Albert. Conductor; *b.* Petrograd, Apr. 23, 1882. 1911, cond., Petrograd Opera; 1914, London Phil.; 1921, g. cond., New York Symph.; 1923, Rochester Symph. Orch.; 1924, *t.* Eastman Sch., Rochester.

Coates, Eric. English composer, violist; *b.* Hucknall, Aug. 27, 1886. 1906, R. A. M. 1907, toured S. Africa *w.* Hambourg String Quartet. 1918, retired to compose many orch. suites; songs, incl. *Mill o' Dreams.*

Coates, John. English tenor; *b.* Bradford, Jun. 29, 1865. 1894, Savoy; 1895-1900, in comic opera in U. S.; 1900, created *Claudio* in Sanford's *Much Ado;* 1901-1916, sang opera in Berlin, Paris, London; 1906, Cin. May Fest.; after war service resumed career as recitalist.

Cobb, Gerhard Francis. Composer; *b.* Netlestead, Eng., Oct. 15, 1838; *d.* Cambridge, Eng., Mar. 31, 1904.

Coenen, Franz. Violinist; *b.* Rotterdam, Dec. 26, 1826; *d.* 1904. *p.* Vieuxtemps.

Coenen (*Kay-nen*), **Johannes Meinardus.** Conductor, composer; *b.* Hague, Jun. 28, 1824; *d.* Amsterdam, Jan. 9, 1899. Comp. symph., operas, chamb. mus.

Coerne (*Kern*), **Louis Adolphe.** Composer; *b.* Newark, N. J., Feb. 27, 1870; *d.* Norwich, Conn., Sept. 11, 1922. 1905, Ph.D., Harvard, first time conferred in Amer. for mus. thesis; 1906, opera, *Zenobia,* prod. Bremen, first German production of an Amer. work; 1915, prof., Conn. Coll., New London. Industrious composer of the old school, with output of over 200 wks. in all forms.

Cole, Rossetter Gleason. Composer, teacher; *b.* Clyde, Mich., Feb. 5, 1866; *d.* Chicago, 1935. *p.* Bruch. 1888, A.B., U. of Mich.; 1913, A.M.; 1890-2, scholarship *w.* Max Bruch. David Bispham's recitations of his setting of *King Robert of Sicily* made it his best known work.

Coleridge-Taylor, Samuel. English composer; *b.* London, Aug. 15, 1875; *d.* Croydon, Sept. 1, 1912. Negroid apostle of color; 1890-7, R. C. M. *u.* Stanford; 1897, first wks. perf. by Joachim in Berlin; 1898, won recognition *w. Hiawatha* mus. to Longfellow's text; 1904, visited U. S., and had many performances of his wks. Opus numbers reach 82, embracing all forms. His short chorus, *The Viking's Song,* is much used.

Colles, Henry Cope. English music critic; *b.* 1879. Edu., R. C. M., London; 1905, mus. critic, *The Academy;* 1911, mus. critic, London *Times;* 1919, *t.* R. C. M.; dir., Cheltenham Ladies' Coll.; 1923, ed., Grove's Dict.; 1923, g.-critic, New York *Times*.

Collinge, Channon. Conductor; *b.* Yorkshire, Jul. 4, 1878; *d.* N. Y. hospital, Jan. 15, 1936. Cond., Cathedral House on C. B. S. Father of Patricia C., actress.

Collins, Edward. Pianist, composer; *b.* Joliet, Ill. *p.* Ganz. 1912-13, toured U. S., *w.* Schumann-Heink; 1914, asst. cond., Wagner Fest., Bayreuth; *t.* Chicago Mus. Coll.

Colonne, Jules Jude (called Edouard Judas). French conductor; *b.* Bordeaux, Jul. 24, 1838; *d.* Mar. 28, 1910. Edu., Paris Cons. 1873, fd. Colonne concerts. Cond. Berlioz, *Damnation of Faust* over 200 times. At death, succ. by Gabriel Pierne.

Combs, Gilbert Raynolds. Music educator; *b.* Phila., Jan. 5, 1863; *d.* ib., Jun. 14, 1934. Edu., Eastburn Acad., Phila.; 1931, Mus.D., Capitol Coll., Columbus, O.; 1885, fd. Combs Cons. of Mus., Phila.

Conant, John Willis. Organist, pianist, teacher; *b.* Nashua, N. H., Dec. 20, 1866. *p.* Lavallee. 1884-90, Boston; 1890-92, *t.* Meadville (Pa.) Cons.; since 1913, dir. of mus., Nat'l. Cath. Sch., Wash., D. C.

Concone (*Kon-ko-ne*), **Giuseppe (Joseph).** Composer, teacher; *b.* Turin, It., 1810; *d.* ib., Jun. 1, 1861. Comp. operas and pf. pcs., but is best recalled by his *Vocalises,* universally used by singers.

Congdon, Charles Harris. Song leader, author; *b.* Nelson, Pa., Dec. 18, 1856; *d.* Mar. 23, 1928. Originated *w.* Robert Foresman, a system of teaching mus. to children in pub. schs., discarding the "scale-method" and substituting pure song material; official song-leader Progressive Party. Author of *Congdon Music Readers* (1908-23).

Coninck, Jacques-Felix de. Pianist, composer; *b.* Antwerp, May 18, 1791; *d.* ib., Apr. 25, 1866. Comp. pf. pcs.

Connell, Horatio. Baritone, teacher; *b.* Phila., Mar. 15, 1876. *p.* Stockhausen, Ger. 1916, *t.* Chautauqua; *t.* Curtis Inst., Phil.; 1935, *t.* Juilliard Grad. Sch., N. Y.

Conradi (*Con-rah-dce*), **August.** Organist, composer; *b.* Berlin, Jun. 27, 1821; *d.* ib., May 26, 1873. Assoc. of Liszt. Comp. operas and symph. wks.

Consolo, Ernesto. Pianist; *b.* London, Sept. 15, 1864; *d.* Florence, Mar. 21, 1931. Edu., Liceo Mus. di Santa Cecilia, Rome, *u.* Sgambati. Concertized in Europe and U. S.; prof., Cherubini R. Inst. of Mus., Florence.

Converse, Charles Crozat. Composer; *b.* Warren, Mass., Oct. 7, 1832; *d.* Highwood, N. J., Oct. 18, 1918. 1895, LL.D., Rutherford Coll.; partner in Burdette Organ Co. Comp. symph. wks., incl. *American Overture;* also some famous hymns, incl. *What a Friend We Have in Jesus.*

Converse, Frederick Shepard. Composer; *b.* Newton, Mass., Jan. 5, 1871. 1893, A.B., Harvard; 1901-7, *t.* ib.; 1924, *t.* N. E. Cons.; 1910, his opera, *Pipe of Desire,* was the first Amer. work prod. at the Met. Op. Comp. symph. wks., incl. *Festival of Pan,* and *La Belle Dame;* oratorio, *Job;* violin concerto, chamb. mus.

Cooke, Benjamin. Organist, composer; *b.* London, 1734; *d.* ib., Sept. 14, 1793. A celebrated glee writer.

Cooke, Henry. Singer, composer; *b.* Westminster, *c.* 1604; *d.* ib., Jul. 13, 1672. "Master of the Children" in the Chapel Royal during reign of Charles II. 1642, commissioned captain in the Royalist forces.

Cooke, James Francis. Editor; *b.* Bay City, Mich., Nov. 14, 1875. 1930, Mus.D., U. of Penna.; 1918, Pres., Presser Foundation.

Coombs, Charles Whitney. Organist, composer; *b.* Bucksport, Me., Dec. 25, 1859. 1887-91, org., Amer. Ch., Dresden; 1908, org., St. Luke's Ch., N. Y. Comp. cantata, *Vision of St. John;* ch. mus., songs.

Cooper, Emil. Conductor; *b.* Odessa, Dec. 20, 1879. 1900, cond., Kiev; 1906, Moscow Imperial Opera. During revolution fd. Leningrad Phil.

Coote, Charles. Composer; *b.* London, 1809; *d.* ib., 1880. Comp. of an immense amount of popular dance mus. ("Coote and Tinney").

Copland, Aaron. Pianist, composer, writer; *b.* Brooklyn, N. Y., Nov. 14, 1900. St. Rubin Goldmark, Nadia Boulanger. 1925, *Music for the Theatre* intro. by Koussevitzky *w.* Boston Symph. Lecturer, New Sch. for Soc. Research. Comp. symph. for organ and orch.; dance symph.; symph. ode; concerto for piano and orch.; wks for str. q., and piano.

Copp, Evelyn Ashton (née Fletcher). Teacher; *b.* Woodstock, Ont., 1872. Exponent of new methods in kindergarten and primary mus. instruction. 1897, *t.* N. E. Cons.; then fd. own studios.

Coquard (*Co-car*), **Arthur.** French composer; *b.* Paris, May 26, 1846; *d.* ib., Aug. 20, 1910. *p.* C. Franck. Comp. operas from *l'Epée du Roi* (1884) to *La Troupe Jolicoeur* (1902); mus. critic, *Echo de Paris.* Author of biog. of César Franck.

Corder, Frederick. English composer; *b.* London, Jan. 26, 1852; *d.* ib., Aug. 21, 1932. *p.* Macfarren. 1888, curator, R. A. M., strongly influencing many British composers. 1887, opera, *Nordisa* perf. Liverpool. Comp. operas, orch. and pf. pcs. Author technical wks., and biography of Liszt. Son, Paul W., prof. comp., R. A. M., since 1907.

Corelli (*Ko-rel-lee*), **Arcangelo.** Violinist, composer; *b.* Fusignano, It., Feb. 12, 1653; *d.* Rome, Jan. 10, 1713. Father of modern violin playing. 1672, visited Paris; 1680-1685, traveled in Germany, where he gained the favor of the Elector of Bavaria. Comp. chamb. mus., and many wks. for violin.

Cornelius, Peter. German poet and composer; *b.* Mainz, Dec. 24, 1824; *d.* ib., Oct. 26, 1874. Only appreciated after his death, on the publication of his literary wks. His opera, *Barber of Bagdad* is said to have suggested to Wagner certain ideas utilized in *Die Meistersinger*.

Cornell, John Henry. Organist theorist; *b.* N. Y., May 8, 1828; *d.* ib., Mar. 1, 1894. Author of numerous technical treatises.

Corona, Leonora. Soprano; *b.* Dallas, Tex., Oct. 14, 1903. *p.* Lilli Lehmann. 1923, debut in *Mefistofele,* at Castellaniare, It.; 1927, Met. Op., N. Y.

Coronaro, Gaetano. Italian composer; *b.* Vicenza, Dec. 18, 1852; *d.* Milan, Apr. 5, 1908. Comp. operas, incl. *Enoch Arden;* also instr. mus. His brothers, **Antonio,** and **Gellio Benvenuto,** were also composers.

Corri, Domenico. Composer, conductor; *b.* Rome, Oct. 4, 1746; *d.* Hampstead, Eng., May 22, 1825. Established mus. publishing house in London, *w.* his son-in-law, Dussek. Comp. operas, songs.

Cortot, Alfred. French pianist; *b.* Niyon, Switz., Sept. 26, 1877. Edu., Paris Cons. Cond., Bayreuth; dir. of orch. Ecole Normal, Paris; 1902, cond., Th. du Château d'Eau, giving first performances in Paris of *Parsifal, Tristan, Gotterdammerung, St. Elizabeth* (Liszt), *Requiem* (Brahms); estab. world famous trio, *w.* Jacques Thibaud and Pablo Casals; 1907, prof. pf. Cons. succ. Pugno; 1918, first tour of U. S. Author of articles on Debussy and Faure in *Revue Musicale*.

Costa, Sir Michael Andrew Agnus. Conductor, composer; *b.* Naples, Feb. 4, 1808; *d.* Hove, Eng., Apr. 29, 1884. Of his compositions, the oratorio *Eli* has most nearly survived.

Costa, Pasquale Mario. Italian composer; *b.* Naples, Jul. 24, 1858; *d.* Monte Carlo, Sept. 27, 1933. Edu., Naples Cons.; 1881, to London, in recitals of his own wks. Comp. numerous songs to It. and Neapolitan texts; stage wks., incl. *L'Histoire d'un Pierrot;* operettas.

Costa-Carrera, Francisco. Spanish violinist; *b.* Barcelona, Feb., 1891. Edu., R. Cons., Brussels. 1914, soloist at concert at which Granados introd. his opera *Goyescas;* cond., Monteux's orch.; toured U. S. and Egypt.

Cottlow, Augusta. Pianist, teacher; *b.* Shelbyville, Ill., Apr. 2, 1878. *p.* Busoni. Concertized in Rus. and the Continent; 1920, settled in U. S.; 1912, *m.* Edgar A. Gerst, of Berlin.

Couperin, Armand Louis. Organist; *b.* Fr., 1725; *d.* Paris, 1789. Comp. harpsichord sonatas.

Couperin, François. Organist, claveçinist, composer; *b.* Paris, Nov. 10, 1668; *d.* ib., 1733. As a composer for the claveçin, or harpsichord, he may be reckoned one of the fathers of modern piano mus.

Courboin, Charles Marie. Organist; *b.* Antwerp, Apr. 2, 1886. 1902, org., Ant. Cath.; 1904, org., St. Paul's, Oswego, N. Y.; 1917-18, Munic. org., Springfield, Mass.; concertized extensively; 1919, perf. Widor's Sixth Symph. (dedicated to him) *w.* Phila. Orch. *u.* Stokowski; 1935, org., Ch. of Ress., Rye, N. Y.

Courvoisier (*Koor-vwah-see-ay*), **Carl.** Violinist; *b.* Basel, Switz., Nov. 12, 1846; *d.* Liverpool, Apr., 1908. Writer on violin playing; comp. symph. wks.

Courvoisier, Walter. Composer; *b.* Riehen, Switz., Feb. 7, 1875. *t.* Munich Acad. of Mus. Son-in-law of Ludwig Thuille. Comp. opera, *Launcelot and Elaine* (1917); also symph. and mus. wks.

Coussemaker (*Koos-ma-kaire*), **Charles Edmond Henri de.** Writer, historian; *b.* Bailleul, Fr., Apr. 19, 1835; *d.* Bourbourg, Jan. 10, 1876. Authority on mus. and musicians of the Middle Ages.

Coward, Henry. English conductor; *b.* Liverpool, Nov. 26, 1849. Exceptional chorus cond.; dir., Sheffield Fest., and others; *w.* Yorkshire Chorus, toured in Canada and round the world. Comp. cantatas, part-songs. Author of articles and books on choral technic.

Cowell, Henry. Composer, pianist, writer; *b.* Menlo Park, Cal., Mar. 11, 1897. Edu., U. of Cal. Originator of a new idiom and a harmony, elucidated in book, 1930, *New Musical Resources.* Collaborated in invention of Theremin. Publisher of *New Music,* magazine. *h.* California. Comp. orch. wks., incl. *Synchrony;* chamb. mus., incl. *Quartet Pedantic;* piano pcs.

Cowen, Sir Frederic Hymen. Composer; *b.* Kingston, Jamaica, Jan. 29, 1852; *d.* London, Oct. 6, 1935. Comp. waltz at six years of age; an operetta, *Garibaldi,* at eight; cantata, *Rose Maiden,* before 21. 1878, visited U. S.; 1882, Scandinavian symph. perf. in Vienna; 1888, cond., Liverpool Phil. Orch.; also mus. dir., Melbourne Centennial Exhibition. Comp. operas, two oratorios, *The Deluge* and *Ruth;* cantatas, symphonies, chamb. mus., and songs.

Cowles, Eugene Chase. Operatic basso; *b.* Stanstead, Can., Jan. 17, 1860; *d.* (?) Washington, Jan. 17, 1932. 1879, to U. S.; 1888, naturalized; 1888, sang in first perf. of *Robin Hood, w.* Bostonians; 1901, *w.* Alice Nielsen, in London. Comp. songs, incl., *Forgotten.*

Cowles, Frederic Albert. Musical educator; *b.* Columbus, Ky., Nov. 26, 1881. Fd. and dir., Louisville Cons. of Mus.

Cowper, Harry Mattingly (Holmes Cowper). Tenor soloist; *b.* Dundas, Ont., Can., Mar. 4, 1870; *d.* Des Moines, Ia., Jul. 7, 1934. Soloist *w.* leading choral and oratorio socs. 1897-1900, *t.* Amer. Cons. of Mus.; 1900-02, Sherwood Sch., Chicago; 1909-34, dean, Coll. Fine Arts, Drake U., Des Moines.

Craft, Marcella. Soprano; *b.* Indianapolis, 1880. 1901-1914, sang in Europe, incl. Munich Royal Op.; 1914-17, concertized in U. S.; 1917-18, San Carlo Op.

Craig, David Scheetz. Writer; *b.* Phila., Jul. 24, 1869. Ed., *Music and Musicians,* Seattle.

Cramer, Johann Baptist. Pianist, composer; *b.* Mannheim, Feb. 24, 1771; *d.* London, Apr. 16, 1858. Fd. mus. publishing business in London. Famous for his piano *études*.

Cras, Jean. French composer; *b.* Brest, 1879. *p.* Henri Duparc. 1922, lyric drama, *Polypheme,* awarded Grand Prix de la Ville de Paris. Comp. wks. about the sea; str. qs.; songs; piano pcs.

Crawford, Ruth Porter. Composer; *b.* East Liverpool, O., Jul. 3, 1901. St., Amer. Cons. 1924-29, *t.* Amer. Cons.; 1930, Guggenheim Fellowship. Comp. *String Quartet, Sonata for Violin and Piano, Chant for Women's Chorus,* pf. pcs., and songs.

Crescentini (*Cresh-en-tee-nee*), **Girolamo.** Singer; *b.* Urbania, It., Feb. 2, 1766; *d.* Naples, Apr. 24, 1846. Celebrated artificial soprano. *t.* Naples Cons. Author of vocal method.

Creser, William. Organist, composer; b. York, Eng., Sept. 9, 1844. Examiner for Trinity Coll. of Mus., London. Comp. oratorios, chamb. mus., organ pcs.

Crimi, Giulio. Tenor; b. Paterno, May 10, 1885. Debut, Treviso, in Catalani's *Wally*. Created tenor part in Zandonai's *Francesca da Rimini* (Turin), and in Puccini's *Tabarro* and *Gianni Schicchi* (N. Y.).

Crist, Bainbridge. Composer, teacher; b. Lawrenceburg, Ind., Feb. 13, 1883. p. Paul Juon. Comp. pf. pcs., and songs especially to Oriental texts. h. Cape Cod, Mass.

Cristofori, Bartolomeo di F. Inventor of the piano; b. Padua, It., May 4, 1653; d. Florence, Mar. 17, 1731.

Crivelli, Domenico. Singer, teacher of singing; b. Brescia, It., 1794; d. 1856. Author of a *Method* for singers.

Croft, William. Composer; b. Nether-Eatington, 1678; d. Bath, Eng., Aug. 14, 1727. Org. of Westminster Abbey and of the Chapel Royal. Comp. anthems, sonatas, songs, hymn-tunes.

Crooks, (Alexander) Richard. Operatic tenor; b. Trenton, N. J., Jun. 26, 1900. 1922, concert debut, w. N. Y. Symph. Orch.; 1927, opera debut, Hamburg, Ger.; 1934, Met. Op. H., N. Y.

Cross, Michael H. Organist, composer; b. Philadelphia, Pa., Apr. 13, 1833; d. ib., Sept. 26, 1897.

Crotch, William. Composer; b. Norwich, Eng., Jul. 5, 1775; d. Taunton, Dec. 29, 1847. Principal, R. A. M. Comp. oratorios, anthems, glees, organ and piano pcs.

Crouch, Frederick William Nicholas. 'Cellist, composer; b. London, Jul. 31, 1808; d. Portland, Me., Aug. 18, 1896. 1849, to U. S.; served in Confederate army u. Stonewall Jackson; taught mus. in Baltimore. Comp. 2 operas, and many songs, incl., *Kathleen Mavourneen*.

Crusell, Bernhard Henrik. Clarinet virtuoso, composer; b. Nystadt, Fin., Oct. 17, 1775; d. Stockholm, Swed., Jul., 1838. Early comp. of the Finnish school, in opera, chamb. mus., songs.

Cui (*Kwee*), **Cesar Antonovitch.** Russian composer; b. Vilna, Jan. 18, 1835; d. Petrograd, Mar. 14, 1918. A prominent composer of the slavonic school. Comp. operas, incl., *The Captain's Daughter*, after Pushkin; also songs and instr. pcs. Best known by *Orientale* for violin.

Culbertson, Sascha. Violinist; b. Dec. 29, 1893. p. Sevcik. 1908, debut, Vienna; 1921, debut, New York.

Cunningham, Claude. Baritone; b. Manchester, Va., 1880. 1903, toured with Patti on her last farewell. Author of essays.

Curry, Arthur M. Composer, teacher; b. Chelsea, Mass., Jan. 27, 1866; d. 1908. p. MacDowell. 1914, t. Berlin; 1915, t. N. E. Cons. Comp. symph. wks., pf. pcs., and songs.

Curschmann, Karl F. Composer; b. Berlin, Jun. 21, 1804; d. Langfuhr, Aug. 24, 1841. Comp. opera, and many songs.

Curtis, Natalie (Mrs. Paul Burlin). Writer on Indian and negro music; b. N. Y.; d. Paris, Oct. 23, 1921 (in auto accident). p. Busoni (Berlin). In Arizona, became interested in Indian folklore, and compiled the *Indians' Book*, a collection of 200 songs culled from 18 tribes. Also a collection of negro mus., Hampton (Va.) Inst. (1917).

Curwen, John. English minister and singing-school teacher; b. Heckmondwike, Nov. 14, 1816; d. Manchester, May 26, 1880. Taking as a basis the system introd. by Sarah Ann Glover, he evolved what is known as the Tonic Sol-fa method; organized the Tonic Sol-fa Coll.; estab. publishing house to make available mus. in that notation. Work continued by son, John Spencer C. (1847), son's wife, Annie Jessie C., and grandson, John Kenneth C. (1881).

Cusins, Sir William George. Organist, pianist; b. London, Oct. 14, 1833; d. Remonchamps, Fr., Aug. 31, 1893. Org., Queen's Private Chapel; cond., Phil. Orch. Comp. oratorio, *Gideon*; piano concerto, overtures.

Cutter, Benjamin. Violinist, composer; b. Woburn, Mass., Sept. 6, 1857; d. Boston, May 10, 1910. Taught many years at New England Cons. Comp. cantata, mass, violin mus.

Cuzzoni (*Coot-so-nee*), **Francesca.** Soprano; b. Parma, It., c. 1700; d. Bologna, 1770. The bad-tempered singer who caused Handel so much difficulty in his London performances. Rivalled by Bordoni, she was imprisoned for debt, and died in poverty.

Czerny (*Chair-nee*), **Karl.** Composer, pianist; b. Vienna, Feb. 20, 1791; d. ib., Jul. 15, 1857. p. Beethoven. t. Liszt. Comp. pf. studies.

Czerwonky (*Tchair-vong-ky*), **Richard Rudolph.** Violinist, composer; b. Birnbaum, Posen, May 23, 1886. p. Berlin Hochschule, u. Joachim. Former conc.-m., Minneapolis Symph.; t. Bush Cons., Chicago. Comp. chamb. mus., concerto for violin, violin pcs.

Czibulka (*Chee-bool'kah*), **Alphonse.** Composer; b. Szeges-Várallya, Hun., May 14, 1842; d. Vienna, Oct. 27, 1894. Comp. operettas, salon mus.

D

Dacre, Harry. English songwriter brought to America by Tony Pastor, veteran variety impresario of America. *Daisy Bell*, about "the bicycle built for two" was his first American song; sung by Kate Lawrence to sensational London success, reported to have been played at wedding of Duke of York.

Daffner, Hugo. Conductor, composer, critic; b. Munich, Jun. 2, 1882. Comp. operas, symph., chamb. mus. Author of critical wks. on mus., incl. *Salome, Her Place in Poetry and Art*.

Dalayrac, Nicholas. Composer; b. Muret, Fr., Jun. 13, 1753; d. Paris, Nov. 27, 1809. 1800, Legion of Honor. Comp. sixty operas.

Dalcroze, Emile Jaques. Composer, teacher; b. Vienna, Jul. 6, 1865, of Swiss parentage. 1910, fd. school at Hellerau, nr. Dresden, the first to teach eurhythmic dancing; later fd. schools in Geneva, Paris, London. Comp. operas, violin concerto, str. q., children's songs.

Dallier, Henri. French organist and composer; b. Rheims, 1849; d. Paris, Dec. 23, 1934. p. César Franck. 1908, prof., Paris Cons.; 1878-1905, org., St. Eustache, Paris; then succ. G. Fauré at the Madeleine. Comp. masses, cantatas, choruses, chamb. mus., violin and piano pcs.

Dalmores, Chas. Operatic tenor; b. Nancy, 1871. Edu., Paris Cons. 1890, horn player in Colonne Orch.; 1894, t. horn, Lyons Cons.; 1899, debut as baritone, Rouen; 1908, Man. Op.; 1910, Chicago Op.

Dambois, Maurice. 'Cellist, composer; b. Liege, 1889. 1910, t. Liege Cons.; 1917, to U. S. w. Ysaye. Comp. chamb. mus., songs.

Damoreau (*Dah-mo-ro*), **Laure Cinthie, née Montalant** (known as Cinti-Damoureau). Soprano; b. Paris, Feb. 6, 1801; d. ib., Feb. 25, 1863. Contemporary with Sontag and Malibran; Rossini wr. revisions of his wks. to utilize her vocal range. 1826-35, Opéra-Comique, Paris; 1843, toured U. S.; 1834-56, prof., Paris Cons.

Damrosch, Frank. Conductor, teacher; b. Breslau, Ger., Jun. 22, 1859; d. N. Y., 19—. Son of Leopold D.; cond. various mus. societies in N. Y.; supervisor of mus. in public schools; fd. Peoples' Chorus; fd. Institute of Musical Art.

Damrosch, Leopold. Violinist, conductor; b. Posen, Rus., Oct. 22, 1832; d. N. Y., Feb. 15, 1885. 1873, fd. Oratorio Soc.; 1878, fd. N. Y. Symph. Soc. Comp. violin concerto, fest. overture, and songs.

Damrosch, Walter Johannes. Conductor, composer; b. Breslau, Ger., Jun. 30, 1862, son of Leopold D. Cond. of Wagnerian opera at Met. Op. H. Revived N. Y. Symph. Soc., fd. by father, and cond. it for many years under patronage of H. H. Flagler. Merged it with N. Y. Phil. Symph. in 1930 to devote his attention to radio broadcasting. m. daughter of James G. Blaine. Comp. operas, *Scarlet Letter, Cyrano de Bergerac*, and incid. mus. to several stage wks. Enjoyed a long career in N. Y.

Dana, Charles Henshaw. Organist, composer; b. West Newton, Mass., Feb. 1, 1846; d. Worcester, Mass., Feb. 5, 1883. Comp. ch. mus.

Dana, Lynn Boardman. Pianist, teacher; b. Middleport, N. Y., Oct. 15, 1875. Succ. father, William H. D., as dir. Dana's Mus. Inst., Warren, O.

Dana, William Henry. Teacher; b. Warren, O., Jun. 10, 1846; d. ib., Mar., 1913. Fd. Dana's Mus. Inst., Warren.

Danbé, Jules. Violinist, conductor, composer; b. Caen, Nov. 16, 1840; d. Vichy, Nov. 10, 1905. 1899, cond., Opéra-Comique. Comp. violin pcs. and variations on popular melodies. Author of a violin method.

Dancla (*Dahnk-lah*), **Jean Baptiste Charles.** Violinist, composer; b. Bagnières, Fr., Dec. 19, 1817; d. Tunis, Africa, Nov. 8, 1907. Comp. orch. wks. Author of technical studies for violin.

Daniels, Mabel Wheeler. Composer; b. Swampscott, Mass., Nov. 27, 1878. Gr., Radcliffe; st. Thuille, Munich. 1911, won 2 NFMC prizes for song and part song; 1917, cantata, *Peace With a Sword*, perf. Handel and Haydn Soc., Boston. Comp. orch. pcs., pf. pcs., songs. Author of *An American Girl in Munich*.

Danks, Hart Pease. Composer; b. New Haven, Apr. 6, 1834; d. Philadelphia, Oct. 20, 1903. Comp. popular songs and hymns, incl., *Silver Threads Among the Gold*.

Dannreuther (*Dan-roi-ter*), **Edward George.** Conductor, pianist, writer; b. Strassburg, Nov. 4, 1844; d. London, Feb. 12, 1905. Edu. in Cincinnati and Leipzig; 1863, London; 1895, prof., R. A. M. Distinguished advocate of the modern school and an early champion of Wagner. Frequent tours to U. S. Author of many critical wks.

Dannreuther, Gustav. Violinist; b. Cincinnati, Jul. 21, 1853; d. N. Y., Dec. 19, 1923. Edu., Berlin Hochschule. 1882, cond., Buffalo Phil. Soc.; 1894-1917, dir., Dannreuther Quartet; t. Vassar Coll. Author of pedagogical wks.

Daquin (*Dak-kan*), **Louis Claude.** Organist, composer; b. Paris, Jul. 4, 1694; d. ib., Jun. 15, 1772. Comp. cantata, *La Rosa*; also pcs. for harpsichord.

Dargomiszki (*Dar-go-mish-ky*), **Alexander Sergevitch.** Pianist, composer; b. Toula, Rus., Feb. 14, 1813; d. Petrograd, Jan. 29, 1869. His opera, *The Stone Guest*, on the same subject as *Don Giovanni*, embodied Balakireff's principles so well that he called it "The Gospel." Comp. operas, *Esmeralde* and *Roussalka*; songs.

David (*Dah-veed*), **Felicien Cesar.** Composer; b. Cadenet, Fr., Apr. 3, 1810; d. St. Germain-en-Laye, Fr., Aug. 29, 1876. Traveled extensively in the East; 1862, Legion d'Honneur; 1867, won prize for opera, *La Saphir*; 1869, succ. Berlioz in Acadamie. His principal work is the symph. ode, *Le Desert*.

David, Ferdinand. Violinist, composer; b. Hamburg, Jun. 19, 1810; d. Klosters, Switz., Jul. 18, 1873. p. Spohr. Conc.-m., Gewandhaus Orch. u. Mendelssohn; t. Leipzig Cons. when organized; t. Joachim and Wilhemj. Comp. opera, *Hans Wacht*; 2 symphs.; 5 concertos, caprices, études, variations for the violin. Author of an historic *Violin Method*.

Davidoff (*Dah-vee-dof*), **Karl.** 'Cellist, composer; b. Goldingen, Rus., Mar. 17, 1838; d. Moscow, Feb. 15, 1889. t. and dir., Petrograd Cons. Comp. orch. wks., violoncello solos and concertos, chamb. mus., songs. Author of a 'cello method.

Davies, Benjamin Grey. Tenor; b. Pontardawe, Wales, Jan. 6, 1858. Singer in oratorio, and concert; frequent tours to U. S.; 1891, sang in première of Sullivan's *Ivanhoe*.

Davies, David Thomas Ffrangcon. Baritone; b. Bethesda, Wales, Dec. 11, 1860. Opera, oratorio, and concert. 1898-1901, Berlin; 1903, prof., R. A. M.

Davies, Sir Henry Walford. Organist, composer; b. Oswestry, Eng., Sept. 6, 1869. Edu., Royal Coll. Mus.; org., Temple Ch., London; 1922, Knighted for service to Eng. mus.; succ., Elgar as "Master of Mus. to his Majesty"; best known by his stage work, *Everyman* (1904, Leeds F.).

Davis, Howard Clarke. School music supervisor; b. Lynn, Mass., May 4, 1881. 1931, head of sch. mus. dept., Villa Maria Coll., Erie, Pa.

Davison, James William. Music critic; b. London, Oct. 5, 1813; d. Margate, Eng., Mar. 24, 1885. 1846-79, critic, London *Times*. Wr. analytical notes for the Monday concerts.

Day, Dr. Alfred. Theorist; b. London, Jan., 1810; d. ib., Feb. 11, 1849. Author of *Treatise on Harmony*.

Dayas, Karin. Pianist; b. Finland. Awarded Liszt prize, Weimar. p. Carl Friedberg, Cologne. Soloist with symph. orch. in Finland, France, Germany, and United States. t. Cin. Cons.

Dayas (*Di-as*), **William Humphries.** Pianist; b. New York, Sept. 12, 1864; d. Manchester, May 3, 1903. p. Liszt. 1890, t. Helsingfors Cons.; 1894, N. Y. Comp. chamb. mus., songs.

De Ahna (*Day-ah-nah*), **Heinrich Karl Hermann.** Violinist; b. Vienna, Jun. 22, 1835; d. Berlin, Nov. 1, 1892. p. Mayseder. Prof., Berlin Hochschule; mem., Joachim Quartet.

De Avirett, Abby. Pianist, teacher; b. Austin, Tex., 1881. p. Godowsky. Mem., Pro Musica; mem., Hollywood Bowl Mus. Comm., Los Angeles.

DeBoeck (*De-book*), **Auguste.** Organist, composer; *b.* Merchtem, Bel., May 9, 1865. *t.* Brussels Cons. Comp. operas, orch., chamb. mus., organ.

Debussy, Achille Claude. Composer, pianist; *b.* St.-Germain-en-Laye, Aug. 22, 1862; *d.* Paris, Mar. 26, 1918. 1884, gr., Paris Cons.; won Prix de Rome with cantata, *L'Enfant Prodigue,* an academic work. When his next work, *Printemps,* was submitted, its harmonic audacity created a scandal in the jury. Later wks., *L'apres-midi d'un faune, La mer, Nocturnes, Iberia,* all delicately scored, were hideously dissonant to the conservatives. 1902, his opera, *Pelleas and Melisande,* was jeered at its Opera-Comique première, yet within a few years it became almost popular. Some of his most exquisite pastel shades of tonal colorings are to be found in his piano pcs., and songs, many of which became exceedingly popular. Yet no composer so completely disorganized the mus. thinking of the world, and dominated its development for a quarter of a century as did Debussy, the John-the-Baptist of ultra-modernism, compared to which his own mus. is now sane and conservative, and imbued with compelling and insinuating charm.

DeCisneros, Eleanora (née Broadfoot). Contralto; *b.* N. Y., Nov. 1, 1880; *d.* ib., Feb. 3, 1934. 1900, debut, Met. Op. H.; 1906, Manhattan Op.; created rôle, *Clytemnestra* in *Elektra* for Richard Strauss in Milan première; 1910, sang in inaugural perf. of Chicago Opera Co.; 1914, Paris; 1916, Havana.

Defrere, Desiré. Baritone. 1926, Chicago Opera; 1931, *m.* Hilda Hopkins Burke; 1935, Stage Dir., Met. Op.

De Gogorza, Emilio Eduardo. Baritone, teacher; *b.* Brooklyn, N. Y., May 29, 1874. *p.* Agramonte. *t.* Curtis Inst. of Mus.

De Haan, Willem. Composer; *b.* Rotterdam, 1849. Comp. orch., cantatas, operas.

de Kontski, Antoine. Pianist, composer; *b.* Cracow, Aus., Oct. 27, 1817; *d.* Ivanitshi, Rus., Dec. 7, 1899. Comp. pf. pcs., of a style once celebrated, as in *The Awakening of the Lion.*

DeKoven, (Henry Louis) Reginald. Composer; *b.* Middletown, Conn., Apr. 3, 1859; *d.* Chicago, Jan. 17, 1920. At several periods he was a newspaper critic. His light opera, *Robin Hood,* appears to enjoy an enduring popularity. It was played over the U. S. in the Nineties by The Bostonians. Other wks. incl. grand operas, *Canterbury Pilgrims* (1917), and *Rip van Winkle* (1919), numerous comic operas, songs and incid. pcs.

Delamarter, Eric. Conductor, composer, organist; *b.* Lansing, Mich., Feb. 18, 1880. *p.* Widor. Mus. critic of several Chicago newspapers; org., Fourth Presby. Ch.; 1918, assist. cond., Chicago Symph. Orch.; Comp. incid. mus. for Winthrop Ames N. Y. production of Maeterlinck's *The Betrothal;* also symph. and chamb. wks., and pcs. for organ.

Delaney, Robert Mills. Composer; *b.* Baltimore, Md., Jul. 24, 1903. St., Nadia Boulanger. 1928-29, *t.* State Normal Coll., Santa Barbara, Cal.; 1929-30, Guggenheim Fellowship; 1931-32, *t.* Concord Summer Sch. of Mus.; 1934, head, Dept. of Mus., Francis W. Parker Sch., Chicago. Comp. *Violin Sonata, First String Quartet, Suite for Orchestra,* songs.

De Lange, Samuel. Organist, composer; *b.* Rotterdam, 1840; *d.* Stuttgart, 1911. Comp. organ pcs., chamb. mus.

De Lara (-Cohen), Isodoro. Composer; *b.* London, Aug. 9, 1858; *d.* 1935. Comp. ten operas.

Deldevez (*Del-de-vay*), **Edouard Marie Ernest.** Violinist, composer; *b.* Paris, 1817; *d.* ib., 1897. Comp. operas, ballets, symph., ch. mus.

De Leone, Francesco Bartholomeo. Composer; *b.* Ohio, 1887. 1924, won Bispham and NFMC medals for opera, *Alglala,* prod. Cleveland. Comp. operettas, cantatas, songs, pf. pcs.

Delibes (*Day-leeb*), **Clément Philibert Léo.** Composer; *b.* St. Germain-du-Val, Fr., Feb. 21, 1836; *d.* Paris, Jan. 16, 1891. Edu., Paris Cons. *u.* Adam. Comp. exquisite ballets, incl. *Coppélia, Sylvia,* and operas, notably *Lakmé.*

Delius (*Day-li-us*), **Frederick.** Composer; *b.* Bradford, Eng., Jan. 29, 1863; *d.* Fr., Jun. 10, 1934. Spent boyhood in Florida orange-grove; 1885 against parental opposition to a mus. career, *t.* mus. in Danville, Va.; 1886, Leipzig Cons.; 1888, to Paris; 1899, London program of D. wks. Comp. operas, *Koanga* and *A Village Romeo and Juliet;* orch. wks., incl., *Appalachia, Brigg Fair, A Mass of Life,* and *On Hearing the First Cuckoo of Spring,* some with voices. In his wks., one senses the colorful but final twilight of Romanticism; Wagner in retrospect, in an embracive but unimitative synthesis. England was slow to recognize his genius, probably because of an aloof and forbidding personality.

Dell 'Orifice (*Oh-re-fee-che*), **Giuseppe.** Composer; *b.* Ortona, It., 1848; *d.* Naples, 1889. Comp. operas of modern flavor.

Delmas, Marc. Composer; *b.* St. Quentin, Mar. 28, 1885; *d.* Paris, Dec. 30, 1931. *p.* Vidal. 1919, *Prix de Rome;* 1911, lyric legend, *Anne-Marie,* won *Prix Rossini;* 1919, *Prix Chartier* for chamb. wks. Also comp. pf. pcs.

Delna, Marie. Contralto; *b.* Paris, 1875; *d.* ib., 1932. *p.* Laborde. 1892, Opéra-Comique; 1898-1901, Opéra; 1910, Met. Op., N. Y.

De Luca, Giuseppe. Baritone; *b.* Rome, Dec. 25, 1876. 1897, debut, Piacenza; 1915, Met. Op. Many royal decorations.

Delune (*Deh-leen*), **Louis.** Conductor, composer; *b.* Charleroi, Bel., Mar. 15, 1876. Comp. pf. concerto, cantatas, songs.

Del Valle de Paz, Edgardo. Pianist, composer, teacher, editor; *b.* Alexandria, Egypt, Oct. 28, 1861; *d.* Florence, Apr. 5, 1920. 1896, fd. *La Nuova Musica.* Comp. orch., pf. pcs., songs.

Demarest, Clifford. Composer, organist; *b.* Tenafly, N. J., Aug. 12, 1874. Comp. anthems, organ pcs., pf. pcs., songs.

DeMol, Pierre. 'Cellist, composer; *b.* Brussels, Nov. 7, 1825; *d.* Alost, Jul. 2, 1899. Comp. operas, cantatas, mass, chamb. mus.

DeMunck, Ernest. 'Cellist, composer; *b.* Brussels, Bel., Dec. 21, 1840; *d.* London, 1915. *m.* Carlotta Patti. 1893, prof., R. A. M.

Dennée (*Den-nay*), **Charles Frederick.** Pianist, composer; *b.* Oswego, N. Y., Sept. 1, 1863. Forty years on piano faculty of N. E. Cons. Comp. light operas, chamb. mus., many songs and pf. pcs., incl. teaching materials and editorial compilations. Assoc. ed., *University Course of Music Study.* Entire career assoc. *w.* Boston.

Densmore, John Hopkins. Composer; *b.* Somerville, Mass., Aug. 7, 1880. Edu., Harvard, Harvard Law. Comp. songs, cantata, pf. pcs., band and orch.

Denza (*Den-tsah*), **Luigi.** Composer; *b.* Castellamare, It., Feb. 24, 1846; *d.* London, Jan. 23, 1922. 1898, prof., R. A. M. Comp. opera, *Wallenstein,* and some 600 Neapolitan songs, incl. the famous *Funiculi-funicula.*

dePachmann, Vladimir. Pianist; *b.* Odessa, Jul. 27, 1848; *d.* Rome, Jan. 7, 1933. Edu., Vienna Cons. 1869, first concert tour in Rus.; 1877, Ger.; 1891, visit Amer.; has frequently toured U. S.; eminent Chopin interpreter.

DePhillippe, Dora. Operatic soprano; *b.* Paris, Fr. Created rôle of *Mme. Butterfly* (sang it 350 times); 1913-14, Chicago Op.

Deppe (*Dep-peh*), **Ludwig.** Pianist, composer, teacher; *b.* Alverdissen, Ger., Nov. 7, 1828; *d.* Pyrmont, Sept. 5, 1890. Comp. symph., songs. Author of technical treatise on pf. playing.

De Reszke (*Resh-keh*), **(Meczislaw) Edouard.** Operatic basso; *b.* Warsaw, Dec. 23, 1855; *d.* ib., 1917. Brother of Jean De R. Historic dramatic basso.

De Reszke, Jean. Operatic tenor; *b.* Warsaw, Jan. 14, 1852; *d.* Paris, Apr. 3, 1925. *p.* Sbriglia. 1885, sang première of Massenet's *Le Cid;* 1891-1901, Met. Op., N. Y.; the greatest dramatic tenor of his time. After retirement, became teacher of many celebrated singers.

DeSabata, Victor. Conductor, composer; *b.* Trieste, Apr. 10, 1892. Cond., symph. concerts at La Scala, Milan; 1927, g.-cond., Cincinnati Symph. Orch.; cond., première of Respighi's *Church Windows,* Milan; 1916, opera, *Il Macigno,* prod. La Scala. Comp. orch. and chamb. mus.

Dessoff, Marguerite. Choir conductor; *b.* Vienna, Jun. 11, 1894. Edu., Frankfort Cons.; fd., Dessoff choirs of Vienna, and later in N. Y.

Després (*Day-pray*), **Josquin.** Composer; *b.* Hainault, *c.* 1450; *d.* Condé, Fr., Aug. 27, 1521. The first contrapuntal composer to bring real mus. beauty into counterpoint. Luther said of him, "Josquin rules the notes, others are ruled by them."

Destinn, Emmy (*née Kittl*). Soprano; *b.* Prague, Boh., Feb. 26, 1878; *d.* ib., 1930. 1910-16, Met. Op.

Destouches (*Day-toosh*), **André Cardinal.** Composer; *b.* Paris *c.* 1672; *d.* ib., 1749. Comp. operas, ballets.

Destouches, Franz Seraph von. Composer; *b.* Munich, Jan. 21, 1772; *d.* ib., Dec. 10, 1844. Comp. operas, incid. mus.

Deswert (*Dehs-vair*), **Jules.** 'Cellist, composer; *b.* Louvain, Aug. 15, 1843; *d.* Ostend, Feb. 24, 1891.

Dethier, Edouard. Violinist; *b.* Liège, 1885. 1906, *t.* Inst. Mus. Art, N. Y.

Dethier, Gaston M. Organist, pianist, teacher; *b.* Liege, 1875. St. Liege Cons. 1894, org., St. Francis Xavier, N. Y.; 1907, *t.* organ and piano, Inst. of Mus. Art, N. Y.

Dett, R. Nathaniel. Negro composer, teacher; *b.* Drummondsville, Ont., Oct. 11, 1882. St. Amer. Cons. of Mus., Harvard U. 1920, Bowdoin prize for essay on "Emancipation of Negro Music"; Pres., Nat'l. Assoc. of Negro Musicians; *t.* Hampton Institute, Hampton, Va. Comp. songs; arr., negro spirituals.

deVore, Nicholas. Organist, editor, composer; *b.* Enon, O., May 19, 1882. *p.* Aviragnet. Edu., Bucknell U.; Cent. Coll. Phys. and Surgs., Indianapolis; 1903, org., Meridian St. M. E. Ch., Indianapolis; 1905, dir., Northern Cons. Mus., Portland, Ore.; 1907, asst. cond., Ocean Grove (N. J.) Fest.; 1908, org., Unity Ch., Brooklyn; 1910, staff-corr. *Musical America;* 1917, first pres., Nat'l. Acad. of Mus.; 1919, exec. ed., *University Course of Music Study;* 1923, prod. first laboratory talking movies; 1926-32, as dir. of research, Nat'l. Broadcasting Co., built world's first and largest mus. lib. for broadcast use; 1935, ed., *The Musician;* also mus. ed., *Whole World Series* of D. Appleton-Century Co. Comp. piano and violin pcs., songs, anthems.

DeVoto, Alfred. Pianist, teacher; *b.* 1875; *d.* Roxbury, Mass., Nov. 24, 1933. Pianist of Boston Symph. Orch.; mem., Boston Mus. Commission; many years *t.* and trustee, New Eng. Cons., Boston.

Devrient (*Deh-vree-ong*), **Philipp Eduard.** Baritone, author; *b.* Berlin, Aug. 11, 1801; *d.* Karlsruhe, Oct. 4, 1877. Author of a history of German dramatic art, memoirs of Mendelssohn, and librettos, incl. Marschner's *Hans Heiling.*

Dezède (*Dezaides*). Composer; *b.* Lyons, Fr., *c.* 1740; *d.* Paris, 1792. Comp. 18 operas and operettas.

Diabelli (*Dee-a-bel-lee*), **Anton.** Composer; *b.* Mattsee, Aus., Aug. 6, 1781; *d.* Vienna, Apr. 7, 1858. Best known by his easy piano duets, and as the composer of a theme on which Beethoven wr. variations.

Diaghilev (*Dyah'-gee-lef*), **Sergei Pavlovich.** Ballet impresario; *b.* Novgorod, Rus., Mar. 19, 1872. Fd. celebrated ballet; toured world; commissioned the comp. of many modern ballets, incl. most of the Stravinsky ballets.

Diamond, David. Composer; *b.* U. S. Edu., Eastman Sch. Mus. *p.* Roger Sessions. Won Paul Whiteman prize for chamb. orch. work. 1936, represented on Hans Lange's "modern program" with Phil. Chamb. Orch.

Diaz, Rafaelo. Tenor; *b.* San Antonio, Tex., May 16, 1888. *p.* Sabatini. 1911, Boston Op.; 1914, Met. Op.

Dibdin, Charles. Composer, singer; *b.* Southampton, Eng., *c.* Mar. 4, 1745; *d.* London, Jul. 25, 1814. Prod. popular plays interspersed with mus. such as *The Padlock, The Waterman, The Quaker.* His fame rests upon his sea-songs, lyrics which gained for him the title of the "Tyrtaeus of the British Navy." 1802, in recognition of the national importance of these songs the government bestowed upon him a pension of $500 a year.

Dickinson, Clarence. Conductor, organist; *b.* Indiana, May 7, 1873. *p.* Vierne. 1909, org., St. James' Ch., Chicago; 1912, org., Brick Ch., N. Y.; *t.* Union Theological Seminary; dir. of Mendelssohn Glee Club, succ. F. Damrosch. Comp. vocal solos and choruses, organ symph., organ and str. wks. Compiler of choral collectors.

Dickinson, Edward. Author, historian; *b.* Springfield, Mass., Oct. 10, 1853. Writer on musical history. 1893-1922, prof., Oberlin (O.) U.

Dickson, Ellen. Composer; *b.* Woolwich, Eng., 1819; *d.* Lyndhurst, Eng., Jul. 4, 1878. Comp. songs, *u.* pseud. "Dolores."

Diémer (*Dee-ay-mair*), **Louis.** Composer, pianist; *b.* Paris, Feb. 14, 1843; *d.* ib., 1920. 1887, prof., Paris Cons., succ. Marmontel. Comp. chamb. mus., concerto, pf. pcs.

Diepenbrock (*Deep-en-brock*), **Alfons.** Composer, teacher; *b.* Amsterdam, Hol., Sept. 2, 1862; *d.* ib., Apr. 5, 1921. Comp. vocal and orch. wks., songs.

Diet (*Deet*), **Edmond Marie.** Composer; *b.* Paris, Sept. 25, 1854. *p.* César Franck. Comp. operas, ballets.

Dilling, Mildred. Harpist, teacher; *b.* Marion, Ind. *p.* Henriette Renié. 1920, debut, Paris.

Dillon, Fannie (Charles). Pianist, composer; *b.* Denver, Colo., Mar. 16, 1881. *p.* Godowsky. 1924, fd., Woodland Th., Fawnskin, Big Bear Lake. Comp. orch., chamb. mus., pf. pcs., songs.

Dippel, Johann Andreas. Tenor, impresario; *b.* Kassel, Ger., Nov. 30, 1866; *d.* Los Angeles, May 13, 1932. Wagnerian opera singer; former co-dir., Met. Op.; 1910-13, g. mgr., Chicago Op. Said to have been able on a moment's notice to sing any one of 200 rôles, some in either Ger., Fr., or It. Prod. *The Lilac Domino* for N. Y. run.

Ditters (Ditters von Dittersdorf), Karl. Violinist, composer; *b.* Vienna, Nov. 2, 1739; *d.* Rothlotta, Boh., Oct. 24, 1799. Comp. comic operas, incl. *Doktor und Apotheker;* also ch. mus., symph., quartets, sonatas, songs. Author of an autobiography.

Divine, Grace. Mezzo-soprano; *b.* Wyoming, O., Feb. 14, 1906. 1924, debut, Century Th., N. Y.; 1928, Met. Op.

Dobrowen, Issai. Conductor; *b.* Nijni Novgorod, 1894. 1919, cond., Grand Theatre, Moscow; 1922, cond., Dresden Op.; 1933, cond., San Francisco Symph. Orch.

Dobson, E. Aldrich. Flutist, composer; *b.* U. S., 1896. Edu., N. E. Cons. Won Endicott prize for orch. work. Descendant from Cherokee chieftains. Writes original wks. in Indian idiom.

Doebber (*Deb-ber*), **Johannes.** Composer; *b.* Berlin, Mar. 28, 1866. Comp. light operas.

Doehler (*Day-ler*), **Theodor.** Pianist, composer; *b.* Naples, Apr. 20, 1814; *d.* Florence, Feb. 21, 1856. Comp. salon mus. and *études*.

Doering, Karl. Pianist, composer; *b.* Dresden, Jul. 4, 1834. Known for his technical studies for piano.

Doerner (*Dair-ner*), **Armin W.** Pianist, teacher; *b.* Marietta, O., Jun. 22, 1851. *t.* Coll. of Mus., Cincinnati, for many years.

Dohnanyi (*Dokh-nahn-yee*), **Ernst von.** Pianist, composer, conductor; *b.* Pressburg, Hun., Jul. 27, 1877. 1894, edu., Royal Hun. Acad.; 1897, debut, as concert pianist, Berlin; 1897-1901, toured U. S. and Europe in virtuoso recitals; 1908, prof., Berlin Hochschule; 1916, dir., Cons. of Budapest; 1919, cond., Budapest Phil. Comp. symph. wks., chamb. mus., operas, pantomime, *Pierrette's Veil,* and smaller wks.

Dolmetsch, Arnold. Violinist; *b.* Le Mans, 1858. *p.* Vieuxtemps. *t.* Dulwich Coll., London; expert on ancient instruments and their mus.; 1902-9, Chickering fact., Boston; 1911-14, Gaveau fact., Paris; 1914, to London.

Donati, Baldassaro. Composer; *b.* Venice, *c.* 1530; *d.* ib., Jun., 1603. Comp. madrigals, motets.

Donaudy, Stefano. Composer; *b.* Palermo, Feb. 21, 1879; *d.* Naples, May 2, 1925. Known for operas *Sperduti nel Buio* (Palermo, 1907), *Ramuntcho* (Milan, 1921), and *La Fiamminga* (Naples, 1922); also chamb. mus., songs.

Donizetti (*Don-ee-tset-tee*), **Gaetano.** Composer; *b.* Bergamo, Nov. 29, 1797; *d.* ib., Apr. 8, 1848. A shining light of the Rossini school of Italian opera. Comp. twenty operas before he met with success. *Anna Bolena, Lucia di Lammermoor,* and *Belisario* brought him into notice, and thereafter he turned out successful operas with ease and rapidity, distinguished by a wealth of fascinating melody and a ready appreciation of the picturesque. Of seventy operas, *Don Pasquale, L'Elisir d'Amore, La fille du régiment* and *Lucrezia Borgia* may be mentioned as the freshest and most original in conception and execution.

Donley, William Henry. Organist; *b.* New Haven, Apr. 20, 1863. Concertized throughout U. S., and at Buffalo and St. Louis Expo.; drew plans for over 300 organs; org., Seattle; dir., S. People's Chorus.

Dont (*Dunnt*), **Jakob.** Violinist; *b.* Vienna, Mar. 2, 1815; *d.* ib., Nov. 18, 1888. *p.* Vienna Cons., *u.* Hellmesberger. 1873, prof., Cons.; *t.* L. Auer. Comp. *études,* of present value.

Doppler, Albert Franz. Flutist, composer; *b.* Lemberg, Oct. 16, 1821; *d.* Vienna, Jul. 27, 1883. Opera comp.

Doppler, Arpad. Conductor, composer, teacher; *b.* Pesth, Hun., Jun. 5, 1857. Comp. opera, *Much Ado About Nothing;* suites, songs. *h.* Stuttgart, Ger.

Doppler, Karl. Flutist, conductor; *b.* Lemberg, Aus., 1826; *d.* Stuttgart, Mar. 10, 1900. Opera comp. Brother of Albert F. D.

Doret (*Doh-ray*), **Gustave.** Conductor, composer, essayist; *b.* Aigle, Switz., Sept. 20, 1866. 1888, Paris Cons.; 1893, cond., Concerts d'Harcourt; 1925, cond., opera, succ. G. Faure. Comp. operas, songs, dramatic legend, *Alienor;* cantatas, incid. mus.

Dorn, Edouard. See Roeckel.

Dorn, Heinrich. Composer, pianist; *b.* Königsberg, Nov. 14, 1804; *d.* Berlin, Jan. 10, 1892. Comp. salon mus.

Douglas, Charles Winfred. Pianist, organist; *b.* Oswego, N. Y., Feb. 15, 1867. 1891, Mus.B., Syracuse U.; 1892-3, New York; 1894-7, Denver; 1907-10, Fond du Lac; 1914-16, Gen. Theo. Sem., N. Y.; 1917, mus. dir., Sisterhood of St. Mary. Comp. masses, assoc. ed., *Episcopal Hymnal.* Author, wks. on aesthetics and history.

Douty, Nicholas. Organist, tenor, writer; *b.* Philadelphia, Apr. 14, 1870. Notable Bach singer, esp. *w.* Bethlehem Bach Fest. Comp. organ, pf., songs. Contrib. to magazines, incl. *New Music Review* and *Musician.* Pres., Musicians Mus. Soc., Phila.

Dowland, John. Composer, lute-player; *b.* Westminster, Eng., 1562; *d.* ib., 1626. Mentioned by Shakespeare in one of his poems. A celebrated madrigal writer.

Downes, Olin. Music critic; *b.* Evanston, Ill., Jan. 27, 1886. 1907, Boston *Post;* 1933, New York *Times;* author, *The Lure of Music* (1918).

Draeseke (*Dray-zeck-eh*), **Felix August Bernhard.** Composer; *b.* Coburg, Ger., Oct. 7, 1835; *d.* Dresden, Ger., Feb. 26, 1913. 1876-d., prof., Dresden Cons. 1912, Ph.D., Berlin U. Comp. operas, oratorios, symph. and ch. mus. Author of theoretical wks. A modernist who turned reactionary.

Dragonetti (*Drah-go-net-tee*), **Domenico.** Double-bass player; *b.* Venice, Apr. 7, 1763; *d.* London, Apr. 16, 1846. Distinguished virtuoso on the double-bass.

Drangosch, Ernesto. Pianist, composer; b. Argentine, 1882. p. Humperdinck. 1905, dir., Buenos Aires Cons. Comp. pf. concerto, pf. pcs., songs.

Drdla, Franz. Violinist, composer; b. Saar, Aus., Sept. 25, 1868. p. Hellmesberger. Cond., Vienna; concert tour to U. S., and remained. Comp. violin pcs., incl., *Souvenir*, popularized by Kubelik.

Dresel (*Dreh-zel*), **Otto.** Composer, pianist; b. Andernach, Ger., 1826; d. Beverly, Mass., Jul. 26, 1890. p. Mendelssohn. 1852-90, taught in Boston.

Dresser, Paul. Songwriter of the nineties; b. Sullivan, Ind.; d. 1906. 1896, his brother, Theodore Dreiser, the novelist, suggested the immortalizing of the Wabash River, thereby inspiring the historic ballad, *On the Banks of the Wabash, Far Away*. Greatest popular balladist after Foster. Distributed tremendous royalties from more than 100 popular ballads to many down-and-out artists, and died in poverty. Terre Haute (Ind.) erected memorial park and monument in his honor.

Dressler, Louis Raphael. Organist, composer; b. New York, Dec. 8, 1861; d. ib., Nov. 8, 1933. Comp. songs, anthems.

Dreyschock (*Dry-shock*), **Alexander.** Pianist, teacher; b. Zak, Boh., Oct. 15, 1818; d. Venice, Apr. 1, 1869. t. of many Bohemian musicians.

Drigo (*Drē'gō*), **Richard.** Italian violinist; comp. violin pcs., incl., *Harlequin's Serenade* and *Valse Bluette*.

Dubensky, Arcady. Composer, violinist, conductor; b. Rus., 1890. Edu., Moscow Cons., u. Ilyinsky. 1916, opera, *Romance*, perf. by Imp. Op.; 1921, violinist w. N. Y. Phil. Symph. Orch.; 1927, cond. his *Russian Bells*, w. N. Y. Symph.; *The Raven* and *Fugue for Eighteen Violins*, intro. by Stokowski and Phila. Symph. h. New York. Comp. opera, orch. wks., chamb. mus., incl., *Caprice for Piccolo-Flute*.

Dubois (*Du-bwah*), **Clément François Théodore.** Composer; b. Rosnay, Fr., Aug. 24, 1837; d. Paris, Jun. 11, 1924. 1861, Prix de Rome, Paris Cons.; 1895-1905, dir., Paris Cons., succ. Ambroise Thomas. Comp. oratorios, incl., *Paradise Lost;* operas, incl., *Frithjof;* orch. wks., incl., *Adonis;* pf. pcs., organ pcs., songs—irreproachable but uninspired mus. Completed Reber's Harmony course.

Dubourg (*Dü'boōr*), **Matthew.** Violinist; b. London, 1703; d. ib., Jul. 3, 1767. p. Geminiani. Conc.-m., Handel's orch; t. John Clegg.

Dufay, Guillaume. Composer; b. Hainault, Fr., c. 1400; d. Cambrai, Fr., Nov. 27, 1474. Leader among early French contrapuntists. Said to have introduced the white (outlined) notes.

Dukas (*Du-kah*), **Paul.** Composer, critic; b. Paris, Oct. 1, 1865; d. N. Y., May 17, 1935. Edu., Paris Cons. 1897, prod., *l'Apprenti Sorcier*, symph. scherzo, once thought modern, and now almost a popular classic; 1907, prod. opera, *Ariane et Barbe-Bleue*, one of the masterpieces of the French repertoire, in which the mus. boldly dominates the drama. Comp. sonata and variations for piano, and other wks. Contrib., *Revue Musicale*.

Dulcken (*Dool-ken*), **Ferdinand Q.** Pianist, organist, composer; b. London, Jun. 1, 1837; d. New York, 1902.

Dumesnil, Maurice. Celebrated French pianist; many highly successful concert tours through South America and the United States. t. Fillion Studios, Pittsburgh.

Dunham, Arthur. Organist, conductor, composer; b. Bloomington, Ill., Mar. 8, 1875. p. Widor. 1895-1924, org., Sinai Cong., Chicago; 1909, *Symphonic Fantasy*, for organ and orch., perf. Thomas Orch. Comp. organ wks., anthems and songs.

Dunham, Henry Morton. Organist, teacher; b. Brockton, Mass., Jul. 27, 1853. N. E. Cons., Boston.

Dunhill, Thomas Frederick. English composer; b. Hampstead, Feb. 1, 1877. Edu., R. C. M. t. Eton Coll.; 1905, t. R. C. M.; 1907-19, gave Thomas Dunhill Concerts in London; 1922, gave concert Brit. mus. in Belgrade. Comp. mainly chamb. mus., songs.

Dunkley, Ferdinand Luis. Organist, composer; b. London, Jul. 16, 1869. p. Parry, London. 1893, mus. dir., St. Agnes Sch., Albany; 1920, Birmingham, Ala. Comp. ballad, *Wreck of the Hesperus*, for chorus and orch., anthems, pf. pcs., songs.

Dunn, James Philip. Organist, composer; b. New York, Jan. 10, 1884. p. MacDowell. Comp. symph. p., *We*, based on Lindbergh flight; choral cantata, *The Phantom Drum;* opera, *The Galleon;* symph. and chamb mus., pf. pcs., songs.

Dunn, John. Violinist, composer; b. Hull, 1866. Edu., Leipzig Cons. u. Schradieck; 1882, one of the leading concert artists of Europe; 1902, first to introduce Tschaikowsky violin concerto in England. Comp. set of cadenzas to the Beethoven concerto, a violin concerto, sonata, and pcs., incl., *Berceuse*.

Dunstable, John. Famous English composer of fourteenth and early fifteenth century.

Duparc, Henri Fouques. Composer; b. Paris, Jan. 21, 1848; d. ib., Feb. 12, 1933. p. César Franck. Comp. in large forms, but best known by his songs. Excessively exacting, destroyed many mss.

Dupin, Paul. Composer; b. Roubaix, Fr., Aug. 14, 1865. At 21, abandoned a trade for a career of poverty and mus. Comp. six hundred wks., mostly in mss., and frowned upon by the critics. Life in Rue de L'Annonciation beset by adversity and obscurity. Comp. opera, *Marcelle;* orch. wks., incl., *Symphonie Populaire;* 40 *Poèmes* for str. q., and 370 *Canons*.

Dupont, Gabriel. Modern opera composer; b. Caen, Fr., 1878; d. 1914. Tragic life, fought lung disease and died in World War. 1904, opera, *La Cabrera*, won Sonzogno prize; 1914, last work, *Antar*, rehearsals interrupted by war, prod., 1921, w. success.

Dupré, Marcel. Organ virtuoso, composer; b. Rouen, May 3, 1886. p. Widor. At Paris Cons., won many prizes: 1905, pf.; 1907, organ; 1909, fugue; 1914, Prix de Rome. Succ. Widor as org., St.-Sulpice, and Louis Vierne at Notre-Dame. Remarkable for memory and improvisations. 1920, gave series ten Bach recitals at Paris Cons., all from memory. Frequent tours to U. S.

Dupuis, Albert. Composer; b. Verviers, Bel., Mar. 1, 1877. Dir., Verviers Cons. Comp. operas, incl., *Jean-Michel*.

Dupuis (*Du-pwee*), **Sylvain.** Composer; b. Liége, Bel., Nov. 9, 1856; d. Bruges, Oct., 1931. Comp. operas, *Moina, Cour d'Ognon;* also cantatas and orch. wks. 1911, dir., Liége Cons.

Durand (*Doo-rah*), **Auguste Frederic.** Violinist; b. Poland, 1770. p. Viotti. Toured Germany, and settled as conc.-m., Brussels opera.

Durante (*Doo-ran-teh*), **Francesco.** Composer; *b.* Frutta Maggiore, It., Mar. 15, 1684; *d.* Naples, Aug. 13, 1755. Comp. operas in the old Italian style.

Dushkin, Samuel. Violinist; *b.* Poland. *p.* Auer. 1825, to U. S.

Dussek (*Doo-shek*), **Franz.** Composer; *b.* Chotebor̆, 1736; *d.* Prague, 1799. Mozart completed *Don Giovanni* (1787) in his house. For his wife (née Josepha Harnbacher) Mozart comp. scena "Bella mia fiamma" and Beethoven "Ah, perfido!"

Dussek, Johann Ladislaus. Pianist, composer; *b.* Czaslav, Boh., Feb. 9, 1761; *d.* St. Germain-en-Laye, Fr., Mar. 20, 1812. Held in high estimation as a pianist, both in Paris and in London. Wr. twelve concertos, quintets, quartets, trios, sonatas, etc.

Dussek, Sophia. Pianist, singer, harpist; 1775-18—. Wife of J. L. D.

Dutton, Theodora (Blanche Ray Alden). *d.* Northampton, Mass., Dec. 5, 1934.

Duvernoy (*Du-vairn-wah*), **Jean B.** Pianist, composer, teacher; *b.* Paris, *c.* 1797; *d.* Passy, Fr., 1880. Best known by his piano studies.

Dux, Claire. Singer; *b.* nr. Bydgoszcz, Pol., Aug. 2, 1890. Edu., Milan; 1909, debut, Cologne; 1911-18, sang with Caruso at Berlin Royal Opera H.; 1923, Chicago Op.

Dvorák (*Dvor-zhak*), **Antonin.** Composer; *b.* Mülhhausen, Boh., Sept. 8, 1841; *d.* Prague, May 1, 1904. Edu., Prague mus. sch. Awarded government stipend to pursue composer's career. 1892-95, dir., Nat. Cons., New York; 1896, dir., Prague Cons. One of the most gifted composers of the modern school. Comp. symph., choral, chamb. mus., pf. pcs., songs. Comp., *Spectre's Bride, New World* symph., piano quintet, are exceptionally notable, in a list embracing practically every form. Popular immortality is insured by the *Humoreske* and *Songs My Mother Taught Me*.

Dwight, John S. Writer; *b.* Boston, May 13, 1813; *d.* ib., Sept., 1893. 1832, gr., Harvard as Unitarian minister, but became mus. *t.;* 1837, fd., Harvard Mus. Assoc. As ed. of *Dwight's Journal of Music* he became the most influential mus. critic of his time.

Dykema, Peter W. Musical æsthetician; *b.* Grand Rapids, Nov. 25, 1873. 1896, *t.* mus., U. of Mich.; 1913, prof., U. of Wis.; 1924, prof., pub. sch. mus., Teachers' Coll., Columbia U. Author, *Community Music*.

Dykes, Rev. John Bacchus. Composer; *b.* Kingston-upon-Hull, Eng., Mar. 10, 1823; *d.* St. Leonards-on-Sea, Eng., Feb. 22, 1876. Celebrated as a writer of hymn-tunes.

E

Eames, Emma. Soprano; *b.* Shanghai, China, Aug. 13, 1867. *p.* Marchesi. 1889, Paris Op.; 1891, Covent Garden; 1891, Met. Op. *w.* deReszke brothers.

Eames, Henry Purmont. Pianist, composer; *b.* Chicago, Sept. 12, 1872. Dir., Cosmopolitan Sch. of Mus. and Dramatic Arts, Chicago; Gr., Northwestern U.; *p.* Sherwood. 1894, toured U. S. *w.* Reményi; 1906, Mus.D., Cornell; 1908, *t.* U. Mus. Sch., Lincoln, Neb.; 1912, *t.* Cosmopolitan Sch. Mus., Chicago; 1913-19, mus. ed., Brunswick records; 1923-28, Amer. Cons., Chicago; 1928, prof., Scripps Coll., Claremont, Cal. Comp. pageants, choral wks., songs.

Earhart, Will. Public school music educator; *b.* Franklin, O., Apr. 1, 1871. 1900-12, Richmond, Ind.; 1912, Pittsburgh; 1913, prof., U. of Pittsburgh; 1920, Mus.D. Author of educational wks.

Eastman, George. Musical philanthropist; *b.* Waterville, N. Y., Jul. 12, 1854; *d.* Rochester, Mar. 20, 1932. Fd. Eastman Sch. of Mus., Rochester. Gave seventy-five millions to educational philanthropies.

Easton, Florence. Soprano; *b.* Middlesboro, Yorkshire, Eng., 1879. 1904-07, Savage Op. Co.; 1907-12, Royal Op., Berlin; 1913-15, Hamburg Op.; 1916-17, Chicago Op.; since 1917, Met. Op.

Eberhardt, Goby. Violinist, composer; *b.* Germany, 1852. Author of Violin Method. Comp. of numerous operas.

Eberhardt, Nelle Richmond. Librettist; *b.* Detroit. Wr. lib., *Shanewis,* prod., Met. Op. (1918).

Eberl (*Ay-berl*), **Anton.** Pianist, composer; *b.* Vienna, Jun. 13, 1766; *d.* ib., Mar. 15, 1807. Friend of Mozart; published own works *u.* Mozart's name. Comp. symph., operas, pf. pcs., songs.

Ebert (*Ay-bert*), **Ludwig.** 'Cellist, composer; *b.* Kladrau, Boh., 1834; *d.* Coblenz, Ger., 1908. Comp. 'cello wks.

Eccarius-Sieber, Artur. Piano teacher, critic; *b.* Gotha, Ger., May 23, 1864; *d.* Berlin, Jun. 30, 1919. 1886, Gotha; 1888, Zurich; 1891, fd. Swiss Acad. of Mus.; 1916, Berlin, mus. critic, *Signale.* Author methods, pf. and violin, and theoretical treatises.

Eck, Franz. Violinist; *b.* Mannheim, 1774; *d.* Strassburg, 1804. Concert violinist of excellent reputation; *t.* Spohr.

Eckert, Karl Anton Florian. Composer; *b.* Potsdam, Dec. 7, 1820; *d.* Berlin, Oct. 17, 1879. Best known by his songs.

Eckstein, Louis. Opera impresario, patron of music; *b.* Milwaukee, Feb. 10, 1865; *d.* Chicago, Nov. 21, 1935. 1912-1932, sponsor of Ravinia Park Summer Op., Chicago, at a personal loss of upwards of a million dollars; 1928, decorated cavalier by King Victor Emmanuel III; 1932, mem. bd. dir. Met. Op., N. Y.

Eddy, Hiram Clarence. Organist, teacher; *b.* Greenfield, Mass., Jun. 23, 1851. *p.* Dudley Buck. Concert org. In concert career of half a century probably gave more organ recitals than any touring perf. in the history of the instrument. Pub. collections of organ mus.

Edwards, George. Composer; *b.* Fargo, N. D., Aug. 22, 1884; *d.* San Francisco, Jun. 24, 1925. His comp. much perf. in Cal.

Edwards, Gus. Songwriter; 1905, wrote, *w.* Vincent Bryan, at Smoker of Nat. Democratic Club, for immediate use, the song, *Tammany,* which has refused to die.

Edwards, Julian. Composer; *b.* Manchester, Eng., Dec. 11, 1855; *d.* Yonkers, N. Y., Sept. 15, 1910. 1888, to U. S. Comp. operas, incl., *King Reni's Daughter;* cantatas, and many operettas, incl. *Dolly Varden* (1901) and *Princess Chic* (1900).

Eeden (*Ay-den*), **Jean Baptiste van den.** Composer; *b.* Ghent, Dec. 26, 1842. 1878, dir., Mons Cons. Comp. cantatas, oratorios, operas, orch.

Eggeling, Georg. Composer, teacher; *b.* Brunswick, Ger., Sept. 24, 1866. 1890-1900, *t.* Breslaur's Piano Seminary; 1900, fd., Inst. of Mus. in Berlin. Comp. teaching pcs. for piano.

Ehlert (*Ay-lert*), **Louis.** Composer, writer; *b.* Königsberg, Jan. 23, 1825; *d.* Wiesbaden, Jan. 4, 1884.

Ehrlich (*Air-likh*), **Alfred Heinrich.** Pianist, composer, writer; *b.* Vienna, Oct. 5, 1822; *d.* Berlin, Dec. 29, 1899. Ed. of Tausig's *Daily Studies.*

Ehrman, Mary Bartholomew. Composer; *b.* Cincinnati, Dec. 19, 1862. 1881, gr., Bartholomew Sch., Cin. Comp. children's songs, incl., *Sleepy Songs for Sleepy Eyes.*

Eichberg, Julius. Violinist, conductor, composer; *b.* Düsseldorf, Ger., Jun. 13, 1824; *d.* Boston, Jan. 18, 1893. 1859, settled in Boston; became mus. sup. in pub. sch. Comp. operettas, incl., *Doctor of Alcantara;* violin pcs., and songs, incl., *To Thee, O Country.*

Eichborn, Hermann Ludwig. Waldhorn virtuoso, inventor, writer; *b.* Breslau, Oct. 30, 1847; *d.* Bozen, 1918. Comp. songs, comic operas, orch. pcs., songs. Writer on instruments.

Eichheim, Henry. Violinist, composer; *b.* Chicago, Jan. 3, 1870. Gr., Chicago Mus. Coll.; 1890-1912, mem., Boston Symph.; 1927, *Oriental Impressions,* pub., SPAM; symph. pcs., *Java,* perf. Boston Symph. Comp. ch. mus.

Eijken (*Eye-ken*), **Heinrich.** Composer; *b.* Elberfeld, Ger., Jul. 19, 1861; *d.* Berlin, Aug. 28, 1908. Comp. songs w. orch. and choruses. Author of Harmony treatise, revised by Leichlentritt (1911).

Eijken, Jan Albert van. Organist; *b.* Ammersfoort, Hol., Apr. 26, 1823; *d.* Elberfeld, Ger., Sept. 24, 1868. Organ comp.

Eisenberg, Jacob. Pianist, writer; *b.* St. Louis, Feb. 19, 1894. Author of *Weight and Relaxation, The New Hanon,* and other technical treatises.

Eisenberger, Severin. Pianist; *b.* Poland. St. Heinrich Ehrlich in Berlin, Leschetizky in Vienna. Soloist w. most of important orch. of Europe and America; 1935-36, appeared w. Cin. Symph., *u.* Goossens, and Cleveland Symph., *u.* Rodzinsky. *t.* Cincinnati Cons.

Eisfeld, Theodor. Conductor; *b.* Wolfenbüttel, Ger., Apr. 11, 1816; *d.* Wiesbaden, Sept. 2, 1882. *p.* Reissiger. 1839, cond., Wiesbaden Th.; 1843, cond., Concerts Viviennes, Paris; 1848, cond., Phil. Orch., N. Y.; 1851, fd. notable series of chamb. mus. concerts; 1857, first cond., Brooklyn Phil. Soc.; 1858, one of few survivors from burning of S. S. Austria in midocean, which compelled his retirement in 1866. He exerted a strong influence on early Amer. mus. development.

Eitner, Robert. Musicographer; *b.* Breslau, Oct. 22, 1832; *d.* Templin, Ger., Feb. 2, 1905. 1869-1904, edited, *Monatshefte für Musikgeschichte;* 1899-1904, author, *Dictionary of Biographical and Bibliographical Sources,* 10 Vols.

Elgar, Sir Edward William. Composer; *b.* Broadheath, Eng., Jun. 2, 1857; *d.* Marl Bank, Feb. 23, 1934. Largely self-taught; leader of the modern British sch. 1885-9, org., St. George's Ch., Worcester; 1905-8, prof., Birmingham U.; 1906, to U. S. for perf. of *Gerontius* and *Apostles* by N. Y. Oratorio Soc.; 1904, Knighted; 1905, Mus.D., Yale; many other awards and decorations. The ever-popular *Salut d'Amour* was an early work. 1902, comp. *Pomp and Circumstance* for coronation of King Edward VII. *Land of Hope and Glory* has almost become the Brit. nat'l. anthem. Comp. also cantatas, incl., *King Olaf,* and *Caractacus;* overtures, incl., *In the South;* orch. suite, *Enigma Variations;* symph. p., *Falstaff;* two symphonies; 'cello and violin concertos; songs and part-songs.

Elie, Justin. Conductor, composer; *b.* Haiti, 1882; *d.* New York, 1932. St. Paris Cons. Fd., mus. sch., in Haiti. Spent many years in New York. Comp. salon mus. for small orch., incl., *Old Mountain Legends, Babilon, Kas Kaya, A Tropical Rhapsody.*

Elkus, Albert. Composer; *b.* U. S., 1894. 1935, won Juilliard Publication award for orch. work, *Impressions From a Greek Tragedy.* Comp. chamb. mus., choral pcs.

Ella, John. Violinist, writer; *b.* Thirsk, Eng., Dec. 19, 1802; *d.* London, Oct. 2, 1888. The possible originator of analytical program notes. Newspaper critic. Author, biographical wks.

Ellicott, Rosalind Frances. Pianist, composer; *b.* Cambridge, Eng., Nov. 14, 1857. Comp. orch., cantatas, chamb. mus.

Ellis, Mary. Operatic soprano; *b.* New York. 1918, debut, Met. Op. in *Suor Angelica;* 1924-25, played in original prod. of *Rose Marie,* N. Y.

Elman, Mischa. Violinist; *b.* Talnoje, Rus., Jan. 20, 1891. 1902-4, St. Petrograd Cons. *u.* Auer, getting waiver of bar against Jewish students. 1904, debut, Berlin; 1905, London; 1908, N. Y. Phenomenal youthful success as virtuoso. *h.* N. Y.

Elsenheimer, Nicholas J. Composer, teacher; *b.* Wiesbaden, Ger., Jun. 17, 1866; *d.* Ger., Jul. 12, 1935. 1890, *t.* Coll. of Mus., Cin.; 1907, *t.* Granberry Pf. Sch., N. Y. Comp. cantatas, part-songs.

Elson, Arthur. Writer; *b.* Boston, Nov. 18, 1873. 1895, gr., Harvard; 1897, gr., M. I. T. Author, critical wks., incl., *Book of Musical Knowledge.*

Elson, Louis C. Writer, historian; *b.* Boston, Apr. 17, 1848; *d.* Boston, Feb. 14, 1920. *t.* theory, N. E. Cons. Author, many books on mus. history. Ed., *University Musical Encyclopedia.*

Elterlein (really Gottschald), **Ernst.** Writer; *b.* Elterlein, Ger., Oct. 19, 1826. By profession a jurist. Analyst of Beethoven's sonatas.

Elvey, Sir George Job. Composer, organist; *b.* Canterbury, Mar. 27, 1816; *d.* Windlesham, Eng., Dec. 9, 1893. 1835, org., St. George's, Windsor; 1871, Knighted. Comp. principally ch. mus.

Emerson, Luther Orlando. Composer; *b.* Parsonfield, Me., Aug. 3, 1820; *d.* Hyde Park, Mass., Sept. 29, 1915. Comp. easy anthems and sacred songs.

Emery, Stephen Albert. Theorist, pianist, teacher; *b.* Paris, Me., Oct. 4, 1841; *d.* Boston, Apr. 15, 1891. 1867-d., *t.* N. E. Cons. Comp. 150 songs, pf. pcs., and studies. Author of textbooks.

Emmanuel, Maurice. French composer, musicologist; *b.* Bar-sur-Aube, May 2, 1862; *d.* Limburg, Ger., Jul. 12, 1935. Edu., Paris Cons. Since 1909, *t.* mus. hist. at Cons., succ. Bourgault-Ducoudray. Comp. violin pcs., chamb. mus., songs.

Emmerich, Robert. Composer, choral conductor; *b.* Hanau, Ger., Jul. 23, 1836; *d.* Baden-Baden, Ger., Jul. 17, 1891. Comp. symph., cantata, operas.

Emmett, Daniel Decatur. Pioneer minstrel and songwriter; b. Mt. Vernon, O., 1815; d. ib., Jun. 27, 1904. Ran away from h. w. a circus; 1843, fd., Virginia Minstrels, toured U. S. and Eng.; 1858-65, joined Bryant's Minstrels; 1859, wrote *Dixie,* which in 1860 became a campaign song. With outbreak of Civil War, it was appropriated as the war song of the South, despite its Northern origin.

Enesco, Georges. Violinist, composer, conductor; b. Dorohoiû, Roumania, Aug. 19, 1881. Edu., Paris C ⌐s. u. Fauré. Touring violin virtuoso; occasional g. cond. at Bucharest. 1898, *Poème Roumain* introd. Concerts Colonne. Best known for his *Roumanian Rhapsodies* for orch. Comp. orch. and chamb. mus. wks.; a lyric drama, *Oedipus;* piano and violin pcs.

Engel, Carl. Composer, editor, librarian; b. Paris, 1883. 1905, to Amer. as ed. of Boston Mus. Co.; 1917, succ. Sonneck, U. S. Libr. of Cong., then as ed. *Musical Quarterly,* and finally as pres., G. Schirmer, Inc. Comp. songs to verses of Amy Lowell: *Opal, A Decade, A Sprig of Rosemary.*

Engel, Karl. Writer, historian; b. Thiedenweise, Ger., Jul. 6, 1818; d. London, Nov. 17, 1882. Eminent writer on mus. and mus. instruments.

Engel, Lehman. Composer. Comp. incl., opera score for *Medea,* to be sung and mimed; also mus. for the Amer. dancers of the Martha Graham, Doris Humphrey sch.

Engelmann, Hans. Pianist, composer; b. Berlin, Jun. 16, 1872; d. Phila., May 5, 1914. p. Herman Mohr. 1891, to U. S. Comp. of easy salon mus., incl., *Melody of Love.*

Englander, Ludwig. Operetta composer; b. Austria, 1859; d. Far Rockaway (N. Y.), Sept. 13, 1914. 1882, to N. Y. Comp. many operettas, prod. at the old Casino Theatre in N. Y., incl. *The Strollers* (1901), *The Casino Girl, The Jewel of Asia.*

English, Granville. Pianist, composer; b. Louisville, Ky. p. Borowski. Mus.B., Chicago Mus. Coll. Comp. *Hunting Song, The Ugly Duckling,* and numerous wks. for violin, piano and voice.

Enna, August. Composer; b. Nakskov, Den., May 13, 1860. Gade secured for him a gov't. stipend for study abroad. 1892, opera, *Hexen,* prod. Copenhagen. Comp. *Komedianter,* the latest of ten operas; symph., chamb. mus., pf. pcs., songs.

Eppert, Carl. Composer, conductor; b. Carbon, Ind., Nov. 5, 1882. 1907-14, in Berlin, st., Hugo Kaun and Nikisch. t. Wis. Coll. Mus., Milwaukee. Comp. chamb. mus., choruses, orch. wks., incl., *A Symphony of the City.*

Erard, Sebastian. Piano-maker; b. Strassburg, Apr. 5, 1752; d. Aug. 5, 1831. Made notable improvements in the action of the harp.

Erb, J. Lawrence. Organist, educator, writer; b. Reading (Pa.), Feb. 5, 1877. 1914, prof., U. of Ill.; 1926, dir. mus., Conn. Coll. for Women, New London; ex-pres., Mus. Teachers' Nat'l. Assoc. Author of *Life of Brahms.*

Erb (*Airb*), **Marie Joseph.** Organist, composer; b. Strasburg, Alsace, Oct. 23, 1860. p. Widor. t. Strassburg Cons. Comp. operas, ch. mus., organ and pf. pcs., and songs.

Erben (*Air-ben*), **Robert.** Composer; b. Troppau, Ger., Mar. 9, 1862. 1900, Berlin. Comp. operas, incl., *Enoch Arden.*

Erdmannsdörfer, Max von. Conductor; b. Nuremberg, Ger., 1848; d. Munich, 1905. Comp. cantatas, incl., *Seelinde,* orch., chamb. mus.

Erkel, Alexander (Alexius). Composer; b. Pesth, 1846; d. ib., Oct. 14, 1900. Son of Franz E. Comp. operettas.

Erkel (*Air-kel*), **Franz (Ferencz).** Composer; b. Bekesgyula, Nov. 7, 1810; d. Pesth, Jun. 15, 1893. 1837, cond., Hun. Nat'l. Th.; 1853, fd., Buda. Phil. Soc.; fd., Hun. Nat'l. Op. Of his nine operas, *Hunyadi Laszlo* (1844), and *Bank Ban* (1861) were successes; also wr. patriotic songs.

Erlanger (*Air-lan-zhair*), **Camille.** Composer; b. Paris, May 25, 1863; d. ib., Apr. 24, 1919. p. Delibes. 1888, Prix de Rome. Comp. operas, incl., *Forfaiture* (1921); symph., choral mus.

d'Erlanger, Friedrich, Baron. Composer; b. Paris, May 29, 1868. Family of Paris bankers. German father, American mother. 1890, became British subject. Comp. operas, chamb. mus.; used pseud. F. Regnal.

Ern, Henri. Violinist; b. 1863. p. Joachim. Prof., Coll. of Mus., Cincinnati, O.

Ernst (*Airnst*), **Heinrich Wilhelm.** Violinist, composer; b. Brünn, Aus., May 6, 1814; d. Nice, Oct. 14, 1865. p. De Bériot. Virtuoso of international repute. Comp. violin concerto; 2 str. q.; and pcs. incl., the *Elégie.*

Erskine, John. Author, educator, pianist; b. N. Y., Oct. 5, 1879. 1900, A.B., Columbia; 1901, A.M.; 1903, Ph.D.; 1919, LL.D., Norwich U.; 1923, Litt.D., Amherst; 1929, L.H.D., Hobart Coll.; 1929, Litt.D.; 1931, Mus.D., U. of Bordeaux; 1900-28, prof., Columbia U.; 1928, pres., Juilliard Sch. of Mus.; 1935, mem. bd. dir., Met. Op. Author of poems, novels, and serious literary wks.

Ertel (*Air-tel*), **Jean Paul.** Composer, writer; b. Posen, Jan. 22, 1865; d. Berlin, Mar., 1933. p. Liszt. 1898, LL.D. Comp. symph., incl., *Harald;* operas, incl., *Gudorun;* chamb. mus., organ, pf. pcs., songs, symph. p. Mus. critic, Berlin *Localanzeiger.*

Eslava y Elizondo, Don Miguel Hilarion. Composer; b. Burlada, Sp., Oct. 21, 1807; d. Madrid, Jul. 23, 1878. 1844, dir., R. Chapel, Madrid; 1854, dir., Madrid Cons. Most influential Spanish musician of his epoch; but his mus. is of no modern interest. Comp. ch. mus.; operas. Author of methods, and theoretical treatises.

Esposito, Michele. Pianist, composer; b. Naples, Sept. 29, 1855; d. Dublin, 1929. Edu., Naples. 1878, Paris; 1882, prof., R. A. M., Dublin. Ed. of Italian classics. Won many prizes for compositions, operas, cantatas, symph., chamb. mus.

Esser, Heinrich. Composer; b. Mannheim, Jul. 15, 1818; d. Salzburg, Jun. 3, 1872. Comp. operas, orch., chamb. mus., songs.

Essipoff, Annette Nicolaievna. Pianist; b. Petrograd, Feb. 1, 1851; d. ib., Aug. 18, 1914. A virtuoso of international repute. p. Leschetizky. 1874, London; 1875, Paris; 1876, U. S. 1880, m. Leschetizky (div. 1890). 1893-d., prof., Petrograd Cons.

Evans, Frederic Shailer. Educator; b. Shailerville, Conn. Gr., Leipzig Cons. 1889-1932, prof. and dean, Cin. Cons.; 1932, retired.

Evans, Frederick Vance. Basso, teacher; b. Des Moines, 1883. 1913, dean of mus., Lawrence Coll., Appleton, Wis.

Evans, George ("Honeyboy"). Song writer; wr. *In the Good Old Summer Time,* to text by Ben Shields. Interpolated by Blanche Ring in *The Defender,* opening in Columbia Th., Boston, marking the first accidental public use of the "runway" built for rehearsal purposes; ten front rows of Harvard students joined in the chorus, and were thereafter known as the "Blanche Ring Angel Chorus." The song has refused to die, and in another generation it became the campaign song of Alfred E. Smith.

Eyken. See **Eijken.**

Eymieu (*Eye-myay*), **Henri.** Composer, writer; b. Saillans, Fr., May 7, 1860. Comp. operetta, oratorio, pf. pcs., songs. Ed., *Le Ménestrel,* Paris.

Eysler, Edmund. Austrian operetta composer; b. Vienna, Mar. 12, 1874. Edu., Vienna Cons. Wr. many operettas. Success due chiefly to Girardi, a popular Viennese idol, in the leading rôles.

F

Fabini, Eduardo. Violinist, composer; b. Mataojo de Solís, Uruguay, May 18, 1883. *p.* Thomson, Brussels. 1907, fd., Cons. of Mus. of Urag.; 1927, *Campo* and *La Isla de los Leibos,* perf. in Met. Op. Concert, and recorded by Victor. Comp. pf. and violin pcs., arr. for orch.

Faccio, Franco. Composer, conductor; b. Verona, Mar. 8, 1841; d. Monza, It., Jul. 21, 1891. Considered greatest conductor after Mariani. Comp. operas, incl., *Amleto.*

Faelten, Carl. Pianist, teacher; b. Ilmenau, Ger., Dec. 21, 1846; d. Boston, Jul. 20, 1925. 1877, t. Frankfort Cons., u. Raft; 1882, t. Peabody Cons., Balt.; 1890-7, dir., N. E. Cons.; 1897, w. his brother (Reinhold, b. ib., Jan. 17, 1856) fd. F. Pf. Sch., Boston. Authors of primary instruction books.

Fagan, Barney. World famous Irish buck and wing dancer. *My Gal Is a High Born Lady,* written to the rhythm of a broken bicycle pedal, brought him fame; also riches to the Chicago publisher to whom he sold it for $100.

Fairchild, Blair. Composer; b. Mass., Jun. 23, 1877. 1899, A.B., Harvard. *p.* Paine; Widor. 1903, h. Paris. Comp. orch. poems, incl. *Zal* (1918); pcs., incl., *Tamineh;* ballet-phantom, *Dame Libellule* (1921); chamb. mus.; songs.

Fairclough, George Herbert. Organist, educator; b. Hamilton, Ont., Jan. 30, 1869. Org., St. John's, St. Paul, Minn.; prof., U. of Minn.

Fairlamb, James Remington. Organist, composer; b. Philadelphia, Pa., Jan. 23, 1837; d. New York, Apr., 1908. Comp. operas and sacred mus.

Faisst (*Fyst*), **Immanuel Gottlob Friedrich.** Organist, theorist; b. Esslington, Ger., Oct. 13, 1823; d. Stuttgart, Jun. 5, 1894. Comp. cantatas, motets, organ mus.

Falcke, Henri-Oscar. Pianist; b. Paris, Feb. 27, 1866; d. ib., 1901. Author of text books on arpeggio playing.

Faleni, Arturo. Argentine composer; b. Chieti, It., 1877. 1897, to Buenos Aires, and fd. Verdi Inst. of Mus. Comp. *Overture in D; Fantasia;* mus.-p., *Il Terremoto;* pf. pcs., and songs.

Fall, Leo. Composer; b. Olmütz, Moravia, Aus., Feb. 2, 1873; d. Vienna, Sept. 16, 1925. *p.* Vienna Cons., *u.* Fuchs. Comp. operettas, incl., *The Dollar Princess* (1907, 600 perf.) and *The Eternal Waltz* (1912).

Falla (*Fy-ya*), **Manuel de.** Spanish composer; b. Cadiz, Andalusia, Nov. 23, 1876. Edu., Madrid Cons., *u.* Felippe Pedrell. 1905, achieved world fame by prize-winning opera, *La Vida Bréve,* prod., Nice (Apr. 2, 1913), Paris (1914), Madrid (1915). Comp. ballets, *El Amor Brujo* and *The Three-Cornered Hat;* piece for pf. and orch., *Nights in the Gardens of Spain;* orch. and chamb mus. wks.; pf. pcs., and songs.

Faltin, Richard Frederick. Composer, conductor; b. Danzig, Jan. 5, 1835; d. Helsingfors, 1918. Mus. dir., Helsingfors U.; leading figure in French musical life prior to rise of Finnish nationalists in the nineties. Comp. organ pcs., songs.

Faltis, Emmanuel. Composer, conductor; b. Lanzow, Boh., May 28, 1847; d. Breslau, Aug. 14, 1900. Comp. songs, masses.

Famintzin, Alexander. Composer, critic; b. Kalouga, Rus., Oct. 24, 1841; d. Petrograd, Jul. 6, 1896. Comp. opera, *Sardanapal,* orch. wks.

Fanelli, Ernest. Composer; b. Paris, Jun. 29, 1860; d. ib., 1919. A tragic destiny; ahead of his time and always poor. Composed orch. suites and chamb. mus.

Faning, Joseph Eaton. Composer, conductor; b. Helston, Eng., May 20, 1850. Comp. symph., the *Holiday* overture, songs, part-songs, incl., *The Miller's Wooing.*

Farina, Carlo F. Violinist; b. 1580. 1625, Court musician at Dresden. Comp. violin solos, and was first to adopt the virtuoso style in writing.

Farinelli, Carlo B. Singer; b. Naples, Jan. 24, 1705; d. Bologna, Jul. 15, 1782. One of the greatest of the old It. male sopranos.

Farjeon, Harry. Composer; b. Hohokus, N. J., May 6, 1878; grandson of Joseph Jefferson. Comp. chamb. mus., pf. pcs., song cycles.

Farkas, Edmund. Composer, teacher; b. Puszta-Monostor, Hun., 1852. *t.* Siebenbürgen Cons. Comp. orch. wks., chamb. mus., and many national Hungarian operas.

Farley, Roland. Composer; b. Aspen, Colo. Edu., Colo. State Sch. for Blind. St., Leipzig Cons. Comp. songs.

Farmer, Henry. Violinist, composer; b. Nottingham, May 13, 1819; d. ib., Jun. 25, 1891. Comp. masses, violin concerto.

Farmer, John. English madrigal composer, late sixteenth century.

Farmer, John. Organist, composer; b. Nottingham, Aug. 16, 1836; d. Oxford, Jul. 17, 1901. Nephew of Henry F. Comp. oratorio, the fairy opera, *Cinderella,* a comic cantata, chamb. mus.

Farnaby, Giles. English virginal composer, early seventeenth century.

Farnam, Lynnwood. Organist, pianist; b. Sutton, Que., Jan. 13, 1885; d. N. Y., Nov. 23, 1930. St., R. C. M. 1904, org., St. James, Montreal; 1920, org., Holy Communion, N. Y.; *t.* Curtis Inst. of Mus. A brilliant recitalist.

Farnsworth, Charles Hubert. Organist, educator; b. Cesaria, Turk., Nov. 29, 1859; d. N. Y., 193–. 1876, org., Worcester, Mass.; 1888, *t.* U. of Colo.; 1901, *t.* Teachers Coll., Columbia U.; 1913-14, pres., M. T. N. A. Author of treatises on pub. sch. mus.

Farrant, Richard. English composer, end of sixteenth century.

Farrar, Geraldine. Soprano; *b.* Melrose, Mass., Feb. 28, 1882. 1901, Berlin R. Op.; 1909, Met. Op., N. Y.; 1915, prod. *Carmen* for cinemas.

Farwell, Arthur. Composer, writer; *b.* St. Paul, Minn., Apr. 23, 1872. *Wa-Wan Press,* to introduce mus. of the New England modernists of the period. 1901-18, critic on *Musical America,* and dir. of Mus. Sch. Settlement. 1918, dir. mus., U. of Cal. Comp. orch. wks. and piano pcs. largely based on Indian themes.

Faulkes, William. Organist, composer; *b.* Liverpool, Eng., Nov. 4, 1863; *d.* ib., Jan. 25, 1933. Blind. Comp. orch., organ, chamb. mus.

Fauré (*Fo-ray*), **Gabriel Urbain.** Organist, composer; *b.* Pamiers, Fr., May 13, 1845; *d.* Paris, Nov. 4, 1924. Edu. in Niedermeyer's sch. as an org., *u.* Saint-Saëns. Followed organist's career for years, while comp. mus. of secular and almost exotic flavor. His acceptance came gradually, and his lyric drama, *Pénélope* was not prod. in Paris until 1913, after its première at Monte Carlo. 1905, appointed dir., Paris Cons. Comp. in all forms, but excelled in vocal and chamb. mus., for which his intimate style was eminently adaptable.

Faure (*Fawer*), **Jean Baptiste.** Baritone, composer; *b.* Moulins, Fr., Jan. 15, 1830; *d.* Paris, Nov. 9, 1914. Brilliant career in opera. Vocal *t.,* Paris Cons. Comp. many songs, incl., *The Palms.*

Favarger (*Fah-vahr-zhair*), **Rene.** Pianist, composer; *b.* Paris, 1815; *d.* Étretat, Fr., Aug. 3, 1868. Comp. salon mus.

Fay, Amy. Pianist, teacher; *b.* Bayou Goula, Miss., May 21, 1844. *p.* Liszt. Author of *Music Study in Germany.*

Fayrfax, Robert. Composer; *b.* Bayford, Eng., 1470; *d.* St. Albans, Eng., Feb., 1529.

Fearis, J. S. Composer; *b.* Richmond, Iowa, 1871; *d.* Lake Geneva, Wis., Sept. 2, 1932. 1893, settled in Chicago. Comp. ch. mus., and ballads. Best known by *Beautiful Isle of Somewhere,* sung at McKinley's funeral.

Federlein, Gottfried Heinrich. Organist, composer; *b.* New York, Dec. 31, 1883. Son of Gottlieb F. Org. in N. Y. ch. Comp. organ wks., ch. mus., songs.

Federlein, Gottlieb Heinrich. Organist, violinist, vocal teacher; *b.* Bavaria, 1835; *d.* Presser Home, Phila., Dec. 29, 1922. 1880, to U. S. Author of vocal method, violin method, and essays on *The Wagner Trilogy.*

Feinberg, Samuel Eugenievitch. Russian composer and pianist; *b.* Odessa, May 26, 1890. 1911, gr., Moscow Cons. Comp. pf. sonatas, pf. pcs., and songs.

Felix, Hugo. Composer; *b.* Vienna, Nov. 19, 1866; *d.* Hollywood, Aug. 25, 1934. Comp. operettas, incl., *Madame Sherry.*

Fenaroli, Fedele. Composer, teacher; *b.* Lanciano, It., Apr. 25, 1730; *d.* Naples, Jan. 1, 1818. *t.* Cimarosa, Zingarelli, Mercadante.

Feo (*Fa-o*), **Francesco.** Composer; *b.* Naples, *c.* 1865; *d.* ib., *c.* 1740. Comp. operas, incl., *Zenobia.*

Fernandez-Caballero (*Fair-nan-deth*). Composer; *b.* Murcia, Sp., Mar. 14, 1835; *d.* Madrid, Feb. 20, 1906. Comp. zarzuelas.

Ferrabosco. Italian family of contrapuntal composers, sixteenth century. **Alfonso F.** Comp. *ayres.* Pub., London, 1609.

Ferrari, Benedetto. Composer, poet; *b.* Reggio, It., 1597; *d.* Modena, It., 1681. Op. comp. and theorbo player.

Ferrari, Carlo. 'Cellist, composer; *d.* Parma, It., 1789. Intro. the high thumb positions. Comp. 'cello pcs.

Ferrari, Domenico. Violinist, composer; *d.* Paris, 1780. Comp. violin sonatas.

Ferrari, Gabriella. Pianist, composer; *b.* It., 1851. *t.* Paris. Comp. operas, orch. wks.

Ferrari, Giacomo. Composer; *b.* Roveredo, It., 1759; *d.* London, Dec., 1842. Accompanist to Marie Antoinette. Comp. operas.

Ferrari, Rodolfo. Conductor; *b.* Staggia (Modena), It., 1865; *d.* Rome, Jan. 10, 1919. Edu., Bologna Acad., *u.* Busi. 1891, created *Amico Fritz* (Mascagni) in Rome; cond., Communale Theatre, Bologna, for 11 seasons. Cond., Met. Op., *u.* Conreid.

Ferrari, Sera Carlotta. Composer; *b.* Lodi, It., Jan. 27, 1837. Comp. operas, songs.

Ferrata, Giuseppe. Pianist, composer; *b.* Gradoli, It., Jan. 1, 1865; *d.* New Orleans, Mar. 28, 1928. 1885, *p.* Sgambati; also Liszt. 1892, to U. S.; 1908, won prizes, Pittsburgh Art Soc. for st. q. and other wks.; 1910, pf. *t.* Newcomb Coll., Tulane U., New Orleans. Decorated by King of Portugal and King of Italy. Comp. many songs, incl., *The Unseen Garden;* also pf. pcs., incl., *Serenata Romanesca.*

Ferron, Adolphe. Composer; *b.* Vienna, May 21, 1855. Operetta comp.

Ferroni, Vincenzo. Composer, teacher; *b.* Tramutola, It., Feb. 17, 1858. 1888, prof., Royal Cons., Milan, succ. Ponchielli. 1889, won Sonzogno prize *w.* opera, *Rudello.* Comp. operas, chamb. mus.

Ferroud, Pierre Octave. Composer, pianist; *b.* Chasselay, Lyon, Fr., Jan. 6, 1900. 1921, *Sarabande,* for orch., intro. by Witkowski. 1922, *p.* Florent Schmitt, Lyon. 1924, *Foules,* perf. in Paris; also by N. Y. Phil. Comp. orch. wks., incl., *Au Parc Monceau;* chamb. mus., incl., *Andante Cordial;* choral mus., pf. pcs., two-piano pcs., songs.

Fesca, Alexander Ernst. Composer; *b.* Carlsruhe, May 22, 1820; *d.* Brunswick, Ger., Feb. 22, 1849.

Fétis (*Fay-tees*), **François Joseph.** Historian, theorist; *b.* Mons, Mar. 25, 1784; *d.* Brussels, Mar. 26, 1871. 1818, prof., Paris Cons.; 1827, fd., *Revue Musicale;* dir., Brussels Cons. Author of theoretical treatises, and the monumental work, *Biographie universelle des musiciens et bibliographie générale de la musique.*

Février (*Fev-ree-ay*), **Henri.** Composer; *b.* Paris, Oct. 2, 1875. Mus. critic, *La Renaissance.* Comp. opera, *Monna Vanna* (1909); *Ghismonda* (1918); and operettas.

Février, Henri Louis. Claveçin composer; *b.* Abberville, *c.* 1750.

Fibich, Zdenko. Composer; *b.* Seborschitz, Boh., Dec. 21, 1850; *d.* Prague, Oct. 15, 1900. *p.* Jadassohn. 1875, cond., Prague Op.; 1878, cond., Russian Church, Prague; one of the most important of Czech composers. Born in the midst of a forest. Comp. operas, *Bukovin, Blanik, Bride of Messina, Sarka;* symph. p., *Othello;* symph. chamb. mus., 376 pf. pcs. Experimented *w.* songs, melodrama, music to spoken words in dramatic trilogy, *Hippodamia.* Popularly known by *Poëme.*

Fiebach (*Fee-bahk*), **Otto.** Organist, composer; *b.* Ohlau, Ger., Feb. 9, 1851. Prof., Königsberg U. Comp. operas, incl., *Die Lorelei.*

Fiedler, Arthur. Conductor; *b.* Boston, Dec. 17, 1894. 1925, fd., Boston Sinfonietta; 1930, cond., "pop" concerts of Boston Symph. Orch., Cecilia Soc., Boston Male Choir, MacDowell Club Orch., and the Esplanade concerts.

Fiedler (*Feed-ler*), **August Max.** Pianist, conductor; *b.* Zittau, Ger., Dec. 31, 1859. 1908-12, cond., Boston Symph.; 1916, cond., Essen Orch. Comp. symph., and chamb. mus.

Field, John. Pianist, composer; *b.* Dublin, Ire., Jul. 26, 1782; *d.* Moscow, Jan. 11, 1837. *p.* Clementi. Spent life in Rus. as perf. and *t.* In his nocturnes, he may be counted the forerunner of Chopin.

Fielitz (*Feel-its*), **Alexander von.** Composer, teacher; *b.* Leipzig, Dec. 28, 1860; *d.* Bad Salzeing, Ger., Aug. 5, 1930. *t.* Stern Cons., Berlin; 1905, *t.* Chicago Mus. Coll.; 1906, cond., Chicago Symph. Orch.; 1918, ret. to Stern Cons. Comp. operas, song cycles, incl., *Eiland;* pf. pcs.

Fillmore, John Comfort. Pianist, teacher, writer; *b.* New London, Conn., Feb. 4, 1843; *d.* ib., Aug. 15, 1898. 1867-8, dir., Oberlin Coll.; 1884, fd., Milwaukee Sch. of Mus.; 1895, dir. mus., Pomona Coll. Investigated Omaha Indian mus. Author of a *History of Music,* a history of the piano and its music, and theoretical wks.

Filtz, Anton. 'Cellist, composer; *b.* Bohemia, 1730; *d.* Mannheim, 1760. Comp. symph., chamb. mus.

Finck, Henry Theophilus. Writer, music critic; *b.* Bethel, Mo., Sept. 22, 1854; *d.* N. Y., Oct., 1926. 1876, gr., Harvard u. Paine. Attended first Bayreuth fest., and became a Wagner advocate. 1881, mus. ed., N. Y. *Evening Post.* Author of mus. treatises, incl., *Wagner and His Works, Paderewski and His Art, Edvard Grieg.*

Fioravanti (*Fee-oh-rah-van-tee*), **Valentino.** Composer; *b.* Rome, Sept. 11, 1764; *d.* Capua, Jun. 16, 1837. Comp. fifty operas, incl., *La Cantatrice Villane.* Succ. by his son, **Vincenzo.** (1799-1877.)

Fiorillo, Dante. Composer; *b.* New York, Jul. 4, 1905. 1935, Guggenheim Fellowship; 1936, reappointed. Comp. *Suite for String Quartet, Prelude and Fugue, Music for Chamber Orchestra.*

Fiorillo (*Fee-o-ril-lo*), **Federigo.** Violinist, composer; *b.* Brunswick, Ger., 1753; *d.* Paris *c.* 1823. Comp. *études* for the violin which have become classics.

Fiqué (*Fee-kay*), **Karl.** Pianist, composer, teacher; *b.* Bremen, Ger., Apr. 17, 1867. 1887, fd. sch. in Brooklyn. Comp. operettas.

Fischel, Max. Violin teacher; *p.* Cesar Thomson. *t.* Chicago Mus. Coll. Author of technical wks. on violin.

Fischer, George. Music publisher; *b.* Dayton, O., Sept., 1876. As head of J. Fischer & Bro., New York, has discovered and encouraged many composers of promise.

Fischhof, Robert. Pianist, composer; *b.* Vienna, 1858. *t.* Vienna Cons. Comp. opera, *Der Bergkönig.*

Fisher, William Arms. Composer; *b.* San Francisco, Apr. 27, 1861. 1897, mus. ed., Ditson, Boston. Comp. songs, incl., *Under the Rose.*

Fissot (*Fees-so*), **Alexis Henri.** Pianist, composer; *b.* Amiens, Fr., Oct. 24, 1843; *d.* Paris, 1896. 1887, prof., Paris Cons. Comp. pf. mus.

Fitelberg (*Feet-el-bairg*), **Grzegorz.** Violinist, composer, conductor; *b.* Livonia, Oct. 18, 1879. 1907, cond., Warsaw Phil. Orch.; 1912, cond., Vienna Imperial Op.; 1914, cond., Pavlova and Fokine ballet in Rus.; 1896, won prize for violin sonata; 1901, won Zamoyski prize for pf. trio. Comp. symph. and chamb. mus., and songs.

Fitzwilliam, Count Richard. Bequeathed to Cambridge U. a valuable collection of early Eng. virginal mus.

Flagler, Isaac van Vleck. Organist; *b.* Albany, N. Y., May 15, 1844; *d.* Mar. 16, 1909. 1879-84, *t.* Syracuse U.; 1885, Cornell. Comp. organ pcs. Compiled collections.

Flagstad, Kirsten. Soprano; *b.* Osk, Nor., 1895. *p.* her mother. 1913, debut, Oslo Op.; 1928, Gothenburg Op.; 1933, Bayreuth; 1935, Met. Op. Her Amer. debut was a sensational triumph.

Fleck, Henry Thomas. Music educator; *b.* Buffalo, N. Y., Apr. 28, 1863. 1883, A.B., Upper Canada Coll., Toronto; 1900-33, prof. mus., Hunter Coll., N. Y.

Fleischer, Friedrich Gottlob. Song composer; *b.* Köthen, Ger., 1722; *d.* Brunswick, Ger., 1806.

Fleischer, Oscar. Musicologist; *b.* Zörbig, Ger., Nov. 2, 1856. Installed Royal collection of ancient instruments. Author, many books on mus.

Fleischer, Reinhold. Organist. composer; *b.* Dahsau, Ger., Apr. 12, 1842; *d.* 1904. Comp. cantata, *Holda;* organ pcs., songs.

Flemming, Friedrich Ferdinand. Physician, composer; *b.* Neuhausen, Ger., Feb. 28, 1778; *d.* Berlin, May 27, 1813. Comp. male chorus pcs., incl., *Integer Vitæ.*

Flesch, Carl. Violinist; *b.* Moson, Hun., Oct. 9, 1873. 1896-1901, *t.* Bucharest Royal Cons.; 1903-8, *t.* Amsterdam Cons.; 1921, *t.* Berlin Hochschule. A distinguished virtuoso. Ed. of violin editions. Author of a violin method.

Fletcher, Alice Cunningham. Writer; *b.* Boston, Mass., 1845; *d.* Washington, Apr. 6, 1923. Gave life to Indian welfare work and research. 1882, assist. in ethnology, Peabody Museum; 1891, awarded Thaw Fellowship. Author of *A Study of Omaha Music* and other monographs.

Fletcher, Percy E. Composer; *b.* Derby, Eng., Dec. 12, 1879; *d.* Farnborough, Sept. 1, 1932. Comp. orch. pcs., choral, chamb. mus., operettas, incl., *Chin-Chin-Chow.*

Fleury, Louis. French flutist; *b.* Lyons, 1878; *d.* Paris, June 21, 1926. St., Paris Cons. *u.* P. Taffanel. Since 1905, dir., Société Moderne d'Instruments à Vent. Career chiefly devoted to spreading knowledge of Eng. mus. on the continent.

Flexer, Dorothea. Contralto; *b.* Allentown, Pa., Sept. 2, 1903. 1926, Met. Op.

Flodin, Karl. Composer, writer; *b.* Wasa, Fin., Jul. 10, 1858. 1878-1905, Helsingfors, as mus. critic, and ed. of the *Post.* An authority on Finnish mus. 1907, to Buenos Aires. Comp. scena *Helena;* incid. mus. to Hauptmann's *Hannele.* Author of biographies, incl., *Sibelius.*

Floersheim (*Flairs-hime*), **Otto.** Composer, writer; *b.* Aix, Ger., Mar. 2, 1853; *d.* Geneva, Nov. 30, 1917. 1875, to N. Y.; 1880-94, ed., *Musical Courier;* 1895, to Berlin. Comp. pf. pcs., and small orch. wks.

Flondor, Theodor Johann von. Composer; *b.* Roumania; *d.* nr. Berlin, Jun. 24, 1908. Comp. opera and operetta.

Floridia, Pietro (Barona Napolino di San Silvestro). Composer, conductor; *b.* Modena, It., Mar. 5, 1860; *d.* N. Y., Aug. 16, 1932. 1904, to U. S.; 1906-8, Coll. of Mus., Cin.; 1908-10, N. Y. Comp. operas, symph., pf. pcs., songs.

Florio, Caryl (Pseud. of William James Robjohn). Singer, organist, composer; *b.* Tavistock, Eng., Nov. 3, 1843; *d.* Morgantown, S. C., Nov. 21, 1920. 1875-82, cond., opera in N. Y., and Havana; 1896-1901, org., Vanderbilt Estate, Biltmore, N. C., yet died in poverty in a sanitarium. Comp. operas, operettas, cantatas, symph. wks., pf. pcs., songs.

Flotow, Friedrich von. Composer; *b.* Teutendorf, Ger., Apr. 27, 1812; *d.* Darmstadt, Jan. 24, 1883. Comp. operas, incl., *Alessandro Stradella* and *Martha*.

Flynn, Joe. Variety performer, partner of Frank B. Sheridan; wr., *Down Went McGinty,* a historic popular success.

Foerster, Adolph Martin. Composer, teacher; *b.* Pittsburgh, Feb. 2, 1854; *d.* ib., 1927. Comp. *Faust* overture, symph. p., *Thusnelda,* orch., chamb. mus., pf. pcs., songs.

Foerster, Alban. Composer, violinist; *b.* Reichenbach, Ger., Oct. 23, 1849; *d.* Neustretitz, 1916; *t.* Neustretitz Cons. Comp. operas, chamb. mus., songs.

Foerster, Joseph. Composer, teacher; *b.* Osojnitz, Boh., Feb. 22, 1833; *d.* Prague, Jan. 3, 1907. Comp. masses.

Foley ("Signor Foli"), **Allan James.** Bass; *b.* Cahir, Ire., Sept. 7, 1835; *d.* Southport, Eng., Oct. 20, 1899. Distinguished in opera and concert; toured U. S.

Folville, Juliette. Pianist, violinist, composer; *b.* Liége, Jan. 5, 1870; 1898-1914, *t.* Liége Cons. Comp. opera, *Atala;* cantatas, violin concerto, suites.

Fonaroff, Vera. Violinist; *b.* Russia. Edu., R. C. M. *p.* Franz Kneisel. 1896, to U. S.; 12 years *w.* Olive Mead Quartet; 1923, *t.* Inst. of Mus. Art, N. Y.; 1929, *t.* Curtis Inst. of Mus.

Fontova, Conrado. Argentine composer; *b.* Barcelona, 1865; *d.* Buenos Aires, 1923. *p.* Van Dam. Cond., Blankenbergen orch. concerts; 1888, *Austria-España* perf. at Universal Exhibition of Barcelona. Later, acted as accompanist for brother, Leon.

Foote, Arthur. Veteran American composer, organist; *b.* Salem, Mass., Mar. 5, 1853. 1874, A.B., Harvard; 1875, A.M., *u.* Paine; 1886, orch. suite, op. 15, perf., Boston Symph.; 1898, pf. quintet perf., Kneisel Quintet; 1909-12, pres., A. G. O.; 1878-1910, org., First Ch., Boston; 1919, Mus.D., Trinity Coll.; 1925, Dartmouth. Dean of the conservative school in New England for half a century. Comp. symph. prologue, *Francesca da Rimini,* cantatas, orch., and piano suites, chamb. mus., songs, and pf. pcs.

Ford, Thomas. Composer; *b.* England, *c.* 1580; *d.* London, 1648. Comp. part-songs, canons, rounds, instr. mus.

Forkel, Johann N. Organist, writer, historian; *b.* Meeder, Ger., Feb. 22, 1749; *d.* Göttingen, Ger., Mar. 17, 1818.

Formes, Karl Joseph. Bass; *b.* Mühlheim-on-the-Rhine, Ger., Sept. 7, 1816; *d.* San Francisco, Cal., Dec. 15, 1889. Distinguished operatic singer.

Forsyth, Cecil. Composer, writer; *b.* Greenwich, Eng., Nov. 30, 1870. Edu., R. C. M. 1914, to U. S. Comp. orch., chamb. mus., comic operas, songs. Author of treatise on Instrumentation.

Forsyth, Wesley Octavius. Pianist, teacher; *b.* Toronto, Jan. 26, 1863. *p.* Jadassohn. 1892, *t.* Toronto. Comp. pf. pcs., songs.

Foster, Fay. Vocal teacher, composer; *b.* Leavenworth, Kan. *p.* Sherwood. *t.* Ogontz Sch., Phila. Comp. songs, incl., *Dusk in June;* choruses.

Foster, Muriel. Contralto; *b.* Sunderland, Eng., Nov. 22, 1877. Distinguished in oratorio and concert. 1903, première, Elgar's *Apostles;* 1904-05, Amer. tour, incl., Worcester fest.; 1906, retired.

Foster, Myles Birket. Organist, composer; *b.* London, Nov. 29, 1851; *d.* Dec. 18, 1922. *p.* Sullivan. Comp. cantatas and anthems.

Foster, Stephen Collins. Composer; *b.* Pittsburgh, Pa., Jul. 4, 1826; *d.* New York, Jan. 13, 1864. Wr. words and mus. of 175 popular songs, incl., *My Old Kentucky Home* and *Old Folks at Home.* Foremost Amer. balladist. 1935, cornerstone laid for F. memorial in Pittsburgh.

Fourdrain, Felix. Composer; *b.* Nice, 1880; *d.* Paris, Oct. 24, 1923. Comp. operas, incl., *Vercingetorix;* also operettas, pf. pcs., songs.

Fowles, Ernest. Theorist; *b.* Eng., 1864; *d.* Caterham, Surrey, Eng., Dec. 9, 1932. Fellow, R. A. M.; 1928-31, four U. S. tours in lectures on mus. theory.

Fox, Felix. Piano teacher; *b.* Breslau, May 25, 1876. Edu., Leipzig Cons. On Helbig prize, to Philipp, Paris. 1897, debut, Paris, playing MacDowell's mus. 1898, fd., Fox-Buonamici Sch., Boston (now Fox School). Officier d'Académie.

Fox, George. Baritone, composer; *b.* Eng., 1854. Opera and cantata comp.

Fox, J. Bertram. Teacher, composer; *b.* Stamford, Conn. *p.* Max Spicker. *t.* Inst. of Mus. Art, N. Y. Comp. pf. pcs., incl., *Eventide, Starlight.*

Fox, Oscar J. Song writer; *b.* Texas. 1904, to San Antonio. Specializes in Cowboy songs, incl., *Hills of Home,* with which Wilbur Evans won the 1927 Atwater-Kent scholarship.

Fox-Strangways, Arthur Henry. Musical journalist and writer; *b.* Norwich, Eng., Sept. 14, 1859. Edu., Wellington Coll. 1887-1910, asst. master there, and 1893-1901, dir. of mus.; 1920, fd., English quarterly, *Music and Letters.*

Fraemcke, August. Pianist, teacher; *b.* Hamburg, Mar. 23, 1870; *d.* N. Y., Jan. 18, 1933. 1900-d., dir., N. Y. Coll. of Mus.

Fragerolle (*Frazhe-rol*), **Georges Auguste.** Composer; *b.* Paris, Mar. 11, 1855; *d.* ib., 1920. Comp. operettas, patriotic songs.

Franchetti (*Frang-ket-tee*), **Baron Alberto.** Renowned Italian composer; *b.* Turin, It., Sept. 18, 1860. Edu., Munich *u.* Rheinberger. Comp. chamb. mus., and orch. wks., but best known for his operas, incl., *Germania* and *Asrael; Cristofore Colombo* was written for City of Genoa for perf. in 1892, at fourth Centenary commemorating discovery of America.

Franchomme (*Fran-shom*), **Auguste.** 'Cellist; *b.* Lille, Fr., Apr. 10, 1808; *d.* Paris, Jan. 22, 1884. Remarkable technician.

Franck (*Frahng*), **César Auguste.** Organist, composer, teacher; *b.* Liége, Dec. 10, 1822; *d.* Paris, Nov. 8, 1890. 1872, prof., Paris Cons., where through the influence of his pupils, he became virtually the father of the modern French school. His relatively meagre list of comp. is among the greatest of our mus. heritages: the *D Minor Symphony*, the violin *Sonata;* the oratorios, incl., *The Beatitudes;* and pcs. for pf., organ, and songs.

Frankenberger, Heinrich Friedrich. Violinist, composer; *b.* Wümbach, Ger., Aug. 20, 1824; *d.* Sonderhausen, Nov. 22, 1885. Comp. operas, songs, pf. pcs.

Franz, Robert. Composer; *b.* Halle, Jun. 28, 1815; *d.* ib., Oct. 24, 1892. One of the first and most sincere of the songwriters, whose greatness is found in his simplicity.

Frederick the Great, of Prussia. Flutist, patron of music, composer; *b.* Berlin, 1712; *d.* Potsdam, 1786. Comp. an opera, *Il Re Pastore;* overture, flute pcs.

Freeman, Henry Lawrence. Negro composer; *b.* Cleveland, 1875. Comp. six operas, symph. p.

Freer, Eleanor Everest. Composer; *b.* Philadelphia, 1864. Fd., Amer. Op. Soc. of Chicago. Comp. ten operas, songs, and pf. pcs.

Fremstad, Olive Nayan. Soprano; *b.* Stockholm, *c.* 1872. *p.* Lilli Lehmann. 1895, Berlin; 1896, Bayreuth; 1879, Vienna; 1903, Met. Op., N. Y. Leading Wagnerian soprano of her epoch.

Frescobaldi, Girolamo. Organist, composer; *b.* Ferrara, It., *c.* Sept. 9, 1583; *d.* Rome, Mar. 2, 1644. Org., St. Peter's, Rome.

Freudenberg (*Froy-den-bairg*), **Wilhelm.** Composer; *b.* Neuwied, Ger., Mar. 11, 1838. 1925, Cond., Berlin Symph. Comp. operas, and overtures.

Freund, John Christian. Editor; *b.* London, Nov. 22, 1848; *d.* Mt. Vernon, N. Y., Jun. 3, 1924. 1871, to U. S.; 1894, fd., *Music Trades;* 1904, fd., *Musical America.*

Fried, Oskar. Composer, conductor; *b.* Berlin, Aug. 10, 1871. Comp. choral wks., and chamb. mus.

Friedberg, Carl. Pianist, teacher; *b.* Bingen, Ger., Sept. 18, 1872. *p.* Rubinstein. *t.* Juilliard Gr. Sch.

Friedenthal, Albert. Pianist; *b.* Bromberg, Ger., Sept. 25, 1862; *d.* Batavia, Dutch East Indies, Jan. 17, 1921. 1913, author of *Music, Dancing and Poetry Amongst the American Creoles,* and other wks. Many tours as virtuoso pianist.

Friedheim (*Freed-hime*), **Arthur.** Pianist, composer, teacher; *b.* Petrograd, Oct. 26, 1859; *d.* N. Y., Oct. 19, 1932. *p.* Rubinstein and Liszt. 1897, to Chicago Mus. Coll.; 1897, opera, *The Dancer,* prod., Karlsruhe. Comp. pf. concerto, pcs., songs.

Friedlander, Max. Eminent musicologist; *b.* Brieg, Silesia, Oct. 12, 1852; *d.* Berlin, May 2, 1934. Authority on German folk song. 1911, exchange prof., Harvard. Discovered 100 Schubert mss. Lectured in many Amer. colleges.

Friedman, Ignace. Pianist, composer; *b.* Cracow, Aus., Feb. 14, 1882. *p.* Leschetizky. 1920, to U. S. Comp. songs, piano wks.

Fries, Wulf. 'Cellist, teacher; *b.* Garbeck, Ger., Jan. 10, 1825; *d.* Boston, Apr. 29, 1902. Distinguished concert artist.

Friml, Charles Rudolf. Pianist, composer; *b.* Prague, Dec. 7, 1881. To U. S., as accompanist for Jan Kubelik. Comp. fifteen light operas, incl., *Firefly, Katinka,* and *Rose Marie;* also piano and violin pcs.

Friskin, James. Composer, pianist; *b.* Glasgow, Mar. 3, 1886. St., R. C. M., *u.* Stanford. 1914, to N. Y.; 1916, N. Y. debut. Comp. pf. and instr. pcs.

Fritze, Wilhelm. Pianist, composer; *b.* Bremen, Feb. 17, 1842; *d.* Stuttgart, Oct. 7, 1881. Comp. oratorios, symph., concertos.

Froberger, Johann Jacob. Organist, composer; *b.* Halle, 1605; *d.* Héricourt, Fr., May 7, 1667. A distinguished comp. in his day, whose wks. were studied by Bach.

Frontini, F. Paolo. Composer; *b.* Catania, It., Aug. 6, 1860. *t.* Catania Cons.

Frugatta, Giuseppe. Pianist, composer; *b.* Bergamo, It., May 26, 1860. 1891, *t.* Milan Cons. Comp. chamb. mus., pf. pcs., and études.

Fry, William H. Composer, critic; *b.* Phila., Sept. 10, 1813; *d.* Santa Cruz, Cal., Sept. 21, 1864. Son of publisher of *National Gazette.* His opera, *Leonora,* prod., Jun. 4, 1845, at Chestnut St. Th., Phila., was the first publicly perf. Amer. grand op., *and in English!* 1858, revived in N. Y., and sung in Italian. As mus. critic for N. Y. *Tribune,* he did *not* review his own work. Comp. also few symph.

Frysinger, J. Frank. Organist, composer; *b.* Hanover, Pa., 1878. *p.* Wolstenholme. 1909, org., York, Pa.; 1911, *t.* U. Sch. of Mus., Lincoln, Neb.; 1918, Augustana Coll., Rock Island, Ill. Comp. org., pf. pcs., songs.

Fuchs (*Fooks*), **Albert.** Composer; *b.* Basel, 1858; *d.* Dresden, 1910. Comp. violin concerto, *Hungarian Suite,* choruses.

Fuchs, Johann Nepomuk. Conductor, composer; *b.* Frauenthal, Aus., May 5, 1842; *d.* Vienna, 1899.

Fuchs, Robert. Composer, teacher; *b.* Frauenthal, Aus., Feb. 15, 1847. *t.* Vienna Cons.; *t.* Gustav Mohler; friend of Brahms, who admired his *Serenades.* Comp. symph., mass, choruses, operas.

Fugère, Lucien. Operatic baritone; *b.* Paris, Jul. 22, 1848; *d.* 1935. 1920, gala perf. at Opéra-Comique to celebrate the 50th anniversary of his debut. Comic effects by vocal devices were called *fugères,* after him.

Führer (*Fear-er*), **Robert.** Organist; *b.* Prague, Boh., Jun. 2, 1807; *d.* Vienna, Nov. 28, 1861. Comp. masses.

Fuller-Maitland, John Alexander. Writer, historian; *b.* London, Apr. 7, 1856; *d.* Carnforth, Mar. 30, 1936. 1882, A.M., Cambridge, *u.* Stanford. Ed., second edition, Grove's *Dictionary of Music.* 1889-1911, mus. critic, *London Times.* Author of many biographical wks.

Fumagalli (*Foo-ma-gahl-lee*), **Luca.** Pianist, composer; *b.* Inzago, It., 1837; *d.* Milan, Jun., 1908.

Fumi (*Foo-mee*), **Vincesiao.** Conductor, composer; *b.* Montepulciano, It., Oct. 20, 1823; *d.* Florence, Nov. 20, 1880. Comp. opera, orch. wks.

Fursch-Madi (*Foorsh-Mah-dee*), **Emmy.** Operatic soprano; *b.* Bayonne, Fr., 1847; *d.* Warrenville, N. J., Sept. 20, 1894.

Furst, William Wallace. Operetta composer; *b.* Baltimore, 1852; *d.* Freeport, L. I., Jun. 11, 1917. Comp. incid. mus. for Belasco plays, and a series of operettas, incl., *Princess Nicotine.*

Furtwangler, Wilhelm. Conductor; *b.* Berlin, Jan. 25, 1886. 1915, succ. Bodansky at Mannheim; 1919, Vienna Tonkünstler; 1920-2, cond., Berlin State Op., succ. R. Strauss; 1922, cond., Leipzig Gewandhaus and Berlin Phil., succ. Nikisch; 1925, g.-cond., N. Y. Phil.; 1934, banished for 6 mos. by Nazi Government; 1936, engaged to succ. Toscanini as cond., N. Y. Phil. Symph. Orch., but withdrew because of anti-Nazi agitation. One of the greatest cond. of his era.

Fux (*Fooks*), **Johann Joseph.** Theorist; *b.* Hirtenfeld, Aus., 1660; *d.* Vienna, Feb. 13, 1741. Author of *Gradus ad Parnassum,* a text-book on counterpoint which has afforded the basis for most of the succeeding wks. on the subject.

G

Gabriel, Chas. H. Writer of gospel songs; *b.* ——; *d.* Hollywood, Sept. 14, 1932. *Glory Song* said to have sold 30 million copies. Wr. *Brighten the Corner Where You Are.*

Gabriel (*Gah-bree-el*), **Richard.** Organist, conductor; *b.* Zackenzin, Ger., Sept. 3, 1874. Comp. choral mus.

Gabrieli, Andrea. Organist; *b.* Venice, *c.* 1510; *d.* ib., 1586. Org., St. Mark's Cath. An early It. comp.

Gabrieli, Giovanni. Organist, composer; *b.* Venice, 1557; *d.* ib., Aug. 12, 1612. Succ. uncle, Andrea G., as org., St. Mark's.

Gabrilowitsch, Ossip. Pianist, conductor; *b.* Petrograd, Feb. 7, 1878. *p.* Leschetizky. 1896-1909, world tour as pf. virtuoso; 1909, cond., Vienna Konzertverain; 1918, cond., Detroit Symph. *m.* Clara Clemens, daughter of Mark Twain. Comp. pf. pcs., songs.

Gade (*Gah-de*), **Niels Wilhelm.** Composer; *b.* Copenhagen, Den., Feb. 22, 1817; *d.* ib., Dec. 21, 1890. A disciple of Mendelssohn. Comp. symph., overtures, opera, choral wks., chamb. mus., all of a strongly marked Scandinavian character.

Gadsby, Henry R. Organist, composer; *b.* London, Dec. 15, 1842; *d.* Putney, Nov. 11, 1907. Comp. anthems.

Gadski, Johanna. Soprano; *b.* Anclam, Ger., Jun. 15, 1871; *d.* Berlin, Feb. 23, 1932. 1895-1914, Met. Op. *m.* Capt. Hans Tauscher, a German agent. Died as a result of automobile accident. Eminent interpreter of Wagnerian rôles.

Gagliano (*Gal-yah-no*), **Marco da.** Composer; *b.* Gagliano, It., *c.* 1575; *d.* ib., Feb. 24, 1642.

Gagnebin, Henri. Composer, organist; *b.* Liége, Bel., Mar. 13, 1886. Edu., Schola Cantorum, Paris, *u.* d'Indy. 1910-16, org., Eglise de la Redemption; 1925, prof., Lausanne Cons. Mus.; later, dir., Geneva Cons.; 1919, *String Quartet* perf. Comp. orch. wks., incl. *Symphony in F;* choral wks., incl. *St. Francis d'Assise;* and chamb. mus.

Gail (*Ghile*), **Edmée Sophia.** Composer; *b.* Paris, Aug. 28, 1775; *d.* ib., Jul. 24, 1819. Comp. operas, songs.

Gaines, Samuel Richards. Composer, conductor; *b.* Mich., 1869. Org., Old Shawmut Ch., Boston; 1928, cond. first perf. of his oratorio, *The Vision,* in Texas; 1930, cond. first perf. of his *Fantasy on Russian Folk Songs,* at Maine Fest.

Gaito, Constantino. Argentine composer; *b.* Buenos Aires, 1878. Pub. first comp. when 11. Edu., Cons. of Naples, *u.* Platania. 1900, ret. to Buenos Aires, and fd. Gaito Inst. Comp. operas, orch. wks., pf. pcs., and songs.

Gale, Clement Rowland. Organist, composer; *b.* Kew, England, Mar. 12, 1862; *d.* N. Y., May 10, 1934. Edu., Exeter Coll., Oxford; 1884, gr. in arts; 1889, in mus.; 1890-1900, org., Calvary Ch., N. Y.; 1900-10, All Angels'; 1910, Christ Ch.; 1902, *t.* Guilmant Organ Sch. Comp. part-songs, anthems, organ and piano pcs.

Gale, Walter C. Organist; *b.* Cambridge, Mass., Sept. 5, 1871. 1891, gr., C. C. N. Y.; 1893, org., Holy Trinity, N. Y.; 1900-05, All Souls; Since 1905, Broadway Tabernacle; *t.* Miss Spence's Sch. for Girls.

Gales, Weston. Organist; *b.* Elizabeth, N. J., Nov. 5, 1877. *p.* Widor. 1902-08, org., Christ Ch., N. Y.; 1908-13, Emmanuel Ch., Boston; 1914, fd., Detroit Symph. Orch., and cond. it till 1918.

Galin (*Gah-lang*), **Pierre.** Theorist, teacher; *b.* Samatan, Fr., 1786; *d.* Bordeaux, Aug. 31, 1821. Devised a system of sight singing by the use of numerals instead of the syllables *do, re, mi.*

Galitzin, Prince George. Composer; *b.* Petrograd, 1823; *d.* ib., 1872. Comp. masses, orch. fantasies, choral wks.

Galli, Amintore. Writer, music critic, composer; *b.* Rimini, It., Oct. 12, 1845; *d.* ib., Dec. 8, 1919. Mus. critic, *Il Secolo;* ed., Sonzogno; *t.* Verdi Cons., Milan; for half-century one of the strongest influences in It. mus. development. Comp. operas, oratorios.

Gallico, Paolo. Pianist, teacher, composer; *b.* Trieste, May 13, 1868. Edu., Vienna Cons. 1892, mus. ed., Schirmer's, N. Y.; 1921, NFMC prize for dramatic oratorio, *The Apocalypse.* Comp. opera, operettas, pf. pcs., studies.

Galli-Curci (*Gahl-lee-coor-chee*), **Amelita (Mrs. Homer Samuels).** Soprano; *b.* Milan, Nov. 18, 1889. Distinguished coloratura singer of extreme range. 1910, Rome; 1916, Chicago Op.; later, Met. Op.

Gallo, Fortune. Opera impresario; *b.* It., 1911. Fd., San Francisco Op. Co., bringing Leoncavallo from It., to cond. Dir., San Carlo Op. Co.

Galloway, Tod Buchanan. Composer; *b.* Oct. 13, 1863; *d.* Columbus, O., Dec. 12, 1935. A prominent jurist, whose songs have gone around the world.

Gallup, Miner Walden. Pianist, composer; prof., Milliken U., Decatur, Ill.

Galuppi (*Gah-loop-pee*), **Baldassaro.** Composer; *b.* Burano, It., Oct. 18, 1706; *d.* Venice, Jan. 3, 1785. Mentioned by Browning. Comp. toccatas in Italian classical style.

Ganapol, Boris. Teacher; *b.* Svenigorodka, Rus., Jul. 10, 1865; *d.* Detroit, Jun. 14, 1934. Edu., Imperial Cons., Kiev. Debut *w.* Kiev Op. Co.; fd.-dir., Ganapol Sch. of Mus. Art, Detroit, succ. by his widow.

Gandolfi, Alfredo. Baritone; *b.* Torino, It., May 18, 1889. San Francisco Op.; Met. Op.

Gandolfi, Riccardo Cristoforo Daniele Diomede. Composer; *b.* Voghera, It., Feb. 16, 1839; *d.* Florence, 1920. *p.* Conti. Comp. opera, orch. wks.; devoted to historical studies.

Ganne (*Gahnn*), **Louis Gaston.** Composer, conductor; *b.* Bruxières-les-Mines, Fr., Apr. 15, 1862; *d.* Paris, 1923. Comp. light operas, popular piano mus., songs.

Gänsbacher (*Gehns-bakh-er*), **Johann B.** Composer; *b.* Sterzing, Aus., May 8, 1778; *d.* Vienna, Jul. 13, 1844.

Gantvoort, Arnold Johann. Teacher; *b.* Amsterdam, Hol., Dec. 6, 1857. Dir., Coll. of Mus., Cin.

Ganz (*Gahntz*), **Rudolph.** Pianist, composer, conductor; b. Zurich, Feb. 24, 1877. p. Busoni. 1921, cond., St. Louis Symph. Orch.; 1934, pres., Chicago Mus. Coll. Comp. symph., over 200 songs, and piano pcs. Distinguished virtuoso.

Ganz, Wilhelm. Composer, pianist; b. Mainz, Nov. 6, 1833; d. London, 1914. Wr. fantasias and teaching pcs. of a style largely outworn.

Garcia (*Gar-thee-a*), **Manuel.** Teacher of singing; b. Madrid, Mar. 17, 1805; d. London, Jul. 1, 1906. For many years a London vocal teacher. Invented the laryngoscope.

Garcia, Manuel del Popolo Vincente. Singer, teacher; b. Seville, Jan. 21, 1775; d. Paris, Jun. 9, 1832. 1825, intro. It. op. in N. Y. Father of Viardot-Garcia, Maria Malibran and Manuel (1805).

Garcin (*Gar-sang*), **Jules Auguste.** Violinist, conductor, composer; b. Bourges, Fr., Jul. 11, 1830; d. Paris, Oct. 10, 1896. Comp. violin pcs.

Garden, Mary. Soprano; b. Aberdeen, Scot., Feb. 20, 1877. Brought up in U. S. St. violin at six; piano at twelve. Famous opera singer. 1900, debut in *Louise* at Opéra-Comique, Paris; 1907, Manhattan Op. H., N. Y.; 1910, Chicago Op.; 1921, dir., Chicago Op.; t. Chicago Mus. Coll.

Gardiner, H. Balfour. Composer; b. London, Nov. 7, 1877. Comp. symph., chamb. mus., songs.

Gardner, Samuel. Violinist, composer; b. Rus., 1892. p. Kneisel. 1918, won Pulitzer prize for str. q.; 1918, won Loeb prize for symph. p., *New Russia;* 1929, orch. piece, *Broadway,* perf., Boston Symph.

Garrett, George Mursell. Organist, composer; b. Winchester, Eng., Jun. 8, 1834; d. Cambridge, Apr. 8, 1897. Comp. oratorios, cantatas, and virile ch. mus.

Garrison, Mabel. Soprano; b. Baltimore, Md. St. Peabody Cons. of Mus. 1914-22, Met. Op.

Gartlan, George H. Director, educator; b. New York City. p. Aronson. Hd. sch. mus. dept., Inst. of Mus. Art, N. Y.; dir. mus., N. Y. Bd. of Edu.

Gast, Peter. Pseud. of Heinrich Köselitz (q. v.). Friend of Nietzsche, who published N's letters under this *nom de plume.*

Gastaldon, Stanislas. Composer; b. Turin, Apr. 7, 1861. Mus. critic, *Nuovo Giornale,* Florence. Comp. operas, incl., *Mala Pusqua* (1890, Rome); pf. pcs., popular ballads, incl., *Musica Proibita,* which sold 500,000 copies.

Gastinel, Leon. Composer; b. Côte d'Or, Fr., Aug. 15, 1823; d. Paris, 1906. Comp. oratorios, overtures, symph., comic operas.

Gates, Lucy. Soprano; b. St. George, Utah. p. Herbert Witherspoon. 1909, debut, Berlin Royal Op.; 1915, fd., Lucy Gates Op. Co.

Gatti-Casazza, Giulio. Impresario; b. Ferrara, It., Feb. 3, 1869. 1898-1908, artistic dir., La Scala; 1908-1935, gen. dir., Met. Op., N. Y.

Gatty, Sir Alfred Scott. Composer; b. Ecclesfield, Eng., Apr. 25, 1847. Comp. operettas, songs.

Gatty, Nicholas Comyn. Organist, composer, conductor; b. Bradfield, Eng., Sept. 13, 1874. Comp. operas, and mus. pcs.

Gaubert, Philippe. Conductor, composer, flutist; b. Cahors, Jul. 4, 1879. 1919, succ. Messager as cond., Conservatoire concerts, Paris; 1920, cond., Paris Opéra. Comp. symph., chamb. mus.

Gaul, Alfred Robert. Composer, organist; b. Norwich, Eng., Apr. 30, 1837; d. Birmingham, Sept. 13, 1913. Best known as comp. of cantata, *The Holy City.*

Gaul, Harvey Bartlett. Organist, composer, teacher, critic; b. New York, Apr. 11, 1881. 1910, t. Carnegie Inst. of Tech., Pittsburgh; mus. critic, *Post* and *Sun.* Comp. organ pcs., songs, cantatas and choruses.

Gauthier, Eva. Mezzo-soprano; b. Ottawa, Can., Sept. 20, 1885. p. Schoen-René. 1909, operatic debut in *Carmen,* at Royal Opera, Pavia. Toured Canada and England w. Emma Albani. Specialized in songs of modern composers. First to introduce jazz on concert program.

Gaviniés (*Ga-veen-yes*), **Pierre.** Violinist, composer; b. Bordeaux, May 26, 1728; d. Paris, Sept. 9, 1800. First violin teacher at Paris Cons. when fd. in 1794. Comp. violin pcs. of considerable technical difficulty, but valuable to advanced students.

Gavronski (*Gah-vron-skee*), **Woitech.** Conductor, composer; b. Sejmony, Pol., Jun. 27, 1868; d. 1913. 1903, Warsaw; 1892, Paderewski prize for 1st str. q.; 1903, Moscow prize for 2nd str. q. Comp. symph., two operas, 4 str. q.; pf. pcs., songs.

Gay, John. Librettist; b. Barnstable, Devon, 1685; d. London, Dec. 4, 1732. 1732, prod., *The Beggar's Opera,* virtually a compilation.

Gay, Maria. Prima donna; b. Barcelona, Jun. 13, 1879. Imprisoned at sixteen for singing a revolutionary song, she devoted herself to singing. Heard at a Pugno concert (1902), she was engaged for the Brussels opera. 1908, Met. Op., N. Y.; 1910, Boston; 1913, Chicago.

Gaynor, Jessie Lovel (née Smith). Composer; b. St. Louis, Feb. 17, 1863; d. Webster Grove, Mo., Feb. 20, 1921. Comp. sch. operettas, and songs for children. Known popularly by her *Slumber Boat.*

Gaztambide (*Gath-tam-bee-deh*), **Joaquin.** Composer, teacher; b. Tuleda, Sp., Feb. 7, 1823; d. Madrid, Mar. 25, 1870. Originated the "grand zarzuela." 1856, fd., Teatro de la Zarzuela. Comp. forty successful zarzuelas, incl., *La Mensajera* (1849).

Gear, George Frederick. Pianist, teacher, composer; b. London, May 21, 1857. Comp. chamb. mus., operettas.

Gebhard, Heinrich. Pianist, composer; b. Sobernheim, Ger., Jul. 25, 1878. Comp. piano pcs.

Gédalge (*Zhay-dalzh*), **André.** Teacher, composer; b. Paris, Dec. 27, 1856. t. Paris Cons. From his counterpoint class came Ravel, Florent Schmitt, Honegger, Darius Milhaud, and the French modernists. Comp. symph., opera comique, chamb. mus. Author of a *Traité de la Fugue.*

Geehl, Henry Ernest. English composer, pianist, conductor; b. London, Sept. 28, 1881. Wr. excellent pf. mus., and songs.

Gehrkens, Karl Wilson. Educator; b. Kelleys Island, Ohio, Apr. 19, 1882. Edu., Oberlin Cons. of Mus. 1907, t. ib.; 1925, ed., *School Music,* and M. T. N. A. *Proceedings.* Author of technical treatises.

Geibel, Adam. Organist, composer; b. Neuenheim, Ger., Sept. 15, 1855; d. Phila., Aug. 3, 1933. 1862, to U. S.; 1897, fd. music publishing house. Blind. Comp. choruses, cantatas, songs, incl., *Sleep, Kentucky Babe.*

Geisler, Paul. Composer, conductor; *b.* Stolp, Ger., Aug. 10, 1856; *d.* Posen, Apr. 3, 1919. 1902, Royal Mus. Dir., Posen. Comp. operas, symph. p., pf. pcs., songs.

Gelink (*Geh-lee-nek*), **Joseph.** Composer; *b.* Selcz, Boh., Dec. 3, 1758; *d.* Vienna, Apr. 13, 1825. Comp. variations.

Geminiani (*Jem-ee-nee-ah-nee*), **Francesco.** Violinist, composer; *b.* Lucca, *c.* 1674; *d.* Dublin, Sept. 17, 1762. One of the great It. violin virtuosi of the eighteenth century. Is credited with the authorship of the first violin method, pub., London, 1740.

Genée, Franz F. R. Operetta librettist, composer; *b.* Danzig, Feb. 7, 1823; *d.* Baden, Jun. 15, 1895. Wr. librettos for Millöcher, von Suppé, and Johann Strauss. Of his several operettas, the best known is *Nanon* (Vienna, 1877). Prod. at the N. Y. Casino in 1886, by Heinrich Conreid, before he became mgr. of Met. Op., it ran for 150 perf. *w.* Pauline Hall and Francis Wilson.

Genss, Hermann. Pianist, composer; *b.* Tilsit, Ger., Jan. 6, 1856. *t.* San Francisco. Comp. orch., choral, chamb. mus.

Gentle, Alice. Soprano, teacher; 1917, debut, La Scala, Milan; 1919, Met. Op.

Georges (*Zhorzh*), **Alexandre.** Organist, composer; *b.* Arras, Fr., Feb. 25, 1850. *t.* Niédermeyer School, Paris. Comp. operas, incid. mus.

Gerardy (*Zhay-rar-dee*), **Jean.** 'Cellist; *b.* Spa, Bel., Dec. 7, 1878. Extensive concert tours, incl. U. S.

Gericke (*Geh-ri-ke*), **Wilhelm.** Conductor; *b.* Graz, Styria, Apr. 18, 1845; *d.* Vienna, Oct. 27, 1925. 1874, dir., Gesellschaft der Musikfreunde; sub-con., *u.* Richter in Vienna; 1884-9, 1898-1906, cond., Boston Symph. Orch., which under him reached front rank.

Gerlach, Theodor. Composer, conductor; *b.* Dresden, Ger., Jun. 25, 1861. Comp. *Epic Symphony;* the opera, *Matteo Falcone;* and lesser wks.

German, J. Edward. Violinist, composer; *b.* Whitchurch, Eng., Feb. 17, 1862. Edu., R. A. M. Devoted his early life to theatre, hence made first success in incid. mus. to plays, chiefly the three dances from his mus. to Sir Henry Irving's *Henry VIII.* He completed Sullivan's *Emerald Isle* and followed with several original operettas, incl., *Tom Jones* (1907); also *Fallen Fairies,* to libretto of W. S. Gilbert. 1928, Knighted. Comp. some effective if not profound symph. and choral comp.

Germer (*Gair-mer*), **Heinrich.** Pianist, teacher; *b.* Sommersdorf, Ger., Dec. 30, 1837; *d.* Dresden, Jan. 4, 1913. Author of educational wks.

Gernsheim (*Gairns-hime*), **Friedrich.** Pianist, composer; *b.* Worms, Ger., Jul. 17, 1839; *d.* Berlin, Sept. 11, 1916. 1874-90, dir., Rotterdam Cons.; 1890-7, *t.* Stern Cons., Berlin. Comp. pf. concerto, quartets, cantata, *Salamis;* symph. wks., incl., *Prologue to a Tragedy.*

Gershwin, George. Composer, pianist; *b.* Brooklyn, N. Y., Sept. 28, 1898. Charles Hambitzer his only teacher. Evolved from Tin-Pan Alley pianist to a jazz-carpenter, but with *Rhapsody in Blue,* established jazz as a serious medium. Has since strengthened his position as one of the more vital of Amer. comp., with additional symph. jazz wks., incl., *Piano Concerto in F,* and *An American in Paris.* With *Porgy and Bess,* the first Amer. Folk-Opera, his claim to serious attention is confirmed. Comp. also many Broadway mus. comedies and cinema successes, incl., *Strike Up the Band,* and *Of Thee I Sing.*

Gerster (*Gair-ster*), **Etelka.** Soprano; *b.* Kaschau, Hun. Jun. 25, 1857; *d.* Berlin, 1920. Fd. sch. for singers in Berlin.

Gerville, Réache Jeanne. Contralto; *b.* Fr., 1882; *d.* N. Y., 1915. 1911, Manhattan Op.; 1913, Chicago Op.

Geselschap, Marie. Pianist; *b.* Batavia, Java, 1874. *t.* Munich; a notable ensemble player.

Gevaërt (*Geh-vahrt*), **François A.** Theorist, composer; *b.* Huysse, Bel., Jul. 31, 1828; *d.* Brussels, Dec. 24, 1908. Author of text-book on harmony.

Ghys, Joseph. Violinist, composer; *b.* Ghent, Bel., 1801; *d.* Petrograd, 1848. Best known for his arr. of *Amaryllis,* the air attributed to Louis XIV.

Gialdini (*Zhyal-dee-nee*), **Gioldino.** Conductor, composer; *b.* Pescia, It., Nov. 10, 1843. Comp. buffo operas.

Giannini, Dusolina. Soprano; *b.* Phila. *p.* Marcella Sembrich. 1923, debut, New York; 1935, Met. Op.

Giardini (*Zhyar-dee-nee*), **Felice de.** Violinist, conductor, composer; *b.* Turin, It., Apr. 12, 1716; *d.* Moscow, Dec. 17, 1796. *p.* Sornis; a brilliant virtuoso.

Gibbons, Christopher. Organist; *b.* London, Aug. 22, 1615; *d.* ib., Aug. 20, 1676. Son of Orlando G.

Gibbons, Orlando. Organist, composer; *b.* Cambridge, 1583; *d.* Canterbury, Jun. 5, 1625. 1604, org., Royal Chapel; 1623, org., Westminster Abbey. A notable madrigal writer, but even more celebrated as comp. of ch. mus.

Gibert (*Zhee-bair*), **Francisco Xavier.** Composer; *b.* Granadella, Sp.; *d.* Madrid, Feb. 27, 1848. A priest.

Gieseking, Walter. Pianist; *b.* Hanover, Ger. *p.* Karl Leimer. 1920, Berlin. 1926, N. Y.

Gigli (*Zheel'-ye*), **Beniamino.** Tenor; *b.* It., Mar. 20, 1890. *p.* Rosati. 1915, debut, Rovigo. 1920, Met. Op., N. Y.

Gigout (*Zhee-goo*), **Eugène.** Organist, composer; *b.* Nancy, Mar. 23, 1844; *d.* Paris, Dec. 30, 1926. *p.* Niédermeyer. *m.* N's daughter, and joined faculty. 1886, fd. organ sch.; 1911, prof., Paris Cons. Organ comp. of distinction.

Gil (*Zhil*), **Francisco Assis.** Teacher, theorist; *b.* Cadiz, Sp., 1829. Prof., Madrid Cons.

Gilbert, Fred. English song writer. 1891, wr. *The Man That Broke the Bank at Monte Carlo.* Interpolated by Wm. Hoey, at opening of Hoyt's "A Parlor Match" (for eighth season, at Bijou Th., 1892) its success was electric.

Gilbert, Harry M. Organist, pianist, composer; *b.* Paducah, Ky. *p.* Alberto Jonas. Accompanist for David Bispham. Org., Fifth Ave. Presby. Ch., N. Y. Comp. songs.

Gilbert, Henry Franklin Belknap. Composer; *b.* Somerville, Mass., Sept. 26, 1868; *d.* Chicago, May 20, 1928. 1889, *p.* MacDowell. 1918, ballet pantomime, *Dance in Place Congo,* perf. Met. Op.; 1921, *Six Indian Sketches,* perf. Boston Symph. Orch. Comp. many orch. wks., pf. pcs., and songs. One of America's unique geniuses, who never quite achieved the success he merited.

Gilchrist, William Wallace. Composer, vocal teacher, conductor; *b.* Jersey City, Jan. 8, 1846; *d.* Easton, Pa., Dec. 20, 1916. Edu., U. of Penn. Org., choirmaster, *t.* and cond., in Phila. Fd., Phila. Mendelssohn chorus; cond., Phila. orch., predecessor of the present Phila. Symph.; 1882, won Cin. Fest. prize, with *Psalm XLVI.* Also comp. cantata, *Song of Thanksgiving,* for chorus and orch., 2 symph., songs, anthems, and part-songs for women's voices.

Gillet (*Zhĕ'-yā*), **Ernest.** Composer, 'cellist; *b.* Paris, Sept. 13, 1856. Edu., Paris Cons. *t.* London. Comp. salon mus., best known by the once popular *Loin du bal.*

Gillette, James Robert. Organist; *b.* Roseboom, N. Y., May 30, 1886. 1913, B.M., Syracuse U.; 1923, prof. org., Carleton Coll.

Gilman, Lawrence. Author, music critic; *b.* Flushing, L. I., Jul. 5, 1878. Author of critical wks. on mus. Since 1932, member of staff, *North American Review,* N. Y.; since 1923, mus. critic, N. Y. *Tribune,* succ. Krehbiel; annotator of program of N. Y. Phil. Orch.

Gilmore, Patrick Sarsfield. Historic bandmaster; *b.* nr. Dublin, Ire., Dec. 25, 1829; *d.* St. Louis, Mo., Sept. 24, 1892. 1869, cond. celebrated Peace Jubilee in Boston, *w.* chorus of 10,000, orch. of 1,000, an anvil chorus of 100 firemen in red shirts, and cannon fired from the conductor's stand by electric buttons, in a coliseum seating 50,000; attended by Pres. U. S. Grant and innumerable notables.

Gilson (*Zheel-song*), **Paul.** Composer; *b.* Brussels, Jun. 15, 1865. Leading Belgian composer. Since 1909, inspector of mus. edu. in Belgium. Comp. operas, incl., *Princess Sunshine* (1903); symph., cantatas, and small pcs. Author of theoretical wks.

Giordani (*Zhyor-dah-nee*), **Tomaso.** Composer, vocal teacher; *b.* Naples, 1744; *d.* Ferma, Jan. 4, 1798.

Giordano (*Zhyor-dah-no*), **Umberto.** Italian operatic composer; *b.* Foggia, It., Aug. 27, 1867. *Andre Chénier* first established his world fame, première Mar. 26, 1896, at La Scala, Milan, and quickly repeated all over the world. 1924, comp. opera on Sam Benelli's *La Cena della beffe.* Comp. also *Mala, Vita, Regina Diaz, Fedora, Siberia,* and *Mme. Sans-Gene.*

Giorzo (*Zhyor-tsa*), **Paolo.** Composer; *b.* Milan, 1838; *d.* Seattle, May 4, 1914. Comp. marches, ballets, ch. mus.

Girard, Narcisse. Conductor, opera impresario; *b.* Nantes, Jan. 27, 1797; *d.* Paris, Jan. 16, 1860. One of the historic general directors of the Paris Opéra.

Gittelson, Frank. Violinist; *b.* Phila., Jun. 12, 1896. *p.* Flesch. 1913, debut, Berlin, Gabrilovitch conducting; 1914, debut, Phila. Symph.; 1919, *t.* Peabody Cons.

Giucci, Carlos. Pianist, composer; *b.* Montevideo, 1904. *p.* Ignacio Friedman. Comp. *Candombe,* perf. by Benno Moiseivitsch. Comp. pf. pcs. in the Spanish idiom.

Giuglini (*Zhyul-yee-nee*), **Antonio.** Tenor; *b.* Fano, It., 1827; *d.* Pesaro, It., Oct. 12, 1865.

Gladstone, Francis E. Organist, composer; *b.* nr. Oxford, Eng., Mar. 2, 1845. Prof., R. C. M.

Glareanus (*Glah-reh-ah-noos*), **Henricus.** Teacher, theorist; *b.* Glarus, Switz., Jun., 1488; *d.* Freiburg, Mar. 26, 1563. Author of treatises on medieval mus.

Glazounoff (*Glah-zoo-nof*), **Alexander Constantinovitch.** Composer; *b.* Petrograd, Aug. 10, 1865; *d.* Paris, Mar. 21, 1936. Edu., Polytechnic Inst. *p.* Rimsky-Korsakoff. An extremely precocious talent, his first symph. was perf. by Balakireff in 1882; 1906, dir., Petrograd Cons. Violin concerto perf. by Zimbalist at N. Y. debut; 1929, cond. gala concert of his wks. at Met. Op., N. Y., and toured U. S. Comp. also eight symph., symph. p., ballet, *Raymonda;* chamb. mus., pf. pcs., and songs.

Gleason, Frederick Grant. Composer, teacher; *b.* Middletown, Conn., Dec. 17, 1848; *d.* Chicago, Dec. 6, 1903. *p.* Dudley Buck. *t.* Eleanor Everest Freer, Mortimer Wilson, and many Amer. comp. of his generation. 1896, symph. p., *Edris,* based on novel by Marie Corelli, perf. by Th. Thomas *w.* Chicago Orch. Comp. cantata, *Culprit Fay,* also operas, incl., *Otho Visconti,* and *Montezuma.* In his will, he stipulated that his remaining operas be sealed until fifty years after his death.

Glière, Reinhold Moritzovitch. Composer; *b.* Kieff, Jan. 11, 1875. Prof. of comp., Moscow Cons. Comp. symph., chamb. mus., pf. pcs., songs.

Glinka, Mikhail Ivanovitch. Composer; *b.* Novospaskoï, Rus., Jun. 1, 1804; *d.* Berlin, Feb. 15, 1857. Russia's first Nationalist. 1836, prod. opera, *Life for the Czar,* his most historic work. Outside of Rus., best known by concert wks., *La Jota Aragonese,* and *Kamarinskaja.*

Glover, Charles W. Composer; *b.* London, Feb., 1806; *d.* ib., Mar. 23, 1863. Comp. popular songs and duets.

Glover, Sarah Ann. Teacher, writer; *b.* Norwich, Eng., 1785; *d.* Malvern, Oct. 20, 1867. Early exponent of the *tonic sol-fa* system.

Glover, Stephen. Composer; *b.* London, 1812; *d.* ib., Dec. 7, 1870. Comp. many popular ballads.

Glover, William Henry. Violinist, composer; *b.* London, 1819; *d.* New York, 1875. 1868, N. Y. mus. critic.

Gluck (*Glook*), **Alma** (pseud. of Reba Fierson). Soprano; *b.* Bucharest, Roumania, May 11, 1886. Opera and concert artist; *m.* Efrem Zimbalist, violinist.

Gluck, Christoph Willibald. Composer; *b.* Weidenwang, Ger., Jul. 2, 1714; *d.* Vienna, Nov. 15, 1787. Studied mus. in Prague, Vienna, and Milan. Wr. some successful operas in the conventional It. style of the period. With the comp. of *Orfeo ed Eurydice,* Gluck entered upon his career as a reformer of opera, writing an important chapter in the history of mus. Gluck triumphed in a memorable contest *w.* Piccinni.

Gniessin, Michael. Composer; *b.* Rostov-on-Don, Rus., Jan. 23, 1883. Edu., Petrograd Cons., *u.* Rimsky-Korsakoff and Glazounoff. 1908, orch. tone-poem, *After Shelley,* perf. by Alex. Siloti. Later, prof. at Moscow Cons. Called "Jewish Glinka," for his operas, *Youth of Abraham* and the *Maccabeans.* Comp. also orch. wks.; and chamb. mus., incl. sonata, *Ballade for 'Cello;* and many characteristic songs.

Gobbaerts, Jean Louis. Composer; *b.* Antwerp, Bel., Sept. 28, 1835; *d.* Saint-Gilles, Bel., May 5, 1886. Comp. easy piano teaching mus., under the names of "Streabbog," "Ludovic" and "Levi."

Godard (*Go-dar*), **Benjamin.** Composer; *b.* Paris, Aug. 18, 1849; *d.* Cannes, Fr., Jan. 10, 1895. Comp. operas, incl., *Jocelyn,* containing his famous *Berceuse;* violin pcs., incl., *Adagio Pathetique;* the violin *Concerto romantique;* besides symph. and chamb. mus., pf. pcs., songs.

Goddard, Arabella. Pianist; *b.* Saint-Servan, Brittany, Jan. 12, 1836; *d.* Fr., 1922. A distinguished Eng. concert artist.

Godefroid (*Gode-frwah*), **Félix.** Harpist, composer; *b.* Namur, Bel., Jul. 24, 1818; *d.* Villers-sur-Mer, Bel., Jul. 8, 1897. Comp. pcs. for harp and piano.

Godfrey, Charles. Bandmaster; *b.* Kingston, Eng., Nov. 22, 1790; *d.* London, Dec. 12, 1863. Bandmaster, Coldstream Guards.

Godfrey, Charles, 2nd. *b.* London, Jan. 17, 1839. Bandmaster, Royal Horse Guards.

Godfrey, Charles, 3rd. British bandmaster; *b.* London, 1867; *d.* ib., 1935.

Godfrey, Daniel. Bandmaster, composer; *b.* Westminster, Eng., Sept. 4, 1831; *d.* Beeston, Eng., Jun. 30, 1903. Famous for his military band.

Godfrey, Sir Dan. Conductor; *b.* London, 1868. 1890, cond., London Military Band; 1893, cond., Bournemouth Municipal Orch. Distinguished g.-cond. of London Orch., and international authority on band mus.

Godowsky, Leopold. Pianist, composer; *b.* Vilna, Pol., Feb. 13, 1870. 1884-5, toured U. S.; 1887-90, *p.* Saint-Saëns; 1890-1900, *t.* U. S.; 1900-09, *t.* Berlin; 1909-12, *t.* Vienna; 1912, to U. S. Comp. long list of pf. wks., incl., 46 *Miniatures,* for pf., 4 hands. Phenomenal technician; authority on modern piano technic.

Goepp (*Gepp*), **Philip Henry.** Writer, composer; *b.* New York, Jun. 23, 1864. 1884, A.B., Harvard; 1892, *t.* Phila.; 1900-21, wr. analytical program notes for Phila. Symph.

Goetschius, Percy. Theorist, teacher, composer; *b.* Paterson, N. J., Aug. 30, 1853. Edu., Stuttgart Cons. 1890, *t.* Syracuse U.; 1892, N. E. Cons.; 1905, *t.* Inst. of Mus. Art, N. Y. Author of textbooks on harmony, counterpoint, composition. Comp. overtures, orch. suites, ch. mus., organ and piano wks.

Goetz (*Gets*), **Hermann.** Composer; *b.* Königsberg, Ger., Dec. 17, 1840; *d.* Hottingen, Switz., Dec. 3, 1876. Comp. opera on *The Taming of the Shrew;* also a symph.

Goldbeck, Robert. Pianist, composer; *b.* Potsdam, Apr. 19, 1839; *d.* St. Louis, May 16, 1908. 1857, N. Y.; 1867, co.-fd., N. E. Cons. Life full of changes. Comp. operas, cantatas, chamb. mus., songs. Author of theoretical wks.

Golde, Walter. Voice teacher; *b.* Brooklyn, N. Y. St., Vienna Cons. Accompanist for Richard Bonelli, Mischa Elman, Jacques Thibaud. *t.* New York. Comp. songs.

Goldmark, Carl. Composer; *b.* Keszthely, Hun., May 18, 1830; *d.* Vienna, Jan. 3, 1915. Comp. operas incl., *Queen of Sheba, Cricket on the Hearth,* and *Winter's Tale; Rustic Wedding* symph., and other orch. wks.

Goldmark, Rubin. Composer, teacher; *b.* N. Y., Aug. 15, 1872; *d.* ib., Mar. 6, 1936. Nephew of Carl G. *t.* comp., Juilliard Grad. Sch. Long a member of Bohemian club. As a teacher of composition strongly influenced many Amer. composers, incl., Robert Runel Bennel, Charles N. Grant, and others. 1910, won Paderewski prize for pf. q.; 1925-36, prof., Juilliard Gr. Sch. Comp. *Theme and Variations* for orch., overture, *Hiawatha;* symph. p., *Samson and Delilah;* cantata, and chamb. mus.

Goldschmidt, Otto. Conductor, pianist, composer; *b.* Hamburg, Ger., Aug. 21, 1829; *d.* London, Feb. 24, 1907. 1851, accompanist for Jenny Lind, on first Amer. tour (*m.* her in 1852).

Gollmick, Adolf. Pianist, violinist, composer; *b.* Frankfort, Feb. 5, 1825; *d.* London, Mar. 7, 1883.

Golschmann, Vladimir. Conductor; *b.* Paris, Dec. 16, 1893. 1919, fd., Concerts Golschmann, Paris, introd. wks. of younger Fr. comp. 1924, g.-cond., N. Y. Symph.; 1925, **cond.**, St. Louis Symph., succ. Ganz.

Goltermann, G. E. 'Cellist, composer; *b.* Hanover, Aug. 19, 1824; *d.* Frankfort, Dec. 29, 1898. Comp. 'cello concerto.

Gomes, Antonio Carlos. Brazilian composer; *b.* Campinas, Brazil, Jul. 11, 1836; *d.* Belem, Brazil, May 19, 1896. 1861, opera, *Noite do Castello,* prod. Rio de Janeiro; 1870, *Il Guarany,* prod. La Scala, Milan, accl. by Verdi; 1891, *Condor,* première, La Scala. Comp. many other operas, symph. wks., incl., *Colombo,* and misc. pcs.

Gompertz, Richard. Violinist; *b.* Cologne, Apr. 27, 1859. *p.* Joachim. *t.* Cambridge, Eng.; 1883, prof., R. C. M.; fd. G. Str. Q.; 1899, to Dresden.

Goodrich, Alfred John. Theorist, author, teacher; *b.* Chilo, O., May 8, 1847; *d.* Paris, May 25, 1920. Author of textbooks on mus. comp.

Goodrich, Frederick William. Organist, composer; *b.* London, 1867. Prof., U. of Oregon; pres., Ore. Mus. T. Assoc.

Goodrich, John Wallace. Organist, conductor, teacher; *b.* Newton, Mass., May 27, 1871. *p.* Widor. 1897, *t.,* dean, dir., N. E. Cons., Boston.

Goodson, Katherine. Pianist; *b.* Watford, Eng., Jun. 18, 1872. *p.* Leschetizky. A leader among women pianists of her epoch. Toured U. S. 1903, *m.* Arthur Hinton (q. v.).

Goodwin, Emina Beatrice. Pianist, writer; *b.* Manchester, Eng., Dec. 5, 1867. *p.* Clara Schumann. 1904, fd. London trio. Author, *Hints on Technique and Touch in Piano Playing.*

Goossens, Eugene. Conductor; *b.* London, May 26, 1893. Son of comp. of same name (*b.* 1867). Asst. cond., Sir Thomas Beecham's Queen's Hall Orch.; cond., première of Stanford's opera, *The Critic;* 1921, fd. own orch., devoted to new and unfamiliar mus.; 1922, Covent Garden; 1926, the Diaghilev Ballet; also g.-cond., N. Y. Symph. Orch.; 1931, cond., Cin. Symph. Orch. Comp. orch. wks.

Goovaerts, Alphonse Jean Marie André. Composer, historian; *b.* Antwerp, May 25, 1847; *d.* Brussels, Dec. 25, 1922. 1866, city librarian, Antwerp; 1887, keeper of state archives, Brussels. Author of musicological wks.

Goria, A. E. Pianist, composer; *b.* Paris, Jan. 21, 1823; *d.* ib., Jul. 6, 1860. Comp. salon mus.

Gordon, Jacques. Violinist; *b.* Rus. *p.* Kneisel. *t.* Amer. Cons. of Mus., Chicago.

Gordon, Westell. 'Cellist, composer, tenor; *b.* London. Comp. popular songs.

Gorno, Albino. Pianist, composer; *b.* Casalmorano, It., *c.* 1859; *d.* Cincinnati, Nov. 28, 1931. Edu., Milan Cons. 1881, to U. S., as accompanist for Patti; 1882, *t.* Coll. of Mus., Cincinnati. Comp. wks. for pf., and pf. w. orch.; cantatas, operettas. Author of technical treatises.

Gorter, Albert. Composer; *b.* Nuremberg, Ger., Nov. 23, 1862. Cond., Mainz. Comp. operas, orch. wks.

Goss, Sir John. Organist, composer; *b.* Fareham, Eng., Dec. 27, 1800; *d.* London, May 10, 1880. Edu., Chapel Royal. 1838, org., St. Paul's Cath.; 1872, Knighted. Comp. anthems. Author of *Introduction to Harmony.*

Goss-Custard, Reginald. English organist; *b.* St. Leonards-on-Sea, Mar. 29, 1877. 1902-14, org., St. Margaret's, Westminster. 1916, toured U. S.; 1922, org., St. Michael's, London.

Gossec, François Joseph. Composer; *b.* Vergnies, Bel., Jan. 17, 1734; *d.* Passy, Fr., Feb. 16, 1829. Fd., symph. mus. in Fr.; perfected the orch. technic. 1762, cond., private orch. of Prince Conti, at Chantilly; 1773, fd., *Concerts Spirituals;* 1780, cond., Paris Op. Assisted in organizing of Paris Cons. Comp. operas and symph. of repute in their day. Chiefly remembered today by a *Gavotte* for violin; also arr. for piano.

Gottschalk, Louis Moreau. Pianist, composer; *b.* New Orleans, La., May 8, 1829; *d.* Rio de Janiero, Brazil, Dec. 18, 1869. Jewish Creole parentage. The original matinée idol. Comp. operas and symph. wks., and piano pcs., incl., *Last Hope,* his most popular work.

Götze (*Get-ze*), **Karl.** Composer; *b.* Weimar, 1836; *d.* Madgeburg, Jan. 14, 1877. Comp. symph. p., operas.

Goudimel, Claude. Composer; *b.* Vaison, Fr., *c.* 1505; *d.* Lyons, Aug. 24, 1572. Comp. ch. mus.

Gould, Herbert Bingham. Basso cantante; *b.* Saranac, Mich., Jun. 12, 1886. 1922-23, Chicago Op.; 1927, Cin. May fest.

Gounod (*Goo-no*), **Charles François.** Composer; *b.* Paris, Jun. 17, 1818; *d.* ib., Oct. 17, 1893. Edu., Paris Cons. 1859, opera, *Faust,* established his reputation. Comp. other operas, incl., *La Reine de Saba, Roméo et Juliette;* oratorios, *Rédemption, Mors et Vita;* cantatas, anthems, and sacred songs, some to English texts.

Gow, George Coleman. Author, teacher; *b.* Ayer, Mass., Nov. 27, 1860. 1889, *t.* Smith Coll.; 1895, prof., Vassar Coll. Comp. songs, part-songs. Author of technical treatises.

Gow, Niel. Violinist; *b.* Inver, Scot., Mar. 22, 1727; *d.* ib., Mar. 1, 1807. Notable for his performances of Scottish dance tunes.

Graben-Hoffman, Gustav. Composer; *b.* Bnin, Ger., Mar. 7, 1820; *d.* Potsdam, May 20, 1900. Ballad comp.

Grace, Harvey. English organist, writer; *b.* Romsey, Jan. 25, 1874. 1918, ed., *Musical Times.* Comp. organ pcs., songs.

Graedener, Hermann. Composer, teacher; *b.* Kiel, May 8, 1844. 1892-1913, prof., Vienna U., then pensioned. Comp. symph., chamb. mus. Son of Karl G.

Graedener, Karl. Composer; *b.* Rostock, Ger., Jan. 14, 1812; *d.* Hamburg, Jun. 10, 1883. Comp. symph., oratorios, concerto.

Graener, Paul. Composer; *b.* Berlin, Jan. 11, 1872. Largely self-taught. 1896, to London, cond., Haymarket Th.; *t.* R. A. M.; 1920, prof., Leipzig Cons.; 1925, resigned, and settled in Berlin, to comp. seriously; 1934, awarded Beethoven Prize of Prus. Acad. of Arts; 1935, succ. Richard Strauss, as pres., League of Ger. Comp. Comp. orch. wks., incl., *Sinfonietta;* opera, incl., *Das Narrangericht;* chamb. mus., choral mus., incl., *Wiebke Pogwisch;* pf. pcs., violin pcs., and songs.

Graham, George Farquhar. Writer; *b.* Edinburgh, Scot., Dec. 29, 1789; *d.* ib., Mar. 12, 1867. An authority on Scotch mus.

Grainger, Percy. Pianist, composer; *b.* Melbourne, Australia, Jul. 8, 1882. *p.* Busoni. 1892, began career as prodigy; 1900, concertizing in London, intro. Grieg *Concerto* at Leeds Fest., Grieg conducting; 1912, own wks. for orch. intro. Queen's Hall; 1915, to U. S.; became citizen; *h.* White Plains, N. Y. Specializes in folk-music. Comp. orch. wks., incl., *In a Nutshell;* choral wks., incl., *Sir Eglamore;* pf. pcs., transcriptions, songs.

Gram, Hans. Composer, organist; 1790, org., Brattle St. Ch., Boston; 1791, comp. first orch. score published in U. S., *The Death Song of an Indian Chief.*

Grammann, Karl. Composer; *b.* Lübeck, Ger., Mar. 3, 1844; *d.* Dresden, Jan. 30, 1897. Comp. opera, symph., cantata, violin concerto.

Granados y Campina, Enrique. Composer, pianist; *b.* Lerida, Sp., Jul. 27, 1867; *d.* Mar. 24, 1916, on steamer Sussex, torpedoed in English Channel, while enroute home from première of opera, *Goyescas,* at Met. Op., N. Y. Comp. many pf. wks., with some symph. mus.

Granberry, George Folsom. Piano teacher; Disciple of Faelten methods in primary piano study. Dir., Granberry Sch. of Mus., N. Y., and Summer Sch. of Mus., U. of Georgia. Author of *Musical Development Through Sight, Touch and Hand.*

Grandval, Maria de Reiset. Composer; *b.* Saint-Rémy des Monts, Fr., Jan. 20, 1830; *d.* Paris, Jan. 15, 1907. Comp. operas, orch. wks.

Graninger, Charles Albert. Organist, pianist, teacher; *b.* Cincinnati, O., Jan. 2, 1861. *t.* Coll. of Mus., Cincinnati.

Grant-Schaeffer, George Alfred. Organist, composer, vocal teacher; *b.* Williamstown, Ont., 1872. 1908-21, *t.* Northwestern U.

Grasse, Edwin. Violinist, composer; *b.* New York, Aug. 13, 1884. 1901, gr., Brussels Cons., *u.* Thomson; 1902, debut, Berlin Phil.; 1903, debut, N. Y., in Brahms concerto. Comp. symph., concerto, chamb. mus., and many pcs. for the violin. Became blind in infancy. Career largely in N. Y.

Grau, Maurice. Impresario; *b.* Brünn, Aus., 1849; *d.* Paris, Mar. 14, 1907. 1867, gr., Columbia Law Sch.; 1872-1883, managed tours of Rubinstein, Wieniawski, Sarah Bernhardt, Offenbach, Salvini, and Clara Louise Kellogg; 1891-1903, gen. Mgr., Met. Op., N. Y.

Graun, Johann Gottlieb. Violinist; *b.* Wahrenbruck, Ger., *c.* 1698; *d.* Berlin, Oct. 27, 1771. *p.* Pisendel and Tartini. In the service of Frederick the Great; cond., Royal Orch.; *t.* Friedemann Bach.

Graupner, Johann Christian Gottlieb. Conductor, oboist; *b.* Verden, Ger., Oct. 6, 1767; *d.* Boston, Apr. 16, 1836. 1791, played in Haydn's orch. in London; 1795, to Charleston, U. S.; 1798, to Boston; 1810, fd. Phil. Soc.; 1815, fd. Handel and Haydn Soc. *w.* Thomas Smith Webb and Asa Peabody. Known as the father of Amer. orch. mus.; also originated the vogue of Negro minstrelsy, singing *The Gay Negro Boy* in character at end of second act of *Oroonoko,* Dec. 30, 1779, at Federal St. Th., Boston, in costume and accompanying himself on the banjo, with which he became acquainted in Charleston.

Gray, Alan. English organist, composer; *b.* York, Dec. 23, 1855; *d.* Cambridge, Eng., Sept. 27, 1935. Edu., Trinity Coll., Cambridge. 1883-92, mus. dir., Wellington Coll.; 1893-12, cond., C. U. M. S.; 1922-3, Pres., R. C. O., London. Comp. cantatas, incl., *Arethusa,* and anthems.

Grazzini, Reginaldo. Composer; b. Florence, It., Oct. 15, 1848; d. Venice, 1906. Comp. cantatas, masses, symph., opera.

Greatorex, Thomas. Organist; b. N. Wingfield, Eng., Oct. 5, 1758; d. Hampton, Jul. 18, 1831. Wr. tunes still found in the hymn books.

Greene, Herbert Wilber. Vocal teacher; b. Holyoke, Mass., 1860. 1885, fd., Met. Coll. of Mus., w. Chas. B. Hawley; 1900, fd., Brookfield Center (Conn.) Summer Sch.; 1895, pres., M. T. N. A.

Greene, Maurice. Organist, composer; b. London, 1695; d. ib., 1755. Projected the great *Cathedral Music* collection, afterward completed by Boyce.

Gregoir (*Gre-gwahr*), **Edouard.** Composer, writer, historian; b. Turnhout, Bel., Nov. 7, 1822; d. Wyneghem, Jun. 28, 1890. Comp. opera, but fame rests on large output of musicological investigations.

Gresser, Emily. Violinist; b. Newark, N. J., Mar. 11, 1896. p. Sam Franko. 1914, début, New York; toured in U. S. and Europe; several seasons w. Mme. Yvette Guilbert.

Gretchaninoff, Alexander. Composer; b. Moscow, Oct. 25, 1864. 1881, entered Petrograd Cons., st. Rimsky-Korsakoff; 1903, opera, *Dobrynia Nikitich*, prod. w. Chaliapin. Comp operas, orch. wks., incl., *Scherezade;* chamb. mus.; sacred choral mus., incl., *Three Liturgies of St. John Chrysostom,* and old Rus. sacred melodies; songs, incl., *Snowflakes.* After revolution, domiciled in Paris.

Grétry (*Gray-tree*), **André Ernest Modeste.** Composer; b. Liége, Feb. 18, 1741; d. Montmorency, Fr., Sept. 24, 1813. A prolific and once celebrated writer of Fr. operas.

Grey, Frank Herbert. Conductor, composer; b. Phila., Nov. 15, 1883. Edu., Harvard U. Cond. of mus. comedies. Comp. pf. pcs., songs, incl., *Mother o' Mine.*

Grieg, Edvard Hagerup. Pianist, composer; b. Bergen, Nor., Jun. 15, 1843; d. ib., Sept. 4, 1907. Edu., Leipzig Cons. As org., in Copenhagen, came under the influence of Gade. Comp. piano concerto, three violin sonatas, many pf. pcs., and songs, all with pronounced Norwegian flavor. Best known by his *Peer Gynt Suite,* and the song, *I Love Thee,* written for his wife, Nina (1845-1935).

Griffes, Charles Tomlinson. Composer; b. Elmira, Sept. 17, 1884; d. Tarrytown, Apr. 9, 1920. p. Humperdinck. 1908, t. Hackley Sch., Tarrytown. His untimely death was a serious loss to Amer. mus. Comp. orch. work, *The Pleasure Dome of Kubla Khan;* poem for flute and orch.; piano, *Roman Sketches;* three tone pictures; many songs.

Griffis, Elliot. Composer, pianist, teacher; b. Boston, Mass. St. Dr. Horatio Parker. 1920-23, t. Grinnell Coll., Ia.; 1924, Brooklyn Settlement Sch. Comp. *Sunlight and Shadows,* piano sonata, songs.

Grimm, C. Hugo. Organist, teacher, composer; b. Zanesville, Ohio, Oct. 31, 1890. p. van der Stucken. 1927, N. F. M. C. prize, for *Erotic Poem,* perf. Chicago Symph.; 1930, MacDowell Club prize for choral wk., *Song of Songs;* t. Cin. Cons. of Mus.; son of Carl W. G. Comp. symph. p.; other choral wks.; organ pcs., and songs.

Grimm, Carl William. Pianist, organist, teacher; b. Dayton, O., Jun. 8, 1863. Prin., Carl W. Grimm Corr. Sch. of Harmony; since 1893, t. in Cincinnati; 1931, comp., *Sonata Allegro* for pf.; author textbooks: *Modern Harmony,* etc.

Grisar (*Gree-zahr*), **Albert.** Composer; b. Antwerp, Bel., Dec. 26, 1808; d. Asnières, Fr., Jun. 15, 1869. Comp. operas

Griselle, Thomas. Composer. 1928, awarded R. C. A.-Victor prize for *Two American Sketches.*

Grisi (*Gree-zee*), **Giulia.** Soprano; b. Milan, Jul. 28, 1811; d. Berlin, Nov. 29, 1869. A celebrated prima donna, famed for voice and beauty.

Grodsky, Boleslaus. Composer; b. Petrograd, Oct. 13, 1865. Comp. pf. pcs.

Grove, Sir George. Writer; b. Clapham, Eng., Aug. 13, 1820; d. Sydenham, May 28, 1900. Author of a series of analytical programs for the Crystal Palace Concerts. 1883, first principal, R. C. M.; upon its inauguration was knighted. As ed. of a *Dictionary of Music and Musicians,* he rendered a lasting service to the cause of mus.

Grovlez, Gabriel. Pianist, composer; b. Lille, Fr., 1879. 1914, cond., Paris Opera; 1921, cond., Chicago Op.; prod. ballet, *Au vrai arbre de Robinson.* Comp. orch. wks., ballets, pf. pcs., songs.

Gruenberg (*Green-bairg*), **Eugene.** Violinist, teacher; b. Lemberg, Oct. 30, 1854. 1899, t. N. E. Cons. Comp. symph., ballet, violin pcs. Author of educational wks. for the violin.

Gruenberg, Louis. Composer, pianist; b. Rus., Aug. 3, 1883. 1885, to U. S.; 1933 (Jan. 7), opera, *Emperor Jones,* prod. Met. Op. Travels much, abroad 25 times; prefers N. Mexico for h. Comp. operas, orch. wks., incl., *Jazz Suite, Enchanted Isle, Music to an Imaginary Ballet;* chamb. mus., incl., *Daniel Jazz,* quintet.

Gruenfeld (*Green-felt*), **Alfred.** Pianist, composer; b. Prague, Boh., Jul. 4, 1852; d. Vienna, 1924. Distinguished as a Mozart player. Comp. operettas, and pf. pcs., incl., *Romance.*

Gruenfeld, Heinrich. 'Cellist; b. Prague, Apr. 21, 1855; d. Berlin, Aug. 26, 1931. A distinguished virtuoso. Brother of Alfred G.

Grunn, Homer. Pianist, teacher, composer; b. W. Salem, Wis., May 5, 1880. St. Berlin. 1903-7, t. Chicago Mus. Coll.; 1910, fd. Brahms Quintet in Los Angeles. Comp. orch. and pf. pcs., incl., *Hopi Indian Dance.*

Gruppe, Paulo Mesdag. Violoncellist; b. Rochester, N. Y. 1891, p. Casals. 1909, to U. S.; t. Arnold Volpe Cons.; fd. Gruppe Trio.

Grützmacher (*Greetz-macher*), **Friedrich.** 'Cellist; b. Dessau, Ger., Mar. 1, 1832; d. Dresden, Feb. 23, 1903. Distinguished virtuoso.

Guarnerius, Giuseppe (Joseph) Antonio. Violin maker; b. Jun. 8, 1683; d. c. 1742. The greatest of the Italian violin makers.

Gudehus (*Goo-de-hoos*), **Heinrich.** Tenor; b. Altenhagen, Ger., Mar. 30, 1845; d. Dresden, Oct. 9, 1909. Eminent in Wagnerian opera rôles. 1882, created rôle of *Parsifal* in Bayreuth; 1891, in N. Y. German Op.

Guglielmi (*Gool-yel-mee*), **Pietro.** Composer; b. Marsa di Carrara, It., May, 1727; d. Rome, Nov. 19, 1804. Comp. operas, ch. mus.

Gui, Vittoria. Conductor; b. Rome, Sept. 14, 1885. 1907, cond., San Carlo, Naples; 1925, gen. mus. dir., Turino; 1933, cond., *Florentino Mai.*

Guidi (*Gwee-dee*), **Scipione.** Violinist; b. Venice, 1884. Edu., Milan Cons. Fd. Guidi Trio, London; mem. New York Trio.

Guido d'Arezzo (*Gwee-do dar-ret-so*). Theorist, teacher; b. Arezzo, It., c. 995; d. c. 1050. Devised a system of mus. notation; the first to use the syllables *ut, re, mi, fa, sol, la.*

Guilford, Nanette. Soprano; b. New York, Aug. 17, 1907. Debut, Met. Op. at 17, after a year in mus. comedy. 1928, *m.* Max Rosen, violinist (divorced).

Guilmant (*Geel-mong*), **Félix Alexandre.** Organist, composer; b. Boulogne, Mar. 12, 1837; d. Meudon, Fr., Mar. 30, 1911. Distinguished concert org., and teacher. Comp. organ sonatas and pcs. Published his own mus.

Guimera, Angal. Lyric writer; d. 1924. A poet whose wks. are much set to mus. Author of *Tema Baixa*, on which is based the libretto of d'Albert's *Tiefland.*

Guion, David Wendel Fentress. Pianist, composer; b. Ballinger, Tex. *p.* Leopold Godowsky. Dir., Southwestern Sch. of Fine Arts, Dallas. Comp. pf. pcs., arr. negro spirituals, and folk melodies, incl., *Turkey in the Straw.*

Guiraud (*Gee-ro*), **Ernest.** Composer; b. New Orleans, Jun. 23, 1837; d. Paris, May 6, 1892. Son of Jean Bapt. G. 1876, prof., Paris Cons. Comp. operas-comiques, ballets, incl., *Gretna Green* (1873); orch., pf. pcs. Author, *Treatise on Instrumentation.*

Gumbert (*Goom-bairt*), **Ferdinand.** Composer; b. Berlin, Apr. 22, 1818; d. ib., Apr. 6, 1896. Comp. songs, operettas.

Gungl (*Goongl*), **Johann.** Composer; b. Zsàmbék, Hun., Mar. 5, 1828; d. Fünfkirchen, Nov. 27, 1883. Nephew of Joseph G. Comp. dance melodies, once popular.

Gungl, Joseph. Composer; b. Zsàmbék, Hun., Jan. 1, 1810; d. Weimar, Jan. 31, 1889. Comp. dances, marches.

Gunn, Glenn Dillard. Pianist, critic; b. Topeka, Kan., 1874. *p.* Teichmuller. 1896-99, Asst. to Teichmuller; 1920, fd. Gunn Sch. of Mus., Chicago; 1901-03, mus. critic, Chicago *Journal;* 1903-10, Chicago *Inter-Ocean;* 1910-14, Chicago *Tribune;* since 1914, Chicago *Herald and Examiner.*

Gura, Eugene. Baritone; b. Pressern, Boh., Nov. 8, 1842; d. Munich, Aug. 26, 1906. Opera and concert singer.

Gura, Hermann. Baritone; b. Breslau, Apr. 5, 1870. *t.* singing. 1911-16, Stage Dir. of Komische Op., Berlin.

Gurlitt (*Goor-lit*), **Cornelius.** Composer; b. Altona, Ger., Feb. 10, 1820; d. ib., Jun. 17, 1901. Historian of the fine arts; best known by his teaching pcs. for piano.

Gutheil-Schoder, Marie. Opera singer; b. Weimar, Feb. 10, 1874; d. Thuringea, 1935. 1891-1900, Hoftheater, Weimar; 1900, Vienna Op. One of the chief interpreters of Mahler's wks.

Gutmann (*Goot-mahn*), **Adolphe.** Pianist, composer; b. Heidelberg, Jan. 12, 1819; d. Spezia, Oct. 27, 1882. Friend and *p.* Chopin; wr. many pf. pcs.

Gyrowetz (*Gee-ro-vetz*), **Adalbert.** Composer; b. Budweis, Boh., Feb. 19, 1763; d. Vienna, Mar. 19, 1850. Comp. symph., opera.

H

Haake, Charles J. Piano teacher; b. Chicago. Mus.B., Northwestern U. *p.* Ottokar Malek. 1910-26, *t.* Northwestern U.; 1927, *t.* Amer. Cons.

Haake, Gail Martin. Piano teacher; b. Liscon, Ia. St. Chicago Mus. Coll. 1912-26, *t.* Northwestern U.; 1927, *t.* Amer. Cons. of Mus.

Haba, Alois. Composer, violinist; b. Vyzovice, Moravia, Jun. 21, 1893. Edu., Prague Cons.; Berlin Hochschule, *u.* Franz Schreker. 1921, *Symphonic Fantasy,* for piano and orch., perf. at Dusseldorf. Notably an experimenter with quarter-tone mus. *h.* Prague. Engaged in comp. opera and *Neue Erde* (unfinished). Comp. operas, incl., *Die Mutter; Choral Suite;* orch. pcs., incl., *Der Weg des Lebens;* chamb. mus., incl., *Second Quarter-Tone Quartet;* and pcs. for quarter-tone piano.

Habeneck (*Ab-nek*), **François Antoine.** Violinist, conductor; b. Mézieres, Fr., Jan. 23, 1781; d. Paris, Feb. 8, 1849. 1828-1848, cond., Société des Concerts du Conservatoire, a celebrated orch. series fd. by him.

Haberbier (*Hah-behr-beer*), **Ernst.** Pianist, composer; b. Königsberg, Oct. 5, 1813; d. Bergen, Nor., Mar. 12, 1869. Comp. salon mus., pf. études.

Habert, Johannes Evangelista. Organist, composer; b. Oberplan, Boh., Oct. 18, 1833; d. Gmunden, Ger., Sept. 1, 1896. Comp. masses, organ pcs.

Habich, Eduard. Baritone; b. Sept. 3, 1889. 1935, Met. Op., N. Y.

Hackett, Charles. Tenor; b. Worcester, Mass. Debut, Genoa Op.; first Amer. tenor to sing at La Scala; 1919, Met. Op.; Chicago Civic Op.

Hackett, Karleton Spalding. Music critic; b. Brookline, Mass., Oct. 8, 1867; d. Chicago, Oct. 7, 1935. 1888-9, Harvard U.; 1893, Chicago U.; 1906, Mus. critic, Chicago *Evening Post;* pres., Amer. Cons. Mus.

Hackh, Otto Christoph. Composer, pianist; b. Würtemberg, Sept. 30, 1852; d. Brooklyn, 1917. *t.* New York. Comp. piano pcs., songs, dance mus.

Hadley, Henry Kimball. Composer, conductor; b. Somerville, Mass., Dec. 20, 1871. St. Munich; cond., Cologne op., Ger.; 1909, cond., Seattle Symph.; 1911, San Francisco Symph.; 1920, asst. cond., N. Y. Phil.; frequent g.-cond. of fests. and orch. concerts; 1917, op. *Azora,* prod. Chicago op.; 1918, won Soc. Amer. Singers prize *w.* op., *Bianca;* 1920, *Cleopatra's Night,* prod. Met. Op. Comp. symph., ballet suites, cantatas, tone poems, incl. *Culprit Fay;* chamb. wks., and small pcs.

Haesche (*Heh-sheh*), **William Edward.** Violinist, pianist, composer; b. New Haven, Conn., Apr. 11, 1867; d. Virginia, 1929. *t.* Yale U. Comp. symph. wks., cantatas, violin pcs.

Hagel (*Hah-gel*), **Carl.** Conductor, violinist; b. Voigstedt, Ger., Dec. 12, 1847. *t.* Munich. Comp. orch., chamb. wks.

Hagel, Richard. Conductor, violinist; b. Erfurt, Ger., Jul. 7, 1872. Son of Carl H. *t.* Brunswick, Ger.

Hageman, Richard. Conductor, teacher, composer; b. Leewarden, Hol., Jul. 9, 1882. 1898, asst. cond., Amsterdam Royal Op.; 1906, to U. S. *w.* Yvette Guilbert; 1918-21, asst. cond., Met. Op., N. Y.; 1935, cond., Chicago Op. Coach and accompanist to leading singers. Comp. songs.

Hagemann, François Willem. Organist, conductor; b. Zütphen, Hol., Sept. 10, 1827. Comp. pf. mus.

Hagemann, Maurits Leonard. Composer, teacher; b. Zütphen, Sept. 25, 1829. Comp. oratorio, cantatas.

Hagen, Adolf. Conductor; b. Bremen, Sept. 4, 1851; d. Dresden, 1917. Operetta comp. Lives Dresden, Ger.

Hagen, Theodor. Composer, writer; b. Hamburg, Apr. 15, 1823; d. New York, Dec. 21, 1871. Comp. pf. pcs., songs.

Hager, Johannes (really **Hasslinger**). Composer; b. Vienna, Feb. 24, 1822; d. ib., Jan. 9, 1898. p. Mendelssohn.

Hägg (*Hegg*), **Gustav W.** Organist, composer; b. Wisby, Swed., Nov. 28, 1867. Org., Stockholm. A virtuoso perf. Comp. chamb. mus., organ and piano pcs.

Hägg, Jacob Adolf. Composer; b. Gothland, Nor., Jun. 27, 1850; d. 1902. Comp. *Northern Symphony,* piano and organ wks., songs.

Hahn, Adolph. Musical educator; b. Indianapolis, Ind., Jan. 13, 1875; d. Cincinnati, Apr. 1, 1934. 1890, gr., Cin. Coll. of Mus.; 1923-31, dir., Cin. Coll. of Mus.

Hahn, Jacob H. Pianist, teacher; b. Philadelphia, Dec. 1, 1847; d. Detroit, 1902. Fd. Detroit Cons. Comp. piano wks. and songs.

Hahn, Reynaldo. Composer; b. Caracas, Venezuela, Aug. 9, 1874. 1885, st. Paris Cons.; 1898, *L'Ile de Reve,* prod. Opéra-Comique. Comp. opera, *Nausicaa,* incid. mus., symph. p., piano wks., and songs, incl. *l'Heure Exquise.*

Hale, Philip. Organist, critic, musicologist; b. Norwich, Vt., Mar. 5, 1854; d. Boston, Nov. 30, 1934. Edu., Andover Acad.; 1876, gr., Yale; 1885-7, p. Guilmant, Paris; 1901, annotator for Boston Symph. programs; 1903, mus. critic, Boston *Herald;* 1928, M.A., Dartmouth; 1933, M.A., Harvard. Foremost Amer. mus. critic of his generation.

Halévy (*Ah-leh-vee*), **Jacques François Fromental Elie** (correctly **Lévi**). Composer; b. Paris, May 27, 1799; d. Nice, Fr., Mar. 17, 1862. Son-in-law of Meyerbeer. Opera writer of the French sch. Principal work, *La Juive.*

Halir (*Hah-leer*), **Carl.** Violinist; b. Hohenelbe, Boh., Feb. 1, 1859; d. Berlin, Dec. 21, 1909. p. Joachim. 1894, prof., Hochschule; mem. Joachim Quartet.

Hall, Charles King. Organist, composer; b. London, 1845; d. ib., Sept. 1, 1895. Comp. ch. mus., operettas.

Hall, Marie (Mary Paulina). Violinist; b. Newcastle, Eng., Apr. 8, 1884. p. Sevcik. Distinguished woman concert violinist.

Hall, Walter Henry. Organist, choral director; b. London, Apr. 25, 1862; d. New York, Dec. 11, 1935. 1896-1914, org., St. James Ch., New York; also for a time, Cath. of St. John the Divine; 1909-1930, prof., Columbia U.; fd. Brooklyn Oratorio Soc.

Hallé (*Hal-leh*), **Sir Charles.** Pianist, conductor; b. Hazen, Ger., Apr. 11, 1819; d. Manchester, Eng., Oct. 25, 1895. During his career of forty-seven years he rendered invaluable service to mus., chiefly as a fest. cond., and by the concerts of his famous Manchester Symph., that after his death became the Hallé Orch.

Hallé, Lady v., **Neruda.**

Hallén, Johan Anders. Composer, music critic; b. Gothenburg, Swed., Dec. 22, 1846. 1909, prof., Stockholm Cons. Leader of new Swedish sch. Comp. operas, cantatas, symph., violin, and songs.

Haller, Michael. Organist, teacher; b. Neusalz, Ger., Jan. 31, 1840; d. Ratisbon, Ger., Jan. 4, 1915. t. counterpoint; comp. sacred mus.

Hallström (*Hahl-straym*), **Ivar.** Composer; b. Stockholm, Jun. 5, 1826; d. ib., Apr. 10, 1901. Comp. operas, cantatas, operettas.

Hallwachs (*Hall-vakhs*), **Carl.** Composer, conductor; b Darmstadt, Sept. 15, 1870. Cond., Cassel. Comp. opera, choruses, songs.

Halm (*Hahlm*), **Anton.** Composer; b. Altenmarkt, Aus., Jun. 4, 1789; d. Vienna, Apr., 1872. A friend of Beethoven; comp. piano études, chamb. mus.

Halstead, Margaret. Soprano; b. Pittsfield, Mass. Met. Op., N. Y.

Halvorsen, Johann. Norwegian violinist, composer; b. Drammen, 1864; d. ib., 1935. p. César Thompson. 1899, cond., Christiania Op. Comp. concerto and three suites for the violin, and a cantata for the coronation of King Haakon (1906).

Ham, Albert. Organist, composer; b. Bath, Eng., 1858. p. Pyne. 1883, F. R. C. O.; 1894, Mus.D., Dublin U.; 1906, Mus.D., Toronto U.; 1893-97, org., Taunton, Eng.; 1897, org., St. James Cath., Toronto. Comp. cantatas, choruses, anthems, part-songs, and marches.

Hamblen, Bernard. Composer, organist; b. England, Jul. 14, 1877. 1911, Montreal; 1917, N. Y. Comp. songs.

Hambourg, Boris. 'Cellist; b. Voronez, Dec. 27, 1884. St., Hoch Cons. 1903, toured w. Mark H. through Australia and New Zealand; 1904, Eng.; 1906, Ger.; 1910, Amer.; fd. Cons. in Toronto w. father and brother Jan. Comp. 'cello pcs.

Hambourg, Jan. Violinist; b. Voronez, Aug. 27, 1882. p. Ysaÿe. t. Toronto; 1935, t. Paris. Ed. restored edition of the Bach sonatas (Oxford, 1934).

Hambourg, Mark. Pianist; b. Bogutschar-Noronez, Rus., Jun. 1, 1879. 1888, debut, Moscow; world tours incl., U. S. A distinguished virtuoso.

Hamerik, Asger. Pianist, composer; b. Copenhagen, Apr. 8, 1843; d. Fredericksburg, Jul. 13, 1923. p. Berlioz. 1872-98, dir., Peabody Cons., Baltimore; 1898, ret. to Copenhagen; 1890, knighted by King of Denmark; 1870, opera, *Vendetta,* prod., Milan. Comp. 7 symph., 4 operas, chamb. mus.

Hamilton, Anna Heuermann. Composer, educator; b. Chicago. p. Clarence Eddy; t. Fulton, Mo. Comp. beginners pcs.

Hamilton, Clarence Grant. Pianist, writer, teacher; b. Providence, R. I., Jun. 9, 1865. 1904, prof., Wellesley Coll. Author of educational treatises.

Hamilton, Harley. Violinist, conductor; b. Oneida, N. Y., 1861; d. Los Angeles, May 14, 1933. 1898, fd. L. A. Symph. Orch.; 1916, retired by deafness; succ. by Adolf Tandler.

Hammerstein, Oscar. Impresario; b. Berlin, 1847; d. N. Y., 1919. A cigarmaker who had a passion for prod. op., and against great handicaps built more op. houses than any one man in the history of op., yet failed in the end through the violent opposition he aroused on the part of the millionaire sponsors of the Golden Horseshoe. 1888-1900, he built the Harlem Op. H., Columbus Th., Harlem Mus. Hall, Murray Hill Th., the first Manhattan (1892), Olympia, Victoria, Harris and Republic Theatres. When starting to prod. real grand op. he built (1906) the Manhattan Op. H.; (1908) Phila. Op. H.; (1911) London Op. H.; (1913) Amer. Op. H. (now Lexington Ave. Op. H.). At the Manhattan, he introd. to N. Y., Fr. and modern Ger. operas, (*Louise, Pelleas and Melisande, Salome, Electra*) and an entire new galaxy of stars, incl., Mary Garden, Trentini, Renaud and numerous others whose names became household words.

Hammond, Laurens. Inventor; *b.* Evanston, Ill., Jan. 11, 1895. 1916, gr., Cornell U. Invented the electric organ that bears his name.

Hammond, Richard. Composer; *b.* England, 1896. Edu., Yale U. Comp. orch. wks., incl., *Six Chinese Fairy Tales, Voyage to the East;* chamb. mus., pf. pcs., songs. Fd. Composers' Mus. Corp.

Hammond, William Churchill. Organist; *b.* Rockville, Conn., Nov. 25, 1860. *p.* S. P. Warren. 1885, org., Second Cong. Ch., Hartford; 1890, *t.* organ, Smith Coll.; from 1900, head of Mus. dept., Mt. Holyoke Coll.

Hampton, Hope. Soprano; *b.* Houston, Tex. 1928, debut, Phila. Op., in *Manon.*

Hanchett, Henry G. Pianist, writer, teacher; *b.* Syracuse, Aug. 29, 1853; *d.* Siasconset, Mass., Aug. 19, 1918. Author of wks. on piano study.

Hand (*Hahnt*), **Ferdinand Gotthelf.** Writer; *b.* Plauen, Boh., Feb. 15, 1786; *d.* Jena, Ger., Mar. 14, 1851. Author of wks. on mus. esthetics.

Handel, George Frederick. Composer; *b.* Halle, Ger., Feb. 23, 1685; *d.* London, Apr. 14, 1759. A precocious genius. 1705, his first opera, *Almira,* perf. at Hamburg; 1708, to Italy; 1712, to England, where he comp. and prod. some forty-two operas. Due perhaps to the changing taste of the period, he went bankrupt. 1737, turned his attention to oratorio. After 7 successful oratorios, he prod. *The Messiah* (1741), which was not appreciated at its first representation, but has gained in favor during all the intervening years. 1742, *Samson;* 1746, *Judas Maccabæus;* 1748, *Solomon;* 1752, *Jephthah,* in which year he became blind. He was buried in Westminster Abbey. His compositions reach to an unbelievable total, covering every form. The layman knows him as the composer of Handel's *Largo.*

Hannsens, Charles Louis. Composer; *b.* Ghent, Bel., May 4, 1777; *d.* Brussels, May 6, 1852. Comp. operas, masses. Charles Louis (Jr), his son (*b.* Ghent, Jul. 12, 1802; *d.* Brussels, Apr. 8, 1871); also comp. operas, ballets, symph.

Hanon (*Hah-nong*), **Charles Louis.** Pianist; *b.* Rem-sur-l'Aire, Fr., 1820; *d.* Boulogne-sur-Mer, 1900. Comp. studies for piano of permanent value.

Hanscom, E. W. Organist, composer; *b.* Durham, Me., Dec. 28, 1848. Comp. songs, anthems.

Hansen, Robert Emil. 'Cellist, composer; *b.* Copenhagen, Den., Feb. 25, 1860. Dir., Jutland Phil. Orch. Comp. orch., chamb. mus.

Hanslick, Eduard. Musicologist; *b.* Prague, Sept. 11, 1825; *d.* Vienna, Aug. 6, 1904. 1849, LL.D., Vienna U.; critic, *Wiener Zeitung;* his philosophy, contained in *Vom Musicolisch Schönen,* supported by a virile, witty pen, made him the persecutor of Wagner, Hugo Wolf, and Bruckner, and the success of Brahms, due largely to him. Wagner's *Beckmesser* was to have been called *Hans Lick,* but he thought better of it.

Hanson, Howard. Conductor, composer, teacher; *b.* Wahoo, Neb., Oct. 28, 1896. Won fellowship, Amer. Acad. in Rome. 1919-21, prof., Coll. of Pacific, Cal.; 1924, dir., Eastman Sch. of Mus., Rochester; cond., Rochester Symph.; g.-cond., N. Y. Phil., also Cleveland, San Francisco, Chicago, Boston, Los Angeles and St. Louis Orchestras. Feb. 10, 1934, première of opera, *Merry Mount,* at Met. Op. Comp. dozen major orch. wks., incl., *Nordic Symphony;* concerto for organ and orch., choral, and chamb. mus., and many pf. pcs.

d'Harcourt Eugene. Composer, writer; *b.* Paris, 1855; *d.* ib., 1918. A mus. propagandist; built concert hall, and organized Concerts d'Harcourt. Comp. operas, symph. wks., songs.

d'Hardelot (*Ar-de-low*), **Guy (Mrs. W. T.) Helen Rhodes, née Guy.** Composer; *b.* Hardelot Castle, nr. Boulogne, Fr., 1858; *d.* N. Y., Jan. 7, 1936. Edu., Paris Cons.; encouraged by Gounod; 1896, to U. S. *w.* Calvé. Comp. songs, incl. *Sans Toi.*

Harker, F. Flaxington. Organist, conductor; *b.* Aberdeen, Scot., Sept. 4, 1876. 1914, org., Richmond, Va. Comp. cantatas, anthems, organ pcs.

Harling, W. Franke. Composer, pianist; *b.* London, 1887. Edu., London Acad. of Mus. 1888, to U. S.; 1916, prize for symph. ballade, *Miracle of Time,* perf. Newark Fest.; 1925, opera, *A Light from St. Agnes,* prod. Chicago Op.; 1926, opera, *Deep River,* prod. Phila. Comp. songs and music for the motion pictures.

Harmati (*Ahr-mah-tee*), **Sandor.** Conductor; *b.* Budapest, Jul. 9, 1892; *d.* Flemington, N. J., Apr. 3, 1936. *p.* Hubay. 1919, mem., Letz Q.; 1925-1930, Omaha Symph. Orch.; g.-cond., Pasdeloup Orch., Paris, and Berlin Phil.; cond., Orch.; 1933, cond., Westchester Fest.; 1935, prof., Bard Coll., Annondale-on-Hudson. Comp. orch. wks., incl., *Symphonic Poem;* chamb. mus., str. q., violin pcs., songs.

Harner, George F. Composer, organist; *b.* Lawrence, Mass., 1862. *p.* Rheinberger. 1887-93, Boston. Comp. anthems, pf. pcs., songs.

Harris, Charles K. Song writer; *b.* Poughkeepsie, N. Y., May 1, 1865; *d.* N. Y., Dec. 22, 1930. A starving banjo teacher in Milwaukee (Wis.), he comp. *After the Ball,* introduced (1892) by J. Aldrich Libby, at Milwaukee perf. of Hoyt's "A Trip to Chinatown," which swept the country by storm. He became his own publisher, and the sales ran into the millions. Was a New York music publisher for fifty years.

Harris, Clement Hugh Gilbert. Composer; *b.* Wimbledon, Eng., Jul. 8, 1871; *d.* Pentepigadia, Greece, Apr. 23, 1897. Comp. orch., chamb. mus., songs.

Harris, Roy. Composer; *b.* Lincoln City, Okla., Feb. 12, 1898. Mostly self-taught; st., Nadia Boulanger. 1935, overture, *Johnny Comes Marching Home,* perf. Phil. Orch., u. Klemperer. *t.* Westminster Choir Sch., Princeton. Comp. orch. wks., incl., *Andante, Symphony;* chamb. mus., concerti.

Harris, William Victor. Composer, teacher of singing; *b.* New York, Apr. 27, 1869. Comp. songs.

Harrison, Julius Allen Greenway. Conductor; *b.* Stourport, Worcestershire, Mar. 26, 1885. Cond., Beecham Op. Co.; 1925, cond., Handel Soc., succ. Goossens. Comp. orch. wks., cantatas, chamb. mus.

Harriss, Charles Albert Edwin. Organist, composer; *b.* London, Dec. 15, 1862. Org., Ottowa. Comp. opera, cantata, ch. mus.

Harrold, Orville. Tenor; *b.* Delaware Co., Ind.; *d.* Darien, Conn., Oct. 23, 1933. Discovered by Schumann-Heink, was taken by Oscar Hammerstein, and prepared for Gr. Op., u. Oscar Saenger; debut, Manhattan Op., in *Pagliacci;* sang leading tenor rôles in London; 1919, Met. Op.; later sang in vaudeville. Never realized his early promise.

Hartmann, Arthur Martinus. Violinist, composer; *b.* Maté Szalka, Hun., Jul. 23, 1881. Distinguished New York violin teacher. Comp. violin transcriptions and songs.

Hartmann, Emil. Composer; *b.* Copenhagen, Feb. 21, 1836; *d.* ib., Jul. 19, 1898. Son of J. P. E. H. Comp. operas, incl., *The Corsicans;* ballet, cantata, symph., concertos.

Hartmann, Johann Peter Emil. Composer; *b.* Copenhagen, Den., May 14, 1805; *d.* ib., Mar. 10, 1900. Rather overshadowed by his son-in-law, Gade (q. v.). Comp. Danish operas, symph. wks.

Hartog, Edouard de. Composer; *b.* Amsterdam, Aug. 15, 1828; *d.* The Hague, Nov., 1909. Comp. orch., chamb. mus.

Hartvigson, Anton. Pianist; *b.* Aarhus, Den., Oct. 16, 1845. *t.* Copenhagen.

Hartvigson, Fritz. Pianist; *b.* Grenaa, Den., May 31, 1841; *d.* Copenhagen, 1919. *t.* R. C. M., London.

Harty, Sir Herbert Hamilton. Conductor; *b.* Hillsborough, Ire., Dec. 4, 1879. First gained repute as cond. London Symph. Orch. 1920, cond., Hallé Orch., Manchester; 1924, brought Hallé Orch. to London for series of symph. concerts which were sensationally successful; 1934-5, g.-perf. *w.* Amer. symph. organizations. Comp. *Irish Symphony, Comedy Overture;* tone-poem, *With the Wild Geese;* cantata, *Mystic Trumpeter,* and many songs, written for his wife, Agnes Nicholls.

Harvard, Sue. Soprano; *b.* Wales. To N. Y., age of 3; soloist leading orchs., U. S.; formerly Met. Op.

Harwood, Basil. Organist, composer; *b.* Woodhouse, Glos., Eng., Apr. 11, 1859. 1887-92, Ely Cath.; 1892-1909, Oxford. Ed., *Oxford Hymn Book.* Comp. cantatas, and organ wks.

Hasse (*Hahs-seh*), **Johann Adolph.** Composer; *b.* Bergedorf, Ger., Mar. 25, 1699; *d.* Vienna, Dec. 16, 1783. Opera comp. His wife, née Faustina Bordoni, mezzo-soprano (*b.* Venice, 1693; *d.* ib., Nov. 4, 1783). A celebrated prima donna *u.* Handel in London.

Hasselmans, Louis. Conductor, 'cellist; *b.* Paris, Jul. 25, 1878. 1905, cond., Lamoreaux Orch., Paris; 1907, fd. Hasselmans concerts, Paris; 1909-1911, cond., Opéra Comique; 1911-1913, cond., Montreal Op.; 1913-1914, Marseilles Concerts Classiques; 1915-1920, Chicago Op.; 1920, Met. Op., N. Y.

Hassler (*Hahss-ler*), **Hans Leo.** Organist, composer; *b.* Nuremberg, Ger., 1564; *d.* Frankfort, Ger., Jun. 8, 1612. One of the first German musicians to go to It. for study. Comp. sacred and secular wks.

Hastings, Frank Seymour. Composer; *b.* Mendham, N. Y., May 31, 1853; *d.* ——. Comp. principally songs.

Hastings, Thomas. Writer, composer; *b.* Washington, Conn., Oct. 15, 1784; *d.* New York, May 15, 1872. Associate of Lowell Mason. 1858, Mus.D., N. Y. U. Comp. a thousand hymn-tunes, incl., *Toplady.*

Hatch, Edith. Pianist, teacher, composer; *b.* Aberdeen, Miss. Edu., Cin. Cons. of Mus., and Matthay, London; 1919, *m.* W. W. Jamesson. Comp. pf. teaching pcs. Assoc. *w.* sister, *Mabel Lee H.*

Hatton, John Liptrot. Composer; *b.* Liverpool, Oct. 12, 1809; *d.* Margate, Sept. 20, 1886. 1844, opera, *Pascal Bruno,* prod. Vienna. Comp. incid. mus. to many of Shakespeare's plays; also oratorio, *Hezekiah;* ch. mus., songs. Author of a song collection.

Hattstaedt (*Haht-stet*), **John James.** Pianist, teacher; *b.* Monroe, Mich., Dec. 29, 1851; *d.* Chicago, 1931. Dir., Amer. Cons. of Mus., Chicago. Author of *Manual of Musical History.*

Haubiel, Charles. Composer, pianist, teacher; *b.* Delta, O., Jan. 30, 1892. *p.* Ganz. *t.* pf., N. Y. U. Comp. symph. pcs., *Karma,* Schubert centennial prize; suite for strings and woodwind; piano pcs., songs.

Hauck (*Howk*), **Minnie.** Soprano; *b.* New York, Nov. 16, 1852; *d.* Lucerne, Feb. 6, 1920. Sang in U. S. and Europe.

Haupt, Karl. Organist, theorist; *b.* Kuhnau, Ger., Aug. 25, 1810; *d.* Berlin, Jul. 4, 1891. Dir., Inst. for Ch. Mus., Berlin.

Hauptmann, Moritz. Theorist; *b.* Dresden, Oct. 13, 1792; *d.* Leipzig, Jan. 3, 1868. Distinguished teacher of harmony at Leipzig Cons.

Hausegger, Siegmund von. Composer, conductor; *b.* Graz, Aus., Aug. 16, 1872. 1893, one-act opera, *Helfried,* prod. in Graz; cond., Munich. Comp. orch. wks., incl., *Barbarossa,* and *Wieland the Smith,* and some notable songs.

Hauser (*How-zer*), **Miska.** Violinist, composer; *b.* Pressburg, Hun., 1822; *d.* Vienna, Dec. 9, 1887. *p.* Kreutzer. Comp. violin pcs., mostly of Hungarian character.

Havens, Charles Arthur. Organist, composer; *b.* Essex, N. Y., 1842. Comp. ch. mus.

Havens, Raymond Lester. Pianist; *b.* Providence, R. I., Apr. 30, 1891. 1905, debut, Boston; 1928, *t.* Boston U.

Hawkins, Sir John. Historian; *b.* London, Mar. 30, 1719; *d.* ib., May 21, 1789. An original mem. of the Madrigal Society, of the Academy of Ancient Mus., and of Dr. Johnson's club. Hawkin's *General History of the Science and Practice of Music* is a monument of patient research, and a storehouse of unusual information.

Hawley, Charles Beach. Composer; *b.* Brookfield, Conn., Feb. 11, 1858; *d.* Red Bank, N. J., Dec. 29, 1915. Comp. songs, incl., *The Sweetest Flower That Blows;* part-songs, anthems.

Hawley, Stanley. Composer; *b.* Ilkeston, Eng., May 17, 1867; *d.* ib., Jun. 13, 1916. Comp. recitations with mus., incl., Poe's *The Bells.*

Hawthorne, Alice. Pseudonym of Septimus Winner (q. v.).

Haydn, Johann Michael. Composer; *b.* Rohrau, Aus., Sept. 14, 1737; *d.* Salzburg, Aug. 10, 1806; brother of Joseph H. Comp. ch. mus.

Haydn, Joseph. Composer; *b.* Rohrau, Aus., Mar. 31, 1732; *d.* Vienna, May 31, 1809. Pupil in the choir-school of Church of St. Stephen, Vienna, until his seventeenth year. On the verge of destitution, he entered the service of Porpora, a renowned It. comp. of the period. At twenty-eight, appointed kapellmeister to Prince Esterhazy, Eisenstadt, Hungary. For thirty years he spent the greater part of the year at the country-seat of the Esterhazy's, discharging the duties of his position, and writing an immense quantity of mus., incl. more than a hundred symph., quartets, trios, fifteen masses, an oratorio, eighteen operas, and many miscellaneous items. While thus leading a life of tranquil industry, his reputation spread far and wide. His visits to England, undertaken somewhat unwillingly, were veritable triumphs. After his return to Vienna, he prod. the oratorios *The Creation* (1797), and *The Seasons* (1801). An amazingly prolific comp., his wks. total 148 symph., 83 quartets, 24 trios, 19 operas, 5 oratorios, 24 concertos, 15 masses, 44 piano sonatas, and many unclassified compositions. He created the modern symph. and str. q., and may well be called the father of instrumental mus.

Hayes, Catherine. Soprano; *b.* Limerick, Oct. 25, 1825; *d.* Sydenham, Aug. 11, 1861. Created a furore by her singing of Irish airs.

Hayward, Dolores. Piano teacher; *b.* United States. St. Inst. of Mus. Art, N. Y. 1921, *t.* Harcum Sch., Bryn Mawr, Pa.; 1923, Warrenton (Va.) Country Sch.; 1924-28, Finch Sch., N. Y. Dir., Kiniya Summer Colony, N. H.

Heacox, Arthur Edward. Music educator, author; *b.* Baraboo, Wis., Jul. 22, 1867. 1893, *t.;* 1902, prof., Oberlin Cons.

Heap, Charles Swinnerton. Pianist, composer; *b.* Birmingham, Apr. 10, 1849; *d.* ib., Jun. 11, 1900. Comp. cantatas, oratorio, *The Captivity;* pf. pcs., songs.

Heckscher, Celeste de Longpre (née Massey). Composer; *b.* Phila., 1860. 1911, pantomime, *Dance of the Pyrenees,* perf. Phila. Orch. Comp. symph. wks., pf. pcs., songs.

Hedden, Warren Rosecrans. Organist, composer; *b.* N. Y., Dec. 25, 1861. 1908-9, warden A. G. O.; 1913, dir., Guild exams., in 20 cities.

Heermann, Hugo. Violinist; *b.* Heilbronn, Mar. 3, 1844; *d.* Merano, It., Nov. 6, 1935. Distinguished virtuoso; 1861, gr. Brussels Cons. *p.* deBeriot, Joachim. 1864-1904, conc.-m., Frankfort Museum Gesellschaft; 1906-9, *t.* Chicago Mus. Coll.; 1909-12, conc.-m., Cincinnati Symph.; 1912, *t.* Geneva (Switz.) Cons.; said to have intro. Brahms *Concerto* to N. Y., Paris, and Australia.

Hegar (*Hay-gar*), **Friedrich.** Conductor, composer; *b.* Basel, Switz., Oct. 11, 1841. 1875-1915, fd., dir., Zurich Cons.; 1907, dir., Hochschule, Berlin, succ. Joachim Comp. oratorios, incl., *Manasse,* a violin concerto, chamb. mus., songs.

Hegedus (*Hay-ge-doosh*), **Ferenc.** Violinist; *b.* Fünfkirchen, Feb. 26, 1881. *p.* Hubay. 1906-7, toured U. S., playing the Gillott Guarnerius.

Heger, Robert. Conductor, composer; *b.* Strassburg, Aug. 19, 1886. 1907, cond., Strassburg Op.; 1911, Vienna Volksoper; 1913-21, Nuremburg Op.; 1921, Munich Op.; g.-cond., Covent Garden, London. Comp. opera, symph., instr. pcs.

Hegner, Anton. 'Cellist; *b.* Copenhagen, Mar. 2, 1861; *d.* New York, Dec. 4, 1915.

Hegner, Otto. Pianist; *b.* Basel, Switz., 1876; *d.* Hamburg, Feb. 22, 1907. 1888, debut as prodigy, but later won a considerable reputation.

Heidingsfeld, Ludwig. Conductor, composer; *b.* Jauer, Ger., Mar. 24, 1854. Dir., Danzig (Ger.) Cons. Comp. orch. pcs., operettas.

Heifetz, Jascha. Violinist; *b.* Vilna, Lith., Feb. 2, 1899. *p.* Auer. 1917, to U. S.; 1929, *m.* Florence Vidor, movie star; 1926, Chevalier, Legion of Honor. A consummate artist with a flawless technique.

Heilman, William Clifford. Composer; *b.* Penn., 1877. Comp. orchestral tone-poem, *By the Porta Catania;* orchestral suite, songs and piano pcs.

Hein, Carl. Music educator; *b.* Rendsburg, Ger., Feb. 2, 1864. 1890, to Amer.; 1900, co-fd., now pres., N. Y. Coll. of Mus.

Heinrich, Max. Baritone, teacher; *b.* Chemnitz, Ger., Jun. 14, 1853; *d.* New York, Aug. 8, 1916. 1873, to U. S. as teacher; 1882-8, concertized; 1888-93, *t.* R. A. M., London; 1894-1903, *t.* Boston; 1903-10, *t.* N. Y. Eminent as a lieder singer. Comp. songs; wr. translations of song texts; author of *Correct Principles of Classical Singing.* Julia H., his daughter (*d.* 1919), sang (1915-*d.*) at Met. Op.

Heinroth, Charles. Organist, teacher; *b.* Jan. 2, 1874. 1897-1907, org., Ch. of the Ascension, N. Y.; 1907, dir. mus., Carnegie Inst., Pittsburgh; 1934, prof., C. C. N. Y.

Heise, Peter Arnold. Composer; *b.* Copenhagen, Den., Feb. 11, 1830; *d.* ib., Sept. 12, 1879. Comp. two operas; songs.

Hekking, Anton. 'Cellist; *b.* The Hague, Sept. 7, 1856; *d.* Bordeaux, Jan., 1926. A distinguished virtuoso.

Helfenbein, Ladislas. Pianist, composer; *b.* Budapest, Hun., Jun. 18, 1901. *p.* Carl Friedberg, Josef Lhevinne. A prominent New York concert artist and teacher. Comp. pf. wks., songs.

Heller, James G. Composer, Rabbi; *b.* New Orleans, 1892. *p.* E. Stillman Heller. 1929, *Three Aquatints,* for str. q., chosen by S. P. A. M.; Rabbi, Plum Street Temple, Cin.; writes program notes for Cin. Orch.

Heller, Stephen. Pianist, composer; *b.* Pesth, May 15, 1814; *d.* Paris, Jan. 15, 1888. Comp. fantasias, études, polonaises, and salon pcs. for piano.

Hellmesberger, Joseph. Violinist, conductor, composer; *b.* Vienna, Apr. 9, 1855; *d.* ib., Apr. 26, 1907. One of a family of violinists; his grandfather was the teacher of Joachim. His father (1828-1893), was prof., Hochschule from 1851. He was the teacher of Brodsky and Kreisler. Of his operettas, *Das Veilchenmädl,* is best known.

Helmholtz, Hermann Ludwig Ferdinand von. Physicist; *b.* Potsdam, Ger., Aug. 31, 1821; *d.* Charlottenburg, Ger., Sept. 8, 1894. 1871-*d.,* prof. of physics, Berlin U. Rendered valuable service to mus. by his work on sound and acoustics, *The Sensations of Tone.*

Helsted, Eduard. Violinist, composer; *b.* Copenhagen, Den., Dec. 8, 1816; *d.* ib., 1900. Comp. ballets.

Helsted, Gustaf Carl. Composer, teacher; *b.* Copenhagen, Den., Jan. 30, 1857. Prof. comp., Copenhagen Cons. Comp. symph., suite, songs, pf. wks.

Hemington, Francis. Organist, choral conductor; *b.* London, Aug. 22, 1866. 1885, assoc. Royal Coll. Orgs., London; 1910, Mus.D., N. Y. Cons. of Mus.; 1894, fd.-dir., Oak Park Sch. of Mus.; 1923, dir., Pilgrim Choral Soc., Chicago.

Hempel, Frieda. Soprano; *b.* Leipzig, Jun. 26, 1885. Successful opera and concert singer. 1907-12, Berlin Op.; 1912-1932, Met. Op., N. Y.

Hemphill, Melvin. Singer; *b.* Avalon, Pa., 1909. *p.* Mario Ancona. St., Pittsburgh Mus. Inst.; sang in Gilbert and Sullivan operettas, *u.* Winthrop Ames, N. Y.; 1930, debut, Naples, in *Traviata;* 1936, recital debut, Town Hall, N. Y.

Henderson, William James. Writer, music critic; *b.* Newark, N. J., Dec. 4, 1855. Mus. critic, N. Y. *Sun* (*Herald*) since 1902. Author of *Modern Musical Drift, Forerunners of Italian Opera,* and other books on mus.

Hendriks, Francis Milton. Pianist, composer; *b.* N. Y., Nov. 28, 1883. *p.* Godowsky, Berlin. 1922, Mus. M., Denver Coll. Mus.; dir. pf. dept., Denver Coll. of Mus. Comp. 64 wks. for pf., voice, orch.

Henkel, Heinrich. Pianist, composer; *b.* Fulda, Ger., Feb. 16, 1822; *d.* Frankfort, Apr. 10, 1899. Comp. technical exercises for piano, violin pcs.

Henriques (*Hen-ree-kes*), **Fini Valdemar.** Violinist, composer; *b.* Copenhagen, Den., Dec. 20, 1867. *p.* Svendsen. Opera, *Völand Smed,* and ballet, *Little Mermaid,* prod. Copenhagen. Comp. chamb. mus., violin pcs., pf. pcs.

Henschel (*Hen-shel*), **Sir Isidor Georg.** Baritone, conductor, composer, teacher; *b.* Breslau, Ger., Feb. 18, 1850; *d.* Aviemore, Scot., Sept. 10, 1934. 1881-84, first cond., Boston Symph.; 1885, cond., London Symph.; 1930, g.-cond., Boston Symph., commemorating its fiftieth anniversary. Retired to London as *t.* singing; 1914, knighted by King George. Comp. operas, oratorios, instrumental pcs., and many songs, incl., *Morning Hymn.* His wife, *Lilian Bailey* (1860-1901), an Amer. soprano, shared his fame through their joint recitals.

Hensel, Fanny Cäcilia. Pianist, composer; *b.* Hamburg, Nov. 14, 1805; *d.* Berlin, May 14, 1847. A sister of Mendelssohn.

Hensel, Octavia (Mrs. G. A. Fonda). Writer.

Henselt, Adolph von. Pianist, composer; *b.* Schwabach, Ger., May 12, 1814; *d.* Warmbrunn, Ger., Oct. 10, 1889. Comp. pf. concerto, a second pf. part to Cramer's *Études;* many pf. pcs., incl. *If I Were a Bird,* piano pcs., and useful studies.

Hentschel, Theodor. Conductor, composer; *b.* Schirgiswalde, Ger., Mar. 28, 1838; *d.* Hamburg, Dec. 19, 1892. Comp. operas, *The King's Page, Lancelot;* overtures, marches.

Herbeck, Johann. Conductor, composer; *b.* Vienna, Dec. 25, 1831; *d.* ib., Oct. 28, 1877. Dir., Vienna Op. Comp. symph., chamb. mus., songs.

Herbert, Victor. 'Cellist, conductor, composer; *b.* Dublin, Ire., Feb. 1, 1859; *d.* New York, May 26, 1924. Grandson of Samuel Lover. St., 'cello in Ger. 1882, played 'cello in Strauss' Orch., Vienna; 1883-6, Stuttgart; 1886, Met. Op., N. Y.; 1894, perf. *2nd Concerto, w.* N. Y. Phil. Orch.; 1889, assoc. cond., Worcester fest., for which he comp. cantata, *The Captive;* 1898-1904, cond., Pittsburgh Symph. Opera, *Natoma,* première Feb. 21, 1911, Phila.; *Madeline,* one act, Jan. 24, 1914, Met. Op. Chief fame rests on his light operas, the *Serenade, Babes in Toyland, Mlle. Modiste.* Comp. orch. pcs., *Suite Romantique, Irish Rhapsody,* and *Panamèricana;* also piano pcs., and songs. First pres. of the Amer. Soc. of Composers, Authors and Publishers.

Heritte-Viardot (*Ay-rit-Vee-ar-doe*), **Louise.** Teacher of singing, composer; *b.* Paris, Dec. 14, 1841. *t.* Heidelberg. Comp. operas, songs.

Herman, Reinhold Ludwig. Composer, conductor; *b.* Prenzlau, Ger., Sept. 21, 1849. 1887, *t.* Union Theol. Sem.; 1898, cond., Handel and Haydn Soc., Boston; 1900, to Berlin. Comp. operas, orch. wks., songs.

Hermann, Friedrich. Violinist, composer, teacher; *b.* Frankfort, Feb. 1, 1828; *d.* Leipzig, Sept. 27, 1907. Comp. orch., chamb. mus.

Hermann, Robert. Composer; *b.* Berne, Switz., Apr. 29, 1869; *d.* Ambach, Bav., 1912. Comp. symph., overture, quintet, songs.

d'Hermanoy, Alice (Mrs. Charles Henri Lauwers). Operatic soprano. 1910, Brussels; 1921, Chicago Op.

Hernandez (*Her-nan-deth*), **Pablo.** Organist, composer; *b.* Saragossa, Sp., Jan. 25, 1834. Org., Madrid. Comp. organ wks., symph., overture, zarzuelas.

Hernando, Rafael. Composer; *b.* Madrid, May 31, 1822. *t.* Madrid. Comp. zarzuelas, masses.

Hérold, Louis Joseph Ferdinand. Composer; *b.* Paris, Jan. 28, 1791; *d.* ib., Jan. 19, 1833. As chorus master at the Paris Op., his greatest influence was upon the ballet, through his compositions in that form. Finally he found a satisfactory librettist and prod. the two greatest operas, *Zampa* (1831), *Le Pré aux Clercs* (1932), out of the twenty he comp.

Hertz, Alfred. Conductor; *b.* Frankfort-on-Main, Jul. 15, 1872. 1891, cond., Stadt-Th., Halle; 1892-1895, Altenburg; 1899, London; 1899-1902, Breslau; 1902-1915, Met. Op., N. Y.; 1903, cond., first perf. of *Parsifal* given outside of Bayreuth; also première of Parker's *Mona* and Damrosch's *Cyrano;* 1915-1930, cond. of San Francisco Symph. Orch.

Hervé (*Air-vay*), (pseud. for Florimond Ronger). Composer, conductor; *b.* Arras, Fr., Jun. 30, 1825; *d.* Paris, Nov. 4, 1892. Operetta comp.

Hervey, Arthur. Composer, writer; *b.* Paris, Jan. 26, 1885; *d.* ib., 1922. Comp. operas, orch. wks., songs. Author of books on mus.

Herz (*Hairtz*), **Henri.** Pianist, composer; *b.* Vienna, Jan. 6, 1806; *d.* Paris, Jan. 5, 1888. *t.* Paris Cons.; 1845-51, toured U. S.; an artist of dazzling technic. Comp. 8 pf. concertos and 200 pieces—all forgotten save for his volume of *Scales.*

Herzog, George. Teacher, writer; *b.* Hungary, Dec. 11, 1901. St., U. of Berlin; 1931, Ph.D., Columbia U.; 1930-32, research in Anthropology, U. of Chicago; 1932, Yale U.; 1935, Guggenheim Fellowship.

Herzog, Sigmund. Pianist; *b.* Budapest, Hun. *p.* Rafael Joseffy. 1925, *t.* Inst. Mus. Art, N. Y.

Herzogenberg, Baron Heinrich von. Pianist, composer; *b.* Graz, Aus., Jun. 10, 1843; *d.* Wiesbaden, Ger., Oct. 9, 1900. *m.* Elizabeth Stockhausen, pianist. Comp. symph., chamb. mus., vocal wks.

Heseltine, Philip. Composer, writer; *b.* London, Oct. 30, 1894; *d.* ib., Dec. 17, 1930. Fd., *The Sackbut;* author, *F. Delius,* and other biographies, *u.* pseud. of Peter Warlock Comp. some orch. and chamb. mus., and many songs. 1923, Str. q., won Carnegie award.

Hess, Ludwig. Tenor, composer; *b.* Marburg, Ger., Mar. 23, 1871. Edu. as comp., later became singer. 1912-14, toured U. S.; 1917-20, cond., Königsberg; 1920, to Berlin. Comp. symph., the epic *Ariadne,* and many songs.

Hess, Myra. Pianist; *b.* London. *p.* Matthay. Since 1922-23, frequent tours of U. S.

Hess, Willy. Violinist; *b.* Mannheim, Jul. 14, 1859. *p.* Joachim. 1903, *t.* R. A. M., London, succ. Sauret; 1904, asst. cond., Boston Symph.; 1910, *t.* Hochschule, Berlin, succ. Halir.

Hesse (*Hes-seh*), **Adolf Friedrich.** Organist; *b.* Breslau, Ger., Aug. 30, 1808; *d.* ib., Aug. 5, 1863. Distinguished perf. Comp. organ pcs.

Hesselberg, Edouard Gregory. Pianist, teacher, composer; *b.* Rus., May 3, 1870. *t.* Toronto Cons. of Mus. Comp. two orch. suites, many pf., and violin pcs.

Hesser, George Ernest. Music educator; *b.* Crestline, O., Feb. 25, 1883. 1924, M. Pd., Cin. Cons. of Mus.; 1927, Dr. Pd.; 1921-30, dir. mus., pub. schs. of Indianapolis; 1930, same in Cin.; also *t.* U. of Cin. Author and ed., texts and collections.

Heuberger (*Hoy-bair-gher*), **Richard.** Composer, writer; b. Graz, Aus., Jun. 18, 1850; d. Vienna, Nov., 1914. Comp. operas, cantatas, ballets, orch. wks.

Heubner (*Hoyb-ner*), **Konrad.** Composer; b. Dresden, 1860; d. Coblenz, Jun. 7, 1905. Comp. orch., chamb. mus.

Heuschkel (*Hoysh-kel*), **Johann Peter.** Oboist, pianist; b. Eisfeld, Ger., Jan. 4, 1773; d. Biebich, Ger., 1853. t. Weber.

Hewitt, James. Early American composer and harpsichordist; b. Dartmoor, Eng., Jun. 4, 1770; d. probably in N. Y., 1827. 1798, purchased N. Y. branch of Carr's Musical Repository, and estab. a publishing business. Wr. opera, *Tammany*, prod. under auspices of Tammany Soc., predecessor of Tammany Hall, so named after legend of Indian Chief Tammany, the society's patron.

Hewitt, John Hill. Newspaper man, poet, song writer; b. N. Y., Jul. 11, 1801; d. Baltimore, 1890. Edu., West Point, w. Robert E. Lee, Polk, Jackson. Became itinerant newspaper man, poet, often called "Father of the American Ballad," a somewhat exaggerated claim. Yet won poetry contest against Edgar Allen Poe, starting a life-long feud. Comp. over 300 songs.

Hey (*High*), **Julius.** Teacher of singing; b. Irmelshausen, Ger., Apr. 29, 1832; d. Munich, Apr. 23, 1909. Aimed to fd. a Ger. sch. of singing to meet the demands of the Wagner mus. dramas.

Heydler, Charles. Violinist, 'cellist, music educator; b. Cleveland, O., May 20, 1861. Dir., Cleveland Cons. of Mus.; mem., Phil. Str. Q.

Heyman, Henry. Violinist, teacher; b. Oakland, Cal., Jan. 13, 1855. 1870, p. David. 1870-5, violinist, Gewandhaus Orch.; 1877, ret. to San Francisco; 1881, conc.-m., San Francisco Phil. Orch.; the dean of violinists on the Pacific Coast. Received dedication of Saint-Saëns' *Élégie*, and Jadassohn's *Romanza*.

Hier, Ethel Glenn. Pianist, composer; b. Cincinnati. p. Marcian Thalberg. 1908, debut, Cin. Comp. piano pcs.

Hierapolis, Leo De. Baritone; b. Eng., Mar. 22, 1891. p. Harry Rowe Shelley. 1921, debut, Montreal Gr. Op., in *Il Trovatore*; 1931, Phila. Gr. Op.; 1928, soloist, St. Patrick's Cath., N. Y. Comp. sacred mus.

Hildach, Eugen. Baritone, composer; b. Wittenberg, Ger., Nov. 20, 1849. Career divided w. Anna H., née Schubert, as duet recitalists, and teachers of singing. Comp. songs and duets, incl., *Passage Bird's Farewell*.

Hilf, Arno. Violinist; b. Bad Elster, 1858; d. ib., 1909. p. Schradieck. 1878, prof., Moscow Cons. u. Nicholas Rubinstein; 1892, prof., Leipzig Cons., succ. Brodsky; a phenomenal player, famous for ensemble playing.

Hill, Edward Burlingame. Composer; b. Cambridge, Mass., Sept. 9, 1872. Edu., and t. Harvard U. Symph. intro. by Koussevitsky and Boston Symph.; 1934, *Sextette for Wind and Piano*, intro. Pittsfield Fest. Comp. orch. wks., choral, incl., *Nuns of Perpetual Adoration*; chamb. mus.

Hill, Junius Welch. Pianist, teacher; b. Hingham, Mass., Nov. 18, 1840. Prof. of Mus. at Wellesley Coll. for a number of years. Lives Los Angeles, Cal.

Hill, Thomas Henry Weist. Violinist; b. London, Jan. 23, 1828; d. ib., Dec. 25, 1891.

Hill, Ureli Corelli. Conductor, violinist; b. ——, 1802; d. (suicide) Paterson, N. J., Sept. 2, 1875. 1835-7, st., Spohr. 1838, perf. *St. Paul*; 1842, fd. N. Y. Phil. Orch., and cond. for five years.

Hille (*Hil-le*), **Gustav.** Violinist, composer; b. Jerichow, Ger., May 31, 1851. t. Phila. Comp. violin pcs.

Hillemacher, Paul. b. Paris, Nov. 25, 1852; d. Versailles, Aug. 13, 1933, and **Lucien.** b. Paris, Jun. 10, 1860; d. ib., Jun. 2, 1909. Composers. Two brothers working together; comp. several operas, and signed their wks. with the single name P. L. H.

Hiller, Ferdinand. Composer; b. Frankfort, Oct. 24, 1811; d. Cologne, May 10, 1885. Fd. Cologne Cons. Comp. symph., oratorios, *Destruction of Jerusalem*, and *Saul*; six operas, overtures, sonatas, songs.

Hiller, Johann Adam (real name, **Huller**). Conductor; b. Wendisch-Ossig, Prus., Dec. 25, 1728; d. Leipzig, Jun. 16, 1794 (1804). 1776, estab. Concerts Spirituels in Ger., similar to those in Paris; 1781-1785, cond., Leipzig Gewandhaus Orch. Known as the fd. of the German *Singspiel*, a form of comic opera.

Himmel, Friedrich Heinrich. Composer; b. Treuenbrietzen, Ger., Nov. 20, 1765; d. Berlin, Jun. 8, 1814.

Hinckley, Allen Carter. Bass; b. Gloucester, Mass., Oct. 11, 1877. Gr. U. of Penn. 1903-8, Hamburg Op.; 1905-7, Bayreuth; 1908-11, Met. Op.; 1912, Chicago Op.; 1917, t. Kansas City Cons.

Hindemith, Paul. Composer, violinist (violist); b. Hanau, Ger., Nov. 16, 1895. Edu. Hochs Cons., Frankfort, u. Arnold Mendelssohn. 1915-23, conc.-m., then cond., Frankfurt Op.; fd. Amar Str. Q.; 1922-24, chamb. wks. perf., Salzburg Fest.; 1925, *Kammermusik* perf., Venice Fest. of ISCM.; 1931 (Nov. 13), concerto for "Trautorium" perf., Berlin; 1931 (Nov. 21), *Unaufhörliche* perf., Berlin. Comp. opera, incl., *Cardillac*; orch. wks., notable chamb. mus., piano, violin, 'cello pcs., and songs.

Hinshaw, William Wade. Opera singer, impresario; b. Union, Ia., Nov. 3, 1867. p. Gadski. 1895-99, dean of mus., Valpariso U.; 1899, operatic debut, St. Louis, in *Faust*; 1909, fd., International Grand Op. Co., Chicago; 1910-13, Met. Op., N. Y.

Hinton, Arthur. Composer; b. Beckenham, Eng., Nov. 20, 1869. p. Sauret. m. Katharine Goodson. Comp. symph., violin concerto, piano concerto, operettas, oratorios, chamb. mus., pf. pcs., songs.

Hipsher, Edward Ellsworth. Editor; b. Caledonia, O., Mar. 28, 1871. Edu., R. A. M., London. 1913-20, mus. dir., Morris Harvey Coll.; 1920, asst. ed., *Étude*.

Hobrecht (*Obrecht*). Composer; b. Utrecht, Hol., c. 1430; d. Antwerp, 1506. Famous contrapuntal comp. of masses and motets.

Hochstein, David. American violinist; b. Rochester, Feb. 16, 1892; d. France, Oct. 15, 1917. p. Sevcik. Won Austrian State Diploma at Vienna Meisterschule. A promising talent. Killed in the Battle of the Argonne.

Hodges, Edward. Organist; b. Bristol, Jul. 20, 1796; d. Clifton, Sept. 1, 1867. 1839-63, org., Trinity Ch., New York. Comp. anthems and services.

Hoesslin, Franz von. Conductor; b. Munich, Dec. 31, 1885. 1922, cond., Berlin State Op.; also at Bayreuth.

Hoffman (Andrews), Richard. Pianist, teacher; b. Manchester, Eng., May 24, 1831; d. Mt. Kisco, N. Y., Aug. 17, 1909. p. Liszt. 1847, to U. S., played at Jenny Lind debut; 1854, first Amer. perf. Chopin *Concerto*. Comp. pf. pcs., anthems, songs, and many transcriptions.

Hoffmann, Ernst Theodor Amadeus Wilhelm. Composer, writer; *b.* Königsberg, Ger., Jan. 24, 1776; *d.* Berlin, Jun. 25, 1822. Celebrated as a critic and author. His criticisms were admired by Beethoven and Schumann. Comp. operas, ballet, mass, symph., chamb. wks.

Hofmann, Heinrich Karl Johann. Pianist, composer; *b.* Berlin, Jan. 13, 1842; *d.* Gross Tabarz, Ger., Jul. 16, 1902. *p.* Kullak. 1882, mem., Berlin Akademie. Comp. operas, symph., chamb. wks., songs, after the Mendelssohnian style.

Hofmann, Josef Casimir. Pianist; *b.* Cracow, Aus., Jan. 20, 1876. 1887, prodigy pianist, toured U. S., but interfered *w.* by the SPCC.; 1894, resumed career; 1899, ret. to U. S.; 1928, dir., Curtis Inst., Phila. Under pseud. Michel Dvorsky, prod. several comp., incl. *Cromaticon.*

Hogarth, George. 'Cellist, writer; *b.* Lauderdale, Scot., 1783; *d.* London, Feb. 12, 1870. Author of interesting books on mus. His eldest daughter *m.* Charles Dickens. His father-in-law was George Thomson, the London publisher.

Hol, Richard. Organist, conductor; *b.* Amsterdam, Jul. 23, 1825; *d.* Utrecht, May 14, 1904. Comp. symph., opera, masses.

Holbrooke, Josef Charles. Composer; *b.* Croydon, Eng., Jul. 6, 1878. 1893, edu., R. A. M. 1900, *The Raven,* intro. Augustus Mann at Crystal Palace; 1904, *Queen Mab,* intro. Leeds Fest. Author, *Contemporary British Composers.* Comp. opera, orch. wks., ballets, chamb. mus.

Holden, Oliver. Composer, vocal teacher; *b.* Shirley, Mass., Sept. 18, 1765; *d.* Charlestown, Mass., Sept. 14, 1844. Earliest Amer. comp. whose mus. has survived on its merits. Comp. hymn tune, *Coronation,* to "All Hail the Power"; 1792, issued *The American Harmony;* 1797, engaged by Isaiah Thomas, publisher, to edit the *Worcester Collection.*

Holländer, Alexis. Composer, conductor; *b.* Ratibor, Ger., Feb. 25, 1840. *t.* Kullak's Acad. Comp. pf., quintet, pcs., songs.

Holländer, Gustav. Violinist; *b.* Leobschütz, Ger., Feb. 15, 1855; *d.* Berlin, Dec. 6, 1915. 1894-d., dir., Stern Cons. Comp. violin pcs.

Holländer, Victor. Composer, conductor; *b.* Leobschütz, Ger., Apr. 20, 1866. Brother of Gustav H. Comp. operettas.

Hollins, Alfred. Organist; *b.* Hull, Sept. 11, 1865. Blind from birth. 1886-8, soloist *w.* leading U. S. orchestras; 1907-9, toured Australia and S. Africa. Comp. organ and pf. pcs.

Hollmann, Joseph. 'Cellist; *b.* Maestricht, Hol., Oct. 16, 1852. A distinguished virtuoso for whom Saint-Saëns wr. his *2nd 'Cello Concerto.*

Holmberg, Gustaf Fredrik. Violinist, music educator; *b.* Aug. 17, 1872. 1891, to U. S.; 1908, *t.* Oklahoma U.; 1921, cond., Okla. City Symph. Orch. 1920, author, *Elementary Theory of Music* for high schs.

Holmés (*Ol-maze*), **Augusta Mary Anne.** Composer; *b.* Paris, Dec. 16, 1847; *d.* ib., Jan. 28, 1903. Irish parentage. *p.* César Franck. In childhood a brilliant pianist. Comp. symph., operas, songs, incl., *En Chemin.*

Holmes, Guy Earl. Composer; *b.* Baraboo, Wis., Feb. 14, 1873. Flute soloist *w.* Weldon's Band; dir., *Ben Hur* Band; dir., Vogel's Minstrels; *t.* Prior's Cons., Danville, Ill.; fac. mem., Vandercook Sch. of Mus. Comp. over 50 military marches, songs, and saxophone pcs.

Holst, Gustav von. Composer, pianist, organist, trombonist; *b.* Cheltenham, Eng., Sept. 21, 1874; *d.* London, May 25, 1934. 1893, gr., R. C. M.; dir., Morley Coll.; *t.* R. C. M.; 1928, visited U. S. Comp. orch. wks., incl., *The Planets;* opera, chamb. mus., and choral wks., incl., *Ode to Death;* and an unbelievably long list of wks. in all forms.

Holyoke, Samuel. Early American musician, composer, teacher; *b.* Boxford, Mass., 1762; *d.* Concord, N. H., 1816. Wr. *Harmonia Americana* (1791); hymn tune, *Arnheim,* and many songs.

Homer, Louise Dilworth, née Beatty. Contralto; *b.* Pittsburgh, Pa., 1872. 1899, Covent Garden; 1900-19, Met. Op. Her daughter, Louise H., in Met. Op. (1936).

Homer, Sidney. Composer; *b.* Boston, Dec. 9, 1864. *p.* Rheinberger. Comp. songs, incl., *Banjo Song,* sung by his wife, Louise H., also organ and pf. pcs.

Honegger, Arthur. Composer, violinist; *b.* Havre, Fr., Mar. 10, 1892. 1912, gr., Paris Cons., u. Widor; also *p.* Vincent d'Indy. Leader of the "French-six." 1921, perf. of ballet, *Horace Victorieux,* marked his fruition. First publication in U. S., 1933, *Movement Symphonique, No. III,* perf. Boston Symph. *w.* Koussevitsky. Comp. orch. wks., incl., *Pacific 231;* choral and chamb. mus., and pcs. for piano.

Hood, Helen. Composer; *b.* Chelsea, Mass., Jun. 28, 1863. Comp. chamb. mus., violin pcs., songs.

Hoogstraten, Willem van. Conductor; *b.* Utrecht, Mar. 18, 1884. First gained repute by a Brahms festival in Vienna, and a Mozart festival in Salzburg. 1911, *m.* Elly Ney, the pianist. 1921, g.-cond., New York Phil.; cond., summer concerts at Lewisohn Stadium; 1925, cond., Portland (Ore.) Symph. Orch., appointed on the death of Theodore Spiering. Frequent g.-cond. in Europe and Amer.

Hooker, Brian. Librettist; *b.* New York. Edu., Yale U. 1903-05, *t.* English, Columbia U.; 1905-09, Yale U.; since 1915, Columbia U.

Hope-Jones, Robert. Inventor; *b.* Hooton Grange, Eng., Feb. 9, 1859; *d.* Rochester, N. Y., Sept. 13, 1914. An electrical engineer who pioneered in developing the electric action pipe organ; inventor of the unit organ. 1903-05, *w.* Austin Organ Co.; 1905-07, Skinner Company; 1907, formed Hope-Jones Organ Co., Elmira, N. Y. (taken over by Wurlitzer in 1910).

Hopekirk, Helen. Pianist, composer, teacher; *b.* Edinburgh, Scot., May 20, 1856. *p.* Leschetizky. 1883, *m.* William Wilson, and emi. to U. S.; 1891-7, world tours; *t.* N. E. Cons.; 1919, ret. to Eng. Comp. orch., pf. concerto, pcs.

Hopkins, Edward John. Organist, composer; *b.* Westminster, Eng., Jun. 30, 1818; *d.* London, Feb. 4, 1901. 1831, sang at coronation of William IV, and 1897, in Victoria's jubilee. Comp. ch. mus.

Hopkinson, Francis. Composer; *b.* Phila., Sept. 21, 1737; *d.* ib., May 9, 1791. A.M., LL.D., from U. of Penn.; invented improvements in harpsichord; America's first comp. A lawyer by profession. Signator to the Declaration of Independence. Friend of George Washington.

Hopper, De Wolf. Comic opera comedian; *b.* N. Y., Mar. 30, 1858; *d.* Kansas City, Sept. 23, 1935. Assoc. *w.* Amer. comic opera history from *Hazel Kirke* (1880) to *Student Prince* (1928). Remembered for his six wives, and his reciting of *Casey at the Bat.*

Hornemann, Johann Ole Emil. Composer; *b.* Copenhagen, Den., May 13, 1809; *d.* ib., May 29, 1870. Ballad comp.

Horner, Charles Francis. Music educator; *b.* Menomonee, Wis., Aug. 1, 1878. St. Law; fd. and pres., Redpath-Horner Chautauquas, and Redpath-Horner Lyceum Bur.; owner, Lyceum-Central Bur.; pres., Horner-Witte Concert Bur.; 1914, fd.-pres., Horner Inst. Fine Arts, now Kansas City-Horner Cons.

Horowitz, Vladimir. Pianist; *b.* Rus., Oct. 1, 1903. 1928, first Amer. tour.

Horsley, Charles Edward. Organist, composer; *b.* London, Dec. 6, 1822; *d.* New York, Mar. 4, 1876. Comp. orch., chamb. mus. Son of H. W. H.

Horsley, Henry William. Organist, composer; *b.* London, Nov. 15, 1774; *d.* ib., Jun. 2, 1858. Comp. sacred mus.

Horvath, Geza. Composer, pianist, teacher; *b.* Komáron, Hun., May 27, 1868. Comp. pf., teaching pcs.

Hoschna, Karl. Composer; *b. c.* 1870; *d.* N. Y., Dec. 23, 1911. 1896, to U. S. Comp. many operettas, incl., *Madame Sherry* (1910) *w.* Lena Abarbanell.

Hosmer, Elmer Samuel. Composer, teacher; *b.* Mar., 1862. *t.* R. I. Coll. of Edu., Providence. Comp. three cantatas, anthems, songs.

Hosmer, Lucius E. Composer; *b.* Acton, Mass., Aug. 14, 1870; *d.* Jefferson, N. H., May 11, 1935. Comp. comic operas, orch. pcs., incl., *Southern Rhapsody;* and songs.

Howard, John Tasker. Writer, composer; *b.* Brooklyn, Nov. 30, 1890. Gr., Williams Coll.; former mg.-ed., *The Musician.* Author of *Our American Music* (1930), and biographies of *Stephen Foster* and *Ethelbert Nevin.*

Howard, Kathleen. Operatic contralto; *b.* Canada. Eng. parents, naturalized U. S. citizen. *p.* de Reszke. 1907, debut, Metz Op.; 1913, Royal Op., London, *u.* Nikisch; leading contralto, Century Op., N. Y.; 1916, Met. Op. Author, 1918, *Confessions of an Opera Singer;* 1928, ed., *Harper's Bazar,* New York.

Howells, Herbert. Composer, conductor; *b.* Lydney, Eng., Oct. 17, 1892. 1912, edu., R. Coll. Mus., *u.* Stanford. 1912, *Mass in the Dorian Mode,* intro. Westminster Cath.; 1913, *Concerto in C-Minor,* intro. by Stanford at Queen's Hall; 1920, *t.* R. Coll.; 1921, cond., Cape Town; 1923, toured Canada and U. S. Comp. orch. wks., incl., *Paradise Rondel;* chamb. mus., incl., *Rhapsodic Quintet;* choral, piano and organ pcs.

Howland, William. Vocal teacher; *b.* Worcester, Mass., May 1, 1871. 1900-14, head of vocal dept., U. of Mich. Sch. of Mus.; 1914, dir. vocal dept., Detroit Inst. of Mus. Art; fd.-dir., Northwestern Choral Club.

Hoyt, Charles H. Boston music and drama critic; turned playwright (1891), he interpolated *The Bowery* in waning play *A Trip to Chinatown,* extending the run to 650 consecutive perf. Bowery merchants vainly protested against the song, but it became a historic seller. The music was written by Percy Gaunt, his mus. dir.

Hrimaly (*Ri-mahl-ee*), **Adalbert.** Violinist, conductor, composer; *b.* Pilsen, Boh., Jul. 30, 1842; *d.* Vienna, Jun. 17, 1908. 1869, *t.* Moscow Cons. Comp. the opera, *Die verzauberte Prinz,* violin pcs., and studies.

Hubay (*Hoo-bye*), **Jeno.** Violinist, composer; *b.* Budapest, Sept. 15, 1858; *d.* Locz, Czechoslovakia, Jul. 13, 1925. 1882, *t.* Brussels Cons., succ. Wieniawski; 1866-*d.*, *t.* and dir., Budapest, Cons. Comp. operas, incl., *Der Geigenmacher von Cremona* (1893), violin pcs.

Huber, Frederick R. Music director; *b.* Baltimore, Jan. 12, 1881. Edu., Peabody Cons. of Mus. Municipal dir. of mus. for the city of Baltimore; dir., Radio Station WBAL.

Huber (*Hoo-ber*), **Hans.** Composer; *b.* Schönewerd, Switz., Jun. 28, 1852; *d.* Locarno, Dec. 25, 1921. 1876-1918, dir., Basle Cons. Leading figure in Swiss mus. during his epoch. Comp. symph., cantatas, concertos, chamb. mus.; also operas, *Kudrun, Der Simplicius.*

Hubermann (*Hoo-ber-man*), **Bronislaw.** Violinist; *b.* Czenstochowa, Pol., Dec. 19, 1882. 1896-7, toured U. S., as prodigy; 1893, as mature artist, was soloist of Phil. *u.* Richard Strauss. Famous virtuoso.

Huberti (*Hoo-bair-tee*), **Gustave Léon.** Composer, teacher; *b.* Brussels, Apr. 14, 1843; *d.* ib., Jun. 28, 1911. Comp. oratorios, symph., concertos.

Hucbald. Theorist; *b.* Flanders *c.* 840; *d.* 930.

Hüe (*Hwee*), **Georges Adolphe.** Composer; *b.* Versailles, Fr., May 6, 1858. 1879, Prix de Rome. Comp. five operas, symph., instr. pcs., and songs. Popularly known by his song, *J'ai pleuré en Rêve.*

Hueffer (*Heef-fer*), **Francis.** Writer; *b.* Münster, Ger., May 22, 1843; *d.* London, Feb. 19, 1889. 1878, critic, London *Times.* Author of *Richard Wagner and the Music of the Future, The Troubadours, Musical Studies,* and other wks. on mus.

Huehn, Julius M. Operatic baritone; *b.* Revere, Mass., Jan. 12, 1910. Edu., Carnegie Inst. Tech., Juilliard Grad. Sch.; Chicago Gr. Op.; 1934, Met. Op.

Huerter, Charles Joseph. Organist, composer; *b.* Brooklyn, N. Y., Jan. 10, 1885. Edu., Royal Acad., Berlin. 1917, org., Syracuse, N. Y. Comp. 300 instr. pcs., and songs.

Hughes, Adella Prentiss. Orchestra manager; *b.* Cleveland, O., Nov. 29, 1869. 1890, A.B., Vassar; organizer, Cleveland Orch., and its mgr. since 1898. 1920, dec., Order of General Haller's Swords (Poland).

Hughes, Edwin. Pianist, teacher; *b.* Washington, Aug. 15, 1884. *p.* and asst., Leschetizky. *t.* Munich; 1916, to U. S.; 1919-22, *t.* Inst. of Mus. Art, N. Y. Gives two-piano concerts *w.* wife, Jewel Bethany Hughes; conducts master classes; New York's leading piano teacher.

Hughes, Royal Delaney. Professor of music; *b.* Cuba, Ill., Sept. 13, 1884. 1918, A.M., Monmouth (Ill.) Coll.; 1924-5, John Knowles Paine travelling fellow, Harvard; st., Sorbonne and Ecole Normale de Musique, Paris; 1926, Ph.D., Harvard; 1925, prof. mus., Ohio State U., Columbus.

Hughes, Rupert. Composer, author; *b.* Lancaster, Mo., Jan. 31, 1872. Author of books on mus. and musicians; popular novelist; comp. songs.

Hugo, John Adam. Composer; *b.* Conn., Jan. 5, 1873. 1919, opera, *The Temple Dancer,* prod. Met. Op. Comp. symph., piano concerto, instr. pcs., songs.

Huhn (*Hune*), **Bruno.** Organist, composer; *b.* London, Aug. 1, 1871. 1891, to N. Y. Comp. sacred and secular songs and choral mus.; best known by song, *Invictus.*

Hull, Alexander. Composer, teacher; *b.* 1887. 1908, dir. mus., Pacific Coll., Newberg, Ore. Comp. symph.; orch. suite *Java,* for piano and orch.; piano sonata; comp. operas, *Paola and Francesca,* and *Merlin and Vivien.*

Hull, Arthur Eaglefield. Writer, teacher; *b.* Market Harborough, Eng., 1876. Author of wks. on mus. biography, criticism, harmony. Ed. of *Dictionary of Modern Music and Musicians.*

Hullah, John Pyke. Organist, composer, teacher; *b.* Worcester, Eng., Jun. 27, 1812; *d.* London, Feb. 21, 1884. A zealous advocate of the Wilhem method of class instruction, and of mus. for the masses. Comp. operas, songs. Author of text books.

Hüllmandel (*Heel-man-del*), **Nicholas-Joseph.** Pianist, composer; *b.* Strassburg, Alsace, 1751; *d.* London, Dec. 19, 1823. Comp. piano pcs.

Humfrey, Pelham. Composer; *b.* London, 1647; *d.* Windsor, Eng., Jul. 14, 1674. Famous English comp. during reign of Charles II.

Humiston, William Henry. Organist, composer, conductor; *b.* Marietta, O., Apr. 27, 1869; *d.* N. Y., 1923. 1912-23, asst. cond. and program annotator N. Y. Phil. Orch. Comp. *Southern Fantasy,* overture to *Twelfth Night;* dramatic scene for soprano, chorus and orch.; songs.

Hummel (*Hoom-mel*), **Ferdinand.** Pianist, composer; *b.* Berlin, Sept. 6, 1855. Comp. operas, chamb. wks.

Hummel, Johann Nepomuk. Pianist, composer; *b.* Pressburg, Hun., Nov. 14, 1778; *d.* Weimar, Oct. 17, 1837. *p.* Mozart. A celebrated virtuoso in his day. Comp. masses, operas, cantatas, chamb. mus., and much piano mus., little of which has modern value.

Humperdinck (*Hoom-per-dink*), **Engelbert.** Composer; *b.* Siegburg, Ger., Sept. 1, 1854; *d.* Neustrelitz, Sept. 28, 1921. Awarded Mozart, Mendelssohn and Meyerbeer stipends, 1885-1920; taught in various Cons. Opera *Hänsel und Gretel,* made him one of the conspicuous comp. of his day. *Königskinder,* a later success, had its première in N. Y. Comp. many other operatic and choral wks. One of the most successful of the Wagnerian disciples.

Huneker, James Gibbon. Writer, author; *b.* Phila., Pa., Jan. 31, 1860; *d.* Brooklyn, Feb. 9, 1921. *p.* and asst. to Joseffy. Brilliant essayist on mus., art, and literature. Critic on New York newspapers, chiefly *The Sun.* Author of many books. Issued his memoirs under title of *Steeplejack* (1921).

Hunkins, Sterling. 'Cellist; *b.* San Jose, Cal., 1907. 1929, mem., N. Y. Chamb. Mus. Soc.; 1935, *t.* Dalcroze Inst.

Hünten (*Hin-ten*), **Franz.** Pianist, composer; *b.* Coblenz, Ger., Dec. 26, 1793; *d.* ib., Feb. 22, 1878. 1821-37, *t.* Paris. A fashionable virtuoso, and popular comp. of chamb. mus., and salon pcs. for piano.

Huré, Jean. Composer; *b.* Gien (Loiret), Fr., Sept. 17, 1877. 1898, fd. Normal Sch. of Mus., Paris. Comp. technical pf. and organ wks.; piano and violin sonata; 2 str. quartets; 2 pf. and 'cello sonatas.

Huss, Henry Holden. Piano teacher, composer; *b.* Newark, N. J., Jun. 21, 1862. Long career in N. Y. as teacher, and in lecture-recitals *w.* Hildegard Hoffman Huss. Comp. orch. wks., songs with orch., violin and piano concertos, chamb. mus., and songs.

Hutcheson, Ernest. Pianist; *b.* Melbourne, Jul. 20, 1871. 1898, Berlin; 1900, *t.* Peabody Cons., Baltimore; dean, Juilliard Sch. of Mus., N. Y. Comp. tone-poem, *Merlin and Vivien,* piano concerto, pf. pcs.

Hüttenbrenner (*Hit-ten-bren-ner*), **Anselm.** Pianist; *b.* Graz, Aus., Oct. 13, 1794; *d.* ib., Jun. 5, 1868. Comp. symph., overtures, masses, operas, chamb. wks., fugues.

Hyatt, Nathaniel Irving. Pianist, organist, composer; *b.* Lansingburgh, N. Y., 1865. Comp. overture, *Enoch Arden,* chamb. wks., piano mus., songs.

Hyllested, August. Pianist, composer; *b.* Stockholm, Swed., Jun. 17, 1858. *p.* Liszt. 1886, asst. dir., Chicago Mus. Coll. Comp. piano wks., songs, orch. wks.

I

Ibert, Jacques. Composer, pianist; *b.* Paris, Aug. 15, 1890. 1919, won Prix de Rome *w.* cantata, *Le Poète et la Fée.* Comp. orch. wks., incl., symph.-p., *Ballad of Reading Gaol,* and *Les Escales;* opera, incl., *Angélique;* ballets, choral and chamb. mus., and pcs. for piano.

Igumnov (*I-goom-noff*), **Konstantin.** Pianist, teacher; *b.* Lebediana, Rus., May 1, 1873. 1909, prof., Moscow Cons.

Iliffe, Frederick. Organist, composer; *b.* Smeeton-Westerby, Eng., Feb. 21, 1847. 1908, examiner, Oxford U. Comp. oratorio, symph., choruses *w.* orch., chamb. wks.

Iljinsky (*Il-yin-ski*), **Alexander Alexandrovitch.** Composer; *b.* Tsarskoë-Selo, Rus., Jan. 24, 1859. 1885, prof., Moscow Cons. Comp. orch. suites, symph., cantatas, incid. mus., opera, and smaller wks. Popularly known by a little *Berceuse* for piano.

Imbert (*Am-bair*), **Hugues.** Writer; *b.* Nièvre, Fr., 1842; *d.* Paris, 1905. Author of anecdotal wks. on mus. subjects.

Incledon, Charles Benjamin. Tenor; *b.* St. Kevern, Eng., Feb. 5, 1763; *d.* Worcester, Eng., Feb. 11, 1826. Famous ballad singer. 1817-8, toured U. S.

d'Indy (*Dandy*), **Paul Marie Theodore Vincent.** Pianist, composer; *b.* Paris, Mar. 27, 1851; *d.* ib., Dec. 2, 1931. St., Lavignac; ardent disciple of César Franck. 1875, *Jean Hungade,* intro. Concerts Populaires *w.* Pasdeloup; fd. *w.* Franck, Société Nationale de Musique; fd. of Schola Cantorum, Prof. Paris Cons. Comp. symph. p., *La Forêt Enchantée, Saugefleurie, Istar,* the *Wallenstein Triptich;* symph., cantatas, the Druidic opera, *Fervaal;* the symbolic *L'Étranger,* and the lighter *Attendez-moi-sous l'orme.*

Ingelius, Axel Gabriel. Composer; *b.* Säkyläska, Fin., Oct. 26, 1822; *d.* Rystad, Fin., Mar. 2, 1868. Comp. songs of a national character.

Inzenga, José. Composer; *b.* Madrid, Sp., Jun. 4, 1828; *d.* ib., Jul., 1891. Comp. zarzuelas.

Ippolitov-Ivanov, Michael. Conductor, composer; *b.* Gatchina, Rus., Nov. 19, 1859; *d.* Moscow, Jan. 28, 1935. 1876-82, edu., Cons. St. Petersburg, *w.* Rimsky-Korsakoff. 1893, prof., Moscow Cons.; 1899, cond., Moscow Private Op.; pres., Union of Soviet Composers; 1934, awarded Order of the Red Banner. Comp. operas, and orch. wks., incl., *Caucasian Sketches.*

Ireland, John. Composer; *b.* Bowden, Eng., Aug. 13, 1879. Edu., R. Coll. Mus. 1917, *Second Violin Sonata,* intro. by Albert Sammons and William Murdoch. Comp. songs, notably *Spleen, Sea Fever,* and *A Shropshire Lad;* orch. wks., incl., *The Forgotten Rite;* chamb. mus., pf. pcs.

Isaac (*Ee-sahk*), **Heinrich (Arrigo Tedesco).** Composer; *b. c.* 1450; *d. c.* 1517. German contrapuntal school.

Isouard (*Ee-swar*), **Nicolo.** Composer; *b.* Island of Malta, Dec. 6, 1775; *d.* Paris, Mar. 23, 1818. Opera comp.

Istel, Edgar. Composer, author; *b.* Mainz, Ger., Feb. 23, 1880. 1920, Madrid. Author of more than twenty books on mus. Comp. operas and songs.

Iturbi, Jose. Conductor, pianist; *b.* Valencia, Nov. 22, 1895. Celebrated piano virtuoso. G.-cond., Lewisohn Stadium, N. Y.; Mexico City, Phila.

Ivanoff, Michael Michailovitch. Composer; *b.* Moscow, Sept. 23, 1849. Comp. four operas, orch. wks., ballet, pf. pcs., songs.

Ives, Charles. Composer; *b.* Danbury, Conn., Oct. 20, 1874. Edu., Yale, *u.* Horatio Parker. 1898-1930, business career, *w.* music as an avocation. Composes in a thoroughly iconoclastic and anarchistic tonal idiom, incl., symph. wks., chamb. mus., piano pcs., and songs.

d'Ivry (*Eev-ree*), **Richard Marquis.** Composer; *b.* Beaune, Fr., Feb. 4, 1829; *d.* Hyères, Fr., Dec. 18, 1903. Opera comp.

J

Jacchia, Agide. Musical director; *b.* Lugo, It., Jan. 5, 1875. Gr., Rossini Cons., *u.* Mascagni. 1902, to U. S., asst. cond., Mascagni Op. Co.; 1922, naturalized citizen; 1907-9, toured U. S. *w.* Milano Op. Co.; 1914, mus. dir., Century Op. Co., N. Y.; 1917-26, cond., Boston Symph., "Pops"; 1920, dir., Boston Cons. of Mus. Comp. cantatas, arr., songs.

Jackson, Leonora. Violinist; *b.* Boston, Feb. 20, 1879. *p.* Joachim. Successful concert artist in Europe and U. S.

Jackson, William. Organist, composer; *b.* Exeter, Eng., May 28, 1730; *d.* ib., Jul. 12, 1803. Comp. ch. mus.

Jacobsen (*Yä'-kōb-sĕn*), **Sascha.** Violinist; *b.* Russia. *p.* Kneisel.

Jacobi, Frederick. Composer; *b.* San Francisco, May 4, 1891. St., Berlin Hochschule, *u.* Paul Juon. 1913-17, asst. cond., Met. Op.; 1926, *String Quartet on Indian Themes,* perf. at International Fest. at Zurich, won award of SPAM (1935); *Indian Dances,* intro. Stokowski and Phila. Symph. *h.* Northampton, Mass. Comp. orch. wks., incl., *Eve of St. Agnes;* choral, *The Poet in the Desert;* chamb. mus., incl., the *String Quartet on Indian Themes.*

Jacobsohn (*Yah-cob-soan*), **Simon E.** Violinist, teacher; *b.* Mitau, Rus., Dec. 24, 1839; *d.* Chicago, Oct. 3, 1902. Edu., Leipzig. 1872, conc.-m. *u.* Th. Thomas; *t.* Coll. of Mus., Cin.; *t.* Chicago Mus. Coll. The teacher of many eminent Amer. violinists.

Jacoby (*Yah-co-bee*), **Georges.** Violinist, composer; *b.* Berlin, 1840; *d.* London, 1906. Comp. operas, ballets, etc.

Jadassohn (*Yad-das-zon*), **Salomon.** Pianist, teacher, theorist; *b.* Breslau, Aug. 13, 1831; *d.* Leipzig, Feb. 1, 1902. Comp. symph., vocal wks., chamb. mus. Author of wks. on harmony and other subjects which are in world-wide use.

Jaell (*Yale*), **Alfred.** Pianist, composer; *b.* Trieste, It., Mar. 5, 1832; *d.* Paris, Feb. 27, 1882. Brilliant player.

Jagel, Frederick. Tenor; *b.* Brooklyn, N. Y., Jun. 10, 1897. 1923-27, st., Milan, It.; 1924, debut, Livorno; 1927, Met. Op.; also Ravinia Op. Co.

Jahn (*Yahn*), **Otto.** Writer; *b.* Kiel, Ger., Jun. 16, 1813; *d.* Göttingen, Ger., Sept. 9, 1869. Philologist and archæologist, comp. and writer on mus. His *Life of Mozart* is his most important contribution to mus. literature.

Jähns, Friedrich Wilhelm. Vocal teacher, conductor, historical student; *b.* Berlin, 1809; *d.* ib., 1888. *t.* of singing. He made a hobby of collecting materials relating to Ch. Maria von Weber, which collection was bought (1883) by the Berlin Royal Library, thus making him a Weber specialist. He wr. *C. M. von Weber in Seinen Werken,* and many articles. Comp. also chamb. mus., and songs.

Jakobowski, Edward. Composer of *Erminie*. This comic opera, prod. in 1886 at the Comedy Th., N. Y., ran for 1,256 perf. The producer, Rudolph Aronson, is said to have paid the comp., $120,000 in royalties. The comp. not recorded in any of the mus. encyclopedias. The Jakobowski appears to have been a pseudonym, some say for E. Belville—which may also be another pseudonym. The comp. is reported as *b.* in London in 1858, from Viennese parents of Polish extraction, and to have been edu., at the Vienna Cons. Three other wks. of record were unsuccessful, but *Erminie* made history for three decades, and is still a lively corpse. It was revived as lately as 1921.

James, Philip. Composer, conductor; *b.* Jersey City, Mar. 17, 1890. 1908, debut as cond., Albert Hall, London; cond. of Bamberger Little Symph. Orch., at WOR; prof. of Mus., N. Y. U.; 1932, won NBC prize *w.* Station WJZBX, a satirical suite. Comp. 12 orch. wks., 32 choral wks., chamb. mus., and songs.

Janacek, Leos. Composer, pianist, organist; *b.* Hukvaldy, Moravia, Jul. 3, 1854; *d.* ib., Aug. 12, 1928. 1874, st., Prague Coll. Organ Playing. Fd., Organ Sch. at Teacher's Sch.; 1919, dir., Brunn Cons. Best known by opera, *Jenufa,* intro. Brunn, 1904; Prague, 1916; Vienna, 1918, *w.* great success. Comp. orch. wks., incl., *Taras Bulba;* opera, chamb. mus.

Janiewicz (*Yah-ne-a-vitch*), **Felix.** Violinist; *b.* Vilna, Lithuania, 1762; *d.* Edinburgh, Scot., 1848. Often spelled: Yanie-wicz; friend of Mozart; entered mus. publishing business in Liverpool. 1813, to London, helped to fd. the Phil. Soc.

Jankó (*Yang-ko*), **Paul von.** Inventor; *b.* Totis, Hun., Jun. 2, 1856; *d.* Constantinople, 1919. *p.* Vienna Cons. Inventor of a new keyboard, bringing the keys within a smaller span than the present keyboard, and enabling all scales and arpeggios to be fingered alike.

Janotha (*Yah-no-ta*), **Natalie.** Pianist; *b.* nr. Warsaw, Jun. 8, 1856; *d.* The Hague, Jun. 12, 1932. Court pianist at Berlin. A much-decorated person. Translated Kleczinski's *Chopin* into English and German.

Janowka, Thomas Balthasar. *b. c.* 1660. Author of the first mus. dictionary (excepting perhaps that of Tinctor) *Clavis ad thesaurum magnae artis musicae* (1701).

Jansa (*Yan-sa*), **Léopold.** Violinist; *b.* Wildenschwert, Boh., Mar. 23, 1795; *d.* Vienna, Jan. 24, 1875. Comp. *études* for violin.

Janssen, Werner. Composer, conductor; *b.* New York, Jun. 1, 1900. 1928, *New Year's Eve in New York,* perf. Cleveland Symph., in Mecca Temple, N. Y.; 1930, won Guggenheim scholarship; toured Europe as g.-cond., in Berlin, Budapest, Helsingfors, Riga, Rome and Turin; 1934-35, g.-cond., New York Phil. Comp. orch., and chamb. mus.

Janssens, Jean François. Composer; *b.* Antwerp, 1801; *d.* ib., 1835. Comp. operas, symph.

Jarecki (*Yar-esk-ee*), **Heinrich.** Conductor, composer; *b.* Warsaw, Pol., Dec. 6, 1846; *d.* Lemberg, 1918. Comp. operas, orch. wks.

Jarecki, Tadeusz. Composer; b. Lemberg, 1889. p. Taneief. 1912-13, t. Dalcroze Inst., Moscow; 1918, won Coolidge prize, Berkshire Fest., for str. q.; naturalized Amer. citizen. Comp. orch., chamb. mus., songs of ultra-modern tendencies.

Järnefelt (*Yair-neh-felt*), **Edvard Armas.** Composer; b. Viborg, Fin., Aug. 14, 1869. Cond., Stockholm Royal Op. Comp. overtures, suites, symph. p., and small pcs., incl. a popular *Berceuse*.

Jarno (*Yar-no*), **Georg.** Composer; b. Buda-Pesth, Hun., Jun. 3, 1868; d. Breslau, 1920. Opera comp.

Jarvis, Charles H. Pianist, teacher; b. Phila., Pa., Dec. 20, 1837; d. ib., Feb. 25, 1895. 1862, fd. chamb. mus. series that in 30 years presented 800 wks. Bequeathed his library to Drexel Inst.

Jaspar, Maurice. Pianist; b. Liége, Bel., Jun. 20, 1870. t. Liége Cons. Comp. pf. pcs., songs.

Jehin (*Zhay-ang*), **François.** Violinist; b. Spa, Bel., Apr. 18, 1839; d. Montréal, Fr., May 29, 1899.

Jehin, Léon. Conductor, composer; b. Spa, Bel., Jul. 17, 1853. Cond., Monte Carlo.

Jenkins, Cora W. b. Pittsford, Vt. p. Goetschius. 1898, fd.-dir., Mus. Sch., Oakland, Cal., said to be largest on Pacific Coast. Comp. pf. pcs.

Jenkins, David. Conductor, composer; b. Trecastell, Wales, Jan. 1, 1849. Lived many years in retirement at Aberystwith, Wales. Comp. oratorios, cantatas.

Jensen (*Yen-sen*), **Adolph.** Composer; b. Königsberg, Ger., Jan. 12, 1837; d. Baden-Baden, Ger., Jan. 23, 1879. Notable as a song writer as well as a comp. of originality in many forms, but best known for his songs, incl., *O Press Thy Cheek*.

Jentsch (*Yentsh*), **Max.** Pianist, composer; b. Ziesar, Ger., Aug. 5, 1855; d. Stendal, 1918. t. Vienna. Comp. orch., and piano wks.

Jepson, Harry Benjamin. Organist, composer; b. New Haven, Conn., Aug. 16, 1870. p. Widor. 1895, dir., Yale U. Choir; 1906, prof., Yale. Comp. orch., *Rhapsodie*; fantasia for org. and orch.; org. sonatas, cantatas, male choruses.

Jepson, Helen. Operatic soprano; b. Titusville, Pa. 1930, gr., Curtis Inst., Phila.; 1928, operatic debut, Phila. Civic Orch., in Strauss's *Ariadne auf Naxos*; 1930, Phila. Gr. Op.; 1931, m. George Possell, flautist; 1934, debut, Met. Op. w. Lawrence Tibbett in John Lawrence Seymour's *In the Pasha's Garden*.

Jeritza, Maria. Soprano; b. Brunn, Aus., 1893. p Marcella Sembrich. 1910, debut, Olmutz, Aus.; 1912, Vienna Op.; Budapest Op.; Covent Garden, London; 1921, Met. Op., N. Y. 1935, m. Winifred Sheehan, movie magnate.

Jimenez (*Yi-may'-neth*), **Jeronimo.** Composer; b. Seville, Sp., Oct. 10, 1854; d. Madrid, Feb. 20, 1923. Zarzuela and orch. comp.

Jiranek (*Yee-rah-nek*), **Aloys.** Composer, teacher; b. Ledec, Boh., Sept. 3, 1858. t. Kharkov, Rus. Comp. opera, orch., chamb. mus.

Jiranek, Josef. Pianist; b. Ledec, Boh., Mar. 24, 1855. t. Prague Cons. Comp. technical wks. for the piano.

Joachim (*Yo-a-kheem*), **Joseph.** Violinist; b. Kittsee, Hun., Jun. 28, 1831; d. Berlin, Aug. 15, 1907. 1843, t. Leipzig Cons.; 1850, cond., Weimar; 1854, cond., Hanover; dir., Hochschule, Berlin. One of the foremost violin teachers of his generation. Fd. Joachim Quar. Author of a violin *Method*.

Johns, Clayton. Pianist, composer; b. Newcastle, Del., Oct. 24, 1857. Comp. *Berceuse* and *Scherzino* for strings; choruses, pf. pcs., and many popular ballads.

Johns, Louis Edgar. Pianist; b. Pittsburgh, Sept. 27, 1886. p. Humperdinck. t. Stattin, Ger.; 1915, t. Skidmore Coll., Saratoga Springs, N. Y.

Johnson, Edward. Tenor, impresario; b. Guelph, Ont., Can. 1929, LL.D., U. of Western Ont.; st., Vincenzo Lombardi, Florence, It.; debut, Teatro Verdi, Padua, in *Andrea Chenier*; sang five seasons at La Scala, Milan; 1914, creator of *Parsifal* in It., and new rôles by Puccini, Alfano, Pizzetti, Zandonai, Montemezzi, Deems Taylor's *The King's Henchman* and *Peter Ibbetson*; 1922, naturalized U. S. citizen; 1920, Chicago Op.; 1922, Met. Op.; 1935, impresario, Met. Op., succ. late Herbert Witherspoon.

Johnson, Herbert. Tenor, composer; b. Middletown, Conn., 1861; d. Boston, Jul. 21, 1904. Comp. sacred songs.

Johnson, Horace. Composer; b. Mass., 1893. p. Bainbridge Crist. Orch. suite, *Imagery*, perf. Goossens. Comp. symph. p., pf. pcs.

Johnson, John Rosamond. Pianist, organist, composer; b. Jacksonville, Fla., Aug. 11, 1873. St. N. E. Cons.; 1894, debut, Boston; 1912-13, dir. mus., Hammerstein Op. H., London; 1914, t. Settlement Sch. for Colored People, N. Y. Comp. mus. for Cole and Johnson's *Shoo-Fly Regiment*, *Red Moon*, Bert Williams' *Mr. Load of Koal*; arr. Negro spirituals; over 300 popular songs; 1921, made sub-chief Iroquois Indian Tribe.

Johnstone, Arthur Edward. Composer, music editor; b. London, May 13, 1860. As mus. ed., Amer. Bk. Co., he wr. over 1,000 sch. songs and pf. pcs.; w. H. W. Loomis, ed., *Lyric Music Series* of sch. readers; devised system of pf. instruction w. use of player rolls. 1915, concert overture for organ and orch., perf. Chicago Symph. Now dean Braun Schs. of Mus., Wilkes-Barre, Pa.

Jomelli, Jeanne. Dramatic soprano; b. Holland; d. S. F., Aug. 29, 1932. Debut, La Scala; 1906-17, Met. Op., N. Y.

Jomelli (*Yo-mel-lee*), **Niccolo.** Composer; b. Averna, It., May 10, 1714; d. Naples, It., Aug. 25, 1774. Opera comp.

Jonas (*Ho-nas*), **Alberto.** Pianist, teacher; b. Madrid, Sp., Jun. 8, 1868. 1894-8, t. U. of Mich.; 1898-1904, dir., Detroit Cons.; 1905-14, t. Berlin; 1914, t. N. Y. Ed. of a monumental *Master School of Modern Piano Virtuosity*.

Joncières (*Zhon-see-ehr*), **Felix Ludger Victorin de.** Composer; b. Paris, Apr. 12, 1839; d. ib., Oct. 26, 1903. Comp. operas; an earlier champion of Wagner.

Jones, Alton. Pianist; b. Fairfield, Neb., Aug. 3, 1899. 1919, Mus.B., Drake U.; 1921, gr., Inst. Mus. Art, N. Y.; 1925, debut, Aeolian Hall, N. Y.; 1921, t. Inst. of Mus. Art, N. Y.; 1929, head pf. dept., Columbia U. Summer Sch.

Jones, Sydney. Operetta composer; b. Leeds, Eng., 1869. After writing a number of successful ballads, he turned his attention to the popular stage, and produced a dozen operettas, at least one of which, *The Geisha* (1896), achieved a world success. It ran to 760 perf. in London.

Jongen, Joseph. Organist, composer; b. Liége, Bel., Dec. 14, 1873. 1897, won Prix de Rome; 1900, *Symphony*, intro. by Ysaye in Brussels; 1920, dir., Brussels Cons. Comp. orch., chamb. mus., ch. mus., organ pcs.

Jordan, Jules. Tenor, composer; *b.* Willimantic, Conn., Nov. 10, 1850; *d.* Providence, R. I., 1927. 1895, Mus.D., Brown U. Comp. opera, *Rip Van Winkle,* and cantatas, but is known best by his songs.

Joseffy (*Yo-sef-fee*), **Rafael.** Pianist, teacher; *b.* Hunfaln, Hun., Jul. 3, 1853; *d.* New York, Jun. 24, 1915. Distinguished virtuoso. *p.* Liszt. For many years fac. mem. National Cons. of Mus., N. Y. Comp. technical wks., and pf. pcs. Ed. of an edition of the Chopin pf. wks.

Josephson (*Yo-sef-son*), **Jacob Axel.** Composer, organist; *b.* Stockholm, Mar. 27, 1818; *d.* Upsala, Mar. 29, 1880. Comp. vocal wks.

Josten, Werner. Composer; *b.* Eberfeld, Ger., Jun. 12, 1888. *p.* Dalcroze. 1923, prof., Smith Coll.; 1929, *Ode for St. Cecilia's Day,* perf. Worcester Fest.; *Jungle,* by Koussevitsky *w.* Boston Symph; 1933, *Concerto Sacro,* perf. by Stokowski *w.* Phila. Symph. Comp. ballets, incl., *Batoula, Joseph and His Brethren;* orch. and choral wks.

Jouret (*Zhoo-ray*), **Léon.** Composer; *b.* Asch, Bel., Oct. 17, 1828; *d.* Brussels, Bel., 1905. Comp. operas, cantatas.

Journet (*Zhoor-nay*), **Marcel.** Bass; *b.* Grasse, Fr., Jul. 25, 1870; *d.* Vittel, Fr., Sept. 6, 1933. 1901-1908, Met. Op. H.; 1914, Chicago Op.

Juch (*Yookh*), **Emma Antonia Joanna.** Soprano; *b.* Vienna, Jul. 4, 1865. 1861, edu., U. S. 1882, sang in opera in London; 1883-6, N. Y. *u.* Mapelson; 1886-7, *u.* Th. Thomas; 1889-90, fd., Emma Juch Op. Co., and toured U. S. and Mexico.

Juhan, Alexander. Violinist, composer; *b.* probably in Charleston. Son of early Amer. piano maker. 1783, appeared in Phila. as cond. of Andrew Adgate's concerts.

Jullien (*Zhool-leang*), **Jean Lucien Adolphe.** *b.* Paris, Jun. 1, 1845. Paris mus. critic.

Jullien, Louis Antoine. Conductor; *b.* Sisteron, Fr., Apr. 23, 1812; *d.* Paris, Mar. 14, 1860. Estab. reputation as cond. and comp. of dance mus., and *w.* his excellent orch. gave fine perf. of classical wks. 1853-4, toured U. S.; died in an insane asylum.

Junck (*Yoongk*), **Benedetto.** Composer; *b.* Turin, It., Aug. 24, 1852. 1875, to Milan. Comp. chamb. mus., songs.

Jungmann (*Yoong-man*), **Albert.** Composer; *b.* Langensalza, Ger., Nov. 14, 1824; *d.* Vienna, Nov. 7, 1892. Comp. salon mus.

Juon (*Zhoo-on*), **Paul.** Composer; *b.* Moscow, Mar. 9, 1872. Edu., Moscow Cons., *u.* Arensky, 1903, *Second Symph.,* intro. Weiningen; 1906, prof., Hochschule, Berlin. Comp. symph. and chamb. mus.; piano and violin pcs. Popularly known by *Berceuse,* a masterful miniature played by Heifitz.

K

Kaan-Albest, Heinrich von. Pianist; *b.* Tarnopol, Aus., May 29, 1852. 1890, *t.* Prague Cons.; since 1907, dir., succ., Dvořák. Comp. operas, orch., a ballet, and small wks.

Kahn, Robert. Composer; *b.* Mannheim, Ger., Jul. 21, 1865. 1903, *t.* Berlin Hochschule; intimate friend of Joachim and Brahms. Comp. chamb. mus., songs.

Kaiser (*Ki-zer*), **Henri Alfred.** Composer; *b.* Brussels, Mar. 1, 1872. *p.* Bruckner. *h.* London. Comp. ballets, operas, incl., *Stella Maris;* symph.

Kajanus, Robert. Conductor; *b.* Helsingfors, Dec. 2, 1856; *d.* ib., Jul. 6, 1933. 1882, estab. Helsingfors choral soc.; 1886, fd., Helsingfors Phil. Orch.; 1897, dir., Helsingfors Cons.; 1932, cond., Queen's Hall, London, program devoted to Sibelius, whose wks. he intro. to the world.

Kalbeck, Max. Writer; *b.* Breslau, Jan. 4, 1850; *d.* Vienna, 1921. Wr. librettos for Henschel, Poldini, and Von Fielitz operas; and new original texts for several Mozart and Gluck operas. Author, Wagnerian studies, and a historic biography of Brahms (1904-14).

Kalinnikov, Vassili Sergeievitch. Composer; *b.* Voina, Rus., Jan. 13, 1866; *d.* Yalta, Rus., Jan. 11, 1900. Comp. symph. p., incl., *The Nymphs;* cantatas, pf. pcs.

Kalisch, Paul. Tenor; *b.* Berlin, May 6, 1855. 1888, *m.* Lilli Lehman. 1884, Munich Op.; 1887, Met. Op., N. Y.

Kalkbrenner, Friedrich Wilhelm Michael. Pianist, composer; *b.* Berlin, 1788; *d.* Paris, Jun. 10, 1849. Not a great artist, but a thorough technician, and was long a fashionable teacher in London. Comp. concertos, and much chamb. mus. *w.* pf., and technical wks.

Kalliwoda, Johann Wenzel. Violinist, composer; *b.* Prague, Boh., Mar. 21, 1800; *d.* Karlsruhe, Ger., Dec. 3, 1866. Comp. symph., overtures, 2 operas, much chamb. mus., and many violin pcs.

Kalman, Emmerich. Composer; *b.* 1882. Comp. a dozen or more popular Viennese operettas, incl., *Sari* and *Countess Maritza.*

Kamienski, Matthias. Composer; *b.* Oedenburg, Hun., Oct. 13, 1734; *d.* Warsaw, Pol., Jan. 25, 1821. 1778, prod. the first opera in Polish.

Kaminski, Heinrich. Composer; *b.* Tiengen, Black Forest, Jul. 4, 1886. Edu., U. Heidelberg. *p.* Paul Juon. 1924, *Geistliche Lieder,* intro., Salzburg Fest.; opera, *Jurg Jenatch,* notable. *h.* Isartal, nr. Munich. Little known in Amer. Comp. orch. wks., incl., *Concerto Grosso;* opera, chamb. mus., choral mus.

Kappel, Gertrude. Soprano; *b.* Halle, Ger., Sept. 1, 1893. Edu., Leipzig Cons. 1911, debut, Hanover, Vienna, Paris; 1922, Met. Op.; concerts. Especially notable in Wagnerian rôles.

Karasowski (*Kar-a-sof-ski*), **Moritz.** Writer; *b.* Warsaw, Sept. 22, 1823; *d.* Dresden, Apr. 30, 1892. Polish mus. historian.

Karg-Ehlert, Sigfrid. Organist, composer; *b.* Oberndorf, Ger., Nov. 21, 1879; *d.* Leipzig, Apr., 1933. Comp. orch., chamb. mus., but best known by his wks. for the organ.

Kargonoff, Genari. Composer; *b.* Kvarelia, Caucasus, May 12, 1858; *d.* Rostov, Rus., Apr. 12, 1890. Comp. piano wks.

Karlowicz, Miecyslav. Composer; *b.* Wiszniewo, Lithuania, Dec. 11, 1876; *d.* Zakopane, Galicia, Feb. 10, 1909. Comp. orch. mus.

Kaschperov, Vladimir. Teacher of singing, composer; *b.* Simbirsk, Rus., 1827; *d.* Romanzevo, Rus., Jul. 8, 1894. Opera comp.

Kashin, Daniel Nikititch. Composer; *b.* Moscow, 1773; *d.* ib., 1844. Comp. operas, cantatas, patriotic songs. Ed. two important collections of Rus. folk-songs.

Kashkin, Nicolai Dmitrievitch. Writer; *b.* Voronesk, Rus., Dec. 9, 1839. Russian critic and historian. Author, *Recollections of Tschaikowsky* (1896) and *Outline of Russian Music History* (1908). Lives Moscow.

Kaskel, Karl Freiherr von. Composer; b. Dresden, Ger., Oct. 10, 1866. 1900, to Munich. Comp. operas, incl., *Die Nachtigal* (1910).

Kastalsky, Alexander Dimitrievitch. Composer; b. Moscow, 1856. Contributed much to development of Rus. liturgical mus. Comp. sacred mus., piano wks.

Kastner, Johann Georg. Composer; b. Strassburg, Mar. 9, 1811; d. Paris, Dec. 19, 1867. Opera comp., and distinguished author of mus. treatises.

Kate (*Kah-teh*), **André ten.** 'Cellist, composer; b. Amsterdam, May 22, 1796; d. Haarlem, Jul. 27, 1858. Comp. operas, chamb. mus., part-songs.

Kauffmann, Fritz. Conductor, composer; b. Berlin, Jun. 17, 1855. 1889, cond., Magdeburg. Comp. orch., chamb. wks.

Kaun (*Kown*), **Hugo.** Composer; b. Berlin, Mar. 21, 1863; d. ib., Apr. 2, 1932. 1887-92, t. Milwaukee (Wis.); 1902, t. Berlin; 1922, prof., Klindworth-Scharwenka Cons., Berlin. Comp. operas, symph., chamb. and choral wks., and many songs.

Kayser, Heinrich Ernst. Violinist, teacher; b. Altona, Ger., Apr. 16, 1815; d. Hamburg, Jan. 17, 1888. Comp. technical studies for the violin.

Keiser (*Ki-zer*), **Reinhard.** Composer; b. Teuchern, Ger., Jan. 12, 1674; d. Hamburg, Sept. 12, 1739. 1697-1734, dir., Hamburg, Op., where he prod. 115 wks. Young Handel played in his orch. Comp. many *singspiele*.

Kéler-Bela (Albert von Kéler). Conductor, composer; b. Bartfeld, Hun., Feb. 13, 1820; d. Wiesbaden, Ger., Nov. 20, 1882. Comp. brilliant dance mus., and violin pcs.

Keller, Matthias. Composer; b. Ulm, Ger., Mar. 20, 1818; d. Boston, 1869. Comp. Amer. hymn, *Angel of Peace*, to a text by Oliver Wendell Holmes, for Gilmore's Peace Fest. in Boston.

Keller, Walter. Music educator, organist, composer; b. Chicago, Feb. 23, 1873. *p.* Gleason. 1899, t. Northwestern U.; 1906, dir., Sherwood Mus. Sch., Chicago; 1903-18, org., St. Vincent de Paul's; 1912, dean of Mus., De Paul U.; cond., première of Gleason's *Otho Visconti*. Comp. comic opera, *Crumpled Isle*; melodrama, *Alaric's Death*; organ pcs., songs.

Kelley, Edgar Stillman. b. Sparta, Wis., Apr. 14, 1857. Edu., Stuttgart; LL.D., U. of Cin. Achieved success in Germany, and on return to U. S. was awarded a residence fellowship at Western Coll., Oxford, O.; t. comp., Cin. Cons. of Mus. Comp. symph., and chamb. mus., the light opera, *Puritania*; incid. mus. to *Macbeth* and *Ben Hur*, and misc. pcs. Author, *Chopin, the Composer*.

Kelley, Jessie (Mrs. Edgar Stillman K.). Music educator; b. Chippewa Falls., Wis. 1910, dir. mus., Western Coll., Oxford, O.; 1911, lect. Cin. Cons. Hon. pres., Natl. Fed. Mus. Clubs.

Kellog, Clara Louise. Soprano; b. Sumterville, S. C., Jul. 1, 1842; d. New Hartford, Conn., May 13, 1916. 1861-87, sang in opera in N. Y. and London, part of the time in her own company. 1887, m. Carl Strakosch, her manager, and retired.

Kelly, Eleanor. Music supervisor; b. Medina, Mich., Aug. 28, 1879. 1920, dir., Cons. of Mus., Hillsdale (Mich.) Coll.

Kennedy, Steven. Pseudonym of **Melvin Hemphill** (q. v.).

Kerker, Gustave. Operetta composer; b. Westphalia, Feb. 28, 1857. 1880, mus. dir., N. Y. Casino, then at its greatest popularity as the home of comic opera in Amer. Comp. several operettas, one of which attained a moderate success, *The Belle of New York*, but in London had a run of 697 perf.

Kern, Carl Wilhelm. Composer; b. Schlitz, Ger., Jun. 4, 1874. t. St. Louis. Comp. salon pcs. for pf., songs.

Kern, Jerome David. Composer; b. N. Y., Jan. 27, 1885. St., N. Y. Coll. of Mus. Comp. operettas, incl., *Oh, Boy!* (1917), *Sally* (1920), *Sunny* (1925), *Sweet Adeline* (1929), *Cat and the Fiddle* (1931), *Show Boat* (1927) and the screen play, *I Dream Too Much* (1935, w. Lily Pons). 1929, library of first editions brought over $1,500,000 at auction.

Kernochan, Marshall Rutgers. Composer; b. N. Y., Dec. 14, 1880. t. Tuxedo, N. Y. Comp. cantata, *The Foolish Virgins*; choral numbers, songs.

Kes, Willem. Conductor, composer; b. Dordrecht, Hol., Feb. 16, 1856; d. Munich, 1934. 1888, cond., Concertgsbourn, Amsterdam; 1896-8, cond., Glasgow Scottish Orch., succ. Henschel; 1905, dir., Coblentz Cons. Comp. symph., and small pcs.

Kettenus (*Ket-nus*), **Aloys.** Violinist, composer; b. Verviers, Bel., Feb. 22, 1823; d. London, Oct. 3, 1896. Comp. opera, *Stella Monti*; violin mus.

Ketterer, Eugène. Pianist, composer; b. Rouen, Fr., Jul. 7, 1831; d. Paris, Dec. 18, 1870. Edu., Paris Cons. Comp. salon mus.

Keurvels, Edward H. J. Conductor, composer; b. Antwerp, Bel., 1853; d. ib., 1916. 1882, cond., Sch. Flamand, Antwerp; prod. première of Benoit's *Charlotte Corday*. Comp. operas, cantatas.

Keussler (*Koyss-ler*), **Gerhard von.** Conductor, composer; b. Schwanenburg, Livonia, Jul. 6, 1874. 1920, cond., Hamburg Phil. Comp. symph. p.

Key, Francis Scott. Baltimore lawyer. Wr. text of *Star Spangled Banner* on deck of British flagship during bombardment of Ft. McHenry on Sept. 13, 1814, whence he went u. flag-of-truce seeking release of Dr. Beans, a physician of Marlborough, Md. The words were written to the meter of the *Ode to Anacreon*, generally attributed to John Stafford Smith, but equally possible to have been written for him, or his predecessor at Chapel Royal, Samuel Arnold, by Handel, then in London. Many verses have been set to this tune.

Khachaturjan, Aram. Composer; b. Tiflis, Rus., 1904. 1934, gr., Moscow Cons., u. Miascowski. Comp. *Symphony*, E minor, and piano concerto.

Khrennikov, Tichon. Composer; b. Russia. Edu., Moscow Cons., u. Shebalin. 1935, *Symphony*, perf. Moscow Broadcasting Orch.

Kidson, Frank. Writer; b. Leeds, Nov. 15, 1855. Historian and collector of folk-songs.

Kiel (*Keel*), **Friedrich.** Composer; b. Puderbach, Ger., Oct. 7, 1821; d. Berlin, Sept. 14, 1885. 1870, prof., Hochschule, Berlin. Comp. choral wks. of large dimensions, and chamb. mus.

Kienzl (*Keenzel*), **Wilhelm.** Composer; b. Waizenkirchen, Aus., Jan. 17, 1857. Edu., Prague Cons.; st., Rheinberger in Munich; friend of Liszt and Wagner. 1893, head of Munich opera; 1893, retired to Vienna; 1886, opera, *Urvasi*, prod. at Dresden; 1894, opera, *Evangelimann*, intro. w. success.

Kiesewetter (*Keeze-vet-ter*), **Raphael Georg.** Writer; b. Holleschau, Aus., Aug. 29, 1773; d. Vienna, Jan. 1, 1850. An amateur musicologist, and author of many books on mus. history.

Kilenyi, Edward. Violinist, composer; b. Békésszentràndràs, Hun., Jan. 25, 1884. Edu., Cologne Cons. 1913, Mosenthal Fellowship, Columbia U., N. Y.; 1914, A.M. Comp. str. q., overture to a play by Kleist; one-act Amer. opera, violin pcs., songs.

Kimball, Josiah. Composer; b. Topsfield, Mass., Feb., 1761; d. ib., Feb. 26, 1826. Comp. hymn tunes.

Kinder, Ralph. Organist; b. Manchester, Eng., Jan. 27, 1876. Since 1899, org., Holy Trinity, Phila.; cond., choral socs.; popular recitalist. Comp. organ and choir mus.

Kindler, Hans. Conductor; b. Rotterdam, Jan. 8, 1893. After several years as g.-cond. in Paris, Brussels, Vienna, Prague, Rome and Milan, came to U. S.; 1930, cond., National Symph. Orch., Washington, D. C.

King, Oliver A. Pianist, composer; b. London, 1855. 1880-3, toured U. S.; 1893, prof., R. A. M. Comp. symph., overtures, cantatas, anthems, but best known by his song *Israfel*.

Kinkeldey, Otto. Organist, musicologist; b. N. Y., Nov. 27, 1878. 1900, A.M., N. Y. U.; 1909, Ph.D., U. Berlin; 1909-14, t. U. of Breslau; 1915, head mus. div., N. Y. Pub. Lib.; 1923, prof., Cornell U.

Kinscella, Hazel Gertrude. Author, composer; b. Nora Springs, Ia.; (Mrs. Samuel K., d., 1935). Originated the Kinscella method of teaching piano in pub. sch. classes. Author of *Essentials of Piano Technique* (1921).

Kircher, Athanasius. Writer; b. Geisa, Ger., May 2, 1602; d. Rome, Nov. 28, 1680. His books are filled with curious information on mus.

Kirchner, Theodor. Pianist, composer; b. Neukirchen, Ger., Dec. 10, 1823; d. Hamburg, Ger., Sept. 18, 1903. Prolific piano comp.

Kirksmith, Karl. Violoncellist. Edu., Hochschule, Berlin; mem. Czerwonky Quartet; t. Cin. Cons. of Mus.

Kirnberger, Johann Philipp. Theorist; b. Saalfeld, Ger., Apr. 24, 1721; d. Berlin, Jul. 27, 1783.

Kistler, Cyrill. Composer; b. Gross-Autingen, Ger., Mar. 12, 1848; d. Kissingen, Ger., Jan. 2, 1907. Comp. operas, in ponderous style of the Wagner imitators. Author of a student's dictionary, and theoretical treatises.

Kitson, C. H. Music educator. Prof., U. of Dublin. Author of *The Art of Counterpoint* (1907), one of the best of the English treatises on the subject.

Kittl, Johann Friedrich. Composer, teacher; b. Vorlik, Boh., May 8, 1809; d. Lissa, Ger., Jul. 20, 1868. 1843-65, dir., Prague Cons. Comp. operas, symph. wks.

Kitzler, Otto. 'Cellist, composer; b. Dresden, Mar. 26, 1834; d. Gratz, 1915. 1868-98, dir., Brünn; teacher of Bruckner. Comp. orch., pf. pcs. Author of *Recollections* (1904) containing letters from Brahms, Bruckner and Wagner.

Kjerulf (*Khyair-oolf*), **Halfdan.** Composer; b. Christiania, Nor., Sept. 15, 1815; d. ib., Aug. 11, 1868. On a government stipend, attended Leipzig Cons., studied u. Richter. 1850, t. Christiania. Close friend of Björnson and Grieg. Wr. poetic pf. pcs., and many beautiful songs.

Klauser (*Klow-zer*), **Julius.** Teacher, writer; b. New York, Jul. 5, 1854; d. Milwaukee, Wis., Apr. 23, 1907. Son of Karl K. Author of treatises on harmony.

Klauser, Karl. Editor, teacher; b. Petrograd, Aug. 24, 1823; d. Farmington, Conn., Jan. 4, 1905. 1850, to U. S. Ed. of *Famous Composers*.

Klauwell, Otto Adolf. Writer, composer; b. Langensalza, Ger., Apr. 7, 1851; d. Cologne, 1917. 1874, Ph.D., Leipzig U. Author of historical and critical wks. Completed Jensen's revision of Cherubini's *Counterpoint* (1896). Comp. overtures.

Kleeberg (*Klay-bairg*), **Clotilde.** Pianist; b. Paris, Jun. 27, 1866; d. Brussels, Feb. 7, 1909. Brilliant concert artist. m. Charles Samuel, the sculptor.

Kleefeld (*Klay-felt*), **Wilhelm.** Composer, teacher; b. Mayence, Apr. 2, 1868. 1904, prof., Berlin U. Ed. of German editions of operas. Comp. opera, *Anarella* (1896), pf. pcs., songs.

Kleffel, Arno. Composer; b. Pössneck, Ger., Sept. 4, 1840; d. Berlin, 1913. Orch. comp.

Kleiber, Erich. Conductor; b. Vienna, Aug. 5, 1890. 1923, dir., Berlin State Op.; intro. Berg's *Wozzeck*, Krenek's *Leben des Orestes*, Weinberg's *Schwanda*.

Klein, Bruno Oscar. Composer, teacher; b. Osnabrück, Ger., Jun. 6, 1858; d. New York, Jun. 22, 1911. 1878, org., St. Francis Xavier's, New York; t. Nat. Cons. of Mus. Comp. opera, *Kenilworth* (prod., Hamburg, 1895), overture, orch., sonatas, ch. mus., pf. pcs., songs.

Kleinmichel, Richard. Pianist, composer; b. Posen, Ger., Dec. 31, 1846; d. Charlottenburg, Ger., Aug. 18, 1901. Comp. operas, symph., pcs.

Klemperer, Otto. Conductor; b. Breslau, 1885. 1909, cond., Hamburg opera, on recommendation of Gustav Mahler; 1934, cond., N. Y. Phil., and Los Angeles Symph.

Klenau (*Klay-now*), **Paul August von.** Leading Danish conductor, composer; b. Copenhagen, Den., Feb. 11, 1883. 1902-07, Berlin Hochschule, u. Thuille. 1908, asst. cond., Stuttgart, u. Max von Schillings; fd., Copenhagen Phil.; 1924, cond., Delius Fest. at Frankfurt. h. Copenhagen. Comp. opera, incl. *Sulamith*; ballet, choral, chamb. mus., piano pcs.

Klengel, Julius. 'Cellist, composer; b. Leipzig, Sept. 24, 1859; d. ib., Sept. 24, 1929. t. Leipzig. Comp. 'cello and chamb. mus., 'cello pcs.

Klengel, Paul K. Pianist, violinist, composer; b. Leipzig, Ger., May 13, 1854. t. Leipzig. Comp. violin pcs., songs.

Klicka, Joseph. Organist; b. Klattau, Boh., Dec. 15, 1855. Comp. orch., organ pcs.

Klindworth (*Klint-vort*), **Karl.** Pianist, teacher, conductor; b. Hanover, Ger., Sept. 25, 1830; d. Oranienberg, Jul. 27, 1916. p. Liszt. 1854-68, London; 1868-84, pf. prof., Moscow Cons.; 1885, opened pf. sch. in Berlin, w. Hans von Bulow; 1893, consol. w. Scharwenka Sch. Co-cond., w. Joachim of first season of Berlin Phil. Orch. Comp. pf. pcs., but most notable as ed. of complete Chopin edition.

Klose, Friedrich. Composer; b. Karlsruhe, Ger., Nov. 29, 1862. 1907, prof., Munich Cons. Comp. opera, *Ilsebil*, symph. p., *Das Leben ein Traum,* organ wks.

Klughardt (*Kloog-hart*), **August.** Conductor; b. Köthen, Ger., Nov. 30, 1847; d. Dessau, Ger., Aug. 3, 1902. Comp. overtures, symph., operas, and smaller wks.

Knappertsbusch, Hans. Conductor; *b.* Elberfeld, Mar. 12, 1888. 1912, cond., Wagner fest. in Holland; 1913, cond., Elberfeld Op.; 1919-1922, Dessau Op.; 1922, Munich State Op.

Kneisel, Franz. Violinist; *b.* Bucharest, Rou., Jan. 26, 1865; *d.* U. S., Mar. 26, 1926. 1885, to U. S. as conc.-m., Boston Symph. Orch.; 1886, estab. the famous Kneisel Quartet; 1905, *t.* Inst. Mus. Art, N. Y.; 1936, bronze bust, by Kitson, unveiled at Juilliard Sch.

Kniese (*Knee-zeh*), **Julius.** Conductor; *b.* Roda, Ger., Dec. 21, 1848; *d.* Dresden, Apr. 22, 1905. Comp. tone-poem, songs.

Knight, Joseph Philip. Singer, song writer; *b.* Bradford-on-Avon, Eng., Jul. 26, 1812; *d.* Great Yarmouth, Eng., Jun. 1, 1887. 1839, spent one year in U. S.; returned to service of Ch. of Eng., and eventually became Bishop of Exeter. Comp. songs., incl., *Rocked in the Cradle of the Deep.*

Knipper, Lyof. Composer; *b.* Tiflis, Rus., Dec. 16, 1898. 1930, *The Legend of a Plaster God,* his op. 1, perf., Stokowski *w.* Phila. Symph. Comp. chiefly for orch., also opera, ballet, chamb. mus.

Knoch, Ernest. Conductor; *b.* Karlsruhe, Aug. 1, 1875; Asst. cond. *u.* Felix Mottl; 1898, dir., Strassburg Op.; 1904, asst. cond., Bayreuth; 1904-1914, cond. of opera at Essen, Cologne, Elberfeld, Rotterdam; 1914, cond., Century Op. Co., N. Y.; since 1916, g.-cond., Wagner fest.

Knorr, Ivan. Composer; *b.* Mewe, Ger., Jan. 3, 1843; *d.* Frankfort, 1916. Dir., Frankfort Cons. Comp. opera, chamb. mus. Author of wks. on harmony.

Kobbé (*Kob-bay*), **Gustav.** Writer, critic; *b.* New York, Mar. 4, 1857; *d.* ib., Jul. 27, 1918. 1883, mus. critic to Bayreuth for N. Y. *World,* to review first *Parsifal* perf. Writer on Wagner. Author of mus. novels, and books on mus.

Koch, Friedrich E. Composer; *b.* Berlin, Jul. 3, 1862. Cond., Berlin. Comp. operas, symph., oratorio.

Kochanski, Paul. Violinist; *b.* Poland, 1877; *d.* N. Y., Jan. 2, 1934. *p.* Mlynarski. 1926, *t.* Juilliard Sch., N. Y.

Kochetov (*Kok-e-toff*), **Nicolai.** Composer, critic; *b.* Oranienbaum, Rus., Jul. 8, 1864. Comp. opera, symph., etc.

Kocian (*Ko-tsee-yahn*), **Jaroslav.** Violinist; *b.* Wildenschwert, Boh., Feb. 22, 1884. *p.* Sevcik. 1901, toured U. S.

Koczalski (*Kot-chall-skee*), **Raoul.** Pianist, composer; *b.* Warsaw, Pol., Jan. 3, 1885. Comp. operas.

Kodaly, Zoltan. Composer; *b.* Keczkemet, Hun., Dec. 16, 1882. 1900, st., Budapest Cons.; 1906, prof., Budapest Cons.; assoc. *w.* Bela Bartok in folk-song research. Comp. opera, incl., *Hary Janos;* chamb. mus., incl., *Serenade for Violin and Viola;* choral, piano pcs., songs, and many arr. of Hun. folk-songs.

Koehler (*Kay-ler*), **Louis.** Teacher, composer; *b.* Brunswick, Ger., Sept. 5, 1820; *d.* Königsberg, Feb. 16, 1886. Best known by his piano *Method.*

Koehler, Moritz. Conductor, composer; *b.* Altenburg, Ger., Nov. 29, 1855. Cond., Imperial Op., Petrograd. Comp. orch., chamb. wks.

Koehler, Wilhelm. Teacher, composer; *b.* Wümbach, Ger., May 22, 1858. *t.* Hamburg. Comp. masses, motets.

Koelling (*Kei-ling*), **Carl W. P.** Composer; *b.* Hamburg, Ger., Feb. 28, 1831; *d.* Chicago, May 3, 1914. Comp. opera, salon pcs. for pf.

Koemmenich, Louis. Composer, conductor; *b.* Elberfeld, Ger., Oct. 4, 1866; *d.* N. Y., 1922. *p.* Dvořák. 1890, cond., Brooklyn Saengerbund. Comp. choruses and songs.

Kolar, Victor. Composer, conductor; *b.* Pesth, Feb. 12, 1888. 1915-1919, asst. cond., on N. Y. Symph. Soc., *u.* Walter Damrosch; 1919, asst. cond., Detroit Symph. Orch., *u.* Ossip Gabrilowitsch. Comp. *Americana,* symph. suite; *Hiawatha* and *A Fairy Tale,* symph. p.; *Lyric Suite,* for orch.

Kolatchevski (*Koh-laht-cheff-skee*), **Michael Nikolaievitch.** Composer; *b.* Oct. 2, 1851. Rus. orch. comp.

Konius, George Eduardovitch. Composer, teacher; *b.* Moscow, Rus., Sept. 30, 1862. Orch. and ballet comp.

Kopecky, Ottokar. Violinist; *b.* Chotebor, Boh., Apr. 29, 1850; *d.* Hamburg, 1917. *t.* Hamburg Cons.

Koptiaiev (*Kop-tya-yeff*), **Alexander Petrovitch.** Composer, author; *b.* Petrograd, Oct. 12, 1868. Comp. orch., pf. pcs. Author of critical and biographical wks.

Kopylov (*Kop-ee-loff*), **Alexander.** Composer; *b.* Petrograd, Jul. 14, 1854; *d.* ib., Feb. 20, 1911. *p.* Rimsky-Korsakoff. Comp. orch., chamb. mus., and pf. pcs., incl., *A Raindrop.*

Korbay (*Kor-bye*), **Francis Alexander.** Tenor, composer; *b.* Pesth, Hun., May 8, 1846; *d.* London, Mar. 9, 1913. 1871-1904, gave song recitals in U. S. Comp. orch. pcs., best known by songs based on Hun. folk material, as *Mohack's Field.*

Korestchenko, Arseni Nikolaievitch. Composer; *b.* Moscow, Rus., Dec. 18, 1870. Comp. operas, orch. pcs.

Korgueff, Serge. Violinist, teacher. *p.* Auer. Prof., Petrograd Cons., succ. Auer; 1926, *t.* Boston Cons.

Korngold, Erich Wolfgang. Composer; *b.* Brünn, Aus., May 29, 1897. Son of Julius K., celeb. mus. critic. Boy prodigy as comp. 1908, *Der Schneemann,* prod., Vienna Court Op.; 1921, opera, *Die Tote Stadt,* intro. to America by Maria Jeritza at Met. Op.; 1935, to U. S. as mus. dir. to Hollywood cinema producers.

Kortschak, Hugo. Violinist, teacher; *b.* Graz, Aus., Feb. 24, 1884. Edu., Prague Cons., *u.* Sevcik. Conc.-m., Berlin Phil.; 1912, conc.-m., Chicago Symph.; 1917, fd., Berkshire Q.; *t.* Yale U. Mus. Sch.; *t.* Neighborhood Mus. Sch., N. Y.

Koschat (*Kosh-at*), **Thomas.** Bass, composer; *b.* Viktring, Aus., Aug. 8, 1845; *d.* Vienna, May 19, 1914. Comp. Corinthian folk-songs. Best known by melody, *Forsaken.*

Köselitz, Heinrich. Composer; *b.* Annaberg, Ger., Jan. 10, 1854; *d.* ib., Aug. 15, 1918. Comp. operas, symph., chamb. mus., songs.

Koss, Henning von. Composer; *b.* Lautow, Ger., Dec. 13, 1855. Mus. critic in Berlin. Comp. songs.

Kotek, Joseph. Violinist, composer; *b.* Kamenez-Podolsk, Rus., Oct. 25, 1855; *d.* Davos, Switz., Jan. 4, 1885. Comp. violin pcs.

Kotzschmar (*Kotsh-mar*), **Hermann.** Organist, teacher; *b.* Finsterwalde, Ger., Jul. 4, 1829; *d.* Portland, Me., Apr. 15, 1908. Municipal organ in Portland (Me.) is a memorial to him, erected by Cyrus H. W. Curtis, of Phila.

Kotzwara (*Kots-vah-ra*), **F.** Violinist; *b.* Prague, Boh., 1750; *d.* London, Sept. 2, 1791. Comp. *The Battle of Prague,* and descriptive piece of this genre.

Koussevitzky, Serge Alexandrovitch. Conductor; *b.* Tver, Rus., Jul. 21, 1874. Edu., Berlin Hochschule as double-bass virtuoso, and toured extensively. 1907, inaugurated Koussevitzky concerts in Moscow, and toured the remote sections of Rus., earning enormous fame. 1916-20, Soviet dir., Russian state orch.; 1920-24, estab. Concerts Koussevitzky in Paris, introducing modern Rus. wks.; 1924, cond., Boston Symph. Orch.; 1924, Legion of Honor of France; 1926, Mus.D., Brown U.; 1929, LL.D., Harvard; 1909, fd., "Musical Editions," a Paris publishing house devoted to Rus. wks. Comp. concerto for double bass and orch.

Kovarovic (*Ko-var-zho-vic*), **Karl.** Composer; *b.* Prague, Boh., Dec. 9, 1862; *d.* ib., Dec. 6, 1921. 1900-*d.*, cond., Natl. Th., Prague. Comp. opera.

Kozeluch (*Kohz-e-lookh*), **Johann Anton.** Composer; *b.* Wellwarn, Boh., Dec. 13, 1738; *d.* Prague, Boh., Feb. 3, 1814. Comp. operas, oratorios, masses.

Kozeluch, Leopold. Composer; *b.* Wellwarn, Boh., 1752; *d.* Vienna, May 7, 1818. Edu., Prague. 1792, Imperial comp., succ. Mozart. Comp. operas, ballets, 30 symph., 70 chamb. wks.

Kramer, A. Walter. Composer, critic; *b.* New York, Sept. 23, 1890. 1910, A.B., Coll. City N. Y. Ed., *Musical America. h.* New York. Comp. orch. wks., incl., *Two Sketches;* chamb. mus., incl., *Elegy in C-Sharp Minor;* songs, piano pcs., and transcriptions.

Kramm, Georg. Composer; *b.* Cassel, Dec. 21, 1856; *d.* Düsseldorf, Oct., 1910. Comp. operas, symph.

Krauss, Clemens. Conductor; *b.* Vienna, Mar. 31, 1893. 1921, cond., Vienna State Op., and Tonkunstlerverein; 1924-1929, Frankfort Op.; 1929-1934, Vienna State Op.; 1934, Berlin State Op.; g.-cond., Munich and Salzburg Fest.; 1929, g.-cond., N. Y. Phil. and Phila. Symph. Orch.

Krebs, Johann Ludwig. Organist, composer; *b.* Buttelstädt, Ger., Feb. 10, 1713; *d.* Altenburg, Ger., Jan., 1780.

Krebs, Karl August. Pianist, conductor; *b.* Nuremburg, Jan. 16, 1804; *d.* Dresden, May 16, 1880. Distinguished cond.

Krebs, Marie. Pianist; *b.* Dresden, Dec. 5, 1861; *d.* ib., Jun. 27, 1900. Toured U. S.

Krehbiel, Henry Edward. Author, critic; *b.* Ann Arbor, Mar. 10, 1854; *d.* N. Y., Mar. 20, 1923. 1909, Mus.D., Yale. A distinguished career as a mus. critic, for years on the N. Y. *Tribune.* Author of book on biography and aesthetics of mus.

Krehl (*Krayl*), **Stephan.** Composer, author; *b.* Leipzig, Ger., May 7, 1864; *d.* ib., 1924. 1902, prof., Leipzig Cons. Comp. chamb. mus. Author of theoretical wks.

Kreisler, Alexander von. *b.* Russia. *p.* Glazounoff. Cond., Tiflis Op.; *t.* Cin. Cons. Mus.

Kreisler, Fritz. Violinist; *b.* Vienna, Feb. 2, 1875. *p.* Hellmesberger. 1888-89, toured U. S., *w.* Moritz Rosenthal; 1899, debut, Berlin. Distinguished virtuoso. Spent greater part of his time in U. S. Comp. operettas, violin pcs., incl., *Caprice Viennois.*

Krenek, Ernest. Composer; *b.* Vienna, Aug. 23, 1900. *p.* Schreker. 1924, *Der Sprung uber den Schatten,* prod., Frankfurt; 1925, cond., Prus. State Theatre in Cassel; 1926, *Jonny Spielt Auf!* controversial jazz-opera, intro., Cassel; also at Met. Op., N. Y.; 1935, opera, *Jazz, the Negro and the Women. h.* Vienna. Married daughter of Gustav Mahler. Comp. orch wks., and chamb. mus.

Kretschmer, Edmund. Composer; *b.* Ostritz, Ger., Aug. 31, 1830; *d.* Dresden, Ger., Sept. 13, 1908. Comp. orch., vocal wks.; best known by operas, incl., *Henry the Lion.*

Kreutzer (*Kroy-tser*), **Conradin.** Composer; *b.* Messkirch, Ger., Nov. 22, 1780; *d.* Riga, Rus., Dec. 14, 1849. Comp. operas, incl., *Das Nachtlager von Granada;* and part-songs for male voices.

Kreutzer, Rodolphe. Violinist, composer; *b.* Versailles, Fr., Nov. 16, 1766; *d.* Geneva, Jan. 6, 1831. 1795-1825, prof., Paris Cons.; court violinist to Napoleon and Louis XVIII. Beethoven dedicated to him his Kreutzer sonata; joint author *w.* Baillot of the Violin Method used at newly fd. cons. Comp. operas, violin concertos, duets, but his *Forty-two Études* or *Caprices* are a familiar and indispensable companion to every violinist.

Kreyn, Alexander. Composer; *b.* Nizhny-Novgorod, Oct. 20, 1883. 1912-17, st., Moscow Cons.; 1918-22, State Mus. Dept.; 1921, assoc. *w.* Gniessen in nat'l. Jewish movement. Best known for *Five Preludes* for orch., intro., 1928, by Stokowski *w.* Phila. Orch. Comp. orch. wks., incl., *Salome;* chamb. mus., incl., *Poem;* choral mus., incl., *Kaddish.*

Kreyn, Gregory. Composer; *b.* 1879. *p.* Paul Juon. Brother of Alexander K.

Kriens, Christian. Conductor, composer, violinist; *b.* Germany, Apr. 29, 1881; *d.* Hartford, Conn., 1934. Abandoned teaching, after many years in New York, to cond orch. in Hartford Broadcasting station. Comp. two orch. suites, *In Holland, In Brittany;* symph., songs and instr. pcs.

Kroeger (*Kray-gher*), **Ernest Richard.** Pianist, teacher, composer; *b.* St. Louis, Mo., Aug. 10, 1862; *d.* ib., Apr. 7, 1934. 1887-*d.,* dir. mus., Forest Park U., St. Louis; ex-pres., M. T. N. A. Comp. symph., and chamb. wks., and pf. pcs.

Krohn, Ilmari Henrik Reinhold. Organist, composer, writer; *b.* Helsingfors, Nov. 8, 1867. Prof., Helsingfors U. Comp. opera, oratorio, songs, part-songs.

Kroll, William. Violinist; *b.* N. Y., Jan. 30, 1901. *p.* Franz Kneisel. 1922, gr., Inst. of Mus. Art, N. Y., winning Morris Loeb prize. 1923-9, mem., South Mountain Q., and Elshuco Trio; 1932, fd. Kroll Sextet; 1934, mem., N. Y. Chamb. Mus. Soc.; 1936, mem. Coolidge Q. Comp. chamb. mus., violin pcs.

Kroyer, Theodor. Musicologist; *b.* Munich, Sept. 9, 1873. 1892, Ph.D., Munich U.; 1902, prof., Kaim U. Comp. orch. wks. Author of treatises on mus.

Krug (*Kroog*), **Arnold.** Composer; *b.* Hamburg, Oct. 16, 1849; *d.* ib., Aug. 4, 1904. Comp. symph., best known by fantasias for pf., based on opera melodies.

Krug, Joseph (Krug-Waldsee). Conductor, composer; *b.* Waldsee, Ger., Nov. 8, 1858. Prof., Magdeburg. Comp. symph., suite, operas, choral wks.

Kruger, George. Pianist, teacher. Pres., San Francisco M. T. A.

Kruis, M. H. van't. Organist, composer; *b.* Oudewater, Hol., Mar. 8, 1861. *t.* Rotterdam Mus. Sch.; 1886, fd.-ed., *Het Orgel.* Comp. opera, *De Bloem van Island;* overtures, symph. Author of *Summary of Music History* (1892).

Krumpholz, Johann Baptist. Harpist; *b.* Prague, 1745; *d.* Paris, Feb. 19, 1790. Celebrated virtuoso and comp. for harp.

Krumpholz, Wenzel. Violinist; *b.* 1750; *d.* Vienna, May 2, 1817. Friend of Beethoven.

Kubelik, Jan. Violinist; *b.* Michle, Jul. 5, 1880. Edu., Prague Cons., *u.* Sevcik. 1898, toured world. Decorated or honored by almost every country. A meteoric career, playing a Paganini repertoire. Owner of the "Emperor" Stradivarius.

Kücken (*Kick-en*), **Friedrich Wilhelm.** Composer; *b.* Bleckede, Ger., Nov. 16, 1810; *d.* Schwerin, Ger., Apr. 3, 1882. Comp. operas, and many popular songs.

Kufferath (*Koof-e-raht*), **Hubert Ferdinand.** Pianist, composer; *b.* Mühlheim, Ger., Jun. 11, 1818; *d.* Brussels, Bel., Jun. 23, 1896. 1872-*d.*, *t.* Brussels Cons. Comp. chamb. mus. Author of a Method for singing.

Kuhe (*Koo-eh*), **Wilhelm.** Pianist, arranger; *b.* Prague, Boh., Dec. 10, 1823; *d.* London, Oct. 8, 1912.

Kuhlau, Friedrich. Composer; *b.* Uelzen, Ger., Sept. 11, 1786; *d.* Copenhagen, Mar. 12, 1832. Best known for pf. teaching pcs.

Kuhnau, Johann. Organist, composer; *b.* Geising, Boh., 1660; *d.* Leipzig, Jun. 5, 1722. One of the earliest German sonata comp.

Kühner (*Kee-ner*), **Conrad.** Composer, music editor; *b.* Markt-Streufdorf, Ger., Mar. 2, 1851. Comp. pf. mus.

Kühner, Vassili. Composer; *b.* Stuttgart, Apr. 1, 1840; *d.* Vilna, Lithuania, Aug., 1911. Comp. operas, symph., chamb. mus.

Kulenkampff (*Koo-len-kamf*), **Gustav.** Composer; *b.* Bremen, Aug. 11, 1849; *d.* Berlin, 1921. Comp. operas, incl., *Der Page*.

Kullak (*Kool-lak*), **Franz.** Pianist, teacher; *b.* Berlin, Apr. 12, 1844; *d.* Dec. 9, 1913. Son of Theodor K.

Kullak, Theodor. Pianist, composer, teacher; *b.* Krotoschin, Ger., Sept. 12, 1818; *d.* Berlin, Mar. 1, 1882. Fd. two conservatories in Berlin. 1861, awarded title Royal Professor. Comp. pf. pcs., of salon type.

Kullman, Charles. Tenor; *b.* New Haven, Conn., 1903. Edu., Yale U., Juilliard Sch., Amer. Cons. in Fontainebleau, Fr.; *t.* Smith Coll.; 1929-33, Berlin St. Op.; 1934, soloist, Verdi *Requiem u.* Toscanini in Vienna; 1935, Met. Op., N.Y.

Kummer (*Koom-mer*), **Franz August.** 'Cellist, composer; *b.* Meiningen, Ger., Aug. 5, 1797; *d.* Dresden, May 22, 1879. A distinguished concert artist.

Kunwald, Ernst. Austrian conductor; *b.* Vienna, Apr. 14, 1868. Edu., Leipzig Cons., *u.* Jadassohn. 1900-1, cond., *The Ring*, Madrid; 1902-5, cond., Frankfort Op.; 1905-6, cond., Kroll Summer Op., Berlin; 1906, Stadttheater, Nuremberg; 1907-12, Phil. Orch., Berlin; 1912, cond., Cin. Symph. Orch. and Cin. May Fest.; 1920, dir., Symph. Concerts, Königsberg.

Kurenko, Maria. Soprano; *b.* Tomsk, Sib. 1914, gr., Moscow Cons.; 1918, debut, Moscow Op.; 1925, Chicago Op.; concert, radio.

Kurth (*Koort*), **Martin Alexander Otto.** Composer; *b.* Triebel, Ger., Nov. 11, 1846. Comp. operas, cantatas, symph.

Kuryllo, Adam. Violinist, teacher; *b.* Krakow, Pol. *p.* Kneisel. 1920-22, cond., Thorn Symph. Orch. in Poland; 1924, *t.* N.Y.

L

Labarre (*Lah-bar*), **Théodore.** Harpist, composer; *b.* Paris, Mar. 5, 1805; *d.* ib., Mar. 9, 1870.

Labitzky (*La-bit-shki*), **Josef.** Composer, violinist; *b.* Schönfeld, Boh., Jul. 4, 1802; *d.* Carlsbad, Ger., Aug. 18, 1881. Comp. salon pcs., incl., *The Alp-Maid's Dream*.

Lablache (*La-blash*), **Luigi.** Bass; *b.* Naples, It., Dec. 6, 1794; *d.* ib., Jan. 23, 1858. A world-wide reputation as an operatic artist.

Lachmund, Carl Valentine. Pianist, composer; *b.* Booneville, Mo., Mar. 27, 1857; *d.* Yonkers, Feb. 20, 1928. 1875, gr., Cologne Cons. *p.* Liszt. *t.* Scharwenka Cons.; 1880, toured U.S. *w.* Wilhelmj; fd. own sch. in N.Y. Comp. orch. pcs., incl., *Japanese Overture*; trio for harp, violin and 'cello.

Lachner (*Lakh-ner*), **Franz.** Composer; *b.* Rain, Ger., Apr. 2, 1803; *d.* Munich, Jan. 20, 1890. Comp. orch. suites, songs.

Lachner, Ignaz. Composer, organist, conductor; *b.* Rain, Ger., Sept. 11, 1807; *d.* Hanover, Feb. 24, 1895. Brother, Franz and Vincenz L.

Lachner, Vincenz. Composer, conductor; *b.* Rain, Ger., Jul. 19, 1811; *d.* Carlsruhe, Ger., Jan. 22, 1893.

Lack (*Lahk*), **Théodore.** Pianist, composer; *b.* Quimper, Fr., Sept. 13, 1846; *d.* Paris, 1921. Comp. salon pcs. for pf., incl., *Idilio*.

Lacombe (*Lah-com*), **Louis.** Composer; *b.* Bourges, Fr., Nov. 26, 1818; *d.* St. Vaast-la-Hougue, Fr., Sept. 30, 1884. Comp. symph., chamb. mus., operas.

Lacombe, Paul. Composer; *b.* Carcassonne, Fr., Jul. 11, 1837. Comp. orch. wks., pf. pcs., incl., *Aubade printanière*.

Ladmiraul (*Lad-mee-row*), **Paul Emile.** Composer; *b.* Nantes, Fr., Dec. 8, 1877. Comp. orch., choral wks., pf. pcs., songs.

La Forge, Frank. Pianist, composer; *b.* Rockford, Ill., 1879. *p.* Leschetizky. Accompanist to Schumann-Heink, Sembrich, and others; vocal teacher, N.Y. Comp. songs.

Lahee, Henry. Organist, composer; *b.* Chelsea, Eng., Apr. 11, 1826; *d.* London, Apr. 29, 1912. Comp. cantatas.

Lahee, Henry Charles. Writer; *b.* London, Jul. 2, 1856. Author of biographical and critical wks.

Lajtha, Ladislas. Composer; *b.* Budapest, Jun. 30, 1892. 1913, Folk-Music Dept., Hun. Natl. Museum, and prof., Hun. Natl. Cons.; 1929, dir., Mus. Bureau, Internatl. Inst. Intellectual Coop.; 1930, *Third String Quartet*, intro. in Amer. at Coolidge Fest. in Wash. Comp. ballet, *Lysistrata*; and chamb. wks., all in a modern and radical idiom.

Lake, Harold. *d.* London, Aug. 5, 1933. Under pseud. of Harold Harford, wr. text of *I Hear You Calling Me*.

Lalo (*Lah-lo*), **Edouard Victor Antoine.** Composer; *b.* Lille, Fr., Jan. 27, 1823; *d.* Paris, Apr. 22, 1892. Comp. operas, incl., *Le roi d'Ys*; suites, and two violin concertos, incl., *Symphonie espagnole*.

Laloy (*Lah-lwah*), **Louis.** Musicologist; *b.* Grey, Haute-Saône, Fr., 1874. 1905, fd., *Mercure Musical,* later the S.I.M. Bulletin; one of the first to champion Debussy; 1921, lect. Sorbonne; gen. sec., Paris Opéra.

Lambert (*Lahm-bair*), **Alexander.** Pianist, teacher; *b.* Warsaw, Nov. 1, 1862; *d.* N.Y., Jan. 31, 1929. 1887, dir., N.Y. Coll. of Mus. Taught many celebrated pupils. Author of a pf. *Method*.

Lambert, Constant. Composer; *b.* London, Eng., Aug. 23, 1905. Edu., R. C. M., *u.* Vaughan Williams. 1926, ballet, *Romeo and Juliet,* comp. for Diaghilev's Rus. Ballet. Comp. orch. wks., incl., *Prize Fight* and *Rio Grande;* chamb. mus., piano pcs., and songs.

Lambert, Lucien. Pianist, composer; *b.* Paris, 1861. Opera comp.

Lambeth, Henry Albert. Organist, conductor; *b.* Gosport, Eng., Jan. 16, 1822; *d.* Glasgow, Jun. 27, 1895. Dir., the celebrated Lambeth Choir.

Lambillote (*Lam-bee-yot*), **Louis.** Writer, composer; *b.* Charleroi, Fr., Mar. 27, 1797; *d.* Vaugirard, Fr., Feb. 27, 1855. Comp. ch. mus.

Lambord, Benjamin. Organist, composer; *b.* Portland, Me., Jun. 10, 1879; *d.* Lake Hopatcong, N. J., Jun. 6, 1915. *p.* MacDowell, at Columbia U.; 1905, won Mosenthal Fellowship. 1912, fd.-cond., Modern Mus. Soc., N. Y. A conspicuous talent cut short at an early age. Comp. opera, *Woodstock;* songs *w.* orch.; *Verses from Omar* for chorus and orch.; pf. trio, pf. pcs., songs, part-songs.

Lambrino, Télémaque. Pianist; *b.* Odessa, Oct. 27, 1878. *p.* Carreño. 1919, *t.* Klindworth-Scharwenka Cons., Berlin.

Lamond, Frederic A. Pianist; *b.* Glasgow, Scot., Jan. 28, 1868. *p.* Liszt. 1917, prof., Hague Cons.; a distinguished concert artist. Comp. symph., chamb. mus.

Lamoureux (*Lah-moo-reuh*), **Charles.** Conductor; *b.* Bordeaux, Sept. 21, 1834; *d.* Paris, Dec. 21, 1899. 1873, fd., Société de l'Harmonie Sacree; 1872-1877, asst. cond., Cons. concerts; 1877, cond., Paris Opera; 1881, fd.-cond., Concerts Lamoureux.

Lampe (*Lahm-peh*), **Walther.** Composer; *b.* Leipzig, Ger., Apr. 28, 1872. 1920, prof., Munich Cons. Comp. orch., chamb. mus.

Lamperti (*Lam-pair-tee*), **Francesco.** Teacher of singing; *b.* Savona, It., Mar. 11, 1813; *d.* Como, It., May 1, 1892. 1850-75, prof., Milan Cons. Author, Method for Singing.

Landowska, Wanda. Pianist; *b.* Warsaw, 1877. St., Warsaw Cons. 1900-13, *t.* Schola Cantorum, Paris; 1913, dir., harpsichord class, Berlin Hochschule. Comp. orch. wks., pf. pcs., songs.

Lane, Eastwood. Composer; *b.* Brewerton, N. Y. Edu., Syracuse U. Asst. Concert Dir., Wanamaker Auditorium, N. Y.; assoc. as comp. *w.* Paul Whiteman and Denishawn Ballet. Comp. pf. pcs., songs.

Lang, Benjamin J. Pianist, composer, conductor, teacher; *b.* Salem, Mass., Dec. 28, 1837; *d.* Boston, Apr. 3, 1909. *t.* Arthur Foote, Ethelbert Nevin; cond., Handel and Hayden Soc., Boston. Comp. oratorio, symph. and chamb. wks.

Lang, Margaret Ruthven. Composer; *b.* Boston, Nov. 27, 1867. Daughter of B. J. L. Comp. overtures, arias *w.* orch., and successful songs and piano pcs. Career identified *w.* Boston.

Lange (*Lang-eh*), **Gustav.** Composer; *b.* Schwerstedt, Ger., Aug. 13, 1830; *d.* Wernigerode, Ger., Sept. 19, 1889. Comp. salon pcs. for pf., incl., *Flower Song.*

Lange, Hans. Conductor, violinist; *b.* ——. Asst. cond., Frankfort *Museumgesellschaft,* *u.* Mengelberg; 1923, asst. conc.-m. and cond., N. Y. Phil.; 1931, cond., N. Y. Phil.; 1935, cond., Phil. Chamb. Orch.

Lange-Müller (*Lang-eh-Mil-ler*), **Peter Erasmus.** Composer; *b.* Frederiksberg, Den., Dec. 1, 1850; *d.* Copenhagen, 1926. Comp. operas, a symph., 200 songs, and choruses.

Langenus, Gustave. Clarinetist; *b.* Malines, Bel., Aug. 6, 1883. Edu., Brussels Cons. 1902, toured Europe *w.* Sousa's Band; 1903-7, mem., Queen's Hall Orch., London, *u.* Wood; 1907-10, mem., Duke of Devonshire's Orch.; 1910, mem., N. Y. Symph. Orch.; 1914, mem., N. Y. Chamb. Mus. Soc. Author of a *Method* for Clarinet. Comp. clarinet pcs.

Langert (*Lahng-airt*), **Johann August Adolf.** Conductor, composer; *b.* Coburg, Ger., Nov. 26, 1836; *d.* ib., Mar. 16, 1924. Comp. operas, incl., *Dornröschen.*

Langhans, Wilhelm. Writer; *b.* Hamburg, Sept. 21, 1832; *d.* Berlin, Jun. 9, 1892. Comp. symph., chamb. mus. Author treatises on mus.

Lanner, Josef F. K. Composer, violinist; *b.* Vienna, Apr. 12, 1801; *d.* ib., Apr. 14, 1843. Alternated *w.* Johann Strauss as cond. of Court mus.

Laparra, Raoul. Composer; *b.* Bordeaux, Fr., May 13, 1876. Comp. operas, incl., *La Habanera,* prod. Met. Op. (1924).

de Lara, Isidore. Composer; *b.* London, Aug. 9, 1858. Comp. operas, incl., *Messalina.*

Larsen, Alfred Ferdinand Olaf. Violinist, director; *b.* Nodebo, Den., Dec. 12, 1877. Fd., Larsen Violin Sch.; 1910, fd., Burlington Symph. Orch.; also Larsen Str. Q., and Beethoven Piano Trio; 1920, prof., Middlebury Coll.

Lashanska, Hulda (Mrs. Harold A. Rosenbaum). Lyric soprano; *b.* N. Y., Mar. 15, 1892. *p.* Marcella Sembrich. Soloist *w.* leading U. S. orch.

Laska, Gustav. Contrabass player, composer; *b.* Prague, Boh., Aug. 23, 1847. Comp. symph., concerto, opera, masses.

Lassalle (*Lah-sal*), **Jean Louis.** Bass; *b.* Lyons, Fr., Dec. 14, 1847; *d.* Paris, Sept. 7, 1909. 1869, debut, Liége. Distinguished opera singer.

Lassen (*Lahs-sen*), **Eduard.** Composer, conductor; *b.* Copenhagen, Apr. 13, 1830; *d.* Weimar, Jan. 15, 1904. 1861-95, court cond., Weimar, succ. Liszt. Comp. operas, orch., choral, vocal wks.

Lasso, Orlando di (Orlandus Lassus). Composer; *b.* Mons, Bel., 1532 (1530?); *d.* Munich, Jun. 14, 1594. A contrapuntal leader; foremost of Netherland comp.

La Tombelle (*Lah Tom-bel*), **Fernand de.** Composer; *b.* Paris, Aug. 3, 1854. 1900, prof., Schola Cantorum, Paris. Comp. orch. suites, organ pcs.

Lauber (*Lou-ber*), **Joseph.** Pianist; *b.* Ruswil, Switz., Dec. 25, 1860. Prof., Geneva Cons. Comp. symph., cantatas, and vocal wks.

Lavallée (*Lah-vah-leh*), **Calixa.** Pianist, composer; *b* Verchères, Can., Dec. 28, 1842; *d.* Boston, Jan. 21, 1891. 1881, soloist on Etelka Gerster's first U. S. tour. Comp. pf. pcs., incl., *Schmetterling.*

Lavignac (*Lah-veen-yak*), **Albert.** Writer; *b.* Paris, Jan. 22, 1846; *d.* ib., May 29, 1916. 1882, dean, Paris Cons. Author of many important wks., incl., the great French encyclopedia of mus.

Lavigne (*Lah-veen*), **Antoine Joseph.** Oboist; *b.* Besançon, Fr., Apr. 23, 1816; *d.* Manchester, Eng., Aug. 1, 1886. An oboe virtuoso of great repute.

Law, Andrew. Composer, writer; *b*: 1748; *d*. 1821. One of America's first mus. critics. In his collections he was the first Amer. choral arr. to give the melody to the soprano rather than the tenor.

Lawrence, Marjorie. Soprano; *b*. Australia. Leading dramatic soprano of Paris Op.; 1935, debut, Met. Op., as *Brunnhilde* in Wagner's *Walküre*.

Lazarus, Henry. Clarinetist; *b*. London, 1815; *d*. ib., 1895. A distinguished virtuoso.

Lazzari (*Lai-zahr-ree*), **Silvio.** Composer; *b*. Bozen, Aus., Dec. 31, 1857. *p*. Giraud. Cond., Monte Carlo Op. Comp. symph. p., operas, vocal and instr. ensemble wks.

Lazzari, Virgilio. Opera-basso; *b*. Assisi, It., Apr. 20, 1887. 1912, debut, Rome; 1918, Chicago Op., Ravinia Park, and La Scala; 1933, Met. Op., N. Y.

Lebert (*Lay-bairt*), **Siegmund.** Composer, pianist, teacher; *b*. Ludwigsburg, Ger., Dec. 12, 1822; *d*. Stuttgart, Dec. 8, 1884. Fd., Stuttgart Cons. Joint author of Lebert and Stark *Method*.

LeBorne (*Luh-born*), **Fernand.** Composer, music critic; *b*. Paris, Mar. 10, 1862. Staff mem., *Le Monde Artiste*. Comp. operas, incl., *Les Girondins;* orch. wks.

Lebrun (*Luh-breen*), **Paul Henri Joseph.** Composer; *b*. Ghent, Apr. 21, 1861. 1890, prof., Brussels Acadamie. Comp. opera, prize symph.

Le Carpentier (*Le' Car-pong-tee-eh*), **Adolphe-Clair.** Composer, pianist; *b*. Paris, Feb. 17, 1809; *d*. ib., Jul. 14, 1869. Comp. technical wks. for pf.; also fantasias on operatic airs.

Leclair, Jean Marie. Composer, violinist; *b*. Paris, May 10, 1697; *d*., ib., Oct. 22, 1764. Mysteriously assassinated. Sometimes called the "French Tartini." Comp. opera, ballets, 48 violin sonatas and other chamb. mus.

Lecocq (*Le-kok*), **Alexandre Charles.** Composer; *b*. Paris, Jun. 3, 1832; *d*. Clifton, Guernsey, Feb. 15, 1911. Also reported as *d*. Paris, Oct. 25, 1918. Edu., Paris Cons. Collaborated *w*. Bizet; won Offenbach prize. Comp. more than fifty comic operas, incl., *La Fille de Mme. Angot*. The New York production ran for 61 perf. at the Casino, in 1890, featuring Eva Davenport.

Lecouppey (*Le-coop-pay*), **Félix.** Composer, pianist; *b*. Paris, Apr. 4, 1811; *d*. ib., Jul. 5, 1887. 1837, prof., Paris Cons. Best known for *études* and teaching pcs.

Le Duc, Alphonse. Flutist, pianist; *b*. 1804; *d*. Paris, 1868. Comp. some 1,300 *études* and pf. pcs.

Lefébure-Wély (*Le-fah-byoor-Va-lee*), **Louis James Alfred.** Organist, composer; *b*. Paris, Nov. 13, 1817; *d*. ib., Dec. 31, 1869. Famous for his improvisation on the organ. Comp. opera, symph., chamb. mus., organ and pf. pcs., incl., *Titania* and *The Monastery Bells*.

Lefébvre (*Luh-fay-vr*), **Charles Édouard.** Composer; *b*. Paris, Jun. 19, 1843; *d*. Aix-les-Bains, 1917. 1895, prof., Paris Cons. Comp. operas, cantatas.

Leginska (*Liggins*), **Ethel.** Pianist, conductor; *b*. Hull, Eng., Apr. 13, 1883. *p*. Leschetizky. Toured as piano virtuoso. 1924, started conducting. First woman to direct leading orch., incl., N. Y. Phil. and Boston Symph.

Lehar, Franz. Operetta composer; *b*. Komorn, Aus., Apr. 30, 1870. Edu., Prague Cons. Comp. a grand opera, but the success of a comic opera kept him in that field. World-renown came *w*. *The Merry Widow* (1905). A later work, *Paganini* (1930), had 1,500 perf. in Europe. Comp. some twenty other operettas.

Lehmann (*Lay-man*), **Amelia.** Folksong collector, appearing on title-pages as "A. L." Mother of Liza L.

Lehmann, George. Violinist; *b*. New York, Jul. 31, 1865. Author, *The Violinist's Lexicon*.

Lehmann, Lilli. Soprano; *b*. Würzburg, Ger., Nov. 24, 1848; *d*. Berlin, May 17, 1928. Famous Wagnerian opera singer. 1885-90, Met. Op., N. Y. Author of several books.

Lehmann, Liza (Elizabetta Nina Maria Frederika). Soprano, composer; *b*. London, Jul. 11, 1862; *d*. ib., Sept. 19, 1918. Daughter of Amelia L. 1894, *m*. Herbert Bedford (q. v.). Comp. song cycles, incl., *In a Persian Garden*.

Lehmann, Lotte. Soprano; *b*. Perleberg, Ger. 1916, debut, Vienna; 1930-31, to Amer. *w*. Chicago Civic Op.; Met. Op.; Hon. mem., State Op., Vienna; Chevalier Legion of Honor (France).

Leichtentritt, Hugo. Composer, musicologist; *b*. Pleschen, Ger., Jan. 1, 1874. Edu., Harvard, *u*. Paine. 1895-8, Berlin Hochschule; 1901, Ph.D., Berlin; *t*. Klindworth-Scharwenka Cons.; 1934, *t*. Harvard U.; 1935, prof., musicology, N. Y. U. Comp. symph. and chamb wks., and many songs. Author of biography of *Busoni*, and many books on mus.

Leighton, George A. Composer, pianist. *p*. Hugo Kaun. Org., Cincinnati; is music critic, Cincinnati *Enquirer;* dir. of ed., Cin. Cons. of Mus. Comp. pf. pcs., songs, choral wks. Author of *Harmony, Analytical and Applied*.

Lekeu (*Luh-kay*), **Guillaume.** Composer; *b*. Neusy, Bel., Jan. 20, 1870; *d*. Angers, Fr., Jan. 21, 1894. *p*. C. Franck. The gifted but short-lived comp. of several orch. wks., a violin sonata, and some pf. pcs., and songs.

Lemaire, Jean Eugéne Gaston. Composer; *b*. France, Sept. 9, 1854. Comp. orch., ballet mus., pf. pcs., songs, incl., *Vous dausez, Marquise*.

Lemare (*Le-mahr*), **Edwin Henry.** Organist, composer; *b*. Ventnor, Eng., Sept. 9, 1865; *d*. Los Angeles, Sept. 24, 1934. Important concert org. 1902-05, Municipal org., Pittsburgh; 1917, San Francisco; 1920, Portland, Me.

Lemmens, Nicholas Jacques. Organist, composer; *b*. Zoerle-Parwys, Bel., Jan. 3, 1823; *d*. Malines, Bel., Jan. 30, 1881. 1849, prof., Brussels Cons.; celebrated concert org. Comp. symph. and organ mus. in a flamboyant style now outmoded. Popularly known by a descriptive piece, *The Storm*.

Lemoine, Henri. Pianist, teacher; *b*. Paris, Oct. 21, 1786; *d*. ib., May 18, 1854. Continued mus. publishing business fd., 1793, by his father, Antoine Marcel L. (1763-1817). Comp. études and a pf. *Method*.

Lemont, Cedric Wilmot. Pianist, teacher, composer; *b*. Fredericton, N. B., Dec. 15, 1879. Gr., N. E. Cons. 1916, *t*. Chicago Inst. of Mus. Comp. pf. pcs., violin, ch. mus., songs.

Lenaerts (*Le-narts*), **Constant.** Composer, conductor; *b*. Antwerp, Mar. 9, 1852. Prof., Antwerp Cons. Comp. cantatas.

Lendvai (*Lend-vye*), **Erwin.** Composer, teacher; *b*. Budapest, Jun. 4, 1882. 1919, prof., Klindworth-Scharwenka Cons., Berlin. Comp. opera, symph., fest. march.

Lenepveu (*Le-nep-vay*), **Charles Ferdinand.** Composer; *b*. Rouen, Fr., Oct. 4, 1840; *d*. 1910. Comp. operas, incl., *Velleda;* cantatas, chamb. mus.

Lent, Sylvia. Violinist; *b.* Washington, D. C. *p.* Auer, in Amer. Toured Europe; 1923, N. Y. debut.

Leo (*Lay-o*), **Leonardo.** Composer, teacher; *b.* Brindisi, It., Aug. 5, 1694; *d.* Naples, Oct. 31, 1744. One of the leaders of the 18th century Neapolitan sch. Comp. 70 operas.

Léonard (*Lā′-ō-năr*), **Hubert.** Violinist; *b.* Bellaire, nr. Liége, Apr. 7, 1819; *d.* Paris, May 6, 1890. Edu., Paris Cons. *u.* Habeneck. Prof., Brussels Cons., succ. de Bériot. He was a brilliant player excelling in staccato and arpeggios. Teacher of Marsick, Dengremont, Marteau, César Thomson. Author of important studies for violin.

Leonard, Isabel. Singing teacher; *b.* N. Y., 1870. *p.* William Mason. *t.* Spence Sch.

Leoncavallo (*Lay-on-ka-val-lo*), **Ruggiero.** Composer; *b.* Naples, Mar. 8, 1858; *d.* Florence, Aug. 9, 1919. His first opera, *Tommaso Chatterton*, a failure when first prod., was later revived *w.* success. He produced a historic trilogy, *Crepusculum*, dealing *w.* the Italian Renaissance, in which he was encouraged by Wagner, whom he devotedly admired. His reputation rests on the two-act opera *I Pagliacci* (1892), other operas, incl., *Trilby*, *Zaza*, also two subjects also treated by Puccini, viz., *Bohême* and *Tosca*.

Leopold, Ralph Herman. Pianist; *b.* Pottstown, Pa., Feb. 14, 1884. *p.* Mme. Stepanoff. Debut, Berlin Phil. Orch.; 1914, New York debut; *t.* Mannes Mus. Sch., N. Y. Lecturer on Wagner.

Leps, Wassili. Composer; *b.* Russia, 1870. 1894, to U. S.; 1909, opera, *Hoshi-San*, perf. in Phila.

Leroux (*Le-roo*), **Xavier Henri Napoleon.** Composer; *b.* Velletri, It., Oct. 11, 1863; *d.* Paris, 1919. Comp. orch. wks., but best known by. his operas, incl., *La Reine Fiammette*, and *Le Chemineau*.

Leschen (*Les-shen*), **Christoph Friedrich.** Composer; *b.* Vienna, 1816; *d.* ib., May 4, 1899. Comp. operas, symph., songs.

Leschetizky (*Leh-she-tit-ski*), **Theodor.** Pianist, composer, teacher; *b.* Lancut, Aus., Jun. 22, 1830; *d.* Dresden, Ger., Nov. 17, 1915. *t.* of Paderewski, Gabrilowitsch, Mark Hambourg; the most celebrated pianoforte teacher of his time.

Leslie, Grace. Contralto; *b.* Grafton, Mass. *p.* Ivan Morawski, Boston; debut, ib.; soloist, major symphs.; operatic debut, Washington Natl. Gr. Op.; Phila. Civic Op.; European debut, Berlin; also radio.

Leslie, Henry D. Composer, conductor; *b.* London, Jun. 18, 1822; *d.* Llansaintfraid, Wales, Feb. 4, 1896. 1855, cond., Leslie Choir. Comp. choral wks.

Lester, Thomas William. Organist, composer; *b.* Leicester, Sept. 17, 1889. 1911-14, mus. critic, Chicago *Record-Herald*; 1913, org., Second Ch. of Christ, Chicago. Comp. str. q., cantatas; violin, 'cello, organ and piano pcs.

Lesueur (*Le-swear*), **Jean François.** Composer; *b.* Drucat-Plessiel, Fr., Feb. 15, 1760; *d.* Paris, Oct. 6, 1837. Prof., Paris Cons. Comp. operas, masses, oratorios.

Letz, Hans. Violinist; *b.* Mar. 18, 1887. Edu., Berlin Hochschule. 1911, conc.-m., Chicago Symph. Orch.; 1914, second violin, Kneisel Quartet; 1917, fd., Letz Quartet.

Leuning, Otto. Composer; *b.* Milwaukee, 1900. 1914-7, st., Munich. 1917-20, Zurich Cons.; 1922-5, *t.* in Chicago; 1925-8, *t.* Eastman Sch. of Mus.; 1930-2, Guggenheim Fellowship; 1933, mus. dept., Bennington Coll. Comp. opera, *Evangeline*, and 38 major symph., and chamb. mus. wks.

Leva (*Lay-vah*), **Enrico di.** Pianist, composer; *b.* Naples, It., Jan. 19, 1867. Comp. operas, songs.

Levi, Hermann. Conductor; *b.* Giessen, Nov. 7, 1839; *d.* Munich, May 13, 1900. 1859, Saarbrucken Op.; 1861, Rotterdam Op.; 1864, Karlsruhe; 1872-1896, estab. world fame as Kapellmeister at Munich; cond., *Parsifal* première Bayreuth, Jul. 28, 1882. Directed the mus. at Wagner's funeral.

Levin, Sylvan. Conductor; *b.* Baltimore. Asst. cond., Phila. Symph. Orch., *u.* Leopold Stokowski; 1934, cond., York (Pa.) Symph. Orch.

Levitzki, Mischa. Pianist; *b.* Kiev, Rus., May 25, 1898. *p.* Dohnanyi. 1914, debut, Berlin; 1916, Amer. debut, Aeolian Hall; 1921-22, Australia-New Zealand tour; 1925, tour, Orient; concertizes U. S. annually.

Levy (*Lay-vee*), **Alexandre.** Composer; *b.* San Paulo, Brazil, Nov. 10, 1864; *d.* ib., Jan. 17, 1892. Comp. chamb. mus., pf. pcs., utilizing folk themes, as in *Variation on a Brazilian Theme*.

Levy, Heniot. Composer, pianist; *b.* Poland, Jul. 19, 1879. 1905, *t.* Amer. Cons. of Mus., Chicago. Comp. chamb. mus., violin, pf., pcs.

Leybach (*Ly-bakh*), **Ignace.** Composer, pianist; *b.* Gambsheim, Alsace, Jul. 17, 1817; *d.* Toulouse, Fr., May 23, 1891. Comp. salon mus., incl., *Fifth Nocturne*.

Lhévinne (*Lay-vin*), **Josef.** Pianist; *b.* Moscow, Dec. 14, 1874. *p.* Safonoff. 1889, debut, Moscow Symph., *u.* Rubinstein; 1895, Rubinstein prize; 1900, *t.* Tiflis; 1902, *t.* Moscow Cons.; 1906, to U. S. Brilliant concert artist.

Liadoff (*Lya-doff*), **Anatole Constantinovitch.** Composer; *b.* Petrograd, May 11, 1855; *d.* Novgorod, Aug. 28, 1914. *b.* Rimsky-Korsakoff. 1878, prof., Petrograd Cons. Comp. orch., pf. mus.

Liapounoff (*Lya-poo-noff*), **Sergei.** Composer, conductor, pianist; *b.* Jaroslav, Rus., Nov. 30, 1859; *d.* Paris, Nov. 11, 1924. 1910, prof., Petrograd Cons.; mem., Imperial folksong commission. Comp. orch., and pf. wks., incl. a pf. concerto; also pf. pcs., *études*, songs.

Lichey (*Likh-eye*), **Reinhold.** Organist, composer; *b.* Liegnitz, Ger., Mar. 26, 1879. Brilliant organ virtuoso. Comp. organ pcs.

Lichtenberg (*Likh-ten-bairg*), **Leopold.** Violinist, teacher; *b.* San Francisco, Nov. 22, 1861; *d.* Brooklyn, May 16, 1935. *p.* Wieniawski. 1899, *t.* Natl. Cons., N. Y. Ed. of violin editions.

Lichtmann, Sina. Pianist, educator; *b.* Odessa, Oct. 30, 1891. St., Teichmuller, Leipzig; Vienna Meisterschule, *u.* Godowsky. 1910, debut *w.* Vienna Symph.; 1914, fd. Lichtmann Piano Inst., N. Y.; dir., Master Inst. of United Arts; board of dir., Roerich Museum.

Lie (*Lee*), **Sigurd.** Composer; *b.* Norway, May 23, 1871; *d.* Christiania, Nor., Sept. 30, 1904. Comp. orch., pf. pcs., songs.

Liebling (*Leeb-ling*), **Emil.** Pianist, composer, teacher; *b.* Pless, Ger., Apr. 12, 1851; *d.* Chicago, Jan. 20, 1914. Eminent teacher in Chicago for many years.

Liebling, Georg Lothar. Pianist, composer; *b.* Berlin, Jan. 22, 1865. Comp. orch., piano.

Liebling Leonard. Music critic; *b.* N. Y., Feb. 7, 1874. 1897, gr., C. C. N. Y. 1902, staff mem., 1911, ed., *Musical Courier;* mus. critic, N. Y. *American.* Comp. chamb. wks., pf. pcs., librettos, incl., *Balkan Princess, Vera Violetta, Girl and the Kaiser.*

Lilienthal, Abraham Wolf. Composer; *b.* N. Y., Feb. 13, 1859. *t.* New York. Comp. chamb. mus., songs.

Limbert, Frank L. Conductor, teacher, composer; *b.* New York, Nov. 15, 1866. 1901, *t.* Dusseldorf Cons. Comp. orch., chamb. wks.

Lincke, Paul. Composer; *b.* Berlin, Nov. 7, 1866. Comp. operettas, small pcs., incl., *Glow Worm.*

Lind, Jenny. Prima-donna soprano; *b.* Stockholm, Swed., Oct. 6, 1820; *d.* Malvern, Eng., Nov. 2, 1887. Brought to U. S. by P. T. Barnum, in sensational debut at Castle Garden, N. Y., Sept. 11, 1850. Made many tours, everywhere exciting enthusiasm by her operatic impersonations, and still more by her singing of simple national melodies.

Lindblad, Adolf. Composer; *b.* Löfvingsborg, Swed., Feb. 1, 1801; *d.* ib., Aug. 23, 1878. Comp. orch., vocal wks.; called the "Swedish Schubert."

Lindegren, Johan. Composer; *b.* Ullared, Swed., Jan. 7, 1842; *d.* Stockholm, Jun. 8, 1908. An authority on ch. mus.

Linden, Karl van der. Composer; *b.* Dordrecht, Hol., Aug. 24, 1839. Comp. overtures, cantatas.

Linder, Gottfried. Composer; *b.* Ehringen, Ger., Jun. 22, 1842; *d.* Stuttgart, 1918. Comp. operas and chamb. mus.

Lindner, Eugen. Composer; *b.* Leipzig, Ger., Dec. 11, 1858; *d.* Wiemar, 1915. Comp. operas and songs.

Lindpainter (*Lint-pint-ner*), **Peter Joseph von.** Conductor, composer; *b.* Coblenz, Ger., Dec. 9, 1791; *d.* Lake of Constance, Aug. 21, 1856. Comp. operas, symph., ch. mus. His most widely known comp. is the celebrated song, *The Standard Bearer.*

Liney, George. Composer; *b.* Leeds, Eng., 1798; *d.* London, Sept. 10, 1865. Comp. operas, songs.

Liney, Thomas. Composer; *b.* Wells, Eng., 1732; *d.* London, Nov. 19, 1795. Comp. stage wks., songs.

Liney, William. Composer; *b.* London, 1771; *d.* ib., May 6, 1835. Comp. many glees and songs.

Linley, Thomas. Violinist; *b.* Bath, Eng., May, 1756; *d.* Lincolnshire, Aug. 7, 1778. *p.* Nardini; intimate friend of Mozart; esteemed player in London; career cut short by drowning.

Lipinski, Karl J. Composer, violinist; *b.* Radzyn, Pol., Nov. 4, 1790; *d.* nr. Lemberg, Dec. 16, 1861. Friend of Paganini.

Lischin (*Lish-in*), **Gregory.** Composer; *b.* 1854; *d.* Petrograd, Jun. 27, 1888. Comp. operas, incl., *Don César de Bazan.*

Lissenko, Nicolai. Composer; *b.* Grinzkky, S. Rus., Mar. 22, 1842; *d.* Kiev, Rus., Nov. 11, 1912. Comp. operas, cantatas, choruses; collected Ukrainian folk-songs.

List, Emanuel. Basso; *b.* nr. Vienna. Brought to U. S. as a child; Amer. citizen (naturalized); debut, Vienna Op.; Berlin St. Op.; Covent Garden, London; Bayreuth; Met. Op., N. Y.

Listemann, Bernhard. Violinist, teacher; *b.* Schlotheim, Ger., Mar. 25, 1839; *d.* Chicago, Feb. 11, 1917. Eminent Chicago teacher for many years.

Liszniewski, Karol. Pianist; *b.* Poland. *p.* Mikuli. LL.D., U. of Lemberg. *t.* Cin. Cons. of Mus.

Liszt (*List*), **Franz.** Pianist, composer; *b.* Raiding, Hun., Oct. 22, 1811; *d.* Bayreuth, Ger., Jul. 31, 1886. *p.* Czerny. 1848, cond., court orch., Weimar, which became one of the vital mus. centers of the Continent through his presentation of new operatic and symph. wks. Early exponent of Wagner. Marvelous skill as a pianist. Distinguished as a comp., also as an author of merit. Will always be known as the comp. of the *Liebestraum* and the *Hungarian Rhapsodies.* Comp. symph. wks. Newman wrote a biography of him (1935).

Litolff, Henry Charles. Pianist, composer; *b.* London, Feb. 6, 1818; *d.* Paris, Aug. 6, 1891. *p.* Moscheles. 1851, *m.* widow of G. M. Meyer, mus. pub.; developed famous firm of H. Litolff, and gave it to adopted stepson (Theodor, 1839-1912) and returned to professional life in Paris. Comp. operas; five concerto-symph.; and many pf. pcs., and *études.*

Ljungberg, Gota. Operatic soprano; *b.* Sundsvall, Oct. 4, 1893. Edu., Stockholm. 1912, *m.* M. H. Stangenberg, opera impres. 1924, Covent Garden, London; 1932, Met. Op., debut as *Sieglinde.*

Lloyd, Charles Harford. Organist, composer; *b.* Thornbury, Eng., Oct. 16, 1849; *d.* Slough, 1919. 1914, org., Chapel Royal. Comp. cantatas, songs.

Lloyd, Edward. Tenor; *b.* London, Mar. 7, 1845; *d.* Mar. 31, 1927. Eminent oratorio singer.

Lobe (*Lo-beh*), **Johann Christian.** Theorist, writer, flutist; *b.* Weimar, May 30, 1797; *d.* Leipzig, Jul. 27, 1881. Fd., Sch. of Mus., Weimar; 1846, ed., *Allgem Musikae Zeitung,* Leipzig. Author of theoretical treatises.

Locatelli, Pietro. Composer, violinist; *b.* Bergamo, It., 1693; *d.* Amsterdam, Apr. 1, 1764. *p.* Corelli. Comp. violin sonatas and *Caprices.*

Lockwood, Albert. Pianist; *b.* Troy, N. Y., Apr. 3, 1871; *d.* Ann Arbor, Mich., Nov. 9, 1933. *p.* Leschetizky. 1892, gr., Leipzig Cons. Concertized Europe and U. S.; 1900-*d.*, head pf. dept., U. Sch. of Mus., Ann Arbor.

Loeffler (*Lef-ler*) **Charles Martin Tornov.** Violinist, composer; *b.* Mühlhausen, Alsace, Jan. 30, 1861; *d.* Medford, Mass., May 19, 1935. *p.* Joachim, Leonard. Mem. of Pasdeloup Orch.; 1885-1903, shared first desk of Boston Symph. *w.* Franz Kneisel; retired to pursue comp. 1926, Mus.D., Yale, and numerous other honors. 1923, won North Shore Fest. prize *w. Memories of My Childhood.* Comp. *Divertimento* for violin and orch., 'cello concerto, chamb., and orch. wks., incl., *La Mort de Tintagiles,* and *A Pagan Poem;* all in a conservative modern idiom.

Loeillet (*Loy-ay*) [**Loelly**], **Jean Baptiste.** Flutist; *b.* Ghent, Bel., *c.* 1650; *d.* London, 1728. Comp. chamb. mus., flute and harpsichord pcs.

Loesser, Arthur. Pianist; *b.* N. Y. Edu., Columbia U., Inst. Mus. Art, N. Y. 1913, debut, Berlin; toured *w.* Maud Powell, Mischa Elman, Schumann-Heink; soloist, maj. orch.; 1919-20, *t.* Inst. Mus. Art; 1926, *t.* Cleveland Inst. Mus.

Loew (*Lave*), **Joseph.** Composer, pianist; *b.* Prague, Jan. 23, 1834; *d.* ib., Oct. 5, 1886. Comp. piano, teaching pcs.

Logier (*Lo-jeer*), **Johann Bernhard.** Flutist; *b.* Kassel, Ger., Feb. 9, 1777; *d.* Dublin, Ire., Jul. 27, 1846. 1814, patented the "Chiroplast," an apparatus for estab. the hand-position at the pf. keyboard; also a system of class teaching, widely used and prominently advocated, but which was the subject of much controversy. 1826, retired to Dublin w. considerable wealth.

Logroscino (*Log-ro-shee-no*), **Nicolo.** Composer; *b.* Naples, It., *c.* 1700; *d.* ib., 1763. A pioneer comp. of opera buffa.

Lolli, Antonio. Violinist, composer; *b.* Bergamo, It., *c.* 1730; *d.* Palermo, 1802. 1775-8, in Petrograd, in court service *u.* Catharine II. Toured most of Europe. Popular, but of unsound musicianship.

Loomis, Clarence. Composer, teacher; *b.* Sioux Falls, S. Dak., Dec. 13, 1889. 1929, opera, *Yolanda of Cypress*, prod., Chicago and N. Y. Comp. four operas, and pf. concerto.

Loomis, Harvey Worthington. Composer; *b.* Brooklyn, N. Y., Feb. 5, 1865; *d.* Boston, Dec. 25, 1930. Principal *p.* of Dvořàk, while in U. S.; last years spent in Boston as ed. for C. C. Birchard, where he prod. hundreds of orig. wks., and adaptations, employing several pseudonyms. Comp. mus. pantomimes, operas, cantatas, chorus collections, songs.

Lopatnikoff, Nikolai. Composer; *b.* Reval, Rus., Mar. 16, 1903. St., Leningrad Cons., *u.* Schitomirski. 1917, expelled from Rus., to Helsingfors, Finland; 1920, to Heidelberg, st. *u.* Ernest Toch; 1929, *Piano Concerto*, perf. in Berlin, and *String Quartet* in Karlsruhe. 1933, domiciled in Helsingfors. Comp. symph., and chamb. wks., opera, and piano pcs., all widely performed in Europe and U. S.

Lora, Arthur. Flutist; *b.* Novale, It., Mar. 11, 1903. 1924, gr., Inst. Mus. Art, N. Y. 1925, mem., N. Y. Chamb. Mus. Soc.; *t.* Inst. Mus. Art.

Lorenz, Karl Adolf. Organist, composer; *b.* Köslin, Ger., Aug. 13, 1837. 1866-1910, cond., Stettin, succ. Loewe. Comp. oratorio, operas, chamb. mus.

Lortzing, Gustav Albert. Composer; *b.* Berlin, Oct. 23, 1801; *d.* ib., Jan. 21, 1851. Comp. operas, incl., *Czar und Zimmermann*.

Löschhorn (*Lesh-horn*), **Albert.** Pianist, composer; *b.* Berlin, Jun. 27, 1819; *d.* ib., Jun. 4, 1905. Best known by his piano studies.

Loth, L. Leslie. Pianist, composer; *b.* Richmond, Va., Oct. 28, 1888. *p.* Alberto Jonas, Berlin. 1908, debut, Richmond; 1908-14, recitals and soloist w. maj. orch. in Europe; 1918, *t.* New York. Comp. symph., chamb. mus., pf. pcs.

Lotti, Antonio. Organist, composer; *b.* Venice, *c.* 1667; *d.* ib., Jan. 5, 1740. Comp. operas, songs., incl., *Pur dicesti o bocca bella,* which is still in the repertoire of most singers.

Loud, John Hermann. Organist; *b.* Weymouth, Mass., Aug. 26, 1873. 1889-90, st., N. E. Cons. of Mus.; 1895, ch. and concert org. and *t.*, Boston.

Lover, Samuel. Composer, poet; *b.* Dublin, Feb. 24, 1797; *d.* St. Heliers, Island of Jersey, Jul. 6, 1868. 1846, visited U. S. Wr. librettos for Balfe. Comp. songs, popular in his day.

Löwe (*Lay-veh*), **Johann Karl Gottfried.** Organist, composer; *b.* Halle, Ger., Nov. 11, 1796; *d.* Kiel, Apr. 20, 1869. Comp. oratorios, operas, part-songs, chamb. mus. His fame rests on his ballads, incl., *Edward*.

Lucas, Clarence. Composer, author; *b.* Niagara, Can., Oct. 19, 1866. 1889, *t.* Toronto Cons.; 1891-3, *t.* Utica Cons.; 1903, ed., Chappell, London; 1909-25, editorial contrib., *Musical Courier*. Comp. operas, orch., songs. Author, *The Story of Musical Form*.

Lucca (*Look-kah*), **Pauline.** Soprano; *b.* Vienna, Apr. 25, 1841; *d.* Paris, Feb. 28, 1908. 1861, Berlin Op., *u.* Meyerbeer; 1872-4, to U. S.; 1874, Vienna Op., and toured all of Europe.

Luckstone, Isidore. Accompanist and vocal teacher; *b.* Baltimore, Md., Jan. 29, 1861. Toured w. Camilla Urso, Eduard Remenyi, Sembrich, Nordica, Melba, Kreisler, Schumann-Heink; 1925, *t.* mus. dept., N. Y. U. Comp. popular concert songs.

Luders, Gustav. Operetta composer; *b.* Germany, 1866. w. Frank Pixley, Chicago librettist, prod. a series of mus. comedy successes, incl., *Prince of Pilsen* (Boston, 1902; London, 1904—160 perf.), and *The Sho-Gun*.

Lugert, Josef. Violinist, teacher, composer; *b.* Frohnau, Boh., Oct. 30, 1841. 1868, prof., Prague Cons. Comp. symph., chamb. wks.

Lully (*Lool-lee*), **Jean Baptiste de.** Violinist, composer; *b.* Florence, Nov. 29, 1639; *d.* Paris, Mar. 22, 1687. Brought to France as a boy; rose from a scullion to chief mus. of Louis XIV. 1671, dir., Gr. Op., Paris. Regarded as fd. of Fr. opera.

Lumbye (*Loom-bee*), **Hans C.** Composer; *b.* Copenhagen, May 2, 1810; *d.* ib., Mar. 20, 1874.

Lund, Charlotte. Soprano, lecturer; *b.* Oswego, N. Y., Dec. 27, 1880. *p.* Goetschius, Jean de Reszke. Author, *Miniature Opera Series;* fd. and pres., N. Y. Opera Club.

Lunn, Louisa Kirkby. Contralto; *b.* Manchester, Eng., Nov. 8, 1873; *d.* London, Feb. 17, 1930. Edu., R. C. M., London. 1902, Met. Op.; 1904, Savage's *Parsifal;* 1906-8, Met. Op.; 1912-14, Australia; 1915, Covent Garden, and concert tours in Europe.

Lussan (*Lis-sang*), **Zélie de.** Soprano; *b.* New York, 1863. 1894-5, 1900-01, Met. Op. 1907, *m.* Fronani, pianist, and retired.

Luther, Martin. Composer; *b.* Eisleben, Ger., Nov. 10, 1483; *d.* ib., Feb. 18, 1546. Estab. congregational singing as a regular part of the ch. service. Comp. hymns, incl., *Ein' Feste Burg*.

Lutkin, Peter Christian. Organist, composer, conductor; *b.* Thompsonville, Wis., Mar. 27, 1858; *d.* Evanston, Ill., Dec. 27, 1931. 1891, fd.-dean, Sch. of Mus., Northwestern U., Evanston, Ill. Comp. ch. mus.

Lutz, Wilhelm Meyer. Composer; *b.* Männerstadt, Ger., 1822; *d.* London, Jan. 31, 1903. Comp. comic operas.

Lux (*Looks*), **Friedrich.** Organist, composer; *b.* Ruhla, Ger., Nov. 24, 1820; *d.* Mainz, Ger., Jul. 9, 1895. Cond., Dessau Court Th. Comp. four operas.

Luzzi (*Loot-si*), **Luigi.** Composer; *b.* Olevano di Lomellina, It., Mar. 28, 1828; *d.* Stradella, It., Feb. 23, 1876. Comp. operas, symph., songs, incl., *Ave Maria*.

Lvoff, Alexis. Composer; *b.* Reval, Rus., Jun. 6, 1799; *d.* Kovno, Rus., Jan. 7, 1871. Comp. operas, violin wks.; best known as comp. of *Russian National Hymn*.

Lyford, Ralph. Composer; *b.* Mass., 1882; *d.* Ohio, 1927. 1926, won Bispham medal for opera, *Castle Agrazant,* prod., Cin.; 1917, N. F. M. C. prize for *Concerto,* for piano and orch.

Lyne, Felice. Soprano; *b.* Kansas City, 1891. A remarkable coloratura. 1911, *w.* Hammerstein in London; Chicago Op.

Lynes, Frank. Organist, composer; *b.* Cambridge, Mass., May 16, 1858; *d.* Bristol, N. H., Jun. 24, 1914.

Lyon, James. Early American composer, Presbyterian minister; *b.* Newark, 1735; *d.* Machias, Me., 1794. Author of *Urania* (1761), a collection of psalm tunes, which contained tune, *America,* to sacred words.

Lysberg (really **Bovy**), **Charles Samuel.** Composer; *b.* Lysberg, Switz., Mar. 1, 1821; *d.* Geneva, Feb. 15, 1873. Comp. popular piano pcs., incl., *Awakening of the Birds.*

M

Maas (*Mahs*), **Joseph.** Tenor; *b.* Dartford, Eng., Jan. 30, 1847; *d.* London, Jan. 16, 1886. Toured U. S. *w.* Kellogg Eng. Op. Co.

Maas, Louis Philipp Otto. Pianist, teacher; *b.* Wiesbaden, Jun. 21, 1852; *d.* Boston, Sept. 18, 1889. *p.* Liszt. 1880, *t.* N. E. Cons., Boston. Comp. symph., chamb. mus.

Mabellini (*Mah-bel-lee-nee*), **Teodulo.** Composer; *b.* Pistoja, It., Apr. 2, 1817; *d.* Florence, It., Mar. 10, 1897. Comp. operas, oratorios, cantatas.

Macbeth, Allan. Organist, composer; *b.* Greenock, Scot., Mar. 13, 1856. 1890, prin., Sch. of Mus., Glasgow Athenaeum. Comp. cantatas, chamb. wks., pf. pcs.; popularly known by pf. piece, *Forget-Me-Nots.*

Macbeth, Florence. Soprano; *b.* Mankato, Minn., 1891. *p.* Yeatman Griffith. 1914, Amer. debut, as Rosina in *The Barber of Seville,* Chicago Grand Op. Co.

MacCunn, Hamish. Composer, conductor; *b.* Greenock, Scot., Mar. 22, 1868; *d.* London, Aug. 2, 1916. Comp. choral wks., operas, pf. pcs., songs.

MacDonough, Glen. Writer; *d.* Stamford, Mar. 30, 1924. *m.* Daughter of Joe Jefferson. Reporter on N. Y. *World.* Librettist of *Babes in Toyland,* and other operettas.

Macdougall, Hamilton Crawford. Organist, teacher, composer; *b.* Warwick, R. I., Oct. 15, 1858. 1900-27, *t.* Wellesly Coll.

MacDowell, Edward Alexander. Pianist, composer; *b.* N. Y., Dec. 18, 1861; *d.* ib., Jan. 23, 1908. Studied in Paris and Germany; wks. first played and championed by his teacher, Teresa Carreño. 1881-1882, pf. *t.,* Darmstadt Cons.; 1896-1904, prof., Columbia U. Ranks historically as Amer. foremost comp. The MacDowell Colony in Peterborough, N. H., fd. in his honor, affords ideal working surroundings for creative artists. Comp. incl., symph. p., orch. suites, choruses, piano concertos, suites, sonatas, études and pcs. for piano, and songs. Popularly known by his piano piece, *To a Wild Rose.*

MacDowell, Marian Nevins (Mrs. E. A.). Pianist, lecturer; *b.* N. Y. Leader in MacDowell Memorial Colony, Peterborough, N. H.

Macfarlane, William Charles. Organist, composer; *b.* London, Eng., Oct. 2, 1870. *p.* S. P. Warren. 1900-12, org., St. Thomas Ch., N. Y.; 1912-19, city org., Portland, Me. Comp. cantata, anthems and organ pcs.

Macfarren, Sir George Alexander. Composer, theorist; *b.* London, Mar. 2, 1813; *d.* ib., Oct. 31, 1887. Comp. operas, oratorios, cantatas, ch. mus., symph., chamb. mus., songs.

Macfarren, Walter C. Pianist, teacher; *b.* London, Aug. 28, 1826; *d.* ib., Sept. 2, 1905. Brother of G. A. M.

Machado (*Mah-chah'-do*), **Augusto.** Composer; *b.* Lisbon, Port., Dec. 27, 1845; *d.* ib., Mar. 28, 1924. *t.* Lisbon Cons. Contemporary Portuguese opera comp.

Mackenzie, Sir Alexander Campbell. Conductor, composer; *b.* Edinburgh, Scot., Aug. 22, 1847; *d.* London, Apr. 28, 1935. 1888, dir., R. A. M. In the front rank of English musicians. Comp. cantatas, incl., *Jason;* oratorio, *The Rose of Sharon;* operas, incl., *Colomba;* much orch. mus.

Mackenzie, Tandy. Singer; *b.* Hana, Maui, Hawaiian Islands, Mar. 10, 1892. *p.* William Thorner. 1921, concert debut *w.* Titta Ruffo at Waldorf-Astoria Hotel, N. Y; 1922-24, three tours of U. S.

Maclean, Alick (Alexander Morvaren). Composer, conductor; *b.* Eton, Eng., Jul. 20, 1872. Mus. dir., Scarborough, Eng. Comp. operas, incl., *Quentin Durward.*

MacLennan, Francis. Tenor; *b.* Bay City, Mich., 1879; *d.* Port Washington, L. I., Jul. 17, 1935. *p.* Henschel. 1902, debut, London; 1904-6, Savage's Op.; 1906-12, Berlin; 1912-15, Berlin; 1915-17, Chicago; 1917, Met. Op. 1904, *m.* Florence Easton.

MacMillan, Ernest. Composer, conductor, organist; *b.* Mimico, Ont. Edu., Oxford and Toronto U. 1919-25, org., Eaton Memorial Ch., Toronto; 1926, principal, Toronto Cons. of Mus.; since 1927, dean of mus., Toronto U.

Macmillen, Francis. Violinist; *b.* Marietta, O., Oct. 14, 1885. St. Joachim, César Thomson, Flesch, Auer. 1903, concert debut, Brussels; 1906, Amer. debut, Carnegie Hall, N. Y.

MacPhail, William. Violinist, teacher; *b.* Glasgow, Nov. 18, 1881. *p.* Sevcik. 1907, debut, Minn.; dir., MacPhail Sch. of Mus., Minn.

Macpherson, Charles. Organist, composer; *b.* Edinburgh, Scot., May 10, 1870; *d.* London, May 28, 1927. 1916, org., St. Paul's Cath., London; pres., R. C. O.; prof., R. A. M. Comp. orch., chamb. mus.

Macpherson, Charles Stewart. Composer, writer; *b.* Liverpool, Eng., Mar. 29, 1865. Comp. symph., overtures. Author of text-books on theoretical subjects.

MacPherson, Joseph Tant. Bass-baritone; *b.* Nashville, Tenn., Jun. 7, 1900. *p.* G. S. de Luca. 1926, Met. Op., N. Y.

Macy, James Cartwright. Composer; *b.* New York, Jun. 27, 1845; *d.* Somerville, Mass., 1918. Comp. cantatas, ch. mus., pf. pcs., songs.

Maddy, Joseph E. Violinist, teacher, conductor; *b.* Wellington, Kan., Oct. 14, 1891. *p.* Czerwonky. Played *w.* Minneapolis, St. Paul, and Wichita Symph. Orch.; 1915, presented mus. fest., Wellington, Kan.

Maelzel (*Mayl-tsel*), **Johann Nepomuk.** Inventor; *b.* Ratisbon., Ger., Aug. 15, 1772; *d.* Jul. 21, 1838. Friend of Beethoven, for whom he made ear trumpets. Invented the metronome now in common use; came to U. S., and died at sea en route to Cuba.

Maganini, Quinto. Composer, flutist, conductor; *b.* Fairfield (Cal.), Nov. 30, 1897. Fd. and cond., N. Y. Chamb. Symph. Orch., presenting unfamiliar old and new wks.

Maggini (*Mad-jee-nee*), **Giovanni Paolo.** Violin maker; b. Botticino Marino, It., Aug. 25, 1580; d. Brescia, It., c. 1632. Work highly esteemed.

Magnard (*Man-yar*), **Lucien Denis Gabriel Alberic.** Composer; b. Paris, Jun. 9, 1865; d. Baron, Oise, Sept. 3, 1914. p. of d'Indy. Comp. symph., opera, chamb. mus.

Mahler, Gustav. Conductor, composer; b. Kalischt, Boh., Jul. 7, 1860; d. Vienna, May 18, 1911. 1908, cond., Met. Op., N. Y.; 1909-10, cond., N. Y. Phil. Soc. Known for his nine large symph., some of them w. solo voices and chorus.

Maier, Guy. Pianist; b. Buffalo, N. Y., Aug. 15, 1892. p. Schnabel. Plays in two-piano combination w. Lee Pattison.

Maillart (*My-yar*), **Louis.** Composer; b. Montpellier, Fr., Mar. 24, 1817; d. Moulins, Fr., May 26, 1871. Opera comp.

Mailly (*My-yee*), **Alphonse Jean Ernest.** Organist, composer; b. Brussels, Bel., Nov. 27, 1833; d. ib., 1918. Comp. orch. wks., organ pcs.

Main, Hubert Platt. Gospel hymn writer; b. Ridgefield, Conn., Aug. 17, 1839; d. Newark, N. J., Oct. 7, 1925. Pioneer gospel hymn writer of 1,000 tunes. Fd. of Bigelow & Main, song book pubs., whose *Gospel Songs*, volumes 1-6, made history.

Major (*Mah-yor*), **Julius Jacques.** Pianist, composer; b. Kaschau, Hun., Dec. 13, 1859. t. Buda-Pesth. Comp. orch., chamb. wks.

Malaschkin, Leonid Demitrievitch. Composer; b. Russia, 1842; d. Moscow, Feb. 11, 1902. Collected Ukrainian folksongs. Comp. ch. mus., pf. pcs.

Malat (*Mah-laht*), **Jan.** Composer; b. Alt-Bunzlau, Boh., Jun. 16, 1843. Czech opera comp.

Malcolm, Alexander. Writer; b. Edinburgh, Scot., 1687; d. c. 1721. Author of *A Treatise of Musick* (Edinburgh, 1721).

Malibran (*Mahl-ee-brahn*), **Maria Felicita.** Contralto; b. Paris, Mar. 24, 1808; d. Manchester, Eng., Sept. 23, 1836. Daughter of Manuel Garcia. 1825-7, w. him in N. Y. One of the greatest opera singers of her epoch.

Malipiero, G. Francesco. Composer; b. Venice, It., Mar. 18, 1882. p. Bossi. 1920, String Quartet won Coolidge prize; 1932, *Concerti,* world première w. Fritz Reiner and Phila. Symph. Orch.; 1934, *Symphony,* perf., ISCM Fest., at Florence. Comp. opera, symph., and chamb. mus. wks.

Malling, Jörgen. Composer; b. Copenhagen, Den., Oct. 31, 1836; d. ib., Jul., 1905. Comp. songs, piano wks., operas.

Malling, Otto Waldemar. Composer; b. Copenhagen, Jun. 1, 1848; d. ib., 1915. Brother of Jörgen M. Comp. orch., chamb. wks.

Mancinelli (*Man-chin-el-lee*), **Luigi.** Composer, conductor; b. Orvieto, It., Feb. 5, 1848; d. Rome, Feb. 2, 1921. 1894-1902, cond., Met. Op. Comp. numerous operas.

Mandl, Richard. Composer; b. Prossnitz, Aus., May 9, 1859; d. Vienna, 1918. Orch. comp.

Manén, Joan de. Violinist, composer; b. Barcelona, Sp., Mar. 14, 1883. A phenomenal player w. modern tendencies as a comp. Comp. operas, symph., violin concerto.

Mankowitz, David. Violinist, violist; b. N. Y., Jun. 11, 1910. 1930, gr., Inst. Mus. Art, N. Y. 1929, mem., Perole Str. Q.; 1933, mem., N. Y. Chamb. Mus. Soc.

Mann, Johann Gottfried. Conductor, composer; b. Hague, Hol., Jul. 15, 1858; d. Coudewater, Hol., Feb. 10, 1904. Comp. for stage and orch.

Mannes, David. Violinist, conductor; b. N. Y., Feb. 16, 1866. 1898, m. Clara, sister of Walter Damrosch. 1902-11, conc.-m., N. Y. Symph. Orch.; dir., Mus. Sch. Settlement; cond. symph. concerts at Met. Museum of Art; dir., Mannes Mus. Sch.

Mannes, Leopold Damrosch. Composer, teacher; b. N. Y., 1899. Grandson, Leopold Damrosch. p. Scalero. 1924, Walter Scott Foundation fellowship; 1925, Pulitzer prize; 1926, Guggenheim fellowship; t. David Mannes Mus. Sch., N. Y. Comp. orch. and chamb. mus., songs.

Manney, Charles Fonteyn. Composer; b. Brooklyn, N. Y., Feb. 8, 1872. 1898, assoc. ed., Ditson, Boston. Comp. cantatas, songs.

Manns, Sir August Friedrich. Conductor; b. Stolzenburg, Ger., Mar. 12, 1825; d. Norwood, Eng., Mar. 1, 1907. 1885, cond., Crystal Palace, London. During his fifty years of service he increased the orch. to symph. proportions, and intro. to London audiences the modern symph. repertoire. In 1901, he celebrated his 14,000th public appearance. One of England's most historic cond.

Mansfield, Orlando Augustine. Organist, composer; b. Horningsham, Eng., Nov. 28, 1863. Edu., London Coll. of Mus. 1892-1912, examiner at London Coll. of Mus.; 1912-18, Wilson Coll., Chambersburg, Pa.; 1918-20, Brenau Coll., Gainesville, Ga.; 1905, Mus.D., Toronto U. Comp. piano and organ pcs., cantatas, songs.

Manville, Edward Britton. b. New Haven, Conn., 1879. p. William C. Carl. 1897-8, org., Grace P. E. Ch., New Haven; 1898-1905, 1st Cong. Ch., South Norwalk; 1905-12, First Baptist Ch., Franklin, Pa.; 1912-17, Woodward Ave. Bapt. Ch., Detroit; 1919-31, Woodward Ave. Pres. Ch., Detroit; 1914, Detroit Inst. Mus. Art; president, since 1922.

Mapleson, Henry. Impresario; b. London, Feb. 17, 1851. Edu., St. Mary's Coll. Assoc. w. father for many years in prod. of opera at Covent Garden and Drury Lane, London; also Acad. of Mus., N. Y.

Maquarre (*Mah-kar'*), **André.** Flutist, composer, conductor; b. Molenbeck, Bel., 1875. Mem., Boston Symph. Comp. opera, *Dolores, Indian Suite;* fantaisie, *On the Sea Cliffs.*

Marcello (*Mahr-chel-lo*), **Benedetto.** Composer; b. Venice, It., Aug. 8, 1686; d. Brescia, It., Jul. 24, 1739. Made an historic mus. setting of the first fifty Psalms.

Marchant, Arthur William. Organist, composer; b. London, Oct. 18, 1850; d. Stirling, 1921. 1880-2, org., Denver (Colo.) Cath.; 1895, org., St. John's, Dumfries, Scot. Comp. ch. mus., songs.

Marchesi de Castrone (*Mahr-kay'-zee*), **Mathilde de C. (née Graumann).** Teacher of singing; b. Frankfort, Ger., Mar. 24, 1821; d. London, Nov. 18, 1913. A famous singing teacher in Paris, Vienna and London; taught Gerster, Melba, Eames, Calve and her daughter, Blanche, who from 1899-1909, sang in U. S. Wr. vocalises; also an *Autobiography.*

Marchetti (*Mahr-ket'-tee*), **Filippo.** Composer; b. Bologna, It., Feb. 26, 1831; d. Rome, Jan. 18, 1902. Opera comp.

Marcosson, Sol. Violinist; b. Louisville, Ky., Jun. 10, 1869. p. Joachim. 1893-94, N. Y. Phil. Club; 1895-96, conc.-m., Cleveland Symph. Orch.; dir., Marcosson Mus. Sch., Cleveland.

Marcoux, Vanni. Operatic baritone; b. Turin, Jun. 12, 1879. 1899, debut, Nice; 1905-12, Covent Garden, London; 1912, Boston Op.; 1913, Chicago Op. Co.

Maréchal (*Mahr-ay-shal*), **Charles Henri.** Composer; b. Paris, Jan. 22, 1842; d. ib., 1935. Comp. operas, sacred mus.

Marenzio (*Mah-ren'-tsee-oh*), **Luca.** Composer; b. Coccaglia, It., c. 1556; d. Rome, Aug. 22, 1599. Famous 16th century madrigal writer.

Maretzek, Max. Impresario, composer; b. Brünn, Aus., Jun. 28, 1821; d. Staten Island, N. Y., May 14, 1897. 1848, cond., opera in N. Y., Havana and Mexico. Comp. opera, *Sleepy Hollow*, based on the Irving legend.

Marinuzzi, Giuseppe Gino. Conductor; b. Palermo, Mar. 24, 1882. 1920, dir., Chicago Op., succ. Campanini; 1922, cond., La Scala, Milan.

Mario (*Mah'-ree-o*), **Giuseppe.** Tenor; b. Cagliari, It., Oct. 17, 1808; d. Rome, Dec. 11, 1883. Retired in 1867 after a triumphant career as an operatic artist. 1854 and 1872, sang in U. S. Of him Meredith, in a poem, said: "and Mario can sooth, with a tenor note, the souls in Purgatore."

Mario, Queena. Soprano; b. Akron, O., Aug. 21, 1896. Newspaper writer; studied art, then singing w. Sembrich. 1918-21, San Carlo Op.; 1922, Met. Op., N. Y. 1925, m. Wilfred Pelletier.

Markevitch, Igor. Composer; b. Kiev, Rus., Jul. 27, 1912. p. Nadia Boulanger. 1929, *Concerto Grosso*, prod. in Paris; 1931, cond. his *Rebus* in Paris. Domiciled in Paris. Comp. symph. and chamb. mus.

Marks, James Christopher. Organist; b. Cork, Ire., Jul. 29, 1863. Edu., Trinity Coll., Dublin. 1904-29, org., Ch. of Heavenly Rest, N. Y.; 1929, Christ Ch., Brooklyn.

Marmontel, Antoine. Pianist, composer, teacher; b. Clermont-Ferrand, Fr., Jul. 18, 1816; d. Paris, Jan. 17, 1898. 1837-87, prof., Paris Cons. Comp. salon pcs., studies, and a pf. *Method*. Author of a *History of the Piano* (1885).

Marpurg (*Mahr-poorkh*), **Friedrich Wilhelm.** Theorist; b. Seehausen, Ger., Nov. 21, 1718; d. Berlin, May 22, 1795. Author of many technical treatises.

Marschalk (*Mahr-schalk*), **Max.** Composer; b. Berlin, Apr. 7, 1863. Comp. operas, incid. mus. to dramas, incl., Maeterlinck's *Sœur Beatrice*; songs.

Marschner (*Marsh-ner*), **Heinrich August.** Composer; b. Zittau, Ger., Aug. 16, 1795; d. Hanover, Dec. 14, 1861. p. Bruckner. Companion of Weber and Spohr in estab. the German romantic opera. Comp. a dozen operas, incl., *Hans Heiling*; also chamb. mus., songs.

Marsh, William John. Organist, composer; b. Liverpool, Jun. 24, 1880. p. J. Clement Standish. 1904, org., Fort Worth, Tex.; 1924, wr. State song, *Texas, My Texas*. Comp. pf. pcs., and songs.

Marshall, Charles. Operatic tenor; b. Auburn, Me., Sept. 15, 1886. p. Lombardi, Sr. 1920, Amer. debut, as *Otello*, Chicago Op.

Marshall, John Patton. Educator, organist, writer, lecturer; b. Rockport, Mass., Jan. 9, 1877. p. MacDowell, Chadwick. 1903, dean, Coll. of Mus., Boston U.

Marsick, Martin Pierre Joseph. Violinist, teacher; b. Liége, Bel., Mar. 9, 1848; d. Paris, Nov., 1924. p. Joachim. Prof., Paris Cons., once Massart; 1895-6, toured U. S. Comp. 3 violin concertos, and pcs.

Marston, George W. Composer, organist, teacher; b. Sandwich, Mass., May 23, 1840; d. ib., Feb. 2, 1901. 1859, Portland, Me. Comp. ch. mus., pf. pcs., and songs.

Marteau, Henri. Composer, violinist, editor; b. Rheims, Mar. 31, 1874; d. Lichtenberg, Oct. 4, 1934. 1884, debut w. Vienna Phil. Soc.; 1907, prof., Hochschule, succ. Joachim.

Martens, Frederick H. Author; b. N. Y., Jul. 6, 1874; d. Mountain Lakes, N. J., Dec. 18, 1932. Wr. Books on mus. and song poems.

Martin, Easthope. Song composer; b. Stourport, Worcestershire, 1882; d. London, Oct. 20, 1925. Frequent visitor to U. S. Wr. songs, incl., *Come to the Fair*.

Martin, Frank. Composer; b. Geneva, Sept. 15, 1890. Fd. Technicum Moderne de Musique, Geneva; mus. critic, *Tribune de Genève*; prof., Dalcroze Inst. Comp. orch. wks., incl., *Suite*, and *Les Dithyrambes*; chamb. mus., operatic and choral wks.

Martin, Sir George Clement. Organist, composer; b. Lambourn, Eng., Sept. 11, 1844; d. London, Jun. 23, 1916. 1888-1916, org., St. Paul's, London; 1883, prof., R. C. M.; 1895, prof., R. A. M.; 1897, knighted. Comp. anthems, hymns, services.

Martinelli, Giovanni. Tenor; b. Montagnana, Oct. 22, 1885. 1910, debut, Milan; 1912, created rôles in Zandonai's *Melenis*, Wolf-Ferrari's *Jewels of the Madonna*; Giordani's *Madame Sans-Gêne*, and Granados' *Goyescas*; 1913, Met. Op., N. Y.

Martini (*Mar-tee-nee*), **Giambattista (called Padre Martini).** Composer, theorist; b. Bologna, It., Apr. 24, 1706; d. ib., Oct. 4, 1784. During his day regarded as the greatest living authority on mus. matters.

Martini, Nino. Tenor; b. Verona, It., 1905. 1929, to U. S. for cinemas. 1934, debut, Met. Op. in *Aida*.

Martinu, Bohuslav. Composer; b. Policka, Czechoslovakia, Dec. 8, 1890. p. Josef Suk. 1932, prize *String Quartet*, perf., Wash., D. C. Comp. opera, *Les Jeux de la St. Vierges*; orch. wks., chamb. mus. h. Paris.

Martucci (*Mar-toot-chee*), **Giuseppe.** Pianist, composer; b. Capua, It., Jan. 6, 1856; d. Jun. 1, 1909. 1874, t.; 1902, dir., Bologna Cons. Comp. symph., chamb. mus., and many pf. pcs.

Marty, Georges Eugène. Composer; b. Paris, May 16, 1866; d. ib., Oct. 11, 1908. Comp. operas, orch. wks.

Marwick, Dudley. Operatic basso; b. Hartford, Conn., Aug. 25, 1898. 1935, Met. Op., N. Y.

Marx, Adolf Bernhard. Theorist; b. Halle, Ger., May 15, 1795; d. Berlin, May 17, 1866. Not a success as a comp., but wr. many valuable theoretical and critical wks.

Marx, Joseph. Composer, teacher; b. Graz, Austria, May 11, 1882. Ph.D., U. of Graz. 1922, dir. Acad. Mus., Vienna. Comp. orch. wks., incl., *Romantic Concerto*, for pf.; chamb. mus., choral mus.

Marzials, Theodor. Composer; b. Brussels, Bel., Dec. 21, 1850; d. London, 1920. 1870, mus. section, British Museum. Comp. many popular ballads, incl., *Leaving, Yet Loving*.

Marzo (*Mahr-tsoh*), **Eduardo.** Composer, teacher; b. Naples, It., Nov. 29, 1852; d. 1929. 1867, to N. Y. as prodigy pianist; later accompanist for Sarasate, and others. Comp. operettas, songs, and ch. mus.

Mascagni (*Mas-kahn'-yee*), **Pietro.** Composer; *b.* Leghorn, It., Dec. 7, 1863. Son of a baker, and intended by his father for the legal profession. St. Instituto Luigi Cherubini *u.* Alfredo Soffredini. 1879, prod. *Symphony* and *Kyrie;* 1885, cond., Cerignole; 1895-1902, cond., fest. of orch. mus. in Rome; 1890, Milan Cons., won Sonzogno prize *w. Cavalleria Rusticana,* prod., Costanzi Th., Rome, *w.* tremendous success; 1902, toured Amer. as cond. of opera company, playing his own wks.; again in 1910. Career chiefly identified *w.* Rome.

Mason, Daniel Gregory. Teacher, composer; *b.* Brookline, Mass., Nov. 30, 1873. Son of Henry, fd., Mason & Hamlin pianos. 1895, gr., Harvard; 1913, st., Vincent d'Indy; 1914, prof., Columbia U.; 1932, *Symphony in A Major,* intro., N. Y. Phil. Comp. orch. wks., chamb. mus., piano pcs., songs.

Mason, Edith Barnes. Soprano; *b.* St. Louis, Mar. 22, 1893. 1912, Boston Op.; 1913-15, Paris; 1915, Met. Op., N. Y.

Mason, Lowell. Teacher, hymn composer; *b.* Medfield, Mass., Jan. 8, 1792; *d.* Orange, N. J., Aug. 11, 1872. An epoch making figure in Amer. mus. development, pioneering in mus. for the masses. 1855, Mus.D., N. Y. U., the first conferring of that degree by an Amer. U. *Handel and Haydn Soc. Collection of Sacred Music* netted him in royalties $30,000. Estab. Mason & Hamlin piano manufacturers *w.* brother Henry. Pioneer in introd. mus. study in pub. schs. 1832, fd. Boston Acad. of Mus. 1834, called first convention of mus. teachers. 1853, estab. N. Y. Normal Inst. Home in Orange Mts., N. J., called *Silver-Spring,* immortalized by his son, William, as the title of his most popular pf. comp. Made many collections, chiefly of sacred mus. Popularly known for his hymn, *My Faith Looks Up to Thee.*

Mason, Luther Whiting. Teacher; *b.* Turner, Me., Apr. 31, 1828; *d.* Buckfield, Me., Jul. 14, 1896. Compiler, *The National Music Course.* 1865-1880, mus. inst., Boston pub. sch.; 1880-83, in Japan.

Mason, Morton Freeman. Organist, composer, teacher; *b.* Natick, Mass., Sept. 12, 1859. Comp. orch., chamb. mus. Pres., Musicians' Club of Los Angeles.

Mason, Stuart. Pianist, teacher; *b.* Weymouth, Mass. *p.* Isidor Philipp. 1910, debut, Boston; *t.* N. E. Cons. Comp. orch. wks., chamb. mus., piano pcs.

Mason, William. Pianist, composer, teacher; *b.* Boston, Jan. 24, 1829; *d.* New York, Jul. 14, 1908. Son of Lowell M. *p.* Liszt. 1854, first Amer. tour of pianist in unassisted recitals. The foremost pf. teacher of his day; *t.* of W. S. B. Mathews and William Sherwood. Evolved the method, "Elastic Finger Touch," and wr. *Mason's Touch and Technic,* historic among pf. methods.

Massé (*Mahs-say*), **Victor (Félix Marie).** Composer; *b.* l'Orient, Fr., Mar. 7, 1822; *d.* Paris, Jul. 5, 1884. 1866-80, prof., Paris Cons. Comp. operettas, incl., *La Reine Topaze,* and *Les noces de Jeannette;* also grand operas, incl., *Paul et Virginie.*

Massenet (*Mas-nay*), **Jules Emile Frédéric.** Composer; *b.* Montaud, Fr., May 12, 1842; *d.* Paris, Aug. 13, 1912. 1863, Prix de Rome, *w.* cantata, *David Rizzio.* Comp. some 25 operas, incl., *Don César de Bazan, Le roi di Lahore, Hérodiade, Manon, Le Cid, Werther, Thaïs, Le Jongleur de Notre-Dame, Don Quixote;* also orch. pcs., 200 songs.

Maszynski (*Mahs-chin-skee*), **Peter.** Composer; *b.* Warsaw, 1855. 1880, *t.* Warsaw Inst. Comp. orch., chamb. mus.

Materna (*Mah-tair-nah*), **Amalie.** Soprano; *b.* St. Georgen, Aus., Jul. 10, 1845; *d.* Vienna, 1918. Celebrated Wagnerian operatic singer.

Mathews, Blanche Dingley. *b.* Auburn, Me.; *d.* Denver, Jun. 25, 1932. Widow W. S. B. Mathews.

Mathews, William Smith Babcock. Writer, teacher; *b.* New London, N. H., May 8, 1837; *d.* Denver, Col., Apr. 1, 1912. *p.* William Mason. A strong educational influence in Amer. mus. Ed., *Mathews Graded Course,* a history-making series.

Mathieu (*Ma-thee-ay*), **Emile Louis Victor.** Composer; *b.* Lille, Fr., Oct. 16, 1844. 1898, dir., Ghent (Bel.) Cons. Comp. operas, orch. wks.

Mattei (*Mat-tay-ee*), **Tito.** Composer; *b.* Campobasso, It., May 24, 1841; *d.* London, Mar. 30, 1914. Comp. operas, instr. mus., songs, incl., *Dear Heart.*

Matthay (*Mat-tay*), **Tobias Augustus.** Pianist, teacher, writer; *b.* London, Feb. 19, 1858. 1876, prof., R. A. M., London; 1900, fd. Matthay Sch. Famous as piano teacher and writer on piano technic. Comp. orch., chamb. wks.

Mattheson (*Mat-te-son*), **Johann.** Composer, conductor, writer; *b.* Hamburg, Ger., Sept. 28, 1681; *d.* ib., Apr. 17, 1764. Comp. operas, oratorios, masses, cantatas. Author of many historical wks.

Matthews, H. Alexander. Composer, organist; *b.* Cheltenham, Eng., Mar. 26, 1879. *t.* Phila. Comp. cantatas, organ pcs., part-songs, songs.

Matthews, John Sebastian. Organist, composer; *b.* Cheltenham, Eng., 1870; *d.* Providence, Jul. 23, 1934. Edu., Trinity Coll., London. 15 years org., St. Peter's Ch., Morristown, N. Y.; 1916, org., Grace Ch., Providence. Comp. choral mus., cantatas, anthems, part-songs.

Matzenauer, Margaret. Mezzo-soprano; *b.* Temesvar, Hun., Jun. 1, 1881. 1901, debut in *Oberon,* Stadttheater, Strassburg; 1904-11, Hoftheater, Munich; 1911, Met. Op., N. Y.

Mauke (*Mow-keh*), **Wilhelm.** Composer, critic; *b.* Hamburg, Ger., Feb. 25, 1867. 1895, mus. critic, Munich *Zeitung.* Opera and song comp.

Maurel, Barbara. Mezzo-soprano, teacher; *b.* Alsace. *p.* de Reszke. 1918-19, Boston Op.

Maurel (*Mo-rel*), **Victor.** Baritone; *b.* Marseilles, Fr., Jun. 17, 1848; *d.* N. Y., Oct. 22, 1923. One of the most distinguished opera singers of his epoch. Created rôles in Verdi's *Otello,* and *Falstaff.* Appeared in all the great houses in the world, incl., Met. Op., N. Y. After retiring from the stage had a great career as a teacher and coach. Author of numerous books on singing.

Maurice (*Mo-reece*), **Alphonse.** Composer; *b.* Hamburg, Apr. 14, 1856; *d.* Dresden, Jan. 26, 1905. Chorus comp.

Maurice, Pierre. Composer; *b.* Geneva, Switz., 1868. Comp. operas, orch., pf. pcs.

Mauricio, Nunes Garcia, Padre José. Brazilian organist; *b.* Rio de Janeiro, Sept. 22, 1767; *d.* ib., Apr. 18, 1830. 1798-d., mus. dir., Cath. of R. de J. Historic musician of Brazil. Comp. 200 wks., incl., masses.

Maxwell, Leon Ryder. Music educator; *b.* Medford, Mass., Sept. 15, 1883. St., N. E. Cons. of Mus. 1905-08, mus. supv., Mass. pub. sch.; 1909, dir., Sch. of Mus., Newcomb Coll., Tulane U.

Maybrick, Michael (pseudonym Stephen Adams). Baritone, composer; *b.* Liverpool, Jan. 31, 1844; *d.* Buxton, Eng., Aug. 25, 1913. His brother was the husband of Mrs. Maybrick, of the celebrated English murder case. Comp. popular English ballads, incl., *The Holy City, A Warrior Bold.*

Mayer (*My-er*), **Charles.** Pianist, composer; *b.* Königsberg, Mar. 21, 1799; *d.* Dresden, Jul. 2, 1862. A brilliant pianist.

Mayer, Joseph Anton. Composer, theorist; *b.* Pfullendorf, Ger., 1855. 1890, prof., Stuttgart Cons. Comp. operas, oratorio.

Mayer, Wilhelm (pseudonym M. Rémy). Composer; *b.* Prague, Boh., Jun. 10, 1831; *d.* ib., Jan. 22, 1898. Comp. symph. wks.

Mayerhoff (*My-er-hofe*), **Franz.** Composer, conductor; *b.* Chemnitz, Jan. 17, 1864. 1911, appointed Royal prof., Leipzig. Comp. symph. wks., cantatas, songs.

Mayseder (*My-say-der*), **Joseph.** Violinist, composer; *b.* Vienna, Oct. 26, 1789; *d.* ib., Nov. 21, 1863. Comp. violin concertos, and pcs.

Mazas (*Mah-zas*), **Jacques Féréol.** Violinist, composer; *b.* Béziers, Fr., Sept. 23, 1782; *d.* ib., 1849. Comp. *études* for violin.

Mazzinghi (*Mat-zin-ghee*), **Joseph.** Composer; *b.* London, Dec. 25, 1765; *d.* Bath, Jan. 15, 1844. Comp. operas, glees.

McAll, Reginald Ley. Organist; *b.* Bocking, Eng., Aug. 20, 1878. St., Peabody Cons. of Mus.; 1900, A.B., Johns Hopkins; 1903-17, organ expert, Estey Organ Corp.; 1902, org., Ch. of Covenant, N. Y.; 1924, fd. Training Sch. in Ch. Mus., N. Y.

McBride, Robert G. Composer, pianist, teacher; *b.* Tucson, Ariz., Feb. 20, 1911. *t.* mus., Bennington Coll., Vt.; 1935, Mus. M., U. of Ariz. Comp. symph. wks., incl., *Prelude to a Tragedy,* and *Mexican Rhapsody;* also violin sonata, chamb. wks., piano pcs., and songs.

McCollin, Frances. Composer; *b.* Phila., 1892. Blind. Comp. chamb., choral mus.

McConathy, Osbourne. Music educator; *b.* Bullitt Co., Ky., Jan. 15, 1875. 1893-1903, mus. supv., pub. schs., Louisville; 1903-13, Chelsea, Mass.; 1913-25, *t.* Northwestern U.; 1922, Pres., M. T. N. A.

McCormack, John. Tenor; *b.* Athlone, Ire., Jun. 14, 1884. *p.* Signor Sabatini. 1907, London debut in *Cavalleria Rusticana;* 1909, Manhattan Op. Co.; later, Chicago Grand Op. Co., Met. Op. Co., Monte Carlo Op. Co.

McCormic, Mary. Soprano; *b.* Belleville, Ark. St., Northwestern U. 1921, debut as Michaela in *Carmen w.* Mary Garden; 1922, Italian debut at Asti, in *Cavalleria Rusticana.* 1931, *m.* Prince Serge Mdivani.

McCoy, William J. Composer; *b.* Crestline, O., Mar. 15, 1848; *d.* Oakland, Oct. 15, 1926. Chamb. mus., opera, violin concerto, orch. pcs.

McCutcham, Robert Guy. Music educator; *b.* Mt. Ayr, Iowa, Sept. 13, 1877. St., Berlin and Paris. 1904-10, *t.* Baker U.; 1912-13, dir., Summer Sch. of Mus., Mt. Lake Park, Md.; 1919-27, dir., Summer Sch. of Mus., Bay View, Mich.; 1928-29, Winona Lake, Ind.

McKinley, Carl. Organist, composer. *p.* Goldmark. 1917, B.A., Harvard. 1923-27, org., Capitol Th., N. Y.; mus. dir., Center Cong. Ch., Hartford, Conn.; 1927, Guggenheim Fellowship.

Mead, Olive. Violinist; *b.* Cambridge, Mass., Nov. 22, 1874. Fd. Olive Mead Str. Q.

Meader, George Farnham. Opera singer; *b.* Minneapolis, Minn., Jul. 6, 1888. 1908, LL.B., U. of Minn. 1910, debut, Leipzig; 1920, Met. Op., N. Y.

Medtner, Nicholaus. Composer, pianist; *b.* Moscow, Dec. 24, 1879. 1900, gr., Cons. Toured Europe as pianist; 1909-10, prof., Moscow Cons.; 1922, world tour. Comp. chamb. mus., pf. pcs., songs.

Mees, Arthur. Conductor; *b.* Columbus, O., Feb. 13, 1850; *d.* N. Y., 1923. Cond., Worcester, Mass., Fest., and numerous choral soc. and fest.; 1887-96, program annotator, N. Y. Phil. Orch.

Mehlig (*May-lig*), **Anna.** Pianist; *b.* Stuttgart, Ger., Jul. 11, 1843. *p.* Liszt. 1869, toured U. S.

Méhul (*May-ill*), **Étienne Nicholas.** Composer; *b.* Givet, Fr., Jun. 22, 1763; *d.* Paris, Oct. 18, 1817. Comp. operas, incl., *Joseph.* The overture, *Le Jeune Henri,* his greatest work still figures on concert programs.

Meinardus (*My-nar-doos*), **Ludwig.** Composer, writer; *b.* Hooksiel, Ger., Sept. 17, 1827; *d.* Bielefeld, Ger., Jul. 10, 1896. Oratorio comp.

Meisle, Kathryn. Contralto; *b.* Phila., Oct. 12, 1899. 1917, *m.* Calvin M. Franklin. 1923, debut as Erda in *Siegfried,* Chicago Civic Op.; soloist, Boston, Chicago, Minneapolis, Detroit, Phila. Symph.; Met. Op., N. Y.

Melartin, Erkki Gustaf. Composer; *b.* Kexholm, Fin., Feb. 7, 1875. 1895, prof., Helsingfors Cons. Comp. opera, *Aino;* symph., chamb. mus., songs.

Melba, Nellie. (Mrs. Nellie Porter Armstrong, née Mitchell; pseudonym derived from Melbourne, her birthplace). Soprano; *b.* Melbourne, Australia, May 19, 1861; *d.* ib., Feb. 23, 1931. One of the most distinguished opera singers of her era. 1886, London; 1887, Brussels; 1889, Petrograd; 1891, La Scala, Milan; 1892, Chicago World's Fair; 1893, Met. Op., N. Y.

Melcer, Henryk. Composer; *b.* Kalisch, Pol., Sept. 21, 1869; *d.* in battle, Galicia, 1915. 1908, cond., Warsaw Phil. Comp. operas, pf., concertos, chamb. mus.

Melchior, Lauritz. Tenor; *b.* Copenhagen, Mar. 20, 1890. Edu., Melchior's Sch., Copenhagen. 1913, debut as baritone, Copenhagen Op.; 1918, as tenor; 1925, Covent Garden; 1926, Met. Op., N. Y.

Melius, Luella. Soprano; *b.* Appleton, Wis., Aug. 21, 1892. 1913, Chicago Civic Op. Co.

Meltzer, Charles Henry. Writer; *b.* London, 1852; *d.* N. Y., Jan. 14, 1936. Mus. critic, New York *American.* Translator of operatic texts, and exponent of opera in English.

Melville, Emily. Singer, actress; *b.* 1850; *d.* San Francisco, May 20, 1932. Played *Ophelia* to Booth's *Hamlet; w.* John McCall organized Emilie Melville Op. Co., and toured U. S., So. Africa, China, Japan; lost singing voice and turned to dramatics; 1928, as *Fanny Cavendish,* in *The Royal Family,* in San Francisco, her last appearance.

Mendelssohn, Arnold. Composer; *b.* Ratibor, Boh., Dec. 26, 1855; *d.* Darmstadt, 1929; Grand-nephew of Félix Mendelssohn. Comp. operas, incl., *Der Bärenhäuter,* and *Die Minneburg;* cantatas, incl., *Pandora.*

Mendelssohn-Bartholdy, Félix. Composer; *b.* Hamburg, Ger., Feb. 3, 1809; *d.* Leipzig, Nov. 4, 1847. Son of a banker and grandson of the Jewish philosopher, Moses Mendelssohn. Early showed talent for mus., and was given every educational advantage. 1833, already possessed of a European reputation, appointed mus. dir., Düsseldorf; 1835, ret. to Leipzig, as cond., Gewandhaus concerts; 1835-1841, prod. piano concerto in D minor, the *42nd* and *114th Psalms*, str. q. in E minor, overture to *Ruy Blas*, trio in D minor, *Hymn of Praise*, the latter written to commemorate the 400th anniversary of the invention of printing from movable types, by Gutenberg. 1841-1847, *St. Paul, Walpurgis Night, Elijah, Christus*, the C minor trio. The *Midsummer Night's Dream* mus., *w.* its immortal *Wedding March*, was composed at eighteen. His greatest service to mus. was his discovery and revival of the wks. of Bach, after a century of neglect. He was a great g.-cond., and exhausted his energy *w.* his incessant wanderings.

Mengelberg, Willem. Conductor; *b.* Utrecht, Hol., Mar. 28, 1871. 1895, cond., Concertgebow Orch., Amsterdam; 1911-1914, cond., London Symph. Orch., and Royal Phil.; 1922-1931, cond., New York Phil.; 1931, resumed former Amsterdam post.

Mengewein (*Meng-eh-vine*), **Karl.** Composer; *b.* Zaunroda, Ger., Sept. 9, 1852; *d.* Berlin, Apr., 1908. Comp. *singspiele*, cantatas.

Menter, Sophie. Pianist; *b.* Munich, Ger., Jul. 29, 1846; *d.* ib., 1918. 1872-87, wife of 'cellist Popper. 1883-87, prof., Petrograd Cons. Comp. *Ungarische Zigeunerweisen* for pf. and orch., instrumented by Tschaikowsky.

Mercadante, Francesco Saverio. Composer; *b.* Altamura, It., Jul. 17, 1795; *d.* Naples, Dec. 17, 1870. Comp. operas in the Rossini style; symph., ch. mus., incl., *Seven Last Words;* 1840, dir., Naples Cons., succ. Zingarelli; 1862, became totally blind.

Merikanto, Oskar. Organist, composer; *b.* Helsingfors, Fin., Aug. 5, 1868; *d.* ib., Feb. 17, 1924. Organ virtuoso. Comp. operas, incl., *The Maid of Pohja;* organ, pf., pcs., songs.

Merkel (*Mair-kel*), **Gustav Adolf.** Organist, composer; *b.* Oberoderwitz, Ger., Nov. 12, 1827; *d.* Dresden, Ger., Oct. 30, 1885. Comp. many organ pcs., once popular, and an organ *Method*.

Merö, Yolando. Pianist; *b.* Budapesth, Aug. 30, 1887. 1903, debut, Dresden Phil.; 1908, prof., Pesth Cons. 1909, *m.* Hermann Irion.

Merrill, Barzille Winfred. Music educator; *b.* Elgin, Ill., May 20, 1864. *p.* Joachim. 1888-93, dir., Tacoma Acad. Mus.; 1895-1900, Merrill Sch. of Mus., Atlanta; 1903-19, head dept. orch. mus., Ia. State Teachers Coll.; 1921, dean, Sch. of Mus., U. of Indiana.

Mertens, Joseph. Composer; *b.* Antwerp, Feb. 17, 1834; *d.* Brussels, 1901. Comp. Flemish operas.

Merulo (*Mer'-oo-lo*), **Claudio.** Organist, composer; *b.* Correggio, It., Apr. 8, 1533; *d.* Parma, May 4, 1604. Comp. madrigals, organ pcs.

Merz (*Mairts*), **Karl.** Teacher; *b.* Bensheim, Ger., Sept. 10, 1836; *d.* Wooster, O., Jan. 30, 1890. 1854, to U. S.; 1861, mus. dir., Oxford Coll., and 1882, Wooster, O., U.; 1873, ed., Brainard's *Musical World*. His library went to the Carnegie Inst., Pittsburgh. Author of text wks.

Méssager (*Mes-sah-zha*), **André.** Conductor, composer; *b.* Montluçon, Fr., Dec. 30, 1853; *d.* Paris, Feb. 24, 1929. 1880, cond., Theatre Eden, Brussels, and 1882-4, choirmaster, St. Marie's; 1884-9, cond., Paris Opéra Comique; 1901-07, artistic dir., Covent Garden, London; 1907-14, Paris Op.; 1918, toured U. S. *w.* a French symph. orch.; cond. of conservatoire concerts. Comp. symph. wks., operas and operettas, incl., *Veronique*.

Messner, Joseph. Conductor; *b.* Schwaz-Tyrol, Aus., Feb. 27, 1893. 1926, choirmaster, Salzburg Cath.; cond., choral perf. at Salzburg Fest.; g.-cond., Warsaw Phil., Vienna Phil.

Mestdagh, Karel. Composer; *b.* Bruges, Bel., Oct. 22, 1850. Comp. orch. wks.

Metcalf, John W. Song writer; *b.* Illinois, 1856; *d.* Oakland, Cal., Jul. 15, 1926. 1881, gr., Leipzig Cons. First dir. of mus. dept., Stanford U. Wrote many songs, incl., *Absent*.

Metternich, Princess Pauline Sandor. Amateur musician and patron of music; *b.* Vienna, 1836; *d.* ib., Sept. 28, 1921. Wife of Prince M., Austrian Ambas. to Court of Napoleon III. Daughter of Count Moriz Sandor. Instrumental in getting first Paris perf. of *Tannhauser*. Said, "Paris is hissing Wagner today, but in 25 years they will acclaim him."

Metz, Theodore. Minstrel conductor; *b.* Mar. 14, 1848; *d.* Jan. 12, 1936. 1896, comp. *Hot Time in the Old Town Tonight* for McIntyre & Heath perf. at Old Town, La. It became the soldiers' marching song during the Spanish-American War, and the campaign song of Theodore Roosevelt, I., throughout his career. A historic popular success.

Metzdorff, Richard. Composer; *b.* Danzig, Ger., Jun. 28, 1844; *d.* Berlin, 1919. Cond., Hamburg; dir., pf. sch. Comp. operas, symph.

Meyer, Leopold von. Pianist; *b.* Vienna, Dec. 20, 1816; *d.* Dresden, Ger., Mar. 5, 1883. 1845-68, frequent tours to U. S., playing his own salon pcs.

Meyerbeer, Giacomo. Composer; *b.* Berlin, Sept. 5, 1791; *d.* Paris, May 2, 1864. *p.* Abbé Vogler. Comp. operas, which were marred by their excellent pedantry. Under the influence of Rossini, he forsook the methods of Vogler for the more attractive style of the Italians, and prod. several successful operas. Later, he again changed his style, and *w.* Scribe as librettist, prod. the series of grand operas, *Robert le Diable, Les Huguenots, Le prophète, L'Étoile du Nord, Dinorah,* and *l'Africaine,* upon which his fame as a comp. chiefly rests.

Meyer-Helmund, Erik. Composer; *b.* Petrograd, Apr. 25, 1861. Comp. operas, songs., incl., *The Magic Song*.

Meyer-Olbersleben, Max. Composer, teacher; *b.* Olbersleben, Ger., Mar. 5, 1850. Prof., Würzburg Cons.

Meysenheym, Cornelie. Teacher, singer; *b.* The Hague, Mar. 29, 1847; *d.* Nesconset, L. I., Dec. 31, 1923. 1872-94, at Roy. Op. H., Munich, sang in 950 perf. of more than 100 operas; 1904-08, faculty of Met. Sch. of Op., N. Y.

Miaskovsky, Nikolai. Composer; *b.* Novogeorgievsk, Rus. (now Poland), Apr. 20, 1881. 1906, Petrograd Cons., *u.* Glière; 1921, prof., Moscow Cons. Comp. chamb. mus., orch. wks., pf. pcs., songs.

Middelschulte, Wilhelm. Organist, composer; *b.* Werne, Ger., Apr. 3, 1863. *p.* August Knabe. 1891-5, org., Cath. of Holy Name, Chicago; 1899, St. James Ch.; 1899, dir. and prof., Wisconsin Cons. of Mus., Milwaukee; 1902, solo org. Cin. May Fest. Comp. organ concerto, toccata, Bach arr.

Mielck (*Meelk*), **Ernest.** Composer; *b.* Viborg, Fin., Oct. 24, 1877; *d.* Locarno, It., Oct. 22, 1899. Comp. orch. mus.

Miersch, Paul Friedrich Theordore. Composer, 'cellist; *b.* Ger., Jan. 18, 1868. 1892, solo 'cellist, N. Y. Symph. Comp. *Indian Rhapsody* for orch., songs and pcs. for violin and 'cello.

Miessner, William Otto. Music educator; *b.* Huntingburg, Ind., May 26, 1880. Edu., Cin. Coll. of Mus. 1900-04, mus. superv., Booneville, Ind.; 1904-09, Connersville; 1909-14, Oak Park; dir., Miessner Inst. of Mus., Chicago.

Mignard (*Min-yar*), **Alexander Konstantinovitch.** Composer; *b.* Warsaw, Aug. 13, 1852. Comp. operas, orch. wks.

Mignone, Francisco. Pianist, composer; *b.* São Paulo, Brazil, Sept. 3, 1897. Edu., São Paulo Cons.; 1920, State Scholarship to Milan. Comp. symph. wks., incl., *Caramuru, Suite Campestre;* operas, incl., *Cantabria;* pf. pcs., songs.

Migot, Georges. Composer; *b.* Paris, Feb. 27, 1891. St. Bouval, Ganaye. 1913, Cons., *u.* d'Indy. Paralyzed in war, 1914, found solace in comp. *h.* Paris. Comp. orch. wks., incl., *Les Agrestides;* chamb. mus., incl., *Dialogue;* choral mus., pf. pcs.

Miguez, Leopoldo. Brazilian composer; *b.* 1850; *d.* 1902. 1901, opera, *I Salduni,* première Rio de J. Comp. symph. wks.

Mikorey, Franz. Composer; *b.* Munich, Jun. 3, 1873. 1919, dir., Helsingfors Op. Comp. operas, incl., *King of Samarcand;* concerto.

Milhaud, Darius. Composer; *b.* Aix, Fr., Sept. 4, 1892. Edu., Paris Cons., *u.* d'Indy. 1917, attaché, Rio de Janeiro; 1922, toured U. S. Author of articles and books on Fr. mus. Comp. theatre mus., incl., *Proteus;* orch. wks., incl., *Symphonic Suite;* chamb. mus., pf. pcs., songs.

Millard, Harrison. Composer; *b.* Boston, Nov. 27, 1830; *d.* Sept. 10, 1895. Comp. ch. mus.

Miller, Horace Alden. Music educator; *b.* Rockford, Ill., Jul. 4, 1872. 1896, Mus.B., Oberlin, O., Cons. of Mus.; 1904, *t.* Cornell Coll. Cons. of Mus.

Miller, Leo C. Pianist. *p.* Busoni. Piano teacher and choral cond. in St. Louis, Mo.

Milligen, Simon van. Composer, music critic; *b.* Rotterdam, Hol., 1849. Critic, Amsterdam *Handelsblad.* Comp. operas, incl., *Brinio.*

Millocher, Karl. Composer; *b.* Vienna, May 29, 1842; *d.* ib., Dec. 31, 1899. Edu., Vienna Cons. Comp. 14 operettas, incl., *The Beggar Student* (N. Y., 1885-6, 110 perf.), *The Black Hussars, Poor Jonathan* (N. Y., 1891, 208 perf., starring Lillian Russell and Jeff. de Angelis). His royalties are said to have reached $50,000 a year.

Mills, Charles Henry. Organist, teacher; *b.* Nottingham, Eng., Jan. 29, 1873. 1911, Mus.D., McGill U., Montreal. 1892-3, concert tour of U. S. as pianist; 1908-14, *t.* U. of Ill.; 1914, U. of Wis. Comp. songs, anthems, choral wks.

Mills, Frederick Allen ("Kerry"). Violin player turned song writer; *b.* Detroit. New York publishers refused *At a Georgia Camp Meeting,* so he published it himself. The first of the cake-walk tunes, anticipating the fox-trot vogue by many years.

Mills, Sebastian B. Pianist, teacher; *b.* Cirencester, Eng., Mar. 13, 1838; *d.* Wiesbaden, Ger., Dec. 21, 1898. 1856, to U. S. Gave first Amer. perf. of Liszt's E-flat Concerto. *t.* of Homer Bartlett. Taught in New York for many years. Comp. many pf. pcs.; best known by his *Tarantelle.*

Mincus, Ludwig. Violinist, composer; *b.* Vienna, 1827. 1872, *w.* Petrograd Op. Ballet composer, an assoc. of Délibes in comp. of *La Source.*

Mischakoff, Mischa. Violinist; *b.* Proskourov, Rus. Gr., Imperial Cons., St. Petersburg. 1918-20, prof., Government Cons., Nizhni-Novgorod; 1920-21, conc.-m., Moscow Grand Op.; 1921-22, Warsaw Phil. Orch.; 1922, to U. S.; 1924-27, conc.-m., N. Y. Symph. Orch.; 1927-29, Phila. Orch.; 1930, Chicago Symph. Orch. Head violin dept., Chautauqua Inst., N. Y.

Missa, Edmond Jean Louis. Composer; *b.* Rheims, Fr., Jun. 12, 1861; *d.* Paris, 1910. Opera comp.

Miura, Tamaki. Soprano; *b.* Japan. St. Tokio Cons. Sang at Imperial Th., Tokio; Covent Garden, London; Chicago Civic and Manhattan Opera Companies.

Mlynarski (*Mlin-ars-ki*), **Emil.** Conductor, composer; *b.* Wirballen, Pol., Jul. 18, 1870; *d.* Warsaw, Apr. 5, 1935. 1898, Paderewski prize for violin *Concerto,* D-minor. Comp. violin pcs.; best known by *Mazurka.*

Mohr, Adolf. Composer; *b.* Munich, Sept. 23, 1841. Comp. operas, incl., *Die Lorelei.*

Mohr, Hermann. Composer, teacher; *b.* Nieustadt, Ger., Oct. 9, 1830; *d.* Phila., May 26, 1896. 1886, *t.* Phila. Mus. Acad. Comp. male choruses, chamb. mus.

Moiseiwitsch, Benno. Pianist; *b.* Odessa, Feb. 22, 1890. *p.* Leschetizky. 1908, debut, Reading, Eng.; 1909, Queen's Hall, London; frequent tours of U. S., and Australia.

Molinari, Bernardino. Conductor; *b.* Rome, Apr. 11, 1880. 1912, cond., Augusteo, Rome, giving fest. devoted to Scarlatti, Beethoven, Saint-Saëns, Debussy, and others; 1928, g.-cond., New York Phil., and other orch.

Molique (*Mo-leek*), **Wilhelm Bernhard.** Violinist, composer; *b.* Nuremberg, Oct. 7, 1802; *d.* Kannstatt, Ger., May 10, 1869. Best known by his violin concertos. Comp. str. q., symph., masses, oratorio.

Mollenhauer, Emil. Violinist, conductor; *b.* Brooklyn, Aug. 4, 1855; *d.* Boston, Dec. 10, 1927. Cond., Handel and Haydn Soc., and Boston Fest. Orch.

Moller, J. C. Composer, organist, pianist, editor; *b.* probably in London. 1790, appeared in N. Y. as harpsichordist; 1793, org. in Zion's Ch., Phila., and opened mus. store and sch.; N. Y. P. L., has some of his manuscript wks.

Molloy, James Lyman. Composer; *b.* Cornlore, Ire., 1837; *d.* Wooleys, Eng., Feb. 4, 1909. Comp. popular ballads, incl., *Love's Old Sweet Song.*

Monckton, Lionel. Composer; *b.* London, 1862; *d.* ib., Feb. 15, 1924. Comp. operetta, *The Quaker Girl* (1910), ran for 536 perf. in London; *The Arcadians* (1909), ran for 809 perf. in London; prod. in N. Y. (1910) *w.* Julia Sanderson, for a long run. Also collab. *w.* Ivan Caryll in *The Circus Girl* and other operettas.

Monestel, Alexander. Organist, composer; *b.* San Jose, Costa Rica, Apr. 26, 1865. 1917, org., St. John Baptist, Brooklyn. Comp. 14 masses.

Moniuszko, Stanislaus. Composer; *b.* Ubil, Rus., May 5, 1820; *d.* Warsaw, Pol., Jun. 4, 1872. Prolific comp. of operas, cantatas, violin and pf. pcs., and 400 songs. 1892, Warsaw Mus. Soc. fd. section to collect and publish his complete wks.

Monsigny (*Mong-seen-ye*), **Pierre Alexandre.** Composer; b. Fauquembergue, Fr., Oct. 17, 1729; d. Paris, Jan. 14, 1817. Comp. operas, ballets.

Montemezzi (*Mon-te-met-zee*), **Italo.** Italian operatic composer; b. Verona, It., May 31, 1875. St., Milan Cons. 1905, opera, *Giovanni Gallurese*, prod., Turin; 1913, world fame w. opera to Sam Benelli's *l'Amore dei Tre Re*, prod. Milan; also at Met. Op., N. Y.

Monteux, Pierre. Conductor; b. Paris, Apr. 4, 1875. 1916, toured Amer. w. Rus. ballet; 1917-1919, cond., Met. Op.; 1918-1924, cond., Boston Symph. Orch., succ. Karl Muck; 1935, cond., San Francisco Symph. Orch.

Monteverde (*Mon-te-vair-de*), **Claudio.** Composer; b. Cremona, It., May 18, 1567; d. Venice, Nov. 29, 1643. Inventor of the free style of comp. and pioneer in the path that led to the modern opera; the first to use unprepared dissonances. His improvement of the orch. gained for him the title of "the father of instrumentation." His innovations were successfully employed in his operas, *Ariana* and *Orfeo*. Comp. much sacred mus., the greater part of which is lost. His influence on comp. of his day was marked, and the results of his work have been lasting.

Moór, Emanuel. Composer; b. Hun., c. 1862; d. Montreux, Switz., Oct. 21, 1931. m. Winifred Christie. Comp. operas, 7 symph., chamb. mus.

Moore, Douglas. Composer; b. Long Island, 1893. Gr., Yale. p. d'Indy, Nadia Boulanger. 1926, awarded Pulitzer Fellowship; 1928, assoc. prof., Columbia, on Joline Foundation; 1923, *The Museum Pieces*, for orch., prod., Cleveland Orch.; 1924, *Barnum Suite*, prod., Cleveland Orch. Also comp. symph. p., *Moby Dick*; incid. mus. to *Twelfth Night*, and *Much Ado About Nothing*; also Negro spirituals.

Moore, Earl Vincent. Music educator; b. Lansing, Mich., Sept. 27, 1890. p. Widor. 1912, A.B., U. of Mich.; 1915, A.M. Since 1914, with U. Sch. of Mus., Ann Arbor; since 1923, dir.; dir., Ann Arbor Fest. Comp. organ and choral mus.

Moore, Edward Colman. Music editor; b. Fond du Lac, Wis., Jan. 22, 1877. 1899, A.B., Yale; 1902, LL.B., Northwestern U.; 1909-21, mus. critic, Chicago *Daily Journal*; 1921, Chicago *Tribune*.

Moore, Grace. Soprano; b. Jellico, Tenn., Dec. 5, 1901. Ran away from sch. and joined traveling concert co.; 1923, sang in Irving Berlin's *Music Box Review*; 1928, debut, Met. Op., as *Mimi* in *Bohëme*.

Moore, Mary Carr. Composer, teacher; b. Memphis, Tenn. 1912, opera, *Narcissa*, prod., Seattle, ran 14 perf. and received David Bispham medal. 1932, première, opera *Rizzio*, Shrine Auditorium, Los Angeles.

Moore, Thomas. Composer; b. Dublin, Ire., May 28, 1779; d. Devizes, Eng., Feb. 25, 1852. Wr. or adapted many of the airs which he sang to his *Irish Melodies*.

Morales, Olallo Juan Magnus. Composer, conductor; b. Almeria, Sp., Oct. 13, 1874. t. Stockholm Cons. Comp. orch. wks.

Moranzoni, Roberto. Conductor; b. Bari, It., Oct., 1882. p. Mascagni. 1901, cond., Teatro Costanzi, Rome; later, Bologne, Milan, Turin; Grand Opera and Champs Elysees, Paris; 1910, Met. Op., N. Y.; Chicago Civic Op.

Morgan, George Washbourne. Organist; b. Gloucester, Eng., Apr. 9, 1822; d. Tacoma, Wash., Jul., 1892. 1855-68, org., Grace Ch., N. Y.; 1870-82, Brooklyn Tabernacle; 1876, recitalist at Phila. Centennial Expo.

Morgan, John Paul. Organist; b. Oberlin, O., Feb. 13, 1841; d. Oakland, Cal., Jan., 1879. A talented but short-lived musician; fd. Oberlin Cons. Translator of Richter's *Harmonie* (1867).

Morgan, Maud. Harpist; b. New York, Nov. 22, 1864. Daughter of G. W. M. Debut in Ole Bull concert.

Morgana, Nina. Operatic soprano; b. Buffalo, N. Y., Nov. 15, 1895. 1921, m. Bruno Zirato. 1919, toured w. Caruso; 1920, debut, Met. Op., as Gilda in *Rigoletto*; 1926, Colon Op., Buenos Aires; 1929, San Francisco and Los Angeles Operas.

Mörike, Eduard. Conductor; b. Stuttgart, Aug. 16, 1877. Asst. cond., Bayreuth; asst. Richard Straus w. first Paris perf. of *Salome*; 1925, cond., Dresden *Singakademie*.

Morlacchi (*Mor-lah-kee*), **Francesco.** Composer; b. Perugia, It., Jun. 16, 1784; d. Innsbruck, Aus., Oct. 28, 1841. 1810, dir., It. Op. at Dresden. Comp. 25 operas, oratorios.

Morley, Thomas. Composer; b. London, 1557; d. ib., c. 1602. Contributed much to the development of vocal mus. in Eng.

Mornington, Garret Wellesley, Lord. Composer; b. Dangan, Ire., Jul. 19, 1735; d. London, May 22, 1781. Father of Duke of Wellington. Comp. ch. mus., glees, madrigals.

Morris, Harold. Composer; b. San Antonio, Tex., 1890. Edu., U. Tex., and Cin. Cons. 1916, located in New York; 1918, *Poem*, perf., Ysaye w. Cin. Symph; 1931, cond., *Piano Concerto* w. Boston Symph. Comp. piano concerto, orch., and chamb. mus., pf. pcs.

Morse, Charles Frederic. Organist, teacher; b. Mishawaka, Ind., Mar. 26, 1881. p. Guilmant. Co-fd., Detroit Inst. of Mus. Art; org., Grosse Pt. Memorial Ch.; cond., Orpheus and Madrigal Clubs.

Morse, Charles Henry. Organist, teacher; b. Bradford, Mass., Jan. 5, 1853. 1901-18, first prof. mus., Dartmouth Coll.

Morse, Woolson. Composer; b. Boston, 1858; d. N. Y., May 3, 1897. Wr. several operettas, but had one success in *Wang*, which at first was a failure u. another title. He also painted the scenery and directed the production.

Mortelmans, Lodewik. Composer; b. Antwerp, Bel., Feb. 5, 1868. Comp. symph., *Germania*; cantatas, songs.

Moscheles (*Mosh-e-les*), **Ignaz.** Pianist, composer; b. Prague, May 30, 1794; d. Leipzig, Mar. 10, 1870. p. Albrechtsberger. 1821-1846, dir., London Phil.; 1846, called by Mendelssohn to head pf. dept., Leipzig Cons. Comp. symph., 8 pf. concertos, chamb. mus., 30 songs, and many pf. *études*. Translated Schindler's *Life of Beethoven*.

Mosenthal (*Mo-zen-tahl*), **Joseph.** Organist, composer; b. Kassel, Ger., Nov. 30, 1834; d. New York, Jan. 6, 1896. Cond., Mendelssohn Glee Club, N. Y. Comp. ch. mus., and male choruses, incl., male voice cantata, *Thanatopsis*.

Mossolov, Alexander. Composer; b. Kiev, Rus., Jul. 29, 1900. 1921, st., Moscow Cons. u. Glière. 1926, *Quartet*, intro. International Fest. Modern Mus.; 1930, *Iron Foundry*, prod. at Liége. Comp. operas, incl., *The Hero*; orch. wks., incl., *Dammerung*; cantatas, chamb. mus.

Moszkowski (*Mosh-kof-ski*), **Moritz.** Pianist, composer; b. Breslau, Ger., Aug. 23, 1854; d. Paris, Mar., 1925. Comp. symph. p., *Jeanne d'Arc;* opera, *Boabdil;* many pf. pcs., songs.

Mottl, Felix. Conductor; b. Vienna, Aug. 24, 1856; d. Munich, Jul. 2, 1911. Cond., Vienna *Wagnerverein;* 1875, asst. cond. in first Bayreuth perf.; 1880-1892, Karlsruhe Phil.; 1886, chief cond. at Bayreuth; 1907, cond. Munich Op.; 1903-04, visited N. Y. to cond. *Parsifal,* but because of protests of the Wagner family did not do so.

Mouton (*Moo-tong*), **Jean.** Contrapuntal composer in the early sixteenth century.

Mozart (*Mo-tsart*), **Leopold.** Composer, violinist; b. Augsburg, Aus., Nov. 14, 1719; d. Salzburg, Aus., May 28, 1787. Father of Wolfgang Amadeus Mozart. Comp. ch. mus., oratorios, operas. Author of a *Violin School* which went through many editions in various languages.

Mozart, Maria Anna. Pianist; b. Salzburg, Aus., Jul. 30, 1751; d. ib., Oct. 29, 1829. Daughter of Leopold Mozart. Toured Europe w. her brother as a mus. prodigy.

Mozart, Wolfgang Amadeus. Composer, pianist; b. Salzburg, Aus., Jan. 27, 1756; d. Vienna, Dec. 5, 1791. 1768, commissioned by the Emperor Joseph II to write a comic opera, *La Finta Semplice.* 1781, comp. *Idomeneo;* 1786, *Figaro.* During the five years between 1786 and his death Mozart poured out a marvellous flood of masterpieces, *Don Giovanni, Magic Flute, Cosi fan tutte, Clemenza di Tito;* the three great symph. in E flat major, G minor, and C major (*Jupiter, the Requiem*), and a stupendous mass of mus. of all kinds. During his thirty-six years he is known to have written at least 626 wks., among which are 22 masses, 17 organ sonatas, 40 offertories, 10 cantatas, 23 operas, 22 sonatas for the piano, 45 sonatas for the piano and violin, 49 symph., and 55 concertos, besides quartets, trios, songs. One of the greatest and most unfortunate geniuses of mus. history.

Mraczek (*Mrat-chek*), **Joseph Gustav.** Composer; b. Brünn, Aus., Mar. 12, 1878. 1908, prof., Brünn Cons. Comp. opera, *The Dream;* symph. p., *Max und Moritz.*

Muck (*Mook*), **Karl.** Conductor; b. Darmstadt, Ger., Oct. 22, 1859. 1906-8 and 1912-18, cond., Boston Symph. Interned during World War, and deported for anti-neutral activities.

Mugellini (*Moo-jel-lee-nee*), **Bruno.** Pianist, composer; b. Piacenza, It., Dec. 24, 1871; d. Bologna, It., Jan. 15, 1912. Comp. orch., chamb. mus.

Muhlmann, Adolf. Opera singer; b. Schiriwa, Rus., Jan. 1, 1867. Edu., Odessa Cons. Debut, Breslau Op.; 1898, Royal Op., Petrograd; 1899-1907, Covent Garden, London; 1899-1912, Met. Op., N. Y.; 1923, fd. Muhlmann Sch. of Opera, Chicago.

Müller (*Mil-ler*), **Carl Christian.** Composer, teacher; b. Meiningen, Ger., Jul. 3, 1831; d. New York, Jun. 4, 1914. Cond. orch., Barnum's Museum, N. Y.; 1875-95, t. N. Y. Coll. of Mus.

Mumma, Archie A. Composer; b. Dayton, O., 1909. p. Schola Cantorum, Paris. Made study of bird calls and embodied them in comp., pf. pcs., and songs.

Muris, Jean de. French writer on music in early fourteenth century.

Murska (*Moorska*), **Ilma de.** Soprano; b. Croatia, Aus., 1836; d. Munich, Jan. 16, 1889. Opera singer. 1880, t. N. Y.

Mussorgsky (**Moussorgsky**), **Modest.** Composer; b. Karev, Rus., Mar. 28, 1839; d. Petrograd, Mar. 28, 1881. Comp. operas, incl., *Boris Godunov;* orch. wks., pf. pcs., songs, all marked by crude strength. With Balakirev, Borodin, Cui, and Rimsky-Korsakoff he helped to create a national Russian school.

Muzio, Claudia. Soprano; b. Pavia, It., 1892. p. Mme. Casaloni. 1912, debut, *Manon,* at Arezzo; 1916, debut, Met. Op., as *Tosca.*

Mysliweczek (*Mis-leh-veh-chek*), **Josef.** Composer; b. Prague, Boh., Mar. 9, 1737; d. Rome, Feb. 4, 1781. Comp. orch., chamb. mus.

N

Nabokoff, Nicolas. Composer; b. Russia, 1903. p. Rebikoff. 1927, comp. *Ode* for Diaghilev ballet; 1929, *Lyric Symphony,* perf. in Paris by Monteux; ballet *La Vie de Polichinelle,* prod. at Paris opera; 1933, to U. S. on Barnes Foundation Scholarship; 1934, oratorio, *Job,* perf., Worcester Fest; 1935, ballet, *Union Pacific,* perf. by Monte Carlo Russian Ballet Co.

Nachez, Tivadar. Composer, violinist; b. Pesth, Hun., May 1, 1859. 1880, Paris; 1889, London; 1916, Santa Barbara, Cal. Comp. concertos, violin pcs., incl., *Gypsy Dance.*

Nadworney, Devora. Contralto; b. N. Y. 1925, debut, Chicago Civic Op.; Natl. concert tour as prize winner Natl. Fed. of Mus. Clubs; first voice to go over radio network.

Nägeli (*Nay-gel-lee*), **Johann Georg.** Composer, writer; b. Zürich, Switz., May 27, 1773; d. ib., Dec. 26, 1836. Author text wks. on singing.

Nanini (*Na-nee-nee*), **Giovanni.** Composer; b. Vallerano, It., c. 1540; d. Rome, Mar. 11, 1607.

Napravnik, Eduard Frantsovitch. Composer, conductor; b. Bejst, Boh., Aug. 24, 1839; d. Petrograd, 1916. 1863, cond., Petrograd Op., succ. Liadoff. Comp. operas, overtures, chamb. wks.

Nardini (*Nar-dee-nee*), **Pietro.** Violinist, composer; b. Fibiana, It., 1722; d. Florence, It., May 7, 1793. Comp. 6 violin concertos, chamb. mus.

Nash, Frances (Mrs. E. M. Watson). Pianist; b. Omaha, Neb. St., Europe. 1918, debut; soloist major Amer. orch.

Naumann (*Nou-man*), **Emil.** Writer, historian; b. Berlin, Sept. 8, 1827; d. Dresden, Jun. 23, 1888. Author of a *History of Music.*

Navratil (*Nav-rah-teel*), **Karl.** Composer; b. Prague, Boh., Apr. 24, 1867; d. Vienna, Apr. 6, 1914. Comp. symph., piano and violin concertos, symph. p., the opera, *Salammbo.*

Nebelong (*Nay-be-long*), **Johann Hendrik.** Organist, composer; b. Copenhagen, Nov. 9, 1847. Virtuoso player. 1885, fd. Organists' Union.

Nedbal, Oskar. Violinist, conductor, composer; b. Tábor, Boh., Mar. 26, 1874; d. Zagreb, Jugo-Slavia, Dec. 24, 1930. 1906-19, cond., Vienna Tonkünstler Orch. Comp. operettas, ballets, orch. wks.

Neefe (*Nay-feh*), **Christian Gottlob.** Organist; b. Chemnitz, Feb. 5, 1748; d. Dessau, Jan. 26, 1798. Cond., Bonn.; t. of Beethoven. Comp. stage wks., violin, pf. wks.

Neff, Fritz. Composer; b. Durlach, Ger., Nov. 20, 1873; d. Munich, Oct. 3, 1904. Comp. chorus, orch.

Neidlinger (*Nide-ling-er*), **William H.** Organist, composer; *b.* Brooklyn, Jul. 20, 1863; *d.* 1924. Became interested in child psychology, and fd. sch. for sub-normal children. Comp. songs, children's songs, cantatas, operettas, ch. mus.

Neitzel (*Nite-zel*), **Otto.** Composer, author; *b.* Falkenberg, Ger., Jul. 6, 1852; *d.* Cologne, 1920. 1885, *t.* Cologne Cons.; mus. critic, *Zeitung;* 1906-7, lecture tour to U. S. Comp. operas, instr. pcs.

Nelson, Edgar Andrew. Organist, teacher; *b.* Chicago, Mar. 14, 1882. Edu., Bush Cons., Chicago. 1895, org., Chicago; 1909, org., First Presby. Ch., Oak Park; 1925, dir., Bush Cons.; 1920, decorated, Order of Vasa by King of Sweden.

Nepomuceno, Alberto. Brazilian composer; *b.* Ceara, Brazil, 1864; *d.* Rio de Janeiro, 1920. *t.* Natl. Inst., Rio de Janeiro. Comp. operas, orch. wks., and songs, incl., *Amor Indeciso.*

Neri (*Nay-ree*), **Filippo.** Composer; *b.* Florence, Jul. 21, 1515; *d.* Rome, May 26, 1595. Priest in whose oratory sacred mus. developed into oratorio.

Neruda, Wilma (sometimes known as **Normann-Neruda**). Violinist; *b.* Brünn, Aus., Mar. 29, 1839; *d.* Berlin, Apr. 15, 1911. 1864, *m.* Ludwig Normann. 1888, *m.* Sir Charles Hallé. 1889, concert tour to Australia and U. S.

Nessler, Victor. Composer; *b.* Baldenheim, Alsace, Jan. 28, 1841; *d.* Strassburg, May 28, 1890. Comp. operettas, once popular, incl., *Trumpeter of Säkkingen.*

Nesvera, Joseph. Composer; *b.* Proskoles, Boh., Oct. 24, 1842; *d.* Olmütz, 1914. Comp. operas, symph., suites, pf. pcs., songs.

Netzorg, Bendetson. Pianist, teacher; *b.* Mecosta, Mich., Apr. 26, 1888. *p.* Hugo Kaun. *t.* Berlin, two years; *t.* Detroit. Comp. pf., choral, organ wks.

Neuendorff (*Noy-en-dorf*), **Adolf.** Conductor; *b.* Hamburg, Ger., Jun. 13, 1843; *d.* New York, Dec. 4, 1897. 1877, cond. first Amer. prod. of *Die Walküre* at N. Y. Acad. of Mus.; 1878, succ. Th. Thomas as cond., N. Y. Phil. Comp. operas, incl., *Rat Charmer of Hamelin.*

Neukomm (*Noy-kom*), **Sigismund Chevalier von.** Composer; *b.* Salzburg, Aus., Jun. 10, 1778; *d.* Paris, Apr. 3, 1858. *p.* Haydn. Comp. 1,000 wks. in all forms.

Neupert (*Noy-pert*), **Edmund.** Pianist, composer; *b.* Christiania, Apr. 1, 1842; *d.* New York, Jun. 22, 1888. 1882, to U. S. Comp. pf., *études,* salon pcs.

Neuville (*Nuh-vil*), **Valentin.** Composer; *b.* Rexpoede, Bel., 1863. Org, St. Nizier, Lyons, Fr. Comp. operas, symph., chamb. mus.

Nevada (really **Wixom**), **Emma.** Soprano; *b.* Alpha, nr. Nevada City, Cal., 1862. 1883, Paris op.; 1884, Acad. of Mus., N. Y., *w.* Mapleson, alternating rôles *w.* Patti.

Neve (*Na-veh*), **Paul de.** Composer; *b.* Steglitz, Ger., Jan. 24, 1881. Comp. operas, incl., *Harald der Taucher.*

Nevin, Arthur Finley. Composer; *b.* Edgewater, Pa., Apr. 27, 1871. Brother Ethelbert N. Comp. opera, *Poïa,* on an Indian subject; symph. and chamb. wks. Career largely in Middle West.

Nevin, Ethelbert. Composer; *b.* Edgeworth, Pa., Nov. 25, 1862; *d.* New Haven, Conn., Feb. 17, 1901. One of the unique comp. of the Amer. sch., the importance of whose career was indicated in the publication of his biography, by John Tasker Howard (1935). Known to fame as the composer of the *Rosary* and *Narcissus.* Output consisted almost entirely of songs and pf. pcs.

Nevin, George Balch. Composer; *b.* Shippensburg, Pa., Mar. 15, 1859; *d.* Easton, Pa., Apr. 17, 1933. Comp. sacred and secular vocal mus.

Nevin, Gordon Balch. Organist, composer; *b.* Easton, Pa., May 19, 1892. Son of George B. N. *t.* and org., Johnstown, Pa. Comp. org. pcs., secular songs, and pf. suite, *Moods from Nature.* Author, organ textworks.

Newman, Ernest. Writer; *b.* Liverpool, Eng., Nov. 30, 1868. 1906, mus. critic, Birmingham *Daily Post.* Author of numerous biographical and critical books, incl., *The Man Liszt* (1935).

Ney, Elly. Pianist; *b.* Bonn, Ger. *p.* Leschetitzky, in Vienna. 1921-22, first Amer. tour; makes annual tours, Europe and Amer., soloist major orch.; 1928, intro. Toch *Concerto* in Amer.

Nicholl, Horace Wadham. Organist, composer; *b.* Tipton, Eng., Mar. 17, 1848; *d.* N. Y., 1922. 1871, org., Pittsburgh; 1878, St. Mark's, N. Y.; 1883, ed., Schirmer. Comp. symph., organ mus. Author of work on *Harmony.*

Nicodé (*Nee-ko-day*), **Jean Louis.** Pianist, composer; *b.* Jerczik, Ger., Aug. 12, 1853; *d.* Dresden, 1919. Comp. symph. p., often with voices; many instr. pcs., songs.

Nicolai, Karl Otto Ehrenfried. Composer; *b.* Königsberg, Ger., Jun. 9, 1810; *d.* Berlin, Apr. 11, 1849. Comp. ch. mus., and operas, incl., *Merry Wives of Windsor.*

Nicolau, Antonio. Conductor, composer; *b.* Barcelona, Sp., Jun. 8, 1858. Dir., Barcelona Cons. Opera and orch. comp.

Nicolini (*Nik-o-lee-nee*), **Ernest Nicolas.** Tenor; *b.* St. Malo, Fr., Feb. 23, 1834; *d.* Pau, Fr., Jan. 19, 1898. 1866, London; 1881, New York. 1886, *m.* Adelina Patti.

Niecks (*Neeks*), **Frederick.** Writer; *b.* Düsseldorf, Ger., Mar. 3, 1845; *d.* Edinburgh, Jun. 24, 1924. Prof., Edinburgh U. Author of *Dictionary of Musical Terms, History of Program Music, Chopin as Man and Musician.*

Niédermeyer (*Nee-ay-der-may-er*), **Louis.** Composer, teacher; *b.* Nyon, Switz., Apr. 27, 1802; *d.* Paris, Mar. 13, 1861. *p.* Moscheles. 1821, *t.* Geneva; 1854, revived Choron's Sch. (suspended, 1830), as École de Musique Religieuse; now government subsidized, as École Niédermeyer; 1857, fd. *La Maîtrise, w.* Ortigue as ed.

Nielsen (*Neel-sen*), **August Carl.** Composer; *b.* Nörre-Lyndelse, Den., Jun. 9, 1864; *d.* Copenhagen, Oct. 2, 1931. Dir., Copenhagen Cons. Comp. operas, incl., *Maskaraden;* symph., choral, chamb. mus.

Nielsen, Ludolf. Composer; *b.* Nörre-Tvede, Zeeland, Jan. 29, 1876. Comp. opera, *Isabella;* misc. pcs.

Nikisch, Arthur. Conductor; *b.* Szent Miklos, Hun., Oct. 12, 1855; *d.* Leipzig, Jan. 24, 1922. 1889, cond., Boston Symph.; 1895, cond., Leipzig Gewandhaus; 1912, toured U. S. as cond., London Symph.; 1901, prof., Leipzig Cons.

Nilsson, Christine. Soprano; *b.* Wexio, Swed., Aug. 20, 1843; *d.* Copenhagen, Nov. 22, 1921. Played violin and flute at fairs; as protégée of Baroness Leuhusen. St. *u.* Berwald. 1864, debut, Paris opera as Violetta in Verdi's *Traviata;* 1872, Strakosch Op. Co., New York.

Noble, Thomas Tertius. Organist; *b.* Bath, Eng., May 5, 1867. 1889, gr. R. Coll. Mus., London; 1917, hon. M.A., Columbia; 1926, hon. Mus. Doc., Trinity Coll., Hartford; 1931, hon. Mus. Doc., Archbishop of Canterbury. Org. in English Cath. 1913, org., St. Thomas' Ch., N. Y. Comp. organ mus., anthems, incl., *Souls of the Righteous.*

Nodermann, Presben Magnus Christian. Composer; *b.* Hjörring, Den., Jan. 11, 1867. 1903, dir., Lund Cath. Comp. operas, incl., *King Magnus;* misc. pcs. Author of a work on *Hymnology.*

Nohl, Karl F. L. Writer; *b.* Iserlohn, Ger., Dec. 5, 1831; *d.* Heidelberg, Dec. 15, 1885. Author of a history of mus. and biographical wks.

Nolan, Michael. Irish comedian. Comp. *Little Annie Rooney,* and sang it in London mus. halls; song intro. in U. S. by Annie Hart in *The Bowery Girl* about 1887, prior to enactment of international copyright law; hence made fortunes for N. Y. publishers, none of which Nolan shared.

Norden, Norris Lindsay. Organist, conductor; *b.* Phila., Pa., Apr. 24, 1887. 1911, A.M., Columbia. Org., N. Y., and Phila.; 1912, fd. Aeolian Choir, Phila.; cond., Pa. Choral Soc.; *t.* 1924-26, Curtis Inst.; 1929, *t.* Germantown Acad.

Nordica, Lillian [Norton]. Soprano; *b.* Farmington, Me., May 12, 1859; *d.* Batavia, Java, May 10, 1914. Edu., N. E. Cons., Boston. 1881, Petrograd; 1882, Paris; 1887, Covent Garden; 1888, Met. Op., N. Y.; 1910, Boston Op. The leading artist of her epoch, especially distinguished in Wagnerian rôles.

Nordqvist, Johann Conrad. Conductor; *b.* Venersborg, Swed., Apr. 11, 1840. 1908, *t.* Stockholm Cons. Comp. orch., pf. pcs., songs.

Nordraak, Rikard. Composer; *b.* Christiania, Nor., Jun. 12, 1842; *d.* Berlin, Mar. 20, 1876. Influenced Grieg toward nationalism. Comp. songs, incid. mus., pf. pcs., songs.

Noren, Heinrich Gottlieb. Violinist, composer; *b.* Graz, Aus., Jan. 6, 1861. Orch. comp. Lives Berlin.

Norris, Homer A. Organist, composer, theorist; *b.* Wayne, Me., Oct. 4, 1860; *d.* N. Y., Aug. 14, 1920. Comp. symph. wks., and cantatas. Author of text-books on harmony and counterpoint.

Noskowski (*Nos-koff-ski*), **Sigismund.** Composer; *b.* Warsaw, Pol., May 2, 1848; *d.* Aug., 1909. Comp. operas, symph., chamb. mus.

Nottebohm, Martin Gustav. Writer; *b.* Lüdenscheid, Ger., Nov. 12, 1817; *d.* Graz, Aus., Oct. 29, 1882. Author of thematic catalogue of Schubert wks.

Nouguès (*Noo-ghes*), **Jean.** Composer; *b.* Bordeaux, Fr., 1876; *d.* Europe, 1932. Comp. operas, incl., *Quo Vadis* (1909).

Nourrit (*Noo-ree*), **Adolphe.** Tenor; *b.* Paris, Mar. 3, 1802; *d.* Naples, Mar. 8, 1839. 1827-37, prof., Paris Cons. Created rôles in *William Tell, La Juive, Les Huguenots,* and many other operas.

Novacek (*No-va-chek*), **Ottokar.** Violinist, composer; *b.* Fehertemplom, Hun., May 13, 1866; *d.* New York, Mar. 3, 1900. 1891, mem., Boston Symph. Comp. orch., chamb. mus., etc.

Novaes, Guiomar. Pianist; *b.* Brazil, 1895. St., Paris Cons.; *u.* Isidor Philipp. Concert tours of Europe and the Amers.

Novak, Viteslav. Composer; *b.* Kamenitz, Boh., Dec. 5, 1870. 1909, prof., Prague Cons. Comp. operas, symph., chamb. mus., songs.

Novello, Clara Anastasia. Soprano; *b.* London, Jun. 10, 1818; *d.* Rome, 1908.

Novello, Vincent. Composer; *b.* London, Sept. 16, 1781; *d.* Nice, Fr., Oct. 9, 1861. Co-fd., London Phil.; 1811, fd. mus. publishing house, Novello & Co., London.

Novoviejski (*No-vo-vyes-ki*), **Felix.** Composer; *b.* Wartenburg, Feb. 7, 1877. 1918, to Posen. Comp. operas, symph. wks., organ pcs.

O

Oakeley, Sir Herbert Stanley. Composer, organist; *b.* Ealing, Eng., Jul. 20, 1830; *d.* Edinburgh, Oct. 26, 1903. 1876, knighted by Queen Victoria. Comp. org. pcs., cath. service, anthems, songs.

Oberhoffer, Emil. Conductor; *b.* nr. Munich, 1867. *p.* Isidor Philipp. 1895, to U. S.; 1903-22, cond., Minneapolis Symph.; prof., U. of Minn.

Oberleithner (*O-ber-lite-ner*), **Max von.** Composer; *b.* Mährisch-Schönberg, Boh., Jul. 11, 1868. Comp. operas, incl., *Aphrodite.*

O'Carolan, Turloch. Singer; *b.* Newtown, Ire., 1670; *d.* Alderford, Ire., Mar. 25, 1738. One of the last and greatest of the Irish bards. Comp. songs.

Ochs (*Ox*), **Siegfried.** Conductor, composer; *b.* Frankfort, Apr. 19, 1858. 1882, fd. Phil. Chorus, Berlin. Comp. comic opera, songs.

Ochs, Traugott. Pianist, composer; *b.* Altenfeld, Ger., Oct. 19, 1854; *d.* Berlin, 1919. 1911, fd. school, Berlin.

Odington, Walter de. Writer; *b.* England, *c.* 1250; *d. c.* 1316. A monk. Inventor of measured notes.

Oehmler, Leo. Pianist, music editor; *b.* Pittsburgh, Aug. 15, 1867; *d.* Pasadena, Nov. 3, 1930.

Oelsner (*Els-ner*), **Bruno.** Composer; *b.* Neudorf, Ger., Jul. 29, 1861. 1882, *t.* Darmstadt Cons. Comp. operas, cantatas, songs.

Oesten (*Ays-ten*), **Theodor.** Pianist, composer; *b.* Berlin, Dec. 31, 1813; *d.* ib., Mar. 16, 1870.

Oetting, William H. Organist, composer; *b.* Pittsburgh, Oct. 14, 1875. St., Berlin. Org. soloist, pres. and dir., Pittsburgh Mus. Inst.

Offenbach, Jacques. Composer; *b.* Cologne, Ger., Jun. 21, 1819; *d.* Paris, Oct. 5, 1880. 1849, cond., Th. Francaise; 1855-66, owner-dir., Bouffes Parisiens; 1872-6, managed Gaité; 1876-7, toured U. S. Comp. 100 stage wks., comic operas, incl., *La Fille du Tambour-Major, Orphée aux Enfers, La Belle Hélène,* and the serious opera, *Les Contes d'Hoffmann.*

O'Hara, Geoffrey. Singer, composer; *b.* Berrian Springs, Mich., Feb. 2, 1888. News reporter; teacher of English. Wr. *K-K-K-Katy,* popular during World War; also, *Give a Man a Horse.*

Okeghem, Jean de. Composer; *b.* Termonde, Bel., *c.* 1430; *d.* Tours, Fr., 1496. Contrapuntal comp.

Olcott, Chauncey. Song writer, ballad singer; *b.* Buffalo, Jul. 21, 1860; *d.* Monte Carlo, Mar. 18, 1932. Wr. *Mother Machree* and *My Wild Irish Rose.*

Oldberg, Arne. Composer, pianist; *b.* Youngstown, O., Jul. 12, 1874. *p.* Rheinberger. 1899, pf. *t.* Northwestern U Comp. symph., overtures, concertos and chamb. mus.

Olheim, Helen. Contralto; b. Buffalo, N. Y. 1935, debut, Met. Op., N. Y.

Oliver, Henry Kemble. Composer; b. Beverly, Mass., Nov. 24, 1800; d. Boston, Aug. 10, 1885. Comp. hymns., incl., *Federal Street.*

Ollone, Max d'. Composer; b. Besançon, Fr., Jun. 13, 1875. Comp. operas, chamb. mus.

Olsen, Ole. Composer, conductor; b. Hammerfest, Nor., Jul. 5, 1850. 1878, cond., Musekförening, Christiania, succ. Svendsen. Comp. operas, symph., violin pcs. Lives Stockholm, Swed.

Olszewska, Maria. Opera singer; b. Bavaria. Hamburg Op.; Vienna Op., *u.* Strauss; 1928, Chicago Op.; 1932-33, Met. Op. H.

Ondricek (*On-dri-chek*), **Franz.** Violinist; b. Prague, Boh., Apr. 29, 1859; d. Milan, Apr. 12, 1922. Edu., Paris Cons. 1896, toured U. S.; 1910, *t.* Vienna Cons. Comp. violin pcs. Author of violin *Method.*

O'Neill, Norman. Composer; b. London, Mar. 14, 1875; d. ib., Mar. 3, 1934. Comp. orch., chamb. mus., songs.

Onslow, George. Composer; b. Clermont-Ferrand, Fr., Jul. 27, 1784; d. ib., Oct. 3, 1852. Comp. operas, symph., and 100 chamb. mus. wks. A wealthy comp. whose wks. were much played during his lifetime.

Opienski, Heinrich. Composer; b. Cracow, Jan. 13, 1870. 1905, cond., Warsaw Op. Comp. opera, *Maria;* misc. pcs. Author of many wks., incl. three books on Chopin (1910).

Ormandy, Eugene. Conductor; b. Budapest, Nov. 18, 1899. 1921, cond., Capitol Th., New York; g.-cond., Phila. Orch.; 1931, cond., Minneapolis Symph. Orch.; 1936, cond., Phil. Symph. Orch., succ. Leopold Stokowski.

d'Ormeville, Carlo. Librettist, impresario, journalist; b. Rome, 1842; d. Milan, 1924. 1871, dir., Khedival Th., Cairo, at world première of *Aïda;* later dir., Colon Th., Buenos Ayres. Wr. libretto of Marchetti's *Ruy Blas,* and Catalani's *Loreley.*

Ornstein, Leo. Pianist, composer; b. Kremenchug, Rus., Dec. 11, 1895. St., Puchalski, at Kiev Cons. Comp. orch., chamb., pf. mus.

Orth (*Ort*), **John.** Pianist, composer; b. Annweiler, Ger., Dec. 2, 1850; d. Boston, May 3, 1932. *p.* Liszt. 1875, *t.* Boston. Comp. pf. pcs.

Orth, Lizette Emma née Blood. Pianist, composer; b. c. 1863; d. Boston, Aug. 14, 1913. Liszt interpreter, and lecture-recitalist. 1883, *m.* John O. Comp. pf. teaching and salon pcs., songs, operettas for children.

Ortmann, Otto Rudolph. Music educator; b. Baltimore, Md., Jan. 25, 1889. Edu., Johns Hopkins; 1917, gr., Peabody Cons.; 1913-28, *t.* Baltimore; 1920-24, *t.* Johns Hopkins; 1928, dir., Peabody Cons. Author, pf. text wks.

Osborne, George Alexander. Pianist, teacher; b. Limerick, Sept. 24, 1806; d. London, Nov. 16, 1893. *p.* Fétis. 1826, *t.* Paris; friend of Chopin and Berlioz; 1843, *t.* London. Comp. chamb. mus. Collab. *w.* deBériot in 33 pf.-violin duets.

Osgood, George Laurie. Composer, teacher; b. Chelsea, Mass., Apr. 3, 1844; d. Godalueing, Eng., 1923. 1866, A.B., Harvard. 1872, *t.* singing, Boston; 1893, retired to Eng. Comp. songs, part-songs.

Osterzee, Cornelia van. Composer; b. Batavia, Java, Aug. 16, 1863. Comp. opera, orch., chamb. mus.

Ostrcil (*Ostr-chil*), **Ottokar.** Composer; b. Prague, Boh., Feb. 25, 1879; d. ib., Aug., 1935. *p.* Fibich. Prof., Czecho-Slavic Acad. of Commerce. Comp. operas to Czech texts, symph., chamb. mus.

Oswaldo, Henrique. Composer; b. Rio de Janeiro, 1852, of Swiss parentage. Comp. chamb. mus., pf. pcs., songs.

Otterstroem (*Ot'-ter-strum*), **Thorvald.** Composer; b. Copenhagen, Den., Jul. 17, 1868; d. Chicago, 19—. Comp. orch. and chamb. mus., and piano pcs. Career chiefly assoc. *w.* Chicago.

Otto, Ernst Julius. Composer; b. Königstein, Ger., Sept. 1, 1804; d. Dresden, Ger., Mar. 5, 1877. Comp. operas, ch. mus., part-songs, pf. pcs.

Ouseley, Sir Frederick Arthur Gore. Organist, composer, theorist; b. London, Aug. 12, 1825; d. Hereford, Eng., Apr. 6, 1889. 1862, Mus.D., Camb. Comp. oratorios, *Hagar* and *St. Polycarp;* anthems, organ pcs., chamb. mus. Author, treatises on harmony, and theoretical subjects.

P

Pache, Johannes. Composer; b. Bischofswerda, Ger., Dec. 9, 1857; d. Limbach, Ger., Dec. 24, 1897. Comp. choruses for men's voices.

Pachulski (*Pak-hool-ski*), **Heinrich.** Composer; b. Lasa, Rus., Oct. 16, 1859. 1886, *t.* Moscow Cons. Comp. orch., pf. pcs.

Pacini (*Pah-chee-nee*), **Giovanni.** Composer; b. Catania, It., Feb. 17, 1796; d. Pescia, It., Dec. 6, 1867. Comp. 80 operas, sacred chamb. mus. Author of *Autobiography,* twice revised and frequently republished.

Pacius (*Pah-che-oos*), **Fredrik.** Violinist, composer; b. Hamburg, Ger., Mar. 19, 1809; d. Helsingfors, Fin., Jan. 9, 1891. Comp. operas, choruses.

Paderewski, Ignaz Jan. Pianist, composer; b. Kurilowka, Pol., Nov. 18, 1860. One of the greatest of piano virtuosos. *p.* Leschetizky. 1887, debut, Vienna; 1888, Paris; 1890, London; 1891, America; 1919, elected first President of Republic of Poland. Comp. opera, *Manru; Polish Symphony;* pf. concerto, misc. pcs. d. June 29, 1941.

Paër (*Pah-air*), **Ferdinando.** Composer; b. Parma, Jun. 1, 1771; d. Paris, May 3, 1839. 1807, court comp. to Napoleon; 1812-27, dir., Italian op., Paris. Comp. 43 operas.

Paganini, Nicolo. Violinist, composer; b. Genoa, It., Oct. 27, 1782; d. Nice, Fr., May 27, 1840. 1828, toured Europe, *w.* sensational success. His immense command of the resources of his instrument, combined *w.* a remarkable appearance, and a manner suggesting secrecy and mystery, caused many to regard him as "possessed of the devil." A wealth of uncanny tradition has gathered round his memory, despite which he was doubtless the greatest virtuoso of violin history. He left many compositions of brilliant style and full of technical difficulties.

Page, Nathaniel Clifford. Composer, editor; b. San Francisco, Oct. 26, 1866. Mus. ed. *w.* C. Fischer and O. Ditson Comp. light opera, cantatas, orch. mus., pf. pcs., songs.

Paine, John Knowles. Organist, composer; b. Portland, Me., Jan. 9, 1839; d. Cambridge, Mass., Apr. 25, 1906. p. Herman Kotzschmar. 1862, prof., Harvard U., teacher of Arthur Foote, Coerne, Converse, Carpenter, and many others. First Amer. comp. in large forms, whose wks. won recognition abroad, and have survived his generation. 1888, comp., *Song of Promise* for Cin. Fest.; 1904, incid. mus. for Sophocles' *Aedipus Tyrannus*, won gold medal at Berlin unveiling of Wagner monument; 1909, comp. *Hymn to the West* for St. Louis Expo.; also comp. pf. and organ pcs., songs.

Paisiello (*Pah-ees-yello*), **Giovanni.** Composer; b. Taranto, It., May 9, 1741; d. Naples, It., Jun. 3, 1816. Comp. over 100 operas for Naples and Petrograd. Many books have been written about him.

Paladilhe (*Pal-a-dee-ye*), **Émile.** Composer; b. Montpellier, Fr., Jun. 3, 1844; d. Paris, Jan., 1926. Comp. operas, orch. wks., songs, incl., *Psyche*.

Paldi, Mari. Composer; b. Michigan. p. Hiller, Paris. t. Caruthers Sch., Chicago.

Palestrina (*Pal-es-tree-na*), **Giovanni Pierluigi da.** Composer; b. Palestrina, It., 1526; d. Rome, Feb. 2, 1594. A singer in the Pontifical Chapel u. Pope Julius III; afterward comp. to the chapel. 1571, chapel-master of St. Peter's. He is held in reverence as one of the greatest masters of plain-song. His severely grand wks. are still the standard by which is measured the mus. of the modern Roman Church.

Palmer, Horatio R. Conductor; b. Sherburne, N. Y., Apr. 26, 1834; d. Nov., 1907. 1887-91, dean of mus., Chautauqua Inst. Author of chorus collections, and text wks. on chorus singing.

Palmgren, Selim. Pianist, composer; b. Björneborg, Fin., Feb. 16, 1878. 1909-12, cond., orch. at Abo; 1919, t. Helsingfors. Comp. operas, pf. pcs., incl., *May Night*.

Pals, Leopold van der. Composer; b. Petrograd, Jul. 5, 1884. Comp. orch., chamb. mus., violin pcs.

Panizza, Ettore. Composer, conductor; b. Buenos Aires, Aug. 12, 1875. 1889, cond., op. in It. houses; 1907-1913, cond., Covent Garden, London; 1916, cond., La Scala, Milan; 1933, cond., Met. Op., New York. Comp. opera, *Aurora*.

Panofka, H. Teacher of singing, composer; b. Breslau, Ger., Oct. 3, 1807; d. Florence, It., Nov. 18, 1887. Comp. violin pcs., songs. Author of exercises for singers.

Panseron, A. Teacher of singing, composer; b. Paris, Apr. 26, 1796; d. ib., Jul. 29, 1859. Comp. of vocal studies.

Panzner, Karl. Conductor; b. Teplitz, Boh., Mar. 2, 1866; d. Düsseldorf, 1924. 1909-10, cond., Hamburg Phil. Orch.

Papi, Gennaro. Conductor. 1906, chorusmaster, San Severo di Puglia; g.-cond., Milan, Warsaw, London; 1917, cond., Met. Op., N. Y.

Papini, Guido. Violinist, composer; b. Camagiore, It., Aug. 1, 1847; d. London, Oct. 3, 1912. 1893, prof., Dublin R. Acad.; 1896, t. London. Comp. violin concerto, chamb. mus., violin pcs. Author of a violin *Method*.

Papperitz, Benjamin Robert. Organist, composer; b. Pirna, Ger., Dec. 4, 1826; d. Leipzig, Sept. 29, 1903. Comp. organ pcs., anthems.

Pâque (*Pahk*), **Marie Joseph Leon Desiré.** Pianist, teacher; b. Liége, May 21, 1867. t. Paris. Comp. operas, symph., chamb. mus.

Paradis, Maria Teresa von. Composer; b. Vienna, May 15, 1759; d. ib., Feb. 1, 1824. Blind from fifth year. Toured extensively. Comp. operas, chamb mus.

Paradisi (Paradies), Pietro Domenico. Composer; b. Naples, 1710; d. Venice, 1792. Comp. operas, pf. pcs.

Paray, Paul. Conductor, musicologist, critic, composer; b. Treport, May 24, 1886. 1921, cond., Lamoureaux Orch., Paris. Comp. operas, chamb. mus., teaching pcs. for piano.

Parepa-Rosa, Euphrosyne [Parepa de Boyescu]. Soprano; b. Edinburgh, May 7, 1836; d. London, Jan. 21, 1874. p. her mother, a sister of Edwin Seguin. 1852, Madrid; 1857, London; 1865-71, U. S.; 1867, m. Carl Rosa; fd. own troupe and gave opera in English; 1873, Cairo. A strong, sympathetic voice, of a range of 2½ octaves. Distinguished oratorio singer.

Parish-Alvars, Elias. Harpist, composer; b. Teignmouth, Eng., Feb. 28, 1810; d. Vienna, Jan. 25, 1849.

Parker, Henry Taylor. Music critic; b. Boston, 1867; d. ib., Mar. 30, 1934. 1905-d., Boston *Transcript*.

Parker, Horatio. Composer; b. Auburndale, Mass., Sept. 15, 1863; d. New Haven, Conn., Dec. 18, 1919. Edu., Munich. 1894, prof. of mus., Yale U. Comp. symph. wks.; the Met. Op. prize work, *Mona* (1912); NFMC prize opera, *Fairyland* (1915); oratorio, *Hora Novissima*; cantatas, anthems, songs, and organ pcs.

Parker, James Cutler Dunn. Organist, teacher, composer; b. Boston, Jun. 2, 1828; d. Brookline, Mass., Nov. 27, 1916. t. Arthur Whiting; org., Trinity Ch., Boston; fac., N. E. Cons. Comp. cantatas, anthems and songs.

Parratt, Sir Walter. Organist, composer; b. Huddersfield, Eng., Feb. 10, 1841; d. Windsor, Mar. 30, 1924. 1916, mus. dean, London U.; 1892, knighted; 1894, Mus.D., Oxford. Comp. organ pcs., anthems, songs.

Parry, Sir Charles Hubert Hastings. Composer; b. Bournemouth, Eng., Feb. 27, 1848; d. Littlehampton, 1918. 1894, dir., R. A. M.; 1898, knighted; 1903, baronet; 1899-1908, prof., Oxford. Comp. over fifty choral wks., incl., *Judith* (Birmingham, 1888), *Hymn to the Nativity* (Hereford, 1912), symph., chamb. mus., pf. pcs., songs. Author of *Evolution of the Art of Music,* and many wks. on mus.

Parry, Joseph. Composer; b. Merthyr-Tydvil, Wales, May 21, 1841; d. Penarth, 1903. Son of a laborer, but won distinction as comp. of operas, contatas, overtures.

Parsons, Albert Ross. Teacher, pianist; b. Sandusky, O., Sept. 16, 1847; d. Mt. Kisco, N. Y., Jun. 14, 1933. p. Tausig. The leading N. Y. pf. teacher of his day.

Pasdeloup (*Pah-de-loo*), **Jules Étienne.** Conductor; b. Paris, Sept. 15, 1819; d. Fontainebleau, Aug. 13, 1887. 1851, fd. Société des jeune artistes du Conservatoire.

Pasmore, Henry Bickford. Music educator; b. Wis., Jun. 27, 1857. Edu., Leipzig Cons. 1885, m. May Stanton. Of six children, four are musicians. t. Stern Cons., Berlin; t. Stanford U. Comp. opera, orch. pcs., songs.

Pasta, Giuditta. Soprano; b. Saronno, It., Apr. 9, 1798; d. Lake Como, It., Apr. 1, 1865. For her Pacini comp. *Niobe* (1826), Donizetti *Anna Bolena* (1830), Bellini *Norma* (1831). v. Sketches by Bossini and Angeloni (1833).

Patey, Janet Monach, née Whytock. Contralto; b. London, May 1, 1842; d. Sheffield, Eng., Feb. 28, 1894. Celebrated British oratorio and concert singer. 1866, m. John George P. (1835-1901), concert baritone. 1871, toured U. S.

Paton, Mary Anne. Soprano; *b.* Edinburgh, Oct., 1802; *d.* Chapelthorpe, Eng., Jul. 21, 1864. 1824, sang in English première of Weber's *Freischütz.* 1824, *m.* Lord William Pitt Lenox; 1831, *m.* Joseph Wood, tenor. 1833-37, toured U. S. in joint recitals.

Patterson, Frank. Composer, author; *b.* Philadelphia, 1871. *p.* Rheinberger, Munich. 1925, opera, *The Echo,* perf. N. F. M. C. conv., Portland'; 1929, opera, *Beggar's Love,* perf., Matinée Musicale. Author of *Practical Instrumentation* and other treatises.

Patti (*Pah-tee*), **Adelina.** Soprano; *b.* Madrid, Sp., Feb. 10, 1843; *d.* Wales, Sept. 27, 1919. Daughter Salvatore Patti, an Italian tenor. Raised by sister, Carlotta, in New York. 1859, New York debut in *Lucia di Lammermoor,* a great success; 1861, London; 1862, Paris; probably the greatest singer of the 19th century, a career lasting forty years, closing with increasingly pathetic farewell tours. Built a famous castle. Retired to Craig-y-Nos, in Wales.

Patti, Carlotta. Soprano; *b.* Florence, It., 1840; *d.* Paris, Jun. 27, 1889. Concert coloratura. Debarred from opera by lameness.

Pattison, John Nelson. Composer, pianist; *b.* Niagara Falls, N. Y., Oct. 22, 1845; *d.* Jul., 1905. Comp. *Niagara* symph. for orch. and band; pf. pcs.

Pattison, Lee Marion. Pianist; *b.* Grand Rapids, Wis., Jul. 22, 1890. 1910, gr., N. E. Cons. Mus. 1913, debut, Boston; 1919, Paris; 1920, London; 1914-18, *t.* N. E. Cons.; plays two-piano recitals *w.* Guy Maier. Comp. pf. pcs., songs.

Patton, Frederick Henry. Baritone; *b.* South Manchester, Conn., Oct. 2, 1888. Concert and oratorio; 1919, opera; 1926-31, Cin. Op.; 1925-29, Phila. Op.; 1927-29, Met. Op.

Pauer (*Pow-er*), **Ernst.** Pianist, teacher, writer; *b.* Vienna, Dec. 21, 1826; *d.* Jugenheim, May 9, 1905. *p.* W. A. Mozart, Jr. 1852, ed. of the classics for London publishers. Author, books on mus. subjects. Comp. operas, pf. pcs.

Pauer, Max von. Pianist; *b.* London, Oct. 31, 1866. Dir., Stuttgart Cons.

Paumgartner, Bernard. Conductor; *b.* Vienna, Nov. 14, 1887. 1910, cond., Vienna Tonkunstler; cond., Mozarteum Orch., Salzburg Fest.

Paur, Emil. Conductor; *b.* Czernowitz, Aug. 29, 1855; *d.* Mystek, Czechoslovakia, Jun. 7, 1932. 1880, Kapellmeister, Mannheim; 1893, cond., Boston Symph. Orch.; 1898-1902, cond., New York Phil., and Wagnerian cond., Met. Op.; 1904-1910, cond., Pittsburgh Symph. Orch.; 1910, returned to Germany to dir. Berlin State Op.

Pavloska, Irene. Opera singer; *b.* of Rus. and Pol. parents in St. Johns, P. Q. 1914, prima donna in *Sari w.* Henry Savage; 1915, Chicago Op.

Pavlowa, Anna. Danseuse; *b.* Russia; *d.* The Hague, Jan. 23, 1931. The most celebrated of the ballerinas of modern Rus. 1920, toured U. S.

Peace, Albert Lister. Organist; *b.* Huddersfield, Eng., Jan. 26, 1844; *d.* Mar. 14, 1912. 1897, city org., Liverpool, Eng. Ed., *Scottish Hymnal.* Comp. cantatas, organ pcs.

Pearce, Charles William. Organist, composer; *b.* Salisbury, Eng., Dec. 5, 1856; *d.* Wimborne, 1929. 1908-12, dean of mus., London U. Notable as an examiner. Author of text wks.

Pearsall, Robert Lucas de. Composer; *b.* Clifton, Eng., Mar. 14, 1795; *d.* Lake Constance, Aug. 5, 1856. Comp. madrigals, part-songs.

Pease, Alfred H. Pianist, composer; *b.* Cleveland, O., May 6, 1838; *d.* St. Louis, Mo., Jul. 13, 1882. Comp. pf. pcs., songs.

Pedrell, Felipe. Composer; *b.* Tortosa, Sp., Feb. 19, 1841; *d.* Barcelona, Aug., 1923. Prof., R. Cons., Madrid. Author of historical wks. Comp. operas, orch. wks.

Pedrotti, Carlo. Composer; *b.* Verona, It., Nov. 12, 1817; *d.* ib., Oct. 16, 1893. Comp. operas.

Pembaur, Joseph. Composer; *b.* Innsbruck, Aus., May 23, 1848; *d.* ib., 1923. Comp. orch. mus., songs.

Pembaur, Joseph, Jr. Pianist; *b.* Innsbruck, Aus., Apr. 20, 1875. Prof., Leipzig Cons.

Penfield, Smith Newell. Organist, teacher, composer; *b.* Oberlin, O., Apr. 4, 1837; *d.* New York, Jan. 7, 1920. Comp. orch. and chamb. wks., pf. pcs., songs.

Penn, Arthur A. Composer; *b.* Eng., 1880. 1903, to U. S. Comp. ballads, incl., *Smilin' Through,* the song that inspired Jane Cowl to write a play of that name.

Perabo, Johann Ernst. Pianist, teacher; *b.* Wiesbaden, Nov. 14, 1845; *d.* West Roxbury, Oct. 29, 1920. *p.* Moscheles. 1865, New York; 1866, Boston. Comp. pf. pcs.

Perfall, Karl, Freiherr von. Composer; *b.* Munich, Ger., Jan. 29, 1824; *d.* ib., Jan. 15, 1907. Opera comp.

Perger, Richard von. Composer; *b.* Vienna, Jan. 10, 1854; *d.* ib., Jan. 11, 1911. Comp. operas, chamb. mus.

Pergolesi (*Per-go-lay-zee*), **Giovanni Battista.** Composer; *b.* Jesi, It., Jan. 3, 1710; *d.* Pozzuoli, It., Mar. 16, 1736. Edu., Naples Cons. Comp. operas, ch. mus., incl., *Stabat Mater,* completed a few days before his death.

Peri (*Pay-ree*), **Jacopo.** Composer, singer, lutenist; *b.* Florence, Aug. 20, 1561; *d.* ib. *c.* 1630. Of noble birth. Comp. *Dafne,* the first real opera, and *Euridice,* thereby affording models for a new style of stage representation.

Perkins, Charles C. Author; *b.* Boston, Mar. 1, 1823; *d.* Windsor, Vt., 1886. 1843, gr., Harvard. Pres., Handel and Haydn Soc. A notable patron of mus. in Boston; promoted building of Boston Mus. Hall.

Perkins, Henry Southwick. Teacher, composer; *b.* Stockbridge, Vt., Mar. 20, 1833; *d.* Chicago, Jan. 20, 1914. Comp. chorus mus.

Pero, Alexander. Teacher, composer, music editor. *t.* theory, New York Sch. of Mus. and Art.

Perosi (*Pa-ro-zee*), **Lorenzo.** Composer; *b.* Tortona, It., Dec. 20, 1872. St., Mus. Lyceum in Rome. 1888, Milan Cons.; 1896, ordained priest; 1898, mus. dir., Sistine Chapel, Rome; 1897-99, perf. of Trilogy of oratorios: *Transfiguration, Raising of Lazarus,* and *Resurrection of Christ,* estab. his fame; 1905, "Perpetual Master of the Pontifical Chapel," by papal decree. Comp. choral, orch. wks., incl., *Florence. Venice.*

Perosi, Marziano. Composer; *b.* It., 1875. Brother of Lorenzo P. Comp. opera, *Last Days of Pompeii.*

Perry, Edward Baxter. Pianist; *b.* Haverhill, Mass., Feb. 14, 1855; *d.* Camden, Me., Jun. 13, 1924. Blind; said to have originated the lecture recital. 1881-3, prof., Oberlin Coll.; 1917, *t.* Woman's Coll., Montgomery, Ala. Author of *Descriptive Analyses of Piano Works,* and other books on mus. Comp. pf. pcs.

Peschka-Leutner (*Loit-ner*), **Minna.** Soprano; *b.* Vienna, Oct. 25, 1839; *d.* Wiesbaden, Jan. 12, 1890. Eminent in opera and concert. 1872-1881, to U. S.

Pessard (*Pes-sar*), **Émile Louis Fortune.** Composer; *b.* Paris, May 28, 1843; *d.* ib., 1917. Comp. operas, chamb. mus., songs.

Peters (*Pay-ters*), **Guido.** Pianist, composer; *b.* Graz, Aus., Nov. 29, 1866. 1905, *t.* Vienna Cons. Comp. 3 symph., chamb. mus.

Petersilea (*Pay-ter-sil-e-a*), **Carlyle.** Pianist, teacher; *b.* Boston, Jan. 18, 1844; *d.* Tropico, Cal., Jun. 11, 1903.

Peterson-Berger (*Pay-ter-son Bair-ger*), **Olof Wilhelm.** Composer, conductor; *b.* Ullangar, Swed., Feb. 27, 1867. 1896, mus. critic, *Dageus Nyheter.* Comp. operas, incl., *Ran.* Author of wks. on Wagner.

Petrie, Henri Willem. Minstrel turned songwriter; *b.* Zeist, 1856; *d.* Dresden, 1914. Wr., *Asleep in the Deep,* intro. by John Early of Haverly Troubadours, McVicker's Th., Chicago, in 1898. Popular sale followed only after its publication in 1899 as a supplement in a N. Y. newspaper.

Petrucci (*Pe-troo-chee*), **of Fossombrone.** Invented the printing of mus. from movable type in It. *c.* 1500.

Petschnikov, Alexander. Violinist; *b.* Jeletz, Rus., Feb. 8, 1873; *d.* Munich. 1913, *t.* Munich R. Acad.

Peyser, Herbert F. Music critic; *b.* New York, Aug. 6, 1886. Edu., Columbia U. 1909, corresp., *Musical America;* 1929, European corresp., N. Y. *Times.*

Pfefferkorn, Otto W. G. Pianist, teacher. Dir., Brenau (Ga.) Coll. Cons.

Pfeiffer (*Pfay-fair*), **Georges Jean.** Pianist; *b.* Versailles, Fr., Dec. 12, 1835; *d.* Paris, Feb. 14, 1908. Comp. symph., chamb. mus.

Pfeiffer, Theodor. Pianist, teacher; *b.* Heidelberg, Oct. 20, 1853. Author of educational wks.

Pfitzner, Hans Erich. Composer; *b.* Moscow, May 5, 1869; *d.* Ger., 1935. German parentage. 1886, Hoch Cons., Frankfurt. 1890, *t.* Coblenz Cons.; 1908-16, dir., Opera and Cons., Strassburg; 1913, Ph.D., U. Strassburg; 1919, cond., *Munich Konzertverein;* 1920, gen. mus. dir. of Bavaria; 1917, dramatic legend, *Palestrina,* prod., Munich. Comp. opera, orch. wks., chamb. mus.

Pfitzner, Heinrich. Composer, pianist. Former dir. of mus. dept., Shorter Coll., Rome, Ga.

Pfohl, Ferdinand. Writer, composer; *b.* Elbogen, Boh., Oct. 12, 1863. 1892, critic, Hamburg *Nachrichten;* 1908, *t.* Vogt Cons., Hamburg. Comp. orch. mus., symph. p. Author of biographical wks. on mus., opera guides. Lives Hamburg, Ger.

Phelps, Ellsworth C. Organist, composer; *b.* Middletown, Conn., Aug. 11, 1827; *d.* Brooklyn, 1913. 1857, mus. supv., Brooklyn Schs. Comp. *Hiawatha* symph., sacred opera, *David,* piano pcs., songs.

Phile, Philip. Violinist, conductor; *d.* Phila., 1793. 1784, advertised concert in Phila. Probably comp. of mus. of *Hail Columbia,* to text by Joseph Hopkinson, son of Francis (q. v.) then called the *President's March,* publ. by Benjamin Carr, bearing picture of Adams, president-elect. Soloist at first Uranian concert. Played in orch. in N. Y. and Phila.

Philidor (really **Danican**), **François André Danican.** Composer; *b.* Dreux, Fr., Sept. 7, 1726; *d.* London, Aug. 31, 1795. Comp. operas.

Philipp, Isidor. Pianist, teacher, composer; *b.* Buda-Pesth, Hun., Sept. 2, 1863. Prof., Paris Cons.; 1935, cond., master class, Chicago Mus. Coll. Author of technical studies for the piano and pf. pcs.

Phillips, Adelaide. Contralto; *b.* Stratford-on-Avon, Eng., 1833; *d.* Carlsbad, Ger., Oct. 3, 1882. Edu. in U. S. 1854-81, opera prima donna in Europe and U. S.

Piatti, Alfredo Carlo. 'Cellist; *b.* Bergamo, It., Jan. 8, 1822; *d.* ib., Jul. 19, 1901. Comp. 'cello pcs.

Piccinni (*Pit-chee-nee*), **Niccolo.** Composer; *b.* Bari, It., Jan. 16, 1728; *d.* Passy, Fr., May 7, 1800. Gluck's rival in Paris, by whom he was eventually defeated. A comp. of recognized talent, but important not so much for his operas, of which he wrote many, as for the controversies in which he figured.

Pick-Mangiagalli, Riccardo. Composer; *b.* Strakonitz, Boh., Jul. 10, 1882. Of Italian parentage. Edu., Milan Cons. 1913, stage-work, *Il Salice D'Oro,* prod., La Scala; 1918, *Il Carillon Magico;* 1920, prod., Met. Op. Comp. orch., opera, and chamb. mus., pf. pcs., songs.

Pierné, Henri Constant Gabriel. Composer, conductor, organist, teacher; *b.* Metz, Aug. 16, 1863. Edu., Paris Cons., *u.* Massenet and César Franck. 1882, cantata, *Edith,* won Prix de Rome. Succ. Franck as org., Sainte Clotilde Ch., Paris; 1903, cond., Colonne concerts; 1912, cond., Colonne Orch.; 1925, mem., Academie des Beaux-Arts. Comp. choral wks., operas, orch. wks., chamb. mus., pf. and harp pcs., songs.

Pierson [**Pearson**], **Henry Hugo.** Composer; *b.* Oxford, Eng., Apr. 12, 1815; *d.* Leipzig, Ger., Jan. 28, 1873. 1844, prof., Edinburgh U.; 1847, Hamburg, Ger.; 1852, oratorio, *Jerusalem,* prod., Norwich, Eng., Fest. Comp. operas, ch. mus., songs, some under pseudonym of Edgar Mansfeldt.

Pijper, Willem. Composer; *b.* Zeist, Utrecht, Sept. 8, 1894. St., Holland. 1918-23, mus. critic, *Utrechter Tagblatt;* 1926, dir., Utrecht Wind Sextet; *t.* Amsterdam High Sch., and Cons. Since 1925, ed., *Die Muziek.* 1921, *First Violin Sonata,* perf., Eng., by Peggy Cochrane and Arthur Sanford. Comp. orch. wks., chamb. mus., choral mus.

Pinelli, Ettore. Violinist, conductor; *b.* Rome, Oct. 18, 1843. 1877, co-fd., *w.* Sgambati, of Liceo Musicale, Rome.

Pinsuti, Ciro. Composer, singing teacher; *b.* Sinalunga, It., May 9, 1829; *d.* Florence, Mar. 10, 1888. 1856, prof., R. A. M., London. Comp. 3 operas, and 250 songs in the ballad style, incl., *Bedouin Love Song.*

Pirani, Eugenio di. Pianist, composer; *b.* Bologna, It., Sept. 18, 1852. 1901, toured for five years *w.* Alma Webster Powell, his pupil; 1904, fd. Powell and Pirani Mus. Inst., Brooklyn. Comp. opera, orch., chamb. mus.

Pisk, Paul. Composer, musicologist; *b.* Vienna, May 16, 1893. Edu., *Gymnasium,* Vienna, *u.* Julius Epstein; 1911-16, U. Vienna, *u.* Guido Adler. 1922, mus. leader, Volkshochschule, Vienna; 1931-3, *t.* Summer Austrian-American Cons., Mondsee. Comp. orch. wks., chamb. mus., choral, pf. pcs., songs.

Piston, Walter. Composer; *b.* Rockland, Me., Jan. 20, 1894. Edu., Harvard U.; st., Nadia Boulanger, Paris. 1926, chamb. work perf., S. M. I. concert in Paris; *t.* Harvard; 1928, *Symphonic Piece,* perf., Koussevitzky and Boston Symph.; 1932, *Orchestral Suite,* perf., Stokowski; 1933, Yaddo, Saratoga, Rochester Fest.; 1934, *String Quartet, No. I,* featured by Roth Q. Comp. orch. wks., chamb. mus.

Pitt, Percy. Composer, conductor; *b.* London, Jan. 4, 1870; *d.* Eng., Nov. 22, 1932. 1915-1920, cond., Beecham Op. Co.; 1920-1924, British Natl. Op.; 1922, artistic dir., British Broadcasting Co.; 1924, mus. dir., Covent Garden Syndicate. Comp. symph. p., *Oriental Rhapsody;* incid. mus.

Pittrich, George Washington. Conductor, composer; *b.* Dresden, Feb. 22, 1870. Cond., Nuremberg Op. Comp. opera, incid. mus.

Piutti, Karl. Organist, composer; *b.* Elgersburg, Ger., Apr. 30, 1846; *d.* Leipzig, 1902. 1874-83, *t.* Wells Coll., Aurora, N. Y. Comp. organ wks.

Pixley, Frank. Operetta librettist; *b.* Chicago, 1868; *d.* San Diego, Dec. 31, 1920. Wr. librettos of *Burgmaster, Prince of Pilsen, King Dodo, Grand Mogul.*

Pizzetti, Ildebrando. Composer; *b.* Parma, It., Sept. 20, 1880. Edu., Parma Cons. 1908, *t.* Cons.; 1909, *t.;* 1918, dir., Florence Cons.; 1932, dir., Milan Cons.; 1923, opera, *Debora e Jaele,* prod., La Scala. Toscanini intro. wks. extensively. 1930, Amer. tour as pianist and g.-cond. Comp. opera, choral, orch. wks., chamb. mus., pf. pcs., songs.

Pizzi (*Pit-see*), **Emilio.** Composer; *b.* Verona, It., Feb. 2, 1862. 1897-1900, dir., Bergamo Inst.; 1900, London. Comp. operas, incl., *Gabriella* (1893), written for Patti.

Plaidy (*Pli-dy*), **Louis.** Pianist, teacher; *b.* Wermsdorf, Ger., Nov. 28, 1810; *d.* Grimma, Ger., Mar. 3, 1874. Best known for his technical studies for piano.

Planquette (*Plang-ket*), **Robert Jean.** Composer; *b.* Paris, Jul. 31, 1848; *d.* ib., Jan. 28, 1903. Comp. songs and light orch. pcs., and some 25 comic operas, incl., *The Chimes of Normandy* (Paris, 1877; London, 1878—705 perfs.); *Rip Van Winkle* (1881); *Nell Gwynne* (1884); and *Paul Jones* (1889).

Platania, Pietro. Composer; *b.* Catania, It., 1828; *d.* Naples, 1907. Comp. symph.

Pleyel (*Pli-el*), **Ignaz Joseph.** Composer; *b.* Ruppertsthal, nr. Vienna, Jun. 1, 1757; *d.* Paris, Nov. 14, 1831. 1792, persecuted by the revolutionists, he escaped (1795) to Paris, where (1807) he estab. the piano manufactory of Pleyel et Cie. He was later joined by Kalkbrenner (1824) and Chopin (1831). Comp. an opera, symph., chamb. mus., violin studies, and some duets for two violins that are still used.

Pochon, Alfred. Violinist; *b.* Lausanne, Switz. (Amer. citizen). Gr., Geneva Acad.; st., Liége Cons., Bel.; ed., writer, comp., soloist throughout Europe; 1903, mem. Flonzaley Quartet.

Podbertsky, Theodor. Composer; *b.* Munich, Ger., Nov. 16, 1846; *d.* ib., Oct. 5, 1913. Comp. male choruses.

Pohlig, Karl. Composer, conductor; *b.* Teplitz, Feb. 10, 1864. Asst. cond., Vienna State Op., *u.* Mahler; 1897, Kapellmeister, Coburg; 1900, dir., Stuttgart Op. and Symph.; 1907-1912, cond., Phila. Symph. Orch.; returned to Germany, cond., Hamburg Op.

Poise (*Pwahs*), **Jean Alexandre Ferdinand.** Composer; *b.* Nimes, Fr., Jun. 3, 1828; *d.* Paris, May 13, 1892. Prod. 15 operettas, incl., *Voisin.*

Polacco, Giorgio. Conductor; *b.* Venice, Apr. 12, 1875. Opera cond., Buenos Aires, Rio de Janeiro, La Scala, Milan; 1906, San Francisco; 1911, selected by Puccini to direct Savage prod. of *Girl of the Golden West;* 1915-1920, cond., Met. Op. H., N. Y.; 1920-30, cond., Chicago Op

Poldini (*Pol-dee-nee*), **Eduard.** Composer; *b.* Buda-Pesth, Hun., Jun. 13, 1869. Comp. fairy plays, the short comic opera, *Vagabond and Princess* (1903), and attractive salon pcs. for piano, incl., *Poupee Valsante.*

Pole, William. Writer, theorist; *b.* Birmingham, Eng., Apr. 22, 1814; *d.* London, Dec. 3, 1900. Wr. valuable wks. of a scientific character.

Polko, Elise née Vogel. Writer; *b.* Dresden, Jan. 13, 1822; *d.* Munich, May 15, 1899. Author of many historical wks. on mus.

Pollak, Egon. Conductor; *b.* Prague, May 3, 1879; *d.* ib., Jun. 14, 1933. 1905, cond., Bremen Stadtteater; 1910-1912, Leipzig; 1917, Frankfort; 1932, cond., Hamburg Op.

Polleri (*Pol-lay-ree*), **Giovanni Battista.** Organist, composer, teacher; *b.* Genoa, It., 1855. 1877-94, in U. S.; 1898, dir., Genoa Cons. Comp. masses, organ, pf. pcs.

Pollitzer, Adolf. Violinist; *b.* Pesth, 1832; *d.* London, 1900. 1861, *t.;* 1890, prin., London Acad. of Mus. Comp. violin concerto.

Pommer, William Henry. Composer, director; *b.* St. Louis, Mar. 22, 1851. 1907, dir. of mus., U. of Missouri. Comp. sonata for violin and piano; quintet for strings.

Ponchielli (*Pon-ke-el-lee*), **Amilcare.** Composer; *b.* Cremona, It., Aug. 31, 1834; *d.* Milan, Jan. 16, 1886. Comp. operas, incl., *La Gioconda* (1876), his best known work.

Pond, Silvanus Billings. Music publisher; *b.* Worcester, Mass., 1792; *d.* 1871. Piano maker in Albany. 1832, entered publishing business as Firth, Pond & Co., and became principal publisher of Stephen Foster songs; later Wm. A. Pond & Co.

Poniatowski (*Pon-ya-tof-ski*), **Prince Josef Michal Xavery Franciszek Jan.** Tenor, composer; *b.* Rome, Feb. 20, 1816; *d.* London, Jul. 4, 1873. 1848, Tuscan diplomat to Paris; 1870, followed Napoleon III to Eng. Comp. It. operas, songs in English.

Pons, Lily. Soprano; *b.* Cannes, Apr. 16, 1904. *p.* Paris Cons., 1st prize in piano at 16 years; actress; 1928, debut, Mulhouse (Fr.); 1931, debut, Met. Op., N. Y., in *Lucia.*

Ponselle, Carmela (family name **Ponzillo**). Mezzo-soprano; *b.* Schenectady, N. Y., Jun. 7, 1892. 1926, debut, Met. Op. as *Amneris* in *Aida;* active in radio.

Ponselle, Rosa Melba. Dramatic soprano; *b.* Meriden, Conn. Sister of Carmela P. 1918, debut, Met. Op. *w.* Caruso in *La Forza del Destino.*

Pontoglio (*Pon-tol-yo*), **Cipriano.** Composer; *b.* Grumello del Piano, It., Dec. 25, 1831; *d.* Milan, It., Feb. 23, 1892. Comp. operas.

Popoff, Ivan Gregorovitch. Composer; *b.* Ekaterinodar, Rus., 1859. 1900, dir., Stavropol (Caucasus) Mus. Sch. Comp. symph. mus., songs.

Popper, David. 'Cellist; *b.* Prague, Boh., Jun. 18, 1846; *d.* Aug. 7, 1913. 1868, solo 'cellist, Vienna Op. 1872, *m.* Sophie Menter, pianist. 1873, concert tours; 1896, prof., Natl. Acad., Pesth. Comp. 'cello wks., *études,* chamb. mus.

Porpora, Niccolo Antonio. Teacher, composer; *b.* Naples, It., Aug. 19, 1686; *d.* ib., Feb., 1766. Eminent as teacher and cond. Known as the fd. of the old It. sch. of *bel canto.* Haydn came under his influence. Comp. 50 operas, oratorios, chamb. mus.

Porter, Frank Addison. Pianist, teacher; b. Dixmont, Me., Sept. 13, 1859. 1884, t. N. E. Cons., Boston. Author of *Piano Course,* and text wks.

Posselt, Ruth. Violinist; b. Medford, Mass. 1923, debut, Carnegie Hall, N. Y.; frequent soloist w. major symphs.

Potter, Philip Cipriani Hambly. Pianist, composer; b. London, Oct. 2, 1792; d. ib., Sept. 26, 1871. 1832, prin., R. A. M. Comp. symph., chamb. mus., pf. pcs. Ed. Mozart wks.

Pottgiesser (*Pot-gee-ser*), **Karl.** Composer, writer; b. Dortmund, Ger., Aug. 8, 1861. Comp. operas, oratorios.

Pougin (*Poo-zhan*), **Arthur** [pen name of **François-Auguste Arthur Paroisse-Pougin**]. Writer, violinist; b. Châteauroux, Fr., Aug. 6, 1834; d. Paris, Aug. 8, 1921. Author of critical biographical, and historical wks.

Poulenc, Francis. Composer; b. Paris, Jan. 7, 1899. St., Ricardo Viñes. 1917, mem., "French Six"; *Rapsodie Nègre* intro. at Vieux Colombier. 1919, *Cocardes,* songs to poems by Jean Cocteau. Comp operatic wks., incl., *Le Gendarme Incompris;* chamb. mus., orch. and choral wks., pf. pcs., songs.

Poulet, Gaston. Conductor; b. Paris, Apr. 10, 1892. Fd. Poulet String Quartet; also Association des Concerts Poulet, which gives concerts at the Sarah Bernhardt Theatre, Paris.

Powell, John. Composer, pianist; b. Richmond, Va., Sept. 6, 1882. 1902, st., Leschetizky, Vienna. 1907, debut w. Vienna Tonkunstler. After tour, 1912 Amer. debut, Richmond; 1918, *Negro Rhapsody,* perf., Damrosch. h. Richmond. Comp. orch. and choral wks., chamb. mus., pf. pcs.

Powell, Maud. Violinist; b. Peru, Ill., Aug. 22, 1868; d. Jan. 8, 1920. One of the foremost women violinists of her time. 1904, m. H. Godfrey Turner, her manager.

Praetorius, Michael. Writer; b. Kreuzberg, Ger., Feb. 15, 1571; d. Wolfenbüttel, Feb. 15, 1621. Comp. *Syntagma Musicum.*

Präger (*Prayger*), **Ferdinand.** Pianist, teacher; b. Leipzig, Ger., Jan. 22, 1815; d. London, Sept. 1, 1891. 1831, Hague; 1834, London; corr., *Neu Zeitschrift;* a Wagner partisan. Comp. symph., chamb. mus. Author of much discussed *Wagner As I Knew Him* (1885).

Pratt, Harry Rogers. Music educator; b. Wellesley Hills, Mass., Jan. 7, 1886. 1905, gr. Harvard; 1905-6, N. E. Cons. 1891-1900, boy-soprano soloist; 1916-21, org., Hartford, Conn.; 1921-23, mus. dir., Lake Placid Fd.; 1923, t. U. of Virginia.

Pratt, Silas Gamaliel. Pianist, composer; b. Addison, Vt., Aug. 4, 1846; d. Pittsburgh, Pa., Dec., 1916. Comp. opera, *Zenobia;* cantatas, symph. mus.

Pratt, Waldo Selden. Organist, writer; b. Philadelphia, Nov. 10, 1857. Author of a *History of Music.*

Preyer, Carl Adolph. Composer; b. Pforzheim, Ger., Jul. 28, 1863. 1893, prof.; 1915, assoc. dean, Sch. Fine Arts, U. of Kansas. Comp. études, pf. pcs.

Price, Carl F. Organist, editor. b. New Brunswick, N. J., May 16, 1881. 1902, A.B., Wesleyan U.; 1927-1936, lect. on Hymnology, Drew U. Comp. hymn-tunes, anthems, cantatas. Edited hymn collections, incl., *Songs of Life, Hymns for Worship.* Author of books on hymnology, incl., *Curiosities of the Hymnal.*

Proch (*Prokh*), **Heinrich.** Teacher of singing, composer; b. Böhmisch-Leipa, Boh., Jul. 22, 1809; d. Vienna, Dec. 18, 1878. Comp. opera, operettas, songs., incl., the noted set of vocal variations w. flute obligato.

Prochazka, Rudolf, Freiherr von. Composer, writer; b. Prague, Boh., Feb. 23, 1864. Imperial Hauptmann for Prague district. Author of many books about mus. Comp. operas, songs, chamb. mus.

Prokofieff, Serge. Composer; b. Ekaterinoslav, Rus., Apr. 23, 1891. Prodigy at five; st., Glière; 1904-10, edu., St. Petersburg Cons. After revolution, sought refuge in London, U. S., Paris; 1921, opera, *Love of Three Oranges,* world première, Chicago Op. Comp. orch. wks., operas, ballets, choral and chamb. mus., pf. pcs., songs.

Proksch, Josef. Composer; b. Reichenberg, Boh., 1794; d. Prague, 1864. Fd. Sch. of Mus., Prague; succeeded by his son, Theodor (1843-76) and daughter, Marie (1836-1900). Comp. pf. wks. Author of text wks.

Proschowski, Frantz James Edward. Vocal teacher; b. Copenhagen, Jun. 29, 1868. 1886, to U. S.; 1921, fd. Sch. of Singing, Chicago; 1930, t. Chicago Mus. Coll. Author, text wks.

Protheroe, Daniel. Composer, conductor; b. Wales, Nov. 24, 1866; d. Chicago, Feb. 24, 1934. 1886, cond., Welsh Singer Societies in U. S. Comp. choruses, cantatas, symph. p., string quartets, ch. mus. Compiled hymnal for Welsh Presby. Ch., and Ritual Music for Scottish Rite.

Prout, Ebenezer. Composer, theorist; b. Oundle, Eng., Mar. 1, 1835; d. London, Dec. 5, 1909. 1871-74, ed., *Monthly Musical Record;* 1894, prof., Dublin U. Comp. chamb. mus., organ concerto, dramatic cantatas. Best known by his books on harmony, orchestration.

Prudent (*Proo-dong*), **Émile.** Pianist, composer; b. Angoulême, Fr., Apr. 3, 1817; d. Paris, May 13, 1863. Comp. salon pcs. for pf.

Prume, François Hubert. Violinist, composer; b. Stavelot, Bel., Jun. 3, 1816; d. Liége, Jul. 14, 1849. 1844, t. Liége Cons.; extensive tours. Comp. violin concertos and pcs., incl., 5 *études* w. orch. accomp.

Pruwer, Julius. Conductor; b. Vienna, Feb. 20, 1874. 1894-1896, cond., Cologne Op.; 1896, city dir. of mus., Breslau; 1907, toured Ger. w. Breslau forces in Richard Strauss' *Salomé;* 1925, cond. popular concerts of Berlin Phil.

Puccini (*Poot-chee-ne*), **Giacomo.** Composer; b. Lucca, It., Jun. 22, 1858; d. Nov. 29, 1924. Foremost of modern It. opera comp. Comp. operas, incl., *Le Villi* (1884), *Edgar* (1889), *Manon Lescaut* (1893), *La Bohême* (1896), *Tosca* (1900), *Madame Butterfly* (1904), and *The Girl of the Golden West* (New York, 1910), *La Condine* (1917), *Il Tabarro, Suor Angelica, Gianni Schicchi* (1918).

Puchalski (*Pu-khal-ski*), **Vladimir Viatcheslavitch.** Composer; b. Minsk, Rus., Apr. 2, 1848. Orch. comp. 1876-1913, dir., Kiev Cons.

Puchat (*Poo-kat*), **Max.** Composer; b. Breslau, Jan. 8, 1859; d. Karwendal Mts., 1919. 1903-05, cond., Milwaukee Musikverein; 1910, fd. own sch., Breslau. Comp. symph. p., chamb. mus.

Pugnani (*Poon-ya-nee*), **Gaetano.** Violinist, composer; b. Turin, It., Nov. 27, 1731; d. ib., Jun. 15, 1798. p. Tartini; taught Viotti. Comp. 7 operas, 9 violin concertos, many pcs., chamb. mus.

Pugni (*Poon-yee*), **Cesare.** Composer; *b.* Milan, It., 1805; *d.* Petrograd, Jan. 26, 1870. 1825, Milan; 1851, Petrograd. Comp. 10 operas, 300 ballets, 40 masses.

Pugno (*Poon-yo*), **Stéphane Raoul.** Pianist, composer; *b.* Montrouge, Fr., Jun. 23, 1852; *d.* Moscow, Rus., Jan. 3, 1914. 1892-1901, prof., Paris Cons.; 1897, toured extensively, incl., U. S. A sterling pianist. Comp. operas, comic operas, pf. pcs.

Purcell, Henry. Organist, composer; *b.* Westminster, Eng., 1658; *d.* ib., Nov. 21, 1695. One of a family of musicians. Edu., Chapel Royal. Org., Westminster Abbey. Wr. anthems while still a choir-boy. Comp. operas, incl., *Dido and Æneas, The Fairy Queen;* incid. mus. to plays; songs, sonatas, odes, ch. mus.

Pyne, James Kendrick. Organist; *b.* Bath, Eng., Feb. 5, 1852. Eminent recitalist. 1875, org., St. Mark's, Phila., but returned to Eng. as org. Manchester Cath. (1875-1908). His father: **John Kendrick P.** Organist; *b.* London, Aug. 21, 1810; *d.* ib., Mar. 2, 1893. His grandfather: **James Kendrick P.** Tenor; *b.* 1785; *d.* 1857.

Q

Quadflieg, Gerhard Jakob. Organist; *b.* nr. Aix, Ger., Sept. 27, 1854; *d.* Elberfeld, 1915. Comp. masses, motets, etc.

Quantz, Johann Joachim. Flutist, composer; *b.* Oberscheden, Ger., Jan. 30, 1697; *d.* Potsdam, Ger., Jul. 12, 1773. Taught Frederick the Great.

Quarles, James Thomas. Organist, music educator; *b.* St. Louis. *p.* Widor. *t.* Cornell U.; 1923; *t.* U. of Missouri; 1924, fd.-dean, Sch. Fine Arts, U. of Missouri.

Quilter, Roger. Composer; *b.* Brighton, Eng., Nov. 1, 1877. Comp. orch. *Serenade,* songs.

R

Raabe, Peter. Conductor, writer; *b.* Frankfort, Nov. 27, 1872. 1907, cond., Weimar; 1920, cond., Aix-la-Chappelle; 1935, pres., Reich Mus. Chamb., succ. Richard Strauss. Author of wks. regarding Liszt.

Rabaud, Henri Benjamin. Conductor, composer; *b.* Paris, Nov. 10, 1873. *p.* Massenet. 1894-1918, cond., Paris Op.; 1918-20, cond., Boston Symph. Orch.; 1920, dir., Paris Conservatoire. Comp. operas, incl., *Marouf* (1911), symph. mus.

Rachmaninoff, Sergei Vassilievitch. Pianist, conductor, composer; *b.* Novgorod, Rus., Apr. 2, 1873. 1912, dir., Mamontov Op., and Royal Op., Moscow. Comp. many orch. wks., pf. pcs., and songs. His symph. p., *Isle of the Dead,* after the Bocklin picture, is in the repertoire of all the leading orchs.; his popular fame rests on the celebrated *Prelude in C-sharp Minor* for pf. Following the Rus. Revolution, he sought domicile in New York. A world-renowned pf. virtuoso. *d.* March 28, 1943.

Radecke, Albert Martin Robert. Composer; *b.* Dittmansdorf, Ger., Oct. 31, 1830; *d.* Wernigerode, Ger., Jun., 1911. Comp. symph., chamb. mus.

Radeglia (*Ra-del-ya*), **Vittorio.** Composer; *b.* Constantinople, 1863. It. opera comp.

Radoux (*Rah-doo*), **Charles.** Composer; *b.* Liége, Bel., Jul. 30, 1877. Son of J. T. R. 1900, *t.* Liége Cons. Comp. opera *Oudelette,* choral wks., instr. pcs.

Radoux, Jean Théodore. Composer; *b.* Liége, Bel., Nov. 9, 1835; *d.* ib., Mar. 20, 1911. 1872, dir., Liége Cons. Comp. operas.

Raff, Joseph Joachim. Composer; *b.* Lachen, Ger., May 27, 1822; *d.* Frankfort, Ger., Jun. 25, 1882. Assoc. of Liszt, and von Bülow. 1877, dir., Frankfort Cons. Comp. five symph., incl., *Im Walde* and *Lenore;* operas, overtures, chamb. mus., songs. Known to every violinist by his *Cavatina.*

Raif (*Rife*), **Oscar.** Pianist, teacher; *b.* Zwolle, Hol., Jul. 31, 1847; *d.* Berlin, Jul. 29, 1899. Eminent teacher. Comp. piano concerto.

Raisa, Rosa. Prima donna soprano; *b.* Bialystok, Pol., May 30, 1893. St., Naples Cons., w. Mme. Marchesi. 1913, debut, La Scala; 1914, Chicago Op.; 1925, chosen by Puccini to create rôle of *Turandot* at La Scala.

Rameau, Jean Philippe. Theorist, composer; *b.* Dijon, Fr., Sept. 25, 1683; *d.* Paris, Sept. 12, 1764. An eminent theorist who did much for the science of modern harmony. Comp. operas, ballets.

Randegger, Alberto. Teacher of singing, composer; *b.* Trieste, It., Apr. 13, 1832; *d.* London, Dec. 17, 1911. Comp. operas, cantatas, songs.

Randegger, Giuseppe Aldo. Pianist, composer, teacher; *b.* Naples, It., Feb. 17, 1874. Fd. Randegger Cons., N. Y. C., and Randegger Trio. Comp. opera, orch. wks., pf. pcs., songs.

Randolph, Harold. Pianist, organist; *b.* Richmond, Va., Oct. 31, 1861. 1885, *t.*; 1898, dir., Peabody Cons., Baltimore, Md.

Rapee, Erno. Conductor; *b.* Budapest, Jun. 4, 1891. 1926, cond., Roxy Theatre; 1934, cond., Radio City Theatres.

Rappoldi, Edouard. Violinist, teacher; *b.* Vienna, Feb. 21, 1839; *d.* Dresden, May 16, 1903.

Ratez, Émile Pierre. Conductor, composer; *b.* Besançon, Fr., Jan. 5, 1851; *d.* Lille, Fr., 1905. 1891, head, Lille Mus. Sch. Comp. operas, concertos.

Rath (*Raht*), **Felix von.** Composer; *b.* Cologne, Ger., Jun. 17, 1866; *d.* Munich, Ger., Aug. 25, 1905. Comp. concerto, pf. pcs.

Rathaus, Karol. Composer; *b.* Tarnopol, Pol., Sept. 16, 1895. St., Franz Schreker in Vienna and Berlin. 1927, opera, *Der Letzte Pierrot,* prod., Berlin State Op.; 1931, *Fremde Erde,* prod. Berlin State Op. Comp. opera, orch. wks., choral, chamb. mus.

Rauchenecker (*Rouk-en-eck-er*), **Georg Wilhelm.** Violinist, composer; *b.* Munich, Mar. 8, 1844; *d.* Jul. 17, 1906. Comp. operas, incl., *Don Quixote;* symph., chamb. mus.

Ravel, Maurice. Pianist, composer; *b.* Ciboure, Fr., Mar. 7, 1875. Edu., Paris Cons. 1910, *L'Heure Espagnole,* prod., Opéra Comique. Comp. *Scheherezade* overture, suite *La Mere l'Oye,* in modern radical style. Popularly known by *Bolero,* for orch.

Ravina (*Rah-vee-na*), **Jean Henri.** Pianist, composer; *b.* Bordeaux, Fr., May 20, 1818; *d.* Paris, Sept. 30, 1906. *t.* Paris. Comp. salon pcs. for piano.

Raway, Erasme. Composer; *b.* Liége, Bel., 1850; *d.* ib., 1918. Comp. operas, symph. mus.

Reber (*Ray-bair*), **Napoléon Henri.** Composer, theorist; *b.* Mühlhausen, Alsace, Oct. 21, 1807; *d.* Paris, Nov. 24, 1880. Comp. symph., chamb. mus., operas, songs.

Rebicek (*Reb-i-chek*), **Josef.** Violinist, conductor, composer; *b.* Prague, Boh., Feb. 7, 1844; *d.* Berlin, Mar. 24, 1904. 1897-1903, cond., Berlin Phil. Orch. Comp. orch., violin mus.

Rebikoff, Vladimir Ivanovitch. Composer; *b.* Krasnojarsk, Sib., Jun. 1, 1866. Comp. operas, melodramas, pf. wks.

Redman, Harry Newton. Composer; *b.* Illinois, 1869. Comp. sonatas, quartets, pf. pcs., songs.

Reed, Clare Osborne (Mrs. Charles B. Reed). Music educator; *b.* Plymouth, Ind. A.B., Chicago Mus. Coll. *p.* Leschetizky. 1901-30, fd.-dir., Columbia Sch. of Mus., Chicago.

Reed, William Henry. Conductor, violinist, teacher; *b.* Frome, Eng., Jul. 29, 1877. Comp. *Suite Venétienne.*

Reeves, John Sims. Tenor; *b.* Woolwich, Eng., Sept. 26, 1818; *d.* Worthing, Eng., Oct. 25, 1900. Leading English oratorio and ballad singer of his epoch. 1896, toured South Africa.

Reger (*Ray-ger*), **Max.** Composer; *b.* Brand, Ger., Mar. 19, 1873; *d.* Jena, Ger., May 11, 1916. Comp. organ, chamb. mus., and orch. wks. One of the most skilled contrapuntists and virile modernists of the German sch. A large output of wks. in all forms except opera.

Rehberg (*Ray-bairg*), **Willi.** Pianist, composer; *b.* Morges, Switz., Sept. 2, 1863. 1907, *t.* Hoch Cons., Frankfort, Ger.; 1921, dir., Basel Cons. Comp. violin sonata, and pf. sonatas.

Reicha, Anton Joseph. Theorist, composer; *b.* Prague, Boh., Feb. 27, 1770; *d.* Paris, May 28, 1836.

Reichardt (*Rike-hart*), **Alexander.** Tenor, composer; *b.* Packs, Hun., Apr. 17, 1825; *d.* Boulogne, Fr., Mar. 14, 1855.

Reichardt, Johann F. Composer, writer; *b.* Königsberg, Ger., Nov. 25, 1752; *d.* Halle, Ger., Jun. 27, 1814.

Reichardt, Louise. Composer, teacher of singing; *b.* Berlin, 1778; *d.* Hamburg, Nov. 17, 1826. Comp. excellent songs, incl., *In the Time of Roses.*

Reichwein, Leopold. Conductor, composer; *b.* Breslau, Ger., May 16, 1878. 1913, cond., Vienna Op. Comp. operas.

Reinecke, Carl Heinrich Carsten. Composer, conductor; *b.* Altona, Ger., Jun. 23, 1824; *d.* Leipzig, Mar. 10, 1910. 1860, cond., Gewandhaus, Leipzig; dir., Leipzig Cons.

Reiner, Fritz. Conductor; *b.* Pesth, Dec. 19, 1888. 1909, chorusmaster, Pesth Komische Op.; 1911-1914, cond., Volksoper; 1914-1921, cond., Dresden Op.; 1922-1931, cond., Cin. Symph. Orch.; g.-cond., Rome, Phila., Los Angeles; g.-cond., Phila. Op.

Reinhardt, Heinrich. Operetta composer; *b.* Pressburg, Apr. 13, 1865. Mus. critic, *Neues Wiener Journal;* known by his one successful work, *The Spring Maid* (Vienna, 1901; Boston, 1910). Comp. several other operettas.

Reinhold, Hugo. Composer; *b.* Vienna, Mar. 3, 1854. Prof., Vienna Academie. Comp. orch., chamb. mus., pf. pcs.

Reinthaler (*Rine-tahl-er*), **Carl Martin.** Composer, organist; *b.* Erfurt, Ger., Oct. 13, 1822; *d.* Bremen, Feb. 13, 1896.

Reisenauer (*Ryz-en-ow-er*), **Alfred.** Pianist; *b.* Königsberg, Ger., Nov. 1, 1863; *d.* Libau, Rus., Oct. 31, 1907. *p.* Liszt. Virtuoso pianist. Many world tours, incl., U. S.

Reiser, Alois. Composer; *b.* Prague, 1884. 1905, to U. S. Comp. tone-poems, *Triton, Summer Evening; Slavic Rhapsody* for orch.; opera, *Gobi;* chamb. mus.

Reissiger, Karl Gottlieb. Composer, conductor; *b.* nr. Wittenberg, Ger., Jan. 31, 1798; *d.* Dresden, Ger., Nov. 7, 1859. Comp. chamb. mus.; facile, but lacking in originality.

Reissmann, August. Writer, composer; *b.* Frankenstein, Ger., Nov. 14, 1825; *d.* Berlin, Dec. 1, 1903. Orch. comp.

Reiter (*Ry-ter*), **Josef.** Composer; *b.* Austrian Tyrol, Jan. 19, 1862. Comp. symph., overtures.

Rellstab, Heinrich F. L. Writer; *b.* Berlin, Apr. 13, 1799; *d.* ib., Nov. 27, 1860.

Remenyi, Eduard. Violinist; *b.* Miskolcz, Hun., Jul. 17, 1830; *d.* San Francisco, Cal., May 15, 1898. One of the most noted artists of his time. 1851, first visit to U. S.

Remy, Alfred. Musicologist; *b.* Elberfeld, Ger., Mar. 16, 1870. 1905, A.M., Columbia U., N. Y. 1895-7, mus. critic, *Vogue;* prof., Greek, Ger.

Renaud, Albert. Composer; *b.* Paris, 1855. Orch. and opera comp.

Renaud, Maurice Arnold. Baritone; *b.* Bordeaux, Fr., 1862; *d.* Paris, Oct. 16, 1933. Eminent in opera, and Wagner's dramas in French. 1906-10, Intro. to N. Y. by Oscar Hammerstein at Manhattan Op.

Rendano, Alfonso. Composer; *b.* Carolei, It., Apr. 5, 1853; *d.* Rome, 1931. Comp. operas, piano pcs.

Respighi, Ottorino. Composer; *b.* Bologna, It., Jul. 9, 1879. Edu., Liceo, *u.* Martucci; also Rimsky-Korsakoff, St. Petersburg. 1913, *t.* Liceo Reale di S. Cecilia, Rome, succ. Enrico Bossi as principal. Comp. *Trilogy* for orch., perf. Toscanini; operas, incl., *Semirama;* suite for strings and organ; chamb. mus.

Rethberg, Elizabeth. Soprano; *b.* Schwarzenberg, Saxony. St., Royal Cons. of Mus. 1922, debut at Met. Op. H., as *Aida.*

Reuss (*Royse*), **August.** Composer; *b.* Liliendorf, Aus., Mar. 6, 1871. Comp. chamb. mus., opera, orch. wks., songs.

Reuss, Eduard. Pianist; *b.* New York, 1851; *d.* Dresden, Ger., Feb. 18, 1911. *p.* Liszt. Author, Liszt biography.

Reuter, Rudolph Ernest. Pianist; *b.* N. Y. C. Edu., Royal Acad. Mus., Berlin. 1909, won Mendelssohn prize. 1910, debut, Hamburg Symph. Orch.; 1910-1913, prof. Imperial Acad. Mus., Tokyo; 1913-1921, *t.* Chicago Mus. Coll.

Reyer (*Ray-er*), **Louis Étienne Ernest.** Composer; *b.* Marseilles, Fr., Jan. 1, 1823; *d.* Toulon, Fr., Jan. 15, 1909. Comp. operas, incl., *Salammbô.*

Reznicek (*Rezh-ni-chek*), **Emil Nikolaus von.** Composer; *b.* Vienna, May 4, 1861. St., Leipzig Cons. *u.* Jadassohn and Reinecke. 1894, opera, *Donna Diana,* prod., Prague; 1931, *Dance Symphony,* intro., by Kleiber, in N. Y.; 1920, *t.* Berlin Hochschule. Comp. operas, incl., *Till Eulenspiegel;* the radical symph. p., *Schlemihl;* also chamb. mus.

Rheinberger, Joseph Gabriel. Organist, composer; *b.* Vaduz, Ger., Mar. 17, 1839; *d.* Munich, Ger., Nov. 25, 1901. 1859, prof., Munich Cons., and taught many famous Amer. pupils. Comp. a large volume of wks. in all forms, but many of his organ and chamb. mus. wks. are still played.

Rhene-Baton. Composer, conductor; *b.* Courseulles-sur-mer, Calvados, Sept. 5, 1879. 1910, cond., French mus. fest. at Munich; 1912, cond., Diaghilev Ballet, in London, Paris and South Amer.; 1918-1923, cond., Pasdeloup concerts, Paris.

Rhys-Herbert, William. Organist, teacher, composer; *b.* Wales, Oct. 3, 1868; *d.* Chicago, Oct. 3, 1921. Comp. operettas for schs.; songs, cantatas.

Ricci (*Rit-chie*), **Luigi.** Composer; *b.* Naples, It., Jun. 8, 1805; *d.* Prague, Boh., Dec. 31, 1859. **Federico.** Composer; *b.* Naples, It., Oct. 22, 1809; *d.* Conegliano, It., Dec. 10, 1877. Two brothers who comp. operas, separately, and together; their best success was *Crispino e Comare.*

Richards, Henry Brinley. Pianist, composer; *b.* Camarthen, Wales, Nov. 13, 1817; *d.* London, May 1, 1885. Comp. salon mus.

Richards, Lewis Loomis. Pianist; *b.* St. Johns, Mich., Apr. 11, 1881. Edu., Roy. Cons. Mus., Brussels. 1927, *t.* Mich. State Coll.; dir., Mich. State Inst. Mus. and Applied Arts.

Richardson, Alfred Madeley. Organist, composer, writer; *b.* Southend, Jun. 1, 1868. Edu., Oxford. Cond., Worcester Orch. Soc.; *t.* Juilliard Sch. of Mus., N. Y. Author of *Fundamental Counterpoint,* and other theoretical and aesthetic wks.

Richter, Ernst Friedrich Eduard. Theorist, composer; *b.* Gross Schönau, Ger., Oct. 24, 1808; *d.* Leipzig, Ger., Apr. 9, 1879. After holding various other appointments was made cantor of the Thomasschule at Leipzig. Widely known as a theorist.

Richter, Hans. Conductor; *b.* Raab, Hun., Apr. 4, 1843; *d.* Bayreuth, Ger., Dec. 5, 1916. Cond. famous Richter Concerts in London; also Bayreuth Festivals.

Riedel (*Ree-del*), **Fürchtegott Ernst August.** Conductor, composer; *b.* Chemnitz, Ger., May 22, 1855. 1888, dir., Musikverein, Plauen. Cantata comp.

Riegger, Wallingfort. Composer; *b.* Albany, Ga., Apr. 29, 1885. 1907, gr., Inst. Mus. Art; st., Berlin Hochschule; identified *w.* modern mus.; ISCM; active Yaddo festivals; 1929, *Study in Sonority,* intro., Stokowski w. Phila. Orch. Comp. orch., chamb. mus., pf. pcs.

Riemann (*Ree-man*), **Karl Wilhelm Julius Hugo.** Writer, historian; *b.* Grossmehlra, Ger., Jul. 18, 1849; *d.* Leipzig, 1919. Most prolific of Ger. writers on mus. Author of *Dictionary of Music and Musicians.*

Riemenschneider, Albert. Organist, conductor; *b.* Berea, O., Aug. 31, 1878. *p.* Widor. Dir., Baldwin Wallace Cons. Mus.; cond., master class at Balboa Park.

Riemenschneider, Georg. Organist, conductor, composer; *b.* Stralsund, Ger., Apr. 1, 1848; *d.* Breslau, 1913. 1889-98, cond., Breslau Orch. Comp. opera, orch., organ, pf., wks.

Ries (*Rees*), **Ferdinand.** Pianist, composer; *b.* Bonn, Ger., Nov. 29, 1784; *d.* Frankfort, Ger., Jan. 13, 1838. *p.* Beethoven; also, son of Franz Anton R., the teacher of Beethoven. Prolific comp. in all forms, but not greatly inspired.

Ries, Franz. Composer, violinist; *b.* Berlin, Apr. 7, 1846; *d.* Naumberg, Thuringia, Jun. 20, 1932. Gave up strain of virtuoso career to become mem. of the firm of Ries & Erler, Berlin mus. publishers. One of his four suites for violin and pf. is known to every violinist. Comp. chamb. mus., songs.

Rieti, Vittorio. Composer; *b.* Alexandria, Egypt, Jan. 28, 1898. 1924, Concerto for Wind and Orch., intro. by Casella at Prague. 1925, *Barabau* ballet, prod., London, *u.* Diaghilev. Since 1925, Rome and Paris, his two homes. Comp. orch. wks., ballet, opera, chamb. mus.

Riga (*Ree-ga*), **François.** Composer; *b.* Liége, Jan. 21, 1831; *d.* Brussels, Jan. 18, 1892. Comp. male chorus mus.

Righini (*Re-ghee-nee*), **Vincenzo.** Composer, conductor; *b.* Bologna, It., Jan. 22, 1756; *d.* ib., Aug. 19, 1812. Comp. 20 operas, and other vocal and chamb. mus.

Rimbault, Edward Francis. Organist, writer; *b.* London, Jun. 13, 1816; *d.* ib., Sept. 26, 1876. Eminent ed. of collections of sacred and secular writings.

Rimini, Giacomo. Baritone; *b.* Verona, It. 1917, Chicago Op. Co.

Rimski-Korsakoff, Nicolai Andreievitch. Composer; *b.* Tikhvin, Rus., Mar. 18, 1844; *d.* Petrograd, Jun. 21, 1908. Eminent Rus. comp. Comp. operas, incl., *The Snow Maiden* (1882), *Le Coq d'Or* (1910); also suite-symph., incl., *Antar, Scheherezade;* chamb. mus., songs.

Rinck, Johann Christian Heinrich. Organist, composer; *b.* Elgersburg, Ger., Feb. 18, 1770; *d.* Darmstadt, Aus. 7, 1846. Author of a famous book of instruction in organ-playing.

Riseley, George. Organist, conductor; *b.* Bristol, Eng., Aug. 28, 1845. 1893, *t.* R. A. M.; cond., orch. and choral societies.

Ritter, Alexander. Violinist; *b.* Narva, Rus., Jun. 27, 1833; *d.* Munich, Ger., Apr. 12, 1896. Comp. operas, symph. p.; influenced Richard Strauss toward modernism.

Ritter, Frederic Louis. Teacher; *b.* Strassburg, Alsace, Jun. 22, 1834; *d.* Antwerp, Bel., Jul. 22, 1891. 1874, prof., Vassar Coll.

Ritter, Théodore (properly **Bennet**). Pianist; *b.* Paris, Apr. 5, 1841; *d.* ib., Apr. 6, 1886. *p.* Liszt. Comp. salon mus.

Rivé-King, Julie. Pianist; *b.* Cincinnati, O., Oct. 31, 1857. *p.* Liszt. Distinguished concert pianist.

Robeson, Paul. Concert singer, actor; *b.* Princeton, N. J., Apr. 9, 1898. Edu., Columbia U. 1923, in *Emperor Jones;* also in *Black Boy, Porgy,* and *All God's Chillun.*

Robyn, Alfred George. Organist, composer; *b.* St. Louis, Mo., Jun. 29, 1860; *d.* N. Y., 1935. Comp. mus. comedies, songs.

Rochlitz, Johann Friedrich. Writer; *b.* Leipzig, Ger., Feb. 12, 1769; *d.* ib., Dec. 16, 1842. His correspondence *w.* Goethe pub., 1887.

Rockstro, William Smyth. Writer; *b.* North Cheam, Eng., Jan. 5, 1823; *d.* London, Jul. 2, 1895. Historian; an authority on ecclesiastical mus.

Rode, Jacques Pierre Joseph. Violinist; *b.* Bordeaux, Fr., Feb. 16, 1774; *d.* Damazon, Fr., Nov. 25, 1830. Known for his *études* for violin.

Rodgers, Richard. Musical comedy composer; *b.* N. Y., 1902. Edu., Columbia U. Of several mus. comedies, his greatest success was *A Connecticut Yankee* (1927), based on a Mark Twain story.

Rodrigo, Joaquin. Composer; *b.* Sagunto, Sp., Dec. 22, 1902. 1918, gr., Valencin Coll. for the Blind. 1927, *p.* Paul Dukas. 1934, orch. work, *For the Flower of the Blue Lily,* perf., Madrid Symph. Orch.; 1935, id. Amer. première by Iturbi at Stadium, N. Y.; 1935, prof. mus. hist., Madrid Natl. Coll. for the Blind, and awarded traveling fellowship by Acad. de Bellas Artes.

Rodzinski, Artur. Conductor; *b.* Spalato, Dalmatia, 1894. 1925-9, asst. cond. *w.* Phila. Symph., *u.* Stokowski; 1929-1933, cond., Los Angeles Phil.; 1933, cond., Cleveland Symph. Orch. Prod. in Cleveland, Shostakowitch opera, *Lady Macbeth of Mzenzk.*

Roeckel, Joseph Leopold. Composer; *b.* London, Apr. 11, 1838; *d.* 1908. Used pseudonym, Edward Dorn. Comp. songs, piano pcs.

Roeder, Carl M. Pianist, teacher; *b.* N. Y. C., 1870. *p.* Harold Bauer. *t.* Juilliard Graduate Sch.; mus. dir., Barrington Sch. for Girls.

Roeder (*Ray-der*), **Martin.** Composer, teacher of singing; *b.* Berlin, Apr. 7, 1851; *d.* Cambridge, Mass., Jun. 10, 1895. Comp. operas, incl., *Vera;* symph. p., songs.

Roentgen (*Rent-ghen*), **Julius.** Pianist, conductor, composer; *b.* Leipzig, Ger., May 9, 1855. 1885, co-fd.; 1913, dir., Amsterdam Cons. Comp. symph., concertos.

Roger-Ducasse, Jean Jules Amable. Composer; *b.* Bordeaux, Fr., Apr. 18, 1875. 1892, ent., Paris Cons.; 1897-1903, st., Faure. *h.* Paris. *t.* Parisian schs. and Cons. Comp. orch. wks., opera, chamb. mus., piano pcs., songs.

Rogers, Bernard. Composer; *b.* New York, 1893. Edu., Inst. of Mus. Art, N. Y. *p.* Ernest Bloch. Guggenheim Fellowship; Pulitzer Scholarship; Eastman Publication Subsidy; *t.* of comp., Eastman Sch. of Mus., Rochester. Comp. symph. wks., incl., *Adonais* and *To the Fallen;* also chamb. mus.

Rogers, Clara Kathleen. Operatic soprano, writer; *b.* Cheltenham, Eng., Jan. 14, 1844; *d.* Apr. 8, 1931. 1871, to U. S. Author of books on the voice and singing. Comp. violin sonata, songs and pf. pcs.

Rogers, James Hotchkiss. Composer, critic; *b.* Fairhaven, Conn., Feb. 7, 1857. *p.* Widor. 1883-1932, org., Unitarian Ch., and Euclid Ave. Temple, Cleveland; critic, Cleveland *Plain Dealer;* 1932, retired to California. Comp. cantatas, organ sonatas, pf. pcs., chorus, anthems, and songs.

Romaniello, Luigi. Pianist; *b.* Naples, 1860; *d.* Buenos Ayres, 1917. Comp. orch., pf. pcs., incl., *Pene d'Amore.*

Romberg, Andreas Jakob. Violinist, composer; *b.* Vechta, Ger., Apr. 27, 1767; *d.* Gotha, Ger., Nov. 10, 1821. Comp. operas, symph., choral wks. *w.* orch.

Ronald, Sir Landon (properly **Russell**). Composer, pianist, conductor; *b.* London, Jun. 7, 1873. Accompanist for Melba. Since 1908, cond. of Royal Albert Hall Orch.; 1910, prin., Guild Hall Sch. Comp. of many songs, incl., *Down in the Forest.*

Root, George Frederick. Composer, teacher; *b.* Sheffield, Mass., 1820; *d.* Bailey's Island, Me., Aug. 6, 1895. 1853, after study in Europe, joined Lowell Mason's Sch., N. Y.; 1859, joined Root & Cady, Chicago mus. publ.; 1872, dir. mus., Chicago U. Wr. Amer. Civil War songs, incl., *Battle Cry of Freedom.*

Ropartz, Joseph Guy Marie. Composer, writer; *b.* Guingamp, Fr., Jun. 15, 1864. Comp. orch., chamb. mus.

Rore (*Ro-re*), **Cipriano de.** Composer; *b.* Malines, Bel., 1516; *d.* Parma, Sept., 1565. Comp. madrigals, motets.

Rosa, Carl August Nicolas (Karl Rose). Impresario; *b.* Hamburg, Ger., Mar. 21, 1842; *d.* Paris, Apr. 30, 1889. Appeared in public as violinist when eight years old. 1867, *m.* Euphrosyne Parepa. Fd. Carl Rosa Opera Co., giving English versions of foreign operas.

Rosellen, Henri. Pianist, composer; *b.* Paris, Oct. 13, 1811; *d.* ib., Mar. 18, 1876. Comp. salon mus.

Rosenfeld, Leopold. Composer; *b.* Copenhagen, Den., Jul. 21, 1850; *d.* ib., Jul. 19, 1909. Comp. choral wks., pf., violin pcs., songs.

Rosenhain (*Ro-sen-hine*), **Jacob.** Pianist; *b.* Mannheim, Ger., Dec. 2, 1813; *d.* Baden-Baden, Ger., Mar. 21, 1894. Comp. salon mus.

Rosenthal (*Ro-sen-tahl*), **Moritz.** Pianist; *b.* Lemberg, Aus., Dec. 18, 1862. Celebrated virtuoso. Five tours to U. S., 1887, 1896, 1898, 1906, 1923.

Ross, Hugh. Conductor; *b.* Langport, Eng., Aug. 21, 1898. 1921, g.-cond., London and Oxford; 1932, cond., Winnipeg Male Choir; g.-cond., Minneapolis Symph. Orch.; 1927, cond., Schola Cantorum, New York.

Rossini (*Ros-see-nee*), **Gioachino Antonio.** Composer; *b.* Pesaro, It., Feb. 29, 1792; *d.* Paris, Nov. 13, 1868. From the production of *Tancredi* in 1813, which marked the beginning of Rossini's European reputation, to 1829, he wr. a succession of brilliantly successful operas, finishing his career as an operatic comp. *w. William Tell,* his best work. His only comp. thereafter was his *Stabat Mater.*

Roth, Philip. Composer, music teacher; *b.* probably in Germany; *d.* Phila., 1804. 1771, appeared in concert in Phila., for benefit of John M'Lean. The claim that he wr. the *President's March* is unverified.

Rothier, Leon. Basso; *b.* Rheims, Fr., Dec. 26, 1874. St., Natl. Cons. Mus., Paris. 1910, Met. Op. H.

Rothwell, Walter Henry. Composer, conductor; *b.* London, Sept. 22, 1872; *d.* Los Angeles, Mar. 13, 1927. 1905-1907, asst. cond., Hamburg Op., *u.* Mahler; toured U. S. *w.* Savage Op.; 1908-1915, cond., St. Paul Symph. Orch.; 1917, g.-cond., Cincinnati, Detroit; 1919, cond., Los Angeles Phil.

Rotoli, Augusto. Composer, teacher of singing; *b.* Rome, Jan. 7, 1847; *d.* Boston, Nov. 26, 1904. 1885, *t.* N. E. Cons.; 1896, ch. mus., St. James. Comp. a mass, many songs.

Rouget de Lisle (*Roo-zhay du Leel*), **Claude Joseph.** Composer; *b.* Lons-le-Saulnier, Fr., May 10, 1760; *d.* Choisy-le-Roi, Fr., Jun. 26, 1836. An officer of engineers. Comp. songs, incl., *The Marseillaise.*

Rousseau (*Roos-soh*), **Jean Jacques.** Theorist, writer; *b.* Geneva, Switz., Jun. 28, 1712; *d.* Paris, Sept. 3, 1778. Comp. operas, songs.

Rousseau, Samuel Alexandre. Composer; *b.* Neuve-Maison, Fr., Jun. 11, 1853; *d.* Paris, Oct. 1, 1904. Comp. operas, masses, psalms.

Roussel (*Roos-sel*), **Albert Charles Paul.** Composer, teacher; *b.* Turcoing, Fr., Apr. 5, 1869. 1902-14, *t.* Schola Cantorum, Paris. Comp. symph., chamb. mus., songs.

Rowbotham, John Frederick. Writer; *b.* Edinburgh, Scot., Apr. 18, 1854. Author of mus. histories and biographies.

Roze, Marie Hippolyte (née Ponsin). Soprano; *b.* Paris, Mar. 2, 1846; *d.* ib., Jul., 1926. 1877-80, toured U. S. 1877, *m.* Henry Mapleson. A famous *Carmen.* 1883-9, mem., Carl Rosa Op. Co.

Rozkosny, Joseph Richard. Pianist, composer; *b.* Prague, Boh., Sept. 22, 1833. Comp. operas, piano pcs., songs.

Rôzycki, Ludomir von. Conductor, teacher, composer; *b.* Warsaw, Pol., 1833. 1908-18, cond., Lemberg Op. Comp. operas, symph. p.

Rubini (*Roo-bee-nee*), **Giovanni Battista.** Tenor; *b.* Romano, It., Apr. 7, 1795; *d.* Mar. 2, 1854. Celebrated opera singer. Sang *u.* Rossini. Toured *w.* Liszt.

Rubinstein, Anton Gregorovitch. Pianist, composer; *b.* Wechwotynecz, Rus., Nov. 28, 1829; *d.* Petrograd, Nov. 20, 1894. Famous concert virtuoso. 1872, visited U. S.; 1862, fd.-dir., Petrograd Cons. As a pianist considered second only to Liszt. Comp. symph., operas, piano concertos, chamb. mus., songs and piano pcs.

Rubinstein, Nikolai Gregorovitch. Pianist; *b.* Moscow, Rus., Jun. 2, 1835; *d.* Paris, Mar. 23, 1881. Dir., Moscow Cons. An excellent artist, but, owing to his distaste for travel, little known outside of Rus. Assoc. *w.* Tschaikowsky.

Rückauf (*Rick-ouf*), **Anton.** Composer; *b.* Prague, Boh., Mar. 13, 1855; *d.* Schloss Alt-Erlaa, Aus., Sept. 19, 1903. Comp. opera, chamb. wks.

Rudersdorff, Hermine. Soprano, teacher of singing; *b.* Ivanovski, Rus., Dec. 12, 1822; *d.* Boston, Feb. 26, 1882. 1871-2, sang at Boston Peace Jubilees; *t.* Boston. *m.* Maurice Mansfield. Mother of Richard M. (1857-1907), the actor.

Rudhyar, Dane. Composer; *b.* Paris, Mar., 1895. 1911, gr. Sorbonne. Author of *Debussy and the Cycle of Musical Civilization* (1911), and biography of *Debussy* (1913). 1916, to U. S. *Dance Poems,* prod., Met. Op. Comp. orch. wks., piano pcs., songs.

Rudnick, Wilhelm. Organist, composer; *b.* Damerkow, Ger., Dec. 30, 1850. Comp. oratorios, organ pcs.

Rudorff, Ernst Friedrich Karl. Conductor, composer; *b.* Berlin, Jan. 18, 1840. Comp. orch., pf. wks.

Ruefer (*Reef-er*), **Philippe.** Pianist, composer; *b.* Liége, Bel., Jun. 7, 1844. *t.* Stern Cons., Berlin. Orch. comp.

Ruegger (*Ree-ger*), **Elsa.** 'Cellist; *b.* Lucerne, Switz., Dec. 6, 1881; *d.* Chicago, Feb. 19, 1924. 1899, toured U. S. 1909, *m.* Edmund Lichtenstein, violinist.

Rueter (*Ree-ter*), **Hugo.** Composer, teacher of singing; *b.* Hamburg, Ger., Sept. 7, 1859. 1897, cond., Matthias-Claudius Gymnasium, Hamburg. Comp. operas, chamb. mus., songs.

Ruffo (*Roof-fo*), **Titta.** Baritone; *b.* Pisa, It., 1877. A notable singing actor. 1912, Chicago Op.

Ruggieri (*Rood-jya-ree*), **John Baptist.** Violin-maker; *b.* Cremona, It., 1700; *d. c.* 1725.

Ruggles, Carl. Composer; *b.* Mass., 1876. Edu., Harvard, *u.* Spalding. Comp. orch. wks., incl., *Men and Angels.*

Rumford, R. H. Kennerly. Baritone; *b.* London, Sept. 2, 1870. Popular ballad singer. 1900, *m.* Clara Butt, contralto. 1913, toured U. S. in joint recitals.

Rummel (*Room-mel*), **Franz.** Pianist; *b.* London, Jan. 11, 1853; *d.* Berlin, May 3, 1901. 1878, 1886, 1898, toured Amer. at Rubinstein's suggestion. *m.* daughter of S. F. B. Morse, inventor of the telegraph.

Rummel, Walter Morse. Composer; *b.* Berlin, Jul. 19, 1887. Son of Franz R. Comp. chamb. mus., pf. pcs., songs.

Runciman, John F. Writer; *b.* England, 1866; *d.* London, Apr. 11, 1916. 1894, mus. critic, London *Saturday Review.* Biased and bitter criticisms won him many enemies. Author of books on mus., and writer on mus.

Rung (*Roong*), **Frederik.** Composer; *b.* Copenhagen, Den., 1854; *d.* ib., 1915. Opera and orch. comp.

Russell, Alexander. Pianist, teacher; *b.* Franklin, Tenn., Oct. 2, 1880. *p.* Widor. Prof., Syracuse U.; 1917, *t.* Princeton U.

Russell, Henry. Organist; *b.* London, Dec. 24, 1813; *d.* ib., Dec. 7, 1900. *p.* Rossini. 1833, org., Presby. Ch., Rochester. As concert singer, of Jewish extraction, he intro. to N. Y. the tricks of applause-getting, and was characterized by the press as a charleton. Gave "farewell" recitals for two years, and (1841) returned to Eng. Comp. many songs, incl., *Woodman, Spare That Tree,* and *The Old Sexton.* In 1889, his *Life on the Ocean Wave* became official song of the British Royal Marines. Of his two sons, Henry (1871-), became the opera impresario, later assoc. *w.* opera in Boston, and Landon Ronald (q. v.) a British comp. of note.

Russell, Lillian. Operetta soprano; *b.* Clinton, Ia., Dec. 4, 1861; *d.* Pittsburgh, Jun. 6, 1922. Lectured on how to live 100 years. *m.* Alex. P. Moore, ed., Pittsburgh *Leader.*

Russell, Louis Arthur. Writer, teacher; *b.* Newark, N. J., Feb. 24, 1854; *d.* ib., Sept. 5, 1925. Author of educational wks. on piano playing and singing.

Rust (*Roost*), **Friedrich Wilhelm.** Violinist, composer; *b.* Dessau, Ger., 1739; *d.* ib., 1796. Comp. violin wks.

Ryan, Charlotte (Griffith). Soprano; *b.* Sharon, Pa. Edu., Boston Cons. Mus. 1922, Met. Op. H.

Rybner (*Reeb-ner*), **Peter Martin Cornelius.** Pianist, composer; *b.* Copenhagen, Den., Oct. 26, 1855. *p.* Liszt. 1904-19, prof., Columbia U., succ. MacDowell. Daughter, Cornelia, also a comp. Comp. orch., chamb. mus., pf. pcs., songs.

Ryder, Arthur Hilton. Organist; *b.* Plymouth, Mass., Apr. 30, 1875. Edu., Harvard. 1894-99, org., St. Stephen's Ch., Boston; 1901-04, org., Grace Ch., Providence, R. I.; 1916-24, org., Quincy, Mass.; 1924, St. Paul's Ch.

Ryder, Thomas P. Organist, composer; *b.* Cohasset, Mass., Jun. 29, 1836; *d.* Somerville, Mass., Dec. 2, 1887. Comp. salon pcs.

Ryelandt, Joseph. Composer; *b.* Bruges, Bel., Apr. 7, 1870. Comp. orch., chamb. mus.

S

Saar (*Sahr*), **Louis Victor Franz.** Composer, teacher; *b.* Rotterdam, Hol., Dec. 10, 1868. 1894, accompanist, Met. Op. H.; *t.* Natl. Cons.; 1906-17, *t.* Coll. of Mus., Cin.; 1917, *t.* Chicago Mus. Coll. Comp. orch., chamb. mus., songs.

Sabata, Victor de. Composer; *b.* Trieste, It., Apr. 10, 1892. Edu., Milan Cons. 1912, *Suite* for orch., perf., Augusteo, Rome; *Juventus and Gethsemane*, perf. in U. S. by Toscanini; 1917, opera, *Il Macigno*, prod., La Scala; 1930, g.-cond., N. Y. Symph. Comp. opera, orch. wks., chamb. mus., violin pcs.

Sacchini (*Sak-kee-ne*), **Antonio Maria Gasparo.** Composer; *b.* Naples, It., Jul. 23, 1734; *d.* Paris, Oct. 8, 1786. Comp. 60 operas, incl., *Œdipe à Colone* (1786), which had 600 perf. at the Paris Op. during the next 60 years.

Sachs (*Sakhs*), **Hans.** Poet, composer; *b.* Nuremberg, Ger., Nov. 5, 1494; *d.* ib., Jan. 19, 1576. Most famous of the Meistersingers.

Sachsenhauser, Theodor. Composer; *b.* Germany, Jul. 27, 1866; *d.* Munich, Ger., Feb. 25, 1904. Comp. orch., chamb. mus., pf. pcs., songs.

Saerchinger, Cesar. Writer; *b.* Aix-la-Chapelle, 1884. 1914-17, managing ed., *The Art of Music;* 1918, ed., *International Who's Who in Music;* 1913, critic, *Current Opinion;* European mus. correspondent, N. Y. *Times.*

Saenger, Oscar. Singing teacher; *b.* Brooklyn, Jan. 5, 1868; *d.* Washington, D. C., Apr. 20, 1929. 1889, *t.* Natl. Cons. of Mus., N. Y. Taught many successful opera singers, incl., Riccardo Martin and Orville Harrold.

Safonoff, Wassili. Pianist, conductor; *b.* Istchery, Rus., Feb. 6, 1852; *d.* Kislovodsk, Cancausus, Rus., Mar. 13, 1918. 1890-1905, dir., Russian Mus. Soc. concerts in Moscow; 1906-1909, cond., N. Y. Phil. Orch.; 1911, returned to Rus. as dir. of RMS concerts in Petrograd. A frequent g.-cond. in Eng. Unique in his non-use of a baton in conducting.

Sahla, Richard. Violinist, conductor; *b.* Graz, Aus., Sept. 17, 1855. 1888, court cond., Bückeburg, Ger. Comp. violin concertos.

Sahlender, Émil. Conductor, composer; *b.* Ibenhain, Ger., Mar. 12, 1864. Cond., Harmonie, Heidelberg. Comp. opera, orch. mus.

Sainton (*San-tong*), **Prosper Philippe.** Violinist; *b.* Toulouse, Fr., Jun. 5, 1813; *d.* London, Oct. 17, 1890. 1845, prof., R. A. M., London.

Sainton-Dolby, Charlotte Helen. Contralto; *b.* London, May 17, 1821; *d.* ib., Feb. 18, 1885. Celebrated as singer and as a song comp.

Saint-Saëns (*San-Sah-ohn*), **Charles Camille.** Composer, pianist, organist, critic; *b.* Paris, Oct. 9, 1835; *d.* Algiers, Dec. 16, 1921. Evinced mus. talent at early age. Edu., Paris Cons. *w.* Halévy. 1853, org., St. Merri; 1858, Le Madeleine; 1913, dec., Legion of Honor. One of the most prolific comp. of mus. history. Comp. operas, incl., *Samson and Delilah,* and *Henry VIII;* symph. wks., pf. and violin concertos, chamb. mus. Foremost French comp. of conservative sch. Wr. numerous critical wks.

Salaman, Charles. Pianist; *b.* London, Mar. 3, 1814; *d.* ib., Jun. 23, 1901.

Saldoni, Don Baltazar. Composer, teacher of singing; *b.* Barcelona, Jan. 4, 1807; *d.* 1890. Comp. zarzuelas.

Saléza (*Sa-lay-za*), **Luc Albert.** Tenor; *b.* Bruges, Bel., Oct. 18, 1867; *d.* Paris, Nov. 26, 1916.

Salieri (*Sal-ya'-ree*), **Antonio.** Composer; *b.* Legnano, It., Aug. 19, 1750; *d.* Vienna, May 7, 1825. Comp. operas, chamb. mus.

Salmon, Alvah Glover. Pianist, composer; *b.* Southold, N. Y., Sept. 23, 1868; *d.* Boston, Oct., 1916.

Salmon, Felix. 'Cellist; *b.* London, Eng. Edu., R. C. M., London. 1909, debut, London; *t.* Juilliard Sch. of Mus., N. Y.; Curtis Inst. of Mus., Phila.

Salo (*Sah-lo*), **Gasparo da.** Violin-maker; *b.* Brescia, It., 1542; *d.* ib., Apr. 14, 1609. Earliest of eminent It. makers.

Salome, Theodore Cesar. Composer, teacher; *b.* Paris, Jan. 20, 1834; *d.* ib., 1896. 1869, org., la Trinité, Paris, succ. Guilmant; *t.* Paris Cons. Comp. symph., chamb. mus., organ pcs., incl., *Offertoire in D flat.*

Salomon, Johann Peter. Violinist, conductor; *b.* Bonn, Ger., Jan., 1745; *d.* London, Nov. 25, 1815. 1871, he induced Haydn to visit Eng.; 1874, for him Haydn comp. *The Creation.*

Salter, Mary Elizabeth Turner. Composer; *b.* Peoria, Ill., Mar. 15, 1856. Edu., Boston Coll. of Mus. 1881, *m.* Sumner Salter. 1876-1892, ch. and concert singer; 1879-81, *t.* Wellesley Coll. Comp. 200 songs, incl., *The Cry of Rachel.*

Salter, Sumner. Organist; *b.* Burlington, Ia., Jun. 24, 1856. *t.* Williams Coll. Comp. anthems.

Salvayre, Gervais Bernard Gaston. Composer; *b.* Toulouse, Fr., Jun. 24, 1847; *d.* ib., 1916. Opera comp.

Samara, Spiro. Composer; *b.* Corfu, Greece, Nov. 29, 1861; *d.* Athens, 1917. Comp. operas, incl., *Flora Mirabilis.*

Samaroff, Olga. Pianist; *b.* San Antonio, Tex., Aug. 8, 1882. Former wife of Leopold Stokowski. Distinguished concert artist. *t.* Juilliard Sch.

Samazeuilh (*Sam-az-weeye*), **Gustave.** Composer; *b.* Bordeaux, Fr., 1877. Comp. orch., chamb. mus.

Saminsky, Lazare. Composer, conductor; *b.* Vale-Gotzulovo, Oct. 27, 1882. 1909, g.-cond., Petrograd Cons. Orch., in concert of his own wks.; again in Moscow, in 1913, on invitation of Koussevitzky; 1923-29, cond. fest. of modern mus. in Paris; choral dir., Temple Emanu-El, New York.

Sammarco, Mario. Baritone; *b.* Palermo, Dec. 13, 1873; *d.* Milan, Jan. 24, 1930. Sang at many premières, incl., *Andrea Chenier, Zaza, Germania, Natoma.* 1907-10, Manhattan Op., N. Y.; 1910, Chicago Op.

Sammond, Herbert Stavely. Organist, conductor; *b.* Milwaukee, Wis., Dec. 4, 1871. Org., Middle Collegiate Ch., N. Y.; cond., Morning Choral of Brooklyn; Flushing (N. Y.) Oratorio Soc.

Samuel, Adolphe Abraham. Composer; *b.* Liége, Jul. 11, 1824; *d.* Ghent, Sept. 11, 1898. Comp. operas, symph. wks.

Samuel, Harold. Pianist; *b.* London, May 23, 1879. Foremost Bach interpreter of his epoch.

Sanchez de Fuentes, Eduardo. Composer; *b.* Havana, 1878. 1918, opera, *Doreya,* prod., Havana. Comp. songs, incl., *Tu.*

Sanctis, Cesare de. Composer; *b.* Albano, It., 1830. Comp. masses, fugues.

Sanderson, Sibyl. Soprano; *b.* Sacramento, Cal., Dec. 7, 1865; *d.* Paris, May 16, 1903. 1894, created *Thaïs,* comp. for her by Massenet; 1895, sang in N. Y.

Sanderson, Wilfred Ernest. Organist, song composer; *b.* 1878; *d.* London, Dec. 11, 1935. Comp. ballads.

Santley, Charles. Baritone; *b.* Liverpool, Eng., Feb. 28, 1834; *d.* London, 1922. Eminent in opera, oratorio, concert. 1891, toured U. S. Author mus. treatises, incl., *The Art of Singing* (1908). Comp. songs, under pseudonym of Ralph Betterton.

Sapellnikoff, Wassily. Pianist, composer; *b.* Odessa, Rus., Nov. 2, 1868. 1897-9, *t.* Moscow Cons. Comp. opera, pf. pcs.

Sarasate (*Sah-ra-sah-te*), **Pablo de (Pablo Martin Meletón S. Navascuez).** Violinist, composer; *b.* Pamplona, Sp., Mar. 10, 1844; *d.* Biarritz, Fr., Sept. 20, 1908. World renowned violinist, for whom Lalo comp. *Symph. Espagnole,* and Bruch, his 2nd *Concerto.* Pamplona has a Sarasate Museum. Comp. violin pcs., incl., *Zigeunerweisen.*

Sargent, Harold Malcom Watts. Conductor; *b.* Stamford, Lincolnshire, Apr. 29, 1895. 1921, g.-cond., Queen's Hall Promenade Concert, in program of own compositions; 1924, cond., first perf. of Vaughan-Williams opera, *Hugh, the Drover;* g.-cond., of English orch.

Sarti (*Sar-tee*), **Giuseppe.** Composer; *b.* Faenza, It., Dec. 28, 1729; *d.* Berlin, Jul. 28, 1802. Comp. thirty operas, ch. mus.

Satie, Erik Alfred Leslie. Composer; *b.* Honfleur, Fr., May 17, 1866; *d.* Paris, Jul. 2, 1925, in poverty. 1883, Paris Cons. Friend of Debussy. His contemporaries said he wr. "crazy" mus. 1905, at the age of forty, ent. Schola Cantorum. *p.* d'Indy. 1910, guided birth of "French Six," now called "The Father of Modernism." Comp. in the impressionistic style for orch.

Satter, Gustav. Composer; *b.* Vienna, Feb. 12, 1832. Comp. opera, symph. wks., incl., tone-picture, *Washington.*

Sauer (*Sour*), **Emil.** Pianist, composer; *b.* Hamburg, Ger., Oct. 8, 1862. Distinguished artist. *p.* Liszt. Frequent tours of U. S. Comp. pf. concertos, chamb. mus., pf. pcs., songs.

Sauret (*So-ray*), **Émile.** Violinist, composer; *b.* Dun-le-Roi, Fr., May 22, 1852; *d.* London, Feb. 12, 1920. Edu., Paris Cons. and Brussels. *p.* deBériot. One of the leading violin virtuosos of his epoch. 1890-1903, *t.* Chicago Mus. Coll. Comp. violin concertos and misc. pcs.

Savart (*Sav-ahr*), **Felix.** Acoustician; *b.* Mézieres, Fr., 1791; *d.* Paris, 1841. Estab. relationship between pitch and vibratory frequencies.

Sawyer, Charles Pike. Editor; *b.* 1855; *d.* N. Y., May 8, 1935. Mus. ed., New York *Evening Post.*

Sax, Antoine. Instrument-maker; *b.* Dinant, Fr., Nov. 6, 1814; *d.* Paris, Feb. 4, 1894. Co-inventor (*w.* his father) of the saxophones. 1857, *t.* saxophone at Paris Cons.

Sbriglia (*Sbril-ya*), **Giovanni.** Teacher of singing; *b.* Naples, 1840; *d.* Paris, Feb. 20, 1916. Teacher of Nordica, the deReszkes, and many other famous singers. 1865, to U. S.; 1875, to Paris.

Scalchi (*Skahl-kee*), **Sofia.** Contralto; *b.* Turin, It., Nov. 29, 1850. 1882-1896, in U. S.

Scalero, Rosario. Violinist, composer; *b.* Moncalieri, It., Dec. 24, 1870. *p.* Wilhelmj. 1917, *t.* Mannes Sch., N. Y.; 1931, *t.* Curtis Inst., Phila.

Scaria (*Scah-ree-ah*), **Emil.** Bass; *b.* Graz, Aus., Sept. 18, 1840; *d.* Dresden, Ger., Jul. 22, 1886. 1882, chosen by Wagner for première of *Parsifal;* 1884, Met. Op., N. Y.

Scarlatti, Alessandro. Composer; *b.* Trapani, It., 1659; *d.* Naples, Oct. 24, 1725. Pioneer It. opera comp.

Scarlatti, Giuseppi Domenico. Harpsichordist, composer; *b.* Naples, Oct. 26, 1685; *d.* ib., 1757. Son of Alessandro S. Developed principles of modern piano technic. Comp. 10 operas, 350 harpsichord pcs.

Schad, Joseph. Pianist, composer; *b.* Steinach, Ger., Mar. 6, 1812; *d.* Bordeaux, Fr., Jul. 4, 1879. Comp. salon pcs.

Schaefer, Alexander Nikolaievitch. Conductor, composer; *b.* Petrograd, Sept. 11, 1866. Comp. operas, symph., chamb. mus.

Schaefer, Dirk. Composer, teacher; *b.* Rotterdam, Nov. 25, 1873. 1894, won Mendelssohn prize; 1904, *t.* Amsterdam. Comp. orch., chamb. mus., songs.

Schalk, Franz. Conductor; *b.* Vienna, May 27, 1863; *d.* ib., Sept. 3, 1931. *p.* Bruckner. 1907-1911, cond., Covent Garden, London; 1914-1918, asst. cond., Vienna Op., *u.* Richard Strauss; 1924, succ. Strauss as cond.; one of the fd. of the Salzburg Fest.

Scharfenberg, William. Editor, pianist, teacher; *b.* Cassel, Ger., Feb. 22, 1819; *d.* Quogue, L. I., N. Y., Aug. 8, 1895. 1838, to N. Y.; 1845, fd. Scharfenberg & Luis, mus. pubrs.; 1863-6, pres., N. Y. Phil. Soc.; 1866, to Cuba; returned to N. Y. as ed. of Schirmer's Library. Comp. pf. pcs. for teaching.

Scharrer, August. Conductor, composer; *b.* Strassburg, Alsace, Oct. 18, 1866. Comp. symph., incl., *Per Aspera ad Astra.*

Scharwenka (*Shar-ven-ka*), **Franz Xaver.** Pianist, composer; *b.* Samter, Ger., Jan. 6, 1850; *d.* Berlin, Dec. 7, 1924. Toured extensively as piano virtuoso. Fd. Cons. in New York; 1898, co-fd., Klindworth-Scharw. Cons., Berlin. Comp. operas, orch. wks., pf. pcs., incl., *Polish Dance.*

Scharwenka, Ludwig Philipp. Composer; *b.* Samter, Ger., Feb. 16, 1847; *d.* Bad Neuheim, Jul. 16, 1917. Co-fd., Klindworth-Scharw. Cons., Berlin. Comp. pf. pcs.

Schaub (*Shoub*), **Hans F.** Composer; *b.* Frankfort, Ger., Sept. 22, 1880. 1914, *t.* Hamburg; mus. critic, *The Correspondent.* Comp. operetta, orch. wks., violin pcs.

Schauffler, Robert Haven. Writer; *b.* Brünn, Aus., Apr. 8, 1879. Son of Amer. missionaries. 1902, A.B., Princeton. 'Cellist, tennis player, soldier, sculptor. Author of many wks. on mus., incl., *Beethoven—The Man Who Freed Music* (1929).

Scheel (*Shale*), **Fritz.** Conductor; *b.* Lübeck, Ger., Nov. 7, 1852; *d.* Philadelphia, Mar. 12, 1907. 1895-99, fd.-cond., San Francisco Orch.; 1900-5, cond., Phila. Orch.

Scheidt (*Shite*), **Samuel.** Organist, composer; *b.* Halle, Ger., 1587; *d.* ib., Mar. 14, 1654. One of the most celebrated players of his time; fd. of new organ style.

Scheinpflug (*Shine-pfloog*), **Paul.** Conductor, composer; *b.* Loschwitz, Ger., Sept. 10, 1875. 1920, cond., Duisberg. Comp. *Spring* symph., overture to a drama.

Schelling, Ernest Henry. Pianist; *b.* Belvedere, N. J., Jul. 26, 1876. *p.* Leschetizky. Virtuoso career thwarted by neuritis, then auto accident. 1903, *Suite Fantastique,* intro., Mengelberg in Amsterdam; 1923, *Victory Ball,* intro., Stokowski; cond., Children's Concerts *w.* N. Y. Phil.; 1935, cond., Baltimore Symph. Orch.

Schenk, Peter. Pianist, composer; *b.* Petrograd, Feb. 23, 1870. Comp. operas, incl., *Actea;* symph., chamb. wks.

Scherchen, Hermann. Conductor; *b.* Berlin, Jun. 21, 1891. 1918, fd., *Neue Musikgesellschaft,* Berlin; 1921, cond., New Grotrian-Steinweg Orch., Leipzig; 1928, cond., Königsberg Phil.; cond., annual fest. of International Soc. of Modern Mus.; first to inaugurate a master-class for conductors.

Scheve, Edward Benjamin. Composer; *b.* Germany, Feb. 13, 1865; *d.* America, 1924. 1888, to U. S. Comp. symph., pf. concerto, oratorios, anthems, pf. pcs., songs.

Schikaneder (*Shik-a-na-der*), **Emanuel Johann.** Bass; *b.* Ratisbon, Ger., 1751; *d.* Vienna, Sept. 21, 1812. Friend of Mozart. Author of librettos, incl., *Magic Flute.*

Schillinger, Joseph. Composer; *b.* Kharkov, Rus., Sept. 1, 1895. 1914, ent. St. Petersburg Cons., *u.* Tchernov. 1918-24, *t.* State Cons., Kharkov; 1922, *t.* State Inst. Mus. Edu., Leningrad; 1927, to New York; 1928, *March of the Orient,* intro. by Sokoloff and Cleveland Symph.; 1929, *Symphonic Rhapsody,* intro., Stokowski and Phila. Symph.; *Airphonic Suite,* for R. C. A. Theremin and orch., intro., Sokoloff, Cleveland. Comp. orch. wks., chamb. mus., pf., 'cello pcs.

Schillings, Max von. Composer, conductor; b. Düren, Ger., Apr. 19, 1868; d. Berlin, Jul. 24, 1933. 1919, gen. dir., Berlin Op.; u. Hitler, cond., Charlottenburg; 1930, toured U. S., cond. of German Grand Op. Co. Comp. operas, incl., *Ingwelde, Mona Lisa* (Stuttgart, 1915); orch. wks., songs w. orch.

Schindler, Anton Felix. Violinist; b. Medl, Aus., 1796; d. Bockenheim, Ger., Jan. 16, 1864. An early biographer of Beethoven.

Schindler, Kurt. Conductor; b. Berlin, Feb. 17, 1882; d. New York, Nov. 16, 1935. 1902, cond., Stuttgart Op.; 1903, Warzburg; 1905-1908, asst. cond., Met. Op., N. Y.; 1909, fd. MacDowell Chorus; 1912-1926, cond., Schola Cantorum. Editorial adviser to G. Schirmer, mus. publishers.

Schipa, Tito. Operatic tenor; b. Lucca, It., Jan. 2, 1890. 1919, Chicago Op.

Schjelderup (*Skyel-der-oop*), **Gerhard.** Composer; b. Christiania, Nor., Nov. 17, 1859. Comp. mus. dramas, orch. wks., in radical modern style.

Schlaeger (*Shlay-ger*), **Hans.** Conductor, composer; b. Filskirchen, Aus., Dec. 5, 1820; d. Salzburg, Aus., May 17, 1885. Opera and orch. comp.

Schlesinger, Daniel. Teacher; b. Germany, 1799; d. N. Y., 1839. p. Fr. Ries and Moscheles. Early Amer. musician of influence. Out of a memorial concert following his death, grew the movement that led to the founding of the N. Y. Phil. Orch.

Schlesinger (*Shlay-sing-er*), **Sebastian B.** Composer; b. Hamburg, Ger., Sept. 24, 1837; d. Nice, Fr., Jan. 8, 1917. Comp. pf. pcs., songs.

Schlieder, Fred W. Organist, composer; b. Foreston, Ill., Jan. 22, 1873. p. Guilmant. t. Phila. Cons., and Union Theological Seminary.

Schloesser (*Schles-ser*), **Karl Wilhelm Adolph.** Pianist, teacher; b. Darmstadt, Ger., Jan. 1, 1830; d. Dorking, 1913. 1854-1903, t. R. A. M.

Schmid, Joseph. Organist, composer; b. Munich, Ger., Aug. 30, 1868. 1891, org., Munich Cath. Comp. opera, masses, organ wks.

Schmidt, Friedrich. Organist; b. Hartefeld, Ger., Mar. 5, 1840. Comp. masses, motets.

Schmidt, Gustav. Conductor, composer; b. Weimar, Sept. 1, 1816; d. Darmstadt, Feb. 11, 1882. Opera comp.

Schmidt, Karl. Writer, teacher; b. Friedberg, Ger., Jul. 10, 1869. Writer on singing.

Schmitt, Aloys. Pianist, teacher; b. Erlenbach, Ger., Aug. 26, 1788; d. Frankfort, Ger., Jul. 25, 1866. Comp. operas, oratorios, pf. concertos, chamb. mus., but best known by his *Études* and *Method*.

Schmitt, Florent. Composer; b. Blamont, Fr., Sept. 28, 1870. Edu., Paris Cons., u. Fauré. 1897, won Prix de Rome; 1909, *Quintet*, intro., Paris; 1922-24, dir., Lyons Cons.; 1932, toured Amer. Comp. highly impressionistic modern mus. in all forms.

Schmitz, E. Robert. Pianist, teacher; b. Paris, Fr. Edu., Paris Cons. 1919, toured U. S. 1920, fd. Pro Musica.

Schnecker, Peter August. Organist, composer; b. Hesse-Darmstadt, Ger., Aug. 26, 1850; d. New York, Oct. 3, 1903. Comp. cantatas, organ wks., violin pcs., songs.

Schneerson, Grigori. Soviet musician and critic; b. Siberia. Edu., Moscow, u. Medtner. Sec., International Music Bureau; contrib., *Moscow Daily News*.

Schneevoigt, George Sennart. Conductor; b. Viborg, Nov. 8, 1872. 1904-1908, cond., Kaim Orch., Munich; 1912, cond., Helsingfors Symph. Orch.; 1918, fd. Oslo Phil. Orch.; 1924, g.-cond., Boston Symph. Orch.; cond., Los Angeles Phil.

Schneider, Edward Faber. Composer; b. Omaha, Neb., 1872. Comp. mus. drama, *Autumn* symph.

Schneider, Johann Christian Friedrich. Composer; b. Altwaltersdorf, Ger., Jan. 3, 1786; d. Dessau, Nov. 23, 1853. Comp. oratorios, cantatas, symph.

Schneider, Johann Gottlob. Organist, composer; b. Altgersdorf, Ger., Oct. 28, 1789; d. Dresden, Apr. 13, 1864. Organ virtuoso.

Schnyder von Wartensee, Xaver. Composer, teacher; b. Lucerne, Switz., Apr. 16, 1786; d. Frankfort, Apr. 27, 1868. Comp. symph., pf. sonatas, choruses, songs.

Schoenberg, Arnold. Composer; b. Vienna, Sept. 13, 1874. p. von Zemlinsky; m. his sister. Strongly influenced by Gustav Mahler. Modern iconoclastic. 1907, *First String Quartet*, intro., Arnold Rose Quartet, and violently hissed; 1931, *Theme and Variations*, intro., Stokowski, also hissed; 1932, *Gurrelieder*, intro., Stokowski, and praised. As a teacher, was the inspiration of the late Alban Berg, Anton Webern, and Egon Wels. 1932, exiled from Germany; t. Malkin Sch., Boston; 1935, prof., U. So. Cal. Comp. opera, incl., *Gluckliche Hand*; orch. wks., incl., *Kammersymphonie*; choral mus., chamb. mus.

Schoenefeld (*Sha-ne-felt*), **Henry.** Pianist, composer; b. Milwaukee, Wis., Oct. 4, 1857. 1915, cond., Pac. Coast Ger. Sängerfest. Comp. *Rural* symph., *In the Sunny South*, w. negro tunes, two *American Rhapsodies* for orch.

Schoepf (*Shepf*), **Franz.** Composer; b. Girlan, Tyrol, 1836. 1859, Munic. org., Bozen, Aus. Comp. ch. mus., operas, operettas.

Scholz, Bernhard E. Composer; b. Mainz, Ger., Mar. 30, 1835; d. Munich, 1916. Comp. operas, orch., pf. pcs.

Schradieck (*Shrah-deek*), **Henry.** Violinist, teacher; b. Hamburg, Ger., Apr. 29, 1846; d. Brooklyn, N. Y., Mar. 25, 1918. 1874-83, t. Leipzig Cons.; 1883, t. Coll. of Mus., Cin.; 1894, Natl. Cons. of Mus., N. Y.; 1898, Broad St. Cons., Phila.; 1912, Amer. Inst. Applied Mus., N. Y. Author of technical wks. for the violin.

Schreck, Gustav. Composer; b. Zeulenroda, Ger., Sept. 8, 1849; d. Leipzig, 1918. 1898, prof., Leipzig Cons.; 1909, Ph.D., Leipzig U. Comp. oratorio, orch., vocal wks.

Schreker, Franz. Composer; b. Monaco, It., Mar. 23, 1878; d. Berlin, Mar. 21, 1934. Edu., Vienna Cons., u. Robert Fuchs. 1911, fd. Vienna Phil. Choir; *Der Ferne Klang*, prod., Paris Op. Comp. operas, orch. wks.

Schroeder (*Shra-der*), **Alwin.** 'Cellist; b. Neuhaldensleben, Ger., Jun. 15, 1855; d. Jamaica Plain, Mass., Oct. 17, 1928. 'Cellist of Kneisel Quartet.

Schroeder, Karl. 'Cellist, composer; b. Quedlinburg, Ger., Dec. 18, 1848. Comp. wks. for 'cello and orch.

Schroeder-Devrient (*Shra-der Dev-ree-ong*), **Wilhelmine.** Soprano; b. Hamburg, Ger., Dec. 6, 1804; d. Coburg, Ger., Jan. 21, 1860. A celebrated artist of her epoch. Sang at premières of *Rienzi, Flying Dutchman,* and *Tannhäuser*.

Schubert, Franz. Composer; *b.* Vienna, Jan. 31, 1797; *d.* ib., Nov. 19, 1828. 1808, entered Imperial Convict (free school) at Vienna as choirboy, played violin in the sch. orch; 1813, singing and piano master in the household of Count Esterhazy; 1815, to Vienna. One of the most fertile of comp. Wr. fifteen operas and operettas, five masses and other ch. mus., nine symph., fifteen str. q., besides other chamb. mus., piano pcs., and songs. One of the most lyrical of comp., yet he lived almost wholly unappreciated and in considerable poverty.

Schuberth (*Schoo-bairt*), **Karl.** 'Cellist; *b.* Würzburg, Ger., Feb. 25, 1811; *d.* Zürich, Switz., Jul. 22, 1863. Comp. 'cello pcs., chamb. mus.

Schuch (*Shookh*), **Ernst von.** Conductor; *b.* Graz, Aus., Nov. 23, 1847; *d.* Dresden, May 10, 1914. Distinguished cond.

Schuchardt (*Shookh-art*), **Friedrich.** Composer; *b.* Gotha, Ger., 1876. Comp. opera, oratorio, ch. mus.

Schuecker (*Schoo-eck-er*), **Edmund.** Harpist; *b.* Vienna, 1860; *d.* Bad Kreuznach, 1911. Mem. Vienna, Pittsburgh, Phila., Chicago, and Met. Op. Orchestras.

Schuecker, Heinrich. Harpist; *b.* Vienna, 1868; *d.* Boston, Apr. 17, 1913. Mem., Boston Symph. Orch.

Schuett (*Shet*), **Eduard.** Pianist, composer; *b.* Petrograd, Oct. 22, 1856; *d.* Merano, It., Jul. 26, 1933. Comp. orch. wks., pf. concerto, chamb. mus., and melodious salon pcs. for pf., incl., *A la bien aimée*.

Schulhoff (*School-hof*), **Julius.** Pianist, composer; *b.* Prague, Boh., Aug. 2, 1825; *d.* Berlin, Mar. 13, 1898. Comp. pf., salon pcs.

Schulz (*Shoolts*), **Heinrich.** Composer, teacher; *b.* Beuthen, Ger., Jun. 19, 1838; *d.* Dresden, Mar. 12, 1915. Comp. operas, symph.

Schulz, Johann Abraham Peter. Composer; *b.* Lüneburg, Ger., Mar. 31, 1747; *d.* Schwedt, Ger., Jun. 10, 1800. Developed the German Lied.

Schulz, Karl. Pianist, composer; *b.* Schwerin, Ger., Jan. 3, 1845; *d.* Mannheim, Ger., May 24, 1913. Comp. orch. wks., sacred mus.

Schumann, Clara. Pianist; *b.* Leipzig, Sept. 13, 1819; *d.* Frankfort, May 20, 1896. A pupil of her father, Friedrich Wieck, she toured as a piano virtuoso at eleven. The first to introduce Chopin's mus. to the German public. 1840, *m.* Robert Schumann. Survived him by thirty years, during which she devoted her energies to propaganda for his compositions.

Schumann, Georg Alfred. Composer; *b.* Königstein, Ger., Oct. 25, 1866. Comp. oratorio, *Ruth;* symph. wks., earnest but pedantic.

Schumann, Robert Alexander. Composer; *b.* Zwickau, Ger., Jun. 8, 1810; *d.* Endenich, Ger., Jul. 29, 1856. Injury to his fingers through use of a mechanical device, obliged him to abandon piano practice. Thereupon he concentrated on composition. 1834, fd. *Neue Zeitschrift für Musik;* 1844, cond., Dresden Choral Union; 1850, to Düsseldorf. Here a long-standing affection of the brain became worse, and in 1854, he had to be placed in an asylum. Comp. choral wks., *Paradise and the Peri;* the opera, *Genoveva;* symph., chamb. mus., piano compositions, and a large number of vocal wks. Some of his songs are classed as immortal.

Schumann-Heink, Ernestine. Contralto; *b.* Prague, Boh., Jun. 15, 1861. Eminent career of upwards of 50 years in opera, concert and sound pictures.

Schuppanzigh, Ignaz. Violinist; *b.* Vienna, 1776; *d.* ib., Mar. 2, 1830.

Schurig (*Shoo-rig*), **Volkmar.** Organist, composer; *b.* Aur, Ger., Mar. 24, 1822; *d.* Dresden, 1899. Comp. organ wks., songs.

Schuster (*Shoos-ter*), **Bernhard.** Conductor, composer; *b.* Berlin, Mar. 26, 1870; *d.* Ger., Jan. 13, 1934. Ed., *Die Musik,* Berlin. Comp. opera, symph., choral wks., songs.

Schuster, Joseph. 'Cellist; *b.* Constantinople, May 23, 1905, of Russian parentage. 1915, discovered at Sebastopol by Glazounoff, and edu. Petrograd Cons., *u.* J. Press; 1929, soloist, Berlin Phil., *u.* Furtwangler; 1934, to U. S.; 1936, soloist, N. Y. Phil.

Schütz (*Sheets*), **Heinrich.** Composer; *b.* Köstritz, Ger., Oct. 8, 1585; *d.* Dresden, Ger., Nov. 6, 1672.

Schuyten, Ernest Eugene Emile. Music educator; *b.* Antwerp, Nov. 7, 1881. Edu., Royal Cons., Brussels. 1911, to U. S.; 1919, fd. New Orleans Cons. of Mus. and Dramatic Arts; cond., New Orleans Symph.

Schwalm (*Shvalm*), **Robert.** Conductor, composer; *b.* Erfurt, Ger., Dec. 6, 1845; *d.* Königsberg, 1912. Comp. opera, oratorio, chamb. mus., male choruses.

Schweitzer, Albert. Organist; *b.* Alsace, Jan. 14, 1875. An unusual personality, eminent as theologian, physician, organist, author, and expert authority on organ building. He studied medicine in order to become a medical missionary to the French Congo. He studied music and the organ on account of his musicological interest in Bach. Known as a world authority on Bach. Author of a *Life of Bach.* Ed. of an edition of the *Bach Organ Works*.

Schytte (*Shee-teh*), **Ludwig Theodor.** Composer; *b.* Aarhut, Den., Apr. 28, 1848; *d.* Berlin, Nov. 10, 1909. Comp. salon type pf. pcs., *études*.

Scontrino (*Scon-tree-no*), **Antonio.** Double-bass player, composer; *b.* Trapani, It., May 17, 1850; *d.* Florence, 1922. 1892, *t.* Royal Inst. of Mus., Florence. Comp. operas, orch. wks., pf. pcs., songs.

Scott, Cyril Meir. Composer; *b.* Oxton, Eng., Sept. 27, 1879. Edu., Hochschule. 1900, *Heroic Suite,* and *First Symphony,* perf., Hans Richter in Liverpool; 1934, won *Daily Telegraph* prize for *Festival Overture*. Comp. symph., chamb. wks., pf. pcs., songs. An exponent of the modern sch.

Scott, John Prindle. Composer; *b.* Norwich, N. Y., Aug. 6, 1891; *d.* Syracuse, N. Y., Dec. 2, 1932. Comp. sacred songs.

Scotti, Antonio. Baritone; *b.* Naples, It., Jan. 25, 1866; *d.* ib., Feb. 26, 1936. 1899, Met. Op., New York.

Scriabin (*Skryah-been*), **Alexander Nikolaievitch.** Pianist, composer; *b.* Moscow, Rus., Jan. 10, 1872; *d.* Petrograd, Apr. 14, 1915. Edu., Moscow Cons.; 1891, Gold Medal. 1898-1904, *t.* Cons. An early modernist, yet often referred to as the Russian Chopin. Comp. symph., orch. *Poème de l'exstase;* piano concertos, pf. pcs.

Sealy, Frank L. Organist; *b.* Newark, N. J., Sept. 13, 1858. *p.* Dudley Buck. 1885, org., N. Y. Symph.; 1885-1921, N. Y. Oratorio Soc.; 1900-18, Fifth Ave. Presby. Ch.

Search, Frederick Preston. 'Cellist; *b.* Pueblo, Colo., 1889. Edu., Leipzig Cons. 1915-16, Amer. Orch., Chicago; 1916-17, Chicago Op. Comp. symph., chamb. wks., 'cello sonatas.

Sebald, Alexander. Violinist, composer; *b.* Pest, Apr. 29, 1869; *d.* Chicago, Jun. 30, 1934. *p.* Cesar Thomson. 1903, Gewandhaus q., Leipzig; 1907, Berlin; 1914, Chicago.

Sebor (*Say-bor*), **Karl.** Composer; *b.* Brandeis, Ger., Aug. 13, 1843; *d.* Prague, May 17, 1903. Comp. opera, chamb. mus.

Sechter (*Sekh-ter*), **Simon.** Organist, theorist; *b.* Friedberg, Boh., Oct. 11, 1788; *d.* Vienna, Sept. 10, 1867. Comp. organ, ch. mus.

Seeboeck (*Say-beck*), **William C. E.** Pianist, composer; *b.* Vienna, 1860; *d.* Chicago, 1907. Comp. opera, pf. pcs., songs.

Seeling (*Say-ling*), **Hans.** Pianist, composer; *b.* Prague, Boh., 1828; *d.* ib., May 26, 1862. Comp. salon, pf. pcs.

Seguin, Ann Childe. Soprano; *b.* London, 1814; *d.* N. Y., Aug., 1888. Wife of A. E. S.

Seguin, Arthur Edward Shelden. Bass; *b.* London, Apr. 7, 1809; *d.* N. Y., Dec. 9, 1852.

Seguin, William Henry. Bass; *b.* London, 1814; *d.* Dec. 28, 1850. Brother of A. E. S.

Seidel, Toscha. Violinist; *b.* Odessa, 1900. *p.* Auer. 1915, debut, Christiania; 1918, to Amer. *w.* Auer.

Seidl (*Sy-dle*), **Anton.** Conductor; *b.* Pesth, Hun., May 7, 1850; *d.* New York, Mar. 28, 1898. 1879-82, cond., Leipzig Op.; 1882, toured Europe; cond., Neumann's company in the *Nibelungen Ring;* 1885, cond., German opera at Met. Op. H., N. Y.; 1891, cond., N. Y. Phil. During his epoch, one of the most beloved of cond. in Amer.

Seiss (*Syse*), **Isidor.** Pianist, composer; *b.* Dresden, Dec. 23, 1840; *d.* Cologne, Sept. 25, 1905. Comp. orch., piano wks.

Sekles, Bernhard. Composer; *b.* Frankfort, Ger., Jun. 20, 1872. St., Hochs Cons., Frankfurt. *t.* 1923; dir., 1908; *Serenade,* intro., Dresden. Comp. symph. p., *The Gardens of Semiramis,* and smaller wks.

Selmer, Johann. Composer, conductor; *b.* Christiania, Nor., Jan. 20, 1844; *d.* Venice, Jul. 22, 1910. Orch., and choral comp.

Sembrich, Marcella [Praxede Marcelline Kochanska]. Soprano; *b.* Wisniewczyk, Aus., Feb. 15, 1858; *d.* N. Y., Jan. 11, 1935. Distinguished in opera and concert. Leading prima donna at Met. Op. during her epoch. *t.* Curtis Inst., Phila.

Semet (*Seh-may*), **Théophile Aimé Émile.** Composer; *b.* Lille, Fr., Sept. 6, 1824; *d.* Corbeil, Fr., Apr. 15, 1888. Opera comp.

Senkrah (really Harkness), Alma Loretta. Violinist; *b.* Williamson, N. Y., Jun. 16, 1864; *d.* Weimar, Ger., Sept., 1900.

Serafin, Tullio. Conductor; *b.* Cavarzere, It., Sept. 8, 1878. 1900, cond., Ferrara; 1903, Turin; 1906, Rome; 1909, La Scala, Milan; 1924-1935, cond., Met. Op., N. Y.; 1935, dir., Teatro Reale, Rome.

Serov, Alexander Nikolaievitch. Composer; *b.* Petrograd, Jan. 23, 1820; *d.* ib., Feb. 1, 1871. Comp. operas, incl., *Judith;* orch., pf. pcs. Author of essays.

Serrao (*Ser-rah'-o*), **Paolo.** Composer; *b.* Filadelfia, It., 1830; *d.* Naples, Mar., 1907. Teacher of Martucci and Giordano. Comp. operas.

Serrao y Ruiz, Emilio. Pianist, composer; *b.* Vittoria, Sp., Mar. 13, 1850. Comp. opera.

Servais (*Ser-vay*), **Adrien François.** 'Cellist, composer; *b.* Hal, Bel., Jun. 6, 1807; *d.* ib., Nov. 26, 1877. Comp. 'cello pcs.

Servais, Joseph. 'Cellist, teacher; *b.* Hal, Bel., Nov. 23, 1850; *d.* ib., Aug. 29, 1885. Son of A. F. S. 1872, *t.* Brussels Cons.; mem., Hubay Quartet; played the Princess Yusupov Stradivarius 'cello, inherited from his father. Comp. str. q.

Sessions, Roger. Composer; *b.* Dec. 28, 1896. 1915, gr. Harvard; st., Yale Mus. Sch., *u.* Horatio Parker. 1922, *t.* Cleveland Inst. Mus.; 1925, to Europe. 1934, commissioned by Stokowski to comp. symph. Well schooled, but an extreme modernist. Comp. symph., concerto for violin and orch., pf., organ pcs.

Sevcik (*Sef-chik*), **Ottokar.** Violinist, teacher; *b.* Horazdowitz, Boh., Mar. 22, 1852; *d.* Pisek, Jan. 18, 1934. Edu., Prague Cons. 1875, *t.* Kief Cons.; 1909, *t.* Vienna Acad.; eminent teacher of Kubelik, Kocian, Ondricek, and other celebrated artists. Comp. celebrated technical system.

Severac, Déodat de. Composer; *b.* St. Felix de Caraman, Fr., Jul. 20, 1873; *d.* Céret, 1921. Comp. mus. dramas, incl., *Le Coeur du Moulin;* symph. p., incl., *Nymphs at Twilight*.

Severn, Edmund. Composer, conductor, violinist; *b.* England, Dec. 10, 1862; *d.* Cleveland, Jan. 16, 1936. 1866, to U. S. Comp. fest. overture, orch. p., *Lancelot and Elaine,* and *Heloise and Abelard;* orch. suite, *From Old New England;* ch. mus., and many violin pcs.

Sevitzky, Fabien. Conductor; *b.* Wyshny, Rus., Sept. 30, 1893. 1925, fd. Phila. Chamber Sinfonietta.

Seydel, Irma. Violinist; *b.* Boston, Sept. 27, 1896. *p.* Loeffler. 1909, appeared *w.* Stadtisches Orch., Cologne. Frequent appearances *w.* Boston Symph. Orch.

Seyffardt (*Sy-fardt*), **Ernst Hermann.** Composer; *b.* Crefeld, Ger., May 6, 1858. *t.* Stuttgart Cons. Comp. symph., choral, chamb. wks., songs.

Seyfried (*Sy-freed*), **Ignaz Xaver Ritter von.** Composer; *b.* Vienna, Aug. 15, 1776; *d.* ib., Aug. 27, 1841.

Seymour, Harriet Ayer. Pianist, teacher; *b.* Chicago. Edu., Royal Acad., Stuttgart. *t.* Inst. of Mus. Art and Settlement Mus. Sch., N. Y.

Sgambati, Giovanni. Pianist, composer; *b.* Rome, May 18, 1843; *d.* ib., Dec. 15, 1914. Comp. symph., chamb. mus., pf. wks.

Shakespeare, William. Teacher of singing, composer; *b.* Croydon, Eng., Jun. 16, 1849; *d.* London, Nov. 1, 1931. An eminent London vocal teacher. Author of a text work on singing.

Shakespeare, William, Jr. Teacher of singing; *b.* London, 1880; *d.* Cincinnati, Aug. 8, 1933.

Shapleigh, Bertram. Composer; *b.* Boston, 1871. Comp. operas, symph., ch. mus., songs; mostly of oriental flavor.

Sharlow, Myrna. Soprano; *b.* Jamestown, N. D. Mem., Royal Op., Covent Garden, London; Chicago Civic Op.; San Carlo Op.; Met. Op.

Sharnova, Sonia. Contralto; *b.* Chicago, Ill., May 2, 1900. 1925, operatic debut, Nice, Fr.; 1930, Chicago Op.

Shavitch, Vladimir. Conductor; b. South Amer., Jul. 20, 1888. 1923, cond., Rochester Phil.; 1924, cond., Syracuse Symph. Orch.; 1929, cond., Moscow State Op.

Shaw, Frank Holcomb. Music educator; b. Paxton, Ill., May 8, 1884. 1907-10, t. Monmouth Coll.; 1910-12, Cornell Coll., Mt. Vernon, Iowa; 1924, dir., Oberlin Cons.

Shaw, William Warren. Vocal teacher; b. Mattoon, Ill. p. Baragli. t. U. of Vermont Summer Sch.; t. voice, U. of Pa.

Shelley, Harry Rowe. Organist, composer; b. New Haven, Conn., Jun. 8, 1858. Comp. opera, cantatas, songs, organ mus., anthems, incl., *Hark, Hark My Soul*.

Shepard, Frank Hartson. Organist, theorist; b. Bethel, Conn., Sept. 20, 1863; d. Orange, N. J., Feb. 25, 1913. Author of harmony text-books.

Shepard, Thomas Griffin. Organist, composer; b. Madison, Conn., Apr. 23, 1848; d. Brooklyn, 1905. Comp. cantatas, anthems.

Shepherd, Arthur. Teacher, composer; b. Paris, Idaho, Feb. 19, 1880. p. Chadwick. Cond., Salt Lake, Utah; prof. of comp., N. E. Cons.; 1929, critic, Cleveland *Press*; t. Western Reserve U., Cleveland; 1902, won Paderewski prize for *Ouverture Joyeuse*; 1909, won NFMC prize for pf. sonata; 1927, *Triptych* for soprano and str. q., won award of SPAM. Comp. orch. wks., incl., *Horizons*; a cantata, piano sonata and songs.

Sherman, Leander S. Music dealer, patron of music; b. Boston, Apr. 29, 1847; d. S. F., Apr. 5, 1926. Mus. clerk; 1870, entered mus. business; 1879, co-fd., w. Major C. C. Clay, of Sherman, Clay & Co.; 1920, retired.

Sherwood, William Hall. Pianist, teacher; b. Lyons, N. Y., Jan. 31, 1854; d. Chicago, Jan. 7, 1911. p. Liszt. Distinguished concert artist. 1897, fd. Sherwood Mus. Sch., Chicago.

Shield, William. Composer; b. Wickham, Eng., Mar. 5, 1748; d. London, Jan. 25, 1829. Comp. ballad operas, once highly popular.

Shilkret, Nathaniel. Conductor; b. New York, Jan. 1, 1895. Cond., R. C. A.-Victor Co., and many radio programs.

Shostakowitch, Dmitri. Composer; b. Leningrad, Sept. 25, 1906. 1919-25, Cons. 1934, *Lady Macbeth of Mtsensk*, perf., Rus.; Amer., 1935, perf. Cleveland, u. Rodzinsky and Met. Op. The most conspicuous disciple of Sovietism in mus. Comp. opera, orch. wks., chamb. mus., ballets.

Shure, R. Deane. Composer, pianist, organist; b. Chillisquaque, Pa. Mus. B., Oberlin Cons.; dir. of mus., American U., Washington.

Sibelius (*See-bay-lee-ous*), **Jean.** Composer; b. Tavastehus, Fin., Dec. 8, 1865. St., law; 1889, to Berlin; 1900, awarded stipend by government of Finland; 1901, dir., Heidelberg Fest. In 1935, considered the foremost living comp. Comp. six symph., orch. legends on *Kalevala* subjects, suites *Carelia*, and *King Christian IV*, choral, pf., organ wks., incl., *Valse Triste* and *Finlandia*.

Siboni, Ernst Anton Waldemar. Pianist, composer; b. Copenhagen, Den., Aug. 26, 1828; d. ib., Feb. 22, 1892. Orch. comp.

Sicard (*See-car*), **Michael.** Violinist, conductor; b. Odessa, Rus., 1868. Comp. orch., chamb. mus.

Sick, Theodor Bernhard. Composer; b. Copenhagen, Den., Nov. 7, 1827; d. ib., 1893. Comp. chamb. mus.

Sieber, Ferdinand. Teacher of singing, composer; b. Vienna, Dec. 5, 1822; d. Berlin, Feb. 19, 1895. Author of studies for voice training.

Sieveking (*See'-ve-king*), **Martinus.** Pianist; b. Amsterdam, Mar. 24, 1867. p. Leschetizky. Artist of distinction. Toured w. Patti; 1893, t. Lincoln, Neb.; 1915, fd. Sch. of Mus., New York. Author of a pf. *Method*. Comp. violin, pf. pcs.

Silas (*See-laz*), **Eduard.** Pianist, composer; b. Amsterdam, Aug. 22, 1827; d. London, Feb. 8, 1909. Comp. orch. wks., piano concerto, oratorio, organ, pf. pcs.

Silber, Sidney. Pianist, teacher; b. Waupun, Wis., Mar 9, 1881. p. Leschetizky. t. U. Sch. Mus., Lincoln, Neb.; t. Sherwood Mus. Sch., Chicago.

Silbermann, Gottfried. Piano-maker; b. Kleinbobritzsch, Ger., 1683; d. Aug. 4, 1753. One of the earliest German makers.

Silberta, Rhea. Pianist, vocal coach, lecturer; b. Pocahontas, Va. Edu., Chicago Mus. Coll., Inst. of Mus. Art. Managed opera company playing in Newark and Phila. for two years. Comp. pf. pcs., and songs.

Silcher, Philipp Friedrich. Composer; b. Schnaith, Ger., Jun. 27, 1789; d. Tübingen, Ger., Aug. 26, 1860. Author of *Collection of German Folksongs*, in 12 vols.; also text work on *Harmony*.

Siloti, Alexander. Pianist, conductor; b. Kharkov, Rus., Oct. 10, 1863. p. Liszt. t. Safonoff. Distinguished virtuoso and teacher. 1898, visited U. S.; 1922, t. Juilliard Sch., N. Y.

Silver, Alfred J. Composer; b. Dec. 20, 1870. Comp. ch. organ mus.

Silver (*Seel-vair*), **Charles.** Composer; b. Paris, Feb. 16, 1868. Comp. opera, incl., *Le Clos*.

Simon (*See-mon*), **Anton.** Composer; b. France, 1851. Comp. operas, ballets, orch., chamb. wks.

Simonetti, Achille. Violinist, composer; b. Turin, It., Jun. 12, 1859. Comp. salon pf. pcs., incl., *Madrigal*.

Sinding, Christian. Composer; b. Kongsberg, Nor., Jan. 11, 1856. Edu., Leipzig Cons. 1884, *Quintet in E-Minor*, first work of note; 1916, awarded thirty thousand crowns by government as successor to Grieg. Comp. orch. wks., *Episodes Chevaleresques*; opera, *The Holy Mountain*; chamb. mus., pf. pcs., songs.

Singelée (*Sanj-lay*), **Jean Baptiste.** Violinist, composer; b. Brussels, Sept. 25, 1812; d. Ostend, Sept. 29, 1875. Comp. violin teaching pcs.

Singer, Otto. Violinist; b. Dresden, Sept. 14, 1863. Piano 4-hands transcr. of orch. wks.

Sinigaglia (*Sin-i-gal-ya*), **Leone.** Composer; b. Turin, It., Aug. 14, 1868. Edu., Vienna. 1901, *Concerto for Violin and Orchestra*, intro. in It.; 1907, overture, *Le Baruffe Chiozzotte*, intro., Toscanini in Milan. Comp. orch., chamb. mus., violin pcs.

Sink, Charles Albert. b. Westernville, N. Y., Jul. 4, 1879. 1904, A.B., U. of Mich. 1904-1907, sec. U. Sch. of Mus., U. of Mich.; 1907-27, bus. mgr.; 1927, pres.

Siskovsky, Jaroslav. Violinist; b. Cleveland, Aug. 8, 1888. p. Auer in Petrograd. 1913, mem. Vienna Tonkünstler orch.; 1920, mem. N. Y. Chamb. Mus. Soc.

Sitt, Hans. Violinist, conductor; *b.* Prague, Boh., Sept. 21, 1850; *d.* Leipzig, 1922. 1883, *t.* Leipzig Cons. Comp. orch., chamb. mus., violin pcs., songs.

Sivori (*See-vo'-ree*), **Ernesto Camillo.** Violinist; *b.* Genoa, It., Oct. 25, 1815; *d. ib.*, Feb. 18, 1894. *p.* Paganini.

Sjögren (*Shya-gren'*), **Johann Gustav Emil.** Organist, composer; *b.* Stockholm, Swed., Jun. 16, 1853; *d. ib.*, Mar. 3, 1918. Comp. cantata, orch., chamb. wks., songs, incl., *Der Vogt von Tenneberg;* pf. pcs., incl., *Erotikon,* and *Novellette,* and 80 songs.

Skilton, Charles Sanford. Composer; *b.* Northampton, Mass., Aug. 16, 1868. 1889, A.B., Yale. 1903-15, dean, Sch. Fine Arts, U. of Kan. Comp. orch. wks., incl., *Suite Primeval, Legend;* operas, incl., *Kalopin, The Sun Bride;* incid. mus. for *Electra;* oratorio, *The Guardian Angel.*

Skroup (*Skroop*), **Frantisek.** Composer; *b.* Vosicz, Boh., Jun. 3, 1801; *d.* Rotterdam, Feb. 7, 1862. Pioneer comp. of Bohemian national operas.

Skuhersky, Franz Zdenko. Composer, theorist; *b.* Opocno, Boh., Jul. 31, 1830; *d.* Budweis, Aug. 19, 1892. Opera comp.

Slivinski, Joseph von. Pianist; *b.* Warsaw, Pol., Dec. 15, 1865. *p.* Leschetizky. 1893, toured in U. S.

Sloper, Lindsay. Pianist, composer; *b.* London, Jun. 14, 1826; *d. ib.*, Jul. 3, 1887. Comp. pf. pcs., studies, songs.

Smallens, Alexander. Conductor; *b.* Petrograd, 1889. 1911, asst. cond., Boston Op.; cond., Century Op., N. Y.; Colon Op., Buenos Aires; Natl. Th., Havana; 1919-22, cond., Chicago Op., where he cond. the world première of Prokofieff opera, *Love of Three Oranges,* at composer's request; 1923-30, cond., Phila. Op.; 1934-35, cond., Summer Op. at Lewisohn Stadium, N. Y.

Smareglia (*Smah-rel-ya*), **Antonio.** Composer; *b.* Pola, Aus., May 5, 1854. Opera comp.

Smart, Sir George Thomas. Composer, conductor; *b.* London, May 10, 1776; *d. ib.*, Feb. 23, 1867.

Smart, Henry. Organist, composer; *b.* London, Oct. 26, 1813; *d. ib.*, Jul. 6, 1879. Brother of George T. S. Comp. organ mus., anthems, sacred songs.

Smetana (*Sme'tah-nah*), **Friedrich.** Composer; *b.* Leitomischl, Boh., Mar. 2, 1824; *d.* Prague, May 12, 1884. 1886, cond., Prague Op.; 1874, retired on account of deafness, finally became insane and was confined in the same sanitarium that had harbored Schumann. Comp. orch. wks., strongly nationalistic, incl., *The Moldau;* also operas, incl., *The Bartered Bride.*

Smith, Alice Mary (Mrs. Meadows-White). Composer; *b.* London, May 19, 1839; *d. ib.*, Dec. 4, 1884. Comp. symph., chamb. mus., vocal wks.

Smith, David Stanley. Conductor, organist, composer; *b.* Toledo, Jul. 6, 1877. Gr. Yale U., *u.* Parker. 1920, prof., Yale U. Sch. of Mus., succ. Parker; cond., New Haven Symph. Orch.; 1912, symph., *F Minor,* perf., Chicago Symph.; 1918, symph., *D Major,* perf., Norfolk Fest. Comp. opera, *Merrymount;* symph., chamb. mus.

Smith, Edward Sydney. Composer, pianist; *b.* Dorchester, Eng., Jul. 14, 1839; *d.* London, Mar. 3, 1889. Comp. salon pf. pcs.

Smith, Gerrit. Organist; *b.* Hagerstown, Md., Dec. 11, 1859; *d.* New York, Jul. 21, 1912. Comp. cantata, *David;* songs, pf. pcs.

Smith, Harry Bache. Operetta librettist; *b.* Buffalo, 1860; *d.* Atlantic City, Jan. 2, 1936. Dramatic critic, playwright; author of librettos for *Robin Hood, Wizard of the Nile, Countess Maritza,* and some seventy-five mus. comedies and operettas.

Smith, Moses. Music critic; *b.* Chelsea, Mass., Mar. 4, 1901. 1921, A.B., Harvard. 1922-23, asst. mus. critic, Boston *Post;* 1924, Boston *Evening American;* Boston correspondent, *Musical Courier.*

Smith, Roy Lamont. Pianist, composer; *b.* U. S., 1882. *t.* Cadek Cons., Chattanooga, Tenn.

Smith, Samuel Francis. Lyricist; *b.* 1808; *d.* 1895. 1832, in Andover, Mass., wr. text of *America,* while not conscious of the British origin of the tune. Jul. 4, 1932, centenary of first perf., celebrated in Park St. Ch., Boston.

Smith, Warren Storey. Composer, critic, editor; *b.* Brookline, Jul. 14, 1885. 1908, gr. Faelton Pf. Sch.; 1908-19, *t.* ib.; 1902, *t.* N. E. Cons.; 1924, mus. critic, Boston *Post.*

Smith, Wilson George. Composer; *b.* Elyria, O., Aug. 19, 1855. Mus. critic, Cleveland, O. Comp. pf. pcs., songs.

Smulders (*Smool-ders*), **Karl Anton.** Composer, teacher; *b.* Maestricht, Hol., May 8, 1863. *t.* Liége Cons. Comp. symph., concertos, pf. pcs., songs.

Smyth, Ethel Mary. Composer; *b.* London, Apr. 23, 1858. Edu., Leipzig Cons. 1893, *Mass in D,* perf., Albert Hall, by Barnby; 1906, opera, *Les Waufrageurs,* prod., Leipzig; 1920, decorated "Dame," equivalent of knighthood. Comp. several operas, mass, chamb. mus.

Södermann (*Say-der-man*), **August Johan.** Composer; *b.* Stockholm, Jul. 17, 1832; *d. ib.*, Feb. 10, 1876. Comp. operettas, part songs.

Sodero, Cesare. Conductor, composer; *b.* Naples, Aug. 2, 1886. Cond. opera at fourteen; cond., San Carlo Op., and Aborn English Op.; 1926, first cond. of radio opera, WEAF; cond. first world première of an opera via radio, in his own *Ombres Russe.*

Sokalski, Peter Petrovitch. Writer, composer; *b.* Kharkov, Rus., Sept. 26, 1832; *d.* Odessa, Mar., 1887. Comp. operas, incl., *Mazeppa;* authority on Russian folk-mus.

Sokalski, Vladimir. Composer; *b.* Heidelberg, Apr. 6, 1863. Comp. orch., chamb. mus.

Sokoloff, Nikolai Grigorovitch. Conductor, violinist; *b.* Kiev, May 28, 1886. Edu., Yale. *p.* Loeffler. 1898, violinist w. Boston Symph. Orch; 1916, cond., San Francisco Symph. Orch.; 1918-1928, cond., Cleveland Symph. Orch.; 1935, dir. of all Federal WPA mus. projects.

Sokolov (*Sok-o-loff*), **Nikolai Alexandrovitch.** Composer; *b.* Petrograd, May 26, 1859. 1896, *t.* Petrograd Cons. Comp. chamb. wks., ballet, incid. mus. to *The Winter's Tale.*

Solomon, Edward. Composer; *b.* London, 1853; *d. ib.*, 1895. Second husband of Lillian Russell. Comp. operettas, incl., *Billie Taylor* (1880), *The Nautch Girl* (1891).

Soloviev (*So-lo'vyef*), **Nicolai Theopemtovitch.** Composer, teacher, music critic; *b.* Petrosadovsk, Rus., May 9, 1846. 1874, prof., Petrograd Cons. Comp. operas, orch. wks.

Soltys, Miecyslav. Composer, teacher; *b.* Lemberg, Aus., Feb. 7, 1863. 1901, dir., Lemberg Cons. Comp. Polish operas.

Somborn, Theodor Karl. Composer, teacher; b. Barmen, Ger., Nov. 16. 1851. 1913, prof., Munich Cons. Comp. operas.

Somerset, Lord Henry Richard Charles. b. England, Dec. 7, 1849; d. Florence, Oct. 11, 1932. Son of 8th Duke of Beaufort. Comp. many songs, incl., *Where'er You Go.*

Somervell, Arthur. Composer; b. Windermere, Eng., Jun. 5, 1863. 1883, A.B., Cambridge. Comp. orch. wks., cantatas, songs.

Sommer, Hans (Pseud. of **Hans Friedrich August Zincken**). Composer; b. Brunswick, Ger., Jul. 20, 1837; d. ib., 1922. 1857-84, t. Brunswick Tech. H. S. co-fd., w. R. Strauss and M. Schillings, of Union of German Composers, a performance rights society. Comp. operas, incl., *Lorelei, Der Waldschratt;* songs.

Sonneck, Oscar George Theodore. Musicologist; b. Jersey City, N. J., Oct. 6, 1873; d. New York, Oct. 30, 1928. 1902-1917, dir., Mus. Section, Library of Congress; 1917, mus. ed., Schirmer, N. Y.; 1915, fd. *Musical Quarterly.* Author *Monograph on Star Spangled Banner.* Comp. songs.

Sonnleithner (*Son-light-ner*), **Christoph.** Composer; b. Szegedin, Hun., May 28, 1734; d. Vienna, Dec. 25, 1786.

Sontag, Henriette Gertrude Walpurgis. Soprano; b. Coblenz, Ger., Jan. 3, 1806; d. Mexico, Jun. 17, 1854. Historic prima donna; sang at premières of Weber's *Euryanthe* (1823), and Beethoven's *Ninth Symphony* (1824), and *Missa Solemnis.* m. Count Rossi, and was given title by King of Prussia. 1848, after revolution, resumed career; d. from cholera.

Sormann, Alfred Richard Gotthelf. Composer, pianist; b. Danzig, May 16, 1861; d. Berlin, 1913. t. Stern Cons., Berlin.

Soro Barriga, Enrique. Composer; b. Concepción, Chile, 1884. Edu., Milan, at expense of Chilean gov't. 1904, won composition prize, R. Cons. of Mus., Milan; 1908, dir., Natl. Cons., Santiago de Chile; g.-cond., U. S. and other countries of the Americas. Comp. pf. concerto, chamb. mus., songs, pf. pcs., incl., *Romance in D.*

Sousa, John Philip. Composer; b. Washington, D. C., Nov. 6, 1854; d. Reading, Pa., Mar. 5, 1932. Amer. bandmaster. The popularity of his marches won him the title of "The March King." Comp. ten comic operas, and 100 marches.

Sowerby, Leo. Composer, organist; b. Grand Rapids, Mich., May 1, 1895. 1921, awarded Amer. Acad. Fellowship at Rome. 1925, t. Amer. Cons. of Mus., Chicago; org., St. James Ch.; 1918, orch. suite, *A Set of Four,* prod., Chicago Orch.; 1918, *Come Autumn Time,* prod., New York Symph.; 1918, *The Serenade,* for str. q., prod., Berkshire Quartet; 1922, symph., *From the Northland,* prod., Chicago Symph. Comp. also, *From the Prairie,* 'cello concerto; *Florida,* a suite; oratorio, chamb. mus., and some "classical jazz" wks. for Paul Whiteman.

Spadoni, Giacomo. Conductor; b. Imola, It. Edu. Bologna Cons. 1910, cond. American tour of Mascagni; 1911, cond. Chicago Op.; 1935, Met. Op.

Spaeth, Sigmund. Music critic, lecturer; b. Philadelphia, Apr. 10, 1885. 1910, Ph.D., Princeton. 1913, lit. ed., G. Schirmer; 1914-18, critic, N. Y. *Evening Mail;* 1919, editorial staff, N. Y. *Times;* 1930, edu. dir., Community Concerts; 1932, lecture tours, as "The Tune Detective." Author of *The Common Sense of Music,* and many books on mus. appreciation.

Spalding, Albert. Violinist, composer; b. Chicago, Aug. 15, 1888. Distinguished virtuoso. Comp. violin concerto, sonatas, and pcs.

Spalding, Walter Raymond. Organist, teacher; b. Northampton, Mass., May 22, 1865. p. Rheinberger. 1895, prof., Harvard U. Author of text wks. on mus.

Spanuth (*Spahn-oot*), **August.** Composer, writer; b. Hanover, Ger., Mar. 15, 1857; d. Berlin, 1920. 1906, t. Stern Cons., Berlin; 1907, ed. of the *Signale.* Comp. pf. pcs., songs.

Speaks, Oley. Composer, baritone; b. Canal Winchester, O., Jun. 28, 1876. Comp. over 250 songs, incl., *On the Road to Mandalay* and *Sylvia.*

Spelman, Timothy Mather. Composer; b. Brooklyn, Jan. 21, 1891. 1913, S.B., Harvard. Comp. operas, *La Magnifica, The Sunken City;* pantomime, *Snowdrop;* also chamb. mus.; many songs, to poems by his wife, Leolyn Louise Everett.

Spencer, Vernon. Pianist, composer; b. Durham, Eng., Oct. 10, 1875. 1903, t. Nebraska Wesleyan U. Cons.; 1911, t. Los Angeles.

Spicker, Max. Conductor, teacher; b. Königsberg, Ger., Aug. 16, 1858; d. New York, Oct. 15, 1912. 1882, cond., Beethoven Männerchor, N. Y.; 1895, t. Natl. Cons.; 1898-1910, ch. mus., Temple Emanu-El; mus. ed., Schirmer. Comp. orch., choral mus., songs.

Spielter, Hermann. Composer; b. Germany, Apr. 26, 1860. 1880, to U. S.; 1897, t. N. Y. Coll. of Mus. Comp. cantatas, choruses, sonata for 'cello and piano.

Spiering, Theodore. Violinist, teacher, conductor; b. St. Louis, Mo., Sept. 5, 1871; d. Germany, Sept., 1925. p. Joachim. 1893-1905, t. Chicago Mus. Coll.; toured w. Spiering Quartet; 1905-9, in Europe; 1909, to N. Y. Phil. w. Mahler, as conc.-m. and asst. cond. Ed., technical wks. for the violin, incl., *Studies in the Positions.*

Spindler, Fritz. Pianist, composer; b. Würzbach, Ger., Nov. 24, 1817; d. Dresden, Dec. 26, 1905. Comp. piano teaching pcs.

Spinelli, Nicolo. Composer; b. Turin, It., Jul. 29, 1865; d. Rome, Oct. 18, 1909. Comp. operas, incl., *A Basso Porto.*

Spitta (*Shpitta*), **Julius August Philipp.** Historian; b. Wechold, Ger., Dec. 27, 1841; d. Berlin, Apr. 13, 1894. Best known for his important biography of Bach.

Spofforth, Reginald. Composer; b. Southwell, Eng., 1770; d. London, Jun. 6, 1864. Famous writer of glees.

Spohr, Louis. Violinist, composer, conductor; b. Brunswick, Ger., Apr. 5, 1784; d. Kassel, Ger., Nov. 22, 1859. Recognized as foremost violinist of his time, and the virtual fd. of the modern sch. of violin playing. As g.-cond. of Royal Phil., London, he made history by intro. the baton, instead of conducting with a violin bow. 1822, court cond., Kassel. Comp. 8 operas, incl., *Jessonda;* 5 oratorios, incl., *The Last Judgment;* 9 symph., 43 quartets, 5 quintets, 5 double quartets, duets for two violins, violin concertos.

Spontini (*Spon-tee-nee*), **Gasparo Luigi Pacifico.** Composer; b. Majolati, It., Nov. 14, 1774; d. ib., Jan. 24, 1851. 1800, cond., Palermo; 1810-12, cond., It. opera at Odèon, Paris; 1820, Kapellmeister at Berlin. Comp. operas of a spectacular nature, modeled after Gluck, incl., *La Vestale* and *Ferdinand Cortez.*

Sporck, Georges. Composer; b. Paris, Apr. 9, 1870. Comp. symph. p., chamb. mus., songs.

Spross, Charles Gilbert. Pianist, composer; *b.* Poughkeepsie, N. Y., Jan. 6, 1874. *p.* Xaver Scharwenka. Accompanist to Melba, Amato, Schumann-Heink, Gluck, Destinn, Gadski. Comp. songs, cantatas, choruses, pf. pcs.

Stainer, Sir John. Organist, composer; *b.* London, Jun. 6, 1840; *d.* Verona, It., Mar. 31, 1901. 1888, knighted; 1889, prof., Oxford U. Comp. cantatas, incl., *The Daughter of Jairus,* and *St. Mary Magdalen;* anthems, songs, incl., *Love Divine.* Author of numerous theoretical treatises.

Stamaty (*Sta-mah-tee*), **Camille Marie.** Pianist, composer; *b.* Rome, Mar. 23, 1811; *d.* Paris, Mar. 19, 1870. Author of technical studies.

Stamitz, Johann Wenzel Anton. Violinist; *b.* Deutschbrod, Boh., Jun. 19, 1717; *d.* Mannheim, Ger., Mar. 27, 1757. 1745, as cond. of Mannheim Orch., he developed the "Mannheim School of Conducting," and made a sensational tour of Germany *w.* his orch. Comp. symph., chamb. wks.

Stanford, Sir Charles Villiers. Composer; *b.* Dublin, Ire., Sept. 30, 1852; *d.* London, Mar., 1924. *p.* Reinecke. 1872, org., Trinity College, Cambridge; 1883, prof., R. A. M. Comp. operas, *The Veiled Prophet,* and *Savonarola;* symph., cantatas, *Battle of the Baltic,* and *The Revenge;* chamb. mus., songs.

Stanley, Albert Augustus. Organist, composer, conductor; *b.* Manville, R. I., May 25, 1851; *d.* Ann Arbor, Mich., Mar. 19, 1932. 1888, prof., U. of Michigan. Comp. symph., *The Soul's Awakening;* symph. p., *Atis.*

Stanley, Helen. Opera singer; *b.* Cincinnati, O., Feb. 24, 1889. 1911-12, Royal Op., Wurzburg; 1912-16, Chicago Op.; 1923-26, Civic Op., Phila.

Stark, Ludwig. Pianist, teacher; *b.* Munich, Jun. 19, 1831; *d.* Stuttgart, Mar. 22, 1884. Co-author of the historic Lebert and Stark *Method.*

Stasny, Carl Richard. Pianist, teacher; *b.* Mainz, Ger., Mar. 16, 1855. *t.* N. E. Cons.

Stasny, Ludwig. Composer; *b.* Prague, Feb. 26, 1823; *d.* Frankfort, Ger., Oct. 30, 1883. Opera comp.

Stassévitch, Paul. Violinist, pianist; *b.* Simferopol, Crimea, Rus., May 5, 1894. *p.* Auer. 1919, to U. S.; 1924, N. Y. debut as violinist and pianist *w.* State Symph. Orch.; *t.* David Mannes Mus. Sch., N. Y.

Staudigl, Joseph. Bass; *b.* Mollersdorf, Aus., Apr. 14, 1807; *d.* nr. Vienna, Mar. 28, 1861. Sang in première of *Elijah* (1846). His son: **Joseph, Jr.** Baritone (*b.* Vienna, Mar. 18, 1854; *d.* Karlsruhe, 1916). 1884-6, Met. Op., N. Y.

Stavenhagen, Bernhard. Pianist, conductor; *b.* Greiz, Ger., Nov. 25, 1862; *d.* Geneva, Switz., Dec. 26, 1914. *p.* Liszt. 1894-5, toured U. S.; 1901-4, dir., Munich Cons. Comp. pf. concertos.

Stcherbatcheff (*Schair-bah-chef*), **Nicolai Vladimirovitch.** Composer; *b.* Russia, Aug. 24, 1853. Comp. orch. wks., pf. pcs.

Stearns, Theodore. Composer; *b.* Berea, O., Jun. 10, 1880; *d.* Los Angeles, Nov. 1, 1935. 1923, opera, *The Snowbird,* prod., Chicago Op.

Stebbins, George C. Hymn writer; *b.* East Carlton, N. Y., Feb. 26, 1846. Author, *The Northfield Hymnal,* and other hymn collections.

Steggall, Charles. Organist; *b.* London, Jun. 3, 1826; *d.* ib., Jun. 7, 1905. Comp. ch. mus.

Steggall, Reginald. Composer; *b.* London, Apr. 17, 1867. Son of Charles S. Comp. scenas, symph.

Stehle (*Shtay-le*), **J. Gustav Eduard.** Organist, composer; *b.* Steinhausen, Ger., Feb. 17, 1839; *d.* St. Gale, 1915. Comp. sacred and secular cantatas *w.* orch.

Steibelt (*Sty-belt*), **Daniel.** Pianist, composer; *b.* Berlin, 1765; *d.* Petrograd, Sept. 20, 1823. Comp. operas, pf. concertos. Author of technical studies for pf.

Steinbach (*Stine-bak*), **Emil.** Conductor; *b.* Lengenrieden, Ger., Nov. 14, 1849; *d.* Mayence, Dec. 6, 1919. 1871-7, Kappelmeister at Mannheim; 1893, cond., Wagnerian opera at Covent Garden, London. Comp. orch. and chamb. wks.

Steinbach, Fritz. Conductor; *b.* Grünfeld, Ger., Jun. 17, 1855; *d.* Munich, Aug. 13, 1916. Cond., Mannheim and Meiningen; 1902-14, cond., Gürzenich concerts.

Steindel, Bruno. 'Cellist; *b.* Zwickau, Saxony, Aug. 29, 1869. 1889-92, solo 'cellist, Phil. Orch., Berlin; 1892, Chicago Symph. Orch.; Chicago Op.

Steiner, Williams Kossuth. Organist; *b.* Pittsburgh, Pa., Jun. 9, 1874. 1904-25, org., Rodelph Shalom Temple, Pittsburgh; dir., Germer Piano Sch. Comp. anthems, organ, pf. pcs.

Stenhammar, Wilhelm. Composer; *b.* Stockholm, Swed., Feb. 7, 1871. Comp. symph., orch. ballads, cantatas.

Stephan, Rudolf. Composer; *b.* Worms, Ger., Jul. 29, 1887; *d.* in battle in Fr., Sept. 29, 1915. Comp. opera, orch., chamb. mus.

Stephens, Percy Rector. Conductor, voice teacher; *b.* Chicago, Ill., Sept. 24, 1876. 1921, *m.* Jeannette Vreeland. 1897, *t.* New York. Prominent in investigations of Amer. Acad. of Teachers of Singing, through Carnegie Foundation.

Stephens, Ward. Organist, composer; *b.* Louisville, Ky., Sept. 9, 1872. *p.* Scharwenka. 1896, Paris debut as pianist; accompanist to Yvette Guilbert, Schumann-Heink, Matzenauer, Kreisler, Chaminade, Kubelik, Melba, Alda, Sembrich. Comp. symph., light operas, songs.

Sterling, Antoinette. Contralto; *b.* Sterlingville, N. Y., Jan. 23, 1850; *d.* London, Jan. 9, 1904. *p.* Garcia. 1871-73, soloist in Beecher's Ch., Brooklyn; removed to Eng., she became a leading ballad interpreter. For her Sullivan wr., *The Lost Chord,* and Cowen, *The Better Land.* 1875, toured Amer.; 1893, toured Australia, where her husband died—John MacKinlay.

Sternberg, Constantin (Ivanovitch Elder) von. Pianist, composer; *b.* Petrograd, Jul. 9, 1852; *d.* Phila., Mar. 31, 1924. *p.* Liszt. 1877, toured from Siberia to Egypt *w.* Desirée Artôt; 1880, toured U. S. *w.* Wilhelmj; 1886, *t.* Atlanta, Ga.; 1890, fd. own sch., Phila. Comp. orch., piano pcs.

Sterner, Ralfe Leech. Vocal teacher; *b.* Lock Haven, Pa., Feb. 26, 1883. 1902, fd. N. Y. Sch. of Mus. and Arts.

Stewart, Humphrey John. Composer, organist; *b.* London, May 22, 1856; *d.* San Diego, Dec. 18, 1932. 1886, to California; 1898, Mus.D., U. of Pacific; 1901-3, org., Trinity Ch., Boston; 1915, munic. org., San Diego, Cal. Comp. opera, operettas, orch. suites, *Montezuma* and *Scenes in California;* choral wks., ch. mus., songs.

Stewart, Sir Robert Prescott. Organist, teacher; *b.* Dublin, Dec. 16, 1825; *d.* ib., Mar. 24, 1894. Prof., Trinity Coll., Dublin.

Stiedry, Fritz. Conductor; *b.* Vienna, Oct. 11, 1883. 1914, cond., Berlin Op.; 1924, succ. Weingartner at Vienna Op.; 1928, returned to Berlin Op.

Stiehl (*Steel*), **Heinrich.** Organist, composer; *b.* Lübeck, Ger., Aug. 5, 1829; *d.* Reval, Rus., May 1, 1886. Comp. chamb. mus., pf. pcs., songs.

Stierlin (*Steer-lin*), **Johann Gottfried Adolf.** Bass, composer; *b.* Adenau, Ger., Oct. 14, 1859. *t.* Münster, Ger., Cons. Comp. operas.

Still, William Grant. Negro composer; *b.* Woodville, Miss., May 11, 1895. Edu., Wilberforce U.; Oberlin Coll.; N. E. Cons., *u.* Chadwick. 1933, awarded Guggenheim Fellowship to study abroad. Comp. symph. p., *Darker America, From the Land of Dreams;* symph., *Africa;* songs.

Stirling, Elizabeth. Organist, composer; *b.* Greenwich, Eng., Feb. 26, 1819; *d.* London, 1895. Comp. organ wks., songs.

Stock, Frederick. Conductor, composer; *b.* Jülich, Ger., Nov. 11, 1872. 1900, asst. cond., Theodore Thomas Orch., Chicago; 1905, cond., changing the name to Chicago Symph. Orch.

Stockhausen, Julius. Baritone, teacher of singing; *b.* Paris, Jul. 22, 1826; *d.* Frankfort, Ger., Sept. 22, 1906. Eminent oratorio and lieder singer; and as a teacher.

Stoessel, Albert. Conductor, violinist, composer; *b.* St. Louis, Oct. 11, 1884. During World War, served as bandmaster; 1921, cond., Oratorio Soc. of New York; 1923, head of mus. dept., N. Y. U.; 1930, *t.* Juilliard Grad. Sch.; dir., Worcester, Westchester County and Chautauqua Fest. Comp. symph. portrait, *Cyrano de Bergerac;* also songs, choruses, and pf. and violin pcs.

Stoeving (*Stay-ving*), **Carl Heinrich Paul.** Violinist, writer, teacher; *b.* Leipzig, May 7, 1861. Author of technical wks. on violin and violin playing.

Stöhr (*Stair*), **Richard.** Composer; *b.* Vienna, Jun. 11, 1874. Comp. symph., chamb. mus., choruses.

Stojowski (*Sto-yof-ski*), **Sigismund Denis Antoine.** Pianist, teacher, composer; *b.* Strelzy, Pol., May 14, 1870. *p.* Paderewski. 1905-11, *t.* Inst. of Mus. Art, N. Y.; 1911-17, *t.* von Ende Mus. Sch. Comp. orch., pf. wks.

Stokes, Richard Leroy. Music critic; *b.* Parke County, Ind., Nov. 30, 1882. 1903-14, feature writer, St. Louis *Post-Dispatch;* 1914-26, mus. and drama critic, ib.; 1926-31, mus. critic, N. Y. *Evening World.* Author of libretto of Howard Hanson's opera, *Merry Mount.*

Stokowski (*Sto-kof-ski*), **Leopold Anton Stanislau.** Conductor; *b.* London, Apr. 18, 1882. 1905-8, org., St. Bartholomew's, New York; 1909-12, cond., Cin. Symph. Orch.; 1912-36, cond., Phila. Symph. Orch.

Storace, Stephen. Composer; *b.* London, Jan. 4, 1763; *d.* ib., Mar. 19, 1796. Comp. many operatic wks.

Stradella, Alessandro. Composer; *b.* Naples, 1645; *d.* Genoa, Jun. 16, 1681. Early opera comp. of eminence.

Stradivari (Stradivarius), Antonio. Violin-maker; *b.* Cremona, 1644; *d.* ib., Dec. 18, 1736. One of the great violin makers of It.

Straesser (*Stray-ser*), **Ewald.** Composer; *b.* Burscheid, Ger., Jun. 27, 1867; *d.* Stuttgart, Apr., 1933. *t.* Stuttgart Cons. Comp. orch., chamb. mus.

Strakosch (*Strah-kosh*), **Maurice.** Pianist, impresario; *b.* Lemberg, Aus., 1825; *d.* Paris, Oct. 9, 1887. Taught Adelina Patti. 1848, to U. S.; *m.* Amalia, sister of Adelina Patti; 1857-60, manager, N. Y. Acad. of Mus.; 1860, to Europe, leaving management of his U. S. productions in hands of his brother, **Max.** *b.* 1834; *d.* New York, Mar. 17, 1892.

Stransky, Josef. Conductor; *b.* Humpoltz, Boh., Sept. 9, 1872; *d.* N. Y., Mar. 6, 1936. *p.* Bruckner. 1898-1903, cond., Royal Op., Prague; 1903-10, cond., Hamburg Op.; 1911-23, cond., N. Y. Phil Orch.; 1923-24, cond., State Orch., N. Y., from which he resigned to pursue his art interests in association *w.* the Wildenstein Galleries.

Straram, Walter. Conductor; *b.* London, Jul. 9, 1876; *d.* Paris, Nov. 24, 1933. 1909, asst. cond., Manhattan Op., N. Y.; later, fd. Walter Straram Concerts, Paris.

Stratton, Stephen Samuel. Writer, critic; *b.* London, Apr. 19, 1840; *d.* Birmingham, 1906. Author of biographical wks.

Straube, Karl. Organist; *b.* Berlin, Jan. 6, 1873. Distinguished virtuoso and conductor. 1918, org., Thomasschule, Leipzig. Exponent of Bach and Reger.

Straus (*Strous*), **Oscar.** Composer; *b.* Vienna, Apr. 6, 1870. Comp. operettas, incl., *Chocolate Soldier;* orch. mus.

Strauss (*Strous*), **Eduard.** Conductor; *b.* Vienna, 1835; *d.* ib., Dec. 29, 1916. Comp. dance mus. Son of Johann S.

Strauss, Johann. Composer, conductor; *b.* Vienna, Mar. 14, 1804; *d.* ib., Sept. 25, 1849. The head of the celebrated Strauss family whose dance music charmed the world.

Strauss, Johann (2d). Composer, conductor; *b.* Vienna, Oct. 25, 1825; *d.* ib., Jun. 3, 1899. Son of Johann S.

Strauss, Joseph. Conductor; *b.* 1827; *d.* Warsaw, Pol., Jul. 22, 1870. Son of Johann S.

Strauss, Richard. Composer; *b.* Munich, Ger., Jun. 11, 1864. 1886-89, cond., Munich Op.; 1889-95, Weimar. His wks. aroused heated discussions by their innovations, but in a few years became conservative in contrast to the ultra-moderns. Comp. operas, incl., *Salome, Elektra,* and *Der Rosenkavalier;* symph. wks., incl., *Death and Transfiguration, Till Eulenspiegel, Don Quixote, Ein Heldenleben.* 1935, aroused new commotion by another opera, *The Silent Woman,* to libretto by Stefan Zweig. In face of Nazi criticism, resigned all posts, incl., pres., Reich Mus. Chamb., and chairman, League of Composers.

Stravinsky, Igor Fedorovitch. Composer; *b.* Oranienburg, Rus., Jun. 5, 1882. St., law; diverted to mus. by Rimsky-Korsakoff; 1910, ballet, *L'Oiseau de Feu,* for Diaghilev. Comp. ballets, orch. wks., chamb. mus., pf. pcs.

Strelezki (*Stre-lets-ki*), **Anton** (pseudonym of **A. A. Burnand**). Composer; *b.* Croydon, Eng., Dec. 5, 1859. Lived in U. S. for a number of years.

Strickland, Lily. Composer; *b.* Anderson, S. C., Jan. 28, 1887. Comp. song cycles, reminiscent of her life in India; pf. concerto, orch. suite, *Carolina;* best known by song, *Lindy Lou.*

Stringfield, Lamar. Flutist, composer, conductor; *b.* Raleigh, N. C. *p.* Barrère. 1927, cond., Washington Natl. Op. Comp. symph., vocal, instr., chamb. wks.

Stringham, Edwin J. Composer; *b.* Kenosha, Wis., Jul. 11, 1890. Edu., Northwestern Mus. Sch. 1914-15, dir., Grand Forks (N. D.) Mus. Sch.; 1920-29, dean, Denver Coll. Mus.; critic, Denver *Post;* 1929, scholarship, Royal Acad. at Rome. *p.* Respighi. 1930, *t.* Teacher's Coll., Columbia U.; *t.* Juilliard Sch.; mus. ed., American Book Co. Comp. during Summer in MacDowell Colony at Peterborough; orch. wks., incl., *Visions;* songs.

Strong, George Templeton. Composer; *b.* New York, 1855(6). *p.* Jadassohn. Taught one year in N. E. Cons., and returned to Europe, where he remained. Comp. symph. wks., incl., *Sintram;* cantatas, songs and pf. pcs.

Strube, Gustav. Violinist, conductor, composer; *b.* Ballenstedt, Ger., Mar. 3, 1867. Fd.-cond., Baltimore Symph. Orch.; *t.* Peabody Cons. Comp. symph. p., *Lorelei* and *Echo et Narcisse;* opera, *The Captive.*

Strungk (*Stroongk*), **Nikolaus Adam.** Violinist, composer; *b.* Celle, Ger., *c.* 1640; *d.* Dresden, 1700. Early opera comp.

Stuart, Leslie (pseud. of **T. A. Barrett**). English church organist, operetta composer; *b.* Southport, 1864. Comp. *Floradora,* the success of which was *Tell Me, Pretty Maiden,* first a duet, then a sextet. In 1900, the Floradora "sextet" became New York's greatest matrimonial bureau, and more than 70 girls were utilized to keep the sextet intact during its run of over 500 performances.

Stueckgold, Grete. Soprano; *b.* London. 1927, Met. Op. Co.

Stults, Robert Morrison. Song writer; *b.* 1862; *d.* Ridley Park, Pa., Mar. 24, 1933. Comp. ballads, incl., *Sweetest Story Ever Told.*

Sturani, Giuseppe. Conductor; *b.* Ancona, It., Nov. 15, 1877. Edu., Cons. of Mus., Bologna. 1907-10, cond., Manhattan Op.; 1913, Met. Op.; 1913-20, Chicago Op.; 1927, Met. Op.

Sudds, William F. Composer; *b.* London, Mar. 5, 1843; *d.* Gouverneur, N. Y., Sept. 25, 1920. Comp. sacred mus., pf. pcs.

Suk (*Sook*), **Josef.** Violinist, composer: *b.* Křečovic, Boh., Jan. 4, 1874; *d.* Prague, May 29, 1935. Edu., Prague Cons., *u.* Anton Dvořàk. Fd. Bohemian String Quartet. Comp. overtures, chamb. wks., incl., *The Fairy Tale* suite, pf. pcs.

Sullivan, Sir Arthur Seymour. Composer; *b.* London, May 13, 1842; *d.* ib., Nov. 22, 1900. Edu. as choir-boy at Chapel Royal. 1856, won Mendelssohn Scholarship, which included three years at Leipzig. First attracted attention by his mus. to *The Tempest;* also by cantata, *Kenilworth;* the oratorios, *The Prodigal Son, The Martyr of Antioch,* and *The Golden Legend.* He ed. the Episcopal Hymnal, and added many noble tunes, incl., *Onward, Christian Soldiers;* also comp. many anthems and songs, notably *The Lost Chord.* Yet in another world he achieved an even greater fame, and became the link between the comic opera of Offenbach and the mus. comedy of Victor Herbert and his successors. The Gilbert and Sullivan operettas are unique and unmatched in the realm of mus. and literature and seem destined for immortality. There are some fifteen of them, incl., *Patience, Pinafore,* and *Iolanthe.*

Sullivan, Joseph J. Variety show comedian; *b. c.* 1850. *c.* 1885, intro. first song of its kind, *Where Did You Get That Hat?* at Miner's Eighth Ave. Th., N. Y.

Summy, Clayton F. Music publisher; *b.* 1853; *d.* Hinsdale, Ill., Feb. 10, 1932. Patron of mus. in Chicago; fd. mus. publishing house.

Sundelius, Marie. Soprano; *b.* Karlstad, Swed. 1929, Mus.D., Rollins Coll.; 1910, debut, Boston; 1913, Met. Op., N. Y.

Suppé (*Soo-pay*), **Franz von.** Composer; *b.* Spalato, Aus., Apr. 18, 1820; *d.* Vienna, May 22, 1895. Comp. over 200 comic operas, incl., *Fatinitza, Boccaccio,* and *Schöne Golathea.*

Surette, Thomas Whitney. Author, composer; *b.* Concord, Mass., Sept 7, 1862. Comp. operettas. Author of text-books on mus. study.

Süssmayer (*Sees-my-er*), **Franz Xaver.** Composer; *b.* Schwanenstedt, Aus., 1766; *d.* Vienna, Sept. 17, 1803.

Suter, Hermann. Composer, conductor; *b.* Kaiserstuhl, Switz., Apr. 28, 1870; *d.* Basil, Jun. 22, 1926. Cond., Basil Mus. Fest. Comp. orch., chamb. mus.

Svendsen, Johann Severin. Composer, conductor; *b.* Christiania, Nor., Sept. 30, 1840; *d.* Copenhagen, Den., Jun. 13, 1911. Edu., Leipzig Cons., at expense of Norwegian government; 1872-7, cond., Christiania; 1883-1908, cond., Copenhagen. Comp. symph., chamb. mus. Best known by *Romance in D,* for violin and orch.

Swarthout, Donald M. Pianist, organist; *b.* Pawpaw, Ill., Aug. 9, 1884. 1911-4, *t.* Milliken Cons., Decatur, Ill.; 1922, *t.* U. of Kansas. Comp. pf. pcs.

Swarthout, Gladys. Mezzo-soprano; *b.* Deepwater, Mo., Dec. 25, 1904. Edu., Bush Cons. of Mus., Chicago; 1924-25, Chicago Civic Op.; 1927-29, Ravinia Op.; 1929, Met. Op.

Sweelinck (*Svay-link*), **Jan Pieterszoon.** Organist, composer; *b.* Amsterdam, 1562; *d.* ib., Oct. 16, 1621. The most distinguished organist of his time.

Swift, Newton. Pianist, teacher; *b.* Spring Lake, N. Y., Jul. 23, 1871. 1897, *t.* Boston. Comp. teaching pf. pcs.

Szanto, Theodore. Pianist; *b.* Vienna, 1877; *d.* Paris, Mar., 1934. Edu., Pesth, Acad. Comp. violin sonata, pf. pcs.

Szekely (*Shek-e-ly*), **Imré.** Pianist, composer; *b.* Matyasfalva, Hun., May 8, 1823; *d.* Pesth, Apr. 1, 1887. Comp. pf. wks., chamb. mus.

Szumowska (*Shoo-mof-ska*), **Antoinette.** Mrs. **Joseph Adamowski** (q.v.).

Szymanowski, Karol von. Composer; *b.* Timashovka, Ukrainia, 1883. Edu., Warsaw, *u.* Noskowski. 1907, to Berlin; 1919, exiled from Rus. to Warsaw; 1930, *Stabat Mater* perf., Modern Mus. Fest., Liége. Comp. orch. wks., masques, opera, choral, chamb. mus., pf. pcs., songs.

T

Tabrar, Joseph. Popular song writer; *b.* London, Nov. 5, 1857; *d.* ib., Aug. 22, 1931. Said to have written words and mus. to 1,000 popular songs, incl., *Daddy Won't You Buy Me a Bow-wow-wow?* which circled the world at the turn of the century.

Tadolini, Giovanni. Composer; *b.* Bologna, It., 1793; *d.* ib., Nov. 19, 1872. Comp. operas, canzonettas.

Taffanel, Claude Paul. Conductor; *b.* Bordeaux, Sept. 16, 1844; *d.* Paris, Nov. 22, 1908. 1892-1908, cond., Paris Op., and Conservatoire concerts.

Talbot, Howard [correctly **Munkittrick**]. Conductor, composer; *b.* Yonkers, N. Y., 1865. Edu., R. C. M., London. 1900, cond., London Th. Comp. operettas, incl., *A Chinese Honeymoon* (1899).

Talexy, Adrien. Pianist, composer; *b.* 1821; *d.* Paris, Feb., 1881. Comp. operettas, salon pcs.

Talley, Marion Nevada. Opera singer; *b.* Nevada, Mo., Dec. 20, 1906. *p.* La Forge. Feb. 17, 1926, debut, Met. Op., N. Y., as Gilda in *Rigoletto;* appeared four seasons, 75 performances, leading rôles in 7 operas; 1929, retired to wheat ranch.

Tallis, Thomas. Organist, composer; *b. c.* 1525; *d.* London, Nov. 23, 1585. Comp. ch. mus.

Tamagno (*Ta-mahn-yo*), **Francesco.** Tenor; *b.* Turin, It., 1851; *d.* Varese, It., Aug. 31, 1905. Most celebrated tenor of his age. 1887, sang at première of Verdi's *Otello;* 1890-94, Met. Op., N. Y.

Tamberlik, Enrico. Tenor; *b.* Rome, Mar. 16, 1820; *d.* Paris, Mar. 15, 1889. Celebrated opera singer. Toured U. S.

Tamburini, Antonio. Bass; *b.* Faenza, It., Mar. 28, 1800; *d.* Nice, Fr., Nov. 9, 1876. Assoc. of Grisi and Lablache.

Taneiev (*Tan-e-yef*), **Sergei Ivanovitch.** Pianist, composer; *b.* Russia, Nov. 25, 1856; *d.* Moscow, Jun. 19, 1915. Comp. four symph., the dramatic trilogy, *Oresteia;* chamb. mus., songs. Author of theoretical wks.

Tansman, Alexander. Composer; *b.* Lodz, Poland, Jun. 12, 1897. *p.* Pierre Rytel, in Warsaw. 1920, concert of his wks., Paris; 1921, *Impressions* for orch., intro. by Vladimir Golschmann; 1926, to Austria; 1927, to Germany; 1928, to America; 1932, world tour. Comp. operas, orch. wks., chamb. mus., pf. pcs.

Tan'sur, William. Organist, composer; *b.* Dunchurch, Eng., *c.* 1700; *d.* St. Neot's, Eng., Oct. 7, 1783.

Tapper, Thomas. Writer; *b.* Canton, Mass., Jan. 28, 1864. 1904-7, ed., *The Musician;* 1911, Litt.D., Bates Coll. Author of educational mus. wks.; 1928, pres., Nat'l. Acad. of Music.

Tartini (*Tar-tee-ne*), **Giuseppe.** Violinist, composer; *b.* Pirano, It., Apr. 12, 1692; *d.* Padua, It., Feb. 16, 1770. 1728, fd. famous violin sch., Padua. Author of treatises on violin playing. Comp. violin sonatas, incl., *The Devil's Trill.*

Tasca, Baron Pier Antonio. Composer; *b.* Noto, It., ·1863. Opera comp.

Taubert (*Tou-bairt*), **Karl Gottfried Wilhelm.** Pianist, composer; *b.* Berlin, Mar. 23, 1811; *d. ib.,* Jan. 7, 1891. Comp. operas, symph., chamb. mus., 300 songs.

Taubmann (*Toub-mann*), **Otto.** Conductor, composer; *b.* Hamburg, Ger., Mar. 8, 1859. 1898, mus. critic, *Börsen-Courier.* Comp. orch., choral mus.

Tausig (*Tou-sig*), **Karl.** Pianist; *b.* Warsaw, Pol., Nov. 4, 1841; *d.* Leipzig, Jul. 17, 1871. Liszt's greatest pupil. Comp. technical studies for pf. and transcriptions.

Taylor, Deems. Composer; *b.* N. Y., Dec. 22, 1885. Edu., N. Y. U. From jack of all trades, incl., vaudeville and carpentering, became, 1921, mus. ed., N. Y. *World;* first noticed by *Through the Looking Glass,* suite for orch., which was widely perf.; 1925, retired to compose exclusively; *Jurgen* commissioned and intro. by Damrosch and N. Y. Symph. Orch.; 1926, to Switz.; comp. to book by Edna St. Vincent Millay, *King's Henchman;* 1927, prod., Met. Op.; 1930, short-time, ed., *Musical America.* Comp. opera, incl., *Peter Ibbetson;* also choral, orch. wks., piano pcs.

Taylor, Franklin. Pianist, writer; *b.* Birmingham, Eng., Feb. 5, 1843; *d.* London, 1919. Author of wks. on piano playing.

Taylor, Raynor. Organist, composer; *b.* England, 1747; *d.* Phila., 1825. As choir boy in Chapel Royal, attended Handel's funeral; his hat fell into the grave and was buried. 1792, org., St. Anne's Ch., Annapolis, Md.; 1793-1825, org., St. Peter's Ch., Phila.; 1820, fd. Mus. Fund Soc. Comp. much mus., some of which is in current use.

Tcherepnine, Alexander. Composer; *b.* St. Petersburg, Jan. 8, 1899. *p.* Liadoff. 1917, dir., Tiflis Op. Exiled from Rus., to Paris. 1923, *First Piano Concerto,* intro., Monte Carlo Orch.; 1928, opera, *Ol-Ol,* prod., Weimar; 1934, New York; 1933, world tour; 1934, to U. S. Comp. opera, ballet, orch. wks., chamb. mus., pf. pcs., songs.

Tecktonius, Leo. Pianist; *b.* Kenosha, Wis., May 10, 1882; *d.* Paris, Aug. 24, 1932. Has made frequent recital tours to U. S.

Telemann, Georg Philip. Organist, composer; *b.* Madgeburg, Ger., Mar. 14, 1681; *d.* Hamburg, Jul. 25, 1767.

Tellefsen, Thomas Dyke Aclaud. Pianist, composer; *b.* Drontheim, Nor., Nov. 26, 1823; *d.* Paris, Oct., 1874. *p.* Chopin.

Telva, Marion. Contralto; *b.* St. Louis, Dec. 26, 1897. 1921, Met. Op.; 1928, San Francisco Op.; 1934, Met. Op.

Temple, Hope (Mme. André Méssager). Composer; *b.* Ireland. Comp. ballads, incl., *An Old Garden.*

Templeton, John. Tenor; *b.* Kilmarnock, Scot., Jul. 30, 1802; *d.* London, Jul. 2, 1886. Successful opera and concert, especially in Scottish songs; 1832, sang in première of Meyerbeer's *Robert;* 1845-6, lecture-recital tour in U. S.

Terhune, Anice (née Stockton). Composer; *b.* Hampden, Mass. 1901, *m.* Albert Payson Terhune. Comp. over 100 songs and pf. pcs. for children.

Ternina (*Ter-nee-na*), **Milka.** Soprano; *b.* Vezisce, Aus., Dec. 19, 1864. Eminent Wagnerian singer. 1899-1904, Met. Op., N. Y.

Terschak, Adolf. Flutist, composer; *b.* Hermannstadt, Aus., 1832; *d.* Breslau, Ger., 1901. Comp. 150 wks. for flute.

Tessarin, Francesco. Composer; *b.* Venice, Dec. 3, 1820. Opera comp.; friend of Wagner.

Tetrazzini (*Tet-ra-tsee-ne*), **Luisa.** Soprano; *b.* Florence, Jun. 29, 1871. Early success in San Francisco. 1907, Manhattan Op., N. Y.; 1913-4, Chicago Op. Famous coloratura singer.

Thalberg (*Tahl-berg*), **Sigismund.** Pianist, composer; *b.* Geneva, Switz., Jan. 7, 1812; *d.* Naples, Apr. 27, 1871. *p.* Hummel. Famous for legato and cantabile effects, though superficial. 1856-7, toured U. S. Comp. pf. wks., and *Études.*

Thayer, Alexander Wheelock. Writer; *b.* South Natick, Mass., Oct. 22, 1817; *d.* Trieste, It., Jul. 15, 1897. Author of a famous biography of Beethoven.

Thayer, Arthur Wilder. Composer, conductor; *b.* Dedham, Mass., Aug. 26, 1857. Comp. songs.

Thayer, Whitney Eugene. Organist; *b.* Mendon, Mass., Dec. 11, 1838; *d.* Burlington, Vt., Jan. 27, 1889. Ed., *Organist's Journal.* Comp. organ pcs., and studies.

Thayer, William Armour. Organist; *b.* Brooklyn, Oct. 5, 1874; *d. ib.,* Dec. 9, 1933. *t.* Adelphi Coll., Brooklyn. Comp. songs, incl., *My Laddie.*

Thibaud (*Tee-bo*), **Jacques.** Violinist; *b.* Bordeaux, Fr., Sept. 27, 1880. Celebrated Paris virtuoso. Frequent tours of U. S., incl., 1903, 1917.

Thiebaut (*Tee-bo*), **Henri.** Composer, teacher; *b.* Schaerbeck, Bel., Feb. 4, 1865. Fd. mus. sch., Brussels. Comp. orch. wks., songs.

Thierfelder (*Teer-fel-der*), **Albert Wilhelm.** Composer; *b.* Mühlhausen, Alsace, Apr. 30, 1846. Comp. operas, symph. wks.

Thiériot (*Tee-air-yo*), **Ferdinand.** Conductor, composer; *b.* Hamburg, Apr. 7, 1838; *d.* ib., 1919. Comp. orch., chamb. mus.

Thoma (*To-mah*), **Rudolf.** Composer, teacher; *b.* Lohsewitz, Ger., Feb. 22, 1829; *d.* Breslau, Oct. 21, 1908. Comp. operas, oratorios.

Thomas, Arthur Goring. Composer; *b.* Ralton Park, Eng., Nov. 21, 1851; *d.* London, Mar. 20, 1892. Comp. operas, incl., *Esmeralda* (1883); cantatas, songs, incl., *A Summer Night*.

Thomas (*To-mah*), **Charles Louis Ambroise.** Composer; *b.* Metz, Alsace, Aug. 5, 1811; *d.* Paris, Feb. 12, 1896. Edu., Paris Cons. 1871, dir., ib. Comp. operas, incl., *Mignon,* and *Hamlet;* ch., chamb. mus., pf. pcs., songs.

Thomas, John Charles. Baritone; *b.* Meyersdale, Pa., Sept. 6, 1890. 1930, Chicago Op.; 1935, Met. Op.

Thomas, Theodore. Conductor; *b.* Esens, Ger., Oct. 11, 1835; *d.* Chicago, Jan. 4, 1905. 1845, to U. S., estab. first permanent orch. and toured U. S.; 1873, org., Cincinnati Fest.; 1876, cond., Phila. Cent. Exp.; 1877, cond., N. Y. Phil.; 1891, fd. Chicago Symph. Orch.; 1893, as cond., World's Fair concerts, commissioned Richard Wagner and Thomas Paine to write a Centennial March. An epic figure in Amer. mus. development.

Thomé (*To-may*), **François Luc Joseph [Francis Lucien].** Composer; *b.* Port Louis, Mauritius, Oct. 18, 1850; *d.* Paris, Nov. 16, 1909. Comp. operas, operettas, chamb. mus., pf. pcs., incl., *Simple Confession,* songs.

Thompson, John W. Organist; *b.* Leland, Mich., Dec. 21, 1867. 1894, gr., Leipzig Cons. 1890, prof. mus., Knox Cons. of Mus., Galesburg, Ill.

Thomson, César. Violinist, teacher; *b.* Liége, Mar. 17, 1857; *d.* Lugano, Sept. 27, 1931. Teacher of well-known violinists. 1882, *t.* Liége Cons.; 1898, *t.* Brussels Cons., succ. Ysaye; 1914, *t.* Paris Cons.

Thomson, Virgil. Composer; *b.* Kansas City, 1896. Edu., Harvard; to Paris on Naumberg Fellowship. *p.* Nadia Boulanger. Collab. on *Four Saints in Three Acts* (1934, Hartford, Conn., and New York). Comp. orch. wks., choral, opera, chamb. mus., piano, organ pcs., songs, incl., settings for Gertrude Stein's poems.

Thornton, James. Pioneer vaudeville monologist, song writer. 1888, the year of the blizzard, wr., *She May Have Seen Better Days.* The fruit of a night celebration on Jul. 4, 1896, was *My Sweetheart's the Man in the Moon,* first intro. at Orpheum Th., San Francisco.

Thuille (*Too-il-leh*), **Ludwig Wilhelm Andreas Marie.** Composer; *b.* Bozen, Ger., Nov. 30, 1861; *d.* Munich, Feb. 5, 1907. 1883, *t.* Munich Cons. Comp. operas, incl., *Lobetanz;* orch., chamb. mus.

Thursby, Emma Cecilie. Soprano; *b.* Brooklyn, Feb. 21, 1857; *d.* N. Y., Jul. 4, 1931. Distinguished concert singer.

Tibbett, Lawrence Mervil. Baritone; *b.* Bakersfield, Cal., Nov. 16, 1896. *p.* LaForge. 1923, debut, Met. Op. H.

Tichatschek (*Tik-a-chek*), **Joseph Aloys.** Tenor; *b.* Ober-Weckelsdorf, Boh., Jul. 11, 1807; *d.* Dresden, Ger., Jan. 18, 1886. Sang at premières of *Rienzi* (1842) and *Tannhäuser* (1845). Favorite of Wagner.

Tiersot (*Tyair-so*), **Jean Baptiste Élisée Julien.** Writer, composer; *b.* Bourg, Fr., Jul. 5, 1857. 1883, librarian, Paris Cons.; 1909, succ. Weckerlin as chief. Comp. symph. p., *Sire Halewyn.* Author of many books on mus.

Tietjens (*Teet-yens*), **Therese Johanna Alexandra.** Soprano; *b.* Hamburg, Jul. 17, 1831; *d.* London, Oct. 3, 1877. Celebrated opera singer. 1876, to U. S.

Tiffany, Marie. Soprano; *b.* Chicago, Ill. *p.* Schoen-Rene. 1916, Met. Op., N. Y.

Timm, Henry Christian. Pianist, choral conductor; *b.* Hamburg, 1811; *d.* N. Y., 1892. 1835, to N. Y.; 1847-64, pres., N. Y. Phil.; org., St. Thomas Ch.

Tinctoris, Johannes. Writer; *b.* Poperinghe, Bel., *c.* 1446; *d.* Nivelles, Fr., 1511.

Tinel, Edgar. Composer; *b.* Sinay, Bel., Mar. 27, 1854; *d.* Brussels, Bel., Oct. 28, 1912. 1896, *t.* Brussels Cons.; 1909, dir., ib., succ. Gavaert. Comp. oratorios, incl., *Franciscus.*

Tirindelli, Pier Adolfo. Violinist; *b.* Conegliano, It., May 5, 1858. *p.* Massart. 1896, *t.* Cin. Cons. of Mus. Comp. operas, songs.

Tobani, Theodore Moses. Composer, arranger; *b.* Hamburg, 1855; *d.* Jackson Heights, L. I., Dec. 12, 1933. Arr. for orch. Comp. small pcs., incl., *Hearts and Flowers.*

Toch, Ernest. Composer; *b.* Vienna, Dec. 7, 1887. St., medicine; edu., Vienna Cons. for few months; largely self-taught. 1910, won Mozart and Beethoven prizes, and definitely chose mus. career; 1913, *t.* Mannheim Hochschule; 1932, to U. S., intro. pf. *Concerto, w.* Koussevitzky; 1933, exiled from Ger., to London; 1934, to U. S.; *t.* New School for Social Research. Comp. orch. wks., opera, chamb. mus., pf. pcs., songs.

Tofft, Alfred. Composer; *b.* Copenhagen, Den., Jan. 2, 1865. Comp. opera pf. and violin pcs., songs.

Tokatyan, Armand. Tenor; *b.* Alexandria, Egypt, Feb. 12, 1898. 1921, to U. S.; 1922, Met. Op., N. Y.

Tomaschek, Johann Wenzel [Jan Václav Tomasek]. Pianist, teacher; *b.* Skutsch, Boh., Apr. 17, 1774; *d.* Prague, Apr. 3, 1850.

Tombelle, Ferdinand de la. Composer; *b.* Paris, Aug. 2, 1854. Comp. organ mus.

Tommasini, Vincenzo. Composer; *b.* Rome, Sept. 17, 1880. Edu., Liceo S. Cecilia. 1902, to Berlin; toured U. S.; 1913, prize for opera, *Uguale,* prod. Teatro Costanze, Rome; 1916, orch. work, *Chiari di Luna,* intro., Toscanini; 1917, choreographic comedy on themes of D. Scarlatti, *Good Humored Ladies,* prod., Diaghilev Ballet in Rome. Comp. operas, ballets, orch. wks., chamb. mus., songs.

Tonassi, Pietro. Composer; *b.* Venice, Sept., 1801; *d.* ib., Nov. 4, 1877. Comp. ch. mus.

Torchi (*Tor-kee*), **Luigi.** Musicologist, composer; *b.* Mordano, It., Nov. 7, 1858; *d.* ib., 1920. First ed., *Revista Musicale Italiana.* Author of many books on mus. Comp. operas, incl., *La Tempestaria;* symph. wks.

Torrance, Rev. George William. Composer; *b.* Rathmines, Ire., 1835; *d.* Kilkenny, 1907. Oratorio comp.

Toscanini, Arturo. Conductor; *b.* Parma, It., Mar. 25, 1867. World famous cond. and opera dir. 1896-1904, La Scala, Milan; 1908-14, Met. Op., N. Y.; 1921-28, La Scala; 1930-36. cond., N. Y. Phil.-Symph. Soc. Orch.

Toselli, Enrico. Composer; *b.* 1883; *d.* Florence, Jan. 15, 1926. 1900, as *wunderkind*, toured U. S.; 1907, *m.* ex-Crown Princess Louise of Saxony (*b.* 1870); 1912, divorced by her on grounds of insanity, after elopement w. her son's tutor. Comp. popular pf. pcs., incl., celebrated *Serenade*.

Tosti, Francesco Paolo. Composer, teacher of singing; *b.* Ortona, It., Apr. 9, 1846; *d.* Rome, Dec. 2, 1916. 1870, *t.* of Royal family, Rome; 1880, *t.* of Royal family, London; 1894, *t.* R. A. M.; 1908, knighted; 1913, retired to Rome. Celebrated comp. of ballads, incl., *Goodbye*.

Tourjée (*Toor-zhay*), **Eben.** Teacher; *b.* Warwick, R. I., Jun. 1, 1834; *d.* Boston, Apr. 12, 1891. 1867, fd. N. E. Cons. of Mus.; a strong advocate of class instruction; 1876, first pres., M. T. N. A.; co-ed., *Methodist Hymnal*.

Tournemire (*Toorn-mere*), **Charles Arnould.** Organist, composer; *b.* Bordeaux, Jan. 22, 1870. *p.* d'Indy. 1898, org., St. Clothilde, succ. Pierné. Comp. symph., chamb. mus., organ pcs.

Tours, Berthold. Violinist, composer; *b.* Rotterdam, Hol., Dec. 17, 1838; *d.* London, Mar. 11, 1897. Comp. ch. mus., pf. pcs., songs. Author of a violin *Method*.

Tours, Frank E. Composer, conductor; *b.* London, Sept. 1, 1877. Son of Berthold T. 1897, cond., Stanford's *Shaemus O'Brien;* 1904, cond., DeKoven Operetta Co. Comp. operettas, songs, incl., *Mother O' Mine*.

Tourte (*Toort*), **François.** Violin bow-maker; *b.* Paris, 1747; *d.* ib., Apr., 1835. Most celebrated of bow-makers.

Tovey, Donald Francis. Pianist, composer; *b.* Eton, Eng., Jul. 17, 1875. Comp. pf. concerto.

Towers, John. Vocal teacher, litterateur; *b.* Manchester, Eng., Feb. 18, 1836; *d.* Presser Home, Jan. 18, 1922. Org. of churches in all parts of Eng. and U. S. Said to have had 91,000 biographical notes at time of death. Author of *28,015 Operas* (1905), and several books on mus.

Trebelli-Bettini, Zelia (properly **Gilbert**). Mezzo-soprano; *b.* Paris, Nov. 12, 1838; *d.* Etretât, Fr., Aug. 18, 1892. 1863, sang Siebel in first London perf. of *Faust; m.* tenor, Bettini, later divorced; 1884, toured U. S. *w.* Abbey Troupe. Opera singer.

Tréville (*Tray-ville*), **Yvonne de.** Soprano; *b.* Galveston, Tex., Aug. 25, 1881. Sang in opera in Paris, Stockholm, Russia, Egypt, Bucharest, and many other European capitals; 1912, to U. S., as a concert singer.

Trnecek (*Trne-chek*), **Hans.** Composer; *b.* Prague, Boh., May 16, 1858; *d.* ib., Mar. 28, 1914. Concert harpist; expert perf. on the Jankó keyboard. Comp. operas, orch. wks.

Trotter, Thomas Henry Yorke. Teacher, conductor; *b.* Nov. 6, 1854; *d.* London, Mar. 11, 1934. 1887, M.A., New Coll., Oxford; 1892, Mus. Doc.; cond. first perf., Schumann's *Manfred* and Mendelssohn's *Athalie* in Eng.; 1915, prin., London Acad. of Mus.

Truette, Everett Ellsworth. Organist, teacher, composer; *b.* Rockland, Mass., Mar. 14, 1861; *d.* Brookline, Mass., Dec. 16, 1933. Concert organist. Comp. ch. mus., organ pcs.

Tryon, Winthrop Pitt. Music critic; *b.* Cape Elizabeth, Me., Jun. 10, 1869. 1892, A.B., Harvard. 1908, mus. critic, *Christian Science Monitor*.

Tschaikowsky (*Chy-kof-sky*), **Peter Ilyitch.** Composer; *b.* Wotkinsk, Rus., May 7, 1840; *d.* Petrograd, Nov. 6, 1893. Edu., Petrograd Cons. 1866-77, *t.* Moscow Cons.; 1876, reviewed first Bayreuth fest. for *Russky Viedomosty;* 1888, government stipend to comp. exclusively; 1891, visited U. S. The greatest of the Russians, and the least Nationalistic. Comp. six famous symph., operas, chamb. mus., pf. and violin concerti, pf. pcs., songs.

Tscherepnine, Nikolai Nikolaievitch. Conductor; *b.* Petrograd, May 15, 1873. Cond., Marinsky Th., Moscow; cond., Opéra Comique, Paris, where he intro. Rimsky-Korsakoff's *Snow Maiden;* 1909-1919, cond., Diaghilev Ballet. Comp. opera, orch. wks., ballet, choral, chamb. mus., pf. pcs., songs.

Tua (*Too-ah*), **Teresina (Marie Felicita).** Violinist; *b.* Turin, It., May 22, 1867. Distinguished virtuoso. 1887, toured U. S.

Tuckerman, Samuel Parkman. Organist; *b.* Boston, Feb. 11, 1819; *d.* Newport, R. I., Jun. 30, 1890.

Tuckey, William. Organist, conductor; *b.* England, 1708; *d.* New York, 1781. 1755, inaugurated choir sch. in Trinity Ch., N. Y.; 1766, played at dedication of St. Paul's Chapel; 1770, cond., first Amer. perf. Handel's *Messiah*, two years prior to its first perf. in Germany. His comp. have not survived.

Turina, Joaquin. Composer; *b.* Seville, Dec. 9, 1882. Edu., Schola Cantorum, *u.* d'Indy. 1907, *Quintet,* perf., Quatuor Parent; 1911, *String Quartet,* perf. Quatuor Touche; 1912, *Procesion del Rocio,* perf., Paris; 1914, *t.* Natl. Cons. of Mus., Madrid. Comp. operas, orch. wks., chamb. mus., songs.

Turner, Alfred Dudley. Pianist, teacher; *b.* St. Albans, Vt., Aug. 24, 1854; *d.* ib., May 7, 1888. *t.* N. E. Cons. Comp. chamb. mus., and piano pcs.

Turner, Arthur Henry. Organist, conductor; *b.* Meriden, Conn., Feb. 6, 1873. 1918, municipal org., Springfield, Mass.; 1922, org. and dir., Springfield Symph. Orch.

Turpin, Edmund Hart. Organist, composer; *b.* Nottingham, Eng., May 4, 1835; *d.* London, Oct. 25, 1907. Comp. ch. mus.

Tutkovski, Nicolai Apollonovitch. Pianist; *b.* Lipowetz, Rus., Feb. 17, 1857. Comp. symph. wks.

Tye, Christopher. Organist, composer; *b.* Westminster, Eng., *c.* 1508; *d.* 1572. Comp. ch. mus.

Tyndall, John. Scientist; *b.* nr. Carlow, Ire., Aug. 2, 1820; *d.* Dec. 4, 1893. Eminent acoustician. Author of *Sound*.

Twaddell, William Powell. Organist; *b.* Philadelphia, Aug. 17, 1879. *p.* Mrs. A. M. Virgil. 1922, dir. mus., Durham, N. C., public schools.

U

Ulibishev (*Oo-lib-i-sheff*), **Alexander von.** Writer; *b.* Dresden, 1795; *d.* Nijni-Novgorod, Rus., Jan. 24, 1858. Author of a biography of Mozart.

Ulrich (*Ool-rik*), **Hugo.** Composer; *b.* Oppeln, Ger., Nov. 26, 1827; *d.* Berlin, May 23, 1872. Comp. orch., chamb. mus.; arr. orch. wks. for pf.; an obvious genius thwarted by adversity.

Upton, George Putnam. Writer, critic; *b.* Boston, Oct. 25, 1834; *d.* Chicago, 1919. 1860, critic, Chicago *Tribune*. Author of critical books on mus.

Urban (*Oor-bahn*), **Heinrich.** Violinist, composer; *b.* Berlin, Aug. 27, 1837; *d.* ib., Nov. 24, 1901. Orch. comp.

Uribe, Holguin Guillermo. Composer; *b.* Colombia, Central Amer. *p.* d'Indy. Dir., Natl. Cons. of Colombia; cond., Bogotá Symph. Orch. Comp. chamb. mus.

Urso (*Oor-so*), **Camilla.** Violinist; *b.* Nantes, Fr., Jun. 13, 1842; *d.* New York, Jan. 20, 1902. 1874, toured Australia; 1895, South Africa; 1896, to U. S. Celebrated concert virtuoso.

Urspruch (*Oor-sprukh*), **Anton.** Pianist, composer; *b.* Frankfort, Ger., Feb. 17, 1850; *d.* ib., Jan. 11, 1907. *p.* Liszt. Comp. operas, pf. mus.

V

Vaccai (*Vah-kah-ee*), **Niccolo.** Composer; *b.* Tolentino, It., Mar. 15, 1790; *d.* Pesaro, It., Aug. 5, 1848. Celebrated singing teacher. Author of technical wks. for the voice.

Valle de Paz, Edgar del. Composer; *b.* Alexandria, Egypt, Oct. 18, 1861. Orch. comp.

Valle-Riestra, Jose. Peruvian composer; *b.* Lima, 1859. *p.* Gédalge, Paris. Uses old Inca themes in operas (*Ollanta*, prod., Lima, 1901), and pf. pcs.

Van Cleve, John Smith. Pianist, teacher; *b.* Maysville, Ky., Oct. 30, 1851; *d.* New York, 1918. Blind.

Vanderpool, Frederick William. Composer; *b.* New York, May 8, 1877. *p.* Louis Koemminich. Comp. songs., incl., *Values.*

Van der Stucken, Frank Valentin. Composer, conductor; *b.* Fredericksburg, Tex., Oct. 15, 1858; *d.* Hamburg, Aug. 19, 1929. 1895, dir., Coll. of Mus., Cin.; and cond., Cin. Symph. Orch. Comp. orch. wks.

Van Dyck, Ernst Marie Hubert. Tenor; *b.* Antwerp, Bel., Apr. 2, 1861; *d.* ib., Sept. 3, 1923. Eminent Wagner interpreter. 1898-1902, Met. Op., N. Y.

Van Emden, Harriet. Soprano; *b.* Milwaukee, Wis. *p.* Sembrich. 1921, debut, New York; 1922-26, toured Europe; *t.* Curtis Inst. of Mus.

Van Gordon, Cyrena. Opera singer; *b.* Camden, O., 1913. Chicago Civic Op.

Van Grove, Isaac. Pianist, composer; *b.* Philadelphia, Sept. 5, 1892. Edu., Chicago Mus. Coll. 1921-27, asst. cond., Chicago Op. Co.; 1925-31, mus. dir., Cin. Zoo Opera Co.; 1929-30, mus. dir., Amer. Op. Co.; 1931, cond., Chicago Civic Op.; *t.* Chicago Mus. Coll. David Bispham medal for opera, *The Music Robber.*

van Hoogstraten, Willem. Conductor; *b.* Utrecht, Hol., Mar. 18, 1894. Edu., Cologne Cons. 1911, *m.* Elly Ney. 1920, to U. S.; 1922, cond., Stadium Concerts, N. Y.; 1925, cond., Portland (Ore.) Symph. Orch.

Van Katwijk, Paul. Pianist, conductor; *b.* Rotterdam, Dec. 7, 1885. *p.* Godowsky. 1912, *t.* Christian Coll., Columbia, Mo.; 1914-18, *t.* Drake U., Des Moines, Iowa; 1919, *t.* Southern Methodist U., Dallas, Tex.; 1925, cond., Dallas Symph. Orch.

Van Rooy, Anton (Antonius Maria Josephus). Baritone; *b.* Rotterdam, Hol., Jan. 12, 1870; *d.* Munich, Nov. 28, 1932. 1898-1908, Met. Op., N. Y.

Van Vechten, Carl. Author, music critic; *b.* Cedar Rapids, Iowa, Jun. 17, 1880; 1903, Ph.B., U. of Chicago. 1906-7, 1910-13, asst. mus. critic, N. Y. *Times*. Author, *Music After the Great War, Music and Bad Manners; Music of Spain.*

Van Vliet, Cornelius. 'Cellist; *b.* Rotterdam, Sept. 1, 1886. 1901, mem., Amsterdam Concertgebouw; 1908-11, solo 'cellist, Vienna Op.; 1912, Minneapolis Symph. Orch.; 1919-29, N. Y. Phil. Orch.

Van Zandte, Marie. Soprano; *b.* New York, Oct. 8, 1861; *d.* Cannes, 1920. 1880-85, Opéra Comique, Paris; 1891-97, Met. Op., N. Y.; 1898, *m.* Tchernoff, Moscow. For her Delibes comp., *Lakme* (1883).

Varese, Edgar. Composer; *b.* Paris, Dec. 22, 1885. Edu., Schola Cantorum, u. d'Indy. 1907, won Bourse Artistique of City of Paris; 1916, to U. S.; 1921, fd. International Comp. Guild; 1923, *Hyperprism*, intro., Stokowski, *w.* Phila. Orch. Comp. orch. wks., chamb. ensembles.

Vavrinecz (*Vav-ri-netch*), **Mauritius.** Composer; *b.* Czegled, Hun., Jul. 18, 1858. 1886, ch. mus., Pesth Cath. Comp. operas, masses, symph. wks.

Vecsey (*Vesh-ey*), **Franz von.** Violinist; *b.* Buda-Pesth, Hun., Mar. 23, 1893; *d.* Rome, Apr. 6, 1935. Distinguished virtuoso. 1905, toured U. S.

Venth, Carl. Composer; *b.* Germany, Feb. 16, 1860. 1880, to U. S. Comp. two operas, orch., chamb. mus., choruses, songs.

Veracini (*Veh-ra-chee-nee*), **Francesco Marie.** Violinist, composer; *b.* Florence, c. 1685; *d.* nr. Pisa, 1750. Eminent virtuoso of the It. classical sch. Comp. operas, violin sonatas.

Verbrugghen, Henri. Conductor, violinist; *b.* Brussels, Aug. 1, 1874; *d.* Northfield, Minn., Nov. 12, 1934. *p.* Ysaye. 1903, asst. cond., Scottish Orch., Glasgow, *w.* Cowen; fd. Violin Quartet; 1922-31, cond., Minneapolis Symph. Orch., succ. Oberhoffer; 1932, faculty, Carleton Coll.

Verdi (*Vair-dee*), **Giuseppe.** Composer; *b.* Le Roncole, It., Oct. 10, 1813; *d.* Milan, Jan. 27, 1901. Edu., Milan, where he was considered lacking in talent. Later amassed great repute by his operas, incl., *Ernani, Rigoletto, Trovatore, Traviata, Aida, Otello, Falstaff,* which enjoyed an immense vogue all over the world. He ranks as the greatest It. comp. of his epoch, and one of the foremost musicians of the nineteenth century.

Verhey, Theodoor H. F. H. Composer, teacher; *b.* Rotterdam, 1848. 1870, *t.* Rotterdam. Comp. operas, chamb. mus.

Verrees, Leon. Organist, composer; *b.* Turnhout, Bel., Dec. 9, 1893. 1916, gr., Cons. of Antwerp, as 'cellist; 1918, diploma in organ. 1920, asst. to Lynnwood Farnam; 1923, org., St. Luke's, Scranton; 1935, won A. G. O. prize for *Choral Prelude on St. Anne.*

Vesque von Püttlingen, Johann. Composer; *b.* Opole, Pol., Jul. 23, 1803; *d.* Vienna, Oct. 30, 1883. Comp. operas, songs.

Vettori, Elda. Soprano; *b.* Italy. 1926, debut, Met. Op., N. Y., as Santuzzi in *Cavalleria Rusticana.*

Viadana, Lodovico. Composer; *b.* Viadana, It., 1564; *d.* Gualtieri, It., May 2, 1645. Comp. vocal, instr. pcs.

Vianesi (*Vee-a-nay-zee*), **Auguste Charles Léonard François.** Conductor; *b.* Legnano, It., 1837; *d.* New York, 1908. 1883-92, cond., Met. Op., N. Y.

Viardot-Garcia, Michelle Ferdinande Pauline. Mezzo-soprano; *b.* Paris, Jul. 18, 1821; *d.* ib., May 18, 1910, daug. of M. Garcia; *m.* Viardot, her manager. St. pf. u. Liszt, but afterward achieved a brilliant success as a singer in It. opera at London and Paris. Sang at première of Meyerbeer's *Prophète* (1849), and Gounod's *Sapho* (1851); to her Schumann dedicated his *Liederkreis* (Op. 24). 1863, *t.* Paris Cons. Comp. operas and 60 songs. Author of *Singing Method.*

Victor, H. B. Composer; b. London. 1774, emigrated to Phila.; 1778, ed. first Amer. Method, or teaching course, *The Compleat Instructor*.

Vidal (*Vee-dahl*), **Paul Antonin.** Composer; b. Toulouse, Fr., Jun. 16, 1863; d. Paris, Apr. 9, 1931. 1906, cond. opera concerts. Comp. operas, ballets, songs.

Vierne, Louis Victor Jules. Organist, composer; b. Poitiers, Oct. 8, 1870. p. César Franck. 1900, org., Notre-Dame, Paris. Comp. symph., choral, chamb. wks., but best known by his organ wks.

Vieuxtemps (*Vyu-ton*), **Henri.** Violinist; b. Verviers, Bel., Feb. 20, 1820; d. Mustapha, Algiers, Jun. 6, 1881. p. deBériot. 1846-52, court violinist, Petrograd. 1857, to U. S. w. Thalberg; 1870, w. Nilsson; 1871, t. Brussels Cons.; 1873, stroke ended career, but he continued to teach for a time. Comp. four violin concertos, and many brilliant and effective violin pcs., incl., the once popular *Ballade et Polonaise*.

Vilbac, Alphonse Charles Renaud de. Pianist, organist; b. Montpellier, Fr., Jun. 3, 1829; d. Brussels, Bel., Mar. 19, 1884. Comp. operas, pf. pcs.

Villa-Lobos, Hector. Composer; b. Rio de Janeiro, Mar. 5, 1886. Mus. dir. in Rio de Janeiro public schools. 1923, to Paris in concert of his wks.; also perf. by Stokowski; 1935, pf. suite, *The Baby's Family*, comp. for her two children, perf. by Guiomar Novaes, in N. Y. Comp. opera, orch. wks., choral, chamb. mus., pf. pcs.

Villebois (*Veel-bwah*), **Constantin Petrovitch.** Composer; b. Petrograd, May 17, 1817; d. Warsaw, Jun. 30, 1882. Comp. operas, songs.

Vincent, Henry Bethuel. Organist, composer; b. Denver, Colo., Dec. 28, 1872. p. Sherwood. 1904-23, official org., Chautauqua Inst. Comp. oratorio, operettas, anthems, organ and pf. pcs., songs.

Vinée (*Vee-nay*), **Anselme.** Composer; b. Loudun, Fr. Comp. orch. suites, *Paysage* and *Bretagne*; chamb. mus., songs.

Viotta, Henri. Conductor, writer; b. Amsterdam, Hol., Jul. 16, 1848; d. ib., Apr. 15, 1933. 1896-1917, dir., Hague Cons., succ. Nicolai. Ed., *Caecilia*. Author of *Lexicon der Teonkunst*, and other books on mus. Comp. orch. mus.

Viotti, Giovanni Battista. Violinist, composer; b. Fontanetto da Pó, It., May 23, 1753; d. London, Mar. 3, 1824. Son of a blacksmith, became protégé of Pugnani, and toured extensively. 1782-92, musician to Marie Antoinette. Banished to London, then to Hamburg. 1819-22, dir., Paris Op. Altogether a turbulent career, but the greatest perf. of his epoch. Often called "the father of modern violin playing." Comp. 29 concertos, 21 str. quartets, 50 duos, 18 sonatas, and misc. pcs.

Virgil, Antha Minerva. Piano pedagogue; b. Elmira, N. Y. Inventor of Tekniklavier, a practise keyboard; intro. constant use of metronome in practice; 1891, fd. Virgil Pf. Sch. 1878, m. Almon Kincaid Virgil (b. Erie, Pa., Aug. 13, 1842; d. Florida, Oct. 15, 1932), who she divorced and who founded a rival sch.

Vitali, Giovanni Battista. Composer; b. Cremona, c. 1644; d. Modena, It., Oct. 12, 1692. Comp. instr. wks.

Vivaldi, Antonio. Violinist, composer; b. Venice, c. 1680; d. ib., 1743. Comp. 40 operas, 150 violin concertos, and many pcs., incl. a famous *Chaconne*. Bach used 16 of his *Concertos* as the basis for more extended development.

Vleeshouwer, Albert de. Composer; b. Antwerp Bel., Jun. 8, 1863. Opera and orch. comp.

Vogel, Friedrich Wilhelm Ferdinand. Organist, composer; b. Havelberg, Nor., Sept. 9, 1807; d. Bergen, Nor., 1892.

Vogel, Charles Louis Adolphe. Composer; b. Lille, Fr., May 17, 1808; d. Paris, 1892. Comp. 7 operas, chamb. mus., pf. pcs., songs, incl., revolutionary air, *The Three Colors* (1830).

Vogl, Heinrich. Tenor; b. Munich, Ger., Jan. 15, 1845; d. ib., Apr. 20, 1900. Eminent Wagner interpreter. Sang at premières of *Rheingold* and *Walküre*. 1868, m. Theresa Thoma (b. 1845), who sang at Munich Op. (1865-92).

Vogler, Abbé Georg Joseph. Organist, composer; b. Würzburg, Ger., Jun. 15, 1749; d. Darmstadt, Ger., May 6, 1814. Celebrated for his improvising on the organ, probably the one to whom Robert Browning makes reference in a poem. Comp. an incredible quantity of mus. in all forms. Author of many technical books on mus. A radical iconoclast who aroused much ridicule.

Vogrich, Max Wilhelm Karl. Pianist, composer; b. Hermannstadt, Aus., Jan. 24, 1852; d. New York, Jun. 10, 1916. Toured world. 1878, first visit to U. S. w. Wilhelmj; 1886-1902, New York, editorial work for Schirmer Library. Comp. operas, incl., *Buddha;* oratorios, anthems, and many wks. in all forms.

Vogt, Jean. Pianist, composer; b. Liegnitz, Ger., Jan. 17, 1823; d. Eberswalde, Ger., Jul. 31, 1888. 1871-73, t. New York. Comp. oratorio, chamb. mus., pf. études and pcs.

Volbach, Fritz. Conductor; b. Wipperfürth, Ger., Dec. 17, 1861. Comp. operas, symph. wks., pcs. Author of many books on mus.

Volckmar, Wilhelm Valentin. Organist, composer; b. Hersfeld, Ger., Dec. 26, 1812; d. Homberg, Ger., Aug. 29, 1887. Organ virtuoso. Comp. 20 organ sonatas, misc. pcs. Author of *Methods*.

Volkmann, Friedrich Robert. Composer; b. Lommatzsch, Ger., Apr. 6, 1815; d. Pesth, Oct. 30, 1883. Comp. symph., chamb. wks., many pcs.

Volpe, Arnold. Composer, conductor; b. Russia, Jul. 9, 1869. 1898, to U. S.; fd. Lewisohn Stadium Concerts, N. Y. Comp. violin pcs., songs.

Von Doenhoff, Albert. Pianist, composer, lecturer; b. Louisville, Ky. p. Scharwenka. Comp. trio, pf. pcs., études.

Von Ende, Herwegh. Violinist, teacher; b. Milwaukee, Wis., Feb. 16, 1877; d. N. Y., Jan. 13, 1919. 1893 t. Chicago; 1895, Berlin; 1899, The Hague; 1900, m. Adrienne Remenyi, daug. of famous violinist; toured U. S.; 1903, t. N. Y.; 1910, fd. Von Ende Sch., N. Y.

Von Kunits, Luigi. Violinist; b. Vienna, Jul. 30, 1870. 1906, cond., Pittsburgh; 1910-12, to Vienna; 1912, t. Can. Acad. of Mus., Toronto; ed., *Canadian Journal of Music*. Comp. violin wks., songs. Author of books on mus.

Votipka, Thelma. Soprano; b. Cleveland. Edu. Oberlin Cons. 1920, Chicago Op.; 1935, Met. Op.

Vreuls, Victor. Composer; b. Verviers, Bel., Feb. 4, 1876. t. Schola Cantorum, Paris. Comp. symph. wks.

Vuillaume (*Vwee-yome*), **Jean Baptiste.** Violin-maker; b. Mirecourt, Fr., Oct. 7, 1798; d. Paris, Mar. 19, 1879. Eminent French maker; expert on old It. violins.

W

Wachs (*Vaks*), **Étienne Victor Paul.** Pianist, composer; *b.* Paris, Sept. 19, 1851. Comp. pf. salon pcs., once much used for teaching.

Wachtel, Theodor. Tenor; *b.* Hamburg, Mar. 10, 1823; *d.* Frankfort, Nov. 14, 1893. Celebrated opera tenor. 1871, 1875, visited U. S.

Waelput (*Vahl-poot*), **Hendrik.** Conductor, composer; *b.* Ghent, Bel., Oct. 26, 1845; *d.* ib., Jul. 8, 1885. *t.* Antwerp Cons. Comp. symph., cantatas.

Waelrant, Hubert. Composer, teacher; *b.* Tingerloo, Bel., *c.* 1517; *d.* Antwerp, Nov. 19, 1595. Eminent musician of the Netherlands contrapuntal sch.

Wagenaar, Bernard. Violinist, composer; *b.* Arnhem, Hol., Aug. 18, 1894. 1920, mem. N. Y. Phil. Orch. Comp. instr. mus.

Wagenaar (*Vah-ge-nahr*), **Johann.** Organist, composer; *b.* Utrecht, Hol., Nov. 1, 1862. 1919, dir., The Hague Acad. of Mus. Comp. cantatas, chamb. mus.

Wagenseil (*Vah-gen-sile*), **Georg Christian.** Composer; *b.* Vienna, Jan. 15, 1715; *d.* ib., Mar. 1, 1777. Comp. 15 operas, 30 symph. misc. wks.

Wagner (*Vahg-ner*), **Richard.** German composer and librettist; *b.* Leipzig, Ger., May 22, 1813; *d.* Venice, Feb. 13, 1883. Edu., U. of Leipzig. An overture and symph. successfully perf. at Gewandhaus, he wr. an opera, *Die Feen.* 1836, cond. his opera, *Das Liebesverbot,* at Magdeburg. 1839, to Paris, where amidst much hardship he completed *Rienzi* and *The Flying Dutchman;* 1842, to Dresden, where a perf. of *Rienzi* won him the appointment as kapellmeister; 1845, prod. *Tannhäuser;* wr. *Lohengrin;* 1849, involved in the Revolution, he escaped to Weimar, then Paris, and Zürich. He interrupted his great project of the *Nibelungen* cycle of operas to comp. *Tristan und Isolde,* prod. in Munich, Jun. 10, 1865; *The Meistersinger* was prod. in Munich, Jun. 23, 1868; 1871, settled in Bayreuth; 1876, the crowning point in his life in the perf. of the *Nibelungen* cycle; 1882, *Parsifal* prod. Few musicians have achieved greater fame nor exerted a greater influence upon the development of opera, representing the culmination of romanticism. He originated the *leitmotif* and the musico-dramatic cult.

Wagner, Siegfried. Composer, conductor; *b.* Triebschen, Switz., Jun. 6, 1869; *d.* Bayreuth, Aug. 4, 1930. Son of Richard W. 1924, visited U. S. Has comp. operas, and other wks. Never fully accepted as successor to his father.

Wakefield, Henriette. Contralto; *b.* New York City. At 18, debut *w.* Met. Op., N. Y., continuing 5 years.

Waldteufel (*Vahlt-toy-fel*), **Émile.** Composer; *b.* Strassburg, Alsace, Dec. 9, 1837; *d.* Paris, Feb. 16, 1915. Celebrated waltz comp.

Walker, Edyth. Contralto; *b.* Hopewell, N. Y., 1870. 1903-6, Met. Op., N. Y.; 1912-17, Munich Op.

Walker, Ernest. Organist, writer; *b.* Bombay, India, Jul. 15, 1870. 1899-1902, ed., *Musical Gazette;* 1900, *t.* Balliol Coll., Oxford. Comp. chamb. mus., songs.

Wallace, William. Composer; *b.* Greenock, Scot., 1860. 1905, sec., Soc. of British Comp. Comp. symph. wks., operas, misc. pcs.

Wallace, William Vincent. Composer, violinist; *b.* Waterford, Ire., Jun. 1, 1814; *d.* Chateau de Bages, Fr., Oct. 12, 1865. Discouraged w. artistic life, became a world traveler. 1845, returned to Eng. and prod. his famous opera, *Maritana,* followed by *Matilda of Hungary;* 1850, lost savings in pf. mfg. in N. Y.; 1860, ret. to London, and prod. *Lurline, The Amber Witch, The Desert Flower.*

Wallaschek, Richard. Writer; *b.* Brünn, Aus., Nov. 16, 1860; *d.* Vienna, 1917. *t.* Vienna Cons.; 1896-1909, mus. critic, *Die Zeit.* Author of wks. on early mus.

Wallenstein, Alfred. Conductor, 'cellist; *b.* Chicago, Oct. 7, 1898. *p.* Klengel, Leipzig. 1914, 'cellist, San Francisco Symph.; 1920-1928, Chicago Symph.; 1928, New York Phil.; 1935, cond., Wallenstein Symphonietta; also mus. dir. of radio station WOR.

Wallnoefer (*Val-nay-fer*), **Adolf.** Composer, singer; *b.* Vienna, Apr. 24, 1854. 1897, Met. Op., N. Y. Comp. songs, choral wks.

Walter, Bruno (originally **Schlesinger**). Conductor; *b.* Berlin. 1876, came early under influence of Mahler. 1914-22, cond., Munich Op.; 1922, g.-cond., N. Y. Symph.; 1925, cond., Berlin-Carconenburg Op.; 1932, co-cond., N. Y. Phil. Orch. Comp. symph., chamb. mus., songs.

Walton, William. Composer; *b.* Oldham, Eng., Mar. 29, 1902. 1912-8, Christ Coll., Oxford, as chorister. 1923, first *String Quartet,* perf., Salzburg by ISCM; 1926, *Portsmouth Point,* perf., Zurich Fest.; 1931, *Belshazaar's Feast,* perf., Vienna Mod. Mus. Fest. Comp. orch. wks., choral, chamb. mus.

Wambach, Emile Xaver. Violinist, composer; *b.* Arlon, Luxembourg, Nov. 26, 1854. 1912, dir., Antwerp Cons., succ. Block. Comp. orch. wks., opera, oratorios.

Ward, Frank Edwin. Organist, composer; *b.* Wysax, Pa., Oct. 7, 1872. *p.* MacDowell. 1902-13, org., St. Paul's Chapel, Columbia U.; 1917, NFMC prize for str. q. Comp. orch. wks., sonatas, instr. pcs., songs.

Ware, Harriet. Composer; *b.* Waupun, Wis., Sept. 26, 1877. Comp. cantata, *Sir Olaf;* songs.

Warlock, Peter. Pseudonym of **Philip Heseltine** (q. v.).

Warner, H. Waldo. Composer; *b.* Northampton, Eng., Jan. 4, 1874. 1907, one of fd. of London Str. Q.; *t.* violin and comp. in London. Won many prizes. Comp. orch. wks., chamb. mus., songs.

Warren, Richard Henry. Conductor, organist, composer; *b.* Albany, N. Y., Sept. 17, 1859; *d.* S. Chatham, Mass., Dec. 3, 1933. 1886-1905, org., St. Bartholomew's Ch., N. Y.; 1907, Ch. of Ascension, N. Y. Comp. operettas, cantata, orch. wks., str. q.

Warren, Samuel Prowse. Organist; *b.* Montreal, Can., Feb. 18, 1841; *d.* New York, Oct. 7, 1915. 1868-94, org., Grace Ch., N. Y. Comp. songs, anthems, organ mus.

Wassilenko (*Vas-si-len-ko*), **Sergei.** Composer; *b.* Moscow, 1872. Comp. orch. wks., cantatas.

Wathall, Alfred G. Organist, composer; *b.* Nottingham, Eng., Jan. 30, 1880. *t.* Northwestern U. Comp. operettas, incl., *Sultan of Sulu* (1903).

Watson, Frank Campbell. Organist, editor, composer; *b.* N. Y., Jan. 22, 1898. M.A., Trinity Coll., Hartford. Asst. ed., *University Course of Music Study.* Comp. symph. wks., masses, operettas. Author of *Modern Elementary Harmony.*

Watson, Mabel Madison. Pianist, composer; *b.* Elizabeth, N. J. *p.* I. Philipp. Comp. pf. and violin pcs.

Watson, Michael William. Composer; *b.* Newcastle-on-Tyne, Eng., Jul. 31, 1840; *d.* London, Oct. 3, 1889. Comp. popular ballads, incl., *Babylon*.

Weaver, Paul John. Music educator; *b.* Reedsville, Wis., Jul. 8, 1889. 1911, A.B., U. of Wis. 1911-12, dir. of mus., Racine (Wis.) Coll.; 1915-19, pub. sch. supv., St. Louis; 1919-29, dir. mus., U. of N. Car.; 1929, *t.* Cornell U.

Webb, Frank Rush. Organist; *b.* Covington, Ind., Oct. 8, 1851. Edu., N. E. Cons. 1873-76, org., St. Paul's Cath., Indianapolis; 1876-83, Trinity M. E. Ch., Lima, O.; 1883-1910, dir., Sch. of Mus., Stuart Hall, Staunton, Va.; 1910-23, Webb Advertising Agency.

Webbe, Samuel. Composer; *b.* Minorca, 1740; *d.* London, May 25, 1816. Wr. 12 volumes of glees.

Webbe, Samuel (2d). Composer, organist; *b.* London, 1770; *d.* Liverpool, 1843. Org., London. Comp. glees. Author of harmony text book.

Weber (*Vay-ber*), **Carl Maria Friedrich Ernest, Freiherr von.** Composer; *b.* Eutin, Ger., Dec. 18, 1786; *d.* London, Jun. 5, 1826. 1800, first opera, *Das Waldmädchen*, prod., Chemnitz, Ger.; 1804, to Breslau, to commence opera entitled *Rübezahl,* the overture to which figures in programs as *Ruler of the Spirits.* After unsettled life he achieved success at Leipzig as pianist and comp., and became cond. Prague Op. In Dresden, he wr. the operas *Preciosa, Freischütz* (1821), *Euryanthe,* and *Oberon,* which made him famous. Shortly before his death he went to London to supervise the production of *Oberon.*

Weber, Gottfried. Theorist, writer; *b.* Freinsheim, Ger., Mar. 1, 1779; *d.* Kreuznach, Ger., Sept. 21, 1839. Author of text-books.

Webern, Anton von. Composer; *b.* Vienna, Dec. 3, 1883. *p.* Schoenberg. 1908-14, cond., German and Viennese opera houses; 1918-21, active in Vereine fur Musikalische Privataufführungen; 1927, cond., radio orch. in Vienna; 1929, BBC annual g.-cond.; 1932, g.-cond., Barcelona. Comp. orch. wks., chamb., choral mus., pf. pcs., songs.

Weckerlin (*Veck-er-lan*), **Jean Baptiste Théodore.** Composer; *b.* Gebweiler, Alsace, Sept. (Nov.) 9, 1821; *d.* Trottberg, Alsace, May 20, 1910. 1869-1909, librarian, Paris Cons., succ. Felicien David. Comp. operettas, choral wks. Authority on folk-mus. Author of *History of Instrumentation.*

Wegelius (*Vay-gay-li-us*), **Martin.** Composer, conductor; *b.* Helsingfors, Fin., Nov. 10, 1846; *d.* ib., Mar. 22, 1906. Orch. comp.

Wehle (*Vay-leh*), **Karl.** Pianist; *b.* Prague, Boh., Mar. 17, 1825; *d.* Paris, Jun. 3, 1883. Comp. salon, pf. pcs.

Weidig (*Vy-dig*), **Adolf.** Composer, teacher; *b.* Hamburg, Nov. 28, 1867; *d.* Hinsdale, Ill., Sept. 24, 1931. *t.* Amer. Cons., Chicago. Comp. tone-poem, *Semiramis;* violin pcs., choruses, songs.

Weidt (*Vite*), **Heinrich.** Composer; *b.* Coburg, Ger., 1828; *d.* Graz, Aus., Sept. 16, 1910. Comp. operas, operettas.

Weigl (*Vy-gel*), **Joseph.** Composer; *b.* Eisenstadt, Hun., Mar. 28, 1766; *d.* Vienna, Feb. 3, 1846. Comp. operas, melodramas, masses.

Weigl, Taddäus. Composer, librarian; *b. c.* 1774; *d.* Vienna, Feb. 10, 1844.

Weil, Irving. Music critic; *b.* New York, Jul. 26, 1878. St. Sorbonne, Paris. 1910, mus. critic, New York *Evening Journal;* 1928-29, mus. critic, *Musical America.*

Weil, Oscar. Pianist, composer; *b.* Columbia Co., N. Y., 1839. Comp. pf. pcs., songs.

Weill, Kurt. Composer; *b.* Dessau, Ger., Mar. 2, 1900. *p.* Berlin Hochschule, *u.* Humperdinck. Dir., Ludenscheid Op. Comp. *Three-Groschen Opera;* orch. wks., choral, chamb. mus.

Weinberg, Jacob. Composer; *b.* Odessa, Rus., Jul. 1, 1879. Edu., Moscow Cons., *u.* Taneiev. 1915, *t.* Odessa Imp. Cons.; 1921, exiled to Jerusalem; 1926, *The Pioneers,* Phila. Sesqui-Cent. prize; 1926, *t.* N. Y. Coll. of Mus. Comp. orch. wks., opera, choral, chamb. mus., piano, violin, 'cello pcs., songs.

Weinberger, Jaromir. Composer; *b.* Prague, 1896. *p.* Max Reger. 1922, *t.* Cons. at Ithaca, N. Y.; 1925, Op.-dir., Natl. Th., Bratislava; 1927, opera, *Schwanda der Dudelsackpfeifer,* prod. Czech Natl. Th., Prague; 1931, prod., Met. Op., N. Y. Comp. orch. wks., opera.

Weiner, Leo. Composer; *b.* Budapest, Apr. 16, 1885. 1901, edu., Landesakademie; *t.* ib.; 1921, *String Quartet in F-sharp Minor* won Coolidge prize; 1922, perf. Washington (D. C.). Comp. orch. wks., chamb. mus., pf. pcs.

Weingartner (*Vine-gart-ner*), **Paul Felix Edler von Münzberg.** Composer, conductor; *b.* Zara, Aus., Jun. 2, 1863. 1881, ent. Leipzig Cons. as protégé of Liszt. 1884, opera, *Sakuntala,* prod. Weimar Court Th.; 1891, cond., Royal Symph. Concerts, Berlin; 1908-27, cond., Vienna Phil.; 1927, Basil Cons.; cond., Basil Symph. Orch. Comp. symph. wks., operas, misc. wks.

Weis (*Vise*), **Karel.** Composer; *b.* Prague, Boh., Feb. 13, 1862. Comp. operas, operettas.

Weisbach, Hans. Conductor; *b.* Germany, Jul. 19, 1885. 1911, asst. cond., Frankfort Rühlschen Gesangverein; 1919, Hagen; 1924, Barmen Konzertgesellschaft; 1926, cond., Dusseldorf Op.

Weiss, Adolph. Composer; *b.* Baltimore, Sept. 12, 1891. *p.* Schoenberg. Bassoon-player *w.* Amer. Symph. Orch.; one of organizers of Conductorless Symph.; 1932, won Guggenheim Fellowship. Comp. orch. wks., chamb. mus., pf. pcs., songs.

Weissheimer (*Vise-hime-er*), **Wendelin.** Conductor; *b.* Osthofen, Ger., 1836; *d.* Nuremberg, Jun. 16, 1910. Comp. operas, orch. wks.

Weitzmann (*Vites-man*), **Karl Friedrich.** Teacher, writer; *b.* Berlin, Aug. 10, 1808; *d.* ib., Nov. 7, 1880. Author of a history of the piano and piano-playing.

Wellesz, Egon. Composer; *b.* Vienna, Oct. 21, 1885. *p.* Schonberg. 1908, Ph.D., U. of Vienna. 1913, *t.* ib. Comp. opera, ballet, orch. wks., chamb. mus., pf. pcs., songs.

Wells, John Barnes. Tenor, composer; *b.* Wilkesbarre, Pa., Oct. 17, 1880; *d.* Roxbury, Mass., Aug. 8, 1935. Edu., Syracuse U. Comp. songs.

Wendland, Waldemar. Composer; *b.* Liegnitz, Ger., May 10, 1873. Comp. operas, incl., *The Tailor of Malta* (1912).

Wennerberg, Gunnar. Composer; *b.* Lidköping, Swed., Oct. 2, 1817; *d.* Leckö, Swed., Aug. 22, 1901. Comp. oratorios, settings of the *Psalms,* songs.

Weprik, Alexander. Composer; *b.* Lodz, Rus., Jul. 23, 1899. Edu., Leipzig Cons., *u.* Max Reger. 1923, *t.* Moscow Cons.; dances and *Songs of the Ghetto,* perf. leading symphs., incl., Toscanini and Phil. Orch. Comp. orch. wks., chamb. mus., pf. pcs., songs.

Wermann (*Vair-man*), **Friedrich Oskar.** Organist, composer; *b.* Neichen, Ger., 1849; *d.* Dresden, Ger., 1906. Comp. cantatas.

Werrenrath, Reinald. Baritone; *b.* Brooklyn, N. Y., Aug. 7, 1883. *p.* Victor Maurel. 1919, debut, Met. Op., N. Y., as Silvio in *Pagliacci*.

Wesley, Samuel Sebastian. Organist, composer; *b.* London, Aug. 14, 1810; *d.* Gloucester, Eng., Apr. 19, 1876. Eminent org. and Bach player.

Westendorf, Thomas Paine. Song writer; *b.* Virginia, *c.* 1860. Comp. *I'll Take You Home Again, Kathleen*.

Westmeyer, Wilhelm. Composer; *b.* Iburg, Ger., Feb. 11, 1827; *d.* Bonn, Ger., Sept. 3, 1880. Comp. operas, symph. wks.

Wetz (*Vetz*), **Richard.** Pianist, conductor; *b.* Gleiwitz, Ger., 1875; *d.* Erfurt, Ger., Jan. 16, 1935. Comp. opera, orch. wks., songs.

Wetzler, Hermann Hans. Conductor, composer; *b.* Frankfort, Ger., Sept. 8, 1870. 1897-1901, org., Trinity Ch., N. Y.; 1902-5, cond. orch. concerts, N. Y.; 1905, dir., Hamburg Op.; 1919, cond., Cologne. Comp. orch., pf. wks.

Whelpley, Benjamin Lincoln. Organist, composer; *b.* Eastport, Me., Oct. 23, 1864. Comp. pf. and violin pcs., songs.

White, C. A. Teacher, composer; *b.* Michigan, 1830. Gave up post as teacher in Naval Acad., Newport, to become a mus. publisher; later fd. White-Smith. 1883, comp. *Marguerite,* intro. by Denman Thompson, in *The Old Homestead,* at Boston Th. First song to intro. the repeat echo. Became sensationally popular for a generation.

White, Maude Valérie. Composer; *b.* Dieppe, Fr., Jun. 23, 1855. Comp. songs, incl., *How Do I Love Thee*.

Whitehill, Clarence Eugene. Baritone; *b.* Marengo, Ia., Nov. 5, 1871. *p.* Sbriglia, Paris. 1900, operatic debut, Brussels; 1903-08, Cologne Op. H.; 1909, Met. Op., N. Y.

Whitehouse, Horace. Organist, conductor; *b.* West Bromwich, Eng., Jan. 25, 1881. 1904, gr., N. E. Cons. 1909-18, *t.* Washburn Coll., Topeka, Kan.; 1918-21, *t.* Ohio Wesleyan U.; 1926-27, dir., Coll. of Mus., U. of Colo.; 1927, prof., Northwestern U.

Whithorne, Emerson. Composer; *b.* Cleveland, Sept. 6, 1884. *p.* Leschetizky. 1917-24, critic, *Pall Mall Gazette;* 1925, exec. ed., Art. Pub. Soc.; 1923, *New York Days and Nights,* perf., Salzburg Fest.; 1925, *In the Court of the Pomegranates,* intro., Colonne concerts, Paris; 1927, *Poem* for piano and orch., intro., Walter Gieseking; 1928, *Fata Morgana,* intro., N. Y. Phil.; 1929, *Quintet* for piano and strings, perf., Coolidge Fest. in Washington (D. C.); 1928, to China to study Chinese mus.; 1936, *Second Symph.,* perf., Toscanini and N. Y. Phil. Orch.

Whiting, Arthur Battelle. Pianist; *b.* Cambridge, Mass., Jun. 20, 1861. Comp. overture, chamb. mus., song cycles, incl., *Floriana*.

Whiting, George Elbridge. Organist, composer; *b.* Holliston, Mass., Sept. 14, 1842; *d.* Boston, Oct. 14, 1923. *t.* N. E. Cons. Comp. cantatas, incl., *Henry of Navarre*.

Whitmer, Thomas Carl. Organist, choirmaster; *b.* Pa., Jun. 24, 1873. Org., Sixth Presby. Ch., Pittsburgh; fd. *Dramamount,* colony nr. Hudson River, N. Y. Comp. *Spiritual Music Dramas, Syrian Ballet* for orch.; *Choral Rhapsody* for soli, chorus and orch.; pf. and organ pcs., songs, anthems.

Whitney, Myron William. Bass; *b.* Ashby, Mass., Sept. 5, 1836; *d.* Sandwich, Mass., Sept. 19, 1910. Distinguished opera and oratorio singer.

Whitney, Samuel Brenton. Organist, composer; *b.* Woodstock, Vt., Jun. 4, 1842; *d.* ib., Aug. 3, 1914. 1871-1908, org., Ch. of Advent, Boston. Comp. ch. mus.

Wickede (*Vee-kay-deh*), **Friedrich von.** Composer; *b.* Dömitz, Ger., Jul. 28, 1834; *d.* Schwerin, Ger., Sept. 11, 1904. Comp. operas, orch., pf. wks.

Wickenhausser, Richard. Composer, conductor; *b.* Brünn, Aus., Feb. 7, 1867. 1907-11, dir., Vienna Singakademie. Comp. vocal, chamb. wks.

Widor (*Vee-dor*), **Charles Marie.** Organist, composer; *b.* Lyons, Fr., Feb. 21, 1845. *t.* Paris Cons.; org., St. Sulpice. The most powerful influence of his period on organ playing throughout the world. Comp. operas, orch. wks., organ symph., chamb. mus., songs.

Wieck (*Veek*), **Friedrich.** Pianist, teacher; *b.* Pretzsch, Ger., Aug. 18, 1785; *d.* Dresden, Oct. 6, 1873. Eminent piano teacher. 1815, at Leipzig; 1840, at Dresden. Father of Clara, wife of Robert Schumann.

Wiedermann, Karl Friedrich. Organist, composer; *b.* Görisseiffen, Ger., Dec. 25, 1856; *d.* Berlin, 1918. Comp. overture, chamb. wks., songs.

Wiemann (*Vee-man*), **Robert.** Conductor, composer; *b.* Frankenhausen, Ger., Nov. 4, 1870. 1910. mus. dir., Stettin. Comp. orch., choral, chamb. wks.

Wieniawski (*Vyen-yof-ski*), **Henri.** Violinist, composer; *b.* Lublin, Pol., Jul. 10, 1835; *d.* Moscow, Rus., Apr. 12, 1880. Edu., Paris Cons. Frequent concert tours throughout world. 1872, *w.* Rubinstein to U. S. Comp. violin concertos and pcs.

Wihtol (*Vee-tol*), **Joseph Ivanovitch.** Composer; *b.* Wolmar, Rus., Jul. 26, 1863. 1919, fd., Riga Cons. Comp. orch. wks., misc. pcs., songs. Collected and arr. over 100 Lettish folk-songs.

Wilcox, John C. Voice teacher; *b.* Sebewaing, Mich., May 5, 1870. Edu., Mehan Sch. Vocal Art, Detroit. 1903-06, *t.* New York; 1907-27, dir., Wilcox Studios, Denver; 1927, dir., Denver Coll. Mus.

Wild, Harrison Major. Organist, conductor; *b.* Hoboken, N. J., Mar. 6, 1861. Cond., Apollo Club, Chicago; org., Grace Ch.

Wilhar (*Vil-har*), **Franz S.** Conductor, composer; *b.* Senoschetsche, Boh., 1852. Comp. operas, masses, pf. pcs., songs.

Wilhelmj (*Vil-hel-my*), **August Emil Daniel Ferdinand.** Violinist; *b.* Usingen, Ger., Sept. 21, 1845; *d.* London, Jan. 22, 1908. Edu., Leipzig, *u.* F. David. 1876, conc.-m., first Bayreuth perf's.; 1878, toured U. S. and around the world; 1894, prof. Guildhall Sch., London. Comp. chamb. mus., violin pcs., and arr. A celebrated virtuoso.

Wilke (*Vil-ke*), **Franz.** Composer, conductor; *b.* Callies, Ger., Sept. 3, 1861. 1910-19, cond., Greiz Phil. Orch.

Willeke, Willem. 'Cellist; *b.* Holland, 1878. 1907-17, mem., Kneisel Quartet, N. Y.

Williams, Alberto. Composer, educator; *b.* Buenos Ayres, Nov. 23, 1862. Fd.-dir., Cons. of Mus. *w.* 92 branches throughout Argentina; 1900, orch. concert of his wks. given in Berlin. Comp. symph. wks., chamb. mus., 150 pt. pcs., and many songs.

Williams, H. J. Song writer; *b.* Eng., 1873; *d.* Coventry, Eng., Feb. 23, 1924. Cripple from birth and never saw Tipperary, yet wr. *It's a Long Long Way to Tipperary*, which sang its way around the world.

Williams, Ralph Vaughan. Composer; *b.* Down Ampney, Eng., Oct. 12, 1872. Edu., Royal Coll. Mus., *u.* Stanford. 1907, *Toward the Unknown Region*, perf., Leeds Fest.; 1910, *Sea Symphony*, perf., London; 1914, *Geoffry Toye*, perf., London Symph.; 1918, *t.* R. C. M. Comp opera, ballet, orch. wks., choral, chamb. mus., songs.

Willis, Richard Storrs. Composer, organist; *b.* Boston, Feb. 10, 1819; *d.* Detroit, Mich., May 7, 1900. Song comp.

Willmers (*Vil-mers*), **Heinrich Rudolf.** Pianist, composer; *b.* Berlin, Oct. 31, 1821; *d.* Vienna, Aug. 24, 1878. Comp. brilliant pf. mus.

Wilm (*Vilm*), **Nicolai von.** Composer; *b.* Riga, Rus., Mar. 4, 1834; *d.* Wiesbaden, Ger., Feb. 20, 1911. Comp. chamb. mus., pf. teaching pcs.

Wilson, Francis. American comic opera star, impresario, author; *b.* Phila., Feb. 7, 1854; *d.* N. Y., Oct. 7, 1935. Won world fame in *Erminie*. Notable career for fifty years, in assoc. *w.* Charles Frohman, deWolf Hopper, and *w.* his own company. First pres., Actors Equity. Author of books, incl., *The Eugene Field I Knew;* also plays, incl., *The Dancing Master*.

Wilson, Grenville Dean. Composer, teacher; *b.* Plymouth, Conn., Jan. 26, 1833; *d.* Nyack, N. Y., Sept. 20, 1897. Comp. salon pcs. for pf.

Wilson, Mortimer. Composer, conductor; *b.* Chariton, Iowa, Aug. 6, 1876; *d.* New York, Jan. 27, 1932. *p.* of Fredk. Grant Gleason, and Max Reger. Cond., Atlanta (Ga.) Symph.; cond. his *In My Youth*, *w.* N. Y. Phil. Won prizes for orch. overtures for motion picture use. Comp. mus. setting for Douglas Fairbanks pictures, incl., *Thief of Bagdad*. First known as comp. of *In Georgia*, piano cycle. Comp. orch. wks. and pf. pcs. Ed. staff of *University Course of Music Study*. Author of text wks., *The Rhetoric of Music*, and a course in orch. training. Career largely assoc. *w.* New York.

Wilson, Raymond. Pianist, teacher; *b.* Oxford, Pa., Apr. 18, 1888. *p.* Ganz. 1912, *t.* Skidmore Coll.; 1914, *t.* Syracuse U.; 1921, *t.* Eastman Sch., Rochester.

Wiltberger, August. Composer, teacher; *b.* Sobernheim, Ger., Apr. 17, 1850. Comp. oratorios.

Winderstein (*Vin-der-stine*), **Hans Wilhelm Gustav.** Composer, conductor; *b.* Lüneburg, Ger., Oct. 29, 1856. 1896, cond. his own orch. in Leipzig. Unable to resume after World War.

Windheim, Marek. Operatic tenor; *b.* Warsaw, Pol. Met. Op.; concert, radio, legitimate stage.

Winkler (*Vink-ler*), **Alexander Adolfovitch.** Pianist, composer; *b.* Kharkov, Rus., Mar. 3, 1865; *d.* Petrograd, 1935. Comp. chamb. mus.

Winner, Septimus. Early American ballad composer. Under the pseud., Alice Hawthorne, wr., *Listen to the Mocking Bird*, and *Whispering Hope*, historic popular successes of the post Civil War epoch.

Winter (*Vin-ter*), **Peter von.** Composer, conductor; *b.* Mannheim, Ger., 1754; *d.* Munich, Ger., Oct. 17, 1825. Comp. operas, operettas, oratorios, masses.

Witek (*Vit-ek*), **Anton.** Violinist; *b.* Saaz, Boh., Jan. 7, 1872; *d.* Winchester, Mass., Aug. 19, 1933. 1909, conc.-m., Boston Symph. Orch.

Witherspoon, Herbert. Bass, teacher of singing; *b.* Buffalo, N. Y., Jul. 21, 1873; *d.* N. Y., May 10, 1935. 1895, concert and oratorio singer; 1908-16, Met. Op.; 1928, pres., Chicago Mus. Coll.; 1935, gen. dir., Met. Op., but fell dead at his desk before season opened.

Woelfl (*Velfl*), **Joseph.** Composer, pianist; *b.* Salzburg, 1772; *d.* London, May 21, 1812. *p.* Leopold Mozart. Concertized extensively. Comp. 9 operas, 15 str. q., 30 violin sonatas, and many other wks. in all forms.

Woikowsky-Biedau (*Voi-koff-sky Bee-dow*), **Victor Hugo von.** Composer; *b.* Nieder-Arnsdorf, Ger., Sept. 2, 1866. Comp. operas, songs.

Wolf (*Voolf*), **Hugo.** Composer; *b.* Windischgräz, Aus., Mar. 13, 1860; *d.* Vienna, Feb. 22, 1903. Comp. opera, *Der Corregidor;* the incomplete *Manuel Venegas;* chamb. wks., symph. p.. incl., *Penthesilea;* best known by his songs.

Wolf, William A. Music educator; *b.* Lancaster, Pa., Jun. 16, 1879. *p.* Busoni. 1903, Mus. B., U. of N. Y. 1913, fd.-dir., Wolf Inst. of Mus., Lancaster, Pa.

Wolfe, James. Basso; *b.* Riga, Latvia, Apr. 27, 1890. 1897-1910, Breslau Op.; 1920, to U. S.; 1923, Met. Op., N. Y.

Wolf-Ferrari, Emanno. Composer; *b.* Venice, Jan. 12, 1876. St., art in Rome; then mus., *w.* Rheinberger, in Munich. 1899, oratorio, *La Sulamita*, perf., Phil. Soc. of Venice; 1900, opera, *Cenerentola*, prod. Teatro Fenice; 1909, *Secret of Suzanne*, perf., Munich; 1902, dir., Liceo Benedetto Marcello, Venice; 1912, visited U. S. Comp. opera, choral wks., chamb. mus.

Wolle, John Frederick. Organist, conductor; *b.* Bethlehem, Pa., Apr. 4, 1863; *d. ib.*, Jan. 12, 1933. Fd., Bach Fest., Bethlehem, Pa.

Wollenhaupt, H. A. Pianist, composer; *b.* Schkeuditz, Ger., Sept. 27, 1827; *d.* New York, Sept. 18, 1863. Comp. salon pf. pcs.

Wolstenholme, William. Organist, composer; *b.* Blackburn, Eng., Feb. 24, 1865; *d.* London, Jan. 23, 1931. Blind. Eminent recitalist. 1908, toured U. S. Comp. chamb. mus., organ pcs.

Wood, Sir Henry Joseph. Conductor; *b.* London, Mar. 3, 1870. Cond., Queen's Hall Concerts, London; 1904, visited U. S.; 1908, declined cond. post *w.* Boston Symph. Orch.

Wood, Mary Knight. Composer; *b.* Easthampton, Mass., Apr. 7, 1857. Comp. attractive songs, a piano trio, etc. Lives New York.

Woodbury, Isaac Baker. Editor, hymn writer; *b.* Beverly, Mass., 1819; *d.* Columbia, S. C., 1858. 1851, ed., *N. Y. Musical Review;* suffered from ill health, and died at thirty-nine. His collections, such as *The Dulcimer*, attained great sale. Comp. songs and hymn tunes.

Woodhouse, George. Piano teacher; *b.* London. Important teacher in London. 1936, *t.* master class, Chicago Mus. Coll. Author of technical wks. for piano. Inventor of *Mutano*, a resilient mute piano keyboard.

Woodman, Raymond Huntington. Organist, composer; *b.* Brooklyn, N. Y., Jan. 18, 1861. 1880-1935, org., First Presby. Ch., Brooklyn; *t.* Packer Inst. Comp. organ wks., anthems, songs.

Work, Henry Clay. Composer; *b.* Middletown, Conn., Oct. 1, 1832; *d.* Hartford, Conn., Jun. 8, 1884. 1855, mus. typographer for *Root and Cady*. Wr. many historic songs, incl., *Grandfather's Clock,* and the great temperance song, *Father, Dear Father, Come Home With Me Now*. Always a fiery abolitionist, he won immortal anathema from the South by his war song, *Marching Through Georgia*.

Wormser (*Vorm-ser*), **André Alphonse Toussaint.** Composer; *b.* Paris, Nov. 1, 1851. Comp. operas, pantomimes, symph. wks.

Wüllner (*Vil-ner*), **Franz.** Conductor, composer; *b.* Münster, Ger., Jan. 28, 1832; *d.* Braunfels, Ger., Sept. 7, 1902. Comp. choral-orch. wks., masses, chamb. mus.

Wüllner, Ludwig. Baritone; *b.* Münster, Ger., Aug. 19, 1858. Son of Franz W. 1908-10, toured U. S. *w.* Coenrad van Bos. Famous dramatico-lyric interpreter of Lieder.

Wurm (*Voorm*), **Marie J. A.** Pianist; *b.* Southampton, Eng., May 18, 1860. Noted as improvisator. Comp. concerto, chamb. mus., pf. pcs.

Wyman, Addison P. Pianist, composer; *b.* Cornish, N. H., Jun. 23, 1832; *d.* Washington, Pa., Apr. 15, 1872. Comp. popular salon pf. pcs.

Y

Yaw, Ellen Beach. Soprano; *b.* Boston, N. Y., Sept. 18, 1868. Phenomenally high voice, *w.* range of almost 4 octaves. 1910, *m.* Vere Goldthwaite. 1910, Met. Op., N. Y.; Sir Arthur Sullivan comp. *Rose of Persia* for her; 1905-9, sang in European opera houses. Concertized extensively. Retired to Covina, Cal.

Yon, Pietro Alessandro. Organist, composer; *b.* Italy, Aug. 8, 1886. 1907, org., St. Francis Xavier Ch., N. Y. Toured extensively as concert org. Comp. wks. for organ and orch., organ pcs., incl., *Gesu Bambino;* songs.

York, Francis Lodowick. Organist, teacher; *b.* Ontonagon, Mich., 1861. *p.* Guilmant. 1822, A.B., U. of Mich.; 1883, A.M., 1892-96, *t.* U. Sch. of Mus.; 1896-1909, *t.* State Normal Cons., Ypsilanti, Mich.; 1902-27, dir., Detroit Cons. of Mus.; chairman board, Detroit Inst. of Mus. Art.

Yost, Gaylord. Violinist, teacher, composer; *b.* Fayette, O., Jan. 28, 1888. St., Detroit Cons. 1915-21, *t.* Indianapolis Coll. of Mus.; 1921, prof., Pittsburg Mus. Inst.; 1935, fd., Yost Str. Q. Comp. pcs. for the violin. Contrib. to mus. journals on technical subjects. Author, *Yost System of Violin Technic*.

Youmans, Vincent. Operetta, composer; *b.* New York, 1899. Comp. operettas, incl., *No, No, Nanette!* (1925, 321 perf.).

Yradier (*Ee-rah-di-er*), **Sebastian.** Composer; *b.* Spain, *c.* 1815; *d.* Vittoria, Brazil, 1865. Comp. about 35 popular ballads, incl., *La Paloma*.

Ysaye (*Ee-zi-eh*), **Eugéne.** Violinist, conductor; *b.* Liége, Jul. 16, 1858; *d.* Brussels, May 12, 1931. Toured Europe and America. Among the foremost violinists of his epoch. 1918, cond., Cin. Symph. Orch.

Z

Zach, Max Wilhelm. Violinist, conductor; *b.* Lemberg, Aus., Aug. 31, 1864; *d.* St. Louis, 1921. Cond., St. Louis Symph. Orch.

Zacharewitsch, Michael. Violinist; *b.* Ostrov, Rus., Aug. 26, 1873. *p.* Ysaye. Played Tschaikowsky Concerto at age of 12, comp. cond.; 1904, debut, London; soloist *w.* European orch.; 1926, toured U. S.

Zachau (*Zakh-ow*), **Friedrich Wilhelm.** Organist, composer; *b.* Leipzig, Nov. 19, 1663; *d.* Halle, Aug. 14, 1721. Teacher of Handel.

Zajicek-Blankenau (*Zah-yi-chek*), **Julius.** Composer; *b.* Vienna, Nov. 2, 1877. Opera comp.

Zandonai, Riccardo. Composer; *b.* Sacco, It., May 28, 1883. Edu., Pesaro Liceo, *u.* Mascagni. 1908, opera, *Il Grillo Sul Farolare,* prod., Turin, commissioned by Ricordi; 1914, *Francesca da Rimini,* prod., Milan. Comp. opera, orch. wks., choral, chamb. mus.

Zanella, Amilcare. Pianist, composer; *b.* Monticelli d'Ongnia, It., Sept. 26, 1873. 1892, toured S. Amer.; 1905, dir., Liceo Rossini, Pesaro, succ. Mascagni. Comp. operas, symph., pf. wks. *w.* orch., chamb. mus.

Zaremba, Nicolai Ivanovitch. Theorist; *b.* Vityebsk, Rus., 1824; *d.* Petrograd, Apr. 8, 1879. 1867-71, dir., Petrograd Cons., succ. A. Rubinstein. Comp. oratorio.

Zaremba, Vladislav Ivanovitch. Teacher, composer; *b.* Podolia, Rus., Jun. 15, 1833. Comp. pf. pcs., songs. Collector of folk-songs.

Zarembski, Jules de. Pianist; *b.* Schitomir, Pol., Feb. 28, 1854; *d. ib.,* Sept. 15, 1885. *p.* Liszt. *t.* Brussels Cons. Comp. pf. pcs., études.

Zarlino, Giuseppe. Theorist; *b.* Chioggia, It., Mar. 22, 1517; *d.* Venice, It., Feb. 14, 1590.

Zarzycki (*Tsar-tsits-ky*), **Alexander.** Pianist, composer; *b.* Lemberg, Aus., Feb. 21, 1831; *d.* Warsaw, Pol., Nov. 1, 1895. 1879, dir., Warsaw Cons. Comp. pf. and violin pcs., songs.

Zaslawsky, Georges. Conductor. 1920, g.-cond., Berlin, Paris, Prague, Buenos Aires; 1927, fd. short-lived Beethoven Symph. Orch.; returned to Europe.

Zeisler, Fanny Bloomfield. Pianist; *b.* Bielitz, Aus., Jul. 16, 1863; *d.* Chicago, Aug., 1927. *p.* Leschetizky. Concertized throughout Europe; *t.* Chicago.

Zelenski, Ladislaus. Composer; *b.* Gowdkowizy, Pol., Jul. 6, 1837; *d.* Cracow, Jan. 26, 1921. Comp. operas, chamb. mus., masses, cantatas.

Zelter, Karl Friedrich. Composer, teacher; *b.* Berlin, Dec. 11, 1758; *d. ib.,* May 15, 1832. Teacher of Mendelssohn. Bitter critic of Beethoven.

Zemlinsky, Alexander von. Composer, conductor; *b.* Vienna, Oct. 14, 1872. Edu., Vienna Cons., *u.* Robert Fuchs. 1906, first cond., Vienna Volksoper; 1908, of Vienna Hofoper; teacher of Schönberg, Korngold; 1920, dir., new German Musikakademie in Prague; 1927, cond., Berlin State Op. Banned from Germany. 1933, opera, *Kreidekreis,* prod. Prague. Comp. opera, orch. wks., chamb. mus.

Zerrahn, Carl. Conductor; *b.* Malchow, Ger., Jul. 28, 1826; *d.* Milton, Mass., Dec. 29, 1909. 1854-95, cond., Handel and Haydn Soc., Boston.

Zichy, Geza (Count Vassony-Kaö). Pianist; *b.* Sztara, Hun., Jul. 23, 1849; *d.* Budapesth, Jan. 15, 1924. Best known as one-armed pianist, having lost his right arm in a hunting accident. Comp. operas, incl., *Rakoczy Trilogy*.

Ziegfeld, Florenz. Music educator; *b.* Jever, 1841; *d.* Chicago, May 20, 1923. *p.* Moscheles. 1867, fd., Chicago Mus. Coll.

Ziegler, Edward. Music critic; *b.* Baltimore, Md., Mar. 25, 1870. 1902, mus. critic, N. Y. *American;* 1903-8, N. Y. *World;* 1908-17, N. Y. *Herald;* 1917-20, adm. sec., Met. Op., N. Y.; 1920, asst. gen. mgr.

Ziehn, Bernhard. Theorist; *b.* Erfurt, Ger., Jan. 20, 1845; *d.* Chicago, Sept. 8, 1912. 1868, *t.* Chicago. Author of text-books on harmony and composition.

Zielinski, Jaroslav de. Pianist, composer; *b.* Galicia, Aus., Mar. 31, 1847; *d.* Jul. 25, 1922. Comp. orch. wks., pf. pcs.

Zientarski, Romualdo Grigorievitch. Composer; *b.* Plozk, Pol., 1831; *d.* Warsaw, Pol., 1874. Prolific orch. and oratorio comp., amounting to 600 titles.

Zientarski, Victor. Composer; *b.* Warsaw, Pol., 1854. Comp. pf. wks., songs.

Zilcher, Hermann. Pianist, composer; *b.* Frankfort, Ger., Aug. 18, 1881. Won Mozart prize; 1920, dir., Würzburg Cons. Comp. violin, pf. pcs.

Zimbalist, Efrem. Violinist, composer; *b.* Rostov, Rus., Apr. 9, 1889. *p.* Auer. 1907, debut, Berlin, and toured Europe; 1910, debut, N. Y. 1914, *m.* Alma Gluck, singer. Comp. violin pcs.

Zimmerman, Agnes. Pianist; *b.* Cologne, Jul. 5, 1847. Comp. chamb. mus., pf. pcs.

Zingarelli, Niccolo Antonio. Composer, violinist; *b.* Naples, Apr. 4, 1752; *d.* ib., May 5, 1837. 1813, dir., Naples Cons.; maestro at Naples Cath. Comp. operas. ch. mus.

Zoellner (*Tsell-ner*), **Heinrich.** Composer; *b.* Leipzig, Jul. 4, 1854. 1908, cond., Antwerp Op. Comp. operas, choral, symph. wks.

Zoellner, Jos. Violinist; *b.* Brooklyn, 1862. *t.* Etterbeck, Bel.; formed quartet, *w.* daughter and 2 sons, and toured U. S. Settled in Cal.

Zois (*Tso-is*), **Hans (Freiherr von Zois-Edelstein).** Composer; *b.* Graz, Aus., Nov. 14, 1861. Comp. operas, operettas.

Zoyotarev, Vassilly Andreievitch. Composer; *b.* Taganrog, Rus., Feb. 23, 1879. 1900, *t.* Moscow Cons. Comp. orch., chamb. mus., pf. pcs.

Zucca, Mana. Pianist, composer; *b.* N. Y., Dec. 25, 1891. At 11 toured U. S.; 1909, toured Europe. Comp. over 400 wks. for voice, violin, 'cello, piano, chorus, symph. orch.

Zumpe, Hermann. Conductor; *b.* Taubenheim, Ger., Apr. 9, 1850; *d.* Munich, Sept. 3, 1903. Comp. operas, operettas.

Zumsteeg, Johann Rudolf. 'Cellist, composer; *b.* Sachsenflur, Ger., Jan. 10, 1760; *d.* Stuttgart, Jan. 27, 1802. Comp. operas, ch. mus., ballads.

Zuschneid, Karl. Conductor, composer; *b.* Oberglogau, Ger., May 29, 1854. 1907-17, dir., Mannheim Hochschule. Comp. choruses *w.* orch.

Zweers (*Tsvairs*), **Bernard.** Composer; *b.* Amsterdam, May 18, 1854. 1895, prof., Amsterdam Cons. Comp. symph. wks., masses, cantatas, songs.

PRONOUNCING DICTIONARY
OF MUSICAL TERMS

DIRECTIONS FOR PRONUNCIATION

All Italian, French and German words are written out phonetically, on the following system:

A as in *far*, represented by *ah*.

The Continental *e* has the sound of *a* in *fare*; it is represented by *eh*.

The Continental *i* has the sound of *e* in *deer*; it is represented by *ee*.

The following vowel sounds have no equivalents in English: French *e*, when not accented, something like the vowel sound in *love*. German *o* (*o* modified, or *Umlaut*) has nearly the same sound. German *u* is about half-way between the sound of *o* in *love* and *e* in *deer*. *O* and *u* have the same sound as in English, the *u* sound being represented by *oo*, as in *cool*. Italian *ae* has the sound of long *i* in English. German *a* is the equivalent of *a* in *air*. German *eu* is sounded like *oi* as in *toil*.

The following consonantal sounds have no English equivalents: German hard gutteral *ach* and soft gutteral *ag*. The French sound of *j* is represented by *zh* as nearly as possible. The French nasals *an*, *en*, *in*, *on*, can be represented but very unsatisfactorily in English only by adding a final *g*.

Whenever *ch* is found it is to be sounded like *ch* in *chair*. *C* always has this sound in Italian when followed by *i* or *e*. The Italian *ch*, on the contrary, always has the sound of *k*, or *c* hard, and is thus represented. The Italian *zz* has the sound of *ts* or *ds*, and is thus represented.

With this explanation of the phonetic system adopted to represent the foreign sounds, it is believed that the reader will find no difficulty in acquiring their proper pronunciation.

A PRONOUNCING DICTIONARY OF MUSICAL TERMS

A

A. The 6th of the normal major scale; the 1st of the normal minor scale; the standard by which the orchestra is tuned, given by the oboe.

A, A (It. and Fr.) (*ah*). At, in, by, for, with.

Ab (Ger.). Off. This word is used in organ music to signify the discontinuance of certain stops.

Abacus harmonicus (Lat.). A table of notes; also the arrangement of the keys and pedals of an instrument.

A ballata (It.) (*ah bal-lah'-tah*). In the style of a ballad.

Abandon (Fr.) (*ah-ban'-dong*). Without restraint.

A battuta (It.) (*ah bat-too'-tah*). As beaten; strictly in time.

Abbandonatamente (It.) (*ahb-bahn-do-nah-tah-men'-teh*). Vehemently; violently.

Abbandono (It.) (*ahb-bahn-do'-no*). With passionate expression; with abandon.

Abbellimento (It.) (*ab-bel-lee-men'-to*). Embellishment.

Abbellitura (It.) (*ab-bellee-too'-ra*). Embellishment. Both are derived from—

Abbellire (*abbel-lee'-reh*). To ornament.

Abbreviamenti (It.). Abbreviations in musical notation.

Abbreviation. A system frequently employed in music, by which a portion of a technical term is made to stand for the whole. The following is a list of the abbreviations in most common use; the explanation of each term may be found on reference to the words themselves in their proper places:

Accel.	} Accelerando
Accel⁰	
Acc.	
Accom.	} Accompaniment
Accomp.	
Accres.	Accresciamento
Adg⁰ or ad⁰	Adagio
Ad l.	} Ad libitum
Ad lib.	
Affett⁰	Affettuoso
Affrett⁰	Affrettando
Ag⁰	} Agitato
Agit⁰	
All⁰	Allegro
Allgtt⁰	Allegretto
All' ott.	} All' ottava
All' 8va	
Al seg.	Al segno
And^no	Andantino
And^te	Andante
Anim⁰	Animato
Arc.	Coll arco, or arcato
Ard⁰	Ardito
Arp⁰	Arpeggio
A t.	
A tem.	} A tempo
A temp.	
Aug.	By Augmentation
B.	{ Bass (voice) / Bassoon / Contre bass
B. C.	Basso continuo
Brill.	Brillante
C. B.	Col basso
C. D.	Colla destra
C. S.	Colla sinistra
Cad.	Cadence
Cal.	Calando
Can.	Cantoris
Cant.	Canto
Cantab.	Cantabile
Cello	Violoncello
Cemb.	Cembalo
Ch.	Choir organ
Chal.	Chalameau
Clar.	Clarinet
Clar^tto	Clarinetto
Clar.	Clarino
Co. so.	Come sopra
Col C.	Col canto
Col otta	Coll' ottava
Col. vo.	Colla voce
Con esp.	Con espressione
Cor.	Cornet or horn
Cres⁰	} Crescendo
Cresc.	
C. S.	Colla sinistra
C. 8va	Coll' ottava
C⁰ 1mo	Canto primo
Co. 1mo	Come primo
C^to	Concerto
D.	Destra, droite
D. C.	Da capo
Dec.	Decani
Decres.	Decrescendo
Delic.	Delicamente
Dest.	Destra
Diap.	Diapasons
Dim.	By diminution
Dim.	Diminuendo
Div.	Divisi
Dol.	Dolce
Dolcis.	Dolcissimo
Dopp. ped.	Doppio pedale
D. S.	Dal segno
Energ.	Energicamente
Espr.	} Espressivo
Espres.	
F. or for	Forte
Fag.	Fagotto
Falset.	Falsetto
Ff. or Fff.	Fortissimo
Fl.	Flauto

729

Abbreviation	Meaning
F. O.	Full Organ
F. Org.	Full Organ
Forz.	Forzando
Fz.	Forzando
G.	Gauche
G. O.	Great Organ
G. Org.	Great Organ
Gt.	Great Organ
Gr.	Grand
Grand°	Grandioso
Graz°	Grazioso
Hauptw.	Hauptwerk
Hptw.	Hauptwerk
H. W.	Hauptwerk
Haut.	Hautboy
H. C.	Haute contre
Intro.	Introduction
Inv.	Inversion
L.	Left
Leg.	Legato
Legg°	Leggiero
L. H.	Left Hand
Lo.	Loco
Luo.	Luogo
Lusing.	Lusingando
M.	Manual
Main	Manual
Mano	Manual
Maest°	Maestoso
Magg.	Maggiore
Man.	Manuals
Manc.	Mancando
Man^{do}	Mancando
Marc.	Marcato
M. D.	Mano diritta / Main droite / Mano destra
M. G.	Main gauche
M. M.	Maelzel's Metronome
M. M. ♩=92	The beat of a quarter-note is equal to the pulse of the pendulum of the Metronome said to be Maelzel's, with the weight set at 92.
M. P.	Mezzo piano
MS.	Manuscript or Mano sinistra
Men.	Meno
Mez.	Mezzo
Mf. or Mff.	Mezzo forte
Mod^{to}	Moderato
Mus. Bac.	Bachelor of Music
Mus. Doc.	Doctor of Music
M. V.	Mezzo voce
Ob.	Oboe, or Hautbois
Obb.	Obbligato
Oberst.	Oberstimme
Oberw.	Oberwerk
Obw.	Oberwerk
Oh. Ped.	Ohne Pedal
Org.	Organ
8va	Ottava
8^a	Ottava
8va alta	Ottava alta
8va bas.	Ottava bassa
P.	Piano
Ped.	Pedal
Perd.	Perdendosi
P. F.	Piu forte
Piang.	Piangendo
Pianiss.	Pianissimo
Pizz.	Pizzicato
P^{mo}	Pianissimo
PP.	Pianissimo
PPP.	Pianississimo
PPPP.	Pianississimo
1ma	Prima (volta)
1mo	Primo
4^{tte}	Quartet
5^{tte}	Quintet
Rall.	Rallentando
Raddol.	Raddolcendo
Recit.	Recitative
Rf., rfz., or rinf.	Rinforzando
R. H.	Right Hand
Ritar.	Ritardando
Riten.	Ritenuto
S.	Senza
𝄋	A sign
Scherz.	Scherzando
2da	Seconda (volta)
2do	Secondo
Seg.	Segue
Sem.	Sempre
Semp.	Sempre
7^{tt}	Septet
6^{tt}	Sestet
Sfz.	Sforzando
Sinf.	Sinfonia
Smorz.	Smorzando
S. Int.	Senza interruzione
S. S.	Sensa sordini
S. sord.	Sensa sordini
Sos.	Sostenuto
Sos^t	Sostenuto
Spir.	Spiritoso
S. T.	Senza tempo
Stacc.	Staccato
St. Diap.	Stopped Diapason
String.	Stringendo
Sw.	Swell Organ
Sym.	Symphony
T.	Tenor, tutti, tempo, tendre
T. C.	Tre corde
Tem.	Tempo
Tem. 1°	Tempo primo
Ten.	Tenuto
Timb.	Timballes
Timp.	Timpani
Tr.	Trillo
Trem.	Tremolando
3°	Trio
Tromb.	Trombi
Tromb.	Tromboni
T. S.	Tasto solo
U.	Una
U. C.	Una corde
Unis.	Unisoni
V.	Voce
V.	Volti
Va.	Viola
Var.	Variation

ABBREVIATION—Vcllo   731   ACCORDATURA

Vcllo . . . . Violoncello
Viv. . . . . Vivace
Vo. . . . .⎫
Vno. . . . .⎬ Violino
Viol⁰ . . . .⎭
V. S. . . . . Volti subito
Vni . . . .⎫ Violini
VV. . . . .⎭

There are other abbreviations employed in manuscript or printed music, the chief of which are as follows:

In time, a dash with a figure above signifies the length of the pause in bars, *e.g.*:

In notes, the trouble of writing a passage in full is saved by the use of abbreviations, *e.g.*:

Repetition phrases are thus shortened:

Abbreviations, by signs, of musical graces:
The Turn,

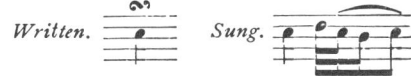

The back Turn,

Passing shake,

Beat,

Shake,

Abgestossen (Ger.) (*ap-geh-stoss-en*) [from *abstossen*, to knock off]. Detached; staccato.

Absolute Music. Music independent of words, scenery, acting or "programme."

A capella (*cah-pel'-la*). In church style, *i. e.*, vocal music, unaccompanied.

A capriccio (*cah-pritch'-eo*). Capriciously; without regard to time in performance or to form in construction.

Accelerando (It.) (*at-chel-leh-ran-do*). Hastening the movement (tempo).

Accent. The stress which recurs at regular intervals of time. Its position is indicated by upright strokes called *bars*. The first note inside a bar is always accented. When the bars contain more than one group of notes, which happens in compound time, other accents of lesser force occur on the first note of each group; these are called *secondary* or *subordinate* accents, whilst that just inside the bar is termed the *primary* or *principal* accent. Other accents can be produced at any point by the use of the sign ⟩——— or *sf*. The throwing of the accent on a normally unaccented portion of the bar is called *syncopation*. A proper grouping of accents will produce rhythm. It is considered a fault if an accented musical note falls on a short syllable.

Acciaccatura (It.) (*at-cheea-ca-too'-ra*). A short grace note, written thus: ♪ takes the place in the harmony of the note it precedes; is played rapidly. [From **Acciaccare** (*at-chee-ac-cá-reh*), to crush or jam together.]

Accidentals. All signs for raising or depressing letters that are not found in the signature.

Accolade (Fr.) (*ac-co-lahd*). A brace enclosing two or more staves. { [From Latin *ad*, to; *collum*, the neck.] To embrace.

Accompagnamento (It.) (*ac-com-pan-ya-men-to*), **Accompagnement** (Fr.) (*ac-com-pang-mongt*), **Accompaniment.** The separate part or parts that accompany a solo or chorus; generally instrumental, but a vocal solo with vocal accompaniment is frequently met with.

Accompaniment ad libitum (Lat.). An accompaniment that may be omitted without injury to the musical effect.

Accompanist or Accompanyist. One who plays or sings an accompaniment to a solo.

Accoppiato (It.) (*ac-cop-pee-ah'-to*). Coupled or joined together.

Accord (Fr.). A chord; agreement in pitch. Mode of tuning a string instrument.

Accordatura (It.) (*ac-cor-da-too'-ra*). The mode of tuning string instruments, as violin, guitar, etc.

Accordion. A small, portable instrument with free reeds.

Achtel (Ger.). Eighth-note.

Achtel Pause (*pow-ze*). Eighth-rest.

Acoustics (*a-koos-tics*) [from Greek *akuo*, to hear]. The science of sound; that which treats of the cause, nature, and phenomena of sound as a branch of physical science.

Action. The mechanism by means of which the hammers of the piano and the valves and stops of the organ are controlled by the performer.

Acuta (Lat.). Acute. A mixture-stop in the organ.

Acute. Pitched high; the opposite of grave.

Adagietto (It.) (*a-da-jee-et'-to*). Diminutive of Adagio; not so slow as Adagio.

Adagio (It.) (*a-da'-jee-o*). Slowly; also a name given to a movement written in that time.

Adagio assai (*as-sah-e*), **Adagio di molto** (*dee mol-to*). Very slowly.

Adagio cantabile (*can-tah'-bee-leh*). Very slow and sustained, as if being sung.

Adagio patetico (*pa-teh'-tee-co*). Slow and with pathos.

Adagio pesante (*peh-san'-teh*). Slow and weighty.

Adagio sostenuto (*sos-teh-noo-to*). Slow and sustained.

Adagissimo (It.). Superlative of Adagio. More than usually slow; very slow indeed.

Added Sixth. A name given to the subdominant chord with the 6th over its fundamental added, thus: F A C D. This explanation of this combination is not now generally accepted.

Addolorato (It.) (*ad-do-lo-rah'-to*). Sorrowful; dolorous.

A demi-jeu (*deh-mee-zheoo*). With half force or play. A direction to use half the power of the instrument, generally used of the organ.

A deux cordes (*doo-cord*). On two strings.

A deux mains (*doo-mang*). By or for two hands.

A deux temps (*doo-tahm*). In 2/4 time.

Adirato (It.) (*ad-ee-rah'-to*). Angrily; irritated.

Adjunct Keys or Scales. Those a fifth above and fifth below the given key or scale. Related scales. The scales or keys of the dominant and subdominant.

Adjunct Notes. Short notes, not essential to the harmony, occurring on unaccented parts of a bar. [Cf. *Auxiliary Notes, Passing Notes.*]

Ad libitum (Lat.). At will. (1) In passages so marked, the time may be altered at the will of the performer. (2) Parts in a score that may be omitted.

A dur (Ger.) (*dure*). A major.

Æolian. The name of one of the Greek scales; also of one of the ecclesiastical scales. Identical with modern A minor without sharped seventh.

Æolian Harp. A shallow, oblong box with gut-strings set in motion by the wind, generally made to fit a window with the lower sash raised enough to admit it. The strings should be tuned in unison.

Äussere Stimmen (Ger.) (*ois-eh-reh stimmen*). The outer parts, as soprano and bass in a chorus, or violin and violoncello in a quartet.

Äusserst (Ger.). Very; extremely.

Äusserst rasch (*rash*). Very quick.

Affabile (It.) (*af-fah'-bee-leh*). Pleasing; affably; agreeably.

Affannato (It.) (*af-fah-nah'-to*) [from *affanno*, anxiety]. Distressfully.

Affannosamente (It.) (*af-fah-no-sah-men'-teh*). Restlessly.

Affannoso (It.) (*af-fah-no-so*). Mournfully.

Affettuosamente (It.) (*af-fet-too-o-sa-men-teh*), **Affetuoso** (It.) (*af-fet-too-o-so*). Affectionately.

Affinity. Connected by relation. Relative keys.

Afflitto (It.) (*af-flit'-to*). Sadly; afflictedly.

Affrettando (It.) (*af-fret-tan'-do*), **Affrettate** (It.) (*af-fret-tah'-teh*), **Affrettore** (It.) (*af-fret-to'-reh*). Hastening the time.

Agevole (It.) (*a-jeh'-vo-leh*), **Agevolezza** (It.) (*a-jeh-vo-letz'-ah*). With lightness or agility.

Agilmente (It.) (*a-jil-men'-teh*), **Agilmento** (It.). In a lively, cheerful manner.

Agitamento (It.) (*a-jee-tah-men'-to*). Restlessness.

Agitato (It.) (*a-jee-tah'-to*). Agitated. To sing or play in an agitated, hurried manner.

Air. A tune, song, melody.

Ais (Ger.) (*a-iss*). A sharp.

A la. In the manner of, as **a la chasse** (*shass*). Like a hunt; hunting song.

A la mesure (Fr.) (*meh-zoor*). In time. Same as *A tempo* and *A battuta*.

Alberti Bass. Broken chords arranged thus:

So called from the name of its reputed inventor, Domenico Alberti.

Al' loco. At the place. Used after the direction to play 8th higher or lower.

Al piacere. See *A piacere*.

Al rigore di (or **del**) **tempo** (*ree-go-reh dee tempo*). In strict time.

Al scozzese (*scots-zeh-zeh*). In Scotch style.

Al segno (*sen-yo*). To the sign. A direction to return to the sign 𝄋. **D'al segno,** from the sign, is used with the same intention.

All' antico (*an'-tee-ko*). In ancient style.

All' ottava (*ot-tah-vah*). When *over* the notes, play octave higher than written; when *under,* an octave lower. In orchestral scores it means that one instrument is to play in octaves with another.

All' unisono. At unison.

Alla (It.). Written Al. or All. before words beginning with a vowel. Like; in the style of.

Alla breve (It.) (*al-lah breh'-veh*). This was originally 4/2 rhythm, so called from the fact that one *breve*, or double-whole-note, filled each measure. To-day the term is more generally applied to 2/2 rhythm, marked 𝄵.

Alla caccia (It.) (*cat-chia*). In hunting style.

Alla camera (It.) (*ca'-meh-rah*). In chamber-music style.

Alla capella. In church style. Also *A capella*.

Alla deritta. By degrees.

Alla hanacca (*ha-nak-ka*). In the manner of a hanacca.

Alla marcia (*mar'-chee-a*). In march style.

Alla mente (*men-teh*). Extemporaneous.

Alla militare (*mee-lee-tah-reh*). In military style.

Alla moderno. In modern style.

Alla Palestrina. In the style of Palestrina, *i.e.*, strict C. P. without instrumental accompaniment.

Alla polacca. Like a polacca or polonaise.

Alla quinta. At the fifth.

Alla rovescio (*ro-veh'-shee-o*). By contrary motion or reverse motion, as when a phrase is imitated with the movement of the intervals inverted. Example:

Alla siciliana (*see-chee-lee-ah'-nah*). In the style of a Siciliana, *q. v.*
Alla stretta. Like a stretto, *q. v.*
Alla turca. In Turkish style.
Alla zingaro. In Gypsy style.
Alla zoppa. Lamely; halting.
Allegramente (It.) (*al-leh-grah-men'-teh*). Joyfully.
Allegretto (It.) (*al-leh-gret'-to*). Diminutive of *Allegro*. (1) Slower than Allegro. (2) A movement in this time.
Allegrettino (It.) (*al-leh-gret-tee'-no*). Diminutive of *Allegretto*. (1) Not so fast as Allegretto. (2) A short Allegretto movement.
Allegro (It.) (*al-leh-gro*). (Lit., joyful.) Quick, lively. The word is occasionally employed to describe a whole movement of a quartet, sonata, or symphony. In music it is sometimes qualified as:
   Allegro agitato (It.). Quick and in an excited manner.
   Allegro assai (It.). Literally, fast enough. A quicker motion than simple allegro.
   Allegro commodo or comodo (It.). An easy, graceful allegro.
   Allegro con brio (It.). Quickly and with spirit.
   Allegro con fuoco (It.). Rapidly and with fire.
   Allegro con moto (It.). With sustained joyfulness.
   Allegro con spirito (It.). Joyfully and with spirit.
   Allegro di bravura (It.). A movement full of executive difficulties intended to exhibit the capacity of the singer or player.
   Allegro di molto (It.). Exceedingly quick.
   Allegro furioso (It.). Rapidly and with fury.
   Allegro giusto (It.). In quick but steady time.
   Allegro ma grazioso (It.). Lively and with graceful motion.
   Allegro ma non presto (It.). Rapidly, but not too fast.
   Allegro ma non tanto (It.). Quickly, but not too much so.
   Allegro ma non troppo (It.). Lively, but not too fast.
   Allegro moderato (It.). Moderately quick.
   Allegro molto (It.). Very quick.
   Allegro risoluto (It.). Lively and with firmness and decision.
   Allegro veloce (It.). Lively and with speed.
   Allegro vivace (It.). Lively and brisk.
   Allegro vivo (It.). Quick and lively.
Allemande (Fr.) (*almain, allemaigne*). A German dance (or some authorities say French), originally in duple time. Adopted as one of the movements in the Suite by Bach, Handel, and others, and written in 4/4 time.
Allentamento (It.) (*al-len-tah-men-to*), **Allentato** (It.) (*al-len-tah-to*), **Allentando** (It.) (*al-len-tan-do*). Giving way; slackening the time.
Allmählig (Ger.) (*all-may-lig*). Gradually; by degrees.
Alpenhorn or **Alphorn.** A wooden horn slightly curved, 4 to 8 feet long, used by the Swiss herdsmen.
Alt (Ger.). The alto voice or part.
Alt-Clarinette. Alto clarinet. Its pitch is a 5th below the ordinary clarinet.
Alt-Geige. The viola.
Alt-Oboe. Oboe de caccia, *q. v.*
Alt-Posaune (*po-zow-neh*). Alto trombone.
Alterato (It.) (*al-teh-rah'-to*), **Altéré** (Fr.) (*al-teh-reh*). Changed; altered.

Altered. Said of intervals, the normal condition of which in a scale or chord is changed
Alternativo (It.) (*al-ter-nah-teé-vo*). An alternate. A part of a movement to be played alternately with others. This name is frequently given to the second trio of a Scherzo in chamber music when (as is unusual) a second trio is added.
Altissimo (It.). The highest.
Alto (It.). High, loud. Originally applied to high male voices, now generally to the lowest female voice. Also applied to the viola (or tenor violin).
Alto Clef. The C clef on the third line, used for the viola, alto trombone, and (in Europe) for the alto voice.
Altra, Altre, Altri, Altro (It.) (masculine and feminine forms in the singular and plural). Other, others.
Amabile (It.) (*ah-mah'-bee-leh*). Amiably, sweetly, tenderly.
Amarevole (It.) (*ah-mah-reh'-vo-leh*). Sad, bitter.
Amateur (Fr.) (*a-mah-toor*). A lover of art. Generally applied to one who does not follow it professionally.
Ambrosian Chant. The system of church music introduced by Ambrose of Milan in the fourth century.
Ambrosian Hymn. A name given to the Te Deum on account of the belief—now known to be erroneous—that it was written by Ambrose of Milan.
Âme (Fr.) (*am*). Soul. The French name for the sound-post of instruments of the violin family.
American Organ. The English name for American reed organs, in which the air is drawn through instead of being forced through the reeds, as in the usual European system.
A mezza voce (It.) (*met-za vo-chee*). With half voice.
A moll (Ger.). A soft, *i. e.,* A minor.
Amorevole (It.) (*a-mor-eh'-vol-eh*), **Amorevolmente** (It.), **Amorosamente** (It.), **Amoroso** (It.). Lovingly; tenderly; amorously.
Amusement (Fr.) (*a-mooz-mong*). A light composition; a divertimento.
Anche (Fr.) (*onsh*). A reed of organ-pipe, or mouth-piece of oboe, clarionet, etc. **Jeu-d'anche**, reed-stop. **Ancia** (It.) (*an-chee-ah*). Italian form of the same word.
Anche (It.) (*an-keh*). Also; yet; still.
Anche piu moto. Still or yet faster.
Ancor (It.). Also; yet; still; used in the same way as Anche.
Ancora (It.). Again. Fr., *encore*.
Andächtig (Ger.) (*an-daych-tig*). Devoutly.
Andamento (It.) (*an-da-men'-to*). Movement; the coda to a long fugue theme frequently dropped in the "working out."
Andante (It.) [from *andare*, to walk or go slowly]. A slow movement; quiet, peaceful tempo.
Andante affettuoso. Slow, with tenderness.
Andante cantabile (*can-tah'-bee-leh*). Slow and singing.
Andante con moto. Slow, but with a little motion.
Andante grazioso. Slow and graceful.
Andante maestosc. Slow and majestic.
Andante non troppo or **ma non troppo.** Slow, but not too slow.
Andante pastorale. Slow, in pastoral style.
Andante sostenuto (It.) (*sos-teh-noo'-to*). Slow, with smoothness.
Andantemente (It.). Like an Andante.
Andantino (It.) (*an-dan-tee'-no*). A diminutive of *Andante*. A little faster than Andante (some say slower, but the Italian dictionaries say faster).
Anelantemente (It.) (*ah-neh-lan-teh-men'-teh*). Ardently; eagerly.

Anfang (Ger.). Beginning.

Anfangsgründe (Ger.). Rudiments.

Anfangs-Ritornel (Ger.). Introductory symphony.

Angenehm (Ger.) (*an'-geh-nehm*). Pleasing; agreeable.

Anglaise (Fr.) (*on-glehs*), **Anglico** (It.) (*an'-glee-ko*). The English country dance.

Angel'ica (Lat.). The vox angelica.

Angel'ique (Fr.) (*on-jeh-leek*). Voix angelique, angel voice, name of an organ-stop. Also called Voix Céleste (Fr.) (*vo-a seh-lest*). Celestial voice.

Angosciosamente (It.) (*an-go-shee-o-sa-men'-teh*), **Angoscioso** (It.) (*an-go-shee-o'-so*). Painfully; with anguish.

Anhang (Ger.) [*anhängen*, to hang to]. Coda.

Anima (It.) (*ah'-nee-mah*), **Animato** (It.) (*ah-nee-mah'-to*), **Animando** (It.). Soul; spirit; life; lively with animation.

Animosamente (It.) (*ah-nee-mo-sah-men'-teh*), **Animosissimo** (It.) or **Animosissamente**. Very energetic; boldly.

Animoso (It.). Spiritedly; energetically.

Anlage (Ger.) (*an-lah'-geh*). The plan of a composition.

Anleitung (Ger.) (*an-ley'-toong*). Direction; guidance; preface.

Anmuth (Ger.) (*an-moot*). Sweetness; grace; charm.

Anmuthig (Ger.). Sweetly; gracefully.

Ansatz (Ger.). (1) Attack. (2) Position of mouth in singing. (3) Position of lips in blowing a wind instrument. See *Embouchure*.

Anschlag (Ger.). Touch, as applied to piano and other keyed instruments.

Anschwellen (Ger.) (*an-shvel-len*). To increase in loudness; crescendo.

Antecedent [Lat. *ante, cado,* to fall before]. The subject or theme proposed for imitation; the subject of a fugue. The reply or imitation is called the consequent.

Anthem, * **anthĕme,** * **ăntĕm,** *s.* [In A. S. *antefen*, a hymn sung in alternate parts, an anthem; O. Fr., *anthame, antene, antienne, antevene;* Prov., *antifene, antifona;* Sp. and It., *antifona;* Low Lat., *antiphona;* from Gr. ἀντίφωνον (*antiphōnon*), an antiphon, an anthem; ἀντίφωνος (*antiphōnos*), sounding contrary, . . . responsive to; ἀντί (*anti*), opposite to, contrary to; φωνή (*phōnē*), a sound, a tone.]

(1) Originally: A hymn sung "against" another hymn; in other words, a hymn in alternate parts, the one sung by one side of the choir, the other by the other.

"*Anthem*, a divine song sung alternately by two opposite choirs and choruses."—*Glossog. Nov.* 2d ed. (1719)

(2) *Now:* A portion of Scripture or of the Liturgy, set to music, and sung or chanted.

There are three kinds of anthems: (1) A verse anthem, which in general has only one voice to a part; (2) a full anthem with verse, the latter performed by single voice, the former by all the choir; (3) a full anthem, performed by all the choir.

Anthropoglossa [Gr. *anthropos*, man; *glossa*, the tongue]. Like the human voice; the vox humana stop in the organ.

Anticipation [Lat. *ante*, before; *capio*, to take]. To introduce a note belonging to the next chord before leaving the preceding chord.

Antiphon [Gr. *anti*, against; *phoneo*, to sing]. A short sentence or anthem sung before and after the psalter for the day.

Antiphony. The responsive singing of two choirs generally placed on opposite sides of the chancel, one called the Decani, on the Dean's side of the chancel, the other the Cantoris, on the precentor's or leader's side. The verses of the psalms are sung by the choirs alternately, but the Gloria by the united choirs.

Anwachsend (Ger.) (*an-vach-sent*). Swelling; crescendo.

Aperto (It.) (*ah-pehr-to*). Open. Direction to use the damper ("loud") pedal.

A piacere (*pee-ah-cheh'-reh*), or **Al piacer**, or **A piacimento** (*pee-ah-chee-men'-to*). At pleasure.

A poco a poco (It.). Little by little.

A poco piu lento (It.). A little slower.

A poco piu mosso (It.). A little faster.

Appassionata (It.) (*ap-pas-sion-ah'-tah*), **Appassionamento** (It.). With strong passion or emotion.

Appassionatamente (It.). Impassioned.

Appenato (It.) (*ap-peh-nah'-to*). Distressfully.

Applicatur (Ger.) (*ap-plee-ka-toor'*). The fingering of a musical instrument.

Appoggiando (It.) (*ap-pod-je-an'-do*). Leaning upon; suspended notes.

Appoggiato (It.). Retardations; syncopations.

Appoggiatura (It.) (*ap-pod-jea-too'-rah*). To lean against. An ornamental note foreign to the harmony, one degree above or below a member of the chord, always on an accent or on a beat. It takes half the value of the note it precedes, but if the note it precedes is dotted, it takes two-thirds of its value.

The modern practice is to write as rendered, thus avoiding any confusion between the appoggiatura and the acciaccatura.

A punto (It.). Accurate, strict time.

A punto d'arco (It.). With the point of the bow.

A quatre mains (Fr.) (*katr-mang*). For four hands.

A quattro mani (It.) (*kwat-tro mah-nee*). For four hands.

Arcate (It.) (*ar-kah'-to*). With the bow; a direction to resume the bow after pizzicato.

Arco (It.). The bow.

Ardente (It.) (*ar-den-teh*). Ardent; fiery.

Ardente (Fr.) (*ar-dongt*). Ardently.

Ardito (It.) (*ar-dee-to*). Ardently; boldly.

Aretinian Syllables. *Ut, re, mi, fa, sol, la,* given by Guido Aretinus to the hexachord. *Ut* was changed to *do*, as being a better vowel for solmization.

Aria (It.) (*ah'-ree-ah*). Air; song. In form the aria consists of three members: Part I, a more or less elaborate melody in the tonic key. Part II, another melody in a related key. Part III, a repetition of the first melody, to which a coda is generally added.

Aria buffa (It.) (*boof'-fah*). An aria with humorous words.

Aria concertante (It.) (*con-cher-tan'-teh*). An aria with obbligato accompaniment of instruments.

Aria di bravura (It.) (*dee-brah-voo'-rah*) or **d'abilita** (*d'ah-bee-lee-tah*). An aria with difficult, showy passages.

Aria fugato (It.) (*foo-gah'-to*). An aria with an accompaniment written in fugue style.

Aria parlante (It.) (*par-lan'-teh*). Literally a speaking aria, one in which the music is designed for declamatory effect. The aria parlante was the precursor of the recitative.

Arietta (It.) (*ah-ree-et'-ta*). A small aria, less elaborate than the aria.

Arioso (It.) (*ah-ree-o'-so*). A short melody at the end of or in the course of a recitation.

Armonia (It.) (*ar-mo'-nee-ah*). Harmony.

Armoniosamente (It.) (*ar-mo-nee-o-sa-men'-teh*), **Armonioso** (It.) (*ar-mo-nee-o'-so*). Harmonious; harmoniously.

Arpa (It.) (*ar'-pah*). Harp.

Arpège (Fr.) (*ar-pehzh'*), **Arpeggio** (It.) (*ar-ped-jeeo*). In harp style. In piano music a direction to play the notes of a chord in rapid succession from the lowest upward. Indicated by

A reversed arpeggio is indicated by

In old music the arpeggio is sometimes indicated thus:

Arpeggiando (It.) (*ar-ped'-jee-an-do*). In harp style.

Arpeggiato (It.) (*ar-ped-jee-a'-to*). Arpeggiated.

Arrangement (Fr.) (*ar-ranzh-mong*). A piece of music written for one or more instruments or voices adapted to other instruments or voices. Also called Transcription.

Ar'sis (Gk.). The unaccented or up beat; the reverse of Thesis, the accented or down beat.

Articolato (It.) (*ar-tik-ko-lah'-to*). Articulated distinctly.

Artig (Ger.) (*ahr-teech*). Neat, pretty, unaffected.

As (Ger.). A flat. **As dur** (*doohr*), A flat major. **As moll**, A flat minor.

Assai (It.) (*as-sah'-ee*). Very, extremely, as Allegro assai, very fast. Adagio assai, very slow.

Assez (Fr.) (*as-seh*). Rather, as **Assez vite** (*veet*), rather quick, or quick enough.

Assoluto (masc.), **Assoluta** (fem.) (It.) (*as-so-loo'-to*). Absolute. Applied to the leading singers of an opera troupe, as Prima donna assoluta, first lady absolute; Prima uomo assoluto, first man absolute.

A suo arbitrio (*soo-oh ar-bee'-tre-o*). At your will.

A tempo (*tem'-po*). In time. A direction to resume strict time after *Rall.* or *Rit., q. v.*

A tempo giusto (*joos'-to*). In strict time.

A tempo rubato (*roo-bah'-to*). In stolen time, *i. e.*, retarding and hurrying the time irregularly.

A tre corde (*tray*). On three strings.

Attacca (It.) (*at-tak'-ka*). Attack. Begin the next movement with slight or with no pause.

Attacca subito (It.) (*soo-bee-to*). Attack quickly, without pause.

Attacco (It.), **Attaque** (Fr.) (*at-tak'*). The motive or theme of an imitation or short fugal subject.

Attaquer (Fr.) (*at-tak-keh*). Same as *Attacca*.

Attack. The manner of beginning a phrase or piece; refers generally to the promptness or firmness of the performer or performers.

Attendant Keys. The keys of the 4th and 5th above, and the relative minors of the principal key and these two major relations, as   C F G
Rel. minors   A D E

Aubade (Fr.) (*o-bad'*). Morning music; the opposite of *Serenade,* evening music.

Audace (Fr.) (*o-dass*). Bold, audacious.

Aufführung (Ger.) (*owf-fee-roonk*). Performance; representation of an opera.

Aufgeregt (Ger.) (*geh-rehgt*). With agitation.

Aufgeweckt (Ger.) (*geh-vekt*). With animation.

Aufhalten (Ger.) (*hol-ten*). To suspend (of dissonances). Also, to hold back or retard (of time).

Aufhaltung (Ger.) (*hol-toonk*). Suspension.

Auflösen (Ger.) (*leh-zen*). To let loose; resolve a dissonance.

Auflösungszeichen (Ger.) (*leh-soonks-tzeich-en*). Releasing sign; the ♮.

Aufschlag (Ger.). Up beat.

Aufschwung (Ger.) (*owf-shvoonk*). Soaring, elevation.

Aufstrich (Ger.). Up bow.

Auftakt (Ger.). The unaccented part of the measure, or the fraction of a measure, at the beginning of a piece.

Augmentation. When the theme of a fugue or imitation is given in notes of double or quadruple the length of those in its original form.

Augmented. (1) Any interval greater than perfect or major. (2) A theme written in notes of greater value than in its original form.

Augmented Sixth Chord. Called also extreme sharp sixth; superfluous sixth; when formed thus, A♭ C F♯, the Italian sixth; thus, A♭ C D F♯, the French sixth; thus, A♭ C E♭ F♯, the German sixth.

Augmenter (Fr.) (*og-mong-teh*). To increase in force. Same as *Crescendo*.

Ausarbeitung (Ger.) (*ows'-ar-bye-toonk*). Development; the working out of a fugue or sonata, etc.

Ausdruck (Ger.) (*drook*). Expression.

Ausdrucksvoll (Ger.). With expression; literally, full of expression.

Ausführung (Ger.) (*fee-roonk*). Execution; manner of performance.

Ausweichung (Ger.) (*veich-oonk*). Literally, evasion; modulation; change of key.

Authentic. The Ambrosian scales. A melody that lies between the keynote and its octave is called authentic. One that lies between the fourth below and the fifth above the keynote is called plagal. These terms are only used in the ecclesiastical modes.

Authentic. The church scales beginning and ending on any given tonic (except B).

Authentic Cadence. Tonic preceded by dominant.

Autoharp. A modern instrument resembling a zither, of easy performance. The plectrum is drawn across all the strings at once, and those that it is not desired to sound are silenced by a series of dampers controlled by the left hand of the player.

Auxiliary Note. Grace note; appoggiatura.

Auxiliary Scales. Related scales.

B

B. The seventh or leading tone of the natural major scale; in German, the note or key of B♭, B♮ being called H.

Baborak or **Baboracka.** A Bohemian dance.

Backfall. An ornament in harpsichord or lute music, written ♪ played

Badinage (Fr.) (*bah-dee-naje*). Banter; raillery.

Bagatelle (Fr.) (*bah-gah-tell*). A trifle; a name frequently given to short pieces of music.

Bagpipe. An instrument consisting of a leather bag into which air is forced either from a bellows or by the mouth of the player; furnished with from two to four pipes, one pipe with double reed pierced with holes, upon which the melody is played, called in Scotland the chanter; the remaining pipes, with single reeds, called drones, sound continuously the first and fifth of the scale or first, fifth and octave.

Bajadere or **Bayadere** (*by-a-dehr*). East Indian dancing girl.

Bakkia (*bak-kee-ah*). A Kamchadale dance.

Balabile (It.) (*bah-lah-bee'-leh*). Any piece of music written for dancing purposes.

Ballad. A simple song, originally a song to accompany dancing; derived from the low Latin word *ballare*, to dance; in its French form, *ballade*, it is used by modern composers as a title for extended lyric compositions, as the ballades of Chopin.

Balladenmässig (Ger.) (*bal-la'-den-meh-sich*). In ballad style.

Ballad-opera. An opera made up of simple songs, and without recitative.

Balafo (*bah-lah-fo*). An African instrument resembling the xylophone; a South American variety is called the marimba.

Balalaika (Russ.) (*bah-lah-lye'-ka*). A Russian guitar with three or four strings, the body triangular.

Ballata (It.). A ballad.

Ballerina (It.) (*bal-leh-ree'-nah*). A female ballet dancer.

Ballet (Eng.), called also *Fa-la*. An old form of part song in simple counterpoint.

Ballet (Fr.) (*bal-leh*). A combination of music and dancing, designed to tell a story in pantomime.

Balletto (It.) (*bal-let'-to*). A ballet. Used as a name for a movement by Bach.

Ballo (It.). A dance; a ball.

Ballo in maschera (*mas-keh-rah*). Masked ball.

Band. (1) A company of instrumentalists. (2) The term is used to distinguish the various groups of instruments in the orchestra; as, string band, wood band, brass band. (3) The commonest use of the word is as applied to a company of players on brass instruments. (4) A band composed of wood and brass instruments is called a harmony band.

Band (Ger.) (*bont*). A volume; a part.

Banda (It.) (*ban-dah*). A band.

Bandola (*ban-do'-lah*). A variety of mandolin.

Bandora (Fr.) (*ban-do'-rah*), **Bandore** (Eng.), **Pandoura** (Gk). An obsolete instrument of the guitar family.

Bandurria (Span.) (*ban-door-ree-ah*). A variety of guitar with wire strings.

Banger, Bania, Banja, Banjo. An instrument resembling a guitar, with a circular body, consisting of a broad hoop of wood covered with parchment, generally provided with five strings. The modern banjo is furnished with frets and with a screw mechanism to tighten the parchment.

Bar. A line drawn across the staff or staves to divide the music into portions of equal duration. The portion enclosed between two bars is called a measure. The almost universal custom of musicians, however, is to use *bar* in the sense of measure.

Barbaro (It.) (*bar'-bah-ro*). Savagely; ferocious.

Barbiton (Gk.). (1) A variety of lyre. (2) A string instrument resembling the violoncello (obsolete).

Barcarole, Barcarolle (Fr.) (*bar-ca-rol*), **Barcarola** (It.) (*bar-ca-ro-lah*), **Barcaruola** (It.) (*bar-ca-roo-o-la*). A boat-song; gondolier's song; vocal or instrumental compositions in the style of the Venetian gondoliers' songs.

Barem (Ger.) (*bah-rehm*). A soft organ-stop; closed pipes of eight- or sixteen-foot tone.

Bargaret (Fr.) (*bar-gah-reh*), **Barginet** (Fr.) (*bar-zhee-neh*), **Berginet** (Fr.) (*behr-zhee-neh*), **Bergiret** (Fr.) (*behr-zhee-reh*). A shepherd's song; pastoral song. From *berger* (Fr.), a shepherd.

Baribasso (It.). A deep bass voice.

Bariolage (Fr.) (*bah-ree-o-laje*). A medley; a series of cadenzas.

Baritenor. A low tenor.

Baritone. A brass instrument; a clarionet of low pitch; an obsolete variety of the viol family; the male voice ranging between bass and tenor (also written barytone); the F clef on the third line (not used now).

Barocco (It), **Barock** (Ger.), **Baroque** (Fr.) (*ba-rok*). Irregular; whimsical; unusual.

Barquade, Barquarde (Fr.) (*bar-kad, bar-kard*). Same as *Barcarole*.

Barré (Fr.) (*bar-reh'*). In guitar playing, pressing the first finger of the left hand across all the strings; the finger acts as a temporary "nut," raising the pitch of the strings.

Barre (Fr.) (*bar*). Bar.

Barre de répétition. A double bar with repeat marks.

Bas dessus (Fr.) (*bah-des-soo'*). The mezzo-soprano voice.

Base. Old way of writing bass.

Bass, Basso (It.), **Basse** (Fr.), **Bass** (Ger.). Low; deep.

Basse chantante (Fr.) (*shan-tont*). Baritone voice.

Basse chiffrée (Fr.) (*shif-freh*). Figured bass.

Basse continué (Fr.). Same as *Figured Bass*.

Basse de cremone (Fr.) (*creh-mone*). Bassoon.

Basse d'harmonie (Fr.) (*d'ar-mo-nee*). The ophicleide.

Basse de hautbois (Fr.). The English horn.

Basse de viole (Fr.). Violoncello.

Basse de violon. The double bass.

Basse taille (Fr.) (*tah-ee*). Baritone voice.

Bass-bar. A strip of wood glued to the belly of instruments of the violin family under the lowest string.

Bass Clef. The F clef on the fourth line.

Bass-Flöte (Ger.) (*fla-teh*). A low-pitch flute.

Bass-Geige (Ger.). The violoncello.

Bass-Pommer (Ger.). An obsolete ancestor of the bassoon.

Bass-Posaune (Ger.) (*po-zow-neh*). Bass trombone.

Bass-Schlüssel (Ger.) (*schlis-sel*). Bass clef.

Bass-Stimme (Ger.) (*stim-meh*). Bass voice or part.

Bass Tuba. A brass instrument of low pitch.

Bass Viol. The largest viol of a set or "chest" of viols.

Bass Voice. The lowest male voice.

Basset Horn. A variety of the clarionet, ranging from F below bass staff to C above treble staff; rich quality of tone; a favorite of Mozart, who used it in several of his operas and in his Requiem Mass.

Bassetto (It.). An eight- or sixteen-foot reed-stop in the organ; obsolete name for viola.

Basso (It.). The lowest part; a bass singer.

Basso buffo (It.). A comic bass singer.

Basso cantante (It.) (*can-tan'-teh*). A vocal or singing bass.

Basso concertante (It.) (*con-cher-tan'-teh*). The principal bass that accompanies solos and recitatives.

Basso continuo (It.). A figured bass.

Basso obbligato (It.) (*ob-blee-gah'-to*). An essential bass; one that may not be dispensed with.

Basso ostinato (It.) (*os-tee-nah'-to*). Literally, obstinate bass; a continuously repeated bass with constant variation of the upper parts; generally used as the foundation of that member of the suite called the Passacaglio.

Basso profundo (It.). A very deep, heavy bass voice.

Basso ripieno (It.) (*ree-pee-eh'-no*). A "filling up" bass. See *Ripieno*.

Bassoon, Basson (Fr.), **Fagotto** (It.), **Fagott** (Ger.). A wood-wind instrument with double reed; the bass of the wind band; compass from B♭ below bass staff to B♭ in treble staff (two or three higher notes are possible).

Basson quinte (Fr.) (*kangt*). A bassoon a fifth higher than the preceding.

Bâton (Fr.). (1) The stick used by a conductor; also, figuratively, his method of conducting. (2) A pause of several measures, signified thus

12

in modern music, viz.: one or two heavy diagonal lines with figures over to indicate the number of bars rest.

Batterie (Fr.) (*bat-teh-ree*). (1) The roll on the drum. (2) Repeated or broken chords played staccato. (3) Striking instead of plucking the strings of the guitar.

Battuta (It.) (*bat-too'-tah*). A measure or bar.

Bauerpfeife (Ger.) (*bower-pfifeh*). An 8-foot organ-stop of small scale.

Baxoncillo (Sp.) (*bah-hon-theel'-yo*). Open diapason.

Bayadere. See *Bajadere*.

Bayles (Sp.) (*bahl-yehs*). Comic dancing songs.

Bearings or **Bearing Notes.** The notes first tuned by an organ- or piano-tuner as a guide to the rest.

Beat. (1) The motion of the hand or baton by which the time (rate of movement) of a piece is regulated. (2) The equal parts into which a measure is divided. (3) The throbbing heard when two sounds not exactly in unison are heard together. (Beats are also produced by other intervals.)

Bebung (Ger.) (*beh-boonk*). Trembling; an effect obtained on the obsolete clavichord by rapidly vibrating the finger up and down without raising it from the key; the tremolo-stop in an organ.

Becken (Ger.). Cymbals.

Begeisterung (Ger.) (*be-geis'-te-roonk*). Spirit; excitement.

Begleitung (Ger.) (*be-glei'-toonk*). Accompaniment.

Beklemmt (Ger.) (*beh-klemt'*). Anxious; oppressed.

Bell. (1) A cup-shaped metal instrument. (2) The cup-shaped end of brass and some wood instruments.

Bell Diapason, Bell Gamba. Organ-stops with bell-shaped mouth.

Bellezza (It.) (*bel-let'-za*). Beauty of expression.

Bellicosamente (It.) (*bel-le-co-sa-men'-teh*). In a warlike manner; martially.

Belly. The upper side of instruments of the violin and guitar families.

Bémol (Fr.) (*beh-mol*). The sign ♭.

Ben (It.) (*behn*). Well; as, **ben marcato**, well marked.

Bene placito (It.) (*beh-neh pla-chee'-to*). At pleasure.

Béquarre or **Bécarre** (Fr.) (*beh-kar*). The sign ♮.

Berceuse (Fr.) (*behr-soos*). A cradle-song; lullaby.

Bergomask or **Bergamask.** A lively dance in triple time.

Bes (Ger.) (*behs*). B double flat.

Bestimmt (Ger.). With energy; con energia.

Bewegt (Ger.) (*beh-vehgt'*). Moved; with emotion; con moto.

Bewegung (Ger.) (*beh-veh'-goonk*). Motion.

Bien-chanté (Fr.) (*be-ang-shong-teh*). Literally, well sung; smoothly; cantabile.

Bifara (Lat.). An organ-stop; same as *Vox angelica;* two pipes not in perfect unison.

Binary Form. A movement founded on two principal themes.

Binary Measure. A measure with two beats.

Bind. A tie. The same sign, when over two or more notes on different degrees, is called a slur.

Bis (Lat.). Twice. When placed over a short passage, inclosed thus, ⌒ Bis signifies that it is to be played twice.

Bit. A small piece of tube used to lengthen the trumpet or other brass instrument to alter the pitch.

Bizzarramente (It.) (*bid-zarra-mente*), **Bizzaria** (It.) (*bid-zarria*), **Bizzaro** (It.) (*bid-zarro*). Bizarre; fantastic; odd; droll.

Blanche (Fr.) (*blongsh*). A half-note; minim.

Blanche pointée (*poin-teh*). A dotted half-note.

Blase-Instrument (Ger.) (*blah-zeh*). Wind instrument.

Bob. A technical term in bell ringing.

Bocca (It.). The mouth. **Con bocca chiusa** (*kee-oo-sa*), with closed mouth; humming.

Bocca ridente (It.) (*ree-den'-teh*). Smiling mouth; the proper position of the mouth in singing.

Bocktriller (Ger.). A bad trill. (Literally, goat's bleat.)

Bois (Fr.) (*bo-a*). Wood. **Les bois,** the wood wind.

Bolero (Sp.) (*bo-leh-ro*). Spanish dance in ¾ time; also called **Cachuca** (*ka-choo-ka*).

Bombard, An 8 or 16-foot reed-stop in the organ.

Bombardon. A large, deep-toned brass instrument.

Bouché (masc.), **Bouchée** (fem.) (Fr.) (*boo-sheh*). Closed. Applied to organ-stops with closed mouth.

Bouffe (Fr.) (*boof*). Comic.

Bourdon. (1) A closed organ-stop of 16 or 32-foot tone. (2) In France also 4 and 8-foot stops, analogous to the stop diapason, are so called. (3) A drone bass. (4) The largest bell of a chime.

Bourrée (Fr.) (*boo-reh*). A rapid dance ¼ or ¾ time, frequently used as one of the movements in a suite.

Bow. (1) The implement of wood and horse-hair by means of which the strings of the violin family of instruments are set in vibration. (2) The rim of a bell.

Bowing. (1) The art of managing the bow. (2) The signs indicating the way in which the bow is to be used.

Brabançonne (Fr.) (*bra-ban-sonn*). The Belgian national air.

Brace. The sign { used to join two or more staves.

Bransle (Fr.) or **Branle** (*brongl*), **Brawl.** An ancient French dance in 4/4 time.

Bratsche (Ger.) (*bratch-eh*). The viola. Corruption of the Italian **Braccia** (*brats-chia*), the arm-viol.

Bravo (masc.) (It.), **Brava** (fem.) (*bra-vah*), **Bravi** (plu.) (*bra-vee*). Literally, brave. Used to applaud performers, meaning "well done."

Bravura (It.) (*bra-voo'-rah*). Boldness; brilliancy. A composition designed to exhibit the powers of the performer.

Break. (1) The point at which the register of the voice changes. (2) The point at which the lower octave is resumed in compound organ-stops. (3) The point where the quality of the tone changes in wood instruments (of the clarionet family especially).

Breit (Ger.) (*bright*). Broad; stately.

Breve [from Lat. *brevis*, short]. Formerly the shortest note; now the longest, equal in value to two whole notes. Made

Bridge. A piece of wood resting on the sound-board or resonance box, upon which the strings of piano, violin, guitar, etc., rest.

Brillante (Fr.) (*bree-yant*), **Brillante** (It.) (*breel-lan-teh*). Brilliant.

Brindisi (It.) (*brin-dee'-zee*). Drinking song in 3/4 or 3/8 time, so written as to resemble the Tyrolese Jodl.

Brio (It.) (*bree-o*). Fire; spirit.

Brioso (It.). Cheerfully; briskly; joyfully.

Broken Cadence. An interrupted cadence.

Broken Chords. See *Arpeggio*.

Brumm-Stimmen (Ger.). Humming voices; con bocca chiusa.

Bruscamente (It.) (*broos-ka-men'-teh*). Roughly; strongly accented.

Brustwerk (Ger.) (*broost-vehrk*). The pipes in the organ belonging to the swell or choir organ.

Buca (It.), **Schall-Loch** (Ger.). The sound-hole of a guitar, mandolin, etc.

Buccolica (It.) (*buk-ko'-li-ka*), **Bucolique** (Fr.) (*boo-ko-leek*). In a rustic style.

Buffo (masc.), **Buffa** (fem.). A comic opera, or air, or singer.

Bugle. (1) A straight or curved hunting horn. (2) A keyed horn, generally made of copper. Chiefly used for military signals.

Burden. Old name for the refrain or chorus to a song.

Burletta (It.). A musical farce.

Busain. A 16-foot reed-organ stop.

C

C. The first note in the natural major scale. Middle C, the C lying between the fifth line of the bass staff and first line of the treble staff; the C clef or always signifies this C.

Cabaletta (It.). ("A little horse," so called from the rapid triplet accompaniment generally used with it.) A vocal rondo, the theme often repeated with elaborate variations.

Cabinet-d'orgue (Fr.) (*ca-bee-neh-d'org*). Organ case.

Cabinet Organ. A reed organ (American) in which the air is drawn instead of forced through the reeds.

Cabinet Piano. An old-style lofty upright piano.

Caccia (It.) (*cat'-chia*). Hunting chase.

Cachucha (Sp.) (*ca-choo'-cha*). The same as *Bolero*.

Cadence [from Lat. *cado*, to fall]. The end of a phrase, part, piece. The principal cadences are as follows: whole, or perfect, dominant to tonic; half, or imperfect, tonic to dominant; deceptive, dominant to subdominant or submediant.

Plagal cadence, subdominant to tonic. In the perfect cadence the dominant is generally preceded by the 6-4 of the tonic; in the half cadence the 6-4 of the tonic before the dominant which is the final; half and deceptive cadences are used in the course of a piece; perfect and plagal at the end. The Phrygian cadence consists of the following chords:

A long, brilliant, vocal or instrumental flourish introduced just before the close, or before the return of the principal theme, is also called a cadence (in Italian, cadenza).

Cadenz or **Kadenz** (Ger.). Cadence.

Cadenza (It.). A cadence. The Italian word is generally used when applied to the kind of passage described above.

Ça-ira (Fr.) (*sah-era*). That will do; lit., that will go. A revolutionary song in France.

Caisse (Fr.) (*case*). A drum.

Caisse claires (*clare*). Kettle drums. **Grosse Caisse**, large drum.

Caisse roulante. Side or snare drum.

Cal'amus (Lat.). A reed. From this are derived the words **Chalumeau** (Fr.) (*sha-loo-mo*), the first register of the clarionet, and **Shawm**, an obsolete reed instrument used in the Bible as the translation of a Hebrew instrument.

Calan'do (It.) [from *calare*, to go down or decrease]. Getting both slower and softer.

Calandrone (It.) [*calandra*, a lark]. A small reed instrument resembling the clarionet.

Cala'ta (It.). A lively dance in 2/4 time.

Calcan'do (It.) [from *calcare*, to tread upon]. Hurrying the time.

Call. A military signal, given by drum or bugle.

Calma (It.). Calm, quiet.

Calma'to (It.). Calmed, quieted.

Calore (It.) (*kal'-o-reh*). Warmth, passion.

Caloro'so (It.). Warmly, passionately.

Cambiata (It.) (*camb-ya'-ta*) [from *cambiare*, to change]. **Nota cambiata**, changing note; a dissonant struck on the accent.

Camera (It.) (*ka'-meh-ra*). Chamber. **Musica di camera**, chamber music.

Camminan'do (It.) [from *camminare*, to travel or walk]. Walking, flowing. Same as *Andante*.

Campa'na (It.). A bell.

Campanello (It.) (*kam-pah-nel'-lo*). A small bell.

Campanet'ta (It.). Instrument consisting of a series of small bells tuned to the musical scale, played either with small hammers held in the hands, or by means of a keyboard.

Campanology. The art of making and using bells.

Canaries. A lively dance in ⅜ time, of English origin.

Can'crizans [Lat. *cancer*, a crab]. A term applied to a canon in which the "follower" takes the theme backward.

Canon (Lat.). Law or rule. (1) The measurement of the ratios of intervals by means of the monochord. (2) A musical composition in which each voice imitates the theme given out by the leading voice; this imitation may be at any interval above or below, or may begin at any point of the theme. There are many varieties of the canon. The following are the most important, if any importance attaches to such dry productions: **Close Canon**, the entrance of the voices indicated by a sign; the parts not written out. **Open Canon**, the reverse of this; *i. e.*, written in full. **Finite Canon**, one with an ending. **Infinite Canon**, one without an ending.

There are also canons by augmentation, by diminution, by inversion, by retrogression (cancrizans), etc., etc.

Canonic Imitation. See *Canon*.

Cantabile (It.) (*can-tah'-bee-leh*) [from *cantare*, to sing]. In a singing style.

Cantan'do (It.). Singing.

Canta'ta. (1) A mixture of aria and recitative for one voice. (2) A short oratorio, or a secular work in oratorio form, sung without costume or action.

Cantatore (It.) (*can-ta-to'-reh*). A singer, male.

Cantatrice (It.) (*can-ta-tree'-cheh*). A singer, female.

Cantilina (Lat.). (1) A folk-song. (2) A solfeggio. (3) A smooth-flowing melody. (4) Anciently the Cantus firmus.

Canticle (Lat.). (1) A song of praise. **Cantico** (It.), **Cantique** (Fr.) (*kan-teek*), **Lobgesang** (Ger.) (*lope-ge-zang*). (2) The parts of Scripture—Te Deum and Benedicite Omina Opera—that form the chief part of the musical service of the Protestant Episcopal Church.

Cantino (It.). See *Chanterelle*.

Canto (It.). The air; the melody; upper part.

Canto a capella (It.). Sacred music.

Canto fermo (It.). Cantus firmus.

Canto figura'to (It.). Florid melody; melody with variations.

Canto primo (It.). First soprano.

Canto recitativo (It.). Declamatory singing.

Canto ripieno (It.) (*ree-pe-eh'-no*). Additional soprano chorus parts.

Canto seconda (It.). Second soprano.

Cantor (Lat.), **Kantor** (Ger.). A precentor.

Cantore (It.). A singer; chorister.

Cantoris (Lat.). The side of a cathedral choir (the north) where the cantor sits is called the cantoris; the opposite side is called the decani side, where the dean sits.

Cantus (Lat.). Song.

Cantus ambrosia'nus (Lat.). Plain song.

Cantus firmus. The plain song or chant.

Cantus mensura'bilis (Lat.). Measurable song; name given to music when first written with notes of definite length.

Canzona (It.) (*cant-so'-na*). (1) A part song in popular style. (2) An instrumental composition in the old sonata form. (3) An indication of lively, rapid movement.

Canzonette (Fr.) (*can-so-net*), **Canzonetta** (It.), **Canzonet** (It.). A short part song.

Capella (It.). Church. **Alla capella,** in church style.

Capellmeister (Ger.) (*ka-pel'-meis'-ter*). Master of the chapel; the head of the musical establishment of a noble or princely house.

Capellmeister-Musik (Ger.). Music made to order without inspiration is so called in Germany.

Capo (It.). Head; beginning. **Da capo,** from the beginning.

Capodastro (It.). Same as *Capo tasto*.

Capo tasto (It.). Head stop. A clamp which is screwed on the finger-board of the guitar, so as to "stop" all the strings, thus raising the pitch to any degree desired.

Capriccietto (It.) (*ca-pree-chee-et'-to*). A little caprice.

Caprice (Fr.) (*ca-prees'*), **Capriccio** (It.) (*caprit'-chio*). A whim; freak; composition without form. In German, Grille.

Caricato (It.) (*ca-ree-ca'-to*). Overloaded with display.

Carillon (Fr.) (*car-ee-yong*). (1) A set of bells played by hand or by machinery. (2) A mixture-stop in the organ.

Carilloneur (Fr.) (*ca-ree-yo-nure*). One who plays the carillon.

Carmagnole (Fr.) (*car-man-yole*). A wild song and dance of the French Revolution.

Carol. A song of praise, usually sung at Christmas and at Easter.

Carola (It.). See *Carmagnole*.

Carrée (Fr.). A breve.

Carressant (Fr.) (*ca-res-sawnt*), **Carrezzando** (It.) (*car-retz-zan'-do*), **Carrezzevole** (It.) (*car-retz-zeh'-vo-leh*). In a caressing manner.

Cassa grande (It.). The large drum.

Cassatio (It.) (*cas-sa-shio*). A suite; cassation.

Castanets, from *castagna* (It. *castanya*, a chestnut), **Castagnette** (It.) (*cas-tan-yet-teh*), **Castanettes** (Fr.) (*cas-tan-yet*), **Castañuelas** (Sp.) (*cas-tan-yu-eh-las*). Small wooden clappers used to mark the rhythm.

Catch. A species of canon so contrived that the meaning of the words is distorted.

Catena di trilli (It.) (*cat-teh-na dee trillee*). A chain or succession of trills.

Catgut. The usual name for gut-strings, made in reality from sheeps' intestines.

Catlings. The smallest lute strings.

Cattivo tempo (It.) (*cat-tee-vo*). The weak beat; literally, bad beat.

Cauda (Lat.). The tail or stem of a note.

Cavalet'ta (It.). See *Cabaletta*.

Cavalet'to (It., little horse). (1) Small bridge. (2) The break in the voice.

Cavatina (It.) (*cah-vah-tee'-nah*). A short air; a song without a repetition of the first member.

C Clef. See *Clef*.

Cebell. A theme consisting of alternate passages of high and low notes, upon which "divisions" or variations were played on the lute or viol.

Celere (It.) (*cheh'-leh-reh*). Quick, rapid.

Celerita (It.) (*che-leh'-ree-tah*), **con.** With speed.

Celeste (Fr.). Celestial. The soft pedal of the piano.

Cello (It.) (*chel-lo*). Abbreviation of violoncello.

Cembalo (It.) (*chem'-ba-lo*). Harpsichord; piano.

Cembalist (It.) (*chem-ba-list*). A pianist.

Cembanella or **Cennamella** (It.). A flute or flageolet.

Cercar la nota (It.) (*cher-car la no-ta*). To slur or slide from one note to the next. Same as *Portamento*.

Ces (Ger.) (tsehs). C♭.

Chacona (Sp.) (*cha-co'-na*), **Ciaconna** (It.) (*chea-con'-na*), **Chaconne** (Fr.) (*sha-con*). A slow dance in 3/4 time, written on a ground bass of eight measures, sometimes introduced in the suite.

Chair Organ. Choir organ.

Chalameau (*shah-lah-mo*) or **Chalumeau** (Fr.). See *Calamus*.

Chamber Music. Vocal or instrumental music suitable for performance in small rooms. Generally applied now to sonatas, trios, quartets, etc., for instruments.

Change of Voice. (1) Passing from one register to another. (2) The change from the child's to the adult's voice in boys. Generally occurs between fourteen and seventeen years of age.

Changes. The various melodies produced by the various ways in which a chime is rung.

Change Ringing. The art of ringing chimes.

Changing Chord. A chord struck with a bass that is not a member of the chord.

Changing Notes (nota cambiata, It.). Dissonant notes struck on the beat or accent; appoggiaturas.

Chanson (Fr.) (*shan-song*). A song, a part song; formerly a part song resembling a madrigal.

Chansonnette (Fr.) (*shan-son-net*). A little song.

Chant. A form of composition in which reciting notes alternate with phrases sung in time. There are two forms of chant, Anglican and Gregorian. The Anglican chant may be single, *i. e.*, with the reciting notes and two inflections (phrases in time), or double, that is, the length of two single chants. The Gregorian chant consists of: (1) The intonation. (2) The dominant or reciting note. (3) The mediation (analogous to the inflection, but not in strict time). (4) The dominant again. (5) Ending or cadence. The chant was undoubtedly first sung to metrical words, therefore was as rhythmic as a modern melody. This rhythmic character has been lost by adapting prose words to it.

Chant (Fr.) (*shawnt*). Song; melody; tune; vocal part.

Chantant (Fr.) (*shong-tawnt*). Singing. **Café chantant**, a café where singing is part of the entertainment.

Chanter. (1) A singing priest. (2) The melody pipe of the bagpipe.

Chanterelle (Fr.) (*shong-ta-rell*). The highest string of the violin, viola, and violoncello; also of the guitar and lute.

Chanteur (Fr.) (*shong-ture*). A singer (male).

Chanteuse (Fr.) (*shong-toose*). A singer (female).

Chant pastoral (Fr.). Shepherd's song.

Characters. The signs used in written music.

Characterstimme (Ger.). Lit., character voice; any solo-stop on the organ.

Characterstücke (Ger.) (*ka-rak'-ter-stee-ke*). Character pieces; descriptive music, as the pastoral symphony.

Chasse, à la (Fr.) (*a la shass*). In the hunting style.

Chef d'attaque (Fr.) (*shef d'at-tak*). The chorus leader, or leading instrument of any division of the orchestra.

Chef d'oeuvre (Fr.) (*shef d'oovr*). Master-work.

Chef d'orchestre (Fr.) (*shef d'or-kestr*). Conductor of the orchestra; leader.

Chest of Viols. A "chest" containing two trebles, two tenors, and two basses. Called also "consort of viols."

Chest Tone. The lowest register of the voice—male or female.

Chevalet (Fr.) (*she-va-leh*). Bridge of string instruments.

Chiara (It.) (*ke-ah-rah*). Clear, pure.

Chiaramente (It.) (*ke-ah-rah-men'-teh*). Clearly, distinctly.

Chiarezza (It.) (*ke-ah-ret'-za*), **con**. With clearness.

Chiarina (It.) (*ke-ah-ree'-na*). Clarion.

Chiave (It.) (*ke-ah'-veh*). Key or clef.

Chica (Sp.) (*chee-ka*). Old Spanish dance. The original of Giga, Jigue, and Jig.

Chiesa (It.) (*ke-eh'-sa*). Church. **Concerto da chiesa**, a church concert. **Sonata da chiesa**, a church sonata.

Chime. A set of bells, generally five to ten. To chime; to play a set of bells by striking them with hammers or by swinging their clappers. **Chime Ringing** is to swing the bells themselves.

Chirogymnast, Chiroplast. Obsolete machines for strengthening the fingers of pianists and keeping them in position.

Chitarra (It.) (*kit-tah'-rah*). Guitar.

Choeur (Fr.) (*koor*). Chorus, choir.

Choir. (1) A company of church singers. (2) The part of the church appropriated to the singers. In English churches (Anglican) the choir is divided into two parts, called the decani, or choir on the dean's side, and cantori, or choir on the cantor's side. When chanting, they usually sing antiphonally, joining in the "gloria." In anthems the words decani and cantoris are printed to indicate which side is to sing a given part.

Choir Organ. One of the divisions of the organ, the manual for which is generally the lowest. Was originally called chair organ; called in France *prestant*.

Chor (Ger.) (*kore*). Chorus, choir; a number of instruments of the same kind.

Choragus (Lat.). (1) Leader of a chorus. (2) A musical official at Oxford University, England.

Choral. (1) For a chorus. (2) An old form of psalm-tune.

Choral Service. A service of which singing is the most prominent part.

Chord, Akkord (Ger.), **Accord** (Fr.), **Accord** (It.). A combination of three or more sounds—common or perfect chord, or triad. Consists of any sound with its third and fifth; it is called major when the interval from one (or root) to three contains two whole tones; minor, when it contains a tone and a half; diminished, if there are three whole tones from one to five; augmented, if there are four whole tones from one to five. A chord is inverted when its root is not at the bass; chords with more than three letters are dissonant chords, called chords of the seventh if they contain four letters, chords of ninth if they contain five letters, etc., etc. Chords bear the name of the degree of the scale upon which they are written: First, tonic; second, supertonic; third, mediant; fourth, subdominant; fifth, dominant; sixth, submediant; seventh, leading note or diminished chord.

Chorister. A chorus- or choir-singer; a precentor.

Chorus. (1) A company of singers. (2) The refrain of a song. (3) A composition for a company of singers. (4) The mixture-stops in an organ.

Chromatic, Chromatisch (Ger.), **Chromatique** (Fr.), **Cromatico** (It.). (1) Sounds foreign to the key. (2) A scale, consisting of half-tones. Chromatic chord, one including foreign sounds. Foreign to the key; chromatic interval, one not found in the major scale; chromatic half-tone, changing the pitch without changing the letter, as C, C♯.

Church Modes. The scales derived from the Greek, in which Gregorian music or plain songs are written.

Cimbal. A dulcimer; harpsichord.

Cimbali (It.) (*chim-ba-lee*). Cymbals.

Cimbalo (It.) (*chim'-ba-lo*). See *Cembalo*. Also a tambourine.

Cimbel (Ger.) (*tsim-bel*). A mixture-stop in the organ.

Cink (Ger.) (*tsink*), **Cinq** (Fr.) (*sank*). A small reed-stop in the organ.

Cinque pace (Fr.) (*sank pace*). An old French dance. In old English, sink a pace.

Circular Canon. One which ends a half-tone higher than it begins, consequently will, if repeated often enough, go through all the keys.

Circulus (Lat.). A circle; the old sign for what was called perfect time, three beats in the measure; for imperfect time, two beats in the measure, the circle was broken in half, thus, C. It is from this the sign for common time is derived; it is not as is generally supposed the letter C.

Cis (Ger.) (*tsis*). C sharp.

Cithara (Lat.). An ancient lute.

Citoli. Old name for the dulcimer.

Civetteria (It.) (*chee-vet-tee'-rea*), **con.** With coquetry.

Clairon (Fr.). Clarion.

Clangtint. A term introduced by Tyndall to designate the quality of sounds (translation of Ger. *Klangfarbe*); means much the same thing as the French word *timbre*.

Claque bois (Fr.) (*clack boa*). The xylophone; in German, Strohfiedel; straw fiddle. Italian, Organo di legno. Graduated strips of hard wood laid on supports made of straw, played by striking with small hammers held in the hands.

Clarabella. An eight-foot soft organ-stop.

Clarabel Flute. The same stop when of four-foot tone.

Clarichord. An old variety of the harpsichord.

Clarinet or **Clarionet** (a little clarion). A wind instrument with a beating reed, invented in 1654 by Denner. The compass of the clarinet is from E third space bass to the second C above the treble (the highest octave is rarely used). Clarinets are made in several keys; those used in the orchestra are in C, B♭ and A; the B♭ clarinet sounds a whole tone lower than the written notes, the A clarinet a minor third lower; alto and bass clarinets are also used, the former in F and E♭, the latter an octave below the ordinary clarinet. The clarinet has four well-marked registers: the first, or chalumeau, extends from the lowest note to the octave above; second to B♭ in treble staff; third to C above treble staff; fourth the rest of the compass.

Clarinetto (It.), **Klarinette** (Ger.), **Clarinette** (Fr.). The clarinet.

Clarino (It.) (*clah-ree-no*). Clarion or trumpet; an organ-stop; four-foot reed.

Claviatur or **Klaviatur** (Ger.) (*kla-fee-a-toor'*). Keyboard.

Clavicembalo (It.) (*cla-vee-chem'-ba-lo*). Keyed dulcimer; the harpsichord.

Clavichord. An instrument resembling a square piano. The strings were vibrated by forcing wedge-shaped pieces of brass called tangents against them. By depressing the keys, the tangent acted both as a means of vibrating the string and as a bridge. When the finger was raised, the string was damped by a piece of woolen cloth wrapped round it, between the tangent and the pin-block. The chief interest in this obsolete instrument is the fact that it was the favorite of J. S. Bach.

Claviçon (Fr.) (*cla-vee-soong*) [from Lat. *clavis,* a key]. The harpsichord.

Clavicytherium. A variety of harpsichord.

Clavier or **Klavier** (Ger.) (*klah-feer'*). (1) Keyboard. (2) Used as a name for the pianoforte.

Clavier (Fr.) (*klah-vee-eh*). An organ manual.

Clavierauszug (Ger.) (*klah-feer-ows-tsoog*). A pianoforte score or edition.

Clef [from Lat. *clavis,* a key]. A sign placed on the staff to indicate the names and pitch of the sounds. Three clefs are used in modern music: (1) The treble or G clef, also called violin clef; this is now always placed on the second line. (2) The C clef:

this clef, when on first line, is called soprano clef; on second line, mezzo-soprano clef; on third line, alto clef, also viola or alto trombone clef; on fourth line, tenor clef; used also for upper notes of violoncello and bassoon. The C clef always signifies middle C; that is, C that lies between the fifth line bass staff and first line treble staff. Bass or F clef, placed on the fourth line, occasionally on the third, when it is called the baritone clef; used for bass voices and all bass instruments.

Cloche (Fr.) (*closh*). A bell.

Clochette (Fr.) (*closhet'*). A small bell.

Close Harmony. When the sounds forming the chords are drawn together as much as possible.

No. 1, close harmony; No. 2, open harmony.

Coda (It.). "Tail." A passage added after the development of a fugue is finished, or after the "form" of a sonata, rondo, or any other composition has been completed, to produce a more satisfactory close.

Codetta (It.). A short coda.

Cogli stromenti (It.) (*col-yee stro-men'-tee*). With the instruments.

Coi (*coee*), **Col, Coll', Colla, Colle, Collo** (It.). With the.

Col arco. With the bow. Used after the direction "pizzicato."

Col basso. *With the bass.*

Col canto. With the melody.

Col legno (It.) (*col-lane-yo*). With the wood; a direction to strike the strings of the violin with the back of the bow.

Colla parte. With the principal part.

Colla voce. With the voice. In score writing, to save the labor of re-writing a part which is to be played by two or more instruments. It is usual to write the part for one instrument, for instance, the violin, and write the words *col violino* on the staff appropriated to the other instrument.

Colophony. Rosin.

Colorato (It.) (*co-lo-rah'-to*). Florid.

Coloratura (It.) (*co-lo-rah-too'-rah*). Florid passages in vocalization.

Come (It.) (*coh-meh*). As; like.

Come prima (It.) (*coh'-meh pree'-mah*). As at first.

Comes (Lat.) (*co-mes*). The answer to the subject, dux of a fugue. *Dux* means leader; *comes,* follower.

Comma. The difference between a major and a minor tone.

Commodamen'te, Commodet'ta (It.). Quietly; leisurely; without hurry.

Commodo (It.) (*com-mo'-do*). At a convenient rate of motion.

Common Chord. The combination of any sound (called the root) with its major or minor 3d and perfect 5th.

Common Meter, or Ballad Meter. A stanza, consisting of alternate lines of four and three iambuses; as,

How blest is he who ne'er consents
By ill advice to walk.

Common Time. Two beats, or any multiple of two beats, in the measure. The signs 2/4, C, ₵, 4/1 (2/2, 2/1, 4/8 rare) indicate simple common time; 6/4, 6/8, 12/8 indicate compound common time, 6/4 being compounded from two measures of 3/4; 6/8 from two measures of 3/8; and 12/8 from four measures of 3/8 time.

Compass. The complete series of sounds that may be produced by a voice or instrument.

Compiacevole (It.) (*com-pea-cheh'-vo-leh*). Agreeable; pleasing; charming.

Complement. The interval which, being added to another, will make an octave. A complementary interval is found by inverting any given interval that is less than an octave.

Composer, Componista (It.), **Componist** or **Komponist** (Ger.). One who composes music.

Composition. The sounds that make up the series of a mixture- or other compound organ-stop.

Composition Pedal or **Knob.** A mechanism worked by the foot or by pressing a button with the finger, which throws on or off certain combinations of stops in the organ.

Compound Intervals. Intervals greater than the octave.

Compound Times. Those formed by adding together several measures of simple time. 6/4, 6/8, 12/4, 12/8 are compound common, having an even number of beats; 9/4, 9/8 are compound triple, having an odd number of beats.

Con (It.). With.

Concert. Any musical performance other than dramatic.

Concertante (It.) (*con-cher-tan'-teh*). A composition in which two or more parts are of equal importance.

Concerted Music. Music for several voices or instruments, or for voices and instruments combined.

Concertina. A small free-reed instrument somewhat like the accordion, but far superior.

Concertmeister (Ger.). Concert master; the leader or conductor of the orchestra.

Concerto (It.) (*con-cher'-to*), **Conzert** (Ger.), **Concert** (Fr.) (*con-sehr*). A composition designed to display the capabilities of one instrument accompanied by others.

Concert spirituel (Fr.) (*con-sehr spiri-too-el*). An association in Paris for the performance of sacred music, vocal and instrumental, founded 1725.

Concertstück (Ger.) (*steek*). Concert piece; concerto.

Concitato (It.) (*con-chee-tah'-to*). Agitated.

Concord. Agreeing. Literally, chording with.

Concordant. (1) Agreeing with. (2, Fr.) The baritone voice.

Conductor. The director or leader of a chorus or orchestra.

Cone Gamba. An organ-stop with bell-shaped top.

Conjunct (Lat., *con-junctus*). Joined together. Adjacent sounds in the scale.

Conjunct Motion. Moving by steps.

Consecutive. Two or more of the same intervals in succession.

Consecutive Fifths. Two voices or parts moving together a fifth apart.

Consecutive Octaves. Two voices or parts moving together an octave apart. Consecutive fifths and octaves are forbidden by the laws of composition, but the prohibition is frequently disregarded by the best writers.

Consequent. The answer to a fugue subject; comes.

Consolante (It.) (*con-so-lan'-teh*). Soothing.

Consonance. Literally, sounding together. Those intervals that enter into the composition of the common chord and its inversions, viz., major and minor 3d and 6th, perfect 4th and 5th, and octave. The major and minor 3d and 6th are called imperfect consonances, being equally consonant, whether major or minor. The perfect 4th, 5th, and 8th are called perfect because any alteration of them produces a dissonance; *i.e.*, an interval that requires resolution. N. B.—This definition of consonance applies only to the modern tempered scale.

Con sordini (It.) (*sor-dee'-nee*). With the mute. (1) In piano music, with soft pedal. (2) Instruments of the violin family: a direction to fasten on the bridge a small implement of wood or metal which has the effect of deadening the tone. (3) Brass instruments: a direction to place a cone-shaped piece of wood covered with leather in the bell, which has the same effect.

Consort. A chest of viols.

Contra (It.). Against (it); in compound words, means an octave below, as contra-bass, contra-fagotto.

Contra danza (It.). Country dance.

Contralto (It.). The lowest female voice, usually called alto.

Contraposaune. A 16- or 32-foot reed-organ stop.

Contrapuntal. Belonging to counterpoint.

Contrapuntist. One skilled in counterpoint, or who writes on the subject of counterpoint.

Contratenor. The highest male voice.

Contra violone (It.) (*vee-o-lo'-neh*), **Contra basse** (Fr.). Double bass.

Countertenor. The developed falsetto. See *Alto*.

Convict of Music. An institution for musical instruction. [Lat., *convictus*, an associate, from *convivere*, to live together.]

Cor (Fr.). A horn.

Cor Anglais (*ong-lay*). English horn; a variety of the hautboy, sounding a fifth lower.

Corale (It.) (*co-rah'-leh*). A choral.

Coranto (It.), **Courante** (Fr.). An old dance in triple time, used as a movement in the suite.

Corda (It.). String. **Una corda, Due corde, Tre corde** or **Tutte corde**, one string, two strings, three strings, all the strings, are directions for the use of the pedal in Grand *p. f.* that shifts the action so as to strike one, two, or all of the strings allotted to each key.

Cornamusa (It.) (*corna-moo-sa*), **Cornemuse** (Fr.) (*corn-moos*). Bagpipe.

Cornet, Cornetto (It.), **Zinke** (Ger.). (1) Originally a coarse-toned instrument of the hautboy family. (2) A compound stop in the organ. (3) **Cornet-à-pistons**, a brass instrument of the trumpet family. (4) Echo cornet, a compound organ-stop with small scale pipes, usually in the swell.

Corno (It.). Horn; the French horn, or **Waldhorn** (Ger.). The horn of the orchestra.

Corno alto. High horn. **Corno basso**, low horn.

Corno di bassetto. Basset horn.

Corno di caccia. Hunting horn.

Corno Inglese. Cor Anglais.

Cornopean. Same as *Cornet* (brass); a reed-stop on the organ, 8-foot tone.

Coro (It.). Chorus.

Corona (It.). "Crown"; a pause.
Corrente (It.) (*cor-ren'-teh*). Coranto.
Cotillion (Fr., Cotillon, *co-tee-yon'*). A dance with numerous figures, originally rather lively, now much the same as the Quadrille.
Couched Harp. The spinet.
Count. The beats in the measure are called counts, from the practice of counting the time.
Counterpoint [from Latin *contra-punctus*, against the point]. Notes were originally called points, hence when another set of points were added above or below the points of the theme, they were called counterpoints. In modern use counterpoint may be defined as the art of making two or more parts move together with such freedom that they seem to be independent, each one with a design of its own.
Counter-subject. A theme employed in conjunction with the principal theme in a fugue.
Coup d'archet (Fr.) (*coo d'ar-shay*). A stroke of the bow.
Coupler. A mechanism in the organ, by means of which the keys of two manuals are joined so that the depression of the keys of one causes the depression of the corresponding keys of the other. **Pedal Coupler** joins pedal keys to one of the manuals. **Octave Coupler** causes the octave above or below each key struck to sound either on the same or on another manual.
Couplet (Fr.) (*coo-play*). Stanza; ballad.
Couplet (Eng). A pair of rhyming lines. Two notes played in the time of three of the same denomination.
Cracovienne (Fr.). Polacca.
Cremona. (1) A town in Italy celebrated for its violin makers. (2) A violin made in Cremona. (3) A soft 8-ft. reed-organ stop (corrupted from *Krummhorn*).
Crescendo (It.) (*cray-shen-do*). Abbreviation, *cres.*, sign: ⟨ to increase in loudness [from It. *crescere*, to increase].
Crescendozug (Ger., hybrid of It. and Ger.). The swell box of the organ.
Croche (Fr.) (*crosh*). An eighth-note.
Crotchet. A quarter-note.
Crowd, Crouth, Crood, Crooth. An ancient string instrument played with a bow. Of celtic origin.
Crush Note. Appoggiatura.
Cue. The last note of one voice or instrument, written in the part of another as a guide to come in.
Cuivre (Fr.). Brass. **Faire cuivrer** (*fare koo-e-vreh*), a direction to produce a rattling, metallic note on the horn by inserting the hand part way in the bell.
Cuvette (Fr.) (*koo-vet'*). The pedal of a harp.
Cyclical Forms. Forms of composition in which one or more themes return in prescribed order, as sonata, rondo, etc.
Cymbals (*Becken*, Ger., *Piatti*, It.). (1) Discs of metal clashed together or struck with drumsticks, used in the orchestra and in military music. (2) A shrill compound stop in the organ.
Czakan (*cha-kan*). A cane flute.
Czardas (*char-dash*). A Hungarian dance with sudden alterations of tempo.
Czimbel (*chim-bel*). A dulcimer strung with wire strings; a national instrument in Hungary.
Czimken (*chim-ken*). A Polish dance.

D

D. Second letter in the natural scale; the third string of the violin; second string of viola or cello; abbreviation of Da or Dal; from D. C., da capo, D. S., dal segno.
Da (It.). From.
Da ballo (It.). In dance style.
Da camera (It.). Chamber music.
Da capella (It.). Church music.
Da capo (It.). From the beginning; abbreviated D. C.
Da capo al fine. From the beginning to the word fine (*fee-neh*), the end, or a double bar with ⌒ over it.
Da capo al segno (It.) (*sehn-yo*). From beginning to the sign 𝄋
D. C. al 𝄋 e poi la coda. From the beginning to the sign, then the coda.
D. C. senza repetitione (*reh-peh-tee-shee-o-neh*) means the same as above.
D. C. senza replica (It.) (*sehntza reh'-plee-cah*). From the beginning without repeating the parts.
Daina or **Dainos.** A Lithuanian love-song.
Damper. A mechanism in the piano to stop the vibration of the strings when the finger is raised from the key.
Damper Pedal. The miscalled loud pedal, a mechanism controlled by the foot for raising all the dampers at once from the strings.
Danse. A piece of music meant to accompany rhythmical movements of the body.
Darabookka. An Arabian drum.
Dash. (1) A line drawn through a figure (𝄒) in figured bass signifies the note must be raised chromatically. (2) A short stroke over a note, signifying it is to be played staccato.
Daumen (Ger.) (*dow-men*). The thumb.
D dur (Ger.). D major.
Début (Fr.) (*deh-boo*). A first appearance.
Decani (Lat.). (1) The dean's side in a cathedral. (2) That part of a choir that occupies the dean's side.
Deceptive Cadence. One in which the dominant chord is not followed by the tonic.
Decima (Lat.). An organ-stop pitched an octave above the tierce.
Deciso (It.) (*deh-chee'-so*). Decided; energetically.
Declamando (It.) (*deh-cla-man'-do*). In declamatory style.
Declamation. The correct enunciation of the words in singing, and their rhetorical accent.
Decres. Abbreviation of **Decrescendo** (It.) (*deh-creh-shen'-do*). To decrease in volume of sound. Sign: ⟩
Decuplet. A group of ten notes played in the time of eight of the same denomination.
Defective. The diminished 5th is sometimes so called.
Degree. From one letter to the next, a degree may be a half-tone, minor second; whole tone, major second; tone and a half, augmented second.
Del, Della, Delli, Dello (It.). Of the.
Deliberatamente (It.). Deliberately.

Deliberato (It.) (*deh-lee-beh-rah'-to*), **con.** With deliberation.
Delicatamente (It.). Delicately; gently.
Delicatezza (It.) (*deh-lee-cah-tetza*), **con.** With delicacy.
Delicatissimo (It.). Exceedingly delicate.
Delicato (It.) (*deh-lee-cah-to*). Delicate.
Délie (Fr.) (*deh-lee-a*). The reverse of legato. Literally, not tied.
Delirio (It.) (*deh-lee-reeo*), **con.** With frenzy.
Demi-baton (Fr.) (*deh-mee-bah-tong*). A rest of two measures.
Demi-croche (Fr.) (*crosh*). A sixteenth-note.
Demi-jeu (Fr.) (*zheu*). Half play; a direction in organ-playing to use half the power of the instrument.
Demi-pause (Fr.). A half-rest.
Demi-semi-quaver. Thirty-second note.
Demi-soupir (Fr.) (*soo-peer*). Eighth-rest.
Derivative. Any chord of which the root is not at the bass, an inverted chord.
Des (Ger.). D flat.
Descant or **Discant.** (1) The earliest attempts at adding other parts to a cantus were called descant. (2) The highest part (soprano) in vocal music.
Des dur (Ger.) D♭ major.
Desiderio (It.) (*deh-see-dee'-rio*). Longing.
Des moll (Ger.). D♭ minor.
Dessus (Fr.) (*des-soo*). The soprano part in vocal music.
Destinto (It.) (*deh-stin-to*). Distinct.
Desto (It.). Sprightly; briskly.
Destra (It.). Right. **Mano destra,** the right hand. **Mano sinistra,** the left hand. **Colla destra,** with the right. A direction in piano music.
Détaché (Fr.) (*deh-tash-eh*). Detached; staccato.
Determinato (It.). Resolutely; with determination.
Detto (It.). The same. **Il detto voce,** the same voice.
Development. [In German, *Durchführung.*] (1) The technical name of that part of a sonata form which precedes the return of the principal theme. In the development both the themes are used in fragments mixed with new matter, the object being to present the musical thought in every possible aspect. (2) The working out of a fugue.
Devoto (It.). Devout.
Devozione (It.) (*deh-vot-see-o'-neh*), **con.** With devotion.
Di (It.) (*dee*). By, with, of, for. **Di bravura,** with bravura. Literally, with bravery.
Diana (It.), **Diane** (Fr.). A morning serenade; aubade.
Diapason (Gr.). (1) An octave. (2) An organ-stop of 8-foot pitch, open or closed (stopped). (3) The standard pitch, A = 435 vibrations per second, not yet universally adopted.
Diatonic. (1) The major and minor scales. Strictly speaking, the modern harmonic minor is not purely diatonic, owing to the presence of the augmented 2d between 6 and 7. (2) Diatonic chords, melody, progressive modulation, are those in which no note foreign to the scale in which they are written appears. [From Gr. *dia-teino,* to stretch; referring to the string of the canon or monochord.]
Di colto (It.). Suddenly.
Diecetto [It.) (*dee-chetto*). A composition for ten instruments.
Dièse (Fr.) (*dee-ehs*). A sharp.
Difficile (It.) (*dif-fee'-chee-leh*), **Difficile** (Fr.) (*dif-fi-seel*). Difficult.
Di gala (It.). Merrily.
Diluendo (It.) [*diluere,* to dilute]. Wasting away; decrescendo.

Diminished. (1) Intervals less than minor or perfect. (2) A chord with diminished 5th, as on the 7th of the scale or the 2d of the minor scale. (3) Diminished 7th chord, a chord composed of three superimposed minor thirds, as B D F A♭.
Diminuendo (It.). Same as *Decrescendo.*
Diminution. In canon and fugue, when the answer (comes) is given in notes of half (or less) the value of those in the subject (dux).
Di molto (It.). Very much. **Allegro di molto,** very fast.
Direct. (1) A sign ∿ placed at the end of a staff to indicate what is the first note on the next page. (2) In MS. music it indicates that the measure is completed on the next line.
Direct Motion. Both (or all) parts ascending or descending together.
Dis (Ger.). D sharp.
Discant. See *Descant.*
Discord. Cacophony; noise. Used incorrectly for dissonance. Dissonance is musical, but discord never is.
Disinvolto (It.). Free; naturally; easily.
Disjunct Motion. Moving by skips.
Dis moll (Ger.). D♯ minor.
Disperato (It.), **Con disperazione** (*dis-peh-ratz-eo'-neh*). Despairingly; with desperation.
Dispersed Harmony. When the members of the chords are separated widely.
Disposition. (1) Of a chord, the order in which its members are arranged. (2) Of a score, the order in which the instruments are arranged on the page. (3) Of an orchestra, the positions assigned to the different instruments.
Dissonance. An interval, one or both of whose members must move in a certain way to satisfy the ear. All augmented and diminished intervals, seconds, sevenths, and ninths, are dissonances.
Ditty. A short, simple air, originally with words that contained a moral.
Divertimento (It.) (*dee-ver-tee-men'-to*), **Divertissement** (Fr.) (*dee-vehr-tiss-mong*). (1) A pleasing, light entertainment. (2) A composition or arrangement for the piano; this is the most usual meaning. (3) A suite or set with a number of movements for instruments, called also a serenata.
Divisi (It.). Divided; a direction that the string instruments must divide into two masses or more, as may be indicated by the composer.
Divisions. An old name for elaborate variations.
Divoto (It.). See *Devoto.*
D moll (Ger.). D minor.
Do. (1) The first note in the natural scale in Italy; this syllable was substituted for *ut,* the first of the Guidonian syllables; *ut* is still retained in France. (2) In the "movable do" system of singing, the keynote of every scale is called *do.*
Dodecuplet. A group of twelve notes played in the time of eight of the same denomination.
Doigter (Fr.) (*doy-zeh*). See *Fingering.*
Dolcan, Dulciana. Soft eight-foot open organ-stop.
Dolce. A stop of same character as dulciana, but softer.
Dolce (It.) (*dol-cheh*). Sweet.
Dolcemente, con dolcezza (It.) (*dol-chet-zah*). With sweetness.
Dolciano, Dolcino (It.), **Dulcan** (Ger.). Dulciana stop.
Dolcissimo (It.) (*dole-chis-see-mo*). As sweet as possible.
Dolente (It.). Afflicted.
Dolentimente (It.). Mournfully; afflictedly.

Dolzflöte (Ger.) (*dolts-fla-teh*). (1) The old German flute with six holes and one key. (2) A soft eight-foot organ-stop.

Domchor (Ger.) (*dome-kor*). Cathedral choir.

Dominant. (1) The fifth note in the scale. (2) The reciting note in Gregorian chants.

Dominant Chord. The major triad on the fifth of the major or minor scale.

Dominant Key. The usual key in which the second theme of a sonata or rondo in major mode is written.

Dominant Seventh. The seventh over the root added to the dominant chord.

Dopo (It.). After.

Doppio (It.) (*dop'-pee-o*). Double, as *doppio movemento*, double movement, *i. e.*, twice as fast.

Dorian. A Greek or ecclesiastical mode, D to D.

Dot. (1) A dot after a note or rest increases its duration one-half; a second dot increases the duration one-half of the first dot

(2) A dot over a note signifies that it is to be played or sung staccato. (3) Dots combined with slur

in music for bow instruments signify the notes are to be played with one motion of the bow with a slight stop after each note; in piano music, to raise the arm with stiff wrist after each note or chord and let it fall lightly from the elbow on the next. (4) Dots over a note thus signify that the note is to be repeated by subdivision into as many notes as there are dots.

Double. (1) An old name for *variation*. (2) An octave below the standard pitch, as double bass, double diapason, double bassoon.

Double (Fr.) (*doobl*). A variation on a minuet; in Italian, *alternativo*.

Double Bar. Two single bars placed close together signifying: (1) The end of a part or piece. (2) A change of key or of time signature. (3) In hymn-tunes the end of a line.

Double Bass. The violone [It., *vee-o-lo-neh*, Fr., *contra-basse*]. The largest of the violin family. Two kinds are in use, one with three strings tuned:

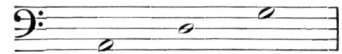

one with four strings tuned:

The pitch is an octave below the written notes.

Double Bassoon. A bassoon of 16-foot pitch.

Double Bourdon. An organ-stop of 32-foot tone.

Double Chant. See *Chant*.

Double Counterpoint. A counterpoint so contrived that it may be placed either above or below the theme, without producing any forbidden intervals. A double counterpoint is said to be at the octave when, if written above the theme, it may be moved down an octave; at the 10th, if it may be moved down a tenth; at the 12th, if it may be moved down a twelfth. Double counterpoint may also be at the 9th and 11th, but the former are much more used.

Double Croche (Fr.) (*doobl crosh*). A sixteenth-note.

Double Diapason. An organ-stop of 16-foot tone.

Double Drum. A drum struck at both ends.

Double Flat, ♭♭, depresses a letter a whole tone.

Double Main (*mang*). Octave-coupler in the organ.

Double Sharp, ✕ raises a letter a whole tone.

Double Stop. In violin music, playing simultaneously on two strings.

Double Tonguing. Playing repeated staccato notes on the flute, cornet, etc., by a movement of the point of the tongue against the roof of the mouth.

Double Touche (*toosh*). A contrivance for regulating the depth of the descent of the keys of the harmonium.

Doublette (Fr.) (*doo-blet*). A two-foot organ-stop, the 15th, or a compound stop of two ranks.

Doucement (Fr.) (*doos-mong*). Sweetly, softly.

Doux (Fr.) (*doo*). Sweet, soft.

Down Beat. The first beat in the measure; the principal accent in the measure.

Down Bow. In instruments of the violin family, the motion of the bow from the nut to the point. The sign is ⊓ or ∧. In French the word *tirez* (*tee-reh*), draw.

Doxology [from Greek *doxa*, praise; *lego*, to proclaim]. A short ascription of praise to the Trinity, metrical or otherwise.

Drammatico (It.), **Drammaticamente** (It.). Dramatic; in dramatic style.

Drängend (Ger.) (*drayn'-gent*). Hurrying; accelerating.

Dritta (It.). The right hand.

Droit or **Droite** (Fr.) (*droa*). Right hand.

Drone. The pipe that sounds one note continuously in the bagpipe.

Drum. An instrument of percussion, the body hollow, made of wood or metal, one or both ends being covered with vellum or parchment drawn tight by braces. Three kinds of drum are used in modern music: (1) The kettle drum; this is the only one that may be tuned to definite pitch; a pair are generally used in the orchestra, tuned usually to the 1st and 5th of the key. (2) The snare drum or side drum, with parchment at both ends; that at one end is crossed by several thick gut-strings that rattle when the drum is struck on the other end by the pair of drumsticks. (3) The long drum, double drum, *grosse caisse*, used chiefly in military music; struck on both ends.

Drum Slade. A drummer.

Due (It.) (*doo-eh*). Two. **A due**, by two; that is, divide, when marked over a string part in the orchestra; but when over a wind instrument part it means that both of the pair are to play the notes.

Due corde (It.). Two strings. In violin music, means that the note is to be played on the open string and as a stopped note simultaneously. The only notes that may be so played on the violin are:

sometimes signified by writing them as above.

Duet, Duo (Fr.), **Duetto** (It.). A composition for two voices or instruments or for two performers on the piano or organ.

Duettino (It.) (*doo-et-tee'-no*). A little duet.

Dulciana. A soft, open, 8-foot organ-stop; flue pipes; in some foreign organs, a soft reed-stop.

Dulcimer. (1) An instrument consisting of an oblong or square box strung with wire strings, struck by small hammers held in the hands of the performer. (2) A small toy instrument, in which strips of glass or metal are used instead of wire strings, played in the same way.

Duolo (It.) (*doo-o'-lo*), **con doloroso** (It.), **con dolore** (It.) (*do-lo'-reh*). Plaintively; mournfully.

Duple. Double. **Duple Time,** two beats in the measure.

Dur (Ger.) (*duhr*). Literally, hard; major.

Dur (Fr.). Hard; coarse; rough.

Duramente (It.) (*doo-ra-men'-teh*). Roughly.

Durchführung (Ger.) (*doorch'-fee-roonk*). The working out; development of a sonata or fugue. See *Development*.

Durchkomponirt (Ger.) (*doorch'-kom-po-neert*). Composed through. Applied to a song that has a separate setting for each stanza.

Durezza (It.) (*doo-retz-a*), **con.** With sternness.

Dur-moll Tonart (Ger.). Major-minor scale or mode; a diatonic scale with major 3d and minor 6th.

Duro (It.), **Durante** (It.). Harshly.

Düster (Ger.) (*dees-tehr*). Gloomy; mournful; sad.

Dux (Lat.). Leader; the theme of a fugue.

E

E. (1) The third of the natural major scale, fifth of the natural minor. (2) The first or highest string (chanterelle) of the violin. (3) The fourth or lowest string of the double bass.

E. (It.) (*eh*). And; when the word that follows begins with a vowel, **ed** (*ehd*).

Ebollimento or **Ebollizione** (It.) (*eh-bol-litz-ee-o'-neh*). Boiling over; sudden expression of passion.

Ecclesiastical Modes. The scales called also Ambrosian and Gregorian, in which plain song and plain chant are written. They differ from the modern diatonic in the position of the half-tones; their position depends upon the initial note of the scale.

Échelle (Fr.) (*eh-shel*). A scale.

Echo Organ. A set of pipes in old organs enclosed in a box.

Éclat (Fr.) (*eh-claw*). Fire; spirit.

Éclogue or **Eglogue** (Fr.) [from Greek εκλεγο to select]. A pastoral; a poem in which shepherds and shepherdesses are the actors.

École (Fr.) (*eh-cole*). A school or style of music.

Écossais (Fr.) (*ek-cos-seh*) or **Écossaise** (*ek-cos-saze*) (1) In the Scotch style. (2) A lively dance.

Eguale (It.) (*eh-gwah-leh*). Equal; steady.

Egualmente. Equally; steadily.

Einfach (Ger.). Simple. **Einfachheit,** simplicity in construction.

Einfalt (Ger.). Simplicity in manner. **Mit Einfalt,** in a simple, natural manner.

Einleitung (Ger.) (*ein-lei-toonk*). Leading in; introductory.

Einschlafen (Ger.). Diminish in power and movement.

Eis (Ger.) (*eh-is*). E sharp.

Eisteddfod (Welsh) (*ice-steth'-fod*). In modern usage a musical contest for prizes.

Eleganza (It.) (*eh-lee-gantza*), **con.** With grace.

Elegy. A mournful poem commemorating the dead.

Elevato (It.) (*eh-leh-vah'-to*). Elevated; exalted.

Eligiac. In the style of an elegy.

Embellishment. The ornaments of melody, as trill, turn, mordent, etc.

Embouchure (Fr.) (*om-boo-shoor*). (1) The mouth-piece of a wind instrument. (2) The position and management of the mouth and lips of the player.

E moll (Ger.). E minor.

Empater les sons (Fr.) (*om-pahteh leh song*). Literally, to strike the sounds together; to sing extremely legato.

Empfindung (Ger.) (*emp-fin-doonk*). Emotion; passion.

Emporté (Fr.) (*om-por-teh*), **Empressé** (Fr.) (*om-pres-seh*). Hurried; eager; passionate.

Encore (Fr.) (*ong-core*), **Ancora** (It.). Again; a demand for the re-appearance of a performer; the piece sung or played on the re-appearance of the performer.

Energia (It.) (*eh-nur-jea*), **con.** With energy.

Energico, Energicamente, Energisch (Ger.). Energetic; forcibly.

Enfatico (It.) (*en-fa'-tee-ko*). Emphatic; decided.

Enfasi (It.) (*en-fah'-see*), **con.** With emphasis.

Engelstimme (Ger.). Angel voice; a soft organ-stop; vox angelica.

Enharmonic. In modern music, a change of the letter without changing the pitch, as, C♯, D♭.

Enharmonic Modulation. A modulation in which the above change takes place, as,

Ensemble (Fr.) (*ong-sombl*). Together. (1) The union of all the performers. (2) The effect produced by this union. (3) The manner in which a composition for many performers is "put together."

Entr'acte (Fr.) (*on-trakt*). Between the acts; music performed between the acts of a drama.

Entrata (It.), **Entrée** (Fr.). Entry; introduction, prelude; the first movement of a serenata.

Entschlossen (Ger.) (*ent-shlos-sen*). Resolute; resolutely.

Entusiasmo (It.) (*ehn-too'-see-as-mo*), **con.** With enthusiasm.

Eolian or **Æolian.** (1) One of the Greek and ecclesiastical scales. (2) A species of harp played on by the wind.

Epicède (Fr.), **Epecedio** (It.) (*ep-ee-cheh'-dee-o*). A funeral dirge.

Epinette (Fr.). A spinet.

Episode. The parts of a fugue that intervene between the repetitions of the main theme.

Epithalamium. A wedding song.

E poi (It.). And then; after.

Equabile (It.) (*eh-qua-bee-leh*). Equal; steady.

Equabilmente. Equally; steadily.

Equal Voices. A composition is said to be for equal voices when written for men's only or women's only. When male and female voices are combined the music is said to be for mixed voices.

Equisono (It.). Equal sounding; unison.

Equivocal Chords. Dissonant chords that are common to two or more keys, or that may be enharmonically substituted for each other, as the diminished 5th chord, diminished 7th chord, and augmented 6th chord.

Ergriffen (Ger.). Affected; moved.
Ergriffenheit. Emotion.
Erhaben (Ger.). Lofty; sublime.
Erhabenheit. Sublimity.
Ermattet (Ger.). Exhausted.
Ernst (Ger.). Earnest; serious.
Eroica (It.) (*eh-ro'-ee-ka*). Heroic.
Erotic. Amatory. [Gr. *Eros,* Cupid.]
Ersterbend (Ger.). Dying away; morendo.
Es (Ger.). E flat.
Es dur (Ger.). E flat major.
Es-es (Ger.). E double flat.
Es moll (Ger.). E flat minor.
Espagnuolo (It.) (*ehs-pan-yu-olo*). In Spanish style.
Espirando (It.). Dying away.
Espressione (It.) (*ehs-pres-see-o-neh*), **con.** With expression.
Espressivo (It.). Expressive.
Essential Dissonances. Those that are added to the dominant chord. Auxiliary notes of all kinds are non-essential dissonances.
Essential Harmony. The harmony independent of all melodic ornaments, etc.
Estinguendo (It.) (*es-tin-guen-do*). As soft as possible.
Estinto (It.). Dying away; extinguishing.
Estravaganza (It.) (*es-trah-vah-gantza*). A fanciful composition; a burlesque.
Étoffé (Fr.). Full; sonorous.
Étouffée (Fr.). Stifled; damped.

Étude (Fr.) (*eh-tood*). A study, lesson.
Etwas (Ger.) (*et-vos*). Somewhat; as, **etwas langsam,** somewhat slow.
Euphonium. A large brass instrument of the saxhorn family, used in military bands; a free reed-stop in the organ, sixteen-foot pitch.
Euphony [Gr., *eu,* good; *phone,* sound]. Well-sounding; agreeable.
Exercise. (1) A study designed to overcome some special difficulty or strengthen special muscles. (2) A lesson in harmony, counterpoint, or composition. (3) A composition written as a thesis for the obtaining of a degree.
Exposition. The giving out of the subject and answer by all the voices in turn at the opening of a fugue.
Expression. The performance of music in such a manner as to bring out all its emotional and intellectual content. Intelligent, appreciative performance.
Expression (Fr.). The name of a harmonium stop.
Extempore (Lat.) (*ex-tem'-po-reh*). The gift of playing music composed as it is played.
Extemporize. To play unpremeditated music.
Extended Harmony. Reverse of close harmony, *q. v.*
Extension. (1) Violin playing, to reach with the fourth or first finger beyond the "position" in which the hand may be. (2) In piano music, spreading the hand beyond the "five-finger" position.
Extraneous Modulation. A modulation to a distant or non-related key.
Extreme. The outside parts, as bass and soprano.
Extreme. Used by many writers on harmony in the sense of augmented; as, extreme 2d or 5th or 6th.

F

F. The fourth or subdominant of the natural major or minor scale.
Fa. The fourth of the syllables adopted by Guido, called the Aretinian syllables. In "Movable Do" system the fourth of any scale.
Fa bemol (Fr.). F flat.
Fa burden, Falso bordone (It.), **Faux bourdon** (Fr.). (1) An ancient species of harmonization, consisting of thirds or sixths added to the cantus. (2) A drone bass like a bagpipe.
Facile (Fr.) (*fa-seel*), **Facile** (It.) (*fah-chee-leh*). Easy.
Facilment (Fr.) (*fa-seel-mong*), **Facilmente** (It.) (*fa-cheel-men-teh*). Easily; fluently.
Facilité (Fr.). Made easy; an easy version of a difficult passage.
Facture (Fr.) (*fak-toor*), **Fattura** (It.) (*fat-too-rah*). Literally, the making. The construction of a piece of music; the scale of organ-pipes.
Fa dièse (Fr.) (*dee-ehs*). F sharp.
Fagotto (It.), **Fagott** (Ger.). Bassoon (so called from its resemblance to a fagot or bundle of sticks). A double-reed instrument of great utility in the orchestra. Compass, three octaves (and over) from B♭ below the bass staff.
Fagottone (It.) (*fag-got-to'-neh*). Double bassoon.
Faible (Fr.) (*faybl*). Weak. **Temps faible,** weak beat.
False Cadence. A deceptive cadence.

False Fifth. A name for the diminished fifth.
False Relation. When a note sounded by one voice is given in the next chord, altered by ♯, ♭, or ♮, by another voice, thus:

Falsetto (It.). The highest register of the voice.
Fandango (Sp.). A rapid dance in triple time.
Fanfare (Fr.), **Fanfara** (It.). A brilliant trumpet call or flourish; a brass band.
Fantasia (It.), **Fantasie** (Ger.), **Fantaisie** (Fr.). A composition that is not in any of the regular forms; often used of pianoforte arrangements of themes from operas.
Fantasia, Free. The name sometimes given to that part of a sonata that comes after the double bar; the Durchführung or development.
Fantasiren (Ger.) (*fan-ta-see-ren*). To improvise.
Fantastico (It.), **Fantastique** (Fr.). Fantastic; grotesque.
Farandola (It.), **Farandole** or **Faraudole** (Fr.). A rapid dance in 6/8 time, Southern France and Italy.
Fascia (It.) (*fashiah*). A tie.
F Clef. See *Clef.*
F dur (Ger.). F major.
Feierlich (Ger.). Festal; pompously; grandly; **solemnly.**
Feld (Ger.). Field; open air.

Feldmusik. Military music.

Feldton. The key of E♭, often used for military band music.

Fermata (It.) [from *fermare*, to stay]. A pause. ⌢ A cessation of accompaniment and time, while a soloist executes a cadenza.

Fermato, Fermamente (It.). Firmly; decidedly.

Feroce (It.) (*feh-ro'-cheh*). Wild; fierce.

Ferocita (It.) (*feh-ro'-chee-tah*), **con.** With ferocity.

Fertig (Ger.). Quick; ready; nimble.

Fertigkeit. Dexterity; technical skill.

Fervente (It.) (*fer-ven'-ieh*). Fervent; vehement.

Fes (Ger.). F flat.

Fest (Ger.). Festival.

Fest (Ger.). Fast; fixed.

Fester Gesang. Canto firmo.

Festgesang. Festival song.

Festivo (It.) (*fes-tee'-vo*). Festive; solemn.

Festivamen'te (It.). Festively; solemnly.

Festivita (It.) (*fes-tee'-vee-ta*), **con.** With joyfulness.

Festo'so (It.). Gay; joyful.

Feuer (Ger.) (*foy-ehr*). Fire.

Feuerig (Ger.). Fiery.

F-holes. The openings in the belly of instruments of the violin family; so called from their shape, *f*.

Fiacco (It.) (*fee-ak'-ko*). Weak; faint.

Fiasco (It.). A failure; breakdown. Literally, "a flask."

Fiato (It.). Breath.

Fiddle. This word and "violin" both come from the same root—the Low Latin word *vitula*.

Fidicen (Lat.). A harp or lute player. [From Lat. *fides*, a string, and *cano*, to sing.]

Fidicinal. A general term for string instruments.

Fiedel (Ger.). Fiddle.

Fieramente (It.). Proudly; fiercely.

Fiero (It.) (*fee-eh-ro*), **Fier** (Fr.) (*fee-eh*), proud; fierce.

Fife, Fifre (Fr.), **Piffero** (It.), **Querpfeife** (Ger.) (*kvehr-pfei-feh*). A small flute without keys, an octave higher than the flute, used in conjunction with drums for military purposes.

Fifteenth. An organ-stop of 2-foot pitch; open; metal.

Fifth. (1) An interval which includes five letters. (2) The dominant of the key.

Figure. (1) A form of accompaniment maintained without change. (2) A repeated melodic phrase. (3) Sequence.

Figured Bass, Basso figurato (It.), **Basse chiffre** (Fr.). A bass with figures over it (or under it) to indicate the chord each note is to bear. Invented as a species of musical shorthand it has been retained as a means of teaching harmony, although its warmest advocates admit its inadequacy to the indication of modern harmony.

Filar la voce (It.) (*feelar-la-vocheh*), **Filer la voix** (Fr.) (*fee-leh-la-voa*). To sustain a sound with even tone. Literally, to spin like a thread.

Fin (Fr.) (*fang*), **Fine** (It.) (*fee-neh*). End.

Finale (It.) (*fee-nah-leh*). Final. The last movement of a sonata or symphony or of the act of an opera.

Fingerboard. The upper side of the neck of string instruments, generally a thin strip of ebony against which the strings are pressed by the fingers of the left hand.

Fingering. The art of using the fingers systematically when playing an instrument; the marks or figures that indicate what fingers are to be used.

Fingersetzung (Ger.). Fingering.

Finto (It.). A feint; applied to a deceptive cadence.

Fioretto (It.) (*fee-o-ret-to*). An ornament.

Fiorito (It.) (*fee-o-ree-to*). Florid.

Fiorituri (It.) (*fee-o-ree-too-ree*). Embellishments; **florid** passages.

Fis (Ger.). F sharp. **Fisfis** or **Fisis**, F double sharp.

Fis dur. F sharp major.

Fis moll. F sharp minor.

Fixed Do. *Do* used as the name of C; movable *do* is *do* used as the keynote of any scale.

Flageolet. A small pipe blown at the end; an organ-stop of 2-foot pitch.

Flageolet Tones. The harmonic sounds produced by touching lightly the strings of violin, etc.

Flat. The sign of depression (♭) lowers the letter a half-tone.

Flautando, flautato (It.). Flute-like; in violin playing, a direction to produce flageolet tones.

Flautino (It.) (*flau-tee-no*). A small flute; a piccolo.

Flue Stops. Organ stops, the pipes of which are constructed on the same principle as the whistle or flageolet.

Flute, Flauto (It.) (*flau-to*), **Flöte** (Ger.) (*flateh*). (1) One of the most important of orchestral instruments; a cylindrical tube blown at a hole in the side called the embouchure. The modern flute, constructed on the Boehm system, is very much superior to the older instrument in both tone and tune. Its compass is from

(2) An organ-stop of 8 or 4-foot pitch; in French organs a general name for flue stops. There are many varieties of the flute, the major part of which are now either obsolete or used as names for organ-stops, as flauto traverso, transvere or German flute; flute d'amour, a soft-toned organ-stop; flute harmonique, an overblown flute, the pipe of which is twice the length necessary to produce the sound it is made to give.

F moll. F minor.

Foco (It.). Fire. **Con foco** or **fuoco,** with fire.

Focoso. Fiery; ardently.

Foglietto (It.) (*fol-yet'-to*). The part used by the leader of the violins in the orchestra, containing cues, etc., of the other instruments, sometimes used by the conductor in place of a score.

Fois (Fr.) (*foa*). Time; as, **première fois,** first time.

Folia (Sp.), **Follia** (It.). A Spanish dance. Elaborate variations are called Follias de España, in French, Folies de'Espagne, meaning "follies of Spain" (a pun on the word folia), which has become a proverbial expression for trifles.

Fonds d'orgue (Fr.) (*fond-dorg*). The 8-foot flue-stops of the organ. The foundation stops.

Foot. (1) A poetic measure or meter. (2) A drone bass. (3) The unit used in determining the pitch of organ pipes, the standard being 8-foot C,

the lowest note on the manuals of the modern organ. An open pipe must be eight feet long to produce this sound, if closed it must be four feet long. Applied to other instruments it signifies that their pitch corresponds with that of the organ diapasons, that is, it is the same as the written note. All the violin family are of 8-foot pitch, except the double bass, which is of 16-foot pitch, that is, the notes sound an octave lower than written. The flute, hautboy, clarionet, and bassoon are also of 8-foot pitch. Of brass

Forlana (It.), **Fourlane** (Fr.) (*foor-lan*). A dance somewhat similar to the tarantella.

Form. The number, order, and key relation of the several themes that are combined to make an extended composition, such as the sonata, rondo, symphony, concerto, etc. The lyric or dance form is the germ from which all varieties of instrumental music have been developed. The simplest form of lyric melody may be thus divided: Motive, two measures; Section, two motives; Phrase, two sections; Sentence, two phrases; Period, two sentences, making sixteen measures in all. The lyric form may be extended indefinitely by the addition of new periods in related keys. One of the most usual is the addition of a new period in the key of the dominant, subdominant, or relative minor, followed by a repetition of the first period. This is called the Aria Form. It was formerly largely used in vocal music, and is now one of the most usual forms for the lighter class of piano music. The following outlines of sonata and rondo forms give their main characteristics. The sonata form is the form of the symphony, and of the trio, quartet, etc., for string instruments, or for piano with strings, or other instruments. The same is the case with the rondo; this form is frequently used for the final movement.

Outline of Sonata Form in Major Key
FIRST HALF.

1st Theme.	2d Theme.
Tonic key.	Dominant key.

SECOND HALF

	1st Theme.	2d Theme.
Development.	Tonic key.	Tonic key.

Sonata in Minor Key
FIRST HALF

1st Theme.	2d Theme.
Tonic.	Relative major.

SECOND HALF

	1st Theme.	2d Theme.
Development.	Tonic.	Parallel major.

Frequent deviations may be found from the foregoing schemes. The intervals between the themes are filled with transition passages or modulations so constructed as to heighten the effect of the theme that follows; codas are frequently added after both appearances of the second theme.

Modern Rondo Form, Major Key
FIRST HALF

1st Theme.	2d Theme.	1st Theme.
Tonic.	Dominant.	Tonic.

SECOND HALF

3d Theme.	1st Theme.	2d Theme.	Coda.
Sub-dom.	Tonic.	Tonic.	Made from 1st
Rel. minor.			theme or all
Parallel minor.			the themes.

For an example of this kind see Beethoven's No. 2 Sonata of the three dedicated to Haydn, last movement.

Same Form of Rondo in Minor Key
FIRST HALF

1st Theme.	2d Theme.	1st Theme.
Tonic.	Relative major.	Tonic.

SECOND HALF

3d Theme.	1st Theme.	2d Theme.	Coda.
Sub-dom. and	Tonic.	Tonic major.	Minor.
relative major.			

See last movement of Sonata Pathétique—Beethoven.

Forte (It.) (*for-teh*). Loud. **Fort** (Fr.), **Stark** (Ger.). **Meno forte**, less loud. **Mezzo forte** (M. F.), half loud. **Piu forte**, louder. **Poco forte**, a little loud; rather loud. **Sempre forte**, always loud. **Forte stop**, a mechanism worked by the feet or the knee, or a draw-stop, by means of which the whole power of the harmonium, organ, etc., may be put on at once.

Forte possibile (It.) (*pos-see'-bee-leh*), **Fortissimo** (It.). Loud as possible.

Fortemente (It.). Loudly; forcibly.

Forza (It.) (*fortza*), **con**. With force.

Forzando (It.) (*fortzando*). Forcing the sound; emphasizing a certain note, indicated by $<$, $\wedge$, *fz, sfz*.

Forzato (It.) (*fortzato*), **Sforzando, Sforzato**. All have the same meaning as *Forzando*.

Fourniture (Fr.). A mixture-stop in the organ.

Fourth. (1) An interval embracing four letters. (2) The subdominant of the scale.

Française (Fr.) (*frong-says*). A dance in triple time.

Francamente (It.) (*frank-a-men'-teh*). Frankly; boldly.

Franchezza (It.) (*fran-ket'-za*), **Franchise** (Fr.) (*frong-shees*). Freedom; confidence.

Freddamente (It.). Frigidly; coldly.

Fredezza (It.) (*freh-det'-za*), **con**. With coldness.

Free Fugue. One that does not conform to strict rules.

Free Parts. Parts added to a canon or fugue that take no part in its development.

Free Reed. See *Reed*.

Free Style. The reverse of strict contrapuntal style.

French Horn. See *Horn*.

French Sixth. The augmented 6th with augmented 4th and major 3d.

French Violin Clef. The G clef on the first line (obsolete).

Frets. Pieces of wood, metal, or ivory, set across the fingerboard of some string instruments, raised slightly above its surfaces, to regulate the pitch of the sounds; the finger is pressed on the string behind the fret, which then acts as a bridge.

Fretta (It.), **con**. With haste; hurry.

Frisch (Ger.). Fresh; lively.

Fröhlich (Ger.). Gay; cheerful.

Frottola (It.). A comic ballad.

Fuga, Fugue (It.), **Fuge** (Ger.) (*foo-geh*). [From Lat., *fuga*, flight]. The parts seeming to fly one after another; the highest development of counterpoint; a composition developed from one or two (sometimes three) short themes, according to the laws of imitation. The chief elements of a fugue are: (1) Subject, or theme. (2) Answer, imitation of theme at 5th above or below. (3) Counter-subject, an additional theme which accompanies the main theme. (4) Episodes; these connect the various repetitions of the theme together. (5) Organ point, generally used before the stretto. (6) Stretto, a drawing together of the subject and answer; the stretto is often written on an organ point. (7) Coda, the free ending after the development is completed. Although all these things enter into the fugue, it is not necessary that every fugue should include all of them. There are many varieties of fugue now happily relegated to the limbo of musical antiquities. The most important are the Real fugue, in which the subject and answer are identical, and the Tonal fugue, in which an alteration must be made in the theme to prevent its going out of the key. In the tonal fugue the subject moves from the tonic to the dominant, or the reverse. The answer must move from dominant to tonic, or the reverse.

Fugara. An open, metal pipe organ-stop, generally of 4-foot tone.

Fugato. In fugue style. **Aria fugato,** a song with fugue-like accompaniment.

Fughetto (It.). A slightly developed fugue.

Full Cadence. Perfect cadence. See *Cadence.*

Fundamental. The generator or root of a chord.

Fundamental Bass. The roots of the harmonics on which a piece is constructed.

Fundamental Position. A chord with its root at the bass.

Funèbre (Fr.) (*foo-nebr*), **Funerale** (It.) (*foo-neh-rah'-leh*). Funereal; dirge-like.

Fuoco (It.) (*foo-o'ko*). Fire. **Con fuoco,** with fire.

Furia (It.) (*foo'-re-ah*), **con.** With fury.

Furibundo (It.), **Furioso** (It.). Furiously; savagely.

Furlano (It.). See *Forlana.*

Furniture. A mixture-stop in the organ.

Furore (It.) (*foo-ro'-reh*), **con.** With fury; passion.

Fusée (Fr.) (*foo-seh'*). A slide from one sound to another.

G

G. (1) The fifth or dominant of the natural major scale. (2) The fourth or lowest string of the violin. (3) The third string of the viola and violoncello; the first string of the double bass. (4) The letter represented by the G or treble clef. (5) Abbreviation for Gauche (Fr.) (*gawsh*), left

Gagliarda (It.) (*gal-yar-dah*), **Gailliarde** (Fr.) (*gah-yard*). A favorite dance in 3/4 time resembling the minuet.

Gai (Fr.) (*gay*), **Gaja** (It.) (*gayah*), **Gaiment** (Fr.) (*gay-mong*), **Gajamente** (It.) (*gay-a-men-teh*). Gay; merry; gaily; merrily.

Gala (It.) (*gah-lah*), **di gala.** Finely; bravely. Literally, in fine array.

Galamment (Fr.) (*gal-lah-mong*), **Galantemente** (It.) (*galant-eh-men-teh*). Gracefully; freely; gallantly.

Galant (Ger.) (*gah-lant'*), **Galante** (Fr.) (*gah-longt*), **Galante** (It.) (*gah-lan-teh*). Free; gallant; graceful.

Galliard. See *Gagliarda.*

Galop (Fr.) (*gah-lo*), **Galopade** (Fr.) (*galo-pahd*), **Galopp** (Ger.). A rapid, lively dance in 2/4 time.

Gamba (It.) [the leg]. (1) See *Viol di gamba.* (2) An organ-stop of eight-foot pitch; in German, **Gambenstimme.**

Gamma. The Greek letter g, Γ; in ancient music the letter G, first line bass staff; in the hexachord system this sound was called *gamma ut,* from whence comes gamut, a scale.

Gamme (Fr.) (*gahm*). A scale; gamut.

Gang (Ger.). Passage.

Ganz (Ger.) (*gants*). Whole. **Ganze Note,** whole note.

Garbo (It.). Gracefulness; refinement.

Gassenhauer (Ger.) (*gas-sen-how-er*). Lit., running the streets. An old dance in 3/4 time.

Gauche (Fr.) (*gawsh*). Left. **Main gauche,** left hand.

Gavot (Fr.) (*gah-vo*), **Gavotte** (*gah-vot*), **Gavotta** (It.). An old dance in ₵ time; lively, yet dignified. Frequently introduced in the suite.

G Clef. See *Clef.*

Gedeckt (Ger.) [from *decken,* to close]. Closed; the stopped diapason.

Gedehnt (Ger.). Slow; stately.

Gedicht (Ger.). Poem.

Gefallen (Ger.) (*geh-fal-len*). Pleasure. **Nach Gefallen,** at will. See **Bene placito** and **A piacere.**

Gefühl (Ger.) (*geh-feel*). Feeling. **Mit Gefühl,** with feeling.

Gegensatz (Ger.) (*geh-gen-sats*). The second theme in a sonata. Lit., the against or contrary theme; **Hauptsatz** being the chief or principal theme.

Gehalten (Ger.) (*geh-hal-ten*). Held; sustained; tenuto.

Gehend (Ger.) (*geh-end*). Going; andante. **Etwas gehend** (con moto), with motion.

Geige (Ger.). Fiddle; violin.

Geigenprincipal. An organ-stop of 8- or 4-foot pitch.

Geist (Ger.). Spirit; mind; genius.

Geistlich (Ger.). Sacred; spiritual.

Gelassen (Ger.). Tranquil; calm.

Gemächlich (Ger.) (*geh-mehch-lich*). Easy; convenient.

Gemächlich commodo. Not too fast.

Gemässigt (Ger.) (*geh-mehs-sicht*). Moderate. Lit., measured.

Gemshorn. An 8- or 4-foot organ-stop with horn-like tone.

Gemüth (Ger.) (*geh-meet'*). Heart; soul; feeling.

Gemüthlich (Ger.). Feelingly; heartily.

Generator. Root; fundamental of a chord.

Genere (It.) (*je'-neh-reh*), **Genre** (Fr.) (*zhongr*). Style; class; mode.

Generoso (It.) (*jeh-neh-ro'-so*). Freely; frankly.

Gentille (Fr.) (*zhong-til*), **Gentile** (It.) (*jen-tee-leh*). Graceful; delicate. **Con gentilezza** (It.) (*jen-tee-letza*), with grace; nobility.

German Flute. See *Flute.*

German Sixth. See *Augmented Sixth.*

Ges (Ger.). G flat.

Gesang (Ger.) (*geh-zong'*). Singing [from *singen,* to sing]; song; melody; air.

Gesangverein (Ger.). Singing society.

Geschmack (Ger.). Taste. **Mit Geschmack,** with taste. **Geschmackvoll,** tasteful.

Geschwind (Ger.) (*geh-shvint'*). Fast; presto.

Gesteigert (Ger.). Raised; exalted in volume; louder; crescendo.

Getragen (Ger.) (*geh-tra-gen*). Sustained. [*Tragen,* to bear up.] Sostenuto.

Gezogen (Ger.) (*geh-tso-gen*) [from *ziehen,* to drawl]. Prolonged; sustained.

Ghazel or **Gazel.** A short Persian poem, used by Hiller as a name for short pianoforte pieces, in which a simple theme constantly occurs.

Ghiribizzo (It.) (*gee-ree-bitz'-o*). Whim; grotesque.

Giga (It.). Jig; a rapid dance in 6/8 time, used as the final movement in the suite, where it is often developed in fugue form.

Giochevole (It.) (*jee-o-keh'-vo-leh*), **Giocondosa** (It.) (*jee-o-kon-do-sah*), **Giocoso** (It.) (*jee-o-co-so*), **Giocondezza** (It.) (*jee-o-con-detza*). Joyful; merry; sportive; happy; mirthful.

Gioja (It.) (*jeo-ya*), **con**. With joy.

Giojante (It.) (*jeo-yan-teh*), **Giojosamente** (It.) (*jeo-yos-a-men-teh*), **Giojoso** (It.) (*jeo-yo-so*). Joyous; mirthfully.

Gioviale (It.) (*jeo-ve-ah'-leh*). Jovial.

Giovialita (It.) (*jeo-vee-ah-lee-tah*), **con**. With joviality.

Gis (Ger.) (*ghiss*). G sharp.

Giubilio (It.) (*jew-bee-leo*). Jubilation.

Giubilioso (It.) (*jew-bee-lee-oso*). Jubilant.

Giustezza (It.) (*jews-tet'-za*), **con**. With exactness.

Giusto (It.) (*jewsto*). Strict; exact.

Glee. A composition for three or more voices without accompaniment. The glee differs from the madrigal, its predecessor, in being constructed more on the harmonic than the contrapuntal system; *i. e.*, admits dominant, dissonances, and second inversions. The glee is the most distinctive form of English music. The best glees belong to the eighteenth century and the first part of the nineteenth. They have been largely superseded by the part song.

Gli (It.) (*lee*). The.

Glide. (1) To connect two sounds by sliding. (2) A modern variety of the waltz.

Glissando, Glissato, Glissicato, Glissicando (It.). To play a scale on the pianoforte by drawing the finger along the keys. Only possible in the natural scale. In violin playing, to slide the finger rapidly from one "stop" to the next.

Glissé (Fr.) (*glis-seh*). See *Glissando*.

Glisser (Fr.) (*glis-seh*). To slide.

Glockenspiel (Ger.). Bell play; a small instrument consisting of bells tuned to the diatonic scale, played by small hammers or by means of a keyboard. Steel bars are sometimes used in place of bells.

Cong. A pulsatile instrument consisting of a disc of bronze, struck with drumstick with soft head.

Gorgheggi (It.) (*gor-ghed'-je*). Florid singing, with runs, trills, etc.

Grace Note. See *Appoggiatura*.

Graces. The ornamental notes first used in harpsichord playing; they are now nearly all obsolete, or if used are written in full by the composer.

Gracieux (Fr.) (*grah-see-oo*), **Gracieuse** (Fr.) (*grah-see-oos*), **Gracile** (It.) (*gra-chee-leh*). Graceful; delicate.

Gradevole (It.) (*grah-deh'-vo-leh*). Grateful.

Graduellement (It.) (*grah-doo-el-mong*). By degrees.

Gran cassa (It.). Great drum; long drum.

Gran gusto (It.), **con**. With grand expression.

Gran tamburo (It.). The big drum.

Grand barré (Fr.). See *Barré*.

Grand jeu (Fr.) (*zheu*), **Grand choeur** (*koor*). Full organ.

Grand Piano. Properly, the long, wing-shaped pianoforte with keyboard at the wide end; commonly applied to all varieties of piano with three strings to each key.

Grande orgue (Fr.) (*org*). Great organ.

Grandezza (It.) (*gran-det'-za*), **con**. With grandeur.

Grandioso (It.) (*gran-de-o'-so*). Grandly.

Grave [Fr., *grahv*; It., *grah-veh*]. Deep in pitch; slow; solemn.

Gravecembalum (Lat.), **Gravicembalo** (It.), (*gra-vee-chembalo*). The harpsichord.

Gravement (Fr.) (*grahv-mong*), **Gravemente** (It.) (*grah-veh-men-teh*). Slowly; seriously.

Gravita (It.) (*gra-vee-tah*), **con**. With dignity.

Grazia (It.) (*grat-se-a*), **con**. With grace; elegance.

Grazioso (It.) (*grat-si-oso*), **Graziosamente** (*grat-si-osa-men-teh*). Gracefully; elegantly.

Great Octave. The sounds from

Great Organ. The division of an organ that contains the most powerful stops, generally operated by the middle keyboard or manual, the upper being the swell organ, the lower the choir organ.

Greater. Major; as, greater third, greater sixth. In old usage the major scale is called the scale with the greater third.

Greek Music. The Greek system of music is still a subject of controversy about which very little is known. The best attempts at its elucidation may be found in Chappel's "History of Music" and Munro's "Greek Music." Its interest is purely antiquarian.

Gregorian Chant. See *Plain Song*.

Groppo (It.), **Groppetto** (It.). A turn; a group.

Grosse (Ger.) (*gros-seh*). (1) Major, applies to intervals. (2) Great or grand, as, grosse Sonate. (3) An octave below standard pitch, as, grosse Nazard, an organ-stop an octave below the twelfth.

Grosse-caisse, Gros tambour. See *Drum*.

Grosso (It.). Great; large; as, grosso concerto.

Grottesco (It.) (*grot-tes'-ko*). Grotesque; comic.

Ground Bass. A bass of four or eight bars, constantly repeated, each time with varied melody and harmony. The ground bass was generally used as the basis of the chaconne and passacaglio.

Group. (1) A series of rapid notes grouped together. (2) One of the divisions of the orchestra, as string group, brass group, wood group.

Gruppo, Grupetto. See *Groppo, Groppetto*.

G-Schlüssel (Ger.) (*gay-shlues-sel*). G clef.

Guaracha (Sp.) (*gwah-rah'-chah*). A lively Spanish dance in triple time.

Guerriero (It.) (*gwer-rech'-ro*). Martial; warlike.

Guida (It.) (*gwee-dah*). Guide; the subject of a canon or fugue.

Guidonian Hand. A diagram consisting of a hand, with the syllables written on the tips of the fingers and on the joints, intended to assist in memorizing the hexachord scales.

Guidonian Syllables. The syllables applied by Guido to the notes of the hexachord, *ut, re, mi, fa, sol, la.* When the octave scale was adopted *si* was added for the seventh note; *ut* was changed to *do* as a better syllable for vocalizing.

Guitar. A string instrument with fretted fingerboard, played by plucking the strings with the fingers of the right hand, one of the oldest and most widespread of instruments. It probably originated in Persia, where it is called *tar* or *si-tar*, passed from thence to Greece, and to the rest of Europe and North Africa. The guitar now in general use is called the Spanish guitar. It has six strings tuned thus:

but their actual sound is an octave below the written notes.

Gusto (It.), **con**. With taste.

Gustoso. Tastefully.

Gut. The material (sheep's entrails) of which violin, guitar, and other strings are made, commonly called catgut.

Gut (Ger.) (*goot*). Good. **Guter Taktteil**, lit., good bar part; the accented part of the bar.

H

H. Abbreviation for Hand. **Hah** (Ger.), the note B♮, B♭ being called B (*bay*). It is this system of nomenclature that makes possible the fugues on the name of Bach, written by Bach, Schumann, and others:

B A C H

Hackbrett (Ger.). Literally, chopping-board. The dulcimer.
Halb (Ger.) (*halp*). Half.
Halbe Cadenz (Ger.). Half cadence.
Halbe Note. Half-note.
Halber Ton. Half-tone.
Half-Note.
Half-Rest.
Half-Shift. On the violin, the position of the hand between the open position and the first shift.
Half-Step. Half-tone.
Half-Tone. The smallest interval in modern music.
Hallelujah (Heb.). The Greek form **Alleluia** is often used. "Praise ye Jehovah."
Halling. A Norwegian dance in triple time.
Hals (Ger.). Neck, as of violin, guitar, etc.
Hammerklavier (Ger.). A name for the P. F. (used by Beethoven in the great sonata, Op. 106).
Hanacca. A Moravian dance in 3/4 time, somewhat like the polonaise.
Hardiment (Fr.) (*har-dee-mong*). Boldly.
Harmonic Flute. See *Flute*.
Harmonic Scale. The series of natural harmonics; the scale of all brass instruments without valves or pistons.
Harmonic Stops. Organ-stops with pipes of twice the standard length pierced with a small hole at the middle, causing them to sound the first overtone instead of the sound that the whole length would produce.
Harmonica. (1) An instrument invented by Benjamin Franklin, the sounds of which were produced from glass bowls. (2) An instrument consisting of plates of glass struck by hammers. (3) A mixture-stop in the organ.
Harmonici (Lat.) (*har-mon'-i-see*). The followers of Aristoxenus, as opposed to the **Canonici** (*ka-non-i-see*), the followers of Pythagoras. The former taught that music was governed by its appeal to the ear, the latter that it was a matter for mathematical and arithmetical study only.
Harmonicon. A toy instrument with free reeds, blown by the mouth.
Harmonics, Overtones, Partial Tones. (1) The sounds produced by the division of a vibrating body into equal parts; it is upon the presence or absence and relative intensity of the overtones that the quality of the sound depends. Open pipes, strings, brass instruments, and instruments with double reed (bassoon and hautboy) give the following series:

$$\begin{array}{ccccccccc} & 1 & 2 & 3 & 4 & 5 & 6 & 7 & 8 & 9 \\ C & C & G & C & E & G & B\flat & C & D & E, \text{ etc.} \\ \text{generator} & & \tfrac{1}{2} & \tfrac{1}{3} & \tfrac{1}{4} & \tfrac{1}{5} & \tfrac{1}{6} & \tfrac{1}{7} & \tfrac{1}{8} & \tfrac{1}{9} & \tfrac{1}{10} \end{array}$$

Closed pipes and beating reeds (clarionet) omit all the even numbers in this series. (2) The sounds produced on the violin by touching the string lightly at one of the points of division; those produced by thus touching the open string are called natural harmonics. Artificial harmonics are produced by stopping the string with the first finger and touching it lightly with the fourth, at the interval of a fourth above; the resulting harmonic is two octaves above the stopped note. In writing music this is indicated by writing thus:

Played.   *Effect.*

The lozenge-shaped notes indicate the notes to be lightly touched. Natural harmonics are frequently used on the harp, guitar, and mandolin.

Harmonie-Musik (Ger.). Harmony music; music for wind instruments. A band composed of brass and wood instruments is called a harmony band.

Harmonist. One who is an expert in the art of harmony.

Harmonium. A keyboard instrument with free reeds. It differs from the reed organ in that the air is forced through instead of drawn through the reeds, giving a stronger, rougher quality of tone. In harmonium music, published in Europe, the stops are indicated by figures placed in a circle. Each stop is divided at the middle. The figure in circle, placed below the bass staff, refers to the lower half of the stop; above the treble staff, to the upper half. The cor anglais and flute form one stop, marked ① below for cor anglais, ① above for flute.

2 means bourdon, below; clarionet, above.
3 means clarion, below; piccolo, above.
4 means bassoon, below; hautboy, above.

Harmony [from Gr. *harmo*, to join]. The art of combining sounds. The study of harmony in its fullest extent is that which treats of the combination of sounds, consonant and dissonant, and their succession. The so-called laws of harmony have all been arrived at empirically, hence have been subject to change, each new composer of sufficient originality and genius modifying them to suit his purposes. Harmonic combinations may be either consonant or dissonant. The consonant combinations consist of the common (perfect) chord and its derivatives. The dissonant combinations all include some dissonant interval, viz., 7th or 2d, augmented 4th, diminished or augmented 5th, augmented 6th or diminished 3d, or 9th. The movement of consonant combinations is perfectly free; that of dissonant combinations is subject to the rules governing the resolution of the dissonant sounds they contain. Two classes of dissonances are recognized: (1) Those that belong to the overtone series, called essential; (2) those that result from the employment of suspensions, retardations, changing and passing notes.

Harp. A string instrument of very ancient origin, probably first suggested by the bow. The earliest forms of Egyptian harps resemble that weapon, the front bar or support being wanting. The modern harp, by means of contrivances for altering the tension of the strings, controlled by pedals, has the complete chromatic scale. The harp is extensively used in the modern orchestra; its clear, "glassy" tones form a striking and effective contrast to the rest of the orchestra. It is most effective when used to give "arpeggios," or broken chords, particularly in soft passages. Scales are ineffective on the harp, and the chromatic scale is impossible. The compass of the modern harp extends from the second C♭ below the bass staff to the second F♭ above the treble staff, six and one-half octaves. The natural harmonics, produced by touching the middle of the string lightly with one hand, are extremely effective in very soft passages.

Harpe (Fr.), **Harfe** (Ger.). The harp

Harpsichord, Harpsicol, Clavicin (Fr.), **Cembalo** (It.), **Clavicembalo** (It.), **Flügel** (Ger.). A string instrument with keyboard, in shape like the modern grand piano. The sound was produced by pieces of quill, leather, or tortoise-shell, which scratched across the strings when the keys were struck. Harpsichords were often made with two rows of keys and with stops, by means of which the tone might be modified.

Haupt (Ger.) (*howpt*). Head; chief; principal.

Hauptmanuel. Great organ.

Hauptnote. Essential note in a turn, mordent, etc.

Hauptsatz. Principal theme in a sonata or rondo, etc.

Hauptwerk. Great organ.

Hautbois (Fr.) (*ho-boa*). See *Oboe*.

Hautbois d'amour. A small variety of the hautboy.

H dur (Ger.). B major.

H moll (Ger.) (*hah moll*). B minor.

Head. The membrane of a drum; the peg-box of violin, guitar, etc.

Head Voice. See *Voice*.

Heftig (Ger.). Impetuous. Literally, heavily.

Heimlich (Ger.). Mysteriously; secretly.

Heiss (Ger.). Ardent.

Heiter (Ger.). Clear; calm.

Heptachord [Gr., *hepta*, seven; *korde*, string]. A scale or lyre with seven diatonic sounds.

Herabstrich or **Herstrich** (Ger.). Down bow.

Heraufstrich or **Hinaufstrich** (Ger.). Up bow.

Hidden Fifths or **Octaves.** Called also concealed. These occur when two parts or voices take a 5th or 8th in parallel motion.

The rule forbidding hidden 5ths and 8ths is now very little regarded.

His (Ger.). B sharp.

Hoboe, Hoboy. See *Oboe*.

Hochzeitsmarsch (Ger.) (*hoch-tseits*). Literally, high time. A wedding march.

Hohlflöte (Ger.) (*hole-fla-teh*). Hollow flute; an organ-stop of 8-foot tone, soft, full quality; a stop of the same character a fifth above the diapason is called **Hohlquinte** (*kvin-teh*).

Holding Note. A sustained note; a pedal point.

Homoph'ony, Homophon'ic, Homoph'onous [Gr., *homo*, one or single; *phonos*, sound]. Music in which one part (melody) is the most important factor, the remaining parts being entirely subsidiary, that is, simply accompaniment.

Horn [It., *Corno;* Fr., *Cor;* Ger., *Horn* or *Waldhorn*]. A generic term for instruments of brass or other metal, wood, or animal horns sounded by means of a cup-shaped mouth-piece. In modern usage applied only to the orchestral horn, called also French horn. A brass instrument with a long, narrow tube bent into a number of circular curves, with a large bell. The modern horn is provided with pistons, which make it a chromatic instrument. The custom is now almost universal of using the horn in F, the part for which is written a fifth higher than the actual sounds. Before the application of pistons to the horn its part was always written in C, and the key was indicated by writing: Corni in B♭ or E♭, etc., as the case might be. Many composers retain this method of writing, but the horn-players generally transpose the part *a vista* to suit the F-horn.

Horn Band. In Russia, a band of performers, each one of whom plays but one sound on his horn.

Hornpipe. An old English dance of a lively, rapid character.

Horn-Sordin (Ger.). A contrivance placed in the mouth of the horn to deaden the tone.

Humoresque (Fr.) (*oo-mo-resk*), **Humoreske** (Ger.). A caprice; humorous, fantastic composition.

Hunting Horn [Fr., *Cor de Chasse;* It., *Corno di Caccia*]. The horn from which the orchestral horn was developed.

Hymn Tune. A musical setting of a religious lyric poem, generally in four parts.

I

Idée fixée (Fr.) (*e-deh fix-eh*). Fixed idea; a name given by Berlioz to a short theme used as the principal motive of an extended composition.

Idyl [Fr., *Idylle;* Gr., *Eidullion*]. A small image or form; a short, tender piece of music generally of a pastoral character.

Il piu (It.) (*eel peu*). The most. **Il piu forte possibile**, as loud as possible.

Imitando (It.). Imitating; as, **Imitando la voce**, imitating the voice; a direction to the instrumentalist to imitate the vocalist.

Imitation. A device in counterpoint; a musical phrase being given by one voice is immediately repeated by another voice. There are many varieties of imitation: (1) By augmentation, when the imitating part is in notes of twice or four times the value of those in the theme. (2) By diminution, when the value of the notes is reduced one-half or one-fourth. (3) By inversion, when the intervals are given by the imitating part in inverted order. Imitation is called Canonic when the order of letters and intervals is exactly repeated, thus:

C D E F   G A B C

Strict, when the order of letters only is repeated, as:

C D E F   A B C D

Free, when the theme is slightly altered, but not enough to destroy the resemblance. The theme is called the antecedent; the imitation, the consequent. There are other varieties of imitation, but they are now generally obsolete, being more curious than musical.

Immer (Ger.). Ever; continuously; always.

Impaziente (It.) (*im-pah-tse-en-teh*). Impatient; restless.

Impazientemente (It.). Vehemently; impatiently.

Imperfect Cadence. Same as *Half Cadence*.

Imperfect Consonance. Major and minor thirds and sixths.

Imperfect Fifth. The diminished fifth.

Imperioso (It.). Imperiously; with dignity.

Impeto (It.) (*im'-peh-to*), **con.** With impetuosity.

Impetuoso (It.), **Impetuosamente** (It.). Impetuously.

Implied Intervals. Those not expressed in the figuring.

Imponente (It.) (*im'-po-nen-teh*). Emphatic; pompous.

Impromptu. (1) An extemporaneous performance. (2) A piece of music having the character of an extemporaneous performance.

Improvisation. Unpremeditated music.

Improvise. To play unpremeditated music.

Improviser (Fr.) (*im-pro-vee-seh*), **Improvvisare** (It.). To extemporize.

Improvvisatore (It.). An improviser (male).

Improvvisatrice (It.) (*im-prov-vi-sa-tree-cheh*). An improviser (female).

In alt (It.). The notes in the first octave above the treble staff.

In altissimo (It.). All notes above the octave *in alt*.

In nomine (Lat.). In the name; a sort of free fugue.

Incalzando (It.) (*in-cal-tsan-do*). To chase; pursue hotly, with constantly increasing vehemence.

Indeciso (It.) (*in-deh-chee-so*). With indecision; hesitating.

Infinite Canon. See *Canon*.

Inganno (It.). Deceptive. **Cadenza inganno,** deceptive cadence.

Inner Parts. The parts that are neither at the top nor the bottom, as the alto and tenor in a chorus.

Inner Pedal. A sustained note in an inner part.

Innig (Ger.). Heartfelt; fervent.

Innigkeit (Ger.), **mit.** With fervor; intense feeling.

Inniglich (Ger.). See *Innig*.

Inno (It.). Hymn.

Innocente (It.) (*in-no-chen'-teh*), **Innocentemente.** Innocent; natural.

Innocenza (*inno-chent'-sah*), **con.** With artlessness.

Inquieto (It.) (*in-quee-eh-to*). Unquiet; restless.

Insensibile (It.) (*in-sen-si-bee-leh*), **Insensibilmente** (It.). By imperceptible degrees; gradually.

Insistendo (It.), **Instante** (It.), **Inständig** (Ger.). Urgent; pressing.

Instrument. Any mechanical contrivance for the production of musical sounds. Instruments are classified as follows: String instruments, wind instruments, pulsatile instruments. String instruments are divided into bow instruments, violin class; instruments the strings of which are plucked by the fingers—harp, guitar, etc.; plectral, *i. e.*, the strings struck by a rod or thin strip of wood, metal, etc., as mandolin, zither; strings struck by hammers held in the hand—cymbal; strings struck by hammers operated by keyboard—pianoforte. Wind instruments are divided as follows: (1) Vibrating column of air—flutes and flue-stops of organ. (2) Single reed—clarionet, saxophone, basset horn, reed-stops in the organ. (3) Double reed—oboe, bassoon. (4) Free reed—harmonium, vocalion, cabinet organ. (5) Brass instruments in which the lip of the player acts as a reed—trumpet, horn, etc. Pulsatile instruments—drums, triangles, cymbals, bells, xylophone. The small or chamber orchestra includes the following instruments: String—first violins, second violins, violas, violoncellos, contrabassi. Wood-wind—pair of flutes (It., *flauti*), pair of hautboys (It., *oboi*), pair of clarionets (It., *clarionetti*), pair of bassoons (It., *fagotti*). Brass-wind—pair of trumpets (sometimes omitted (It., *clarini*), pair of horns (It., *corni*), pair of kettle-drums (It., *timpani*). The addition of three trombones changes this to the full or grand orchestra, which is often augmented by the addition of the following instruments: Wood-wind—piccolo or octave flute, English horn (It., *corno Inglese*), alto or bass clarinet, double bassoon (It., *contra fagotto*). In the brass quartet the horns are increased to four, and the alto, tenor, and bass trombones are added and the bass trombone reinforced by the bass tuba. Three or more kettle-drums are frequently employed, also the following pulsatile instruments: large drum, snare drum, triangle, and cymbals. The harp has almost become an essential in the modern orchestra, whether large or small.

Instrumentation. The art of using a number of instruments in combination; the manner of arranging music for the orchestra.

Instrumento or **Stromento** (It.). An instrument.

Instrumento or **Stromento di corda** (It.). String instrument.

Instrumento or **Stromento di fiato** (It.). Wind instrument.

Interlude, Intermède (Fr.) (*in-ter-made*), **Intermedio** (It.) (*in-ter-meh-deo*). A short piece of music between the acts of a drama or the verses of a hymn.

Intermezzo (It.) (*in-ter-medzo*). An interlude; a short movement connecting the larger movements of a symphony or sonata.

Interrupted Cadence. See *Cadence*.

Interval. The difference in pitch between two sounds. The name of an interval is determined by the number of letters it includes (counting the one it begins with and the one it ends with). Seconds may be minor (E, F), major (E, F♯), augmented (E♭, F♯). Thirds may be minor (E, G), major (E, G♯), diminished (E, G♭). Fourths may be perfect (E, A), augmented (E, A♯), diminished (E, A♭). The inversion of an interval produces one of the opposite kind except when it is perfect. Inversion of minor 2d produces major 7th, and since all intervals lie within the octave, and the octave contains twelve half-tones, it follows that an interval and its inversion must together make an octave or twelve half-tones. Intervals are further divided into consonant and dissonant, the consonant into perfect and imperfect. The perfect consonances are the 4th, 5th, and octave. They are called perfect because any alteration of them produces a dissonance. The imperfect consonances are the major and minor 3d and 6th, called imperfect because equally consonant whether major or minor. All other intervals are dissonant, that is, one or both the sounds forming them must move in a certain direction to satisfy the ear. If the dissonant is minor or diminished the sounds must approach each other (except minor 2d); if major or augmented they must separate (except major 7th, which may move either way). Intervals are augmented when greater than major or perfect. Intervals are diminished when less than major or perfect. The prime or unison is often called an interval and if altered, as C C♯, is called an augmented unison or prime; it is more properly a chromatic semitone. Natural intervals are those found in the major scale. Chromatic intervals are those found in the harmonic minor scale and in chords that include sounds foreign to the scale or key.

Intimo (It.) (*in'-tee-mo*). Heartfelt; with emotion.

Intonation. (1) The correctness or incorrectness of the pitch of sounds produced by the voice or by an instrument. (2) The notes which precede the reciting notes of the Gregorian chant.

Intoning. In the Anglican Church the singing of prayers, etc., in monotone.

Intrada (It.). An introduction or interlude.

Intrepido (It.) (*in-tre-pee-do*), **Intrepidezza, con** (It.) (*in-treh-pee-detza*), **Intrepidamente** (It.) (*in-treh-pee-da-men-teh*). Boldly; with daring; dashingly.

Introduction. A preparatory movement to a piece of music symphony, oratorio, etc., sometimes very short, sometimes a long, elaborate movement in free style.

Introduzione (It.) (*in-tro-doo-tse-oneh*). Introduction.

Introit. A short anthem sung before the administration of the communion in the Protestant Episcopal Church; in the Roman Catholic Church before the celebration of the mass.

Invention. A name given by Bach to a set of thirty pieces in contrapuntal style.

Inversion. (1) Of intervals. See *Interval*. (2) Of chords, when any member of the chord but the root is used as a bass. (3) Of themes. See *Imitation*.

Ira (It.) (*e-rah*), **con.** With anger.

Irato (It.) (*e-rah'-to*). Angrily.

Irlandais (Fr.) (*ir-lan-day*). In the Irish style.

Ironico (It.) (*e-ron'-e-co*), **Ironicamente** (It.). Ironically; sardonically.

Irresoluto (It.) (*ir-reh-so-lu'-to*). Undecided; irresolute.

Islancio (It.) (*is-lan'-chee-o*). Same as *Slancio*.

Istesso (It.). Same. **L'istesso tempo,** the same time, *i.e.* rate of movement.

Italian Sixth. See *Augmented Sixth*.

Italienne (Fr.) (*e-ta-lee-en*), **Italiano** (It.) (*e-tal-yah-no*) In Italian style.

J

Jack. The short, upright piece of wood at the end of the key of the harpsichord or spinet, to which the quill was attached which struck the strings.

Jagdhorn (Ger.) (*yagd-horn*). Hunting horn.

Jägerchor (Ger.) (*yay-ger-kore*). Hunting chorus.

Jaleo (Sp.) (*hak-leh-o*). A Spanish dance in triple time.

Janko Keyboard (yanko). The invention of Paul Janko, arranged like a series of steps, six in number. Each key may be struck in three places, some on the 1st, 3d and 5th steps, the rest on the 2d, 4th, and 6th, thus enabling the performer to select the most convenient for the passage to be executed. The chief advantages claimed for this keyboard are: that all scales may be fingered alike; that the thumb may be placed on any key, black or white; that the extended chords are brought within easy reach.

Janissary Music. Instruments of percussion, as small bells, triangles, drums, cymbals.

Jeu (Fr.) (*zhoo*). Literally, play. A stop on the organ.

Jeu d'anche (*d'ongsh*). Reed stop.

Jeu de flute. Flue stop.

Jeu demi (*deh-mee*). Half power; mezzo forte.

Jeu doux (*doo*). Soft stops.

Jeu forts (*fort*). Loud stops.

Jeu grand. Full organ.

Jeu plein (*plane*). Full power.

Jig [It., *Giga;* Fr. and Ger., *Gigue;* comes either from Geige, an obsolete variety of fiddle, or from Chica, a rapid Spanish national dance]. Now a rapid rustic dance of no fixed rhythm or figures. In the classic suite the jig is the last movement, written in $\frac{6}{8}$ time and often very elaborately treated in fugal form.

Jodeln (Ger.) (*yo-deln*). A manner of singing cultivated by the Swiss and Tyrolese; it consists of sudden changes from the natural to the falsetto voice.

Jota (Sp.) (*ho-ta*). A Spanish national dance in triple time.

Jour (Fr.) (*zhoor*). Day. An open string is called corde à jour.

Jubal (Ger.) (*yoo-bal*). An organ-stop of 2- or 4-foot pitch.

Jungfernregal (Ger.) (*yung-fern-reh-gal*). See *Vox angelica*.

Just Intonation. Singing or playing in tune.

K

Kalamaika (*ka-la-my-ka*). A Hungarian dance; rapid $\frac{2}{4}$ time.

Kammer (Ger.). Chamber.

Kammerconcert. Chamber concert.

Kammermusik. Chamber music.

Kammerstil. Chamber-music style.

Kammerton. Concert pitch.

Kanon, Kanonik (Ger.). See *Canon*.

Kanoon. A Turkish dulcimer, played like the psalterion by means of plectra attached to thimbles.

Kantate (Ger.). Cantata.

Kapellmeister (Ger.). The leader of a band or chorus attached to a royal or noble household.

Kapellmeister-Musik (Ger.). A contemptuous term for music that is dull and unoriginal, while it may be correct and pedantic.

Keckheit (Ger.). Boldness. **Mit Keckheit,** with boldness.

Kehrab or **Kehraus** (Ger.). Lit., turn out. The last dance at a ball.

Kent Bugle. A wind instrument generally made of copper, with cup-shaped mouthpiece, furnished with keys. It was named in honor of the Duke of Kent.

Keraulophon [from Gr., *keras,* horn; *aulos,* flute; and *phone,* sound]. A soft flue-stop of 8-foot pitch.

Keren. A Hebrew trumpet.

Kettle-drum. A half-sphere of copper, the head made of vellum, which may be tightened or loosened by means of screws or braces. The kettle-drum is the only drum from which sounds of definite pitch may be obtained. They are generally used in pairs in the orchestra, and are tuned to the tonic and dominant of the key, but modern writers adopt various other methods of tuning; it is also quite usual now to use three drums. The larger drum may be tuned to any note from

The smaller

In old scores the drum part was always written in C and the sounds wished were indicated by writing Timpani in F, B♭, etc. The modern custom is to write the actual sounds.

Key. (1) A series of sounds forming a major or minor scale. See *Scale*. (2) A piece of mechanism by means of which the ventages of certain wind instruments, as flute and clarionet, are closed or opened. (3) A lever by which the valves of the organ are opened or the hammers of the pianoforte put in motion.

Klangfarbe (Ger.). Lit., sound-color. Quality of tone; timbre (Fr., *tambr*).

Klavier or **Klaviatur** (Ger.) (*kla-feer', klah-fee-a-toor'*). Keyboard.

Klavierauszug. Pianoforte arrangement.

TABLE OF SIGNATURES AND NAMES OF ALL THE MAJOR AND MINOR KEYS

Key-signature.	English.	German.	French.	Italian.	
	C-major / A-minor	C dur / A moll	Ut majeur / La mineur	Do maggiore / La minore	Natural key.
	G-major / E-minor	G dur / E moll	Sol majeur / Mi mineur	Sol maggiore / Mi minore	
	D-major / B-minor	D dur / H moll	Ré majeur / Si mineur	Re maggiore / Si minore	
	A-major / F-sharp minor	A dur / Fis moll	La majeur / Fa dièse mineur	La maggiore / Fa diesis minore	
	E-major / C-sharp minor	E dur / Cis moll	Mi majeur / Ut dièse mineur	Mi maggiore / Do diesis minore	Keys with sharps
	B-major / G-sharp minor	H dur / Gis moll	Si majeur / Sol dièse mineur	Si maggiore / Sol diesis minore	
	F-sharp major / D-sharp minor	Fis dur / Dis moll	Fa dièse majeur / Ré dièse mineur	Fa diesis maggiore / Re diesis minore	
	G-flat major / E-flat minor	Ges dur / Es moll	Sol bémol majeur / Mi bémol mineur	Sol bemolle maggiore / Mi bemolle minore	
	D-flat major / B-flat minor	Des dur / B moll	Ré bémol majeur / Si bémol mineur	Re bemolle maggiore / Si bemolle minore	
	A-flat major / F-minor	As dur / F moll	La bémol majeur / Fa mineur	La bemolle maggiore / Fa minore	
	E-flat major / C-minor	Es dur / C moll	Mi bémol majeur / Ut mineur	Mi bemolle maggiore / Do minore	Keys with flats.
	B-flat major / G-minor	B dur / G moll	Si bémol majeur / Sol mineur	Si bemolle maggiore / Sol minore	
	F-major / D-minor	F dur / D moll	Fa majeur / Ré mineur	Fa maggiore / Re minore	

Keyboard, Klavier (Ger.) (*kla-feer*). The rows of keys of the organ or piano; those for the hands are called manuals, for the feet, pedals.

Keynote. The sound or letter with which any given scale begins; tonic. See *Scale*.

Kinderscenen (Ger.) (*kin-der-stsa-nen*). Child-pictures; a name given by Schumann to a collection of little pieces for the piano.

Kinderstück (Ger.). Child's piece.

Kirchenmusik (Ger.). Church music.

Kirchenstil. Church style.

Kirchenton. Ecclesiastical mode.

Kit, Pochette (Fr.), **Taschengeige** (Ger.). A small pocket-fiddle used by dancing-masters.

Klaviermässig. Suited to the piano.

Klaviersatz. In pianoforte style.

Klavierspieler. Pianist.

Klein (Ger.). Small; minor.

Klein gedeckt. Small stopped diapason.

Knee-stop. A lever controlled by the knees of the performer, used in the harmonium or cabinet organ either to operate the swell or to put on or off the full power of the instrument.

Koppel (Ger.). A coupler. **Koppel ab,** coupler off. **Koppel an,** coupler on.

Kosakisch (Ger.). Cossack dance in 2/4 time.

Kraft (Ger.). Force; power.

Kräftig (Ger.). Vigorous; powerfully.

Krakowiak (*kra-ko-viak*). Cracovienne.
Kreuz (Ger.) (*kroyts*). A sharp.
Kriegerisch (Ger.). Martial.
Kriegerlied (Ger.). War-song.
Krummhorn (Ger.). Crooked horn; the cremona stop.
Kunst (Ger.). Art.
Kunstlied (Ger.). An artistic song; the reverse of a popular song or Volkslied.
Kurz (Ger.) (*koorts*). Short; staccato.
Kurz und bestimmt. Short and emphatic.
Kyrie [Gr., *Lord*]. The first word of the mass; used as a name for the first division.

L

L. H. Abbreviation for left hand; in German, *linke Hand*.
La. The sixth Aretinian syllable; the name in French and Italian of the sound A.
Labial [Lat., *labium*, lip]. A flue-stop.
Labialstimme (Ger.). A flue-stop.
Lacrimoso or **Lagrimoso** (It.) [from *la grima*, tear]. Tearfully; mournfully.
Lamentabile, Lamentabilmente, Lamentando, Lamentevolmente, Lamentevole, Lamentato [It., from *lamentare*, to lament]. Mournfully; complainingly.
Lancers. The name of a variety of the contra dance.
Ländler (Ger.) (*laynd-ler*). A slow waltz of South German origin.
Langsam (Ger.). Slow. **Etwas langsam,** rather slow (poco adagio). **Ziemlich** (*tseem-lich*) **langsam,** moderately slow (andante). **Sehr langsam,** very slow (adagio).
Language. The diaphragm of a flue-pipe.
Languendo (It.) (*lan-gwen'-do*), **Languente** (It.) (*lan-gwen'-teh*) [from *lan-guire*, to languish], **Languemente** (It.) (*lan-gweh-men'-teh*). In a languishing style.
Largamente (It.). Broadly; slowly; with dignity.
Largando (It.). Gradually slower and broader.
Largement (Fr.) (*larzh-mong*). Largamente.
Larghetto (It.) (*lar-get-to*). Rather slow.
Larghissimo (It.) (*lar-gis-sim-mo*). Slowest possible time.
Largo (It.). Lit., large; broad. Very slowy, stately movement is indicated by this term.
Largo assai. Slow enough.
Largo di molto. Very slow.
Largo ma non troppo. Slow, but not too much so.
Larigot (Fr.) (*larigo*). An organ-stop of 1⅓-foot pitch, that is, a twelfth-stop.
Lauftanz (Ger.). Running dance; the coranto.
Launig (Ger.) (*low-nig*). Gay; light; facile.
Lavolta (It.). An old Italian dance resembling the waltz.
Lay [Ger., *Lied*; Fr., *lai*]. A song.
Leader. Conductor; principal violinist in an orchestra; principal clarionet in a wind band; principal cornet in a brass band.
Leading Motive. In German, *Leitmotiv*, q. v.
Leading Note. The 7th note of a scale; in the major scale the 7th is naturally a half-tone below the keynote, in the minor scale it is naturally a whole tone below, and must be raised by an accidental (see *Minor Scale*); called also subtonic.
Leaning Note. See *Appoggiatura*.
Leap. To move from one tone to another more than one degree distant; the reverse of diatonic or chromatic.
Lebendig (Ger.) (*leh-ben'-dig*), **Lebhaft** (Ger.) (*lehb'-hahft*). Lively; with animation.
Ledger Line. See *Leger Line*.
Legato (It.) (*leh-gah'-to*), **Legando** (It.) (*leh-gan'-do*) [from *legare*, to tie or bind]. Passages thus marked are to be played with smoothness, without any break between the tones. *Legatissimo*, as smooth as possible, the notes slightly overlapping. Legato is indicated by this sign ⌒ called a slur. The proper observance of Legato is of the utmost importance in phrasing.
Legatura (It.) (*leh-gah-too'-ra*). A tie.
Legatura di voce (*de-vo-cheh*). A group of notes sung with one breath; a vocal phrase.
Legend, Légende (Fr.) (*leh-zhend*), **Legende** (Ger.) (*leh-ghen'-deh*). A name given to an extended lyric composition, somewhat in the manner of "program music." [*Cf.* Chopin's Légendes.]
Léger, Lègere (Fr.) (*leh'-zhehr*). Light.
Leger Line. Short lines used for notes which are above or below the staff.
Légèrment (*leh-zhehr-mong*). Lightly.
Leggeramente (*led-jehr-a-men'-teh*). Lightly.
Leggerezza (It.) (*led-jeh-ret'-za*). Lightness.
Leggero (*led-jeh-ro*), **Leggiero** (*led-jee-ro*). Light; rapid.
Leggiadramente (It.) (*led-jah-drah-men'-teh*), **Leggiaramente** (*led-jah-rah-men'-teh*), **Leggiermente** (*led-jeer-men'-teh*). All these terms (derived from the same root—*leggiere*, light, quick, nimble) indicate a light, rapid style of performance without marked accent.
Legno (It.) (*lehn-yo*). Wood. **Col legno,** with the wood. A direction in violin playing to strike the strings with the wooden part of the bow.
Leicht (Ger.). Light; easy.
Leichtbewegt (Ger.) (*beh-vehgt*). Light; with motion.
Leidenschaft (Ger.). Passion; fervency.
Leidenschaftlich (Ger.). Passionately.
Leierkasten. Barrel-organ.
Leiermann. Organ-grinder.
Leise (Ger.) (*lei'-seh*). Soft; piano.
Leiter (Ger.). Ladder. **Tonleiter,** tone-ladder; scale.
Leitmotiv (Ger.). Leading motive; a name given by Wagner to certain striking phrases used to indicate certain emotions, characters, or situations.
Leitton (Ger.). Leading note.
[NOTE.—*ei* in German is sounded like *eye* in English.]
Lenezza (It.) (*leh-net'-za*). Gentleness.
Leno (It.) (*leh'-no*). Faint; feeble.
Lentamente (*len-tah-men-teh*). Slowly.
Lentando. Growing slower; retarding.
Lentezza (*len-tet-za*). Slowness.
Lento (It.). Slow, between adagio and grave.
Lesser. Minor is sometimes so called, as key of C with lesser third; C minor.

Lesson. A name used in England for the suite, or the various members of it.

Lesto (It.) (*leh'-sto*). Lively; brisk.

Letter Name. The letter used to designate a degree of the scale, key of piano or organ, line or space of the staff.

Levé (Fr.) (*leh-veh*). Raised; up beat.

Leyer or **Leier** (Ger.). Lyre.

Liaison (Fr.) (*lee-eh-song*). A tie.

Libellion. A variety of music-box.

Liberamente (It.) (*lee-beh-ra-men'-teh*), **Librement** (Fr.) (*leebr-mong*). Freely.

Libretto (It.) (*lee-bret-to*). Little book; the book of an opera or oratorio, etc.

License, Freiheit (Ger.), **Licence** (Fr.), **Licenza** (It.) (*lee-chentza*). An intentional disregard of a rule of harmony or counterpoint.

Liceo (It.) (*lee-cheh'-o*). Lyceum; academy of music.

Lie (Fr.) (*lee-eh*). Tied; bound; legato.

Lieblich (Ger.). Sweet; lovely.

Lieblich gedacht. Stopped diapason.

Lied (Ger.) (*leed*). Song. **Durchkomponirtes Lied** (all through composed), a song with different melody, etc., to every stanza. **Strophenlied,** the same melody repeated with every stanza. **Kunstlied,** art song; high class of song. **Volkslied,** people's song; national song.

Lieder-Cyclus. Song-circle (as Schubert's Müllerin).

Liederkranz. A singing-society.

Liederkreis. Song circle; collection of songs.

Liederspiel. Song-play; operetta; vaudeville.

Liedertafel (song-table). A social singing-society.

Ligato. See *Legato*.

Ligature. A tie. See *Legatura*.

Ligne (Fr.) (*leen*), **Linea** (It.) (*lee'-neh-ah*), **Linie** (Ger.) (*lee-nee-eh*). Line.

Lingua (It.) (*ling-wah'*). Tongue; reed of organ-pipe.

Linke Hand (Ger.). Left hand.

Lip. The upper and lower edges of the mouth of an organ pipe. **To lip,** the act of blowing a wind instrument.

Lippenpfeife or **Labialpfeife** (Ger.). A flue pipe-organ.

Lira (It.) (*lee'-ra*). Lyre.

Lirico (It.) (*lee'-ree-co*). Lyric.

Liscio (It.) (*lee'-sho*). Smooth.

L'istesso (It.) (*lis-tes'-so*). See *Istesso*.

Litany [from Gr., *litaino*, to pray]. A form of prayer consisting of alternate petitions and responses by priest and people, frequently sung or chanted.

Livre (Fr.) (*leevr*). Book. **A libre ouvert,** 'at open book"; to sing or play at sight.

Lobgesang (Ger.). Song of praise.

Loco (It.). Place; play as written. Used after *8va*.

Lontano (It.), **Da lontano.** As if from a distance.

Lösung or **Auflösung** (Ger.) (*lay-soonk*) [from Ger., *lösen*, to free]. Resolution.

Loud Pedal. A name for the damper-pedal.

Loure (Fr.) (*loor*). (1) A slow dance in $\frac{6}{4}$ or $\frac{3}{4}$ time. (2) An old name for a variety of bag-pipe.

Louré (Fr.) (*looreh*). Legato; slurred.

Low. (1) Soft. (2) Deep in pitch.

Lugubre [Fr., *loo-goobr*; It., *loo-goo-breh*]. Mournful.

Lullaby. Cradle song; berceuse.

Lunga (It.). Long. **Lunga pausa,** long pause.

Luogo (It.). See *Loco*.

Lusingando (It.) (*loos-in-gan'-do*), **Lusingante** (It.) (*loo-sin-gan'-teh*), **Lusinghevolmente** (It.) (*loo-sing-eh-vol-men'-teh*), **Lusinghiere** (It.) (*loo-sin-gee-eh-reh*). Coaxing; caressing; seductive. [From It., *lusingare*, to coax or flatter.]

Lustig (Ger.) (*loos-tig*). Merry; gay; lively.

Lute, Luth (Ger.) (*loot*). A string instrument of the guitar family of very ancient origin. It was brought into Europe by the Moors. In shape it resembled the mandolin, and was strung with from six to twelve or more strings of gut. The bass strings were wire-covered and did not pass over the fingerboard. For several centuries the lutes held the foremost place as fashionable instruments. They were made of several sizes. The larger varieties were called Theorbo, Arch Lute, or Chittarone. Music for the lute was written in a system of notation called tablature, *q. v.*

Luth (Ger.) (*loot*). Lute.

Luthier (Ger.) (*loot-eer*). A lute-maker; also given to makers of all string instruments of the guitar or violin families.

Luttosamente. Mournfully. [From It., *luttare,* to mourn; struggle.]

Luttoso (It.) (*loot-to-so*). Mournful.

Lyre. A Greek string instrument of the harp family.

Lyric. Song-like. In poetry, a short poem of a simple, emotional character. The term has been borrowed by music to designate musical works of like character.

Lyric Form. A composition the themes of which are not treated in the manner of the rondo or sonata, *q. v.*

Lyric Stage. The operatic stage. This term will hardly apply to the modern "music drama."

M

M. Abbreviation for Mano or Main, the hand.

M. D. Abbreviation for Main Droite or Mano Destra, the right hand.

M. F. Abbreviation for Mezzo Forte, half loud.

M. G. Abbreviation for Main Gauche, left hand.

M. M. Abbreviation for Maelzel's Metronome.

M. V. Abbreviation for Mezzo Voce.

Ma (It.). But.

Machine Head. The screw and wheel contrivance used instead of pegs in the guitar, etc.

Madre (It.) (*mah'-dreh*). Mother; the Virgin Mary.

Madrigal. A word of uncertain origin. A name given to contrapuntal compositions in any number of parts. They differ from the motet only in being written to secular words, generally amatory. This style of composition was cultivated with great success in England in Elizabeth's reign.

Maesta (It.) (*mah'-es-ta*), **con, Maestade** (*mah'-es-tah-deh*), **con, Maestevole** (*mah'-es-ta-vo-leh*), **Maestevolmente** (*vol-ment-e*), **Maestosamente** (*mah'-es-to-sah-men'-teh*). All mean the same thing: Dignified; with dignity.

Maestoso (It.) (*mah-es-to-so*). Majestic; with dignity.

Maestrale (It.) (*mah-es-trah-leh*). "Masterful"; the stretto of a fugue when written in canon.

Maestro (It.) (*mah-es-tro*). Master.

Maestro al cembalo. Old term for conductor of orchestra, so called because he conducted seated at the cembalo, or harpsichord.

Maestro del coro. Master of the chorus or choir.

Maestro del putti (*del poot'-tee*). Master of the boys (choir boys).

Maestro di capella. Chapel-master; choir-master; name also given to the conductor of the music in the household of a great personage.

Magadis (Gr.). A string instrument tuned in octaves.

Magas (Gr.). A bridge.

Maggiolata (It.) (*madjo-lah'-tah*). A spring song (from Maggio—May).

Maggiore (It.) (*mad-jo'-reh*), **Majeur** (Fr.) (*mah-zhoor*), **Dur** (Ger.) (*duhr*). Major.

Maggot. Old English name for a short, slight composition of fanciful character.

Magnificat (Lat.). Doth magnify; opening word of the hymn of the Virgin Mary.

Main (Fr.) (*mang*). Hand. **M. D.** or **droite**, right hand; **M. G.** or **gauche**, left hand.

Maitre (Fr.) (*mehtr*). Master.

Maitrise (Fr.) (*meh-trees*). A cathedral music school.

Majestätisch (Ger.) (*mah-yes-tay'-tish*). Majestically.

Major (Lat.). Greater.

Major Chord or **Triad.** One in which the third over the root is major, *i. e.*, two whole tones above the root.

Major Scale. One in which the third of the scale is a major third above the keynote. **Major Key,** or **Mode,** or **Tonality,** has the same meaning.

Malinconia (It.) (*mah-lin-co-nee'-a*), **Malinconico, Malinconoso, Malinconioso, Malinconicamente.** Melancholy; in a sad, melancholy manner.

Mancando (It.) [from *mancare,* to want; fail]. Decreasing; dying away in loudness and speed.

Manche (Fr.) (*mansh*), **Manico** (It.) (*mah'-nee-ko*). Handle; neck of violin, etc.

Mandola (It.), **Mandora.** A large mandolin.

Mandolin, Mandolino (It.) (*man-do-lee-no*). A string instrument of the lute family, strung with eight wire strings tuned in pairs; the tuning same as the violin; played by means of a small plectrum; fingerboard fretted like the guitar.

Mandolinata (It.). Resembling the mandolin in effect.

Manichord [from Lat., *manus,* hand; *chorda,* string]. Supposed to be the earliest form of a string instrument, with keyboard, possibly the same as the clavichord.

Manier (Ger.) (*mah-neer'*). A harpsichord grace.

Maniera (It.) (*man-yeh'-ra*). Manner; style.

Männerchor (Gr.) (*man'-ner-kor*). A men's chorus.

Männergesangverein. Lit., men's song-union.

Mano (It.). Hand. **D.** or **destra**, right hand; **S.** or **sinistra**, left hand.

Manual [from Lat., *manus,* hand]. An organ keyboard.

Marcando, Marcato. Decided; marked; with emphasis.

Marcatissimo. As decided as possible.

March, Marche (Fr.) (*marsh*), **Marcia** (It.) (*mar-chee-a*), **Marsch** (Ger.) (*marsh*). A composition with strongly marked rhythm, designed to accompany the walking of a body of men. Marches vary in tempo from the slow, funeral march to the "charge." The following are the principal varieties: Parade March (Ger., *Paraden-Marsch;* Fr., *pas-ordinaire*); Quick-march or Quickstep (Ger., *Geschwind-Marsch;* Fr., *pas redoublé*); Charge (Ger., *Sturm-Marsch;* Fr., *pas-de-charge*). The funeral march and parade march are generally in $\frac{4}{4}$ time; the quick marches often in $\frac{6}{8}$ time.

Mark. A sign, *q. v.*

Markiert (Ger.) (*mar'-keert*), **Marqué** (Fr.) (*mar-kay*). See *Marcato.*

Marseillaise (Fr.) (*mar-sel-yase*). The French national song, composed by Rouget de Lisle.

Martelé (Fr.) (*mar-tel-leh'*), **Martellato** (It.) (*mar-tel-lah'-to*). Hammered. In piano music indicates a heavy blow with stiff wrist; in violin music, a sharp, firm stroke.

Marziale (It.) (*mart-se-a'-leh*). Martial.

Maschera (It.) (*mas-kay'-ra*). A mask.

Mascherata (It.) (*mas-kay'-ra-ta*). Masquerade.

Masque. Mask. A species of musical and dramatic entertainment founded on mythical or allegorical themes.

Mass, Missa (Lat.), **Messa** (It.), **Messe** (Fr. and Ger.). The communion service in the Roman Catholic Church. In music, that portion of the service consisting of the Kyrie, Gloria, Sanctus and Agnus Dei, which are sung. The word mass is generally explained as being derived from the words *"Ite missa est,"* used to dismiss non-communicants before the service. High Mass is used on feasts and festivals. Low Mass on ordinary occasions, sometimes without music.

Mässig (Ger.) (*may'-sig*). Moderate; moderato.

Massima (It.). Whole note.

Master Chord. The dominant chord.

Master Fugue. One without episodes.

Master Note. The leading note.

Masure (*mah-soo-re*), **Masurek. Masurka, Mazurka.** A Polish dance in $\frac{3}{4}$ time.

Matelotte (Fr.). A sailors' hornpipe dance in $\frac{2}{4}$ time.

Matinée (Fr.) (*ma-tee-neh'*). A morning concert.

Mean. Old name for an inner part in music for voices; also for inner strings of viol, lute, etc. The C clef was also called the mean clef.

Measure. (1) Old name for any slow dance. (2) The portion of music enclosed between two bars. (3) Rhythm. (4) Tempo.

Mechanism, Mecanisme (Fr.), **Mechanik** (Ger.) (1) A mechanical appliance. (2) Technical skill.

Medesimo (It.) (*mee-deh'-see-mo*). The same as. **Medesimo tempo,** the same time.

Mediant. The third degree of the scale.

Mediation. That part of a chant (Anglican) between the reciting note and the close.

Meisterfuge (Ger.). See *Master-fugue.*

Meistersänger or **Meistersinger** (Ger.). Mastersinger. The Meistersängers were the successors of the minnesingers. Chief among them was Hans Sachs, the hero of Wagner's opera, "Die Meistersinger." The Meistersänger first appeared in the 14th century. They were for the most part workingmen, differing in this respect from the minnesingers, who numbered royal and noble singers in their ranks. The Meistersänger became extinct in 1839, when their last society in Ulm was dissolved.

Melancolia (It.), **Mélancholic** (Fr.). See *Malinconia.*

Mélange (Fr.) (*meh-lonzh*). A medley.

Melisma (Gr.). (1) A song; melody. (2) A run; roulade.

Melismatic. Florid vocalization. A melismatic song is one in which a number of notes are sung to one syllable, as in the florid passages in Handel's solos.

Melodeon. The precursor of the cabinet organ; an instrument with free reeds, operated by suction.

Melodia (It.). (1) Melody. (2) An organ-stop of 8- or 4-foot pitch; soft, flute-like quality.

Melodic. Pertaining to melody, as opposed to harmonic.

Melodico, Melodicoso (It.). Melodiously.

Mélodie (Fr.). Melody; air.

Melodrama. A play abounding in romantic and dramatic situations, with or without musical accompaniment. Melodramatic music is music used to accompany and "intensify" the action of a drama. The term is also applied to instrumental music abounding in startling changes of key or sudden changes of loud and soft.

Melody. An agreeable succession of single sounds, in conformity with the laws of rhythm and tonality. In music for voices the melody is generally in the soprano, or, if for male voices, in the first tenor, but there are many exceptions to this. In orchestral music it is even less necessary that the melody should be in the highest part, as the varying "tone color" of the instruments used is enough to give it the necessary prominence.

Melograph. A mechanical device for recording improvisation on the pianoforte. Many attempts have been made to produce such a machine, but with only partial success.

Melopiano. A pianoforte in which a continuous tone was produced by a series of small hammers which struck rapidly repeated blows on the strings. Invented by Caldara in 1870. It was re-invented in 1893 by Hlavàc of St. Petersburg, and exhibited at the Columbian Exposition, where it attracted great attention.

Melos (Gr.). Melody. Used by Wagner as a name for the recitative in his later works.

Même (Fr.) (*mame*). The same.

Men. (It.). Abbreviation for **Meno,** less; as, **Meno mosso,** slower, less motion.

Menestral (Fr.). Minstrel; Troubadour.

Ménétrier (Fr.) (*meh-neh'-tree-eh*). A fiddler.

Mente (It.) (*men-teh*). Mind. **Alla mente,** improvised.

Menuet (Fr.) (*me-noo-eh*), **Menuett** (Ger.), **Minuetto** (It.). Minuet; a slow, stately dance in $\frac{3}{4}$ time, retained as one of the members of the sonata, quartet, symphony, etc., until Beethoven changed it into the scherzo.

Mescolanza (It.) (*mes-co-lant'-sa*). A medley.

Messa di voce (It.) (*messa-dee-vo-cheh*). Swelling and diminishing on a sustained sound; literally, "massing of the voice."

Mestizia (It.) (*mes-tit'-sia*), **con.** With sadness.

Mesto (It.) (*mehs-to*). Gloomy; mournful.

Mestoso, Mestamente. Mournfully; sadly.

Mesure (Fr.) (*meh-soor*). Measure. **A la mesure,** in time.

Metal Pipes. Organ-pipes made of tin, zinc, etc.

Metallo (It.). Metal; a metallic quality of tone. **Bel metallo di voce,** fine, "ringing" quality of voice.

Meter or **Metre** [Gr., *metron*, a measure]. Properly belongs to poetry, from whence it is transferred to music. In poetry it has two meanings: (1) As applied to a group of syllables; (2) as applied to the number of these groups in a line. English prosody recognizes four groups of syllables, called feet: (1) The Iambus, consisting of a short or unaccented syllable followed by a long or accented syllable as, be-fore; (2) the Trochee, which is just the reverse, as mu-sic; (3) the Anapest, two short followed by a long, as, re-pro-duce; (4) the Dactyl, which is just the reverse, as, cear-ful-ly. As applied to lines (verses), **Long Meter** signifies four iambic feet in every line; **Common Meter** (also called **Ballad Meter**) an alternation of four and three iambic feet; **Short Meter,** two lines of three feet, one of four, and one of three in every stanza. Trochaic, Anapestic, and Dactyllic Meters are indicated by figures giving the number of syllables in each line, as 8, 6, 8, 6, etc. It is important to the musician to become thoroughly familiar with prosody, lest he fall into the too common error of setting short syllables to the accented beats of the measure, or the reverse.

Method, Méthode (Fr.) (*meh-tode*), **Metodo** (It.). (1) System of teaching. (2) Manner of using the voice, or of performing on an instrument.

Metronome [Gr., *metron*, measure; *nomos*, rule]. A mechanical device for determining the time-value of the beat. The one in ordinary use is attributed to Maelzel, whose name it bears. It consists of a pendulum with two bobs, one of which is movable, driven by clockwork; back of the movable bob is a graduated scale. It is used as follows: If the metronomic indication at the beginning of a piece of music in $\frac{4}{4}$ time is ♩ = 100 (¼-note equal to 100), the movable bob is slid along the rod until it is opposite the figures 100, the pendulum is set in motion, and one swing—indicated by a sharp click—is allowed to every beat.

Mettez (Fr.) (*met-teh*). Put; in organ music used in the sense of "draw" or "add" any stop or stops.

Mezzo or **Mezza** (It.) (*med-zo*). Half.

Mezzo Aria. A style of singing in which the distinctness of recitative is aimed at; also called **Aria parlante,** "speaking aria."

Mezzo Forte. Half loud.

Mezzo Piano. Half soft.

Mezzo Soprano. The female voice between the alto and soprano.

Mezzo Tenore. A tenor with range of baritone.

Mezzo Voce. Half voice.

Mi (It.) (*mee*). The name of E in French, Italian, and Spanish. **Mi contra fa** (mi against fa), the interval from F to B♮; the tritone; three whole tones.

Middle C. The C half way between the fifth line of the bass staff and first line of the treble staff; the C always indicated by the C clef:

Militairemente (Fr.) (*mee-lee-tehr-mong*), **Militarmente** (It.) (*mee-lee-tar-men-teh*). Military style.

Military Band. Consists of (1) brass instruments only; (2) saxophones; (3) brass instruments and clarionets; (4) brass, wood, and saxophones.

Minaccivole (It.) (*min-nat-chee'-vo-leh*), **Minnacivolmente** (*min-nat-chee-vol-men'-teh*), **Minnacciando** (*min-nat-chee-an'-do*), **Minnacciosamente** (*min-nat-chee-o-sa-men'-teh*), **Minnaccioso** (*min-nat-chee-o'-so*). Menacing; threatening.

Mineur (Fr.) (*mee-noor*). Minor.

Minim. A half-note.

Minnesänger or **Minnesinger** (Ger.). German name for Troubadour; literally, love-singer.

Minor (Lat.). Lesser.

Minor Chord. The third above the root minor.

Minor Interval. One half-tone less than major.

Minor Scale. The third degree, a minor third above the keynote.

Minstrel. See *Troubadour*. Minstrel has been adopted as the name of the imitation Ethiopians who sing songs supposed to be illustrative of the manners and customs of the plantation negroes in the days of slavery.

Minuet. See *Menuet*.

Mise de voix (Fr.) (*meese de vo-a*). See *Messa di voce*.

Mise en scene (Fr.) (*meese ong scayne*). The "getting up"; putting on the stage of a play, opera, etc.

Misteriosamente. Mysteriously.

Misterioso (It.). Mysterious.

Misurato (It.) (*mee-soo-rah'-to*). Measured; in strict time.

Mit (Ger.). With.

Mit Begleitung (*be-gley'-toonk*). With accompaniment.

Mixed Cadence. A close, consisting of subdominant, dominant, and tonic chords, so called because it includes the characteristic chords of both the plagal and authentic cadences, viz.: subdominant and dominant.

Mixed Chorus, Mixed Voices. Male and female voices together.

Mixolydian. See *Mode*.

Mixture. An organ-stop with from three to six small pipes to each note, tuned to certain of the overtones of the fundamental (diapason) used in full organ only.

Mobile (It.) (*mo'-bee-leh*). With motion; mobile.

Mode [Lat., *modus*, manner, way]. (1) A scale in Greek and ecclesiastical music. (2) In modern music used only in conjunction with the terms major and minor, as Major Mode, Minor Mode. **Greek Modes**; the scale system of the Greeks is not yet quite satisfactorily made out. According to Chappel, who is considered the best authority, the succession of whole and half tones was the same in all the modes, their only difference being in pitch. He gives the following as the initial notes of the principal modes: Dorian (the standard mode) D, Phrygian E, Lydian F♯, Mixolydian G. Those modes the initial notes of which are below the Dorian were distinguished by the prefix *hypo*, beneath, as Hypolydian C♯, Hypophrygian B, Hypodorian A. The succession of sounds was like that of the natural scale of A minor. Church (or ecclesiastical), or Gregorian, or Ambrosian modes were derived from the Greek modes, but discarded the chromatic sounds. Thus the Dorian and Phrygian were the same, that is, had the same initial sounds, but the Lydian began on F instead of F♯. There are other differences between the Greek and the Church modes, viz.: The first four are called authentic; those the initial notes of which are below the Dorian are called plagal; each plagal mode is considered as the relative of the authentic mode, beginning a 4th above it. The final of a plagal is always made on the initial note of its related authentic mode. If the interpretation of the Greek modes is to be trusted, the Church modes seem to have arisen from a misunderstanding of the Greek modes.

Moderatamente (*mod-e-rah-tah-men'-teh*). Moderately.

Moderatissimo (*mod-e-rah-tis'-see-mo*). Very moderate.

Moderato (It.) (*mod-e-rah'-to*). Moderate.

Moderazione (It.) (*mo-deh-rat-se-o'-neh*), **con**. With moderation.

Modificazione (It.) (*mo-dee-fee-cat-se-o'-neh*). Modification; light and shade.

Modinha (Port) (*mo-deen'-ya*). Portuguese love-song.

Modo (It.). Mode; style.

Modulation. (1) Gradation of sound in intensity. (2) Change of key or tonality. Diatonic modulation moves from one key to another by means of chords from related keys; chromatic modulation, by means of chords from non-related keys; enharmonic modulation, by substituting ♯ for ♭, or the reverse. A passing or transient modulation is one followed by a quick return to the original key; the signature is not changed in a modulation of this kind. A final modulation is one in which the new key is retained for some time, or permanently; it is generally indicated by a change of signature following a double bar.

Modus (Lat.). Mode; scale.

Moll (Ger.) [Lat., *mollis*, soft]. Minor.

Moll-Akkord. Minor chord.

Moll-Tonart. Minor key or mode.

Moll-Tonleiter. Minor scale; literally, tone-ladder.

Molle (Lat.). Soft; mediæval name for B♭, B♮ being called B durum (hard). The German words for minor and major (*moll, dur*) are derived from these terms, also the French and Italian names for the flat sign, viz., French, *bémol*; Italian, *bemolle*.

Mollemente (It.) (*mol-leh-men-teh*). Softly; sweetly.

Molto (It.). Very much. **Di molto**, exceedingly; as Allegro di molto, exceedingly rapid.

Monferina (It.) (*mon-feh-ree'-nah*). Italian peasant dance in 6/8 time.

Monochord [Gr., *monos*, one; *chorda*, string]. An instrument consisting of a single string stretched over a sound-board, on which is a graduated scale giving the proportionate divisions of the string required for the production of perfect intervals. A movable bridge is placed at the points indicated on the scale. The Monochord was formerly used as a means for training the ear. It is now used only for acoustic experiments.

Monody. (1) A song for a single voice unaccompanied. (2) In modern usage it denotes a composition in which the melody is all-important, the remaining parts simply accompaniment; called also Homophony and Monophony—the antithesis of Polyphony.

Monotone. Recitative on a single sound.

Montre (Fr.) (*mongtr*). Lit., displayed. The open diapason, so called because the pipes are generally placed in the front of the case and ornamented.

Morceau (Fr.) (*mor-so*). A "morsel"; a short piece; an extract.

Mordent, Mordente (It.), **Beisser** (Ger.). A sign indicating a single rapid stroke of the auxiliary note below the principal followed by a return to the principal. Thus:

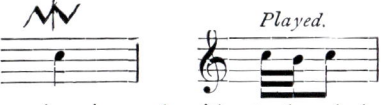

When the sign is used without the dash through it, thus ⁓ it is called an Inverted Mordent, or Pralltriller, and consists of the principal and the auxiliary note above. Thus:

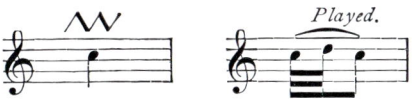

The Mordent proper is not used in modern music, and the word Mordent is now by common usage applied to the inverted Mordent, or Pralltriller.

Morendo (It.) [from *morire, to die*]. Dying away; gradually growing softer and slower.

Morisca (It.). Morris dance.

Mormorando, Mormorevole, Mormorosa (It.). Murmuring.

Morris Dance. A rustic dance of Moorish origin.

Mosso (It.). Moved. **Piu mosso**, faster. **Meno mosso**, slower.

Mostra (It.). A direct ⁓, generally used in manuscript music to indicate an unfinished measure at the end of a brace.

Moteggiando (It.) (*mo-ted-jan'-do*). Bantering; jocose.

Motet, Motett, Motetto (It.). A vocal composition to sacred words in contrapuntal style. The madrigal differs only in being set to secular words. Many modern compositions to sacred words (not metric) are called motets, but would more properly be called anthems.

Motif (Fr.), **Motivo** (It.), **Motiv** (Ger.). Motive. (1) A short, marked musical phrase. (2) A theme for development. See *Leitmotiv*.

Motion, Moto (It.). **Conjunct Motion,** movement by degrees. **Disjunct Motion,** movement by skips. **Direct, Similar, or Parallel Motion,** when two parts ascend or descend together. **Contrary Motion,** when two parts move in opposite directions. **Oblique Motion,** when one part is stationary while the other moves.

Mouth. The opening in the front of an organ flue-pipe.

Mouth-organ. The harmonica; Pandean pipes.

Mouthpiece. In brass instruments the cup-shaped part applied to the lips in oboe, clarionet, etc., the part held between the lips. [Fr., *embouchure;* It., *imboccatura;* Ger., *Mundstück.*]

Movement, Mouvement (Fr.) (*move-mong*). (1) Tempo. (2) One of the members of a sonata, symphony, etc. (3) The motion of a part or parts.

Movimento (It.). Movement; tempo. **Doppio movimento,** double movement; when a change of time signature from ¾ to ₵ occurs, and it is desired to preserve the same rate of movement, or tempo, *i. e.,* the quarter-note beat becomes the half-note beat.

Munter (Ger.). Lively; brisk; allegro.

Murky. An old name for a piece of harpsichord music with a bass of broken octaves.

Musars. Troubadour ballad singers.

Musette (Fr.). (1) A bagpipe. (2) An old dance. (3) In the suite the second part or "trio" of the gavotte, etc., is frequently so called, and is written in imitation of bagpipe music. (4) A soft reed-stop in the organ.

Music, Musica (Lat. and It.), **Musique** (Fr.), **Musik** (Ger.) [from Gr., *mousike,* from *mousa, muse*]. Originally any art over which the Muses presided, afterward restricted to the art that uses sound as its material.

Music Box. An instrument in which steel tongues are vibrated by means of pins set in a revolving cylinder.

Musical Glasses. An instrument consisting of a number of goblets, tuned to the notes of the scale, vibrated by passing a wetted finger around the edge.

Musician. (1) One who makes a livelihood by playing, singing, or teaching music. (2) A member of a regimental or naval band. (3) A composer of music. "Musician" is a very elastic term; it includes every grade from the drummer and fifer to Mozart.

Musikant (Ger.). A vagabond musician.

Musiker, Musikus (Ger.). A musician (Generally used in a derogatory sense.)

Mutation Stop. Any organ-stop not tuned to the diapason or any of its octaves, as the tierce, quint, twelfth, larigot, etc. Stops of this kind (also mixtures, cornets, sesquialteras) are used for the purpose of "filling up" the volume of tone and giving it greater brilliancy.

Mute [It., *sordino;* Fr., *sourdine;* Ger., *Dämpfer*]. A small contrivance of wood or metal placed on the bridge of the violin, etc., to deaden the sound; a cone or cylinder of pasteboard, leather, or wood placed in the bell of a brass instrument for the same purpose.

Mutig (Ger.) (*moo-tig*). Bold; spirited; vivace.

N

Nacaire (Fr.) (*nah-kehr'*). A large drum.

Nacchera (It.) (*nak-keh'-rah*). Military drum.

Nach (Ger.). After; according to; resembling.

Nach Belieben. At pleasure; ad libitum.

Nach und nach. By degrees; poco a poco.

Nachahmung. Imitation.

Nachdruck. Emphasis.

Nachlassend. Retarding.

Nachsatz. Closing theme; coda.

Nachspiel. Postlude.

Nachthorn (Ger.). Night-horn. An organ-stop; large-scale closed pipes, generally 8-foot tone.

Naïf (Fr.), masc. (*nah-if*), fem. **Naïve** (*nah-eve*). Simple; natural; unaffected.

Naiv (Ger.) (*nah-if*). See *Naïf*.

Naïvement (Fr.) (*na-eve-mong*). Artless.

Naïveté (Fr.) (*na-eve-teh*). Simplicity.

Naker. A drum. (Obsolete.)

Narrante (It.) (*nar-ran-teh*). Narrating. A style of singing in which especial attention is given to distinctness of enunciation, rather than to musical effect.

Nasard, Nazard, or **Nassat.** An organ-stop tuned a twelfth above the diapason.

Nason Flute. A soft, closed stop, 4-foot pitch.

Natural. A sign ♮ which restores a letter to its place in the natural scale. In the ancient system of music the only changeable note in the scale was B. The sign for that sound was ♭, the old form of the letter; it signified the sound we call B flat and was called B rotundum, *i. e.,* round B. When it was to be raised a half tone a line was drawn downward at the right side, thus ♮, and it was called B quadratum, *i. e.,* square B. In our modern music these have been retained as the signs for flat and natural.

Natural Horn or **Trumpet.** Those without valves or slides. The sounds produced are called natural harmonics, and are the same as may be produced by touching lightly a vibrating string at any point that will cause it to divide into equal parts, as 2, 3, 4, etc.

Natural Major Scale. The scale of C major.

Natural Minor Scale. A-minor; also any minor scale with unchanged 6th and 7th.

Natural Pitch. The sounds produced by flute, clarionet, etc., without overblowing. The flute, oboe, and bassoon overblow at the octave above their fundamental. The clarionet at the 12th.

Naturale (It.) (*nah-too-rah'-leh*), **Naturel** (Fr.) (*nah-too-rel'*). Natural; unaffected.

Neapolitan Sixth. A name given to a chord consisting of the subdominant with minor 3d and minor 6th, as F, A♭, D♭; used in both major and minor keys.

Neben (Ger.) (*neh'-ben*). Subordinate; accessory.

Neben-Dominant (Ger.). The dominant of the dominant.

Neben-Gedanken (Ger.). Accessory themes.

Nebensatz (Ger.). An auxiliary theme in sonata, etc.

Nebenwerk. The second manual of the organ.

Neck [Ger., *Hals;* Fr., *manche* (mongsh)]. The "handle" of violin, guitar, etc.; on its top is the fingerboard; at its end, the peg-box.

Negli (It.) (*nehl-yee'*), **Nei, Nel, Nell, Nella, Nelle, Nello.** In the manner of.

Negligente (It.) (*neg-lee-gen'-teh*). Careless.

Negligentimente (It.) (*neg-lee-gen-te-men-teh*). Carelessly.

Negligenza (*neg-lee-gent-sa*), **con.** With carelessness.

Nel battere (It.) (*bat-teh-reh*). At the beat.

Nel stilo antico. In the antique style.

Nenia or **Nænia** (Lat.). A funeral dirge.

Nettamente (It.) (*nett-a-men-teh*). Neatly; clearly.

Netto (It.). Neat; exact.

Neuma, Neumes. Signs used in mediæval notation.

Nineteenth. An organ-stop; two octaves and a fifth above the diapason.

Ninth. An interval one degree beyond the octave, being the second removed an octave; it may, like the second, be minor, major, or augmented. The minor and major ninths are essential dissonances, that is, sounds derived from the fundamental; with the augmented ninth the lower sound is really the ninth, thus, G, B, D, F, A or A♭, are overtones of G, but C, D♯ arise from B, D♯, F♯, A, C, chord of ninth. A chord consisting of root major 3, perfect 5, minor 7, and major or minor ninth may have either major or minor ninth in major keys, but only the minor ninth in minor keys.

Nobile (It.) (*no-bee-leh*). Noble; grand.

Nobilita (It.) (*no-bee'-lee-ta*), **con.** With nobility.

Nobilmente (It.) (*no-bil-men-teh*). Nobly.

Noch (Ger.). Still; yet; as, **noch schneller,** still faster.

Nocturne (Fr.) (*noc-toorn*), **Notturno** (It.), **Nachtstück** or **Nokturne** (Ger.) (*nok-toor'-neh*). Literally, night-piece; a quiet, sentimental composition, usually in Lyric form, but under the title Notturno important compositions for several instruments or full orchestra have been written containing several movements.

Nocturns. Night services in the R. C. Church, at which the psalms are chanted in portions, also called nocturns.

Node. A line or point of rest in a vibrating body. A node may be produced in a vibrating string by touching it lightly. (*Cf.* under Natural Horn.) The sounds thus produced, called harmonics, are often used on instruments of the violin family and on the harp.

Noël (Fr.) (*no-el*), **Nowell** (Eng.). "Good news"; "Gospel." Christmas eve songs or carols.

Noire (Fr.) (*no-ar*). Black; quarter note.

Nonet [It., *nonetto;* Ger., *Nonett*]. A composition for nine voices or instruments.

Nonuplet. A group of nine notes to be played in the time of six or eight of the same value.

Normal Pitch. The pitch of a sound, generally A or C, adopted as a standard. This standard for the sound A, second place, has varied from 404 vibrations per second in 1699 to 455 in 1859. By almost universal consent the modern French pitch is now adopted, viz., A = 435 vibrations per second.

Notation. The various signs used to represent music to the eye, as staff, clefs, notes, rests, etc. The earliest attempts at the representation of musical sounds of which we have any knowledge were made by the Greeks, who used the letters of their alphabet, modified in various ways to represent the series of sounds they employed. Their series of sounds is supposed to have begun on the note A, first space in the bass clef. From this system music has retained the name of A for this sound. The next development was the adoption of a series of signs called neumæ. These signs, although curiously complicated, were yet very defective in precision, being inferior to the letters as indications of pitch. The great want, both of the letter system and the neumæ, was that neither gave any indication of the duration of the sounds. The next step was the adoption of the staff. At first use was made only of the spaces between the lines, and, as notes had not yet been invented, the syllables were written in the spaces; this gave exactness to the relative pitch of the sounds but no indication of their duration. The next step was to use the lines only, indicating the sounds by small square notes called points. The letter names of the lines, of which eight was the number, were indicated by Greek letters placed at the beginning. This, though an improvement on the plan of dislocating the syllables, was still wanting in that no duration was indicated. This desideratum was secured by the invention of the notes, attributed to Franco of Cologne. Invention was now on the right track. The expression of pitch and relative duration were now determined with exactness. The system of notation now in use is substantially the same, modified and improved to meet the requirements of modern musical complexity.

Note. A sign which, by its form, indicates the relative duration of a sound, and by its position on the staff the pitch of a sound.

Notenfresser (Ger.). "Note devourer." A humorous title for a ready sight-reader; generally implies one whose playing is more notes than music.

Nourri (Fr.) (*nour-ree*). Nourished; *un son nourri,* a well-sustained sound. Generally applied to vocal sounds.

Novelette. A name invented by Schumann and given by him to a set of pieces without formal construction, with numerous constantly changing themes, giving expression to a very wide range of emotions.

Novemole (Ger.) (*no-veh-mo'-leh*). Nonuplet.

Nuance (Fr.) (*noo-ongs*). Shading; the variations in force, quality, and tempo, by means of which artistic expression is given to music.

Number. (1) A movement of a symphony or sonata. (2) A solo, chorus, or other separate part of an opera or oratorio, etc. (3) A given piece on a concert programme. (4) The "opus" or place in the list of an author's works as to order of composition.

Nunsfiddle [Ger., *Nonnen-Geige*]. Called also Tromba Marina. An instrument with a distant resemblace to a double bass, furnished with one string and a peculiarly constructed bridge. The harmonic sounds only are used. It gets its name from the fact that it was formerly used in Germany and France in the convents to accompany the singing of the nuns.

Nuovo (It.) (*noo-o'-vo*), **Di nuovo.** Over again; repeat.

Nut [Ger., *Sattel,* saddle; Fr., *sillet,* button; It., *capo tasto,* head-stop]. (1) The ridge at the end of the fingerboard next the peg-box; its purpose is to raise the strings slightly above the fingerboard of instruments of violin and guitar families. (2) [Ger., *Frosch,* frog; Fr., *talon,* heel]. The piece at the lower end of violin bow, etc., in which the hair is inserted and tightened or slackened by means of a screw

O

O (It.). Or; also written **od**.

Ob. Abbreviation of oboe and obbligato.

Obbligato (It.) (*ob-blee-gah'-to*). An essential instrumental part accompanying a vocal solo.

Ober (Ger.) (*o'-behr*). Over; upper.

Oberwerk. The uppermost manual of an organ.

Obligé (Fr.) (*o-blee-zheh*). Obbligato.

Oblique Motion. When one part is stationary while the other ascends or descends.

Oboe (It.) (*o-bo-eh*), plural, oboi (*o-bo-ee*); (Fr.) **Hautbois** (*ho-boa*); (Eng.) **Hautboy** or **Hoboy** [from the French word which means, literally, "high-wood"]. A wind instrument with double reed, formerly the leading instrument in the orchestra, filling the place now taken by the violins. A pair are generally employed in the modern orchestra. The oboe is one of the most ancient and widely disseminated of musical instruments. It is the general opinion of students of antiquity that many of the instruments called by the general name "flute" by the Greeks were oboi.

Oboe. A reed-stop in the organ, of 8-ft. pitch, voiced to resemble the oboe.

Oboe d'amore (It.) (*dah-mo'-reh*). Oboe "of love"; a small soft-toned oboe.

Oboe di caccia (It.) (*cat'-cheea*). Oboe of the chase; a large oboe, used formerly as a hunting signal.

Oboist, Oboista (It.). An oboe player.

Ocarine, Ocarina (It.). A small wind instrument of terra cotta, with flute-like quality of tone,—more of a toy than a musical instrument.

Octave, Ottava (It.), **Oktave** (Ger.). (1) The interval between a given letter and its repetition in an ascending or descending series. The diapason of the Greeks. (2) An organ-stop of 4-ft. pitch.

Octave Flute. The piccolo.

Ottava bassa. An octave lower than written; the sign: 8va Ba..............

Ottava alta (It.). At the octave above; indicates that the passage is to be played an octave higher than written, indicated by the sign: 8va..............
A return to the natural position of the notes is signified by the word *loco* (place), or frequently by the cessation of the dotted line, thus: 8va..............

Octet, Octuor, Ottetto (It.), **Oktett** (Ger.), **Octette** (Fr.). A composition for eight solo voices or instruments.

Octo basse (Fr.). A large double bass going a third lower than the ordinary instrument, furnished with a mechanism of levers and pedals for stopping the strings—an important addition to the orchestra.

Octuplet. A group of eight notes played in the time of six of the same value.

Ode Symphonie (Fr.). Choral symphony.

Odeon (Gr.), **Odeum** (Lat.). A building in which public contests in music and poetry were held. In modern use as a name for a concert-hall or theater.

Oder (Ger.). Or.

Œuvre (Fr.) (*oovr*). Work; opus.

Offen (Ger.). Open.

Offertory, Offertorio (It.), **Offertoire** (Fr.) (*of-fer-twar*), **Offertorium** (Ger. and Lat.). (1) The collection of the alms of the congregation during the communion service. (2) The anthem or motet sung by the choir at this time. (3) A piece of organ music performed during this time.

Ohne (Ger.) (*o'-neh*). Without, as ohne Ped., without pedal.

Olio [Sp., *olio*, from Lat., *olla*, pot. A mixture of meat, vegetables, etc., stewed together]. Hence, a medley of various airs; a potpourri.

Olivettes (Fr.) (*o-lee-vet*). Dance after the olive harvest.

Omnes or **Omnia** (Lat.). All. Same as *Tutti*.

Omnitonic, Omnitonique (Fr.). All sounding, *i. e.*, chromatic; applied to brass instruments.

Ondeggiamento (It.) (*on-ded-ja-men'-to*), **Ondeggiante** (It.) (*on-ded-jan'-teh*), **Ondulation** (Fr.) (*on-doo-lah-siong*), **Ondulé** (Fr.) (*on-doo-leh*), **Ondulieren** (Ger.) (*on-doo-lee'-ren*). Waving, wavy; undulating; tremolo.

Ongarese (It.) (*on-gah-reh'-seh*). Hungarian.

Open Diapason. See *Diapason*.

Open Harmony. An equidistant arrangement of the notes of the chords.

Open Notes. (1) The sounds produced by the strings of a violin, etc., when not pressed by the finger. (2) The natural sounds of horn, trumpet, etc., *i. e.*, without valves.

Open Pipe. An organ-pipe without stopper.

Open Score. One in which each voice or instrument has a separate staff assigned to it.

Open Strings. See *Open Notes* (1).

Opera (It.) [from Lat., *opus*, work]. A combination of music and drama in which the music is not merely an incidental, but the predominant element. The opera originated in an attempt to revive what was supposed to be the manner in which the classic Greek drama was performed. The efforts of the group of musical enthusiasts who made this attempt culminated in the production of "Euridice," in 1600, the first Italian opera ever performed in public. The ground being broken, new cultivators soon appeared, and the new plant grew rapidly. Peri, the composer of "Euridice," was succeeded first by Gagliano, then by Monteverde—one of the great names in music. In his hands the opera developed with extraordinary rapidity. Before the close of the 17th century a host of opera writers appeared, led by Scarlatti. The next important development in the form of opera was made by Lulli, the court musician of Louis XIV. No very striking advance was now made until Handel appeared. He did little in the way of developing the form, but infused so much genius into the received form that it gave it a new life. In this respect Handel resembled Mozart, who, at a later stage of the development of the opera, was quite satisfied to take the then received form, which his genius sufficed to make immortal. The first decided departure from the traditional form was made by Gluck, whose theory of dramatic music is strongly akin to the modern theory of Wagner. The opera since Mozart has grown with so much luxuriance, in such a diversity of forms, that even a slight sketch of it would be impossible in our limits. Appended will be found the names of the principal varieties.

Opera Buffa. Comic opera. (Fr., *Opéra Bouffe*.)

Opéra Comique (Fr.). Comedy (not comic) opera.

Opera drammatica (It.). Romantic opera. In modern German usage the term "Musikdrama" has been adopted to distinguish the modern from the old form of opera.

Opera Seria. Grand opera; serious opera; tragic opera.

Operetta (It.). An opera with spoken dialogue.

Ophicleide, Oficleide (It.) [from Gr., *ophis*, snake, and *kleis*, key. Lit., "keyed snake," in allusion to its contorted shape]. A large brass instrument of the bugle family, *i. e.*, with keys, now little used. The best example of its use by a great composer will be found in Mendelssohn's "Midsummer Night's Dream" music.

Oppure (It.) (*op-poo'-reh*). See *Ossia*.

Opus (Lat.). Work; used by composers to indicate the order in which their works were written.

Oratorio (It.) [from Lat., *oratorius*, pertaining or belonging to prayer; a place for prayer]. A composition consisting of solos and concerted pieces for voices, the theme of which is taken from the Bible or from sacred history. The name arose from the fact that St. Philip Neri gave discourses intermingled with music in his oratory about the middle of the 16th century. The term Oratorio is also used for secular works written on the same plan, such as Haydn's "Seasons," and Bruch's "Odysseus," but is manifestly inappropriate. The oratorio is descended from those middle-age dramatic performances founded on biblical or moral themes, known as mysteries, moralities, or miracle plays. It took its rise about the same time as the opera, from which it differs chiefly in that it affords an opportunity for the highest developments of the contrapuntal art, whereas the opera is essentially monodic. The oratorio has not gone through the manifold changes and diversities that have marked the development of the opera, nor has it attracted anything like the number of composers that have devoted themselves to the opera. The first writer of any prominence in this field was Carissimi. He was followed by A. Scarlatti; then Handel appeared and stamped for all time the form of the oratorio. His great contemporary, Bach, equaled if he did not surpass him, but in a different style. Handel has had but two successors worthy to be named with him—Haydn and Mendelssohn, each of whom has stamped a new character on the oratorio without descending from the high plane on which this class of composition should stand. The taste for the oratorio seems to be on the wane, as no composer of any mark has of late years devoted his attention to it.

Orchestra, Orchestre (Fr.), **Orchester** (Ger.) [from Gr., *orchester*, a dancer]. Originally the place where the dancing took place in the Greek theater. (1) The place where the instrumentalists are placed. (2) The company of instrumentalists. (3) The collection of instruments used at any performance. See *Instrument*.

Orchestrate. To write music for the orchestra.

Orchestration. The art of writing for the orchestra.

Orchestrion. A mechanical organ designed to imitate, by means of various stops, the instruments of the orchestra.

Ordinario (It.) (*or-dee-nah'-ree-o*). Usual; ordinary; as tempo ordinario, the usual time, used in the sense of moderate.

Organ, Organo (It.), **Orgue** (Fr.), **Orgel** (Ger.) [from Gr., *organon*, tool, implement, instrument]. An instrument consisting of a large number of pipes grouped according to their pitch and quality of tone into "stops." A large bellows supplies the compressed air or "wind" to the various air-tight boxes called sound-boards, on which the pipes are placed. By means of a key mechanism the "wind" is allowed to enter the pipes corresponding to any given pitch at will. The set or sets of pipes it is desired to sound are controlled by means of "registers," which, when drawn, allow the "wind" to enter the pipes of the "stop," the name of which is marked on the knob of the register. Organs are built with from one to four, and even more, "manuals," or keyboards, placed one above the other. Three manuals is the usual number. The lowest is called the "choir organ," the middle the "great organ," the upper the "swell organ." When a fourth manual is added it is called the "solo manual," a fifth the "echo organ"; there is also a keyboard for the feet called the "pedal organ."

Organ Point, Point d'orgue (Fr.), **Orgelpunkt** (Ger.). A succession of harmonies belonging to the key, written over a prolonged holding of the dominant or tonic, or both; an organ point is generally at the bass.

Organetto (It.). Small organ; bird-organ.

Organum (Lat.), **Organon** (Gr.). An early attempt at part-writing in which the parts moved in fourths or fifths with each other.

Orguinette. A small mechanical reed-organ.

Orpharion. A lute with wire strings.

Osservanza (It.) (*os-ser-van'-tsa*), **con.** With care; with exactness.

Ossia (It.) (*os'-see-a*). Or else; otherwise; as ossia piu facile, or else more easily.

Ostinato (It.) (*os-tee-nah'-to*). Obstinate. **Basso ostinato** is a name given to a frequently repeated bass with a constantly varied counterpoint, called also ground bass; frequently used by the old composers as the foundation for the passacaglio.

Otez (Fr.) (*o-teh*). Take off; a direction in organ music to push in a given register.

Ottavino (It.) (*ot-ta-vee-no*). The piccolo.

Ottavo (It.). See *Octave*.

Ottetto (It.). See *Octet*.

Ou (Fr.) (*oo*). See *Ossia*.

Ouvert (Fr.) (*oo-vehr*). Open. See *Open Notes*. **A livre ouvert**, literally, "at open book"; at sight.

Overblow. To blow a wind instrument in such a manner as to make it sound any of its harmonics. In the organ a pipe is overblown when the air-pressure is too great, causing it to sound its octave or twelfth.

Overspun. Said of strings covered with a wrapping of thin wire.

Overstring. Arranging the stringing of a piano in such a way that one set crosses the rest diagonally.

Overtone. The sounds produced by the division of a vibrating body into equal parts.

Overture, Overtura (It.), **Ouverture** (Fr.), **Ouverture** (Ger.). A musical prelude to an opera or oratorio. Independent compositions are also written under the name of concert overtures, generally with some descriptive title. In its highest form the overture is developed in the sonata form without repeating the first part. Many overtures are nothing but a medley of airs in various tempos.

Ovvero. See *Ossia*.

P

P. Abbreviation for piano. Soft (positive degree).

PP. Abbreviation for piu piano. Softer (comparative degree).

PPP. Abbreviation for pianissimo. Softest (superlative degree).

P. F. Abbreviation for pianoforte (when capital letters are used). **p. f.** Abbreviation for poco forte, a little loud; or piu forte, louder. In French organ music P. signifies positif, *i. e.*, choir-organ.

Padouana (It.) (*pah-doo-ah'-nah*), **Paduana, Padovana, Padovane** (Fr.) (*pah-do-van*). See *Pavan*.

Pæan (Gr.). A song of triumph, originally in praise of Apollo.

Paired Notes. A succession of thirds, sixths or eighths on the piano.

Palco (It.). The stage of a theater.

Pallet. The valve that controls the admission of "wind" to the pipes of the organ, harmonium, etc.

Pallettes (Fr.). The white keys of the piano, etc. The black keys are called *feintes* (faints).

Pandean Pipes or **Pan's Pipes.** The syrinx; a series of small pipes made from reeds, sounded by blowing across the open top. An instrument of unknown antiquity and universal use. The ancient Peruvians carved them out of stone. The Fijians and the South American Indians make them with a double set of pipes—one set open, the other closed at one end, thus producing octave successions.

Pantalon (Fr.). One of the numbers in a set of quadrilles. The old set of quadrilles consisted of five or six numbers called: (1) pantalon; (2) été; (3) poule; (4) pastourelle; (5) finale. If there were six, the other was called trénis.

Parallel Keys. The major and minor scales beginning on the same keynote.

Parallel Motion. When two parts or voices ascend or descend together.

Paraphrase. An elaborate arrangement of a piece of music for the piano, originally written for the voice, or for some other instrument. An orchestral paraphrase is a like arrangement of a vocal or pianoforte composition.

Parlando, Parlante (It.) (*par-lan'-do, par-lan'-teh*). Declaiming; singing in recitative style; playing in imitation of vocal recitative.

Part. (1) The series of sounds allotted to a single voice or instrument, or a group of voices or instruments of identical kind in a musical composition. (2) One of the counterpoints of a polyphonic composition for piano or organ, as a three- or four-part fugue. (3) One of the divisions of an extended form as indicated by double bars.

Part-Song. A composition for equal or mixed voices, unaccompanied, consisting of a melody to which the other parts are subordinated, in this respect differing from the glee and madrigal, which are contrapuntal, *i. e.,* all the parts are of equal importance.

Part-Writing. Counterpoint.

Partial Tones. See *Overtone.*

Partita (It.) (*par-tee'-tah*). See *Suite.*

Partition (Fr.) (*par-tee'-syong*), **Partitur** (Ger.) (*par-tee-tour'*), **Partitura** (It.) (*par-tee-too'-rah*), **Partizione** (It.) (*par-teetz-eo'-neh*). [From It., *partire,* to divide.] In allusion to the division by bars of the page; in English "scoring"; an orchestral or vocal score.

Paspy [from Fr., *passepied*], **Passamezzo** (It.) (*passa-med'-so*). A dance resembling the minuet, but more rapid in its movement.

Passacaglio (It.) (*pas-sa-cal'-yo*), **Passacaglia** (*pas-sa-cal'-ya*), **Passecaille** (Fr.) (*pass-ca-ee*), **Passe-rue** (Fr.) (*pass-roo*), **Passa-calle** (Sp.) (*pas-sa-cal'-leh*), **Gassenhauer** (Ger.) (*gas-sen-how-er*). Literally, "running the street." An old dance in triple time, generally written on a ground bass.

Passage. (1) A musical phrase. (2) The figure of a melodic sequence. (3) A brilliant run or arpeggio.

Passaggio (It.) (*pas-sad'-jeo*). Passage.

Passing Note. An ornamental melodic note foreign to the harmony; when these notes fall on the beat or the accent they are called changing notes.

Passione (It.). Passion-music; a musical setting of the closing scenes in the life of the Saviour in the form of an oratorio, originally with dramatic action. The Oberammergau passion-play is a survival of this custom.

Passione (It.) (*pas-se-o'-neh*), **Passionato** (It.) (*nah-to*), **Passionatamente** (It.), **Passioné** (Fr.) (*pas-si-o'-neh*), **con.** With passion; intensity; impassioned; with intense passion.

Pasticcio (It.) (*pas-tit'-che-o*), **Pastiche** (Fr.) (*pas-tish*). A "composition" made up of airs, etc., borrowed from different sources.

Pastoral, Pastorale (It.) (*pas-to-rah'-leh*). (1) A rustic melody in 6/8 time. (2) Used to designate an extended composition intended to portray the scenes and emotions of rustic life, as pastoral symphony, pastoral sonata.

Pastorella (It.) (*pas-to-rel'-lah*), **Pastorelle** (Fr.) (*pas-to-rel*). A little pastoral.

Pastourelle. A figure in the quadrille. See *Pantalon.*

Pateticamente (It.) (*pa-teh-tee-cah-men'-teh*), **Patetico** (It.) (*pa-teh'-tee-co*), **Pathétiquement** (Fr.) (*pa-teh-teek-mong*), **Pathétique** (Fr.) (*pa-teh-teek*). Pathetic; pathetically.

Patimento (It.) (*pah-tee-men-to*). Suffering. **Con espressione di patimento,** with an expression of suffering.

Patouille (Fr.) (*pah-too-ee*). Claquebois; xylophone.

Pauke (Ger.) (*pow-keh*), pl., **Pauken.** Kettle-drum.

Pausa (It.) (*paw-sa*), **Pause** (Fr.) (*paws*). A rest or pause; a bar's rest.

Pavan. A stately dance in 4/4 time. The name is derived either from *pavo,* a peacock, in allusion to its stately character, or from *pavana,* the abbreviated form of *Padovana,* the Latin name of Padua, where the dance is said to have originated.

Pavana (It.), **Pavane** (Fr.). Pavan.

Paventato (It.) (*pa-ven-tah'-to*), **Paventoso** (*pa-ven-to-so*) [from Lat., *pavidus,* fearing]. Timid; with fear; timidly.

Pavillon (Fr.) (*pa-vee-yong*). The bell of a horn, clarionet, etc.

Pavillon chinois (*shee-no-a*). A staff of small bells. **Flute à pavillon,** an organ-stop with "bell-mouthed" pipes.

Pedal, abbreviated **Ped.** [from Lat., *pes,* a foot]. (1) Any mechanism controlled by the foot; in the piano, the contrivance for raising the dampers; also that for shifting the action (una-corda). In square and upright pianos, the soft pedal, when depressed, interposes small strips of soft leather between the hammers and strings. The sostenuto pedal is a contrivance by means of which one or more sounds in the lower register of the piano may be prolonged at will. In the organ, the keyboard for the feet, the levers for opening and closing the swell (swell pedal) and for operating various groups of stops (combination pedals).

Pedal Check. A mechanism in the organ, controlled by a hand-knob, which prevents the movement of the pedals **Crescendo Pedal,** a mechanism in the organ by means of which the full power may be put on or off. **Balancing Swell Pedal** is one that remains in whatever position it may be when the foot leaves it.

Pedal Harp. The mechanical contrivances by means of which certain strings are tightened or slackened to change the key, as F#-ped., B♭-ped., etc.

Pedal Pipes. The organ-pipes sounded by the pedal keyboard.

Pedal Point or **Organ Point.** See *Organ Point.*

Pédale (Fr.). Pedal.

Pedale doppio (It.) (*peh-dah'-leh dop'-yo*). Pedal in octaves; organ music.

Pedalflügel (Ger.). A grand piano with pedal keyboard.

Peg. The wooden or metal pins around which one end of the strings of the violin, etc., are wound, by turning which the pitch of the strings is raised or lowered; in the pianoforte they are generally called pins.

Pensieroso (It.) (*pen-see-eh-ro'-so*). Pensive; thoughtful.

Pentatone. An interval of five whole tones; augmented 6th.

Pentatonic Scale. See *Scale.*

Per (It.) (*pehr*). For, or by; as, **Per il violino,** for the violin.

Percussion Stop. A hammer which, striking the reed of a harmonium or organ-pipe, causes it to vibrate promptly when the key is depressed.

Percussive Instruments. Drums, cymbals, triangles, etc.

Perdendo (It.) (*pehr-den'-do*), **Perdendosi** (*pehr-den-do'-see*) [from *perdere*, to lose]. Gradually dying away, both in speed and power. (Abbr., Perd. or Perden.)

Perfect Cadence. See *Cadence*.

Perfect Concord. Root, minor or major 3d, and perfect 5th.

Perfect Consonances. See *Interval*.

Périgourdine (Fr.) (*peh-ree-goor-deen*), **Périjourdine** (*peh-ree-zhoor-deen*). An old French dancing-song in ¾ time.

Period, Période (Fr.) (*peh-ree-ode*), **Periodo** (It.) (*peh-ree-o-do*). A complete musical sentence, generally eight measures.

Perlé (Fr.) (*per-leh*), **Perlend** (Ger.), "Pearled," like a string of pearls. A metaphorical expression for a clear, delicate execution; also a direction that the passage is to be played in a "pearly" manner.

Pesante (It.) (*peh-san'-teh*). Heavy; weighty.

Petite (Fr.) (*peh-teet*). Small; little.

Petite Flute. The piccolo.

Petite mesure à deuz temps. ⅔ time.

Petite Pedale. Soft pedal in organ music.

Petites Notes. Grace notes.

Petto (It.). Chest.

Peu à peu (Fr.). (This sound cannot be reproduced in English; it resembles *oo*, but is not so broad.) Little by little; by degrees.

Pezzi (It.) (*pet-see*). Pieces.

Pezzi concertanti. (1) Concerted pieces. (2) A "number" of an opera, concert, etc.

Pezzi di bravura (*bra-voo-ra*). Showy, brilliant pieces.

Pezzo (It.) (*pet'-so*). A piece; phrase. Beethoven uses the following sentence as a direction in one of his pianoforte sonatas: "Questo pezzo si deve trattare con piu gran delicatezza"—Every phrase must be treated with the greatest delicacy.

Pfeife (Ger.) (*pfei-feh*). Pipe; fife.

Phantasie (Ger.). See *Fantasia*.

Phantasieren (Ger.) (*fan-ta-see'-ren*). To improvise.

Phantasiestück. A piece devoid of form.

Phrase. Technically, an incomplete musical sentence.

Phrasing. The art of dividing a melody into groups of connected sounds so as to bring out its greatest musical effect, including also the placing of accent—cres. and decres., rall. and accel., rubato, etc.—and in pianoforte music, the varieties of touch. In vocal music, it refers chiefly to the breathing places; in violin music, to the bowing.

Phrygian Mode. One of the Greek scales, generally supposed to be E—E. In the ecclesiastical scales, the octave scale from

Phrygian Cadence.

Physharmonica. (1) The predecessor of the melodeon. (2) A free reed-stop in the organ.

Piacere, à (It.) (*pe-aht-cheh'-reh*). At pleasure, *i. e.*, the tempo at the will of the performer.

Piacevole (It.) (*pe-aht-cheh'-vo-leh*). Smoothly; quietly.

Piacevolezza (It.) (*pe-aht-cheh-vo-let'-za*), con. With smoothness.

Piacevolmente (It.) (*pe-aht-cheh-vol-men'-teh*). Smoothly.

Piacimento (It.) (*pe-aht-chee-men'-tō*). See Piacere.

Pianette (Fr.), **Pianino** (It.) (*pee-ah-nee-no*). A small piano; upright piano.

Piangendo (It.) (*pee-an-jen'-do*), **Piangevole** (*pee-an-jeh'-vo-leh*), **Piangevolmente** (*pee-an-jeh-vol-men'-teh*). "Weeping"; plaintively wailing.

Piano (It.) (*pee-ah'-no*). Soft. (Abbreviation, P.; pianissimo, PP.)

Pianoforte (It.) (*for'-teh*). In common usage, piano, without the forte. An instrument strung with steel wire (formerly brass wire was largely used), provided with a keyboard; the depression of the keys causes the hammers to strike the strings. The name pianoforte was given to it because the volume of sound was under the control of the performer. Three forms of pianoforte are made: The grand piano [in Fr., *piano à queue*, lit., "piano with a tail"; Ger., *flügel*, in allusion to its wing shape]; the square, and the upright. The pianoforte is descended from the dulcimer in the same sense that the harpsichord is descended from the psalterion. In form the dulcimer and psalterion were identical, differing only in that the former was played by means of hammers, the latter by means of "plectra." The adaptation of mechanism to control the hammers developed the piano out of the dulcimer, and the adaptation of mechanism to control the plectra" developed the harpsichord out of the psalterion. The hammer action was first made practically effective by Cristofori of Padua, in 1711. About the same time an English monk, "Father Wood," made one in Rome. This instrument came into the possession of the celebrated Fulke Greville, and became well known as Mr. Greville's pianoforte. In 1717, a German youth of eighteen, named Schröter, invented the pianoforte independently; his invention was copied by Silberman of Strasburg, who submitted two of his instruments to Bach, who liked the mechanism but not the tone, preferring that of the clavichord. The growth of the pianoforte has been rapid since the beginning of the nineteenth century, and has reached a point beyond which it hardly seems possible to advance.

Piatti (It.) (*pe-at'-tee*). Cymbals.

Pibroch. A sort of fantasia for the bag-pipe of the Scotch Highlanders; supposed to represent the incidents of a fight.

Piccolo. A small flute an octave higher than the ordinary flute; a 2-foot organ-stop.

Piccolo-piano. A small upright pianoforte.

Picco-pipe. A small instrument resembling a flageolet; gets its name from an Italian peasant, Picco, who produced astonishing results from it.

Piece. A composition; a single instrument, as, "a band of twenty pieces."

Pièce (Fr.) (*pee-ace*). A member of a suite, *q. v.*

Pieno (It.) (*pe-eh'-no*). Full.

Pietoso (It.) (*pe-eh-to'-so*), **Pietosamente** (*pe-eh-to-sa-men'-teh*). Tender; pitiful; tenderly.

Pifferaro (It.) (*pif-feh-rah-ro*). A player on the piffero.

Piffero or **Piffaro** (It.). Old form of the hautboy, still used in Italy. The same form of instrument exists all through Asia—probably the "*aulos*" of the Greeks.

Pincé (Fr.) (*pang-seh'*). (1) Pinched. See *Pizzicato*. (2) A mordent.

Pipe. The tubes of wood or metal in the organ. They are classified as follows: Open pipes, open at the top; closed or stopped pipes, with a movable plug; flue pipes, those constructed on the principle of the whistle or flageolet; reed pipes, those in which a beating reed is combined with the pipe. Pipes are also classified by length, the open diapason being the standard. An open pipe must be eight feet long to sound

A closed pipe four feet long gives the same sound; both are said to have an 8-foot tone. If a pipe has a 4-foot tone, its sound is an octave higher than the diapason; if a 2-foot tone, it is two octaves above the diapason.

Piqué (Fr.) (*pee-keh'*). A manner of bowing the violin, indicated by combined slur and dots:

Piquieren (Ger.) (*pik-ee'-ren*). To play piqué.

Piston (Fr.), **Ventil** (Ger.). Valve; a device used in brass instruments to lengthen the tube, thus depressing the pitch.

Pitch. Relative pitch is the interval between a given sound and some other sound. Absolute pitch is the number of vibrations per second necessary to produce a given sound. Standard pitch is the number of vibrations per second adopted as the pitch of a given sound. The standard (now almost universal) is = 435.
which is known as the French "diapason normal." Between 1699 and 1859 the standard rose from 404 to 455.

Pitch Pipe. A wooden pipe used to give the keynote. A small tube containing a free reed is now generally used.

Piu (It.). More; as, **Piu forte**, louder.

Piva (It.) (*pee-vah*). A bagpipe; also a piece of music in imitation of the bagpipe.

Pizzicato (It.) (*pits-e-cah'-to*), **Pincé** (Fr.), **Gekneipt** (Ger.). Lit., "pinched." A direction in music for bow instruments to pluck the strings with the finger, as in the guitar. (Abbr., **Pizz.**)

Placidamente (It.) (*plah-chee-dah-men'-teh*). Placidly; quietly.

Placido (It.) (*plah-chee'-do*). Placid; quiet.

Plagal Cadence. From subdominant to tonic:

Plagal Scales or **Modes.** In the ecclesiastical system, those scales beginning a fourth below the authentic scales, but ending on the keynotes of their related authentic scales. They are distinguished by the prefix *hypo* [Gr., ὑπο, below], as Dorian (authentic) D-D, ending on D; Hypodorian (plagal) A-A, ending on D.

Plain Chant. Plain song. **Cantus planus,** or **Cantus choralis** (Lat.), the early music of the church, written in the ecclesiastical modes (also called Ambrosian) and Gregorian scales. In the 12th century the unrhythmic melodies of the early forms of plain song were largely superseded by the rhythmic cantus mensurabilis, or measured song, which came into existence upon the invention of notes by Franco of Cologne. Before this invention the musical rhythm depended entirely on the rhythm of the words to which it was sung.

Plainté (Fr.). Elegy; lament.

Plaisanterié (Fr.) (*play-zong-te-ree*). A lively fantasia in which various dance-tunes are introduced.

Planxties. Laments; music of Irish harpers to celebrate the departed.

Plectrum [Gr., *plectron*]. A small rod of metal, bone, ivory, etc., or a flat strip of wood or tortoise shell, or a ring with a projecting piece, used to strike the strings of the lyre, Japanese guitar, mandolin, zither, etc.

Plein jeu (Fr.) (*plane zhoo*). Full power; full organ.

Pneuma (Gr.). Breath. See *Neumæ*.

Pneumatic Action. A contrivance in large pipe-organs by means of which a small bellows, called pneumatic bellows, is made to do the work of opening the palettes in place of the fingers.

Pochettino (It.) (*po-ket-tee-no*). Very little.

Pochetto (It.) (*po-ket'-to*). A little; (not so much as *Poco*).

Pochissimo (It.) (*po-kis-see-mo*). The "least little bit"; as **Cres. pochissimo,** the least degree louder.

Poco (It.). A little; rather; as, **Poco lento,** rather slow.

Poco a poco. By degrees; as, *Rall. poco a poco*.

Poggiato (It.) (*pod-je-ah'-to*). Dwelt upon; lit., leaned upon.

Poi (It.) (*po'ee*). Then; afterward. **P. poi f.,** soft, then loud.

Point (Fr.) (*po-ang*). A dot (Eng.). A phrase for imitation.

Point d'orgue (Fr.). Pedal point.

Pointé (Fr.) (*po-ang-teh*). Dotted.

Poitrine (Fr.) (*po-a-treen*). Chest. **Voix de poitrine,** chest voice.

Polacca. A Polish dance in $\frac{3}{4}$ time; polonaise.

Polka. A dance in time, originated among the peasants of Bohemia.

Polka Mazurka. A mazurka danced with the polka-step.

Polonaise. See *Polacca*.

Polska. Swedish dance in triple time.

Polyphonic [from Gr., *polus*, many; and *phone*, a voice]. Music written contrapuntally, as opposed to music written harmonically with a single melody.

Polyphony. "Many voices." Counterpoint in several parts.

Pommer. A large instrument of the hautboy family; bombard.

Pomposamente (It.) (*pom-po-sah-men'-teh*). Dignified; majestic.

Pomposo (It.). Pompous.

Ponderoso (It.). Ponderous; strongly marked.

Ponticello (It.) (*pon-tee-chel-lo*). The bridge of the violin, etc.

Portamento (It.) (*por'tah-men'-to*). Sliding or "carrying" the voice from one sound to another; also on bow instruments, sliding the finger along the string from one place to another.

Portando la voce. Same as *Portamento*.

Porte de voix (Fr.). (1) Portando la voce. (2) An obsolete grace in harpsichord music.

Portunal Flute. Organ-stop with wooden pipes which "flare," *i. e.*, get wider from the mouth to the top.

Portunen (Ger.) (*por-too'-nen*). The bourdon stop.

Posatif (Fr.) (*po-sa-teef*). The choir organ.

Posato (It.) (*po-sah'-to*), **Posément** (Fr.) (*po-seh-mong*). Quiet; sedate; grave.

Posaune (Ger.) (*po-zown-eh*). The trombone; a powerful reed-stop in the organ, of 8-, 16-, or 32-foot pitch.

Position. (1) Of chords. The common chord may be written in three positions, called the octave, tierce, and quint.

Octave. Tierce. Quint.

As given in this example it is called the close position of the chord; the following example is called the open position:

(2) On instruments of the violin and guitar family, "Position" refers to the part of the fingerboard on which the left hand is placed.

Possibile (It.) (*pos-see'-bee-leh*). Possible; as, **Il piu forte possibile,** as loud as possible.

Postlude, Postludium (Lat.), **Nachspiel** (Ger.), **Clôture** (Fr.). The concluding voluntary on the organ; lit., afterplay.

Potpourri (Fr.) (*po-poor-ee*). A number of tunes strung together.

Poule, la. See *Quadrille*.

Poussé (Fr.) (*poos-seh*). "Push." Up bow.

Prächtig (Ger.) (*praych-tig*). Grand; majestic.

Pralltriller (Ger.).

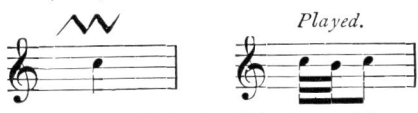

Played.

now commonly called the Mordent. The sign for the mordent proper is ∧∧. It always means that the auxiliary note is to be below the principal. When the line that crosses the sign was omitted it was called the Inverted Mordent or Pralltriller. The original form of the mordent is never used by modern writers.

Precentor. In the English Church, the clerical head of the choir; his side of the chancel is called the cantoris side. In the Scotch Presbyterian Church, the singer who stands in front of the pulpit and "gives out" the psalm tunes.

Precipitoso (It.), **Precipitato** (It.), **Precipitazione, con** (It.), **Precipitamente** (It.), **Precipité** (Fr.). A rapid, precipitate, hurried style of execution.

Prelude, Preludium (Lat.), **Vorspiel** (Ger.). An introduction; an opening voluntary; a composition which may or may not be in some regular form.

Premier (Fr.) (*preh-mee-eh*). First. **Première fois,** first time.

Preparation. The prolongation, in the same voice, of a sound from one chord in which it is a member into a chord in which it is not a member.

Prepared Trill. One preceded by a grace-note or turn.

Pressante (It.) (*pres-san'-teh*), **Pressieren** (Ger.) (*pres-see'-ren*), **Pressez** (Fr.) (*pres-seh*). Pressing on; hurrying.

Prestant (Ger. and Fr.). 4-foot metal open stop. Same as *Principal*.

Prestezza (It.) (*pres-tet'-za*), **con.** With rapidity.

Prestissimo (It.) (*pres-tis'-see-mo*), **Prestissimamente** (It.) (*pres-tis-se-ma-men'-teh*). As fast as possible.

Presto (It.). Fast.

Prick-song. Old name for written music. The first notes used were small, square marks without stems, called pricks, or points.

Primary Accent. The first member of the measure. When there are two or more accents in the measure, the first is the primary, the rest are called secondary.

Prima donna. First lady; the leading soprano.

Prima vista. At first sight.

Prima volta. First time; lit., first turn.

Prime. The first note of a scale; keynote; the generator of an overtone series; unison.

Primo (masc.), **Prima** (fem.) (It.) (*pree-mo, pree-ma*). First.

Primo tenore. First tenor.

Principal (Eng.). 4-foot open metal stop.

Principale (It.) (*prin-chee-pah-leh*), **Principal** (Fr.), **Prinzipal** (Ger.). The open diapason.

Probe (Ger.) (*pro-beh*). Rehearsal.

Program or **Programme.** A list of compositions to be performed at a musical entertainment.

Program-music. Music designed to "tell a story," or illustrate some action or event.

Progression. (1) Melodic—from note to note. (2) Harmonic—from chord to chord.

Progressive Stop. An organ-stop in which the number of pipes to each key increases as the pitch rises; a variety of mixture-stop.

Prontamente (It.) (*prom-tah-men'-teh*), **Promptement** (Fr.) (*prompt-mong*). Promptly; exactly; strictly.

Pronto (It.). Prompt; strict.

Pronunziato (It.) (*pro-nuntz-ee-ah'-to*), **Prononcé** (Fr.) (*pro-nong-seh*). Pronounced; emphatic. **Ben pronunziato** (It.), **Bien prononcé** (Fr.), well marked; strongly accented.

Prova (It.). Rehearsal.

Psaltery, Psalterium (Lat.), **Salterio** (It.), **Psalterion** (Fr.), **Psalter** (Ger.) [from Gr., *psaltein*, to harp]. Ancient instrument, consisting of a square, oblong, or triangular flat box, with wire strings stretched across it, played by the fingers, each of which is armed with a ring with a short projecting plectrum. The same instrument is called a dulcimer when played by two small hammers, held one in each hand.

Pulsatile. Instruments played by drumsticks or by clashing them together; as drums, cymbals, etc. [From Lat., *pulsare*, to beat.]

Pulse. A beat.

Punkt (Ger.) (*poonkt*). Dot; point.

Punta (It.) (*poon'-tah*). The point. **Colla punta d'arco,** with the point of the bow.

Puntato (It.) (*poon-tah'-to*). Pointed; staccato.

Purfling. The thin strips of wood (a white strip between two black) around the border of the back and belly of the violin, etc.

Pyramidon. An organ-stop with pipes shaped like an inverted pyramid, closed at top. From its peculiar shape a pipe not three feet long will produce 16-foot C.

Pyrophone [from Gr., *pur*, fire, *phone*, sound]. An instrument the sounds of which are produced by gas jets burning just inside of the lower end of glass tubes open at both ends. Invented by Kastner.

Q

Quadrate, B quadratum, *i. e.,* B squared. Old name for B♮—retained as the sign for a ♮.

Quadratum (Lat.). A breve □.

Quadrible or **Quatrible.** An ancient species of counterpoint, consisting of a succession of 4ths over a cantus.

Quadrille. A "square dance." See *Pantalon.*

Quadruple Counterpoint. A four-part counterpoint so constructed that the parts may change places without involving any false progressions.

Quadruple croche (Fr.) (*crosh*). A 64th-note.

Quadruplet. A group of four notes played in the same time of three or six of the same value.

Quality of Tone [Ger., *Klangfarbe* or *Tonfarbe;* Fr., *Timbre;* It., *Timbro*]. That which enables us to distinguish between different instruments. The character of a tone quality depends largely upon the presence or absence and relative intensity of its overtones; thus, the tone of a clarionet differs entirely from that of a violin, although all violins and all clarionets do not sound alike. The differences in tone quality that are found among violins, for example, depend on other factors, as the construction, material, weight of strings, individuality of the performer, and many more. The tone qualities of the voice are dependent largely on the accurate contact of the vocal cords, the size and shape of the cavity of the mouth and nostrils, and the management of the breath.

Quart. Interval of 4th. [It. and Lat., *Quarta.*]

Quart (Fr.) (*kart*). Quarter.

Quart de soupir (*soo-peer*). A 16th-rest.

Quart de mesure (Fr.) (*meh-zoor*). A 4th-rest.

Quartfagott (Ger.). A bassoon a 4th lower than the ordinary instrument.

Quartflöte (Ger.). A flute a 4th higher than the ordinary instrument.

Quarte du ton (Fr.) (*kart doo tong*). A 4th of the scale; subdominant.

Quarter Note ♩

Quartet. A composition for four solo performers. **String Quartet** is composed of first and second violins, viola, and violoncello. **Piano Quartet** is composed of violin, viola, violoncello, and piano. **Vocal Quartet** may be either for male or female or mixed voices.

Quartett (Ger.) (*kvar-tet'*), **Quatuor** (Fr.) (*qua-too-or*), **Quartetto** (It.) (*quar-tet'-to*). Quartet in English, sometimes spelled quartette.

Quartole (Ger.) (*kvar-to'-le*). Quadruplet.

Quasi (It.) (*quah'-see*). As if; in the manner of; like; as, *Quasi allegro,* like allegro; *Quasi sonata,* resembling a sonata.

Quatre mains (Fr.) (*katr mang*). For four hands.

Quatrible. See *Quadrible.*

Quattro mani (It.) (*quat-tro man-nee*). Four hands.

Quatuor. See *Quartet.*

Quaver. An eighth-note.

Querflöte, (Ger.) (*kvehr-fla'-teh*), **Flauto traverso** (It.). "Cross-flute." The flute played by blowing across it, as distinguished from the old flute, blown at the end.

Queue (Fr.) (*koo*). Tail-piece of violin; stem of a note.

Quickstep. A rapid march, generally in $\frac{6}{8}$ time.

Quinable. An old species of counterpoint, consisting of a succession of fifths above the cantus.

Quint. (1) A 5th. (2) An organ-stop a 5th above the diapason.

Quint Viola. An organ-stop of the Gamba species a 5th or 12th above the diapason.

Quintaton. An organ-stop so voiced that it gives two sounds—the fundamental and the 12th. The pipes are of metal, slender and closed.

Quinte (Ger.) (*kvin-teh*). (1) The interval of a 5th. (2) The E-string of the violin.

Quintet. A composition for five solo performers. The string quintet generally consists of first and second violins, first and second violas, and violoncello; occasionally two violoncellos are used, in which case it is called a Violoncello Quintet to distinguish it from the former. The Piano Quintet consists of a string quartet and the piano.

Quintole (Ger.) (*kvin-to'-leh*). A group of five notes to be played in the time of four of the same value.

Quintuor (Fr.) (*kang-too-or*), **Quintetto** (It.), **Quintett** (Ger.) (*kvin-tet*). Quintet, or quintette.

Quintuplet. Quintole.

Quire and Quirester. Old English for choir and chorister.

Quodlibet (Lat.) (*quod-lee'-bet*). "What you will." A performance in which every participant sings or plays a different tune; an impromptu fantasia; a musical jest.

R

R. Abbreviation for Right. In French organ music, for Recit. (swell manual).

Rabbia (It.) (*rab'-be-a*), **con.** With fury.

Rackett or **Rankett.** An obsolete instrument resembling the double bassoon; a 16- or 18-foot stop in old organs.

Raddolcendo (It.) (*rad-dol-chen'-do*), **Raddolcente** (*rad-dol-chen'-teh*), **Raddolcito** (*rad-dol-chee'-to*). Growing gradually softer and sweeter.

Radiating Pedals. A fan-shaped arrangement of the pedal keys of the organ; the narrow end of the fan farthest from the organ. Radiating pedals are generally "concave" at the same time, that is, the pedals at the sides are higher than those in the middle.

Radical Bass. The root of a chord.

Rallentamento (It.) (*ral-len-ta-men'-to*). Slower. Same as *Piu lento,* or *Meno mosso.*

Rallentando (It.) (*ral-len-tan'-do*), **Rallentato** (*ral-len-tah'-to*), **Rallentare** (*ral-len-tah'-reh*). Gradually slower. Abbreviation for the above, **Rall.**

NOTE.—Rallentando and Ritenuto, although both mean to "get slower," differ somewhat in the manner of using them: Rallentando being used at the end of a piece (movement); Ritenuto in the course of a piece, followed by "A Tempo," when the original pace is to be resumed. Ritardando is used in the same way as Ritenuto. Abbreviation for both is *Rit.*

Rank. A row of organ-pipes belonging to one stop. Mixture-stops are of 2, 3, 4, 5, or 6 ranks, according to the number of pipes that "speak" for each key.

Rant. An old dance. In scotland many dance-tunes are called rants.

Ranz des vaches (Fr.) (*rongs deh vash*). Lit., "row of cows." Tunes played or sung by the Swiss as cattle calls. (In Ger., *Kuhreihen.*) As the Alpine horn is a simple tube, the melodies played on it are formed from the natural harmonic notes. When the *ranz des vaches* are sung, the melodies are varied by adding the characteristic Jodel. Many of these melodies are of great antiquity and exceeding beauty.

Rapidamente (It.) (*rah-pid-a-men'-teh*). Rapidly.

Rapidita (It.) (*rah-pid'-ee-tah*), con. With rapidity.

Rapido (It.) (*rah'-pee-do*). Rapid.

Rasgado (Sp.). In guitar-playing, a direction to sweep the strings with the thumb.

Rattenuto (It.) (*rat-teh-noo'-to*), **Rattenendo** (It.) (*rat-teh-nen-do*). Holding back the movement.

Rauschquinte (Ger.) (*rowsh'-kvin-teh*). A two-rank mixture-stop.

Rauscher (Ger.) (*row-sher*) [from *rauschen*, to rustle]. A repeated note on the piano.

Ravvivando il tempo (It.) (*rav-vee-van'-do*). Lit., "reviving the time." Resuming the original tempo after a rall. or rit.

Re. The second Aretinian syllable; the note D in French, Italian, and Spanish. In tonic sol-fa spelled **Ray.**

Real Fugue. One in which the subject and answer are identical, as opposed to *Tonal Fugue, q. v.*

Rebab, Rebec, Rebeck, Rebibe, Rebible. One of the precursors of the violin in the middle ages.

Recheat. A hunting signal sounded on the horn to recall the hounds.

Recht (Ger.). Right.

Recitando (It.) (*reh-chee-tan'-do*), **Recitante** (*reh-chee-tan'-teh*). In the style of a recitative.

Recitative (*res-i-ta-teev'*), **Recitatif** (Fr.) (*reh-see-ta-teef'*), **Recitativo** (It.) (*reh-chee-ta-tee'-vo*), **Recitativ** (Ger.) (*reh-see-ta-tiv'*). Declamatory singing, resembling chanting somewhat, and supposed, when invented in 1600, to be a revival of Greek art. Abbreviation **Recit.**

Recitative Accompaniment. The string band is generally used to accompany Recitative. If the accompaniment is at all elaborate the freedom of the singer is greatly curtailed. Modern writers frequently use the whole resources of the orchestra to accompany Recitative.

Recitativo secco. Dry Recitative was accompanied very sparingly with chords. It was customary at one time, during the pauses of the voice, for the violoncello to execute impromptu flourishes.

Reciting Note. In Gregorian chant, the dominant, being the note on which the greater part of the reciting is done.

Recorder. An obsolete instrument of the flageolet family; also an old name for the flute.

Redita (It.) (*reh-dee'-ta*). A repeat.

Redowa, Redowak, Redowazka. A Bohemian dance in ¾ time.

Redundant. Same as *Augmented*.

Reed, Zunge (Ger.) (*tsoon'-geh*), **Anche** (Fr.) (*onsh*), **Ancia** (It.) (*an'-che-a*). The technical name for the small thin strip of metal, cane, or wood, the vibration of which causes the sound of a variety of instruments. There are three kinds of reeds: (1) The single beating reed of instruments of the clarionet family; also of the reed-stops of the organ. (2) The double reed of the hautboy and bassoon family, also of the bagpipe; these two varieties are never used except in conjunction with a tube or pipe. (3) The free reed of the cabinet-organ, vocalion, etc. This reed may be used with or without a tube. The effect of the tube when combined with the free reed is analogous to that of a resonator, *i. e.*, the vibration of the contained air is sympathetic, whereas in the other cases the vibration of the reed is controlled by the column of air.

Reed Instruments. Those in which the sound is produced by the vibration of a reed in the mouthpiece.

Reel. A lively dance, nationalized in Ireland and Scotland; supposed to be of Danish origin, as the same kind of dance is found under the Danish name of Hreol.

Refrain. Burthen. (1) The chorus at the end of every stanza of some ballads. (2) The drone of a bagpipe. (3) The tune sung as an accompaniment to dancing.

Régales de bois (Fr.) (*reh-gal de bo-a*). See *Xylophone*.

Regals, Rigals, Rigoles. Small, portable organs with one or two sets of pipes, carried by a strap round the neck of the player, who worked the bellows with his left hand and manipulated the keyboard with the right.

Register. (1) Same as stop, or rank of pipes. (2) The projecting knobs on which the names of the stops are marked. (3) The compass of a voice. (4) One of the divisions of the voice; as, chest register, head register.

Registration. The combinations and successions of stops used by an organist in the performance of a piece.

Règle de l'octave (Fr.) (*regl de loc-tav*). See *Rule of the Octave.*

Relative Chord. A chord whose members are found in the scale.

Relative Key. One whose tonic chord is one of the common chords found in the scale.

Religioso (It.) (*reh-lee-jo'-so*), **Religiosamente** (*reh-lee-jo-sa-men'-teh*). In a devotional manner.

Relish. An obsolete harpsichord grace.

Remote Key. A non-related key.

Remplissage (Fr.) (*rom-plis-sazh*). Filling up. (1) The inner parts. (2) Sometimes used in the same sense as "development" (*durchführung*) in the sonata or rondo. (3) Non-essential (ripieno) parts. (4) Used in a contemptuous sense of a clumsy, overloaded composition.

Rendering. A modern term which is supposed to mean more than saying one "played" or "sang."

Repeat. A double bar with dots, thus 𝄁 signifies that the part before the double bar is to be repeated. If the dots are on both sides 𝄆𝄇 it signifies that the parts before and after the double bar are to be repeated.

Repercussion. The re-entry of subject and answer in a fugue, after an episode.

Repetition. (1) The reiteration of a note or chord. (2) A pianoforte action invented by Erard, which admits of the re-striking of a note before the key has risen to its normal position. (3) The re-entry of one of the principal themes of a sonata or rondo.

Répétition (Fr.) (*reh-peh-tis-yong*). A rehearsal.

Repetizione (It.) (*reh-peh-titz-e-oh'-neh*). Repetition.

Replicate. The recurrence of the same letter in an ascending or descending series; the octave repetitions of a given letter.

Reply, Répons (Fr.) (*reh-pong*), **Réponse** (Fr.) (*reh-pongs*), **Report.** The "answer" to a fugue subject or theme for imitation.

Reprise (Fr.) (*reh-prees*). (1) A repeat. (2) The re-entry of the principal theme in the second part of a sonata; also called **Rentrée** (*rong-treh*).

Requiem (Lat.). "Rest." The first word in the mass for the dead, hence called requiem mass.

Resin or Rosin. The clarified gum of the pitch pine.

Resolution. The movement of a dissonant to a consonant sound.

Rests. Signs indicating silence of the same duration as the notes for which they stand. In all varieties of time the whole rest is used to indicate a silence of one measure.

| Whole Rest | Half Rest | Quarter Rests | Eighth Rest | Sixteenth Rest | Thirty-second Rest | Sixty-fourth Rest |

Three forms of quarter-rest are found. No. 1 is generally found in music printed from type, Nos. 2 and 3 in engraved music. No. 2 is the most convenient form in MS. In orchestral parts a rest of two measures is indicated thus:

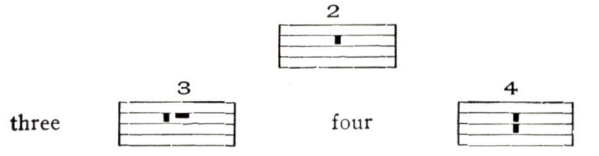

three (3)   four (4)

Any number of measure rests may be expressed by combining these three signs, but when the number exceeds six it is generally expressed thus: (9) a heavy diagonal line with numeral above it.

Retardation. The prolonging of a sound which is a member of one chord into a chord in which it is not a member, thus producing a dissonance. See *Resolution*.

Reverie. A sentimental name used by some modern writers for composition of like character, generally in lyric form.

Rhapsodie or **Rhapsody** [from Gr., *rhabdos*, a staff]. The Rhapsodists were wandering reciters who carried a long staff. The term is now applied to an irregular, formless composition which "wanders" from one theme, or key, or tempo to another at the will of the composer.

Rhythm. (1) The recurrence of accents at equal intervals of time. (2) The repetition of a group of sounds (not necessarily melodic) at equal intervals of time. This is an illustration of the first meaning:

This, of the second:

The first may be called the essential rhythm; it is never destroyed, no matter how much it may be divided by the second or ideal rhythm, thus the essential rhythm of the following passage is 1' 2 3; the ideal rhythm varies with each measure:

Rhythm is the first essential of melody; without it we have only an aimless rising and falling of sounds. The essential rhythm is a fixed quantity which will bear very little tampering with. Witness the generally unsatisfactory effect of those compositions in which alternate measures of two and three units are used. Its pace may be changed by acceleration or retardation provided the rhythmical unit is maintained. The ideal rhythm, or rhythm of the melody, is, on the other hand, completely under the composer's control, provided that its melodic motives, phrases, etc., may be "measured" by the rhythmical units adopted as the "time signature."

Ricercata (It.) (*ree-cher-cah'-ta*). A species of fugue very highly elaborated.

Rigadoon. A rapid dance of French origin, generally in $\frac{4}{4}$ time.

Rigore (It.) (*ree-go'-reh*), **con**, **Rigoroso** (*ree-go-ro'-so*). With rigor; exactly; in strict time.

Rilasciando (It.) (*ree-lah-she-an'-do*), **Rilasciante** (*ree-lah-she-an'-te*). Relaxing the time; retarding.

Rimettendo (It.) (*ree-met-ten'-do*). Holding back; retarding.

Rinforzando (It.) (*rin-for-tzan'-do*), **Rinforzare** (*rin-for-tzah'-reh*), **Rinforzato** (*rin-for-tzah'-to*). Lit., re-enforcing. Placing a strong accent on a note or passage.

Ripieno (It.) (*ree-pee-eh'-no*). "Filling up." A part that is not essential to the score, added to increase the volume of a tutti.

Ripigliare (It.) (*ree-peel-yah'-reh*), **Riprendere** (*ree-pren'-deh-reh*). To resume.

Ripresa (It.) (*ree-preh'-sah*), **Riprese** (It.). A repeat; the sign 𝄋.

Risentito (It.) (*ree-sen-tee'-to*). With energetic expression.

Risolutamente (It.) (*ree-so-lu-ta-men'-te*). Resolutely.

Risoluto (It.) (*ree-so-lu'-to*). Resolute.

Risoluzione (It.) (*ree-so-loot-ze-o-neh*), **con**. With resolution.

Risvegliato (It.) (*ris-vehl-ya-to*). Animated; lively.

Ritardando (It.) (*ree-tar-dan'-do*), **Ritardato** (*ree-tar-dah'-to*), **Ritenuto** (*ree-ten-oo'-to*), **Ritenente** (*ree-ten-en'-teh*). Holding back; retarding. Abbreviation **Rit**.

Ritmo (It.). See *Rhythm*.

Ritmo a due battate. Of two measures.

Ritmo a tre battate. Of three measures. The following passage, which, being written in $\frac{3}{4}$ (scherzo) time, looks like a six-bar phrase, is in reality a two-bar phrase, founded on the triple unit:

Ritmo a tre battate.

written in $\frac{9}{8}$ time; or it may be written in $\frac{3}{4}$ time with triplets.

This example is analogous to the oft-quoted one in the scherzo of Beethoven's ninth symphony.

Ritornella (It.) (*ree-tor-nel'-la*). Interlude; chorus; burden; tutti in the old concertos.

Robusto (It.) (*ro-bus'-to*). Robust; bold.

Roger de Coverley. Old English country dance in $\frac{3}{4}$ time.

Röhrflöte (Ger.) (*rare'-fla-teh*). Reed-flute; a flute-stop in the organ.

Rôle (Fr.) (*roll*). The part in an opera or play assigned to any performer.

Roll, Wirbel (Ger), **Rollo** (It.), **Roulement** (Fr.). The tremolo produced on the drum by the rapid alternation of blows with the drumsticks. On the kettle-drum the roll is produced by single alternating blows; on the side drum, by double alternating blows.

Romance. (1) A ballad. (2) An instrumental piece in lyric form, of romantic character; often used as the slow movement of a sonata, etc.

Romanesca (It.) (*ro-ma-nes'-ca*), **Romanesque** (Fr.) (*ro-man-esk*). Same as *Galliard*.

Romantic. A vague term for that form of art in which the emotional content is considered as of more importance than the form. The term "romantic" is often used as opposed to classic; but the application of "classic" is as vague as is that of "romantic." The element of time seems to be an essential of classicism, the work of a living author never being considered classic. The term romantic may be defined as roughly dividing the music written on harmonic principles from that written before the principles of harmonic combination and succession were discovered; but already the romantic school has been sub-divided into what may be called the classic-romantic and the new-romantic; but since every "new" thing must in time become "old," this last school must, when its day is past, give place to a newer romanticism.

Rondo, Rondeau (Fr.). One of the forms of composition characterized by the return of the first theme after the presentation of each new theme. The modern rondo partakes of the character of the sonata form, in that its second theme is repeated in the tonic key, having been first given in the dominant key. The following schemes exhibit at a glance the usual forms of the rondo:
MAJOR KEY.—I Th. II Th. I Th. || III Th. I Th. II Th. I Th.
          Tonic. Dom. Tonic   Subdom. Tonic. Tonic. Tonic
                             Rel. min.
                             Par. min.
MINOR KEY.—I Th. II Th. I Th. || III Th. I Th. II Th. I Th.
          Tonic. Rel. Tonic   Subdom. Tonic. Tonic Tonic
               major.   of rel. major.   major.

Example of Rondo in Major Key—last movement of Op. 2, No. 2 (Beethoven).
Example of Rondo in Minor Key—last movement of Sonata Pathétique.

Root. The fundamental or generating note of a chord.

Rosalia (It.) (*ros-al-ya*). The repetition of a melodic phrase several times, each time one degree higher or lower than the last. It gets its name from an Italian folk-song, "Rosalia Mia Cara," the melody of which is constructed in this way. Although not considered good writing, many examples may be found in the works of the greatest composers. Three such repetitions are generally considered allowable. In Germany the Rosalia has the ludicrous name of *Schusterfleck* (cobbler's patch), also *Vetter Michel* (Cousin Michel), from its occurrence in a well-known Volkslied, "Gestern Abend war Vetter Michel da."

Rose. The sound-hole in the belly of the guitar, mandolin, etc.

Rosin. See *Resin*.

Rota (Lat.). A round.

Rote. Hurdy-gurdy; vielle.

Roulade (Fr.) (*roo-lad*). A brilliant run; an ornamental flourish.

Round. A variety of canon, the imitation being always at the 8va or unison.

Roundel, Round, Roundelay. A dance in which a ring with joined hands was formed. Roundelay also means a poem with a constantly reiterated refrain or burden.

Rubato (It.) (*roo-bah'-to*). Robbed; stolen. The direction Rubato, or Tempo Rubato, indicates a style of performance in which the rhythmic flow is interrupted by dwelling slightly on certain melodic notes and slightly hurrying others. This style of performance is used with great effect in the modern intensely emotional school of music.

Ruhig (Ger.) (*roo'-ig*). Calm; quiet; tranquilly.

Rule of the Octave. An old formula for putting chords to the diatonic scale, major or minor.

Run. A passage founded on the scale, generally used in vocal music. The run is generally sung to one syllable.

Rusticano (It.) (*rus-tee-cah'-no*). Rustically.

Rustico (It.) (*rus'-tee-co*). Rustic; pastoral.

Rutscher (Ger.) (*root'-sher*). "Slider." Old name for the galopade.

Ruvido (It.) (*roo'-vee-do*). Rough; harsh.

Rythme (Fr.) (*reethm*), **Bien rythmé** (Fr.), **Ben ritmato** (It.). Well marked; exact.

S

S. Abbreviation of **Segno** (sign); **Senza** (without); **Sinistra** (left); **Solo**; **Subito** (quickly).

𝄋 A sign used to point out the place from which a repeat is to be made. Al 𝄋, to the sign; Dal 𝄋, from the sign.

Sabot (Fr.). A "shoe." Part of the mechanism of the double-action harp, consisting of a revolving disk of brass with two projecting studs; when the pedal is depressed the string is caught between the studs and drawn tighter, thus raising its pitch.

Saccade (Fr.) (*sac-cad*). A strong pressure of the violin bow on the strings, causing two or three to sound together.

Sackbut. An old name for a species of the trombone. Sometimes written Sagbut.

Sackpfeife (Ger.). Bagpipe.

Saite (Ger.) (*sy-teh*). A string.

Salicional, Salicet, Salcional [from Lat., *salix*, willow]. A soft, open metal organ-stop.

Salonflügel (Ger.). Parlor grand pianoforte.

Salonstück (Ger.). Parlor piece; salon music.

Saltarello (It.) (*sal-tah-rel'-lo*) [from *saltare*, to leap]. An Italian dance in triple time.

Saltato (It.). "Springing bow" in violin playing.

Salto (It.). A skip. A counterpoint that moved by skips was called C. P. di salto; in Lat., *C. P. per saltem*.

Sambuca. Generally supposed to be an ancient variety of the harp. The Sabeca, mentioned in the Bible (Daniel iii: 5, 7, 10, 15), translated "sackbut" in the English version, is supposed to be the same instrument. The derivation of the word is not known.

Sampogna or **Zampogna** (It.) (*sam-pone'-ya*). Bagpipe.

Sanft (Ger.). Soft.

Sans (Fr.). Without.

Saraband, Sarabanda (It.), **Zarabanda** (Sp.), **Sarabande** (Fr.). A slow, stately dance in $\frac{3}{4}$ time, used as the "slow movement" in the suite. The Saraband is founded on the following rhythm:

One of the finest examples is the song in "Rinaldo," by Handel, "*Lascia ch'io pianga*," which is said to have been written first as a Saraband, and afterward adapted to the words.

Sarrusophone. A brass wind instrument with a double reed like hautboy.

Satz (Ger.). (1) A theme. **Hauptsatz,** principal theme; **Seitensatz,** secondary theme; **Nebensatz,** auxiliary theme; **Schluss-Satz,** closing theme, or coda. (2) A piece; composition.

Saxhorn. A brass instrument with from three to five cylinders or pistons; invented by A. Sax. Saxhorns are made in seven different keys. A saxhorn band consists of "high horn" (or cornet), soprano, alto, tenor, baritone, bass (or tuba), double bass (or bombardon). The "high horn," alto, and bass are in E♭, the others in B♭.

Saxophone. Brass instrument with clarinet mouthpiece, invented by A. Sax. Made in seven sizes, corresponding to the saxhorns, except that there are two of each kind, differing by a whole tone in pitch; thus: Sopranino (high saxophone) in F and E♭, soprano in C and B♭, alto in F and E♭, tenor in C and B♭, baritone in F and E♭, bass in C and B♭. The saxophone is extensively used in France in military bands, but has not as yet found its way into the orchestra, as its tone quality is not of a character to mix well with the rest of the orchestra.

Saxtromba. Brass instrument resembling the saxhorn, but differing in tone quality from having a narrower tube.

Saxtuba. The bass saxhorn.

Sbalzato (It.) (*sbalt-zah'-to*). Impetuously; dashing.

Scale. (1) A succession of ascending or descending sounds. **Major Scale,** a series of sounds with a half-tone between 3-4 and 7-8, reckoning upward. **Minor Scale,** a series of sounds with a half-tone between 2-3 and 5-6 in the natural minor, in the Melodic Minor, 7-8, ascending. The Melodic Minor descends, like the Natural Minor; in the Harmonic Minor there are half-tones between 2-3, 5-6, and 7-8, and a tone and a half between 6 and 7. The Minor Scale sometimes descends with raised 6 and 7. Many examples may be found in Bach's music. **Chromatic Scale,** one formed wholly of half-tones. **Pentatonic Scale** [Gr., *penta,* five, *tonos,* sound], one that omits the 4 and 7. The Pentatonic Scale may be major or minor, thus:

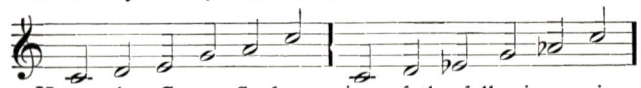

Hungarian Gypsy Scale consists of the following curious succession:

(2) The series of overtones of a simple tube, such as the horn without valves. (3) In organ-pipes, the proportion between the length and the diameter. (4) In the piano, the proportion between the length, weight, and tension of the string and the pitch of the sound it is meant to give. Piano builders include many other points in the term "scale;" those given are the most important.

Scemando (It.) (*shay-man'-do*). See *Diminuendo.*

Scena (It.) (*shay-nah*). (1) A scene. (2) A solo for voice in which various dramatic emotions are expressed.

Scenario (It.) (*shay-nahr'-yo*). (1) The plot of a drama. (2) The book of stage directions.

Scene. (1) See *Scena.* (2) A division of a dramatic performance. (3) A stage-setting.

Schablonenmusik (Ger.). "Pattern" or "stencil" music, *i. e.,* correct, but uninspired.

Schäferlied (Ger.) (*shay'-fer-leet*). Shepherd song; pastoral.

Schäferspiel (Ger.) (*shay'-fer-speel*). Pastoral play.

Schallbecken (Ger.). "Sound bowls"; cymbals. Frequently called **Becken.**

Schalmay, Schalmei (Ger.). A shawm.

Scharf (Ger.). Sharp. A mixture-stop.

Schaurig (Ger.). Weird; dread-inspiring.

Scherz (Ger.) (*sherts*). Droll; playful.

Scherzando (It.) (*sker-tzan'-do*), **Scherzante** (*sker-tzan'-teh*), **Scherzevole** (*sker-tzeh'-vo-leh*), **Scherzoso** (*skertzo'-so*). All derived from *scherzo,* and signifying a light, playful style of performance or composition.

Scherzhaft (Ger.). Funny; amusing.

Scherzo (It.) (*skert'-zo*). A "jest." (1) A piece of music of a sportive, playful character. (2) A symphony or sonata movement of this character, taking the place of the minuet. Haydn first changed the character of the minuet, while still retaining its name, by giving it a light, playful character and more rapid tempo. Beethoven discarded the name and adopted that of *Scherzo,* and still further increased the rapidity of the movement; all that he retained of the minuet was the 3/4 time. Many composers since Beethoven have made still further departure, Scherzi being now written in 6/8 and 2/4 time.

Schiettamente (It.) (*ske-et-ta-men'-teh*). Without ornament.

Schietto (It.) (*ske-et'-to*). Simple; neat.

Schleppend (Ger.). Dragging; retarding.

Schluss (Ger.). End; close.

Schlüssel (Ger.). Key; clef.

Schlussfall (Ger.). Cadence.

Schlussnote (Ger.). Last note.

Schluss-Satz (Ger.). Last movement; last theme; coda.

Schmeichelnd (Ger.). Coaxing; *lusingando.*

Schmelzend (Ger.) (*schmel'-tzend*). Lit., melting; *morendo.*

Schmerz (Ger.) (*schmerts*). Pain; sorrow.

Schmerzlich (Ger.). Painful; sorrowful.

Schnell (Ger.). Quick.

Schneller (Ger.). An inverted mordent (called mordent in modern usage):

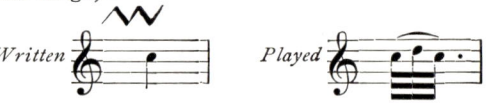

with accent on the first note.

Schottische. A dance in 2/4 time resembling the polka.

Schusterfleck (Ger.). See *Rosalia.*

Schwach (Ger.). Weak; soft.

Schwärmer (Ger.). See *Rauscher.*

Schwebung (Ger.) (*shveh'-boonk*). A beat. (Acoustic;) *i. e.,* produced by the simultaneous vibration of two sounds, especially prominent in unisons and octaves when not in tune.

Schweigezeichen (Ger.) (*schvei-geh-tseich-en*). Lit., "silence sign." A rest.

Schwellen or **Anschwellen** (Ger.). To swell the tone.

Schweller (Ger.). The swell organ.

Schwellton (Ger.). See *Messa di voce.*

Schwellwerk (Ger.). See *Schweller.*

Schwer (Ger.). Heavy; difficult.

Schwermütig (Ger.) (*schvehr'-mee-tig*). Sad; pensive.

Schwindend (Ger.). See *Morendo.*

Schwungvoll (Ger.) (*schvoong'-foll*). With elevated passion.

Scintillante (It.) (*shin-til-lan'-teh*), **Scintillante** (Fr.) (*sintee-yong*). Scintillating; brilliant; sparkling.

Sciolto (It.) (*shol'-to*), **Scioltezza** (*shol-tet'-za*), con, **Scioltamente** (*shol-tah-men'-teh*). Freedom; fluency; with freedom; freely.

Score. See *Partition.*

Scoring. See *Instrumentation.*

Scorrendo (It.) (*skor-ren'-do*), **Scorrevole** (*skor-reh'-vo-leh*). Gliding; glissando.

Scotch Snap. A short note followed by a longer one; thus 𝅘𝅥𝅮𝅘𝅥. borrowed from Hungarian gypsy music.

Scozzese (It.) (*skotz-zeh'-seh*), alla. In Scotch style.

Scroll. The head of the violin, etc.

Sdegno (It.) (*sdehn'-yo*). Scorn; disdain.

Sdegnosamente (It.) (*sdehn'-yo-sa-men'-teh*). Scornfully.

Sdegnoso (It.) (*sdehn-yo'-so*). Scornful.

Sdrucciolando (It.) (*sdroot-sho-lan'-do*). See *Glissando*.

Se (It.) (*seh*). As if.

Sec (Fr.), **Secco** (It.). Dry. See *Recitativo secco*.

Second. 1) An interval embracing adjacent letters. (2) The lower of two equal voices or instruments. (3) The alto in a vocal quartet or chorus.

Seconda Donna. Second lady; the next in rank after the prima donna.

Secondo (It.) (*seh-con'-do*). Second; the lower part in a duet for two voices or instruments; the lower part in a four-hand pianoforte composition.

Seele (Ger.) (*seh'-leh*), **Âme** (Fr.). Soul. The sound-post of the violin.

Seg (It.). Abbreviation of **Segue**, *q. v.*, and of **Segno**.

Segno (It.). See *Signs*.

Segue (It.) (*sehg'-weh*). Follows. **Segue il coro**, the chorus follows.

Seguendo (It.) (*sehg-wen'-do*), **Seguente** (*sehg-wen'-teh*). Following. **Attacca il seguente**, attack what follows.

Seguidilla (Sp.) (*seh-gwee-deel'-ya*). A dance in ¾ time.

Sehnsucht (Ger.). Longing.

Sehnsüchtig (Ger.). Longingly.

Sehr (Ger.). Very.

Semi-breve. A whole note. 𝅝

Semi-chorus. Half the chorus; a small chorus.

Semi-grand. A small (half) grand pianoforte.

Semi-quaver. A sixteenth note.

Semi-tone. A half tone. A chromatic semi-tone changes the pitch without changing the letter; as, C—C♯: a diatonic semi-tone changes both, as, C—D♭.

Semplice (It.) (*sem-plee'-cheh*). Simple.

Semplicimente (It.) (*sem-plee-chee-men'-teh*). Simply; unaffectedly.

Semplicita (It.) (*sem-plee'-chee-tah*), con. With simplicity.

Sempre (It.) (*sem'-preh*). Always.

Sensibile (It.) (*sen-see'-bee-leh*), **Sensible** (Fr.) (*song-seebl*). **Nota sensibile**, the leading note. **Note sensible**, "sensitive" note.

Sensibilita (It.) (*sen-see-bee'-lee-tah*), con. With feeling.

Sentito (It.) (*sen-tee'-to*), **Sentimento** (*sen-tee-men'-to*), con. With feeling; with sentiment.

Senza (It.) (*sen-tza*). Without.

Septet, Septuor. A composition for seven solo voices or instruments.

Septole (Ger.). Septuplet; a group of seven.

Se piace (It.) (*seh pe-ah'-cheh*). "Please yourself." *Ad libitum*.

Sequence, Melodic. The repetition of a melodic phrase at regular intervals. **Harmonic Sequence**, the repetition of a harmonic progression at regular intervals. **Contrapuntal Sequence**, a succession of common chords with roots moving in a regular "pattern."

Melodic Sequence.

Harmonic Sequence.

Contrapuntal Sequence.

Seraphine. A free-reed instrument that preceded the harmonium.

Serenade, Sérénade (Fr.), **Serenata** (It.), **Ständchen** (Ger.). Lit., an evening song. The Italian form, Serenata, is also applied to an instrumental symphonic composition, and by Handel to his cantata "Acis and Galatea."

Sereno (It.) (*seh-reh'-no*). Serene; tranquil.

Serio (It.) (*seh-re-o*). Serious.

Serioso (It.). Gravely; seriously.

Serpent. A nearly obsolete instrument made of wood covered with leather, cup-shaped mouthpiece, finger-holes, and keys.

Service. A musical setting of the canticles, etc., of the Episcopal Church.

Sesqui-altera. A mixture-stop in the organ. In ancient musical nomenclature the following compounds with Sesqui were used:
Sesqui-nona, *i. e.*, the ratio of 9 to 10; minor whole tone.
Sesqui-octava, 8 to 9; major whole tone.
Sesqui-quinta, 5 to 6; minor third.
Sesqui-quarta, 4 to 5; major third.
Sesqui-tertia, 3 to 4; perfect fourth.
Sesqui-tone, a minor third.

Sestet. See *Sextet*.

Sestetto (It.). See *Sextet*.

Sestole. See *Sextuplet*.

Seule (Fr.) (*sool*). Alone.

Seventeenth. An organ-stop sounding the octave of the major 3d above the diapason; called also the tierce.

Seventh. An interval including seven letters. **Seventh Major**, seven letters and eleven half-tones, as C—B. **Seventh Minor**, seven letters and ten half-tones, as C—B♭. **Diminished Seventh**, seven letters and nine half-tones, as C♯—B♭.

Severamente (It.) (*seh-veh-rah-men'-teh*). Severely; strictly.

Severita (It.) (*seh-ver'-ee-ta*), con. With severity; exactness.

Sextet, Sestet, Sestetto (It.), **Sextuor** (Fr.). A composition for six solo voices or instruments.

Sextuplet. A group of six notes occupying the time of four.

Sfogato (It.) (*sfo-gah'-to*) [from *sfogare*, to evaporate]. A soprano voice of thin, light quality and unusually high range is called a soprano sfogato.

Sforzando (It.) (*sfortz-an'-do*) or **Sforzato**, abbreviated **Sf.** or **Sfz.** "Forced." A strong accent immediately followed by piano.

Shake. See *Trill*.

Sharp. The sign, ♯, which raises the pitch of a letter a half tone. Sharp is sometimes used in the sense of augmented, as sharp 6th for augmented 6th; popular name for the black keys of pianoforte and organ.

Sharp Mixture. A mixture with shrill-voiced pipes.

Shawm. See *Calamus*.

Shift. A change in the position of the left hand on the fingerboard of the violin; each shift is a fourth higher than the preceding one.

Si. (1) The note B in French, Italian, and Spanish. (2) The Italian impersonal pronoun, "one," or "they," as, *si piace*, "one" pleases, *i. e.*, as you please.

Siciliana (It.) (*see-cheel-ya'-nah*), **Sicilienne** (Fr.) (*see-see-lee-en*). A pastoral dance in slow 6/8 time; slow movements, vocal or instrumental, are frequently called Sicilianas.

Side Drum. See *Drum*.

Siegeslied (Ger.) (*see'-ges-leed*). Song of victory.

Signs. (Only the most important are here given. Complete information may be obtained by consulting the "Embellishments of Music," by Russell.)

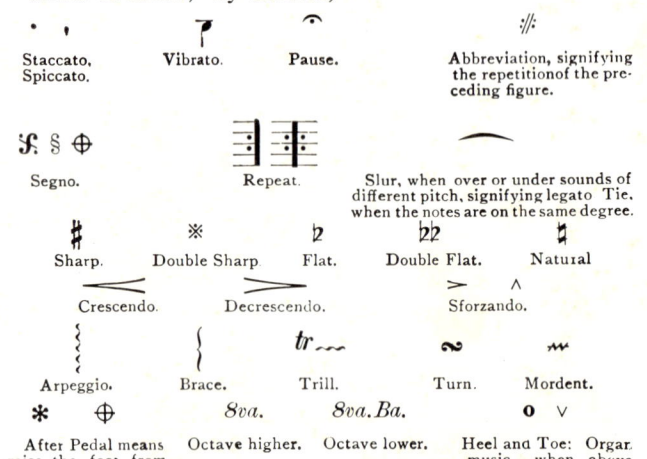

Staccato. Spiccato.	Vibrato.	Pause.	Abbreviation, signifying the repetition of the preceding figure.
Segno.	Repeat.		Slur, when over or under sounds of different pitch, signifying legato Tie, when the notes are on the same degree.
Sharp.	Double Sharp.	Flat. Double Flat.	Natural.
Crescendo.	Decrescendo.	Sforzando.	
Arpeggio.	Brace.	Trill. Turn.	Mordent.
After Pedal means raise the foot from the pedal.	Octave higher.	Octave lower.	Heel and Toe: Organ music — when above the notes, right foot; when below, left foot.

Signature, Signatur (Ger.), **Time.** The signs C, ₵ etc. **Key Signature**, the sharps or flats marked at the beginning of a part or piece.

Simile (It.) (*see-mee-leh*). The same; in the same way.

Sinfonia (It.), **Sinfonie** (Ger.), **Symphonie** (Fr.), **Symphony** [from Gr., *sumphonia*, a sounding together]. Originally had the same meaning that we attach to interval, *i. e.*, two simultaneous sounds. (1) By the early writers of Italian opera it was used in the modern sense of overture. (2) The introduction to a song is still called the symphony. (3) The adaptation of the large forms of composition (sonata and rondo) to the orchestra.

Singend or **Singbar** (Ger.). Singing; cantabile.

Singhiozzando (It.) (*sin-ghee-otz-an'-do*). Sobbingly.

Singspiel (Ger.) (*sing-speel*). "Sing-play." Operetta; an opera without recitatives, the dialogue being spoken. "Der Freischütz," when first produced, was of this character, which may be considered as one of Germany's contributions to the development of the opera, the Italian operas from the beginning being largely composed of recitative. The "Singspiel" form has found its most congenial home and its best exponents in France.

Sinistra (It.). Left.

Sino, Abbr., **Sin.** (It.) (*see'-no*). As far as; used after D. C. or al 𝄋; as **al 𝄋**, **Sin' al fine**, go to the sign, then as far as "fine." **D. C. sin' al 𝄋**, from the beginning as far as the sign.

Sixteenth Note.

Sixth. An interval including six letters.

Sixth Major. Six letters, nine half-tones.

Sixth Minor. Six letters, eight half-tones. **Augmented Sixth**, six letters, ten half-tones. **Diminished Sixth**, six letters, seven half-tones.

Sixty-fourth Note.

Slancio (It.) (*slan'-che-o*), **con.** With impetuosity.

Slargando (It.) (*slar-gan'-do*). Widening; growing slower.

Slargandosi (It.) (*slar-gan-do'-see*). Slower.

Slentando (It.) (*slen-tan'-do*). Gradually slower.

Slide. (1) The movable tube of the trombone. (2) See *Portamento*.

Slur. ⌢ Legato sign. In vocal music signifies that all the notes it includes are to be sung to one syllable.

Smanioso (It.) (*sma-ne-o'-so*). Frantic; raging.

Smaniante (It.) (*sma-ne-an'-teh*). Frantically.

Sminuendo (It.) (*smin-oo-en'-do*), **Sminuito** (*smin-oo-ee'-to*), **Smorendo** (*smo-ren'-do*). Same as *Diminuendo*.

Smorzando (It.) (*smor-tzan'-do*). Lit., "smothering"; morendo.

Snare Drum. See *Drum*.

Soave (It.) (*so-a'-veh*). Sweet.

Soavemente (It.) (*so-a-veh-men'-teh*). Sweetly.

Sogetto (It.). Subject; theme of a fugue.

Sognando (It.) (*sone-yan'-do*). Dreaming; dreamily.

Sol. The note G in Italian, French, and Spanish; fifth Aretinian syllable.

Solenne (It.) (*so-len'-neh*). Solemn.

Solennemente (It.) (*so-len-neh-men'-teh*). Solemnly.

Solennita (It.) (*so-len'-nee-ta*), **con.** With solemnity.

Sol-fa (verb). To sing with the syllables.

Solfeggio (It.) (*solfed-jo*). (1) A vocal exercise. (2) Used by Bach as a name for certain short instrumental pieces.

Solmization. A method of learning to sing by the application of syllables to the scale. The earliest invention of this method of fixing the succession of sounds forming the scale in the memory is attributed to Guido of Arezzo (*ah-rets-o*), who used for this purpose the syllables ut, re, mi, fa, sol, la, having chanced to observe that these syllables—the first in the successive lines of a Latin hymn—were sung to six successive notes which formed a hexachord scale: C, D, E, F, G, A. There were seven hexachord scales, as follows:

First began on G, 1st line bass staff; this was called the hexachordum durum (hard hexachord). Second began on C, a 4th higher. Third began on F, another 4th higher; in this scale B was flat; it was called the hexachordum molle (soft hexachord). Fourth, fifth, and sixth were respectively an octave higher than the first, second, and third, and the seventh was two octaves higher than the first. The first note of every scale was called *ut* (afterward changed to *do*), therefore from its inception "do" was "movable." Various modifications of these syllables have at different times been used for solmization. One extensively used at one time was the practice of using only four of them, viz., mi, fa, sol, la. These were so arranged that *mi* always fell upon the third note in the tetrachord, for example, the scale of C was sol-faed thus:

Tetrachord. Tetrachord.
C D E F | G A B C
sol la mi fa *sol la mi fa*

It was owing to the difficulty and, to ancient ears, harshness of the skip from the *fa* of the lower tetrachord to the *mi* of the upper that the expression, "mi contra fa," came to have a proverbial meaning. This interval, called the tritone (three tones), was by the ancient theorists stigmatized as "tritonus diabolus est." New syllables have at different times been proposed; one scheme of which the syllables were bo, ce, di, ga, lo, ma, ni, was called bocedization; another with da, me, ni, po, hi, la, be, was called damenization. The only modifications and additions to the

Solo (It.) (plural, **Soli**). Alone; a composition in which the principal part is taken by one voice or instrument. **Solo Parts** are those sung or played by single performers as distinguished from chorus or tutti passages.

Somma (It.). Utmost; as **Con somma espressione**, with the utmost expression.

Sonabile (It.) (*so-nah'-bee-leh*), **Sonante** (*so-nan'-teh*). Resonant; sounding; sonorous.

Sonare (It.) (*so-nah'-reh*). To sound; to play upon.

Sonata (It.) (*so-nah'-tah*). "Sound piece." (1) The highest development of musical form. (2) In modern use, an extended composition with several movements for pianoforte, or pianoforte in conjunction with one other instrument. A composition of this class for more than two instruments is called trio, quartet, etc.; for full orchestra, a symphony. The "form" of the sonata (see *Form*) has undergone many modifications since it was first adopted, about the beginning of the 17th century. At first it was applied indifferently to any instrumental piece, such, for example, as were commonly called "airs." Those written for the harpsichord or for viols were called "sonata da camera." Those for the organ (or frequently those for harpsichord or viols, if written in grave style), "sonata da chiesa" (church sonata). The distinguishing characteristic of the modern sonata form is the possession of two themes in different keys (see Scheme in article *Form*). The gradual growth of this binary development may be traced in the works of Kuhnau, Scarlatti, Alberti, Durante, and others. The binary form was first definitely fixed by K. P. E. Bach. The only changes made since have been the immense development given to the form by Beethoven, and the adoption of other keys for the second theme.

Sonata di chiesa (It.) (*key-eh'-sa*). A church sonata; organ sonata.

Sonatilla (It.) (*so-na-til'-la*), **Sonatina** (It.) (*so-na-tee'-na*), **Sonatine** (Fr.) (*so-na-teen*). A short, easy, undeveloped sonata.

Song, Gesang, Lied (Ger.), **Chant** (Fr.), **Canto** (It.). (1) Originally a poem. (2) A musical setting of a poem, especially for one voice. (3) Folk-song (Ger., *Volkshed*). A simple air containing but one member, the words lyrical or narrative (if the poem is a lengthy narrative it is generally called a ballad). (4) Art songs contain several members, and in many cases, as in the songs of Schubert, Franz, Schumann, and others, rise to the highest plane of art expression. The Germans have a word, *durchkomponirt*, which is applied to songs every stanza of which has a separate musical setting, so designed as to exalt and emphasize the expression of the words.

Songs without words, Lieder ohne Worte (Ger.), **Chants sans paroles** (Fr.). A title invented by Mendelssohn and given by him to a set of pianoforte compositions. Songs for several voices are called part-songs. See *Part-Song*.

Sonoramente (It.). Sonorously.

Sonore (It.), **Sonoro** [from Lat., *sonus*, sound]. Sonorous; sounding.

Sonorita (It.) (*so-no'-ree-ta*), **con.** With resonance.

Sopra (It.). On; above; upon.

Soprano (It.), **Sopran** (Ger.), **Dessus** (Fr.) (*des-soo*). The female or boy's voice of the highest range.

Soprano Clef. C clef on the 1st line.

Soprano Sfogato (*sfo-gah'-to*). An unusually high light soprano.

Sordamente (It.). Veiled, dampened, muffled tone.

Sordino (It.) (*sor-dee'-no*). A mute; small instruments of metal, wood, etc., put on the bridge of the violin, etc., to deaden the tone. Pear- or cylinder-shaped mutes of wood, cardboard, or leather are put in the bell of the horn or trumpet with the same object. The use of sordino is indicated by **Con S.**, their removal by **Senza S.**

Sordo (It.). Mute; muffled. **Clarinetto sordo,** muted clarionet.

Sortita (It.) (*sor-tee'-ta*). "Going out." Concluding voluntary; first appearance of any character in an operatic performance.

Sospirando (It.) (*sos-pee-ran'-do*), **Sospiroso** (*sos-pee-ro'-so*), **Sospirante** (*sos-pee-ran'-teh*), **Sospirevole** (*sos-pee-reh'-vo-leh*) [from *sospiro*, a sigh]. Sighing; sobbing; mournful.

Sostenuto (It.) (*sos-teh-noo'-to*), **Sostenendo** (*sos-teh-nen'-do*). Sustained; without haste.

Sotto (It.). Below. **Sotto voce,** in an undertone.

Soubasse (Fr.) (*soo-bass*). A 32-foot organ pedal-stop.

Soubrette (Fr.) (*soo-bret*). A waiting maid; a minor female rôle in comic or comedy opera.

Sound-board. A thin sheet of spruce-pine, or fir, upon which the bridge that supports the strings of the pianoforte rests. The function of the sound-board is to increase the volume of the tone, which it does by taking up the vibration of the string. There are many unsolved problems in the relation which subsists between the string and the sound-board, as to the manner in which this amplification of the sound takes place. It is impossible to form a conception of the complications in the mode of vibration of the sound-board that must take place when, for example, a full chord is struck. Yet all these complications are not only simultaneous, but they obey the changing conditions of the most rapid execution with such swiftness and certainty that not a note is lost or a tone quality obscured.

Sound-box. The body of the violin, guitar, etc. The problems as to the function of the sound-box are even more complicated than those connected with the sound-board, as a sound-box is a combination of a sound-board and an enclosed mass of air, the vibrations of which have an important bearing on the quality and intensity of the tone.

Sound-hole. The orifice or orifices in the upper part, called technically the "belly," of the violin, guitar, etc. In the violin family they are called F-holes, from their resemblance to the letter *f*

Sound-post. A slender, cylindrical, wooden prop between the belly and the back in instruments of the violin family, placed under the foot of the bridge on the side of the highest string.

Sourdine (Fr.) (*soor-deen*). See *Sordino*.

Spaces. The intervals between the lines of the staff or between the leger lines.

Spalla (It.). The shoulder. Used in the sentence, **Viola da spalla,** one of the viols in a "chest."

Spanischer Reiter (Ger). See *Spanisches Kreuz.*

Spanisches Kreuz (Ger.) (*spah-nish-es kroits*). Spanish cross; German name for double sharp ※.

Sparta (It.) (*spar-ta*), **Spartita** (*spar'-ti-ta*). A score. See *Partition.*

Spasshaft (Ger.). Jocose; merry; scherzando.

Spezzato (It.) (*spets-sa'-to*) [from *spezzare,* to break in pieces]. Divided; broken.

Spianato (It.) (*spe-a-nah'-to*). Leveled; tranquillo.

Spianto (It.) (*spe-an-to*). Level; smooth.

Spiccato (It.) (*spik-kah'-to*). Detached; pointed.

Spiel (Ger.) (*speel*). Play.

Spielart. Style; touch.

Spielbar. Playable; well adapted to the instrument.

Spieloper. Operetta; comic opera.

Spieltenor. Light tenor; comic opera tenor.

Spinet. The predecessor of the harpsichord, called also couched harp.

Spirito (It.) (*spee-ree-to*), **con**, **Spiritoso** (*spee-ree-to'-so*), **Spiritosamente** (*spee-ree-to-sa-men'-teh*). With spirit; spirited; lively; animated.

Spitzflöte, Spindelflöte (Ger.). An organ-stop of reed-like quality, 8-, 4-, or 2-foot pitch.

Squilla (It.) (*squil'-la*). Little bell.

Squillante (It.) (*squil-lan'-teh*). Bell-like; ringing.

Stabile (It.) (*stah-bee'-leh*). Firm; steady.

Stac. Abbreviation of Staccato.

Staccatissimo (It.) (*stac-cah-tis'-see-mo*). As detached as possible. The sign for staccatissimo is a pointed dot over the note ♩.

Staccato (It.) (*stac-cah'-to*). Detached; cut off; separated.

Staff or **Stave.** The five lines with their enclosed spaces. Gregorian music is written on a staff of four lines.

Standard Pitch. See *Pitch*.

Ständchen (Ger.). See *Serenade*.

Stark (Ger.). Loud; strong.

Stave. See *Staff*.

Stem, Hals (Ger.), **Queue** (Fr.), **Gambo** (It.). The part of a note consisting of a vertical line; also called tail.

Stentato (It.) (*sten-tah'-to*), **Stentando** (*sten-tan'-do*) [from *stentare*, to labor]. A heavy emphasis combined with a dragging of the time.

Step. From one letter to the next; a degree. **Whole Step**, a whole tone; **Half Step**, half tone; **Chromatic Step**, chromatic half tone.

Sterbend (Ger.) (*stair-bent*). Dying; morendo.

Steso (It.) (*stay-so*). Extended. **Steso moto**, slow movement.

Stesso (It.) (*stes-so*). The same.

Sticcado (It.). Xylophone.

Stil (Ger.) (*steel*), **Stilo** (It.). Style; manner.

Stillgedacht (Ger.). Soft organ-stop with closed pipes; stopped diapason.

Stimmbildung. Voice formation; voice training.

Stimme (Ger.) (*stim'-meh*). (1) Voice. (2) Part. (3) Sound-post. (4) Organ-stop.

Stimmen (verb). To tune.

Stimmung. Pitch, tuning.

Stimmungsbild. "Voicing picture," *i. e.*, a short composition designed to "voice" or express some given mood or emotion, *e. g.*, "Warum," by Schumann.

Stinguendo (It.) (*stin-gwen'-do*) [from *stinguere*, to extinguish]. Fading away; becoming extinguished.

Stirato (It.) (*stee-rah'-to*), **Stiracchiato** (*stee-rak-ke-ah'-to*) [from *stirare*, to stretch]. Retarding the time.

Stop. (1) To press the finger on the string of violin, guitar, etc. **Double Stop**, pressing two strings at once. (2) (noun) A rank or set of organ-pipes. **Draw Stop**, the arrangement of levers by means of which the "wind" is admitted to the various ranks of pipes at will, called also register. **Foundation Stop**, one of 8-foot pitch. **Mutation Stop**, one sounding the major third or perfect fifth, or both, over the fundamental. **Solo Stop**, one with a tone quality suited to the rendition of melody.

Stracino (It.) (*strah-chee'-no*), **Stracicato** (*strah-chee-cah'-to*), **Stracicando** (*strah-chee-can'-do*), **Stracinando** (*strah-chee-nan'-do*). A drag, or slur; sliding from one note to another and at the same time slightly slackening the time.

Strain. Song, air, tune, or a part of one.

Strathspey. A Scotch dance in ¼ time.

Stravagante (It.) (*strah-vah-gan'-te*). Extravagant; fantastic.

Stravaganza (It.) (*strah-vah-gant'-sah*). A fantastic composition.

Streng (Ger.). Rigid; severe.

Strepito (It.) (*streh'-pee-to*), **con**. With noise; fury.

Strepitosamente (It.) (*streh-pee-to-sah-men'-teh*). Furiously.

Strepitoso (It.) (*streh-pee-to'-so*). Furious.

Stretta, Stretto (It.). "A throng." (1) Hurrying the time at the close. (2) In fugue, causing the voices to follow one another at less distance, so that the subject and answer are brought closer together.

Stridente (It.) (*stree-den'-teh*). Strident; noisy; impetuous.

String. Abbreviation for Stringendo.

String. Cords made of wire, catgut, or silk, used for musical instruments.

String Band. The violins, violas, violoncellos, and double bass, also spoken of collectively as the "strings" or the string quartet.

String Instruments. Those in which the tone is reproduced by the vibration of strings. They are classified as follows: 1st, strings plucked by the fingers—harp, guitar, etc.; 2d, strings struck by plectra—mandolin, zither, etc.; 3d, strings vibrated by means of a bow—violin, etc.; 4th, strings struck with hammers—pianoforte, dulcimer, etc.

String Quartet. A composition for two violins, viola, and violoncello.

String Quintet, Sextet, Septet, Octet are formed by combining the string instruments in various proportions.

Stringendo (It.) (*strin-jen'-do*). Hurrying the time.

Strisciando (It.) (*strish-e-an'-do*). Creeping; gliding.

Stromentato (It.). Instrumented; scored; orchestrated.

Stromento (It.) (*stro-men'-to*). Instrument.

Stromento di corda. String instrument.

Stromento di fiato or **di vento.** Wind instrument.

Stück (Ger.) (*stick*). A piece. **Concertstück**, concert piece. **Salonstück**, parlor piece.

Study, Étude (Fr.), **Studio** (It.). (1) A composition designed to facilitate the mastering of some special difficulty. (2) A name often given by modern writers to pieces analogous to the old toccata, *q. v.*

Stufe (Ger.) (*stoo'-feh*). A step; degree of the scale.

Stürmisch (Ger.). Stormy; furioso.

Suave (It.) (*soo-a'-veh*). Sweet.

Suavemente (It.) (*soo-a-veh-men'-teh*). Sweetly.

Suavita (It.) (*soo-ah'-vee-ta*), **con**. With sweetness.

Sub-bass. An organ pedal-stop of 16- or 32-foot tone.

Sub-dominant. The 4th degree of the scale; not called sub-dominant because it is below the dominant, but because it is the same distance below the tonic that the dominant is above.

Sub-mediant. The 6th of the scale.

1. Tonic. 2. Mediant, *i. e.*, half-way to dominant. 3. Dominant. 4. Sub-mediant, *i. e.*, half-way to sub-dominant. 5. Sub-dominant.

Sub-octave. A coupler on the organ that pulls down the keys an octave below those struck.

Sub-principal. Open organ-stop, 32- and 16-foot pitch.

Sub-tonic. The leading note, 7th of the scale.

Subito (It.) (*soo-bee'-to*), **Subitamente**. Quickly. **Volti subito**, abbreviated **V. S.**, turn over quickly.

Subject. The theme of a fugue; any one of the themes of a sonata, rondo, etc.

Subordinate Chords. Those on the 2d, 3d, and 6th of the scale.

Suite (Fr.) (*sweet*). A set or series of movements. The suite originally consisted solely of dance tunes to which "airs" or movements, designated by the tempo terms, allegro, etc., were added. The classical suite contained: 1st, allemand; 2d, coranto; 3d, saraband; 4th, gigue, preceded by a prelude. Occasionally the gavotte, pavan, loure, minuet, etc., may be found with or in place of some of the above dances. According to the rule of the suite, all the movements had to be in the same key.

Suivez (Fr.) (*swee-vey*). Follow; a direction for the accompanist to follow the soloist.

Sujet (Fr.) (*soo-zhay*). Subject.

Sul, Sull, Sulla (It.). Upon; on; by; in violin music a passage to be played on a certain string is marked Sul E, or A, or D, or G, as the case may be.

Sul ponticello (It.). By the bridge; in violin playing, a direction to play with the bow close to the bridge.

Suonata. See *Sonata*.

Superfluous. Same as *Augmented*.

Super-octave. (1) An organ-stop of 2-foot pitch, same as fifteenth. (2) A coupler in the organ that pulls down the keys one octave above those struck.

Super-tonic. The 2d degree of the scale.

Super-dominant. The 6th degree of the scale.

Supplichevole (It.) (*sup-plee-kay'-vo-leh*), **Supplichevolmente** (*sup-plee-kay-vol-men'-teh*). Pleading; supplicating.

Suspension. Tying or prolonging a note from one chord into the following. See *Retardation*.

Süss (Ger.) (*sees*). Sweet.

Sussurando (It.) (*soos-soo-ran'-do*). Murmuring.

Sussurante (It.) (*soos-soo-ran'-teh*). Whisperingly.

Svegliato (It.) (*svehl-ya'-to*). Brisk; lively.

Svelto (It.) (*svel'-to*). Swift; quick; easy.

Swell Organ. A part of the organ enclosed within a box provided with shutters, which are opened and closed by a lever, called the swell-pedal, worked by the foot.

Symphony. See *Sinfonia*.

Symphonic. In the manner of a symphony.

Symphonic Ode. A combination of symphony and chorus, as Beethoven's Ninth Symphony, or Mendelssohn's Lobgesang.

Symphonic Poem. A modern name for an orchestral composition supposed to illustrate a poem or story.

Syncopation. A shifting of the accent, caused by tying a weak beat to a strong beat.

Syrinx. (1) Pandean Pipes, *q. v.* (2) Part of a hymn to Apollo sung in the Pythian games.

T

T. Abbreviation of Tasto, Tenor, Tempo, Tutti, Toe (in organ music)

Taballo (It.). Kettle-drum.

Tablature (Fr.) (*tab-lah-toor*), **Intavolatura** (It.), **Tablatur** (Ger.). An obsolete system of notation used for the lute principally; another form was used for the organ, harpsichord, etc.

Table (Fr.) (*tahbl*). The belly or sound-board.

Table Music. (1) Music intended to be sung by several people sitting around a table. (2) Music appropriate for entertainment during the pauses in the "serious" work of eating and drinking.

Tabor, Taboret, Tabret. A small drum, like a tambourine without the "jingles." It hung in front of the performer, who beat it with one hand and played a "pipe" or flageolet with the other.

Tacet (Lat.), **Tace** (It.) (*tah'-cheh*). Is silent, or be silent"; signifies that the instrument thus marked is silent during the phrase or movement; as **Tromboni tacent,** the trombones are silent.

Tafelclavier (Ger.). Square pianoforte.

Tafelmusik. Table music.

Tail. (1) Stem of a note. (2) The piece of wood to which the strings of the violin, etc. are attached at the base of the instrument.

Taille (Fr.) (*tah-ee*). The tenor voice or part.

Takt (Ger.). Time, as **Im Takt,** a tempo; measure, as **Ein Takt,** one measure (or bar); beat, as **Auftakt,** up beat.

Taktmässig. In time.

Taktstrich. A bar (line, not measure).

Talon (Fr.). The "frog" or heel of the bow.

Tambour (Fr.). (1) A drum. (2) A drummer.

Tambour de basque. Tambourine.

Tamboura, Tambura (also **Pandora**). An Eastern species of the lute.

Tambourin (Fr.) (*tam-boo-rang*). (1) A tabor. (2) A French rustic dance.

Tambourine. A small variety of drum consisting of a hoop of wood or metal about two inches in depth, with a head of parchment. Small circular plates of metal called jingles are inserted in pairs in holes in the hoop, strung loosely on wires. The tambourine is held in the left hand and struck with the fingers or palm of the right hand; used to accompany dancing in Spain, Italy, and Southern France; occasionally used in the orchestra in ballet music. The "roll" is indicated thus { ♪   The "jingle" ♫

Tamburo (It.). Drum; side drum.

Tamburone (It.) (*tam-boo-ro'-neh*). The great drum.

Tam-tam. Gong.

Tändelnd (Ger.) (*tehn-delnd*). Playful.

Tangent. The brass pin in the action of the clavichord that was forced against the string when the key was struck.

Tantino (*tan-tee-no*), very little.

Tanto (It.). So much; as much. **Allegro non tanto,** not so fast; lit., "fast, not too much."

Tanz (Ger.) (*tants*). Dance.

Tanzlieder. Songs to accompany dancing. See *Ballad*.

Tanzstücke. Dancing pieces.

Tanzweisen. Dancing tunes.

Tarantella (It.), **Tarantelle** (Fr.). A rapid dance in 6/8 time; the name is derived from *tarantula* (the poisonous spider). The dance is popularly believed to be a remedy for the bite of this insect.

Tardamente (It.) (*tar-dah-men'-teh*). Slowly.
Tardando (It.) (*tar-dan'-do*). Slowing; retarding.
Tardato (It.) (*tar-dah'-to*). Made slower.
Tardo (It.) (*tar'-do*). Slow; dragging.
Tartini Tone. An undertone produced by the simultaneous vibration of two strings, etc., first observed by Tartini, the violinist. Called also a differential tone.
Tastatur (Ger.) (*tas-tah-toor*). **Tastatura** (It.) (*tas-tah-too'-ra*). Keyboard.
Taste (Ger.) (*tas'-teh*). A pianoforte or organ key; pedal key.
Tastenbrett (Ger.), **Tastenleiter.** Keyboard.
Tastiera (It.) (*tas-tee-eh'-ra*). Fingerboard of violin, guitar, etc. **Sulla Tastiera**, a direction in violin music to play with the bow near the fingerboard—the opposite of *Sul ponticello, q. v.*
Tasto (It.). A "touch." (1) A key. (2) A fret. (3) Touch. (4) Fingerboard. The preceding words from *Tastatur* are all derived from *Tasto*.
Tasto Solo. Literally, "key alone," *i. e.,* one key or note at a time. A direction in figured bass that the notes are to be played without chords, *i. e.,* unison or octaves.
Tattoo or **Taptoo.** The drumbeat ordering soldiers to retire for the night.
Technic, Technik (Ger.), **Technique** (Fr.). The purely mechanical part of playing or singing.
Technicon. A mechanism for strengthening the fingers and increasing their flexibility.
Techniphone. See *Virgil Clavier.*
Tedesco or **Tedesca, alla** (It.). In German style.
Tema (It.) (*teh'-mah*). Theme; subject; melody.
Temperament. The division of the octave. **Equal Temperament.** The modern system of tuning divides the octave into twelve equal parts, called semitones. **Unequal Temperament** (which was formerly used for all keyed instruments, and retained until quite recently for the organ) tuned the natural notes true, and distributed the superfluous interval among the "black" keys. The discovery of the art of equally tempering the scale lies at the foundation of modern music. Without it, the sudden excursions into remote keys would be impossible. Although we have lost something in purity of intonation, the loss is more than made up in the gain of twelve keys, all equally well in tune. Some enthusiasts, generally acousticians, express great dissatisfaction with our modern scale. A sufficient reply is, that the scale that satisfied the ears of, and made possible the music of the great writers from Bach to Beethoven, must of necessity be the best musical scale.
Tempestosamente (It.) (*tem-pes-to'-sa-men'-teh*). Impetuously.
Tempestoso (It.) (*tem-pes-to'-so*). Tempestuous.
Tempête (Fr.) (*tam-peht*). Tempest. A French dance—formerly fashionable—resembling a quadrille.
Tempo (It.). Time. "Tempo" is universally used to signify "rate of movement."
Tempo Indications—

Slow { Largo, Grave, Lento, Adagio.   Moderate { Andante, Moderato, Commodo.

Fast { Allegro, Presto.

Words used to modify the above: *Poco,* a little. Before a word meaning *slow,* signifies an *increase* of speed, as *poco lento,* a little slow; before a word meaning *fast,* it signifies a *decrease* of speed, as *poco allegro,* a little fast. *Piu,* more. Before a word meaning *slow,* signifies a *decrease* of speed, as *piu lento,* slower; before a word meaning *fast,* it signifies an *increase* of speed, as *piu allegro,* faster. *Assai,* very. After a word meaning *slow,* decreases the speed, as *adagio assai,* very slow; after a word meaning *fast,* increases the speed, as *allegro assai. Molto,* much; has the same meaning as *assai.*

THE DIMINUTIVE *Etto*

Slow { Larghetto, a little faster than Largo. Adagietta, a little faster than Adagio.
Fast, Allegretto, a little slower than Allegro.

THE SUPERLATIVE *Issimo*

Slow { Larghissimo, Lentissimo, Adagissimo, } As slow as possible.
Fast { Allegrissimo, Prestissimo, } Fast as possible.

THE DIMINUTIVE *Ino*
slow, Andantino, faster than Andante.

Andante means "going" [from *andare,* to go], therefore Andantino means "going a little." A large number of words are used in conjunction with the tempo indications that refer more to the manner or style of the performance than to the speed, as Appassionata, with passion; Vivace, with life.

The majority of these words are preceded by con, with; as
Con brio . . . with vigor,
Con calore . . with warmth,
Con fuoco . . with fire,
Con moto, etc. . with motion, } After words meaning fast.

Con espressione . with expression
Con dolcezza . with sweetness,
Con dolore . . with sadness,
Con tristezza . with sorrow, } After words meaning slow.

Tempo commodo. Convenient; easy movement.
Tempo di ballo. Dance time.
Tempo giusto. Strict; exact time.
Tempo marcia. March time.
Tempo ordinario. Ordinary; usual.
Tempo primo. First time, used after a ritard. or accel. to indicate a return to the original time.
Tempo rubato. See *Rubato.*
Tempo wie vorher (Ger.). Same as *Tempo primo.*
Temps (Fr.) (*tam*). (1) Time. (2) Beat.
Temps faible or **levé.** Weak beat; up beat.
Temps fort or **frappé.** Strong beat; down beat.
Tendrement (Fr.) (*tondr-mong*). Tenderly.
Tenendo il canto (It.). Sustaining the melody.
Teneramente (It.) (*teh-neh-ra-men'-teh*). Tenderly; delicately.
Tenerezza (It.) (*teh-neh-ret'-za*), **con.** With tenderness, delicacy.
Tenero (It.) (*teh'-neh-ro*). Tender; delicate.
Tenor, Tenore (It.), **Taille** or **Ténor** (Fr.). (1) The highest natural male voice. (2) In the old system of music, the cantus or plain song. (3) A common name for the viola. The word tenor is supposed to be derived from Lat., *teneo,* to hold, as it *held* the melody.
Tenor Clef. C clef on 4th line.
Tenor Violin. Viola.
Tenore buffo. A comic tenor singer.
Tenore di grazia. A "smooth-singing" tenor singer.
Tenore leggiero. A light tenor singer.
Tenore robusto. A vigorous, strong tenor singer.
Tenorino (It.) (*ten-o-ree'-no*). "Little tenor." Falsetto tenor.

Tenorist. A tenor singer; also viola player.

Tenoroon. (1) See *Oboe di caccia*. (2) Any organ-stop of 8-foot tone that does not go below middle C.

Tenuto (It.) (*teh-noo'-to*). Abbreviated **Ten**. Hold; a direction to sustain the notes for their full value. Sign

Tepidita (It.) (*teh-pee'-dee-ta*), **con**. With indifference.

Tepiditamente (It.) (*teh-pee-dee-ta-men'-teh*). Coldly; lukewarmly.

Tercet (Fr.) (*tehr-say*). A triplet.

Ternary Form. Rondo with three themes.

Ternary Measure. Simple triple time.

Tertian. A two-rank stop, sounding the major 3d and 5th in the third octave above the fundamental.

Terz (Ger.) (*terts*), (It.) **Terza**. Third.

Terzetto (It.) (*tert-set'-to*). A vocal trio.

Terzflöte (Ger.). (1) A flute sounding a 3d above the written notes. (2) An organ-stop sounding the major 3d in third octave.

Tessitura (It.) (*tes-see-tu'-rah*). Texture. The general range of the voice included in a given song, etc.

Testo (It.) (*tehs'-to*). Text. (1) The "words" of any vocal composition. (2) The theme or subject.

Tetrachord [from Gr., *tetra, chordon*]. Four strings; hence, a succession of four sounds. The tetrachord always consists of two whole tones and one half-tone. These intervals may be arranged in three ways. The oldest arrangement, called the Pythagorean tetrachord, began with the half-tone, thus:

It is generally supposed that the original four-string lyre (called the tetrachordon) was tuned to these sounds. The addition of another tetrachord, beginning with the highest note of this one, gives the scale of the heptachord, or seven-string lyre, thus:

This is called the scale of conjunct tetrachords, the A being the note common to both. The addition of a note *below* this scale, thus:

gives the original octave scale of the lyre. This scale is the normal Greek scale, called the Dorian. It is doubtless the origin of the modern minor scale. The tetrachord known as Hucbald's had the half-tone in the middle, thus: D E F G.

The *Hexachord scales* (q. v.) were formed from the tetrachord by adding one letter above and one below, thus:

C D E F G A.

In the modern major scale the half-tone lies between the third and fourth letters of the tetrachord, thus: C D E F, and the scale consists of two of these tetrachords separated by a whole tone.

Tetrachordal System. The original name of the *Tonic Sol-fa*, q. v.

Theil or **Teil** (Ger.). A part (portion, not "voice").

Theme, Thème (Fr.) (*tehm*), **Thema** (Ger.) (*teh-ma*) The subject of a fugue; one of the subjects of a sonata or rondo. The subject of a set of variations. The "cantus" to which counterpoint is added.

Theorbo, Théorbe (Fr.). A large variety of lute.

Third. An interval including three letters, and, if major, **two** whole tones; if minor, three half-tones; if diminished, **two** half-tones:

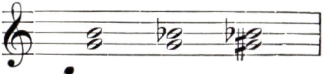

Thirty-second Note

Thorough Bass, Figured Bass, Continued Bass. A system of musical short-hand originally; now used as a means of teaching harmony.

Threnody [Gr. *threnos*]. A song of mourning; dirge.

Thumb Position. Violoncello music; sign , the thumb is laid across the strings, making a temporary bridge.

Tibia (Lat.). The "shinbone." Latin name for the flute, which was originally made from the bone, the name of which it bears.

Tibia Utricularis. Bagpipe.

Tibicen (Lat.). A flute player.

Tie, Fascia (It.), **Bindebogen** (Ger.), **Liaison** (Fr.). A curved line joining two notes on the same degree. The first note is sounded, the second is "held." In old editions, in place of the tie, it was customary to write a single note on the bar-line, equal in value to the two notes that in modern practice are tied. Thus:

Any number of notes may be tied. The sign must be repeated for each one, thus:

The first note is struck, but the sound is prolonged until the time value of all has expired.

Tief (Ger.). Deep; low.

Tierce. (1) A third. (2) An organ-stop. See *Terz*.

Tierce de picardie (Fr.). The major 3d in place of the minor in the final chord of a piece in the minor key. At one time this manner of ending was the rule.

Tierce Position. A common chord with root in bass and third at top.

Timbale (Fr.), **Timballo** (It.). Kettle-drum.

Timbre (Fr.) (*tambr*). Quality of tone. In German *Klangfarbe*, for which *Clangtint* has been proposed as an English equivalent.

Timbrel. Tambourine.

Time. (1) The division of music into portions marked by the regular return of an accent. All varieties of time are founded on two units—the Binary = 1 2, and Ternary = 1 2 3. Time signatures for the most part are formed from figures written like fractions, the upper figure giving the rhythmic units and the number of times the value of the note indicated by the lower figure occurs in the measure. Time is Simple Binary when the upper figure is 2; Simple Ternary, when the upper figure is 3. Compound times are formed by adding together two or more of the time units. When the number of accents resulting from this combination are *even*, it is called Compound Common time; when they are odd, Compound Triple time. Simple Duple time is indicated by this sign . As now used, it always means the value of a whole note in the measure, and is called Alla Capella time. Like all duple times, it must have but one accent in the measure, no matter how the time value of the measure may be divided. The first compound of Duple time, viz., 4/4 time, is often marked **C** and is called Common time, under the impression that the sign is the letter C, whereas it is the old sign for Imperfect time, viz., a broken circle, and originally meant two beats in the measure. Three beats was called Perfect time; the sign was ◯. With the exception of the times with 4 for the upper figure, all the compound times are multiples of the ternary unit, as 6/2, 6/4, 6/8, 12/4, 12/8, 12/16, etc., Compound Common; 9/4, 9/8, 9/16, Compound Triple. The accents in compound times are determined by the number of units in the measure. The first is the strongest, third next, the second is weak, the fourth weaker.

In Compound Triple, the second and third are both weak.

Timidezza (It.) (*tee-mee-det'-za*), **con**. With timidity.
Timorosamente (It.) (*tee-mo-ro-sa-men'-teh*). Timorously.
Timoroso (It.) (*tee-mo-ro'-so*). Timorous; hesitating.
Timpani (It.) (*tim'-pa-nee*). Kettle-drums. Abbreviated **Timp.**
Timpanista (It.). Player on the kettle-drums.
Tirade (Fr.) (*tee-rad*). A rapid run or scale passage.
Tirasse (Fr.) (*tee-rass*). A pedal keyboard that "draws down" the manual keys.
Tirata (It.) (*tee-rah'-tah*). See *Tirade*.
Tirato (It.), **Tiré** (Fr.) (*tee-reh*). "Drawn" bow, *i. e.*, down bow.
Toccata (It.) (*tok-kah'-tah*) [touched, from *toccare*, to touch]. (1) A prelude or overture. (2) A brilliant composition resembling somewhat the modern "Étude" for piano or organ.
Toccatina (It.) (*tok-kah-tee'-nah*). A little toccata.
Toccato (It.). A bass trumpet part.
Todtenmarsch (Ger.) (*tote'-ten marsh*). Funeral march.
Ton (Ger.), **Ton** (Fr.). Tone; sound; pitch; scale.
Tonal Fugue. A fugue in which the answer is slightly changed to avoid modulation.
Tonality. Character or quality of tone; key.
Tonart (Ger.). Key.
Tonbildung. Tone production.
Tondichter. Tone poet.
Tondichtung. Tone poem.
Tone. (1) Sound. (2) Quality of sound. (3) Interval of major second. (4) A Gregorian chant.
Tongue. (1) See *Reed.* (2) (verb) To interrupt the sound of a wind instrument by raising and lowering the tip of the tongue, as in the act of pronouncing the letter T. **Double-tonguing** is produced by a like action of the tip and the middle of the tongue; **Triple-tonguing**, by the tip, the middle, and the tip.
Tonkunst. Tone art; music.
Tonkünstler. Composer; artist in tone.
Tonic. The keynote of a scale, whether major or minor.
Tonic Chord. The common chord of which the tonic is the root.
Tonic Secion. That part of the sonata or rondo that is the principal key; the first theme.
Tonic Sol-fa. A system of musical notation in which the syllables doh, ray, me, fah, soh, lah, te, with certain modifications, are used in place of notes, staff, clefs, and all the ordinary characters of musical notation. The Tonic Sol-fa is based on the assumption, amply proved by experience, that the mental association between a succession of sounds and a succession of syllables helps materially to fix the former succession in the memory. The principle of the Tonic Sol-fa system is as old as the time of Guido; the modern development of it originated with Miss Sarah Ann Glover, of Norwich, England, in 1812, and was perfected by the Rev. John Curwen about thirty years later.
Tonleiter. Tone ladder; scale.
Tonsetzer. Composer; tone setter.
Tonstück. Tone piece; composition.
Tonstufe. Tone step; a degree in the scale.
Tostamente (It.) (*tos-tah-men'-teh*). Quickly.
Tostissimo (It.) (*tos-tis'-see-mo*), **Tostissamente** (*tos-tis-sah-mah-men'-teh*). Fast as possible.
Tosto (It.). Quick. **Piu tosto**, faster.
Touch. (1) The resistance of the keys of the pianoforte or organ. (2) The manner in which a player strikes the keys.
Touche (Fr.) (*toosh*). Digital; key; fret; fingerboard.
Toucher (Fr.) (*too-shay*). To "touch"; play the pianoforte.
Toujours (Fr.) (*too-zhoor*). Always; as, Toujours piano, always soft.
Tradotto (It.) (*trah-dot'-to*). Transcribed; arranged.
Tragen der Stimme (Ger.). Carrying of the voice. See *Portamento*.
Trainé (Fr.) (*tray-nay*). Slurred; legato.
Trait (Fr.) (*tray*). A run; passage; sequence.
Tranquillamente (It.). Quietly; composedly.
Tranquillita, con (It.). With tranquillity.
Tranquillo (It.). Tranquil; quiet.
Transcription. The arrangement of a vocal composition for an instrument, or of a composition for some instrument for another.
Transient Modulation. A short excursion into a non-related key.
Transition. (1) An abrupt modulation. (2) The connecting passages between the themes of a rondo or sonata.
Transpose. To change the key of a composition to one higher or lower.
Transposing Instruments. Instruments whose sounds do not correspond with the written notes; as horns, clarionets, trumpets, etc.
Transverse Flute. See *Flute*.
Trascinando (It.) (*trah-shee-nan'-do*). Dragging; retarding.
Trattenuto (It.) (*trat-teh-noo'-to*). Held back; retarded.
Trauermarsch (Ger.). Funeral march.
Traurig (Ger.) (*trou'-rig*). Mournful; sad.
Traversflöte (Ger.). See *Flute*.
Tre (It.) (*tray*). Three.
Tre corde. Three strings, used in pianoforte music to signify a release of the una-corda pedal.
Treble. (1) The highest part in vocal music for mixed or female voices. (2) The G clef on second line. (3) The first violin in quartet, and the flute, oboe, and clarinet in the orchestra generally.
Treibend (Ger.). Hastening; accelerando.
Tremando (It.) (*treh-man'-do*), **Tremolando** (It.) (*treh-mo-lan'-do*), **Tremolo** (It.) (*treh'-mo-lo*). Abbreviation **Trem.** The rapid reiteration of a note or chord. In music for string instruments written thus:

In pianoforte music:

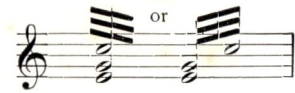

Tremoloso (It.) (*treh-mo-lo'-so*). Tremulously.

Tremulant, Tremolante (It.), **Tremblant** (Fr.) (*tromblont*). A mechanism in the organ that causes the sound to waver.

Tremulieren (Ger.). To trill or to sing. See *Vibrato*.

Trenchmore. An old English dance in $\frac{6}{8}$ time.

Trenise (Fr.). A figure in the quadrille.

Très (Fr.) (*tray*). Very; as, **Très vite,** very fast.

Triad. A chord of three sounds; a common chord, consisting of root, 3d major or minor, and 5th. If the 5th is diminished, it is called a diminished triad; if augmented, an augmented triad.

Maj. Min. Dim. Aug.

Triangle. A pulsatile instrument, consisting of a steel rod bent into an equilateral triangle. Struck with a small steel rod, it gives a very clear penetrating sound.

Trill, Trillo (It,). **Trille** (Fr.), **Triller** (Ger.). The trill, or shake, is the rapid iteration of the written note and the note above, indicated by the sign, *tr*⏜⏜⏜ The trill continues to the end of the waved line. The oldest form or trillo was a mere repetition of a tone. The oldest form of the modern shake was held to be derived from appoggiaturas and their resolutions. Until the time of Beethoven, the trill beginning with upper auxiliary note was most generally used. However, the present method of beginning with the principal tone was gradually gaining the attention of writers.

The trill is generally finished with a turn. The after-turn is usually written out at the close of the trill, but whether or not this be so, the trill is not complete without this closing beat:

To make the trill symmetrical with an after-turn, an additional tone is inserted, just before the close, otherwise there will be a break between the last and the next to the last beats; thus:

This gap beween D and B is filled by the insertion of an additional principal tone, which will make the next to the last beat contain three tones (a triplet); thus:

This makes a satisfactory close to a trill, the two beats (five notes) making a complete turn of quintuplet form.

Many writers call this (quintuplet) the turn of the trill, but properly speaking the after-turn of the trill is only the last beat, the triplet preceding being a real part of the trill. From this it will be seen that the beats of a trill may be either twofold or threefold, and the smallest complete trill, according with the modern acceptation of the correct form of the embellishment, would be with two beats, five notes; thus:

The rapidity of a trill is reckoned by the number of beats, not by the number of tones, sounded within a given note's time. The trill upon a long note has no positive number of beats, this being decided, in case there is no particular accompanying figure, by the character of the composition and also measurably by the ability of the interpreter. The after-turn, however, should always be played in the same time as the trill, regardless of the size of note used for its representation in the notation.

Trinklied (Ger.). Drinking song.

Trio (It.) (*tree-o*). (1) A composition for three voices or instruments. (2) One of the parts of a minuet or march. etc. The origin of its application is very uncertain.

Triole (Ger.), **Triolet** (Fr.). A triplet.

Triomphale (*tree-om-fal*), **Triomphant** (Fr.) (*tri-om-font*), **Trionfale** (*tree-on-fah'-leh*), **Trionfante** (It.) (*tree-on-fan'-teh*). Triumphant; triumphal.

Triple Counterpoint. One so contrived that the three parts may change places, each one serving as bass, middle, or upper part.

Triplet, Triole (Ger.), **Triolet** (Fr.), **Tripla** (It.), or **Tripola.** Three notes played in the time of two of the same value.

Triple Time. See *Time*.

Tristezza (It.) (*tris-tet'-za*), con. With sadness; sadly.

Tritone [Lat., *tritonus*, three tones], **Triton** (Fr.), **Tritone** (It.). The interval of the augmented 4th, as:

Trois (Fr.) (*tro-a*). Three.

Trois temps. Triple time.

Troll [from Ger., *trollen,* to roll about]. (1) (verb) To sing a catch or round. (2) (noun) A catch or round.

Tromba (It.). Trumpet; a brass instrument of piercing, brilliant tone quality.

Tromba marina (It.). Marine trumpet.

Trombetta (It.). A small trumpet.

Trombone, Posaune (Ger.). (1) A brass instrument with a sliding tube, by means of which the pitch may be varied. Three trombones are used in the modern orchestra, viz., alto, tenor, and bass. A smaller trombone formerly used was called the Descant Trombone. (2) A reed stop of 8-, 16-, or 32-foot pitch in the organ.

Trommel (Ger.). Drum.

Trompe (Fr.). Hunting horn.

Trompe de bearn. Jew's-harp.

Trompette (Fr.). Trumpet.

Troppo (It.). Too much. **Allegro non troppo,** "Allegro," not too much.

Troubadour, Trouvère (Fr.), **Trovatore** (It.). The poet musicians of the eleventh century, in southern France, Italy, and Spain. The troubadours originated in Provence. From thence their "gentle art," or "gay science," as it was called, spread over Europe.

Trübe (Ger.) (*tree'-beh*). Gloomy; dismal.

Trumpet. See *Tromba*.

Tuba (Lat.). (1) Trumpet. (2) A bass instrument of the saxhorn family, frequently used with, or in place of, the bass trombone.

Tuba mirabiles (Lat.). Tuba "wonderful." A reed-stop in the organ with heavy wind pressure, 8- or 16-foot tone.

Tumultuoso (It.) (*too-mul-too-o'-so*). Agitated; tumultuous.

Tune. (1) Air; melody. (2) Just intonation.

Tuner. One who adjusts the sounds of an instrument to the standard and relative pitch.

Tuono (It.). (1) Sound. (2) Mode.

Turca, alla (It.). In the Turkish manner.

Turkish Music or **Janissary Music.** Drums, cymbals, gongs, etc., to produce noise.

Turn. (Abridged from Russell's "Embellishments of Music.") The Turn partakes in its delivery somewhat of the character of the composition in which it appears, and should be played (or sung), according to Louis Köhler, broad in slow tempo, light and flowing in brighter movements, and always legato. It may be broadly divided into four classes:

1. The symbol ∞ placed over the note ( ), or the note preceded by the embellishment written in full.

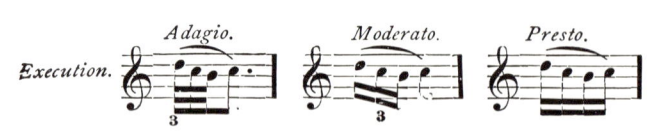

2. A turn between two notes on different degrees (or four small notes between).

3. A turn between two notes of similar pitch.

4. The turn after a dotted note. The delivery of this turn is the same as the third class in its effect, since the dot is simply another way of writing a second similar note.

An exception to this fourth rule is made if the dotted note with turn directly precedes a close (possibly forming part of the cadence) and is followed by two notes of equal value leading up or down to the closing notes of the phrase.

Tutta (It.). All. **Con tutta forza.** With full power.
Tutti (It.) (*too-tee*). In scores, a notification to all the performers and singers to take part.
Tuyau (Fr.). Pipe.
Tuyau d'orgue. Organ pipe.
Tuyau à anche. Reed pipe.
Tuyau à bouche. Flue pipe.
Twelfth. An organ stop sounding the 12th above the diapason.
Tympani. See *Timpani*.
Tyrolienne (Fr.) (*tee-rol-yen*). (1) A Tyrolese song for dancing. (2) Tyrolese song with yodel.

U

U. C. Abbreviation of Una corda, one string.
Übergang (Ger.) (*e'-ber-gangk*). Passage; transition; modulation.
Übung (Ger.) (*e'-boonk*). Exercise; study; practice.
Uguale (It.) (*oo-gwah'-leh*). Equal.
Ugualmente (It.) (*oo-gwahl-men'-teh*). Equally; evenly.
Umfang (Ger.) (*oom-fangk*). Compass.
Umore (It.) (*oo-mo'-reh*), **con.** With humor.
Umstimmung (Ger.) (*oom-stim-moonk*). The change of the pitch of a brass instrument by the addition or change of "crooks"; the change of the pitch of kettle-drums.
Un (It.) (*oon*), **Una** (*oo'-nah*), **Uno** (*oo'-no*). One; as, **Una voce,** one voice.
Un or **Une** (Fr.) (*ong, oon*). One.
Unda maris (Lat.). "Wave of the sea." The vox celestis, an organ-stop, 8-foot pitch, with a tremulous tone.
Unessential Dissonances. Those that occur by suspension, the essential dissonances being the 7th and 9th, and, according to some authorities, the 11th and 13th over the dominant.
Unessential Notes. Passing and changing notes.

Ungarisch (Ger.). Hungarian.
Ungeduldig (Ger.). Impatiently.
Ungestüm (Ger.). Impetuous; con impeto.
Unison. Sounds consisting of the same number of vibrations per second. The term "unison passage" is applied to vocal or instrumental parts in the octave also.
Unisono (It.) (*oo-nee-so-no*). Unison.
Unisson (Fr.) (*oo-nis-song*). Unison.
Un poco (It.). A little.
Un pochino (It.) (*po-kee'-no*), **Un pochettino** (*po-ket-tee'-no*). A very little.
Unruhig (Ger.) (*oon-roo'-ig*). Restless.
Unschuldig (Ger.) (*oon-shool-dig*). Innocent.
Up bow. In violin playing, the motion of the bow from the point to the nut. The sign is ∨; the down bow ⊓.
Ut (Fr.) (*oot*). The note C; the first of the Aretinian syllables, changed in Italy to *do*, a better vowel sound for solfeggio.
Ut (Lat.). As; like. **Ut supra,** as before.

V

V. Abbreviation of Violino, Voce, Volta.
V-cello. Abbreviation of Violoncello.
Vla. Abbreviation of Viola.
Va (It.). Go; as, **Va crescendo,** go on getting louder.
Vacillando (It.) (*vat-chil-lan'-do*). "Vacillating." A direction to play without strict regard to time.
Vago (It.). Vague; dreamy.

Valse (Fr.) (*vals*), **Valce** (It.) (*val-cheh*). Waltz; a dance of German origin in 3/4 time.
Valse à deux temps (Fr.) (*doo tomp*). A species of waltz with two steps to each measure.
Value. The value of a note or rest is its relative duration, the standard being the whole note or rest, which may be divided into half, quarter, eighth, sixteenth, thirty-second

notes, etc. The value of a note is increased one-half by placing a dot after it; a second dot adds to its value an amount equal to half that of the first. The absolute value of a note depends upon the tempo, *i. e.*, rate of movement of the piece in which it occurs.

Valve. See *Piston*.

Variante (Fr.) (*vah-ree-ongt*). A variant; other reading.

Variations, Variationen (Ger.) (*fah-ree-a-tse-o'-nen*), **Variazioni** (It.) (*va-ree-at-zee-o'-nee*). Melodic, rhythmic, and harmonic modifications of a simple theme, each one more elaborate than the last.

Varie (Fr.) (*vah-ree*), **Variato** (It.) (*var-ya'-to*). Varied; with variations.

Varsovienne (Fr.) (*var-so-vee-en*), **Varsovianna** (It.) (*var-so-vee-an'-na*). A dance in ¾ time resembling the mazurka, invented in France.

Vaudeville (Fr.) (*vode-veel*). A light operetta consisting of dialogue interspersed with songs; the name is said to come from Vaux de Vire in Normandy.

Veemente (It.) (*veh-eh-men'-teh*). Vehement; forceful.

Veemenza (It.) (*veh-eh-men'-tza*), **con**. With vehemence.

Velato (It.) (*veh-lah'-to*), **Voce velato**, a veiled voice, *i. e.*, lacking in clearness and resonance.

Vellutata (It.) (*vel-loo-tah'-tah*). Velvety; smooth.

Veloce (It.) (*veh-lo'-cheh*). Rapid; swift.

Velocissimamente (It.) (*veh-lo-chis-see-ma-men'-teh*). Very swiftly.

Velocissimente (It.) (*veh-lo-chis-see-men'-teh*). Swiftly.

Velocita (It.) (*veh-lo'-chee-tah*), **con**. With rapidity.

Ventage. The holes in the tubes of wind instruments, the opening or closing of which by the finger-tip or by valves worked by keys alters the pitch by varying the sounding length of the tube.

Ventil. (1) Valve; piston. (2) In the organ a contrivance for cutting off the wind from a part of the organ.

Venusto (It.) (*veh-noos'-to*). Graceful; fine.

Veränderungen (Ger.) (*fer-an'-de-roong-en*). Variations.

Vergnügt (Ger.) (*fehr-gneegt'*). Pleasant; cheerful.

Verhallend (Ger.). See *Morendo*.

Verlöschend (Ger.) (*fehr-lesh'-end*). See *Morendo*.

Vermittelungsatz (Ger.) (*fehr-mit'-tel-oonk-sotz*). A subsidiary part; episode in sonata, etc.

Verschiebung (Ger.) (*fehr-shee'-boonk*), **mit**. Use "soft pedal."

Verschwindend (Ger.) (*fehr-shwin'-dend*). Dying away.

Versetzung (Ger.) (*fehr-set'-soonk*). Transposition.

Verspätung (Ger.) (*fehr-spay'-toonk*), **Verweilend** (*fehr-wei'-lent*), **Verzögernd** (*fehr-tseh'-gernt*). Delaying; retarding.

Verve (Fr.) (*vehrv*). Spirit. **Avec verve**, with spirit.

Verzweiflungsvoll (Ger.) (*fehr-tsvy'-floonks-foll*). Lit., full of desperation. Despairingly.

Vezzoso (It.) (*vets-so'-so*), **Vezzosamente** (*vets-so-sa-men'-teh*). Beautiful; graceful; gracefully.

Vibration. The rapid motion to and fro that produces the phenomena of sound by setting up a wave-motion in the air.

Vibrato (It.) (*vee-brah'-to*), **Vibrante** (*vee-bran'-teh*). "Vibrating" with strong, "intense" tone; vocal music, heavy accent in piano playing.

Viel (Ger.) (*feel*). Much; many.

Vielle (Fr.) (*vee-el'*). Rote; hurdy-gurdy.

Vier (Ger.) (*feer*). Four.

Vierstimmig. Four-voiced. **Vierfach**, fourfold.

Vif (Fr.). Lively.

Vigorosamente (It.) (*vee-go-ro-sa-men'-teh*). Vigorously; boldly.

Vigoroso (It.) (*vee-go-ro'-so*). Vigor; force.

Villancico (Sp.) (*veel-lan'-thee-co*). Originally a species of song or madrigal, later a motet sung in church at certain services.

Villanella (It.). An ancient Italian folk-song.

Viol. The precursor of the violin. Viols were made in sets of six called a "chest of viols"; the smallest was about the size of the modern viola, and all were provided with frets.

Viola. The alto violin, generally called the tenor. The viola is slightly larger than the violin, and has four strings tuned as follows:

Music for it is written with the C clef on the third line.

Viola da braccia (arm viola), **Viola da gamba** (leg viola), **Viola da spalla** (shoulder viola), **Viola pomposa**. Obsolete varieties of the viola family. The last was the invention of J. S. Bach.

Viole (Fr.). Viola.

Viole d'amor (Fr.) (*d'ah-moor*), **Viola d'amore** (It.) (*d'ah-mo-reh*). A variety of the viola with wire sympathetic strings in addition to the usual gut strings.

Violin, Violon (Fr.), **Violino** (It.), **Fiddle, Geige** (Ger.). The words "violin" and "fiddle" both come from the Latin *vitula* or *fitula*, a mediæval form of string instrument played with a bow. The violin has four strings, tuned as follows:

The strings are of gut, the lowest, or G string, covered with thin wire.

Violin Clef. The G clef on the second line.

Violina. A 4-foot organ-stop with string-like tone.

Violino principale (It.) (*prin-chee-pah'-leh*). The solo violin, or leader of the violins.

Violino ripieno. A violin part only used to fill up the tutti.

Violoncello (It.). The "little violone." The violoncello has four strings of gut, tuned an octave below the viola:

The C and G strings are covered with wire.

Violonar (Fr.). Double bass.

Violonaro (Fr.). See *Octo Bass*.

Violone (It.). The double bass, *q. v.*

Virgil Clavier. A soundless keyboard for practice.

Virginal. A small instrument of the harpsichord family.

Virtuoso (masc.) (It.) (*vir-too-o'-so*), **Virtuosa** (fem.) (*vir-too-o'-sah*). An eminent skilled singer or player. The word was formerly used in the same sense as "amateur."

Virtuos (Ger.), **Virtuosin** (fem.) (Ger.), **Virtuose** (Fr.). Virtuoso.

Vista (It.). Sight. **A prima vista**, at first sight.

Vistamente (It.) (*vis-tah-men'-teh*), **Vitamente** (It.) (*vee-tah-men'-teh*), **Vive** (Fr.) (*veev*), **Vivente** (It.) (*vee-ven'-teh*), **Vivido** (It.) (*vee'-vee-do*), **Vivezza** (*vee-vet-za*), **con**. Lively; briskly; with animation; vividly.

Vivace (It.) (*vee-vah'-cheh*), **Vivacemente** (*vee-vah-cheh-men'-teh*), **Vivacita** (*vee-vah'-chee-tah*), **con**, **Vivacezza** (*vee-vah-chet'-zah*). Lively; rapid; with animation; with vivacity.

Vivacissimo (*vee-vah-chis'-see-mo*). Very lively and fast.
Vivo (It.) (*vee-vo*). Alive; brisk.
Vocal. Belonging to the voice; music meant to be sung or well designed for singing.
Vocalion. A variety of reed organ in which the quality and power of the tone is much modified by resonators.
Vocalise (Fr.) (*vo-cal-ees*), **Vocalizzi** (It.) (*vo-cah-lit'-zee*). Vocal exercises.
Vocalization. (1) The manner of singing. (2) The singing of studies—solfeggio—to one or more vowel sounds.
Voce (It.) (*vo-cheh*). The voice.
Voice. (1) The sound produced by the human organs of speech. (2) A part in a polyphonic composition. There are three well-marked varieties of the male and female voice. Male voices are divided into bass, baritone, and tenor; the analogues in the female voice are alto, mezzo soprano, and soprano.
Voicing. Regulating the quality and power of the tone of organ-pipes.
Voix (Fr.) (*vo-a*). Voice.
Voix celeste (Fr.). Vox angelica.

Volante (It.) (*vo-lan'-teh*). "Flying." The rapid, light execution of a series of notes.
Volkslied (Ger.) (*folks-leed*). Popular song.
Voll (Ger.) (*foll*). Full.
Volonté (Fr.) (*vo-lon-teh*), **A volonté.** At will; a piacere.
Volta (It.). Turn. **Una volta,** first turn or first time.
Volti (It.) (*vol'tee*) (verb). Turn. **Volti subito,** abbreviated V. S., turn over (the page) rapidly.
Voluntary. An organ solo before, during, or after church service, frequently extemporary.
Vordersatz (Ger.) (*for'-der-sots*). Principal theme; sonata.
Vorspiel (Ger.) (*for-speel*). Prelude; overture; introduction.
Vox (Lat). Voice.
Vox celestis, Vox angelica. See *Unda maris*.
Vox humana. An organ-stop imitating the human voice. (Fr. *Voix humane*).
Vuide (Fr.) (*voo-eed*), **Vuoto** (It.) (*voo-o-to*). Open. **Corde vuide, Corda vuide,** open string, *i.e.*, a string of instruments of violin family sounded without being touched by the finger.

W

Waits, Waytes, Waightes. Watchmen who "piped the hours" at night on a species of hautboy called a wait, or shawm. In modern times "Christmas waits" are parties of singers who go from house to house collecting pennies on Christmas Eve.
Waldflöte (Ger.) (*volt-flay-teh*). Forest flute; a 4-foot open organ-stop. **Waldquinte** is a 12th with the same tone quality.
Waldhorn (Ger.). Forest horn; hunting horn; the French horn without valves.
Waltz. See *Valse*.
Walze (Ger.) (*vol'-tseh*). A run, alternately ascending and descending; a "roller."
Wankend (Ger.). Hesitating.
Wärme (Ger.) (*vehr'-meh*). Ardor; warmth.
Wehmut (Ger.) (*veh'-moot*). Sadness.
Wehmütig (Ger.). Sad; melancholy.
Weich (Ger.). Weak; soft; minor.
Weinend (Ger.). Weeping; lamenting.
Well-tempered (**Wohltemperirtes**) **Clavier** (Ger.). A title given by Bach to a set of preludes and fugues in all the keys. See *Temperament*.
Wenig (Ger.). Little; un poco.

Whistle. A small flue-pipe or flageolet; the first step in advance of the pandean pipe, *i. e.*, a tube blown across the top.
Whole Note. 𝅝
Whole Step. A whole tone.
Wie (Ger.). As; the same. **Wie vorher,** as before.
Wiederholung (Ger.) (*wee-dehr-ho'-loonk*). Repetition.
Wiegenlied (Ger.) (*wee'-gen-leed*). Cradle song; berceuse.
Wind Band. (1) The wind instruments in the orchestra. (2) A band composed of wind instruments only, called also a harmony band.
Wolf. (1) The dissonant effect of certain chords on the organ or pianoforte tuned in unequal temperament. See *Temperament*. (2) Certain notes on the violin or other bow instruments that do not produce a steady, pure tone.
Wood-stops. Organ-stops with wooden pipes.
Wood-wind. The flute, oboe, clarionet, and fagotto in the orchestra.
Wuchtig (Ger.). Weighty; emphatic.
Würde (Ger.). Dignity. **Mit Einfalt und Würde,** with simplicity and dignity.
Wütend (Ger.). Raging; furioso.

X Y Z

Xylophone, Strohfiedel (Ger.), **Claquebois** (Fr.), **Gigelira** (It.). An instrument consisting of strips of wood graduated to produce the diatonic scale. They are supported on ropes of straw, etc., and are struck by hammers held one in each hand. An ingenious form of the xylophone is found in Africa, called the marimba. From Africa it was brought to South America, where it has been greatly enlarged by the Negroes of Guatemala.
Yodel, Jodel, Jodeln. See *Jodeln*.
Zampogna (It.) (*zam-pone'-ya*). A bagpipe; also a harsh-toned species of hautboy.

Zapateado (Sp.) (*tha-pah-te-a'-do*). "Stamping." A Spanish dance in which the rhythm is marked by stamping.
Zarabanda (Sp.) (*tha-ra-ban'-da*). See *Saraband*.
Zart, Zärtlich (Ger.). Tender; tenderly; suave.
Zartflöte (Ger.). A soft-toned flute in the organ.
Zeitmass (Ger.). Tempo.
Zelo (It.) (*zeh'-lo*). Zeal; earnestness.
Zelosamente (It.) (*zeh-lo-sah-men'-teh*). Earnestly.
Zeloso (It.) (*zeh-lo'-so*). Zealous; energetic.

Ziemlich (Ger.) (*tseem'-lich*). Moderately. **Ziemlich langsam**, moderately slow.

Ziganka. A Russian peasant dance in 2/4 time.

Zimbalon, Cymbal, Czimbal. The Hungarian dulcimer.

Zingaresca (It.) (*zin-gah-res'-ca*), **Zigeunerartig** (Ger.) (*tsee-goy'-ner-ar-tig*). In Gypsy style.

Zinke (Ger.). Cornet; an obsolete variety of hautboy.

Zither (Ger.) (*tsit'-ter*). A string instrument consisting of a shallow box over which pass two sets of strings—one set of gut for the accompaniment, the other, of steel and brass, pass over a fretted fingerboard; on these the melody is played. The notes are stopped by the left hand, and the melody strings are struck by a plectrum attached to a ring on the thumb of the right hand; the accompaniment is played by the first, second, and third fingers of the right hand.

Zitternd (Ger.). Trembling.

Zögernd (Ger.). Hesitating; retarding.

Zoppo (It.). Lame. **Alla zoppo**, halting; limping; syncopated.

Zukunftsmusik (Ger.). Music of the future. The music of Wagner and his disciples is thus called by both friend and enemy, but with different meanings.

Zunehmend (Ger.). Crescendo.

Zurückhaltend (Ger.) (*tsoo-reek'-hal-tend*). Retarding.

Zwischensatz (Ger.). An episode.

Zwischenspiel (Ger.). "Between play"; interlude.